The SAGE Handbook of

Social Network Analysis

'An outstanding volume that brings together contributions from the world's leading experts on social network analysis. Methods, theory and substantive applications are presented in a clear exposition making this the most comprehensive text available in this rapidly expanding and changing field. For anyone with any interest in social networks this is quite simply a "must have" book.'

Martin Everett, Professor of Social Network Analysis, Manchester University, UK

'There is something for everyone in *The SAGE Handbook of Social Network Analysis*. Whether you are brand new to the field or a seasoned expert, interested in the theoretical under-pinnings of network analysis or the methodological nuts and bolts associated with analyzing the evolution of an affiliation network over time, this book is a must have.'

Michael Schwartz, Chair, Department of Sociology, Stony Brook University, USA

'Over the past decades Social Network Analysis has broadened its scope from anthropology and sociology to all behavioral and social sciences, from social and organizational psychology to management science and economics. This Handbook provides well-founded introductions and overviews for a broad range of social network studies, approaches, and methodology. It is a must for everybody who is interested in the way social network relations evolve, are structured and affect outcomes in any part of our life and society.'

Frans N. Stokman, Professor of Social Science Research Methodology, ICS,
University of Groningen, The Netherlands

The SAGE Handbook of

Social Network
Analysis

Edited by

John Scott and
Peter J. Carrington

Los Angeles | London | New Delhi
Singapore | Washington DC

Contents

Notes on Contributors

Weihua (Edward) An is a PhD candidate in Sociology, doctoral fellow in the Multidisciplinary Program in Inequality and Social Policy at the Kennedy School of Government and a graduate associate in the Institute for Quantitative Social Science and the Fairbank Center for Chinese Studies at Harvard University. He earned a master's degree in Statistics from Harvard (in 2009) and has strong interests in quantitative methods, especially social network analysis, causal inference, and Bayesian statistics. His general substantive interests span a variety of areas, including sociology of health, inequality and social policy and organizations. Currently, he focuses on formal and statistical analysis of peer effects on health and social behaviours, and social-network-based policy interventions. He is working on several projects, including 'Bayesian Propensity Score Estimators: Incorporating Uncertainties in Propensity Score into Causal Inference' (forthcoming in *Sociological Methodology*), 'Instrument Variable Estimates of Peer Effects on Health Behaviors', 'Directionality of Social Ties and the Edge-Reversal Test of Peer Effects' and 'Peer Effects on Adolescent Cigarette Smoking and Social-Network-Based Interventions: Experimental Evidence from China'.

Vladimir Batagelj is Professor of Discrete and Computational Mathematics at the University of Ljubljana. His main research interests are in graph theory, algorithms on graphs and networks, combinatorial optimization, data analysis and applications of information technology in education. With A. Mrvar, he has developed Pajek, http://pajek.imfm.si, a program for analysis and visualization of large networks. He is author and coauthor of several papers published in scientific journals (*CACM, Psychometrika, Journal of Classification, Social Networks, Discrete Mathematics, Algorithmica, Journal of Mathematical Sociology*, etc.) and in proceedings of international conferences. Recently he coauthored two books: *Generalized Blockmodeling* (with P. Doreian and A. Ferligoj) and *Exploratory Network Analysis with Pajek* (with W. de Nooy and A. Mrvar). These books were published in 2005 by Cambridge University Press. The book *Generalized Blockmodeling* was awarded a Harrison White Outstanding Book Award by the Mathematical Sociology Section of the American Sociological Association in 2007.

Matthew Bond is a Senior Lecturer in the Department of Social and Policy Studies, Faculty of Arts and Human Sciences, London South Bank University. His main research interests are the quantitative analysis of corporate political behaviour, corporate charity and the British Establishment.

Stephen P. Borgatti is the Paul Chellgren Chair of Management at the University of Kentucky. His research interests include social network theory and methodology, knowledge management and career trajectories. He is a member of the LINKS Center for Social Network Analysis in Management, and has recently coauthored a piece on network theory in *Science* with his LINKS Center colleagues.

Peter J. Carrington is Professor of Sociology and Legal Studies at the University of Waterloo and editor of *Canadian Journal of Criminology and Criminal Justice*. His current research, the Canadian Criminal Careers and Criminal Networks Study, combines his long-standing interests in social network analysis and in crime and delinquency. Other interests include police discretion and the impact of the Canadian

Youth Criminal Justice Act. His recent articles have appeared in *Criminology, Canadian Journal of Criminology and Criminal Justice,* and *Criminal Justice Policy Review.* With John Scott and Stanley Wasserman, he coedited *Models and Methods in Social Network Analysis* (Cambridge University Press, 2005), which won the 2006 Harrison White Outstanding Book Award, given by the Mathematical Sociology Section of the American Sociological Association.

William K. Carroll is a member of the Sociology Department at the University of Victoria since 1981, and a founding participant in the Graduate Program in Cultural, Social and Political Thought. He currently directs UVic's Interdisciplinary Minor/Diploma Program in Social Justice Studies. His research interests are in the areas of social movements and social change, the political economy of corporate capitalism and critical social theory and method. His recent books include *The Making of a Transnational Capitalist Class* (Zed Books, 2010) and *Corporate Power in a Globalizing World* (Oxford University Press, revised edition, 2010).

Vincent Chua obtained his PhD in Sociology at the University of Toronto. In his dissertation, he examined the sources of several forms of social capital in Singapore and the effects of social capital on occupational success. He has won several academic awards for his dissertation research: the Daniel Grafton Hill Prize, the Ellie Yolles Ontario Graduate Scholarship in Sociology and the Norman Bell Award.

Mario Diani is ICREA Research Professor in the Department of Political and Social Sciences of the Universitat Pompeu Fabra, Barcelona. He has worked extensively on social network approaches to social movements and collective action. His publications include *Social Movements* (with Donatella della Porta, Blackwell, 1999/2006), *Social Movements and Networks* (coedited with Doug McAdam, Oxford University Press, 2003), and articles in leading journals such as *American Sociological Review, American Journal of Sociology, Social Networks* and *Theory and Society.*

Paul DiMaggio is A. Barton Hepburn Professor of Sociology and Public Affairs and the Director of the Center for the Study of Social Organization at Princeton University. His current projects include the development and application of network methods to detect schematic heterogeneity in attitude data and a study of network effects on social inequality. He is coeditor (with Patricia Fernandez-Kelly) of *Art in the Lives of Immigrant Communities in the U.S.* (Rutgers University Press, 2010).

Patrick Doreian is Emeritus Professor of Sociology and Statistics at the University of Pittsburgh and a research faculty member of the Faculty of Social Sciences at the University of Ljubljana. He 'retired' in order to have more time for research and writing. He currently coedits *Social Networks* with Tom Snijders and previously edited *The Journal of Mathematical Sociology* for 23 years. His research interests include social network analysis, network evolution, and macro social change.

Katherine Faust is Professor of Sociology and member of the Institute for Mathematical Behavioral Sciences at the University of California, Irvine. She is coauthor (with Stanley Wasserman) of the book *Social Network Analysis: Methods and Applications* (Cambridge University Press) and of numerous articles about social networks and network methodology. Her current research focuses on comparing network patterns across different forms of social relations and animal species; development of methodology for complex network structures, including constraints and local network properties; and understanding relationships between social networks and demographic processes.

Anuška Ferligoj is Professor at the Faculty of Social Sciences at University of Ljubljana, head of the graduate program on Statistics at the University of Ljubljana and head of the Center of Methodology and Informatics at the Institute of Social Sciences. She has been the editor of the journal *Advances in Methodology and Statistics* (*Metodoloski zvezki*) since 2004 and is a member of the editorial boards of the *Journal of Mathematical Sociology, Journal of Classification, Social Networks, Advances in Data Analysis and Classification, Methodology, Structure and Dynamics: eJournal of Anthropology and Related Sciences, BMS* and *Corvinus Journal of Sociology and Social Polic*y. She was a Fulbright scholar in 1990 to 1991 and a visiting professor at the University of Pittsburgh in 1996 and at the University of Vienna in 2009 to 2010. She was awarded the title of Ambassador of Science of the Republic of Slovenia in 1997 and was given the Simmel Award in 2007 by the International Network for Social Network Analysis (INSNA). In 2010 she received Doctor et Professor Honoris Causa at Eotvos Lorand University (ELTE) in Budapest. She is an elected member of the European Academy of Sociology and the International Statistical Institute. Her interests include multivariate analysis (constrained and multicriteria clustering), social networks (measurement quality and blockmodeling), and survey methodology (reliability and validity of measurement). She is the coauthor of the monograph *Generalized Blockmodeling* (Cambridge University Press, 2005), which obtained the Harrison White Outstanding Book Award in 2007, given by the Mathematical Sociology Section at the American Sociological Association.

Ove Frank, is Emeritus Professor in the Department of Statistics at Stockholm University. From 1971 he held professorships in statistics at the universities of Uppsala, Lund and Stockholm. He also had visiting positions at the University of California–Riverside and Stanford University. He is one of the pioneers of statistical graph theory and he contributed to the development of statistical sampling theory for social networks. He developed probabilistic network models and statistical methods for sampling and estimation in networks. He also made contributions to various problems in combinatorics and information theory. Among his recent publications are contributions to *Encyclopedia of Complexity and Systems Science* (Springer, 2009), *International Encyclopedia of Statistical Science* (Springer, 2010) and *Official Statistics: Methodology and Applications in Honour of Daniel Thorburn* (Department of Statistics, Stockholm University, 2010).

Linton C. Freeman is Research Professor in the Department of Sociology and member of the Institute for Mathematical Behavioral Sciences at the University of California, Irvine. He began working in social network analysis in 1958 when he directed a structural study of community decision making in Syracuse, New York. In 1978 he founded the journal *Social Networks*. Beginning in the 1950s, and continuing on to the present time, one of his continuing areas of interest has been the history of social network analysis.

Sanjeev Goyal is Profesor of Economics at the University of Cambridge and Fellow of Christ's College, Cambridge. He was educated at the University of Delhi and the Indian Institute of Management (Ahmedabad) in India, and at Cornell University in the United States. He has carried out theoretical research in the fields of learning, coordination problems and political economy and industrial organization; and is one of the pioneers in the economic study of networks. His research has appeared in leading international journals such as *Econometrica, Journal of Political Economy, American Economic Review* and the *Review of Economic Studies*. His book *Connections: An Introduction to the Economics of Networks* was published by Princeton University Press in 2007.

Anatoliy Gruzd is Assistant Professor in the School of Information Management at Dalhousie University in Canada. He earned his PhD in Library and Information Science at the University of Illinois at Urbana-Champaign and also holds a MS in Library and Information Science from Syracuse University as well as BS and MS degrees in Computer Science from Dnipropetrovsk National University in Ukraine. His current research includes the development of various automated text-mining techniques and visualization tools for uncovering social networks between online participants based on their digital footprints alone. Recently, he was awarded a $161,000 Social Sciences and Humanities Research Council of Canada grant to study how online social media and networks are changing the ways scholars disseminate information. He is also participating in a $23.2 million NCE collaborative research initiative called the GRAND (GRaphics, Animation and New meDia) network.

Daniel S. Halgin is Assistant Professor of Management at the University of Kentucky, where he is a member of the LINKS Center for Organizational Social Network Analysis. His program of research focuses on social network theory, identity dynamics and research methodologies.

Klaus Hamberger teaches Social Anthropology at the École des Hautes Etudes en Sciences Sociales (Paris, France). He has done fieldwork in Southern Togo and has published on social space and kinship networks.

Robert A. Hanneman is Professor of Sociology at the University of California, Riverside. Much of his work has been in simulation modeling (both systems dynamics and agent-based) as an approach to formal theory construction. He has published on a variety of topics in macro-sociology, political economy and the sociology of education. In the field of social network analysis, he is currently working on empirical projects in market organization and world systems. He is also working on software and algorithms for the modeling of multimodal network data.

Nicholas Harrigan is Assistant Professor of Sociology in the School of Social Sciences and Humanities, Singapore Management University. He works in two overlapping research areas: social networks and the politics of business. He has developed Coevolution Regression Graph Models and has used statistical models to study corporate political strategy in Australia and the United Kingdom.

Caroline Haythornthwaite received her PhD in 1996 from Toronto. She is Director of the School of Library, Archival and Information Studies, University of British Columbia. She joined UBC in August 2010 after 14 years at the University of Illinois at Urbana-Champaign, where she was Professor in the Graduate School of Library and Information Science. In 2009 to 2010, she was Leverhulme Trust Visiting Professor at the Institute of Education, University of London, presenting and writing on 'Learning Networks'. Her research concentrates on information and knowledge sharing through social networks, and the impact of computer media and the Internet on work, learning and social interactions. She has studied social networks of work and media use, the development and nature of community online, distributed knowledge processes, the nature and constraints of interdisciplinary collaboration, and transformative effects of the Internet and Web 2.0 technologies on learning and collaborative practices, and automated processes for analysis of online activity. Her major publications include *The Internet in Everyday Life* (2002, with Barry Wellman); *Learning, Culture and Community in Online Education* (2004, with Michelle M. Kazmer), the *Handbook of E-Learning Research* (2007, with Richard Andrews) and *E-Learning Theory and Research* (2011, with Richard Andrews).

Betina Hollstein is Professor of Sociology at Hamburg University. She was educated at Marburg University and at the Free University Berlin. She has been a lecturer and researcher at the Free University Berlin and at Ludwig-Maximilians-University Munich, and an assistant professor at Mannheim University and Humboldt-University Berlin. Her research interests include social networks, sociology of the life-course, social inequality, and social research methods. Her relevant publications include *Mixed Methods in Social Network Research* (coedited with Silvia Dominguez) and 'Netzwerkveränderungen verstehen. Zur Integration von struktur- und akteurstheoretischen Perspektiven' [Understanding Changes in Personal Networks. Integrating Structural and Actor-oriented Approaches] in *Berliner Journal für Soziologie* (2003).

Michael Houseman is Professor of Religions of Black Africa (Ethnology) at the École Pratique des Hautes Etudes (Paris, France) and was trained in social anthropology at the University of Paris 10-Nanterre. He has done fieldwork in Cameroon, Benin and French Guyana. He has published numerous articles on ritual and on kinship and social organization, is the author (with Carlo Severi) of *Naven or the Other Self. A Relational Approach to Ritual Action* (Brill, 1998) and the editor of *Eprouver l'Initiation* (EPHE, 2008).

Mark Huisman is Assistant Professor in the Department of Sociology at the University of Groningen. His research interests are in applied statistics, statistical models for social networks and methods for nonresponse and missing data. He teaches courses on statistics and multivariate statistical methods.

Ron Johnston is Professor in the School of Geographical Sciences at the University of Bristol, having previously worked at Monash University and the universities of Canterbury, Sheffield and Essex. His main research interests are in electoral studies and urban social segregation and include several studies on neighbourhood effects in voting patterns generated by conversations in social networks. His recent books include (with Charles Pattie) *Putting Voters in Their Place: Geography and Elections in Great Britain* (Oxford University Press, 2006).

Andrew Jorgenson is Macro-Sociologist at the University of Utah. His current research interests include the political-economy and human-ecology of global environmental change, environmental degradation and public health, and the structural determinants of income inequality. His publications have appeared in *Social Forces, Social Problems, Social Science Research, International Sociology, Global Environmental Politics, Organization and Environment* and dozens of other scholarly journals and collections. He also serves as coeditor of the *Journal of World-Systems Research*.

Edward L. Kick is the former Head and now Professor of Sociology in the Department of Sociology and Anthropology at North Carolina State University. His macro-sociological research has examined world-system structure and its impacts on social change, militarization, economic development, inequality, environment, polity, urban and rural community, and food insecurity. Recently, he has examined environmental issues of flood management and global biodiversity. His research has appeared in the *American Sociological Review, American Journal of Sociology, Social Forces, Social Science Research*, and most recently in *Disasters, Organization and Environment* and in handbooks on networks and on globalization. He coedits the *Journal of World-Systems Research*.

David Knoke is Professor of Sociology at the University of Minnesota. He received his Ph.D. in 1972 from the University of Michigan. His primary areas of research and teaching are organizations, networks, and social statistics. He has been a principal investigator on more than a dozen National Science Foundation grants, most recently a project to investigate networks and teamwork of 26 Minnesota Assertive Community Treatment (ACT) teams, a multiprofessional mental-health services program. His recent books, some with coauthors, include *Comparing Policy Networks: Labor Politics in the U.S., Germany, and Japan* (1996), *Organizations: Business Networks in the New Political Economy* (2001), and *Statistics for Social Data Analysis*, 4th ed. (2002), and *Social Network Analysis*, 2nd ed. (2008). In 2008 he received the UMN College of Liberal Arts' Arthur 'Red' Motley Exemplary Teaching Award.

Lothar Krempel is a senior Research fellow at the Max Planck Institute for the Study of Societies in Cologne, Germany, and is Associate Professor (PD) for Empirical Social Science Research at the University of Duisburg, Essen. He has written a book (in German) on network visualization and has applied network visualization technologies in various domains like German capital ties and directory interlocks and world trade and historical networks.

Nan Lin is the Oscar L. Tang Family Professor of Sociology of the Trinity College, Duke University. His academic interests, for more than four decades, have focused on social networks, social support and social capital. He has made efforts to construct theories, devise measurements and conduct empirical research in each research arena. Empirically, he has applied these theories and measurements to the studies of social stratification and mobility, stress and coping, and individual, organizational, and community well-being. He has employed both quantitative (large-scale national surveys, and surveys in organizations and communities) and qualitative (intensive long-term observations in villages, for example) methods. He has authored or edited 11 books (including *Social Capital: A Theory of Social Structure and Action*, Cambridge University Press, 2001), 40 book chapters and numerous journal articles.

Virginie Lopez-Kidwell is a Doctoral Candidate in management at the University of Kentucky and is affiliated with the LINKS International Center for Research on Social Networks in Business. Her research interests include social networks, the role of affect in organizational behaviours, as well as power and dependence in workplace relationships.

Julia Madej was a Researcher at NetLab from 2006 to 2009. She is a graduate of the University of Toronto and is currently an official of the Ministry of Health and Long-Term Care in the Province of Ontario.

Alexandra Marin is Assistant Professor of Sociology at the University of Toronto. Her research interests include the role of social networks and social capital in the labour market and workplace, and social network data collection.

Peter V. Marsden is Harvard College Professor and Edith and Benjamin Geisinger Professor of Sociology at Harvard University. His concern with the measurement of social networks via survey methods is long-standing. Marsden's substantive research interests center on social organization, including social networks, formal organizations, and the sociology of medicine. He has done methodological work on network analysis and survey research. He coedited (with James D. Wright) the *Handbook of Survey Research*, 2nd ed. (Emerald Group Publishing, 2010). He is editing a forthcoming collection of studies of U.S. social trends based on General Social Survey data.

Steve McDonald is Assistant Professor of Sociology at North Carolina State University. His research examines inequality in access and returns to social capital across the life course. His primary focus is on the role that social networks play in reproducing race and gender inequality in the labour market. He has also conducted research on informal mentoring in adolescence and the consequences of these relationships for status attainment in adulthood. Examples of his research can be found in the *American Journal of Sociology, Social Problems, Social Forces, Social Science Research, Sociology of Education* and *Gender and Society*.

Laura A. McKinney is a doctoral candidate in the Department of Sociology and Anthropology at North Carolina State University. Her dissertation research uses cross-national data and structural equation modeling to examine interdependencies among economic, ecological, and social systems that determine sustainability. Her research interests include global and local sustainability, global political economy, environmental sociology, global social change, rural/community development and research methods. Her work has been published in *Organization and Environment, Disasters, Human Ecology Review* and the *International Journal of Comparative Sociology*.

Ann Mische is Associate Professor of Sociology at Rutgers University. Her work combines interpretive and network-analytic approaches to the study of political communication in social movements and democratic politics. Her book *Partisan Publics: Communication and Contention across Brazilian Youth Activist Networks* was published by Princeton University Press in 2007. In addition to her work on Brazil, she has also published theoretical articles in leading sociological journals addressing the relationship between networks, culture, and agency. She is currently beginning a new research project on how individual and collective projections of future possibilities influence interactions and choices in the present.

Charles Pattie is Professor of Geography at the University of Sheffield. His research interests include electoral studies, political participation and the politics of devolution.

Philippa Pattison is Professor of Psychological Sciences at the University of Melbourne. Her research interests include the development of mathematical and statistical models for social and behavioural phenomena, particularly for social networks and network-based social processes. Her current research focuses on the development of stochastic models for social processes and on applications of these models to a diverse range of phenomena, including the evolution of the biotechnology industry in Australia and the spread of infectious diseases.

Mark Riddle is Associate Professor of Sociology at the University of Northern Colorado.

Garry Robins is a mathematical psychologist and social network methodologist in the Department of Psychological Sciences at the University of Melbourne. His research has concentrated on developing exponential random graph models for social networks but he is also involved in a wide range of empirical social network projects. His research has won awards from the Psychometric Society, the American Psychological Association and the International Network for Social Network Analysis. He is a former editor of the *Journal of Social Structure*.

J.P. Sapinski is currently pursuing a PhD in Sociology at the University of Victoria, in British Columbia, Canada. His research focuses on the involvement of private actors and of business organizations in global environmental and climate politics. Before turning to sociology, he obtained a Master's degree in Anthropology from the Université de Montréal, where he studied aboriginal social movements in Mexico.

John Scott is Professor of Sociology at the University of Plymouth and was previously Professor of Sociology at the universities of Essex and Leicester. He has been President, Chair, Secretary, and Treasurer of the British Sociological Association and is a Fellow of the British Academy and an Academician of the Academy of the Social Sciences. He is the author of *Social Network Analysis* (1992 and 2000), editor of *Social Networks: Critical Concepts* (Routledge, 2002) and with Peter Carrington and Stanley Wasserman, of *Models and Methods in Social Network Analysis* (2005). In addition to applications of network analysis in studies of economic sociology (including *Capitalist Property and Financial Power*, 1986, and *Corporate Business and Capitalist Classes*, 1997) he is the author of *Power* (2001), *Social Theory* (2006) and *Conceptualising the Social World* (2011). He is currently completing a book on the early development of British sociology.

Tom A.B. Snijders is Professor of Statistics in the Social Sciences at the University of Oxford and a Fellow of Nuffield College; he also is Professor of Statistics and Methodology at the University of Groningen. His research focuses on methodology for social network analysis, and multilevel modeling. He has a particular interest in modeling network dynamics and has been the originator of the statistical program *SIENA* for analysing network panel data. He is coeditor of *Social Networks*.

Joonmo Son received his PhD in Sociology from Duke University and is currently Assistant Professor of Sociology at the National University of Singapore. His research interests include social capital, social support, network diversity, health and aging, volunteering and comparative sociology. One of his current research projects compares the effect of social support on depression and physical health in the United States, China, and Taiwan. His publications have appeared in *Social Science Research*, *Journal of Health and Social Behavior* and *Sociological Quarterly*.

Lijun Song received her PhD in Sociology from Duke University and is Assistant Professor of Sociology and a participant at the Center for Medicine, Health, and Society at Vanderbilt University. Her scholarly interests focus on causes and consequences of social networks, social integration, social capital, and social support. Her recent publications include 'Social Capital and Health Inequality: Evidence from Taiwan' (2009) in *Journal of Health and Social Behavior*; 'The Effect of the Cultural Revolution on Educational Homogamy in Urban China' (2009) in *Social Forces*; and several book chapters, including 'Social Capital and Health' (2009) in *The New Companion to Medical Sociology*.

Marijtje A.J. van Duijn is Associate Professor of Statistics in the Department of Sociology of the University of Groningen. Her research interests are in the development and application of random effects models for discrete or complex data, such as longitudinal, grouped, or social network data.

Renée C. van der Hulst (1970) is the Director of Bureau Netwerkanalyse (the Netherlands) and specializes in social scientific research, in particular social network analysis in relation to law enforcement, crime prevention, public safety and security. She has been working for several years as a researcher and consultant in this area, and holds a PhD in Sociology and a Master's degree in Social and Organisational Psychology. Her main areas of interest are the study of social networks, and human factors in relation to radicalization, terrorism, and organized crime.

Barry Wellman is a Fellow of the Royal Society of Canada and the past chair of the American Sociological Association's Community and Urban Sociology section and the Communication and Information Technologies section. Wellman holds the S.D. Clark Chair at the Department of Sociology, University of Toronto, where he directs NetLab. He founded the International Network for Social Network Analysis in 1976. The author and coauthor of more than 200 papers, his most recent coedited book is *The Internet in Everyday Life* (with Caroline Haythornthwaite). His coauthored book *Networked* (with Lee Rainie) will be published by MIT Press in 2011.

Douglas R. White is Professor of Anthropology and Mathematical Behavioral Sciences at the University of California, Irvine, and External Faculty at the Santa Fe Institute. He is a recipient of the Distinguished Senior U.S. Scientist Award, Alexander von Humboldt Foundation (Ethnosoziologie). He has published extensively on kinship and social organization and is the author (with Ulla Johansen) of *Network Analysis and Ethnographic Problems: Process Models of a Turkish Nomad Clan* (Lexington, 2005) and the editor of *Structure and Dynamics: eJournal of Anthropological and Related Sciences*.

Howard D. White received his PhD in Librarianship at the University of California, Berkeley, in 1974. He joined Drexel University, where he is Professsor Emeritus. He is known for author-centered bibliometric techniques, examples of which appear in this volume. He and Katherine W. McCain won the best paper award of the American Society for Information Science and Technology in 1998. The society gave him its highest honour, the Award of Merit, in 2004. The following year, he received the Derek Price Medal of the International Society for Scientometrics and Informetrics for contributions to the quantitative study of science.

Acknowledgements

We are grateful to the large number of leading researchers who gave their time to join us in producing this Handbook. Collating the efforts of a large and diverse group of scholars is not always an easy task and we hope that this final version of the Handbook will be a fitting tribute to the generosity and forbearance of our authors. The editors and authors acknowledge with gratitude the permission granted by various copyright holders for the reproduction of extracts from their work, and we are happy to have included the necessary formal acknowledgements at appropriate places in the book. At SAGE we are grateful to Chris Rojek for suggesting the idea of the book and to Jai Seaman for her commitment to the book and patience with us throughout the production process. As network researchers we are also particularly aware of the hidden networks of individuals at SAGE who have labored on our behalf to produce this finished version. Preparation of this book was supported by a grant from the Social Sciences and Humanities Research Council of Canada. We are grateful to Kritika Kaul at Glyph International for her work in copy editing and proofing the manuscript.

John Scott
Peter Carrington

Introduction

Peter J. Carrington and John Scott

The *SAGE Handbook of Social Network Analysis* is the first published attempt to present, in a single volume, an overview of the social network analysis paradigm. It includes accounts of the history, theory and methods of social network analysis, and a comprehensive review of its application to the various substantive areas of work in which cutting-edge research is taking place. We do not intend to repeat in this Introduction the ideas to be found in the various individual chapters, but it is important to provide a brief introduction to the discussions that follow.[1]

THE DEVELOPMENT OF SOCIAL NETWORK ANALYSIS

The date at which researchers on social structure began to explicitly use the idea of a 'social network' is difficult to determine with any precision. While structural thinking has deep roots in the sociological tradition, it was not until the 1930s that researchers and theorists began to employ such ideas to represent the shape and characteristics of social structures.[2] This was especially marked in German sociology, where the 'formal sociology' of Simmel and others emphasised the formal properties of social relations and the investigation of the configurations of social relations that result from the interweaving of actions in social encounters. These writers explicitly adopted a novel terminology and referred to 'points', 'lines' and 'connections' in their analyses and descriptions of patterns of social relations.

These formal ideas influenced many people working in social psychology and psychotherapy, especially when looking at the ways in which the structures of small groups influenced the perceptions and action choices of their individual members. This was most explicit in the work of Lewin (1936) and Moreno (1934), who investigated the 'field' or 'space' of social relations and its characteristics as a 'network' (see also Bott, 1928). Moreno referred to this approach as 'sociometry' and invented the 'sociogram' as a way of visually representing social networks with points and lines. Sociometry became a major field of investigation in education (Jennings, 1948; Gronlund, 1959) and community studies (Lundberg and Lawsing, 1937; Lundberg and Steele, 1938). In social psychology it took the form of an emphasis on 'group dynamics' (Cartwright and Zander, 1953; Harary and Norman, 1953), an approach that was particularly developed at the University of Michigan and, in London, at the Tavistock Institute.

The initial insights into community relations by Lundberg had a wider impact through the work of Warner, who initially cooperated with Mayo in a study of the Hawthorne electrical works in Chicago (Roethlisberger and Dickson, 1939). Although sociometry no doubt had some influence on their visual representations, the Hawthorne researchers were also directly influenced by seeing the electrical wiring diagrams in the Hawthorne factory, seeing these as a metaphor for group relations. Warner went on to investigate community structure in American towns and cities. Influenced by the work of the British anthropologist Radcliffe-Brown, Warner looked at the structure of group relations in large communities and used network diagrams to represent social structure. In his study of the New England town of Newburyport, carried out between 1930 and 1935, Warner presented large-scale community relations in matrix form to represent what he referred to as the 'clique structure' of the city (Warner and Lunt, 1941). In a famous commentary, Homans (1950) advanced on these matrix methods to reanalyze a small clique of women studied by Warner in the southern town of Natchez, Mississippi.

A major advance in social network analysis took place at the University of Manchester in the 1950s, when social anthropologists critical of the emphasis on consensus and harmony in mainstream American sociology sought to recognize conflict and divisions within African and European communities. They were influenced by the 'structuralist' view of society that had been expounded by Radcliffe-Brown since the 1920s; his public lectures delivered in 1937 and 1940 referred explicitly to a 'network of social relations' and 'social morphology' (Radcliffe-Brown, 1940, 1957). The network analysis being developed at the Tavistock Institute and in the work of Warner was the means through which they developed this. This work on African communities was subsequently reported by Mitchell (1969b). This work had a wide influence. In a Norwegian study, Barnes (1954) proposed that the metaphor of the network of relations be taken seriously to explore the warp and weft of community relations, and in a study of kinship in London, Bott (1955, 1956) employed ideas of connectedness and density. Barnes and Bott worked closely with the Manchester researchers and inspired the systematic study by Nadel (1957) as well as Mitchell's (1969a) commentary on this work. The latter provides one of the earliest summaries of a formal social network methodology.

A group of American researchers led by Harrison White had begun to develop and apply a formal methodology for social network analysis by the time that Mitchell published his summary. Building on the work of Lévi-Strauss (1969 [1949]) and his collaborator Weil, White (1963a) had initially used algebra to represent kinship structures. When White moved from Chicago to Harvard University he formed a large and dynamic group of students and associates to develop the network paradigm (see Mullins, 1973: Chapter 10). These researchers included Levine's (1972) work on corporate power as a multidimensional field, Lee's (1969) sociometric study of searches for abortionists, Granovetter's (1973, 1974) investigation of searches for employment, and Mullins's (1973) analysis of modern American sociology. White himself worked with others on algebraic methods for representing and analysing systems of social positions and roles (Lorrain and White, 1971; Boorman and White, 1976; White et al., 1976). This group constituted a new generation of social network researchers who helped to spread social network analysis across the globe.

An important area for the application of social network analysis has been the investigation of corporate power and interlocking directorships. While Sweezy (1939) and others had adopted ad hoc techniques in their early studies for drawing network diagrams of board-level connections, it was not until the 1960s and 1970s that these suggestions were furthered as a result of the technical advances made in social network analysis. A path-breaking paper by Bearden and his colleagues (1975) elaborated on the idea of centrality to explore the power and influence of banks in the American corporate world, connecting with Levine's (1972) documentation of the clusters associated with particular banks and their directors. In the Netherlands, work led by Mokken and Stokman (Helmers et al., 1975) became the basis for an investigation of transnational patterns (Fennema, 1982) and an international comparative investigation (Stokman et al., 1985; see Scott and Griff, 1984). This was extended into a comparative investigation of intercorporate shareholding networks (Scott, 1986) and led to numerous studies in a variety of societies (see the reviews in Scott, 1997, and Carroll and Sapinski, this volume).

Another important area of application has been in the investigation of community structure. Rooted in Warner's studies, it was again a number of researchers influenced by the developments at Harvard who pushed this area forward. Fischer (1977) and Wellman (1979) generated work that completely reoriented the research area. Wellman carried out a series of investigations on the changing structure of communal relations in a Canadian city and examined the role of friendship in social integration. A particular concern was to investigate the changing ways in which people maintained contact: his thesis was that each individual has his or her own 'community', consisting of those to whom the individual is socially connected. Thus, community was reconceptualised as a personal network and liberated from its previous spatial bounds in the neighbourhood (Chua et al., this volume). Wellman has recently explored the impact of electronic means of communication on patterning the structuring and operation of interpersonal networks (Wellman and Hogan, 2006; Gruzd and Haythornthwaite, this volume). This work is connected with network formulations of social support (Song et al., this volume) and has most recently converged with ideas on social capital that developed out of Putnam's (2000) work. The most important contributions to this work have been the reflections of Lin (2001) and Burt (2005; see also Lin et al., 2001).

Numerous other applications have extended social network analysis into the study of political and policy networks (Bond and Harrigan, this volume; Knoke, this volume), social movements (Diani, this volume), criminality and terrorism (Carrington, this volume; van der Hulst, this volume), the world political economy (Kick et al., this volume), cultural, scientific, and scholarly networks (DiMaggio, this volume; Howard White, this volume), economics (Goyal, this volume), geography (Johnston and Pattie, this volume), the impact of peers on attitudes and behaviour (An, this volume) and many other topics, even including animal networks (Faust, this volume).

At the same time, network theory and theories have been developed, including network exchange theory, network flow theory, small world theory, and the strength of weak ties theory (Borgatti and Lopez-Kidwell, this volume). Many researchers have stressed the links between social network analysis and theories of rational choice, but this has often led to a methodological individualism in which structural features become more outcomes of social action. More recent contributions have investigated the relationship between individual agency and the structural features of social networks. White (1992) and Emirbayer (Emirbayer and Goodwin, 1994; Emirbayer, 1997) have made especially important contributions to the theorisation of a 'relational sociology', while Mische (this volume; Mische, 2003; see also Mische, 2007) has developed White's approach to culture and identity to make important connections with the relational orientation (see Emirbayer and Mische, 1998).

Since the late 1970s there has been a huge increase in technical contributions to social network methodology and in its application. Of particular importance have been major studies by Burt (1982), Freeman and his colleagues (1989), Wasserman and Faust (1994) and an introductory text by Scott (2000; originally published in 1991). Edited collections have included those by Wasserman and Galaskiewicz (1994), Brandes and Erlebach (2005) and Carrington et al. (2005).

The most striking development in social network analysis in recent years, however, has been the growth of interest among physicists in applying network ideas to social phenomena (Freeman, this volume; Scott, this volume). This growing interest from outside the social sciences first became apparent in a paper by Watts and Strogatz (1998), which built on Milgram's pioneering work on 'small worlds' (1967; Travers and Milgram, 1969) and the literature on random networks that had grown up around it. Barabási (2002) and Watts (1999, 2003) suggested that these ideas

could be applied to the social world, egregiously ignoring the work on social networks already undertaken by sociologists, anthropologists, economists and political scientists. This lack of awareness of prior research – they proposed, for example, investigations into networks of directorships on the grounds that none had so far been undertaken – surprised and shocked those who had been researching the topics for many years. Reaction in a wider public context was, however, much more favourable. These later researchers' claims to novelty were taken at face value by many journalists and reviewers (see, e.g., Buchanan, 2002) but did create a wider interest in network analysis at a time when practical applications of 'social networking' were also being stimulated by new Web 2.0 technologies.

Freeman's (2004) history of social network analysis undertook a network analysis of citation patterns in research on social networks and showed that the work published by the physicists had rarely cited work by social scientists (see also Freeman, this volume). It also disclosed, however, that social network analysts had been reluctant to engage with the work of the physicists. This division is now breaking down: Watts has moved into sociology, and sociologists have debated the ideas contained in his work. Others such as Barabási, however, still persist in ignoring the work carried out by social scientists during the last century.

The work of the physicists has, however, brought to the forefront of attention a number of issues that received less than their due attention in earlier social network analyses. These physicists had, in particular, stressed network dynamics and change over time, and they helped to develop techniques for investigating these. Such work moves social network analysis beyond the generally static or cross-sectional methods typically used and the new techniques outlined by physicists and social scientists are helping to develop explanations of network processes and to explore processual transformations in network structure.

Social network analysis is a scientific community, or invisible college, with a recognizable intellectual lineage and clusters of researchers based in several centers and loosely linked by cross-cutting collaborations and intercitations (Freeman, 2004). It is also a scientific institution, with dedicated journals (*Social Networks, Journal of Social Structure* and *Connections*), textbooks and handbooks (e.g. Degenne and Forsé, 1994; Wasserman and Faust, 1994; Scott, 2000; Knoke and Yang, 2008), dedicated computer software (van Duijn and Huisman, this volume) and an association (the International Network for Social Network Analysis; see http://www.insna.org/).

Although a well-defined paradigm in its own right, social network analysis is embedded within traditional disciplines such as social psychology, social anthropology, communication science, organizational science, economics, geography and, especially, sociology. Since its 'take-off' in the 1970s, the volume of published research on social networks has grown exponentially (Knoke and Yang, 2008: 1–2), while the number of subject areas in which it is being employed has experienced almost linear growth, from a handful to almost 60 by the year 1999 (Freeman, 2004: 5). Neither the volume of published research nor the expansion of social network analysis into diverse subject areas shows any sign of leveling off.

CENTRAL IDEAS IN SOCIAL NETWORK ANALYSIS

At the heart of social network analysis is the branch of mathematics called graph theory (Harary and Norman, 1953; Harary et al., 1965; Harary, 1969). This is a set of axioms and deductions that originated in Euler's mathematical investigations of the famous problem of the seven bridges of Köningsberg. He explored the problem of whether it was possible to walk through the city crossing each bridge just once and so visiting each of the islands that made up the city. Euler converted this practical problem into an abstract model of points and lines, the points representing the islands and the lines representing the bridges, and showed that there is no solution to the problem: the task is impossible. This proof laid the foundations for studying networks of all kinds as being graphs composed of points and lines.

Social network analysis is a specific application of graph theory in which individuals and other social actors, such as groups, organizations and so on, are represented by the points and their social relations are represented by the lines (Hanneman and Riddle, this volume). This mathematical model formalises the initial insight depicted in Moreno's sociograms. The theorems of graph theory provide a basis for analysing the formal properties of sociograms. It is not, however, necessary to draw sociograms in order to use graph theoretical concepts and measures. Network data on a given social relationship are typically recorded in the form of a square matrix – the 'sociomatrix' – in which the rows and columns of the matrix represent individuals or other social actors and the presence or absence of the social relationship between each pair of individuals is recorded in the cells. Thus, the sociomatrix contains the same information as the corresponding sociogram, taking the rows or columns as its points and the contents of the cells as the presence or absence of lines between pairs of points.

Sociomatrices can be analysed using the operations of matrix algebra. This is a great advantage when analysing large-scale data sets for which it is often difficult to draw a meaningful sociogram, or to analyse it.

While most social network research analyses 'one-mode' networks, in which the rows and columns of the data matrix represent the same set of points, or social actors, some work analyses 'two-mode' or 'affiliation' networks, in which there are two distinct classes of points, and the lines exclusively connect points of one class with points of the other class (Borgatti and Halgin, this volume). Two-mode data are represented by a rectangular matrix, in which the rows represent one type of point and the columns represent the other type. For example, one class of points could be persons and the other type could be events in which they were involved, or organizations to which they belonged; each cell entry would indicate whether the indexed person was related to the indexed event or organization. Two-mode networks can easily be converted to one-mode networks.

Graph theory analyses the formal properties of graphs, which are systems of points and lines between pairs of points. The concept of the graph can be extended to take account of the 'direction' of a line, so as to represent asymmetric relations such as friendship choices made or the flow of influence or resources. It can also take account of the intensity or strength of a relationship by assigning a 'value' to a line in order to represent this; the value can be positive or negative. There can be multiple labelled lines between each pair of points, with each type of line representing a different relationship, or 'type of tie'. Points can also have discrete- or continuous-valued properties, representing the attributes of the actors represented by the points, as in conventional social analysis. The term 'network' is used in mathematics for these extensions of a graph, in which the lines and/or points have properties such as direction, valence, weight, multiplicity and so forth: thus, social network analysis is the analysis of systems of social relationships represented by networks.

From this initial basis of representation, network analysis can measure such things as the overall 'density' of a network and the relative 'centrality' of the various points within it. Centrality measures have typically been used as indicators of power, influence, popularity and prestige. Other network analyses based on graph theory include the investigation of cliques and clusters of points, structural divisions within a social network being seen in terms of the existence of particularly dense or well-connected sub-groupings, or, equivalently, in terms of particularly sparse or poorly connected areas of the network, representing points of potential cleavage. Notions of local clustering, cleavage and centrality have allowed the investigation of intermediary or brokerage roles (Burt, 2005), as well as the development of methods for 'network reduction', in which large, complex networks are 'reduced' to smaller, more manageable realisations (Batagelj, this volume).

While graph theory is the heart of social network analysis, a number of other mathematical models have been employed to highlight specific aspects of network structure. The matrix-based algebraic approach used by Harrison White and others looks not at the properties of individuals and groups but at the structural properties of the social positions (or 'statuses') occupied by individuals and the performed roles that are associated with these positions. These so-called positional approaches – sometimes termed 'block models' (Ferligoj et al., this volume) – use methods of matrix clustering that build on Homans's early suggestions to decompose networks into hierarchical positions of the kind documented by Nadel (1957). These approaches have led to various ways of measuring and analysing the 'structural equivalence' or 'substitutability' of individuals within social positions, and to algebraic modelling of systems of compound social roles (Pattison, this volume), corresponding formally to the more familiar systems of compound kinship roles (mother's brother, wife's father, etc.) developed by ethnographers (Douglas White, this volume; Hamberger et al., this volume).

Networks containing more than 20 or so points are difficult to draw accurately and legibly as sociograms. Multidimensional scaling was one of the earliest ways of eliminating the random jumble of criss-crossing lines in order to display points in a way that retains the spatial patterns inherent in relational data. New techniques such as multiple correspondence analysis and spring embedder algorithms have greatly improved graph drawing, and writers such as Batagelj and his colleagues (De Nooy et al., 2005; see also http://vlado.fmf.uni-lj.si/) and Krempel (2005; this volume) have been exploring alternative bases for network visualisation, including moving images of network change.

Special techniques are generally used to obtain or generate network data. Network data can be difficult to obtain, and they raise unique problems of measurement validity and reliability, as well as particular ethical issues (Marsden, this volume). While the emphasis in social network analysis has been on quantitative data and analyses, qualitative approaches are also used and indeed have characterised much of the foundational anthropological work in social network analysis, as well as a growing body of recent work (Hollstein, this volume).

Standard sampling procedures and statistical procedures such as significance tests, regression, and the analysis of variance cannot usually be employed in social network analysis as their assumption of the independence of observations does not hold for network data: indeed, it is the assumption of the interdependence of social actors that is the basis of network analysis. Frank (this volume) has pioneered the investigation of inference from sampled network data. Conventional statistical models have been adapted for use with network data (van Duijn and Huisman, this volume). Building on work by Frank and Strauss (1986), Wasserman and his colleagues (Wasserman and Pattison, 1996; Pattison and Wasserman, 1999; Robins et al., 1999; Robins, this volume) developed novel statistical techniques by generalising Markov graphs to a larger family of models. Their so-called exponential random graph models – or $p*$ models – define a probability distribution on the set of all networks that can be constructed on a given set of points using specific parameters. Solving the estimating equation for the parameters, which resembles a logistic regression model, provides estimates of the impact of such structural features such as transitivity and reciprocity, as well as of the attributes of the points.

Most recently, agent-based computational methods have been used to explore processes of change in networks, relating structural transformations to the unanticipated consequences of individual-level decision making (see Monge and Contractor, 2003). Knowledge of the rules under which agents make decisions and act can be used to predict broad patterns of change in network structure. Networks change because of the ways in which individual actions are constrained by the structural locations of actors and the wider structural properties of the network, though work on 'small-world' networks has shown that these structural transformations may not be linear in nature. Snijders (this volume; Snijders and van Duijn, 1997; Snijders, 2001, 2005) has developed a powerful approach to this problem in which networks develop through the continual iteration of actions, and in which small, incremental changes can accumulate to a tipping point at which nonlinear transformation in network structure occurs.

CONCLUSION

In preparing this volume, we took the view that social network analysis is a 'paradigm', rather than a theory or a method: that is, a way of conceptualizing and analysing social life that guides the selection of the social behavior data that are studied, influences the way these data are organized for analysis, and specifies the kinds of questions addressed (Leinhardt, 1977: xiii).

In the most general terms, social network analysis is a structuralist paradigm: it conceptualises social life in terms of structures of relationships among actors, rather than in terms of categories of actors. Harrison White's comment that 'subinfeudation reminds one of industrial decentralization' (1963b: 77) highlighted structural rather than categorical parallels, and illustrates the kinds of questions and insights that arise from the study of social networks:

> The same conundrums that baffled them baffle us. Just as William the Conqueror insisted on submission directly to himself from the chief vassals of his loyal lords ... so a wise President seeks loyalty of subcabinet officers directly to himself (White, 1963b: 78).

A social science paradigm is composed of a theory or theories, a methodology or set of commonly employed methods, and a body of empirical research. This volume is organised around that tripartite division. Readers who are experienced in social network analysis can use this volume as a reference book, referring to particular chapters for up-to-date summaries of knowledge and indications of future trends, in a given topic area. Readers who are new to social network analysis may wish to begin with the introductory chapters by Marin and Wellman and by Hanneman and Riddle, before reading chapters on particular topics. Alternately, a newcomer to social network analysis who is interested in a particular topic, such as kinship or terrorism, or in applications of social network analysis in a particular discipline, such as economics, geography or criminology, may prefer to start with the corresponding substantive chapter, referring back to the introductory, conceptual and theoretical chapters as necessary.

In terms of theory, methods and substantive empirical work, this is an exciting time in social network analysis. The *SAGE Handbook of Social Network Analysis* aims to present a one-volume state-of-the-art presentation of contemporary views and to lay the foundations for the further development of the area.

NOTES

1 See also the introductory chapters in this volume by Marin and Wellman, and by Hanneman and Riddle. An earlier version of some sections of this introduction appeared in Scott (2010).

2 Overviews of the history of social network analysis can be found in Scott (2000: Chapter 2) and Freeman (this volume; 2004).

REFERENCES

Barabási, A.-L. (2002) *Linked: The New Science of Networks*. Cambridge, MA: Perseus.

Barnes, J.A. (1954) 'Class and committee in a Norwegian island parish', *Human Relations* 7: 39–58.

Bearden, J., Atwood, W., Freitag, P., Hendricks, C., Mintz, B. and Schwartz, M. (1975) 'The nature and extent of bank centrality in corporate networks', presented at the Annual Meetings of the American Sociological Association. Reprinted in J. Scott (ed.), *Social Networks*. Vol. 3. London: Sage, 2002.

Boorman, S.A. and White, H.C. (1976) 'Social structure from multiple networks II: Role structures', *American Journal of Sociology* 81: 1384–446.

Bott, E. (1955) 'Urban families: Conjugal roles and social networks', *Human Relations* 8: 345–84.

Bott, E. (1956) 'Urban families: The norms of conjugal roles', *Human Relations* 9: 325–41.

Bott, H. (1928) 'Observation of play activities in a nursery school', *Genetic Psychology Monographs* 4: 44–48.

Brandes, U. and Erlebach, T. (eds.) (2005) *Network Analysis: Methodological Foundations*. Berlin: Springer.

Buchanan, M. (2002) *Small World: Uncovering Nature's Hidden Networks*. London: Weidenfeld and Nicolson.

Burt, R.S. (1982) *Towards a Structural Theory of Action*. New York: Academic Press.

Burt, R.S. (2005) *Brokerage and Closure: An Introduction to Social Capital*. New York: Oxford University Press.

Carrington, P.J., Scott, J. and Wasserman, S. (eds.) (2005) *Models and Methods in Social Network Analysis*. Cambridge: Cambridge University Press.

Cartwright, D. and Zander, A. (eds.) (1953) *Group Dynamics*. London: Tavistock.

De N., Wouter, M., Andrej and Batagelj, V. (2005) *Exploratory Social Network Analysis with Pajek*. Cambridge, UK: Cambridge University Press.

Degenne, A. and Forsé, M. (1994) *Les réseaux sociaux. Une approche structurale en sociologie*. Paris: Armand Colin, 1994. Published in English as *Introducing Social Networks*. London: Sage, 1999.

Emirbayer, M. (1997) 'Manifesto for a relational sociology', *American Journal of Sociology* 103: 281–317.

Emirbayer, M. and Goodwin, J. (1994) 'Network analysis, culture, and the problem of agency', *American Journal of Sociology* 99: 1411–54.

Emirbayer, M. and Mische, A. (1998) 'What is agency?' *American Journal of Sociology* 103: 962–1023.

Fennema, M. (1982) *International Networks of Banks and Industry*. The Hague: Martinus Nijhof.

Fischer, C.S. (1977) *Networks and Places: Social Relations in the Urban Setting*. New York: Free Press.

Frank, O. and Strauss, D. (1986) 'Markov graphs', *Journal of the American Statistical Association* 81(395): 832–42.

Freeman, L.C. (2004) *The Development of Social Network Analysis: A Study in the Sociology of Science.* Vancouver: Empirical Press.

Freeman, L.C., White, D.R. and Romney, A.K. (eds.) (1989) *Research Methods in Social Network Analysis.* New Brunswick, NJ: Transaction.

Granovetter, M. (1973) 'The strength of weak ties', *American Journal of Sociology* 78, 6: 1360–80.

Granovetter, M. (1974) *Getting a Job.* Cambridge, MA: Harvard University Press.

Gronlund, N.E. (1959) *Sociometry in the Classroom.* New York: Harper & Bros.

Harary, F. (1969) *Graph Theory.* Reading, MA: Addison-Wesley.

Harary, F. and Norman, R.Z. (1953) *Graph Theory as a Mathematical Model in Social Science.* Ann Arbor, MI: Institute for Social Research.

Harary, F., Norman, R.Z. and Cartwright, D. (1965) *Structural Models: An Introduction to the Theory of Directed Graphs.* New York: Wiley.

Helmers, H.M., Mokken, R.J.R., Plijter, C. and Stokman, F.N. (1975) *Graven naar Macht. Op Zoek naar de Kern van de Nederlandse Economic.* Amsterdam: Van Gennep.

Homans, G. (1950) *The Human Group.* London: Routledge and Kegan Paul, 1951.

Jennings, H.H. (1948) *Sociometry in Group Relations.* Washington, DC: American Council on Education.

Knoke, D. and Yang, S. (2008) *Network Analysis.* 2nd ed. Beverly Hills, CA: Sage.

Krempel, L. (2005) *Visualisierung komplexer Strukturen.* Frankfurt: Campus Verlag.

Lee, N.H. (1969) *The Search for an Abortionist.* Chicago: University of Chicago Press.

Leinhardt, S. (ed.) (1977) *Social Networks: A Developing Paradigm.* New York: Academic Press.

Lévi-Strauss, C. (1969 [1949]) *The Elementary Structures of Kinship,* ed. Rodney Needham. Rev. ed. Boston: Beacon Press. (Originally published as *Les Structures élémentaires de la Parenté.* Paris: Mouton, 1949.)

Levine, J.H. (1972) 'The sphere of influence', *American Sociological Review* 37: 14–27.

Lewin, K. (1936) *Principles of Topological Psychology.* New York: Harper and Row.

Lin, N. (2001) *Social Capital: A Theory of Social Structure and Action.* New York: Cambridge University Press.

Lin, N., Cook, K.S. and Burt, R.S. (eds.) (2001) *Social Capital: Theory and Research.* New Brunswick, NJ: Transaction.

Lorrain, F.P. and White, H.C. (1971) 'Structural equivalence of individuals in social networks', *Journal of Mathematical Sociology* 1: 49–80.

Lundberg, G.A. and Lawsing, M. (1937) 'The Sociography of Some Community Relations', *American Sociological Review* 2: 318–35.

Lundberg, G. and Steele, M. (1938) 'Social attraction-patterns in a village', *Sociometry* 1: 375–419.

Milgram, S. (1967) 'The small world problem', *Psychology Today* 2: 60–67.

Mische, A. (2003) 'Cross-talk in movements: Rethinking the culture-network link', in M. Diani and D. McAdam (eds.), *Social Movements and Networks: Relational Approaches to Collective Action.* Oxford: Oxford University Press.

Mische, A. (2007) *Partisan Publics: Communication and Contention across Brazilian Youth Activist Networks.* Princeton, NJ: Princeton University Press.

Mitchell, J.C. (1969a) 'The concept and use of social networks', in J. Clyde Mitchell (ed.), *Social Networks in Urban Situations.* Manchester: Manchester University Press.

Mitchell, J. (ed.) (1969b) *Social Networks in Urban Situations.* Manchester: Manchester University Press.

Monge, P.R. and Contractor, N.S. (2003) *Theories of Communication Networks.* Oxford: Oxford University Press.

Moreno, J.L. (1934) *Who Shall Survive?* New York: Beacon Press.

Mullins, N.C. (1973) *Theories and Theory Groups in American Sociology.* New York: Harper and Row.

Nadel, S.F. (1957) *The Theory of Social Structure.* Glencoe, IL: Free Press.

Pattison, P. and Wasserman, S. (1999) 'Logit models and logistic regressions for social networks: II. Multivariate relations', *British Journal of Mathematical and Statistical Psychology* 52: 169–93.

Putnam, R.D. (2000) *Bowling Alone: The Collapse and Revival of American Community.* New York: Simon and Schuster.

Radcliffe-Brown, A.R. (1940) 'On social structure', *The Journal of the Royal Anthropological Institute of Great Britain and Ireland* 70: 1–12.

Radcliffe-Brown, A.R. (1957) *A Natural Science of Society.* Chicago: University of Chicago Press.

Robins, G.L., Pattison, P. and Wasserman, S. (1999) 'Logit models and logistic regressions for social networks: III. Valued relations', *Psychometrika* 64: 371–94.

Roethlisberger, F.J. and Dickson, W.J. (1939) *Management and the Worker.* Cambridge, MA: Harvard University Press.

Scott, J. (1986) *Capitalist Property and Financial Power.* Brighton: Wheatsheaf Books.

Scott, J. (1997) *Corporate Business and Capitalist Classes.* Oxford: Oxford University Press.

Scott, J. (2000) *Social Network Analysis.* 2nd ed. London: Sage.

Scott, J. (2010) 'Social network analysis: Developments, advances, and prospects', *Social Network Analysis and Mining* 1, 1.

Scott, J. and Griff, C. (1984) *Directors of Industry.* Cambridge: Polity Press.

Snijders, T.A.B. (2001) 'The statistical evaluation of social network dynamics', in M.E. Sobel and M.P. Becker (eds.), *Sociological Methodology, 2001.* Oxford: Basil Blackwell.

Snijders, T.A.B. (2005) 'Models for longitudinal network data', in Peter J. Carrington, John Scott, and Stanley Wasserman (eds.), *Models and Methods in Social Network Analysis.* Cambridge: Cambridge University Press.

Snijders, T.A.B. and van Duijn, M.A.J. (1997) 'Simulation for statistical inference in dynamic network models', in R. Conte, R. Hegelmann, and P. Terna (eds.), *Simulating Social Phenomena.* Berlin: Springer.

Stokman, F., Ziegler, R. and Scott, J. (eds.) (1985) *Networks of Corporate Power*. Cambridge: Polity Press.

Sweezy, P.M. (1939) 'Interest groups in the American economy', in National Resources Committee, *The Structure of the American Economy*, Part 1, Appendix 13. Reprinted in Paul M. Sweezy, *The Present as History*. New York: Monthly Review Press, 1953.

Travers, J. and Milgram, S. (1969) 'An experimental study of the small world problem', *Sociometry* 32(4): 425–43.

Warner, W.L. and Lunt, P.S. (1941) *The Social Life of a Modern Community*. New Haven: Yale University Press.

Wasserman, S. and Faust, K. (1994) *Social Network Analysis: Methods and Applications*. New York: Cambridge University Press.

Wasserman, S. and Galaskiewicz, J. (eds.) (1994) *Advances in Social Network Analysis*. Beverly Hills, CA: Sage.

Wasserman, S. and Pattison, P. (1996) 'Logit models and logistic regressions for social networks: I. An introduction to Markov random graphs and p*', *Psychometrika* 60: 401–26.

Watts, D.J. (1999) *Small Worlds: The Dynamics of Networks Between Order and Randomness*. Princeton, NJ: Princeton University Press.

Watts, D.J. (2003) *Six Degrees: The Science of a Connected Age*. New York: W. W. Norton.

Watts, D.J. and Strogatz, S.H. (1998) 'Collective dynamics of "small-world" networks', *Nature* 393: 440–42.

Wellman, B. (1979) 'The community question: The intimate networks of East Yorkers', *American Journal of Sociology* 84: 1201–31.

Wellman, B. and Hogan, B. (2006) 'Connected lives: The project', in J. Purcell (ed.), *Networked Neighbourhoods*. London: Springer-Verlag, 2006.

White, H.C. (1963a) *An Anatomy of Kinship*. Englewood Cliffs, NJ: Prentice-Hall.

White, H.C. (1963b) 'Uses of mathematics in sociology', in James C. Charlesworth (ed.), *Mathematics and the Social Sciences*. Philadelphia, PA: American Academy of Political and Social Science.

White, H.C. (1992) *Identity and Control*. Princeton, NJ: Princeton University Press.

White, H.C., Boorman, S.A. and Breiger, R.L. (1976) 'Social structure from multiple networks I: Blockmodels of roles and positions', *American Journal of Sociology* 81: 730–81.

General Issues

Social Network Analysis: An Introduction

Alexandra Marin and Barry Wellman

Social network analysis takes as its starting point the premise that social life is created primarily and most importantly by relations and the patterns formed by these relations. Social networks are formally defined as a set of nodes (or network members) that are tied by one or more types of relations (Wasserman and Faust, 1994). Because network analysts consider these networks to be the primary building blocks of the social world, they not only collect unique types of data, but they begin their analyses from a fundamentally different perspective than that adopted by researchers drawing on individualist or attribute-based perspectives.

For example, a conventional approach to understanding high-innovation regions such as Silicon Valley would focus on the high levels of education and expertise common in the local labour market. Education and expertise are characteristics of the relevant actors. By contrast, a network analytic approach to understanding the same phenomenon would draw attention to the ways in which mobility between educational institutions and multiple employers has created connections between organizations (Fleming et al., 2011). Thus, people moving from one organization to another bring their ideas, expertise and tacit knowledge with them. They also bring with them the connections they have made to coworkers, some of whom have moved on to new organizations themselves. This pattern of connections between organizations, in which each organization is tied through its employees to multiple other organizations, allows each to draw on diverse sources of knowledge. Since combining previously disconnected ideas is the heart of innovation and a useful problem-solving

strategy (Hargadon and Sutton, 1997), this pattern of connections – not just the human capital of individual actors – leads to accelerating rates of innovation in the sectors and regions where it occurs (Fleming et al., 2011).

In this chapter, we begin by discussing issues involved in defining social networks and then go on to describe three principles implicit in the social network perspective. We explain how these principles set network analysis apart from attribute- or group-based perspectives. In the second section, we summarize the theoretical roots of network analysis and the current state of the field, while in the third section we discuss theoretical approaches to asking and answering questions using a network analytic approach. In the fourth section, we turn our attention to social network methods, which we see as a set of tools for applying the network perspective rather than as the defining feature of network analysis. In our concluding section we argue that social network analysis is best understood as a perspective within the social sciences and not as a method or narrowly defined theory.

WHAT IS A SOCIAL NETWORK?

A social network is a set of socially relevant nodes connected by one or more relations. Nodes, or network members, are the units that are connected by the relations whose patterns we study. These units are most commonly persons or organizations, but in principle any units that can be connected to other units can be studied as nodes.

These include Web pages (Watts, 1999), journal articles (White et al., 2004; White, this volume), countries (Kick et al., this volume), neighbourhoods, departments within organizations (Quan-Haase and Wellman, 2006) or positions (Boorman and White, 1976; White et al., 1976; Ferligoj et al., this volume).

Defining which nodes to include in a network analysis often poses an early challenge. A scholar might wish to analyse medical researchers studying heart disease. However, knowing which individuals to consider as researchers in this field can be tricky, especially because many network analysts avoid group-based approaches to understanding the social world.

Laumann et al. (1983) identify three approaches to addressing this boundary specification problem. First, a position-based approach considers those actors who are members of an organization or hold particular formally defined positions to be network members and all others would be excluded. In the example listed above, network members could be researchers employed in hospital cardiology departments or members of a professional association for cardiologists. Second, an event-based approach to defining the boundaries of the network looks at who had participated in key events believed to define the population. For example, this might include researchers who had attended at least two cardiology conferences in the past three years. Third, a relation-based approach begins with a small set of nodes deemed to be within the population of interest and then expands to include others sharing particular types of relations with those seed nodes as well as with any nodes previously added. For example, a relation-based approach might begin with researchers publishing in a key cardiology journal and include their co-authors and collaborators, and those co-authors' co-authors and collaborators, and so on. This relation-based approach is particularly common in the study of egocentric networks, which we discuss later in this chapter (see also Hanneman and Riddle, this volume and Chua et al., this volume). These three approaches are not mutually exclusive, and studies will commonly use a combination of more than one approach to define network boundaries. For example, a network analyst could study only researchers who work in cardiology departments and attend cardiology conferences.

After researchers have identified network members, they must identify the relations between these nodes. These could include collaborations, friendships, trade ties, Web links, citations, resource flows, information flows, exchanges of social support or any other possible connection between these particular units (Wasserman and Faust, 1994). Borgatti et al. (2009) identify four broad categories of relations: similarities, social relations, interactions and flows.

Similarities occur when two nodes share the kinds of attributes frequently studied in variable-based approaches, such as demographic characteristics, attitudes, locations or group memberships. Group memberships (particularly co-memberships and interlocking memberships) are the only similarities frequently treated as relations by network analysts. For example, network analysts have examined the structure of industries by studying networks created by interlocking directorates (Mizruchi and Stearns, 1988; Mintz and Schwartz, 1985; Carroll and Sapinski, this volume).

Social relations include kinship (White, this volume) or other types of commonly defined role relations (e.g., friend, student); affective ties, which are based on network members' feelings for one another (e.g., liking, disliking); or cognitive awareness (e.g., knowing). These are among the ties most commonly studied by personal community analysts. For example, Killworth et al. (1990) study the network of people 'known' by respondents, and Casciaro et al. (1999) study how affective ties (liking) predict cognitive perceptions of network forms.

Interactions refer to behaviour-based ties such as speaking with, helping, or inviting into one's home. Interactions usually occur in the context of social relations, and interaction-based and affective-based measures are frequently used as proxies for one another. For example, researchers may measure discussion networks as proxies for core support networks (Marsden, 1987; McPherson et al., 2006).

Flows are relations based on exchanges or transfers between nodes. These may include relations in which resources, information or influence flow through networks. Like interactions, flow-based relations often occur within other social relations and researchers frequently assume or study their co-existence. For example, Wellman and Wortley (1990) show how social relation ties such as kinship and friendship affect the exchange of different kinds of support and companionship.

GUIDING PRINCIPLES OF NETWORK ANALYSIS

Taking social relations seriously calls for more than knowing how to measure some characteristics of networks, such as the density of their interconnections. It requires a set of assumptions about how best to describe and explain the social phenomena of interest. Network explanations do not assume that environments, attributes or circumstances affect actors independently. Moreover, they do not assume the existence of uniformly cohesive and discretely bounded groups. Finally, network analysis take context so seriously that relations themselves are often analysed in the context of other relations.

Relations, not attributes

Individuals (and organizations, countries, Web pages, etc.) indisputably possess particular attributes. To study the effects of attributes such as race, gender or education – which are inherently contained within and not between actors – researchers sort individuals based on their attributes and determine which outcomes are disproportionately common to individuals with particular attributes. This endeavour treats causation as something that comes from within individuals, with common attributes acting independently on individuals to produce similar outcomes.

By contrast, social network analysts argue that causation is not located in the individual, but in the social structure. While people with similar attributes may behave similarly, explaining these similarities by pointing to common attributes misses the reality that individuals with common attributes often occupy similar positions in the social structure. That is, people with similar attributes frequently have similar social network positions. Their similar outcomes are caused by the constraints, opportunities and perceptions created by these similar network positions.

By studying behaviour as embedded in social networks, social scientists are able to explain macro-level patterns not simply as a large number of people acting similarly because they are similar, but as a large number of people acting on one another to shape one another's actions in ways that create particular outcomes. For example, researchers using an attribute-based approach might find that tough economic times make Mary, John and Susan each cut back on spending. In each case, Mary, John and Susan are independently – without regard to one another or to other people – acted upon by economic conditions and by attributes such as their net worth, financial savvy or internalised norms of frugality. By contrast, social network analysts would argue that understanding how this happens requires understanding how John's, Mary's and Susan's relationships with each other – and with others – affect their views of the economy, their ideas about reasonable spending and their opportunities to save or to splurge. For example, financial knowledge or advice can come from network members (Chang, 2005), and network-based reference groups shape norms of saving or splurging (Zelizer, 1994). While economic choices may be correlated with attributes, this is because

of network positions. In addition to being a more realistic model of causation, a network-based explanation is better able to explain how feedback loops can cause an epidemic of frugality, infecting even those with secure incomes and contributing further to economic troubles in societies.

Networks, not groups

While researchers using a network analytic approach must be concerned with defining the boundaries of the networks they study, they do not treat network embeddedness as binary and they do not treat nodes as belonging only to sets of mutually exclusive groups. It is too easy an oversimplification for researchers seeking to understand the effects of opportunities and constraints afforded to people in various positions to operationalize these positions by dividing research subjects into discrete groups, such as employees in different departments, residents of different city districts or members of different school clubs. Treating these group memberships as having discretely bounded or mutually exclusive memberships makes invisible the importance of differing levels of group membership, membership in multiple groups and cross-cutting ties between groups.

Studying group membership as having a uniform influence on members only makes sense if membership itself is uniform: if every group member shares the same relation to the group. This is rarely the case. Even when something that would be recognised as a 'group' exists, some members are more or less committed, more or less tied to other group members, more or less identified with the group or more or less recognised by others as co-members of the group. For example, people affiliated with universities are sorted into departments, which could be treated as groups. However, to treat group membership as binary and thus uniform ignores distinctions between full-time, adjunct, cross-appointed, visiting and emeritus faculty, to say nothing of students, staff and alumni. While one might argue that the department qua department has particular interests, the extent to which these interests are shared by department members and the extent to which department members influence one another's understandings of their own interests will vary.

A network approach to studying university departments would look instead at the strength and nature of connections of department members: the proportion of the individual's courses that are taught within a department, the funding and resources that flow from department to faculty member, the frequency of attendance at departmental talks or the frequency of socializing with other members. Examining 'groups' in this way has three advantages. First, it allows researchers to think of individuals as embedded in groups to varying degrees and thus differentially subject to the opportunities, constraints and influences created by group membership. Second, it allows researchers to examine variations in group structure, determining which groups are more or less cohesive, which are clearly bounded and which are more permeable. Such a strategy also allows network analysts to define groups empirically rather than a priori. Third, leaving open the questions of cohesion and boundary strength allows network researchers to move beyond studying clearly identifiable groups to studying sets of people who would be less easily identifiable as groups but who nonetheless structure social relations – such as gatherings of old-timers or newcomers at a wind-surfing beach (Freeman et al., 1989).

Approaches that assume mutually exclusive group memberships preclude the study of patterns of multiple group membership or ties to multiple groups. Yet, multiple group memberships are the basis of social structure, creating bridges between some groups and, just as significantly, not creating bridges between others (Blau, 1994; Breiger, 1974; Feld, 1981). Because people exist at the intersections of groups, memberships in multiple groups interact. They exacerbate or mitigate opportunities, constraints and influences offered by single-group memberships and influence the identities of group members. Thus, neglecting varying levels of overlap between social circles precludes the study of the social processes that knit otherwise atomised individuals into a society (Simmel, 1922 [1955]).

Relations in a relational context

Social network analysts study patterns of relations, not just relations between pairs. This means that while relations are measured as existing between pairs of nodes, understanding the effect and meaning of a tie between two nodes requires taking into account the broader patterns of ties within the network (Barnes, 1972). For example, while individual ties provide social support and companionship, the amount of support provided by one person to another is affected by the extent to which support network members know one another (Wellman and Frank, 2001). The nature of relationships between two people may also vary based on their relations with others. For example, understanding relations of support, jealousy and competition between siblings requires understanding and taking into account the relationship of each child to the parents. Parent-child relationships are similarly affected by the relationship each parent has with the other parent (Wellman

and Frank, 2001). Thus, assuming that each pair acts independently hides network processes that are created by larger patterns in the network. For example, bridging is a structural condition where the tie creates a connection between previously unconnected portions of a network. A relationship between Romeo and Juliet constitutes a bridge between the Capulets and Montagues. To identify the tie as bridging, we must know the network of Verona elites well enough to know that the Capulets and Montagues are otherwise unconnected.

THE ORIGINS AND CURRENT STATE OF SOCIAL NETWORK ANALYSIS

Simmelian roots

The primacy of relations over atomised units is an idea much older than the field that has come to be known as network analysis (see Freeman, this volume). Network theorists have found examples of this idea in the work of influential thinkers from Heraclitus to Einstein, and in the work of such giants of sociological theory as Marx, Durkheim, Weber, Goffman and even Parsons (Emirbayer, 1997) – a theorist often associated with the norm-based approach with which network analysis is frequently contrasted (Granovetter, 1985; Wellman, 1988). The primacy of relations is most explicit in the work of Georg Simmel, whose theoretical writings inspired and anticipated major empirical findings in network analysis. Simmel clearly articulates the premise that social ties are primary. Instead of viewing things as isolated units, they are better understood as being at the intersections of particular relations and as deriving their defining characteristics from the intersections of these relations. He argues that society itself is nothing more than a web of relations. There is no 'society' without interactions:

> The significance of these interactions among men lies in the fact that it is because of them that the individuals, in whom these driving impulses and purposes are lodged, form a unity, that is, a society. For unity in the empirical sense of the word is nothing but the interaction of elements. An organic body is a unity because its organs maintain a more intimate exchange of their energies with each other than with any other organism; a state is a unity because its citizens show similar mutual effects. (Simmel, 1908 [1971]: 23)

Here, Simmel argues against understanding society as a mass of individuals who each react independently to circumstances based on their individual tastes, proclivities and beliefs and who create new circumstances only by the simple aggregation of their actions. He argues we should focus instead on the emergent consequences of the interactions of individual actions:

> A collection of human beings does not become a society because each of them has an objectively determined or subjectively impelling life-content. It becomes a society only when the vitality of these contents attains the form of reciprocal influence; only when one individual has an effect, immediate or mediate, upon another, is mere spatial aggregation or temporal succession transformed into society. (Simmel, 1908 [1971]: 24–25)

Based on his belief that the social world is found in interactions rather than in an aggregation of individuals, Simmel argued that the primary work of sociologists is to study patterns among these interactions – which he called forms – rather than to study the individual motives, emotions, thoughts, feelings and beliefs – which he called content. Similar forms can exist and function similarly in diverse content areas, and different forms can emerge within any single content area. Therefore, Simmel argued, sociologists' study of form and content must remain separate. Only by studying similar forms across diverse contents can people truly understand how these forms function as forms and separate the effects of forms from the effects of contents. While a similar argument holds for the study of contents – they can be fully understood only by studying their manifestations in diverse forms – Simmel argued that the sociologist's role is to focus on form because only forms are 'purely social', unlike contents, which frequently exist as individual-level characteristics (Simmel, 1908 [1971]).

Although Simmel developed theories of many types of forms and the consequences of various forms across contents, he did not formalize his theories mathematically as many network analysts do today. However, he did recognize the inherently mathematical logic of his theories. He used geometric metaphors in his writing, and he compared the study of forms to geometricians' ability to analyse pure forms apart from their real-world manifestations (Simmel, 1908 [1971]: 24–25). His influence is apparent in much subsequent network analytic work, such as formalistic 'blockmodelling' described below (White et al., 1976; Boorman and White, 1976; Ferligoj et al., this volume) and Burt's substantive analysis (1992, 2005) of how individuals benefit by knowing two people unknown to each other.

Current state: association, grants and journals

Today, social network analysis has become an interdisciplinary area of study, with its own professional association, annual conference and multiple journals. The International Network for Social Network Analysts (INSNA), founded by Barry Wellman in 1977, has grown from 175 founding members to more than 1,300 members as of February 2011. While sociologists form a plurality of members, the network also includes researchers from anthropology, communications, computer science, education, economics, management science, medicine, political science, public health, psychology and other disciplines. INSNA's annual conference, the International Sunbelt Social Network Conference, attracts more than 500 people each year, to sites rotating in a three-year cycle between the east and west coasts of North America and Europe.

Social network analysis is a thriving research area. Between 1998 and 2007, network-based projects accounted for the fourth largest share of grants dispensed by the Social Science Research Council of Canada, and it was the area receiving the largest per-project grants (Klassen, 2008). Research applying a social network perspective appears in major generalist social science journals such as the *American Journal of Sociology*, *American Sociological Review*, *Social Forces*, *Human Organization* and *Administrative Science Quarterly*, as well as specialised journals, such as *City and Community*, *Work and Occupations* and *Information, Communication and Society*. Three peer-reviewed journals publish social network research exclusively: *Social Networks* (INSNA's flagship journal), *Connections* (an INSNA journal publishing short, timely papers) and the *Journal of Social Structure*, published online.

APPLYING A NETWORK PERSPECTIVE

We have shown thus far that network analysts take patterns of relations between nodes as the primary units for sociological theorizing and research. In this section we describe the ways in which network analysts use this perspective to develop theory, including those analysts who focus exclusively on patterns of relations themselves and those who seek to address substantive issues.

Formalist theories

Formalist theories are primarily concerned with the mathematical form of social networks (see Scott, this volume). These theories study the effects of forms, insofar as they are effects on the form itself, and the causes of these forms, insofar as they are structural. For example, when networks are composed of clusters of densely connected nodes with many ties within clusters and just a small number of ties between clusters, the result is a network in which short paths are available between most pairs of nodes (Watts, 1999).

Because these theories are concerned primarily with pure form – in the mathematical, platonic sense – of networks, they can be studied without the need for empirical data. Mathematical modelling and computer simulations can create networks that allow researchers to observe unfolding patterns of relations that result from particular rules of tie formation or dissolution. For example, Barabási and Albert (1999) simulated networks that were continually joined by new nodes. As nodes joined, they formed ties to existing nodes, particularly to already-popular existing nodes. Based on these simulations, Barabási and Albert showed that this form of preferential attachment creates a Matthew Effect ('For to everyone who has, more will be given', Matthew 25:29; see also Merton, 1968), magnifying popularity gaps and creating networks with power-law distributions. That is, this process of tie formation creates networks where a small number of nodes have huge numbers of ties, while the vast majority of nodes have only a few.

Recently, formalist-based research has received popular exposure in trade books such as *Six Degrees* (Watts, 2003), *Linked* (Barabási, 2002) and *Nexus* (Buchanan, 2002), partly because the approach has interesting real-world applications. For example, the concept of preferential attachment is based on the empirical reality that people meet people through other people. The more people you know, the more people can introduce you to others. Small-world networks also resonate well with the public imagination. The most well-known example of a small-world network is a network formed by co-appearances in movies and television shows. This is a clustered network with clusters created both by career timing (Rudolph Valentino and Dakota Fanning are unlikely to have ever been co-stars), and by actors' specialization within genres. For example, there is a cluster of actors who frequently co-star in romantic comedies: Jennifer Aniston, Hugh Grant, Meg Ryan, Tom Hanks and Julia Roberts. Yet, genre-based clusters are interconnected thanks to genre-hopping actors. For example, Tom Hanks links actors appearing in romantic comedies to those appearing in children's films (*Toy Story*, *Polar Express*), dramas (*Philadelphia*), comedies (*Turner and Hooch*) and film adaptations of pulp fiction conspiracy theories (*The Da Vinci Code*, *Angels and Demons*).

Genre-crossing actors, such as Tom Hanks, Kevin Bacon and many lesser-known genre crossers, make possible the well-known game 'Six Degrees of Kevin Bacon'. While identifying the shortest path to Kevin Bacon may be a challenge (Watts et al., 2002), a path no longer than four degrees exists for the large majority of those appearing on television and in film (Watts, 1999).

Structuralist theories

Structuralist theories are concerned with how patterns of relations can shed light on substantive topics within their disciplines. Structuralists study such diverse subjects as health (Lin and Ensel, 1989; Pescosolido, 1992; Cohen S. et al., 1997, 2001), work (Burt, 1992; Podolny and Baron, 1997; Ibarra, 1993) and community (Fischer, 1982a; Wellman and Wortley, 1990). Structuralists take at least four different approaches to applying the mantra that relations matter.

Defining key concepts in network terms
One approach to applying a network perspective to a substantive area is to take a key concept within that area and define it in network terms. Researchers adopting this approach examine how new understandings of the key concept reframe longstanding debates and call widely accepted findings into doubt. For example, Wellman argued that communities are not geographic areas providing support and services, but are people providing support and services to those to whom they are connected. By thinking of communities as 'personal', meaning that a person's community uniquely consists of the people to whom he is connected, Wellman transformed understandings of how modernity and urban living affect interaction and support (Wellman, 1979; Wellman and Wortley, 1990). This work set the agenda for debates that would follow about how social support networks are changing (Fischer, 1982a; Grossetti, 2005; Hennig, 2007), and how new technology affects communities (Wellman et al., 2006; Boase and Wellman, 2006; Hampton, 2007; Stern, 2008; also see Chua et al., this volume).

Testing an existing theory
Researchers may start from an existing sociological theory. By thinking of relation-based understandings of the theory and testing the resulting hypotheses, these researchers apply a network approach to a theory that may previously have been studied using attribute- or group-based approaches. For example, Wilson's (1978, 1987)

theory of the underclass suggests that as poor African Americans have come increasingly to live in high-poverty neighbourhoods, they have lost connections to people who provide ties to the labour market. Their social isolation contributes to difficulties in finding work, and it hinders social mobility.

Although Wilson's argument speaks of network connections, the evidence presented is still group-based, treating neighbourhoods as monoliths that are connected – or not connected – to the labour market by virtue of the neighbourhood's class composition. Further, by focussing on within-neighbourhood ties, the theory neglects the possibility of out-group ties providing connections to the labour market. However, the story may be more complex. Fernandez and Harris (1992) find that the urban poor do have out-group ties to people committed to labour market participation, while Smith (2005) further finds that what the African American urban poor lack are ties to people in the labour market who are willing to offer assistance in finding jobs. By looking at real patterns of relations rather than assuming a lack of relations based on a perceived lack of opportunity, such research creates a stronger link between theory and data. The original theory – like many social theories that are studied nonetheless from attribute-based or group-based perspectives – is about patterns of relations. Therefore, the theory can be more validly tested using data on relations than data on neighbourhood characteristics.

Looking at network causes of phenomena of interest

Researchers taking this approach ask what kinds of social networks lead to particular outcomes. These outcomes may include finding a job (Granovetter, 1973, 1974) or promotion (Burt, 1997, 1998; Podolny and Baron, 1997; Ibarra, 1997), catching a cold (Cohen et al., 1997, 2001), having a good idea (Burt, 2004), being sexy (Martin, 2005) or knowing about different kinds of culture (Erickson, 1996).

Network-based explanations of substantive outcomes are fundamentally different from explanations that rely on individual-level or group attributes. Social network analysts often have little tolerance for norm-based explanations, norms being precisely the kind of content that Simmel argued was outside the domain of social explanations. Moreover, when causal forces are presumed to be internal or possessed by individuals, the mechanisms frequently are internalised norms or atomised rational actors (Granovetter, 1985). Social network analysts argue that internalised norms are inherently asocial mechanisms.

Therefore, treating such norms as the primary causal mechanism provides asocial or psychological explanations. Rational-actor approaches similarly locate causality within individuals, in this case in an internal process of reason and calculation. Thus, when social network analysts study norms, they are usually not treated as static and internalised but as memes created in response to network positions or that diffuse through social networks (see accounts of adaptation and transmission, below).

At times, social network-based theories do assume some rationality. However, taking social network positions into account tempers this rationality so it is no longer the dominant causal force. Instead, social network analysts argue that differences in available opportunities mean that uniformly rational actors will make different choices and will experience different consequences even when they make the same choices. Moreover, network positions create obligations and commitments that alter the calculus of rationality by promoting trustworthiness and relieving people of the fear that their interaction partners will always be strictly and ruthlessly rational (Granovetter, 1985; Uzzi, 1996).

Researchers using network structure to explain substantive outcomes frequently combine network-based data with more standard kinds of statistical analyses. By taking networks as the units of analysis, researchers can use statistical methods to determine if more densely interconnected networks provide more support than similarly sized but more sparsely connected networks (Wellman and Frank, 2001). By taking network positions as the units of analysis, they can ask if people who are in bridges are more likely to be promoted (Burt, 2005). This combined approach is especially common among researchers studying the networks surrounding individual people (see ego networks, below). By sampling unconnected individuals and collecting data about their social networks, researchers can essentially sample networks and network positions. Ego network data for N randomly selected people are essentially data on N randomly selected networks, one ego network for each respondent. The same data could be treated as data on N randomly selected network positions, using each respondent's position as a unit of analysis (e.g. Wellman, 1979; Fischer, 1982a; Marsden, 1987; McPherson et al., 2006).

Looking at network effects of phenomena of interest

Finally, in addition to studying the effects of particular network properties and positions, social network analysts study the causes of networks

and positions. For example, McPherson and Smith-Lovin (1987) draw from theories of how foci of social interaction shape social networks (Feld, 1981) to argue that participation in demographically segregated voluntary associations causes friendship networks to be filled with demographically similar people. Hampton and Wellman (2003) find that within-neighbourhood relations are more likely to form between neighbours who have access to electronic means of communicating with each other. Like researchers studying the effects of network structures, researchers taking this approach also frequently combine network-based data with statistical approaches, taking positions or networks as their units of analysis.

NETWORK EXPLANATIONS

In this section, we show the mechanisms by which network analysts argue that particular kinds of networks or network positions can cause particular outcomes. We follow Borgatti et al.'s (2009) classification of network arguments into four categories: transmission, adaptation, binding and exclusion (see Borgatti, this volume).

Transmission

Network-based theories frequently treat network ties as pipelines through which many things flow: information about jobs (Granovetter, 1973, 1974), social support (Wellman and Wortley, 1990), norms (Coleman, 1988), workplace identities (Podolny and Baron, 1997), disease (Morris, 1993), immunity to disease (S. Cohen et al., 1997, 2001), material aid (Stack, 1974) or knowledge of culture (Erickson, 1996). Researchers taking this approach study the kinds of networks that result in the most widespread distribution, the network positions most likely to receive flows, and the ways in which different network structures create different patterns of flow under different circumstances. For example, networks leading to people who are neither connected to one another nor connected to the same others provide the best access to new, nonredundant information and ideas (Burt, 1992, 2004, 2005; Hargadon and Sutton, 1997; Granovetter, 1973). On the other hand, networks leading to people who are connected directly to one another transmit consistent expectations and clear norms (Coser, 1975; Coleman, 1988; Podolny and Baron, 1997).

The effects of network structure on the ways in which resources flow through networks may not always be uniform. For example, Bian (1997) finds that where institutional factors make the exercise of influence risky, job opportunities are more likely to flow through strong ties. Gibson (2005a) uses computer simulations to show that having a small number of highly connected nodes can slow the early stages of diffusion when compared to random networks. However, once central actors have been infected, diffusion rates are comparable.

Adaptation

Adaptation occurs when two people make the same choices because they have similar network positions and are thus exposed to similar constraints and opportunities. For example, California winemakers make wines from grapes sourced primarily in one region, allowing them to market their wines as Sonoma County or Napa Valley wines. While blending grapes from different sources may create higher-quality wines, losing place-based appellations would lower the status associated with the wine and cause wine drinkers to react similarly – by drinking something else. Therefore, winemakers are not making decisions about how to blend their wines because they are transmitting knowledge of winemaking to one another but because they are responding to similar network constraints. Maintaining ties to customers requires that they maintain ties with viticultural regions (Podolny, 2005).

Binding

Binding occurs when a network binds together to act as one unit. The actions or outcomes of that action are influenced by the internal structure of the network. For example, Granovetter (1973) argues that communities fighting urban renewal in their neighbourhoods are better able to organize their resistance when their internal networks are less fragmented. When community networks are internally disconnected, information cannot diffuse fully through the network and trust in leaders that is facilitated by indirect connections may never develop. With an internally fragmented structure, the community is less effective, less coordinated and more easily defeated in its attempts at collective action than a community with a more integrated network.

Exclusion

Exclusion occurs when the presence of one tie precludes the existence of another tie, which in turn affects the excluded node's relations with

other nodes. This mechanism is most visible in markets or exchange networks where the availability of alternative partners improves a node's bargaining power. A manufacturing firm with two potential suppliers can negotiate a good price by creating competition between them. When one of those suppliers enters an exclusive contract with another manufacturer, this not only prevents our protagonist firm from buying from that supplier but it also greatly increases the remaining supplier's power to name its own price. Similarly, a person with two potential romantic partners loses access to a potential partner who marries someone else. In addition, this person loses bargaining power with the remaining love interest due to the absence of (immediately visible) alternatives.

STUDYING AND OPERATIONALIZING NETWORKS

Although social network analysis is more than a set of algorithms and methods, analysts have developed unique ways of measuring concepts and analysing relation-based data. These methods have been developed because the key premise of network analysis – that relations are primary – makes it difficult to rely only on analytic tools that treat atomised individuals as primary.

Operationalizing concepts relationally

Studying substantive phenomena from a network perspective requires that at least one theoretically significant concept be defined relationally. This redefinition, together with an examination of its implications, can in itself become a seminal piece of research. However, even where the network definition of a concept is not the primary focus of a project, thinking about how networks cause particular outcomes or what kinds of networks are caused by different forces requires that we map sociological concepts onto particular network forms. For example, we study network density because it is a mathematical expression of concepts such as cohesion, solidarity or constraint, each of which is associated with social processes likely to have particular effects. For example, cohesion and solidarity create identity (Podolny and Baron, 1997) and reinforce norms (Coleman, 1988; Podolny and Baron, 1997). Constraint (Burt, 1992) is a more negative framing of reinforced norms. We study structural equivalence because it is a mathematical expression of the concept of the role (White et al., 1976; Boorman and White, 1976; Ferligoj et al., this volume), and therefore

we expect that those who are structurally equivalent will be subject to similar pressures and opportunities.

Similarly, when we study the effects of phenomena on networks, the results are sociologically significant only insofar as the network measures being affected are sociologically significant. If something causes a network to be fractured such that there is no path between pairs of nodes, the fracture matters only because of the social effects it will have. These consequences might include bringing the Internet to its knees (R. Cohen et al., 2000, 2001) or preventing the widespread transmission of sexually transmitted diseases among teenagers (Bearman et al., 2004). Even a measure as basic as the number of ties that a particular node has is primarily significant for its social implication: a high level of network activity (Freeman, 1979).

COLLECTING NETWORK DATA

Researchers collecting network data must first decide what kinds of networks and what kinds of relations they will study. While there are many kinds of network data, we discuss here only two important dimensions along which network data vary: whole versus ego networks, and one-mode versus two-mode networks. Researchers must make these choices even before they can begin to think about the boundary specification problem discussed above.

Whole networks versus ego networks

Whole networks take a bird's-eye view of social structure, focussing on all nodes rather than privileging the network surrounding any particular node (see Hanneman and Riddle, this volume). These networks begin from a list of included nodes and include data on the presence or absence of relations between every pair of nodes. Two well-known examples are a network where nodes consist of all workers in a factory, showing who plays games with whom (Roethlisberger and Dickson, 1939) and a network of actors appearing on film or television, showing who has co-starred with whom (Watts, 1999).

Researchers using whole network data frequently analyse more than one relation, sometimes collapsing relations into a single network such as workplace networks or support networks (Burt, 1992) and sometimes examining how different relations are used to different effect. For example, Padgett and Ansell (1993) collected data on eight types of relations among elite Florentine families in the fifteenth century to show how the Medici used economic ties to secure political support from geographically neighbouring families, but used marriage and friendship ties with more distant families to build and maintain the family's status.

Egocentric network data focus on the network surrounding one node, known as the ego (see Hanneman and Riddle, this volume). Data are on nodes that share the chosen relation(s) with the ego and on relations between those nodes. Although these networks could extend to the second-order ego network, or nodes sharing relations with nodes related to the ego (e.g., friends of friends), in practice, first-order ego networks are the most commonly studied (e.g., Wellman, 1979; Marsden, 1987; Fischer, 1982a; Campbell and Lee, 1992).

Ego network data can be extracted from whole network data by choosing a focal node and examining only nodes connected to this ego. For example, Burt's (1992, 2005) studies of the effects of network constraint are often based on whole network data, though his measure of constraint is egocentric, calculated by treating each node in the whole network as a temporary ego.

Like whole network data, ego network data can also include multiple relations. These relations can be collapsed into single networks, as when ties to people who provide companionship and emotional aid are collapsed into a single support network (Fischer, 1982; Wellman, 1979). Or each relation can be treated as creating its own network: for example, to examine how the kin content of the networks providing material aid differs from the kin content of socializing networks (Wellman and Wortley, 1990). Unlike whole network analyses, which commonly focus on one or a small number of networks, ego network analyses typically sample large numbers of egos and their networks. Typically, these ego networks are treated as the units of analysis using standard statistical methods. In another approach, alters (members of each ego's network) are treated as the units of analysis, using multilevel methods to take into account dependence created by being tied to common egos (Wellman and Frank, 2001; Snijders and Bosker, 1999).

One-mode data versus two-mode data

Researchers studying whole networks most frequently collect data on a single type of node in networks where every node could conceivably be connected to any other node. Most of the networks they analyse are one-mode networks. However, some research problems, particularly those concerned with group memberships, require the collection and analyses of two kinds of nodes – typically organizations and organization members, or events and attendees. In these two-mode networks or affiliation networks, relations consist of things such as memberships or attendance at events that cannot exist between nodes of the same type: a person can attend an event or belong to an organization, but a person cannot attend or belong to another person and an event cannot attend another event (see Borgatti and Halgin, this volume).

One-mode network data can be derived from two-mode network data by extracting relations that consist of co-membership/co-attendance or relations based on having members of attendees in common (Breiger, 1974). For example, the network of actors who have appeared in movies together (Watts, 1999) is a one-mode network, in which nodes are actors and actors are connected to one another if they have both appeared in a movie or television show together. However, this one-mode network is derived from the analysis of a two-mode network in which one mode consists of actors and the second mode consists of movies and television shows.

Types of ties

Once network types have been chosen and theoretically relevant relations have been identified, researchers must decide how to measure their chosen relations. Relations can be measured as directed or undirected and as binary or valued. Directed ties are those that go from one node to another, while undirected ties exist between two nodes in no particular direction. Advice seeking, information sharing, visiting at home and lending money are directed ties while co-memberships are examples of undirected ties. Directed ties may be reciprocated, as would be the case for two people who visit one another or they may exist in only one direction, as when only one gives emotional support to the other (Plickert et al., 2007). Some kinds of directed ties preclude the possibility of reciprocity: for example, two military officers cannot have command relationships over one another.

Both directed and undirected ties can be measured as binary ties that either exist or do not exist within each dyad, or as valued ties that can be stronger or weaker, transmit more or fewer resources, or have more or less frequent contact. For example, a friendship network can be represented by binary ties that indicate if two people are friends or by valued ties that assign higher or lower scores based on how close people feel to one another, or how often they interact.

As these examples suggest, decisions about whether to measure ties as directed or undirected or as valued or unvalued are sometimes dictated by the theoretical nature of the tie: a co-membership is inherently undirected and authority is inherently directed. However, for many types of ties, decisions to treat ties as directed or undirected, or binary or valued, are pragmatic choices based on available data, expected methods of analyses and the expected theoretical pay-off.

Survey and interview methods

Network data can be collected through observation (Gibson, 2005b), from archives and historical materials (Gould, 1995; Padgett and Ansell, 1993) or from trace observation of electronic communications (Carley, 2006). We discuss survey and interview methods here because collecting social network data from network members directly through surveys and interviews involves challenges unique to social network data (see Marsden, this volume).

Surveys and interviews collecting social network data ask respondents to report with whom they share particular relations. Collecting whole network data can be done by presenting respondents with a list of network members and asking them to indicate the people with whom they share ties. When networks are too large to make a full list feasible or where no complete list is available, respondents are asked to make a list by recalling the people with whom they share the relevant relation. Follow-up questions may ask respondents to rank the importance or strength of their relation to different network members, to choose their most important relations or to provide more detail about their relations. Because whole-network researchers will also be collecting data directly from other network members, respondents need not report on characteristics of their alters or on relations between the people with whom they share relations.

Ego network data are most commonly collected using name generators: survey questions that ask respondents to list the people with whom they share a particular relation (Marsden, 1987, 2005; Burt, 1984; Hogan et al., 2007). Because these alters will not be surveyed directly, respondents must report any characteristics of the relationship or characteristics of the alters that are of interest to researchers. Additional data collected from respondents can include information about ties between network members.

These surveys or interviews can be difficult and burdensome for both respondents and researchers. Ego-network surveys especially – with their repetitive questions about each alter – can be long and boring. In addition, providing the information requested by researchers is difficult. People interpret relations in different ways (Fischer, 1982b; Bailey and Marsden, 1999; Bearman and Parigi, 2004): they forget people with whom they share relations (Brewer, 2000; Brewer and Webster, 1999; Bernard and Killworth, 1977; Killworth and Bernard, 1976; Marin, 2004), they misapprehend relations between their alters

(Freeman, 1992), and they may not know their alters' characteristics (Chen, 1999).

Designing surveys and interviews to collect network data presents related issues. Surveys require complicated patterns of skips and loops, with questions not only being asked or skipped based on previous answers, but questions also being created by incorporating previous responses. Given these challenges, computer-assisted interviewing and computer-based surveying are common (e.g., Hampton, 1999; Marin, 2004; Manfreda et al., 2004). However, continued innovation in survey and interview design using non-computer-based methods of working around these difficulties shows that the analog interview is not dead yet (Hogan et al., 2007).

When researchers are interested in specific properties of social networks that can be measured without knowing the full structure of the network, they sometimes use data collection methods that collect only relevant data. For example, researchers interested in the diversity of the social status of acquaintances (Lin, 1986; Lin and Erickson, 2008; Erickson, this volume), the size of social networks (Killworth et al., 1990), and resource availability within networks (van der Gaag and Snijders, 2005) have developed specialised measures of data collection.

Analysing network data

Once network data have been collected, social network analysts use these data to calculate measures of the properties of network positions, dyads and networks as a whole. Properties of network positions include things such as the number of relations a node has and the extent to which the node is a bridge between other nodes (Freeman, 1979). Dyads can vary in the strength or reciprocity of their ties, the similarity of the two nodes (homophily), their content, the number of relation types shared (multiplexity) or the number of communication media used (media multiplexity).

When studying properties of networks as a whole, researchers can look at such things as the proportion of dyads connected to one another (density), the average path length necessary to connect pairs of nodes, the average tie strength, the extent to which the network is dominated by one central actor (centralization [Freeman, 1979]) or the extent to which the network is composed of similar nodes (homogeneity) or of nodes with particular characteristics (composition), such as the proportion of network members who are women.

In addition, networks can be studied by the ways that they can be divided into subgraphs. For example, networks may consist of multiple components: sets of nodes that are tied directly or indirectly to one another but are not tied directly to nodes in other components. They may also include cliques, in which every node is tied directly to every other node.

Because social network analysts do not take individuals as their units of analysis, quantitative analysis packages designed for individual- or attribute-based analyses are frequently either unsuitable or intolerably clunky for relation-based analyses. In response to this problem, social network analysts have developed a number of software applications to analyse social network data (see van Duijn and Huisman, this volume). The most commonly used are Pajek (Batagelj and Mrvar, 2007; Nooy et al., 2005), UCINet (Borgatti et al., 2002), MultiNet (Richards and Seary, 2006), SIENA (Snijders, 2001), P*/ERGM (Snijders et al., 2006), R (R Development Core Team, 2007; Butts, 2008) ORA (Carley and DeReno, 2006) and Node XL (Smith and the Node XL Development Team, 2009). These packages are designed primarily for studying whole network data. While ego network data can be analysed using network-specific software packages or standard statistical packages such as SAS, SPSS or Stata (Müller et al., 1999), UCINet also includes functions to calculate ego network measures from whole network data.

Applying the network perspective using qualitative methods

Qualitative as well as quantitative modes of research have been used since the outset of social network analysis (see Hollstein, this volume). Indeed, the earliest social network analyses were qualitative, such as Barnes's study of Norwegian fishing crews (1954), in which he invented the term 'social network'; Bott's (1957) demonstration that kinship networks trumped social class in explaining English women's domestic behaviour; and Mitchell's (1969) analysis of South African migrants.

More recently, Stack, in her ethnography of poor families in a Midwestern city in the United States (1974), defined families relationally as 'an organized, durable network of kin and non-kin who interact daily, providing the domestic needs of children and assuring their survival' (p. 31). By defining families based on interactions and exchanges rather than on kin groups or households – two group-based definitions – her research showed the importance of ties across kin groups and households and the ways in which the strength of membership within families varied, with men frequently being less permanently tied than women. It also showed both the fluidity of family memberships – with people sometimes moving between families – and the overlapping nature of families, with people belonging to more than one family group.

Ethnographers and qualitative interviewers continue to inform their work with network perspectives. For example, Menjívar (2000) uses interviews with Salvadoran immigrants in San Francisco to show how network relations are strained and severed when economic conditions and positions preclude meeting obligations of reciprocity. Domínguez and Maya-Jariego (2008) use ethnographic and interview data to demonstrate that networks connecting immigrants and natives of the host country spread culture in both directions, both assimilating immigrants and causing non-immigrants to adopt aspects of the immigrant culture. In a different vein, Tilly's (1984) lifelong corpus of historical analysis emphasised that contentious politics and social movements drew heavily from the relations among participants.

CONCLUSIONS

Social network analysis is neither a theory nor a methodology. Rather, it is a perspective or a paradigm. It takes as its starting point the premise that social life is created primarily and most importantly by relations and the patterns they form. Unlike a theory, social network analysis provides a way of looking at a problem, but it does not predict what we will see. Social network analysis does not provide a set of premises from which hypotheses or predictions can be derived. The primacy of relations over atomised units has no immediately identifiable specific implications for when inequality will rise or fall, how organizations can ensure success, or who is likely to live a long and healthy life. Taken alone, network analysis can offer only vague answers to these questions: relations within and between classes should matter, relations between organizations should matter and health-related and health-influencing relations will matter. Yet these answers serve a function: while they do not tell social scientists the answers to these questions, they provide guidance on where to look for such answers.

ACKNOWLEDGEMENTS

We thank Julie Bowring, Jessica Collins, Robert Di Pede, Sherri Klassen and Paromita Sanyal for their comments on this chapter, and Julia Chae, Stephen Di Pede, Christine Ensslen, Sinye Tang, Yu Janice Zhang and Natalie Zinko for editorial assistance.

REFERENCES

Bailey, S. and Marsden, P.V. (1999) 'Interpretation and interview context', *Social Networks* 21: 287–309.

Barabási, A.-L. and Albert, R. (1999) 'Emergence of scaling in random networks', *Science* 286(5439): 509–12.

Barabási, A.-L. (2002) *Linked: The New Science of Networks*. Cambridge, MA: Perseus.

Barnes, J.A. (1954) 'Class and committees in a Norwegian island parish', *Human Relations* 7: 39–58.

Barnes, J.A. (1972) *Social Networks*. Reading, MA: Addison-Wesley.

Batagelj, V. and Mrvar, A. (2007) 'Pajek: package for large network analysis', University of Ljubljana, Slovenia. http://vlado.fmf.uni-lj.si/pub/networks/pajek/.

Bearman, P.S., Moody, J. and Stovel, K. (2004) 'Chains of affection', *American Journal of Sociology* 110: 44–91.

Bearman, P.S. and Parigi, P. (2004) 'Cloning headless frogs and other important matters: Conversation topics and network structure', *Social Forces* 83(2): 535–57.

Bernard, H.R. and Killworth, P. (1977) 'Informant accuracy in social network data II', *Human Communication Research* 4: 3–18.

Bian, Y. (1997) 'Bringing strong ties back in', *American Sociological Review* 62(3): 366–85.

Blau, P.M. (1994) *Structural Context of Opportunities*. Chicago: University of Chicago Press.

Boase, J. and Wellman, B. (2006) 'Personal relationships: On and off the Internet', in Anita V. and Dan P. (eds.), *Cambridge Handbook of Personal Relationships*. Cambridge: Cambridge University Press. pp. 709–23.

Boorman, S. and White, H. (1976) 'Social structure from multiple networks II: Role structures', *American Journal of Sociology* 81: 1384–446.

Borgatti, S., Everett, M. and Freeman, L. (2002) UCINet 6.0 for Windows. MA: Analytic Technologies. http://www.analytictech.com/.

Borgatti, S., Mehra, A., Brass, D. and Labianca, G. (2009) 'Network analysis in the social sciences', *Science* 323(5916): 892–95.

Bott, E. (1957) *Family and Social Network*. London: Tavistock.

Breiger, R. (1974) 'The duality of persons and groups', *Social Forces* 53: 181–90.

Brewer, D. (2000) 'Forgetting in the recall-based elicitation of personal and social networks', *Social Networks* 22: 29–43.

Brewer, D. and Webster, C. (1999) 'Forgetting of friends and its effects on measuring friendship networks', *Social Networks* 21: 361–73.

Buchanan, M. (2002) *Nexus: Small Worlds and the Groundbreaking Theory of Networks*. New York: W. W. Norton.

Burt, R. (1984) 'Network items and the General Social Survey', *Social Networks*, 6: 293–339.

Burt, R. (1992) *Structural Holes*. Cambridge, MA: Harvard University Press.

Burt, R. (1997) 'The contingent value of social capital', *Administrative Science Quarterly* 42: 339–65.

Burt, R. (1998) 'The gender of social capital', *Rationality and Society* 10: 5–46.

Burt, R. (2004) 'Structural holes and good ideas', *American Journal of Sociology* 110(2): 349–99.

Burt, R. (2005) *Brokerage and Closure: An Introduction to Social Capital*. Oxford: Oxford University Press.

Butts, C. (2008) 'Network: A package for managing relational data in R', *Journal of Statistical Software* 24(2).

Campbell, K. and Lee, B. (1992) 'Sources of personal neighbor networks: Social integration, need, or time?' *Social Forces* 70(4): 1077–100.

Carley, K.M. (2006) 'A dynamic network approach to the assessment of terrorist groups and the impact of alternative courses of action', in *Visualising Network Information* Meeting Proceedings RTO-MP-IST-063, Keynote 1. Neuilly-sur-Seine, France. pp. KN1–1—KN1–10.

Carley, K.M. and DeReno, M. (2006). ORA: Organization Risk Analyzer, ORA User's Guide. Carnegie Mellon University, School of Computer Science, Institute for Software Research, Technical Report, CMU-ISRI-06-113.

Casciaro, T., Carley, K.M. and Krackhardt, D. (1999) 'Positive affectivity and accuracy in social network perception', *Motivation and Emotion* 23: 285–306.

Chang, M.L. (2005) 'With a little help from my friends (and my financial planner)', *Social Forces* 83(4): 1469–97.

Chen, K.K. (1999) 'The networks methodology of proxy-reporting: How well do respondents proxy-report different kinds of information on others, and how do respondents err in making these proxy-reports?' Qualifying paper, Department of Sociology, Harvard University, Cambridge, MA.

Cohen, R., Erez, K., ben-Avraham, D. and Havlin, S. (2000) 'Resilience of the Internet to random breakdowns', *Physical Review of Letters* 85: 4626–28.

Cohen, R., Erez, K., ben-Avraham, D. and Havlin, S. (2001) 'Breakdown of the Internet under intentional attack', *Physical Review of Letters* 86: 3682–85.

Cohen, S., Brissette, I., Skoner, D.P. and Doyle, W.J. (2001) 'Social integration and health: The case of the common cold', *Journal of Social Structure*, http://www.library.cmu.edu:7850/JoSS/cohen/cohen.html.

Cohen, S., Doyle, W.J., Skoner, D.P., Rabin, B.S. and Gwaltney, J.M. (1997) 'Social ties and susceptibility to the common cold', *Journal of the American Medical Association* 277: 1940–44.

Coleman, J.S. (1988) 'Social capital in the creation of human capital', *American Journal of Sociology* 94: S95–S120.

Coser, R.L. (1975) 'The complexity of roles as a seedbed of individual autonomy', in *The Idea of Social Structure: Papers in Honor of Robert K. Merton*. New York: Harcourt Brace Jovanovich.

Domínguez, S. and Maya-Jariego, I. (2008) 'Acculturation of host individuals: Immigrants and personal networks', *American Journal of Community Psychology* 42: 309–27.

Emirbayer, M. (1997) 'Manifesto for a relational sociology', *American Journal of Sociology* 103(2): 281–317.

Erickson, B. (1996) 'Culture, class and connections', *American Journal of Sociology* 102: 217–51.

Feld, S. (1981) 'The focused organization of social ties', *American Journal of Sociology* 86: 1015–35.

Fernandez, R.M. and Harris, D. (1992) 'Social isolation and the underclass', in Adele Harrell and George Peterson (eds.), *Drugs, Crime, and Social Isolation*. Washington, DC: The Urban Institute. pp. 257–93.

Fischer, C.S. (1982a) *To Dwell Among Friends*. Berkeley: University of California Press.

Fischer, C.S. (1982b) 'What do we mean by friend?' *Social Networks* 3: 287–306.

Fleming, L., Colfer, L.J., Marin, A. and McPhie, J. (2011) 'Why the Valley went first: Aggregation and emergence in regional collaboration networks', in John Padgett and Walter Powell (eds.), *Market Emergence and Transformation*. Princeton, NJ: Princeton University Press.

Freeman, L. (1979) 'Centrality in social networks: Conceptual clarification', *Social Networks* 1: 215–39.

Freeman, L. (1992) 'Filling in the blanks: A theory of cognitive categories and the structure of social affiliation', *Social Psychology Quarterly* 55: 118–27.

Freeman, L., Freeman, S. and Michaelson, A. (1989) 'How humans see social groups: A test of the Sailer-Gaulin models', *Journal of Quantitative Anthropology* 1: 229–38.

Gibson, D. (2005a) 'Concurrency and commitment', *Journal of Mathematical Sociology* 29(4): 295–323.

Gibson, D. (2005b) 'Taking turns and talking ties', *American Journal of Sociology* 110(6): 1561–97.

Gould, R. (1995) *Insurgent Identities: Class, Community and Protest in Paris from 1848 to the Commune*. Chicago: University of Chicago Press.

Granovetter, M. (1973) 'The strength of weak ties', *American Journal of Sociology* 78: 1360–80.

Granovetter, M. (1974) *Getting a Job: A Study of Contacts and Careers*. Cambridge, MA: Harvard University Press.

Granovetter, M. (1985) 'Economic action and social structure: The problem of embeddedness', *American Journal of Sociology* 91: 481–510.

Grossetti, M. (2005) 'Where do social relations come from?' *Social Networks* 27: 289–300.

Hampton, K. (1999) 'Computer-assisted interviewing: The design and application of survey software to the Wired Suburb Project', *Bulletin de Méthodologie Sociologique* 62: 49–68.

Hampton, K. (2007) 'Neighborhoods in the network society: The e-Neighbors study', *Information, Communication & Society* 10(5): 714–48.

Hampton, K. and Wellman, B. (2003) 'Neighboring in Netville', *City and Community* 2(3): 277–311.

Hargadon, A. and Sutton, R. (1997) 'Technology brokering and innovation in a product development firm', *Administrative Science Quarterly* 42: 716–49.

Hennig, M. (2007) 'Re-evaluating the community question from a German perspective', *Social Networks* 29(3): 375–90.

Hogan, B., Carrasco, J.-A. and Wellman, B. (2007) 'Visualizing personal networks', *Field Methods* 19(2): 116–44.

Ibarra, H. (1993) 'Personal networks of women and minorities in management', *Academy of Management Review* 18: 56–87.

Ibarra, H. (1997) 'Paving an alternate route: Gender differences in managerial networks', *Social Psychology Quarterly* 60: 91–102.

Killworth, P. and Bernard, H.R. (1976) 'Informant accuracy in social network data', *Human Organization* 35: 269–86.

Killworth, P., Johnsen, E., Bernard, H.R., Shelley, G.A and McCarthy, C. (1990) 'Estimating the size of personal networks', *Social Networks* 12: 289–312.

Klassen, S. (2008) 'Indicators of research success in sociology at the University of Toronto', [presentation to the Faculty] Department of Sociology, University of Toronto.

Laumann, E., Marsden, P. and Prensky, D. (1983) 'The boundary specification problem in network analysis', in Ronald Burt and Michael Minor (eds.), *Applied Network Analysis*. Beverly Hills, CA: Sage. pp. 18–34.

Lin, N. (1986) 'Access to occupations through social ties', *Social Networks* 8: 365–85.

Lin, N. and Ensel, W. (1989) 'Life stress and health', *American Sociological Review* 54: 382–99.

Lin, N. and Erickson, B. (eds.) (2008) *Social Capital*. New York: Oxford University Press.

Manfreda, K.L., Vehovar, V. and Hlebec, V. (2004) 'Collecting ego-centred network data via the Web', *Metodološki zvezki* 1(2): 295–321.

Marin, A. (2004) 'Are respondents more likely to list alters with certain characteristics? Implications for name generator data', *Social Networks* 26: 289–307.

Marsden, P. (1987) 'Core discussion networks of Americans', *American Sociological Review* 52: 122–31.

Marsden, P. (2005) 'Recent developments in network measurement', in Peter Carrington, John S., and Stanley W. (eds.), *Models and Methods in Social Network Analysis*. Cambridge, UK: Cambridge University Press. pp. 8–30.

Martin, J.L. (2005) 'Is power sexy?' *American Journal of Sociology* 111: 408–46.

McPherson, J.M. and Smith-Lovin, L. (1987) 'Homophily in voluntary organizations', *American Sociological Review* 52: 370–79.

McPherson, J.M., Smith-Lovin, L. and Brashears, M. (2006) 'Social isolation in America', *American Sociological Review* 71: 353–75.

Menjívar, C. (2000) *Fragmented Ties*. Berkeley: University of California Press.

Merton, R. (1968) 'The Matthew Effect in science', *Science* 159: 56–63.

Mintz, B. and Schwartz, M. (1985) *The Power Structure of American Business*. Chicago: University of Chicago Press.

Mitchell, J.C. (ed.). (1969) *Social Networks in Urban Situations*. Manchester: Manchester University Press.

Mizruchi, M. and Brewster Stearns, L. (1988) 'A longitudinal study of the formation of interlocking directorates', *Administrative Science Quarterly* 33(2): 194–210.

Morris, M. (1993) 'Epidemiology and social networks', *Sociological Methods and Research* 22: 99–126.

Müller, C., Wellman, B. and Marin, A. (1999) 'How to use SPSS to study ego-centered networks', *Bulletin de Methode Sociologique* 69: 83–100.

Nooy, W.D., Mrvar, A. and Batagelj, V. (2005) *Exploratory Social Network Analysis with Pajek*. Cambridge: Cambridge University Press.

Padgett, J. and Ansell, C. (1993) 'Robust action and the rise of the Medici, 1400–1434', *American Journal of Sociology* 98(6): 1259–319.

Pescosolido, B. (1992) 'Beyond rational choice', *American Journal of Sociology* 97: 1096–138.

Plickert, G., Côté, R. and Wellman, B. (2007) 'It's not who you know, it's how you know them', *Social Networks* 29(3): 405–29.

Podolny, J.M. (2005) *Status Signals*. Princeton, NJ: Princeton University Press.

Podolny, J.M. and Baron, J.N. (1997) 'Resources and relationships', *American Sociological Review* 62: 673–93.

Quan-Haase, A. and Wellman, B. (2006) 'Hyperconnected net work', in Charles Heckscher and Paul Adler (eds.) *The Firm as a Collaborative Community*. New York: Oxford University Press. pp. 281–333.

R Development Core Team (2007) 'R: A language and environment for statistical computing', R Project for Statistical Computing, Vienna, Austria. Version 2.6.1. http://www.R-project.org/.

Richards, W. and Seary, A. (2006) MultiNet for Windows. Version 4.75. http://www.sfu.ca/~richards/Multinet/Pages/multinet.htm.

Roethlisberger, F.J., and Dickson, W.J. (1939) *Management and the Worker*. Cambridge, MA: Harvard University Press.

Simmel, G. (1908 [1971]) *On Individuality and Social Forms: Selected Writings*. Chicago: University of Chicago Press.

Simmel, G. (1922 [1955]) 'The web of group affiliations', in Kurt Wolff (ed.), *Conflict and the Web of Group Affiliations*. Glencoe, IL: Free Press. pp. 125–95.

Smith, M. and the Node XL Development Team (2009) Node XL: Network overview. Version 1.0.1.84. http://www.codeplex.com/NodeXL.

Smith, S.S. (2005) 'Don't put my name on it', *American Journal of Sociology* 111: 1–57.

Snijders, T.A.B. (2001) SIENA. Version 3.1. http://stat.gamma.rug.nl/snijders/siena.html.

Snijders, T. and Bosker, R.J. (1999) *Introduction to Multilevel Analysis*. London: Sage.

Snijders, T., Pattison, P., Robins, G. and Handock, M. (2006) 'New specifications for exponential random graph models', *Sociological Methodology* 36: 9–153.

Stack, C. (1974) *All Our Kin*. New York: Harper & Row.

Stern, M. (2008) 'How locality, frequency of communication, and Internet usage affect modes of communication within core social networks', *Information, Communication & Society* 11(5): 591–616.

Tilly, C. (1984) *Big Structures, Large Processes, Huge Comparisons*. New York: Russell Sage Foundation.

Uzzi, B. (1996) 'The sources and consequences of embeddedness for the economic performance of organizations', *American Sociological Review* 61: 674–98.

van der Gaag, M. and Snijders, T. (2005) 'The resource generator', *Social Networks* 27: 1–27.

Wasserman, S. and Faust, K. (1994) *Social Network Analysis*. Cambridge: Cambridge University Press.

Watts, D. (1999) *Small Worlds*. Princeton, NJ: Princeton University Press.

Watts, D. (2003) *Six Degrees*. New York: W. W. Norton.

Watts, D., Dodds, P. and Newman, M. (2002) 'Identity and search in social networks', *Science* 296: 1302–5.

Wellman, B. (1979) 'The community question', *American Journal of Sociology* 84: 1201–31.

Wellman, B. (1988) 'Structural analysis', in Barry Wellman and S.D. Berkowitz (eds.), *Social Structures*. Cambridge: Cambridge University Press. pp. 19–61.

Wellman, B. and Frank, K. (2001) 'Network capital in a multilevel world', in Nan Lin, K.C. and Ronald B. (eds.), *Social Capital*. Chicago: Aldine De Gruyter. pp. 233–73.

Wellman, B., Hogan, B., Berg, K., Boase, J., Carrasco, J.-A., Côté, R., Kayahara, J., Kennedy, T. and Tran, P. (2006) 'Connected lives: The project' in Patrick Purcell (ed.), *Networked Neighbourhoods*. Guildford, UK: Springer. pp. 157–211.

Wellman, B. and Wortley, S. (1990) 'Different strokes from different folks', *American Journal of Sociology* 96(3): 558–88.

White, H., Boorman, S. and Breiger, R. (1976) 'Social structure from multiple networks I: Blockmodels of roles and positions', *American Journal of Sociology* 81: 730–80.

White, H., Wellman, B. and Nazer, N. (2004) 'Does citation reflect social structure?' *Journal of the American Society for Information Science and Technology* 55(2): 111–26.

Wilson, W.J. (1978) *The Declining Significance of Race*. Chicago: University of Chicago Press.

Wilson, W.J. (1987) *The Truly Disadvantaged*. Chicago: University of Chicago Press.

Zelizer, V.A. (1994) *The Social Meaning of Money*. New York: Basic Books.

3

The Development of Social Network Analysis – with an Emphasis on Recent Events

Linton C. Freeman

In a recent book I reviewed the development of social network analysis from its earliest beginnings until the late 1990s (Freeman, 2004). There, I characterized social network analysis as an approach that involved four defining properties: (1) It involves the intuition that links among social actors are important; (2) it is based on the collection and analysis of data that record social relations that link actors; (3) it draws heavily on graphic imagery to reveal and display the patterning of those links; and (4) it develops mathematical and computational models to describe and explain those patterns.

In that book I reviewed the prehistory of social network analysis. I showed that as early as the thirteenth century, and probably even earlier, people began to produce work that drew on one or more of the four properties listed above. Until the 1930s, however, no one had used all four properties at the same time. The modern field of social network analysis, then, emerged in the 1930s.

In its first incarnation, modern social network analysis was introduced by a psychiatrist, Jacob L. Moreno, and a psychologist, Helen Jennings (Freeman, 2004: Chapter 3). They conducted elaborate research, first among the inmates of a prison (Moreno, 1932) and later among the residents in a reform school for girls (Moreno, 1934).

Moreno and Jennings named their approach *sociometry*. At first, sociometry generated a great deal of interest, particularly among American psychologists and sociologists. But that interest turned out to be short-lived; by the 1940s most American social scientists returned to their traditional focus on the characteristics of individuals.

During the same period another group, led by an anthropologist, W. Lloyd Warner, also adopted the social networks approach (Freeman, 2004: Chapter 4). Their efforts were centered in the Anthropology Department and the Business School at Harvard, and their approach was pretty clearly independent of Moreno's and Jennings's work. Warner designed the "bank wiring room" study, a social network component of the famous Western Electric research on industrial productivity (Roethlisberger and Dixon, 1939). He also involved business school colleagues and anthropology students in his community research. They conducted social network research in two communities, Yankee City (Warner and Lunt, 1941) and Deep South (Davis et al., 1941).

The Warner research group never stirred up as much interest as did Moreno and Jennings. When Warner moved to the University of Chicago in 1935 and turned to other kinds of research, the whole Harvard movement fell apart.

The third version of social network analysis emerged when a German psychologist, Kurt Lewin, took a job at the University of Iowa in 1936 (Freeman, 2004: 66–75). There, Lewin worked with a large number of graduate students and postdocs. Together, they developed a structural perspective and conducted social network research in the field of social psychology (e.g., Lewin and Lippitt, 1938).

The Lewin group moved to the Massachusetts Institute of Technology in 1945, but after Lewin's sudden death in 1947 most of the group moved again, this time to the University of Michigan. This Michigan group made important contributions to social network research for more than 20 years (e.g., Festinger et al., 1950; Cartwright and Harary, 1956; Newcomb, 1961).

One of Lewin's students, Alex Bavelas, remained at MIT where he spearheaded a famous study of the impact of group structure on productivity and morale (Leavitt, 1951). This work was influential in the field of organizational behavior, but most of its influence was limited to that field.

All three of these teams began work in the 1930s. None of them, however, produced an approach that was accepted across all the social sciences in all countries; none provided a standard for structural research.

Instead, after the 1930s and until the 1970s, numerous centers of social network research appeared. Each involved a different form and a different application of the social network approach. Moreover, they worked in different social science fields and in different countries. Table 3.1 lists 13 centers that emerged during those 30 years.[1]

By 1970, then, 16 centers of social network research had appeared. With the development of each, knowledge and acceptance of the structural approach grew. Still, however, none of these centers succeeded in providing a generally recognized paradigm for the social network approach to social science research.

That all changed in the early 1970s when Harrison C. White, together with his students at Harvard, built a seventeenth center of social network research. In my book I described the impact of this group (Freeman, 2004: 127):

> From the beginning, White saw the broad generality of the structural paradigm, and he managed to communicate both that insight and his own enthusiasm to a whole generation of outstanding students. Certainly the majority of the published work in the field has been produced by White and his former students. Once this generation started to produce, they published so much important theory and research focused on social networks that social scientists everywhere, regardless of their field, could no longer ignore the idea. By the end of the 1970s, then, social network analysis came to be universally recognized among social scientists.

Following the contributions of White and his students, social network analysis settled down, embraced a standard paradigm, and became widely recognized as a field of research.

In the late 1990s, however, there was a revolutionary change in the field. It was then that physicists began publishing on social networks.[2] First, Watts and Strogatz (1998) wrote about small worlds. A year later Barabási and Albert (1999) examined the distribution of degree centralities. I ended the earlier account in my book by

Table 3.1   Centers of social network research from 1940 to 1969

Place	Field	Team leaders	Country
Michigan State	Rural sociology	Charles P. Loomis Leo Katz	USA
Sorbonne	Linguistics	Claude Lévi-Strauss André Weil	France
Lund	Geography	Thorsten Hägerstrand	Sweden
Chicago	Mathematical Biology	Nicolas Rashevsky	USA
Columbia	Sociology	Paul Lazersfeld Robert Merton	USA
Iowa State	Communication	Everett Rogers	USA
Manchester	Sociology	Max Gluckman	Great Britain
MIT	Political Science	Ithiel de Sola Pool Manfred Kochen	USA
Syracuse	Community Power	Linton Freeman	USA
Sorbonne	Psychology	Claude Flament	France
Michigan	Sociology	Edward Laumann	USA
Chicago	Sociology	Peter Blau James A. Davis	USA
Amsterdam	Sociology	Robert Mokken	Netherlands

commenting on the entry of Watts, Strogatz, Barabási, and Albert into social network research. I expressed the pious hope that, like all the earlier potential claimants to the field, our colleagues from physics would simply join in the collective enterprise.

That hope, however, was not immediately realized. These physicists, new to social network analysis, did not read previous literature; they acted as if our 60 years of effort amounted to nothing. In a recent article, I contrasted the approach of these new physicists with that of earlier physicists who had been involved in social network research (Freeman, 2008): "Other physicists had already been involved in social network analysis. Notable among these were Derek de Solla Price, Harrison White and Peter Killworth (e.g., Price, 1965, 1976; White, 1970; White et al., 1976; Killworth et al., 2003; Killworth et al., 2006). These physicists read the social network literature, joined the collective effort and contributed to an ongoing research process." But neither Watts and Strogatz nor Barabási and Albert did any of these things. They simply claimed research topics that had always been part of social network analysis and made them topics in physics.

The result was a good deal of irritation (and perhaps a certain amount of jealousy) on the part of many members of the social network research community. Bonacich (2004) put it this way:

> Duncan Watts and Albert-László Barabási are both physicists who have recently crashed the world of social networks, arousing some resentment in the process. Both have made a splash in the wider scientific community, as attested by their publications in high status science journals (*Science, Nature*).... Both have recently written scientific best-sellers: *Six Degrees* ranks 2,547 on the Amazon list, while *Linked* ranks 4,003.

Watts, Strogatz, Barabási, and Albert opened the door. They managed to get a huge number of their physics colleagues involved—enough to completely overwhelm the traditional social network analysts. Their impact, then, was to produce a revolution in social network research. In the present chapter I will focus on that revolution and its aftermath. Here I will review the developments that have occurred since those two articles (by Watts and Strogatz and by Barabási and Albert) were published.

THE ORIGINS OF THE REVOLUTION

The article by Watts and Strogatz (1998) addressed a standard topic in social network analysis: the "small world." Concern with that issue stemmed from one of the classic social network papers, "Contacts and Onfluence," written by Pool and Kochen (1978) in the mid-1950s. It circulated in typescript until 1978 when it was finally published as the lead article in volume 1, number 1, of a new journal, *Social Networks*.

The questions raised by Pool and Kochen concerned patterns of acquaintanceship linking pairs of persons. They speculated that any two people in the United States are linked by a chain of acquaintanceships involving no more than seven intermediaries.

Various students picked up on Pool and Kochen's ideas, including Stanley Milgram, who used them as the basis for his doctoral dissertation on the "small world." Milgram published several papers on the subject, one of which was a popularization that appeared in *Psychology Today* (1967).

Watts and Strogatz cited the *Psychology Today* article as well as a later book edited by Kochen (1989) on the small-world idea. But they apparently did not discover any of the other literature on the subject. In any case, they introduced an entirely new model that was designed to account for both the clustering found in human interaction and the short paths linking pairs of individuals.

The Watts and Strogatz model begins with an attempt to capture clustering—the universal tendency of friends of friends to be friends. They represent links among individuals as a circular lattice like the one shown in Figure 3.1, where each node is an individual and each edge is a social link connecting two individuals. They go on to define an *average clustering coefficient C(p)* that measures the degree to which each node and its immediate neighbors are all directly linked to one another. The structure in Figure 3.1 embodies a good deal of clustering—neighbors of neighbors are, for the most part, neighbors—thus the clustering coefficient $C(p)$ is high. But, at the same time, $L(p)$, the average length of the path linking any two individuals in the whole lattice, is relatively large.

Since $L(p)$ is large, the world represented by this circular lattice is certainly not small. But Watts and Strogatz showed that they could produce a small-world effect—where no individual is very far from any other individual—simply by removing just a few of the links between close neighbors and substituting links to randomly selected others. As Figure 3.2 shows, under those conditions some links span across the lattice. The result is that, as random links are substituted for links to close neighbors, path length $L(p)$ drops abruptly, but the clustering coefficient $C(p)$ is hardly diminished at all. Thus, for the most part, friends of friends are still friends, but the total world has become dramatically smaller.

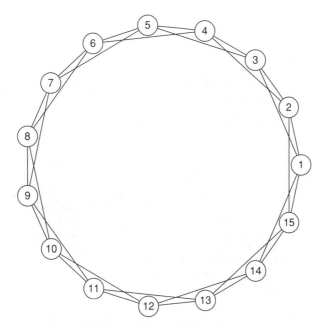

Figure 3.1 A circular lattice with high clustering but long path lengths

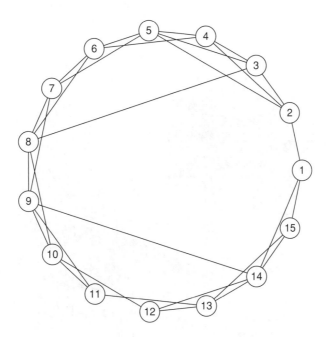

Figure 3.2 A lattice with high clustering and shorter path lengths

The article by Barabási and Albert (1999) also took up a standard network analytic topic: degree distribution. The degree of a node is simply the number of other nodes to which it is directly connected by edges. Much of the earliest research on social networks was focused on the distributions of degrees. Research in sociometry often involved asking people whom they would choose, say, to invite to a party or to work with on a project (Moreno, 1934). As soon as the responses to such questions began to be tallied, it became apparent that the distribution of being chosen was dramatically skewed. A few individuals were chosen extremely often while a large number were chosen rarely, if at all.

Moreno and Jennings (1938) reported two empirical results: (1) such skewed distributions were universally observed, and (2) they departed from expectations based on random choices. As they described it, "A distortion of choice distribution in favor of the more chosen as against the less chosen is characteristic of all groupings which have been sociometrically tested."

Barabási and Albert (1999) studied the distribution of connections in networks that grew as a consequence of adding new nodes. Their examples included links between sites in the World Wide Web, links between screen actors who worked together on films, and links between generators, transformers, and substations in the U.S. electrical power grid. Although Barabási and Albert were apparently unaware of the earlier findings by Moreno and Jennings, they discovered that the connections in the networks they examined were not random. Instead, the links were skewed; there were a few nodes that displayed too many connections and a great many nodes that displayed too few.

Barabási and Albert went on to propose a simple model designed to account for the pattern of skewing they had observed. Consider a collection of existing nodes. Let k_i be the number of links already established to node i. Then let the probability that a new node is going to link to any node i depend on k_i. The model specifies the probability of that link connecting to node i as $P(k_i) k_i^g$, where $2 \leq \gamma \leq 3$.[3] The distribution of connections, then, follows a power law, or as Barabási and Albert characterize it, it is "scale free."

THE GROWTH OF THE REVOLUTION

As a consequence of the interest generated by Watts and Strogatz and by Barabási and Albert, the revolution began in earnest. As Figure 3.3 shows, physicists followed up on the Watts and Strogatz small-world paper. Within five years, the physics community had produced more

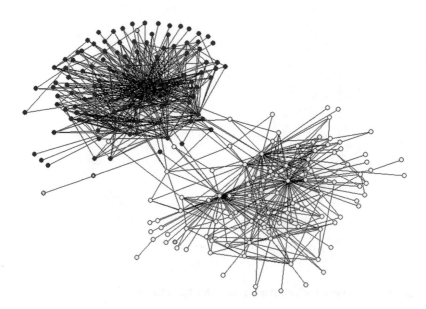

Figure 3.3   Small world publications 1950–2004 (physicists are displayed as black points)

small-world papers than the social network community had turned out in 45 years (Freeman, 2004: 164–66).

Moreover, Figure 3.3 also shows that, at that point, 98 percent of the citations were made within either the physics community or the social network community. For the most part, physicists ignored the earlier work by social network analysts. And social network analysts responded in kind.

Physicists were also quick to follow up on Barabási and Albert's work on degree distributions. According to Google Scholar, their first paper had received over 4,000 citations as of mid-November 2008. But practically none of those citations were produced by social network analysts.

It soon became evident that the physicists' interest in social networks was not going to be confined to small-world phenomena and degree distributions. Members of the physics community quickly began to explore other problems that had traditionally belonged to social network analysts. Nor was that interest restricted to physicists. At the same time, physicists succeeded in getting biologists and computer scientists involved in their efforts. Two main foci of this new thrust involved the study of cohesive groups, or what physicists call *communities,* and the study of the positions that nodes occupy in a network—particularly their centrality. I will review these foci in the next two sections.

COHESIVE GROUPS OR COMMUNITIES

The notion of cohesive groups is foundational in sociology. Early sociologists (Tönnies, 1855/1936; Maine, 1861/1931; Durkheim, 1893/1964; Spencer, 1897; Cooley, 1909/1962) talked about little else. Their work provided an intuitive "feel" for groups, but it did not define groups in any systematic way.

When the social network perspective emerged, however, network analysts set out to specify groups in structural terms. Freeman and Webster (1994) described the observation behind this structural perspective on groups:

Whenever human association is examined, we see what can be described as thick spots—relatively unchanging clusters or collections of individuals who are linked by frequent interaction and often by sentimental ties. These are surrounded by thin areas where interaction does occur, but tends to be less frequent and to involve very little if any sentiment.

Thus, the social ties within a cohesive group will tend to be dense; most individuals in the group will be linked to a great many other group members. Moreover, those in-group ties will tend to display clustering—where, as described above, friends of friends are friends. In contrast, relatively few social ties will link members of different groups, and clustering will be relatively rare.

An early social network analyst, George Homans (1950: 84), spelled out the intuitive basis for the social network conception of cohesive groups:

A group is defined by the interactions of its members. If we say that individuals A, B, C, D, E, ... form a group, this will mean that at least the following circumstances hold. Within a given period of time, A interacts more often with B, C, D, E,... than he does with M, N, L, O, P, ... whom we choose to consider outsiders or members of other groups. B also interacts more often with A, C, D, E, ... than he does with outsiders, and so on for the other members of the group. It is possible just by counting interactions to map out a group quantitatively distinct from others.

Over the years, network analysts have proposed dozens of models of cohesive groups. These models serve to define groups in structural terms and provide procedures to find groups in network data. They all try to capture something close to Homans's intuition in one way or another. Some of them represent groups in terms of on/off or binary links among actors (e.g., Luce and Perry, 1949; Mokken, 1979). Others represent them in terms of quantitative links that index the strength of ties linking pairs of actors (e.g., Sailer and Gaulin, 1984; Freeman, 1992).

Currently, then, we have a huge number of models of cohesive groups. Most of them were reviewed by Wasserman and Faust (1994). Some were algebraic (e.g., Breiger, 1974; Freeman and White, 1993), some were graph theoretic (e.g., Alba, 1973; Moody and White, 2003), some were built on probability theory (e.g., Frank, 1995; Skvoritz and Faust, 1999), and some were based on matrix permutation (e.g., Beum and Brundage, 1950; Seary and Richards, 2003). All, however, were designed to specify the properties of groups in exact terms, to uncover group structure in network data, or both.

Over the years social network analysts have also drawn on various computational algorithms in an attempt to uncover groups. These include multidimensional scaling (Freeman et al., 1987; Arabie and Carroll, 1989); various versions of singular value decomposition, including principal components analysis and correspondence analysis

(Levine, 1972; Roberts, 2000); hierarchical clustering (Breiger et al., 1975; Wasserman and Faust, 1994: 382–83); the max-cut min-flow algorithm (Zachary, 1977, Blythe, 2006); simulated annealing (Boyd, 1991: 223; Dekker, 2001); and the genetic algorithm (Freeman, 1993; Borgatti and Everett, 1997).

In social network research, the general tendency over the years has been to move from binary representations to representations in which the links between nodes take numeric values that represent the strengths of connections. At the same time social network analysts have gradually shifted from building algebraic and graph theoretic models to developing models grounded in probability theory. And, as time has passed, they have relied more often on the use of computational procedures to uncover groups.

A notable exception to this trend can be found in an article by Moody and White (2003). They used graph theory to define *structural cohesion*. They defined structural cohesion "... as the minimum number of actors who, if removed from a group, would disconnect the group." Then they went on to define *embeddedness* in terms of a hierarchical nesting of cohesive structures. This approach represents a new and sophisticated version of the traditional social network model building.

Since the early 1970s, mathematicians and computer scientists had also been interested in groups or communities. They defined that interest in terms of *graph partitioning* (Fiedler, 1973, 1975; Parlett, 1980; Fiduccia and Mattheyses, 1982; Glover, 1989, 1990; Pothen et al., 1990). Social network analysts recognized this tradition when the work by Glover was cited and integrated into the program UCINet (Borgatti et al., 1992). And in 1993 the link in the other direction was made when a team composed of an electrical engineer and a computer engineer, Wu and Leahy (1993), cited the work of a statistician and social network analyst, Hubert (1974). And in 2000 three computer scientists, Flake, Lawrence, and Giles (2000), cited the social network text by Scott (1992).

Until quite recently, however, these efforts did not stir up much interest in the physics community. Instead, the physicists turned to the procedures developed in social network analysis. Girvan and Newman (2002) adapted the social network model of betweenness centrality (Freeman, 1977) to the task of uncovering groups. Their adaptation was based on the betweenness of graph edges, rather than nodes, and the result was a new algorithm for partitioning graphs.

Edge betweenness refers to the degree to which an edge in the graph falls along a shortest path linking every pair of nodes. A path in a graph is a

sequence of nodes and edges beginning and ending with nodes. Girvan and Newman reasoned that since there should be relatively few edges linking individuals in different groups, those linking edges should display a high degree of betweenness. So they began by removing the edge with the highest betweenness, and they continued that process until the graph was partitioned.

Two years later Newman and Girvan (2004) published a follow-up article. Their second paper again focused on edge removal, but this time they introduced an alternative model that had two intuitive foundations. In one, they showed that random walks between all pairs of nodes would determine the betweenness of edges—not just along shortest paths, but along all the paths linking pairs of nodes. The other intuition was motivated by a physical model where edges were defined as resistors that impeded the flow of current between nodes. The edge with the lowest current flow was removed. If that did not yield a partition the process was continued until partitioning did take place. These two models produced the same partitions.

Newman and Girvan went on to show that all of their algorithms always partitioned the data even though some of the partitions might not reflect the presence of actual communities. So they introduced a measure called *modularity*. Modularity is based on the ratio of within-partition ties to those that cross partition boundaries and compares that ratio to its expected value when ties are produced at random. Thus, it provides an index of the degree to which each partition embodies a group- or community-like form.

The result of the two papers by Girvan and Newman was dramatic. Both physicists and computer scientists quickly developed an interest in groups or communities. Radicchi and colleagues (2004) specified two kinds of communities. One was characterized as "strong"; it defined a partition as a community if it met the condition that every node had more within-group ties than cross-cutting ones.[4] The other they characterized as "weak." It proposed that a partition was a community if the total number of ties within each partition was greater than the total number of ties linking nodes in the partition to nodes outside the partition.

Radicci et al. also pointed out that the Girvan and Newman betweenness-based algorithm was computationally slow. So they introduced a new, more efficient measure. They reasoned that edges that bridge between communities are likely to be involved in very few 3-cycles (where friends of friends are friends). So they based their measure on the number of 3-cycles in which each edge is involved, and they showed that their measure had moderate negative correlation with the

Girvan-Newman measure. The number of 3-cycles in which an edge is involved, then, turns out to be inversely related to the betweenness of that edge.

Newman (2004) quickly jumped back in. He, too, was troubled by the slowness of the Girvan-Newman algorithm for finding communities. So he proposed a fast "greedy" algorithm. A greedy algorithm makes the optimal choice at each step in a process, without regard to the long-term consequences of that choice.[5] In this case, Newman proposed starting a process by having each cluster contain a single node. Then, at each stage in the process, the pair of clusters that yields the highest modularity is merged.

The concern with computing speed seems to have started a race to see who could develop the fastest algorithm to cluster nodes in terms of their modularity. A computer scientist, Clauset, working with two physicists, Clauset et al. (2004), was able to speed up Newman's "greedy" algorithm. Two more computer scientists, Duch and Arenas (2005), devised an algorithm to speed it up even more. And in 2006 Newman showed how to gain still more speed by applying singular value decomposition to the modularity matrix. Then, in 2007, a computer scientist, Djidjev, developed a still faster algorithm for constructing partitions based on modularities.

Continuing the search for speed, two other computer scientists, Pons and Latapy (2006), took an entirely different approach. They reasoned that since communities are clusters of densely linked nodes that are only sparsely linked together, a short (two- or three-step) random walk should typically stay within the community in which it is started. They proposed an algorithm that begins with a series of randomly selected starter nodes. Each starter is used to generate a random walk. Then the starters, along with the nodes that are reached, are tallied as linked. The likelihood is that once these results are cumulated, they will display the clustered communities. Finally, two industrial engineers and a physicist, Raghavan, Albert, and Kumara (2007), produced a very fast algorithm based on graph coloring. Nodes begin with unique colors, then, iteratively, each acquires the color of the majority of their immediate neighbors.

Other quite different procedures were also introduced. A physicist and a computer scientist, Wu and Huberman (2004), developed a model based on assuming that edges are resistors, as was the case in the earlier model introduced by Newman and Girvan. But Wu and Huberman's model turns out to be much more complicated and ad hoc. Four physicists, Capocci, Servedio, Caldarelli, and Colaiori (2004), suggested using singular value decomposition to uncover communities. And three others, Fortunato, Latora, and Marchiori (2004), proposed a variation of edge centrality called "information centrality." Their centrality is based on the inverse of the shortest path length connecting each pair of nodes. The physicists Palla et al. (2005) defined communities as cliques and focused on patterning of clique overlap. Reichardt and Bornholdt (2006) used simulated annealing to search for partitions that yield communities that have a large number of ties within groups and a small number of ties that cut across groups.

Some of these ideas, like overlapping cliques and simulated annealing, will be familiar to seasoned social network analysts. Many others, however, are new and several are quite creative. In particular, edge betweenness, modularity, the use of 3-cycles, short random walks, and graph coloring appear to have promise.

Almost all of these contributions focused on building new tools to uncover groups or communities. They all reported applications to data, but for the most part their applications were merely illustrative. The main thrust of this research has been to build better and faster group-finding algorithms. That preoccupation with developing ever-faster algorithms may not seem too important to most social network analysts, but many applications — particularly those in biology — involve data sets that involve connections linking hundreds of thousands or millions of nodes. For those applications, speed is essential.

POSITIONS

Concern with the positions occupied by individual actors has been the second main theme in social network analysis. Four kinds of positions have been defined. First, positions in groups — *core* and *periphery* — have been specified. Second, a good deal of attention has been focused on *social roles*. Third, some attention has also been devoted to the study of the positions of nodes in *hierarchical structures*. And fourth, social network analysts have been concerned with the structural *centrality* of nodes in networks.

Core and peripheral positions in groups were first defined by the early network analysts Davis et al. (1941):

> Those individuals who participate together most often and at the most intimate affairs are called *core members*; those who participate with core members upon some occasions but never as a group by themselves alone are called *primary members*; while individuals on the fringes, who

participate only infrequently, constitute the *secondary members* of a clique. (p. 150)

Various others followed up on this observation, and algorithms for finding core and peripheral positions in groups were proposed by Bonacich (1978), Doreian (1979), Freeman and White (1993), and Skvoretz and Faust (1999). Finally, in a pair of articles, (Borgatti and Everett, 1999; Everett and Borgatti, 2000) two researchers developed a full model of core/periphery structure.

The intuitive idea of social role was introduced by the anthropologist Ralph Linton (1936). The notion was that two individuals who were, say, both fathers of children occupied a similar position as a consequence of their being fathers. They could, it was assumed, be expected to display similar behaviors. This idea was spelled out by Siegfried Nadel (1957) and formalized by Lorrain and White (1971) in their model of *structural equivalence*. In that model, two individuals are structurally equivalent if they have the same relations linking them to the same others.

Other social network analysts concluded that structural equivalence was too restrictive to capture the concept of social role (Sailer, 1978). They were quick to propose other models that relaxed the restrictions of structural equivalence. These include *regular equivalence, isomorphic equivalence, automorphic equivalence*, and *local role equivalence*. These ideas are all thoroughly reviewed in Wasserman and Faust (1994).

The third kind of positional model used in social network analysis is focused on hierarchies or dominance orders. The study of dominance began with Pierre Huber's (1802) observations of dominance among bumblebees. Huber was an ethologist, and most of the research and model building about dominance has remained in ethology. But Martin Landau (1951), who was both an ethologist and a social network analyst, created a formal model of hierarchical structure for social network analysts. Another social network analyst, James S. Coleman (1964), proposed an alternative model. More recently, Freeman (1997) adapted an algebraic model from computer science (Gower, 1977) to be used in social network analysis. And Jameson et al. (1999) took a model from psychology (Batchelder and Simpson, 1988) and applied it to the study of social networks.

The fourth and final kind of model of social position is based on the notion of centrality. Alex Bavelas (1948) and Harold Leavitt (1951) originally developed the idea of structural centrality at the Group Networks Laboratory at the Massachusetts Institute of Technology. Their conception of centrality, based on the distance of each node to all the others in the graph, was used to account for differences in performance and morale in an organization.

Very soon a large number of other conceptions of centrality were introduced. Those based on graph theory were reviewed (Freeman, 1979) and reduced to a set of three. They included Sabidussi's (1966) measure based on *closeness*, Nieminen's (1974) measure based on *degree*, and Freeman's (1977) measure based on *betweenness*.

In addition to these graph theoretic measures, Bonacich (1972, 1987) introduced an algebraic centrality measure. His measure is based on the concept of *eigenstructure*; it is determined by a combination of the degree of a node, the degrees of its neighbors, the degrees of their neighbors, and so on.

The community of physicists has not displayed any major interest in the first three of these kinds of positions developed in social network analysis. Physicist Petter Holme (2005) did write an article about core/periphery structures, and in a review article, Mark Newman (2003) introduced structural equivalence to physicists. Petter Holme and Mikael Huss (2005) reviewed the social network equivalence measures and applied them in the study of protein function in yeast. Finally, Juyong Park and Mark Newman (2005) introduced a new model of dominance and applied it to ranking American college football teams.

The physicists, however, were quick to adopt the ideas about centrality that had been developed in social network analysis, and they immediately passed them on to biologists. Figure 3.4 displays the number of articles on centrality published each year by social network analysts and the number published by physicists and biologists. It is clear that once they began publishing in this area, the physicists and biologists quickly overtook the social network analysts.

In working with centrality, though, the physicists took a very different approach than the one they used when they dealt with the group or community concept. As we saw above, most of their contributions to the study of groups involved the development of new models and the introduction of refined procedures for finding groups. But, with centralities, most of the physicists' work has involved applications; they simply found new problems to which standard centrality measures could be fruitfully applied.

Many of the areas in which physicists applied centrality may seem quite surprising, as only a few of their applications fall into what most outsiders would think of as belonging to physics. These include packet switching on the Internet, electronic circuitry, and the electric power grid (Freeman, 2008).

A great many more of these applications involve areas that traditionally are considered to fall in the

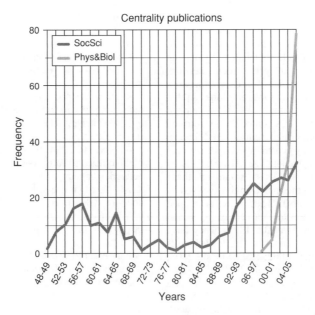

Figure 3.4   Articles on centrality by date and by field (from Freeman, 2008)

domain of social network analysis. These include studies of friendships linking students, contacts among prisoners, email contacts, telephone conversations, scientific collaboration, corporate interlock, and links among sites on the World Wide Web (Freeman, 2008).

By far the most common application of centrality has been to problems in biology. This work was started by physicists (Jeong et al., 2001) who studied interactions among proteins. But, almost immediately, biologists themselves began to use centrality ideas in their research. Two biologists, Wagner and Fell (2001), examined centrality in a study of metabolic networks. A year later, four molecular biologists, Vendruscolo et al. (2002), used centrality in a study of protein folding. These three themes — protein-protein interaction, metabolic networks, and protein folding — have all come to rely heavily on the use of various centrality models and have produced a great deal of research (Freeman, 2008).

SUMMARY AND CONCLUSIONS

In social network analysis we have a field with a long history. It began in the late 1930s and emerged again and again in different social science disciplines and in various countries. In the 1970s all these separate research efforts came

together and merged into a single coherent research effort that embodied a structural perspective.

But in the late 1990s a new kind of situation arose. A completely alien field, physics, embraced the same kind of structural perspective that was embodied in social network analysis. Moreover, a good many of these physicists did not limit their research to the physical realm but studied the patterning of links among social actors. One physicist, Evans (2004), reported on this trend to his fellow physicists: "If you are naturally skeptical about trendy new areas of physics and attempts to mix physics with anything and everything, then the citations of papers in journals of sociology ... and of books on archeology and anthropology ... may just be the last straw!" Thus, though it may not be mainstream physics, at least some physicists have defined social network analysis as a proper part of their discipline.

To understand how this occurred, we need to look at physics and biology in the late 1990s. Both fields were suddenly faced with mammoth amounts of structural data. In physics, data on the Internet became available. These data involve millions of computers, all linked by wires, fiber-optic cables, and wireless connections. And in biology, data on genetic and metabolic networks were being produced by genome research. In both fields investigators were confronted with data on very large networks.

These investigators needed tools – both intellectual and computational – that would help them to grapple with these huge new network data sets. So they turned to a field that had been dealing with network data for 60 years: social network analysis. They drew on ideas from social network analysis and used analytic tools developed in that field. They refined existing tools and developed new ones. Sometimes they reinvented established tools and sometimes they rediscovered known results, but often they contributed important new ways to think about and analyze network data.

More important, at least some of these physicists have become increasingly involved in social network research. They have developed new tools aimed toward the study of social networks (Watts and Strogatz, 1998). They have reanalyzed standard social network data sets (Girvan and Newman, 2002; Holme et al., 2003; Kolaczyk et al., 2007; Newman, 2006).

Physicists have increasingly begun to cite social network articles. Girvan and Newman (2002), for example, cited eight social network articles among their 29 citations. Fortunato et al. (2004) cited nine social network articles in 27 citations. And Holme and Huss (2005) cited five in 34 citations. On the other hand, most social network analysts have resisted citing physicists. Many, I suspect, still view the physicists as "alien invaders."

Physicists have used computer programs produced by social network analysts in their data analyses, and they have produced new programs that include some of the models developed in social network analysis (Freeman, 2008). In addition, a few physicists have attended the annual Sun Belt social network meetings,[6] and a few social network analysts have been invited to the meetings of the physicists.[7] Representatives of each discipline are beginning to publish in journals usually associated with the other.[8] There are even some joint publications (e.g., Reichardt and White, 2007; Salganik et al., 2006).

My earlier hope for rapprochement between physics and social network analysis, it seems, is beginning to take place. All that is required now is that the social network analysts relax their claim to ownership of the field. The physicists are making important contributions to what could easily end up as a collective effort.[9]

NOTES

1 Important publications from each of these centers are listed in Freeman (2004).

2 Scott, in the current volume, also describes the entry of physicists into social network analysis.

His description centers on their theoretical perspective.

3 The Barabási and Albert model, however, turns out to be essentially the same as that proposed by a social network analyst, Derek de Solla Price, in 1976.

4 They did not cite the similar social network models introduced by Sailer and Gaulin (1984).

5 Hierarchical clustering is an example of a greedy algorithm.

6 Freeman (2004: 166) mentions the attendance of the physicists Watts, Newman, and Hoser at social network meetings.

7 The social network analysts Vladimir Batagelj and Linton Freeman were invited to the Summer Workshop in Complex Systems and Networks, put on by physicists in Transylvania in 2007.

8 See, for example, the physicists Watts (1999), Holme, Edling, Liljeros (2004), and Newman (2005) publishing in Social Networks or network analysts Borgatti et al. (2009) appearing in Science.

9 A hopeful sign is that Jeroen Bruggeman (2008) cites 77 reports by physicists in a book about social network analysis.

REFERENCES

Alba, R.D. (1973) 'A graph theoretic definition of a sociometric clique', *Journal of Mathematical Sociology* 3: 113–26.

Arabie, P. and Carroll, J.D. (1989) 'Conceptions of overlap in social structure'. In Freeman, L.C., White, D.R. and Romney, A.K. (eds.), *Research Methods in Social Network Analysis*. George Mason University Press, pp. 367–92.

Barabási, A-L. and Albert, R. (1999) 'Emergence of scaling in random networks', *Science* 286: 509–12.

Batchelder, W.H. and Simpson, R.S. (1988) 'Rating system for human abilities: the case of rating chess skill', *Modules in Undergraduate Mathematics and Its Applications*. Arlington, MA: Consortium for Mathematics and its Applications, Inc. pp. 289–314.

Bavelas, A. (1948) 'A mathematical model for small group structures', *Human Organization* 7: 16–30.

Beum, C.O. and Brundage, E.G. (1950) 'A method for analyzing the sociomatrix', *Sociometry* 13: 141–45.

Blythe, J. (2006) KP 4.3. from http://www.isi.edu/~blythe/KP4.

Bonacich, P. (1972) 'Factoring and weighting approaches to status scores and clique identification', *Journal of Mathematical Sociology* 2: 113–20.

Bonacich, P. (1978) 'Using boolean algebra to analyze the overlapping Memberships', *Sociological Methodology* 15: 101–15.

Bonacich, P. (1987) 'Power and centrality-a family of measures', *American Journal of Sociology* 92(5): 1170–82.

Bonacich, P. (2004) 'The invasion of the physicists', *Social Networks* 26(3): 285–88.

Borgatti, S.P. and Everett, M.G. (1997) 'Network analysis of 2-mode data', *Social Networks* 19(3): 243–69.

Borgatti, S.P. and Everett, M.G. (1999) 'Models of core/periphery structures', *Social Networks* 21(4): 375–95.

Borgatti, S.P., Everett, M.G. and Freeman, L.C. (1992) 'Ucinet, version iv', *Analytic Technology*, Columbia, SC.

Borgatti, S.P., Mehra, A., Brass, D.J. and Labianca, G. (2009) 'Network analysis in the social sciences', *Science* 323: 892–5.

Boyd, J.P. (1991) *Social Semigroups*. Fairfax, VA: George Mason University Press.

Breiger, R.L. (1974) 'The duality of persons and groups', *Social Forces* 53: 181–90.

Bruggeman, J. (2008) *Social Networks*, London: Routledge.

Breiger, R.L., Boorman, S.A. and Arabie, P. (1975) 'An algorithm for clustering relational data, with applications to social network analysis and comparison to multidimensional scaling', *Journal of Mathematical Psychology* 12: 328–83.

Capocci, A., Servedio, V.D.P. and Caldarelli, G. and Colaiori, F. (2004) 'Detecting communities in large networks', *Physica: Statistical Mechanics and Its Applications* 352: 669–76.

Cartwright, D. and Harary, F. (1956) 'Structural balance: a generalization of heider's theory', *Psychological Review* 63: 277–92.

Clauset, A., Newman, M.E.J. and Moore, C. (2004) 'Finding communities in very large networks', *Physical Review E* 70(6): 066111.

Coleman, J.S. (1964) *Introduction to Mathematical Sociology*. New York: Free Press.

Cooley, C.H. (1909/1962) *Social Organization*. New York: Shocken Books.

Davis, A., Gardner, B.B. and Gardner, M.R. (1941) *Deep South*. Chicago: The University of Chicago Press.

Dekker, A. (2001) 'Visualization of social networks using Cavalier', *Proceedings of the 2001 Asia-Pacific Symposium on Information Visualization* 9: 49–55.

Djidjev, H. (2007) 'A fast multilevel algorithm for graph clustering and community detection'. Arxiv preprint arXiv:0707.2387,2007 - arxiv.org.

Doreian, P. (1979) 'On the deliniation of small group structures', *Classifying Social Data*. Hudson, M. (ed.), San Francisco: Jossey-Bass pp. 215–30.

Duch, J. and Arenas, A. (2005) 'Community detection in complex networks using external optimization', *Physical Review* 72: 2027104.

Durkheim, E. (1893/1964) *The Division of Labor in Society*. New York: Free Press.

Evans, T.S. (2004) 'Complex networks', *Contemporary Physics*. 45(6): 455–74.

Everett, M. and Borgatti, S.R. (2000) 'Peripheries of cohesive subsets', *Social Networks* 21(4): 397–407.

Festinger, L., Schachter, S. and Back, K.W. (1950) *Social Pressures in Informal Groups*. New York: Harper & Bros.

Fiduccia, C.M. and Mattheyses, R.M. (1982) 'A linear time heuristic for improving network partitions', *Design Automation* Conference pp. 175–81.

Fiedler, M. (1973) 'Algebraic connectivity of graphs', *Czechoslovak Mathematics Journal* 23: 298–305.

Fiedler, M. (1975) 'A property of eigebvectors of non-negative symmetric matrices and its application to graph theory', *Czechoslovak Mathematics Journal* 25: 619–33.

Flake, G.W., Lawrence, S. and Giles, C.L. (2000) 'Efficient identification of web communities', *Proceedings of t he Sixth International Conference on Knowledge Discovery and Data Mining* New York, NY: ACM Press, pp. 150–60.

Fortunato, S., Latora, V. and Marchiori, M. (2004) 'Method to find community structures based on information centrality', *Physical Review* 70(5): 056104.

Frank, K.A. (1995) 'Identifying cohesive subgroups', *Social Networks* 17(1): 27–56.

Freeman, L.C. (1977) 'A set of measures of centrality based on betweenness', *Sociometry* 40: 35–41.

Freeman, L.C. (1979) 'Centrality in social networks: conceptual Clarification', *Social Networks* 1: 215–39.

Freeman, L.C. (1992) 'On the sociological concept of "group": a empirical test of two models', *American Journal of Sociology* 98: 152–66.

Freeman, L.C. (1993) 'Finding groups with a simple genetic algorithm', *Journal of Mathematical Sociology* 17: 227–41.

Freeman, L.C. (1997) 'Uncovering organizational hierarchies', *Computational and Mathematical Organization Theory* 3: 5–18.

Freeman, L.C. (2004) '*The development of social network analysis: a study in the sociology of science*', Vancouver, B.C.: Empirical Press.

Freeman, L.C. (2008) 'Going the wrong way on a one-way street: centrality in physics and biology', *Journal of Social Structure* 9(2).

Freeman, L.C., Romney, A.K. and Freeman, S.C. (1987) 'Cognitive structure and informant accuracy', *American Anthropologist* 89: 311–25.

Freeman, L.C. and Webster, C.M. (1994) 'Interpersonal proximity in social and cognitive space', *Social Cognition* 12: 223–47.

Freeman, L.C. and White, D.R. (1993) 'Using galois lattices to represent network data', Marsden, P. (ed.), *Sociological Methodology 1993*. Cambridge, MA: Blackwell pp. 127–46.

Girvan, M. and Newman, M.E.J. (2002) 'Community structure in social and biological networks', *PNAS* 99(12): 7821–26.

Glover, F. (1989) 'Tabu search-part I', *ORSA Journal on Computing* 1: 190–206.

Glover, F. (1990) 'Tabu search-part II', *ORSA Journal on Computing* 2: 4–32.

Gower, J.C. (1977) 'The analysis of asymmetry and orthoganality', *Recent Developments in Statistics*. Barra, J., Brodeau, F., and Romier, G. (eds.), Amsterdam: North Holland, pp. 109–23.

Holme, P. (2005) 'Core-periphery organization of complex networks', *Physical Review* 72(4).

Holme, P. and Huss, M. (2005) 'Role-similarity based functional prediction in networked systems: application to the yeast proteome', *Journal of the Royal Society Interface*. 2(4): 327–33.

Holme, P., Edling, C.R. and Liljeros, F. (2004) 'Structure and time evolution of an Internet dating community', *Social Networks* 26: 155–74.

Holme, P., Huss, M. and Jeong, H.W. (2003) 'Subnetwork hierarchies of biochemical pathways', *Bioinformatics* 19(4): 532–38.

Homans, G.C. (1950) *The Human Group.* New York: Harcourt, Brace and Company.

Huber, P. (1802) 'Observations on several species of the genus apis, known by the name of humble bees, and called bombinatrices by linneaus', *Transactions of the Linnean Society of London* 6: 214–98.

Hubert, L. (1974) 'Approximate evaluation techniques for the single-link and complete-link hierarchical clustering procedures', *Journal of the American Statistical Association* 69: 698–704.

Jameson, K.A., Appleby, M.C. and Freeman, L.C. (1999) 'Finding an appropriate order for a hierarchy based on probabilistic dominance', *Animal Behaviour* 57: 991–98.

Jeong, H., Mason, S.P., Barabási, A.L. and Oltvai, Z.N. (2001) 'Lethality and centrality in protein networks', *Nature* 411(6833): 41–42.

Killworth, P.D., McCarty, C., Bernard, H.R. and House, M. (2006) 'The accuracy of small world chains in social networks', *Social Networks* 28: 85–96.

Killworth, P.D., McCarty, C., Bernard, H.R., Johnsen, E.C., Domini, J. and Shelley, G.A., (2003) 'Two interpretrations of reports of knowledge of subpopulation sizes', *Social Networks* 25: 141–69.

Kochen, M. (1989) *The Small World.* Northwood, NJ: Ablex Publishing Co.

Kolaczyk, E.D., Chua, D.B. and Barthelemy, M. (2007) 'Co-betweenness: a pairwise notion of centrality', *Arxiv preprint arXiv:0709.3420, 2007 – arxiv.org.*

Landau, H.G. (1951) 'On dominance relations and the structure of animal societies: some effects of possible social factors', *Bulletin of Mathematical Biophysics* 13: 245–62.

Leavitt, H.J. (1951) 'Some effects of communication patterns on group performance', *Journal of Abnormal and Social Psychology* 46: 38–50.

Levine, J.H. (1972) 'The sphere of influence', *American Sociological Review* 37: 14–27.

Lewin, K. and Lippitt, R. (1938) 'An experimental approach to the study of autocracy and democracy: a preliminary note', *Sociometry* 1(3/4): 292–300.

Linton, R. (1936) *The Study of Man.* New York: D. Appleton-Century Company.

Lorrain, F.P. and White, H.C. (1971) 'Structural equivalence of individuals in social networks', *Journal of Mathematical Sociology* 1: 49–80.

Luce, R.D. and Perry, A. (1949) 'A method of matrix analysis of group structure', *Psychometrika* 14: 95–116.

Maine, H. (1861/1931) *Ancient Law.* London: Oxford University Press.

Milgram, S. (1967) 'The small world problem', *Psychology Today* 22: 61–67.

Mokken, R.J. (1979) 'Cliques, clubs and clans', *Quantity and Quality* 13: 161–73.

Moody, J. and White, D.R. (2003) 'Structural cohesion and embeddedness: a hierarchical concept of social groups', *American Sociological Review* 68(1): 103–27.

Moreno, J.L. (1932) *Application of the Group Method to Classification.* New York: National Committee on Prisons and Prison Labor.

Moreno, J.L. (1934) *Who Shall Survive?* Washington, DC: Nervous and Mental Disease Publishing Company.

Moreno, J.L. and Jennings, H.H. (1938) 'Statistics of social configurations', *Sociometry* 1: 342–74.

Nadel, S.F. (1957) *The Theory of Social Structure.* London: Cohen and West.

Newcomb, T.M. (1961) *The Acquaintance Process.* New York: Holt, Rhinehart, and Winston.

Newman, M.E.J. (2003) 'The structure and function of complex networks', *Siam Review* 45(2): 167–256.

Newman, M.E.J. (2004) 'Detecting community structure in networks', *European Physical Journal* 38(2): 321–30.

Newman, M.E.J. (2006) 'Finding community structure in networks using the eigenvectors of matrices', *Physical Review* 74(3): 19.

Newman, M.E.J. and Girvan, M. (2004) 'Finding and evaluating community structure in networks', *Physical Review* 69: 026113.

Nieminen, J. (1974) 'On centrality in a graph', *Scandinavian Journal of Psychology* 15(4): 332–36.

Palla, G., Derény, I., Farkas, I. and Vicsek, T. (2005) 'Uncovering the overlapping community structure of complex networks in nature and society', *Nature* 435: 814–18.

Park, J. and Newman, M.E.J. (2005) 'A network-based ranking system for U.S. college football', *Journal of Statistical Mechanics: P Theory and Experiment* Vol. P10014.

Parlett, B.N. (1980) 'A new look at the {L}anczos method for solving symmetric systems of linear equations', *Linear Algebra Applied* 29: 323–46.

Pons, P. and Latapy, M. (2006) 'Computing communities in large networks using random walks', *Journal of Graph Algorithms and Applications* 10(2): 191–218.

Pool, I.D. and Kochen, M. (1978) 'Contacts and influence', *Social Networks* 1(1): 5–51.

Pothen, A., Simon, H. and Liou, K-P. (1990) 'Partitioning sparse matrices witheigenvalues of graphs', *Journal of Matrix Analysis Applied* 11(3): 430–52.

Price, D.J. (1965) 'Networks of scientific papers', *Science* 149: 510–15.

Price, D.J. (1976) 'A general theory of bibliometric and other cumulative advantage processes', *Journal of the American Society for Information Science* 27: 292–306.

Radicchi, F., Castellano, C., Cecconi, F., Loretto, V. and Parisi, D. (2004) 'Defining and identifying communities in networks', *Proceedings of the National Academy of Sciences* 101: 2658–63.

Raghavan, U.N., Albert, R. and Kumara, S. (2007) 'Near linear time algorithm to detect community structures in large-scale networks', *Physical Review* 76: 036106.

Reichardt, J. and Bornholdt, S. (2006) 'Statistical mechanics of community detection', *Physical Review* 74: 016110.

Reichardt, J. and White, D.R. (2007) 'Role models for complex networks', *The European Physical Journal* 60: 217–24.

Roberts, J.M. (2000) 'Correspondence analysis of two-mode network data', *Social Networks* 22: 65–72.

Roethlisberger, F.J. and Dickson, W.J. (1939) *Management and the worker*, Cambridge, MA: Harvard University Press.

Sabidussi, G. (1966) 'The centrality index of a graph', *Psychometrika* 31(4): 581–603.

Sailer, L.D. (1978) 'Structural equivalence: meaning and definition, computation and application', *Social Networks* 1: 73–90.

Sailer, L.D. and Gaulin, S.J.C. (1984) 'Proximity, sociality and observation: the definition of social groups', *American Anthropologist* 86: 91–98.

Salganik, M.J., Dodds, P.S. and Watts, D.J. (2006) 'Experimental study of inequality and unpredictability in an artificial cultural market', *Science* 311: 854–56.

Scott, J. (1992) *Social Network Analysis*. Newbury Park, CA: Sage.

Seary, A.J. and Richards, W.D. (2003) 'Spectral methods for analyzing and visualizing networks: an introduction', *Dynamic Social Network Modeling and Analysis*. Breiger, R.L., Carley, K.M., and Pattison, P. (eds.), Washington: The National Academies Press, pp. 209–28.

Skvoretz, J. and Faust, K. (1999) 'Logit models for affiliation networks', *Sociological Methodology* 29: 253–80.

Spencer, H. (1897) *The Principles of Sociology*. New York: Appleton-Century-Crofts Vol I.

Tönnies, F. (1855/1936) *Fundamental Concepts of Sociology*. New York: American Book Company.

Vendruscolo, M., Dokholyan, N.V., Paci, E. and Karplus, M. (2002) 'Small-world view of the amino acids that play a key role in protein folding', *Physical Review* 65(6): 061910–061913.

Wagner, A. and Fell, D.A. (2001) 'The small world inside large metabolic networks', *Proceedings of the Royal Society of London Series B-Biological Sciences* 268(1478): 1803–10.

Warner, W.L. and Lunt, P.S. (1941) *The Social Life of a Modern Community*. New Haven, CT: Yale University Press.

Wasserman, S. and Faust, K. (1994) *Social Network Analysis: Methods and Applications*. Cambridge: Cambridge University Press.

Watts, D.J. (1999) 'Networks, dynamics, and the small-world phenomenon', *American Journal of Sociology* 105: 493–527.

Watts, D.J. and Strogatz, S.H. (1998) 'Collective dynamics of "small-world" networks', *Nature* 393(6684): 440–42.

White, H.C., Boorman, S.A. and Breiger, R.L. (1976) 'Social structure from multiple networks i: blockmodels of roles and positions', *American Journal of Sociology* 81: 730–81.

Wu, F. and Huberman, B.A. (2004) 'Finding communities in linear time: a physics approach', *European Physical Journal* 38(2): 331–38.

Wu, Z. and Leahy, R. (1993) 'An optimal graph theoretic approach to data clustering: theory and its application to image segmentation', *IEEE Transactions on Pattern Analysis and Machine Intelligence* 15: 1101–13.

Zachary, W. (1977) 'An information flow model for conflict and fission in small groups', *Journal of Anthropological Research* 33: 452–73.

4

Network Theory

Stephen P. Borgatti and Virginie Lopez-Kidwell

This chapter is about *network theory*, which in general usage can refer to several different kinds of ideas. For example, both a theory of *tie formation* and a theory of the advantages of *social capital* could be considered network theory. In the tie formation case, network properties serve as the dependent variable, and the theory concerns the antecedents of network phenomena. In the social capital case, the network construct is the independent variable, and the theory considers the consequences of network phenomena. We distinguish between the two kinds of theory by referring to the first (on antecedents) as *theory of networks* and the second (on consequences) as *network theory*.[1] The focus of this chapter is on network theory, which we define as the proposed processes and mechanisms that relate network properties to outcomes of interest.

One approach to writing a chapter on network theory is to simply review the network literature and note that so-and-so argued that network variable X leads to Y while someone else argued that network variable Z leads to W. The problem with this is that theory is more than a system of inter-related variables—it is the reason the variables are related. Theory describes the unseen mechanism that generates an outcome from initial conditions. Our approach, therefore, is to examine well-known network theories and extract the underlying principles or mechanisms they propose. We think of these mechanisms as elemental theoretical memes that are combined in various ways to generate theory. We hope this approach will help identify commonalities across different research efforts and provide conceptual tools for creating new theory.

We start the chapter with detailed accounts of a few well-known network theories that serve as prototypes. We then abstract an underlying generic theory that we call the *network flow model* (where networks are seen as systems of pipes through which information flows), which we argue underlies much of network thinking. As part of this, we introduce a typology of dyadic states and events. Next, we consider examples of network theorizing that stem from a different underlying model, which we call the *network architecture model* (where networks are seen as systems of girders that create structures of dependencies). The two models are then discussed in the light of a typology of network research traditions. We conclude with some general observations about the state of network theorizing.

EXAMPLES OF NETWORK THEORIZING

We start with a detailed account of Granovetter's (1973) strength of weak ties (SWT) theory, using new terminology that facilitates comparison with other theories. Conveniently, the theory is organized as a set of explicit premises and conclusions, as shown in Figure 4.1. The first premise of the theory is that the stronger[2] the tie between two people, the more likely that their social worlds will overlap—that they will have ties with the same third parties, a kind of transitivity.

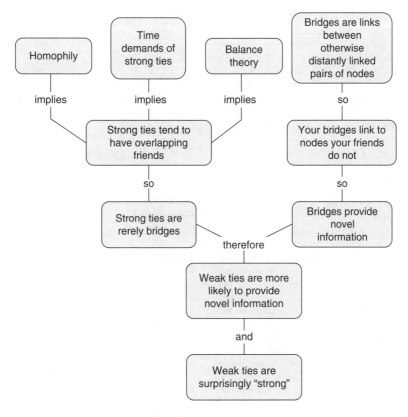

Figure 4.1 Granovetter's (1973) strength of weak ties theory

For example, if A is married to B, and B is close friends with C, the chances are that A and C will at least be acquaintances (see Figure 4.2). The reason for this, Granovetter argues, is that the underlying causes of tie formation have this kind of transitivity built into them. For example, people tend to be *homophilous*, meaning that they have stronger ties with people who are similar to themselves (Lazarsfeld and Merton, 1954; McPherson et al., 2001). Homophily is weakly transitive because if A is similar to B, and B is similar to C, then A and C are likely to share some similarity as well. To the extent ties are caused by similarity, this will induce weak transitivity in the tie structure as well.

Another argument is based on balance or cognitive dissonance theory (Heider, 1958; Cartwright and Harary, 1956; Newcomb, 1961; J. Davis, 1967). If A likes B, and B likes C, A would like to like C as well to avoid dissonance.

The second premise of SWT is that bridging ties are a potential source of novel ideas. A bridging tie is a tie that links a person to people who are not connected to their other friends.[3] The idea is that from a bridging tie a person can hear things that are not already circulating among their other friends. In Figure 4.3, A's tie with G is a bridging tie.[4]

Putting the two premises together, Granovetter reasoned that strong ties are unlikely to be the

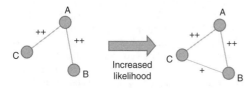

Figure 4.2 One premise of Granovetter's (1973) SWT theory

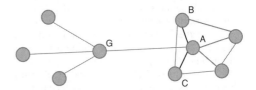

Figure 4.3 Bridging tie from A to G. Removing the tie disconnects the network

sources of novel information. The reason is as follows. First, bridging ties are unlikely to be strong. According to premise 1, if A and G have a strong tie, then G should have at least a weak tie to A's other strong friends. But if this is true, then the tie between A and G cannot be a bridge, since this would imply the existence of many short paths from A to G via their common acquaintances. Therefore, only weak ties can be bridges. Since bridges are the sources of novel information, and only weak ties are bridges, it is the weak ties that are the best potential sources of novel information.[5]

Granovetter uses this theory to explain why people often get or at least hear about jobs through acquaintances rather than close friends. In this sense, the theory is one of individual social capital, where people with more weak ties (i.e., more social capital) are more successful.

Granovetter also applies the theory at the group level, arguing that communities with many strong ties have pockets of strong local cohesion but weak global cohesion. In contrast, communities with many weak ties have weak local cohesion but strong global cohesion. He illustrates the idea in a case study of Boston in which the city assimilated one adjacent community (the West End) but failed to assimilate another (Charlestown). According to Granovetter, Charlestown had more weak ties, which facilitated community-level organizing. The traditional ethnic West End was a bedroom community in which people worked elsewhere; it was fragmented into distinct clusters of very dense strong ties, lacking bridging weak ties. In contrast, Charlestown residents worked in the community and had more opportunities to rub elbows. Thus, a community's diffuse weak-tie structure constitutes group-level social capital that enables the group to work together to achieve goals, such as mobilizing resources and organizing community action to respond to an outside threat.

Another well-known network theory is Burt's (1992) structural holes theory of social capital. Burt argues that if we compare nodes A and B in Figure 4.4, the shape of A's ego network is likely to afford A more novel information than B's ego network does for B. Both have the same number of ties, and we can stipulate that they are of the same strength. But because B's contacts are connected with each other, the information B gets from, say, X may well be the same information B gets from Y. In contrast, A's three ties connect A to three pockets of the network, who may know different things. A's ties connect to three different pools of information (represented by circles in Figure 4.4), while B's ties connect to just one pool. Burt argued that, as a result, A is likely to receive more nonredundant information at any given time than B, which can then be exploited to do a better job or to be the source of "new" ideas.

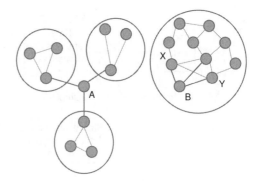

Figure 4.4   Node A has more structural holes than B

Burt's theory may look different from Granovetter's, but the differences are largely in language and focus. In Burt's language, A has more structural holes than B, which means A has more nonredundant ties. In Granovetter's language, A has more bridges than B. But whether we call them nonredundant ties or bridges, the concept is the same, and so are the consequences: more novel information.

Where Granovetter and Burt differ is that Granovetter further argues that a tie's strength determines whether it will serve as a bridge. Burt does not disagree and even provides empirical evidence that bridging ties are weaker in that they are more subject to decay (Burt, 1992, 2002). However, Burt sees tie strength as a mere "correlate" of the underlying principle, which is nonredundancy (1992: 27). Thus, the difference is between preferring the distal cause (strength of ties), as Granovetter does, and the proximal cause (bridging ties), as Burt does. The first yields an appealingly ironic and counterintuitive story line, while the second "captures the causal agent directly and thus provides a stronger foundation for theory" (Burt, 1992: 28). But it is all based on the same underlying model of how networks work, a model that we shall argue underpins a great deal of network theory.

The superficial differences and underlying similarity of weak tie and structural hole theories recall the apparent contradiction between Burt's structural hole argument and Coleman's closure theory of social capital. Burt (1992) argues that communication between an ego's two alters doesn't just reduce information, it constrains ego's behavior. For example, if the alters share information about their interactions with ego, then ego cannot tell substantially different stories to each party, constraining ego's behavior and reducing ego's social capital. In contrast, Coleman (1988) argues that the connections among ego's alters enable the alters to work together to help ego, increasing ego's social capital.

For example, a child benefits from having parents, teachers, neighborhood adults, and so on communicate with each other because this way they can ensure that the child does his homework, avoids danger, etc. But as Burt (2005) points out, the conflict between these views is more apparent than real, as both assume that ties among the child's alters constrain that child. The difference is simply that in Coleman's educational setting, constraint is good, and in Burt's corporate setting, constraint is typically bad. It is really only the (unwise) value-loadedness of the social capital concept that creates contradiction.

Another well-known area of network theorizing is small-world theory. In the 1950s and 1960s, a stream of mathematical research sought to explain coincidences of mutual acquaintanceship (de Sola Pool and Kochen, 1978[6]; Rapoport and Horvath, 1961). The basic thrust of the research was to show that societies were probably much more close-knit than popularly believed. A field experiment by Milgram (1967; Travers and Milgram, 1969) supported this theory, finding that paths linking random Americans were incredibly short. Restarting this stream of research 20 years later, Watts and Strogatz (1998) asked how human networks could have such short average distances, given that human networks were so clustered, a property that was known to lengthen network distances (Rapoport and Horvath, 1961). The answer, Watts and Strogatz showed, was simple: adding even a small number of random ties to a heavily clustered network could radically reduce distances among nodes. The reason was that many of these random ties would be between clusters, which is to say, they were bridges.

Integrating network yheories: the network flow model

In our view, small-world (SW) theory, structural hole (SH) theory, Coleman social capital (CSC) theory, and SWT theory are all elaborations—in different directions and for different purposes—of the same theory. In this section, we deconstruct this theory into three layers: a deep layer that defines the rules of a theoretical universe within which to work, a middle layer that consists of a theorem derived from the rules of the universe, and a surface layer that connects to the variables associated with a specific empirical setting. Together, these create the theory of which SW, SWT, SH and CSC are all different views. We then show how other theorems or derivations from the same set of underlying rules generate different (but not incompatible) theories.

The deep layer consists of a very simple model of how social systems work, which is essentially that they are networks through which information

(or any resource) flows from node to node along paths consisting of ties interlocked through shared endpoints. The element of network paths is important. Paths simultaneously imply both connection and disconnection, with the length of paths indicating the degree of disconnection. We refer to this model as the network flow model, and we conceive of it as a platform for theorizing.

We limit the network flow model to "true" flows in the sense that what arrives at the other end is the same as when it started. Whatever flows through the network may be damaged or changed en route, but it remains basically the same thing. If it starts as gossip, it arrives as gossip, even if the details have changed. The distinction we are making is with a more general sense of flow such as a chain of causality, where, for example, someone misses an appointment and sets off a chain of events that culminate in a civil war. We regard this more general sense of flow as constituting a different model.

The middle layer consists of a bit of reasoning that says that transitivity (closure; clusteredness) slows network flows by increasing path lengths. This reasoning is effectively a theorem derived from the underlying flow model. Because all of the elements of the theorem are drawn from the network flow model, the theorem can be proved (or disproved) mathematically and can be explored via simulation. The network flow model is a closed world in which all the rules are known. Theory, at this level, consists of taking constructs defined on the underlying model (such as betweenness centrality) and relating them to outcomes in the same universe (such as frequency and time of first arrival of something flowing through the network).

The surface layer can be seen as a "personalization" of the theory that ornaments the basic theory with variables drawn from the immediate empirical context and which serve as an interface to general social theory. For example, Granovetter decorates the theory at one end by adding strength of tie as an antecedent to transitivity. Burt decorates the theory at the other end by connecting information flows to personal creativity and producing value. Travers and Milgram suggest that upper-class people are more likely to be key nodes.

The transitivity theorem is just one of many we can derive from the underlying flow model to yield new theory. For example, a different theorem is that, ceteris paribus, nodes with more ties have greater exposure to (i.e., more chances of receiving) whatever is flowing through a network (Freeman, 1979; Borgatti, 1995, 2005). Depending on the flow's usefulness, this should mean better outcomes for nodes with more ties.[7]

We can also reason that it matters how well connected a node's contacts (Bonacich, 1972) are.

A node with five contacts that have no other contacts has little exposure to information flowing through the network. A node whose five contacts are the most central nodes in the network will have great exposure. For example, in a sexual network, many nodes can be monogamous, but their risk of catching a sexually transmitted disease will vary based on how well "connected" their partner has recently been.

If the connectedness of an ego's alters matters, so could other characteristics, including nonstructural attributes, such as wealth, power, or expertise. Being connected to powerful and wealthy people may present more opportunities than being connected to an equal number of people without such resources. This is the basis of Lin's (1982) social resource theory (see also Snijders, 1999), another branch of social capital research.

If we assume that the time it takes for information to move along a network path is proportional to the length of the path, another obvious theorem is that nodes that are closest to all others should, on average, receive flows more quickly (Freeman, 1979; Borgatti, 1995, 2005). When it is beneficial to receive flows before others do (e.g., information on organizational events), nodes with greater overall closeness should perform better.

A well-known theoretical proposition is that nodes positioned along the only or best paths between others may be able to benefit by controlling, filtering, or coloring the flow, as well as charging rents for passing along the flow (Freeman, 1977).

Finally, we can theorize that nodes located in the same general areas (e.g., connected to the same nodes; Lorrain and White, 1971) will tend to hear the same things and therefore have equal access to opportunities provided by network flows (Burt, 1976).

There are many other basic theoretical propositions found in the literature that can be derived from the basic network flow model. The main point is that the network flow model provides a conceptual universe within which we can conceptualize properties (such as clusteredness or centrality) and relate them to other properties (such as probabilities of receiving something flowing through the system). These properties are widely misperceived as elements of methodology (i.e., "measures") that are unconnected to theory, when in fact they are derivations of a model and exist only in the context of a theoretical process.[8]

RELATIONAL STATES AND EVENTS IN THE NETWORK FLOW MODEL

Theories derived from the network flow model distinguish between two kinds of relational or

Figure 4.5 Types of dyadic phenomena

dyadic phenomena, which Atkin (1974, 1977) referred to as *backcloth* and *traffic*. The backcloth consists of an underlying infrastructure that enables and constrains the traffic, and the traffic consists of what flows through the network, such as information. For example, in SWT theory, social ties such as acquaintanceships serve as potential conduits for information.

A more elaborate set of distinctions is illustrated in Figure 4.5, which divides dyadic phenomena into four basic categories: similarities, social relations, interactions, and flows.[9]

The *similarities* category refers to physical proximity, co-membership in social categories, and sharing of behaviors, attitudes, and beliefs. Generally, we do not see these items as social ties, but we do often see them as increasing the probabilities of certain relations and dyadic events. For example, in an organizational setting, Allen (1977) found that communication tends to increase as a function of spatial proximity.

The *social relations* category refers to the classic kinds of social ties that are ubiquitous in network theorizing. We distinguish between two types of social relations: role-based and cognitive/affective. *Role-based* includes kinships and role relations such as *boss of*, *teacher of*, and *friend of*. We use the term *role-based* because these relations are usually institutionalized into rights and obligations, and are linguistically identified as, for example, *friend*, *boss*, or *uncle*. Many are also symmetric or skew-symmetric, such that if A is a friend of B, then B is a friend of A, and if A is the teacher of B, then B is the student of A. Another characteristic of role-based relations is that they are in a weak sense public and objective—a researcher can ask a third party whether two people are friends or have a teacher/student relationship and not receive an automatic "how should I know?" reaction.

The second type of social relation consists of perceptions and attitudes about specific others, such as *knowing*, *liking*, or *disliking*. These evaluations are widely considered private, idiosyncratic, and invisible. They can easily be nonsymmetric: A likes B, but the reverse may or may not be true.

The *interactions* category refers to discrete and separate events that may occur frequently but then stop, such as *talking with*, *fighting with*, or *having lunch with*.

Finally, the *flows* category includes things such as resources, information, and diseases that move from node to node. They may transfer (being only at one place at a time) and duplicate (as in information). Flows matter in most network theories but are generally assumed immeasurable in practice.

In Atkin's view, the four dyadic phenomena all serve as the backcloth for the phenomena to their right. Hence, physical proximity can facilitate the development of certain relationships, and certain relationships permit certain interactions; these in turn provide the vehicle for transmissions or flows. However, it is also clear that phenomena on the right can transform the phenomena on the left, so that people with certain relationships (e.g., spouses) tend to move closer together, and certain interactions (e.g., sex) can change or institutionalize relationships.

Theory based on the network flow model focuses on either social relations or interactions, using these ties to define the network backcloth, which then determines flows. Interactions are transitory, so theory built on them typically conceptualizes them as cumulative and repeated over time, describing them as *recurrent*, *patterned*, or *relatively stable*. In effect, this relation converts into an underlying social relation that is ongoing across interaction episodes.

We emphasize three points based on this discussion. First, much of the flow model exists because we do not measure flows directly.[10] Hence we build theory that links the observable network of social relations to these latent flows. If the flows were directly measurable, we would not need to infer that nodes with more structural holes (or weak ties) would receive more information: we would simply measure the information they got.

Second, much of network flow theory depends on the relative permanence of ties. For example, consider a node that profits from being the broker between otherwise unconnected nodes. This works only if the spanned nodes cannot simply create a tie with each other at will. If a direct tie can always be formed, the importance of paths through a network vanishes, as does the importance of structure in general.

Third, when researching the exploitation of network position by nodes, it is problematic to measure relational *events* such as interactions and flows rather than relational states, because power use can change the event network. For example, if a node tries to extract rents for being between two others, the others may choose a different path (Ryall and Sorenson, 2007; Reagans and Zuckerman, 2008). So the event network we see is not the potential structure defined by underlying relations, but an actualized instance that could change at any time and therefore does not tell us what other paths might have been possible.

THE NETWORK ARCHITECTURE MODEL

As noted earlier, the network flow model is based on what we termed *true* flows of resources, which travel along network paths and are acquired by the nodes encountered along the way, either as capital or as a trait. However, not all network theorizing derives from this underlying model. Consider the image of an entrepreneur usually presented in social resource theory (Lin, 1982, 1999a, 1999b). To be successful, the entrepreneur needs help: rich friends can contribute capital, or experienced friends can convey key knowledge, but often no resources are actually transferred to ego. For example, a legislator can favor a developer by pushing through a bill that allows the developer to utilize previously off-limits land. A judge can decide a case for a friend's benefit. The benefits are real, but contrary to the network flow model, the legislator's and the judge's powers are not transferred to the developer. Rather, work is done on behalf of another, as described by principal/agent theory (Rees, 1985; Eisenhardt, 1989), and this constitutes a different mechanism for achievement.

A similar situation is seen in transactional knowledge theory (Hollingshead, 1998; Argote, 1999; Moreland, 1999), where organizations are seen as distributed knowledge systems in which different bits of the organization's knowledge store are held in different heads. While it is known who knows what, the knowledge can be utilized. However, the knowledge in a node's head may not be actually transferred when it is used. For example, a chemist is tapped to solve a problem involving stereo isomers. The chemist's knowledge of chemistry is not likely to be transferred to others on the project team who may not have a chemistry background. In fact, if the knowledge were transferable, the organization would cease to be a distributed knowledge system, and every member would be a prodigious polymath. Rather, the chemist works in concert with the team or its leader.[11]

These examples imply a mechanism of node success that is slightly different from the procurement of resources through network paths, as in the network flow model. Instead, it is a virtual procurement because instead of transferring their resources, an ego's alters act on behalf of or in concert with ego. Another way to think about this is that the alters act as an extension of ego, together forming a larger, more capable, entity. The nodes act as one, and this coordination not only harnesses the powers of all the nodes but also means that the individual nodes cannot be used against each other. This is the principle behind unions, co-ops, and other collectivities that prevent negotiation with each member individually. The key here is that ties are serving as bonds that bind the nodes together (whether through solidarity or authority), creating a common fate.

We argue that this mechanism is different enough from that of the network flow model to constitute a different model, which we term the *network architecture model*. In defining a separate model that does not include the term "flow," we do not imply that, in the architecture model, information does not flow. To coordinate actions, nodes may well communicate. However, two points should be kept in mind. First, communication is not the only way to achieve coordination (Thompson, 1967). Second, communication, even if plentiful, plays a role in the network architecture model that is different from its role in the network flow model. In the network flow model, it is the value of the flow itself that generates outcomes for the ego that receives it. A manager receives gossip about a failing project and takes steps to disassociate herself from it. In the architecture model, it is the alignment between nodes produced by the flow that yields the outcome.

The case of authority relations—bureaucracy's backbone—is instructive. The "reports to" ties serve as conduits for information flow (e.g., orders going down; reports going up), but this differs from the network flow model both because simply receiving an order is not enriching, and orders are not (usually) repeated down the line, as on a ship. Rather, the orders from A to B are different from those from B to C. Communication is involved, but the coordination, not the message, is the mechanism.

Finally, consider *network exchange theory*, which we regard as the analogue to SWT theory in providing a clear example of a distinctive kind of network theorizing. In the experimental exchange tradition of social network analysis (Cook et al., 1983; Markovsky et al., 1988), researchers have volunteers bargain with each other to distribute points between them, with the goal of amassing as many points as possible across a series of rounds. The participants are placed in a network designed by the experimenters and can negotiate only with people they have been given links to. In each round of the game, participants must divide 24 points with someone they have a tie to. Initially, they tend to make even trades of 12 and 12. Over time, however, those in certain network positions are able to command more favorable terms, such as 13–11, 14–10, and eventually, 23–1. For example, in Figure 4.6a, node X accumulates the most points.

Initially, centrality was thought to be the underlying principle (Cook et al., 1983). However, it was soon discovered that in the network shown in Figure 4.6b, the most central node had no power. Instead, the Zs had the power. The reason was simple: even though X has as many potential trading partners as the Zs, the Zs each have a partner (a Y) that is in a very weak position, whereas X

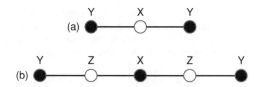

Figure 4.6   Two experimental exchange networks. Light-colored nodes have more power (Allen, Thomas J., *Managing the Flow of Technology,* **figure, page 239, © 1977 Massachusetts Institute of Technology, by permission of The MIT Press)**

has only powerful partners to trade with. Why are the Ys weak? Because whenever their Z makes a deal with someone else, the Y is excluded from that particular round. The Ys depend on the Zs because they lack alternatives. But it is not simply the number of alternatives that matters, because X has just as many alternatives as the Zs. Ultimately, a node's bargaining position is a consequence not only of its alternatives, but also the (lack of) alternatives of its alternatives, which in turn are determined by their own alternatives, virtually ad infinitum.

Note a number of interesting points about the exchange situation. First, while nodes interact and accumulate resources, resources (i.e., points) do not travel along paths of the network; the rules of the game prevent it. This is why centrality measures are useless in predicting outcomes of this experiment—centrality is a construct of the network flow model, and there are no flows here. But even without flows, paths do matter here. For example, adding a node linked to any of the Ys in Figure 4.6b would tend to change X's fortunes considerably. It is, if not a flow, a propagation effect in which being adjacent to a weak node makes a node strong, which in turn weakens others that the node is connected to, which strengthens still others and so on through the network (Bonacich, 1987). Perhaps a better term than *propagation* would be *autocorrelation*, meaning that a node's state is affected by the states of the nodes it is connected to, but not necessarily in the simple manner proposed by the network flow model, in which a node always comes to have the same thing its environment has.[12] Rather, it is more like adaptation, such that nodes react to their environments rather than acquire them.

Network exchange theory may be seen as a special case of network role theory (Borgatti and Everett, 1992b). If we examine a network such as shown in Figure 4.7, it is apparent that nodes *b*, *g*, *d*, and *i* are structurally similar to each other, even if they are not particularly close to each other. Indeed, suppose one were to remove the labels on all nodes in Figure 4.7, pick up the diagram, flip it

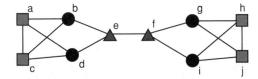

Figure 4.7 Shapes identify nodes that are structurally isomorphic

around on both its vertical and horizontal axes, and then put it back down on the page. Could one reassign the labels correctly? Clearly one could not mistake *b* for *e*, because *b* has a pair of friends (*a* and *c*) who are friends with each other, while none of *e*'s friends are friends with each other. We would also not confuse *b* for *a*, because among *a*'s friends, not one but two pairs are friends with each other. But we could not tell the difference between *b* and *d*, nor *g* and *i*. Similarly, *a, c, h*, and *j* are indistinguishable from each other, as are *e* and *f*; within each of these sets, the nodes are structurally isomorphic.

In a sense, the network in Figure 4.7 has an underlying structure in which the 10 different nodes reduce to just three classes of nodes that share certain characteristic relations with each other. The pattern of relations among classes is shown in Figure 4.8, which presents a reduced model (a *blockmodel* in the language of White et al., 1976) of the network in Figure 4.7. The pattern is that square nodes (the class containing *a, c, h, j*) have ties to both circle nodes and other square nodes; triangle nodes have ties with themselves and with circle nodes; circle nodes connect square nodes to triangle nodes and have no ties among themselves.

In effect, the three classes of nodes play three different structural roles and have three different social environments, and these differences imply different consequences for the nodes occupying those positions. Indeed, returning to experimental exchange networks, Borgatti and Everett (1992a) showed that all experimental results to date confirm that nodes playing the same structural roles obtain the same results, within bounds of statistical variation.

In discussing the flow and architecture models, it is tempting to argue that they rest on two different metaphorical understandings of ties. In the flow model, ties are pipes (or roads, or circuits) through

which things flow (the traffic, the current). In the architecture model, the ties are bonds, ligatures, girders, or bones that bind the network together, creating a structure (like a skeleton) around which the rest of the social system is draped. The bonds serve as the elemental units of structure.

This pipes-and-bonds distinction is not unhelpful, but it is also not quite right. As we have tried to point out, both models typically involve flows of some kind at the dyadic level. It is the style and function of these flows that is different.

GOALS OF NETWORK THEORY

For simplicity of exposition, our discussion of the network flow and architecture models has focused on explaining differences in node (or group) success with respect to performance or rewards. This value-loaded focus is drawn from the *social capital* research tradition, which investigates the benefits of (or aspects of) network position for individuals and groups.

However, social capital is not the only theoretical perspective in the field. The *social homogeneity* perspective seeks network-theoretic explanations for why some nodes share traits with certain others, particularly with respect to behaviors (such as adoption of innovation), beliefs, and attitudes (Borgatti and Foster, 2003).[13]

The network flow model and the architecture model are used in both social capital and social homogeneity studies, providing competing explanations for the same outcomes. Figure 4.9, drawn from Borgatti and Foster (2003), summarizes this discussion as a simple 2-by-2 cross-classification. The rows correspond to the fundamental models and therefore basic explanatory modes. The columns correspond to research traditions, based on their generic goals of explaining variance in performance or similarity of traits. The cells of the table identify specific mechanisms used in each context. We regard these elemental mechanisms as part of the vocabulary of social network theory. We discuss each quadrant in turn.[14]

Underlying model	Social capital	Social homogeneity
Network flow model	Capitalization	Contagion
Network architecture model	Coordination	Adaptation

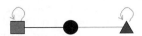

Figure 4.8 Blockmodel of network in Figure 4.7

Figure 4.9 Network functions (mechanisms) by model and research tradition

The top-left quadrant, which uses the network flow model to understand success, is one of the most developed, particularly in organizational research. The key concept is *capitalization*, meaning that nodes acquire ideas, resources, and opportunities through their ties, and this process either directly increases their human capital or increases their ability to exploit their human capital, which in turn contributes to their success in terms of performance and rewards. The capitalization process is evident in work on social support (e.g., Wellman and Wortley, 1990), status attainment (Lin, 1999a), job search information and job-getting (Granovetter, 1973, 1974), knowledge (Borgatti and Cross, 2003; Bouty, 2000), creativity (Perry-Smith and Shalley, 2003; Burt, 2004), mobility (Boxman et al., 1991; Burt, 1997; Seibert et al., 2001), power (Brass, 1984; Kilduff and Krackhardt, 1994), leadership (Brass and Krackhardt, 1999; Pastor et al., 2002), performance (Baldwin et al., 1997; Mehra et al., 2001), and entrepreneurship (Renzulli et al., 2000).[15] The capitalization mechanism can also be seen in group-level research, such as in the work of Bavelas (1950) and Leavitt (1951), showing that communication networks with short distances from each node to a central node (an "information integrator") were better able to solve puzzles involving pooling of information.

The bottom-left quadrant, labeled *coordination*, uses the architectural model to provide an alternative set of explanations for node (or group) success. In this model, networks provide benefits because they can coordinate or "virtually agglomerate" multiple nodes in order to bring all their resources to bear in a coordinated fashion (and avoid being divided and conquered). Different network structures, in combination with contextual rules of the game, create different dependencies and possibilities for coordination (Markovsky et al., 1988; Cook et al., 1983). Work based on these mechanisms includes Burt's (1992) work on the control benefits of structural holes, research on "network organizations" (Miles and Snow, 1986; Powell, 1990; Snow et al., 1992; Jones et al., 1997), research on compliance with norms (Roethlisberger and Dickson, 1939; Mayhew, 1980; Kiuru et al., 2009), and work on the in- and out-groups of leaders (Sparrowe and Liden, 1997). Other work in this tradition is the literature on transactional memory systems (Hollingshead, 1998; Moreland, 1999; Rulke and Galaskiewicz, 2000), in which an individual or group benefits from the knowledge of others without necessarily acquiring that knowledge themselves. At the group level, we have already mentioned Granovetter's (1973) account of communities' differential ability to fight off incorporation by a neighboring city, thanks to having a network structure that facilitated community-wide collaboration.

The top-right quadrant, *contagion*, is the basis for most diffusion research. The basic idea is that nodes essentially become their environments through a process of contamination/infection/staining[16] so that one's location in a network has much to do with one's acquired traits. Both the coordination quadrant and the capitalization mechanisms are about processes in which nodes acquire something flowing through network paths. The difference is that in one case the nodes acquire capital, while in the other they acquire traits.

Network research based on the contagion mechanism includes Coleman, Katz, and Menzel's (1966) classic study, which argued that informal discussions among physicians created behavioral contagion with respect to adopting tetracycline, as well as the study by Davis (1991) arguing that the now-standard corporate practice of "poison pills" spread through corporate board interlocks. The contagion mechanism has been used to explain similarity in job decisions (Kilduff, 1990), the adoption of organizational structures and strategies (DiMaggio and Powell, 1983; Geletkanycz and Hambrick, 1997), disease and immunity outcomes (Morris, 1993; Cohen et al., 1997), decisions to smoke (Christakis and Fowler, 2008), similarity of attitudes and beliefs (Harrison and Carroll, 2002; Sanders and Hoekstra, 1998; Molina, 1995), and the production of consensus through social influence (Friedkin and Johnsen, 1999).

It should be noted that each of these general processes, such as contagion, can be broken down further into micro-mechanisms at the dyadic level. For example, DiMaggio and Powell (1983) discussed *mimetic processes*, in which a firm actively imitates another firm in its environment, and *coercive processes*, where a trait is imposed on a firm, as when a large customer imposes a certain accounting system on a supplier. Within each of these micro-mechanisms we can continue to add detail, such as noting that the likelihood of mimetic processes increases with uncertainty and the need for legitimacy (DiMaggio and Powell, 1983; Galaskiewicz and Wasserman, 1989; Haunschild and Miner, 1997). However, this kind of theorizing belongs to the interface layer discussed earlier and is outside the scope of this chapter.

Finally, the bottom-right quadrant, *adaptation*, uses the architecture model to provide an alternative to network flows for explaining homogeneity. Instead of a node acquiring what is flowing through the network, as in contagion, the node responds or adapts to a set of environmental dependencies. Social homogeneity is explained by the architecture model as *convergent evolution*, similar to the evolutionary process that results in sharks and dolphins having similar shapes. For example, two nodes that are both central in the advice networks of their respective firms may come to have a similar distaste for the phone, because it so often brings more work. Similarly, in structural role theory, nodes are seen as similar if they have ties to similar others, which is to say they have similar environments.

The adaptation mechanism has been used to explain similarity in attitudes (Erickson, 1988), organizational behaviors (Galaskiewicz and Burt, 1991; Haunschild and Miner, 1997; Galaskiewicz and Wasserman, 1989), and organizational isomorphism (DiMaggio, 1986).

DISCUSSION

A frequent confusion about network research has to do with where theory ends and methodology begins. Network analysis is exemplary in the social sciences in basing its theorizing on a fundamental construct—the network—that is both emically meaningful and fully mathematical. Fitted with some fundamental processes, such as flows of resources through paths, the network model is extremely fertile in that it so easily generates distinctive research questions—such as, how does it affect a node to be along the only path between two sets of others?

Furthermore, the "mathematicity" of the network construct means that such research questions are almost automatically expressible in terms of mathematical properties of the network (such as betweenness), and usually are. This makes research questions in the network field highly amenable to empirical, mathematical, and simulation-based exploration. But it also generates an image problem because the same formula that defines the theoretical network property of, say, betweenness, also enables us to measure it in an empirical dataset. Therefore, it appears to be "just" methodology. Yet concepts like centrality are not only theoretical constructs, they embody a basic model of how social systems work.

Confusion also exists regarding what a network is. In our view, at least two fundamental conceptualizations define networks: *nominalist* and *realist* conceptualizations, echoing a well-known distinction by Laumann, Marsden, and Prensky (1989) with regard to data collection. The concept of networks implicit in this chapter and in most academic research has been the nominalist view, which sees networks principally as models rather than things "out there." For a nominalist, a network is defined by choosing a tie, such as friendship, to examine among a set of nodes. So when a nominalist speaks of *multiple networks*, the nominalist is considering different kinds of ties simultaneously, such as a friendship network together with an advice network, both defined on the same set

of nodes. For a nominalist, networks can be disconnected, and indeed the degree of connectedness is just another property of networks that can be theorized about.

In contrast, in the realist perspective (which is often found in applied work), networks are defined as a set of interconnected nodes, which by definition cannot be disconnected. A realist considers multiple networks to mean multiple groups. Indeed, the realist conception of a network tends to be a replacement for or variant of the concept of sociological group. This is especially evident in popular culture, where public entities that would once have been named the "Preservation Society" or "Lexington Trade Association" would today be called the "Preservation Network" and "Lexington Trade Network." Similarly, we speak of terrorist networks rather than terrorist organizations, and medical insurance companies identify doctors as either in- or out-of-network.

In academic work in the realist tradition, *network* typically connotes a group that has more lateral than vertical ties, relies on social or informal ties to achieve coordination, and consists of relatively empowered or autonomous members, whether they are employees in a firm or organizations in a so-called network organization.

A consequence of having these different views is confusion about meaningful research questions. For example, although we have not discussed theories of networks, a reasonable research question for a realist is, "What conditions will cause a network to emerge?" For the nominalist, this question is awkward because networks arise when you define them, even if they are empty of ties. It is not the network that emerges, but rather ties (or, more usefully, it is that properties of the network structure change over time). Similarly, a meaningful methodological question for a realist is, "What are the best relations to ask about in a survey to tap into the network?" For a nominalist, each question corresponds to a different network, and which question is asked depends on the research question. But for the realist, an underlying reality can be detected by well-chosen questions, much like a psychometric scale. Confusion also lies in the concept of a node "belonging to multiple networks." For a realist, this really means that the node belongs to multiple groups. For a nominalist, it is an odd concept—at best it could mean that the node is not an isolate in several different networks defined by different social relations.

A final confusion has to do with the multiple levels of analysis possible in network research and how this relates to traditional micro/macro distinctions. At the lowest level is the dyad. Research at this level is concerned with whether one kind of tie influences another. For example, in economic sociology, a fundamental proposition is that economic transactions are embedded in social relationships (Granovetter, 1985). In knowledge management, Borgatti and Cross (2003) suggested that in order for X to seek information from Y, certain relational conditions must be present.

At the next level is the node. This is the level that receives the most attention in the literature, and it is readily accessible to researchers outside the network tradition. Most of the work reviewed in this chapter is at the node level, such as when the number of structural holes a node possesses is related to the node's performance.

The highest level is the network as a whole.[17] Theorizing at this level is concerned with the consequences for the network of properties of the network's *internal structure*. For example, Johnson, Boster, and Palinkas (2003) argued that work teams with core/periphery structures would have higher morale than teams divided into potentially warring factions. Thus, a property of network structure, core/peripheriness, is related to a network outcome—morale. The network level of analysis should not be confused with whether the nodes themselves consist of collectivities. For example, suppose our nodes are firms, and we theorize that more central firms in an inter-firm alliance network are more profitable. This is a node-level analysis, not a network-level analysis. In contrast, if we theorize that the shape of the alliance network in an industry affects the profitability of the industry as a whole (and we compare across several industries), this is a network-level analysis. Similarly, a study of how the network structure of top management teams affects their performance is also a network-level study.

CONCLUSION

In this chapter, we have sought to explain network theory, and to do so in a way that would facilitate generating new theory. Our approach has been to analyze a few representative network theories and extract from them generic mechanisms or modes of explanation. In so doing, we found it convenient to deconstruct network theories into "layers," where the deepest layer consists of a general model of how things work. This is a model of a system, not of any particular outcome. On top of that are the theorems or propositions that we can derive from the underlying model. The final layer is the interface layer, which connects the network constructs to the concepts of specific research domains.

We argue that two underlying models are in evidence in network theorizing, which we refer to as the network flow model and the network architecture model. The flow model views a social system as a system of nodes interconnected by paths (the backcloth), which carry information or other resources (the traffic). Theories based on the flow model define properties of the backcloth structure and relate these to flow outcomes, such as frequency and time of arrival of something flowing through the network, which are then related to more general outcomes such as status attainment. The architecture model sees network ties as creating structures of interdependency and coordination. Theories based on this model explain how the pattern of interconnections interacts with contextual rules to generate outcomes such as power.

Drawing on Borgatti and Foster (2003), we note that network theorizing can be seen as answering two basic types of research questions, namely why some nodes or groups achieve more (the social capital tradition), and why some nodes or networks are more similar to each other (the social homogeneity tradition). Combining this distinction based on types of outcomes with the distinction between the two explanatory models yields a four-cell cross-classification in which each cell corresponds to a different generic mechanism for explaining outcomes (Figure 4.9): the capitalization mechanism is used to explain success as a function of receiving useful flows through the network; the coordination mechanism explains success via virtually merging with others and preventing adversaries from coordinating with each other; the contagion mechanism explains observed similarity as a function of direct influence or diffusion; and the adaptation mechanism explains similarity as resulting from adaptation to similar social environments.

Our objective has been to analyze network theory into theoretical building blocks that make it easier to create new theory as needed. We hope this will help stem the flow of "cookie-cutter" studies that copy the variables of classic studies but miss the logic of how network properties generate outcomes.

NOTES

Steve Borgatti is Chellgren Chair and Professor of Management, sborgatti@uky.edu. Virginie Lopez-Kidwell is a doctoral candidate in Management, v.kidwell@uky.edu. Both authors are affiliated with the LINKS Center for Network Research in Business (http://www.linkscenter.org/), Dept. of Management, Gatton College of Business and Economics, at the University of Kentucky.

This chapter is based in part on a piece in *Science* (Borgatti et al., 2009) and a piece in *Organization*

Science (Borgatti and Halgin, forthcoming). The present authors are indebted to the coauthors of those pieces as well as to Beth Becky, Travis Grosser, and Brandon Ofem for their critical reviews of the chapter. We would also like to thank Jackie Thompson for her editorial assistance. This work was supported by grant HDTRA1–08–1-0002-P00002 from the Defense Threat Reduction Agency (DTRA).

1 In this terminology, a theory of endogenous network evolution, in which both independent and dependent variables are network properties, would be called a network theory of networks. A psychological theory of tie formation (e.g., homophily) would be labeled a theory of networks, but not a network theory of networks.

2 While Granovetter (1973: 1361) provides a definition of strength of tie, it is useful to realize that any definition of tie strength that preserves the first premise can be used (Freeman, 1979).

3 More technically, a bridge is a tie between A and B, which, if removed, would leave a very long path (if any at all) connecting A to B. A bridge is a shortcut.

4 The second premise was "in the air" when Granovetter was writing. Rapoport and Horvath (1961), in particular, explored this concept in depth.

5 Note that there is no claim that all weak ties are sources of novel information—just the ones that happen to be bridges. Granovetter's point is simply that it is weak ties rather than strong ties that are more likely to be bridges.

6 Original paper written in 1958 and well circulated for 20 years before publication in 1978 in the inaugural issue of *Social Networks*.

7 Similarly, a well-connected node has many opportunities to expose others to what it carries, whether an idea or a disease.

8 Indeed, Borgatti (2005) showed that the well-known formulas for closeness and betweenness centrality give the expected values of key network outcomes (such as frequency and time of arrival) under specific models of flow. They are not generic measures or techniques such as regression, which can be divorced from an underlying model of how things work. Rather, they are rooted in specific network theories of how social systems work.

9 It is useful to note that the two categories on the left make up relational phenomena that, while they exist, exist continuously, like states. The phenomena on the right tend to be transitory and discrete, as in events.

10 This is largely for convenience. For example, it is time-consuming and therefore rare to track a specific bit of information as it moves through a gossip network. However, some settings lend themselves to observing flows, as in the movement of goods in the world economic trade network.

11 However, this is not to imply particular motives such as wanting to help, or being coerced into helping. Space limitations in this chapter prevent us from discussing the micro-theory of these exchanges.

12 We don't use the term "autocorrelation" because it refers to a statistical condition rather than a social process.

13 As Borgatti and Foster (2003) pointed out, modeling variance in outcome and homogeneity in attributes are logically two sides of the same coin but seem to constitute different literatures in the field.

14 This terminology varies slightly from Borgatti et al.'s (2009) and Marin and Wellman's in this volume. What was *transmission* in Borgatti et al. has been subdivided into *capitalization* and *contagion* here. *Binding* and *exclusion* in Borgatti et al. have been combined as *coordination* here. The mechanism of adaptation is the same in both.

15 At the empirical level, much of this work is ego-centered, and therefore might seem to ignore the network path structure that is at the heart of the network flow model. However, in much of this work, the theoretical rationale is built on whole network processes, as in the case of weak tie theory and structural hole theory.

16 We do not intend to imply that what is adopted is "bad." Any attitude, behavior, or belief can be diffused, whether it is positive, negative, or indifferent.

17 To simplify exposition, we have omitted the intermediary level of the subgroup, which shares qualities with both the node and whole network levels.

REFERENCES

Allen, T. (1977) *Managing the Flow of Technology*. Cambridge, MA: MIT Press.

Argote, L. (1999) *Organizational Learning: Creating, Retaining and Transferring Knowledge*. Boston: Kluwer.

Atkin, R.H. (1974) *Mathematical Structure in Human Affairs*. London: Heinemann.

Atkin, R.H. (1977) *Combinatorial Connectives in Social Systems*. Basel: Birkhauser.

Baldwin, T.T., Bedell, M.D. and Johnson, J.L. (1997) 'The social fabric of a team-based M.B.A. program: Network effects on student satisfaction and performance'. *Academy of Management Journal* 40: 1369–97.

Bavelas, A. (1950) 'Communication patterns in task-oriented groups'. *Journal of the Acoustical Society of America* 22: 271–82.

Bonacich, P. (1972) 'Factoring and weighing approaches to status scores and clique identification'. *Journal of Mathematical Sociology* 2: 113–20.

Bonacich, P. (1987) 'Power and centrality: A family of measures'. *American Journal of Sociology* 92: 1170–82.

Borgatti, S.P. (1995) 'Centrality and AIDS'. *Connections* 18, 112–14.

Borgatti, S.P. (2005) 'Centrality and network flow'. *Social Networks* 27: 55–71.

Borgatti, S.P. and Cross, R. (2003) 'A relational view of information seeking and learning in social networks'. *Management Science* 49: 432–45.

Borgatti, S.P. and Everett, M.G. (1992a) 'Graph colorings and power in experimental exchange networks'. *Social Networks* 14: 287–308.

Borgatti, S.P. and Everett, M.G. (1992b) 'Notions of position in social network analysis'. *Sociological Methodology* 22: 1–35.

Borgatti, S.P. and Foster, P.C. (2003) 'The network paradigm in organizational research: A review and typology'. *Journal of Management* 29: 991–1013.

Borgatti, S.P. and Halgin, D.S. (forthcoming) 'Network Theorizing'. *Organization Science.*

Borgatti, S.P., Mehra, A., Brass, D.J. and Labianca, G. (2009) 'Network analysis in the social sciences'. *Science* 323: 892–95.

Bouty, I. (2000) 'Interpersonal and interaction influences on informal resource exchanges between R&D researchers across organizational boundaries'. *Academy of Management Journal* 43: 50–65.

Boxman, E.A.W., De Graaf, P.M. and Flap, H.D. (1991) 'The impact of social and human capital on the income attainment of Dutch managers'. *Social Networks* 13: 51–73.

Brass, D.J. (1984) 'Being in the right place: A structural analysis of individual influence in an organization'. *Administrative Science Quarterly* 29: 518–39.

Brass, D.J. and Krackhardt, D. (1999) 'The social capital of 21st century leaders'. In J.G. Hunt, and R.L. Phillips (eds.), *Out-of-the-Box Leadership,* pp. 179–94. Stamford, CT: JAI Press.

Burt, R.S. (1976) 'Positions in networks'. *Social Forces* 55: 93–122.

Burt, R.S. (1992) *Structural Holes: The Social Structure of Competition.* Cambridge, MA: Harvard University Press.

Burt, R.S. (1997) 'The contingent value of social capital'. *Administrative Science Quarterly* 42: 339–65.

Burt, R.S. (2002) 'Bridge decay'. *Social Networks* 24: 333–63.

Burt, R.S. (2004) 'Structural holes and good ideas'. *American Journal of Sociology* 110: 349–99.

Burt, R.S. (2005) *Brokerage and Closure: An Introduction to Social Capital.* Oxford: Oxford University Press.

Cartwright, D. and Harary, F. (1956) 'Structural balance: A generalization of Heider's theory'. *Psychological Review* 63: 277–93.

Christakis, N.A., and Fowler, J.H. (2008) 'The collective dynamics of smoking in a large social network'. *New England Journal of Medicine* 358: 2249–58.

Cohen, S., Doyle, W.J., Skoner, D.P., Rabin, B.S. and Gwaltney, J.M. (1997) 'Social ties and susceptibility to the common cold'. *Journal of the American Medical Association* 277: 1940–44.

Coleman, J.S. (1988) 'Social capital in the creation of human capital'. *American Journal of Sociology* 94: S95–S120.

Coleman, J.S., Katz, E. and Menzel, H. (1966) *Medical Innovation: A Diffusion Study.* Indianapolis: Bobbs-Merrill.

Cook, K.S., Emerson, R.M., Gillmore, M.R. and Yamagishi, T. (1983) 'The distribution of power in exchange networks: Theory and experimental results'. *American Journal of Sociology* 89: 275–305.

Davis, G.F. (1991) 'Agents without principles? The spread of the poison pill through the inter-corporate network'. *Administrative Science Quarterly* 36: 583–613.

Davis, J.A. (1967) 'Clustering and structural balance in graphs'. *Human Relations* 20: 181–87.

de Sola Pool, I. and Kochen, M. (1978) 'Contacts and influence'. *Social Networks* 1: 5–51.

DiMaggio, P. (1986) 'Structural analysis of organizational fields: A blockmodel approach'. *Research in Organizational Behavior* 8: 335–70.

DiMaggio, P.J. and Powell, W.W. (1983) 'The iron cage revisited: Institutional isomorphism and collective rationality in organizational fields'. *American Sociological Review* 48: 147–60.

Eisenhardt, K. (1989) 'Agency theory: An assessment and review'. *Academy of Management Review* 1: 57–74.

Erickson, B. (1988) 'The relational basis of attitudes'. In B. Wellman and S. Berkowitz (eds.), Social Structures: A Network Approach, pp. 99–121. New York: Cambridge University Press.

Freeman, L.C. (1977) 'A set of measures of centrality based on betweenness'. *Sociometry* 40: 35–41.

Freeman, L.C. (1979) 'Centrality in social networks: Conceptual clarification'. *Social Networks* 1: 215–39.

Friedkin, N.E. and Johnsen, E.C. (1999) 'Social influence and opinions'. *Journal of Mathematical Sociology* 15: 193–205.

Galaskiewicz, J. and Burt, R.S. (1991) 'Interorganization contagion in corporate philanthropy'. *Administrative Science Quarterly* 36: 88–105.

Galaskiewicz, J. and Wasserman, S. (1989) 'Mimetic and normative processes within an interorganizational field: An empirical test'. *Administrative Science Quarterly* 34: 454–79.

Geletkanycz, M.A. and Hambrick, D.C. (1997) 'The external ties of top executives: Implications for strategic choice and performance'. *Administrative Science Quarterly* 42: 654–81.

Granovetter, M. (1973) 'The strength of weak ties'. *American Journal of Sociology* 78: 1360–80.

Granovetter, M. (1974) *Getting a Job: A Study of Contacts and Careers.* Cambridge, MA: Harvard University Press.

Granovetter, M. (1985) 'Economic action and social structure: The problem of embeddedness'. *American Journal of Sociology* 91: 481–510.

Harrison, R.J. and Carroll, G.R. (2002) 'The dynamics of cultural influence networks'. *Computational and Mathematical Organization Theory* 8: 5–30.

Haunschild, P.R. and Miner, A.S. (1997) 'Modes of interorganizational imitation: The effects of outcome salience and uncertainty'. *Administrative Science Quarterly* 42: 472–500.

Heider, F. (1958) *The Psychology of Interpersonal Relations.* New York: Wiley.

Hollingshead, A.B. (1998) 'Distributed knowledge and transactive processes in groups'. In M.A. Neale, E.A. Mannix, and D.H. Gruenfeld (eds.), *Research on Managing Groups and Teams*, 1: 103–23. Greenwich, CT: JAI Press.

Johnson, J.C., Boster, J.S. and Palinkas, L.A. (2003) 'Social roles and the evolution of networks in extreme and isolated environments'. *Journal of Mathematical Sociology* 27: 89–121.

Jones, C., Hesterly, W.S. and Borgatti, S.P. (1997) 'A general theory of network governance: Exchange conditions and social mechanisms'. *Academy of Management Journal* 22: 911–45.

Kilduff, M. (1990) 'The interpersonal structure of decision making: A social comparison approach to organizational choice'. *Organizational Behavior and Human Decision Processes* 47: 270–88.

Kilduff, M. and Krackhardt, D. (1994) 'Bringing the individual back in: A structural analysis of the internal market for reputation in organizations'. *Academy of Management Journal* 37: 87–108.

Kiuru, N., Nurmi, J.E., Aunola, K. and Salmela-Aro, K. (2009) 'Peer group homogeneity in adolescents' school adjustment varies according to peer group type and gender'. *International Journal of Behavioral Development* 33: 65–76.

Laumann, E.O., Marsden, P.V. and Prensky, D. (1989) 'The boundary specification problems in network analysis'. In L.C. Freeman, D.R. White and A.K. Romney (eds.), *Research Methods in Social Network Analysis*, pp. 61–87. Fairfax, VA: George Mason University Press.

Lazarsfeld, P. and Merton, R.K. (1954) 'Friendship as social process: A substantive and methodological analysis'. In M. Berger, T. Abel, and C. Page (eds.), *Freedom and Control in Modern Society*, pp. 18–66. New York: Octagon Books.

Leavitt, H. (1951) 'Some effects of certain communication patterns on group performance'. *Journal of Abnormal and Social Psychology* 46: 38–50.

Lin, N. (1982) 'Social resources and instrumental action'. In P. Marsden and N. Lin (eds.), *Social Structure and Network Analysis*, pp. 131–45. Beverly Hills, CA: Sage.

Lin, N. (1999a) 'Social networks and status attainment'. *Annual Review of Sociology* 25: 467–87.

Lin, N. (1999b) 'Building a network theory of social capital'. *Connections* 22: 28–51.

Lorrain, F. and White, H.C. (1971) 'Structural equivalence of individuals in social networks'. *Journal of Mathematical Sociology* 1: 49–80.

Markovsky, B., Willer, D. and Patton, T. (1988) 'Power relations in exchange networks'. *American Sociological Review* 53: 220–36.

Mayhew, B.H. (1980) 'Structuralism versus individualism: Part 1, Shadowboxing in the dark'. *Social Forces* 59: 335–75.

McPherson, J.M., Smith-Lovin, L. and Cook, J.M. (2001) 'Birds of a feather: Homophily in social networks'. *Annual Review of Sociology* 27: 415–44.

Mehra, A., Kilduff, M. and Brass, D.J. (2001) 'The social networks of high and low self-monitors: Implications for workplace performance'. *Administrative Science Quarterly* 46: 121–46.

Miles, R.E. and Snow, C.C. (1986) 'Network organizations, new concepts for new forms'. *California Management Review* 28: 62–73.

Milgram, S. (1967) 'The small-world problem'. *Psychology Today* 1: 62–67.

Molina, J.L. (1995) 'Analysis of networks and organizational culture: A methodological proposal'. *Revista Española de Investigaciones Sociológicas* 71: 249–63.

Moreland, R.L. (1999) 'Transactive memory: Learning who knows what in work groups and organizations'. In L. Thompson, D. Messick and J. Levine (eds.), *Sharing Knowledge in Organizations*, pp. 3–33. Hillsdale, NJ: Erlbaum.

Morris, M. (1993) 'Epidemiology and social networks'. *Sociological Methods and Research* 22: 99–126.

Newcomb, T.M. (1961) *The Acquaintance Process*. New York: Holt, Rinehart and Winston.

Pastor, J.-C., Meindl, J.R. and Mayo, M.C. (2002) 'A network effects model of charisma attributions'. *Academy of Management Journal* 45: 410–20.

Perry-Smith, J.E. and Shalley, C.E. (2003) 'The social side of creativity: A static and dynamic social network perspective'. *Academy of Management Review* 28: 89–107.

Powell, W.W. (1990) 'Neither market nor hierarchy: Network forms of organization'. *Research on Organizational Behavior* 12: 295–336.

Rapoport, A. and Horvath, W. (1961) 'A study of a large sociogram'. *Behavioral Science* 6: 79–91.

Reagans, R.E. and Zuckerman, E.W. (2008) 'Why knowledge does not equal power: The network redundancy trade-off'. *Industrial and Corporate Change* 17: 903–44.

Rees, R. (1985) 'The theory of principal and agent—part I'. *Bulletin of Economic Research* 37: 3–26.

Renzulli, L.A., Aldrich, H. and Moody, J. (2000) 'Family matters: Gender, networks, and entrepreneurial outcomes'. *Social Forces* 79: 523–46.

Roethlisberger, F. and Dickson, W. (1939) *Management and the Worker*. Cambridge: Cambridge University Press.

Rulke, D.L. and Galaskiewicz, J. (2000) 'Distribution of knowledge, group network structure, and group performance'. *Management Science* 46: 612–26.

Ryall, M.D. and Sorenson, O. (2007) 'Brokers and competitive advantage'. *Management Science* 53: 566–83.

Sanders, K. and Hoekstra, S.K. (1998) 'Informal networks and absenteeism within an organization'. *Computational and Mathematical Organization Theory* 4: 149–63.

Seibert, S.E., Kraimer, M.L. and Liden, R.C. (2001) 'A social capital theory of career success'. *Academy of Management Journal* 44: 219–47.

Snijders, T.A.B. (1999) 'Prologue to the measurement of social capital'. *The Tocqueville Review* 20: 27–44.

Snow, C.C., Miles, R.E. and Coleman, H.J. (1992) 'Managing 21st century organizations'. *Organizational Dynamics* 20: 5–20.

Sparrowe, R.T. and Liden, R.C. (1997) 'Process and structure in leader-member exchange'. *Academy of Management Review* 22: 522–52.

Thompson, J.D. (1967) *Organizations in Action*. New York: McGraw-Hill.

Travers, J. and Milgram, S. (1969) 'An experimental study of the "small-world" problem'. *Sociometry* 32: 425–43.

Watts, D.J. and Strogatz, S.H. (1998) 'Collective dynamics of "small-world" networks'. *Nature* 393: 409–10.

Wellman, B. and Wortley, S. (1990) 'Different strokes from different folks'. *American Journal of Sociology* 96: 558–88.

White, H.C., Boorman, S.A. and Breiger, R.L. (1976) 'Social structure from multiple networks: I. Blockmodels of roles and positions'. *American Journal of Sociology* 81: 730–80.

5

Social Physics and Social Networks

John Scott

Social network analysis has made rapid strides since the 1960s as ever larger numbers of sociologists, and other social scientists, have built and applied the methodological techniques necessary to explore the relational phenomena reported in the various chapters of this Handbook. The ability to describe structural phenomena has advanced considerably beyond the ideas inherited by the researchers of the 1970s. One of the most striking developments in recent years, however, has been the massive growth of interest in social network analysis by researchers working in physics. Because of an apparent decline in the number of soluble theoretical problems that are left to resolve in their own discipline, a growing number of theoretical physicists have begun to explore the implications of some of their mathematical ideas for the explanation of social and economic phenomena. Many of these theorists have made great claims for the novelty of what they are doing and for the explanatory power of their proposed models. The most striking feature of their work, however, is that they present their arguments as novel and distinctive advances from a zero starting point. They know little or nothing of sociological work that preceded them, and they present themselves as initiating a scientific revolution in sociological analysis.

This has not prevented outside commentators, ignorant of sociological work, from being strongly attracted to these social physics publications in large numbers. Its innovations have been lauded in numerous glowing reviews of books in the press and on the Internet. More worrying is the fact that many sociologists unacquainted with social network analysis have also accepted the claims of the social physicists at face value. Those sociologists who have been working in social network analysis, however, have been rather less welcoming. While recognising that a number of important insights and theoretical advances have been made by the social physicists, they have been dismayed by the almost total ignorance shown concerning the vast amount of prior work in social network analysis. The social physicists have moved into sociology in the role of the civilised colonisers of virgin, barbarian territory. Not unnaturally, they have encountered resistance from the native inhabitants, who justifiably feel that their achievements have been disparaged and that they are being dispossessed from the field that they have made their own. So great is the concern, that some network specialists would reject the new social physics out of hand.

This chapter will present an intellectual assessment of the work of the advocates of the new social physics and it will demonstrate the failure of this new work to engage with existing sociological work. I want also to recognise, however, that there is a long and important history of social physics within sociology. Earlier generations of physicists have provided models of analysis that have been developed through an intellectual engagement with social scientists. This history and the debates that constitute it are generally unknown to the present-day proponents of social physics. I aim to show the failures in its historiography and the rather arrogant and dismissive stance towards the social sciences of the new social physicists, but also to recognise the contributions that it can make to the development of social network analysis.

SOCIOLOGY, SOCIAL PHYSICS AND SOCIAL NETWORKS

As is fairly well known, Comte's first choice of name for the new discipline of sociology was, in fact, 'social physics'. In proposing this name he was establishing the idea that the discipline should focus on the systemic organisation of social life and that specific scientific methods were required if these systemic properties were to be properly explored. While some of the early sociologists pursued their work through using an organic model of systems, an approach that gave rise to various forms of 'functionalism', others borrowed directly from classical physics and pursued mechanical models of social systems. In drawing explicitly from physics, and later from chemistry, sociologists held that societies could be seen as systems of forces and energies that could be analysed in terms of their specific equilibrium conditions. The first attempt to construct a social physics in these terms was that of the Belgian statistician Adolphe Quetelet (1848). His attempt was remarkably successful. Indeed, its success appeared to undermine the novelty of Comte's own work and led him to abandon his original preference for the term 'social physics' and to advocate, instead, the neologism 'sociology' in its place. Quetelet sought to discover the laws of association between statistically defined social facts. The interdependence of social facts, he argued, could be studied through the systems of equations that define these laws.

This basic insight was elaborated in economics and in social demography by those who applied concepts of 'force' and 'gravity' in their studies of the social world. Friedrich List and Herman Gossen were early pioneers in this area and their ideas were taken up by Eugen Dühring in Germany and Henry Carey (1858–59, 1872) in the United States. For these writers, labour activity was the human form of physical force or effort. The social interaction of individuals could, therefore, be understood as the resultant of the forces that are inherent in the motions of individuals acting under the influence of 'gravitational' forces of attraction. These forces push and pull individuals, whose movements can, therefore, be analysed in terms of the 'distance' moved in space and time and the 'mass' produced by the total volume and density of activity. This led to the view that the circulation of forces in a social system creates the equilibrium conditions that shape individual actions. Thus, it was held that large social aggregates, which have a greater mass than smaller ones, can exert a strong attractive pull on individuals and so can generate tendencies towards the concentration of individuals in the emerging centres of population.

This basic idea was used to explore migration and urbanism and to explain conquest and the formation of markets and trading monopolies.

One of the most important theorists to develop this approach was Friedrich Engels (1876, 1886), who paradoxically came to his own position through a critical engagement with the work of Dühring. Engels employed the idea of the parallelogram of forces and its equilibrium conditions to establish social physics as a central feature in orthodox Marxism. This general idea has also had a great deal of influence in recent Marxism (see, for example, Althusser, 1962, 1963).

The most important development within the social physics approach was its incorporation of more advanced physical ideas that began to appear from the late nineteenth century. The innovations made by James Clerk Maxwell (1865, 1877) were taken up as social physics by Georg Helm (1887) and Wilhelm Ostwald (1909) in Germany, Ernst Solvay (1904) in Belgium and Nelson Sims (1924) in the United States. Their key innovation was to see labour and other types of social activity not simply as examples of 'force' but as embodiments of the 'energy' that flows around a system and can be both expended and accumulated. Referring to their theoretical standpoint as 'energetics', these theorists held that social systems could be seen as energy fields. These field theories began to influence mainstream social theory during the 1930s through the efforts of Lawrence Henderson (1935, 1938–42), who was popularising the equilibrium theories of Pareto (1916). Henderson's influence was especially apparent in the emerging system theories of Parsons (1945) and the more practical system concepts of George Lundberg (1939) and George Homans (1951; also see Homans and Curtis, 1934). This sociological work was closely associated with marginalist economics and inspired more general applications of rational choice theories to social interaction.

These theoretical advances had a crucial influence on the early development of social network analysis. Kurt Lewin (1936) combined Maxwell's field theories with ideas from Gestalt psychology in his concept of the 'psychic field', a concept designating the system of energising forces or motives at work in the human mind. Equilibrium is established in a psychic field through the processes that were later explored by Fritz Heider (1958) and Leon Festinger (1957) as processes of cognitive 'balance'. Lewin extended the idea of the psychic field to a sociological idea of the social field. This was understood as a system of interpersonal forces, such as pressure, influence and constraint, which are at work within social groups. These ideas echoed and systematised the formal sociology of Georg Simmel (1908), Alfred Vierkandt (1923) and Leopold von Wiese

(1924–29; and see Wiese-Becker 1932), who all used concepts of attraction and repulsion in social situations to model the networks of social relations built through interactions. This complex of arguments was reflected in the sociometric concerns of Jacob Moreno (1934) and eventually led to the emergence of a 'group dynamics' perspective on small-scale networks (Cartwright and Zander, 1953). In parallel with this, Homans (1951) applied his system ideas in a reinterpretation of empirical work on social networks that he used to develop a more general rational choice model (Homans, 1961).

The roots of contemporary social network analysis are to be found in these emerging ideas. Through the 1940s and into the 1950s and 1960s, social network analysts used concepts of distance, density, spatial direction, valence and balance in their studies, and their use of these as their central concepts demonstrated the extent of their debt to the earlier social physics. With the growth of social network analysis, the approach drew more extensively on the sociological concepts of systems, fields and spaces that had developed from the wider system theories of the 1930s that had, like Homans's arguments, been influenced by the Pareto circle. Central to this work was the use of multidimensional scaling and similar methods for embedding relational networks in social space (see, for example, Laumann, 1966; Laumann and Pappi, 1976).

THE NEW SOCIAL PHYSICS

This is the historical context from which I think we can best approach the recent emergence of a new social physics. The new social physics, however, has been constituted by those who lack any awareness that there is a pre-existing research specialisation of social network analysis and that physicists made a number of the early contributions to its development. The leading theorists of the new social physics have been Albert-Lázló Barabási (2002), Mark Buchanan (2002), Duncan Watts (1999, 2003) and Mark Newman (Newman et al., 2006). Their works are connected with wider, and slightly older, theories of complexity and emergence in physical systems (Lewin, 1992; Buchanan, 2000; Strogatz, 2003; Ball, 2004).

Barabási has received the greatest attention and has been the most strident in his views on social network analysis. Barabási's approach to networks relies almost exclusively on the mathematical theory of graphs, the true significance of which he sees as beginning with the 1959 work of Erdös and Renyi on random graph models. His claim is that this was pioneering work that defined the field and that subsequent researchers

into networks have investigated the 'macro complexity' of real networks as an outcome of the random links among their individual elements. Apart from this work, Barabási holds, there has been little work in the biological and human sciences that has been at all concerned with studying networks of relations and their properties. He does note the existence of some empirical work on 'small worlds' from the 1960s, and he makes some brief allusions to the growth of interest in social networks that began at Harvard in the late 1960s and culminated in Granovetter's (1974) work on the strength of weak ties, but he sees nothing beyond this. Small-world and weak-tie research, he argues, focused on clustering rather than randomness and added something important to the basic model of Erdös and Renyi, but he rather strangely observes that these advances 'did not come from sociology or graph theory' (Barabási, 2002: 44): until the 1990s there simply was no network analysis – and certainly no social network analysis – worth speaking of.

In the introduction to an anthology produced by the leading social physicists (Newman et al., 2006) there is a rather more rounded recognition of prior achievements in network analysis. A 'brief history' of the study of networks suggests that this history begins in mathematics and 'more recently' in sociology, also stating that 'Nowhere . . . has graph theory found a more welcome home than in sociology' (Newman et al., 2006: 3). Despite recognising a growing interest in networks by sociologists from the 1950s, however, no citations are given to this work and three textbooks from the 1990s (Scott, 1991; Wasserman and Faust, 1994; Degenne and Forsé, 1994) are the only indication of any familiarity with the literature.

Barabási's strongest and most influential claim – often repeated by other commentators – is that it was not until 1998 that a significant breakthrough occurred in a paper by Duncan Watts and Steven Strogatz (1998). The key innovation in this paper, he held, was that it saw the most efficient networks as combining features of both randomness and clustering. This paper was, he claims, 'the first serious challenge to the view that real networks are fundamentally random' (Barabási, 2002: 51) and it generated a mass of new work among mathematicians and physicists, who were keen to take up its revolutionary implications. The paper was described by Mark Buchanan, a mathematician and science journalist, as 'unprecedented' (2002: 13) and as alluding to 'some deep organizational principles of our world' (2002: 15) that had hitherto been unrecognised by social scientists. Sociologists, in particular, wrongly assumed that 'society' is formed through the random accumulation of social relationships (Barabási, 2002: 62, 64). The mathematical discoveries of Watts and

Strogatz, Barabási held, had highlighted phenomena that are 'unprecedented and unexpected in the context of networks' (Barabási, 2002: 77). They had showed 'a new and unsuspected order within networks' that 'lifted complex networks out of the jungle of randomness' (Barabási, 2002: 77). Buchanan claimed that research by 'mathematicians, physicists and computer scientists', had begun to show that social and all other networks have certain common properties. This led Buchanan to make the extremely strong claim that 'for the first time in history, scientists are beginning to learn how to talk meaningfully about the architecture of networks' (2002: 19).

The discovery by scientists that complex networks are orderly 'represented a serious deviation from everything then [1998] known about networks' (Barabási, 2002: 71, 221). The properties of real networks, including all social networks, have to be seen as expressions of 'strict mathematical laws' (Barabási, 2002: 64). There are 'fundamental laws forcing different networks to take up the same universal form and shape' (Barabási, 2002: 78). The reason why complex systems of all kinds have similar characteristics is that there are necessary and therefore universal structural features in all real networks. Barabási saw his task as the uncovering of these laws.

It has to be said immediately that no sociologists, to the best of my knowledge, have ever thought that complex social networks are purely random phenomena. While some have made analytical use of models of random networks, it is a central, defining idea in sociology that social life is to be seen as structured. Social life is organised and patterned by purposive actions that have unintended, but far from random, consequences.

Unintended and unplanned consequences are not the same as random consequences. The structuring of social life is apparent to most participants on a practical level, and it is difficult to understand what kind of life Barabási may have been leading if he believes that, prior to 1998, all real networks were assumed to be formed as random processes.[1]

Despite these deep reservations about the central claim to originality made in the new social physics, it is important to see what positive discoveries they felt they had established about network structure. Barabási argued that previous researchers had been wrong to assume that networks are always formed through the concatenation of random links. Rather, networks tend to be organised around key brokers or intermediaries who tie other, less well-connected points into the network. Networks, therefore, are organised around 'hubs' or 'connectors', understood as 'nodes with an anomalously large number of links' (Barabási, 2002: 56). It is for this reason, Barabási held, that the distribution of links in a network does not follow a normal distribution. There is, instead, a 'power law' distribution. As in the well-known Pareto curve of income distribution, the majority of points have very few connections, while a small minority have extremely large numbers of connections. As there is no meaningful mean figure of connections, the whole distribution is seen as 'scale-free' (see Figure 5.1). Barabási claims that this methodological research 'gave legitimacy to hubs' as the pivotal points in networks and it highlighted the need to make them a topic of further research (2002: 71).

In an illuminating insight into his research process he states that he came up with a first 'simple and straightforward' mechanism for the

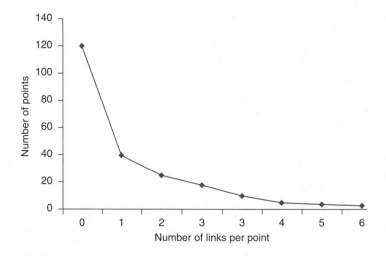

Figure 5.1 A Scale Free Distribution (Artificial Data)

power law during a 15-minute walk between conference rooms and he wrote this up on a five-hour flight back from the conference. The resulting paper was summarily rejected by *Science* without even being sent for peer review: it was, the editor said, neither novel nor of wide interest (Barabási, 2002: 81). He succeeded in getting the paper published only because he telephoned the editor and complained about the decision. Barabási did not, it seems, consider for one moment that the editor may have been correct in the assessment of the paper. As I will show, there are, in fact, good reasons for thinking that the editor was correct when making this original decision.

The basic mathematical law at work in a power law or scale-free distribution, Barabási argued, is simply the law that 'the rich get richer'. Put simply, this is the principle that to he who hath shall be given, that is, the famous 'Matthew Effect' formulated by sociologist Robert Merton (1968), though Barabási was not aware of Merton's work. Barabási describes this as the principle of 'preferential attachment', according to which well-connected points tend to become even better connected over time. Thus, successful people who become more prominent over the course of their careers will accumulate business and professional connections exponentially, while those who fail to build connections will tend to remain unconnected. Colleagues apparently developed this into the idea that the 'fittest' will attract and accumulate connections. One colleague, he reports, came up with a striking extension to this law that stated that 'actors stop acquiring links after retirement' (Barabási, 2002: 89). As a statement of the commonplace, this was, perhaps not such a striking conclusion after all.

THE POWER LAW IN ECONOMIC SOCIOLOGY

The novelty and potentiality of the new social physics can, perhaps, best be assessed in relation to the area that Barabási has highlighted as the one in which it seeks to have the greatest impact. This area is economic sociology. He has claimed that it is only since the appearance of his own work that researchers have started to look at business networks. He holds that economists – he does not even mention sociologists – have studied the economy only as a collection of anonymous and impersonal markets. However, 'Motivated by the renaissance of networks in physics and mathematics' researchers have, since 1999, begun to see the economy as a complex network of companies that are linked to each other by financial ties. This supposed conceptual innovation led Barabási to

formulate his most striking conclusion: 'We have learned that a sparse network of a few powerful directors controls all major appointments in *Fortune* 1000 companies' (2002: 200, 204).

Yet economic sociologists would regard this conclusion as commonplace. The 'discovery' would certainly not have surprised Rudolf Hilferding a century ago. Hilferding demonstrated exactly this phenomenon in 1910, and in some detail, as a central element in his analysis of German finance capital (Hilferding, 1910). Nor would it have surprised John Hobson, who had published his report on economic concentration and interlocking directorships just a few years earlier (Hobson, 1906). Congressional hearings into the Money Trust in the United States produced the report of the Pujo Committee (1913), which came to precisely the same conclusion. These findings were repeated for economy after economy and generated a long-standing research tradition that constantly updated its results. However, despite these well-known predecessors, Barabási presented his findings as a new and significant discovery about corporate networks.

Barabási sees economic concentration as proceeding hand in hand with the formation of 'hubs' of economic power. He holds that in 1999 'the Web was the only network mathematically proven to have hubs' (2002: 79), but by 2001 this had all changed. Barabási reported a new study that showed the distribution of directorships and company connections to follow a scale-free pattern that is associated with the formation of hubs and the clustering of companies around these hubs. This again displays a massive ignorance of economic sociology and the results – conceptual and empirical – of investigations into corporate networks. Studies of interlocking directorships had long ago demonstrated both the phenomenon and the word 'hub'. More than 20 years earlier, Warner and Unwalla (1967) had shown in 1967 that the American corporate network could be seen as a huge national 'wheel' with a New York hub. Less than 10 years later, Jim Bearden and his colleagues (1975) documented the centrality of banks in corporate networks and employed a variety of measures of centrality. Their work was elaborated in that of Mintz and Schwartz (1985), who explicitly used the language of hubs and peaks to describe the patterns of centrality in their data. Clustering, too, was recognised as early as the U.S. National Resources Committee's investigations during the 1930s (Means et al., 1939). The committee's report demonstrated the existence of financial 'interest groups' of interlocked companies and established a long line of research into what later writers called 'spheres of influence'. In the face of all this research, Barabási still felt able to claim that, prior to 1999, 'social network models did not support the existence of hubs' (2002: 130).

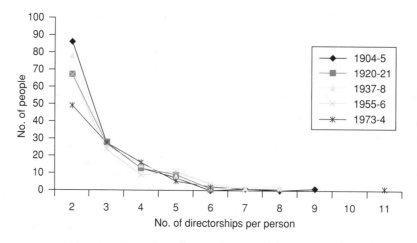

Figure 5.2   Directorships: Scotland, 1904–74

In fact, the phenomenon of the corporate hub was widely recognised and explored in sociological research. Combined with an explicit recognition of the existence of hubs in corporate networks was an almost universal recognition that the distribution of degrees in a network follows a scale-free pattern. It is certainly the case that the terminology of the scale-free distribution or power law was not used, but standard frequency distribution tables were used precisely in order to display this pattern. The evidence was abundant, with supporting data from studies dating back to at least the 1930s. Some examples of this work are shown in Figures 5.2 to 5.5.

Figure 5.2, taken from research published in 1980, shows data for the top 100 companies in Scotland from 1904 to 1974. Charting the number of directorships in these companies held by each director, it shows a clear scale-free pattern. For each of the five periods studied, the number of directorships per person fell rapidly to the point at which hubs – multiple directors with five or more directorships – appear. Similar data for Britain as a whole are shown in Figure 5.3. In this case, directorships in the top 250 companies were analysed with strikingly similar results. The British research formed part of the largest international research project in this area. Using data on the top 250 companies for 1976 in 10 different countries, the project showed a series of comparative measures of network structure. Figure 5.4 shows that each country showed precisely the same

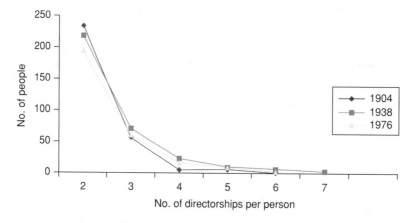

Figure 5.3   Directorships: Britain 1904–76

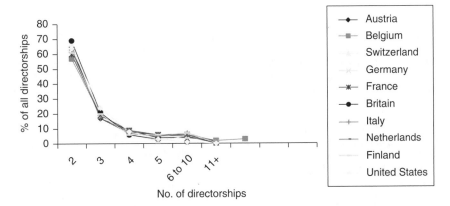

Figure 5.4   Multiple Directorships: Global 1976

scale-free pattern. Figure 5.5 again looks at historical data, this time for the United States, and also shows the scale-free distribution.

Barabási was unaware of the research reported in Figures 5.2 to 5.5. Nor was he aware of many similar studies. This failure to appreciate the long-standing traditions of research was responsible for his belief that he had made startlingly new discoveries and that he was the first to recognise the existence of scale-free distributions in social networks. Not all of the new social physicists were so ignorant of earlier research, though few were aware of its full extent. Buchanan knew of the importance of Mark Granovetter's classic study, which he discusses at some length. Yet he remarkably claims that 'For nearly 30 years, his simple but striking insights . . . remained virtually unnoticed by other scientists' (Buchanan, 2002: 47). This is a truly astonishing statement to make about one of the most cited works in the history of sociology. Buchanan seems, in particular, to have completely missed the extensive use of

Granovetter's work in studies undertaken by Granovetter's Harvard associates during the 1970s and after: work by Michael Schwartz and his colleagues (see, for example, Mintz and Schwartz, 1985; Mizruchi, 1982; Mizruchi and Schwartz, 1987), by Barry Wellman (Wellman and Berkowitz, 1988), and, of course, those by Harrison White and his students and colleagues (White, 1992). Indeed, Granovetter was himself a student and colleague of White and learned a great deal from White's own work on networks that was undertaken earlier in the 1960s (White, 1963).

Why is there such ignorance of relevant sociological work among the new social physicists? It is, perhaps, an unstated assumption that sociologists – not being 'real' scientists – cannot be expected to know how to study the social world scientifically. For this reason, it would seem, they felt that there was simply no point in looking for any sociological work, as nothing worthwhile could have been undertaken. If sociologists are barely safe enough to be let out on their own,

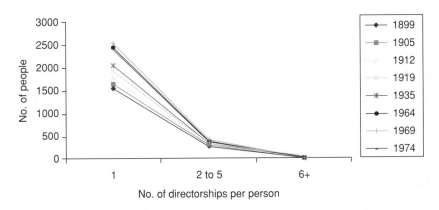

No. of directorships per person

Figure 5.5   Directorships: United States 1899–1974

without the guidance of a real scientist to tell them what they ought to be doing, there is no reason to expect them to have undertaken important work independently.

However, poor research skills must also be recognised as responsible for Barabási's ignorance. He has given some indication of how he came to miss the existing sociological research. Having completed his PhD, and with nothing better to do, he read 'a general audience book on computer science' and came to realise 'how little was known about networks in general' (2002: 219). This was why he began to study the random network models of Erdös. But he did not take the crucial first step of undertaking a systematic bibliographical investigation. He did not undertake the basic literature review that any neophyte PhD candidate in sociology would undertake. Barabási knew where his university library was, as he had borrowed his computer book from it, but he did not seem to have used the library or its catalogues to try to discover what work might already have been carried out. Perhaps this bibliographical failing was why the editor of *Science* had rejected his initial paper so rapidly because of its lack of originality. Barabási discovered nothing on social network analysis except the text by Wasserman and Faust (1994) – though he shows no sign of having read it – and he did not even discover that a journal called *Social Networks* had begun publication in 1978. Nor did he discover that an International Network for Social Network Analysis had been formed around the same time and that it carried an image of a scale-free network on the cover of its regular newsletter. The possibility of searching for material on the Internet also seems to have escaped him completely. Although Barabási's particular specialisation was search engine methods, he did not, apparently, think of typing the word 'networks', or the phrase 'social networks' into a search engine.

Even stranger is the fact that some sociologists have also failed to appreciate the extent of sociological research on social networks and have accepted the physicist's view of network analysis rather than researching the subject for themselves. John Urry (2004), for example, has been heavily influenced by the new social physics. Reviewing the contributions of its advocates, he equates it with social network analysis and then criticises it for its excessive formality and its lack of understanding of the sociological character of the data employed. These criticisms of the new social physics may be well founded, but they misunderstand social network analysis by failing to address it. Relying heavily on popular science books, Urry reiterates the misleading claim that the social physicists are proposing a 'new network analysis'. Strikingly, Urry makes no reference at all to any

studies in social network analysis. He makes a brief nod towards an introductory textbook on methods (Scott, 2000), but he makes no mention of any of the substantive studies that have looked at precisely the issues that he sees as being so important.

PROMISE AND POTENTIAL IN THE NEW SOCIAL PHYSICS

The new social physics, then, has developed largely in ignorance of the achievements made by sociologists working in social network analysis and of the contributions made by earlier generations of social physicists. The much-trumpeted innovations that lie at the heart of their 'revolution' – the power law and hubs – are the well-known and well-established findings of social network analysts. Does this mean that we are dealing simply with a case of the emperor's new clothes: is there nothing substantial in the new social physics? I think it would be a mistake to conclude this. Behind the hype and misplaced enthusiasm there are some important ideas that do make a real and substantial contribution. This contribution can make itself felt, however, only insofar as the social physicists engage with existing work in social network analysis and enter into a proper dialogue with the sociologists and other social scientists who have already begun to move in a similar direction.

The potential contribution of the new social physics is most apparent in the work of Duncan Watts. He is, undoubtedly, the most sophisticated physicist to contribute to the area and he has, albeit rather belatedly, recognised the overstatements of other social physicists. In a review article he noted that the label 'new' science of networks 'may strike many sociologists as misleading, given the familiarity . . . of many of its central ideas' (Watts, 2004: 243). This recognition led Watts to transfer into a Department of Sociology, where he could better develop his ideas.

Watts rejects the view that most real networks are built from random connections and highlights, instead, the fact that they are characterised by a clustering into zones of relatively high density and a differentiation between close ('strong') and more distant ('weak') ties. These features of real networks mean that it is impossible to study network properties from purely 'local' data. Networks have to be investigated through their *global* or overall properties. Watts holds that this can be done best by starting from certain general network principles.

Watts's own theoretical work begins from a recognition of the importance of 'small-world' research.

He asks what structural features the social world must have if it exhibits the characteristics of a small world and he tries to assess the implications of this for sociological analysis. The concept of a small-world network derives from the frequently experienced claim on meeting someone with a mutual acquaintance: 'what a small world!' As a network idea, it originates in experimental studies by Milgram (1967; Travers and Milgram, 1969) in which he investigated the number of links required to connect two people who are unknown to each other. Typically, he found, randomly close individuals are connected by lines of length six.

In his work, Watts attempted to formalise the features of the interesting subset of networks that have this small-world feature. A small-world network is not a 'small' network but one in which the distances between points is optimally low. It is one in which the interweaving and overlapping of connections and a high degree of redundancy in linkages is such that distances are non-transitive. Graphs that are embedded in a Euclidean or other metric space will not show any small-world properties for their metric distances. Thus, small-world phenomena are features of the *relational* properties of a graph and not of its *spatial* properties (Watts, 1999: 41–42). It is possible for two spatially 'distant' people to be connected by a relatively short path.

A 'small-world graph' is one in which there are a large number of 'shortcuts'. A shortcut in a graph is a line that connects two points that would otherwise be distant from each other. Specifically, a line is a shortcut if it reduces the distance between two points otherwise connected at a distance greater than two. Shortcuts are 'wormholes' in a graph. Formally, a shortcut is a line that *does not* complete a triad (see Figure 5.6). A completely connected graph consists only of triads so has no shortcuts – it is made of numerous overlapping one-cliques. A random graph, on the other hand, has neither triads nor shortcuts. The creation of shortcuts, therefore, builds the intermediate range of graphs where small-world properties occur. They are most marked at a certain subrange of the small-world networks. Small-world

graphs are locally clustered but globally sparse – they are 'Granovetter graphs'.

Watts shows that small-world graphs can be defined by the two parameters n and k, where n is the number of points and k is the average degree of the points. These are *mathematical* conditions that apply to *any* type of network, which leads Watts to claim that he is constructing a generic science of networks. The small-world properties of a network do not, in any sense, depend upon the type of connections that are involved. Thus, a social network has small-world properties not because of the type of social relation involved but because of the mathematical relations that define its structure. *If* a social network is formed that has the non-random attributes of a small-world network, *then* certain structural consequences will necessarily follow. While an explanation of the emergence of such a network lies in the sociology of the area under investigation, the explanation of these consequences is to be found in the mathematics of the network.

It is important to be clear about exactly what is being claimed in this argument. If it is claimed – as Barabási often implies – that *any* actual network will, *of necessity*, have certain characteristics, then highly deterministic assumptions are being made about the formation of social relations. If, on the other hand, it is argued that mathematics describes the *constraints* that are inherent in particular structures, then greater scope remains to recognise the autonomy of human agency in social networks.

The implications of this argument are illustrated with an examination of diffusion processes. Despite its rather disappointing neglect of the classic works by Rogers (1962) and by Coleman and his colleagues (1966), he does produce some suggestive conclusions about the intuitive idea that the spread of a disease is faster in networks with shorter path lengths (Watts, 1999: 180). Rather more compelling is his discussion of the development of cooperative relationships and strategic behaviour, where he shows that the possibility of cooperation improves at a particular, though unspecified, level of network connectivity. The most general conclusion that Watts draws from his explorations is that relatively small changes in the connectivity of a network (e.g., adding a small number of shortcuts) can dramatically change its small-world properties and, hence, the ability of its members to communicate or cooperate with each other.

In order to develop this point of view into a generalised theory of network processes, Watts draws on contemporary complexity theories of nonlinear change. The development of network structure, he argues, is a result of gradual, incremental changes that generate sudden 'phase transitions' at critical threshold points. Radical transformation in macro-level structure can result,

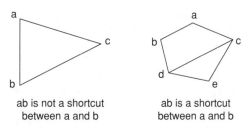

ab is not a shortcut
between a and b

ab is a shortcut
between a and b

Figure 5.6   Shortcuts in networks

unintentionally, from an immediate, situational change at the micro-level. Specifically, the *making* or *breaking* of links in a network as agents pragmatically adjust to their immediate situation creates the shortcuts that enhance the small-world features of the network and alter the way in which it operates at a macro level. Watts shows, for example, that a phase transition that reduces the small-world conditions in the network will disrupt its ability to promote the diffusion of innovations. Individuals in such a fragmentary network that fragments are susceptible to new influences and constraints, but their innovations will never spread very far. On the other hand, the making of extensive links that result in a highly connected network produces a situation in which innovations reverberate around the network in constantly reinforcing cascades that rapidly suffuse the whole network. Watts holds that these threshold points can be predicted on the basis of the purely mathematical properties of the network in question.

The implications of this argument are apparent in the influential study of social capital undertaken by Putnam (2000). A person individually might decide not to go bowling, not to go to church, not to watch the latest repeat of a television show and so on. Each individual thereby reduces the number of links, though in a small world there is high redundancy and the effects of these reductions may be masked until a critical point is reached. This critical point occurs when individual actions have significantly reduced the number of shortcuts. The network begins to lose its small-world properties and people will then find it more difficult to recruit bowling teams, mount political protests and so on. A point may eventually be reached at which the number of shortcuts is so few that the whole network collapses catastrophically. This is the complete collapse in the 'bridging' social capital that Putnam saw as critical for holding networks together.

Similar considerations apply in relation to the board-level recruitment of directors in corporate enterprises. The structural features of networks of interlocking directorships – bank centrality, spheres of influence, centralisation and so on – change in relation to changes in recruitment practices that result from the introduction of new systems of regulation or governance, such as antitrust laws and the limitation of bank interlocking. They change, however, in unintended ways as a consequence of incremental changes in recruitment at the micro level. Company-level decisions about the recruitment of particular directors transform the network through a threshold point and so generate radical, nonlinear changes in patterns of corporate control and intercorporate cohe-

sion (as suggested in Scott and Griff, 1984: 11–12; see also Useem, 1984). In a fragmented network, it is more difficult for knowledge about business conditions to flow through the network and so people will respond to more immediate, local conditions.

Watts does not see these processes deterministically but as describing the constraints on individual agency. He shows that the development of networks and processes within networks is constrained by mathematical features. That is to say, once a small-world network has emerged, then its mathematical properties will constrain, but not determine, the actual relationships formed and so will make particular patterns of development more likely than others to occur. Indeed, this was the basis on which Barabási himself had formulated the Matthew Effect, and it is what corporate researchers argued when describing the formation of bank-centred spheres of influence (Scott and Griff, 1984). Here are to be found the principal implications of the new social physics. The new social physics complement existing approaches by pointing to crucial and significant features of network dynamics. Much research in social network analysis has been static and cross-sectional. Use of the mathematical theorems of small worlds promises a more dynamic understanding of processes of change over time. This perspective has converged with uses of complexity theory and agent-based computational methods to begin to produce more powerful and productive examinations of longitudinal change (see, for example, Monge and Contractor, 2003; see also the special issue of the *American Journal of Sociology*, 2005: 110, 4). The work of Tom Snijders – discussed elsewhere in this handbook – already offers software for modelling dynamic processes in terms of the macro-level, nonlinear consequences of individual, micro-level processes.

We may yet see further contributions from the new social physics that will match the introduction of force and energy in the earlier social physics, but we are not there yet. The exaggerated claims that have been made should not lead us to reject the work as a whole, and we must recognise that some of its practitioners are making important studies in collaborative work. We can hope that others might be willing to work more collegially with social scientists in the future.

NOTE

1 It is also puzzling that Barabási, a pioneering Web user, should have assumed that Internet links are made at random.

REFERENCES

Althusser, L. (1962) 'Contradiction and overdetermination', in Louis Althusser (ed.), *For Marx*. Harmondsworth: Allen Lane.

Althusser, L. (1963) 'On the materialist dialectic', in Althusser, 1962.

Ball, P. (2004) *Critical Mass: How One Thing Leads to Another*. London: Heinemann.

Barabási, A.L. (2002) *Linked: The New Science of Networks*. Cambridge, MA: Perseus.

Bearden, J., Atwood, W., Freitag, P., Hendricks, C., Mintz, B. and Scwhartz, M. (1975) 'The nature and extent of bank centrality in corporate networks', in John Scott (ed.), *Social Networks, Volume 3*. London: Sage, 2002.

Buchanan, M. (2000) *Ubiquity: The New Science That Is Changing the World*. London: Weidenfeld and Nicholson.

Buchanan, M. (2002) *Small World: Uncovering Nature's Hidden Networks*. London: Weidenfeld and Nicolson.

Bunting, D. and Barbour, J. (1971) 'Interlocking directorates in large American corporations, 1896–1964', in John Scott (ed.), *Social Networks, Volume 3*. London: Sage, 2002.

Carey, H.C. (1858–59) *The Principles of Social Science, Three Volumes*. New York: Augustus M. Kelley, 1963.

Carey, H.C. (1872) *The Unity of Law: As Exhibited in the Relation of Physical, Social, Mental, and Moral Science*. New York: Augustus M. Kelley, 1967.

Cartwright, D. and Zander, A. (eds.) (1953) *Group Dynamics*. London: Tavistock.

Coleman, J.S., Katz, E. and Menzel, H. (1966) *Medical Innovation: A Diffusion Study*. New York: Bobbs-Merrill.

Degenne, A. and Forsé, M. (1994) *Introducing Social Networks*. English translation, Beverly Hills: Sage, 1999.

Dooley, P.C. (1969) 'The interlocking directorate', in John Scott (ed.), *The Sociology of Elites, Volume 3*. Aldershot: Edward Elgar, 1990.

Engels, F. (1876) *Anti-Dühring*. Moscow: Foreign Languages Publishing House, 1954.

Engels, F. (1886) *Dialectics of Nature*. Moscow: Progress, 1964.

Festinger, L. (1957) *A Theory of Cognitive Dissonance*. Stanford: Stanford University Press.

Granovetter, M. (1974) *Getting a Job*. Cambridge, MA: Harvard University Press.

Heider, F. (1958) *The Psychology of Interpersonal Relations*. New York: Wiley.

Helm, G. (1887) *Die Lehre Von Der Energie*. Leipzig: Felix.

Henderson, L.J. (1935) *Pareto's General Sociology: A Physiologist's Interpretation*. Cambridge, MA: Harvard University Press.

Henderson, L.J. (1938–42) 'Sociology 23 Lectures', in Bernard Barber (ed.), *L.J. Henderson on the Social System*. Chicago: University of Chicago Press, 1970.

Herman, E.O. (1981) *Corporate Control, Corporate Power*. New York: Oxford University Press.

Hilferding, R. (1910) *Finance Capital*. London: Routledge and Kegan Paul, 1981.

Hobson, J.A. (1906) *The Evolution of Modern Capitalism, Revised Edition*. London: George Allen and Unwin.

Homans, G. (1951) *The Human Group*. London: Routledge and Kegan Paul.

Homans, G. (1961) *Social Behaviour: Its Elementary Forms*. London: Routledge and Kegan Paul.

Homans, G. and Curtis, C.P. (1934) *An Introduction to Pareto: His Sociology*. New York: Knopf.

Laumann, E.O. (1966) *Prestige and Association in an Urban Community*. Indianapolis: Bobbs-Merrill.

Laumann, E.O. and Pappi, F.U. (1976) *Networks of Collective Action: A Perspective on Community Influence Systems*. New York: Academic Press.

Lewin, K. (1936) *Principles of Topological Psychology*. New York: Harper and Row.

Lewin, R. (1992) *Complexity: Life at the Edge of Chaos*. New York: Macmillan.

Lundberg, G. (1939) *Foundations of Sociology*. New York: Macmillan.

Maxwell, J.C. (1865) *A Dynamical Theory of the Electromagnetic Field*. Edinburgh: Scottish Academic Press, 1982.

Maxwell, J.C. (1877) *Matter and Motion*. London: Routledge, 1996.

Means, D.E., Gardner, C., Montgomery, J.M., Clark, A., Hansen, H, and Mordecai E. (1939) 'The structure of controls', in National Resources Committee (ed.), *The Structure of the American Economy*. National Resources Committee of the U.S. Senate. Washington: Government Printing Office.

Merton, R.K. (1968) 'The Matthew Effect in Science', *Science* 159: 56–63.

Milgram, S. (1967) 'The Small World Problem', *Psychology Today* 2: 60–67.

Mintz, B. and Schwartz, M. (1985) *The Power Structure of American Business*. Chicago: University of Chicago Press.

Mizruchi, M.S. (1982) *The American Corporate Network, 1900–1974*. London: Sage.

Mizruchi, M.S. and Schwartz, M. (eds.) (1987) *Intercorporate Relations: The Structural Analysis of Business*. New York: Cambridge University Press.

Monge, P.R. and Contractor, N.S. (2003) *Theories of Communication Networks*. Oxford: Oxford University Press.

Moreno, J.L. (1934) *Who Shall Survive?* New York: Beacon.

Newman, M., Barabási, A.L., and Watts, D.J. (eds.) (2006) *The Structure and Dynamics of Networks*. Princeton, NJ: Princeton University Press.

Ostwald, W. (1909) *Energetische Grundlagen Der Kulturwissenschaften*. Leipzig: Duncker.

Pareto, V. (1916) *A Treatise on General Sociology*. New York: Dover, 1963.

Parsons, T. (1945) 'The present position and prospects of systematic theory in sociology', in Talcott Parsons (ed.), *Essays in Sociological Theory, Revised Edition*. New York: Free Press, 1954.

Pujo, Report (1913) *Money Trust Investigation*. House Subcommittee on Banking and Currency, Washington: Government Printing Office.

Putnam, R.D. (2000) *Bowling Alone: The Collapse and Revival of American Community*. New York: Simon and Schuster.

Quetelet, L.A.J. (1848) *Du Système Sociale Et Des Lois Qui Le Régissent*. Paris: Guillaumin.

Rogers, E. (1962) *Diffusion of Innovations, 5th Edition.* New York: Free Press, 2003.

Scott, J. (1985) *Corporations, Classes and Capitalism, Second Edition.* London: Hutchinson.

Scott, J. (1991) *Social Network Analysis.* London: Sage.

Scott, J. (2000) *Social Network Analysis, Second Edition.* London: Sage.

Scott, J. and Griff, C. (1984) *Directors of Industry.* Cambridge: Polity Press.

Scott, J. and Hughes, M. (1980) *The Anatomy of Scottish Capital.* London: Croom Helm.

Simmel, G. (1908) *Soziologie: Untersuchungen Über Die Formen Der Vergesselshaftung.* Berlin: Düncker und Humblot, 1968.

Sims, N.L. (1924) *Society and Its Surplus: A Study in Social Evolution.* New York: D. Appleton and Co.

Solvay, E. (1904) *L'energétique Consideré Comme Principe D'orientation Rationelle Pour La Sociologie.* Bruxelles: Misch et Thron.

Stokman, F., Ziegler, R. and Scott, J. (eds.) (1985) *Networks of Corporate Power.* Cambridge: Polity Press.

Strogatz, S.H. (2003) *Sync: The Emerging Science of Spontaneous Order.* New York: Hyperion.

Travers, J. and Milgram, S. (1969) 'An experimental study of the small world problem', *Sociometry* 32(4): 425–43.

Urry, J. (2004) 'Small worlds and the new "social physics"', *Global Networks.*

Useem, M. (1984) *The Inner Circle.* New York: Oxford University Press.

Vierkandt, A. (1923) *Gesellshaftslehre.* Stuttgart: F. Enke.

von Wiese, L. (1924–29) *Allgemeine Soziologie Als Lehre Von Dem Beziehungen Und Beziehungsgebilden, Two Volumes.* München: Duncker und Humblot.

Warner, W.L. and Unwalla, D.B. (1967) 'The system of interlocking directorates', in W. Lloyd Warner, Darab B. Unwalla, and Joan H. Trimm (eds.), *The Emergent American Society: Volume 1. Large-Scale Organizations.* New Haven: Yale University Press.

Wasserman, S. and Faust, K. (1994) *Social Network Analysis: Methods and Applications.* New York: Cambridge University Press.

Watts, D. (1999) *Small Worlds: The Dynamics of Networks between Order and Randomness.* Princeton, NJ: Princeton University Press.

Watts, D. (2003) *Six Degrees: The Science of a Connected Age.* New York: W. W. Norton.

Watts, D. (2004) 'The "New" Science of Networks', *Annual Review of Sociology* 30.

Watts, D. and Strogatz, S.H. (1998) 'Collective dynamics of "small-world" networks', *Nature* 393: 440–42.

Wellman, B. and Berkowitz, S. (eds.) (1988) *Social Structures.* New York: Cambridge University Press.

White, H.C. (1963) *An Anatomy of Kinship.* Englewood Cliffs, NJ: Prentice-Hall.

White, H.C. (1992) *Identity and Control.* Princeton, NJ: Princeton University Press.

Wiese, L. and Becker, H.P. (1932) *Systematic Sociology, on the Basis of the Beziehungslehre and Gebildelehre of Leopold Von Wiese, Adapted and Amplified by Howard P. Becker.* New York: Wiley.

6

Social Networks in Economics

Sanjeev Goyal

INTRODUCTION

While Facebook, SecondLife and LinkedIn give networks a definite contemporary resonance, human beings are gregarious by nature and social relations have been studied by economists for a long time. Prominent instances include the study of relative consumption by Veblen (1899) and Dussenbery (1949), and the study of the role of social contacts in labour markets by Rees (1966) and Rees and Schultz (1970). In spite of these works, until the mid-1980's, most studies in economics largely ignored the role of social relations. Instead, economists sought to explain economic phenomena using an approach founded on the idea that human interaction is centralised (takes place in large markets) and anonymous. Moreover, prices (sometimes set by a fictitious Walrasian auctioneer!) were the principal device of coordination among individuals. The theory of general equilibrium and the theory of oligopoly epitomize this paradigm. This state of affairs is reflected in the following lines taken from Granovetter (1985): 'How behaviour and institutions are affected by social relations is one of the classic questions of social theory . . . the utilitarian tradition, including classical and neoclassical economics, assumes rational, self-interested behaviour is affected minimally by social relations'. Much has changed since the mid-1980s; social relations and informal institutions occupy centre stage in economics, today.

A comprehensive overview of this work is clearly beyond the scope of a single chapter. Here, my aim is to develop two general points about this work.[1] The first point is relatively simple: there is now a wide-ranging body of formal – analytical and quantitative – work that rigorously examines the consequences of social relations for economic action. I will illustrate this by discussing how new models of social relations address questions that are at the heart of economics. The second point is more fundamental and closely related to the points discussed in the above quotation. This new research in economics illustrates how institutions and social structure shape and are, in turn, shaped by individual action. In this sense, it constitutes a rigorous and substantive elaboration on the themes explored in the work of Granovetter (1985), Burt (1994) and Coleman (1994), among others.

In this chapter, I restrict myself to economics research in which social structure is mathematically modelled as a network/graph and the focus is on understanding the relation between features of the network – such as centrality, the number and distribution of connections, distance, connectedness – and individual behaviour and aggregate economic outcomes. There is a large body of work in economics that studies informal institutions such as business groups in developing countries, country formation, crime and social interaction, social and personal identity; see, for example, Akerlof (1997), Akerlof and Kranton (2000), Alesina and Spolaore (2003), Dasgupta and Serageldin (1999), Ghatak and Kali (2001), Glasear and Scheinkman (2002), Kali (1999), Rauch and Casella (2001) and Taylor (2000). Due to space constraints, I will not be discussing this work here.

THE CONSEQUENCES OF SOCIAL STRUCTURE

In the last decade, economists have explored the role of social networks in understanding a variety of questions. This section takes up two important economic questions: one, employment and inequality and two, diffusion and innovation.[2] I first discuss research on these issues and then turn to conceptual issues in the empirical identification of network effects.

Unemployment and Wage Inequality

Workers like jobs that suit their skills and location preferences, while firms are keen to hire workers who have the right abilities for jobs. However, workers do not know which firms have vacancies, and finding the right job takes time and effort. Similarly, firms do not know which workers are looking for jobs. Faced with this lack of information, workers look for job advertisements in newspapers and magazines. They also spread the word among their friends and acquaintances that they are looking for a job, and indeed there is substantial evidence that they often get information on job vacancies via their personal connections. A second type of information problem concerns the ability of workers: a person generally knows more about his own ability as compared to a potential employer. Indeed, this asymmetry in information leads workers to invest in signals of their quality (such as educational degrees, certificates, and licenses), and it leads potential employers to ask for references and recommendation letters.[3] Empirical work also shows that referrals (references and recommendation letters) are widely used in the process of matching workers and firms. A letter of reference is only valuable insofar as the employer can trust the writer of the letter; this suggests that the structure of personal connections is likely to play an important role in matching workers and firms.

These observations raise the question of how the pattern of social contacts affects the flow of information about jobs. The flow of information across persons will influence how quickly workers are matched with jobs, which will in turn shape the level of employment The patterns of social connections will also determine who gets information and when; this in turn may determine who gets a job and who is left unemployed, which will have a bearing on the distribution of earnings and overall inequality in a society. I start with a discussion of empirical evidence and then turn to theoretical models of social networks.

Evidence: Social Networks in Labour Markets

Empirical work on the sources of information about jobs and about workers has a long and distinguished history. Early contributions to this body of work include Rees (1966), Myers and Shultz (1951), Rees and Schultz (1970) and Granovetter (1974). These early studies presented evidence for specific geographical locations and/or particular occupations; in recent years, the research covers a wider range of professions and skill levels and a number of countries as well. Taken together, this research establishes that social networks are used extensively across skill levels and across countries in labour markets.

This work has looked at the use of contacts by both employees as well as employers. With regard to the use of personal contacts by workers, the literature has focussed on three themes. One, to what extent do workers rely on personal sources of information in obtaining jobs? Two, how does the use of personal contacts vary with the nature of the job and across countries? Three, how productive is the use of contacts in terms of wages and jobs obtained? Rees (1966), Rees and Shultz (1970) and Granovetter (1974) explored the extensive use of social connections in obtaining information about jobs. In a study of textile works, Myers and Shultz (1951) showed that almost 62 per cent of those surveyed obtained their first job via personal contacts, in contrast to only 15 per cent who obtained their jobs from agencies and advertisements. Similarly, in a widely cited study, Granovetter (1974) showed that almost one half of the people he surveyed received information about their current jobs from personal acquaintances. These findings have inspired an extensive body of empirical research across countries over the years; Granovetter (1994) and Pellizzari (2004) provide an extensive set of references on information sources of job vacancies across countries.

The empirical work on variations in the use of contacts across types of jobs suggests that personal contacts are used less often for higher-salary jobs: in those cases a negative correlation exists between age, education and occupational status and the likelihood of finding one's job through personal contacts. This finding is observed in the 1978 Panel Study on Income Dynamics (Corcoran et al., 1980) and in other studies for the United States; a similar negative correlation is also observed across European countries (Pellizzari, 2004).

A number of papers have studied the effectiveness of personal contacts both with regard to the success of finding a job as well as with regard to the wages obtained. The studies use different methods and have different concerns, so it is difficult to compare them directly. However, a number of the studies find that personal contacts are an efficient way of finding jobs: a higher proportion of jobs found via contacts are likely to be accepted (Blau and Robins, 1990; Holzer, 1988). With regard to the relation between relative wages of jobs found via personal contacts, the evidence here is mixed. Early work by Ullman (1966) suggested that there is a positive relation between wages and hiring via contacts. In more recent work, Pellizzari (2004) finds that in some countries such as Austria, Belgium and the Netherlands there exists a wage premium for jobs found via personal contacts, while in other countries such as Greece, Italy, Portugal and the United Kingdom there exists a wage penalty for jobs obtained via contacts.

Moving on to the other side of the market, there is also evidence about how employers use referrals in their recruitment. Indeed, a study by Holzer (1987) found that over 35 per cent of the firms interviewed filled their last vacancy via referral. Similarly, Marsden and Campbell (1990) in their study of 53 Indiana establishments (in the United States) found that roughly 51 per cent of the jobs had been filled through referrals.

Theoretical Models

I now present two theoretical models that explore the consequences of the use of social networks for employment and inequality. In the first model, the interest is in the transmission of information on job vacancies, while the second model focuses on the use of referrals by firms to hire workers whose quality is unknown.

The model of information transmission on job vacancies is taken from Cálvo-Armengol and Jackson (2004). Individual workers have personal connections and these connections taken together define a social network. Information about new jobs arrives randomly to individuals. If they are unemployed they apply for the jobs; if they are employed and do not need the job, they send this information to their unemployed friends and acquaintances. There is also a chance that someone who is employed may lose his job. The process of job loss, arrival of new job information, the transmission of this information via the network, and the matching of worker to this job, defines a dynamic process the outcome of which is summarised in terms of the employment status of different individuals at any point in time. The interest is in understanding how the properties of the social network affect the employment prospects of individuals.

The analysis of this model yields two main insights. The first insight is that the employment status of individuals in a social network is positively correlated. Empirical work suggests that there is significant correlation in employment status within social communities or geographically contiguous city districts (see, for example, Conley and Topa, 2002; Topa, 2001). Geographical proximity overlaps highly with social connections and so this first insight provides a theoretical account for how local information sharing can generate such correlations in employment status. The second insight is that the probability of finding a job is declining with the duration of unemployment. Duration dependence of unemployment has been widely documented (see, for example, Heckman and Borjas, 1980). The reason that duration dependence arises in a context of social information sharing is that a longer spell of unemployment reveals that a person's social contacts are less likely to be employed, which in turn makes it less likely that they will pass on information concerning vacancies. This in turn lowers the probability of the individual moving out of unemployment and into an employed status.

The second model studies the role of social networks in resolving adverse selection problems in hiring and recruitment. A worker has information on her friends and cohorts, and employees may find it profitable to use such information. The following model taken from Montgomery (1991) takes as its starting point the idea that workers know their own abilities, while potential employers do not know this information. However, working in a firm reveals the ability of the worker to the firm. Now consider a firm who needs to hire a new worker. This firm can place an advertisement in the newspapers and/or it can ask its current employees if they know someone who is suitable for the job. Empirical work suggests that there is considerable similarity in attributes between workers who know each other (see, for example, Rees, 1966; Marsden, 1988). This motivates the idea that a firm with a higher-ability worker expects its current workers to recommend someone of higher ability on average, as compared to a firm whose current employee is of low ability. This difference in expectation may lead some firms to use referrals while others go to the market. If some firms hire via referrals and these referrals pick out higher-ability workers on average, then the ability of workers who go to the market will be lower on average. These differences are reflected in the wages that different workers make. The model explores these ideas and brings out the aggregate implications of social connections for wage inequality and firm profits.

The analysis of this model yields two key insights. The first insight is that workers with more connections will earn a higher wage and that firms who hire through contacts (of their existing higher-quality workers) will earn higher profits. The reason for this relation between connections and wages is simple: more connections implies a higher number of referral wage offers from firms (on average) and this translates into a higher accepted wage (on average). Firms that hire through contacts make higher profits due to imperfect competition between firms (due to a positive probability of a person receiving only one offer); on the other hand, firms hiring workers in the open market are perfect competitors and therefore make zero profits. The second insight is that an increase in the density of social connections raises the inequality in wages. This is a reflection of the lemons effect: an increase in social ties means that more higher-ability workers are hired via referrals, and this lowers the quality of workers who go into the open market, thereby pushing down their wages (relatively).

Social Learning and Diffusion

Technological change is central to economic growth and social development. The process of technological change is complicated and involves many steps starting from basic research and going on to wide-scale adoption. But it is generally agreed that wide diffusion is important for the full gains of a new technology to be realised. This rate of diffusion, however, seems to vary greatly. Consider the following examples:

- The spread of new hybrid seeds has been central to the increase in agricultural productivity over the past century. Classic work by Griliches (1957), Hagerstrand (1967) and Ryan and Gross (1943) document that hybrid corn seeds were adopted over a period of several years in the early twentieth century in the United States. Moreover, diffusion of these seeds displayed clear spatial patterns: initially a small group of farmers adopted the seed, followed by their neighbours adopting it, and this was followed by the neighbours of the neighbours adopting it and so on.[4]
- The period before first prescription of new drugs or medicines by doctors within the same town can range from six months to three years, as observed in the classical study of the spread of a drug, by Coleman et al. (1966).
- The facsimile technology was available in 1843. AT&T introduced wire photo service in 1925. However, fax machines remained a niche product until the mid-1980s. At that point, there was an explosion in the use of fax machines.

The research on the determinants of diffusion suggests that the critical factor in the diffusion of a new technology is the uncertainty about its profitability. Information from governments and firms will alleviate this uncertainty. However, if the technology in question is complicated and involves substantial resources (such as adoption of crops or prescription of medicines) then it is clear that an individual is likely to place much greater faith in information from close friends, colleagues and neighbours, and others in a similar decision situation.

These ideas have inspired a large and ambitious literature on the role of social structure in shaping diffusion and innovation.[5] Let us consider the general framework introduced in Bala and Goyal (1998): suppose that individuals are located on nodes of a network and the links between the nodes reflect information flows between them. At regular intervals, individuals choose an action from a set of alternatives. Actions include the choice of alternative crops, medicines and consumer products. Since they are uncertain about the rewards from different actions, individuals use their own past experience as well as gather information from their neighbours. A variety of issues have been studied by this literature. Here I will focus on the following question: *Are there features of networks that facilitate/hinder the adoption of optimal actions?*

I will restrict attention to connected societies, that is, societies in which every individual is linked either directly or indirectly to everyone else.[6] The first finding is that in such societies every person earns the same payoffs and chooses the same action (except when there are several payoff equivalent actions) in the long run. The intuition for this general result is as follows: if A observes the choices and outcomes experienced by B, then over time she can infer whatever B actually learns from those she is observing. So in the long run A must be able to do as well as B. But in a connected society every pair of individuals mutually observes each other: our reasoning then implies that they must earn equal payoffs in the long run.

This basic result sets the stage for an examination of the role of structure in facilitating/hindering diffusion. Connected societies take on a variety of forms and it is possible to show that some structures get locked into suboptimal actions while others are always able to choose the optimal action in the long run. These examples bring out the following idea: information blockages arise due to the presence of individuals who observe only a few others but are observed by a great many other people. This pattern of linkages is of practical interest as it is empirically observed on the World Wide Web as well as in social communication more generally.

These examples lead to the study of network features that facilitate social learning. The principal finding is that an information network in which individuals learn the optimal actions and earn the maximum payoffs has two general properties. The first property is local independence. Local independence captures the idea that individuals have distinct sources of information and that these distinct sources are relatively important as compared to common sources of information. Local independence facilitates experimentation and gathering of new information. The second property is the existence of links that act as bridges between the distinct sources of information. These bridge links facilitate the diffusion of useful information across a society.[7]

The Identification of Network Effects

We discussed the use of social networks in hiring and job searches and in social learning; more generally, there is evidence for the use of social networks in a variety of social and economic contexts.[8] For the most part, this evidence takes the form of survey data or correlations between networks and outcomes. While this evidence is plausible, establishing causal relations from networks to economic outcomes has proven to be much more difficult. I discuss the conceptual issues involved. Identification of these effects is central to the research programme on networks across the social sciences.

To see why identification of social network effects is difficult let us consider an example from a job search: suppose that we observe that the flow of worker immigrants from country A to country B is positive correlated with the stock of workers from country A in country B. Social networks (e.g. better information in country A about country B, or lower costs of adjustment in a new country) are a natural interpretation for such an observed positive correlation. However, an alternative and equally plausible explanation for the observed correlation is that workers from A have particular skills that are especially in demand in country B. A greater existing stock reflects this better match quality between source country A and destination country B and implies a greater flow. Identification of network effects thus raises delicate problems of inference even in simple contexts.[9]

These issues are at the heart of the large literature on social interactions—see Manski (2000) and Brock and Durlauf (2001) for overviews. Their work argues that a significant part of the variation in behaviour across individuals faced with similar incentives is due to their being a member of one group rather than another (e.g. Glaeser and Scheinkman, 2002; Fafchamps, 2004; Munshi, 2003). This literature seeks to explain behavioural differences across well-defined groups, paying special attention to the difficulty of empirically identifying social interaction effects. In the research on social networks the point of departure is that we look at differences in social connections within a group to understand differences in individual behaviour.

These difficulties on inference are greatly compounded when we begin to study the effects of different aspects of social networks, such as centrality in the network, proximity to others, or the relative connectedness of different individuals.[10] A key new element is that the ties between individual actors are typically endogenous. To see the nature of this problem consider the well-known study on survival and social embeddedness of garment manufacturers in New York by Uzzi (1996). In this study an interesting finding is that survival is positively related to the number of social connections that a firm has. The interpretation is that greater connections (embeddedness) help a firm to share risks more effectively and this in turn leads to greater survival. However, a moment's reflection suggests a natural potential confounding element about the connections: they are not exogenous to the system. Indeed, it is plausible to suppose that firms that are relatively healthy may be better connected than weaker and more vulnerable firms. Thus the positive correlation between connectedness and survival may simply be a reflection of some unobservable characteristics of firms, which are positively related to financial health and survival.

This example points to a key conceptual problem with establishing network effects: the network is itself endogenous and often shaped by individual choice. It may therefore be related in systematic ways to important unobserved individual characteristics. The economics literature has tried to address this problem of identification in a number of different ways. I now briefly discuss some of them and also provide references to related papers. A natural route to addressing the identification issue is to exploit the time structure of the data. This route has been used by Conley and Udry (2008) to study the influence of social networks in the adoption of pineapple in West Africa. Fafchamps and colleagues (2008) exploit the time structure of the data to study the formation of new collaborations in academic research. I elaborate on their strategy to illustrate the use of timing for identification of network effects.

Research collaboration is an environment where much public information is available on individual ability (e.g. publications record, employment history). Consequently we would expect matching frictions to be less prevalent than in other team formation processes. If network proximity affects the formation of new teams even in such a favourable environment, we expect that social networks will also matter for matching processes more generally. It is reasonable to suppose that, to economize on friction costs, individuals will use information easily available in their circle of friends and acquaintances.

Fafchamps et al. (2010) examine data on co-authorship among economists over a 30-year period, from 1970 to 1999. They show that two economists are more likely to publish together if they are close in the network of all economics co-authors. This result is robust and statistically significant. Network distance coefficients are large in magnitude: being at a network distance of 2 instead of 3 raises the probability of initiating a collaboration by 27 per cent. They develop a number of arguments (based on a variety of controls of time invariant as well as time-varying factors) to show that this proximity effect can be interpreted as reflecting flows of information about individuals as well as about the quality of the match. To identify such social network effects, they need to convincingly control for the other confounding factors discussed above.

First, they control for pairwise fixed effects. This takes care of all time-invariant complementarity and social proximity effects, such as similarity in age, place of education, stable research interest and so on. With pairwise fixed effects, identification of network effects is achieved solely from the timing of collaboration, that is, they ask whether, conditional on eventually publishing together, a pair of authors is more likely to initiate a collaboration after they got closer in the network of co-authorship. Second, using the available data they construct control variables for time-varying effects, such as changes in productivity and research interests. This takes care of the most serious time-varying confounding factors. Third, they take up the unobserved time-varying effects (such as non-measurable changes in research interests) that affect the likelihood of collaboration and are correlated with network proximity. Because these effects capture unobserved forces that induce researchers to work together, they should affect the likelihood of all collaborations, not just the first one. In contrast, network effects should only affect the likelihood of the first collaboration between two authors: social networks carry relevant information and create opportunities for face-to-face interaction that may induce two authors to begin to work together; but once two authors have published together, they have a lot of information about match quality and network proximity should no longer matter.

Building on this observation, they conduct a placebo-like experiment by contrasting the effect of network proximity on first and subsequent collaborations. Time-varying confounding factors that are correlated with network proximity should have a similar effect on first and subsequent scientific collaborations; network effects should only affect the first collaboration. Their key finding is that network proximity is only significantly positive for the first collaboration.

THE ORIGINS OF SOCIAL STRUCTURE

I have argued that social structure has profound effects on individual behaviour and payoffs as well as on aggregate social outcomes. We observed that individuals occupying certain positions in a network have access to substantial advantages. For example, two workers with the same ability would earn different wages depending on the number of their personal connections. Similarly, at the aggregate level, two villagers may exhibit very different patterns of adoption of new technology due to differences in social connections. These findings suggest that individual entities – firms, workers, managers or countries – will have an incentive to form connections with others to shape the network in ways that are advantageous to themselves. These general considerations suggest an economic approach in which individuals will trade off the costs and benefits of forming connections.

The strategic aspect of link formation arises from the observation that links between a pair of individual entities will influence the payoffs of others, that is, a link can generate externalities, in ways that are sensitive to the structure of the network. A game of network formation specifies a set of players, the link formation actions available to each player and the payoffs to each player from the networks that arise out of individual linking decisions.

The origins of an economic approach to network formation can be traced to the early work of Boorman (1975), Aumann and Myerson (1988) and Myerson (1991).[11] Boorman (1975) studied a setting in which individuals chose to allocate a fixed set of resources across links; these links yield information on jobs. Larger resource allocation to a link makes it stronger, which in turn yields more information (on average). However, an increase in the number of links that a person has implies that each of her contacts has a lower probability of receiving information. Hence link formation involves private resources and generates externalities on other players. The main finding of Boorman's analysis was that individual linking can generate an inefficient flow of information about jobs and this has implications for the level of employment in an economy. The model studied by Boorman is quite specific but it captures the following general ideas: link formation has costs and benefits for the individual and it also generates externalities on others. These two ideas and the principle of individual optimization together constitute the key conceptual elements in the economic theory of network formation.

The distinctive feature of the economics approach is its emphasis on individual incentives in shaping link formation decisions and therefore in understanding how a network arises out of purposeful individual actions. The central role of individual choice requires that we explicitly take into account the preferences, the knowledge and the rationality of individuals. This explicit formulation in turn permits the examination of a number of normative questions such as whether the networks that arise are good or bad and if something should be done to modify individual incentives to facilitate the emergence of other (better) networks.

These issues can be illustrated through a discussion of the following model, due to Goyal (1993) and Bala and Goyal (2000).[12] There are n individuals, each of whom can form a link with any subset of the remaining players. Link formation is unilateral: an individual i can decide to form a link with any player j by paying for the link. While there are some interesting practical examples of this type of link formation – such as forming links across Web pages, citations, telephone calls, the sending of gifts in the context of social relations – it must be emphasised that the principal appeal of this model is its simplicity. This simplicity is an important virtue as it permits an exploration of a number of important questions concerning the process of network formation and its welfare implications in a straightforward manner. A second feature of the model is that it allows for a fairly general description of payoffs. Individual payoffs are assumed to be increasing in the number of other people accessed via the network and they are falling in the number of links formed by an individual; no assumptions are made on the curvature of the returns to linking.

A third attractive feature of the model is that it yields sharp predictions on the architecture of networks. In particular, simple network architectures such as stars and variants of the star (such as interlinked stars) arise naturally and the economic reasons underlying their emergence is easily understood.[13] Two types of economic pressures have been identified in the literature: distance-related pressures and diminishing returns from linking. Bala and Goyal (2000), Jackson and Wolinsky (1996) and Hojman and Sziedl (2008) show that if payoffs are falling in distance from others, individuals have incentives to get close to others. In addition, if there are diminishing returns then small-world networks are supported by a few links, each formed by a great many people but pointing to only a few key players. This is the foundation of periphery-sponsored star networks.

Moreover, it turns out that equilibrium networks have striking efficiency and distributional properties: stars are efficient but exhibit significant payoff inequality (since the central player typically earns very different payoffs as compared to the peripheral ones). Finally, a study of the dynamics reveals that, starting from any network, a simple process of best responses by individuals leads eventually to the star network; in other words, individuals can through trial and error arrive at a simple social structure that is fully characterized.

The simplicity of the model and the sharpness of its predictions have motivated an extensive theoretical literature that seeks to examine their robustness. The basic model assumes that all players are homogenous in terms of value as well as costs of forming links. More generally, heterogeneity offers a natural way to incorporate the idea of restrictions placed by existing social structures. A simple way to model existing social structure is to suppose that individuals live on islands or belong to groups (Galeotti et al., 2006; Jackson and Rogers, 2005; Johnson and Gilles, 2000). The costs to forming links within a group are lower than the costs of forming links across groups. The idea of group here is very general and may reflect geographic distance, or ethnic, linguistic, or religious difference. The interest is in understanding how such difference shapes the structure of social networks that arise due to individual choice. The analysis of the model suggests that cost differences with regard to linking may lead to relatively more clustering within groups and less across groups. They may also lead to few links across groups, which may be interpreted as 'weak ties'. Finally, within each group, a few individuals may constitute hubs and the hubs across different groups may form connections to create a core. These results illustrate the scope of the general approach to strategic network formation outlined above and also illustrate how choice and existing structure together shape the emergence of a new structure.[14]

TOWARDS A GENERAL SOCIAL THEORY

Social structure is a description of the relations among individuals in a society. At birth, individuals inherit a variety of social relations; while this varies considerably across societies and across history, it will generally include their parents, extended family and the immediate social circle of their parents. As the individual grows and matures, he will choose to retain some of the inherited ties while others will slowly dissolve, and he will form new ties. These choices will take place along with other choices in regard to behaviour along a range of different dimensions. The freedom with which an individual can exercise these different choices will vary across societies and over time. It is likely that in traditional societies with little geographic and economic mobility, the range of choices is more limited than in modern societies. These differences in the space for choice will shape choice and in turn have a bearing on how the social structure evolves over time.

The recent research in economics has made important progress in understanding the processes through which choice is shaped and, in turn, shapes social structure and institutions. I discuss two models to illustrate the scope of this new line of research.[15]

The Co-Evolution of Social Structure and Behaviour

This section considers a dynamic model in which individuals choose actions in interaction with others as well as with whom to interact. Our interest is in understanding how individual behaviour and social structure co-evolve over time.

Consider the following simple framework taken from Goyal and Vega-Redondo (2005):[16] there is a group of players who have the opportunity to play a simple two-action coordination game. Let the two actions be denoted by A and B. This game has two (pure-strategy Nash) equilibria, corresponding to the two actions. Let us suppose that an individual's payoffs are larger if everyone chooses action A as compared to the case when everyone chooses B. However, action B yields an individual high payoff if one half of the population chooses each action (in other words, action B is risk-dominant). Two players can only play with one another if they have a 'link' between them. These links are made by individual initiative. They are also costly to form, in the sense that it takes effort and resources to create and maintain them. A link permits several interpretations; examples include communication links (with messages sent from one person to another), investments of time and effort by two persons in building a common understanding of a research problem, or travel by one person to the location of another to carry out some joint project.

At regular intervals, individuals choose links and actions to maximize (myopically) their respective payoffs. Occasionally, they also make errors or experiment. Our interest is in the nature of long-run outcomes, when the probability of these errors is small. First, we show that, provided the costs of link formation are not too high, any network architecture that is robust enough to be observed a significant fraction of time in the long run must be complete.[17] This implies that partially connected networks are just ephemeral situations in the long run. Second, we find that in long-run states, players always coordinate on the same action, that is, social conformism obtains. However, the specific nature of coordination sharply depends on the costs of link formation. There is a threshold value in the interior of the payoff range such that, if the costs of link formation are below the threshold, players coordinate on the risk-dominant action B. In contrast, if those costs are above that threshold, players coordinate on the efficient action A.

The main insight of this analysis is the role of dynamics of link formation: note that the only social architecture that we observe in the long run is complete, but players' behaviour in the coordination game is different depending on the costs of forming links. Indeed, if the social network was fixed throughout, standard arguments indicate that the risk-dominant action must prevail in the long run (cf. Young, 1998). Thus it is the co-evolution of the links and actions that decisively shapes individual behaviour in our model.

The discussion above focused on coordination games, but a similar approach can be used to study games of conflict. In such games, individuals can condition their links on good behaviour in the past. Deleting a link is then a form of ostracism, while maintaining a link constitutes a gesture of goodwill. There is an interesting line of research that studies co-evolution of social structure and cooperation (see, for example, Mengel and Fosco, 2008; Ule, 2008 and Vega-Redondo, 2006).

Individual Choice, Networks and Markets

Research collaboration among firms takes on a variety of forms (such as joint ventures, technology sharing, cross licensing and joint R&D). In recent years, joint R&D has become especially prominent.[18] Moreover, a general feature of research collaboration is that firms enter into different projects with non-overlapping sets of partners. Thus it is natural to represent collaboration relations as a network. Empirical work shows that the networks of collaboration links exhibit several striking features: the average degree is relatively small (as compared to the total number of firms), the degrees are unequally distributed, the architectures resemble a core-periphery network and the average distance between firms is relatively small. These empirical findings motivate an enquiry into the economic origins and the implications of interfirm research collaboration networks.

A simple model of network formation is developed using the following ideas. Firms compete in a market, and having lower costs is advantageous, as it leads to larger market share and profits. Collaboration between firms is a way to share knowledge and skills and this lowers costs of production. Thus a collaboration between two firms makes them relatively more competitive vis-à-vis other firms. On the other hand, collaboration with other firms involves resources and is costly. So a firm compares the costs and returns from collaboration when deciding on how many links to form. At the heart of the analysis is the issue of how a collaboration link between two firms alters the incentives of other firms to form collaboration links.

These externalities from a collaboration link arise from the disadvantages that a firm suffers in competing with firms that have lower costs. The economic effects of cost differentials depend on the nature of market competition. Thus in the two-way flow of influence between markets and networks it is important to note that the nature of market competition shapes the incentives for collaboration. However, the pattern of collaboration among firms determines the cost structure in an industry and this in turn shapes the nature of market competition.

The following discussion is based on a model due to Goyal and Joshi (2003).[19] Let us first illustrate the ways in which the choice of firms is shaped by and, in turn, shapes the network and the market. To see this in the simplest form consider the two classical models of oligopolistic competition: price competition and quantity competition. Suppose that there is a small but positive cost that must be incurred by both firms that form the link. Goyal and Joshi (2003) show that in a market with price competition, firms will choose to form no links as the competition is too great and the firms that form a link cannot recover the costs of the link. By contrast, in a market with quantity competition, every firm will form a link with every other firm, and the network will be complete! Thus the form of market competition (price or quantity) shapes incentives to form collaboration ties, which in turn shape the nature of competition. An important consequence is that the outcome under quantity competition will exhibit higher quantities and lower prices as compared to the outcome with price competition!

Let us now examine the case of large costs of forming links. Following from the earlier discussion, it is easy to see that in a market with price competition, the same result obtains: no firm will form any links and the empty network is realised. However, in the market with quantity competition we need now to examine the curvature of the marginal returns from collaboration with the possibly large costs of forming links. The key insight here

is that the marginal returns from an additional link to a firm are increasing in its own links and are decreasing in the links of other firms. In a context where the cost of a new link is either constant or only increasing slowly it then follows that an equilibrium network has the dominant group architecture: there is a group of fully linked firms and the rest of the firms are isolated. Moreover, it is possible to show that firms with more degrees have a higher market share and earn higher profits as compared to isolated firms.

Let us explore further the implication of the observation that marginal returns to new links are increasing in the number of own links and decreasing in the links of others. This suggests the possibility that a network may be sustained by transfers from highly linked firms to poorly linked firms.

The main finding is that transfers facilitate the emergence of star and variations on the star network such as interlinked stars. These networks are indeed sustained by the transfers from highly connected core firms to poorly connected peripheral firms. Moreover, these transfers allow the core firms to make larger profits as compared to the peripheral firms.

These findings are obtained in a theoretical framework where firms know the structure of the network as well as the value of linking with other firms, and there is no problem in eliciting efforts from partner firms in a collaboration. These are strong assumptions, as, in actual practice, incomplete information and the attendant incentives problems are likely to be important factors.

In actual practice, a firm is more likely to know about the knowledge and skills of other firms with whom it has had past collaborations. Similarly, individual firms are likely to have significant private knowledge about their own efforts and skills: this private knowledge is likely to create the familiar incentive relating to moral hazard and adverse selection. In the context of research and development, formal contracts will typically not be able to address these problems fully. This suggests that firms may prefer repeated collaboration with existing collaboration partners or with firms about whom they can get reliable information via existing and past common partners. In other words, the network structure of past collaborations may well play an important role in shaping the performance of existing collaborations as well as the pattern of new collaborations.

These considerations constitute key elements in the work of Granovetter (1985) on the social embeddedness of economic activity.[20] Broadly speaking, three questions have been explored in this research. The first question is, what types of firms enter into collaborative agreements and with whom? The second question is, how does the existing pattern of collaboration links relate to the governance structure of a new collaboration partnership (is there a formal contract, or are loose research-sharing agreements used?). The third question is, how is the network position of the partners related to performance of a collaboration link? These questions have been addressed in interesting empirical work in sociology and organization theory; for a survey of this work, see Gulati (2007).

Theoretical research in this area lags behind the empirical work. Gradual building of trust in bilateral links has been explored by economists (see, for example, Ghosh and Ray, 1996).[21] However, in these models an individual only takes part in one interaction at any point in time, and if this relationship breaks down then there is no information flow across different partnerships. In contrast to the above setting, information flow across firms (both about skills as well as about actions) is a key element of the process. The formal study of evolving network relations in a context characterised by informational asymmetries appears to be an open problem.

CONCLUDING REMARKS

Economists have been successful at developing concepts for the study of interaction in small groups (game theory) and interaction among large groups (competitive markets and general equilibrium). Social networks appear to fall in between these two extremes. A social network typically consists of a large number of individuals and any individual interacts only with a small subset of them. The analysis of many actors located within complex networks strains the plausibility of delicate chains of strategic reasoning, which are typical in game theory. Similarly, the 'local' interaction in social networks makes anonymous competitive equilibrium analysis implausible. This tension between the large and the small is fundamental to understanding behaviour at the intersection of markets and social networks. It offers a fertile ground for exciting theoretical work in the years to come.

There is a large body of evidence for the correlation between social networks on the one hand and individual behaviour and outcomes on the other hand. However, establishing a causal link from social networks has proved harder and I have briefly discussed the issues involved. The identification of network effects is an important ongoing research programme in economics but also in many other disciplines such as health, business strategy, organization theory and sociology. The availability of large longitudinal data sets on networks as well as behaviour taken together with continuing improvements in computing power

offer the prospect for major progress on this critical question.

ACKNOWLEDGEMENTS

I thank Bryony Reich, Peter Carrington and John Scott for comments on an earlier draft.

NOTES

1 This chapter builds on the arguments developed in Goyal (2007). The study of networks is one of the most active fields of research in many disciplines; other book-length treatments include Barabási (2002), Gulati (2007), Jackson (2008), Scott (2000), Vega-Redondo (2006), Wasserman and Faust (1994) and Watts (1999).

2 A number of other economic applications have been studied. For effects of networks on research and market competition, see Goyal and Moraga-Gonzalez (2001); for an application to criminal activity, see Ballester et al. (2006); on financial contagion, see Allen and Gale (2000); for the effects of consumer networks on market competition, see Galeotti (2005); on the use of social networks for marketing, see Campbell (2008) and Galeotti and Goyal (2009); for effects of networks on bidding and markets, see Kranton and Minehart (2001); for effects of networks on bargaining power, see Manea (2008).

3 For a classical study of the effects of asymmetric information on the functioning of markets, see Akerlof (1970).

4 For a recent study on the use of social networks in agriculture, see Conley and Udry (2008).

5 See for example, Acemoglu et al. (2008), Bala and Goyal (1998), De Marzo et al. (2003), Ellison and Fudenberg (1993, 1995), Golub and Jackson (2010); for a recent survey of this work, see Goyal (2009).

6 This covers a wide range of structures. A star network (with one central hub), a circle (in which everyone is linked to two others) and the complete network (in which everyone is linked to everyone else) are all instances of connected societies.

7 The bridges may be seen as weak links connecting communities, as Granovetter (1974) found. The above result may then be interpreted as making precise an insight relating to the 'strength of weak ties': societies with many weak ties will exhibit better diffusion of new innovations.

8 For a discussion of this work, see Fafchamps (2003, 2004), Goyal (2007) and Jackson (2008). The empirical study of the architecture of empirical social networks is relatively new in economics. For a study of the evolution of large social networks, see

Goyal et al. (2006). In recent work, Krishnan and Sciubba (2009), Comola (2007) and Mayer and Puller (2008) study the formation of links.

9   For an influential contribution to the study of social networks in international labour migration, see Munshi (2003).

10   However, see Bramoulle et al. (2009) who show that, in contrast to the use of group affiliation data, the use of detailed network data allows stronger identification of contextual network effects. For an interesting attempt at estimation of network effects in education and crime, see Cálvo-Armengol et al. (2008).

11   In recent years, the study of network formation has been a very active field of study in economics and a number of different questions have been explored; see Demange and Wooders (2005) and Dutta and Jackson (2003) for references.

12   This model has been extended in a number of directions by many researchers. Important contributions include Hojman and Szeidl (2008) and Ferri (2004). This model is very close in spirit to the model of connections developed in Jackson and Wolinsky (1996). For a survey of strategic network formation, see Goyal (2007).

13   A star has one central/hub player: all other players form a single link to this central player and have no other links.

14   These theoretical findings have led to a number of experimental investigations of network formation; for a survey, see Kosfeld (2004).

15   See Schelling (1975) for an early attempt at understanding social structure through the lens of individual choice. See Young (1998) for a study of the relations between individual choice and social structure and Kirman (1997) for an early discussion of the network approach to the study of economic activity.

16   In independent work, Droste et al. (1999), Hojman and Szeidl (2006), Jackson and Watts (2002) and Skyrms and Pemantle (2000) study a similar model of co-evolution of social structure and behaviour.

17   In a complete network, every pair of players is directly linked.

18   For a survey of these developments, see Hagedoorn (2002).

19   For related work on networks and markets, see Belleamme and Bloch (2004) and Deroian and Gannon (2006).

20   For an early empirical study on interlocking boards and firm performance, see Carrington (1981).

21   For theoretical work in sociology, see Raub and Weesie (1990).

REFERENCES

Acemoglu, D., Dahleh, M., Lobel, I. and Ozdaglar, A. (2008) 'Bayesian learning in social networks', mimeo. MIT Press.

Akerlof, G. (1970) 'The market for lemons', *Quarterly Journal of Economics* 84(3): 488–500.

Akerlof, G. (1997) 'Social distance and social decisions', *Econometrica* 65: 1005–27.

Akerlof, G. and Kranton, R. (2000) 'Economics and identity', *Quarterly Journal of Economics* 115(3): 715–53.

Alesina, A. and Spolaore, E. (2003) *Size of Nations*. MIT Press.

Allen, F. and Gale, D. (2000) 'Financial contagion'. *Journal of Political Economy* 108(1): 1–34.

Aumann, R. and Myerson, R. (1988) 'Endogenous formation of links between players and coalitions: An application to the Shapley Value', in *The Shapley Value*, A. Roth (ed.), Cambridge University Press. pp. 175–91.

Bala, V. and Goyal, S. (1998) 'Learning from neighbours', *Review of Economic Studies* 65: 595–621.

Bala, V. and Goyal, S. (2000) 'A non-cooperative model of network formation', *Econometrica* 68(5): 1181–231.

Ballester, C., Cálvo-Armengol, A. and Zenou, Y. (2006) 'Who's who in networks. Wanted: The key player', *Econometrica* 74(5): 1403–17.

Barabási, A.L. (2002) *Linked*. Boston: Perseus Books.

Blau, D. and Robins, P.K. (1990) 'Job search outcomes for the unemployed and the employed', *Journal of Political Economy* 98(3): 637–55.

Belleamme, P. and Bloch, F. (2004) 'Market sharing agreements and collusive networks', *International Economic Review* 45(2): 387–411.

Boorman, S. (1975) 'A combinatorial optimization model for transmission of job information through contact networks', *Bell Journal of Economics* 6(1): 216–49.

Bramoulle, Y., Djebbari, H. and Fortin, B. (2009) 'Identification of peer effects through social networks', *Journal of Econometrics* 150(1): 41–55.

Brock, W. and Durlauf, S. (2001) 'Interactions-based models', in Heckman and Leamer (eds.), *Handbook of Econometrics: Volume V*. Amsterdam.

Burt, R. (1994) *The social structure of competition*. Boston: Harvard University Press.

Cálvo-Armengol, A., Patacchini, E. and Zenou, Y. (2008) 'Peer effects and social networks in education'. *Review of Economic Studies*.

Cálvo-Armengol, A. and Jackson, M.O. (2004) 'The effects of social networks on employment and inequality', *American Economic Review* 94(3): 426–54.

Campbell, A. (2008) 'Tell your friends! Word of mouth and percolation in social networks', mimeo, MIT Press.

Carrington, P.J. (1981) 'Horizontal co-optation through corporate interlocks'. Unpublished PhD thesis, University of Toronto.

Coleman, J. (1994) *Foundations of Social Theory*. Cambridge, MA: Harvard University Press.

Coleman, J., Katz, E. and Mentzel, H. (1966) *Medical Innovation: Diffusion of a Medical Drug Among Doctors*. Indianapolis. MN. Bobbs-Merrill.

Comola, M. (2007) 'The network structure of informal arrangements: Evidence from rural Tanzania', mimeo, Universitat Pompeu Fabra.

Conley, T. and Topa, G. (2002) 'Socio-economic distance and spatial patterns in unemployment', *Journal of Applied Econometrics* 17: 303–27.

Conley, T.G. and Udry, C.R. (2008) 'Learning about a new technology: Pineapple in Ghana', *American Economic Review*, to appear.

Corcoran, M., Datcher, L. and Duncan, G. (1980) 'Information and influence networks in labour markets', in G. Duncan and J. Morgan (eds.), *Five Thousand American Families: Patterns of Economic Progress*, Volume 7. Ann Arbor, MI: Institute for Social Research.

Dasgupta, P. and Serageldin, I. (1999) *Social Capital: A Multifaceted Perspective*. Washington: World Bank.

De Marzo, Peter, Dimitri Vayanos and Jerry Zweibel (2003) 'Persuasion bias, social influence, and unidimensional opinions', *Quarterly Journal of Economics* 118: 909–68.

Demange, G. and Wooders, M. (2005) *Group Formation in Economics: Networks, Cubs and Coalitions*. Cambridge University Press.

Deroian, F. and Gannon, F. (2006) 'Quality improving alliances in differentiated oligopoly', *International Journal of Industrial Organization* 24(3): 629–637.

Droste, E., Gilles, R. and Johnson, K. (1999) 'Endogenous interaction and the evolution of conventions', in *Adaptive Behaviour in Economic and Social Environments*, PhD thesis. University of Tilburg.

Dussenbery, J. (1949) *Income, Savings and the Theory of Consumer Behaviour*. Cambridge, MA: Harvard University Press.

Dutta, B. and Jackson, M. (eds.) (2003) *Models of the Strategic Formation of Networks and Groups*. Springer-Verlag.

Ellison, G. and Fudenberg, D. (1993) 'Rules of thumb for social learning', *Journal of Political Economy* 101: 612–44.

Ellison, G. and Fudenberg, D. (1995) 'Word-of-mouth communication and social learning', *Quarterly Journal of Economics* 109: 93–125.

Fafchamps, M. (2003) *Rural Poverty, Risk, and Development*. New York: Elgar Publishing.

Fafchamps, M. (2004) *Market Institutions and Sub-Saharan Africa: Theory and Evidence*. MIT Press.

Fafchamps, M., Goyal, S. and van der, L.M. (2010) 'Matching and network effects', *Journal of European Economic Association* 8(1): 203–231.

Ferri, F. (2004) 'Stochastic stability in networks with decay', mimeo, University of Venice.

Galeotti, A. (2005) 'Consumer networks and search equilibria', *Tinbergen Institute Discussion Paper 2004–75*.

Galeotti, A. and Goyal, S. (2009) 'Influencing the influencers: A theory of strategic diffusion', *Rand Journal of Economics* 40(3): 509–532.

Galeotti, A., Goyal, S. and Kamphorst, J. (2005) 'Network formation with heterogeneous players', *Games and Economic Behaviour* 54(2): 353–372.

Ghatak, M. and Kali, R. (2001) 'Financially interlinked business groups', *Journal of Economics and Management Strategy* 10: 4.

Ghosh, P. and Ray, D. (1996) 'Cooperation in community interaction without information flows', *Review of Economic Studies* 63: 491–519.

Glasear, E. and Scheinkman, J. (2002) 'Non-market interactions', in Dewatripont, Hansen, and Turnovsky (eds.), *Advances in Economics and Econometrics: Theory and Applications*. Cambridge University Press.

Golub, B. and Jackson, M.O. (2010) 'Naive learning and the wisdom of crowds'. *American Economic Journal: Microeconomics* 2(1): 112–149.

Goyal, S. (1993) 'Sustainable communication networks', Tinbergen Institute Discussion Paper', TI, pp. 93–250.

Goyal, S. (2007) *Connections: An Introduction to the Economics of Networks*. Princeton, NJ: Princeton University Press.

Goyal, S. (2009) 'Learning in networks', in *Handbook of Social Economics*, J. BenHabib, A. Bisin, M.O. Jackson (eds.) Elsevier Press.

Goyal, S. and Joshi, S. (2003) 'Networks of collaboration in oligopoly', *Games and Economic Behaviour* 43(1): 57–85.

Goyal, S., van der, L.M. and Moraga-Gonzalez, J.L. (2006) 'Economics: Emerging small world', *Journal of Political Economy* 114: 403–12.

Goyal, S. and Moraga-Gonzalez, J.L. (2001) 'R&D networks', *Rand Journal of Economics* 32(4): 686–707.

Goyal, S. and Vega-Redondo, F. (2005) 'Network formation and social coordination', *Games and Economic Behaviour* 50: 178–207.

Granovetter, M. (1974) *Getting a Job: A Study of Contacts and Careers*. Cambridge, MA: Harvard University Press.

Granovetter, M. (1985) 'Economic action and social structure: The problem of embeddedness', *American Journal of Sociology* 3: 481–510.

Granovetter, M. (1994) *Getting a Job: A Study of Contacts and Careers*. Second Edition. Chicago: University of Chicago Press.

Griliches, Z. (1957) 'Hybrid corn: An exploration in the economics of technological change', *Econometrica* 25: 501–22.

Gulati, R. (2007) *Managing Network Resources*. Oxford, NY: Oxford University Press.

Hagedoorn, J. (2002) 'Inter-firm R&D partnerships: An overview of major trends and patterns since 1960', *Research Policy* 31: 477–92.

Hagerstrand, J. (1967) *Innovation Diffusion as a Spatial Process*. Translated by A. Pred. University of Chicago Press.

Heckman, J. and Borjas, G. (1980) 'Does unemployment cause future unemployment? Definitions, questions and answers from a continuous time model of heterogeneity and state dependence', *Economica* 47: 247–83.

Hojman, D. and Szeidl, A. (2006) 'Endogenous networks, social games and evolution', *Games and Economic Behaviour* 551: 112–30.

Hojman, D. and Szeidl, A. (2008) 'Core and periphery in endogenous networks', *Journal of Economic Theory* 139(1): 295–309.

Holzer, H.J. (1987) 'Hiring procedures in the firms: Their economic determinants and outcomes', *NBER Research Working Paper No 2185*.

Holzer, H.J. (1988) 'Search method use by unemployed youth', *Journal of Labour Economics* 6: 1–20.

Jackson, M.O. (2008) *Social and Economic Networks*. New Jersey: Princeton University Press.

Jackson, M. and Rogers, B. (2005) 'The economics of small worlds', *Journal of European Economic Association* 32(2): 617–27.

Jackson, M. and Watts, A. (2002) 'On the formation of inter-action networks in social coordination games', *Games and Economic Behaviour* 41(2): 265–91.

Jackson, M. and Wolinsky, A. (1996) 'A strategic model of economic and social networks', *Journal of Economic Theory* 71(1): 44–74.

Johnson, C. and Gilles, R. (2000) 'Spatial social networks', *Review of Economic Design* 5: 273–300.

Kali, R. (1999) 'Endogenous business networks', *Journal of Law, Economics and Organization* 15:3.

Kirman, A. (1997) 'The economy as an evolving network', *Journal of Evolutionary Economics* 7: 339–53.

Kosfeld, M. (2004) 'Economic networks in the laboratory: A survey', *Review of Network Economics* 3: 20–42.

Kranton, R. and Minehart, D. (2001) 'A theory of buyer-seller networks', *American Economic Review* 91(3): 485–508.

Krishnan, P. and Sciubba, E. (2000) 'Links and architecture in village economies', *Economic Journal* 119(4): 917–949.

Manea, M. (2008) 'Bargaining in stationary environments', mimeo', Harvard University.

Manski, C. (2000) 'Economic analysis of social interactions', *Journal of Economic Perspectives* 14(3): 115–36.

Marsden, P.V. (1988) 'Homogeneity in confiding relations', *Social Networks* 10: 57–76.

Marsden, P.V. and Campbell, K. (1990) 'Recruitment and selection processes: The organizational side of the job searches', in R. Breiger (ed.) *Social Mobility and Social Structure*. Cambridge University Press, pp. 50–79.

Mayer, A. and Puller, S.L. (2008) 'The old boy (and girl) network: Social network formation on university campuses', *Journal of Public Economics* 92: 329–47.

Mengel, F. and Fosco, C. (2008) 'Cooperation through imitation and exclusion in networks', mimeo, University of Alicante.

Montgomery, J. (1991) 'Social networks and labour-market outcomes: Toward an economic analysis', *American Economic Review* 81(5): 1408–18.

Munshi, K. (2003) 'Networks in the modern economy: Mexican migrants in the U.S. labour market', *Quarterly Journal of Economics* 118(2): 549–97.

Myers, C. and Schultz, G. (1951) *The Dynamics of a Labor Market*. Englewood Cliffs. NJ.

Myerson, R. (1991) *Game Theory: Analysis of Conflict*. Harvard University Press.

Pellizzari, M. (2004) 'Do friends and relatives really help in getting a good job?' *CEP Discussion Paper, no. 623.*

Raub, W. and Weesie, J. (1990) 'Reputation and efficiency in social interactions: An example of network effects', *American Journal of Sociology* 96: 626–54.

Rauch, J. and Casella, A. (2001) *Networks and Markets*. New York: Russell Sage Foundation.

Rees, A. (1966) 'Information networks in labour markets', *American Economic Review* 56: 559–66.

Rees, A. and Schultz, G.P. (1970) *Workers in an Urban Labour Market*. University of Chicago Press.

Ryan, B. and Gross, N. (1943) 'The diffusion of hybrid seed corn in two Iowa communities', *Rural Sociology* 8: 15–24.

Schelling, T. (1975) *Micromotives and Macrobehavior*. New York: Norton.

Scott, J. (2000) *Social Network Analysis*. London: Sage.

Skyrms, B. and Pemantle, R. (2000) 'A dynamic model of social network formation', *Proceedings of the National Academy of Sciences* 97(16): 9340–46.

Taylor, C.R. (2000) 'The old-boy network and the young-gun effect international', *Economic Review* 41(4): 871–91.

Topa, G. (2001) 'Social interactions, local spillovers and unemployment', *Review of Economic Studies* 68(2): 261–95.

Ule, E. (2008) *Partner Choice and Cooperation in Networks: Theory and Experimental Evidence*. Springer.

Ullman, J.C. (1966) 'Employee referrals: Prime tool for recruiting workers', *Personnel* 43: 30–35.

Uzzi, B. (1996) 'The sources and consequences of embeddedness: The network effect', *American Sociological Review* 61(4): 674–98.

Veblen, T. (1899) *The Theory of the Leisure Class*. New York: Macmillan.

Vega-Redondo, F. (2006) 'Building social capital in a changing world', *Journal of Economic Dynamics and Control* 30: 2305–38.

Vega-Redondo, F. (2007) *Complex Social Networks*. Cambridge University Press.

Wasserman, S. and Faust, K. (1994) *Social Network Analysis: Methods and Applications*. Cambridge, NY: Cambridge University Press.

Watts, D. (1999) *Small Worlds: The Dynamics of Networks Between Order and Randomness*. Princeton, NJ: Princeton University Press.

Young, P. (1998) *Individual Strategy and Social Structure*. Princeton, NJ: Princeton University Press.

7

Relational Sociology, Culture, and Agency

Ann Mische

One of the debates surrounding social network analysis has been whether it consists of a method or a theory. Is network analysis merely a cluster of techniques for analyzing the structure of social relationships, or does it constitute a broader conceptual framework, theoretical orientation, or even philosophy of life? In an article two decades ago synthesizing emerging work on social networks, Barry Wellman argued that network analysis goes beyond methodology to inform a new theoretical paradigm: "structural analysis does not derive its power from the partial application of this concept or that measure. It is a comprehensive paradigmatic way of taking social structure seriously by studying directly how patterns of ties allocate resources in a social system" (1988: 20). This paradigm, he goes on to argue, takes relations—rather than individuals, groups, attributes, or categories—as the fundamental unit of social analysis. This argument was taken up a few years later by Mustafa Emirbayer and Jeff Goodwin (1994), who described the new "anti-categorical imperative" introduced by network analysis and explored its relationship to research on cultural and historical change.

While disagreement remains among network analysts regarding this issue, a broader "relational perspective" within sociology has been simmering for the past three decades, often involving scholars who themselves do not use formal network methodology or who use it only marginally in their research. Inspired by such eminent figures as Harrison White and Charles Tilly, this perspective has taken some of the broader theoretical insights of network analysis and extended them to the realms of culture, history, politics, economics, and social psychology. Fundamental to this theoretical orientation (if it can be called that) is not merely the insistence that what sociologists call "structure" is intrinsically relational, but also, perhaps more

deeply, that relational thinking is a way to overcome stale antinomies between structure and agency through a focus on the dynamics of social interactions in different kinds of social settings.

In this chapter, I will explore the historical origins of this perspective and its positioning in broader intellectual networks. While a relational orientation has germinated in a number of different intellectual hubs (and is certainly not limited to sociology),[1] I will focus in particular on the emergence of what might be called "the New York School" of relational sociology during the 1990s and the constitution of a cluster of scholars working in diverse subfields who elaborated this perspective in partially intersecting ways. I go on to explore four distinct ways in which scholars have conceptualized the relationship between networks and culture, with implications for different kinds of substantive research. I argue that these conversations propose a new theoretical agenda that highlights the way in which communicative interaction and the performance of social relations mediate between structure and agency across a wide range of social phenomena.

THE NEW YORK SCHOOL

To explain the emergence of what I am calling the "New York School" of relational analysis, we can use the conceptual framework that was elaborated in its own conversations and debates. New York in the 1990s was home to a set of interstitial spaces of conversation and debate, composing what some within this perspective might call "publics," using a particular networked meaning of that term that I will discuss in more detail below. These publics brought together senior scholars – notably, White and Tilly – who were undergoing intensive reformulation of their own theoretical frameworks, in (sometimes contentious) dialogue with emerging younger scholars who were advancing new theoretical syntheses and critiques, as well as graduate students composing original frameworks for empirical research.

To borrow from two strongly relational (although somewhat discordant) theories of intellectual innovation, these publics were sources of intellectual opposition, energy, and excitement (Collins, 1998), and also of experimental probing of fractal divides in theoretical perspectives, particularly those related to realism and constructivism as well as positivism and interpretivism (Abbott, 2001a). Participants in these discussions were linked by multiple ties that were forged and enacted in a series of partially overlapping discursive settings (workshops, miniconferences, study groups, dissertation committees), facilitated by a set of prominent scholars who were extraordinarily attuned to the democratic exchange of ideas. As participants wrestled with the tensions generated in these conversations, they developed not a unified theory (important differences remain among them), but rather a shared focus on the communicative grounding of network relations and the implications of these relations for understanding dynamic social processes.

To trace the emergence of this perspective, we need to examine the structural holes that it was bridging, as well as the intersecting intellectual streams that gave it a distinctive voice. During the mid-1990s, social network analysis was maturing as a field, with the publication of several handbooks and edited volumes (Wellman and Berkowitz, 1988; Scott, 1991; Wasserman and Faust, 1994), the development of software packages such as UCINet, and the expansion of its professional association, the International Network for Social Network Analysis (founded in 1978, but growing beyond its initial tight-knit base in the 1990s). However, much of the work in the field was highly formal and technical, thus making it relatively inaccessible to non-mathematical researchers who otherwise might have gravitated toward its core ideas. Most cultural theorists saw network analysis as located squarely in the positivist camp, reducing cultural richness to 1s and 0s and lacking attention to processes of interpretation and meaning-construction.

At the same time, the subfield of cultural sociology in the United States was undergoing a rapid expansion and shift in orientation, moving beyond the study of artistic production to encompass practice and discourse more generally. The Culture Section of the American Sociological Association grew from a relatively marginal section in the early 1990s to one of the largest sections by the mid-2000s. Moreover, cultural sociology often overlapped with other subareas, especially political sociology, comparative-historical sociology, and the study of collective behavior and social movements, thus creating significant subfield cross-fertilization. While a handful of researchers in the late 1980s and early 1990s pioneered the use of network analytic techniques to study cultural and historical processes (notably Erickson, 1988, 1996; Carley, 1993, 1994); Bearman, 1993; Mohr, 1994; Gould, 1995), a sizeable gap remained between formal network analysis and more interpretively oriented cultural research.

These streams converged in the mid-1990s in New York City, as a cluster of scholars across several universities in the area engaged in a series of intensive exchanges related to networks, culture, and historical analysis. One center for these debates was Columbia University, where Harrison White arrived from Harvard (via Arizona) in 1988, taking on the directorship of the Paul F. Lazarsfeld Center for the Social Sciences.[2] Under White's leadership, the Lazarsfeld Center sponsored a series of ongoing interdisciplinary workshops on topics including social networks, sociolinguistics, complex systems, and political economy. These workshops brought in outside speakers while sponsoring graduate students and nurturing local research and debate across intersecting intellectual domains. During this period, White began thinking deeply about the origins and transformations of language, involving many young scholars in these discussions.[3]

Likewise, the Graduate Faculty of the New School for Social Research was a sometimes tempestuous hub of interdisciplinary debate. In the mid-1980s, then Dean Ira Katznelson recruited a cluster of top scholars – including Charles and Louise Tilly, Janet Abu-Lughod, Ari Zolberg, Talal Asad, Richard Bensel, Elizabeth Sanders, Eric Hobsbawm, and others – that added new voices to the Graduate Faculty's already strong grounding in normative theories of civil society. Debates between critical theorists, poststructuralists, and structurally oriented historical scholars were frequent and intense, and, as I argue below, helped to push Tilly toward a re-examination of the role of identities, narratives, and discourse in theories of contentious politics, as he developed the synthesis he labeled "relational realism." In 1991, Mustafa Emirbayer arrived at the New School as an assistant professor. While he himself came from a strongly interpretive tradition, he became interested in network analysis from watching his White-inspired peers at Harvard. He and his fellow Harvard alum Jeff Goodwin, who was then at NYU, began writing an article to explore what all this fuss about network analysis was about (Emirbayer and Goodwin, 1994). The conversations sparked by this network of New York area scholars – in dialogue with a broader circle of researchers elsewhere – set the stage for the consolidation of a perspective that crossed a series of fractal divides, linking network relations with discourse, identities, and social interaction.

Harrison White began what might be called his "linguistic turn" in the early 1990s with the publication of his major theoretical statement, *Identity and Control* (1992). White had been preoccupied since the 1970s with the lack of theoretical understanding of what he called "types of ties," the basic measurement unit of the mathematical approach to network analysis that he and his students pioneered at Harvard in the 1970s. In *Identity and Control*, he wrestles with this question by proposing the narrative constitution of social networks. Social ties, he argues, are generated by reporting attempts in relation to contending efforts at control: "a tie becomes constituted by story, which defines a social time by its narrative of ties" (White, 1992: 67). Because ties are multiple, fluid, and narratively constructed (and reconstructed) in relation to evolving time frames, the new challenge for network analysis, White argued, was to understand this link between temporality, language, and social relations.

Fascinated by these connections, he began to probe more deeply into work on language usage, function, and evolution. In conjunction with a group of graduate students, he carried out an intensive reading of sociolinguistics, discourse analysis, and theories of linguistic change. He was especially attuned to work on the link between semantics, grammar, and interaction context (Halliday, 1976, 1978; Goodwin and Duranti, 1992; Schriffen, 1987), as well as studies of tense (Comrie, 1985) and the indexical (or "deictic") nature of language use (Hanks, 1992; Silverstein, 2003). He saw in contextualized grammatical references to time, space, and relations the link between language, networks, and what he called "social times." His attention to linguistic work on code switching (Gumperz, 1982) inspired some of his ideas on switching dynamics between network domain (see below). Moreover, he saw work on "grammaticalization" (Hopper and Traugott, 1993) as important for understanding how language emerges and shifts in relation to usage patterns in particular relational contexts. He also engaged with Bakhtin's (1981, 1986) dialogic theory, seeing the notion of "speech genre" as grounded in a relational semiotics attuned to multiple and shifting ties.

Many of these ideas were elaborated in White's ongoing graduate seminar on "Identity and Control" at Columbia, as well as in the student-organized workshops on sociolinguistics and social networks at the Lazarsfeld Center. These workshops contributed to a series of articles and working papers that focused on the relationship between language, time, and social relations (White, 1993, 1994, 1995) as well as an article with Ann Mische highlighting the disruptive potential of conversational "situations" (Mische and White, 1998). These papers propose the notion of "network domains" as specialized sets of ties and associated story-sets that keep those ties moving forward in time through a continuous process of reflection, reporting, and updating. With the complexity of modern life, White argues, we are continuously forced to switch between multiple network domains (or "netdoms"), thus creating the need for buffering in the transitional zones of "publics."

White's notion of publics is an innovative twist on Goffman's work on interaction in public spaces; within the bubble of publics, participants experience a momentary sense of connectedness due to the suspension of surrounding ties. Such publics can range from silent encounters in an elevator to cocktail parties, carnivals, or protest rallies, all of which involve a provisional equalization of relationships and decoupling from stories and relations around them, which nevertheless may threaten to impinge on and disrupt the situation at hand (White, 1995; Mische and White, 1998). "The social network of the public is perceived as fully connected, because other network-domains and their particular histories are suppressed. Essential to its mechanism is a decoupling of times, whereby time in public is always a continuing present time, an historic present" (White, 1995: 1054). Empirical work building on Goffman's notion of publics has since been developed by several participants in those discussions, including Mische on communicative styles in Brazilian activist publics, Gibson on turn-taking dynamics in managerial groups, Ikegami on Japanese aesthetic publics, and Sheller on black antislavery publics in Haiti and Jamaica (described in more detail below).

Between 1993 and 1996, White organized a series of miniconferences at the Lazarsfeld Center around the themes of time, language, identities, and networks. A broad range of outside scholars took part (see note 4), thus helping cross-fertilize the emerging "relational" perspective.[4] At one of these miniconferences, Mustafa Emirbayer was inspired to write a programmatic statement that systematized some of the ideas that were being discussed in the group. The resulting "Manifesto for a Relational Sociology" (Emirbayer, 1997) draws on pragmatist, linguistic, and interactionist philosophies as well as historical and network analysis to develop a critique of "substantialist" approaches to social analysis. He calls instead for a "transactional" approach focusing on the dynamics of "supra-personal" relations that transcend individual actors, and he discusses the implications of this approach for historical, cultural, and social psychological analysis. This widely cited article has become one of the rallying cries of the "new relational" approach in sociology, articulating its underlying philosophy in an expansive manner that goes beyond the use of mathematical techniques.

While he was working on this article, Emirbayer was also organizing a study group on Theory and Culture at the New School that brought in graduate students and some faculty from the broader New York area (including the New School, Columbia, NYU, Princeton, CUNY, and other schools). Most of the authors discussed by the group were strongly relational in orientation, including Andrew Abbott, Pierre Bourdieu, Hans Joas, Alessandro Pizzorno, William Sewell, Margaret Somers, and Norbert Wiley. This group also discussed drafts of Emirbayer's "Manifesto," as well as a series of related articles exploring the interface between relations and culture. His now-classic article with Jeff Goodwin was followed by an article with Ann Mische that develops a relational theory of human agency, focusing on the embedding of actors in multiple sociotemporal contexts, with varied orientations toward past, present, and future (Emirbayer and Mische, 1998). Emirbayer also published a paper with Mimi Sheller exploring the network composition of publics as interstitial locations for the exchange of ideas (Emirbayer and Sheller, 1999). Sheller (2000) extends these ideas in her comparison of the linguistic markers and network embedding of black antislavery counterpublics in Haiti and Jamaica, showing how these influenced the differing trajectories of post-abolition civil societies.

Several study group participants (including Mische and Sheller) were also students of Charles Tilly at the New School, where they participated in another essential public for discussion of relational sociology: Tilly's Workshop on Contentious Politics. This workshop was started by Chuck and Louise Tilly at Michigan in the 1970s, transplanted to the New School in the late 1980s, and then relocated again when Tilly moved to Columbia in 1996 (with several name changes along the way). This famously democratic workshop drew in faculty and students from the greater New York region, in addition to many notable international scholars. Students and younger researchers presented work-in-progress alongside senior scholars and were encouraged to offer commentary and critique. During the 1990s, Tilly was undergoing an important transition in his thinking, spurred by debates in the workshop as well as challenges he was receiving from normative and poststructuralist scholars at the New School. He was moving from a resolute structuralism

(developed in opposition to the normative orientation of Parsonian functionalism) to a deep engagement with cultural processes of identity formation, storytelling, and boundary construction, rethought in dynamic, relational terms.

While a focus on relations and interaction was integral to Tilly's thinking from the beginning (Diani, 2007; Tarrow, 2008), at the New School he began to pay closer attention to the ways in which such relations are constructed through processes of meaning making. Tilly responded to what he saw as the solipsistic dangers of poststructuralism by, as he described it, "tunneling under the postmodern challenge." As Viviana Zelizer writes, this meant not only recognizing "that a great deal of social construction goes into the formation of entities – groups, institutions markets, selves," but also calling on social scientists "to explain how that construction actually works and produces its effects" (2006a: 531). This is the perspective that Tilly called "relational realism," which he contrasted to "methodological individualism," "phenomenological individualism," and "holism" in a series of broad theoretical statements in the highly productive final decade of his life. He defines relational realism as "the doctrine that transactions, interactions, social ties and conversations constitute the central stuff of social life" (2004: 72; see also Tilly, 1995, 2008a; Somers, 1998).

The evolution of this shift can be seen in a series of essays, books, and working papers that addressed the relational dimensions of identities, narratives, and boundaries (many of which are collected in Tilly, 2004, 2006a). In these papers, he continually stressed that political process is best understood as a "conversation," a trope that captures the dynamic association between discourse, relations, and interaction (Tilly, 1998a). In *Durable Inequality* (1998b), Tilly turns his attention away from contentious politics to look at the relational origins of inequality, focusing on how durable, exclusionary categories emerge as solutions to relational and institutional problems. Early chapter drafts of this book were workshopped by White and others at the Lazarsfeld Center at Columbia – showing again the multiple intersections in the New York milieu. The emphasis on the dynamic dimension of relationships – including discursive mechanisms of attribution, identity activation, and boundary shift – is forcefully expressed in Tilly's collaborative work with Doug McAdam and Sidney Tarrow, *Dynamics of Contention* (McAdam et al., 2001), as well as in a series of other articles describing "relational mechanisms" as key elements in explaining political processes. Tilly's attention to the social dynamics of stories can also be seen in his later popular work, *Why?* (Tilly, 2006b), which describes the relational underpinnings of different kinds of reason giving.

Several other prominent New York area scholars engaged in this local dialogue on culture, relations, and contentious politics, often participating in several of the workshops described above. Karen Barkey (at Columbia) and Eiko Ikegami (at Yale) completed major historical works on the relational dimensions of the transformation of state bureaucratic control in the Ottoman Empire and Japan, respectively (Barkey, 1994; Barkey and van Rossem, 1997; Ikegami, 1995, 2000). Ikegami's second book (2005) builds directly on White's language work by examining the emergence of new forms of civility across aesthetic networks in Tokugawa Japan. Francesca Polletta finished several important books and articles while at Columbia focusing on communicative processes of deliberation and storytelling in political protest; her work has a strongly relational focus, albeit with a more interpretive grounding than either White or Tilly (Polletta, 2002, 2006). Polletta collaborated with Jeff Goodwin and James Jasper (at NYU) in a volume on the role of emotions in social movements (Goodwin et al., 2001); this theme was taken further by Goodwin and Jasper in a series of critical articles challenging the structural bias of social movement theory and arguing for a revived focus on culture, creativity, strategy, and emotions (Goodwin and Jasper, 1999, 2004; see also Jasper, 1997, 2006).

In addition, other Tilly students from the New School and Columbia during that period blend a focus on relations, culture, and interaction without using mathematical network analytic techniques. Javier Auyero (2001, 2003) examines interpretation, performance, and networks in his study of poor people's protest and politics in Latin America, drawing heavily on Tilly's notion of "relational mechanisms." John Krinsky (2007) studies the co-constitution of discourse, relations, and contentious events in struggles over welfare-to-work programs in New York City. Chad Goldberg (2007) examines the reconstruction of the discourse of citizenship through struggles over class, race, and welfare rights. And Victoria Johnson (2008) explores the relationship between organizations, culture, and social relations in her study of the historical transformations of the Paris Opera. In addition to their work with Tilly, these scholars are all strongly influenced by Bourdieu's work on the relational sources of cultural distinction; Goldberg and Johnson co-authored articles with Emirbayer exploring the links between Bourdieu and other branches of research (Emirbayer and Goldberg, 2005; Emirbayer and Johnson, 2008). Goldberg, Johnson, and Krinsky were also participants in the New School Theory and Culture group, along with Mische, Gibson, and Sheller.

Additional scholars arriving at Columbia in the late 1990s helped to cement its position as a hub

for relational sociology. David Stark came to Columbia from Cornell in 1997, bringing a focus on the complex network combinatorics involved in political and economic transitions. Duncan Watts was a postdoctoral fellow in 1997–98 and joined the faculty in 2000, contributing additional mathematical expertise in relation to his work on small-world networks (Watts, 1999). And in 1999 Peter Bearman arrived at Columbia from Chapel Hill, adding an important voice to the local contingent working at the border of networks and culture (see below). Many other Columbia PhDs since 2000 have studied with some combination of White, Tilly, and these relationally oriented scholars.[5] Most of these students have combined attention to networks and discourse in some way, building on the work from the previous decade described above.

In short, the New York area in the 1990s and 2000s was a rich hub of conversation that contributed to a reformulation of the link between networks, culture, and social interaction. I would suggest that we can explain these conceptual innovations by drawing on the core concepts developed in these discussions, described in more detail below. The "publics" convened across these New York universities were characterized by a complex web of overlapping ties (colleagueship, co-authorship, dissertation advising, workshop participation, and study group membership) as well as frequent cross-fertilization by visiting scholars from allied perspectives. The equalizing dynamic that was famously characteristic of White and Tilly is analogous to the "open regimes" – combined with geographic proximity – which institutional scholars have seen as critical to innovation (e.g., Owen-Smith and Powell, 2004). While Columbia and the New School served as key incubators, researchers from area universities (NYU, Princeton, Yale, SUNY, CUNY, Rutgers, Penn, and others) joined in these partially overlapping conversations. What emerged was a perspective that straddled positivist and interpretivist positions, stressing the mutual constitution of networks and discourse, the communicative nature of social ties, and the interplay between multiple relations in social action. As I argue below, these researchers also show how a focus on interaction, performance, and social dynamics helps to mediate (if not resolve) the tension between structure and agency.

FOUR APPROACHES TO THE LINK BETWEEN NETWORKS AND CULTURE

While I have been focusing so far on the emergence in the 1990s of a cluster of scholars in the New York area, this group is embedded in a much broader intellectual network of researchers who have been contributing to discussions about networks, culture, and agency for the past three decades. Although this work is international in scope and has developed in dialogue with the highly relational work of European scholars such as Bourdieu, Luhmann, and Elias (see Fuchs, 2001; Fuhse, 2009; Fuhse and Mützel, 2010), the link between networks and culture has been most clearly elaborated in a set of closely linked American universities. Harvard has repeatedly served as a hub for the development of network analysis since the 1970s; many early scholars linking networks and culture (such as Bearman, Carley, Emirbayer, Goodwin, Gould, Ikegami, Morrill, and Somers) have come out of the second wave of White-inspired conversation in the 1980s. Chicago has been a second hub, housing important debates about contingency, creativity, and multiple networks, while Princeton has been central in linking social ties to culture, institutions, inequality, and economic relations. Toronto, Stony Brook, Arizona, UC Irvine, Michigan, Berkeley, UNC-Chapel Hill, Stanford, and Rutgers have also been important centers for relational sociology at different periods in time.

I will incorporate this expanded group in discussing four distinct ways in which the link between networks and culture has been conceptualized over this period. Because much work in this area is detailed in other chapters in this volume (especially those by Valente and DiMaggio), my analysis will be schematic rather than exhaustive, sketching some of the main analytic tendencies linking culture, networks, and agency. Many of my examples come from the field of social movements and contentious politics, since this is the work I know best; however, work in this area extends to other substantive subfields as well. I will demonstrate how each of these perspectives builds on the shortcomings of the others in constructing a more dynamic, processual account of the culture-network link.

Networks as Conduits for Culture

One of the earliest and most straightforward ways of linking culture with networks has been to see networks as carriers or "pipelines" of social influence, in the form of attitudes, ideas, and innovations. As other chapters discuss in more depth (e.g., Valente in this volume), a variety of mechanisms for the transmission and diffusion of cultural ideas have been proposed by network researchers since the 1950s. These range from simple contact, information flow, and opinion leadership (Katz and Lazarsfeld, 1955) to normative pressure in

relationships (Coleman et al., 1966) to competitive mimicry based on structural equivalence (Burt, 1987). The idea of networks as conduits for cultural transmission has been extended to the diffusion of social movement participation and repertoires of contention, often drawing upon rational choice theories of the critical mass (Granovetter, 1978; Marwell et al., 1988; Oliver and Myers, 2003; Kim and Bearman, 1997). The concept of "tipping points," taken from critical mass theory, has been popularized by Malcolm Gladwell (2000) and has been heavily influential in studies of marketing and consumption, although some tenets of this theory have been recently challenged by Duncan Watts and colleagues using models of influence in small-world networks (Watts and Dodds, 2007; Watts, 1999; see also Gibson, 2005b).

What characterizes these approaches is the assumption that cultural elements (information, ideas, attitudes, practices) are something external to the networks. Network relations serve as conduits of transmission or influence from one node to the next, but the nodes and ties have an existence that is independent of the cultural object, attitude, or practice that travels across them. Social ties contribute to the adoption and diffusion of cultural elements but are not themselves composed by cultural practices. While this approach has provided valuable insights into the dynamics of cultural flows, it is grounded in a limited and substantialist account of the relationship between networks and culture. Network nodes and ties are seen as pre-given and unproblematic, as are the cultural goods that move between nodes; as a result both networks and cultural processes take on a reified quality that eclipses their mutual constitution.

Networks as Shaping Culture (or Vice Versa)

A second major theoretical perspective focuses on the causal relationship between networks and culture, that is, how networks shape culture, or vice versa. While this perspective shares some characteristics with the "cultural conduit" approach – particularly the role of social influence – it places a stronger emphasis on the culturally generative dimension of network structures. There are three main variants of this approach: a focus on network clusters as *incubators* of culture; on network positions as generating categorical identities (or *cat-nets*); and on network *bridges* as a source of cultural resources and creativity. Finally, there has recently been a move in the other direction, showing how cultural factors (such as tastes and moral frameworks) create relational affinities that shape network structure.

The first of these variations, which I'll call the *incubator* approach, focuses on the intense commitments and solidarities generated by location within particular network clusters or enclaves. Alberto Melucci (1989), for example, describes how social movement identities develop in submerged countercultural networks (see also Taylor and Whittier, 1992). Donatella della Porta (1988) notes that tight-knit, strong-tie networks may be especially important for supporting engagement in high-risk activism. Overlapping involvements can intensify the incubator effect (Fernandez and McAdam, 1988; Gould, 1991, 1995; Meyer and Whittier, 1994; Diani, 1995, 2003; Osa, 2001, 2003; Mische, 2003, 2007; Baldassari and Diani, 2007) since densely overlapping relations bring identities, loyalties, and solidarities generated in one network domain (home, neighborhood, religion, school) to bear on another (e.g., social movement mobilization). Friedman and McAdam (1992) argue that strong preexisting ties in social movement networks provide "identity incentives" for social movement participation; McAdam and Paulsen (1993) look at the flip side of this, exploring how salient countervailing identities developed in competing strong-tie networks can impede mobilization.

However, enclaves of strong or overlapping ties are not the only source of identities and discourse; other researchers take what I call the *catnet* approach, building upon the early idea proposed by Harrison White (2008 [1965]) and developed by Tilly (1978) that identities are born from emerging awareness of structural equivalence in network position. For example, Roger Gould (1995) shows how "participatory identities" in nineteenth-century Paris insurrections shifted from class to urban community, based on the changing network positions of participants in relation to work, neighborhood, and the state. Likewise, Peter Bearman (1993) uses blockmodeling techniques to show how the shifting rhetorical orientations of pre–civil war English elites were rooted in changing network positions. In both cases, position in relation to other blocks of actors is an important generator of shared identities and discourse, rather than simply solidarities and pressures within an enclave.

A third approach stresses network intersections, or *bridges*, as creators of cultural resources, contributing to status, mobility, coalition building, and cultural innovation. This can be seen as the opposite of the enclave approach, because it focuses on weak ties, network diversity, and structural holes rather than on dense network clusters (Granovetter, 1973; Burt, 1992). For example, Paul DiMaggio (1987) argues that wide-ranging networks contribute both to diversity in taste and genre differentiation. Bonnie Erickson (1996) builds on this insight by demonstrating that higher-status actors tend to have more diverse cultural repertoires, due to a greater variety in network ties. Recent work on social movements has shown that interorganizational bridging and network desegmentation can contribute to the multivalent symbolism and brokerage activity useful for coalitions (Ansell, 1997; Mische, 1996; Mische and Pattison, 2000; Diani, 2003; Hillmann, 2008). What we consider "good ideas" are often borrowed from other networks, thus making network bridging (or interstitial locations in institutional fields) the key to innovation (Burt, 2004, 2005; Clemens and Cook, 1999; Uzzi and Spiro, 2005; Mische, 2007; Morrill, forthcoming). And Internet communication has made network diversity and weak ties the keys to the emergence of a new "networked individualism" (Wellman et al., 2003; Boase and Wellman, 2006). In these cases, theorists focus on the generation of culture through relational intersections, rather than through intracluster solidarities or categorical positioning.

Finally, recent work turns the causal arrow in the other direction by arguing that cultural tastes, values, and moral frameworks can shape network structure. Building on deeply relational work by Bourdieu (1984) and DiMaggio (1987), Omar Lizardo (2006) takes a "constructionist" approach to the relationship between culture and networks. He argues that "highbrow" cultural tastes are more easily "converted" into exclusionary and solidaristic strong-tie networks than tastes for popular culture, which facilitate weak ties that bridge locations in social space. Vaisey and Lizardo (2009) extend these insights to the realm of moral values, arguing that deep-seated (and largely unconscious) moral worldviews provide the basis for the emotional "click" that leads to the selection of friendship relations, as well as the effort (or lack of effort) that contributes to the cultivation or decay of those ties over time. In both cases, cultural tastes or values shape network structure, rather than the other way around.

What links these approaches is a nuanced examination of the mutual influence between network structures (enclaves, positions, bridges) and cultural elements (identities, tastes, moral values). Networks and culture are seen as autonomous variables that impact each other but that are ontologically distinguishable components of social life. This assumption of causal autonomy simplifies analysis and allows for the use of network measures in models containing cultural indicators. However, it does not go as far as other recent work in seeing networks themselves as composed of cultural processes, as I discuss below.

Networks of Cultural Forms

A third major analytical perspective conceives of culture itself as organized into networks of cultural forms, including concepts, categories, practices, and narrative events. Margaret Somers, for example, describes a "conceptual network" as "a structured relational matrix of theoretical principles and conceptual assumptions." She argues that these networks deeply constrain historical processes of interpretation and concept formation: "concepts cannot be defined on their own as single ontological entities; rather, the meaning of one concept can be deciphered only in terms of its 'place' in relation to the other concepts in its web" (1995: 135–36). Working from this premise, a wide array of scholars has applied formal relational techniques to the study of cultural networks. Some approaches examine the structure of direct connections among cultural elements, while others analyze the "dual" or interpenetrating relations of cultural forms with other kinds of elements (e.g., people, groups, events). Among the varied approaches to this analysis, I'll focus here on two: techniques for cognitive and discursive mapping and analysis of narrative or sequential relations.

Kathleen Carley has been a pioneer in the area of cognitive mapping, beginning with her early work in extracting mental models from cultural texts (Carley and Palmquist, 1992; Carley, 1993, 1994; Carley and Kaufer, 1993). Carley goes beyond conventional content analysis by examining relations between concepts, writing that "the meaning of a concept for an individual is embedded in its relationship to other concepts in the individual's mental model" (Carley and Palmquist, 1992: 602). These mental models, she argues, serve as samples of the representation of the individual's cognitive structure, and they can be analyzed using network analytic measures such as density, consensus, and conductivity (Carley, 1993; Hill and Carley, 1999). More recently, she has examined complex intersections between different kinds and levels of relations, focusing on communication and learning in an "ecology of networks" (e.g., Carley, 1999).

John Mohr has been another pioneer in modeling cultural forms, using blockmodeling and Galois lattices to examine relations between discourse and practice in changing institutional fields. Using a cultural adaptation of the Simmelian notion of "duality" elaborated by Breiger (1974, 2000), Mohr studies the dual association between historical representations of identity categories and poverty relief services (Mohr, 1994; Mohr and Duquenne, 1997), as well as the changing relational logic of affirmative action categories and practices (Mohr and Lee, 2000; Breiger and Mohr, 2004; Mohr et al., 2004). Recently, he has carried his analysis deeper into cultural and institutional theory by applying blockmodeling techniques to Foucault's notion of institutional power (Mohr and Neely, 2009) and co-authoring with Harrison White on the modeling of institutional change (Mohr and White, 2008).

A number of other researchers have applied the notion of duality in mapping cultural elements. Breiger (2000) uses correspondence analysis and Galois lattices to show deep mathematical similarities between the theories of Bourdieu and Coleman. Martin (2000) examines the dual association between the symbolic representation of animals and job occupations in a Richard Scarry children's book, using an entropy-based dispersion measure to reconstruct "the logic of the dispersion of species across the occupational map" (Martin, 2000: 206; see also Martin, 2002). Ann Mische and Philippa Pattison (2000) propose a tripartite version of lattice analysis to examine intersections among political organizations, their projects, and coalition-building events during the Brazilian impeachment movement. King-to Yeung (2005) uses Galois lattices to map relations between meanings attributed to persons and to relationships, showing how a group's "meaning structure" is associated with variation in leadership structure and group stability. John Sonnett (2004) uses correspondence analysis to show the association between genre configurations and boundary drawing in musical tastes. And Craig Rawlings and Michael Bourgeois (2004) demonstrate how the dual association between organizations and credentialing categories differentiate an institutional field into distinct niche positions.

A more temporal approach to cultural mapping uses formal relational methods to analyze the narrative or sequential structure of discourse and interaction. For example, Roberto Franzosi (1997, 2004) has developed a formal methodology for analyzing "semantic grammars," focusing on relations between subjects, actions, and objects. As he argues, such a methodology is intrinsically relational, first for "expressing mathematically the complex relations between words" (1997: 293), but also more substantively in mapping relations among sets of actors, linked by different kinds of historical actions. Charles Tilly (1997, 2008b) combines semantic grammars with network analytic tools, using blockmodeling techniques to compose partitions on sets of actors linked by different kinds of actions (e.g., claim, attack, control, cheer), thus mapping the changing relationships involved in the parliamentarization process in Great Britain (see also Tilly and Wood, 2003; Wada, 2004).

Other mapping strategies focus on the sequential character of narrative and interaction. For example, Peter Bearman and Kate Stovel (2000) treat autobiographical stories as networks of elements linked by connective narrative arcs, and apply network analytic techniques (such as path distance, reach, and centrality) to compare their narrative structures. Bearman et al. (1999) extend this technique to historical "casing," showing how dense clusters of narrative elements (composed of multiple overlapping autobiographical stories) create robust historical cases that are resistant to future reinterpretation. Andrew Abbott's "optimal matching" techniques for comparing sequences of events provide insight into the narrative structure of "cultural models" underlying institutional trajectories (Abbott and Hrycak, 1990; Abbott, 1995; see also Stovel et al., 1996; Blair-Loy, 1999). Several scholars have combined sequences methods with network analysis to show how both networks and careers shift together over time (Giuffre, 1999; Stark and Vedres, 2006).

These techniques are one expression of a broader theoretical perspective linking temporal and relational structures with historical contingency and theories of social change. Such techniques allow us to conceive of historical process, as Abbott describes it, as occurring in "a world of socially structured and generated trajectories linked by occasional turning points: a network in time" (Abbott, 2001b: 253). This perspective focuses on the multiplicity and intersection of social and cultural structures, as well as the resourceful agency of individuals and collectivities in sustaining and transforming those (Sewell, 1992; Emirbayer and Mische, 1998). Network techniques help to show the robust and interlocking nature of cultural structures, as well as the social locations and historical periods in which these can be challenged and reformulated.

Networks as Culture via Interaction

A final major approach to the network-culture link moves beyond the conception of cultural forms as autonomous from networks (and thus capable of being "transmitted" or "incubated" or "transformed" by means of network ties), focusing rather on networks themselves as constituted by cultural processes of communicative interaction. While early work in the symbolic interactionist tradition (Fine and Kleinman, 1983) examined the link between networks, meaning, and group interaction, this connection has recently been revitalized by younger researchers, often in response to the limitations of the methodologies described above. For example, the study of network effects on identities and coalitions begs the question of how actors actively construct relations of solidarity or alliance through the communicative activation (or deactivation) of network ties.

Here I examine how four younger scholars have developed this perspective in recent work. The commonalities in this work are no accident; two of these researchers came out of the New York School described above, and the other two came out of the closely aligned Chicago milieu, both of which have genealogical links to the Harvard hub of relational sociology in the 1970s and 1980s. A recent generation of incubatory workshops (organized by McLean and Mische at Rutgers and Gibson at Penn) has helped to nourish an innovative perspective focusing on the dynamic construction and deconstruction of network relations through temporally unfolding processes of talk and interaction. Strongly influenced by the work of Erving Goffman, this work involves deepening attention to communication, setting, performance, and interaction, showing how these are simultaneously constitutive of and permeated by network relations.

One of the most detailed network appropriations of Goffman can be seen in Paul McLean's (1998, 2007) study of the rhetorical construction of patronage ties and self-presentations in Renaissance Florence. McLean argues that both selves and relations are discursively constructed by patronage seekers when they appeal to notions such as "friendship," "honor," "respect," and "deference." By "keying" (to use Goffman's term) particular dimensions of relationships, they signal the "type of tie" that people strategically hope to activate as they build networks capable of providing them with various kinds of material and social rewards. Note here that in this perspective, networks themselves are the dynamic and changing results of discursive "framing processes," although at the same time position in these networks shapes the kinds of discursive moves one is able and likely to make.

Likewise, Mische (2003, 2007) studies the discursive and performative dynamics of network construction in a multiorganizational field that is itself undergoing change. In her ethnographic and historical study of Brazilian youth activist networks, she maps the trajectories of overlapping institutional affiliations among young activists in student, religious, partisan, professional, NGO, and business groups during a period of democratic reconstruction. She builds on Goffman's notion of "publics" by showing how activists highlight, suppress, segment, and combine dimensions of their multiple identities as they create new settings for civic and political intervention. Extending the concept of "group style" developed by Eliasoph and Lichterman (2003), she analyzes how actors switch between different modes of political communication as they grapple with the relational tensions posed by particular institutional intersections.

A somewhat different appropriation of Goffman can be seen in David Gibson's work on the sequential dynamics of conversation and the ways that these are permeated by different kinds of relationships. Gibson (2003, 2005a) offers a formalization of Goffman's "participation framework," focusing on the moving window of the changing relations between speaker, target, and unaddressed recipients within small-group interaction settings. He shows how conversational dynamics (i.e., who takes the floor, when, and after whom) are affected both by formal institutional hierarchies and by network ties such as friendship and co-work. In this way, he demonstrates how fleeting ties forged through co-involvement in interaction sequences enact preexisting ties of a more durable kind. Like McLean and Mische, he has focused on the strategic and opportunistic dimension of conversation, as speakers pursue goals and build relations by means of particular discursive moves (Gibson, 2000, 2005c).

Finally, McFarland (2001, 2004) analyzes the relation between networks, discourse, and performative interaction in his study of classroom resistance in high school settings. Drawing on the work of Goffman and Victor Turner, he describes how students switch between "social frames" and "person frames" in disruptive dramas that challenge institutional relations in the classroom (McFarland, 2004). In a recent series of articles, he has used network visualization techniques (Moody et al., 2005) to show how different "discursive moves" contribute to the stabilization and destabilization of classroom relations, arguing that it is "through talk that interactional networks shift, stabilize and are potentially undermined" (McFarland and Diehl, 2009: 4).

While the work of these four scholars provide especially vivid examples of the dynamic construction of ties via conversation, others researchers have explored similar patterns. For example, Bearman and Paolo (2004) demonstrate that people segment topic domains in relation to different conversational partners. Smilde (2005, 2007) describes how network-based conversations influence the construction of conversion narratives. Wagner-Pacifici (2000, 2005) examines the performative and discursive composition of moments of relational disruption and transformation, such as standoffs and surrenders. Recent collaborations with Harrison White address the generation of meaning, strategy, and power through switching across "netdoms" (White et al., 2007; Fontevila and White, 2010), extending the theoretical agenda developed during the 1990s in the New York School.[6]

The shared focus in this work on the conversational and performative enactment of ties allows these scholars to elide traditional dichotomies between structure and agency. The study of relational settings, patterns and constraints can be linked to a focus on strategic (and sometimes transformative) maneuvering by motivated, culturally embedded actors. Relations in this conception have durability, in that they have histories, meanings, obligations, and projected futures; yet this durability requires communicative work and is subject to negotiation, contestation, and opportunistic challenge. Both opportunities and constraints result from the fact that multiple relations can potentially enter into play, charging relational settings with tension, drama, and potential for change.

FURTHER LINKS AND DIRECTIONS

The sketch that I have given here of recent developments in relational sociology is certainly not exhaustive or bounded; rather it represents my own situated perspective on a sprawling network of overlapping conversations across several sociological subdisciplines. While network imagery – if not network analytic techniques – is central in most of the work that I have described, it has close kinship with other kinds of relational metaphors that have gained currency among allied scholars, including those of fields, ecologies, and circuits. In closing, I would like to mention several distinct but intersecting streams of research that are also deeply relational and have taken some interesting turns in recent years.

John Levi Martin (2003, 2009), for example, traces the genealogy of the "field" metaphor in social analysis from Lewin and Bourdieu through new institutionalism (Powell and DiMaggio, 1991; see also Fligstein, 2001; Owen-Smith and Powell, 2008; Mohr, 2010). The field perspective, Martin argues, offers an alternative to conventional social science models of causality in its focus on the subjective alignments and propulsive forces involved in social positioning. Work drawing on field imagery includes studies of artistic elites (DiMaggio, 1991, 1992); social movement organizations and repertoires (Ennis, 1987; Klandermans, 1992; Clemens, 1997; Evans, 1997; Armstrong, 2002; Davis et al., 2005; Schneiberg and Lounsbury, 2008); organizational conflict (Morrill, 1995; Morrill et al., 2003); and culinary professionals (Leschziner, 2009). Moreover, the concept of social fields has also been central to relationally oriented historical research that focuses on culture as discourse and positioning (e.g., Spillman, 1995; Steinberg, 1999; Gorski, 2003; Steinmetz, 2008).

Others have studied links across multiple fields, networks, or institutional "ecologies," often focusing on the ways that intersecting relational logics reinforce, constrain, or transform each other.

This idea is central to the pathbreaking work of John Padgett and his collaborators on the coupling and decoupling of relational logics in Renaissance Florence (Padgett and Ansell, 1993; Padgett, 2001; Padgett and McLean, 2006). Many historical sociologists have similarly sought to combine a focus on relational contingency and social structure by analyzing interactions within "relational settings" (Somers, 1993) or between multiple social orders (see reviews of this extensive literature by Clemens, 2007; Adams et al., 2005). Such multiplicity is also addressed in Abbott's (2005) concept of "linked ecologies," in which different institutional arenas are connected through "hinge" strategies that work in both ecologies at once. The ecological metaphor itself is intrinsically relational, with a long history going back to the Chicago School (Abbott, 1999) and recently revived in work on organizational niche formation and population dynamics (Hannon and Freeman, 1989; McPherson et al., 1991).

In addition, recent work in economic sociology stresses the relational dimension of economic exchange, while paying attention to meaning and process. Viviana Zelizer (2004, 2005a, 2005b) describes how differentiated ties ramify into "circuits of commerce" involving "different understandings, practices, information, obligations, rights, symbols, and media of exchange." She argues that these differ from networks, traditionally conceived, in that "they consist of dynamic, meaningful, incessantly negotiated interactions among the sites" (2005a: 293). Other scholars have focused on the moral weighting of exchange relations and their embeddedness in organizations and networks (Fourcade and Healy, 2007; Healy, 2006), as well as on the importance of networks and meanings in economic restructuring (Bandelj, 2008). Harrison White's early work on markets (revamped in his 2004 book) also pays attention to processes of communication, signaling, and meaning production among networks of producers, focusing on local processes of market differentiation and niche production (see also Bothner, 2003; Bothner et al., 2004; Hsu and Podolny, 2005).

Finally, one of the most promising future directions of this work is the recent revival of pragmatist thinking, as informed by this emerging relational perspective (Joas, 1997; Whitford, 2002; Lichterman, 2005; Emirbayer and Goldberg, 2005; Gross, 2009, 2010; Mische, 2007, 2009; Herrigal, 2010). Early statements by Emirbayer (1997) and Somers (1998) make explicit the connection between network thinking and the pragmatist theories of Dewey, Mead, James, Peirce, and others. Likewise, Abbott (1999) reminds us that the roots of American sociology in the Chicago School were pragmatist as well as relational in orientation. In this perspective, the (necessary) tension

between ontology and epistemology (as with that between realism and constructivism, or between structure and agency) becomes productive rather than troubling; something is "real" because it produces actions, which are necessarily grounded in the interpretation of relations. One exciting vein to be tapped is that of pragmatist semiotics, as proposed by Peirce, which focuses on the triadic relation between sign, object, and "interpretant." The interpretant is the product of the action involved in the "addressing" relation, which brings forth new interpretations – and thus, by extension, new relations among actors mediated by interpretations of objects in the world (Emirbayer, 1997). This move helps us transcend the realist-constructivist divide we have inherited from Saussurean semiotics, a move implicit (but not fully elaborated) in Tilly's term "relational realism."[7]

Because most social science research – including much work on culture and networks – is still rooted in Saussurean (and Kantian) antinomies, this poses a number of challenges for the future. I would argue that we need to craft an approach to theory and research that views relations, interpretations, and actions as mutually generative, yet also subject to what Peirce calls the "resistance" of objects in the world. As I have demonstrated in my own work, the formal representations we gain from network analytic techniques provide useful insight into the complex patterning of relationships – and thus the structural opportunities, constraints, and dilemmas actors confront. But these representations need to be complemented by historical, ethnographic, and interview research that examines the communicative interplay, strategic maneuvering, and reflective problem solving carried out by actors in response to these relational tensions and dilemmas.

As Jan Fuhse (2009) argues, this requires attention both to the observable communicative processes that compose networks – which he, like Emirbayer, calls "transactions" – and to the "meaning structure" of networks, grounded in intersubjective expectations as well as systems of categories and the ongoing interpretive work of situated individuals. This approach also builds on recent theories of "situated actions" in multilayered social and institutional contexts (Vaughan, 2002; see also Broadbent, 2003). An important future challenge lies in understanding how the communicative construction of relations is channeled and constrained by institutions, which influence the durability, robustness, and constraining power of social ties (Swidler, 2001; Owen-Smith and Powell, 2008; see also Stinchcombe, 1997).[8] In this light, the practical and communicative construction of such durability – along with the multiple temporalities in which relations are embedded – become in themselves the focus of sociological attention.

The work discussed in this chapter brings us to this threshold and suggests a compelling framework for future research. More than just a set of analytical techniques, the new relational sociology becomes a way of challenging the core theoretical and methodological divides in the discipline. The effervescent "New York moment" described above was one formative conversational hub in a recent movement that returns sociology to its relational and pragmatist roots, while suggesting a new agenda for studying the dynamic interplay of networks and culture.

ACKNOWLEDGEMENTS

I would like to thank Jeff Boase, Phaedra Daipha, Mustafa Emirbayer, Jan Fuhse, David Gibson, Neha Gondal, John R. Hall, Jim Jasper, Corrine Kirchner, John Krinsky, Eloise Linger, Paul McLean, Dan Nexon, Ignacia Perugorría, John Scott, Mimi Sheller, Lyn Spillman, Sid Tarrow, Dianne Vaughan, Viviana Zelizer, and the participants in the Rutgers Workshop on Networks, Culture and Institutions and the Columbia Workshop on Meaning, Language and Sociocultural Processes for their criticisms and suggestions on early drafts of this chapter. Also, thanks to the participants in a rollicking debate on the Contentious Politics listserv that helped me think through the ending to this chapter.

NOTES

1 Additional relational perspectives in adjacent fields include a budding movement in political science (e.g., Nexon and Wright, 2007; Jackson, 2002) as well as important work in science and technology studies (e.g., Knorr Cetina, 2003). Actor network theory as developed by Latour, Callon, Law, and others shares a deep focus on relations as productive of action, including nonhuman objects and sites in its network imagery (see Law and Hassard, 1999; Muetzel, 2009). Other relevant European work includes the systemic and configurational perspectives of Luhmann and Elias (see Fuhse, 2009; Fuchs, 2001), as well as "the new mobilities" literature (Sheller and Urry, 2006), which combines elements from anthropology and cultural studies and resists some of the depoliticizing elements in ANT.

2 In 1999 the name of the Lazarsfeld Center was changed to the Institute for Social and Economic Research and Policy (ISERP), under the direction of Peter Bearman. Other network analysts at Columbia in the late 1980s and early 1990s included Ron Burt (who helped to bring White to Columbia), Eric Leifer,

and Martina Morris, although all three of them had left by the mid-1990s.

3 New York area students centrally involved in discussions about networks and culture at the Lazarsfeld Center during the mid-1990s included David Gibson, Melissa Fischer, Salvatore Pitruzzello and Matthew Bothner (from Columbia); Ann Mische and Mimi Sheller (from the New School); and Shepley Orr, a visiting scholar from Chicago. Earlier students in this ambit who also worked with Burt, Leifer, and Morris included Shin-Kap Han, Holly Raider, Valli Rajah, Andres Ruj, and Hadya Iglic. While my own degree was at the New School (supervised by Tilly), I was a visiting scholar at the Lazarsfeld Center from 1994 to 1998 and I was a postdoc from 1998 to 1999.

4 According to conference records, outside participants in these mid-1990s miniconferences at Columbia included Andrew Abbott, Ron Breiger, Jerome Bruner, Kathleen Carley, Aaron Cicourel, Elisabeth Clemens, Randall Collins, Michael Delli-Carpini, Paul DiMaggio, Mustafa Emirbayer, Robert Faulkner, Michael Hechter, Eiko Ikegami, Walter Mischel, William Ocasio, John Padgett, Philippa Pattison, Richard Schweder, Ann Swidler, Charles Tilly, Chris Winship, Viviana Zelizer, and others.

5 Other Columbia PhDs since 2000 include Delia Baldassari, Matthew Bothner, Andrew Buck, Emily Erickson, Jorge Fontdevila, Fumiko Fukase-Indergaard, Frederic Godart, Hennig Hillman, Jo Kim, Sun-Chul Kim, Jennifer Lena, Denise Milstein, Sophie Mützel, Paolo Parigi, Joyce Robbins, Tammy Smith, Takeshi Wada, Cecilia Walsh-Russo, Leslie Wood, Balazs Vedres, and others. Most of these scholars have highly relational approaches building on the perspective described here; I regret that space constraints keep me from going into detail on them all.

6 See the recent special issue of *Poetics* (2010), edited by Corinne Kirschner and John Mohr, with articles by Frederic Godart and Harrison White, Jorge Fontdevila, John Mohr, Ronald Breiger, and Jennifer Schultz. See also the recent review essay on culture and networks by Mark Pachucki and Ronald Breiger (2010).

7 A nice discussion of the links between Tilly's work and American pragmatist theory can be found in Gross (2010).

8 Arthur Stinchombe notes that both the focus on action and the constraining power of institutions are important for Tilly's view of networks: "Tilly regards neither the links in networks nor the needs of institutions as naturally existing causes, but instead as things brought into existence by human action on the links and nodes that are important for institutions" (1997: 387). While Stinchombe himself has not theorized the link between networks and culture, he is certainly a fellow traveler in this relational perspective; his work on causality, mechanisms, and institutional flows has been influential for both White and Tilly (see Stinchombe, 1991, 2005).

REFERENCES

Abbott, A. (1995) 'Sequence analysis: New methods for old ideas', *Annual Review of Sociology* 21: 93–113.

Abbott, A. (1999) *Department and Discipline: Chicago Sociology at 100*. Chicago: University of Chicago Press.

Abbott, A. (2001a) *Chaos of Disciplines*. Chicago: University of Chicago Press.

Abbott, A. (2001b) *Time Matters: On Theory and Method*. Chicago: University of Chicago Press.

Abbott, A. (2005) 'Linked Ecologies', *Sociological Theory* 23: 245–274, 2005.

Abbott, A. and Alexandra H. (1990) 'Measuring resemblance insequence data: An optimal matching analysis of musicians' careers', *American Journal of Sociology* 96: 144–85.

Adams, J., Clemens, E.S. and Orloff, A.S. (eds.) (2005) *Remaking Modernity: Politics and Processes in Historical Sociology*. Durham, NC: Duke University Press.

Ansell, C.K. (1997) 'Symbolic networks: The realignment of the French working class, 1887–1894', *American Journal of Sociology* 103: 359–90.

Armstrong, E.A. (2002) *Forging Gay Identities: Organizing Sexuality in San Francisco, 1950–1994*. Chicago: University of Chicago Press.

Auyero, J. (2001) *Poor People's Politics: Peronist Networks and the Legacy of Evita*. Durham, NC: Duke University Press.

Auyero, J. (2003) *Contentious Lives: Two Argentine Women, Two Protests, and the Quest for Recognition*. Durham, NC: Duke University Press.

Bakhtin, M.M. (1981) *The Dialogic Imagination: Four Essays*. Ed. Michael Holquist. Trans. Caryl Emerson and Michael Holquist. Austin: University of Texas Press.

Bakhtin, M.M. (1986) *Speech Genres and Other Late Essays*. Trans. by Vern W. McGee. Austin: University of Texas Press.

Baldassari, D. and Mario D. (2007) 'The integrative power of civic networks', *American Journal of Sociology* 113: 735–80.

Bandelj, N. (2008) *From Communists to Foreign Capitalists: The Social Foundations of Foreign Direct Investment in Postsocialist Europe*. Princeton: Princeton University Press.

Barkey, K. (1994) *Bandits and Bureaucrats: The Ottoman Route to State Centralization*. Ithaca, NY: Cornell University Press.

Barkey, K. and Ronan van R. (1997) 'Networks of contention: Villages and regional structure in the seventeenth century Ottoman Empire', *American Journal of Sociology* 102: 5.

Bearman, P. (1993) *Relations into Rhetorics: Local Elite Social Structure in Norfolk, England: 1540–1640*. American Sociological Association, Rose Monograph Series. New Brunswick, NJ: Rutgers University Press.

Bearman, P., Robert F. and James M. (1999) 'Blocking the future: New solutions for old problems in historical social science', *Social Science History* 23(4): 501–33.

Bearman, P.S. and Paolo P. (2004) 'Cloning headless frogs and other important matters: Conversation topics and network structure', *Social Forces* 83(2): 535–57.

Bearman, P.S. and Katherine S. (2000) 'Becoming a Nazi: Models for narrative networks', *Poetics* 27: 69–90.

Blair-Loy, M. (1999) 'Career patterns of executive women in finance: An optimal matching analysis', *American Journal of Sociology* 104: 1346–97.

Boase, J. and Barry W. (2006) 'Personal relationships: On and off the Internet', pp. 709–23 in D. Perlman and A. L. Vangelisti (eds.), *The Cambridge Handbook of Personal Relationships*. Cambridge: Cambridge University Press.

Bothner, M. (2003) 'Competition and social influence: The diffusion of the sixth generation processor in the global computer industry', *American Journal of Sociology* 6: 1175–210.

Bothner, M., Toby S. and Harrison C.W. (2004) 'Status differentiation and the cohesion of social networks', *Journal of Mathematical Sociology* 28: 261–95.

Bourdieu, P. (1984) *Distinction: A Social Critique of the Judgment of Taste* (translated by Richard Nice). Cambridge, MA: Harvard University Press.

Breiger, R.L. (1974) 'The duality of persons and groups', *Social Forces* 53: 181–90.

Breiger, R.L. (2000) 'A tool kit for practice theory', *Poetics*. p. 27.

Breiger, R.L. and John W.M. (2004) 'Institutional logics from the aggregation of organizational networks: Operational procedures for the analysis of counted data', *Computational and Mathematical Organization Theory* 10: 17–43.

Broadbent, J. (2003) 'Movement in context: Thick networks and Japanese environmental networks', pp. 204–29 in *Social Movements and Networks: Relational Approaches to Collective Action*, ed. Mario Diani and Doug McAdam. Oxford: Oxford University Press.

Burt, R.S. (1987) 'Social contagion and innovation: Cohesion versus structural equivalence', *American Journal of Sociology* 92: 1287–335.

Burt, R.S. (1992) *Structural Holes: The Social Structure of Competition*. Cambridge, MA: Harvard University Press.

Burt, R.S. (2004) 'Structural holes and good ideas', *American Journal of Sociology* 110: 349–99.

Burt, R.S. (2005) *Brokerage and Closure: An Introduction to Social Capital*. Oxford: Oxford University Press.

Carley, K. (1993) 'Coding choices for textual analysis: A comparison of content analysis and map analysis', in *Sociological Methodology*, vol. 4, ed. Peter Marsden. Oxford: Blackwell.

Carley, K. (1994) 'Extracting culture through textual analysis', *Poetics* 22: 291–312.

Carley, K. (1999) 'On the evolution of social and organizational networks', in David Knoke and Steve Andrews (eds.), *Special issue of Research in the Sociology of Organizations on Networks In and Around Organizations* 16: 3–30, Stanford, CT: JAI Press.

Carley, K. and Kaufer, D. (1993) 'Semantic connectivity: An approach for analyzing symbols in semantic networks', *Communication Theory* 3: 183–213.

Carley, K. and Michael P. (1992) 'Extracting, representing and analyzing mental models', *Social Forces* 70: 601–36.

Clemens, E.S. (1997) *The People's Lobby: Organizational Innovation and the Rise of Interest Group Politics in the United States, 1890–1925*. Chicago: University of Chicago Press.

Clemens, E.S. (2007) 'Toward a historicized sociology: Theorizing events, processes, and emergence', *Annual Review of Sociology* 33: 527–49.

Clemens, E. and James C. (1999) 'Politics and institutionalism: Explaining durability and change', *Annual Review of Sociology* 25: 441–66.

Coleman, J.S., Katz, E. and Menzel, H. (1966) *Medical Innovation: A Diffusion Study.* Indianopolis: Bobbs-Merril.

Collins, R. (1998) *The Sociology of Philosophies: A Global Theory of Intellectual Ch.* (1985) *Tense.* Cambridge: Cambridge University Press.

Davis, G.F., McAdam, D., Scott, W.R. and Zald, M.N. (eds.) (2005) *Social Movements and Organization Theory.* Cambridge: Cambridge University Press.

della Porta, D. (1988) 'Recruitment processes in clandestine political organizations: Italian left-wing terrorism', in Bert Klandermans, Hans Kriesi, and Sidney Tarrow (eds.), *From Structure to Action.* Greenwich: JAI Press.

Diani, M. (1995) *Green Networks: A Structural Analysis of the Italian Environmental Movement.* Edinburgh: Edinburgh University Press.

Diani, M. (2003) 'Leaders or brokers? Positions and influence in social movement networks', pp. 105–22 in *Social Movements and Networks: Relational Approaches to Collective Action,* ed. Mario Diani and Doug McAdam. Oxford: Oxford University Press.

Diani, M. (2007) 'Review essay: The relational element in Charles Tilly's recent (and not so recent) work', *Social Networks* 29: 316–23.

DiMaggio, P. (1987) 'Classification in art', *American Sociological Review* 52: 440–55.

DiMaggio, P. (1991) 'Constructing an organizational field as a professional project: U.S. art museums, 1920–1940', pp. 267–92 in *The New Institutionalism in Organizational Analysis,* ed. Walter W. Powell and Paul J. DiMaggio. Chicago: University of Chicago Press.

DiMaggio, P. (1992) 'Nadel's paradox revisited: Relational and cultural aspects of organizational structure', pp. 118–42 in *Networks and Organizations,* ed. Nitin Nohria and Robert G. Eccles. Boston: Harvard Business School Press.

Eliasoph, N. and Lichterman, P. (2003) 'Culture in interaction', *American Journal of Sociology* 108: 735–94.

Emirbayer, M. (1997) 'Manifesto for a relational sociology', *American Journal of Sociology* 103: 281–317.

Emirbayer, M. and Goldberg, C. (2005) 'Pragmatism, Bourdieu, and collective emotions in contentious politics', *Theory and Society* 34: 469–518.

Emirbayer, M. and Goodwin, J. (1994) 'Network analysis, culture, and the problem of agency', *American Journal of Sociology* 99: 1411–54.

Emirbayer, M. and Johnson, V. (2008) 'Bourdieu and organizational analysis', *Theory and Society* 37: 1–44.

Emirbayer, M. and Mische, A. (1998) 'What is agency?' *American Journal of Sociology* 103: 962–1023.

Emirbayer, M. and Sheller, M. (1999) 'Publics in history', *Theory and Society* 28: 145–97.

Ennis, J.G. (1987) 'Fields of action: The structure of movements' tactical repertoires', *Sociological Forum* 2: 520–33.

Erickson, B.H. (1988) 'The relational basis of attitudes', pp. 99–121 in *Social Structures a Network Approach,* ed. Barry Wellman and S.D. Berkowitz. Cambridge: Cambridge University Press.

Erickson, B.H. (1996) 'Culture, class, and connections', *American Journal of Sociology* 102: 217–51.

Evans, J. (1997) 'Multi-organizational fields and social movement organization frame content: The religious pro-choice movement', *Sociological Inquiry* 67 (4): 451–69.

Fernandez, R.M. and McAdam, D. (1988) 'Social networks and social movements: Multiorganizational fields and recruitment to freedom summer', *Sociological Forum* 3: 257–382.

Fine, G.A. and Kleinman, S. (1983) 'Network and meaning: An interactionist approach to structure', *Symbolic Interaction* 6: 97–110.

Fligstein, N. (2001) 'Social skill and the theory of fields', *Sociological Theory* 19: 105–25.

Fontdevila, J. and White, H.C. (2010) 'Power from switching across netdoms through reflexive and indexical language', *REDES* vol. 18, #13.

Fourcade, M. and Healy, K. (2007) 'Moral views of market society', *Annual Review of Sociology* 33: 285–311.

Franzosi, R. (1997) 'Mobilization and counter-mobilization processes: From the red years (1919–20) to the black years (1921–22) in Italy. A new methodological approach to the study of narrative data', *Theory and Society* 26: 275–304.

Franzosi, R. (2004) *From Words to Numbers: Narrative, Data, and Social Science.* Cambridge: Cambridge University Press.

Friedman, D. and McAdam, D. (1992) 'Collective identities and activism: Networks, choices, and the life of a social movement', pp. 156–73 in *Frontiers of Social Movement Theory,* ed. Aldon D. Morris and Carol Mueller. New Haven, CT: Yale University Press.

Fuchs, S. (2001) *Against Essentialism.* Cambridge, MA: Harvard University Press.

Fuhse, J.A. (2009) 'The meaning structure of networks', *Sociological Theory* 27: 51–73.

Fuhse, J.A. and Sophie Mützel, S. (eds.) (2010) *Relationale Soziologie: Zur kulturellen Wende der Netzwerkforschung [Relational Sociology: The Cultural Turn in Network Research].* VS Verlag.

Gibson, D. (2000) 'Seizing the moment: The problem of conversational agency', *Sociological Theory* 18(3): 368–82.

Gibson, D. (2003) 'Participation shifts: Order and differentiation in group conversation', *Social Forces* 81 (4): 1135–81.

Gibson, D. (2005a) 'Taking turns and talking ties: Network structure and conversational sequences', *American Journal of Sociology* 110(6): 1561–97.

Gibson, D. (2005b) 'Concurrency and commitment: Network scheduling and its consequences for diffusion', *Journal of Mathematical Sociology* 29: 295–323.

Gibson, D. (2005c) 'Opportunistic interruptions: Interactional vulnerabilities deriving from linearization', *Social Psychology Quarterly* 68(4): 316–37.

Giuffre, K. (1999) 'Sandpiles of opportunity: Success in the art world', *Social Forces* 77: 815–32.

Gladwell, M. (2000) *The Tipping Point: How Little Things Can Make a Big Difference.* New York: Little, Brown.

Godart, F.C. and White, H.C. (forthcoming) 'Switchings under uncertainty: The coming and becoming of meanings', *Poetics.*

Goldberg, C.A. (2007) *Citizens and Paupers: Relief, Rights, and Race, from the Freedmen's Bureau to Workfare.* Chicago: University of Chicago Press.

Goodwin, C. and Duranti, A. (eds.) (1992) *Rethinking Context: Language as Interactive Phenomenon.* Cambridge: Cambridge University Press.

Goodwin, J. and Jasper, J.M. (1999) 'Caught in a winding, snarling vine: The structural bias of political process theory', *Sociological Forum* 14: 27–54.

Goodwin, J. and Jasper, J.M. (2004) *Rethinking Social Movements: Structure, Culture, and Emotion.* Lanham, MD: Rowman & Littlefield.

Goodwin, J., Jasper, J.M. and Polletta, F. (eds.) (2001) *Passionate Politics: Emotions and Social Movements.* Chicago: University of Chicago Press.

Gorski, P.S. (2003) *The Disciplinary Revolution: Calvinism and the Rise of the State in Early Modern Europe.* Chicago: University of Chicago Press.

Gould, R. (1991) 'Multiple networks and mobilization in the Paris commune, 1871', *American Sociological Review* 56: 716–29.

Gould, R. (1995) *Insurgent identities: Class, Community, and Insurrection in Paris from 1848 to the Commune.* Chicago: University of Chicago Press.

Granovetter, M.S. (1973) 'The strength of weak ties', *American Journal of Sociology* 78: 1360–80.

Granovetter, M.S. (1978) 'Threshold models of collective behavior', *American Journal of Sociology* 83: 1420–43.

Gross, N. (2009) 'A pragmatist theory of social mechanisms', *American Sociological Review* 74: 358–79.

Gross, N. (2010) 'Charles Tilly and American Pragmatism', Forthcoming, in *The American Sociologist* (special issue on Charles Tilly, edited by Andreas Koller).

Gumperz, J.J. (1982) *Discourse Strategies.* Cambridge: Cambridge University Press.

Halliday, M.A.K. (1976) *System and Function in Language: Selected Papers.* Ed. G. Kress. London: Oxford University Press.

Halliday, M.A.K. (1978) *Language as Social Semiotic: The Social Interpretation of Language and Meaning.* Baltimore: University Park Press, 1978; London: Edward Arnold, 1978.

Hanks, W.F. (1992) 'The indexical grounds of deictic reference', pp. 43–76 in Charles Goodwin and Alessandro Duranti (eds.), *Rethinking Context: Language as Interactive Phenomenon.* Cambridge: Cambridge University Press.

Hannon, M.T. and Freeman, J. (1989) *Organizational Ecology.* Cambridge, MA: Harvard University Press.

Healy, K. (2006) *Last Best Gifts: Altruism and the Market for Human Blood and Organs.* Chicago: University of Chicago Press.

Herrigal, G.B. (2010) *Manufacturing Possibilities: Creative Action and Industrial Recomposition in the US, Germany and Japan.* Oxford: Oxford University Press.

Hill, V., and Kathleen, C. (1999) 'An approach to identifying consensus in a subfield: The case of organizational culture', *Poetics* 27: 1–30.

Hillmann, H. (2008) 'Mediation in multiple networks: Elite mobilization before the English civil war', *American Sociological Review* 73: 426–54.

Hopper, P.J. and Traugott, E.C. (1993) *Grammaticalization.* Cambridge: Cambridge University Press.

Hsu, G. and Podolny, J.M. (2005) 'Critiquing the critics: An approach for the comparative evaluation of critical schemas', *Social Science Research* 34: 189–214.

Ikegami, E. (1995) *The Taming of the Samurai: Honorific Individualism and the Making of Modern Japan.* Cambridge, MA: Harvard University Press.

Ikegami, E. (2000) 'A sociological theory of publics: Identity and culture as emergent properties in networks', *Social Research* 67: 989–1029.

Ikegami, E. (2005) *Bonds of Civility: Aesthetic Publics and the Political Origins of Japanese Publics.* Cambridge: Cambridge University Press.

Jackson, P.T. (2002) 'Rethinking Weber: Towards a non-individualist sociology of world politics', *International Review of Sociology* 12: 439–68.

Jasper, J. (1997) *The Art of Moral Protest: Culture, Biography, and Creativity in Social Movements.* Chicago: University of Chicago Press.

Jasper, J. (2006) *Getting Your Way: Strategic Dilemmas in the Real World.* Chicago: University of Chicago Press.

Joas, H. (1997) *The Creativity of Action.* Chicago: University of Chicago Press.

Johnson, V. (2008) *Backstage at the Revolution: How the Royal Paris Opera Survived the End of the Old Regime.* Chicago: University of Chicago Press.

Katz, E. and Lazarsfeld, P.F. (1955) *Personal Influence.* Glencoe, IL: Free Press.

Kim, H. and Bearman, P.S. (1997) 'Who counts in collective action? The structure and dynamics of movement participation', *American Sociological Review* 62: 70–93.

Klandermans, B. (1992) 'The social construction of protest and multi-organizational fields', pp. 77–103 in *Frontiers of Social Movement Theory*, ed. Aldon D. Morris and Carol Mueller. New Haven, CT: Yale University Press.

Knorr Cetina, K. (2003) 'From pipes to scopes: The flow architecture of financial markets', *Distinktion* 7: 7–23.

Krinsky, J. (2007) *Free Labor: Workfare and the Contested Language of Neoliberalism.* Chicago: University of Chicago Press.

Law, J., and John H. (1999) *Actor Network Theory and After.* Oxford: Blackwell Publishers.

Leschziner, V. (2009) 'Cooking logics: Cognition and reflexivity in the culinary field', Forthcoming in James Farrer (ed.), *Globalization, Food and Social Identities in the Pacific Region.* Tokyo: Sophia University Institute of Comparative Culture.

Lichterman, P. (2005) *Elusive Togetherness: How Religious Americans Create Civic Ties.* Princeton: Princeton University Press.

Lizardo, O. (2006) 'How cultural tastes shape personal networks', *American Sociological Review* 71: 778–807.

Marwell, G., Oliver, P.E. and Prahl, R. (1988) 'Social networks and collective action: A theory of the critical mass. III', *American Journal of Sociology* 94: 502–34.

Martin, J.L. (2000) 'What do animals do all day? On the totemic logic of class bodies', *Poetics* 27: 195–231.

Martin, J.L. (2002) 'Power, authority, and the constraint of belief systems', *American Journal of Sociology* 107: 861–904.

Martin, J.L. (2003) 'What is field theory?' *American Journal of Sociology* 109: 1–49.

Martin, J.L. (2009) *Social Structures*. Princeton: Princeton University Press.

McAdam, D. and Paulsen, R. (1993) 'Specifying the relationship between social ties and activism', *American Journal of Sociology* 99: 640–67.

McAdam, D., Tarrow, S. and Tilly, C. 2001. *Dynamics of Contention*. Cambridge Studies in Contentious Politics. Cambridge: Cambridge University Press.

McFarland, D.A. (2001) 'Student resistance: How the formal and informal organization of classrooms facilitate everyday forms of student defiance', *American Journal of Sociology* 107(3): 612–78.

McFarland, D.A. (2004) 'Resistance as a social drama—A study of change-oriented encounters', *American Journal of Sociology* 109(6): 1249–318.

McFarland, D.A. and Diehl, D. (2009) 'Cueing orders: Discursive moves and the accomplishment of network forms in classrooms', Unpublished paper.

McLean, P. (1998) 'A frame analysis of favor seeking in the Renaissance: Agency, networks, and political culture', *American Journal of Sociology* 104: 51–91.

McLean, P. (2007) *The Art of the Network: Strategic Interaction and Patronage in Renaissance Florence*. Durham, NC: Duke University Press.

McPherson, M.J. and Ranger-Moore, J.R. (1991) 'Evolution on a dancing landscape: Organizations and networks in dynamic Blau space', *Social Forces* 70: 19–42.

Melucci, A. (1989) *Nomads of the Present: Social Movements and Individual Needs in Contemporary Society*. Philadelphia: Temple University Press.

Meyer, D.S. and Whittier, N. (1994) 'Social movement spillover', *Social Problems* 41: 277–98.

Mische, A. (1996) 'Projecting democracy: The construction of citizenship across youth networks in Brazil', In *Citizenship, Identity, and Social History*, ed. by Charles Tilly. Cambridge: Cambridge University Press.

Mische, A. (2003) 'Cross-talk in movements: Rethinking the culture-network link', pp. 258–80 in *Social Movements and Networks: Relational Approaches to Collective Action*, ed. Mario Diani and Doug McAdam. Oxford: Oxford University Press.

Mische, A. (2007) *Partisan Publics: Communication and Contention across Brazilian Youth Activist Networks*. Princeton: Princeton University Press.

Mische, A. (2009) 'Projects and possibilities: Researching futures in action', *Sociological Forum* 24: 694–704.

Mische, A. and Pattison, P. (2000) 'Composing a civic arena: Publics, projects, and social settings', *Poetics* 27: 163–94.

Mische, A. and White, H.C. (1998) 'Between conversation and situation: Public switching dynamics across network domains', *Social Research* 65: 695–724.

Mohr, J. (1994) 'Soldiers, mothers, tramps, and others: Discourse roles in the 1907 New York City charity directory', *Poetics* 22: 327–57.

Mohr, J. (2010) 'Implicit terrains: Meaning, measurement, and spatial metaphors in organizational theory', Forthcoming in Marc Ventresca, Kamal A. Munir and Michael Lounsbury

(eds.) *The Economic Sociology of Markets and Industries*. Cambridge: Cambridge University Press.

Mohr, J., Bourgeois, M. and Duquenne, V. (2004) 'The logic of opportunity: A formal analysis of the University of California's outreach and diversity discourse', Center for Studies in Higher Education, UC Berkeley, Research and Occasional Papers Series.

Mohr, J. and Duqenne, V. (1997) 'The duality of culture and practice: Poverty relief in New York City, 1888–1917', *Theory and Society* 26: 305–56.

Mohr, J.W. and Lee, H.K. (2000) 'From affirmative action to outreach: Discourse shifts at the University of California', *Poetics* 28/1: 47–71.

Mohr, J.W. and Neely, B. (2009) 'Modeling Foucault: Dualities of power in institutional fields', pp. 203–256 in Renate Meyer, Kerstin Sahlin-Andersson, Marc Ventresca, Peter Walgenbach (eds.), *Ideology and Organizational Institutionalism* (*Research in the Sociology of Organizations, Vol. 27*).

Mohr, J.W. and White, H.C. (2008) 'How to model an institution', *Theory and Society* 37: 485–512.

Moody, J., McFarland, D.A. and Bender-deMoll, S. (2005) 'Dynamic network visualization', *American Journal of Sociology* 110(4): 1206–41.

Morrill, C. (1995) *The Executive Way: Conflict Management in Corporations* Chicago: University of Chicago Press.

Morrill, C. (forthcoming) 'Institutional change through interstitial emergence: The growth of alternative dispute resolution in American law, 1965–1995', In *How Institutions Change*, ed. Walter W. Powell and Daniel L. Jones. Chicago: University of Chicago Press.

Morrill, C., Mayer N. Zald and Hayagreeva Rao (2003) 'Covert political conflict in organizations: Challenges from below', *Annual Review of Sociology* 30: 391–415.

Muetzel, So. (2009) 'Networks as culturally constituted processes: A comparison of relational sociology and actor-network theory', *Current Sociology* 57 (6): 871–87.

Nexon. D. and Wright, T. (2007) 'What's at stake in the American empire debate', *American Political Science Review* 101: 253–71.

Oliver, P.E. and Myers, D.J. (2003) 'Networks, diffusion, and cycles of collective action', pp. 173–203 in Mario Diani and Doug McAdam (eds.), *Social Movements and Networks: Relational Approaches to Collective Action*. Oxford: Oxford University Press.

Osa, M. (2001) 'Mobilizin structures and cycles of protest: Post Stalinist contention in Poland, 1954–1959', *Mobilization* 6: 211–31.

Osa, M. (2003) 'Networks in opposition: Linking organizations through activists in the Polish People's Republic', pp. 77–104 in *Social Movements and Networks: Relational Approaches to Collective Action*, ed. Mario Diani and Doug McAdam. Oxford and New York: Oxford University Press.

Owen-Smith, J. and Powell, W.W. (2004) 'Knowledge networks as channels and conduits: The effects of spillovers in the Boston biotechnology community', *Organization Science* 15(1): 5–21.

Owen-Smith, J. and Powell, W.W. (2008) 'Networks and institutions', pp. 596–623 in Royston Greenwood,

Christine Oliver, Roy Suddaby and Kerstin Sahlin-Andersson (eds.) *The Handbook of Organizational Institutionalism.* New York: Sage.

Pachucki, M.A. and Breiger, R.L. (2010) 'Cultural holes: Beyond relationality in social networks and culture', *Annual Review of Sociology* 36: 205–24.

Padgett, J.F. (2001) 'Organizational genesis, identity and control: The transformation of banking in Renaissance Florence', pp. 211–57 in *Networks and Markets*, ed. James E. Rauch and Alessandra Casella. New York: Russell Sage.

Padgett, J.F. and. Ansell, C.K. (1993) 'Robust action and the rise of the Medici, 1400–1434', *American Journal of Sociology* 98: 1259–319.

Padgett, J.F. and McLean, P.D. (2006) 'Organizational invention and elite transformation: The birth of partnership systems in Renaissance Florence', *American Journal of Sociology* 111: 1463–568.

Polletta, F. (2002) *Freedom Is an Endless Meeting: Democracy in American Social Movements.* Chicago: University of Chicago Press.

Polletta, F. (2006) *It Was Like a Fever: Storytelling in Protest and Politics.* Chicago: University of Chicago Press.

Powell, W.W. and DiMaggio, P.J. (eds.) (1991) *The New Institutionalism in Organizational Analysis.* Chicago: University of Chicago Press.

Rawlings, C.M. and Bourgeois, M.D. (2004) 'The complexity of institutional niches: Credentials and organizational differentiation in a field of U.S. higher education', *Poetics* 32: 411–37.

Sewell, W.H., Jr. (1992) 'A theory of structure: Duality, agency, and transformation', *American Journal of Sociology* 98: 1–29.

Schneiberg, M. and Lounsbury, M.(2008) 'Social movements and institutional analysis', pp. 648–70 in Royston Greenwood, Christine Oliver, Roy Suddaby and Kerstin Sahlin-Andersson (eds.), *The Handbook of Organizational Institutionalism.* New York: Sage.

Schriffen, D. (1987) *Discourse Markers.* Cambridge: Cambridge University Press.

Scott, J. (1991) *Social Network Analysis: A Handbook.* London: Sage.

Sheller, M. (2000) *Democracy After Slavery: Black Publics and Peasant Radicalism in Haiti and Jamaica.* Oxford: Macmillan.

Sheller, Mimi and John Urry. (2006) 'The new mobilities paradigm', *Environment and Planning A* 38: 207–26.

Silverstein, M. (2003) 'Indexical order and the dialectics of sociolinguistic life', *Language and Communication* 233–4: 193–229.

Smilde, D. (2005). 'A qualitative comparative analysis of conversion to Venezuelan evangelicalism: How networks matter', *American Journal of Sociology* 111: 757–96.

Smilde, D. (2007) *Reason to Believe: Cultural Agency in Latin American Evangelicalism.* Berkeley: University of California Press.

Somers, M.R. (1993) 'Citizenship and the place of the public sphere: Law, community, and political culture in the transition to democracy', *American Sociological Review* 58(5): 587–620.

Somers, M.R. (1995) 'What's political or cultural about the political culture concept? Toward an historical sociology of concept formation', *Sociological Theory* 13(2): 113–44.

Somers, M.R. (1998) 'We're no angels: Realism, rational choice, and relationality in social science', *American Journal of Sociology* 104(3): 722–84.

Sonnett, J. (2004) 'Musical boundaries: Intersections of form and content', *Poetics* 32: 247–64.

Spillman, L. (1995) 'Culture, social structure, and discursive fields', *Current Perspectives in Social Theory* 15: 129–54.

Stark, D. and Vedres, B. (2006) 'Social times of network spaces: Network sequences and foreign investment in Hungary', *American Journal of Sociology* 111(5): 1367–412.

Steinberg, M.W. (1999) 'The talk and back talk of collective action: A dialogic analysis of repertoires of discourse among nineteenth-century English cotton spinners', *American Journal of Sociology* 105: 736–80.

Steinmetz, G. (2008) 'The colonial state as a social field', *American Sociological Review* 73: 589–612.

Stinchcombe, A.L. (1991) 'The conditions of fruitfulness of theorizing about mechanisms in social science', *Philosophy of the Social Sciences* 21: 367–88.

Stinchcombe, A.L. (1997) 'Tilly on the past as a sequence of futures', pp. 387–410 in *Roads from Past to Future* (by Charles Tilly). Lanham, MD: Rowman and Littlefield.

Stinchcombe, A.L. (2005) *The Logic of Social Research.* Chicago: University of Chicago Press.

Stovel, K.W., Savage, M. and Bearman, P.S. (1996) 'Ascription into achievement: Models of career systems at Lloyds Bank, 1890–1970', *American Journal of Sociology* 102: 358–99.

Swidler, A. (2001) *Talk of Love: How Culture Matters.* Chicago: University of Chicago Press.

Tarrow, Sidney (2008) 'Charles Tilly and the practice of contentious politics', *Social Movement Studies* 7(3): 225–46.

Taylor, V. and Whittier, N. (1992) 'Collective identity in social movement communities', pp. 104–29 in Aldon D. Morris and Carol Mueller (eds.), *Frontiers of Social Movement Theory.* New Haven, CT: Yale University Press.

Tilly, C. (1978) *From Mobilization to Revolution.* Reading, MA: Addison-Wesley.

Tilly, C. (1995) 'Macrosociology, past and future', pp. 1–3 in *The Relational Turn in Macrosociology: A Symposium.* Working Paper No. 215. New York: Center for Studies of Social Change.

Tilly, C. (1997) 'Parliamentarization of popular contention in Great Britain, 1758–1834', *Theory and Society* 26: 245–73.

Tilly, C. (1998a) 'Contentious conversation', *Social Research* 65: 491–510.

Tilly, C. (1998b) *Durable Inequality.* Berkeley: University of California Press.

Tilly, C. (2004) *Stories, Identities, and Political Change.* Lanham, MD: Rowman & Littlefield.

Tilly, C. (2006a) *Identities, Boundaries, and Social Ties.* Boulder: Paradigm.

Tilly, C. (2006b) *Why?* Princeton: Princeton University Press.

Tilly, C. (2008a) *Explaining Social Processes.* Boulder: Paradigm.

Tilly, C. (2008b) *Contentious Performances.* Cambridge: Cambridge University Press.

Tilly, C. and Wood, L. (2003) 'Contentious connections in Great Britain, 1828–34', pp. 147–72 in *Social Movements and Networks: Relational Approaches to Collective Action*, ed. Mario Diani and Doug McAdam. Oxford: Oxford University Press.

Uzzi, B. and Spiro, J. (2005) 'Collaboration and creativity: The small world problem', *American Journal of Sociology* 111: 447–504.

Vaisey, S. and Lizardo, O. (2009) '"Can cultural worldviews influence network composition?'" *Social Forces* 88: 1595–1618.

Vaughan, D. (2002) 'Signals and interpretive work: The role of culture in a theory of practical action', pp. 28–54 in Karen Cerulo (ed.) *Culture in Mind: Toward a Sociology of Culture and Cognition*. New York: Routledge.

Wada, T. (2004) 'Event analysis of claim making in Mexico: How are social protests transformed into political protests?' *Mobilization* 9(3): 241–57.

Wagner-Pacifici, R.E. (2000) *Theorizing the Standoff: Contingency in Action*. Cambridge, UK: Cambridge University Press.

Wagner-Pacifici, R.E. (2005) *The Art of Surrender: Decomposing Sovereignty at Conflict's End*. Chicago: University of Chicago Press.

Wasserman, S. and Faust, K. (1994). *Social Network Analysis: Methods and Applications*. Cambridge: Cambridge University Press.

Watts, D.J. (1999) 'Networks, dynamics, and the small-world phenomenon', *American Journal of Sociology* 105: 493–527.

Watts, D.J. and Dodds, P.S. (2007) 'Networks, influence, and public opinion formation', *Journal of Consumer Research* 34: 441–58.

Wellman, B. (1988) 'Structural analysis: From method and metaphor to theory and substance', pp. 19–61 in *Social Structures a Network Approach*, ed. Barry Wellman and S.D. Berkowitz. Cambridge: Cambridge University Press.

Wellman, B. and Berkowitz, S.D. (eds.) (1988) *Social Structures a Network Approach*. Cambridge: Cambridge University Press.

Wellman, B., Quan-Haase, A., Boase, J., Chen, W., Hampton, K., Diaz de Isla, I. and Miyata, K. (2003) 'The social affordances of the Internet for networked individualism', *Journal of Computer Mediated Communication* 8:3.

Whitford, J. (2002) 'Pragmatism and the untenable dualism of means and ends: Why rational choice theory does not deserve paradigmatic privilege', *Theory and Society* 31: 325–63.

White, H.C. (1992) *Identity and Control: A Structural Theory of Social Action*. Princeton: Princeton University Press.

White, H.C. (1993) 'Network moves', Revised version of paper prepared for the 'Workshop: Time as a Social Tapestry', Center for the Social Sciences, March 12–13, 1993.

White, H.C. (1994) 'Talk and ties: Change through publics', Unpublished paper.

White, H.C. (1995) 'Network switchings and Bayesian forks: Reconstructing the social and behavioral sciences', *Social Research* 62: 1035–63.

White, H.C. (2004) *Markets from Networks: Socioeconomic Models of Production*. Princeton: Princeton University Press.

White, H.C. (2008) 'Notes on the constituents of social structure: Soc. Rel. 10—Spring '65', *Sociologica* 1/2008: 1–14.

White, H.C., Godart, F.C. and Corona, V.P. (2007) 'Mobilizing identities: Uncertainty and control in strategy', *Theory, Culture & Society* 24(7–8): 181–202.

Yeung, K. (2005) 'What does love mean? Exploring network culture in two network settings', *Social Forces* 84(1): 391–420.

Zelizer, V. (2004) 'Circuits of commerce', pp. 122–44 in Jeffrey C. Alexander, Gary T. Marx, and Christine Williams (eds.), *Self, Social Structure, and Beliefs. Explorations in Sociology*. Berkeley: University of California Press.

Zelizer, V. (2005a) 'Circuits within capitalism', pp. 289–322 in Victor Nee and Richard Swedberg (eds.), *The Economic Sociology of Capitalism*. Princeton: Princeton University Press.

Zelizer, V. (2005b) *The Purchase of Intimacy*. Princeton: Princeton University Press.

Zelizer, V. (2006a) 'Why and how to read *Why?*' *Qualitative Sociology* 29: 531–34.

Substantive Topics

8

Personal Communities:
The World According to Me

Vincent Chua, Julia Madej, and
Barry Wellman

Except for saintly altruists, the world revolves around 'Me'. We keep a mental network map of our friends and enemies. Who are the people I will see today or contact by the Internet or mobile phone? Who can I count on for different kinds of help? Which of my friends and relatives know each other, and which get along with each other?

Networks built around 'Me' – personal communities – have always been with us. But, nowadays, with Facebook and its ilk, people are becoming very aware that communities can consist of a person's network of relationships, wherever such communities are located.

In fact, there are three ways of looking at communities:

- Once upon a time, almost all people believed that communities were rooted in neighbourhoods: the traditional spatially bounded areas in which, at least in principle, most people know each other and can walk or make a short drive to each other's homes.
- Communities can consist of people with a shared interest, such as communities of people who drift cars.
- The less traditional way we discuss here is that personal communities are defined as those connected to the individuals at their centres. From this standpoint, friends, neighbours, kin, acquaintances, co-workers and fellow members of organisations are personal community members and are often connected to each other.

There has been a shift in perception from spatially defined communities to relationally defined communities. These personal communities are social networks defined as an individual set of ties (Figure 8.1). Such personal communities have become more palpably visible with the advent of the Internet. Facebook and similar social media organise people's social worlds in terms of lists of friends and acquaintances.

While some scholars continue to study community in terms of spatially bounded units such as groups, neighbourhoods and villages, others focus on community as an interpenetrating combination of online and offline worlds managed by autonomous individuals at their respective centres (Boase and Wellman, 2006). Hence, the traditional representation of community as a distinct set of local ties is often usefully replaced by looking at personal communities characterised by a combination of local, regional and distant ties, no matter how far-flung (Wellman, 2002).

To be sure, such personal communities have always existed (e.g. Bender, 1978), but their form has changed drastically with time. In an earlier period, personal communities were mostly geographically bound, densely knit and broadly based ties organised around discrete social units such as bars and taverns or neighbourhoods (Keller, 1968). Today, many personal communities are geographically dispersed, sparsely knit and specialised (Wellman, 1979). The growth of social affordances that facilitate personal communication – such as mobile phones, email and social software such as Facebook and Twitter – has radically facilitated this transformation. Where landline phones link households to households, mobile phones and the Internet directly link people,

Figure 8.1   Typical personal community (© Barry Wellman 2011)

giving rise to a contemporary form of community we call 'networked individualism' (Wellman, 2001a, 2001b).

The most persistent concern about contemporary communities has been their alleged decline in the past hundred years. Different commentators have offered different causes for the decline, ranging from industrialisation, capitalism, socialism, urbanisation, bureaucratisation, feminism and technological change (Wellman, 2001b). In 2000, political scientist Robert Putnam argued that Americans were now 'bowling alone' and that civic activities such as voting, social club memberships and family dinners were declining. More recently, McPherson et al. (2006) repeated the caution, showing that the number of people with whom Americans discuss 'important matters' had decreased from 2.8 to 2.1 in the span of two decades from the mid-1980s to the mid-2000s. Putative technological explanations for the alleged decline of community have been proffered since

the time when it was believed that automobiles took people away from face-to-face interactions on streets and streetcars. The culprit du jour is the Internet, with some commentators fearing that excessive use of email, Facebook et al., would lure people away from face-to-face contact and perhaps even ensnare some by causing online addictions (Pope Benedict XVI, 2009; Sigman, 2009).

Yet most studies show that personal communities continue to be a central part of people's lives. The data are consistent from Western Europe, Latin America, China, Japan, Iran, Canada or the United States (Fischer, 1982; Wellman, 1999; Boase et al., 2006; Wellman, 2007). The losses in involvement in formal organisations (such as Rotary Clubs) have been supplanted by more informal means of communicating and socialising, and large networks of specialised ties are flourishing. With Internet and email, distance poses less hindrance as communication comes to be increasingly defined by social accessibility rather than spatial accessibility (Hogan, 2008b; Mok et al., 2010). While personal communities may have gone indoors, from cafés to living rooms and computer screens, this does not mean that community has disappeared. People continue to be social when they are indoors. They chat online with friends, keep up with them via their Facebook pages, tweet them (via Twitter) about where they are going, meet them offline to round out discussions, and then meet online again to talk about other things (Robinson et al., 2002).

In this chapter, we describe the nature of personal communities as well as their characteristics and consequences. For reasons of space, we focus on personal communities in the developed world, but bring in some comparative information from elsewhere.

COMMUNITIES AS PERSONAL COMMUNITIES

Personal community research invokes a certain understanding of 'community'. Instead of regarding communities as bound up with organised institutions such as family, neighbourhood, work or voluntary organisations, personal community research treats communities as 'personal networks'. The personal network approach views networks from the standpoint of an individual (*ego*) managing his or her ties with *alters*. This contrasts with the 'whole network' approach that observes an entire set of ties, such as in a neighbourhood, workplace or organisation.

One practical way to understand the personal network approach is to think about a person's friends on Facebook. His or her personal network would include all fellow Facebook users personally linked to him or her as 'friends' (Hogan, 2008a). These 'friends' may be anyone ranging from an acquaintance barely met, a long-lost friend who has recently contacted you, a neighbour next door or a sibling living within the same house. Because personal networks on Facebook (or of professionally gregarious folks such as politicians or salespeople) can include thousands of weak ties, we follow Hogan's (2008a) distinction here between 'personal networks' and our subject, 'personal communities' that consist of the ties that are meaningful to egos.

Facebook and similar social media have privacy issues. Such is the world we live in that communities have become personal and private and yet, in some ways, significantly publicised

with friends being announced, shared and recommended across networks. It has become quite common among Facebook friends to peruse one another's personal networks during their free time. Facebook and MySpace help to facilitate transitive relations; that is, if Jane knows Bob and Alice, then over time, Bob and Alice will likely get to know each other.

Sharing between networks allows different parts of the social structure to overlap and intersect, with a particular person, or ego, as the focal point. Such intertwining possibly breaks down barriers between groups and unites individuals through the sharing of new information and friendship, creating opportunities for developing diverse personal communities – to have diverse friends is to have diverse experiences and all these add to a broad and enriching life (Erickson, 2003).

The community question

The early nineteenth century was a time of tumultuous change in Western societies. Towns and cottages had quickly evolved into industrial centres and were engaged in the mass production of goods and services. Over time, the production and consumer markets became increasingly specialised, with workers filling unique occupational roles. Scholars and policymakers feared that interpersonal relations would atrophy as relationships specialised, neighbourhoods were flooded with strangers, and people turned to governments and large organisations for support. Social scientists feared that this new role-based approach reduced the quality of interpersonal relations within society, leading to a loss of community (Wellman, 2001b).

While compelling, these fears rarely were based on a systematic evaluation of people's everyday lives. In the 1960s, several ethnographies challenged these fears by highlighting the persistence of tight-knit communities in urban areas such as working-class London (Young and Willmot, 1957), Italian-American 'urban villages', (Gans, 1962) and suburban white America (Gans, 1967).

Although these ethnographies were successful in demonstrating the persistence of community, by adhering to a neighbourhood-based approach, they neglected other important bases of community such as workplaces, voluntary organisations and online worlds. Moreover, by treating communities as coterminous with spatially defined neighbourhoods, they deflected attention away from the large number of friendship and kinship ties that were not local. On a wider scale, globalised communication and extensive air travel now facilitate the growth of transnational networks and entrepreneurial activity across continents (Chen and Wellman, 2009). Immigration need not imply the loss of ties with the home country but rather the expansion of personal communities to include both host and home country ties (Salaff et al., 1999).

The historical trajectory of community formation can be seen as a series of three ideal types, reflecting changes in technology and human mobility (Figure 8.2). The first type, 'little boxes', was especially prevalent before the advent of the telephone. It involved reaching others through traveling by foot (or horseback), trudging from door to door.

In the second type, 'glocalisation', the telephone, car and plane liberated a portion of this constraint and allowed communications to take place between households (Wellman and Tindall, 1993). However, one characteristic of the telephone is that the person on the other side may not actually be the intended recipient but the family member who happens to be nearest the ringing phone. Thus, such interactions – whether mediated by phone, car or plane – were 'place-to-place', involving the entire household.

A third type has proliferated in the past decade. With the widespread use of the Internet and mobile phones, people may be reached directly, creating a situation whereby 'networked individuals' communicate as individuals. Such 'person-to-person' interactions create a unique way of life. They privilege interpersonal interaction among individuals rather than interaction between households. It is common to see individuals conversing on their mobile phones while walking down the street and sending emails through their phones while on the run – not isolated, but connected (see Wellman et al., 2006). With digital media such as the Internet and mobile phone, people remain reachable regardless of their physical location. Whether such accessibility is a boon or a bane remains an open question. While some scholars argue that person-to-person affordances create flexibility in social relations and work schedules, others have pointed to the social control that such affordances create by allowing people to be located and contacted at any time and almost any place (Olson-Buchanan and Boswell, 2006). For example, software such as Google Latitudes can immediately inform people

Little boxes

Glocalization

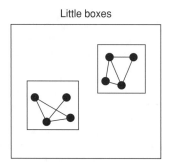
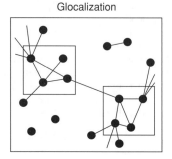

Networked individualism

Figure 8.2   Three forms of networked communities (© Barry Wellman 2011)

about the locations of others in their personal communities.

Personal communities online and offline

Although we often deal with media queries about the supposedly isolating nature of the media (e.g. Anderssen, 2009), research has made it clear that the Internet is in fact seamlessly integrated with personal communities and is rarely a separate second life in itself (Veenhof et al., 2008; Quan-Haase et al., 2002). One over-time study shows that for American adults, the mean number of friends in weekly in-person contact has increased by 20 per cent between 2002 and 2007: from 9.4 to 11.3 friends. At the same time, the median number of friends slightly decreased, from 6 to 5. Taken together, these statistics indicate that while the number of friends slightly decreased for about half of Americans, the number of friends increased appreciably for many Americans (Wang and Wellman, 2010).

This increase may well be related to Internet use, for the increase in the number of friends is greater as the amount of Internet activity increases. For example, heavy Internet users had a 38 per cent increase in the number of friends during this period (from 9.0 to 12.4) while nonusers had a more modest 7 per cent increase (from 9.5 to 10.2). Not only do Internet users have more friends, their friendship networks are growing at an accelerated pace (Wang and Wellman, 2010).

These data suggest that the Internet not only enables people to maintain and strengthen existing ties but it also aids some to forge new ties. The time that people spend online is not reducing time spent in face-to-face contact but rather is redeploying time formerly spent in less social activities such as eating, television watching, and sleeping (Boase et al., 2006; Rainie and Wellman, forthcoming). However, one large Canadian study did show heavy Internet users spending somewhat less time seeing friends and family (Veenhof et al., 2008).

Whether or not there is some time displacement from the Internet, it is now apparent that the addition of Internet and mobile phone communication to traditional face-to-face and phone contact means that there is more overall communication between friends and relatives now than before the coming of the Internet. Interactions via information and communication technologies (ICTs) have become cheaper, quicker and much more efficient than visiting, telephoning, or writing letters the old fashioned pen-to-paper way (Boase et al., 2006; Baron, 2008; Stern,

2008; Collins and Wellman, 2010; Wang and Wellman, 2010).

Analysts continue to fear that online communication will replace face-to-face interaction among individuals (Sigman, 2009). This fear is unfounded, for Internet users usually report that the Internet makes life easier, more social, makes learning easier, and facilitates the connection of members within a personal community (Kraut et al., 2002; Wellman et al., 2006; Veenhof et al., 2008; the many reports at www.pewinternet.org). Most relationships formed via face-to-face interactions during the day are continued and extended via ICTs such as emailing, texting, instant messaging, or calling via mobile phones. Therefore, ICTs add to face-to-face contact, rather than replace it (Boase et al., 2006; Wellman et al., 2006; Wang and Wellman, 2010).

The increasing use of the Internet as a communication medium has made distance less of a limiting constraint on communication. The social affordances associated with email include high velocity and zero additional costs above the monthly rate, the ability to contact many people at once (and for those contacted to respond to one or to many), the ability of communications to be stored and retrieved later, the lack of visual and audio barriers to making contact, and the ease of contacting, replying and forwarding (Wellman, 1999, 2001a, 2001b). This makes communication between people accessible regardless of the distance separating them (Gotham and Brumley, 2002). On average, email contact is less sensitive to distance although other modes of communication are not. Face-to-face contact drops off after a 5-mile cut-off point, phone contact is most sensitive only within 100 miles, and email is largely insensitive to distance (Mok et al., 2010).

The issue of how the Internet affects communication at a distance has become especially salient in the 21st century. Prior to the Internet, migration over long distances meant a disruption to relationships in one's personal community because visits and continuous contact were expensive and cumbersome (Hiller and Franz, 2004). More recently, the notion of transnational community has replaced the old concept of migration as severing social ties. Immigrants and rural people particularly value the Internet's effortless long-distance connectivity (Veenhof et al., 2008; Collins and Wellman, 2010; Stern and Messer, 2009).

For example, the 2003 General Social Survey found that 56 per cent of Canadians aged 25 to 54 who immigrated to Canada between 1990 and 2003 used the Internet in the previous month to communicate with friends, as compared with only 48 per cent of Canadian-born individuals (Veenhof et al., 2008). It is now possible to return home to

Trinidad (Miller and Slater, 2000), the Philippines (Ignacio, 2005), or anywhere else in the world, by virtual visits via webcam, email or the sharing of electronic photographs through online sites such as Facebook and Flickr. It is no longer necessary to rely solely on memories and letters to remain connected with friends and folk back home.

Personal community ties are maintained both online and offline, with relationships formed online spilling into the physical realm and ties in the physical realm continuing as online interactions (Wellman and Haythornthwaite, 2002). Some ties start online and remain online, but they usually constitute only a small part of a person's personal community. American Internet users have on average about four online-only friendship ties (Wang and Wellman, 2010). Critics of involvement with online ties often fail to contextualize the online relationship as a medium of communication, like the telephone, that largely fills the gaps between face-to-face interactions and helps to arrange future meetings (Wellman and Tindall, 1993).

Sites such as Facebook and Twitter are now major sites of communication in North America. They have often superseded email and instant messaging as the main way for students and young adults to keep track and stay connected to their personal communities (Lenhart et al., 2005). In Canada, Facebook adoption within urban centres is especially high. For example, 22 per cent of Toronto's population (aged 18+) have Facebook profiles (Zinc Research and Dufferin Research, 2008).

Such social networking sites do not suppress offline social contact, but they are integrated with it, as many relationships are migratory: moving from being online only to combining online with offline contact. A 38 per cent increase in the number of such migratory friends reported by heavy Internet users, from a mean of 1.6 friends in 2002 to 2.2 in 2007, is one indication of the seamless integration of social networking sites into our daily communication repertoire (Wang and Wellman, 2010). Moreover, the heavy Internet users' number of online-only friends more than doubled: from 4.1 in 2002 to 8.7 in 2007, an increase of 112 per cent (Wang and Wellman, 2010).

COLLECTING PERSONAL COMMUNITY DATA

The two most popular instruments for collecting personal community data are the *name generator* and the *position generator*.

Name generators ask respondents to provide a list of contacts with whom they share one or more criterion relations, such as 'close with' or 'friendship' (Burt, 1984; Marsden, 1987; Wellman, 2001b).

Name generator studies began in the late 1960s. Within a decade, several personal community studies appeared, such as Edward Laumann's Detroit-area study (1973), Barry Wellman's first East York (Toronto) study (1979) and Claude Fischer's Detroit and Northern California studies (Fischer et al., 1977, Fischer, 1982). These studies treated communities as personal communities and found them to have a variety of ties with friends, kin, neighbours and workmates.

Two approaches to collecting name generator information differentially affect which alters are described (Ferligoj and Hlebec, 1999; Straits, 2000). One approach asks respondents who are their 'best friends' (Laumann, 1973) or socially close 'intimates' (Wellman, 1979). The second approach asks respondents to name alters with whom they exchange specific resources, such as borrowing a large sum of money or getting advice on a work-related decision (Fischer, 1982). It yields a somewhat larger and more diversified set of names, although at risk of neglecting those who are socially close but do not provide the kinds of supportive resources that are being examined.

Both name generator approaches focus on the core regions of personal networks, although questions about finding a job usually locate a weaker but important set of ties (Granovetter, 1995). Overall, name generators tend to be biased towards eliciting alters who are socially closer to the respondents, who have known the respondents longer and who know more of the respondents' other alters (Marin, 2004).

Name generators are typically followed up with *name interpreters*, which elicit information about each named contact and the nature of the ego-alter relationship (Marsden, 2005). Name interpreters may include items such as the personal characteristics of the named contact (gender, age, education, socioeconomic background) and the attributes describing the tie, things such as the role-relation connecting ego and alter (whether parent, child, relative, co-worker, friend or spouse etc.), the frequency of contact, level of intimacy, longevity of the tie (Marsden and Campbell, 1984) and the origin of the tie (Fischer, 1982).

Although name generators gather detailed information about individuals in an ego's network, this can be tedious. One innovation has been to use 'participant-aided sociograms' (Hogan et al., 2007). With just paper, pencil and removable tags, this low-technology method requires respondents to place their contacts within a given set of concentric circles, each circle representing a

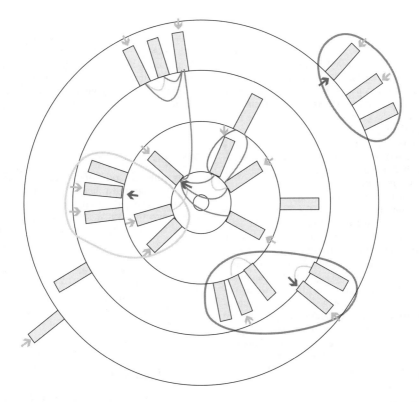

Figure 8.3   Concentric zone paper and pencil way of collecting personal community data (© Barry Wellman 2011)

different level of intimacy (Figure 8.3). While laptop computers were initially used, pretests showed that they made many respondents uncomfortable. Hence, the research team used paper and pencil. Respondents started by providing a list of names, each of which was written on removable Post-It notes. These tags were then placed within the concentric circles and adjusted iteratively as respondents added other names to the chart. This iterative approach induces respondents to think about their alters in relation to one another. Given that people tend to classify alters according to groups (McCarty, 2002) it became relatively easy to collect all the relevant alter information once every name was set in place.

By contrast to the name generator approach, the *position generator* approach asks respondents to report whether or not they have linkages to specific locations in the social structure (Lin and Erickson, 2008). Operationally, the position generator asks respondents if they know any alters occupying a range of low- to high-status occupations: 'lawyer', 'security guard', 'cashier', 'physician', 'secretary', etc. Cultural variations in occupations notwithstanding, position generators should be designed with several principles

in mind: (1) choose occupations that suitably cover a range of low- to high-prestige occupations; (2) select those occupations that have fairly large populations so that respondents have a reasonable chance of knowing a person in that occupational category; (3) ensure that occupations have clear titles that all respondents will understand; (4) create a list that is fairly long because adding more occupations will hardly increase data collection time (Erickson, 2004b).

There are important differences between name generators and position generators. Name generators tend to be more demanding because of the name interpreters that follow. People can usually give detailed reports only on a small number of connections, typically as few as three to five strong ties, and rarely more than a dozen or so (see Lin and Erickson, 2008: 12). By contrast, position generators are easier to administer and are better suited for measuring weak ties. Structurally, weak ties are more likely to bridge race, gender and class divides, and are channels through which individuals gain access to important resources (Granovetter, 1973; Lin and Dumin, 1986; Erickson, 2004a; Moren-Cross and Lin, 2008).

Other ways to collect personal community data include the more recent *contact diary* and *resource generator* approaches. One study using the contact diary approach asked respondents to keep records of every single interpersonal contact daily for three to four consecutive months (Fu, 2008). While a labour-intensive task, the information valuably captures a whole range of strong, medium and weak ties that may not appear in either a name generator or position generator. It is particularly useful for measuring 'seasonal' contacts of weak to medium strength, such as a tax consultant or a summer vacation friend.

The resource generator is another effort to combine aspects of the position generator (its economy and extensive reach) and the name generator (its detailed resource information). A resource generator measures the extent to which an individual has access to specific resources such as whether he or she knows anyone who 'can repair a car', 'play an instrument' or 'has knowledge of literature', etc. One advantage of the resource generator is that it is easier to administer than a name generator and more concrete and directly interpretable than a position generator (van der Gaag and Snijders, 2005; van der Gaag et al., 2008).

WHAT DO PERSONAL COMMUNITIES LOOK LIKE?

Geographically dispersed

Contemporary communities are rarely found within neighbourhoods alone, but they usually include a significant number of network members living as far as an hour's drive or even a few continents away (Fischer, 1982; Wellman et al., 1988; Chen and Wellman, 2009). Short distances remain advantageous because they facilitate face-to-face interactions and exchanges of goods and services. Where such contact is not readily available, there is always the Internet. The Connected Lives study of personal communities in Toronto found that email contact is generally insensitive to distance, though it tends to increase for transoceanic relationships greater than 3,000 miles apart. The study also shows that email has somewhat altered the way people maintain their relationships (Mok et al., 2009). Transnational families see ICTs as improving the overall quantity and quality of contact – they encourage a wider range of kin to become involved in kin work typically performed by women and they strengthen bonds between family members separated by distance (Wilding, 2006). Despite the ostensibly impersonal nature of email, people continue to integrate

their email contact with face-to-face meetings and phone calls in everyday life. With such integration, personal communities are becoming more 'glocalised' – both extensively global and intensely local (Wellman, 2001a, 2001b; Hampton and Wellman, 2002; Hampton and Wellman, 2003; Wellman et al., 2006; Collins and Wellman, 2010).

Sparsely knit

Many personal communities are 'sparsely knit', meaning that most network members are not directly connected with one another. A 1968 study in Toronto found that among socially close intimates, only one-third of all possible alter-to-alter links were present (Wellman, 1979; Wellman et al., 1988). A 1979 re-study in the same area, found density to be even lower, at 0.13, although the study investigated a larger set of alters, including somewhat less socially close ties: the larger the network, the less likely that two alters would be connected (Wellman, 2001b).

Specialised ties

Personal communities are usually specialised, with different community members supplying different kinds of social support (Wellman and Wortley, 1990). In these specialised relationships, the guiding principle is 'tit-for-tit' and not 'tit-for-tat': people tend to reciprocate with the same kind of help that an alter has given to them (Plickert et al., 2007). In general, neighbours are conveniently suited for handling unexpected emergencies because their proximity to ego enables them to react quickly with goods and services (Wellman and Wortley, 1990). Close kinship is a bastion of emotional and long-term support: parents and adult children especially exchange financial aid, emotional aid, large services and small services involving things such as childcare and financial support (Wellman, 1990; Wellman and Wortley, 1990). Spouses supply each other with many types of support (Wellman and Wellman, 1992). Friends are valued as confidants and social companions, especially among singles (de Vries, 1996). They are also valued for the non-redundant information they sometimes provide about job openings (Granovetter, 1995).

A few ties among many

While most Americans can name 200 to 300 alters in their personal networks (McCarty et al., 2001), personal community studies examine at most a small percentage of ties that are intimate and active. Depending on the actual study design, different name generator strategies elicit different kinds and numbers of names (Straits, 2000). Fischer's (1982) Northern California study, which used a diverse set of 10 name generators, elicited a mean of 12.8 names per person, while a more recent study by Hogan et al. (2007) elicited 6 to 66 names. Yet, in neither case do the numbers approach the more than 1,000 names that Boissevain (1974) discovered when he followed two people for a year, or even the 150 ties that British anthropologist Dunbar (1996) posits as the maximum number of members that cohesive groups (such as subsistence villages, nomadic tribes and military units) can successfully accommodate.

People like us

Personal relations are more homogeneous than chance would predict. The circumstances and situations in which individuals find themselves intersect with their personal choices to influence homogeneous networks (Blau, 1977; McPherson and Smith-Lovin, 1987; Marsden, 1988). Egos and alters are typically matched on attributes such as race, class and cultural interests (Lin and Dumin, 1986; Erickson, 1988; Marsden, 1988). Often, these social contexts are already presorted according to some specific set of personal attributes. For example, institutions such as workplaces, schools, neighbourhoods and voluntary organisations tend to bring people of similar education, age, race and gender together, creating a relatively homogeneous pool of 'eligibles' from which choice then exerts its secondary impact (Feld, 1981; Laumann et al., 1994). Depending on the context, some aspects of homophily may be more salient than others. For example, in the United States, racial homophily is a robust phenomenon (Moren-Cross and Lin, 2008).

Yet many ties cut across homogeneous groups, and such ties both help prevent homogeneous clusters from becoming insular and also integrate social systems by providing links between groups (Granovetter, 1973; Laumann, 1973; Ferrand et al., 1999). Homophily on one dimension will not guarantee homophily on other dimensions.

Variation in network composition by individuals' social location

The composition of personal networks differs according to individuals' social locations.

On average, men and women have the same number of alters, but differences exist in the composition and dynamics of these networks. American women tend to have more kin, and they are also active networkers with their kin. Even as dual-income households have become common, women still have more ties with neighbours and extended kin, while men have more ties to coworkers (Fischer, 1982; Wellman, 1985; Marsden, 1987; Moore, 1990). In France, men confide in workmates about as much as they confide in kin while women are three times more likely to confide in kin than in workmates (Ferrand et al., 1999). In Taiwan, women tend to have less access to influential contacts relative to men, because they are less likely to be in the workforce and more likely to be tied down with household obligations (Lin et al., 2001).

Personal communities differ according to stages in life such as the teenaged years, marriage and parenthood. Marriage and early parenthood often entail high levels of commitment to kin, exerting strenuous demands on both time and energy for both spouses (de Vries, 1996). Whereas singles use weekends for socialising with friends, married couples use weekends and weekday evenings for childcare and visits to their parents and in-laws. Particularly for working mothers, there is hardly time after working hours to spend socialising with friends (Hochschild, 1997). When mothers are pressed for time, it is friendship that gives way and kinship that remains (Wellman, 1985).

Age is also an important predictor of network composition. Elderly people tend to have smaller networks because retirement removes an important sphere of non-kin contact in workplaces (Pickard, 1995), and their participation in voluntary organisations declines significantly (Mirowsky and Ross, 1999). Young single people tend to have larger and more diverse networks because they tend to gravitate towards cities (Fischer, 1982) and are more likely to have friend-centered networks (de Vries, 1996).

Personal communities also differ by egos' income, education and ethnicity. The wealthy and educated have more friends and acquaintances than the less well-off (Fischer, 1982; Moore, 1990). People with higher education are more likely to know people from a greater diversity of occupations (Lin and Dumin, 1986) and to know high-status people (Ferrand et al., 1999). Ethnic minorities such as African Americans and Hispanic Americans tend to have lower access to high-status contacts than whites (Lin, 2000; Erickson, 2004a; Moren-Cross and Lin, 2008). African Americans' networks are highly focused on kin and neighbours (Martineau, 1977; Lee et al., 1991). Consequently, their networks tend to be more dense and localised (Stack, 1974; Green et al., 1995).

Variation in networks by national context

Institutional contexts affect the manner in which individuals build their personal communities. Changes in these institutions are usually accompanied by changes in network composition. For example, as the Chinese economy began its shift from socialist to free-market, people became more likely to discuss important matters with friends rather than with co-workers or kin. Within the space of just seven years, the percentage of friends within the observed Tianjin-based networks had increased from 5 per cent in 1986 to 34 per cent in 1993 – a 700 per cent change (Ruan et al., 1997). In an increasingly capitalist economy, Chinese workers have gravitated towards friends and activating new forms of *guanxi* that can serve as better bridges to job opportunities (also see Wellman et al., 2002; Gold et al., 2002). At the same time, with state-driven work-assignment programs being gradually phased out, the role of co-workers has receded, with strong friendship ties becoming more important (Ruan et al., 1997).

East Germany provides another case. Before the fall of the Berlin Wall, East German personal communities were characterised by distinct niche and provisioning components. Whereas the niche component was a set of densely knit ties that the East Germans used circumspectly while exchanging sensitive political views among close friends and relatives, the provisioning component was a set of sparsely knit ties that they used to garner instrumental resources such as job information and financial aid. This changed after the fall of communism when the East Germans' personal communities were no longer linked to highly controlled institutional conditions. As a result, differences between niche and weaker ties began to disappear (Völker and Flap, 2001).

FRIENDSHIP AND KINSHIP IN PERSONAL COMMUNITIES

The upsurge of education and physical mobility in contemporary times has not suppressed the importance of family in personal communities. Kinship continues to be important even among socially mobile people. In the United States, highly educated individuals continue to consult immediate kin on important matters (McPherson et al., 2006). In Tehran, kin remains a central concern

among middle-class Iranians who share social and economic resources amid unstable state conditions (Bastani, 2007). In Toulouse, kin predominate in personal communities, especially among highly educated individuals (Grossetti, 2007). Both kinship and friendship remain important in German modern life, working interdependently with family to provide a range of social and emotional resources to egos (Hennig, 2007). One reason why kinship and friendship are so complementary is that they constitute somewhat distinct systems of activity characterised by relatively unique structural properties, exchange processes and resources.

Differences in structure

Personal communities often contain distinct clusters of activity and interests. Kin may rarely know friends, and some friends may not know each other. At times, segregation allows egos to maintain discreet associations with friends unbeknownst to the ego's inner circle (Hannerz, 1980).

Kinship networks tend to be densely knit clusters with close bonds between network members, while friendship networks tend to be sparsely knit, creating holes within broad network structures. Given that family and friends are important in everyday life, both aspects of network structure are typically found within many personal communities – they are characterised by a dense inner core made of immediate kin and a separate middle and outer core containing a range of close to superficial friendship relations (Wellman and Wortley, 1990; Bastani, 2007; Grossetti, 2007; Hennig, 2007; Hogan, 2008b).

Differences in exchange processes

Kinship and friendship tend to be marked by distinct exchange processes, due in part to the structural contexts in which they are embedded. Because between-kin relations are more likely to revolve around densely knit contexts, these ties are mostly governed by diffuse reciprocity norms, whereby favours given to a beneficiary are not repaid directly by the beneficiary but by other community members (Uehara, 1990).

Differences in resources

Friendship and kinship networks tend to be sources of different kinds of resources (Wellman and Wortley, 1990). Immediate kin are often high on solidarity, trust and commitment, whereas friends and acquaintances often constitute loosely coupled networks that provide channels to things such as job information (Granovetter, 1995). In many instances, friendship networks serve as bridges connecting individuals to different strata of society, thus facilitating social mobility (Bian, 1997; Ferrand et al., 1999; Lin, 2001). Yet the distinction between instrumental friendship and affective kinship is more fluid. Friends often make good social companions and providers of emotional support, while immediate kin can be important sources of instrumental support, particularly in the areas of financial aid and knowledge acquisition (Coleman, 1988; Wellman and Wortley, 1990; Ferrand et al., 1999).

CONSEQUENCES OF PERSONAL COMMUNITIES

Personal community and social support

Personal communities are important to the routine operations of households, crucial to the management of crises, and sometimes instrumental in helping change situations. They provide havens and a sense of belonging and being helped. People count on family and close friends to provide routine emotional aid and small services to help cope with a variety of stresses and strains. For example, when faced with a medical crisis, people typically consult close friends and family. These network members constitute a 'therapy managing group' (Pescosolido, 1992: 1124), and are important partners in the health management process (Pescosolido, 1992; Antonucci and Akiyama, 1995; Rainie and Wellman, forthcoming).

Personal communities can also help to change situations. As conduits through which resources such as money, skills, information and services are exchanged, personal communities can often lead to enhanced life chances such as receiving advice on important matters (Fischer, 1982), having more diverse knowledge (Erickson, 1996) and getting a job (Granovetter, 1995). They are useful for negotiating barriers in everyday life such as formal bureaucratic structures. In pre-market China, close connections with influential friends and family were often invoked to expedite illegal job changes amid tight governmental control (Bian, 1997). During the authoritarian regime in Chile, neighbours provided each other with food and childcare, as well as helped in building homes and finding work (Espinoza, 1999).

Personal community and inequality

While personal communities are channels for the transmission of many benefits, they are also conduits for social control and the reproduction of inequalities. They can be mechanisms through which inequalities are transmitted in the labour market. With many employers preferring to use insider networks in addition to formal hiring methods, personal recommendations have become a popular form of hiring in both high-status and low-status jobs (Burt, 1997; Fernández et al., 2000; Erickson, 2001).

In job searches, information holders with diverse networks (the ego knows others from a wide range of occupations) and specialised networks (the ego knows others within the same industry) are more likely to be aware of job openings, but they do not necessarily identify potential applicants or share these job openings with job seekers (Marin, 2008). Much depends on whether information holders are willing to share their information. Sometimes, they may be reluctant to share because they think that the job seekers are not reliable and will not be good candidates (Smith, 2005).

Homogeneous networks often reproduce inequalities in job searches. For example, male managers are more likely to hire members of their 'old boy networks,' preventing equally qualified women from moving up (Reskin and McBrier, 2000). Here, an overreliance on networks suppresses the impact of meritocratic hiring, preventing women from gaining access to managerial positions. Homogeneous class-stratified networks are especially disadvantageous for lower-status groups, who tend to have relatively little access to higher-status contacts (Ferrand et al., 1999; Lin, 2001). Given their relative lack of education, the job success of lower-status job seekers is often closely bound up with their ability to reach up to more influential contacts.

Personal community and diverse functions

A personal community is typically composed of a dual combination of network arrangements, differentiated roughly by an inner and outer core. The inner core tends to have ties with multiple role relations knotted together in densely knit clusters, while the outer core tends to have specialised ties in sparsely knit network structures (Wellman and Wortley, 1990; Hogan, 2008b). As modern societies have become differentiated, the functions of personal communities have likewise become specialised and diverse. Personal communities have not declined in contemporary times; they have complex structures and processes.

Reflecting modern trends in marketing and community, individuals now shop for support at specialised interpersonal boutiques rather than at general stores. Diverse ties fulfill diverse functions. Strong ties in the form of immediate kin are typically associated with long-term care and small services. Friends, siblings and organisational members, especially those with strong ties, are likely to be social companions. Physically accessible relations are more likely to provide large and small services and women are more likely to provide emotional aid. As necessarily individual managers of their personal communities, people come to learn about what kinds of networks work for what kinds of purposes, and they thereby invest in diverse combinations of relationships according to their priorities and needs in life.

CONCLUSIONS

Personal communities are personal, yet they are also intensively social, spanning continents, social divisions, and other networks. In reality, personal communities are not like the thousands of isolated islands in the Indonesian archipelago. Rather, they overlap with other social networks to create a system of social interactions resembling a loosely coupled but unmistakably linked social whole. The birth and development of communication technologies such as the Internet, email, mobile phones and smartphones now allow people to build communities in new and exciting ways. Because these technologies enable people to talk over large distances as well as keep short-distance ties, distance has become less of a barrier to the cultivation and maintenance of personal communities (Mok et al., 2009).

With the explosive growth of new communications technologies, the contemporary world is undergoing a 'triple revolution': an Internet revolution, a mobile revolution and a social network revolution (Rainie and Wellman, forthcoming). The *Internet revolution* has opened up renewed ways of communicating and finding information. The power of knowledge is no longer the monopoly of professionals, because common folk can now research on the Internet and compare notes with healthcare and financial experts. This Internet revolution is bound up with the *mobile revolution*, which allows individuals to communicate and gather information while on the move. With greater connectivity all around, people can engage their networks and access information regardless of their physical locations. Home bases are still important as sources of ideas and inspiration, but the mobile revolution ensures that people never lose touch with either their home bases or their other important social worlds.

These technological changes are in reciprocal acceleration with the *social network revolution*. While social networks have always been with us, the Internet and mobile revolutions are both weakening group boundaries and expanding the reach, number and velocity of interpersonal ties. Modern individuals have become networked, managing their personal communities with the help of communication technologies as social affordances. Taken together, the personal community approach accurately reflects the habits of modern people who are profoundly and individually mobile and networked.

NOTES

We appreciate the financial support of the Intel Corporation's People and Practices unit, the Social Sciences and Humanities Research Council of Canada and the National University of Singapore. We have learned much from our NetLab colleagues, present and past, at the Department of Sociology, University of Toronto. We thank Natalie Zinko for her editorial help.

REFERENCES

Anderssen, E. (2009) 'Lent's most controversial sacrifice: Facebook', *Toronto Globe and Mail,* March 7.

Antonucci, T. and Akiyama, H. (1995) 'Convoys of social relations', in Rosemary Blieszner and Victoria H. Bedford (eds.), *Handbook of Aging and the Family.* Westport, CT: Greenwood Press. pp. 355–72.

Baron, N. (2008) *Always On.* Oxford: Oxford University Press.

Bastani, S. (2007) 'Family comes first: men's and women's personal networks in Tehran', *Social Networks* 29(3): 357–74.

Bender, T. (1978) *Community and Social Change in America.* New Brunswick NJ: Rutgers University Press.

Benedict XVI, Pope (2009) *Message for the World Day of Communication.* http://www.vatican.va/holy_father/benedict_xvi/messages/communications/documents/hf_ben-xvi_mes_20090124_43rd-world-communicationsday_en.html.

Bian, Y. (1997) 'Bringing strong ties back in: indirect ties, network bridges, and job searches in China', *American Sociological Review* 62(3): 366–85.

Blau, P. (1977) *Inequality and Heterogeneity.* New York: Free Press.

Boase, J., Horrigan, J., Wellman, B. and Rainie, L. (2006) 'The strength of Internet ties', *The Pew Internet and American Life Project.* Washington, DC.

Boase, J. and Wellman, B. (2006) 'Personal relationships: On and off the Internet', in Anita Vangelisti and Dan Perlman (eds.), *Cambridge Handbook of Personal Relationships*. Cambridge: Cambridge University Press. pp. 709–23.

Boissevain, J. (1974) *Friends of Friends*. Oxford: Blackwell.

Burt, R. (1984) 'Network items and the General Social Survey', *Social Networks* 6: 293–339.

Burt, R. (1997) 'The contingent value of social capital', *Administrative Science Quarterly* 42(2): 339–65.

Chen, W. and Wellman, B. (2009) 'Net and jet: the Internet use, travel and social networks of Chinese Canadian entrepreneurs', *Information, Communication and Society* 12(4): 525–47.

Coleman, J. (1988) 'Social capital in the creation of human capital', *American Journal of Sociology* 94: S95–S120.

Collins, J. and Wellman, B. (2010) 'Small town in the Internet society', *American Behavioral Scientist* 53(9): 1344–66.

de Vries, B. (1996) 'The understanding of friendship: an adult life course perspective', in Carol Margai and Susan McFadden (eds.), *Handbook of Emotion, Adult Development and Aging*. San Diego, CA: Academic Press. pp. 249–68.

Dunbar, R. (1996) *Grooming, Gossip, and the Evolution of Language*. London: Faber and Faber.

Erickson, B. (1988) 'The relational basis of attitudes', in Barry Wellman and Stephen Berkowitz (eds.), *Social Structures*. New York: Cambridge University Press. pp. 99–121.

Erickson, B. (1996) 'Culture, class, and connections', *American Journal of Sociology* 102(1): 217–51.

Erickson, B. (2001) 'Good networks and good jobs: the value of social capital to employers and employees', in Nan Lin, Ronald S. Burt and Karen Cook (eds.), *Social Capital: Theory and Research*. New York: Aldine de Gruyter. pp. 127–57.

Erickson, B. (2003) 'Social networks: the value of variety', *Contexts* 2(1): 25–31.

Erickson, B. (2004a) 'A report on measuring the social capital in weak ties', Policy Research Initiative, Ottawa, Canada. pp. 1–16.

Erickson, B. (2004b) 'The distribution of gendered social capital in Canada', in Henk Flap and Beate Völker (eds.), *Creation and Returns of Social Capital*. New York: Routledge. pp. 27–50.

Espinoza, V. (1999) 'Social networks among the urban poor: Inequality and integration in a Latin American city', in Barry Wellman (ed.), *Networks in the Global Village*. Boulder, CO: Westview. pp. 147–84.

Feld, S. (1981) 'The focused organization of social ties', *American Journal of Sociology* 86: 1015–35.

Ferligoj, A. and Hlebec, V. (1999) 'Evaluation of social network measurement instruments', *Social Networks* 21: 111–30.

Fernández, R.M., Castilla, E.J. and Moore, P. (2000) 'Social capital at work: networks and employment at a phone center', *American Journal of Sociology* 105(5): 1288–356.

Ferrand, A., Mounier, L. and Degenne, A. (1999) 'The diversity of personal networks in France', in Barry Wellman (ed.), *Networks in the Global Village*. Boulder, CO: Westview. pp. 185–224.

Fischer, C. (1982) *To Dwell Among Friends*. Berkeley: University of California Press.

Fischer, C., Jackson, R.M., Steuve, C.A., Gerson, K., McCallister, L.J. and Baldassare, M. (1977) *Networks and Places*. New York: Free Press.

Fu, Y.-C. (2008) 'Position generator and actual networks in everyday life: an evaluation with contact diary', in Nan Lin and Bonnie H. Erickson (eds.), *Social Capital*. New York: Oxford University Press. pp. 49–64.

Gans, H. (1962) *The Urban Villagers*. New York: Free Press.

Gans, H. (1967) *The Levittowners*. New York: Pantheon.

Gold, T., Guthrie, D. and Wank, D. (eds.) (2002) *Social Connections in China*. Cambridge: Cambridge University Press.

Gotham, K.F. and Brumley, K. (2002) 'Using space', *City and Community* 1(3): 267–89.

Granovetter, M. (1973) 'The strength of weak ties', *American Journal of Sociology* 78: 1360–80.

Granovetter, M. (1995) *Getting a Job,* 2nd ed. Chicago: University of Chicago Press.

Green, G., Tigges, L. and Browne, I. (1995) 'Social resources, job search, and poverty in Atlanta', *Research in Community Sociology* 5: 161–82.

Grossetti, M. (2007) 'Are French networks different?' *Social Networks* 29(3): 391–404.

Hampton, K. and Wellman, B. (2002) 'The not so global village of Netville', in Barry Wellman and Caroline Haythornthwaite (eds.), *The Internet in Everyday Life*. Oxford: Blackwell. pp. 345–71.

Hampton, K. and Wellman, B. (2003) 'Neighbouring in Netville', *City and Community* 2(4): 277–311.

Hannerz, U. (1980) *Exploring the City*. New York: Columbia University Press.

Hennig, M. (2007) 'Re-evaluating the community question from a German perspective', *Social Networks* 29(3): 375–90.

Hiller, H. and Franz, T. (2004) 'New ties, old ties and lost ties: the use of the Internet in diaspora', *New Media & Society* 6: 731–52.

Hochschild, A.R. (1997) *The Time Bind*. New York: Metropolitan.

Hogan, B. (2008a). 'A comparison of on and offline networks using the Facebook API'. QMSS2: Communication Networks on the Web. Amsterdam, December.

Hogan, B. (2008b) 'Networking in everyday life'. PhD dissertation, University of Toronto, Toronto.

Hogan, B., Carrasco, J.-A. and Wellman, B. (2007) 'Visualizing personal networks: working with participant-aided sociograms', *Field Methods* 19(2): 116–44.

Ignacio, E.N. (2005) *Building Diaspora: Filipino Community Formation on the Internet*. New Brunswick, NJ: Rutgers University Press.

Keller, S. (1968) *The Urban Neighborhood*. New York: Random House.

Kraut, R., Kiesler, S., Boneva, B., Cummings, J., Helgeson, V. and Crawford, A. (2002) 'Internet paradox revisited', *Journal of Social Issues* 58(1): 49–74.

Laumann, E. (1973) *Bonds of Pluralism*. New York: Wiley.

Laumann, E., Gagnon, J., Michael, R. and Michaels, S. (1994) *The Social Organization of Sexuality: Sexual*

Practices in the United States. Chicago: University of Chicago Press.

Lee, B., Campbell, K. and Miller, O. (1991) 'Racial differences in urban neighboring', *Sociological Forum* 6: 525–50.

Lenhart, A., Madden, M. and Hitlin, P. (2005) 'Teens and technology', *Pew Internet and American Life Project*, Washington.

Lin, N. (2000) 'Inequality in social capital', *Contemporary Society* 29(6): 785–95.

Lin, N. (2001) *Social Capital.* Cambridge: Cambridge University Press.

Lin, N. and Dumin, M. (1986) 'Access to occupations through social ties', *Social Networks* 8: 365–83.

Lin, N. and Erickson, B. (2008) 'Theory, measurement, and the research enterprise on social capital', in Nan Lin and Bonnie H. Erickson (eds.), *Social Capital: An International Research Program.* New York: Oxford University Press. 1–24.

Lin, N., Fu, Y.-C. and Hsung, R.-M. (2001) 'The position generator: measurement techniques for investigations of social capital', in Nan Lin, Karen Cook, and Ronald Burt (eds.), *Social Capital: Theory and Research.* New York: Aldine de Gruyter. pp. 57–81.

Marin, A. (2004) 'Are respondents more likely to list alters with certain characteristics?' *Social Networks* 26: 289–307.

Marin, A. (2008) 'Depth, breadth, and social capital'. Paper presented at the American *Sociological Association Annual Meeting*, Boston.

Marsden, P. (1987) 'Core discussions networks of Americans', *American Sociological Review* 52: 122–31.

Marsden, P. (1988) 'Homogeneity in confiding networks', *Social Networks* 10(1): 57–76.

Marsden, P. (2005) 'Recent developments in network measurement', in Peter Carrington, John Scott, and Stanley Wasserman (eds.), *Models and Methods in Social Network Analysis.* Cambridge: Cambridge University Press. pp. 8–30.

Marsden, P. and Campbell, K. (1984) 'Measuring tie strength', *Social Forces* 63: 482–501.

Martineau, W. (1977) 'Informal ties among urban Black Americans', *Journal of Black Studies* 8: 83–104.

McCarty, C. (2002) 'Measuring structure in personal networks', *Journal of Social Structure* 3: 1.

McCarty, C., Killworth, P., Bernard, H.R., Shelley, G.A. and Johnsen, E. (2001) 'Comparing two methods for estimating network size', *Human Organization* 60: 28–39.

McPherson, M. and Smith-Lovin, L. (1987) 'Homophily in voluntary organizations', *American Sociological Review* 52: 370–79.

McPherson, M., Smith, Lovin, L. and Brashears, M. (2006) 'Social isolation in America', *American Sociological Review* 71: 353–75.

Miller, D. and Slater, D. (2000) *The Internet: An Ethnographic Approach.* Oxford: Berg.

Mirowsky, J. and Ross, C.E. (1999) 'Well-being across the life course', in Allan V. Horwitz and Teresa L. Scheid (eds.), *A Handbook for the Study of Mental Health.* Cambridge: Cambridge University Press. 328–47.

Mok, D., Wellman, B. and Carrasco, J.-A. (2010) 'Does distance still matter in the age of the Internet?', *Urban Studies* 47 (13): 2743–83.

Moore, G. (1990) 'Structural determinants of men's and women's personal networks', *American Sociological Review* 55: 726–35.

Moren-Cross, J.L. and Lin, N. (2008) 'Access to social capital and status attainment in the United States', in Nan Lin and Bonnie Erickson (eds.), *Social Capital: An International Research Program.* New York: Oxford University Press. pp. 364–79.

Olson-Buchanan, J. and Boswell, W. (2006) 'Blurring boundaries ', *Journal of Vocational Behavior* 68: 432–45.

Pescosolido, B. (1992) 'Beyond rational choice', *American Journal of Sociology* 97: 1096–138.

Pickard, S. (1995) *Living on the Front Line.* Aldershot: Avebury.

Plickert, G., Côté, R. and Wellman, B. (2007) 'It's not who you know, it's how you know them', *Social Networks* 29(3): 405–29.

Putnam, R. (2000) *Bowling Alone.* New York: Simon and Schuster.

Quan-Haase, A., Wellman, B., Witte, J. and Hampton, K. (2002) 'Capitalizing on the net', in Barry Wellman and Caroline Haythornthwaite (eds.), *The Internet in Everyday Life.* Oxford: Blackwell. pp. 291–324.

Rainie, L. and Wellman, B. (forthcoming) *Networked: The New Social Operating System.* Cambridge, MA: MIT Press.

Reskin, B. and McBrier, D.B. (2000) 'Why not ascription?' *American Sociological Review* 62: 210–33.

Robinson, J.P., Kestnbaum, M., Neustadl, A. and Alvarez, A. (2002) 'The Internet and other uses of time', in Barry Wellman and Caroline Haythornthwaite (eds.), *The Internet in Everyday Life.* Oxford: Blackwell. pp. 244–62.

Ruan, D., Freeman, L., Dai, X., Pan, Y. and Zhang, W. (1997) 'On the changing structure of social networks in urban China', *Social Networks* 19(1): 75–90.

Salaff, J., Fong, E. and Wong, S.-l. (1999) 'Using social networks to exit Hong Kong', in Barry Wellman (ed.), *Networks in the Global Village.* Boulder, Colorado: Westview. pp. 299–329.

Sigman, A. (2009) 'Well connected? The biological implications of social networking', *Biologist* 56(1): 14–20.

Smith, S.S. (2005) 'Don't put my name on it: social capital activation and job-finding assistance among the Black urban poor', *American Journal of Sociology* 111: 1–57.

Stack, C. (1974) *All Our Kin.* New York: Harper & Row.

Stern, M. (2008) 'How locality, frequency of communication, and Internet usage affect modes of communication within core social networks', *Information, Communication, and Society* 11(5): 591–616.

Stern, M. and Messer, C. (2009) 'How family members stay in touch', *Marriage and Family Review* 45.

Straits, B. (2000) 'Ego's important discussants or significant people', *Social Networks* 22: 123–40.

Uehara, E. (1990) 'Dual exchange theory, social networks, and informal social support', *American Journal of Sociology* 96(3): 521–57.

van der Gaag, M. and Snijders, T.A.B. (2005) 'The resource generator', *Social Networks* 27: 1–27.

van der Gaag, M., Snijders, T.A.B. and Flap, H. (2008) 'Position generator measures and their relationship to other social capital measures'. In Nan Lin and Bonnie H. Erickson (eds.), *Social Capital: An International Research Program*. New York: Oxford University Press. pp. 27–48.

Veenhof, B., Wellman, B., Quell, C. and Hogan, B. (2008, December 4) 'How Canadians' use of the Internet affects social life and civic participation'. Connectedness report series. http://www.statcan.gc.ca/pub/56f0004m/6f0004m2008016-eng.pdf.

Völker, B. and Flap, H. (2001) 'Weak ties as a liability: the case of East Germany', *Rationality and Society* 13(4): 397–428.

Wang, H. and Wellman, B. (2010) 'Social connectivity in America', *American Behavioral Scientist* 53 (8): 1148–69.

Wellman, B. (1979) 'The community question', *American Journal of Sociology* 84: 1201–31.

Wellman, B. (1985) 'Domestic work, paid work and net work'. In Steve Duck and Daniel Perlman (eds.), *Understanding Personal Relationships*. London: Sage. pp.159–91.

Wellman, B. (1990) 'The place of kinfolk in community networks', *Marriage and Family Review* 15(1/2): 195–228.

Wellman, B. (ed.) (1999) *Networks in the Global Village*. Boulder, CO: Westview Press.

Wellman, B. (2001a) 'Physical place and cyber place: the rise of personalized networking', *International Journal of Urban and Regional Research* 25(2): 227–52.

Wellman, B. (2001b) 'The persistence and transformation of community: from neighbourhood groups to social networks', Report to the Law Commission of Canada.

Wellman, B. (2002) 'Little boxes, glocalization, and networked individualism', in Makoto Tanabe, Peter van den Besselaar, and Toru Ishida (eds.), *Digital Cities II*. Berlin: Springer. pp. 10–25.

Wellman, B. (2007) 'The network is personal', *Social Networks* 29(3): 349–56.

Wellman, B., Carrington, P. and Hall, A. (1988) 'Networks as personal communities', in Barry Wellman and S.D. Berkowitz (eds.), *Social Structures*. Cambridge: Cambridge University Press. pp. 130–84.

Wellman, B., Chen, W. and Dong, W. (2002) 'Networking Guanxi', in Thomas Gold, Douglas Guthrie, and David Wank (eds.), *Social Connections in China*. Cambridge: Cambridge University Press. pp. 221–41.

Wellman, B. and Haythornthwaite, C. (eds.) (2002) *The Internet in Everyday Life*. Oxford: Blackwell.

Wellman, B., Hogan, B., Berg, K., Boase, J., Carrasco, J.-A., Cote, R., Kayahara, J., Kennedy, T. and Tran, P. (2006) 'Connected lives: the project', in Patrick Purcell (ed.), *Networked Neighbourhoods: The Online Community in Context*. Guilford, UK: Springer. pp. 157–211.

Wellman, B. and Tindall, D. (1993) 'Reach out and touch some bodies', *Progress in Communication Science* 12: 63–94.

Wellman, B. and Wellman, B. (1992) 'Domestic affairs and network relations', *Journal of Social and Personal Relationships* 9: 385–409.

Wellman, B. and Wortley, S. (1990) 'Different strokes from different folks', *American Journal of Sociology* 96: 558–88.

Wilding, R. (2006) 'Virtual intimacies? Families communicating across transnational contexts', *Global Networks* 6(2): 125–42.

Young, M. and Willmott, P. (1957) *Family and Kinship in East London*. Harmondsworth, UK: Penguin.

Zinc Research and Dufferin Research. (2008) 'Canadians and social networking sites'. Toronto: Zinc Research.

9

Social Support

Lijun Song, Joonmo Son, and Nan Lin

Social support, a network-based social phenomenon, has become the focus of research attention in the last three decades. As shown by a search of the Social Sciences Citation Index for articles whose topics include "social support," there were only three such articles in the 1950s and ten in the 1960s. The number rose to 76 in the 1970s. Following this, on average per year, there were 94 such articles in the 1980s, 1,394 in the 1990s, and 2,687 from 2000 to 2008. Social support has attracted burgeoning attention especially in health literature, and the lack of social support is regarded as a potential fundamental cause of disease (Link and Phelan, 1995). In another search of the Social Sciences Citation Index for articles with "social support" and "health" in their topics reports (see Figure 9.1), on average per year, there were less than six articles from 1976 to 1989; the number increased to 445 in the 1990s and dramatically jumped to 1,135 from 2000 to 2008. A few books explored the relationship between social support and its health consequences (Caplan, 1974; Caplan and Killilea, 1976; Cohen and Syme, 1985; Cohen, Underwood et al., 2000; Gottlieb, 1981, 1983; House, 1981; Lin et al., 1986). Many reviews from different disciplinary backgrounds have surveyed the associations of social support with various health-related outcomes (Alcalay, 1983; Berkman, 1984, 2000; Coyne and Downey, 1991; Ell, 1984; Faber and Wasserman, 2002; Green, 1993; House, 1987; Umberson et al., 1988a; Kessler et al., 1985; Schwarzer and Leppin, 1991; Smith et al., 1994; Thoits, 1995; Turner and Turner, 1999).

Despite its substantial popularity and voluminous development, "social support" still stimulates debates on its conceptualization and operationalization. Social support is confounded with other network-based but distinct social factors without clear discrimination, such as social cohesion, social integration, social networks, and social capital. Empirical results on its health returns are abundant but inconsistent across studies. We thus begin this review by clarifying the nature and forms of social support. We then turn to its distinction from and association with other network-based factors. Next, we examine the operation of social support in the social production process of disease and illness. We conclude with a brief discussion of future research directions of social support research. Even though social support is a sociological phenomenon in nature, the existing literature on the topic has been dominated by epidemiologists, psychiatrists, and psychologists, as Umberson et al. (1988a) observed two decades ago. Sociologists are expected to play a crucial role in the advancement of future studies on social support.

CONCEPT OF SOCIAL SUPPORT: NATURE AND FORMS

The idea of social support has achieved great currency since the mid-1970s (for reviews, see Barrera, 1981, 1986; Gottlieb et al., 2000; Dean and Lin, 1977; Gottlieb, 1981; Lin, 1986a;

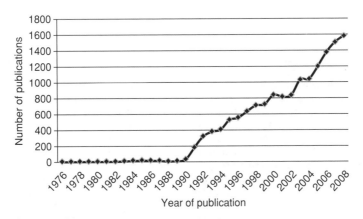

Figure 9.1 Articles with "social support" and "health" in topic: social sciences citation index

Thoits, 1982). Epidemiologist John Cassel, physician and epidemiologist Sidney Cobb, and psychiatrist Gerald Caplan make groundbreaking contributions to its popularity. Cassel and Cobb summarize accumulating empirical evidence on the promising impact of relational factors in health maintenance and promotion, and underscore social support as one such protective antecedent. Cassel (1974, 1976) dichotomizes various social conditions relevant to health from a functionalist perspective: one category protects health, while the other one produces disease. He speaks broadly of social support as the first category, "the protective factors buffering or cushioning the individual from the physiologic or psychological consequences of exposure to the stressor situation" (1976: 113). Cobb (1974, 1976) uses a communication perspective. He (1976) conceives of social support as information, and he classifies three types of information in terms of their functions: information leading a person to believe that he or she is cared for and loved (i.e., emotional support), is esteemed and valued (i.e., esteem support), and belongs to a network of communication and mutual obligation. Similar to Cassel's definition, Cobb argues that the major protective role of social support lies in its moderating effect on life stress instead of its main health effect. In addition, Caplan (1974: 6–7) addresses the concept of the support system as "an enduring pattern of continuous or intermittent ties that play a significant part in maintaining the psychological and physical integrity of the individual over time," and he lists three types of support activities: "The significant others help the individual mobilize his psychological resources and master his emotional burdens; they share his tasks; and they provide him with extra supplies of money, materials, tools,

skills, and cognitive guidance to improve his handling of his situation."

More attempts to conceptualize the substance of social support from different perspectives quickly followed. Dean and Lin (1977) consider social support as functions of primary groups that meet instrumental and expressive needs. Lin and colleagues later reconstruct social support at multiple levels of social networks as "support accessible to an individual through social ties to other individuals, groups, and the larger community" (Lin et al., 1979: 109). Kaplan and colleagues (Kaplan et al., 1977: 54) point out that social support is the content of social ties (i.e., "the meanings that persons in the network give their relationships"), and it is contingent on structural and interactional characteristics of social networks (i.e., anchorage, reachability, density, range, directedness, intensity, and frequency). Henderson (1977) applies attachment theory and views social support as affectively positive social interaction with others under stressful conditions. Gottlieb (1978) lists four forms of informal social support derived from 26 helping behaviors: emotionally sustaining behaviors, problem-solving behaviors, indirect personal influence, and environmental actions. Wellman (1981) dichotomizes the content of social ties. He asserts that social support is only one type of content; the other is nonsupport. He lists five forms of social support derived from 21 interactional strands: doing things, giving and lending things, helping with personal problems, helping with information, and sharing activities, values, interests, and interaction. He also highlights the variation of social support with network properties (i.e., tie strength, tie symmetry, density). Pearlin and colleagues view social support as "the access to and use of individuals, groups, or organizations in dealing with life's vicissitudes" (1981: 340). House and his colleagues define social support as one type of relational content, "the emotionally or instrumentally sustaining quality of social relationships" (Umberson et al., 1988a: 293). Berkman (1984) sees social support as the emotional, instrumental, and financial aid that is obtained from one's social network. More recently, Turner (1999) defines social support as social bonds, social integration, and primary group relations. Cohen and colleagues refer to social support as "any process through which social relationships might promote health and well-being" (Gottlieb et al., 2000: 4).

These different conceptualizations reflect an ambiguous construction of the social support concept. Despite the inconsistent framing, most of these efforts explicitly or implicitly converge on the relationship-based, assisting nature of social support. Based on the above review, we are more attracted to a strict synthetic definition of social support as the aid – the supply of tangible or intangible resources – individuals gain from their network members (Berkman, 1984; House, 1981). This definition narrows down social support to a specific relational content, separates its nature from its preceding social structures such as social networks and social integration, and eliminates its tautological assumption that social support protects against disease and that what fosters health is social support. The stretching of social support as general environmental factors (Cassel, 1976), relational content (Kaplan et al., 1977; Henderson, 1977), or relational process (Gottlieb et al., 2000) paves the way for diverse measurements and mixed evidence, and endangers the unique theoretical value of social support. The functionalist framing of social support (Cassel, 1976; Gottlieb et al., 2000; Henderson, 1977) mixes social support with its consequences, and this overlooks the fact that social support does not always function in a positive direction to meet needs or to intervene between stressors and health. The disease- or stress-related definition (Cassel, 1976; Cobb, 1976; Gottlieb et al., 2000; Henderson, 1977; Pearlin et al., 1981) constrains the significance of social support within the health area, which would be applicable to the production of other consequences and the general stratification process.

Most conceptualizing efforts also converge on multifaceted forms of social support. Social support can be categorized in different ways. In terms of its content, for example, social support can be divided into emotional support (liking, love, empathy); instrumental support (goods and services); informational support (information about the environment); or appraisal support (information relevant to self-evaluation) (House, 1981). In terms of its degree of subjectivity, social support is dichotomized into perceived support and objective or actual support (Caplan, 1979). In terms of the role relationship between the recipient and the donor (Dean and Lin, 1977; LaRocco et al., 1980; Thoits, 1982), social support could be kin-based (e.g., parents, spouses, children, siblings, other relatives) or nonkin-based (e.g., friends, neighbors, co-workers). In terms of its contexts, social support could be routine support within an ordinary situation or nonroutine support within a crisis situation (Lin et al., 1986). Social support is thus a multidimensional construct. Its exhaustive typology is beyond the scope of this chapter. A cross-tabulation following the foregoing strategies produces 32 forms of social support. Also, social support is traditionally used as a single directional concept and refers only to received support, which is support egos get from their network members. Some argue that social support is bidirectional (Pearlin, 1985; Wellman, 1981). Egos not only receive support from alters but also give support to alters or reciprocate support with alters. Providing or reciprocating support has received limited attention. We will focus on received support in the rest of this chapter.

DISTINCTION FROM OTHER NETWORK-BASED CONCEPTS

Theoretical distinction

Social support thus rigorously conceived allows us to distinguish it from other network-based but distinct preconditions of disease and illness such as social cohesion, social integration, social networks, and another recently popular construct, social capital. The health consequences of these four factors have also been well documented (for reviews, see Berkman, 1995; Berkman and Glass, 2000; Berkman et al., 2000; Greenblatt et al., 1982; Landis et al., 1988b; Kawachi et al., 2008; Kawachi and Berkman, 2001; Lin and Peek, 1999; Luke and Harris, 2007; Pescosolido and Levy, 2002; Smith and Christakis, 2008; Song et al., 2010; Stansfeld, 2006). However, the distinction between social support and these factors tends to be blurred in recent health literature. Some put social networks, social integration, and social resources under the rubric of social support (e.g., Elliott, 2000; Lin et al., 1999; Roxburgh, 2006; Turner, 1999). One recent fashionable trend is to subsume social support together with social cohesion, social integration, and social networks under the popular umbrella of social capital (e.g., Carpiano, 2006; Coleman, 1990; Putnam, 2000; Szreter and Woolcock, 2004).

Such an entangled conceptualization jeopardizes the unique heuristic utility of each concept and confounds their causal relationships. To overcome this theoretical issue scholars have attempted to distinguish them from each other (Berkman et al., 2000; Umberson et al., 1988a; House and Kahn, 1985). We have made careful efforts to differentiate them elsewhere (Song and Lin, 2009). To begin, a social network is "a specific set of linkages among a defined set of persons, with the additional property that the characteristics of these linkages as a whole may be used to interpret the social behavior of the persons involved" (Mitchell, 1969: 2). Its simplest form is a dyadic social tie. A social network is not a theory but a perspective (Mitchell, 1974). It provides guides to explore various network properties, their causes, and consequences. Network properties may be objective, including tie attributes such as tie strength and relational contents; structural attributes such as network size; and compositional attributes such as network members' characteristics. They may also be subjective, such as network norms. Specific theories such as social cohesion, social integration, social capital, and social support are derived from the network perspective (Berkman et al., 2000; Lin and Peek, 1999; Pescosolido, 2007). Social cohesion is the degree of social bonds and social equality within social networks, indicated by trust, norms of reciprocity, and the lack of social conflict (Kawachi and Berkman, 2000). Social integration is the extent of participation in social networks, indicated by active engagement in social roles and social activities, and cognitive identification with network members (Brissette et al., 2000). Social capital is resources embedded in social networks, measured as structural positions of one's network members (Lin, 1999a).

Thus conceived (see Figure 9.2), social support is separated from its structural contexts (Dohrenwood and Dohrenwood, 1981; House and Kahn, 1985; Lin et al., 1999). Social cohesion as a norm is more upstream in the causal chain, and it may regulate properties of other network-based

factors. Social integration is positively associated with the quality and quantity of social capital and social support by maintaining old relationships and establishing new relationships. Social capital is a source of social support because network members' resources are drawn for various supportive purposes. Social support may therefore be conceived as a downstream factor subsequent to the operation of social cohesion, social integration, and social capital, and other network features. Certain indicators of social integration, social capital, and other network characteristics may act as proximate measures of social support. The relationship between these network-based factors is indeed reciprocal and dynamic from a longitudinal perspective. For example, the activation process of social support, either satisfying and effective or unsatisfying and ineffective may redirect the degree and form of social integration, reconstruct the availability of social capital, and finally reshape the strength of social cohesion. After clarifying the meaning of these terms, we turn to empirical evidence on the network contingency of social support. Little attention has been paid to the relationship between social cohesion and social support. We review a few studies on the associations of social integration, social capital, and other network features with social support.

Empirical evidence: the network contingency of social support

Social integration fosters the production of social support. Lin and colleagues (Lin et al., 1999) use a community sample of adults. They measure social support based on 40 items in a survey, and they derive four latent factors to respectively indicate perceived instrumental support, actual instrumental support, perceived expressive support, and actual expressive support. As they report, social integration (or participation in community organizations, in their own words) directly leads to more actual instrumental support, indirectly increases all types of support through expanding network size (i.e., the number of weekly contacts), and indirectly produces perceived and actual instrumental support by increasing the chance of the presence of an intimate relationship. Seeman and Berkman (1988) analyze a community sample of older adults. Two types of perceived support, instrumental (i.e., help on daily tasks) and emotional (i.e., talking over problems and decision making), are both positively associated with network size; number of face-to-face contacts; number of proximal ties; having a confidant relationship; and direct contacts with children, friends, and relatives. One specific form of social integration, religious participation, and its linkage to

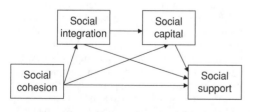

Figure 9.2 A conceptual model of social support and its network-based sources

social support has received much attention. Ellison and George (1994) employ a community sample of adults. Their findings vary with the measurements and the types of actual support. They presented a list to respondents of 13 types of support and asked whether their network members ever offered these types of support. If each type of received support is measured separately as dummy variables, the frequency of religious attendance is positively associated with the supplies of 4 out of 13 types of support: gifts or presents, business or financial advice, house maintenance and repair tasks, and running errands. When they measure received support as a summed score ranging from 0 to 13, the frequency of religious attendance increases the variety of received support only indirectly through expanding the size of networks (i.e., number of nonkin ties, in-person contacts, and telephone contacts). Nooney and Woodrum (2002) focus on religious participation and church-based support. Using a national sample of adults, they find that the frequency of church attendance is positively associated with perceived support from their congregations. Taylor and Chatters (1988) investigate a national sample of African Americans, and report that the frequency of church attendance expands the chance of receiving support from people in the church. In a study of national longitudinal data of adolescents (Petts and Julliff, 2008), social support (i.e., how much adults, teachers, parents, and friends care about them; and how much their family understands them, cares about them, and has fun together) explains away the effect of religious participation on depression.

The positive linkage of social capital to health and economic well-being has been documented (Lin, 1999b; Song et al., 2010). As social capital researchers generally assume, social capital contributes to various returns by providing a higher level of different forms of social support, such as information, influence, social credential, and reinforced identity (Lin, 2001). However, direct examinations of the impact of social capital on social support are very limited if we operationalize social capital strictly as structural positions of network members (Lin, 2001). Empirical results are also mixed. One study examines the relationship between social capital and informational support (Lin and Ao, 2008). It employs a national sample of currently or previously employed adults between 21 and 64 years of age and captures informational support by asking respondents whether they received job information at the time they started their current job. They map positional networks through the position generator that asked respondents to identify contacts, if any, in each of 22 occupational positions at the time they started their current job. Social capital is derived

from three indicators of positional networks: range (i.e., the difference of the highest and lowest prestige scores among the positions that each respondent could access), extensity (i.e., the number of different positions each respondent could access), and upper reachability (i.e., the highest score among accessed positions). They find a significant positive effect of social capital on the receipt of job information. Another study (Wellman and Wortley, 1990) collected information on 29 respondents' active network members in the East York section of Toronto, the total of which is around 335. It finds no association between network members' socioeconomic positions (i.e., education, employment status, and occupational status) and five indicators of actual support (i.e., emotional aid, major services, small services, financial aid, and companionship). In addition, one study explores the influence of social capital on actual support in a natural disaster context (Beggs et al., 1996). The authors interviewed residents in two communities after Hurricane Andrew in Louisiana and collected information on their core networks prior to the disaster and on their actual support as well as support from formal organizations during disaster recovery. They measure 11 network characteristics. Among them, the proportion of alters with less than a high school education reflects structural locations of network members and is the most proximate indicator of social capital. That proportion is positively associated with the receipt of informal recovery support. This finding seems to disconfirm our previous causal argument on the positive association of social capital with social support. As the authors explain, that finding is consistent with previous disaster studies. The underlying rationale is that individuals with less education may possess disaster-relevant occupational skills. Such a finding implies that the function of social capital in the social distribution of social support varies across social contexts.

Apart from social integration and social capital, other network features also shape the process of social support. Haines and Hurlbert (1992) study a community sample of adults. They measure three indicators of perceived support: instrumental (i.e., having enough people to get help), companionship (i.e., having enough people with whom to socialize), and emotional (i.e., having enough people to talk to). The average number of contents per tie decreases instrumental support only for women; the proportion of kin among alters increases instrumental support only for men; and density among alters increases companionship and emotional aid for men only. Wellman and Wortley's East York study (1989) observes that various forms of actual support vary with kinship relations. Parents and adult children offer higher levels of emotional aid, services, and financial aid; siblings especially supplement the provision of services; and extended kin are least supportive and less companionable. They further report (Wellman and Wortley, 1990) that stronger ties, measured as a higher degree of intimacy and voluntary interaction within diverse contexts, supply wider support and offer more emotional aid, small services, and companionship, and that physically accessible ties tend to provide services. They do not find significant associations of actual support with frequency of contact, group's interconnections, and positional similarity between egos and network members. A more recent study (Plickert et al., 2007) investigates determinants of reciprocal exchange of emotional support, minor services, and major services. It reports significant associations between the giving and receiving of emotional support, the giving and receiving of minor services, and the giving and receiving of major services. It also finds partial evidence that giving one type of resource is associated with getting other types of resources in turn. Being a neighbor, a parent, or an adult child is positively associated with reciprocal support of major and minor services. The number of ties is positively associated with reciprocal emotional support. Tie strength does not exert a significant effect. We next review the theoretical and empirical evidence for the role of social support in the social production of disease and illness.

HEALTH RETURNS TO SOCIAL SUPPORT

Theoretical modeling

Social support initially received research attention only as a buffer in the association of stressors with mental health (Cassel, 1976; Cobb, 1976; Kaplan et al., 1977). Most individuals have limited personal capital. When encountering undesirable life events they are expected to use social capital (i.e., personal capital of their network members) to supplement their personal capital through the process of social support. This process may reduce the negative health effects of stressful life events. In the last three decades diverse models linking social support to health have been developed (Barrera, 1986; Berkman, 2000; Gottlieb et al., 2000; Dohrenwend and Dohrenwend, 1981; Ensel and Lin, 1991; Umberson et al., 1988a; Lin, 1986b; Thoits, 1982; Wheaton, 1985). Most of these modeling efforts focus on the health functions of social support in the stressor-distress framework. We attempt to summarize these efforts, extend them beyond that framework, and focus on

the crucial operation of social support. From a social causation perspective, social support has four major roles in the production of health: main effect, mediating effect, indirect effect, and moderating effect. The main effect hypothesis states that social support can protect health net of other social preconditions. In other words, social support adds a unique explanatory power to the social etiology of health and illness. Personal capital such as socioeconomic status is a fundamental cause of disease and illness (Link and Phelan, 1995). Therefore social support, the use of personal capital from network members, is expected to exert a direct health effect as well. The mediating effect hypothesis argues that social support may act as an intermediate variable, and it may intervene in the relationship between its precursors and health consuences. As mentioned earlier, other network-based factors such as social integration or social capital may exert positive health impacts through strengthening social support. Personal resources such as socioeconomic status may have similar indirect health effects by determining the quality and quantity of social support. Stressors could play similar roles by either triggering the use of social support or diminishing its availability. The indirect effect hypothesis holds that social support may prevent disease indirectly by shaping other health risk factors, such as health behaviors, psychological resources, and the physiological system (Berkman et al., 2000; Umberson et al., 1988a). Also, as the prominent job search literature in the area of social stratification assumes (Lin, 2001), social capital advances socioeconomic status attainment through the provision of social support. In this context, social support may exert an indirect health effect by increasing socioeconomic positions that are fundamental causes of disease and illness (Link and Phelan, 1995). The moderating effect hypothesis assumes that social support may mitigate or exacerbate the health effects of other risk factors. For example, disadvantaged individuals with lower personal capital may be more motivated to use social support in the protection of health. In this case social support equalizes the inequality effect of personal capital. On the other hand, advantaged individuals may invest more resources in social networking and may be able to use social support more successfully and more efficiently in their access to health resources. Social support could thus intensify the inequality effect of personal capital. Take the stress paradigm as another example. Social support may ameliorate the negative health effect of stressors by helping individuals successfully deal with undesirable life situations. It may also enlarge that negative effect on mental health especially, for example, by increasing the recipients' psychological burden. Furthermore, from a social selection perspective, health status may also influence the availability and activation of social support (Thoits, 1995). There are two possibilities. On one hand, poorer health may provoke the recognition and mobilization of social support. On the other hand, poorer health may produce lower perceived and received social support, because of resultant higher needs for help or because of its constraint on social interaction with network members. Finally, as mentioned earlier, the mainstream social support literature focuses on received support rather than on providing support. The foregoing theoretical modeling applies to received support. Some have argued for the direct and mediating effect of providing social support on health (Krause et al., 1999). Supporting others may protect health directly through fostering personal control, sustaining a sense of self-worth, maintaining network ties, and improving immune functioning. It may also mediate the relationship between religious practice and health.

Next, we selectively review recent empirical evidence. We include only quantitative studies using a noninstitutionalized sample of adults due to limited space and for the purpose of stronger generalizability and more rigorous theoretical examination (Dean and Lin, 1977). We also choose to highlight varying specifications of social support by summarizing these studies one by one.

Empirical evidence

Most studies explore received support. They employ data from cross-sectional surveys and report inconsistent evidence. The health impact of perceived support receives much more attention, and most studies use data from community surveys. In one study (Ross and Mirowsky, 1989), perceived support (i.e., having someone to talk to or run to for support) has a main negative effect on depression. It mediates some positive effects of marriage and education but not those of family income or race/ethnicity. Perceived support also interacts in a complementary manner with the level of control. The positive depression effect of a low level of control is significantly reduced by access to a higher level of perceived support. Another study (Jackson, 1992) examines four-item perceived spouse support and also four-item perceived friend support. The relationship of support with depression depends on the sources of support and the nature of stressors. Spouse support reduces the depression effect of all five kinds of stressors (i.e., marital strain, parental strain, work strain, economic strain, and physical health strain), while friend support plays similar roles only for three kinds of stressors (i.e., marital

strain, economic strain, physical health strain). Roxburgh (2006) investigates perceived support from co-workers and partners. Partner support exerts a main negative effect on depression for both gender groups and does not have moderating effects. Co-worker support has a main negative effect on depression only for men, and it buffers the positive depression effect of the stressor time pressure only for men. Turner and colleagues (Turner and Lloyd, 1999; Turner and Marino, 1994) measure perceived support from partners, relatives, friends, and co-workers based on 25 items. Perceived support has main negative effects on both depressive symptoms and major depressive disorder. It mediates some effects of gender, age, marital status, and soioeconomic status on depressive symptoms but does not mediate their effects on major depressive disorder. It does not moderate the linkages of stressors, age, sex, marital status, and socioeconomic status to both measures of mental health. Haines and Hurlbert (1992) use three indicators of perceived support: instrumental (i.e., having enough people to get help), companionship (i.e., having enough people with whom to socialize), and emotional (i.e., having enough people to talk to). Among them, only companionship exerts a main negative effect on distress. Only this indicator buffers the effect of stressors. Landerman and colleagues (1989) measure perceived support (e.g., the frequency of feeling lonely, feeling understood, feeling useful, feeling listened to, feeling one has a definite role, knowing what is going on with family and friends, and talking about problems) and satisfaction with social support. The negative interaction effects of those two indicators with life events on depression are significant in linear probability models but not in logistic regression models. Elliott (2000) uses two indicators of social support: emotional support (i.e., presence of a confidant) and social integration (i.e., frequency of social interaction). Both types of social support reduce depressive symptoms and protect physical health, but only for residents of higher-socioeconomic neighborhoods. It is speculated that disadvantaged neighborhoods are less likely to foster social interactions between residents, and residents there are less able to offer support.

Four studies investigate perceived support using national samples. Gorman and Sivaganesan (2007) report that social support (i.e., the frequency of getting social or emotional support) does not exert a main effect on both hypertension and self-reported health. Ferraro and Koch (1994) measure perceived emotional support based on a four-item scale (i.e., feeling loved, feeling listened to, feeling demanded, and feeling criticized). This indicator has a direct positive effect on health status (i.e., subjective health, chronic conditions, activity limitation) for both black and white respondents. In contrast, another study (Lincoln et al., 2003) reports racial/ethnic differences. Their latent social support factor is derived from three indicators (i.e., the extent to which respondents feel that relatives understand the way they feel, appreciate them, and can be relied on for help). Social support exerts a main effect on psychological distress only for African Americans. It mediates the effect of personality only for African Americans in that neuroticism decreases social support. It has an indirect negative effect on psychological distress only for whites in that it increases personal control, which decreases distress. Furthermore, Ross and Willigen (1997) analyze two national data sets simultaneously. Both data sets have information on perceived emotional support (i.e., having someone to turn to for help and talk to), and one on perceived instrumental support (i.e., having someone to help with daily tasks and care in sickness). Social support as a sum of emotional and instrumental support in one data set has a main negative effect on four forms of psychological distress such as depression, anxiety, malaise, and aches and pains. In another data set social support as emotional support exerts a similar effect on all outcomes except for aches and pains. They fail to find evidence from both data sets for social support as a significant mediator between education and distress.

A few studies examine both perceived and actual support. Wethington and Kessler (1986) use a national sample of married adults. They have one indicator of perceived support (i.e., the presence of someone to count on for help), and six indicators of actual support: support from providers, support from spouses, support from close relatives, support from others, emotional support, and instrumental support. For those experiencing undesirable life events, perceived instead of actual support has a direct negative effect on psychological distress. Actual spouse support exerts an indirect effect by increasing perceived support.

Lin and colleagues also examine both perceived and actual support in three cross-sectional studies. One study (Lin et al., 1979) uses a community sample of Chinese American adults. Social support is measured by a nine-item scale (i.e., feelings about the neighborhood, feelings about people nearby, frequency of talking with neighbors, having close friends in D.C. area, interaction with friends from old country, involvement in Chinese activities, involvement in Chinese association, being an officer in Chinese association, and being satisfied with job. It has a main negative effect on psychiatric symptoms. It does

not moderate the effect of stressors. Another study (Lin et al., 1999) distinguishes two components of social support: structural support and functional support. It measures three layers of structural support: belonging relationship (i.e., participation in seven types of formal organizations), bonding relationship (i.e., the number of weekly contacts), and binding relationship (i.e., the presence of an intimate tie). It uses 40 items of social support from which four latent factors are derived: perceived and actual instrumental support, and perceived and actual expressive support. Among these indicators, bonding and binding relationships as well as perceived expressive support and actual instrumental support exert main negative effects on depression. Three layers of structural support also have indirect effects on depression by producing actual instrumental support, and the bonding relationship exerts an indirect effect through enhancing perceived emotional support. The third study (Lin et al., 1985) asked respondents to identify their most important life event in the last six months, then asked them about people they interacted with following that event. This collected information on respondents' support networks. The study measures social support in two ways: the strength of ties and the homophily between egos and helpers, assuming that such indicators capture the quality of social support. As the authors observe, strong ties decrease the negative effect of undesirable life events on depression but only for those in a stable marital status. Age and educational homophily reduce depressive symptoms only for the married, while occupational homophily exerts a similar effect only for the unmarried.

Longitudinal studies are limited and also report mixed evidence. In one study of a two-wave community sample (Thoits, 1984), stable emotional support (i.e., the presence of an intimate relationship) over time directly reduces the level of anxiety and depression at Time 2. It does not interact with stressors. In another study of a two-wave community sample (Pearlin et al., 1981), emotional support (i.e., the presence of someone who provides understanding and advice; intimate exchange with spouses) does not have a main effect on changes in depression over time while decreasing economic strain and increasing mastery. It also does not moderate the relationship between the stressor (i.e., job disruption) and depression. One study uses a four-wave community sample (Aneshensel and Frerichs, 1982). Its latent variable of social support is derived from three measures: number of close friends, number of close relatives, and received socioemotional and instrumental assistance. As it reports, current social support has a main negative effect on current depression at Time 1 and Time 4.

Current social support also has indirect effects on subsequent depression as a result of the impact of current depression on subsequent depression over time. Depression does not seem to influence the social support factor over time. Current stressors result in a higher level of current social support at Time 1 and Time 4, which may imply that stressors trigger the use of social support.

Lin and colleagues (Ensel and Lin, 1991; Lin, 1986b; Lin and Ensel, 1984, 1989; Tausig, 1986) collected a three-wave community sample. Three of their studies use the first two waves of data. One (Lin, 1986b) measures social support as a latent variable derived from 39 items covering community support, network support, confidant support, and instrumental-expressive support. Social support thus measured has a main negative effect on depression and its change over time. It mediates the effect of prior undesirable life events, which indirectly increase depressive symptoms by decreasing social support. It also exerts an indirect effect by suppressing current life events. There is no evidence for the interaction of social support with undesirable life events. In the other two studies (Lin and Ensel, 1984; Tausig, 1986), social support is indicated by a two-item perceived strong-tie support (i.e., perception of having enough close companions or friends). Prior social support and change in social support have a main negative effect on the change in depression over time. Prior social support also has an indirect effect on the change in depression by suppressing the change in undesirable life events. Change in social support mediates some effects of prior social support, prior undesirable life events, the change in undesirable life events, and prior depression, which decreases the change in social support. Furthermore, prior physical health has a positive association with current social support. Two more studies use the three waves of data and measure social support using the foregoing two-item strong-tie support scale. One study (Lin and Ensel, 1989) focuses on physical health. It fails to find a main effect of social support on physical symptoms at Time 3. Social support at Time 2, however, does buffer the effects of stressors and depression at Time 1. The second study (Ensel and Lin, 1991) explores depression. Social support at Time 2 has a main negative effect on depression at Time 3. It also mediates the effect of stressors at Time 1 that decreases social support. The study fails to find evidence for any moderating effect.

In addition, providing support and its health effects receives little attention. For example, Krause and colleagues (1999) examine a national sample of the elderly in Japan. They measure emotional support provided to others based on two items (i.e., how often respondents listen to people who wish to talk about worry or trouble, and how often respondents encourage and comfort people experiencing hardship). Providing emotional support is positively associated with self-reported health for both men and women. It also mediates the positive health effect of religious practice, but only for men.

In summary, the above empirical studies focus on received support. They are concerned more with mental health outcomes than with physical health outcomes. Most studies assume a social causation explanation. They pay more attention to the main and moderating health effect of social support than its mediating and indirect impact. The results of these studies are inconsistent. There is more confirming than disconfirming evidence that social support exerts a direct protective effect on health, mental health in particular. The significance of that effect may vary with samples, outcomes, measures of social support; sociodemographic groups; and even neighborhood contexts. Some studies demonstrate that social support mitigates the effect of psychological resources and stressors, but more studies do not. The importance of the moderating role of social support differs across gender groups, statistical methods, and types of social support. A few studies on the mediating function of social support report that social support may help explain some health effects of sociodemographic and socioeconomic variables, psychological resources, social integration, tie and network attributes, and precedent stressors. Furthermore, social support may act as a precursor and affect health indirectly by influencing psychological resources and reducing stressors. Longitudinal research designs are limited. As a result, the social selection argument receives very little attention. Such limited studies also report conflicting evidence. Aneshensel and Frerichs (1982) do not find an impact of depression on social support, while Lin and colleagues (Lin, 1986b; Tausig, 1986) find that better physical and mental health brings in more social support. In addition, providing support seems to have a direct or mediating effect on health.

CONCLUSION

Social support has triggered a burgeoning multidisciplinary research literature, especially in the area of health during the last three decades. Social support initially arose as a post hoc explanation for the emerging relationships that linked social factors, especially relational factors to health and well-being. Since the appearance of the seminal works, scholars have made significant advances in exploring the substance and dimensions of social support, developing diverse measurement instruments, and examining its multiple functions in the social distribution of health using a variety of data. However, they have accumulated mixed evidence. Further efforts are needed to clarify and expand our current understanding of social support.

Social support is a unique social concept. As is the case with relatively new concepts in social sciences, social support has been defined in diverse ways. The intellectual value of a concept is evaluated not by its widening meaning or its potential role as a panacea, but by its uniqueness and originality. Rather than going as far as Barrera (1986) in proposing the abandonment of the general concept of social support, we suggest a rigorous strategy in which future studies should define social support by its precise nature and the supply of resources from network members and then separate it from its structural preconditions and functional consequences. The priority of a reliable and valid social support scale was recognized decades ago (Dean and Lin, 1977). As the reviewed empirical studies illustrate, the indicators of social support were still quite diverse, probably due to the use of secondary data and post hoc measurements (Berkman, 1984). A strict definition may help us overcome such inconsistency in operational measurements of social support and empirical results.

Social support is a multidimensional factor in its intrinsic features. More theoretical and empirical attention has been paid to received support than providing or reciprocal support. Note that providing or reciprocal support influences health through different mechanisms than received support. Among the literature on received support, there are more studies on perceived than actual support, and on emotional than instrumental or other types of support. Different kinds of support appear to be outcomes of disparate network-based preconditions. Perceived and emotional support seem to have stronger explanatory power in the social distribution of health than other types. To achieve a more complete picture of social support, such multiple kinds of support concepts and measures need to be simultaneously subjected to a rigorous empirical test in order to distinguish their network-based antecedents and further compare their effects on specific health outcomes.

Social support is a distinctive network-based factor. Its precise definition is crucial for a coherent and comprehensive understanding of the general literature from a social network perspective. Various network-based concepts, including social support, are different constructs. Social support is expected to be a meaningful pathway that links other prominent network-derived concepts to our outcomes of interests. Some of the above-reviewed empirical studies use other network terms as proximate measures of social support, but they do not examine social support directly. Their results in making stronger causal inferences regarding social support are limited. Future studies should measure network concepts independently and examine their relationships systematically in a causal sequence. Thus the urgent task in the area of health research is to examine how divergent types of social support mediate the effect of dissimilar network-based antecedents. The application of network analysis to social support research is undoubtedly a promising direction (Hall and Wellman, 1985; Wellman, 1981). The caveat is that social support should be captured more accurately through support-related network instruments than by general network instruments (Bearman and Parigi, 2004).

Social support is dynamic over time rather than being a constant feature (Dean and Lin, 1977; Pearlin, 1985). Most empirical studies are still cross-sectional, which leaves us questioning the robustness of their results. We are also aware of limited information about, for example, how health and well-being shape the availability or mobilization of social support (Thoits, 1995), or how social support and its change may be in a reciprocal causal relationship with the change of other network-based terms. Refined longitudinal research designs are therefore needed to disentangle these complicated causality puzzles.

Finally, social support goes beyond its traditional function as a stress buffer and plays multiple roles in the social organization of health and illness. It may protect health directly or it may protect indirectly by reducing other health risks. It may mediate and moderate health effects of other determinants. There is further but mixed evidence for its direct and moderating effects, and fewer but also conflicting findings for its mediating and direct effect. For a thorough understanding of social dynamics through which social support maintains or changes health status, future studies should explore various models simultaneously in single studies as far as their data allow, and report all relevant results, either confirming or disconfirming.

REFERENCES

Alcalay, R. (1983) 'Health and social support networks: A case for improving interpersonal communication', *Social Networks*, 5: 71–88.

Aneshensel, C.S. and Frerichs, R.R. (1982) 'Stress, support, and depression: A longitudinal causal model', *Journal of Community Psychology*, 10: 363–76.

Barrera, M. Jr. (1981) 'Social support in the adjustment of pregnant adolescents: Assessment issue', in Benjamin H. Gottlieb (ed.), *Social Networks and Social Support*. Beverly Hills: Sage. pp. 69–96.

Barrera, M. Jr. (1986) 'Distinctions between social support concepts, measures, and models', *American Journal of Community Psychology*, 14: 413–45.

Bearman, P. and Parigi, P. (2004) 'Cloning headless frogs and other important matters: Conversation topics and network structure', *Social Forces*, 83: 535–57.

Beggs, J.J., Haines, V.A. and Hurlbert, J.S. (1996) 'Situational contingencies surrounding the receipt of informal support', *Social Forces*, 75: 201–22.

Berkman, L.F. (1984) 'Assessing the physical health effects of social networks and social support', *Annual Review of Public Health*, 5: 413–32.

Berkman, L.F. (2000) 'Social support, social networks, social cohesion and health', *Social Work in Health Care*, 31: 3–14.

Berkman, L.F. and Glass, T. (2000) 'Social integration, social networks, social support and health', in L. F. Berkman and I. Kawachi (eds), *Social Epidemiology*. New York: Oxford University Press. pp. 137–73.

Berkman, L.F., Glass, T., Brissette, I. and Seeman, T.E. (2000) 'From social integration to health: Durkheim in the new millennium', *Social Science & Medicine*, 51: 843–57.

Brissette, I., Cohen, S. and Seeman, T.E. (2000) 'Measuring social integration and social networks', in Sheldon Cohen, Lynn G. Underwood, and Benjamin H. Gottlieb (eds), *Social Support Measurement and Intervention*. New York: Oxford University Press. pp. 53–85.

Caplan, G. (1974) *Support Systems and Community Mental Health*. New York: Behavioral Publications.

Caplan, G. and Killilea, M. (1976) *Support Systems and Mutual Help: Multidisciplinary Explorations*. New York: Grune & Stratton.

Caplan, R.D. (1979) 'Social support, person-environment fit, and coping', in L.A. Ferman and J.P. Gordus (eds), *Mental Health and the Economy*. Michigan: W.E. Upjohn Institute for Employment Research. pp. 89–138.

Carpiano, R.M. (2006) 'Toward a neighborhood resource-based theory of social capital for health: Can Bourdieu and sociology help?' *Social Science & Medicine*, 62: 165–75.

Cassel, J. (1974) 'An epidemiological perspective of psychoso-cial factors in disease etiology', *American Journal of Public Health*, 64: 1040–43.

Cassel, J. (1976) 'The contribution of the social environment to host resistance', *American Journal of Epidemiology*, 104: 107–23.

Cobb, S. (1974) 'Physiologic changes in men whose jobs were abolished', *Journal of Psychosomatic Research*, 18: 245–58.

Cobb, S. (1976) 'Social support as a moderator of life stress', *Psychosomatic Medicine* 38: 300–314.

Cohen, S. and Syme, S.L. (eds) (1985) *Social Support and Health*. Orlando: Academic Press.

Cohen, S., Underwood, L.G. and Gottlieb, B.H. (eds) (2000) *Social Support Measurement and Intervention: A Guide for*

Health and Social Scientists. New York: Oxford University Press.

Cohen, S., Gottlieb, B.H. and Underwood LG. (2000) 'Social relationships and health', in Sheldon Cohen, Lynn G. Underwood, and Benjamin H. Gottlieb (eds), *Social Support Measurement and Intervention: A Guide for Health and Social Scientists*. New York: Oxford University Press. pp. 3–25.

Coleman, J.S. (1990) *Foundations of Social Theory*. Cambridge: Belknap Press of Harvard University Press.

Coyne, J.C. and Downey, G. (1991) 'Social factors and psychopathology: Stress, social support, and coping processes', *Annual Review of Psychology*, 42: 401–25.

Dean, A. and Lin, N. (1977) 'The stress-buffering role of social support: Problems and prospects for systematic investigation', *Journal of Nervous and Mental Disease*, 165: 403–17.

Dohrenwend, S.B. and Dohrenwend, B.P. (1981) 'Life stress and illness: Formulation of the issues', in B.S. Dohrenwend and B.P. Dohrenwend (eds), *Stressful Life Events and Their Contexts*. New York: Prodist. pp. 1–27.

Ell, K. (1984) 'Social networks, social support, and health status: A review', *The Social Service Review*, 58: 133–49.

Elliott, M. (2000) 'The stress process in neighborhood context', *Health & Place*, 6: 287–99.

Ellison, C.G. and George, L.K. (1994) 'Religious involvement, social ties, and social support in a Southeastern community', *Journal for the Scientific Study of Religion*, 33: 46–61.

Ensel, W.M. and Lin, N. (1991) 'The life stress paradigm and psychological distress', *Journal of Health and Social Behavior*, 32: 321–41.

Faber, A.D. and Wasserman, S. (2002) 'Social support and social networks: Synthesis and review', in Judith A. Levy and Bernice A. Pescosolido (eds), *Social Networks and Health*. New York: JAI Press. pp. 29–72.

Ferraro, K.F. and Koch, J.R. (1994) 'Religion and health among black and white adults: Examining social support and consolation', *Journal for the Scientific Study of Religion*, 33: 362–75.

Gorman, B.K. and Sivaganesan, A. (2007) 'The role of social support and integration for understanding socioeconomic disparities in self-rated health and hypertension', *Social Science & Medicine*, 65: 958–75.

Gottlieb, B.H. (1978) 'The development and application of a classification scheme of informal helping behaviours', *Canadian Journal of Behavioural Science*, 10: 105–15.

Gottlieb, B.H. (ed.) (1981) *Social Networks and Social Support*. Beverly Hills: Sage.

Gottlieb, B.H. (1983) *Social Support Strategies: Guidelines for Mental Health Practice*. Beverly Hills: Sage.

Green, G. (1993) 'Editorial review: Social support and HIV', *AIDS Care*, 5: 87–104.

Greenblatt, M., Becerra, R.M. and Serafetinides, E.A. (1982) 'Social networks and mental health: An overview', *American Journal of Psychiatry*, 139: 977–84.

Haines, V.A. and Hurlbert, J.S. (1992) 'Network range and health', *Journal of Health and Social Behavior*, 33: 254–66.

Hall, A. and Wellman, B. (1985) 'Social networks and social support', in S. Cohen and S.L. Syme (eds), *Social Support and Health*. New York: Academic Press. pp. 23–41.

Henderson, S. (1977) 'The social network, support and neurosis: The function of attachment in adult life', *The British Journal of Psychiatry*, 131: 185–91.

House, J.S. (1981) *Work Stress and Social Support*. Reading, MA: Addison-Wesley.

House, J.S. (1987) 'Social support and social structure', *Sociological Forum*, 2: 135–46.

House, J.S. and Robert, L. (1985) 'Measures and concepts of social support', in S. Cohen and S.L. Syme (eds), *Social Support and Health*. New York: Academic Press. pp. 83–108.

House, J.S., Landis, K.R. and Umberson, D. (1988a) 'Social relationships and health', *Science*, 241: 540–45.

House, J.S., Umberson, D. and Landis, K.R. (1988b) 'Structures and processes of social support', *Annual Review of Sociology*, 14: 293–318.

Kaplan, B.H., Cassel, J.C. and Gore, S. (1977) 'Social support and health', *Medical Care*, 15: 47–58.

Krause, N., Berit, I.-D., Jersey, L. and Hidehiro, S. (1999) 'Religion, social support, and health among the Japanese elderly', *Journal of Health and Social Behavior*, 40: 405–21.

Jackson, P.B. (1992) 'Specifying the buffering hypothesis: Support, strain, and depression', *Social Psychology Quarterly*, 55: 363–78.

Kawachi, I. and Berkman, L. (2000) 'Social cohesion, social capital and health', in L.F. Berkman and I. Kawachi (eds), *Social Epidemiology*. New York: Oxford University Press. pp. 174–90.

Kawachi, I. and Berkman, L. (2001) 'Social ties and mental health', *Journal of Urban Health: Bulletin of the New York Academy of Medicine*, 78: 458–67.

Kawachi, I., Subramanian, S.V. and Kim, D. (eds) (2008) *Social Capital and Health*. New York: Springer.

Kessler, R.C., Price, R.H. and Wortman, Camille, B. (1985) 'Social factors in psychopathology: Stress, social support, and coping processes', *Annual Review of Psychology*, 36: 531–72.

Landerman, R., George, L.K., Campbell, R.T. and Blazer, D.G. (1989) 'Alternative models of the stress buffering hypothesis', *American Journal of Community Psychology*, 17: 625–41.

LaRocco, J.M., House, J.S., French, Jr. and John, R.P. (1980) 'Social support, occupational stress, and health', *Journal of Health and Social Behavior*, 21: 202–18.

Lin, N. (1986a) 'Conceptualizing social support', in Nan Lin, Alfred Dean, and Walter Ensel (eds), *Social Support, Life Events and Depression*. Orlando: Academic Press. pp. 17–30.

Lin, N. (1986b) 'Modeling the effects of social support', in Nan Lin, Alfred Dean, and Walter Ensel (eds), *Social Support, Life Events and Depression*. Orlando: Academic Press. pp. 173–209.

Lin, N. (1999a) 'Building a network theory of social capital', *Connections*, 22: 28–51.

Lin, N. (1999b) 'Social networks and status attainment', *Annual Review of Sociology*, 25: 467–88.

Lin, N. (2001) *Social Capital: A Theory of Social Structure and Action*. Cambridge: Cambridge University Press.

Lin, N. and Ao, D. (2008) 'The invisible hand of study: An exploratory study', in Nan Lin and Bonnie Erickson (eds), *Social Capital: Advances in Research*. Oxford University Press. pp.107–32.

Lin, N. and Ensel, W.M. (1984) 'Depression-mobility and its social etiology: The role of life events and social support', *Journal of Health and Social Behavior*, 25: 176–88.

Lin, N. and Ensel, W.M. (1989) 'Life stress and health: Stressors and resources', *American Sociological Review*, 54: 382–99.

Lin, N. and Peek, M.K. (1999) 'Social networks and mental health', in A.V. Horwitz and T.L. Scheid (eds), *A Handbook for the Study of Mental Health: Social Contexts, Theories, and Systems*. Cambridge: Cambridge University Press. pp. 241–58.

Lin, N., Dean, A. and Ensel, W. (1986) *Social Support, Life Events and Depression*. Orlando: Academic Press.

Lin, N., Ensel, W.M., Simeone, R.S. and Kuo, W. (1979) 'Social support, stressful life events, and illness: A model and an empirical test', *Journal of Health and Social Behavior* 20: 108–19.

Lin, N., Woelfel, M.W. and Light, S.C. (1985) 'The buffering effect of social support subsequent to an important life event', *Journal of Health and Social Behavior*, 26: 247–63.

Lin, N., Ye, X. and Ensel, W.M. (1999) 'Social support and depressed mood: A structural analysis', *Journal of Health and Social Behavior*, 40: 344–59.

Lincoln, K.D., Chatters, L.M. and Taylor, R.J. (2003) 'Psychological distress among black and white Americans: Differential effects of social support, negative interaction and personal control', *Journal of Health and Social Behavior*, 44: 390–407.

Link, B.G. and Phelan, Jo.C. (1995) 'Social conditions as fundamental causes of disease', *Journal of Health and Social Behavior*, Extra Issue: 80–94.

Luke, D.A. and Harris, J.K. (2007) 'Network analysis in public health: History, methods, and applications', *Annual Review of Public Health*, 28: 69–93.

Mitchell, J.C. (1969) 'The concept and use of social networks', in J.C. Mitchell (ed.), *Social Networks in Urban Situations*. Manchester, England: Manchester University Press. pp. 1–50.

Mitchell, J.C. (1974) 'Social networks', *Annual Review of Anthropology*, 3: 279–99.

Nooney, J. and Woodrum, E. (2002) 'Religious coping and church-based social support as predictors of mental health outcomes: Testing a conceptual model', *Journal for the Scientific Study of Religion*, 41: 359–68.

Pearlin, L.I. (1985) 'Social structure and processes of social support', in Sheldon Cohen and S. Leonard Syme (eds), *Social Support and Health*. Orlando: Academic Press. pp. 43–60.

Pearlin, L.I., Menaghan, E.G., Lieberman, M.A. and Mullan, J.T. (1981) 'The stress process', *Journal of Health and Social Behavior*, 22: 337–56.

Pescosolido, B.A. (2007) 'Sociology of social networks', in Clifton D. Bryant and Dennis L. Peck (eds), *21st Century Sociology: A Reference Book*. Thousand Oaks: SAGE. pp. 208–17.

Pescosolido, B.A. and Levy, J.A. (2002) 'The roles of social networks in health, illness, disease and healing: The accepting present, the forgotten past, and the dangerous potential for a complacent future', in Judith A. Levy and Bernice A. Pescosolido (eds), *Social Networks and Health*. New York: JAI Press. pp. 3–25.

Petts, R.J. and Jolliff, A. (2008) 'Religion and adolescent depression: The impact of race and gender', *Review of Religious Research,* 49(4): 395–414.

Plickert, G., Côté, R.R. and Wellman, B. (2007) 'It's not who you know, it's how you know them: Who exchanges what with whom?', *Social Networks,* 29: 405–29.

Putnam, R.D. (2000) *Bowling Alone: The Collapse and Revival of American Community*. New York: Simon and Schuster.

Ross, C.E. and Mirowsky, J. (1989) 'Explaining the social patterns of depression: Control and problem solving—or support and talking?', *Journal of Health and Social Behavior* 30: 206–19.

Ross, C.E., and Van Willigen, M. (1997) 'Education and the subjective quality of life', *Journal of Health and Social Behavior* 38: 275–97.

Roxburgh, S. (2006) '"I wish we had more time to spend together . . .": The distribution and predictors of perceived family time pressures among married men and women in the paid labor force', *Journal of Family Issues,* 27: 529–53.

Schwarzer, R. and Leppin, A. (1991) 'Social support and health: A theoretical and empirical overview', *Journal of Social and Personal Relationships,* 8: 99–127.

Seeman, T.E. and Berkman, L.F. (1988) 'Structural characteristics of social networks and their relationship with social support in the elderly: Who provides support', *Social Science & Medicine,* 26: 737–49.

Smith, C.E., Fernengel, K., Holcroft, C., Gerald, K. and Marien, L. (1994) 'Meta-analysis of the associations between social support and health outcomes', *Annals of Behavioral Medicine,* 16: 352–62.

Smith, K.P. and Christakis, N.A. (2008) 'Social networks and health', *Annual Review of Sociology,* 34: 405–29.

Song, L. and Lin, N. (2009) 'Social capital and health inequality: Evidence from Taiwan', *Journal of Health and Social Behavior,* 50(2): 149–63.

Song, L., Son, J. and Lin, N. (2010) 'Social capital and health', in William C. Cockerham (eds), *The New Blackwell Companion to Medical Sociology*. London: Blackwell, pp. 184–210.

Stansfeld, S.A. (2006) 'Social support and social cohesion', in M. Marmot and R.G. Wilkinson (eds), *Social Determinants of Health*. 2nd edition. New York: Oxford University Press. pp. 148–71.

Szreter, S. and Woolcock, M. (2004) 'Health by association? Social capital, social theory, and the political economy of public health', *International Journal of Epidemiology,* 33: 650–67.

Tausig, M. (1986) 'Prior history of illness in the basic model', in Nan Lin, Alfred Dean and Walter Ensel (eds), *Social Support, Life Events and Depression*. Orlando: Academic Press. pp. 267–80.

Taylor, R.J. and Chatters, L.M. (1988) 'Church members as a source of informal social support', *Review of Religious Research,* 30: 193–203.

Thoits, P.A. (1982) 'Conceptual, methodological, and theoretical problems in studying social support as a buffer against life stress', *Journal of Health and Social Behavior,* 23: 145–59.

Thoits, P.A. (1984) 'Explaining distributions of psychological vulnerability: Lack of social support in the face of life stress', *Social Forces,* 63: 453–81.

Thoits, P.A. (1995) 'Stress, coping, and social support processes: Where are we? What next?', *Journal of Health and Social Behavior,* Extra Issue: 53–79.

Turner, R.J. (1999) 'Social support and coping', in A.V. Horwitz and T.L. Scheid (eds), *A Handbook for the Study of Mental Health: Social Contexts, Theories, and Systems*. New York: Cambridge University Press. pp. 198–210.

Turner, R.J. and Lloyd, D.A. (1999) 'The stress process and the social distribution of depression', *Journal of Health and Social Behavior,* 40: 374–404.

Turner, R.J. and Marino, F. (1994) 'Social support and social structure: A descriptive epidemiology', *Journal of Health and Social Behavior,* 35: 193–212.

Turner, R.J. and Turner, J.B. (1999) 'Social integration and support', in C.S. Aneshensel and J.C. Phelan (eds), *Handbook of the Sociology of Mental Illness*. New York: Kluwer Academic Press. pp. 301–20.

Wellman, B. (1981) 'Applying social network analysis to the study of social support', in B.H. Gottlieb (ed.), *Social Networks and Social Support*. Beverly Hills: Sage. pp. 171–200.

Wellman, B. and Wortley, S. (1989) 'Brothers' keepers: Situating kinship relations in broader networks of social support', *Sociological Perspectives,* 32: 273–306.

Wellman, B. and Wortley, S. (1990) 'Different strokes from different folks: Community ties and social support', *American Journal of Sociology,* 96: 558–88.

Wethington, E. and Kessler, R.C. (1986) 'Perceived support, received support, and adjustment to stressful life events', *Journal of Health and Social Behavior,* 27: 78–89.

Wheaton, B. (1985) 'Models for the stress-buffering functions of coping resources', *Journal of Health and Social Behavior,* 26: 352–64.

10

Kinship, Class, and Community

Douglas R. White

INTRODUCTION: KINSHIP NETWORKS AND COHESION

This review presents studies in various world regions. Each uses network analysis software designed explicitly for kinship studies with explicit network measures of cohesion. It presents evidence of fundamental differences in the forms of marital cohesion that show profoundly variable effects over a wide range of social phenomena, regional scales, and diverse cultures. Social cohesion is the basis of mutuality, cooperation, and well-being in human societies (Council of Europe, 2009). It includes the modes by which people are assimilated into societies, how groups hold power, stratify social relations, and manage the flow of resources. Kinship networks embedded in the civil societies of nation-states, in contrast to smaller-scale societies, are far too rarely studied as a basis of social cohesion. Networks, the social tissues of our lives, are only partially visible to us; thus we fail to see how these are wrapped and embedded in larger networks. Thus the importance, as emphasized here, of an explicit science of social network analysis for kinship studies both at local and larger scales. The analyses of cohesive subsets show how kinship networks involve constructions of social class, ethnicity, migration, inheritance, social movements, and other large- as well as small-scale social phenomena.

A *kinship network* is composed of relations of parentage (parent-child *arcs*, oriented by time) and couples (e.g., marriage). The nodes in an Ore-graph (Ore, 1960) are individuals, or, in a P-graph (White and Jorion, 1992), couples and

individuals. The latter embeds the matrimonial or parental couple relation *within* the appropriate nodes: a person from a family of orientation parental-node joins one or more partners to form their own parental-couple node(s) (families of procreation). This makes it easy to trace matrimonial circuits, where one or more couples have common ancestors (see Hamberger et al., 2011: Chapter 35) so the last in their series of marriages (ordered in time), or a single marriage, *relinks* families that were already linked. It is these relinking circuits that create kinship cohesion through marriage. Ore-graphs have to separate the cohesiveness of parent-child 3-cliques (mother-father-child) from the broader of cohesiveness of shared ancestries, which is directly captured by P-graph circuitry. To reconcile these differences, Harary and White (2001) defined a P-system as a parental (kinship) network that orders the inclusion relations, at multiple levels of embedding, of individuals, marriage, nuclear family, descent lines, and cohesive groups. People are in one or more family, one or more marriage, and embedded in groups of higher levels of organization. The higher-order analyses of kinship networks offer integrative perspectives that are more veridical as to how individuals and communities are connected, one that also takes into account how different kinds of groups are embedded in one another.

New ways of imaging and analyzing kinship networks as objects in their own right, with tens to millions of people, make it possible to see social phenomena in ways that open a new series of sociological and anthropological questions.

Ninety-odd case studies of kinship network research among anthropologists and fellow scientists have been contributed on-line (at http://kinsource.net) that enable using these new approaches to gain unexpected insights about "big structures" and "large processes" (Tilly, 1984). These allow us to view marriage and descent, community, class, and other topics through the new lens of kinship cohesion created through marriage. Some main results presented here in regional and historical terms give a sense of spread and variation in social structure. Methods used are developed and reviewed in White and Jorion (1992) and Hamberger et al. (2004: Chapter 35, 2011). The most important of these in terms of kinship translates as bounded structural endogamy (White, 1997), which derives from the general sociological concepts of structural cohesion (White and Harary, 2001; Moody and White, 2003). These methods may prove especially useful in new studies needed to gauge the effects of globalization on kinship networks and the new ways in which kinship networks are implicated in constructions of community, social class, ethnicity, migration, social movements, and other phenomena.

Relinking theorem, cycle rank, and measures of cohesion

Barring sibling unions, marriage cohesion or *relinking* is unavoidable in human populations that are not undergoing population collapse.

Proof

This is self-evident if the average number of children per couple is $k > 2$. For N living people,

the number of their *personal* ancestors relative to the current population grows exponentially each generation back: N/1, 2N/k, 4N/k^2, . . . , N(2^{g-1})/k_{g-1} = N$(2/k)^{g-1}$ for successive ancestral generations g = 1, 2, . . . m. This also holds if $k_g > 2$ for each generation. From generation to generation with $k = 2$ there are N$_g$–N$_{g-1}$ = r new relinkings and more cohesive marriages.

Definition of cycle rank

When the number of (ancestral, m) links in a network surpasses the number of (kinship, n) parental nodes in a network with c components, the *cycle rank* = $m - n + c$ of ancestral links – those involved in relinking marriage cycles, as in Figure 10.1 – will overlap. Here, in P-graph notation, focal marriages A and B (temporally the lowermost nodes where the couple represented by the node was already related *before* the marriage) are shown to have ancestral male♂ or female♀ links that lead to common ancestors (two or more couples could also have several common ancestors by which they are relinked). Keeping track of those links we see that couple A (persons 3 and 4) have a MBD (mother's brother's daughter) marriage and B (6 and 7) have a MZD (mother's sister's daughter) marriage. (In a P-graph the numbered lines represent individuals, offspring of their parental node, and members of their family[ies] of procreation.) Wife 4♀, however, is M of 6♂, so these two cohesive marriages overlap by sharing a common arc. Adding the arcs and nodes of two cycles and removing their overlap is a *graph-union*, as shown for marriage C, where a new matrimonial circuit is created (6–3–1–2–5–7-6) by the A-B union. Cohesive marriage cycles with ancestral overlaps, as in graph D, form *bicomponents* with two or more independent paths between every pair of nodes. This forms a unit

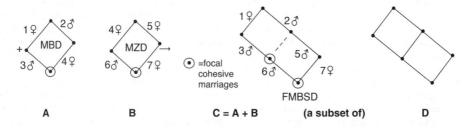

Figure 10.1   Shared-edge cycle unions produce other cycles (e.g., removing the dotted line 4 ♀ in graph C). The *cycle rank* γ (cyclomatic number) is the smallest number of edges that must be removed from a connected graph with *m* edges and *n* nodes. Removal of γ = *m* – *n* + *1* leaves only a tree. In this case γ = 2 for the full graph D (C with line 4 restored). γ is also the minimum number of cycles whose iterative unions produce all the cycles in the graph. The nodes here are couples or families, and the upward-oriented edges link to parental couples

of *structural endogamy*. Pairwise cohesion (White and Newman, 2001) in a kinship graph gives the number of disjoint cohesive paths between pairs of individuals or couples. Thus the persons connected by the dotted parent-child link 4♀ in Figure 10.1 P-graphs C and D have three disjoint paths with others in these marriage circuits, whereas others have only two. Cohesion can thus be measured at the inter-individual or interfamily levels and measured for pairs or identified for groups or subnetworks.

Reconceptualizing endogamy: segregation and cohesion

Mapping the skeleton of kinship networks begins with generative genealogical relationships. Demographers, historians, geneticists, genealogical societies, Mormon baptismal projects, GEDCOM databases, social registers, and many other sources provide massive amounts of genealogical data. They come with varying amounts of other data of variable quality and supplementary contextual data. Anthropologists collect genealogical data of high quality about communities, with protected or historical personal identities, dense ethnography, narrative, or household survey data.

Speaking of endogamy, sociologists think of intermarriage within or between social units as defined by attributes that specify loci of endogamy (community, territory, occupational group, level of wealth, or combinations thereof). This leads to a fractured view of social structure, a myriad of separate attribute-defined groups with varying degrees of overlap depending on the regions studied or how samples are drawn. Surprisingly, endogamy has rarely ever been *defined in terms of the boundaries of emergent network entities* although it is always assumed that endogamous marriages do somehow constitute themselves in this way. But how? One approach is the "segregation measure" game of finding which individual attributes best partition networks to detect endogamous groups. Another is "community detection" (a literature inaugurated by Girvan and Newman, 2002) based on the questionable assumption that communities must be separately partitioned according to maximum density within and minimum density between groups. These are segregative (even segregationist) models. The real world is not so categorical: communities overlap, social modules and roles intersect, individuals are members of multiple communities, and social formations are complex. What "kinds" or aspects of networks actually *define endogamy* rather than merely correlate

densities of endogamy with varying subgroups defined by attributes or partitions?

The bicomponent answer to the question of endogamy (White, 1997) offers a clearly defined and demarcated form of cohesion within a kinship network. A *bicomponent* of a (kinship) network is a(n) (induced) subgraph with a maximal node set <*S*> wherein (1) every pair of nodes is multiply connected through paths among nodes in *S* that have no common intermediaries; (2) these are the *units of structural endogamy*; (3) they conform to a minimal definition of *structural cohesion* (White and Harary, 2001), connectivity-2; and (4) they are a *maximal* unit of *biconnectedness*. Bicomponents don't *partition* a network but may *overlap*, and a higher multipath measure *k* of structural *k-cohesion* allows more overlap. Bicomponent computation is subquadratic (Gibbons, 1885), accomplished in networks of unlimited size.

Similarly, a *cohesive marriage* (marital relinking) is a smaller set <*S*> of nodes in a kinship network, one that includes one or more husband-wife pairs and some of their common ancestors, for which the induced subgraph <*S*> (nodes in *S* and all edges between them) in the network is a *cycle* (White and Jorion, 1992; White, 1997, White, 2004; see also Hamberger et al., 2011: Chapter 35). These are *minimal* units of *biconnectedness* in that (1) every node in a cycle has degree 2, density is minimal; (2) a cycle is only disconnected by removal of two or more nodes; and (3) every pair of nodes is connected by two paths that have no common intermediaries, that is, by one or more cycles.

Given that overlaps of marriage cycles form other cycles, as illustrated in Figure 10.1, with sufficient population growth (Relinking theorem), these will form bicomponents composed of overlapping cohesive marriages, each of which has well-defined boundaries in the population. Empirically, temporally deeper and more accurate memory of fatherhood and motherhood as ancestral ties will expand and densify marriage bicomponents.

Bicomponent scale

We do not see much marital cohesion or structural endogamy (marriage within varying degrees such as those of cousinhood) within the extended families or kindreds of European societies. This is a consequence of the stamping out of polygamy by the Christian church during the Middle Ages and the prohibition of marriages up to six canonical kin degrees. These proscriptions reduced the internal marital cohesiveness of corporate kinship groups and tended to destroy corporate kin groups altogether for all but nobilities, royalties, and merchant elites. "This influence was [most] profound when the Christian church was backed by the state" (Korotayev, 2003: 12).

Historical and ethnographic background of world kinship networks

The influence on features of kinship by world religions – Christian, Islamic, Hindu, Hinayana, and Vajrayana Buddhist (and the extent to which cultures traditionally combined in different proportions Mahayana Buddhism and Confucianist ideology, or varied in the intensity to which Christianity or Islam were combined with local religions that were not world-scale) – was studied by Korotayev and Kazankov (2002) and Korotayev (2003, 2004). Once they had coded the 1,472 societies of the Ethnographic Atlas (Murdock, 1967) for world religion, they found, for the complex societies of Eurasia, that clusters of societies with similar features, purely on the basis of kinship, were extremely well discriminated by world religion. Kinship "systems" and religion (Latin *religio* = bonds) have the capacity to spread, diffuse, and extend cohesion through marriage practices. They can form large-scale subcontinent-level systems in terms of world religion and can form smaller and more variable patchworks in areas of nonworld religions. Lévi-Strauss (1949), for example, identifies huge contiguous areas of matrimonial "dual organization," and regional axes of directed exchange such as brothers-in-law among whom the marriages involve members of one gender moving in a coordinated direction to join their spouses, often counterbalanced by flows of gifts, obligations, or statuses. Other ethnographers (Leach, 1954; subsequent Cambridge scholars) have found that oscillations between directed asymmetric and cyclical exchange along these axes may coordinate with oscillations between the opening (asymmetric exchange) and closing (marriage cycles) of trade routes.

Still, in proximal times and social spaces, at moderate and large territorial scales, and with sufficiently dense sampling, we expect and see structurally endogamous communities in localities all over the world and also local contrasts in varying proportions of emigrants and immigrants and those who marry locally and those who do not. Within multigenerational community kinship networks today, bicomponent cohesion is dissipating in later generations with higher globalization rates of outmigration so that larger frameworks for study are needed to see the effects on more broadly distributed cohesion.

Scalability and organization

Every pair of new descendants that marry in a bicomponent enlarges its structurally endogamous community through marriage although it may be reduced by the forgetting of ancestors. It is easy for the sizes of structurally endogamous communities to grow large and for smaller, denser communities to combine into a larger bicomponent with decreased density. As members of relatively dense socially contiguous communities (territorial, religious, class, etc.) migrate away from their home communities, or marry exogamously, local boundaries of structural endogamy may shrink, altering their local densities.

Features of kinship, however, do not so easily diffuse through marriage. Kinship is linked to beliefs about social rights, privileges, and expectations. The founding charter of Judaism establishes equal rights for younger sons and the sanctity of mothers as the transmitters of the covenant (as discussed for Figure 10.2); Christianity has a belief in the sanctity of the married monogamous couple; Arabic kinship as modified by Islam establishes limits of polygamy and the rights of daughters to inherit half-shares relative to brothers. But kinship establishes an interlock of networks at three levels: the actual ties of marriage and parentage; the separate calculus of the kinship terms; and the role relations established by the moral expectations associated with the kin-naming calculus ("mother," "sister," etc). These normative but individualized expectations (support, love, mediated competition, etc.) apply to particular persons within the marriage and parentage networks. The first two levels have separate generative structures for their respective networks: concatenations of actual ties as social networks and concatenations of terms as semantic networks (Read, 2000). The social ties have their units of network cohesion bounded by bicomponents; the terminological ties have their limits of extension, while the third interlock – role relations – is the mediated outcome of interaction, memory, language, and emotion. Kinship interactions within a community do not establish a kinship "system" that is somehow culturally shared through proximity and diffusion but a pragmatic systematicity (Leaf, 2007) both stronger and restrictive: an *organization* with established members and succession, interlocking roles and expectations, ways of doing things, and ways of adjusting rights, obligations, and differences. It is within communities and organizations, or concrete social institutions where people interact more intensively that "cultures" of shared meanings are formed in beliefs, cognition, the reading of expression, behaviors, and components of structure and dynamics in social

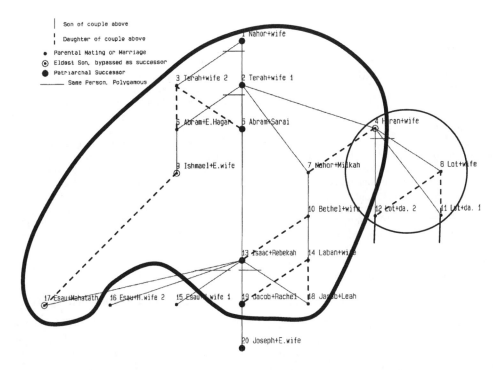

Figure 10.2   Marriage and succession in the Genesis genealogy of Canaan in P-graph format

and kinship networks. Tacit acceptance through usage of the terminology for kin *and* the behavioral interaction within the network of actual parentage and marriage relations solves the coordination problem – who is whom to who and how to collaborate or compete under mediated supervision – for the organization. The boundaries of these organizations, ranging from corporate groups to loose kindreds and even social classes linked through marriage, are tighter and often more exclusive than the well-defined boundaries of structural endogamy. Kinship *organizations*, however, are much less permeable and more resilient than the scalability of bicomponents would suggest.

Sociological and historical examples

Given their organizational characteristics, disjoint communities with the same organization and terminology easily recognize one another as "the same" spatially extensible "zones" of structural similarity that do not blend gradually but have discrete boundaries. The simplest way

to present the relevance of large-scale kinship network analysis for historical and ethnographic sociology – class, community, ethnicity, politics, and economy – is to look at different regions and religions such as Middle Eastern Hebrews and Muslims, European-origin Christians, South Asian Buddhists, and Australians of the Dreamtime.

STRUCTURAL ENDOGAMY WITH CO-DESCENDANT RELINKING (MIDDLE EAST)

Religion and relinking in a historical canaanite lineage

One variant of bicomponent endogamy, along with specific organizational features, is exemplified in Figure 10.2, from the Old Testament example used by White and Jorion (1992: 456) to show how to construct and analyze kinship networks using P-graphs in relation to historical narratives. In Figure 10.2 males are shown as solid lines, and those with several wives (Terah,

Abraham, Lot, Esau, Isaac) have multiple lines connected by a horizontal line below their parental node. Dotted lines are for females, solid circles mark the singles or couples, and the large circles mark the line of patrilineal succession to leadership.

The story behind the lineage in Figure 10.2

The narrative of this lineage of founders of monotheism is often called "the Patriarchs and Matriarchs," the latter renowned for establishing a line of male succession that passes to younger sons, not the elder ones, and recognizing that Judaic religious descent passes through mothers, not fathers. This new pattern of succession, "arranged" by mothers (the Matriarchs), occurs with lineage-mate arranged-marriages of their youngest sons to women in their patrilineage. Marrying women of one's patriline also conveys a double ancestry to one's children, who receive the religious, cultural, and lineage tradition from both the mother and the father. The change of mythological themes from the pre- to post-Abrahamic narratives include greater equality for lineage-endogamous women (the Arabic Father's brother's daughter (FBD) marriage-right, see below) and younger sons favored by their mothers over eldest sons with exogamously political marriages (succession by the most able rather than the eldest). This pattern reoccurs among the Hebrew religious elite and Sumerian, Berber, Maronite, Druze, and Arabic lineages again and again for a period of 4,000 years (Adams, 1966: 81; Korotayev, 2000: 403) up to today, often coinciding with lineage corporations (and is also found among the Merina of Madagascar and other scattered societies, see Barry, 1998, 2008).

The message of this religious-founders network narrative is also marked out by the difference between the nodes in the large bicomponent, marked out within the thick lasso, excluding Lot, versus the smaller encircled bicomponent in which Lot's incestuous fatherhood through his daughters occurs "cohesively." Thus, moral boundaries are symbolized by the immorality of drunkard Lot (with his daughters to wed in Sodom in the biblical story and wife then turned to salt [salty tears?]) reflected by limits to endogamy and the exclusion of his descendants in later generations from the larger bicomponent. Thus, the recognition of the bicomponent, added to the original Figure 10.2 of White and Jorion (1992: 456), clarifies what they called the network "core" of the Canaan genealogy, where the structural endogamy focuses around marriage within a single patrilineage. White et al.'s (1999) *index of relinking* for Figure 10.2 showed marriages in the large bicomponent (structurally endogamous group) were

at 64 percent of maximum (7/11) as contrasted with 56 percent when lineage-member couples *outside* the bicomponent are included.

Hebrew and Islamic social organization, as noted for the "founder" genealogy in Figure 10.2, stem from the same root, according to this tradition, with Ishmael as an ancestor of Mohammed. They have kinship patterns that have continued and been embellished in various ways for over 4,000 years. Network data from a long-term ethnographic field study (Johansen and White, 2002) provides a Turkish case that derives historically from implantation of this system by Arab conquest (although Sunni Turks, with fewer simultaneous marriages, Sunni Arabs, Shi'a Persians, etc., have variant marriage customs, polygyny being more common in rural areas; yet there are broad similarities).

Arab lineages and endoconical clans

An endoconical clan is one where cohesion is generated by marital relinking through remembered ties, like those in Figure 10.2, that go back to a "founder core" of common ancestral roots extending from a compact bicomponent of common ancestors. As defined by White and Johansen (2005: xxxiv), "a loose and flexible system of interpersonal ranking based on respect for age and experience" "allows each family line to bring capable members forward in promoting alternative adaptations." Their monographic study of an Arabized Turkish nomad clan, one of the clans of Aydınlı, shows a social organization very similar to that discussed for the Old Testament lineage core of patriarchs and matriarchs. The scale at which endogamy is viewed here, however, is expanded from a single lineage to a set of lineages integrated by structural endogamy that now includes both marital relinking within and *between* lineages and, at a much lower density, to taking wives from outside clans and smaller, less sustainable families moving out through migration to towns. Families with more siblings and siblings-in-law are more competitive because they have more allies.

Historical background to Arab lineages and endoconical clans

The unusual and distinctive feature of Arabized and Arabic lineages, which Korotayev (2000) has traced out to show correspondence to the limits of the Arabic conquests, is matrimonial relinking within the patriline. These are male rights to marry with lineage members like FBD rather than obligations (hence the frequency of exercise of these rights will vary). The lineage segment that is cohesively reinforced, when this right is exercised, varies according to whether the wife shares a patrilineage ancestor two to five generations back (i.e., first-, second-, third-, or fourth-cousin patrilineal parallel marriage). This creates, and does throughout the entire Arabic and Arabized zone, a whole series of fractally cohesive marriages generated by marriages at different depths and branches of these deep patrilines. (The leadership of classical tribes or clans usually has genealogical scrolls recording ancestries; these lines are memorized in stylized ways in both classical and nonclassical leading tribal families.) The ways that different lineages can be welded together ancestrally again create fractal patterns of ties between lineage pairs or triples. Marriages that family *a* made with *b* and *b* with *c* may be reciprocated, *c* to *b* and *b* to *a*, forming broadcast strong-tie chains of reciprocated ties across pairs, triples, and so forth *between the lineages of these families*. These reciprocated ties may be repeated between same or different branches of the same lineages, or cast anew. White and Johansen (2005) found that in the Aydınlı clan of some 2,000 people (counting ancestors plus others who had settled in towns), these chains formed a navigable network of hubs (White and Houseman, 2002) that connected everyone in the clan by strong (that is, reciprocated) ties. This contrasts with Granovetter's (1973) "strength of weak ties" model where strong ties tend to cluster while the weak ties form the only navigable long-range paths. The strong ties of the endoconical clan thus form a kind of invisible social-highway system, with routes composed of reciprocated ties that provide meeting places for others at different points along the chain, places to get to know more intimately the men and women not only from an ally but the ally's allies who often visit and thus meet in intermediary families. Ideally, every reciprocally linked pair of families on these chains, allies due to the reciprocated exchanges, had relations of intimacy and mutual trust. In Middle Eastern merchant and commercial networks, kinship "highways" of this sort also provide in large part the most common ties for transacting business (Berkowitz et al., 2006).

The Aydınlı society, then, like many in the Arabic region, is a fractally segmentary lineage system (see Peters, 1967 for another classic segmentary lineage study) with subcorporations affiliated with clans and lineages at every fractal level, claiming rights over resources and property through relations of trust based on in-married, lineage-endogamous women. These women are important lineage members who exercise rights in the corporation, and out-married reciprocal

relinking between units at all fractal levels (clan-clan, lineage-lineage, sublineage-sublineage, etc.). Women who marry in from other lineages, to the extent they have reciprocal and repeated marriages, are considered allies and have lineage sisters who are also allies, and are in some sense able to negotiate for their home lineage, if it is allied, thereby gaining greater rights and privilege in their husbands' lineages. In a segmentary system with reciprocal alliances at all these fractal levels, the response to an outside opportunity or threat can begin at one place and spread over time, scaling up to a level that will depend on the magnitude of opportunity or threat. When crimes or offenses are committed, revenge can be mobilized if compensation is not forthcoming, at levels of cooperation that will adjust to the extent of the opposition; and similarly in mobilizing for new cooperative opportunities. Leadership in this context, as among the Aydınlı, can be emergent, with reputation for performance gaining adherence – often for a lifetime – by people's willingness to come to deliberative council in the emergent leader's home. Moreover, this form of organization, very different from Europe, is one that has been used effectively in business, business corporations that involve kinship, and in short- and long-range mercantile trade. It is in this manner that Jewish trading families spread as an ethnic kin-linked diaspora throughout Islamic territories and then into Europe and elsewhere. White and Johansen (2005) explicate how network analytic methods are mobilized to study kinship and complexity in this Judeo-Arabic context.

Preference signatures and genealogical networks of the Greek gods

The possibility of "preference signatures" left by the relative frequency of each type of relinking marriage in kinship networks was investigated by White and Houseman (2002). They rank-ordered kin-type frequencies for dozens of empirical kinship networks for two types of marital relinking: (1) marriage with consanguineal relatives such as FBD or MBD (more generally: *co-descendant marriage* between co-descendants of a common ancestor) and (2) relinking *co-affinal marriage* among multiple descent lines, such as BWB (sister exchange) or ZHZ (brothers marry sisters) in two-family relinkings. Fitting these distributions by simple regression to power-law versus exponential curves (unaware as yet of better procedures, such as to use normalized cumulative probabilities and bootstrap statistics

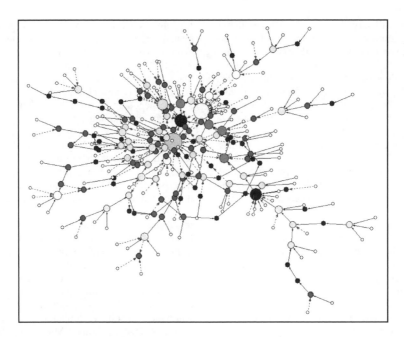

Figure 10.3 "Arab/Hebrew" genealogy of Greek gods *(temporally ordered "ancestrally," center to periphery)* in P-graph format

for curve fitting), they discovered two dominant sortings of societies:

1   Societies with a predominance of co-descendant marriage showed a power-law ranking of co-descendant marriage-type frequencies, indicative of preferential choice, and an exponential ranking of co-affinal marriage-type frequencies, expected where there are no preferences (i.e., random differences in frequencies).
2   Societies with a predominance of co-affinal marriage showed the reverse.

Thus, the overall preference (frequency) for *co-descendant versus co-affinal marriage* tends to correlate with a preference among the marriage types in the preferred class of cohesive marriage types. Within each class, societies might have a similar ranking of preferences, such as FBD as the leading co-descendant marriage preferences.

A subsequent unpublished finding is quite amazing: analysis of the genealogical network of the Greek gods (Newman and Newman, 2003) shows a preference gradient matching that of Aydınlı clan marriages and some other Arabized or Arabic societies, including the gradient first-preference for FBD (see also Barry, 2008). Little is known about the social organization of preclassical Greeks as tribal societies, but this gives a clue. Obviously, Western ideas about the "origins

of Democracy" in Greek city-states should take into account the earlier foundations of Greek societies: "in the archaic period, as in the late bronze-age, Greece belonged to the single cultural and intellectual circle of the Near East," and the names of Greek gods had Hebrew roots (Sealey, 1976: 29). More generally, kinship network analysis may have potentials for historical reconstruction.

STRUCTURAL ENDOGAMY WITH CO-AFFINAL RELINKING (E.G., THE CHRISTIAN WEST)

Here, social class tends to be constituted as distributed marital cohesion and elite pedigrees.

The Christian West

A more horizontal view of kinship ties, with the idea of co-affinal *relinking* and more specific *renchaînement* between pairs of families, was invented and studied by Jolas et al. (1970) as a form of social integration in peasant villages in France and elsewhere in Europe. This has been found to be common in European, Christian, and many other societies where intermarried ancestral lines are relinked by marriage but not by marriage to blood kin. Across many studies, we find that relinkings go beyond local alliances through overlapping ancestries to also form horizontal cycles of intermarriages that repeatedly overlap to form larger cohesive units. When they are large and cohesive social formations, they may be entwined with community, social class, or ethnicity.

Genealogy and pedigree

Many studies of kinship are concerned with pedigree and lineage or lines of vertical descent. This is also a social concern of many elites in establishing boundaries and social identities. Lloyd Warner's Yankee elite ethnographies (1941–1959, 1949) echoed this obsession. Descent group corporations were then the dominant concern of the descent theory school of British anthropology. Warner, one of the foremost ethnographers of an American city, viewed church and voluntary associations as the two great institutional organizations of the United States, one religiously divisive, the other integrative through special interests. In his "beautiful, static, organized community" description, however (as John Phillips Marquand in the novel *Point of No Return* [1949] describes the work of Warner's character, Malcolm Bryant), he neglected not only social change and disorganization but also the organizational role of kinship and marriage in the formation of social class and social strata.

Social class

Max Weber, like most theorists of social class, was not blind to marital relinking: his two basic characteristics of class were endogamy (*social* class; often conflated with prestige hierarchies) and differential access to life chances or access to productive wealth (*economic* class, acquired through inheritance, or achievement indexed by income distinctions).

Some large cohesive formations based on marital relinkings are generationally shallow, with large multiply connected sets of siblings or cousins and no need to go back more than two generations in finding the multiconnected ties among overlapping cycles of affines.

Ethnographic examples for social class
Brudner and White (1997) used P-graph and P-systems analysis (Harary and White, 2001) to move from Jolas et al.'s (1970) more local view

of relinking to a network analysis of how those couples who relinked with one another in an Austrian farmer village formed a giant bicomponent that constituted most (about half) of the community. Further, they showed it was within the bicomponent, whose members inherited land, "in which propertied marriages were an instrument of class formation" (1997: 175), citing Rebel's (1983) distinction between economic and social class in Austrian farming villages. Thus marital relinking at the scale of the entire community was a core feature of the social construction of class as constituted in part by cohesively overlapping relinking marriage cycles. Following White (1997), who coined the term *structural endogamy* for the boundaries of network cohesion created by marriages, Brudner and White showed that the coefficient of covariation between bicomponent membership and "stayers" in the community who inherited parental land and property was highly significant statistically even if underestimated ($R^2 = .29$) because a minority of the community who were "stayers" were not interviewed. Interviewing more of the permanent residents in the community could only have had the effect of magnifying the size estimate for the structurally endogamous group since the exceptions to the hypothesis were almost all those of heirs with missing endogamous links, including the uninterviewed. Simulation analysis (White, 1999) supported the conclusion that marriage relinking among sets of siblings and cousins occurred far more than expected by chance. The Turkish nomads study by White and Johansen (2005), with more complete data, found a higher "structural endogamy-stayers" correlation coefficient R^2, of .90. Here the "stayer" category includes the *larger* families who are more successful in competition for resources. This suggests that a Brudner-White type of "structural endogamy-stayers" correlation at the community level could be very widespread and include many non-European cases.

Analyzing systemic relinking among Guatemalan colonial elites, Casasola Vargas and Alcántara Valverde (Casasola Vargas, 2001; Casasola Vargas and Alcántara Valverde, 2002) showed that both aspects of class elites, social and economic, were recognized family by family by experts in this historical period and as identified concomitantly through network analyses of relinking. Like Brudner and White (1997), these studies showed conformity between the social (endogamously bounded) and economic (wealth and property transmission) aspects of Weberian class. In a direct test of the cohesion/class hypothesis for a society with co-affinal relinking, White (2009) reexamined the San Juan Sur (Turrialba, Costa Rica) farmer village data of Loomis and

Powell (1949) and found that higher levels of structural cohesion (Moody and White, 2003) in kinship visiting patterns among family households correlated with villager judgments of higher social class.

Further examination of structural endogamy and social class (Fitzgerald, 2004) found distinct strata of structural endogamies within the Bevis Marks (Sephardim) Synagogue in London at the levels of crafts people and office workers (horizontal adjacent generation relinking) and elites (generationally deeper relinking), as Berkowitz (1975, 1980), his teacher, had suspected. In contrast, Widmer et al. (1999) found deep ancestral (vertical) relinking and relinking between family lines in among the Geneva Scientists of the seventeenth to nineteenth centuries.

Challenges to pluralism

Once relinkings are analyzed to show the extent of interfamily cohesion at different class levels, the pluralistic theory of interest groups can be challenged by ones that explore how interfamily ties intersect to cohesively integrate a social class with interest groups and diverse political office holding, directorships, and other leadership roles. Systematic use of kinship network data, in the manner of analyzing horizontal social cohesion, can provide a basis for the study of power elites, as Berkowitz suggested (1975, 1980). Here, the identification of cohesive groups provides a basis for causal modeling of historical contingencies. For comparative politics, Doyle (2005: 1) finds the White and Johansen (2005) P-graph framework to provide for "detailed assessment of highly decentralized self-organizing local governance structures" in Central Asia and "unparalleled examination of sub-national political behavior," and European politologists have since begun to do so. Studies of Mexican power elites by Alcántara Valverde (2001) and Gil and Schmidt (1996, 2005) show the interlocking of political power and kinship/marriage networks. Kuper's (2006) P-system study of the families of Bloomsbury found maritally cohesive groups that supported the great English scientific families (e.g., the Darwin-Wedgewood families) and mounted some of the great English scientific, political, and literary projects of the nineteenth and early twentieth centuries.

SIDEDNESS AND SECTIONS

Moieties are a form of matrimonial dual organization that divides a maritally cohesive group into two sides that exchange spouses: that is, into sides

that are mutually exogamous but more globally endogamous.

Dual organization, divides, sides, and cognatic sides

The view that exogamous exchanges between marital moieties must be based on principles of residence or descent (e.g., Fox, 1977: 175–207) needed to create clear-cut named oppositions of local groups (e.g., patrilocal) or (patri- or matri-) lineages assumes that other peoples lack the relational logics for understanding their own networks. This view correlates with the insistence that that "egocentric" kinship terminologies consistent with dual organization – kinterms that systematically distinguish one side, "lines of relatives I can marry," from the other side of unmarriageable relatives – do not entail "sociocentric" organization. The balance theorem of signed graphs (Harary, 1953, 1969), however, applied as a principle of network organization, explains the conditions under which cognition and behavior do converge in this way for egocentric and sociocentric relational classes. It shows for a context of structural endogamy how the consistent individual *practice* of marital sidedness is coterminous with marital sidedness as a network outcome. Four new theorems relating egocentric sidedness in kinship terminology to sociocentric sidedness among consangineally married couples, in relation to their common ancestors, are given by White (2010). The study of empirical kinship networks in the following examples shows that the predicted cognitive-behavioral-network convergence is very common.

Empirical examples for dual organization, divides, sides, and cognatic sides

Divides and sides were defined for P-graphs by White and Jorion (1996: 287–88) solely in terms of principles of balance in signed networks and independently of rules of descent or named moieties. In a P-graph, if links of opposite gender are signed + and –, then *divides* exist in a single generation connected by sibling and sibling-in-law links if the product of signs in marriage cycles is positive. Divides were found to be statistically significant[1] for the Anuta of Polynesia (Houseman and White, 1996). *Sides* extend the principle of balance to marriage cycles across all generations in the network and were found to be statistically significant (p < .0001) by Houseman and White (1998b) for all nine societies in "Dravidian

Amazonia," a region where most societies have sided egocentric categories in their kin terms with published genealogies but no named moieties or dual descent group organization and four other cases from elsewhere with Dravidian kin terms but no moieties. In these 13 cases, "imperfect" sidedness error rates of 1 to 7 percent matched "imperfect" locally sided behavior. Structural cohesion, dual opposition in local and global "balance," and local marriage cycles or "types" of marriage come together in a single package (in a way that is easily tested with empirical kinship networks) where egocentric kin terms and marriage behavior are linked to more global network structures.

Especially troubling to ethnographers is the occurrence of "sidedness" (supposedly based on descent) in complex Eurasian state societies that are cognatic, lacking descent groups, and with monogamy or limited polygyny and inheritance divided between sons and daughters. Leach's (1961) Sinhalese village ethnography put an end to British descent-based theory of kinship corporations by showing that Pul Eliyan productive systems were egocentrically organized and based on marriage alliances. He could not find the coda, however, as to how conflicts and alliances were organized. Houseman and White (1998a) coded his detailed genealogies into P-graphs to test whether Sinhalese two-sided (Dravidian) egocentric kin terms were associated with maritally sided networks in the absence of unilineal descent groups, and found that couples linked through common ancestries included women marrying between opposing sides formed by male succession to ownership. Without a male heir in a family, however, daughters could receive through cognatic inheritance the normally male-transmitted residential compound, fields, and irrigation ditches. The exceptions to male-sidedness were all "diga" marriages (residence with the wife), in which the device to reconcile the contradictions with sidedness was to choose the husband in these cases from a distant village whose sidedness was discounted. Rather than marrying from the "side" of the father, children took their side from the mother's inherited compound.

Generations

Generations in a kinship network are often thought of, alternatively, as relative to ego, as roughly contemporaries of the ego (assuming men and women marry as close to the same age), or as having a different average time span for males and females depending, for example, on how early females marry or have children relative to men,

and on how late men begin (because of male initiations, for example) and go on having children relative to women. The Alyawarra of the central Australian desert (Denham and White, 2005), as a result of two years' fieldwork by Denham, have one of the most complete data sets on kinship networks, actual ages, and use of kinship terminology. Women's average age at childbirth is only two-thirds that of men's paternity so that men's generational time span is 50 percent longer and slower than women. In any society where a large spousal-age difference is present, this will create chains of wives' brothers that move forward in time in augmented-generational increments (and backward in diminished generational increments for sisters' husbands).

Empirical examples for generations

The Alyawarra take siblings and siblings-in-law to define their *generations*, so that generations are most definitely not contemporaries. In Figure 10.4 the two diagonal dash-dotted lines connect marriages in the age-slanted generations of WB (wife's brother) chains (WBWBWB . . .), with vertical solid lines for the patridescent lines of sons and dotted lines veering from the vertical, diagonally down and left, following a recurrent pattern of MBD- or MMBDD-type marriages, and those veering to the right breaking this pattern with other kinds of marriage. The age slant entails that a WF averages a female half-generation older than his DH and a WB averages a female half-generation younger than his ZH.

The brother/sister age-to-marriage variations in vertical heights of lines in Figure 10.4 closely approximate true age, so age differences can be read off the figure. When arranged by classificatory descent lines (1–6 for men), it is possible in this P-graph to see patterns of marriages, all of which are consistent with the marriageable-category memberships of the kinship terminology. In some marriages the wife is older than the husband (e.g., widow marriage), or much younger (e.g., alternating generation, like MBDDD).

Sections

A section system like the marriage classes of the Alyawarra is a matrimonial organization that gives different members of the nuclear family and their spouses – father, mother, children, and children's spouses – four "section" names that govern their marriages and marital sections of their offspring. Governing pairs of names create a permutation group where each parental pair creates children's and their spouses' pairs (Weil, 1949). The naming

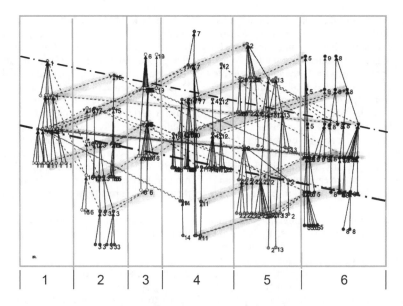

Figure 10.4   Alyawarra age-slanted alternating sibling and sibling-in law generations *(main female lines shaded and two)* in P-graph format

pairs are doubly *sided*, with intersecting male and female sides, and marriages only with their opposites. Sides are not *descent groups*, considering that the section names in both male and female names alternate between generations. This creates an equivalence of alternating generations wherein one can only marry *within the generation* (normally composed of sibling and sibling-in-law chains) or a generation twice removed.

Empirical example for sections

Alyawarra have four sections, each divided into two subsections, and the data show a nearly perfect correspondence between marriage behavior and sections/subsection memberships. In indigenous Australia, where four-, six-, and eight-section systems (or simple sidedness) are nearly universal, ethnographers have tried to model kinship networks as if they had symmetries and regularities beyond the permutation group governance of marital sections. Nearly every mathematical model of Australian kinship networks (e.g., H. White, 1963) has exaggerated symmetries. Kinship network analysis (e.g., with P-graphs) allows networks to be considered as complex relational systems rather than marriage prescriptions for categorical descent lines of men and women. Figure 10.4 is perhaps the only actual-age marriage pattern diagram of an Australian society in existence. Denham et al. (1979) explored the puzzle of how the age difference between spouses

would affect marriage within one's (or an alternating) generation and proposed an idealized double helix model where classificatory lines of females in the MBD diagonal would pass through six classificatory male descent groupings and then cycle over back to the first of these groups, continuing indefinitely while only coded for a finite number of generations in the kinship terminology. Yet, in this small-scale society the possibilities for continuity, like a generation that wraps around from the right side to the left in the next *alternating* generation, are not filled in. There are too few people. In Figure 10.4 there are many breaks where WB links are missing and the WB link pattern does not recur for all the patrilines. Rather than "fill in" imaginary links, as in a double helix model, it is better to consider how such a system works on the ground: when residence is virilocal, with men in the male line living together, then a MBD marriage, within a *parallelogram of female shaded lines bounded left and right by adjacent classificatory male lines*, will link to another group in which one's MB is resident and one's wife was born. In the struggle for survival, this MB group will be a potential place to visit, and an obvious source for exchange and balancing out of resources. The neighboring group in turn may have a similar MB group, to which the ego could be redundantly linked through a wife as an MMBDD relative. In life on the ground, these two-step linkages to a neighbor's and a neighbor's neighbor's groups are sufficient for survival and correspond to the short chains of single or double MBD links in the diagram, where empirical pulses of one or two successive MBD marriages sum to 18 in all in Figure 10.4.

Having temporally ordered time series data is of enormous value in social network analysis, even using heuristic placement of generations (a standard option in Pajek: White, 2008a) and age-difference adjustment that can be done in the absence of known dates of births, marriages, deaths, and other events. (Temporal marriage-date adjustments can be made for FZD marriages, for example, which entail same-age for husband and wife, while MBD does not; MBDDD entails wives' average marriage at half or less the ages of their husbands.) Knowing approximate generations, age differences between individuals, and rough temporal intervals of contemporaneity is a major advantage to kinship network analysis because we can permute marriages randomly or with rules of prohibition (e.g., against marrying prohibited relatives) or with probabilistic biases for *contemporaneous* men and women whose marriages could have been different, like within games of musical chairs. Valid estimates of marriage *preferences or aversions/prohibitions* can be made with the statistical controls explained below (White, 1999), as deviations against this random "musical chair" baseline of controlled "random rewirings".

SIMULATIONS: STRUCTURE AND AGENCY

Permuting only the element of who women marry (alternately, the men) in each generation or contemporaneous period limits the permuted choices to only those marriage opportunities indexed by actual marriages in that generation. This holds constant the demographic composition of descent groups in the male (or alternately, female) lines, the numbers of sons and daughters in each nuclear family, and thus all other structural and demographic features of the observed marriages. The resulting frequencies for each type of marriage (those resulting from the permutated marriages, all else constant), compared with the actual marriage-type frequencies, give appropriate measures of preference or aversion (prohibition) for each type of marriage (White, 1999, 2008b). These can be *departures from the controlled simulation frequencies*, either for sizes of bicomponents or for or against specific types of marriage. This allows a separation of structure and agency by means of empirical criteria. Such measures can also include inferential statistics that improve and refine these results by positing a probabilistic

model of choices over the target set of marriage types, using bootstrap simulation to generate probability distributions evaluated against the data.

Ethnographic example for simulations: structure and agency

For separating structure and agency, structural "signals" that come from limitations of context need not be interpreted in terms of decision-making agency. Table 10.1 gives an example. Here, the ethnographer (Schweizer) recorded four types of cohesive marriage (using the notation here and in Table 10.1 of F = Father, B = Brother, D = Daughter, M = Mother, and Z = Sister: FBD, MBD, FZDD, ZD) among the 19 marriages of Muslim elites in a Javanese village (Sawahan), compared to commoners who had only one such marriage (White and Schweizer, 1998). Is this a difference in marriage preferences or cultural rules or strategies for the two groups? Each group was partitioned into generations, and marriages in each group and generation were randomly rewired using controlled simulation (White, 1999). No marriage frequency was found to significantly differ in frequency from those of random marital rewirings, that is, controlling for difference in the sizes of the groups and thus noting the smaller size of the elite group. In marrying within its status group, each such group will require a proportionate number of spouses, but in a smaller group descended from a common ancestor there will be more co-descendant marriages among the marriages if marriage choices are random. The result would have been different if the elites chose to avoid co-descendant marriages, but they did not. Nor did they prefer them, similar to the commoners, assuming that they followed a preference for *status endogamy*, each preferring to choose spouses from their own groups.

The Austrian village case (analysis of social class, above) studied by Brudner and White (1997) provides an example where controlled ("musical chairs") simulation answered the question: In the competition for heirships how do we know whether some farm family children *choose* to relink or whether relinking occurred by chance? Couldn't the relinking be the product of a random assortment of marriages, relative to inheriting, some persons relinking by chance in a giant component and others not? Permuting women's marriage in each generation, in the latest and prior historical generations surveyed, showed that relinking occurred far more frequently than by chance at single, double, and triple generational depths (i.e., relinking among sets of siblings or cousins in the village) but far less frequently than

Table 10.1   Marriage-type comparisons between Javanese Muslim elites (MusElite) in Dukah Hamlet versus Dukah commoners (DhC) (White, 1999: 13.2, Table 7)

Muslim Elite vs. Dukah Commoners	Presence of the marriage for this kin type		Absence of the marriage for this kin type		Fisher Exact test	Marriage types	Three-way Fisher test
	Actual	Simul.	Actual	Simul.	p=	type	p=
1:MusElite	1	0	4	3	.625	FBD	
* DhCom	0	1	9	12	.591	"	1.00
2:MusElite	1	2	2	3	.714	MBD	
* DhCom	1	0	11	16	.429	"	1.00
3:MusElite	2	1	3	2	.714	FZDD	
* DhCom	0	0	11	0	n.a.	"	1.00
4:MusElite	0	1	6	7	.571	ZD	
* DhCom	0	0	18	24	n.a.	"	1.00
Total MusElite	4	4	15	15	1.00	All	
* Total DhCom	1	1	49	52	1.00	"	1.00

* The three-way Fisher test compares the difference between entries within two 2 x 2 cross-tabs, controlling for the bivariate marginal totals of each pair of variables (White et al., 1983). Given the number of each type of marriage and the numbers in each group, none of these pairs of fourfold tables differ as between the two groups.

by chance for relinkings at greater generational depths. It is obvious that relatives at shallow depth sets would know each other, and could self-select and marry endogamously, excluding relinking with noninheriting members of their sets. Further, it is among the sibling and cousin sets that there is competition for parental inheritances that are not yet decided. Thus, we can conclude that the statistical evidence favors intentional or implicit and strategic decision making, while relinking fails the test for randomness.

INSTITUTIONAL AND COHESION ANALYSIS

Greif (1994, 2006) treats social networks in the context of embedded decision making and a historical context to derive analyses of economic institutions. The systems of co-descendant marriage preferences in the Matriarchs and Turkish nomads examples fall into his "collectivist belief system" societies (Grief, 1994), which are segregated (they individually, socially, and economically interact with members of specific groups), while the systems of co-affinal marriage preferences such as the Austrian farmers example fall into Grief's "individualistic belief system" societies, in which social structure is integrated, economic transactions are conducted among people of different groups, enforcement is achieved through specialized organizations (courts),

and self-reliance is highly valued. The contrast suggests to Greif that the individualistic system may be more economically efficient in the long run. The networks he considers include family relationships, but not kinship networks writ large. He fails to take into account that European kinship networks have a marriage structure that facilitates stratified social classes and dominance by elites. That is very different from systems in which lineages and clans compete and each may have its elites that not only cooperate within groups but have broadcast strong ties for cooperation and exchange. Greif's conclusions may be premature.

The endoconical clans examined here, in contrast, have very high marital relinking indices within their bicomponents (Aydınlı, 66 percent; Canaan, 64 percent) and a power-law spread of ties that balances intensive relinking for close relatives against broadcast links with distant ones. Up close, these look like segregative networks but in fact, in Greif's terms, the "social structure *is* integrated, economic transactions *are* conducted among people of different groups, enforcement *is* achieved through specialized organizations," the difference being that it is not only courts but kinship norms of reciprocity and punishment that are operative. The class-stratified Austrian farming village has a lower relinking index (48%), 60% among farmstead heirs. Counterintuitively, the "kin-based" Australian Alyawarra have the lowest index of relinking, 23 percent, in consequence of the fact that polygynous local family groups are large, but the precious kinship ties between local groups are spread thin, as befits a low-density scarce-resource society, integrating the Aranda linguistic neighbors of the Alyawarra into their bicomponent as well as the Alyawarra themselves.

OVERVIEW AND CONCLUSIONS

Attention to the type of evidence presented here – on how class, political, and religious formations are related to the types and boundaries of marital cohesion and structurally endogamous groups in the kinship networks of different societies – was predicated on expectations from previous research about the effects of cohesive blocks in social formations. This research (motivated by findings *from* kinship studies) examined the effects of variable highest-levels of cohesion of individual, family, or firm for the cohesive blocks to which they belong within networks of various sorts. Moody and White (2003) showed (1) strong effects of levels of cohesion of individual students in their friendship blocks on their reports of attachment to high school and (2) how the cohesive strengths of co-memberships in the cohesive blocks of business alliances align with similarities in the choices of firms in their political party alliances of firms in party politics. The problem of structure and agency for this kind of research finding is disorienting to many social scientists. Does membership in a cohesive group "cause" an individual or firm to alter attitudes or choices? Do similar choices or attitudes "cause" homophilous affiliations? Is the causation circular? Powell et al. (2005), using the Moody-White measurement of structural cohesion, looked at time-lagged effects. They showed that choice of partners for strategic collaborations in the biotech industry was heavily predicated from year to year by level of cohesion in the cohesive blocks to which potential partners belonged the year before but decisions driven by cohesion may be matters of intent (which entails that actors perceive differences in cohesion). For kinship, in the most telling case where bicomponent (more cohesively integrated) members of a farming community tended to be those who inherit productive property, which came first? Knowledge that one is an heir, then the cohesively "local" marriage, or the "local" marriage first, disposing the parents to favor one child over another? In both the biotech and the farming examples, compared to a simulated baseline for "those eligible," convergences of structure (cohesion) and the decision to partner occurred empirically, but were they determined by agency, structural context, or both? A good example is the

contrast within the Indonesian Muslim village (Sawahan) between the relatively few rich elites and the majority of poor commoners. There, the expectation was that *marriage choice* was within one's status group or class, but the simulation, controlling for status endogamy, showed no difference in marriage *structure* although marriage to a relative is far more probable by chance in a smaller group with common ancestry than in a larger group with more distributed ancestry. Context may mask as agency ("we marry X and Y relatives") although agency may operate at a higher level ("we marry our own", status-wise). Network studies need to attend to the multiple network levels at which agency engages.

What we find from kinship data is that preferences or proscriptions in monogamous Christian societies *not to marry a relative* creates horizontal co-affinal relinking at a sufficient spatial scale (given the Relinking theorem) and this *stratum* forms the basis of social class. This is no surprise in the Weberian view, where endogamy is the social tendency in class formation, while inheritance and consolidation of wealth through status endogamy is the economic tendency. This is true for the farming community at a scale of 500 people, half of whom on average, within each sibling group, inherit property and practice structural endogamy within the village, while the other half tend to marry outsiders and immigrate or take up a nonfarming occupation. This is also true for national societies with populations of millions, where subsets of elites (political, intellectual, scientific, occupational) not only practice structural endogamy within the social class they generate by these choices but as a corollary, as a maritally cohesive group, they also wield joint influence over political parties, governance, economic power, and industrial ownership. Similarly, for some countries, such as England, for the class strata of laborers, particularly those who wield particular skills, there is a hereditary component to social and economic class transmission. These two aspects weld together through *structural endogamy cum inheritance*, a combined engine of both structure *and* agency.

Composed within the kinship network, marriage choices (which include the universalistic aspect including the possibility of *leaving one's group*) in the context of structural endogamy are *particularistic* as to whom one marries (i.e., to someone at a particular distance or position within the social network). In societies where *it is commonly a relative who is married*, we Westerners are more apt to ascribe *prescription* or *normative preferences* in marriage. The use of tools for *marriage census* frequencies of different types of marriage (described as cycles or marriage motifs, such as MBD, but including many hundreds of more remote relatives), however, reveals contrastive characteristic probability distributions (White and Houseman, 2002), ones that may tend to be Zipfian in equalizing the sums of close marriage types of higher individual frequency against the sums of lower individual frequencies more of the distant marriage types, thereby indicating overall either co-affinal or co-descendant marriage "preferences."

In many co-descendant marriage Middle Eastern clan structures (like the Aydınlı, the Old Testament Patriarchs and Matriarchs, or the mythical clan of Greek Gods), marital cohesion also distributes widely, as in co-affinal Christian marriage and class systems, but with an important difference: rather than "strength of weak ties," the broader networks are welded by "navigable strong ties" created through reciprocity between local and fractal kinship units with large size inequalities due to polygyny and fecundity. Here, too, as with the Aydınlı, those outside the structurally endogamous cores of communities are more likely to emigrate to cities (structure or agency?).

It is no surprise, then, that the embeddedness structure of kinship groups, integrated by marital cohesion at varying scales, marks out distinctive types of *social organizations* with different scalings of structure, and that these organizations are interlocked with large-scale class, clan and inter-clan, and caste and inter-caste formations (always linked by divisions of labor and occupations), and with political structure, religion, and religious organization. This also provides kinship frameworks, for politologists like Doyle (2005), for "examination of sub-national political behavior . . . the study of comparative politics . . . [and] of inter-governmental organizations, non-governmental organizations, or transnational advocacy networks with state government infrastructure." Korotayev (2003) and the regional case studies examined here show that multiple features of kinship, and network forms of marital cohesion, are closely interlocked with specific historical religions and regions.

For kinship, Weil (1949) was the first to understand that kinship structures are relations among marriages and groups and not just among people, and that even core relational structures, like sections, are easily transformed (e.g., to subsections, and back to sections). How cohesive units in kinship networks are connected to kin terms, norms, and prototypical role expectations is part of the views of social organization discussed by Firth (1951), H. White (1963), and Leaf (2007). Variant kinship networks not only serve as fundamental platforms for historically specific forms of social organization but exhibit general regularities that derive from how they engage with specific network principles (e.g., sidedness and balance

principles, sections, class stratification through relinking, etc.). These support variant social processes, like the effect of horizontal stratification implied by co-affinal marriage relinking on a stratified mode of social class formation (Brudner and White, 1997) that channels wealth transmission, outmigration, and occupational mobility. By considering how selection processes affect changes in network structure in a population, rather than taking Firth's idealized approach to structure, we can study how network structures, organization, and agency interact dynamically at different scales. We now (see 2011: Chapter 35) have the tools, such as P-graphs, Ore-graphs, P-systems, Pajek (Batagelj and Mrvar, 1998, 2008), Puck (Hamberger et al., 2009a, 2009b), Tipp (Houseman and Granger, 2008), R programs (White, 2008a, 2008b) and statistical software (Butts, 2008; Handcock et al., 2008) to do so in a way that changes the landscape of our understanding of the "social" in the social sciences. Bank on the fact that with the global financial meltdown of the economy, kinship, like ecological sustainability, will be more important in people's lives than ever.

ACKNOWLEDGMENTS

I thank Peter Carrington, Martin Doyle, Robert Adams, Lilyan Brudner, and Klaus Hamberger for feedback on this paper, the teams of collaborators on the French kinship projects mentioned in the citations for sharing in the development of the methods, the UC Irvine graduate students cited for dissertation studies, and each of my coauthors of previous kinship studies as cited, for contributing to this study. Funding for many of the projects discussed were supported by NSF Grants SBR-9310033 1993–95 "Network Analysis of Kinship, Social Transmission and Exchange: Cooperative Research at UCI, UNI Cologne, CNRS Paris" and BCS-9978282 1999–2001 "Longitudinal Network Studies and Predictive Social Cohesion Theory." I had support as an SFI External Faculty member from John Padgett, Mark Newman, and many other Santa Fe Institute Research Faculty, who discussed with us the concepts of cohesion used in this paper as they were being developed.

NOTES

1 In a random graph, half the chromatic number $\gamma = m - n + 1$ of independent cycles are expected to have a negative product of signs, so an

appropriate test is given by the binomial theorem. The Par-side Program (White and Skyhorse, 1997) calculates statistical significance as a departure from randomness in the frequencies of balanced and unbalanced cycles.

REFERENCES

Adams, R.McC. (1966) *The Evolution of Urban Society: Early Mesopotamia and Prehistoric Mexico.* Chicago: University of Chicago Press.

Alcántara V.N. (2001) *Kinship, Marriage, and Friendship Ties in the Mexican Power Elite.* PhD Dissertation, Program in Social Networks. University of California, Irvine.

Barry, L.S. (1998) 'Les modes de composition de l'alliance. Le "mariage arabe"' *L'Homme*, 147: 17–50.

Barry, L.S. (2008) *La Parenté.* New York: Ballantine Books.

Batagelj, V. and Mrvar A. (1998) 'Pajek: A program for large networks analysis' *Connections*, 21: 47–57.

Batagelj, V. and Mrvar A. (2008) 'Analysis of kinship relations with Pajek', *Social Science Computer Review*, 26(2): 224–46.

Berkowitz, S.D. (1975) *The Dynamics of Elite Structure: A Critique of C. Wright Mills' "Power Elite" Model.* PhD Dissertation, Brandeis University.

Berkowitz, S. D. (1980) 'Structural and non-structural models of elites', *Canadian Journal of Sociology*, 5: 13–30.

Berkowitz, S.D., Woodward, L.H. and Woodward C. (2006) 'The use of formal methods to map, analyze and interpret *hawala* and terrorist-related alternative remittance systems', *Structure and Dynamics*, 1(2): 291–307.

Brudner, L.A. and White D.R. (1997) 'Class, property and structural endogamy: Visualizing networked histories', *Theory and Society*, 25(2): 161–208.

Butts, C. (2008) 'Social network analysis with sna', *Journal of Statistical Software*, 24(6): 1–51.

Casasola V.S. (2001) *Prominence, Local Power and Family Networks in Santiago de Guatemala: 1630–1820.* PhD Dissertation, Program in Social Networks. University of California, Irvine.

Casasola V.S. and N. Alcántara V. (2002) 'La estrategía matrimonial de la red de poder de Guatemala colonial', in J. Gil Mendieta and Samuel Schmidt (eds.), *Análisis de Redes*: *Aplicaciones en Ciencias Sociales*, Mexico: Universidad National de México. pp. 158–78.

Council of Europe (2009) *Well-being for All – Concepts and Tools for Social Cohesion* (Trends in social cohesion no. 20). Strasbourg, France: Palais de l'Europe.

Denham, W.W., McDaniel, C.K. and Atkins, J.R. (1979) 'Aranda and Alyawarra kinship: A quantitative argument for a double helix model', *American Ethnologist*, 6: 1–24.

Denham, W.W. and White, D.R. (2005) 'Multiple measures of Alyawarra kinship', *Field Methods*, 17: 70–101.

Doyle, T.M. (2005) 'Network analysis for comparative politics', Amazon review of White and Johansen, 2005. http://www.amazon.com/gp/pdp/profile/A3V8ZGN18V6BQ4.

Firth, R. (1951) *Elements of Social Organization.* London: Watts and Co.

Fitzgerald, W. (2004) *Structural and Non-structural Approaches to Social Class: An Empirical Investigation.* PhD Dissertation, Program in Social Networks. University of California, Irvine.

Fox, R. (1977) *Kinship and Marriage.* Harmondsworth: Penguin.

Gibbons, A. (1985) *Algorithmic Graph Theory.* Cambridge: Cambridge University Press.

Gil M.J. and Schmidt, S. (1996) 'The Mexican network of power', *Social Networks*, 18(4): 355–81.

Gil M.J. and Schmidt, S. (2005) *Estudios sobre la Red Política de Mexico.* Mexico: Universidad National de México.

Girvan, K. and Newman, M.E.J. (2002) 'Community structure in social and biological networks', *Proceedings of the National Academy of Sciences USA*, 99: 7821–26.

Granovetter, M. (1973) 'The strength of weak ties', *American Journal of Sociology*, 78(6): 1360–80.

Greif, A. (1994) 'Cultural beliefs and the organization of society: A historical and theoretical reflection on collectivist and individualist societies', *The Journal of Political Economy*, 102(5): 912–50.

Greif, A. (2006) *Institutions and the Path to the Modern Economy: Lessons from Medieval Trade.* Cambridge: Cambridge University Press.

Hamberger, K. and Daillant, I. (2009a) 'L'analyse de réseaux de parenté: concepts et outils', *Annales de Démographie Historique, Parenté et Informatique.*

Hamberger K., Houseman, M. and Grange, C. (2009b) 'La parenté radiographiée: un nouveau logiciel pour le traitement et l'analyse des structures matrimoniales', *L'Homme*, 189.

Hamberger, K., Houseman, M., Daillant, I., White, D.R. and Barry, L. (2004) 'Matrimonial ring structures', *Mathématiques et sciences humaines*, 43(168): 83–121.

Hamberger, K., Houseman, M. and White, D.R. (2011) 'Kinship network analysis', in P. Carrington and J. Scott (eds.), *SAGE Handbook of Social Network Analysis.*

Handcock, M.S., Hunter, D.R., Butts, C.T., Goodreau, S.M. and Morris, M. (2008) 'Statnet: Software tools for the representation, visualization, analysis and simulation of network data', *Journal of Statistical Software*, 24(1): 1–11.

Harary, F. (1953) 'On the notion of balance of a signed graph'. *Michigan Mathematical Journal*, 2: 143–146.

Harary, F. (1969) *Graph Theory.* Reading, MA: Addison-Wesley.

Harary, F. and White, D.R. (2001) 'P-systems: A structural model for kinship studies', *Connections*, 24(2): 22–33.

Houseman, M. and Grange, C. (2008) 'Présentation du programe TIPP'. http://www.kintip.net/content/view/4/2/.

Houseman, M. and White, D.R. (1996) Les structures réticulaires de la pratique matrimoniale', *L'Homme*, 139: 59–85.

Houseman, M. and White, D.R. (1998a) 'Network mediation of exchange structures: Ambilateral sidedness and property flows in Pul Eliya (Sri Lanka)', in T. Schweizer and D.R. White (eds.), *Kinship Networks and Exchange.* Cambridge: Cambridge University Press. pp. 59–89.

Houseman, M. and White, D.R. (1998b) 'Taking sides: Marriage networks and Dravidian kinship in Lowland South America', in M. Godelier and T. Trautmann (eds.), *Transformations of Kinship*. Washington DC: Smithsonian Press.

Johansen, U. and White, D.R. (2002) 'Collaborative long-term ethnography and longitudinal social analysis of a nomadic clan in Southeastern Turkey', in R. van Kemper and A. Royce (eds.), *Chronicling Cultures: Long-Term Field Research in Anthropology*. Walnut Creek, CA: AltaMira Press. pp. 81–99.

Jolas, T., Verdier, Y. and Zonabend, F. (1970) 'Parler famille', *L'Homme*, 10(3): 5–26.

Korotayev, A. (2000) 'Parallel-cousin (FBD) marriage, Islamization, and Arabization', *Ethnology*, 39(4): 395–407.

Korotayev, A. (2003) 'Unilineal descent groups and deep Christianization: A cross-cultural comparison', *Cross-Cultural Research*, 37(1): 132–56.

Korotayev, A. (2004) *World Religions and Social Evolution of the Old World Oikumene Civilizations: A Cross-Cultural Perspective*. Lewiston, NY: Edwin Mellen Press.

Korotayev, A. and Kazankov, A. (2002) 'Regions based on social structure: A reconsideration', *Current Anthropology* 41: 668–90.

Kuper, A. (2006) 'Endogamy, adultery and homosexuality: An ethnographic perspective on the Bloomsbury Group'. http://intersci.ss.uci.edu/wiki/htm/talks.htm.

Leach, E.R. (1954) *Political Systems of Highland Burma: A Study of Kachin Social Structure*. Cambridge: Harvard University Press.

Leach, E.R. (1961) *Pul Eliya, A Village in Ceylon: A Study of Land Tenure and Kinship*. Cambridge: Cambridge University Press.

Leaf, M. (2007) 'Empirical formalism', *Structure and Dynamics*, 2(1): 804–24.

Lévi-Strauss, C. ([1949] 1967) *Les structures élémentaires de la parenté*. 2nd ed. Paris/La Haye: Mouton.

Loomis, C.P. and Powell, R.M. (1949) 'Sociometric analysis of class status in rural Costa Rica – A peasant community compared with an hacienda community', *Sociometry* 12(1/3): 144–57.

Marquand, J.P. (1949) *Point of No Return*. Boston, MA: Little, Brown.

Moody, J. and White, D.R. (2003) 'Structural cohesion and embeddedness: A hierarchical conception of social groups', *American Sociological Review*, 68(1):1–25.

Murdock, G.P. (1967) *Ethnographic Atlas*. Pittsburgh, PA: University of Pittsburgh Press.

Newman, H. and Newman, J.O. (2003) *A Genealogical Chart of Greek Mythology*. Chapel Hill: University of North Carolina Press.

Ore, O. (1960) 'Sex in graphs', *Proceedings of the American Mathematical Society*, 11: 533–39.

Peters, E. (1967 [1991]) *The Bedouin of Cyrenaica: Studies in Personal and Corporate Power*. 2nd ed. J. Goody and E. Marx (eds.). Cambridge: Cambridge University Press.

Powell, W.W., White, D.R., Koput, K.W. and Owen-Smith, J. (2005) 'Network dynamics and field evolution: The growth of interorganizational collaboration in the life sciences', *American Journal of Sociology*, 110(4): 901–75.

Read, D. (2000) 'Formal analysis of kinship terminologies and its' relationship to what constitutes kinship'. *Mathematical Anthropology and Cultural Theory*, 1(1):1–46.

Rebel, H. (1983) *Peasant Classes: The Bureaucratization of Property and Family Relations Under Early Habsburg Absolutism, 1511–1636*. Princeton: Princeton University Press.

Sealey, R. (1976) *A History of the Greek City States, 700–338 B.C.* Berkeley, CA: University of California Press.

Tilly, C. (1984) *Big Structures, Large Processes, Huge Comparisons*. New York: Russell Sage.

Warner, W.L. (1949) *Democracy in Jonesville: A Study of Quality and Inequality*. New York: Harper.

Warner, W.L., Lunt, P.S., Srole, L. and Low, J.O. (1941–1959) *The Social Life of a Modern Community. II: The Status System of a Modern Community. III: The Social Systems of American Ethnic Groups. IV: The Social System of a Modern Factory. V: The Living and the Dead: A Study in the Symbolic Life of Americans*. New Haven: Yale University Press.

Warner, W.L., Meeker, M. and Eells, K. (1949) *Social Class in America: A Manual of Procedure for the Measurement of Social Status*. New York: Science Research Associates.

Weil, A. (1949) 'Sur l'étude algèbrique de certains types de lois de mariage', in C. Lévi-Strauss, *Les structures élémentaires de la parenté*. Paris: Presses Universitaires de France. pp. 279–85.

White, D.R. (1997) 'Structural endogamy and the graphe de parenté', *Mathématiques, informatique, et sciences humaines*, 137: 107–25.

White, D.R. (1999) 'Controlled simulation of marriage systems', *Journal of Artificial Societies and Social Simulation*, 2(3).

White, D.R. (2004) 'Ring cohesion theory in marriage and social networks', *Mathématiques et sciences humaines*, 43(168): 5–28.

White, D.R. (2008a) 'Generation depth partition', http://intersci.ss.uci.edu/wiki/index.php/Generation_depth_partition.

White, D.R. (2008b) 'Software: Kinship simulation', http://intersci.ss.uci.edu/wiki/index.php/Software:_Kinship_simulation.

White, D.R. (2009) 'K-cohesion and kinship', Paper for the Sunbelt Social Networks Conference, San Diego, CA.

White, D.R. (2010) 'Egocentric and sociocentric structure in classificatory kinship systems: Four theorems', *Mathematical Anthropology and Cultural Theory*, 3(6): 1–19.

White, D.R., Batagelj, V. and Mrvar, A. (1999) 'Analyzing large kinship and marriage networks with P-graph and Pajek', *Social Science Computer Review*, 17(3): 245–74.

White, D.R. and Harary, F. (2001) 'The cohesiveness of blocks in social networks: Node connectivity and conditional density', *Sociological Methodology*, 31: 305–59.

White, D.R. and Houseman, M. (2002) 'Navigability of strong ties: Small worlds, tie strength and network topology', *Complexity*, 8(1): 72–81.

White, D.R. and Johansen, U. (2005) *Network Analysis and Ethnographic Problems: Process Models of a Turkish Nomad Clan*. Boston, MA: Lexington Press.

White, D.R. and Jorion, P. (1992) 'Representing and computing kinship: A new approach', *Current Anthropology*, 33(4): 454–63.

White, D.R. and Jorion, P. (1996) 'Kinship networks and discrete structure theory: Applications and implications'. *Social Networks,* 18(3): 267–314.

White, D.R. and Newman, M.E.J. (2001) 'Fast approximation algorithms for finding node-independent paths in networks', Santa Fe Institute Working Paper, 01-07-035.

White, D.R., Pesner, R. and Reitz K. (1983) 'An exact significance test for three-way interaction', *Behavior Science Research,* 18: 103–22.

White, D.R. and Schweizer, T. (1998) 'Kinship, property and stratification in rural java: a network analysis', in T. Schweizer and D.R. White (eds.), *Kinship Networks and Exchange.* Cambridge: Cambridge University Press. pp. 36–58.

White, D.R. and Skyhorse, P. (1997) *Parenté Suite User's Guide, Vol. 1.* UC Irvine. http://eclectic.ss.uci.edu/~drwhite/pdf/PGMAN2-6.pdf.

White, H.C. (1963) *The Anatomy of Kinship.* Englewood Cliffs, NJ: Prentice-Hall.

Widmer, E., Sutter, W.D., Sigris, R. and Fitzgerald, W. (1999) 'The institutionalization of science: Kinship networks of Geneva Scientists', 24th Sunbelt International Social Networks Conference, Chapel Hill, North Carolina.

11

Animal Social Networks

Katherine Faust

Many species of animals are social and engage in associations and interactions with conspecifics. These associations and interactions are components of a species' social organization and, in turn, are prerequisites for the formation of social networks among individuals of the species. This chapter outlines how features of an animal's social network are circumscribed by its social organization (including typical group sizes, demographic composition, patterns of dispersal, spatial proximity and subgrouping arrangements, characteristic types of social interaction, forms of communication, and the social contexts in which interactions take place). Since social organization varies among animal species, it follows that features of social networks also vary.

Tackling the topic of "animal social networks" in a chapter is challenging in light of the range of issues it subsumes and the fact that the number of known animal species is more than one million (Wilson, 1999: 136). However, the number of *social* animals is considerably less than that, perhaps several tens of thousands, though exact numbers are elusive. Given the number of animal species, rather than providing an exhaustive account, this chapter relies on illustrative examples of different forms of social organization and highlights general features that affect social network structure and variability.

The chapter focuses on social networks of nonhuman animals. However, it refers to animal social networks rather than specifying *nonhuman* animal social networks, with the implicit understanding that *Homo sapiens* is included as matter of course. Indeed, ideas that are useful for understanding animal social networks in general are also relevant for understanding human social networks more particularly.

The chapter is organized as follows. The first section presents stylized descriptions of social organization for several animal species. The second section discusses prerequisites for animal social networks including collectivities of individuals, associations or interactions among them, and individual recognizability. The third section describes basic parameters of social organization that circumscribe social networks. The fourth section reviews historical background and more recent insights from empirical studies of animal social networks. The concluding section discusses areas for future investigation.

STYLIZED DESCRIPTIONS OF SOCIAL ORGANIZATION

The social network for a group of animals is constrained by the species' social organization. As Clutton-Brock (1974) observes, "Most species possess characteristic modal patterns of social organization" (539) and these forms of social organization differ between species. Social organization refers to the patterns of relationships between individuals of a population, including typical group sizes, demographic composition (age and sex distributions), patterns of spatial association, extent of communication, typical forms of social interaction, and fluidity of group boundaries (Wilson, 1975; Whitehead, 2008). These aspects of social organization impact how individuals relate to one another and thus constrain features of their social networks. In this context, constrain means that possible social network configurations are limited by aspects of social organization.

As a point of departure for understanding animal social networks it is useful to consider stylized descriptions for several species, or taxa. This overview is intended to highlight both variability between species and suggest common features that operate as structural parameters affecting social networks regardless of species.

Social insects (eusociality): Ants

Social insects — isoptera (termites) and some species of hymenoptera (ants, some bees, and wasps) — represent one "pinnacle" of animal social organization (Wilson, 1975; Grier, 1984). These *eusocial* (truly social) species provide stark examples of extremes of social living; individuals only exist collectively. As a taxa, the ant family Formicidae illustrates eusociality. In ant colonies, castes perform different roles: queen(s) (reproductive female/s), workers (nonreproductive females), and drones (males). Only queens reproduce, while a caste of sterile workers provisions the nest, tends pupae and larvae, and provides defense. Behaviors might be differentiated within castes, for example, by age (Fresneau and Dupuy, 1988; Sendova-Franks et al., 2010). Ants communicate using pheromones (chemical signals) to coordinate activities such as foraging, signaling danger, or tending larvae (Wilson, 1975: 414). Ant species differ in longevity of the queen and means for her replacement, formation of new colonies, group size, and intergroup relations, among other characteristics (Hölldobler and Wilson, 1994).

For ants, a social network probably is most appropriately expressed as relations between and within castes rather than between individuals. Indeed, ants are unlikely to recognize particular individuals (Wilson, 1975: 379). With respect to social networks, important features of eusociality include coresidence of multiple generations, social roles of castes and their relationships, and forms of communication.

Eusociality is found mostly in social insects and is extremely rare in other species. One mammal species provides a provocative exception: parallels to eusociality are seen in the naked mole rat, a subterranean rodent from Kenya, Ethiopia, and Somalia (Jarvis, 1981). A naked mole rat population consists of a single reproductive female along with her immature and adult male and female offspring. Adults cooperatively tend the colony and raise young.

Cooperative breeding: Florida scrub jays

In many bird species the strongest adult social relationships occur in mated pairs, and these bonds might endure for many years. Florida scrub jays (*Aphelocoma coerulescens*) provide an example. Florida scrub jays are a territorial species that practices cooperative breeding. A mated pair raises young and their older male offspring might help defend territory and provide food for younger siblings. Groups average three individuals but can be as large as eight (Goodwin, 1986; Schoech, 1998). Parents distinguish calls of their own offspring from other young (Barg and Mumme, 1994). Generally, females disperse farther from their natal location than do males. Males are more likely than females to remain in or near their natal area, and males might inherit vacated parental territory or move into adjacent areas (Schoech, 1998; Woolfenden and Fitzpatrick, 1978, 1984). This form of social organization, referred to as "group breeding," (Woolfenden, 1975; Woolfenden and Fitzpatrick, 1978) or "cooperative breeding" (Schoech, 1998), is found in a number of bird species (Stacey and Koenig, 1990).

Social network implications of this form of social organization include long-term social bonds between mated pairs, sex-biased dispersal, continued social relations between parents and (male) offspring, helping relations between siblings, and recognition of individuals.

Shoaling: Guppies

Many fish species form schools or congregate in shoals. Guppies (*Poecilia reticulata*) are illustrative. Croft et al. (2004) describe the shoaling network of a guppy population in the Arima River in Trinidad: "shoals are usually small (2–20 fishes) and encounter each other approximately every 14 [seconds]. They also disperse overnight, resulting in the breakdown of shoal composition and a reassembly every morning" (S516). Despite the daily breakdown of shoals, females have preferred associates who are found together more often than expected (Croft et al., 2004; Griffiths and Magurran, 1997, 1998; Morrell et al., 2008) and female associates cooperate in the hazardous activity of inspecting potential predators (Croft et al., 2006). Males are more likely than females to move between shoals.

Important features of guppy social organization include the ability to recognize individuals and associate differentially, assortativity by sex (for females), and sex differences in the spatial extent of movement.

Solitary mammals: Black bears

Species that are generally solitary occupy one end of a continuum of sociality. In solitary animals, individuals spend a considerable portion of time on their own. Examples of relatively solitary species include bobcats (Bailey, 1974), black bears (Rogers, 1987), raccoons (Barash, 1974), red foxes (Barash, 1974), some species of bees and wasps, and many other species. Some solitary species recognize neighbors and respond in different ways to familiar individuals than to strangers. Sociality can also depend on resource availability or point in the life cycle (Barash, 1974) or vary seasonally. Thus, solitariness is a matter of the degree of gregariousness and does not imply that individuals are socially isolated.

Black bears (*Ursus americanus*) illustrate a solitary mammal species. As Rogers (1987) reports for a black bear population in northern Minnesota, females inhabit home ranges and males occupy larger areas that overlap multiple females' ranges. Juveniles leave their natal location and disperse as yearlings, with males moving farther away than females. Independent adult females can inhabit areas near their natal range, and a female black bear might cede some territory to her daughter(s). Females recognize their adult offspring (Larivière, 2001). Black bear females defend territories (Rogers, 1987: 14). Black bears encounter each other at concentrated food locations such as garbage dumps or seasonal food sources where they might form dominance relations (Rogers, 1987).

From the perspective of social networks, important features of black bear social organization include relatively solitary individuals, sex differences in dispersal and territoriality, maternal kinship as a basis for spatial location of females, female recognition of adult offspring, and dominance relations.

Social marine mammals: Bottlenose dolphins

Cetaceans (dolphins, whales, and porpoises) are social marine mammals. As an illustrative species, consider bottlenose dolphins (*Tursiops truncates*), which are found in temperate oceans around the world. The social organization of bottlenose dolphins has been well studied in several populations (Smolker et al., 1992; Lusseau, 2003, 2007; Lusseau and Newman, 2004; Diaz-Lopez et al., 2008; Sayigh et al., 1998; Wells, 2003). Bottlenose dolphins live in pods of several dozen individuals but generally are found in smaller collections (Lusseau, 2003; Smolker et al., 1992). Females associate with their offspring and other females (Smolker et al., 1992; Wells, 2003), whereas males tend to associate with other males. Males can form long-lasting associations or alliances with other males (Wells, 2003; Smolker et al., 1992), and

multiple alliances occasionally join together in super-alliances to monopolize females or to attack other alliances (Connor et al., 1992, 1999). In contrast, the social organization of females is "better described as a network rather than discrete subgroups" (Smolker et al., 1992: 1). Dolphins communicate by whistles that are individually distinctive and recognizable to others over long distances (Sayigh et al., 1998; Janik et al., 2006).

Important features of dolphin social networks include fluid social organization of a large population in which associations are generally in smaller subsets, individually recognizable communication signals, assortativity by sex, long-lasting associations or alliances between males, and networks rather than subgrouping relations between females.

Matrilines: African savannah elephants

A number of mammal species are organized around sets of related females, called *matrilines*. Matrilines consist of an adult female with her juvenile offspring and grown female offspring, or multiple females with their offspring, along with one or more adult males. Females form the core of matrilineal societies.

The social organization of African savannah elephants (*Loxodonta africana*) provides an example. As described by Archie et al. (2006), "For female elephants, 'families' represent one of the most predictable levels of social association. Families are composed of around 2–20 adult females and their immature offspring. . . . [M]ost social interactions, both competitive and affiliative, occur within family groups, indicating that most of the relevant forces shaping female relationships occur there" (p. 120). Since females remain in their natal area whereas males disperse, families contain maternal kin (Archie et al., 2006; Moss and Poole, 1983). Maternal kin form "female bonded kin groups," which might join together in larger "bond groups" of multiple families (Payne, 2003). Elephant social organization consists of a large population of individuals who often associate in smaller subsets, organized in "tiers" (Wittemyer et al., 2005). Genetically related females tend to remain together when the population fissions (Archie et al., 2006). Males disperse from their natal area and have a very different form of organization from females. Males are generally single, found in small unstable groups called "bull groups" (Payne, 2003: 70), or with females, depending on age and reproductive state (Moss and Poole, 1983). Among adult male elephants, there is "little evidence of social structure above the level of one-on-one contests"

(Payne, 2003: 73). Seasonal changes in resource availability affect interactions between family units and larger aggregations (McComb et al., 2001). Elephants communicate over long distances and recognize other individuals (McComb et al., 2000, 2001), leading to "mutual recognition in a large social network" (Payne, 2003: 66). Elephants are long-lived, and older females are important to the group due to their extensive knowledge of natural resources and social relationships (McComb et al., 2001; Payne, 2003).

Social network implications of this form of social organization include individual recognizability, long-distance communication, enduring bonds between related females, sex differences in social organization, fluid organization of a larger population in a multitiered structure, assortativity by age and sex, dominance relations, and importance of older females due to social experience and knowledge.

Many other mammal species have a matrilineal social organization: spotted hyenas (Engh et al., 2005), lions (Pusey and Packer, 1987), and most cercopithecine primates (e.g., macaques [Thierry et al., 2004; Cheverud et al., 1988] and savanna baboons [Cheney and Seyfarth, 2007]).

Male-centered social units: Hamadryas baboons

In contrast to species organized around matrilines, in some species males form the social core. In this form of social organization, males are accompanied by multiple females, who might or might not be related to each other, depending on the species.

In hamadryas baboons (*Papio hamadryas hamadryas*) the basic social unit is the one-male group, consisting of an adult male, one or more adult females, and their offspring (Kummer, 1968; Dunbar, 1983; Swedell, 2002). Multiple one-male groups are found in association to form troops of many dozen individuals, within which males have relatively frequent interactions with each other and coordinate daily movements (Kummer, 1968; Swedell, 2002; Dunbar, 1983). Relationships among adult females can be quite limited (Dunbar, 1983). In hamadryas baboons, both males and females disperse from their natal units and females transfer to different populations (Kummer, 1968; Greenwood, 1980). In some populations, individuals congregate in large aggregations during the night and forage in smaller subsets during the day (Kummer, 1968).

With respect to social networks, important aspects of this form of social organization include different patterns and strengths of social relationships within and between sexes, coordinated activities among males, relatively weak ties between females, and a large population of individuals organized around smaller social units.

Male-centered reproductive units are also found in the closely related species, geladas (Kummer, 1968; Dunbar, 1983). However, despite the superficial similarity, gelada females generally are related to each other, interact frequently with one another, and might join or leave a male together. Thus the social networks of hamadryas baboons and geladas differ in important ways.

Implications for Social Networks

As these descriptions illustrate, there are many different forms of animal social organization. Variability occurs along multiple dimensions (group size, demographic composition, dispersal, and pattern and strength of ties among individuals) with consequences for social network structure. Figure 11.1 shows idealized social networks for some forms of social organization. Although these stylized descriptions gloss over many details, they suggest structural parameters underlying differences in ways that individuals interact and therefore lead us to expect differences in social networks.

PREREQUISITES FOR ANIMAL SOCIAL NETWORKS

Several conditions are required for animals to form a social network. These include collectivities of individuals of the same species along with associations or interactions among them. In addition, a social network representation will likely be most useful when individuals recognize specific others and differentially direct their associations and interactions accordingly.

Collectivities

Sociality is an obvious prerequisite for an animal species to form a social network. This implies that members of the species spend time together and relate to conspecifics in ways that are usefully conceptualized as a social network. This requirement is not as trivial as it first appears. A species might or might not be social; indeed, apart from mating and infant care, many animals are solitary for a substantial portion of their lives (Poole, 1985). However, the distinction between social

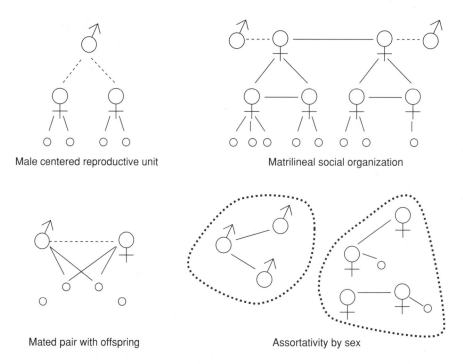

Figure 11.1   Stylized animal social networks. ♀**: Female;** ♂**: Male. Solid lines indicate close social bonds; dashed lines show reproductive pairs. Dotted hulls surround subsets**

and solitary is best viewed as a continuum: in species that are generally solitary, individuals have social contact with others, and in species that are usually social, individuals might spend considerable time alone, especially at particular points in the life cycle (Barash, 1974).

The nature of social groupings varies across species, from populations with relatively fixed membership (langurs or meerkats) to more fluid arrangements (elephants, dolphins, or chimpanzees). As a consequence, exactly how collectivities of individuals are identified can be problematic (Wey et al., 2008; Wolf et al., 2007; Whitehead, 1997). This is especially true for species with flexible forms of social organization, multiple levels of organization in which smaller subsets aggregate into larger populations, or patterns of sociality that vary by age or sex.

From the perspective of animal social networks, it is useful to distinguish collections of individuals that are in close physical proximity but not interacting, communicating, or coordinating their activities, from collections of individuals who associate for longer periods of time, communicate with one another, and coordinate their actions. The first type of collectivity is an *aggregate* (Krause and Ruxton, 2002) or *aggregation* (Whitehead, 2008; Wilson, 1975). An aggregation is a collection of individuals

"gathered in the same place but not internally organized or engaged in cooperative behavior" (Wilson, 1975: 8). Members of an aggregation might be gathered at a seasonal food source but would not otherwise be found together. In contrast, individuals who tend to associate with one another rather than with outsiders over an extended period of time constitute a *population* or *group* (terms vary across disciplines) (Wilson, 1975; Whitehead, 2008).

Understanding a species' grouping patterns presents a challenge in studying animal social organization. In some cases, groupings can be determined by observing space use (Cross et al., 2005), patterns of association among subsets (Cairns and Schweger, 1987), or differences in social interactions within versus between groups (e.g., Hrdy, 1977; Herbinger et al., 2009).

Associations and interactions

Relations between or among individuals are another social network prerequisite, and animals relate to one another in a variety of ways. Close physical proximity, facial expressions, body postures, gestures, dominance displays, physical contact (grooming, hitting), and vocalizations are all types of social behavior. Two general forms of animal sociality are widely used in studying animal social networks (Croft et al., 2008; Wey et al., 2008; Whitehead, 2008). First, *association* is a form of sociality among subsets of individuals indicated by spatial proximity. Associations are useful for detecting subgrouping patterns within a population. Second, *interactions* are dyadic social behaviors, generally directed from one individual to another, which can take on stereotypic forms for a particular species. Interactions are useful for studying social differentiation or dominance orderings among individuals.

Associations

Association is a form of affiliative relationship among subsets of individuals (Smolker et al., 1992; Whitehead, 2008). Associations within a population are not homogeneous since some subsets of individuals tend to differentially associate with one another; they spend considerable time together in close proximity.

Spatial proximity is a basic indicator of differential association and is used to identify subgroup membership and dyadic patterns of association (Smolker et al., 1992; Whitehead, 2008; Slooten et al., 1993; Sailer and Gaulin, 1984; Cross et al., 2005). Obviously, the distance indicating spatial proximity differs between species: "close" for a 32-meter-long blue whale is different from "close" for a few-millimeters-long ant. The operative distance for association depends on distances over which individuals can communicate and coordinate their actions. In practice, associations are determined by examining typical spatial arrangements. Often the distribution of distances between individuals shows discontinuities indicating a distance beyond which individuals are not likely to be associating (Cross et al., 2005; Slooten et al., 1993). For example, Wolf et al. (2007) used spatial proximity to study subgrouping patterns of the Galápagos sea lion. "Operationally, we defined a group using a chain rule . . . such that animals within one body length (between 1 and 2 m) of each other shared the same group" (Wolf et al., 2007: 1294–95).

Associations are especially salient in *fission-fusion* societies (Kerth and König, 1999; Kummer, 1968, 1971; Aureli et al., 2008). In a fission-fusion society members of a larger population usually associate in smaller subsets, which travel and interact relatively independently of others for some time before rejoining the larger group. The composition of subsets during fission events indicates stronger associations between individuals. For example, among African savannah elephants genetically related females tend to remain together during fusion events (Archie et al., 2006). Fission-fusion societies are also found in chimpanzees, hamadryas baboons (Kummer, 1968), kangaroos (Carter et al., 2009), bats (Kerth and König, 1999), dolphins (Smolker et al., 1992), and many other species. Fission-fusion social organization exhibits multiple dimensions of association: variation in social cohesion, subgroup sizes, and subgroup composition (Aureli et al., 2008).

With respect to social networks, patterns of associations indicate whether there are pairs of individuals who tend to associate at rates higher (or lower) than expected by chance, subsets who associate with each other forming cohesive groupings or "communities," or differential assortativity by demographic characteristics (e.g., age/sex classes) (Whitehead, 1999, 2008; Sailer and Gaulin, 1984; Bejder et al., 1998).

Interactions

Social interactions are dyadic who-to-whom behaviors that are generally directed from one individual to another. Examples include both affiliative acts (grooming, contact) and agonistic behaviors (dominance displays, threats, physical contests). Patterns of social interactions in a group can reveal prominent individuals, asymmetries in dyadic arrangements, or overall network structure (such as dominance hierarchies).

Social interactions of a species can be more or less stereotyped, in that characteristic forms of behavior are enacted under specific circumstances. Along with nonsocial acts, these constitute the "behavioral repertoire" of a species (Grier, 1984: 69). A behavioral repertoire is described in an *ethogram*, which includes all behaviors of a species: for example, feeding, movement, and intraspecific interactions (Grier, 1984; Banks, 1982). Of most relevance for animal social networks are the intraspecific social behaviors: the ways in which individuals interact with conspecifics. The following excerpt describes some dyadic agonistic behaviors of the emperor tamarin monkey and shows the level of detail in a typical ethogram (Knox and Sade, 1991: 447, Table II).

"Lunge . . . The tamarin's head and shoulders are rapidly thrust toward another animal. The mouth may be partially opened. The vertebral column is somewhat arched."

"Grab Face . . . The hand is extended toward the face of another tamarin and the claws are used to grab the pelage, which is then immediately released."

"Bat . . . A tamarin swiftly cuffs another tamarin, usually on the face."

"Head Shake . . . The head is rapidly turned from side to side while staring at the target tamarin."

Ethograms enable systematic observation and recording of social interactions between members of a population and thus provide relational data to construct a social network.

Associations and interactions are prerequisite building blocks for social networks since they indicate relations between or among members of a population. However, differential associations or interactions are required for patterned social networks.

Individual recognition

Arrangement of an animal population into a patterned social network presumes that associations and interactions among individuals are not random; some pairs or subsets have a greater or lesser than expected tendency to interact in particular ways. Nonrandom associations or interactions indicate that individuals differentially relate to others and suggest that they can distinguish individuals and act accordingly. Multiple lines of evidence show that, in many species, individuals emit distinctive signals that are recognizable to others, can distinguish familiar individuals from strangers, and know about specific individuals and react in different ways to them. Evidence for these capabilities is widespread.

Many species have distinctive characteristics or signals: for example, vocalizations or scents that are individually recognizable. Bird songs differ among individuals of the same species and can be distinguished by others (Weeden and Falls, 1959). Bottlenose dolphins have "distinctive signature whistles" (Sayigh et al., 1998). Spotted hyenas make individual "whoops" that are recognized by members of their clan (East and Hofer, 1991) and have distinctive anal gland scents (Burgener et al., 2009). Calls of vervet monkeys, including juveniles, are distinctive and recognizable (Cheney and Seyfarth, 1990). Signals and recognition can involve multiple modalities. For example, horses recognize individuals both visually and by the sounds of their whinnies (Proops et al., 2009).

Recognizable differences between individuals result in differentiated patterns of interactions and associations. Guppies recognize and prefer to school with familiar individuals (Griffiths and Magurran, 1997). Cichlid fish react differently to a mate than to a neighbor or strange fish (Balshine-Earn and Lotem, 1998). Mantis shrimp respond differently to individuals who have bested them in agonistic encounters, avoiding water that has been occupied by the winning shrimp (Caldwell, 1979). Red foxes and raccoons resolve dominance disputes with neighbors more quickly than with strangers (Barash, 1974).

That animals recognize particular individuals and react in different ways to them is important for understanding animal social networks. As Heinrich observes from his research on recruitment and social dynamics in ravens, "Almost nothing of the ravens' observed social behavior makes sense without the capacity of individual recognition among their own kind" (2000: A13). Recognition and differential reaction to others indicate substantial cognitive capacities as social actors. In addition, animals of some species know about social relationships between other individuals, a point discussed in more detail below. These capacities lead to interdependencies in social relationships and thus affect social network properties.

Collectivities, associations (or interactions), and the capacity for individual recognition are prerequisites for forming social networks. Beyond these basics, several social structural parameters limit social network configurations that can occur.

PARAMETERS OF SOCIAL ORGANIZATION

Several features of animal social organization provide structural parameters that limit possible social networks in which an animal species can engage. These features vary among species and therefore lead us to expect differences in social networks between species. Topics discussed in this section parallel Wilson's "qualities of sociality" (Wilson, 1975; also Whitehead, 2008).

Group size

In all networks, the number of individuals is a structural parameter that constrains other network properties (Mayhew and Levinger, 1976). Therefore, typical group sizes restrict many features of a species' social network (Lehmann et al., 2007). Indeed, Pollard and Blumstein observe "group size is a core trait defining social systems, social complexity and social structure" (2008: 1683). The size of a group generally refers to the typical population size or "the size of the largest stable exclusive group" (1686). Group size is quite variable (Dunbar, 2003). In a survey of several dozen animal species, Reiczigel et al. (2008: 716) report median observed group sizes ranging from 1 (feeding Adelie penguins; bushbucks) to 300 (American white pelicans). For 50 species of diurnal primates, Pollard and Blumstein (2008: 1693–94) report group sizes ranging from around 4 (agile gibbons) to over 100 (geladas).

Most basically, group size determines the potential number of contacts that an individual can have. Individuals in large groups obviously have more opportunities to interact with conspecifics than do individuals in small groups. In addition, regardless of whether or not interactions take place, group size determines the number of others an individual is exposed to. Group size also governs the number of pairs, triples, and subsets that can be formed from a population, and thus limits subgrouping arrangements. There are more possibilities for fissioning into subsets in large groups than in small groups. Therefore, the social combinations in which individuals of a species can engage depend on the species' typical group sizes.

Demographic composition

The demographic composition of a population refers to the age and sex distribution of its members. This composition is affected by a species' social organization: for example, whether there are monogamous mated pairs, an adult male accompanied by multiple adult females and immature offspring, or matrilines of related females. Social behaviors generally differ by the age and sex of individuals involved, including dependence of infants, differences between sexually mature and immature individuals, age-related participation in dominance hierarchies, and sex differences in forms of interaction. Thus, demographic characteristics are related to the social "roles" of individuals (Blumstein and Armitage, 1997, 1998).

The age and sex distribution of members of a group also affect combinations for associations and interactions and thus relational possibilities in a social network. Availability of partners for affiliative relationships or coalitions depends on population composition. For example, availability of kin as social partners or allies depends on kin group sizes (Silk et al., 2006; Cheney and Seyfarth, 1990). In addition, because individuals of many species tend to associate with others who are similar in age or sex, the demographic composition of a population affects possibilities for assortativity by demographic characteristics.

Dispersal

Social networks depend on interactions between individuals, which in turn require spatial and temporal proximity, therefore factors that affect group membership, movement, and spatial locations also affect social networks. In particular,

dispersal, the departure of individuals from their natal group, affects animal social networks through the capability to maintain associations and interactions.

In most animal species some individuals leave their natal group around the time of sexual maturity or for breeding (Shields, 1987). A consequence of nondispersal is *philopatry*, the tendency for individuals to remain at or near their natal location (Greenwood, 1980; Shields, 1987; Wasser and Jones, 1983). From the perspective of social networks, remaining individuals have the opportunity to retain social relationships with members of their population, including relationships with remaining kin.

Dispersal is related to the permeability of group boundaries and networks since "increased permeability is . . . associated with a reduction in the stability of such interpersonal relationships . . . as dominance hierarchies, coalitions, and kin groups" (Wilson, 1975: 17). Thus, dispersal, especially sex-biased dispersal, has important consequences for social networks, because it fundamentally alters social relationships. Dispersal affects the social network of the dispersing individual (by severing or greatly reducing the frequency of interactions with members of its former group) and dispersing individuals can become socially isolated for a period of time (Wilson, 1975; Colvin, 1983). Dispersal also can be accompanied by striking differences in relative social positions. Spotted hyenas provide an example. A "hyaena clan can be appropriately described as consisting of two classes of animals, a relatively high-ranking natal class, and a relatively low ranking immigrant class" (Smale et al., 1993: 476). However, social isolation of dispersing individuals need not be permanent. In long-lived species where dispersal happens only once (e.g., chimpanzees) close bonds can develop between previously unfamiliar (and unrelated) individuals (Lehmann and Boesch, 2009).

Occasionally, both sexes disperse, but often there is a sex bias such that one sex is more likely than the other to leave (Packer, 1979; Pusey and Packer, 1987; Greenwood, 1980; Shields, 1987). Sex-biased dispersal has important consequences for social organization and networks. For example, in species where males transfer and females remain with their natal group, maternally related kin can form the core of a matrilineal social organization.

Dispersal from a natal group might involve transfer to a different group, and there is evidence that movement between groups is not random (Cheney and Seyfarth, 1983, 1990). Individuals might disperse together (Pusey and Packer, 1987) or join some groups in preference to others (Cheney and Seyfarth, 1983).

Communication

Communication is a social behavior conveying information from one individual to others within range of the signal (McGregor, 2005). Animals have many means of communication, including chemical and olfactory signals (pheromones, scent markings), vocalizations, gestures, facial expressions, and postures. The "amount and pattern" of communication is related to the connectedness of a species' social network (Wilson, 1975: 16). Communication serves many social functions: affiliative gestures of support, indications of status orderings, expressions of location and territory, recruiting allies, or coordinating movement, for example.

As noted above, many animal vocalizations and signals are individually recognizable, so communications are not anonymous. In addition, although communication can be directed from one individual to another, many signals occur in a social context and can be received by all individuals within range of the signal (McGregor, 2005). Thus, communications are observable by bystanders or eavesdroppers who might adapt their own behaviors accordingly.

Social context

Sociality implies that associations and interactions frequently take place within a social context and therefore are observable by others. Individuals not only witness what others do but can intervene and participate. Passive observation includes being a bystander to social interactions or eavesdropping on encounters between others (Chase et al., 2002, 2003; McGregor, 2005; Lindquist and Chase, 2009; Dugatkin, 2001). Bystanders are privy to information about the outcomes of others' interactions and might adjust their own behavior in response. In addition, participants themselves can be influenced by the presence of others, which inhibits or encourages their own interactions. Social context thus provides conditions for social network interdependencies beyond individuals and dyads.

In summary, a number of general features are important components of a species' social organization, social relations, and thus social networks. Some of these parameters, such as group size, demographic composition, patterns of dispersal, extent of communication, and social context, limit possible social network arrangements that can occur. Therefore, animal social networks should be expected to vary in predictable ways with variation in these parameters.

INSIGHTS FROM EMPIRICAL STUDIES OF ANIMAL SOCIAL NETWORKS

This section briefly reviews historical foundations and discusses recent contributions from empirical research on animal social networks.

Historical background and recent contributions

Studies of animal social organization and social networks have a long and fruitful history, dating at least to the early twentieth century. The Norwegian zoologist Schjelderup-Ebbe is widely acknowledged as one of the first people to systematically observe and record patterns of social interactions between individually identified animals, in this case dozens of bird species (Schjelderup-Ebbe, 1922, 1935; Allee, 1938; Price, 1995). His particular interest concerned the observation that pairs of birds often exhibit persistent asymmetry in outcomes such that one generally directs pecks at the other more than the reverse. These dyadic asymmetries are components of pairwise dominance relationships. For a flock of birds, pairwise dominance might or might not align into a consistent linear hierarchy (Noble et al., 1938; Allee, 1938; Schjelderup-Ebbe, 1935). This line of research reputedly gave rise to the phrase "pecking order" (Perrin, 1955). It also spawned numerous studies of social relations in birds, many of which recorded dominance relations using sociograms or sociomatrices (Masure and Allee, 1934; Noble et al., 1938; Marler, 1955).

Around the same time in the social sciences, animal social behavior was often included among topics in standard social psychology texts. (Murchison's 1935 *Handbook of Social Psychology* had seven chapters on nonhuman social systems including Schjelderup-Ebbe's "Social behavior of birds," and Lindzey's 1954 *Handbook of Social Psychology* included Hebb and Thompson's chapter "The social significance of animal studies.") In 1945, an issue of *Sociometry* was devoted to animal social organization. In that volume, Jacob Moreno suggested that "human and nonhuman social structures formed by actual individuals have a characteristic type of organization which differs significantly from structures which are formed by 'chance' or by imaginary individuals. . . . There must be a factor, 'tele,' operating between individuals . . . which draws them to form more positive or negative relations. . . . A parallel process should be demonstrable for non-human groups as well" (1945: 75). In the same volume, the primatologist C. Ray

Carpenter (1945: 57) argued that "to map the pattern or form of a group" required identifying individuals and systematically recording associations and interactions between all animals in the group, advice that has informed studies of animal social networks ever since.

In the field of social networks, largely in the social and behavioral sciences, many people have used social networks to study animal social organization and contributed to methodology (Sailer and Gaulin, 1984; Dow and de Waal, 1989; Freeman et al., 1992; Jameson et al., 1999; Roberts, 1990), theory (Chase, 1974, 1980; Chase et al., 2002; Cheverud et al., 1988), and substance (Sade, 1972, 1989; Sade et al., 1988; Chepko-Sade et al., 1989; Maryanski, 1987; Maryanski and Ishii-Kuntz, 1991). In 1988–89, the journals *Social Networks* and *The American Journal of Physical Anthropology* published special issues on animal social networks.

Behavioral biology, ethology, primatology, and related disciplines are concerned with animal social relations, but explicit use of social network concepts has been more limited. Only recently has the approach come to the forefront. However, many researchers in these fields view patterns of interactions between individuals as critical for understanding animal social organization (e.g., Allee, 1938; Imanishi, 1960; Hrdy, 1977; Goodall, 1971, 1986; Seyfarth, 1977; Fossey, 1983; Cheney and Seyfarth, 1990, 2007; de Waal, 1982; Heinrich, 2000; Wilson, 1975).

Social network studies of animal social organization have increased dramatically in recent years, as seen in a number of books and review articles on the topic (Whitehead, 2008; Croft et al., 2008; Wey et al., 2008; Krause et al., 2007, 2009; Coleing, 2009; Sih et al., 2009). Empirical studies of animal social networks have also increased, with studies of a variety of species: bottlenose dolphins (Lusseau, 2003), African elephants (Wittemyer et al., 2005), guppies (Croft et al., 2004), Grevy's zebras and onagers (Sundrasen et al., 2007), cowbirds (Miller et al., 2008), rhesus macaques (McCowan et al., 2008), pigtailed macaques (Flack et al., 2006), ground squirrels (Manno, 2008), giraffes (Shorrocks and Croft, 2009), yellow-bellied marmots (Wey and Blumstein, 2009), bats (Rhodes et al., 2006), Galápagos sea lions (Wolf et al., 2007; Wolf and Trillmich, 2008), Asian elephants (Coleing, 2009), African buffalos (Cross et al., 2005), Tasmanian devils (Hamede et al., 2009), and kangaroos (Carter et al., 2009), for example.

Empirical studies provide insights into aspects of animal social networks that appear to hold across many species. Some of these insights are summarized in the following sections.

Dominance

Pairwise asymmetry, in which a behavior is generally directed from one individual to another, is widely observed in animal social interactions. Consistency in the direction of agonistic asymmetry can indicate a pairwise dominance relationship. Dominance refers to "an attribute of the pattern of repeated, agonistic interactions between two individuals, characterized by a consistent outcome in favor of the same dyad member and a default yielding response of its opponent rather than escalation" (Drews, 1993: 308). Dominance has been a prominent concern in animal social networks for decades (Schjelderup-Ebbe, 1922; Chase, 1974, 1980; de Vries, 1995, 1998).

Several features of dominance are relevant for social networks. First, dominance relations can be summarized at multiple levels: pairwise directionality; individual position in a dominance ordering; or the extent to which a group adheres to a linear order or other ideal form (e.g., a partial order). Pairwise dominance is indicated by many forms of social interaction, including threats, attacks, displays, victories in contests, or gestures of deferral, which vary across species. The position of an individual in a dominance ordering for a group depends on the others it dominates and their own positions (Clutton-Brock et al., 1979). For a group, pairwise dominance might or might not be consistently ordered; cycles, inconsistencies, and unresolved pairwise orderings occur (Lahti et al., 1994). The dominance pattern for a group can be summarized quantitatively by its departure from linearity (de Vries, 1998) or descriptively, for example, whether it is "despotic" or "egalitarian" (Flack and de Waal, 2004).

Second, once established, the dominance ordering in a group can remain stable for substantial periods of time, especially in populations with relatively consistent membership. Stability tends to be associated with philopatry; dominance relations are more stable among nondispersing individuals. For example, stable dominance hierarchies among females tend to be found in species with male dispersal and female philopatry, such as macaques or savannah baboons (Chapais, 2004; Cheney and Seyfarth, 2007).

Third, dominance relations are often contingent on the social context, presence of observers, or actions of others who intervene or take sides in an encounter. Individual capacities or winner/loser effects are not sufficient to account for near-linear hierarchies (Lindquist and Chase, 2009). Moreover, pairwise dominance orderings formed in isolation from others are unlikely to combine into linear or near-linear hierarchies (Chase et al., 2002). Dependencies among triples, which arise through bystander effects, transitive inference, or systematic interventions, are necessary for near-linearity (Chase, 1974; Lindquist and Chase, 2009; Skvoretz et al., 1996; Dugatkin, 2001). Bystander effects occur when an observer adjusts his or her own behavior in response to outcomes of encounters between other pairs, for instance, attacking the loser rather than the winner from an earlier dyadic encounter. Social context and interventions can reinforce existing hierarchies and even lead to "inheritance" of dominance positions across generations (Cheney, 1977; Horrocks and Hunte, 1983; Chapais, 1988; Engh et al., 2000; Engh and Holekamp, 2003). For example, Chapais observes that among macaques a "female's relative rank is determined by the patterning of interventions by third parties in her conflicts with other females" (2004: 186). Interventions by high-ranking females reinforce the relative standing of individuals they support (their female relatives), contributing to inheritance of dominance rank.

Social roles and important individuals

As the presence of dominance orderings suggests, there is variability among individuals in their social network positions and roles. In addition to position in a dominance hierarchy, individuals can be socially important due to accumulated knowledge of resources or social relationships (African elephant matriarchs [McComb et al., 2001]), network positions that make them effective in interventions during conflicts (policing in macaques [Flack et al., 2006]), or bridging locations between subgroups in a population (young female killer whales [Williams and Lusseau, 2006]).

The importance of individuals is convincingly demonstrated by "knockout" experiments, in which social consequences of removal of particular individuals are studied. For example, Flack et al. (2006) examined effects of removing high-ranking males from captive groups of pigtailed macaques and found that stable affiliative social relations in the group were diminished when these individuals were not present. Network disruption also results from the natural loss of high-ranking individuals (Barrett et al., 2009).

Preferred associations and assortativity

Animal sociality is not homogeneous and is characterized by greater than chance levels of association between some pairs or subsets of individuals (Cheney et al., 1986; Bejder et al., 1998; Croft et al., 2005; Cross et al., 2005; Sundrasen et al., 2007; Whitehead, 1999; Lehmann and Boesch, 2009). Associations show preferred dyadic partnerships (Silk, 2002) or cohesive subsets (Croft et al., 2005; Whitehead, 2008). In addition, associations are often patterned by demographic categories (age and sex classes) such that there is homophily (positive assortativity) along these traits (Conradt, 1998; Whitehead, 1997; Croft et al., 2005). Kinship is also a basis for association in many species, with higher rates of association between related individuals (Cheney et al., 1986; Archie et al., 2006). Dispersal and philopatry affect close associations, with enduring associations more likely among remaining individuals (Wasser and Jones, 1983). Sex bias in dispersal results in sex difference in strength and pattern of relationships, an important feature of many animal social networks (Thierry et al., 2004).

The flip side of preferred associations (strong ties) is social cleavage where ties are weak or absent. For example, Cheney and Seyfarth (1990) observe that in vervet monkeys (a matrilineally organized species with male dispersal) close bonds do not occur between adult males and adult females.

Kinship and nepotism

Kinship is associated with many aspects of animal social networks, including close associations (Archie et al., 2006; Payne, 2003; Wolf and Trillmich, 2008), individual recognition (Cheney and Seyfarth, 1990; Janik et al., 2006), affiliative acts such as grooming (Silk et al., 1999, 2002, 2006), interventions (Cheney and Seyfarth, 1986), helping across generations (Woolfenden and Fitzpatrick, 1978; Jarvis, 1981), alliances (Parsons et al., 2003), inheritance of dominance rank (Cheney and Seyfarth, 2007; Chapais, 1988; Holekamp et al., 2007), and stability of social relationships (Silk et al., 2006). Close bonds and preferential interactions based on kinship are referred to as *nepotism* and provide a primary "axis" of social organization (Silk, 2002).

Genetic relatedness per se is not a necessary condition for some kinship effects. "Adopted" spotted hyenas attain dominance ranks of their adoptive rather than their biological mothers (East et al., 2009) and strong bonds can develop among nonkin in long-lived species such as chimpanzees (Lehmann and Boesch, 2009).

Multiple relations

Individuals of a population interact in many ways, giving rise to multiple social relations.

Multiplexity in these relations takes several forms, including reciprocity (Packer, 1977; Cheney and Seyfarth, 1990; Hemelrijk, 1990), exchange of different social acts (e.g., supporting prior grooming partners or exchanging food for grooming [Cheney and Seyfarth, 1986, 1990; Hemelrijk, 1990; de Waal, 1997; Schino, 2007]), association between kinship and affiliation (see above), or multiple behaviors indicating degrees of agonistic severity (Knox and Sade, 1991). How and why different social relations are associated remain important questions for theoretical understanding of animal social organization and social networks.

In studies of animal social networks, the methodology for relational comparison uses matrix permutations and their extensions (Hemelrijk, 1990; Dow and de Waal, 1989; Knox and Sade, 1991). One might anticipate that statistical models for multirelational social networks will be more widely used in the future.

Complex networks and levels of social organization

Animal social organization is often described as "complex" (Blumstein and Armitage, 1997, 1998; Whitehead, 2008) or consisting of multiple levels of organization (Hill et al., 2008; Wittemyer et al., 2005; Wolf et al., 2007; Croft et al., 2008; Zhou et al., 2005). "Complex" in this context generally connotes differentiated social organization consisting of multiple forms of social behavior in which individuals assume different social roles (Blumstein and Armitage, 1997, 1998). As noted above, social roles differ across age and sex classes and affect patterns of social interactions between individuals. The number of different social roles is one indicator of a species' social complexity (Blumstein and Armitage, 1997, 1998). Observations about layered or multilevel social organization credit the influential conceptual framework of Hinde (1976), linking interactions, relationships, and social structure. In a multilevel society, social units are nested or aggregated from individuals, to pairs, small subsets, and larger populations. For example, male-centered reproductive units of hamadryas baboons (see above) combine into larger populations (Kummer, 1968), or fission-fusion societies (such as African elephants or bottlenose dolphins, described earlier) are organized around large populations of individuals who usually are found in much smaller associations.

From the perspective of social networks, researchers have found that complex social organization suggests that animal social networks will not be well characterized by simple group-level summaries without considering both internal social differentiation and linkages to external social contexts.

Third parties and higher-order network dependencies

As noted in the section on social context, interactions often take place in the presence of other individuals. As a consequence, social acts and dyadic relations are seldom independent of what others do. Animals gain information about others and act accordingly. Bystanders, eavesdropping, triadic configurations, interventions, alliances, coalitions, and redirected aggression are all features of animal social organization. Because these effects entail linkages among multiple social actors, they lead to network dependencies beyond individuals or dyads. These higher-order effects have been well documented in animal social interactions.

Beyond recognizing particular individuals (see above), many species of animals are aware of how other members of their population are related to each other: for example, their relative dominance positions (Chase et al., 2002, 2003; Cheney and Seyfarth, 1990, 2007; Jennings et al., 2009; Holekamp et al., 2007) or whether they have close bonds, such as kinship relations (Cheney and Seyfarth, 2007; Holekamp et al., 2007). This enables social interactions such as bystander effects in which a losing party is more likely to be the target of future attacks (Chase, 1974, 1980; Clotfelter and Paolino, 2003); differential recruitment to coalitions (Silk et al., 2004; Harcourt and de Waal, 1992); displacement of aggression toward relatives of one's prior agonistic opponents (Engh et al., 2005; Cheney and Seyfarth, 1983, 1988); or targeted interventions in support of particular participants (Holekamp et al., 2007; Jennings et al., 2009; van Dierendonck et al., 2009).

These social interdependencies indicate substantial actor capacities for perceiving social relations and altering behaviors in response (Byrne and Whitten, 1988; de Waal and Tyack, 2003; Seyfarth and Cheney, 2000; Lindquist and Chase, 2009; Holekamp et al., 2007). From a social network perspective, this means that simple individual and dyadic summaries are unlikely to provide sufficient accounts of animal social networks; higher-order effects are necessary.

Network instability and change

Despite persistent forms of social organization, animal social networks are not static. Networks change membership and composition through natural demographic events (birth, death, maturation), dispersal (immigration and emigration), and other disruptions (seasonality, ecological shifts, disease outbreaks, anthropogenic effects). These changes have substantial consequences for social networks. A number of examples are informative.

Turnover in membership (e.g., loss through predation) leads to reconfiguration of social relationships as former partners are lost and population sizes change (Carter et al., 2009). Dominance positions in a group change through time and are dynamically associated with individual centrality (Sade et al., 1988). Removal of structurally important individuals (noted above) disrupts affiliative relationships (Flack et al., 2006). Imbalance in demographic distributions might result in group fission (Fedigan and Asquith, 1991), which, along with unresolved dominance relationships, can lead to increased serious aggression or "cage wars" in captive populations (McCowan et al., 2008).

Understanding dynamic network processes is an active research area across disciplines. Given the number of long-term studies of animal social organization this is a promising arena for further investigation.

Comparing social networks

Social organization has been characterized in general ways for various animal taxa; however, systematic formal comparisons of social network structure across species or meta-analyses of multiple cases are rare (Skvoretz and Faust, 2002; Faust and Skvoretz, 2002; Schino, 2001, 2007; Faust, 2007; Bhadra et al., 2009; Kasper and Voelkl, 2009). Social network comparisons suggest that general characterizations of network structure across species are likely to be fruitful, though appropriate methodologies are still emerging. Results include statistical summaries of local structural signatures contrasting "positive" and "negative" relations (Skvoretz and Faust, 2002) or triadic configurations (Faust, 2007); the generality of theoretical predictions about associations between social grooming, status, and kinship (Schino, 2001, 2007); structural patterns characterizing primate networks (Kasper and Voelkl, 2009); and comparative properties of wasps and school rooms (Bhadra et al., 2009).

FUTURE DIRECTIONS

Despite the volume of research on animal social organization, comprehensive studies that explicitly take a social network perspective are relatively rare. The hurdles are daunting but include at least being able to identify individuals, catalog their characteristic forms of social behavior, and systematically record their interactions and associations over time (hopefully, with detailed information about individual characteristics and environmental factors). Despite the hurdles, applications of social network approaches to animal social organization are beginning to blossom in the biological sciences, and there are many fruitful areas for further investigation.

Social animals provide excellent systems in which to investigate hypotheses about social network processes. Controlled comparisons are more feasible, and behavioral, biological, and social data often are more accessible, than for human social systems. Automated social network data collection using sensors (e.g., Hamede et al., 2009) and availability of biological and genetic data (e.g., Parker et al., 1995) should provide important insights into factors associated with social network structure and dynamics.

Extended studies by ethologists and behavioral biologists have yielded rich, detailed, and multifaceted information about animal social organization, and appropriate social network approaches are needed to deal with the substantive and theoretical concerns of those fields. Social network concepts and methods tailored to the study of particular animal species and contexts have been developed for many properties: for example, behavioral sampling (Altmann, 1974), dominance (de Vries et al., 1993), or associations (Cairns and Schwager, 1987; Whitehead, 2008). It seems likely that, in the future, rather than borrowing off-the-shelf methods designed for other kinds of network systems, approaches will be specifically tailored to appropriately study animal social networks, as happened earlier in the social and behavioral sciences. To the extent that these methods address general properties of social organization and social networks, they should also prove useful for studying human social networks.

A broad consideration of animal social networks points a different lens on social networks than is usually used by social and behavioral scientists. In particular, it puts general aspects of sociality at the center of investigation. For example, behavioral biology is concerned with the adaptive basis of sociality. From the perspective of social and behavioral sciences, studying animal social behavior turns attention on general aspects of *social* behaviors and interactions and seeks explanations for the relational basis of social organization, regardless of species.

From the perspective of other kinds of network systems, considering *animal social networks* leads one to distinguish *social* networks from other sorts of networks and to focus on those features that are distinctly characteristic of social situations and social relations. Although network and graph theoretic formalization might be equally appropriate for representing particular aspects of networked physical systems, semantic networks, molecular networks, and social networks, many aspects of sociality, and by implication social networks, probably require theories and theoretical models to appropriately study their social aspects. As a consequence, it is worth attending to aspects of *social* organization that are especially pertinent for understanding *social* networks.

One is then naturally led to ask "What is social about social networks?" I suggest that sociality of animals entails several characteristics that make social networks distinctive. Sociality implies that behavior occurs in a collective context that makes it observable to participants and bystanders alike. Given sufficient perceptual and cognitive capacities, actors acquire information about others and their relationships. When individuals adjust their own behaviors in response to this information and coordinate their actions with others, higher-order network dependencies arise. This means that *social* networks must include network effects and interdependencies beyond individuals and dyads, along with sufficient actor capacities to enable these interdependencies. These features distinguish networks that we quite likely agree are social (enduring patterns of interaction and affiliation among members of a baboon troop) from those we generally agree are not (networks of cracks in a dried mudflat). They leave room for discussion about other networks, such as computer systems, in which nodes are endowed with substantial capabilities for assessing the status of other nodes, monitoring flows, and interacting in ways that respond to states of the network.

Systematic studies of animal social networks give excellent insights into both differences and commonalities across species. In particular, they lead to general insights about social organization that are perhaps lost on researchers who restrict attention to a single species (e.g., on *Homo sapiens*). However, with a few exceptions, researchers in the social and behavioral sciences are largely unaware of major advances in studies of animal social organization and animal social networks. There is considerable room for expanding perspectives. Complementary investigations of social networks by social scientists and behavioral biologists will provide fertile ground for sharing theoretical, substantive, and methodological advances in the future.

REFERENCES

Allee, W.C. (1938) *The Social Life of Animals*. Boston, MA: Beacon Press.

Altmann, J. (1974) 'Observational study of behavior: Sampling methods', *Behaviour*, 49: 227–67.

Anindita, B., Jordán, F., Sumana, A., Deshpande, Sujata, A. and Gadagkar, R. (2009) 'A comparative social network analysis of wasp colonies and classrooms: Linking network structure to functioning', *Ecological Complexity*, 6(1): 48–55.

Archie, E.A., Moss, C.J. and Alberts, S.C. (2006) 'The ties that bind: Genetic relatedness predicts the fission and fusion of social groups in wild African elephants', *Proceedings of the Royal Society B*, 273: 513–22.

Aureli, F., Schaffner, C.M., Boesch, C., Bearder, S.K., Call, J., Chapman, C.A. et al. (2008) 'Fission-fusion dynamics', *Current Anthropology*, 49(4): 627–54.

Bailey, T.N. (1974) 'Social organization in a bobcat population', *Journal of Wildlife Management*, 38(3): 435–46.

Balshine-Earn, S. and Lotem, A. (1998) 'Individual recognition in a cooperatively breeding cichlid: Evidence from video playback experiments', *Behaviour*, 135(3): 369–86.

Banks, E.M. (1982) 'Behavioral research to answer questions about animal welfare', *Journal of Animal Science*, 54: 434–46.

Barash, D.P. (1974) 'Neighbor recognition in two 'solitary' carnivores: The raccoon (Procyon lotor) and the red fox (*Vulpes fulva*)', *Science*, 185(4153): 794–96.

Barg, J.J. and Mumme, R.L. (1994) 'Parental recognition of juvenile begging calls in the Florida scrub jay', *The Auk*, 111(2): 459–64.

Barrett, L., Lusseau, D. and Henzi, S.P. (2009) 'Natural knock-out: Changes in female social networks as a consequence of mortality in female chacma baboons', *American Journal of Physical Anthropology*, 48: 84.

Bejder, L., Fletcher, D. and Brager, S. (1998) 'A method for testing association patterns of social animals', *Animal Behaviour*, 56: 1718–25.

Blumstein, D.T. and Armitage, K.B. (1997) 'Does sociality drive the evolution of communicative complexity? A comparative test with ground dwelling sciurid alarm calls', *The American Naturalist*, 150(2): 179–200.

Blumstein, D.T. and Armitage, K.B. (1998) 'Life history consequences of social complexity: A comparative study of ground-dwelling sciurids', *Behavioral Ecology*, 9(1): 8–19.

Burgener, N., Dehnhard, M., Hofer, H. and East, M.L. (2009) 'Does anal gland scent signal identity in the spotted hyaena?' *Animal Behaviour*, 77(3): 707–15.

Byrne, R. and Whiten, A. (eds.) (1988) *Machiavellian Intelligence: Social Expertise and the Evolution of Intellect in Monkeys, Apes, and Humans*. Oxford: Oxford University Press.

Cairns, S.J. and Schwager, S.J. (1987) 'A comparison of association indices', *Animal Behaviour*, 35: 1454–69.

Caldwell, R.L. (1979) 'Cavity occupation and defensive behaviour in the stomatopod *Gonodactylus festai*: Evidence for chemically mediated individual recognition', *Animal Behaviour*, 27: 194–201.

Carpenter, C.R. (1945) 'Concepts and problems of primate sociometry', *Sociometry*, 8(1): 56–61.

Carter, A.J., Macdonald, S.L., Thomson, V.A. and Goldizen, A.W. (2009) 'Structured association patterns and their energetic benefits in female eastern grey kangaroos', *Macropus giganteus, Animal Behaviour*, 77(4): 839–46.

Chapais, B. (1988) 'Rank maintenance in female Japanese macaques: Experimental evidence for social dependency', *Behaviour*, 104(1/2): 41–59.

Chapais, B. (2004) 'How kinship generates dominance structures: A comparative perspective', in Bernard, Thierry, Mewa Singh, and Werner Kaumanns (eds.), *Macaque Societies: A Model for the Study of Social Organization*. Cambridge: Cambridge University Press. pp. 186–204.

Chase, I.D. (1974) 'Models of hierarchy formation in animal societies', *Behavioral Science*, 19(6): 374–82.

Chase, I.D. (1980) 'Social-process and hierarchy formation in small-groups: A comparative perspective', *American Sociological Review*, 45(6): 905–24.

Chase, I.D., Tovey, C. and Murch, P. (2003) 'Two's company, three's a crowd: Differences in dominance relationships in isolated versus socially embedded pairs of fish', *Behaviour*, 140: 1193–217.

Chase, I.D., Tovey, C., Spangler-Martin, D. and Manfredonia, M. (2002) 'Individual differences versus social dynamics in the formation of animal dominance hierarchies', *Proceedings of the National Academy*, 99(8): 5744–49.

Cheney, D.L. (1977) 'The acquisition of rank and the development of reciprocal alliances among free-ranging immature baboons', *Behavioral Ecology and Sociobiology*, 2(3): 303–18.

Cheney, D.L. and Seyfarth, R.M. (1983) 'Nonrandom dispersal in free-ranging vervet monkeys: Social and genetic consequences', *The American Naturalist*, 122(3): 392–412.

Cheney, D.L. and Seyfarth, R.M. (1988) 'Social and non-social knowledge in vervey monkeys', in Richard Byrne and Andrew Whiten (eds.), *Machiavellian Intelligence: Social Expertise and the Evolution of Intellect in Monkeys, Apes, and Humans*. Oxford: Oxford University Press. pp. 255–70.

Cheney, D.L. and Seyfarth, R.M. (1990) *How Monkeys See the World*. Chicago: University of Chicago.

Cheney, D.L. and Seyfarth, R.M. (2007) *Baboon Metaphysics: The Evolution of a Social Mind*. Chicago: University of Chicago Press.

Cheney, D., Seyfarth, R.M. and Smuts, B. (1986) 'Social relationships and social cognition in nonhuman-primates', *Science*, 234(4782): 1361–66.

Chepko-Sade, B.D., Reitz, K.P. and Sade, D.S. (1989) 'Sociometrics of *Macaca Mulatta* IV: Network analysis of social structure of a pre-fission group', *Social Networks*, 11(3): 293–314.

Cheverud, James, Chepko-Sade, M.B., Diane, D., Malcolm, M. and Sade, D.S. (1988) 'Group selection models with population substructure based on social-interaction networks', *American Journal of Physical Anthropology*, 77(4): 427–33.

Clotfelter, E.D. and Paolino, A.D. (2003) 'Bystanders to contests between conspecifics are primed for increased aggression in male fighting fish', *Animal Behaviour*, 66: 343–47.

Clutton-Brock, T.H. (1974) 'Primate social organization and ecology', *Nature*, 250: 539–42.

Clutton-Brock, T.H., Albon, S.D., Gibson, R.M. and Guinness, F.E. (1979) 'The logical stag: Adaptive aspects of fighting in red deer (*Cervus elaphus L.*)', *Animal Behaviour*, 27(1): 211–25.

Coleing, A. (2009) 'The application of social network theory to animal behaviour', *Bioscience Horizons*, 2(1): 32–43.

Colvin, John. (1983) 'Influences of the social situation on male emigration', in Robert A. Hinde (ed.), *Primate Social Relationships: An Integrated Approach*. Oxford: Blackwell. pp. 160–70.

Connor, R.C., Heithaus, M.R. and Barre, L.M. (1999) 'Superalliance of bottlenose dolphins', *Nature*, 397: 571–72.

Connor, R.C., Smolker, R.A. and Richards, A.F. (1992) 'Dolphin alliances and coalitions', in Alexander H. Harcourt and Frans B.M de Waal (eds.), *Coalitions and Alliances in Humans and Other Animals*. Oxford: Oxford University Press. pp. 415–43.

Conradt, L. (1998) 'Measuring the degree of sexual segregation in group-living animals', *Journal of Animal Ecology*, 67(2): 217–26.

Croft, D.P., James, R. and Krause, J. (2008) *Exploring Animal Social Networks*. Princeton, NJ: Princeton University Press.

Croft, D.P., James, R., Thomas, P.O.R., Hathaway, C., Mawdsley, D., Laland, K.N. and Krause, J. (2006) 'Social structure and co-operative interactions in a wild population of guppies (*Poecilia reticulata*)', *Behavioral Ecology and Sociobiology*, 59(5): 644–50.

Croft, D.P., James, R., Ward, A.J.W., Botham, M.S., Mawdsley, D., and Krause J. (2005) 'Assortative interactions and social networks in fish', *Oecologia*, 143(2): 211–19.

Croft, D.P., Krause, J. and James, R. (2004) 'Social networks in the guppy (*Poecilia reticulata*)', *Proceedings of the Royal Society of London Series B-Biological Sciences*, 271: S516–S519.

Cross, Paul C., Lloyd-Smith, James O. and Getz, Wayne M. (2005) 'Disentangling association patterns in fission-fusion societies using African buffalo as an example', *Animal Behavior*, 69: 499–506.

de Vries, H. (1995) 'An improved test of linearity in dominance hierarchies containing unknown or tied relationships', *Animal Behaviour*, 50: 1375–89.

de Vries, H. (1998) 'Finding a dominance order most consistent with a linear hierarchy: A new procedure and review', *Animal Behaviour*, 55: 827–43.

de Vries H., Netto, W.J. and Hanegraaf, P.L.H. (1993) 'Matman: A program for the analysis of sociometric matrices and behavioural transition matrices', *Behaviour*, 125(3/4): 157–75.

de Waal, F. (1997) 'The chimpanzee's service economy: Food for grooming', *Evolution and Human Behavior*, 19: 375–86.

de Waal, F. (1982) *Chimpanzee Politics: Power and Sex among Apes*. Baltimore, MD: Johns Hopkins University Press.

de Waal, F. and Tyack, P.L. (2003) *Animal Social Complexity: Intelligence, Culture, and Individualized Societies*. Cambridge, MA: Harvard University Press.

Diaz-Lopez, B. and Shirai, J.A.B. (2008) 'Marine aquaculture and bottlenose dolphins (*Tursiops truncates*) social structure', *Behavioral Ecology and Sociobiology*, 62: 887–94.

Dow, M.M. and de Waal, F.B.M. (1989) 'Assignment methods for the analysis of network subgroup interactions', *Social Networks*, 11(3): 237–55.

Drews, C. (1993) 'The concept and definition of dominance in animal behavior', *Behaviour*, 125: 283–313.

Dugatkin, L.A. (2001) 'Bystander effects and the structure of dominance hierarchies', *Behavioral Ecology*, 12(3): 348–52.

Dunbar, R.I.M. (1983) 'Relationships and social structure in gelada and hamadryas baboons ', in Robert A. Hinde (ed.), *Primate Social Relationships: An Integrated Approach*. Oxford: Blackwell. pp. 299–307.

Dunbar, R.I.M. (2003) 'The social brain: Mind, language, and society in evolutionary perspective', *Annual Review of Anthropology*, 32: 163–81.

East, M.L. and Hofer, H. (1991) 'Loud calling in a female-dominated mammalian society: II. Behavioural contexts and functions of whooping of spotted hyaenas, *Crocuta crocuta*', *Animal Behaviour*, 42(4): 651–69.

East, M.L., Höner, O.P., Wachter, B., Wilhelm, K., Burke, T. and Hofer, H. (2009) 'Maternal effects on offspring social status in spotted hyenas', *Behavioral Ecology*, 20(3): 478–83.

Engh, A.L., Esch, K., Smale, L. and Holekamp, K.E. (2000) 'Mechanisms of maternal rank 'inheritance', in the spotted hyaena, *Crocuta crocuta*', *Animal Behaviour*, 60(3): 323–32.

Engh, A.L. and Holekamp, K.E. (2003) 'Maternal rank "inheritance", in the spotted hyena case study', in Frans B.M. de Waal and Peter L. Tyack (eds.), *Animal Social Complexity: Intelligence, Culture, and Individualized Societies*. Harvard, MA: Harvard University Press. pp. 149–52.

Engh, A.L., Siebert, E.R., Greenberg, D.A. and Holekamp, K.E. (2005) 'Patterns of alliance formation and postconflict aggression indicate spotted hyaenas recognize third-party relationships', *Animal Behaviour*, 69: 209–17.

Faust, K. (2007) 'Very local structure in social networks', in *Sociological Methodology* 2007, volume 32, edited by Yu Xie. Cambridge, MA: Basil Blackwell. pp. 209–56.

Faust, K. and Skvoretz, J.V. (2002) 'Comparing networks across space and time, size and species', *Sociological Methodology*, (32): 267–99.

Fedigan, L.M. and Asquith, P.J. (1991) *The Monkeys of Arashiyama: Thirty-Five Years of Research in Japan and the West*. Albany, NY: State University of New York Press.

Flack, J.C. and de Waal, F.B.M. (2004) 'Dominance style, social power, and conflict management: A conceptual framework', in Bernard Thierry, Mewa Singh and Werner Kaumanns (eds.), *Macaque Societies: A Model for the Study of Social Organization*. Cambridge: Cambridge University Press. pp. 157–82.

Flack, J.C., Girvan, M., de Waal, Frans B.M. and Krakauer, D.C. (2006) 'Policing stabilizes construction of social niches in primates', *Nature*, 439(7075): 426–29.

Fossey, Dian. (1983) *Gorillas in the Mist*. Boston, MA: Houghton Mifflin.

Freeman, L.C., Freeman, S.C. and Romney A.K. (1992) 'The implications of social-structure for dominance hierarchies in red deer, *Cervus-Elaphus L.*', *Animal Behaviour*, 44(2): 239–45.

Fresneau D. and Dupuy, P. (1988) 'A study of polyethism in a ponerine ant: *Neoponera apicalis* (Hymenoptera, Formicidae)', *Animal Behaviour*, 36: 1389–99.

Goodall, J. (1971) *In the Shadow of Man*. Boston, MA: Houghton Mifflin.

Goodall, J. (1986) *The Chimpanzees of Gombe*. Cambridge, MA: Belknap.

Goodwin, D. (1986) *Crows of the World*. London: British Museum of Natural History.

Greenwood, P.J. (1980) 'Mating systems, philopatry and dispersal in birds and mammals', *Animal Behaviour*, 28: 1140–62.

Grier, J.W. (1984) *Biology of Animal Behavior*. St. Louis, MO: Times Mirror.

Griffiths, S.W. and Magurran, A.E. (1997) 'Schooling preferences for familiar fish vary with group size in a wild guppy population', *Proceedings of the Royal Society: Biological Sciences*, 264(1381): 547–51.

Griffiths, S.W. and Magurran, A.E. (1998) 'Sex and schooling behavior in the Trinidadian guppy', *Animal Behaviour*, 56: 689–93.

Hamede, R., Bashford, K.J., McCallum, H. and Jones, M. (2009) 'Contact networks in a wild Tasmanian devil (*Sarcophilus harrisii*) population: Using social network analysis to reveal seasonal variability in social behaviour and its implications for transmission of devil facial tumour disease', *Ecology Letters*, 12: 1147–57.

Harcourt, A.H. and de Waal, F.B.M. (eds.). (1992) *Coalitions and Alliances in Humans and other Animals*. Oxford: Oxford University Press.

Heinrich, B. (2000) *Mind of the Raven*. New York: Harper.

Hemelrijk, C.K. (1990) 'A matrix partial correlation test used in investigations of reciprocity and other social interaction patterns at group level', *Journal of Theoretical Biology*, 143: 405–20.

Herbinger, I., Papworth, S., Boesch, C. and Zuberbühler, K. (2009) 'Vocal, gestural and locomotor responses of wild chimpanzees to familiar and unfamiliar intruders: a playback study', *Animal Behaviour*, 78(6): 1389–96.

Hill, R.A., Bentley, R.A. and Dunbar, R.I.M. (2008) 'Network scaling reveals consistent fractal pattern in hierarchical mammalian societies', *Biology Letters*, 4(6): 748–51.

Hinde, R.A. (1976) 'Interaction, relationships and social structure', *Man*, 11(1): 1–17.

Holekamp, K.E., Sakai, S.T. and Lundrigan, B.L. (2007) 'Social intelligence in the spotted hyena (*Crocuta crocuta*)', *Philosophical Transactions of the Royal Society B*, 362: 523–38.

Hölldobler, B. and Wilson, E.O. (1994) *Journey to the Ants: A Story of Scientific Exploration*. Cambridge, MA: Belknap Press.

Horrocks, J. and Hunte, W. (1983) 'Maternal rank and offspring rank in vervet monkeys: An appraisal of the mechanisms of rank acquisition', *Animal Behaviour* 31: 772–82.

Hrdy, S.B. (1977) *The Langurs of Abu: Female and Male Strategies of Reproduction.* Cambridge, MA: Harvard University Press.

Imanishi, K. (1960) 'Social organization of subhuman primates in their natural habitat', *Current Anthropology*, 1(5/6): 393–407.

Jameson, K.A., Appleby, M.C. and Freeman L.C. (1999) 'Finding an appropriate order for a hierarchy based on probabilistic dominance', *Animal Behaviour*, 57: 991–98.

Janik, V.M., Sayigh, L.S. and Wells, R.S. (2006) 'Signature whistle shape conveys identity information to bottlenose dolphins', *Proceedings of the National Academy of Sciences*, 103(21): 8293–97.

Jarvis, J.U.M. (1981) 'Eusociality in a mammal: Cooperative breeding in naked mole-rat colonies', *Science*, 212(4494): 571–73.

Jennings, D., Carlin, C.M. and Grammell, M.P. (2009) 'A winner effect supports third-party intervention behaviour during fallow deer, *Dama dama*, fights', *Animal Behaviour*, 77: 343–48.

Kasper, C. and Voelkl, B. (2009) 'A social network analysis of primate groups', *Primates*, 50(4): 343–56.

Kerth, G. and Konig, B. (1999) 'Fission, fusion and nonrandom associations in female Bechstein's bats (*Myotis bechsteinii*)', *Behaviour*, 136: 1187–202.

Knox, K.L. and Sade, D.S. (1991) 'Social behavior of the emperor tamarin in captivity: Components of agonistic display and the agonistic network', *International Journal of Primatology*, 12(5): 439–80.

Krause, J., Croft, D.P. and James, R. (2007) 'Social network theory in the behavioural sciences: potential applications', *Behavioral Ecology and Sociobiology*, 62(1): 15–27.

Krause, J., Lusseau, D. and James, R. (2009) 'Animal social networks: An introduction', *Behavioral Ecology and Sociobiology*, 63(7): 967–973.

Krause, J. and Ruxton, G.D. (2002) *Living in Groups.* Oxford: Oxford University Press.

Kummer, H. (1968) *Social Organization of Hamadryas Baboons: A Field Study.* Chicago, IL: University of Chicago Press.

Kummer, H. (1971) *Primate Societies: Group Techniques of Ecological Adaptation.* Chicago, IL: Aldine.

Lahti, K., Koivula, K. and Orell, M. (1994) 'Is the social hierarchy always linear in tits', *Journal of Avian Biology*, 25: 347–48.

Larivière, S. (2001) *Ursus americanus. Mammalian Species*, 647: 1–100.

Lehmann, J. and Boesch, C. (2009) 'Sociality of the dispersing sex: The nature of social bonds in West African female chimpanzees, *Pan troglodytes*', *Animal Behaviour*, 77(2): 377–87.

Lehmann, J., Korstjens, A.H. and Dunbar, R.I.M. (2007) 'Group size, grooming and social cohesion in primates', *Animal Behaviour*, 74(6): 1617–29.

Lesley, J.M., Croft, D.P., Dyer, J.R.G., Chapman, B.B., Kelley, J.L., Laland, K.N. and Krause, J. (2008) 'Association patterns and foraging behaviour in natural and artificial guppy shoals', *Animal Behaviour*, 76: 855–64.

Lindquist, W.B. and Chase, I.D. (2009) 'Data-based analysis of winner-loser models of hierarchy formation in animals', *Bulletin of Mathematical Biology*, 71(3): 556–84.

Lindzey, G. (1954) *Handbook of Social Psychology*, Vol. I. Cambridge, MA: Addison-Wesley.

Lusseau, D. (2003) 'The emergent properties of a dolphin social network', *Proceedings of the Royal Society of London Series B-Biological Sciences*, 270: S186–S188.

Lusseau, D. (2007) 'Evidence for social role in a dolphin social network', *Evolutionary Ecology*, 21(3): 357–66.

Lusseau, D. and Newman, M.E.J. (2004) 'Identifying the role that animals play in their social networks', *Proceedings of the Royal Society of London Series B-Biological Sciences*, 271: S477–S481.

Manno, T.G. (2008) 'Social networking in the Columbian ground squirrel, *Spermophilus columbianus*', *Animal Behaviour*, 75(4): 1221–28.

Marler, P. (1955) 'Studies of fighting in chaffinches. (1) Behaviour in relation to the social hierarchy', *The British Journal of Animal Behaviour*, 3: 111–17.

Maryanski, A.R. (1987) 'African ape social-structure: Is there strength in weak ties', *Social Networks*, 9(3): 191–215.

Maryanski, A.R. and Ishii-Kuntz, M. (1991) 'A cross-species application of Bott hypothesis on role segregation and social networks', *Sociological Perspectives*, 34(4): 403–25.

Masure, R.H. and Allee, W.C. (1934) 'The social order in flocks of the common chicken and the pigeon', *The Auk*, 51: 306–25.

Mayhew, B.H. and Levinger, R.L. (1976) 'Size and the density of interaction in human aggregates', *American Journal of Sociology*, 82: 86–110.

McComb, K., Moss, C., Durant, S.M., Baker, L. and Sayialel, S. (2001) 'Matriarchs as repositories of social knowledge in African elephants', *Science*, 292: 491–94.

McComb, K., Moss, C., Sayialel, S. and Baker, L. (2000) 'Unusually extensive networks of vocal recognition in African elephants', *Animal Behaviour*, 59(6): 1103–9.

McCowan, B., Anderson, K., Heagarty, A. and Cameron, A. (2008) 'Utility of social network analysis for primate behavioral management and well-being', *Applied Animal Behaviour Science*, 109(2–4): 396–405.

McGregor, P. (ed.) (2005) *Animal Communication Networks.* Cambridge: Cambridge University Press.

Miller, J.L., King, A.P. and West, M.J. (2008) 'Female social networks influence male vocal development in brown-headed cowbirds, *Molothrus ater*', *Animal Behaviour*, 76(3): 931–41.

Moreno, J.L. (1945) 'The two sociometries, human and subhuman', *Sociometry*, 8(1): 64–75.

Moss, C.J. and Poole, J.H. (1983) 'Relationships and social structure of African elephants', in Robert A. Hinde (ed.), *Primate Social Relationships: An Integrated Approach.* Oxford: Blackwell. pp. 307–13.

Murchison, Carl. (1935) *A Handbook of Social Psychology.* Worcester, MA: Clark University Press.

Noble, G.K., Wurm, A. and Schmidt, M. (1938) 'Social behavior of the black-crowned night heron', *The Auk*, 55(1): 7–40.

Packer, C. (1977) 'Reciprocal altruism in *Papio anubis*', *Nature*, 265: 441–43.

Packer, C. (1979) 'Inter-troop transfer and inbreeding avoidance in *Papio anubis*', *Animal Behaviour*, 27: 1–36.

Parker, P.G., Waite, T.A. and Decker, M.D. (1995) 'Kinship and association in communally roosting black vultures', *Animal Behaviour*, 49(2): 395–401.

Parsons, K.M., Durban, J.W. et al. (2003) 'Kinship as a basis for alliance formation between male bottlenose dolphins, *Tursiops truncatus*, in the Bahamas', *Animal Behaviour*, 66: 185–94.

Payne, K. (2003) 'Sources of social complexity in the three elephant species', in Frans B.M. de Waal and Peter L. Tyack (eds.), *Animal Social Complexity: Intelligence, Culture, and Individualized Societies*. Cambridge, MA: Harvard University Press. pp. 57–85.

Perrin, P. (1955) 'Pecking order', *American Speech*, 30(4): 265–68.

Pollard, K.A. and Blumstein, D.T. (2008) 'Time allocation and the evolution of group size', *Animal Behaviour*, 76: 1683–99.

Poole, T.B. (1985) *Social Behavior in Mammals*. Glasgow: Blackie.

Price, J. (1995) 'A remembrance of Thorleif Schjelderup-Ebbe', *Human Ethology Bulletin*, 10(1): 1–6.

Proops, L., McComb, K. and Reby, D. (2009) 'Cross-modal individual recognition in domestic horses (*Equus caballus*)', *Proceedings of the National Academy of Sciences*, 106(3): 947–51.

Pusey, A.E. and Packer, C. (1987) 'Dispersal and philopatry', in Barbara B. Smuts, Dorothy L. Cheney, Robert M. Seyfarth, Richard W. Wrangham, Thomas T. Struhsaker (eds.), *Primate Societies*. Chicago, IL: University of Chicago Press. pp. 250–66.

Reiczigel, J., Lang, Z., Rozsa, L. and Tothmeresz, B. (2008) 'Measures of sociality: Two different views of group size', *Animal Behaviour*, 75: 715–21.

Rhodes, M., Wardell-Johnson, G.W., Rhodes, M.P. and Raymond, B. (2006) 'Applying network analysis to the conservation of habitat trees in urban environments: A case study from Brisbane, Australia', *Conservation Biology*, 20(3): 861–70.

Roberts, J.M. (1990) 'Modeling hierarchy: Transitivity and the linear ordering problem', *The Journal of Mathematical Sociology*, 16(1): 77–87.

Rogers, L.L. (1987) 'Effects of food supply and kinship on social behavior, movements, and population growth of black bears in northeastern Minnesota', *Wildlife Monographs*, (97): 3–72.

Sade, D.S. (1972) 'Sociometrics of *Macaca-Mulatta*: Linkages and cliques in grooming matrices', *Folia Primatologica*, 18(3–4): 196–223.

Sade, D.S. (1989) 'Sociometrics of *Macaca Mulatta* III: n-path centrality in grooming networks', *Social Networks*, 11(3): 273–92.

Sade, D.S., Altmann, M., Loy, J., Hausfater, G. and Breuggeman, J.A. (1988) 'Sociometrics of *Macaca-Mulatta*.2. Decoupling centrality and dominance in rhesus-monkey social networks', *American Journal of Physical Anthropology*, 77(4): 409–25.

Sailer, L.D. and Gaulin, S.J.C. (1984) 'Proximity, sociality, and observation: The definition of social groups', *American Anthropologist*. 86: 91–98.

Sayigh, L.S., Tyack, P.L., Wells, R.S., Solow, A.R., Scott, M.D. and Irvine, A.B. (1998) 'Individual recognition in wild bottlenose dolphins: A field test using playback experiments', *Animal Behaviour*, 57: 41–50.

Schino, G. (2001) 'Grooming, competition and social rank among female primates: A meta-analysis', *Animal Behaviour*, 62: 265–71.

Schino, G. (2007) 'Grooming and agonistic support: A meta-analysis of primate reciprocal altruism', *Behavioral Ecology*, 115–20.

Schjelderup-Ebbe, T. (1922) 'Beiträge zur Sozialpsychologie des Haushuhns', *Zeitschrift für Psychologie*, 88: 225–52.

Schjelderup-Ebbe, T. (1935) 'Social behavior of birds', in Murchison, Carl (ed.), *A Handbook of Social Psychology*. Worcester, MA: Clark University Press. pp. 947–72.

Schoech, S.J. (1998) 'Physiology of helping in Florida scrub-jays', *American Scientist*, 86: 70–77.

Sendova-Franks, H., Rebecca K., Wulf, B., Klimek, T., James, R., Planqué, R., Britton, N.F. and Franks, N.R. (2010) 'Emergency networking: Famine relief in ant colonies', *Animal Behaviour*, 79(2): 473–85.

Seyfarth, R.M. (1977) 'Model of social grooming among adult female monkeys', *Journal of Theoretical Biology*, 65(4): 671–98.

Seyfarth, R.M. and Cheney, D.L. (2000) 'Social awareness in monkeys', *American Zoologist*, 40(6): 902–9.

Shields, W.M. (1987) 'Dispersal and mating systems: Investigating their causal connections', in B. Diane Chepko-Sade and Zuleyma Tang Halpin (eds.), *Mammalian Dispersal Patterns: The Effects of Social Structure on Population Genetics*. Chicago, IL: University of Chicago Press. pp. 3–24.

Shorrocks, B. and Croft, D.P. (2009) 'Necks and networks: A preliminary study of population structure in the reticulated giraffe (*Giraffa camelopardalis reticulata de Winston*)', *African Journal of Ecology*, 47(3): 374–81.

Sih, A., Hanser, S.F. and McHugh, K.A. (2009) 'Social network theory: New insights and issues for behavioral ecologists', *Behavioral Ecology and Sociobiology*, 63: 975–88.

Silk, J.B. (2002) 'Using the 'F'-word in primatology', *Behaviour*, 139: 421–46.

Silk, J.B., Alberts, S.C. and Altmann, J. (2004) 'Patterns of coalition formation by adult female baboons in Amboseli, Kenya', *Animal Behaviour*, 67: 573–82.

Silk, J.B., Alberts, S.C. and Altmann, J. (2006) 'Social relationships among adult female baboons (*Papio cynocephalus*) II: Variation in the quality and stability of social bonds', *Behavioral Ecology and Sociobiology*, 61: 197–204.

Silk, J.B., Seyfarth, R.M. and Cheney, D.L. (1999) 'The structure of social relationships among female savanna baboons in Moremi Reserve, Botswana', *Behaviour*, 136: 679–703.

Skvoretz, J. and Faust, K. (2002) 'Relations, species, and network structure', *Journal of Social Structure*, 3(3).

Skvoretz, J., Faust, K. and Fararo, T. (1996) 'Social, structure, networks, and E-state structuralism models', *Journal of Mathematical Sociology,* 21(1–2): 57–76.

Slooten, E., Dawson, S.M. and Whitehead, H. (1993) 'Associations among photographically identified Hector's dolphins', *Canadian Journal of Zoology,* 71: 2311–18.

Smale, L., Frank, L.G. and Holekamp, K.E. (1993) 'Ontogeny of dominance in free-living spotted hyaenas: Juvenile rank relations with adult females and immigrant males', *Animal Behaviour,* 46: 467–77.

Smolker, R.A. Richards, A.F., Connor, R.C. and Pepper, J.W. (1992) 'Sex differences in patterns of association among Indian Ocean bottlenose dolphins', *Behaviour,* 123(1–2): 38–69.

Stacey, P.B. and Koenig, W.D. (1990) *Cooperative Breeding in Birds: Long Term Studies of Ecology and Behaviour.* Cambridge: Cambridge University Press.

Sundrasen, S.R., Fischhoff, I.R., Dushoff, J. and Rubenstein, D.I. (2007) 'Network metrics reveal differences in social organization between two fission-fusion species, Grevy's zebra and onager', *Oecologia,* 151(1): 140–49.

Swedell, L. (2002) 'Affiliation among females in wild hamadryas baboons (*Papio hamadryas hamadryas*)', *International Journal of Primatology,* 23(6): 1205–26.

Thierry, B., Singh, M. and Kaumanns, W. (eds.). (2004) *Macaque Societies: A Model for the Study of Social Organization.* Cambridge: Cambridge University Press.

Van Dierendonck, M.C., de Vries, H., Schilder, M.B.H., Colenbrander, B., Porhallsdottir, A.G. and Sigurjonsdottir, H. (2009) 'Interventions in social behaviour in a herd of mares and geldings', *Applied Animal Behaviour Science,* 116(1): 67–73.

Wasser, P.M. and Jones, W.T. (1983) 'Natal philopatry among solitary mammals', *Quarterly Review of Biology,* 58(3): 355–90.

Weeden, J.S. and Falls, J.B. (1959) 'Differential responses of male ovenbirds to recorded songs of neighboring and more distant individuals', *The Auk,* 76(3): 343–51.

Wells, R.S. (2003) 'Dolphin social complexity: Lessons from long-term study and life history', in Frans B.M. de Waal and Peter L. Tyack, (eds.), *Animal Social Complexity: Intelligence, Culture, and Individualized Societies.* Cambridge, MA: Harvard University Press. pp. 32–56.

Wey, T.W. and Blumstein, D.T. (2009) 'Ontogeny of social relations in yellow-bellied marmots', International Sunbelt Social Network Conference, San Diego, CA.

Wey, T.W., Blumstein, D.T., Shen, W. and Jordan, F. (2008) 'Social network analysis of animal behaviour: A promising tool for the study of sociality', *Animal Behaviour,* 75(2): 333–44.

Whitehead, H. (1997) 'Analysing animal social structure', *Animal Behaviour,* 53(5): 1053–67.

Whitehead, H. (1999) 'Testing association patterns of social animals', *Animal Behaviour,* 57(6): F26–F29.

Whitehead, H. (2008) *Analyzing Animal Societies: Quantitative Methods for Vertebrate Social Analysis.* Chicago, IL: University of Chicago Press.

Williams, R. and Lusseau, D. (2006) 'A killer whale social network is vulnerable to targeted removals', *Biology Letters,* 2: 497–500.

Wilson, E.O. (1975) *Sociobiology: The New Synthesis.* Cambridge, MA: Harvard University Press.

Wilson, E.O. (1999) *The Diversity of Life.* New York: Norton.

Wittemyer, G., Douglas-Hamilton, I. et al. (2005) 'The socio-ecology of elephants: Analysis of the processes creating multitiered social structures', *Animal Behaviour,* 69(6): 1357–71.

Wolf, J.B.W., Mawdsley, D., Trillmich, F. and James, R. (2007) 'Social structure in a colonial mammal: Unravelling hidden structural layers and their foundations by network analysis', *Animal Behaviour,* 74: 1293–302.

Wolf, J.B.W. and Trillmich, F. (2008) 'Kin in space: Social viscosity in a spatially and genetically substructured network', *Proceedings of the Royal Society B-Biological Sciences,* 275(1647): 2063–69.

Woolfenden, G.E. (1975) 'Florida scrub jays helpers at the nest', *The Auk,* 92: 1–15.

Woolfenden, G.E. and Fitzpatrick, J.W. (1978) 'The inheritance of territory in group-breeding birds', *BioScience,* 28(2): 104–8.

Woolfenden, G.E. and Fitzpatrick, J.W. (1984) *The Florida Scrub Jay: Demography of a Cooperative-breeding Bird.* Princeton, NJ: Princeton University Press.

Zhou, W.X., Sornette, D., Hill, R.A. and Dunbar, R.I.M. (2005) 'Discrete hierarchical organization of social group sizes', *Proceedings of the Royal Society B-Biological Sciences,* 272(1561): 439–44.

12

Networking Online: Cybercommunities

Anatoliy Gruzd and
Caroline Haythornthwaite

INTRODUCTION

As social creatures, our daily lives are intertwined with others in a wide variety of social networks involving our relatives, friends, co-workers, and a vast array of acquaintances and strangers. It is only natural that our digital lives are also made up of various social structures and networks. As Wellman (2001) noted, "Computer networks are inherently social networks, linking people, organizations, and knowledge" (p. 2031). Our online interactions can complement other communication channels in support of existing social relationships, and they can open up new, exclusively virtual, relationships maintained through online groups, communities, and worlds. Richly nuanced, strong ties can be maintained through the abundant and interconnected media channels now at our fingertips: from the commonplace email to the latest in blogging, microblogging, and mobile texting. While widespread, weak ties can be maintained through discussion lists, Web forums, and social networking sites.

The potential for online communication to change the way we form and manage human and communal interaction was addressed very early in the history of computer-mediated communication by Hiltz and Turoff in *The Network Nation*, first published in 1978. The authors envisioned the world of computer-mediated connection we see today: individuals networked across geography through computer conferencing. While studies in the 1980s concentrated on the transformative effects of information and communication technologies at work (e.g., Galegher et al., 1990;

Fulk and Steinfield, 1990; Sproull and Kiesler, 1991; Dutton, 1996; Rice, 1992), it is not until over 10 years after *The Network Nation* that studies of online communities begin to emerge.

First among these are several major qualitative examinations of online communities: Reid's analysis of the play-based MUD (multi-user dungeon) "Electropolis" environment (Reid, 1995); Baym's examination of a Usenet online group for soap opera fans (see Baym, 2000); and Rheingold's (1993) exploration of the Well community. The Well, which began in 1985, stands as perhaps one of the first social networking sites, specifically created to allow interaction among a widespread group of online participants. Each of these studies addressed the (then) very new, exclusively online, communities. Without directly referring to social networks, each describes how the kinds of relations maintained offline are re-created online, and how interaction in a text-based medium becomes a space where people meet, discuss, play, and create meaningful friendships and communal practices. In the second edition of the *The Virtual Community* (2000), Rheingold directly addresses social networks, bringing in the work of Barry Wellman and Mark Smith.

At the same time that these all-online communities were being examined, major studies of computer-mediated communities were underway that emphasized structure and language in online interaction (Sudweeks et al., 1998; Cherny, 1999; Smith, 1999), the development and expression of social norms (Smith et al., 1996; Kendall, 2002), and social networks online (Rice, 1993, 1994; Haythornthwaite and Wellman, 1998).

By the mid-1990s, real life and online life were beginning to converge. Email was much more commonplace in work settings, the Internet was beginning to make an impact on information and communication practices, personal computers appeared and became less expensive, and efforts to make wired connectivity a taken-for-granted infrastructure were making access easier and more prevalent, and thus more expected. Home connection made its major debut, and the Internet entered the home for work, school, and play. Research and popular views of computing began to recognize and accept the presence of the Internet in everyday life (Wellman and Haythornthwaite, 2002), and studies turned to how online worlds overlapped and complemented offline relations and practices (Kendall, 2002; Rice and Katz, 2001; Hampton, 2003; Hagar and Haythornthwaite, 2005). At a societal level, studies began to document and interpret the way new information and communication technologies (ICTs) created a "digital divide," and contributed to e-inclusion and exclusion from societal benefits (Schement and Curtis, 1997; Katz and Rice, 2002; U.S. National Telecommunications and Information Administration reports starting in 2002, http://www.ntia.doc.gov; Commission of the European Communities, 2005). The social capital arising from online social network connectivity is recognized and included as part of the benefits of community-wide implementations of computer networks (Kavanaugh and Patterson, 2002; Keeble and Loader, 2001).

Since 2000 the rapid proliferation of media types and media accessibility has driven a revolution in communication practices. The online social networking that Constant et al. (1996) observed — that email networks provided access to organization-wide expertise — is now perhaps best represented in the widespread networking achieved through social networking sites: Facebook for the college crowd, Myspace for the working crowd, and LinkedIn for the business crowd; Orkut for Brazil, and Cyworld for Korea (Hargittai, 2007; Donath and boyd, 2004; boyd and Ellison, 2007; with the caveat that clear boundaries in geography and demography are beginning to blur, see statistics presented by the sites themselves).

Through these many means, single-threaded, online communication via email has spread to include information, communication, and document exchange through synchronous and asynchronous online means, constant contact through wireless networks and mobile phones, and multithreaded contact as face-to-face interaction is blended with email, chat, texting, and twittering. Cybercommunities are no longer simple text-based groups but can be supported through the multiple features of a comprehensive online portal such as in knowledge management systems, virtual learning environments, and social networking sites. Network contacts are no longer constrained to single media, and communities can follow individuals as network lists are maintained on multiple devices, and as messages cross platforms from phone to email and back again (Haythornthwaite, 2000; Wellman, this volume).

Social network studies of online communication and community have provided some insight into how relations, ties, and networks are maintained online. Research to date has generally confirmed that ties maintained online are as real as offline ties, entailing mutual trust and disclosure, supporting relations of work, advice, socializing, and social support, and with more relations maintained more frequently and more intensely among strongly versus weakly tied pairs. Along with relational multiplexity, strongly tied pairs also demonstrate "media multiplexity," the use of more media the closer the tie (Haythornthwaite and Wellman, 1998). Computer media also appear to provide a structure for latent ties (i.e., for ties "for which a connection is available technically but [which have] not yet been activated by social interaction" [Haythornthwaite, 2002: 387]). Such structures provide the potential for the information sharing observed by Constant et al. (1996) as well as for the widespread social connectivity of social networking sites.

Analysis of these phenomena using traditional social science methods of interviews and questionnaires has been useful in providing a basis for understanding online social networks, communication, information transfer, and community. Yet many of the studies have been limited to small or relatively small datasets because of difficulties with access to group members, the time and participant effort needed for social network questionnaire completion, and ethical, access, analysis, and interpretation issues relating to online data. The phenomenal growth of online interaction, and the online traces left by all this interaction, begs the use of these data in order to explore and understand the equally rapid changes in means of creating and supporting online social networks. Since a number of reviews are available that give more extensive coverage of the ideas and studies that have informed current social network understanding of cybercommunities, this chapter focuses on what is and can be done to harness the massive quantities of data now being produced online to address questions about social networks and cybercommunities. (For more on communities and cybercommunities from a social network perspective, see Wellman et al., 1996;

Garton et al., 1997; Wellman, 1999, 2001; Rice, 2002; Haythornthwaite, 2007; Hogan, 2008.)

Online network data

Each reply to an email, link to a Web page, posting of a blog, or comment on a Youtube video, leaves a digital trace, a record that explicitly or implicitly connects the poster to another online participant. Each creates a network of attention around topics of interest, common affiliation, communities of practice, or collective action.

The data quantity is impressive: in 2003, Marc Smith estimated 100 million posters in Usenet (Festa, 2003), and a 2008 Wikipedia compilation of sources estimated 4.6 terabytes of data posted *daily* on Usenet. Technorati's (2008) "State of the Blogosphere" indicates 900,000 blogs are created each day, with 184 million people worldwide who have started a blog (23–26 million in the United States), and 346 million blog readers (60–94 million in the United States). Various estimates suggest something on the order of 100 billion emails sent per day (Leggatt, 2007). Even with the caveat that at least half of the email traffic is spam, there remains a remarkable amount of text generated every day. Dealing with the quantities of data becomes even more overwhelming when the problems of interest often require examining multiple platforms (e.g., to explore how communications are distributed across media, or across multiple instances to examine common patterns of exchange, development of shared language and understanding, or emergence of roles and positions).

Thus, it is not surprising that there is an increasing interest in retrieving and analyzing online behavior automatically, using Web and text mining techniques to gain insight into the inner workings of online communities. Discovering details about online social networks has already proven useful in deciding what information is relevant on the Internet, identifying credible Web sites, finding popular resources, and sharing information within a network of trust. Other uses of social network data include conducting viral marketing, identifying and tracking terrorist cells on the Internet, analyzing consumers' perceptions of products, and measuring the effectiveness of political campaigns in online and offline media.

One of the reasons automated discovery of social networks has become so popular is that it tends to be unobtrusive, scalable, and fast and thus avoids the difficulties of obtaining respondent compliance in completing the often burdensome social network questionnaires. Automated network

data collection is also unencumbered with the subjectivity of traditional data collection techniques (e.g., that respondents may provide partial answers, respond in ways they believe make their behavior look better, exaggerate interactions, forget people and interactions, or perceive events and relationships differently from other network members).

The remainder of this chapter explores in depth new ways of revealing and discovering social networks online. The chapter begins by describing various Internet sources of data for these kinds of analyses, then describes the main steps needed to uncover explicit and implicit social ties and common applications where these networks are used. With the necessary limitations of space, the chapter does not address data sources that are already organized in the form of social networks, such as "Friend of a Friend" data, and only briefly addresses email-based social networks since both require very little processing of original data to build a network and have been explored elsewhere (see boyd and Ellison, 2007; Hogan, 2008). The chapter also does not address theoretical perspectives on communication networks (see Monge and Contractor, 2003), semantic networks (e.g., Scott, 2005), or the kinds of "community" revealed by online networks (Haythornthwaite, 2007). Finally, since not all types of data sources are freely accessible on the Internet, we assume that a researcher has acquired legal access to a dataset, is cognizant of the ethical issues and implications of work and its impact on online communities and their members, and, as required, has received the necessary permission from the appropriate ethics review board for the use of the data. (For more on ethical issues, see Ess and the Association of Internet Researchers Ethics Working Committee, 2002; Breiger, 2005.)

INTERNET DATA SOURCES FOR DISCOVERY OF SOCIAL NETWORKS

This section reviews the three most prevalent Internet data types – email, discussion forums, and Web pages – with examples of how social network data discovered from each data type have been used.

Email

Email is one of the data sources most commonly used for social network extraction. It is interesting to network analysts in a number of ways. First, its structure fits easily into a network paradigm.

Email headers provide "To" and "From" data, fitting easily into network considerations of direction of relations. Subject lines (where present) offer a short text that can be used to cluster messages by topic. Even with the limitations of such data – for example, that subject lines may be maintained even after the messages change topic – the subject line provides a simple, text-based indicator of message content that often can be interpreted without further formal analysis. Further, the text of the message provides a wealth of information about the relation being maintained by the actors. This text can be instrumentally counted for indications of engagement – for example, length of the message minus appended replies – and it can be read, coded, or text-mined for keywords, common phrases, tone of communication, etc., in order to gain insight into the topics, ties, roles, and relations being maintained.

Second, the ubiquity of email provides a wealth of data that parallels other kinds of relationships – work, friendship, family ties – suggesting it is viable reflection of person-to-person interaction and ties. Since each email is an instance of a social interaction between two or more people who know (or will know) each other, it is reasonable to assume that the number of emails exchanged between two people is a good indicator of the existence and the strength of their social tie.

Email has also come along significantly as a means for analyzing networks because of access to the large, publicly available real-world Enron email dataset. This dataset has provided a common platform for evaluation of email messages in the context of a contemporary phenomenon of wide interest (i.e., who knew what during the Enron crisis). The Enron email dataset (http://www.cs.cmu.edu/~enron) was made public by the Federal Energy Regulatory Commission during its investigation of the Enron Corporation financial collapse. Since the release of the dataset, a number of studies covering a wide range of organizational research have used this dataset to conduct their studies. In the process, researchers have been able to study and fine-tune their automated network discovery algorithms and their interpretations of various social network analysis (SNA) measures.

Diesner and Carley (2005) used "who talks to whom" networks to compare Enron employees' communication patterns before and during the company's collapse. They found that communication networks during the collapse did not reflect Enron's formal organizational structures: top executives formed a tight clique, perhaps to provide mutual support to each other, and interacted less often with other employees as the company's

collapse progressed. Furthermore, the characteristics of the discovered networks, such as centrality and group cohesion, suggested that "a highly segmented workforce with little cross communication may have been a factor that supported the frauds in Enron" (p. 10). Lim et al. (2007) used the Enron dataset to test automated techniques to detect anomalous behavior in email traffic. Their techniques were able to detect changes in email traffic between the two top-ranked employees and the rest of the company before and during Enron's financial crisis. These Enron network studies have shown the feasibility of analyzing email data in an automated and systematic fashion and how email data can be used to discover connections and roles within groups.

While the ubiquity of email makes it a highly appealing source of data, there are reservations in interpreting social network relations from such data. First, as noted above, access to email may be legally and ethically questionable. While most legal cases have granted the right to email access to owners of the service (e.g., Bloom, 2008; "Who owns your email?" 2005), practical and ethical considerations weigh against automatic data extraction on a day-to-day basis. Most email is sent privately between individuals and thus does not reside in the public domain for researchers. Access must be secured from the organizational owners, and it may also be necessary to obtain permission from each user whose data may be analyzed. This holds true as much for the who-to-whom data as for the subject line and text of the messages. A researcher may also need to negotiate the visibility, anonymity, and distribution of results (e.g., on whether organizational management has access to results). Second, email is often not the only communication means used by actors. Hence, interpretations of behavior need to take into account that email represents only one stream of interaction, not the entirety of a network tie (Haythornthwaite and Wellman, 1998; Haythornthwaite, 2002, 2005).

Online forums

Online forums with threaded discussions are a more easily accessible source of Internet-based communication data than email, and they are also good candidates for automated social network extraction. Since open, online forums are often the communication medium of choice for many groups, there is a wealth of accumulated data that can be used to conduct studies and experiments. Having the ability to automatically discover and represent the various networks that exist within these online forums provides researchers with a window on the collaborative processes in online groups and communities.

Among the numerous types of online forums, Usenet groups and online classes have received the most attention from researchers and generated the most amount of literature on automated analysis. Fisher et al. (2006) used social networks extracted from Usenet discussion groups to identify and characterize populations of participants into four distinct groups: "question and answer," "conversational," "social support," and "flame." Fiore et al. (2002) examined how Usenet participants' posting behaviors (such as the number of postings and the number of newsgroups they subscribed to) were associated with readers' subjective evaluations of them. They found a high correlation between these, with participants who dominated the conversations being viewed more unfavorably than others.

In automated studies of online classes, Reyes and Tchounikine (2005) relied on the "who replies to whom" data to build a communication network of participants in an online class. The researchers argued that participants' centrality and group cohesion are two very important measures for the assessment of learning groups. Using a case study of 15 participants, the researchers demonstrated how a tutor could rely on these measures to assess collaborative learning. In one of the threaded discussions that they studied, group cohesion was extremely low. Upon further investigation, it was discovered that the two participants with the highest centrality were dominating the conversation, a condition that may be undesirable for learning communities where wider-spread contribution is intended, and thus of value to identify. Among more recent work, Cho et al. (2007) explored different social network properties such as degree, closeness, betweenness, and structural holes to find relations between students' positions in the social network and their success in the class to see which measures correlated with final grades. They found that "closeness centrality was significantly associated with students' final grades" (p. 322). In sum, these studies demonstrate that threaded discussion is a good source for extracting communication networks, providing a view of online data that can be useful for studying group dynamics and online communities.

Web pages

Web pages are another important source of social network data on the Internet. The content of Web pages may and often does reveal explicit and implicit connections between people (e.g., through links to a colleague's homepage, names on a homepage, messages on a friend's blog, comments on a picture published by a relative, appearance in the same online publication, or subscription to the same online data feed). All these examples may be used by an automated system to infer social networks. The work in this area is wide and varied due to the seemingly endless variations in the types of Web pages (homepages, personal blogs, news articles, academic publications, etc.). Recent studies include research by Adamic and Adar (2003), who used links between homepages of students at Stanford University and the Massachusetts Institute of Technology to infer real-world connections and communities of students; Chin and Chignell (2007), who used links between comments posted on Canadian Independent Music blogs to identify communities of blog authors and readers; and online resources such as Silobreaker (http://www.silobreaker.com) and Muckety (http://news.muckety.com), which extract social networks from online news, with the aim of developing new browsing and visualization techniques for connections between people in the news.

The rise in online publishing has also made it easier to mine and access citation information on the Internet. Work in bibliometrics and infometrics uses this to discover and study co-author and co-citation networks. To social scientists, this type of network is of interest because of the way it follows and reflects social structures (White et al., 2004). Chen and his colleagues (2001) used co-citation networks extracted from several conference proceedings to conduct a subject domain analysis and provide a more effective user interface to access information in a digital library. Newman (2001) built a co-authorship network to discover collaboration patterns between scientists in physics, biomedical research, and computer science.

Each of these kinds of online data examines different spheres of interaction. Email may be best for examining dyadic and close group relationships where message senders know at least the email address of the recipient(s). Online forums, as well as email traffic on listservs, require less knowledge about those who are part of the conversation, allowing examination of groups with larger, more unknown membership. Web pages provide connectivity information on a much wider scale, drawing connections not just between people, but between organizations, ideas, and knowledge. As such, Web pages may be best for providing insight into the organization of people and knowledge at a wider societal level, across regions, nations, and the globe.

FROM DATA NETWORKS TO SOCIAL NETWORKS

As work progresses in this area, a major issue to be addressed is how to interpret networks derived from online data. For example, how well do networks derived from online transcripts represent "real" or "on-the-ground" social networks, those defined by the complete, multirelational set of interactions and perceptions that make up inter-personal ties? A corollary question is how do we compare what is known about social networks from studies that ask individuals to report on their associations with results from single, abstracted parts of their daily interaction such as the traces left in online conversations? Thus, it is important to ask not only whether online networks are as "real" as offline networks, but also what part of those "real" networks is captured through examining online interactions, and how that part relates to other network capture mechanisms.

In the absence of sufficient empirical data comparing offline to online networks, it is only possible at this point to consider the relationship between the ties revealed from online data and the entirety of an interpersonal relationship. In doing so, we find that different Internet data sources provide different levels of confidence for the identification of meaningful dyadic relationships. For example, while a one-to-one email communication provides data that two people exchanged a message, it does not reveal the nature of the tie. The relationship may be friendship, but it may equally be strictly formal (e.g., supervisor to subordinate), or present only because an automated system has generated emails to the recipient (e.g., notices from discussion lists, marketing materials, or spam). Ensuring that networks derived automatically are viable representations of the kinds of social networks usually derived from asking people about their ties may require additional computational steps, such as examining the text of messages to identify roles and relationships.

"One-to-many" modes of communication such as online forums may provide even less confidence in the depth of the identified dyadic relationship. While an email clearly identifies the intended recipient(s), forum postings do not. As a result, it is difficult to ascertain who exactly is involved in the observed interaction. Therefore, to discover "one-to-one" relationships from "one-to-many" modes of communication, it is necessary to look beyond message addressing. One possible approach is to use text-mining techniques to extract all mentions of personal names in the postings and use these as actual addressee(s) of postings. A recent study of six online classes by Gruzd

(2009) showed that such an approach provides a better reflection of perceived social ties. The study found 40 percent more information was gained about social ties compared to approaches that relied only on "who posted after whom" data derived from position in the threaded discussion. The additional information mostly comes from instances when a poster addressed or referenced somebody who had not previously posted in a particular thread. (Other methods that rely on text-mining techniques to discover social networks are discussed further below.)

Web pages as network data sources present their own set of difficulties. In their raw form, Web pages provide very little information about dyadic relationships. For example, discovering that two people are mentioned on the same Web page as attending the same conference is not sufficient, on its own, to make judgments about their social relationship. Nevertheless, with the proper text-mining tools, Web pages may still reveal explicit or implicit declarations of relationships between two or more people. However, from a programming point of view, the latter is a more challenging task compared to analyzing email communication, because the majority of Web pages are essentially unstructured text that requires a lot more automated processing to discover relational declarations.

One of the ways used to increase confidence in the existence of dyadic relationships found on the Internet is to use a combination of data sources generated by members of the same community. This approach is based on the idea that analyzing different data sources provides more evidence in support (or rejection) of dyadic relationships between members of that community. This method can provide additional insight into the strength of ties; pairs that maintain ties through multiple media are more likely to be strongly tied than those connected via only one medium (Haythornthwaite and Wellman, 1998; Haythornthwaite, 2001).

Several studies have taken the approach of examining multiple online data sources. Stefanone and Gay (2008) relied on both email networks and forum networks to study social interactions of undergraduate students. Matsuo et al. (2006) used self-declared Friend-of-a-Friend networks, Web-mined collaborator networks, and face-to-face meeting networks to build Polyphonet, a community support system for two different conferences. Aleman-Meza et al. (2006) used two social networks – Friend-of-a-Friend networks extracted from pages on the Semantic Web and a co-authorship network derived from the DBLP Computer Science Bibliography – to determine the degree of conflict of interest among potential reviewers and authors of scientific publications.

Although there seems to be an increasing interest in combining datasets, it is not always feasible or possible to collect social network data from multiple sources for any particular online communities. Some groups, particularly distributed groups, may only use one channel of communication. Also, there is still the ongoing research question of how to combine evidence of social relationships from different types of data. However, no matter what the medium or media examined, the problem of extracting social networks is present for all such datasets. The next section describes in more detail the steps used to extract social networks from Internet data and how to address some of the challenges mentioned above.

SOCIAL NETWORK DISCOVERY FROM TEXTUAL DATA ON THE INTERNET

Text-mining techniques have been gaining in sophistication over the past decade. These techniques now offer ways to discover social networks from documents published on the Internet and text-based online communication. In general, to discover social networks from textual data, the following steps are taken:

- *Node Discovery*: All references to people are identified using names, pronouns, and email addresses.
- *Coreference and Alias Resolution*: Ambiguities about people are resolved, for example, differentiating between people with the same name and creating a single identity for those with multiple aliases.
- *Tie Discovery*: Social connections are determined between people identified in the first two steps.
- *Relationship and Role Identification*: The types of ties (e.g., friend, co-worker, classmate, etc.), and relations (e.g., trust, help, agreement, etc.) are identified, and roles (e.g., manager, subordinate, etc.) are assigned for each person based on communication content or patterns.

The following describes each of these four steps and provides examples from the literature.

Node discovery

Node discovery is usually conducted through the discovery of personal names and other references to people found in the text. It is part of a broader task in computational linguistics (CL) called named entities recognition (NER). NER is a set of text-mining techniques designed to discover named entities and the types of connections and relations between them (Chinchor, 1997). In NER, a named entity is defined very broadly. It may be a person, organization, or even a geographic location. NRE is commonly used in various natural language processing (NLP) applications such as machine translation, information extraction, and question answering systems. An example of an application that deals specifically with people's names is anonymization or pseudonymization used to hide sensitive data in private or secret documents such as personal medical records and vital government documents (e.g., Sweeney, 2004; Uzuner et al., 2007).

Since it is relatively easy to find pronouns (e.g., by comparing each word to a list of possible pronouns) and email addresses in text (by matching each word with a string pattern such as [part1]@[part2].[part3]), the following focuses primarily on the discovery of personal names. There are two primary approaches to finding personal names in the text. The first and easiest approach is to look up each word in a dictionary of all possible personal names. If a word is in the dictionary of names, then it is considered to be a name. Examples of electronic dictionaries with English names include the publicly accessible U.S. Census (www.census.gov), the commercial *InfoSphere Global Name* database from IBM, and the Web resource *Behind the Name* (www.behindthename.com). Researchers who have relied on this approach include Harada et al. (2004), and Sweeney (2004).

This approach is easy to implement and run; however, it leaves out names that are not already found in the dictionary. These may be names of non-English origin, informal variations of names, or nicknames. Neither does this approach take into account that in different sentences a word may be a name or just a noun (e.g., "*Page* asked for my help" and "Look at *page* 23"). To make sure that an algorithm finds the name "Page" and ignores the word "page," some researchers consider only capitalized words as potential candidates for personal names and ignore others. However, this restriction is not very practical with informal texts such as computer-mediated communication where names are often not capitalized.

An alternate approach to finding personal names does not require using a dictionary of names. This approach applies linguistic rules or patterns to the content and sentence structure to identify potential names. The linguistic rules and patterns are often built based on characteristic attributes of words such as word frequencies, context words, and word position in the text.

Some work in this direction includes that of Chen et al. (2002) and Nadeau et al. (2006).

In practice, these two approaches are usually used together; for example, finding all names in the dictionary first, and then using linguistic rules or patterns to find names that are not in the dictionary. Using such a hybrid approach, Minkov et al. (2005) reported a 10–20 per cent improvement in accuracy. The downside of a hybrid approach is that it tends to increase the time needed to process the textual data. (For a more detailed survey of modern NER techniques, see Nadeau and Sekine, 2007.)

Coreference and alias resolution

Once names and other words that refer to people (e.g., titles, pronouns, email addresses) are identified, the next step is coreference and alias resolution. The goal of this step is twofold: to group all mentions of the same person together (for example, "*you*," "*John*," "*Mr. Smith*," and *j.smith@mail.net*) and to distinguish between two or more people with the same name. Similar to the previous step of identifying named entities, for coreferencing, computational linguistics (CL) relies on a more general approach based on machine learning (ML) techniques and tries to link not just names, but also any coreferring noun phrases across sentences and documents where noun phrases may refer to people, organizations, or any other objects in the world. CL uses ML techniques to determine the likelihood that a set of noun phrases might refer to the same entity. Likelihood is measured by attributes of noun phrases, such as the distance between noun phrases in the text, lexical similarities, how often phrases collocate with each other, agreement in gender, and semantic meanings, etc. (For recent work in this area, see Culotta et al., 2007; Yang et al., 2008.)

In practice, however, to discover a social network from Internet data, there is usually no need to perform a full coreference and alias resolution. Quite often, resolution among personal names, email addresses, and sometime pronouns is sufficient. Thus, researchers working with Internet data often rely on simple rule-based or string-matching approaches. For example, McArthur and Bruza (2003) approached a pronoun coreference resolution in an email archive by simply replacing pronouns "*I*," "*my*," "*me*" with the sender's name and pronouns "*you*" and "*your*" with the receiver's name. There are also a number of simple but effective methods that match variations of names or email addresses by relying on phonetic encoding and pattern-matching techniques (e.g., Feitelson, 2004; Christen, 2006). For example, a simple rule may state that an email address belongs to a person if it contains either his or her first or last name and the initial of the other. According to this rule, emails that would be attributed to *John Smith* include *john.smith@mail. org, jsmith@mail.net, john@smith.net, s.john@ mail.net*. (For a more in-depth review of personal name-matching techniques, see Reuther and Walter, 2006.)

The second part of this step, alias resolution, requires special attention. Alias resolution can be performed as part of general NER, but it can also be conducted as a standalone procedure; it has a broad range of application in research on authorship, citation analysis, spam detection, author disambiguation in digital libraries, and more. The purpose of the various approaches to alias resolution is to distinguish between two or more people with the same name by identifying the unique "signature" that can be associated with each person. These approaches often rely on either unique linguistic characteristics of a person's writing (e.g., common writing styles, punctuation marks, average length of sentences, expertise keywords, etc.; e.g., Hsiung et al., 2005; Pedersen et al., 2006) or network-based patterns of interactions (e.g., common senders and recipients; e.g., Malin et al., 2005). When extracting social networks from the Internet, alias resolution is often addressed by automatically assigning a set of expertise keywords (e.g., Bollegala et al., 2006) or summaries of several contextual sentences (e.g., Phan et al., 2006) to each name in the text. The assumption is that different people (even with the same name) will be mentioned in different contexts in the text. So the task is reduced to finding a set of discriminating words and semantic features to uniquely describe a particular person.

Finally, in addition to content-based features, coreference and alias resolution in computer-mediated communication can rely on traffic-based features. For example, for threaded discussions, Gruzd and Haythornthwaite (2008a) relied on both types of features to associate names extracted from the content of messages (content-based feature) with the unique identifiers of posters' email addresses found in the posting headers (traffic-based features). All names that were associated with the same email address were considered to belong to the same person. This approach will require modification for communities where users use more than one email address.

Tie discovery

After all network nodes are identified and grouped to represent unique people, the next step is to uncover if, and how, these nodes are interconnected. There are two main methods in the literature for automated discovery of ties based on textual information. One is based on the similarity between users' profiles. A profile is either created manually by a person himself (e.g., a Facebook profile) or pulled out automatically from information on the Internet (e.g., a person's homepage or parts of the text written about that person). A simple way to measure the similarities is to count how many profile items two people have in common (e.g., Adamic and Adar, 2003). Another common approach includes measuring the semantic similarity between words extracted from the profiles. According to this method, two people are considered connected when the value of semantic similarity between their profiles is higher than a predefined threshold. In other words, people are considered to be connected when there is a substantial overlap of words and phrases found in their profiles. (For more on measuring semantic similarity, see Kozima and Furugori, 1993; Maguitman et al., 2005.)

Another method for tie discovery uses a co-occurrence metric to calculate the number of times two names appear in close proximity within the text. This approach is especially popular among researchers using Web pages to build networks. This is because search engines make it easy to count the co-occurrence of two people on Web pages. Matsuo et al. (2006) counted the number of hits from an Internet search engine in response to a query consisting of two names joined via the boolean operator "AND". Kautz et al. (1997) used this approach in their application called ReferralWeb for visualizing and searching social networks on the Web. For threaded discussions, Gruzd and Haythornthwaite (2008a) used the co-occurrence between posters' email addresses found in the posting headers and names found in the body of their messages to reveal learning networks in online classes (also see Haythornthwaite and Gruzd, 2008).

Role and relationship identification

Text-mining techniques have also proven to be useful for identifying roles and relationships in social networks. To perform this task automatically, researchers closely examine the context in which people's names are mentioned in the text. For example, if two names appear in the same sentence with a word like *committee*, then an assumption is made that these two people are members of the same organization, oriented to the same responsibilities.

Due to their rich textual content, Web pages are especially good sources for this kind of analysis.

Matsuo et al. (2007) relied on content-based characteristics – such as the number of co-occurrences of two people's names (e.g., whether their names appear on the same line) or whether a page included particular keywords in the title or first five lines – to automatically derive rules for the identification of the following relationships: (1) co-authors, (2) members of the same lab, (3) members of the same project, and (4) participants in the same conference or workshop. The researchers discovered that to identify "co-authorship" only required checking whether or not the names appeared on the same line in their collection of Web pages.

Mori et al. (2005) assigned these four relationships to two broad categories: common property relationships (when people share a common property such as profession, workplace, hobbies, etc.) and event-participation relationships (when people participate in the same event such as "taking a course" or "watching the same movie"). Common property relationships reflect the well-known principle in sociology called homophily, which holds that people with similar interests are more likely to associate with each other (McPherson et al., 2001). Event-participation relationships are known to social network researchers in studies of two-mode networks. There is an assumption that co-attendance signifies a similarity of interest in the common event, and a similar exposure to knowledge, ideas, or activities presented at the event. Assumptions may also include an increased likelihood that individuals have accomplished interpersonal interaction. An event-participation relationship creates what Haythornthwaite (2002) has called a *latent tie structure*, one that is organized by authorities beyond the individuals involved and yet provides the first (and sometimes required) step for the formation of weak ties, some of which may then build to stronger ties.

The content of emails has also been used to identify relationships or roles automatically. For example, Carvalho et al. (2007) used the content of email messages to identify leadership roles in a set of 34 workgroups. Specifically, to identify the leadership roles, the researchers looked for messages with words that were good indicators of such speech acts as Commit, Request, Deliver, Propose, and Meeting. Using both content-based and traffic-based information together in their study yielded 96 percent accuracy in predicting leadership roles.

Interest in automated social network discovery

Interest in automated social network discovery extends beyond academic researchers. More and more Web applications (often called social Web apps) are using information about users' personal networks to help users find more relevant information, share information with friends, or make better decisions (for a list of applications, see www.programmableweb.com/tag/social). As Web and text-mining techniques become more accessible to an even broader audience, even more applications can be expected that make use of online social network data. Research on how to make text-mining techniques more accessible for use in the discovery of social networks is on the way from a number of researchers cited here, including the lead author of the chapter who has developed a system called Internet Community Text Analyzer (ICTA; available at http://textanalytics.net). A detailed description of this system can be found in Gruzd and Haythornthwaite (2008b).

Industry-led initiatives in this direction by Facebook (http://developers.facebook.com) and Google (http://code.google.com/apis/opensocial) are likely to have an important impact because of their reach. Each company has built a free Web interface that gives Web developers access to the personal networks information of their and their partners' users. This has resulted in an explosion of social Web apps. While most of this newly available data is already pre-organized into a network form, additional processing of the texts produced by these communities, as described above, could reveal even more details about the nature of social ties between their members.

CONCLUSIONS

The chapter reviewed three types of commonly available Internet data sources (emails, online forums, and Web pages) in the context of automated discovery of social networks. Along with a brief discussion of each of the three data types, the chapter provided examples from the literature of how social networks have been discovered and used to study communities that rely on computer-mediated communication. The chapter then discussed the merits of different Internet data sources for revealing "real" dyadic relationships and social networks. Among the data types discussed, the one-to-one nature of email inspires the most confidence in attributing socially significant ties to the revealed network, with Web pages providing the least confidence.

Regardless of the data type, two main approaches are currently being used to extract networks from Internet data. One approach collects and combines evidence about dyadic relationships from multiple Internet sources associated with a particular community. However, this approach is not always practical since additional data sources are often absent or unavailable to the researchers. The other approach is to use Web and text-mining techniques to extract additional information about relationships and social roles through four main steps of node discovery, coreference and alias resolution, ties discovery, and relationship and role identification.

The automated techniques reviewed in this chapter can be used to transform even unstructured Internet data into social network data. With the social network data available, it is much easier to analyze and make judgments about social connections between community members. These automated techniques for social network discovery can be used where more traditional methods for data collection are too costly or impractical, or they can be used in conjunction with traditional methods. This is an exciting, new area of research, and we can expect future studies to provide improved accuracy using Web and text-mining methods and new automated methods to interpret the networks as they are extracted.

REFERENCES

Adamic, L.A. and Adar, E. (2003) 'Friends and neighbors on the web', *Social Networks*, 25(3): 211–30.

Aleman-Meza, B., Nagarajan, M., Ramakrishnan, C., Ding, L., Kolari, P., Sheth, A. P., Arpinar, I. B., Joshi, A. and Finin, T. (2006) 'Semantic analytics on social networks: experiences in addressing the problem of conflict of interest detection', *Proceedings of the 15th International Conference on the World Wide Web* (Edinburgh, Scotland). WWW '06. NY: ACM. pp. 407–16.

Baym, N.K. (2000) *Tune in, Log on: Soaps, Fandom and Online Community*. Thousand Oaks, CA: Sage.

Bloom, E.M. (2008, February 22) 'Who wins the fight over email ownership?' *The National Law Journal*. Retrieved November 1, 2008, from http://www.law.com/jsp/legaltechnology/pubArticleLT.jsp?id=1203602189436.

Bollegala, D., Matsuo, Y. and Ishizuka, M. (2006) 'Extracting key phrases to disambiguate personal names on the web', in A. Gelbukh (ed.), *Computational Linguistics and Intelligent Text Processing*. Berlin: Springer. pp. 223–34.

boyd, D.M. and Ellison, N.B. (2007) 'Social network sites: Definition, history, and scholarship', *JCMC*, 13(1): 210–30. Retrieved March 21, 2009, from http://jcmc.indiana.edu/vol13/issue1/boyd.ellison.html.

Breiger, R.L. (ed.) (2005) 'Ethical dilemmas in social network research', *Social Networks*, 27(2), whole issue.

Carvalho, V.R., Wu, W. and Cohen, W.W. (2007) 'Discovering leadership roles in email workgroups', *Proceedings of Fourth Conference on Email and Anti-Spam* (Mountain

View, CA). Retrieved October 30, 2008, from http://www.ceas.cc/2007/papers/paper-08.pdf.

Chen, C., Paul, R.J. and O'Keefe, B. (2001) 'Fitting the jigsaw of citation: Information visualization in domain analysis', *Journal of the American Society for Information Science and Technology,* 52(4): 315–30.

Chen, Z., Wenyin, L. and Zhang, F. (2002) 'A new statistical approach to personal name extraction', in C. Sammut and A.G. Hoffmann (eds), *Proceedings of the Nineteenth International Conference on Machine Learning.* San Francisco: Morgan Kaufmann. pp. 67–74.

Cherny, L. (1999) *Conversation and Community: Chat in a Virtual World.* Stanford, CA: CSLI Publications.

Chin, A. and Chignell, M. (2007) 'Identifying communities in blogs: Roles for social network analysis and survey instruments', *International Journal of Web Based Communities,* 3(3): 343–65.

Chinchor, N. (1997) 'MUC-7 named entity task definition', *Proceedings of the 7th Message Understanding Conference.* Retrieved October 30, 2008, from http://www-nlpir.nist.gov/related_projects/muc/proceedings/ne_task.html.

Cho, H., Gay, G., Davidson, B. and Ingraffea, A. (2007) 'Social networks, communication styles, and learning performance in a CSCL community', *Computers & Education,* 49(2): 309–29.

Christen, P. (2006) 'Comparison of personal name matching: Techniques and practical issues', *Proceedings of the Workshop on Mining Complex Data, IEEE International Conference on Data Mining.* ICDMW. Washington, DC: IEEE Computer Society. pp. 290–94.

Commission of the European Communities (2005) *eInclusion Revisited.* Retrieved March 21, 2009, from http://europa.eu.int/comm/employment_social/news/2005/feb/eincllocal_en.pdf.

Constant, D., Kiesler, S.B. and Sproull, L.S. (1996) 'The kindness of strangers: The usefulness of electronic weak ties for technical advice', *Organization Science,* 7(2): 119–35.

Culotta, A., Wick, M. and McCallum, A. (2007) 'First-order probabilistic models for coreference resolution', *Proceedings of Human Language Technologies 2007.* Rochester, NY: Association for Computational Linguistics. pp. 81–88.

Diesner, J. and Carley, K.M. (2005) 'Exploration of communication networks from the Enron email corpus', *Proceedings of the 2005 SIAM Workshop on Link Analysis, Counterterrorism and Security,* Newport Beach, CA. pp. 3–14. Retrieved October 30, 2008, from http://research.cs.queensu.ca/home/skill/proceedings/diesner.pdf.

Donath, J. and boyd, D. (2004) 'Public displays of connection', *BT Technology Journal,* 22(4): 71–84.

Dutton, W.H. (1996) (ed.) *Information and Communication Technologies.* Oxford: Oxford University Press.

Ess, C. and the AoIR Ethics Working Committee (2002) 'Ethical decision-making and Internet research', Retrieved March 21, 2009, from www.aoir.org/reports/ethics.pdf.

Feitelson, D.G. (2004) 'On identifying name equivalences in digital libraries', *Information Research,* 8(4): paper 192. Retrieved October 30, 2008, from http://InformationR.net/ir/9–4/paper192.html.

Festa, P. (2003) 'Newsmaker: Microsoft's in-house sociologist', *CNET.* Retrieved March 21, 2009, from http://www.news.com/2008–1082_3–5065298.html.

Fiore, A.T., Tiernan, S.L. and Smith, M.A. (2002) 'Observed behavior and perceived value of authors in usenet newsgroups: Bridging the gap', *Proceedings of SIGCHI.* Minneapolis, MN: ACM. pp. 323–30.

Fisher, D., Smith, M. and Welser, H.T. (2006) 'You are who you talk to: Detecting roles in usenet newsgroups', *Proceedings of HICSS 39.* pp. 59–68.

Fulk, J. and Steinfield, C.W. (eds) (1990) *Organizations and Communication Technology.* Newbury Park, CA: Sage.

Galegher, J., Kraut, R. E. and Edigo, C. (eds) (1990) *Intellectual Teamwork.* Hillsdale, NJ: Lawrence Erlbaum.

Garton, L., Haythornthwaite, C. and Wellman, B. (1997) 'Studying online social networks', *JCMC,* 3(1). Retrieved March 20, 2008, from http://jcmc.indiana.edu/vol3/issue1/garton.html.

Gruzd, A. (2009) 'Name networks: A content-based method for automated discovery of social networks to study collaborative learning', *Proceedings of the Association for Library and Information Science Education Conference.* Denver, CO, January 20–23, 2009. Retrieved October 30, 2008, from http://blogs.iis.syr.edu/alise/archives/168.

Gruzd, A. and Haythornthwaite, C. (2008a) 'Automated discovery and analysis of social networks from threaded discussions', *International Network of Social Network Analysts.* St. Pete Beach, FL, January 22–27, 2008.

Gruzd, A. and Haythornthwaite, C. (2008b) 'The analysis of online communities using interactive content-based social networks (extended abstract)', *Proceedings of the American Society for Information Science and Technology Conference.* 523–27.

Hagar, C. and Haythornthwaite, C. (2005) 'Crisis, farming and community', *Journal of Community Informatics,* 1(3). Retrieved March 21, 2009, from http://ci-journal.net/index.php/ciej/article/view/246/210.

Hampton, K. (2003) 'Grieving for a lost network: Collective action in a wired suburb', *The Information Society,* 19(5): 1–13.

Harada, M., Sato, S. and Kazama, K. (2004) 'Finding authoritative people from the web', *Proceedings of the 4th ACM/IEEE-CS Joint Conference on Digital Libraries.* Tucson, AZ: ACM. pp. 306–13.

Hargittai, E. (2007) 'Whose space? Differences among users and non-users of social network sites', *JCMC,* 13(1), article 14. Retrieved March 21, 2009, from http://jcmc.indiana.edu/vol13/issue1/hargittai.html.

Haythornthwaite, C. (2000) 'Online personal networks: Size, composition and media use among distance learners', *New Media and Society,* 2(2): 195–226.

Haythornthwaite, C. (2001) 'Exploring multiplexity: Social network structures in a computer-supported distance learning class,' *The Information Society,* 17(3): 211–26.

Haythornthwaite, C. (2002) 'Strong, weak and latent ties and the impact of new media', *The Information Society,* 18(5): 385–401.

Haythornthwaite, C. (2005) 'Social networks and Internet connectivity effects', *Information, Communication and Society,* 8(2): 125–47.

Haythornthwaite, C. (2007) 'Social networks and online community', in A. Joinson, K. McKenna, U. Reips, and T. Postmes (eds), *Oxford Handbook of Internet Psychology.* Oxford, UK: Oxford University Press. pp. 121–36.

Haythornthwaite, C. and Gruzd, A. (2008) 'Analyzing networked learning texts', *Proceedings of the Networked Learning Conference.* Halkidiki, Greece, May 5–6, 2008.

Haythornthwaite, C. and Wellman, B. (1998) 'Work, friendship and media use for information exchange in a networked organization', *Journal of the American Society for Information Science,* 49(12): 1101–14.

Hiltz, S.R. and Turoff, M. (1978) *The Network Nation.* Reading, MA: Addison-Wesley.

Hogan, B. (2008) 'Analyzing social networks via the Internet', in N. Fielding, R.M. Lee and G. Blank (eds), *SAGE Handbook of Online Research Methods.* Thousand Oaks, CA: Sage. pp. 141–60.

Hsiung, P., Moore, A., Neill, D. and Schneider, J. (2005) 'Alias detection in link data sets', *Proceedings of the International Conference on Intelligence Analysis.* Retrieved October 30, 2008, from http://www-cgi.cs.cmu.edu/~schneide/hsiung_alias.pdf.

Katz, J.E. and Rice, R.E. (2002) *Social Consequences of Internet Use.* Cambridge, MA: MIT Press.

Kautz, H., Selman, B. and Shah, M. (1997) 'Referral web: Combining social networks and collaborative filtering', *Communications of the ACM,* 40(3): 63–65.

Kavanaugh, A. and Patterson, S. (2002) 'The impact of computer networks on social capital and community involvement in Blacksburg', in B. Wellman and C. Haythornthwaite (eds), *The Internet in Everyday Life.* Oxford, UK: Blackwell. 325–44.

Keeble, L. and Loader, B. (eds) (2001) *Community Informatics: Shaping Computer Mediated Social Relations.* London: Routledge.

Kendall, L. (2002) *Hanging Out in the Virtual Pub.* Berkeley: University of California Press.

Kozima, H. and Furugori, T. (1993) 'Similarity between words computed by spreading activation on an English dictionary', *Proceedings of the Sixth Conference on European Chapter of the Association for Computational Linguistics.* pp. 21–23. Retrieved October 30, 2008, from http://acl.ldc.upenn.edu/E/E93/E93–1028.pdf.

Leggatt, H. (2007, April 12) 'Spam volume to exceed legitimate emails in 2007', *BizReport: Email Marketing.* Retrieved October 30, 2008, from http://www.bizreport.com/2007/04/spam_volume_to_exceed_legitimate_emails_in_2007.html.

Lim, M.J.H., Negnevitsky, M. and Hartnett, J. (2007) 'Detecting abnormal changes in email traffic using hierarchical fuzzy systems', *Proceedings of Fuzzy Systems Conference, 2007. FUZZ-IEEE 2007.* IEEE International. 1–6. Retrieved October 30, 2008, from http://ieeexplore.ieee.org/servlet/opac?punumber=4295328.

Maguitman, A.G., Menczer, F., Roinestad, H. and Vespignani, A. (2005) 'Algorithmic detection of semantic similarity',

Proceedings of 14th International Conference on World Wide Web. Chiba, Japan, May 10–14, 2005. WWW '05. New York: ACM. pp. 107–16.

Malin, B., Airoldi, E. and Carley, K.M. (2005) 'A network analysis model for disambiguation of names in lists', *Computational and Mathematical Organization Theory,* 11(2): 119–39.

Matsuo, Y., Hamasaki, M., Nakamura, Y., Nishimura, T., Hasida, K., Takeda, H., Mori, J., Bollegala, D. and Ishizuka, M. (2006) 'Spinning multiple social networks for semantic web', *Proceedings of the Twenty-First AAAI Conference on Artificial Intelligence.* Menlo Park, CA: AAAI Press.

Matsuo, Y., Mori, J., Hamasaki, M., Nishimura, T., Takeda, H., Hasida, K. and Ishizuka, M. (2007) 'Polyphonet: An advanced social network extraction system from the web', *Web Semantics,* 5(4): 262–78.

McArthur, R. and Bruza, P. (2003) 'Discovery of social networks and knowledge in social networks by analysis of email utterances', *Proceedings of ECSCW 03 Workshop on Moving from Analysis to Design.* Helsinki, Finland. Retrieved October 30, 2008, from http://www.ischool.washington.edu/mcdonald/ecscw03/papers/mcarthur-ecscw03-ws.pdf.

McPherson, M., Smith-Lovin, L. and Cook, J.M. (2001) 'Birds of a feather: Homophily in social networks', *Annual Reviews in Sociology,* 27(1): 415–44.

Minkov, E., Wang, R.C. and Cohen, W.W. (2005) 'Extracting personal names from email: Applying named entity recognition to informal text', *Proceedings of Human Language Technology Conference and Conference on Empirical Methods in Natural Language Processing.* Morristown, NJ: Association for Computational Linguistics. pp. 443–50.

Monge, P.R. and Contractor, N.S. (2003) *Theories of Communication Networks.* Oxford, UK: Oxford University Press.

Mori, J., Sugiyama, T. and Matsuo, Y. (2005) 'Real-world oriented information sharing using social networks', *Proceedings of the 2005 International ACM SIGGROUP Conference on Supporting Group Work.* New York: ACM. pp. 81–84.

Nadeau, D. and Sekine, S. (2007) 'A survey of named entity recognition and classification', *Linguisticae Investigationes,* 30(1): 3–26.

Nadeau, D., Turney, P. and Matwin, S. (2006) 'Unsupervised named-entity recognition: Generating gazetteers and resolving ambiguity', in J.G. Carbonell and J. Siekmann (eds), *Lecture Notes in Computer Science: Advances in Artificial Intelligence.* Berlin: Springer. pp. 266–77.

Newman, M.E.J. (2001) 'Scientific collaboration networks. I. Network construction and fundamental results', *Physical Review E,* 64(1): 64–71.

Pedersen, T., Kulkarni, A., Angheluta, R., Kozareva, Z. and Solorio, T. (2006) 'An unsupervised language independent method of name discrimination using second order co-occurrence features', in A. Gelbukh (ed.), *Computational Linguistics and Intelligent Text Processing.* Berlin: Springer. pp. 208–22.

Phan, X.-H., Nguyen, L.-M. and Horiguchi, S. (2006) 'Personal name resolution crossover documents by a semantics-based approach', *IEICE Transactions on Information and Systems,* E89-D(2): 825–36.

Reid, E. (1995) 'Virtual worlds: Culture and imagination', in S.G. Jones (ed.), *CyberSociety: Computer-Mediated Communication and Community.* Thousand Oaks, CA: Sage. pp. 164–83.

Reuther, P. and Walter, B. (2006) 'Survey on test collections and techniques for personal name matching', *International Journal of Metadata, Semantics and Ontologies,* 1(2): 89–99.

Reyes, P. and Tchounikine, P. (2005). 'Mining learning groups' activities in forum-type tools', *Proceedings of the 2005 Conference on Computer Support for Collaborative Learning: Learning 2005: the Next 10 Years!* Taipei, Taiwan, pp. 509–513.

Rheingold, H. (1993) *The Virtual Community.* Reading, MA: Addison-Wesley.

Rice, R.E. and Katz, J. (eds) (2001) *The Internet and Health Communication.* Thousand Oaks, CA: Sage.

Rice, R.E. (1992) 'Contexts of research on organizational computer-mediated communication', in M. Lea (ed.), *Contexts of Computer-Mediated Communication.* New York: Harvester Wheatsheaf. pp.113–44.

Rice, R.E. (1993) 'Using network concepts to clarify sources and mechanisms of social influence', in G. Barnett and J. W. Richards (eds). *Advances in Communication Network Analysis.* Norwood, NJ: Ablex. pp. 42–52.

Rice, R.E. (1994) 'Network analysis and computer-mediated communication systems', in S. Wasserman and J. Galaskiewicz (eds), *Advances in Social Network Analysis.* Thousand Oaks, CA: Sage. pp. 167–203.

Rice, R.E. (2002) 'Primary issues in Internet use: Access, civic and community involvement, and social interaction and expression', in L. Lievrouw and S. Livingstone (eds), *Handbook of New Media.* London, UK: Sage. pp. 105–29.

Schement, J.R. and Curtis, T. (1997) *Tendencies and Tensions of the Information Age: The Production and Distribution of Information in the United States.* Piscataway, NJ: Transaction Publishers.

Scott, P.B. (2005) 'Knowledge workers: Social, task and semantic network analysis', *Corporate Communications,* 10(3): 257–21.

Smith, C.B., McLaughlin, M.L. and Osborne, K.K. (1996) 'Conduct control on Usenet', *JCMC,* 2(4). Retrieved March 21, 2009, from http://jcmc.indiana.edu/vol2/issue4/smith.html.

Smith, M.A. (1999) 'Invisible crowds in cyberspace', in M.A. Smith and P. Kollock (eds), *Communities in Cyberspace.* London: Routledge. pp. 195–219.

Sproull, L. and Kiesler, S. (1991) *Connections.* Cambridge, MA: MIT Press.

Stefanone, M.A. and Gay, G. (2008) 'Structural reproduction of social networks in computer-mediated communication forums', *Behaviour and Information Technology,* 27(2): 97–106.

Sudweeks, F. McLaughlin, M.L. and Rafaeli, S. (eds) (1998) *Network and Netplay.* Cambridge, MA: MIT Press.

Sweeney, L. (2004) 'Finding lists of people on the Web', *Computer Science Technical Report CMU-CS-03–168.* Carnegie Mellon University, Pittsburg, PA. Retrieved October 30, 2008, from http://reports-archive.adm.cs.cmu.edu/anon/2003/CMU-CS-03–168.pdf.

Technorati (2008) 'State of the Blogosphere', Retrieved October 30, 2008, from http://technorati.com/blogging/state-of-the-blogosphere/.

Uzuner, O., Luo, Y. and Szolovits, P. (2007) 'Evaluating the state-of-the-art in automatic de-identification', *Journal of the American Medical Information Association,* 14(5): 550–63.

Wellman, B. (ed.) (1999) *Networks in the Global Village.* Boulder, CO: Westview Press.

Wellman, B. (2001) 'Computer networks as social networks', *Science,* 293(5537): 2031–34.

Wellman, B. and Haythornthwaite, C. (eds) (2002) *The Internet in Everyday Life.* Oxford, UK: Blackwell.

Wellman, B., Salaff, J., Dimitrova, D., Garton, L., Gulia, M. and Haythornthwaite, C. (1996) 'Computer networks as social networks', *Annual Review of Sociology,* 22: 213–38.

White, H.D., Wellman, B. and Nazer, N. (2004) 'Does citation reflect social structure?', *Journal of the American Society for Information Science and Technology,* 55(2): 111–26.

'Who owns your email?' (2005, January 11) *BBC NEWS.* Retrieved November 1, 2008, from http://news.bbc.co.uk/go/pr/fr/-/2/hi/uk_news/magazine/4164669.stm.

Wikipedia (2008) 'Usenet,' Retrieved October 30, 2008, from http://en.wikipedia.org/wiki/USENET.

Yang, X., Su, J., Lang, J., Tan, C.L., Liu, T. and Li, S. (2008) 'An entity-mention model for coreference resolution with inductive logic programming', *Proceedings of the 46th Annual Meeting of the Association for Computational Linguistics.* Morristown, NJ: ACL. pp. 843–51.

13

Corporate Elites and
Intercorporate Networks

William K. Carroll and J.P. Sapinski

INTRODUCTION

Although systematic network analyses mapping the social organization of business power date only from the 1970s, scholars have explored the relations that link corporations and their directors into corporate elites and intercorporate networks for over a century. Otto Jeidels's (1905) study of the relationship of German banks to industry, the first noteworthy investigation of this kind, discovered 1,350 interlocking directorates between the six biggest banks and industry. He related the interlock network to "a new phase in German industrial development caused by concentration and launched by the economic crisis of 1900" (Fennema and Schijf, 1978: 298). This chapter reviews the empirical work that followed from Jeidels, with an emphasis upon the period since the 1970s, when social scientists turned to network analysis as the primary means of representing the structure of elite and intercorporate relations.

First, some terminology. Networks linking corporations and their directors are known as "two-mode" or "affiliation" networks (see Borgatti, this volume): they contain two kinds of nodes (directors and corporations), with lines running only between one kind and the other. When an individual sits on two corporate boards concurrently, (s)he is said to hold *interlocking directorships* with the two companies, which also means that the directorates of the companies interlock, tying them together at the level of governance. For individuals, interlocking directorships enable participation in governance of multiple

firms, thereby enhancing contacts, influence, and prestige. For firms, interlocking directorates put boards in contact, and may enable coordination of business strategies within an interlocked group. There is a *duality* in networks of directors and the corporate boards on which they sit (Breiger, 1974), which is reflected in this chapter's title. These affiliation networks simultaneously draw together persons and large corporations, and they can be fruitfully analyzed on either level. As such, the study of these networks is relevant to a number of issues, including economic organization and the structure of capitalist classes (Scott, 1985: 2).

Large corporations are governed by boards of directors, elected at annual meetings of shareholders on the basis of one share, one vote – a system that favors owners of large blocks of shares – whether the shares are held by persons, other corporations, or institutional investors. Each corporate directorate is typically made up of both internal executives (insiders) and outside directors who do not hold executive positions in the firm. Individuals who hold interlocking directorships in large corporations include those with only outside directorships as well as executives of firms with which they are principally affiliated. In either case, "their directorships spread throughout the economy, and they form a corporate or business elite" (Scott, 1991: 182). An elite, however, is more than a set of advantaged individuals; it refers to "those who occupy the most powerful positions in structures of domination" (Scott, 2008: 33). As hierarchical organizations controlled by major shareholders, top executives, or some combination of both, large corporations are structures of domination par excellence. However, a corporate elite is different from a capitalist class, though the former, in its coordinated agency as an "organized minority" (Brownlee, 2005), may be the "leading edge" of the latter. "An economic elite," says Scott (2008: 37), "is an inter-organizational group of people who hold positions of dominance in business organizations and who may, under certain circumstances, have certain additional powers available to them." Interlocks figure heavily in creating or reflecting these circumstances. Just as interlocking directorships furnish the basis for a more or less cohesive corporate elite, interlocking directorates create relations between companies that add up to an intercorporate network.

Of course, it was not always so. Although elites and dominant classes have existed for millennia, corporate elites and intercorporate networks are creatures of advanced capitalism, going back only about a century or so, to the merger movements of the late nineteenth and early twentieth centuries that created, in the core regions of world capitalism, today's large corporations or their predecessors (Stanworth and Giddens, 1975). Jeidels's (1905) pioneering work emphasized the formation of networks of interlocking directorships between German industry and banks that accompanied this new phase of concentration. Rudolf Hilferding's (1981 [1910]) conception of finance capital as the symbiotic relation between money capital and industrial capital offered a theorization of the new power structure. On the one hand, banks needed an outlet to invest their accumulated capital; on the other, industry's scale of production had reached the point that only the largest banks could provide sufficient capital. Integration and coordination of the system was managed by a small circle of finance capitalists whose corporate affiliations linked banks with top industrial corporations. In the United States, the first reference to interlocking directorates comes from the Pujo Committee, a congressional investigation set up in 1912 to address the growing concerns about this system of bank power undermining market competition (Scott, 1997: 106). Another investigation directed by Paul Sweezy in the 1930s examined the bases of ownership of corporations, their interlocking directorates, and the control exerted by large banks on them. Sweezy was the first to delineate in the U.S. economy several interest groups among the 200 largest corporations and the 50 largest banks (Sweezy, 1953: 166–67).

Concerns with the concentration of power found another expression in C. Wright Mills's (1956) theory of the power elite, as well as in the work of the Canadian sociologist John Porter (1955, 1957). Both Mills and Porter invoked social networks more as metaphor than as full-fledged research method. Mills argued that corporate interlocking creates, among leading corporate executives and the very rich, an elite that is autonomous from specific property interests. These interlockers, along with shareholders whose investments span many sectors, come to embrace classwide interests that transcend specific property interests (Mills, 1956: 123). Interlocks offer to these elites a potential for exchanging views, consolidating the corporate world by unifying the outlook and policy of the propertied class (ibid.). Porter shared Mills's concerns about the threat to democracy posed by the concentration of economic power. His study of interlocks in Canada revealed a strong relationship between banks and industrial corporations, as bankers sat on industrial boards and vice versa (Porter, 1956: 211). The classic work of G. William Domhoff (1967) also treated social networks more as metaphor than method. His interest in power structures led him to stress the role of elite networks in creating unity. Domhoff's key contribution was to extend the analysis of interlocking to organizations that are part of the policy-planning process, such as business associations, policy forums, and think tanks (see Bond and Harrigan, this volume).

POWER STRUCTURE RESEARCH AND THE TURN TO NETWORK ANALYSIS

The groundwork having been laid in the 1950s and 1960s, "power structure research" came into its own in the 1970s (Domhoff, 1980), as researchers in the United States articulated an alternative to pluralist readings of economic and political power. The debate revolved mainly around the question of the unity and cohesiveness of the corporate elite. Against the pluralist position that market competition precludes elite unity, structuralist researchers used network analysis to reveal elite cohesion, and the capacity for political action.

At the level of individual directors, common participation in civic and political organizations (social clubs, foundations, universities, business associations and forums) as well as on corporate boards was found to foster social cohesion (Domhoff, 1974; Koenig and Gogel, 1981; Moore, 1979). Power structure research showed how individual directors connect, through the many venues where they meet, exchange ideas, and discuss economic as well as political issues. Useem (1978, 1984) identified, as the "dominant segment" of the capitalist class, an "inner circle" of corporate interlockers, directors of multiple firms who possess greater wealth than single-firm directors, have more connections to financial institutions, and show a higher degree of social cohesion and of political influence (Useem, 1978). Elite cohesion, moreover, was shown to have biographical depth. Studies in the United Kingdom indicated that most corporate directors share a similar background of privilege and inherited wealth, and that elites' educational and social backgrounds had become increasingly homogeneous in the twentieth century (Stanworth and Giddens, 1975; Whitley, 1974). Domhoff (1974) drew from experimental research on group dynamics to show that proximity and face-to-face communication enhance group cohesion, which in turn facilitates consensus formation in problem solving. For power structure researchers, the extensive network connecting corporate directors, layered upon personal networks that reach back to common educational and social backgrounds, promoted a common worldview (Koenig and Gogel, 1981), the basis for elite consensus and for concerted political agency (see Bond and Harrigan, this volume).

The findings of power structure researchers also challenged the managerialist position that saw a separation of ownership and control in the evolution of the modern corporation. As ownership became dispersed among many small shareholders, control of the firm was claimed to pass into the hands of disinterested managers (Berle and Means, 1932). If this were so, corporate directors and interlocks would be no more than window-dressing, irrelevant to economic power (Koenig et al., 1979). Power structure researchers questioned managerialism on many counts. On the level of corporations, Zeitlin (1974) analyzed the structure of ownership relations to show that, in the majority of cases, personal shareholding has been replaced by bank and insurance company shareholding, catapulting the latter, not managers, into controlling positions. On the individual level, Pfeffer (1987) argued that managers' goals are tied to their organizations' goals, especially in the case of corporations where top executives directly benefit from the firm's profitability through the shares they hold.

Studies such as these affirmed, in opposition to pluralism and managerialism, that corporations cannot be considered in isolation. They are embedded in a wider system of power through interlocking directorates and other relations. These multilevel relations shape corporate decisions and policies. The accomplishment of power structure research was to move beyond the "aggregative" methods of classic elite analysis, of pluralist political science, and of managerialism alike. These prenetwork approaches studied attributes of units of analysis (individuals or corporations), tacitly assuming the autonomy of the units, but did not systematically examine the structure of relations among them. In contrast, network analysis highlights the relations between units and the ways in which units (whether directors or corporations) are themselves shaped by their positions in systems of interrelations (Berkowitz, 1980).

By 1978, the research literature had burgeoned to the point that Fennema and Schijf, in their authoritative review, could offer a summary statement on the architecture and span of interlock networks in the developed capitalist societies:

> In all cases financial institutions, banks and insurance companies have central positions in the network of interlocking directorates. Another very general result is that in all studies so far almost all the companies are directly or indirectly connected with each other. (p. 327)

Debates within the study of interlocks

As network analysis of interlocks developed roots in the 1970s, internal debates grew within the field. Scott (1985) classifies approaches to the study of interlocks along two dimensions: first, an agent–system axis, and second, an organization-individual axis. The intersection of these two axes define four approaches (see Table 13.1).

The agent-centered approaches correspond for the most part to the prenetwork perspectives reviewed above. Focusing on organizational agents, interlocks become a characteristic of the firm that can be statistically related to performance or profitability. This not only diverts the agenda from questions of power; it fails to see that the goals and decision making of one firm are affected by the other firms with which it has relations of interdependency (Pfeffer, 1987). Focusing on individual agents, interlocks become properties of individuals, to be related to other personal characteristics, like wealth, education, class background and club membership (see Domhoff, 1967, 1974; Whitley, 1974). In reducing the social relations among directors to mere attributes, information on the actual system of interrelations that socially constitute the elite is sacrificed (Scott, 1985: 4).

Table 13.1   Approaches to the study of interlocks (*Networks of Corporate Power*, John Scott)

	Agent	System
Individuals	Social background	Class cohesion
Corporations	Organizational	Intercorporate

Source: Scott (1985: 3)

The main debates that took place in the 1980s were situated at the structural, systemic level, between interorganizational approaches and a "class hegemony" approach that emphasized the integrative function of interlocks for leading members of a dominant class. The former developed along two lines. In viewing corporations as formal organizations and corporate networks as interorganizational fields (Breiger, 1974; Palmer, 1987), some researchers introduced ideas from the sociology of formal organization, as in Allen's (1974) claim that interlocks issue from attempts by organizations to reduce environmental uncertainties by co-opting elites from other organizations and as in Pfeffer's (1987) view that policies and decisions are designed to manage this uncertainty as organizations interlock to secure access to necessary resources from other organizations (cf. Pennings, 1980). Although this analytic lens afforded some insights on how organizational imperatives figure in intercorporate networks, in assimilating the corporation to the broader category of formal organization, its specificity as a key institution of advanced capitalism was lost. Issues of class, power, and capital accumulation have not been taken up by interorganizational researchers, even though these are arguably central to this field of study. (For a review of research on interorganizational networks, see Krackhardt, this volume.)

Other researchers took an *intercorporate* view. In this perspective, interlocks are instrumental means in the accumulation and control of capital. Earlier researchers, often affiliated with old left parties, had taken up this approach, basing their work on Hilferding's view of finance capital as an integration of the financial and industrial forms of capital, placing big banks in central positions within a power structure segmented into "financial groups" of aligned corporations (Aaronovitch, 1961; Menshikov, 1969; Park and Park, 1973 [1962]; Perlo, 1957; Rochester, 1936). Mintz and Schwartz (1985) employed this approach in their study of the power structure of American business in the 1960s. Observing that "large investments create a common fate; both lender and borrower depend heavily upon successful use of capital," (1985: 183) they analyzed how, by controlling flows of capital, banks shape industrial structure, directing capital toward the most profitable or promising lines of investment. In this system of financial hegemony, the largest banks are "vehicles for the class control of the economy" (1985: 254), and their central position in the interlock network reflects their hegemonic role as mediators of intraclass competition and meeting points for finance capitalists. In this formulation, bank-centered interlocks provide the information necessary, at the organizational level, to implement financial hegemony – the broad scan across sectors of the business community. But at the individual level the same interlocks help constitute an elite of finance capitalists: "a cohesive group of multiple directors tied together by shared background, friendship networks and economic interests, who sit on bank boards as representatives of capital in general" (1985: 254).

Finally, the class hegemony perspective saw corporations as "units in a class controlled apparatus of appropriation" (Soref and Zeitlin, 1987: 58). In this view, decision making takes place within a wider network, not of organizations but of individual members of the dominant class, whose particular interests are crystallized not in individual corporations but in control groups (families or financial cliques), and whose general class interests are reinforced by the manifold weak ties of interlocking outside directors. The analysis focuses on individual directors as members of the upper class, on the internal class structure, including the relations between the industrial and financial fractions of the capitalist class, and on how firms are connected through individual board members or corporate and family ownership. Interlocks are considered an expression of class cohesion, allowing for the integration of potentially contradictory interests (financial, industrial, commercial) of the richest families, whose investments span different sectors (Soref and Zeitlin, 1987: 60). In the class hegemony perspective, interlocks serve as channels of communication between individual directors, facilitating a common worldview among them (Koenig and Gogel, 1981), and giving the "inner circle" of interlockers access to a broad resource base from which to exert their hegemony in and beyond business circles (Useem, 1978).

Thus, system-centered approaches broke from the limitations of agent-centered and "aggregative" approaches to corporate elites and intercorporate networks (Berkowitz, 1980). Taking into account the embedded character of corporations and directors, these approaches depicted the power structure as a formation within which elite individuals and capitalist enterprises pursued particular goals while often contributing to wider class-based interests, as in the allocation of investment capital and the solidification of class hegemony. Many authors have stressed the complementarity between these approaches (Koenig and Gogel, 1981; Scott, 1985; Stokman et al., 1988). In combination, they depict corporate interlocks as "traces of power" (Helmers et al., 1975, cited in Fennema and Schijf, 1978) of two sorts: the instrumental power associated with the accumulation of capital and the expressive power associated with class hegemony (Carroll, 2004; Sonquist and Koenig, 1975). This raises a key question, succinctly posed by Mark Mizruchi: what do interlocks do?

What do interlocks do?

In an extensive review of research literature, Mizruchi (1996) considered the causes and consequences of corporate interlocks. Focussing on the local rather than systemic significance of such ties, he noted both corporate and individual-level factors. For instance, interlocks can be created as mechanisms of co-optation or monitoring, as when a bank sends one of its officers to the board of one of its clients. Firms may invite prestigious directors on their boards to enhance their own reputations and contacts. Simultaneously, interlocks result from individual decisions to serve on multiple boards, which can be influenced by the prestige brought by the position, the remuneration, and the possibilities of making useful personal contacts (Mizruchi, 1996: 277). Any one explanation accounts for only a subset of all interlocks (Mizruchi, 1996: 274); hence, the precise significance of a given interlock is highly context-dependent.

In this regard, Scott's (1991: 184) observation that "power in intercorporate networks is based on at least three distinct kinds of intercorporate relation: personal, capital and commercial" has purchase. Commercial relations are simply trading links between buyers and sellers, but personal and capital relations are the main control relations surrounding corporations. Personal relations include interlocking directorships as well as kinship and friendship ties. Capital relations "are the links between business agents that result from shareholdings and from the granting and witholding of credit" (p. 184). While interlock networks open a window onto the social organization of corporate business, they comprise only one type of relation in a multilayered formation. Of particular significance in decoding interlocks as "traces of power" is the tendency, highlighted in the concept of finance capital, for interlocking directorships to be undergirded by capital relations (Scott, 2003: 159), including, in different contexts, intercorporate ownership, family control of multiple firms, institutional shareholding, and the credit relations through which banks exercise allocative power vis-à-vis borrowers.

COMPARATIVE PERSPECTIVES AND THE GLOBAL INTERLOCK NETWORK

By the 1980s, a vast body of empirical research, much of it centered on the United States, had yielded many detailed insights on the structure of intercorporate networks and corporate elites. What was lacking, however, was a comparative-historical perspective that could broaden and deepen knowledge beyond the tacit positing of the United States as the norm. It was in this context that John Scott (1985) produced the second edition of his *Corporations, Classes and Capitalism*, a compendium of research emphasizing the distinct routes that the advanced capitalist countries had taken to the corporate regimes of the late twentieth century, and the implications of those differences for network structure. In the same year, an international research group comparing the structure of intercorporate networks in 10 countries (the United States plus nine European states), published *Networks of Corporate Power* (Stokman et al., 1985). Although structural analysis of corporate interlocks had, since Jeidels, been pursued in various countries and had been advanced significantly by Dutch researchers (see Fennema and Schijf, 1978), these works began to broaden the focus of interlock research and at the same time to afford systematic cross-national comparison.

Drawing on such exemplars as Hilferding's analysis of bank control in Germany and Mintz and Schwartz's study of financial hegemony in the American corporate network, Scott (1985, 1987) noted that the capital relations that undergird interlock networks entail two forms of power: strategic control over specific corporations by means of concentrated blocs of shares and allocative power over capital flows, exercised by financial institutions. Distinct patterns of economic development and corporate law had produced variant configurations of these forms of economic power within national business systems and networks (cf. Whitley, 1999). In Germany, these forms intersected in the big "universal" banks, engendering a network of "oligarchic bank hegemony" in which banks were dominant in both capital allocation and control. In the postwar Japanese system, strategic and allocative power were also combined in discrete, bank-centered enterprise groups whose members held large blocs of shares in each other. In France, Belgium, and Italy, a "Latin model," organized around the extensive shareholdings of rival holding companies, imparted "a granular, group structuring of the economy" and of the network (Scott, 1985: 136). In the Anglo-American system of "polyarchic financial hegemony," which took shape in the aftermath of the Great Depression and was consolidated during the post–World War II boom, large financial institutions held powerful allocative positions opposite industrial firms while institutional investors such as pension funds held blocs of shares that enabled them to function collectively as "constellations of interests," exercising a constraining strategic power upon corporate management. The "polyarchic" character of the Anglo-American system made for an interlock network centralized around major banks and insurance companies, with little to no fractioning of the network into discrete financial groups (Scott, 1985: 129–260). With continuing growth in all advanced capitalist countries of depersonalized, institutional investment, Scott saw "a common move toward bank hegemony of a loosely structured kind" (p. 227).

A stream of comparative research flowed in the wake of these initiatives, and by the time Scott (1997) issued a completely rewritten compendium he was able not only to refine his earlier categories of variant patterns but to add the "post-Communist pattern" of collusive business organization in Eastern Europe and the "Chinese pattern" of corporate cooperation based on fraternal inheritance. More recent comparative studies include Maclean et al.'s (2006) investigation of business elites and corporate governance in France and the United Kingdom, which contrasted the thinness of the British network with the extensive involvement of wealthy families and the state in corporate France. Drawing on Bourdieusian field analysis, these authors explored "the social reality of how power is applied, channelled and contained in both countries" (2006: 164). Although in both cases serving on the boards of charitable institutions, business associations, public bodies, and the like was a mainstream medium for elite networking, the French elite favored service on business associations while the British elite was heavily involved in arts, sport, and private clubs. Maclean et al. argued that "there are powerful, logical economic reasons why individuals rich in contacts are appointed as directors, leading to the self-perpetuating cohesion of the business elite on both sides of the Channel" (2006: 191). Paul Windolf's (2002) study of interlock networks in Europe and the United States also merits attention, not only for its further details on the organization of big business in advanced capitalism but for its attention to post-socialist networks in Eastern Europe. Windolf's analysis of the economic annexation of the former German Democratic Republic by the West German capitalist class – a process that produced an East German network of companies "legally and economically dependent upon western interests" (2002: 163) – raised the larger question of how, in a globalizing world, corporate power is configured on world capitalism's semi-periphery.

In one reply, Ilya Okhmatovskiy's (2005) study of the Russian interlock network evidenced an instructive reversal of the dominant pattern of financial hegemony found in core countries. In the aftermath of the 1998 financial crisis, Russian banks, previous leaders in converting public assets into capital were unable to access foreign capital or even to aggregate the savings of wary householders. They yielded their centrality to giant industrial firms whose resource exports generated deep pools of capital, on which the banks themselves came to depend. The study supported the concept of finance capital as an integration of financial and industrial forms, but showed how, when financial institutions are weak, a few industrial concerns can act as the coordinating centers of financial-industrial groups (2005: 452). Yun Tae Kim (2007), focusing on the level of individual Korean directors, detailed the role of exogamous marriage networks, common educational backgrounds, and exclusive social clubs in knitting together the major chaebol into a cohesive corporate elite with a wide range of connections with state officials, politicians, and the military elite. Although Kim found very little direct involvement of the corporate elite in political parties or the state, a plethora of informal connections "have provided chaebols not only with communication channels, but also with significant power and influence over policy-making" (2007: 34).

If studies such as these suggest that on the semi-periphery the move to impersonal possession and polyarchic financial hegemony is less advanced, other political-economic transformations, beginning in the 1980s, brought changes to the dominant pattern of business organization in core countries. The long-term tendency for capital to internationalize in the form of transnational corporations and financial markets, and the associated accumulation crisis of nationally organized capitalism, furnished favorable terrain for neoliberal policies of deregulation, pursued in the context of the increasingly visible impact of globalization on the structure, and functioning of corporate power. Scott (1997: 252) suggested that, with neoliberal globalization, the disarticulation of national core economies brought a disarticulation to national interlock networks. A study of change in the Canadian network from 1976 to 1996 did find an overall weakening of ties but also a tendency for Canada-based transnationals, both industrial and financial, to become more central in the network. The network became sparser mainly due to corporate governance reforms within the business community, implemented after 1995, which sought both to bolster shareholder rights and to prevent further corporate scandals, under the pressure of intensified international competition (Carroll, 2002a: 367).

Indeed, in the wake of deregulatory policies that rendered corporate business prone to Enron-style scandals and corporate capitalism more susceptible to financial crisis, a governance reform movement was spearheaded by institutional investors in the 1990s and embraced by the Organization for Economic Cooperation and Development in 1998. The thrust of these reforms was to make corporate boards more effective and reliable in generating value for shareholders, the most powerful of whom, within systems of polyarchic financial hegemony, are institutional investors. These objectives dictated a normative ideal for corporate boards: that they be independent from top management, uninfluenced by interests other than shareholders, small enough to function efficiently, and composed of high-performance, well-oriented directors who are directly engaged in the decision-making process (Carroll, 2004: 34; Maclean et al., 2006: 213). Governance reforms reshaped the structure of corporate elites. They encouraged corporations, in the name of efficiency, to reduce the size of boards and to limit the number of directorships that members should hold concurrently; they weakened the basis for interlocks between non-shareholding creditors (typically banks) and debtors; they brought merit-based recruitment practices, opening boardrooms to more women and ethnic minorities (Carroll, 2004). The result, in countries where reforms were vigorously undertaken (but much less so in France [Maclean et al., 2006: 257] and elsewhere), was a thinning of the interlock network (as leaner boards were populated with fewer "big linkers"), a weakening of bank centrality, a modest shift away from patriarchal and toward multicultural board composition, and a decline of the "old boys networks" that had formed the dense core of corporate elites (cf. Carroll, 2004; Davis and Mizruchi, 1999; Heemskerk, 2007; Zweigenhaft and Domhoff, 1998).

Meanwhile, with the ongoing globalization of corporations, network analysis of corporate organization also went global. Key issues informing this strand of analysis have been (1) whether transnational interlocks between firms based in different countries are on the rise while national interlocks contained within countries are declining and (2) the spatial distribution of transnational interlocking. These questions, the second of which we take up later, are crucial to an understanding of the *global* intercorporate network and the *global* corporate elite.

Fennema (1982) made the earliest attempt to analyze a transnational intercorporate network. Mapping the network before and after the generalized international recession of 1973–74, he documented the consolidation of a Euro-North American component but found very few ties extending beyond that heartland of postwar capitalism. Fennema and Schijf's (1985) more extensive network analysis, conducted as part of the 10 countries study (Stokman et al., 1985), clarified that the 1976 Euro-USA network linked the two continents only sparsely, largely through Britain, but that certain pairs of European countries (particularly Germany/Netherlands and Belgium/France) were quite profusely connected.

After a lapse of 17 years, Carroll and Fennema (2002) picked up the thread, with an analysis of Fennema's (1982) 1976 network and comparable data for 1996. They reported only a modest increase in transnational interlocking alongside the persistence of national networks, suggesting strong path dependencies reproducing the patterns of national corporate-elite organization discerned by Scott (1997). Kentor and Jang (2004) purported to show a much more dramatic increase in transnational interlocking between 1983 and 1998; however, questions were raised about the validity of their data (Carroll and Fennema, 2004). Whatever the case, research on the 500 leading corporations in the world in the most recent decade (1996–2006) finds a proliferation of transnational interlockers and a decline in national networkers, particularly in Japan, whose complement of leading corporations plummeted during the 1990s. The transnationalists have profuse ties to each other as well as to various national segments; thus, "in the inner circle of the global corporate elite, transnationalists and national networkers intermingle extensively, 'national' and 'supranational' spaces intersect, and whatever common interest takes shape is likely to blend 'national' and 'transnational' concerns" (Carroll, 2009: 308).

KEY ISSUES

Across the last several decades, researchers have used an eclectic combination of techniques to map corporate networks at different scales and over various time frames. In this section we consider how four analytic issues have been addressed – the duality of corporate networks, questions of temporality, questions of spatiality, and the relation between interlocking directorates and capital relations.

The duality of interlock networks

As we saw above, interlock networks can be fruitfully analyzed as interpersonal networks of directors forming a corporate elite or as intercorporate configurations. Although both approaches shed light on issues of social organization, each reveals only one facet of an inherently dualistic structure (Breiger, 1974), reducible neither to an elite of directors nor to a network of faceless corporations (Carroll, 1984: 249). The challenge has been to devise ways of representing interlock networks as configurations of both individual directors and the corporations they direct.

One approach has been to examine the network in two parallel analyses, as an interpersonal network of directors, linked to each other by virtue of their common corporate affiliations, and as an intercorporate network of interlocking directorates. Applying this strategy to the U.S. network, Bearden and Mintz (1987: 204) discovered "parallels in structure between the corporate and director networks," with regional organization, the merger of institutional and class interests, and the unifying role of big linkers occurring on both levels, and with bank boards serving as key sites in both the director network and the corporate network. Davis and colleagues (2003) also pursued parallel analyses in their small-world study of change in the U.S. corporate network between 1982 and 1999. Although the mean degree of contacts decreased in both the interpersonal and intercorporate networks, at both levels the structure remained a small world, due to the integrative impact of both linchpin boards and linchpin directors: nodes whose ties across clusters create shortcuts that shrink the social space of the network. The remarkable consistency in connectivity, despite decreasing board interlocks, led these researchers to conclude that the small world of the corporate elite may issue less from elite institutions such as private schools and commercial banks and more from simple tendencies for boards to recruit well-connected directors and for directors to prefer well-connected boards (p. 322).

Alternatively, the two levels can be considered in a single analysis of the interpersonal network by assigning to directors, as contextual variables, the attributes of the firms with which they are principally affiliated. Applying this approach to the Canadian network, Carroll (1984) found that industrial and financial firms controlled in Canada were strongly over-represented at the center of the director network and in its principal cliques. The cliques were substantially organized around intercorporate ownership relations, supporting the conclusion that the Canadian corporate power structure revolves around "groups of interlocked capitalists who own and manage supra-corporate blocs of finance capital" (p. 265).

Researchers have also addressed the issue of duality directly by analyzing corporate affiliations as two-mode networks, thereby keeping both levels in view. Levine and Roy (1979) pioneered this approach with their "rubber-band" model, simultaneously clustering directors, and corporations on either side of a set of elastic board affiliations. This approach is limited to relatively small corporate networks, but it can be very revealing when applied to specific corporate empires, as in Carroll and Lewis's (1991) case study of the Brascan enterprise group, which in 1986 included 56 directors of two or more of the 14 major Canadian corporations controlled by or affiliated with the investment company Brascan Limited.

More recently, Alexander explored the boardroom networks of Australian directors, in an intricate two-mode analysis at 1976 and 1996. Following Faust and Wasserman (1993), Alexander (2003: 235) notes that both the interpersonal and intercorporate network have as their common *infrastructure* "the specific subset of memberships of all the interlockers/networkers in the affiliation network," which provides the resources for network connectivity. The patterning of such memberships simultaneously shapes both levels of the network. For instance, if directors tend to clump together on the same boards, as in a configuration built around corporate groups, the network will contain extensive redundancy, with the same directors linking the same boards in a system of "tight" interlocks that will dampen the spread of contacts in the interpersonal network. In the Australian case, although the density of intercorporate relations increased only slightly from 1976 to 1996, redundancy in the infrastructure decreased substantially, creating more networking resources, which increased the interpersonal network's density and drew many more boards into the dominant component.

Temporality and network dynamics

Intercorporate networks and corporate elites arise and persist in the broad sweep of history, and researchers have explored the temporality of these formations using a variety of models and designs. The most basic longitudinal research design depicts network structure at two moments, and interprets patterns of continuity and change in view of social and historical processes that are known to have occurred in the interim, as in Allen's (1974) comparison of the U.S. intercorporate network at 1935 and 1970. A slightly more elaborate longitudinal design incorporates three or more points of observation. Bunting and Barbour (1971) analyzed interlocking directorates among 207 American firms at six points from 1896 to 1964 and reported a decline in both inter-sectoral and intra-sectoral density after 1905, which they attributed to the introduction of anti-trust legislation. As well, Stanworth and Giddens (1975), in their study of the British network at seven points between 1906 and 1970, find that the concentration of firms has increased, along with the number of ties among firms; they also note that the top 50 British firms grew closer to the

City banks since the beginning of the twentieth century. Gilles Piédalue (1976) replicated the snowball-sampling approach of Jeidels (1905) in a study of Canadian corporations from 1900 to 1930 that included four observation points. Like Jeidels, Piédalue began with the big banks and included corporations sharing directors with a bank or firms interlocked with a bank. He was able to show a dramatic expansion of the network, particularly in the first decade, and an increasing degree of interlocking. Mark Mizruchi's (1982) follow-up to Bunting and Barbour examined the U.S. network at seven points from 1904 to 1974, revealing one large cluster of firms dominated by JP Morgan & Co., which divided after 1919 into bank-centerd cliques, with most corporations inhabiting the borders of multiple cliques. More recently, Barnes and Ritter (2001) tracked the thickening and then thinning of the American corporate network at four points from 1962 to 1995, and Barnes (2005), using the same data but examining the interpersonal network, explored the multiple dimensions of the American corporate elite's small world. By assessing how much the addition of extra-corporate affiliations decreased mean geodesic distances among directors, Barnes documented the decline of cultural ties (e.g., to museum and symphony boards) but a steady increase in the integrative role of elite affiliations with policy planning organizations. In line with Useem (1984), these trends depict a corporate elite becoming less concerned with maintaining social or civic ties and much more politically mobilized (cf. Carroll, 2004; Murray, 2006).

Although successive cross-sections allow researchers to pinpoint when major structural changes occur, they do not afford much basis for discerning the dynamics of change. With panel designs it is possible to analyze changes in both the composition of the set of largest corporations and the structure of relations among them. Carroll's (1986) analysis of turnover in the corporate constituents of the Canadian network and the links between them (1946–76) isolated as the stable core the set of multiple-director interlocks that were maintained throughout the three decades among firms that consistently ranked in the Top 100, despite changes in board composition. It was around this stable core that the major structural transformations occurred, as differential rates of accumulation and corporate reorganizations led firms to enter or exit from the Top 100 and as interlocks emerged or disappeared with corporate realignments. Panel design has also been used in assessing the stability of network parameters, as in Mariolis and Jones's (1982) study of relative centrality in the American corporate network, which was found to be extremely stable over the

years 1962, 1964, and 1966, consistent with interpretations of interlocks as indicators of power, interdependence, and communication.

Following from the groundbreaking work of Helmers et al. (1975, cited in Fennema and Schijf, 1978: 324–25), which showed that in the Netherlands in the 1960s interlocks between financial institutions and industrial corporations had a high probability of being restored after retirement, resignation, or death of a director, several studies then employed restoration of broken ties as an indicator of the importance of an interlock to the two linked firms. Ornstein (1984) found that of the 5,354 interlocks among large corporations in Canada broken at some point during the first three postwar decades, 30 percent were restored, but the rate of restoration varied according to several factors. Interlocks carried by executives in one of the interlocked firms, and interlocks that were part of a multiple-interlock relation or a relation of intercorporate ownership between firms, were substantially more likely to be restored. Also, ties among companies controlled domestically were far more likely to be restored than were ties between Canadian- and American-controlled firms. And, after controlling for country of control, industry, and location of head office, financial-industrial interlocks were more likely to be restored than other ties. Richardson (1987) used cross-lagged correlations to show that in the Canadian network the profitability of industrial firms in 1963 predicted the restoration of their interlocks with financial institutions five years later, in a "circular and self-sustaining process" that reinforced companies' original profit position, supporting the theory of finance capital as capital integration.

Palmer's studies of broken ties in the American network found a low rate of restoration, particularly for non-executive interlocks. He concluded that although some interlocks facilitate formal intercorporate coordination, many of them are expressions of class hegemony, as interactions among leading directors and executives create "a loose, but nonetheless very real system of coordination in which firms are instruments of inner circle policy" (p. 70). Stearns and Mizruchi (1986), however, in a panel study that tracked 22 major industrial corporations over three decades, found evidence of "functional reconstitution," in which an industrial firm's broken tie to a financial institution is restored by an interlock to a different financial institution. This suggests that the incidence of purposive, strategic interlocking is higher than that estimated by the "direct" restoration of broken ties. In a complementary investigation using the same database, an event-history analysis of the creation of new interlocks showed that although firms with decreasing solvency and profitability were likely to appoint executives in financial institutions to their boards, all corporations were more likely to make such appointments during upswings in the business cycle, as capital needs expand. Both the specific situation facing a firm and the general context for capital accumulation appear to influence the creation of a financial-industrial interlock (Mizruchi and Stearns, 1988).

Although the bulk of sociological research on corporate networks has been set within the power-structure tradition, some of the most innovative analyses of temporality have explored practices only indirectly related to this central problematic. Galaskiewicz and Wasserman (1981), in a study of a regional corporate network, used Markov chains to model network processes. Focusing on the probability of establishing a linkage and the probability of an asymmetric (executive) linkage becoming reciprocated (or vice versa), they found that norms of reciprocity are not operative in corporate interlock networks, as they are in other interorganizational relations – consistent with the idea that interlocks carried by corporate insiders tend to be relations of influence and power. Diffusion of innovation analysis has also been employed in tracking network effects on speed of adaptation and patterns of prevalence of corporate governance practices. Here, Davis and Greve's (1997) study of the adoption of poison pills and golden parachutes in the American network (1980–86), marking a shift to "investor capitalism," is iconic. They showed how, amid the takeover waves of the 1980s, poison pills spread rapidly through board-to-board diffusion processes "in which firms adopted to the extent that their contacts had done so," but parachutes spread slowly, on the basis of geographical proximity rather than interlocking directorates (p. 29).

More recently, the development of actor-oriented modeling by Tom Snijders and his colleagues (Snijders, this volume; Steglich et al., 2006) has opened new possibilities for systematic analysis of network dynamics. As applied to intercorporate networks, this approach accounts for the changing pattern of inter-firm relations by estimating the underlying rational choices of network actors. For instance, van de Bunt and Groenewegen's (2007) study of collaborative agreements among genomic companies found that firms prefer to start partnerships with high-status (well-connected) companies and with companies that are already members of the same (2-clique) groups as the focal firm. The modeling procedure enabled these researchers to show that an apparent transitivity effect (whereby firms prefer to partner with companies that are already partners of partners) could be accounted for by the preference for high-status partners. Although actor-oriented

modeling has only recently been applied to interorganizational relations, it offers intriguing opportunities to explore how macro-configurations of corporate power are shaped by local, context-dependent decisions of corporations.

The career trajectories of directors and executives present yet another dynamic in the life of corporate networks. In their study of pathways to corporate management in the United States, Useem and Karabel (1986) found that although there are a variety of routes to the top, individuals who become members of the elite's inner circle are those with the greatest amount of both "scholastic" (elite education) and "social" (upper-class background) capital. The core of the elite, the segment most engaged in classwide leadership, appears to be recruited through mechanisms emphasized in Bourdieu's (1984) generalized theory of capital. In a fully longitudinal study of Dutch corporations over two decades (1960–80), Stokman et al. (1988) tracked the careers of the 105 big linkers whose extensive corporate directorships carried most of the network. The typical career pattern involved entering the network as an executive, acquiring several outside directorships, retiring from the executive position but maintaining (some of) the outside directorships, and finally exiting from the network altogether. As corporate boards recruit outside directors from a pool of executives of other large firms, and as executives move through this career sequence, the network is reproduced in its duality, partly on the basis of "permanent economic and financial relations between companies," and partly through recruitment processes that cause "*global* stability of the structure of the network, together with *local* instability of dyadic relations" (p. 203).

Finally, more qualitative approaches have highlighted the contingent, historical, and contextual character of network temporality. Davita Glasberg's (1987) case studies of the assertion of financial hegemony in restructuring insolvent corporations through such mechanisms as stock dumping are of great relevance to the current conjuncture of global capitalist crisis. Equally apposite is Brayshay and colleagues' (2006) qualitative study of "power geometries" in the rescue of Hudson's Bay Company (HBC) by the Bank of England during the last worldwide Depression. Eschewing a large-sample approach, these researchers began from the biography of a single person, Patrick Ashley Cooper, appointed governor of the HBC in 1931 and a director of the Bank of England in 1932, and thereupon assembled a remarkable set of international business contacts. By tracing Cooper's network in depth, through archival documents including his detailed personal diaries and letters, as well as Bank of

England archives, Brayshay et al. constructed a rich longitudinal account of the corporate network and wide range of business- and policy-related practices that were enabled by it. Significantly, Cooper's embeddedness extended well beyond the boardrooms of London. Indeed, among his core group of special confidants were many people who had no overlapping corporate affiliations with him. The authors' sensible conclusion, that "a full reconstruction of an economic actor's array of contacts requires research beyond the stylized mapping of corporate networks" (p. 996), should serve as a challenge to researchers: they should delve into the kind of qualitative depth that can yield insight on specific mechanisms of social power, corporate control, and capital accumulation.

Spatiality

The question of how business networks are configured in space has preoccupied researchers since the consolidation of power structure analysis in the 1970s. The outstanding study from that era is Sonquist and Koenig's (1975) clique analysis of the American network circa 1969. Geocoding each corporation by the city of its headquarters, they found a structure of 32 overlapping cliques and their satellites, most of which were based in particular cities, with New York hosting the largest and most central group. Mintz and Schwartz (1981: 863) soon demonstrated the special position of New York as "the base of a national network of corporate interlocks, uniting regional clusters into a loosely integrated whole." Green's (Green, 1983; Green and Sempel, 1981) subsequent studies of the inter-urban network of corporate interlocks and of institutional stock ownership (Green, 1993) revealed a regionalized network dominated by the cities in which major financial institutions have their headquarters: New York and four secondary urban centers (Chicago, Boston, Los Angeles, and San Francisco). Later, Kono and his colleagues (1998) explored the possibility that local and nonlocal interlocking may have different determinants by examining the relationship between spatial propinquity of corporate headquarters and corporate interlocking among 500 U.S. firms in 1964. Interestingly, firms based in cities with exclusive upper-class clubs were more likely to interlock with each other, suggesting that "the local capitalist class social organization made possible by the colocation of corporate headquarters and upper-class clubs may be an instrument by which corporate elites manage their organizational environments, gaining information, trusted contacts, and access to national networks of elites" (Kono et al., 1998: 904). Of course, the

regionally dispersed pattern of interlocking in the United States should not be abstractly generalized to other social formations. For instance, in Canada the corporate elite has long been centered in two cities – Montreal and Toronto – with the corporate network aligned along a highly integrated Toronto-Montreal axis (Clement, 1975). However, a study of the shifting corporate geography from 1946 to 1996 found that the westward flow of capital brought a plethora of corporate head offices to Calgary and Vancouver, creating a westward drift in the network itself. Still, the continuing preeminence of Toronto and Montreal as centers of finance produced a national network carried substantially by finance capitalists directing eastern-based financials and western-based industrials (Carroll, 2002b; see also, in the British case, Scott and Griff, 1984).

Recently, the geography of corporate networks has been explored at a global level. In a study of the global corporate elite (1996–2006) mentioned earlier, Carroll found a highly regionalized network, most of whose members are entirely embedded in national networks, with transnational interlocking mainly integrating corporate Europe or linking across to North America. Moreover, the growing cohesiveness of corporate Europe and the thinning of the American network shifted the global network's center of gravity, registering the success, from a business standpoint, of European integration, along with the decline of American hegemony (Carroll, 2009).

Several investigations have reached similar conclusions by charting the network of global cities on the basis of intercorporate relations. Using interlock data from 1996, aggregated by city of head office, Carroll (2007) found an inter-urban network in which Paris, London, and New York are particularly central, along with other cities of northeast North America and northwest Europe — the heartland of an Atlantic ruling class, in van der Pijl's (1984) terminology. Alderson and Beckfield's (2004) research on intercorporate ownership relations radiating from the world's 500 largest corporations provided a different vantage point on the world city system. Based on parent-subsidiary ownership relations, Tokyo emerged as the most central point. A follow-up investigation, analyzing change in the centrality of cities between 1980 and 2000, found a substantial reshuffling of the hierarchy and an increasing interurban disparity in centrality. Overall, the parent-subsidiary network of global cities appeared to be reproducing the "old" geography of center-periphery relations in the world-system "in an even more pronounced form" (Alderson and Beckfield, 2007: 34). A finding common to all these studies has been the marginal position of corporations headquartered on global capitalism's semi-periphery. The global corporate elite, the global intercorporate network, and the world city network compose a core-periphery structure in which the Global North continues to dominate (see also Kick et al., this volume).

Capital relations and corporate interlocks

Although this chapter has focused on interlocking directorates, earlier we noted Scott's (2003: 159) thesis that interlocking directorships must be viewed "alongside the capital relations that undergird them." This point, central to an understanding of interlock networks, has been made by numerous researchers in various ways. Ratcliff's (1980) study of 78 commercial banks based in St. Louis evidenced a strong relationship between a bank's centrality in the interlock network and its loans to capitalists. Invoking Hilferding, Ratcliff concluded that the personal union of banking and corporate interests at the center of the capitalist class "is associated with a major flow of loan capital from banks to corporations and other related borrowers" (p. 565).

Although firm-by-firm data on bank loans are not generally available, data on intercorporate ownership have been widely employed in studies of corporate networks. An especially fruitful approach combines ownership and directorship data in the study of enterprises: sets of firms operating under common control, detectable in the coincidence of intercorporate ownership with shared directors. Applying this to the Canadian economy (1972–87), Berkowitz and Fitzgerald (1995) found a five-fold consolidation of enterprises, from 1,456 to 298, representing an enormous centralization of the control of capital, even though the actual number of legally defined large companies hardly changed at all. Windolf's (2002: 42, 69) comparative investigations of American and European corporate networks included ownership ties, and revealed sharp differences, into the 1990s, between continental regimes such as Germany's, where ownership and interlocking often coincide, and the British and American networks, which show few instances of significant intercorporate ownership and little overlap between the networks. Scott's (1986) comparative study of corporate shareholding and financial power in the United Kingdom, United States, and Japan showed that in the mid-1970s most large corporations were not controlled by single interests but were "tied through interweaving share participations into a system of impersonal possession" (p. 200). However, the

precise shape of these systems varied between the Anglo-American pattern of financial hegemony and the Japanese structure of aligned participation in corporate sets (on the latter, see Scott, 1997: 181–95). In the case of Australia, Murray's (2006, 2008) research, considering both interlocking directorates and shareholding in top companies, reached the conclusion that "of themselves interlocks do not reveal the underlying power structures of companies" (Murray, 2008: 17). Indeed, in 2007 six top financial institutions operating in Australia (including Morgan Chase, HSBC, and Citicorp) held 34.1 percent of the market capitalization of the top 300 companies, indicating both an enormous centralization of financial power and a remarkable penetration by transnational capital.

Other research has looked purely at the network of intercorporate ownership ties. The German case was examined in a study by Kogut and Walker (2001) whose longitudinal design (running from 1993 to 1997) enabled a tracking of 101 acquisitions involving the top 550 German companies. Results showed a strong small-world effect, connecting firms through owners and owners through firms (2001: 325) and tendencies for acquisitions to make the network more centralized and for leading financial institutions to act as "brokering owners" in mergers and acquisitions. Grbic (2007) mapped the Japanese bank ownership network from 1988 to 1999, a period of massive restructuring and economic recession, which saw the collapse of major financial institutions. Defining as an ownership tie a block of 2.5 to 5 percent of a bank's share capital (the latter being the legal limit), Grbic compiled the two-mode matrix of relations between Japanese banks and their institutional stockholders (including other banks), and then converted it to a one-mode matrix of institutional shareholders, linked by the number of banks in which they jointly held stakes. He found that nearly all the 80-odd institutional investors formed a single component, whose density approached 0.2 in every year; that the network structure fit a core-periphery pattern, with negligible factionalization; and that core actors were almost entirely financial institutions. Bearing in mind the longstanding division of corporate Japan into corporate sets, Grbic discerned a "dual network . . . of cross-cutting ties linking all banks and insurance firms while underneath exists a system organized by business groups that constitute separate spheres of influence" (p. 486). Studies such as these show how national intercorporate networks continue to be underpinned to some extent by capital relations entailing combinations of allocative power and strategic control, as theorized by Scott (1997).

CONCLUSION

Interlock research has come a long way since Jeidels's groundbreaking research. In the study of economic elites and the structure of corporate power, a variety of approaches has been used. We noted the limitations of focusing only on individual or corporate characteristics, in comparison to systemic approaches that consider the structure of the entire field. Among systemic approaches, we emphasized how the class hegemony and intercorporate perspectives complement each other. The former focuses on the individual directors who, as an organized minority, exercise classwide leadership and control the corporate structure as an "apparatus of appropriation." The latter views interlocks as vectors of inter-firm communication, coordination, influence, and control. Insofar as intercorporate ties entail capital relations, two forms of power have been discerned: strategic control over corporations through ownership of blocs of shares, and control over capital flow exerted by financial corporations. Since the 1980s, interlock research has been enriched through comparative research designs and has started to look beyond national networks to the global level. Questions of network dynamics have been addressed through longitudinal designs and the study of broken and reconstituted ties. The geography of intercorporate networks has also been charted in the various core countries of capitalism and on a global scale.

If in the past few decades the methods of analysis have grown in sophistication, corporate elites and intercorporate networks have hardly remained static in their organizational features. The research literature reviewed above records major structural changes, often catalyzed by economic crises that provoke massive capital reorganizations and, sometimes, new regulatory frameworks. This dynamic of economic crisis and network re-composition, of course, has great relevance to the contemporary scene. The financial meltdown and global recession that took hold in the autumn of 2008 has already transformed the corporate landscape, claiming most of the major U.S. investment banks, for instance. With the collapse of the paper economy, and with widespread calls for re-regulation of corporate capital, the stage seemed set for a resurgent hegemony of whichever amalgamated financial institutions emerge from the crisis, under conditions of renewed state regulation and, in some countries, direct state control. Meanwhile, the growth of giant corporations on the semi-periphery presents another possible source of re-composition in the structure of corporate power. For corporate elites and intercorporate networks, both national and global, what is certain is that change is here to stay.

REFERENCES

Aaronovitch, S. (1961) *The Ruling Class: A Study of British Finance Capital*. London: Lawrence and Wishart.

Alderson, A.S. and Beckfield, J. (2004) 'Power and position in the world city system', *The American Journal of Sociology*, 109(4): 811–51.

Alderson, A.S. and Beckfield, J. (2007) 'Globalization and the world city system: Preliminary results from a longitudinal data set', in P.J. Taylor, B. Derudder, P. Saey and F. Witlox (eds), *Cities in Globalization: Practices, Policies, Theories*. London: Routledge. pp. 21–36.

Alexander, M. (2003) 'Boardroom networks among Australian company directors, 1976 and 1996', *Journal of Sociology*, 39(3): 231–51.

Allen, M.P. (1974) 'The structure of interorganizational elite cooptation: Interlocking corporate directorates', *American Sociological Review*, 39(3): 393–406.

Barnes, R.C. (2005) 'The multiple dimensions of the corporate elite's "small world" from 1962 to 1995', Paper presented at the annual meeting of the American Sociological Association, Philadelphia, August 13–16.

Barnes, R.C. and Ritter, E.R. (2001) 'Networks of corporate interlocking: 1962–1995', *Critical Sociology*, 27(2): 192–220.

Bearden, J. and Mintz, B. (1987) 'The structure of class cohesion: The corporate network and its dual', in M.S. Mizruchi and M. Schwartz (eds), *Intercorporate Relations: The Structural Analysis of Business*. Cambridge: Cambridge University Press. pp. 187–207.

Berkowitz, S.D. (1980) 'Structural and non-structural models of elites: A critique', *Canadian Journal of Sociology*, 5(1): 13–30.

Berkowitz, S.D. and Fitzgerald, W. (1995) 'Corporate control and enterprise structure in the Canadian economy: 1972–1987', *Social Networks*, 17(2): 111–27.

Berle, A.A. and Means, G.C. (1932) *The Modern Corporation and Private Property*. New York: Harcourt, Brace & World.

Bourdieu, P. (1984) *Distinction: A Social Critique of the Judgement of Taste*, Translated by R. Nice. Cambridge, MA: Harvard University Press.

Brayshay, M., Cleary, M. and Selwood, J. (2006) 'Power geometries: Social networks and the 1930s multinational corporate elite', *Geoforum*, 37(6): 986–98.

Breiger, R.L. (1974) 'The duality of persons and groups', *Social Forces*, 53(2): 181–90.

Brownlee, J. (2005) *Ruling Canada: Corporate Cohesion and Democracy*. Halifax: Fernwood Publishing.

Bunting, D. and Barbour, J. (1971) 'Interlocking directorates in large American corporations, 1986–1964', *Business History Review*, 45(3): 317–35.

Carroll, W.K. (1984) 'The individual, class, and corporate power in Canada', *Canadian Journal of Sociology*, 9(3): 245–68.

Carroll, W.K. (1986) *Corporate Power and Canadian Capitalism*. Vancouver: University of British Columbia Press.

Carroll, W.K. (2002a) 'Does disorganized capitalism disorganize corporate networks?' *Canadian Journal of Sociology*, 27(3): 339–71.

Carroll, W.K. (2002b) 'Westward ho? The shifting geography of corporate power in Canada', *Journal of Canadian Studies*, 36(4): 118–42.

Carroll, W.K. (2004) *Corporate Power in a Globalizing World: A Study in Elite Social Organization*. Oxford: Oxford University Press.

Carroll, W.K. (2007) 'Global cities in the global corporate network', *Environment and Planning A*, 39(10): 2297–323.

Carroll, W.K. (2009) 'Transnationalists and national networkers in the global corporate elite', *Global Networks* 9(3): 289–314.

Carroll, W.K. and Fennema, M. (2002) 'Is there a transnational business community?' *International Sociology*, 17(3): 393–419.

Carroll, W.K. and Fennema, M. (2004) 'Problems in the study of the transnational business community: A reply to Kentor and Jang', *International Sociology*, 19(3): 369–78.

Carroll, W.K. and Lewis, S. (1991) 'Restructuring finance capital: Changes in the Canadian corporate network, 1976–1986', *Sociology*, 25(3): 491–510.

Clement, W. (1975) *The Canadian Corporate Elite: An Analysis of Economic Power*. Toronto: McClelland and Stewart.

Davis, G.F. and Greve, H.R. (1997) 'Corporate elite networks and governance changes in the 1980s', *The American Journal of Sociology*, 103(1): 1–37.

Davis, G.F. and Mizruchi, M.S. (1999) 'The money center cannot hold: Commercial banks in the U.S. system of corporate governance', *Administrative Science Quarterly*, 44(2): 215–39.

Davis, G.F., Yoo, M. and Baker, W.E. (2003) 'The small world of the American corporate elite, 1982–2001', *Strategic Organization*, 1(3): 301–26.

Domhoff, G.W. (1967) *Who Rules America?* Englewood Cliffs, NJ: Prentice-Hall.

Domhoff, G.W. (1974) *The Bohemian Grove and Other Retreats: A Study in Ruling-Class Cohesiveness*. New York: Harper & Row.

Domhoff, G.W (ed.) (1980) *Power Structure Research*. Beverly Hills, CA: Sage.

Faust, K. and Wasserman, S. (1993) 'Correlation and association models for studying measurements on ordinal relations', *Sociological Methodology*, 23: 177–215.

Fennema, M. (1982) *International Networks of Banks and Industry*. The Hague: M. Nijhoff.

Fennema, M. and Schijf, H. (1978) 'Analysing interlocking directorates: Theory and methods', *Social Networks*, 1(4): 297–332.

Fennema, M. and Schijf, H. (1985) 'The transnational network', in F. N. Stokman, R. Ziegler and J. Scott (eds), *Networks of Corporate Power: A Comparative Analysis of Ten Countries*. Cambridge: Polity Press. pp. 250–66.

Galaskiewicz, J. and Wasserman, S. (1981) 'A dynamic study of change in a regional corporate network', *American Sociological Review*, 46(4): 475–84.

Glasberg, D. (1987) 'The ties that bind? Case studies in the significance of corporate board interlocks with financial institutions', *Sociological Perspectives*, 30(1): 19–48.

Grbic, Douglas (2007) 'The source, structure, and stability of control over Japan's financial sector', *Social Science Research*, 36(2): 469–90.

Green, M.B. (1983) 'The interurban corporate interlocking directorate network of Canada and the United States: A spatial perspective', *Urban Geography*, 4(4): 338–54.

Green, M.B. (1993) 'A geography of institutional stock ownership in the United States', *Annals of the Association of American Geographers*, 83(1): 66–89.

Green, M.B. and Semple, R.K. (1981) 'The corporate interlocking directorate as an urban spatial information network', *Urban Geography*, 2(2): 148–60.

Heemskerk, E.M. (2007) *Decline of the Corporate Community: Network Dynamics of the Dutch Business Elite*. Amsterdam: Amsterdam University Press.

Helmers, H.M., Mokken, R.J., Plijter, R.C. and Stokman, F.N. (1975) *Graven naar Macht. Op zoek naar de kern van de Nederlandse ekonomie*. Amsterdam: Van Gennep.

Hilferding, R. (1981 [1910]) *Finance Capital: A Study of the Latest Phase of Capitalist Development*, Translated by M. Watnick and S. Gordon. London: Routledge & K. Paul.

Jeidels, O. (1905) 'Das Verhältnis der deutschen Grossbanken zur Industrie mit besonder Berücksichtigung der Eisenindustrie (Relation of the German big banks to industry with special reference to the iron industry)', *Staats- und sozialwissenschaftliche Forschungen*, 24(2): 1–271.

Kentor, J. and Jang, Y.S. (2004) 'Yes, there is a (growing) transnational business community: A study of global interlocking directorates, 1983–98', *International Sociology*, 19(3): 355–68.

Kim, Y.T. (2007) 'Korean elites: Social networks and power', *Journal of Contemporary Asia*, 37(1): 19–37.

Koenig, T. and Gogel, R. (1981) 'Interlocking corporate directorships as a social network', *American Journal of Economics and Sociology*, 40(1): 37–50.

Koenig, T, Gogel, R. and Sonquist, J. (1979) 'Models of the significance of interlocking corporate directorates', *American Journal of Economics and Sociology*, 38(2): 173–86.

Kogut, B. and Walker, G. (2001) 'The small world of Germany and the durability of national networks', *American Sociological Review*, 66(3): 317–35.

Kono, C., Palmer, D., Friedland, R. and Zafonte, M. (1998) 'Lost in space: The geography of corporate interlocking directorates', *The American Journal of Sociology*, 103(4): 863–911.

Levine, J.H. and Roy, W.S. (1979) 'A study of interlocking directorates: Vital concepts of organization', in P.W. Holland and S. Leinhardt (eds), *Perspectives on Social Network Research*. New York: Academic Press. pp. 349–78.

Maclean, M., Harvey, C. and Press, J. (2006) *Business Elites and Corporate Governance in France and the UK*. Basingstoke, UK: Palgrave Macmillan.

Mariolis, P. and Jones, M.H. (1982) 'Centrality in corporate interlock networks: Reliability and stability', *Administrative Science Quarterly*, 27(4): 571–85.

Menshikov, S. (1969) *Millionaires and Managers: Structure of the U.S. Financial Oligarchy*. Moscow: Progress Publishers.

Mills, C.W. (1956) *The Power Elite*. New York: Oxford University Press.

Mintz, B. and Schwartz, M. (1981) 'Interlocking directorates and interest group formation', *American Sociological Review*, 46: 851–69.

Mintz, B. and Schwartz, M. (1985) *The Power Structure of American Business*. Chicago: University of Chicago Press.

Mizruchi, M.S. (1982) *The American Corporate Network: 1904–1974*. Beverly Hills: Sage.

Mizruchi, M.S. (1996) 'What do interlocks do? An analysis, critique, and assessment of research on interlocking directorates', *Annual Review of Sociology* 22: 271–98.

Mizruchi, M.S. and Schwartz, M. (1987) 'The structural analysis of business: An emerging field', in M.S. Mizruchi and M. Schwartz (eds), *Intercorporate Relations: The Structural Analysis of Business*. Cambridge: Cambridge University Press. pp. 3–22.

Mizruchi, M.S. and Stearns, L.B. (1988) 'A longitudinal study of the formation of interlocking directorates', *Administrative Science Quarterly*, 33(2): 194–210.

Moore, G. (1979) 'The structure of a national elite network', *American Sociological Review*, 44(4): 673–92.

Murray, G. (2006) *Capitalist Networks and Social Power in Australia and New Zealand*. Aldershot, UK: Ashgate.

Murray, G. (2008) 'Invisible invaders: Does Australia have a transnational class?' Paper presented at the ISA Forum of Sociology, Barcelona, September 4–8.

Okhmatovskiy, I. (2005) 'Sources of capital and structures of influence: Banks in the Russian corporate network', *International Sociology*, 20(4): 427–57.

Ornstein, M.D. (1984) 'Interlocking directorates in Canada: Intercorporate or class alliance?' *Administrative Science Quarterly*, 29(2): 210–31.

Palmer, D. (1987) 'The dual nature of corporate interlocks', in M. Schwartz (ed.), *The Structure of Power in America: The Corporate Elite as a Ruling Class*. New York: Holmes and Meier. pp. 60–74.

Park, L. and Park, F. (1973 [1962]) *Anatomy of Big Business*. Toronto: James Lewis & Samuel.

Pennings, J.M. (1980) *Interlocking Directorates: Origins and Consequences of Connections Among Organizations' Boards of Directors*. San Francisco: Jossey-Bass.

Perlo, V. (1957) *The Empire of High Finance*. New York: International Publishers.

Pfeffer, J. (1987) 'A resource dependence perspective on interorganizational relations', in M.S. Mizruchi and M. Schwartz (eds), *Intercorporate Relations: The Structural Analysis of Business*. Cambridge: Cambridge University Press. pp. 22–55.

Piédalue, G. (1976) 'Les groupes financiers au Canada 1900–1930 — Étude préliminaire', *Revue d'histoire de l'Amérique française*, 30(1): 3–34.

Porter, J. (1955) 'Elite groups: A scheme for the study of power in Canada', *Canadian Journal of Economics and Political Science*, 21(4): 498–512.

Porter, J. (1956) 'Concentration of economic power and the economic elite in Canada', *The Canadian Journal of Economics and Political Science*, 22(2): 199–220.

Porter, J. (1957) 'The economic elite and the social structure in Canada', *The Canadian Journal of Economics and Political Science*, 23(3): 376–94.

Ratcliff, R.E. (1980) 'Banks and corporate lending: An analysis of the impact of the internal structure of the capitalist class on the lending behavior of banks', *American Sociological Review*, 45(4): 553–70.

Richardson, R.J. (1987) 'Directorship interlocks and corporate profitability', *Administrative Science Quarterly*, 32(3): 367–86.

Rochester, A. (1936) *Rulers of America: A Study of Finance Capital*. London: Lawrence & Wishart.

Scott, J. (1985) 'Theoretical framework and research design', in F.N. Stokman, R. Ziegler and J. Scott (eds), *Networks of Corporate Power: A Comparative Analysis of Ten Countries*. Cambridge: Polity Press. pp. 1–19.

Scott, J. (1986) *Capitalist Property and Financial Power*. Brighton, Sussex: Wheatsheaf Books.

Scott, J. (1987) 'Intercorporate structures in Western Europe: A comparative historical analysis', in M.S. Mizruchi and M. Schwartz (eds), *Intercorporate Relations: The Structural Analysis of Business*. Cambridge: Cambridge University Press. pp. 208–32.

Scott, J. (1991) 'Networks of corporate power: A comparative assessment', *Annual Review of Sociology*, 17: 181–203.

Scott, J. (1997) *Corporate Business and Capitalist Class*. New York: Oxford University Press.

Scott, J. (2003) 'Transformations in the British economic elite', *Comparative Sociology*, 2(1): 155–73.

Scott, J. (2008) 'Modes of power and the re-conceptualization of elites', in M. Savage and K. Williams (eds), *Remembering Elites*. Oxford: Blackwell. pp. 27–43.

Scott, J, and Griff, C. (1984) *Directors of Industry: The British Corporate Network, 1900–1976*. Cambridge: Polity Press.

Sonquist, J.A. and Koenig, T. (1975) 'Interlocking directorates in the top U.S. corporations: A graph theory approach', *The Insurgent Sociologist*, 5(3): 196–230.

Soref, M. and Zeitlin, M. (1987) 'Finance capital and the internal structure of the capitalist class in the United States', in M.S. Mizruchi and M. Schwartz (eds), *Intercorporate Relations: The Structural Analysis of Business*. Cambridge: Cambridge University Press. pp. 56–84.

Stanworth, P, and Giddens, A. (1975) 'The modern corporate economy: Interlocking directorships in Britain, 1906–1970', *The Sociological Review*, 23(1): 5–28.

Stearns, L.B. and Mizruchi, M.S. (1986) 'Broken-tie reconstitution and the functions of interorganizational interlocks: A reexamination', *Administrative Science Quarterly*, 31(4): 522–38.

Steglich, C.E.G., Snijders, T.A.B. and West, P. (2006) 'Applying SIENA: An illustrative analysis of the coevolution of adolescents' friendship networks, taste in music, and alcohol consumption', *Methodology*, 2: 48–56.

Stokman, F.N., van der Knoop, J. and Wasseur, F.W. (1988) 'Interlocks in the Netherlands: Stability and careers in the period 1960–1980', *Social Networks*, 10: 183–208.

Stokman, F.N., Ziegler, R. and Scott, J. (eds) (1985) *Networks of Corporate Power: A Comparative Analysis of Ten Countries.* Cambridge: Polity Press.

Sweezy, P.M. (1953) *The Present as History: Essays and Reviews on Capitalism and Socialism.* New York: Monthly Review Press.

Useem, M. (1978) 'The inner group of the American capitalist class', *Social Problems*, 25(3): 225–40.

Useem, M. (1984) *The Inner Circle: Large Corporations and the Rise of Business Political Activity in the U.S. and U.K.* New York: Oxford University Press.

Useem, M. and Karabel, J. (1986) 'Pathways to top corporate management', *American Sociological Review*, 51(2): 184–200.

van de Bunt, G.G. and Groenewegen, P. (2007) 'An actor-oriented dynamic network approach: The case of interorganizational network evolution', *Organizational Research Methods*, 10: 463–82.

van der Pijl, K. (1984) *The Making of an Atlantic Ruling Class.* London: Verso.

Whitley, R. (1974) 'The city and industry: The directors of large companies, their characteristics and connections', in P. Stanworth and A. Giddens (eds), *Elites and Power in British Society.* London: Cambridge University Press. pp. 66–82.

Whitley, R. (1999) *Divergent Capitalisms.* New York: Oxford University Press.

Windolf, P. (2002) *Corporate Networks in Europe and the United States.* New York: Oxford University Press.

Zeitlin, M. (1974) 'Corporate ownership and control: The large corporation and the capitalist class', *American Journal of Sociology*, 79(4): 1073–119.

Zweigenhaft, R.L. and Domhoff, G.W. (1998) *Diversity in the Power Elite: Have Women and Minorities Reached the Top?* New Haven, CT: Yale University Press.

14

Political Dimensions of Corporate Connections

Matthew Bond and Nicholas Harrigan

INTRODUCTION

Social network analysis (SNA) is (1) a method for analysing the volume and patterns of social relations linking individual actors to each other and (2) a way of theorising social structure and its effects on behaviour. The analysis of corporate political activity, on the other hand, is part of the empirical examination of business politics. They are distinct intellectual endeavours; however, their paths have often crossed and led to mutually beneficial partnerships. Social network analysts have an opportunity to test the utility of their measures and theoretical predispositions in a substantive field of empirical research. Scholars of business politics have relied on SNA for a set of tools suited to the task of operationalising and testing their theories.

In this chapter we review and evaluate these collaborations. We start by outlining the history and contours of the broader research agenda concerned with corporate politics. We then discuss analytic issues involved in conceptualising corporate actors and the relations linking them as a social network. We continue by examining how social network mechanisms and measures have been used in the empirical literature. We conclude by reviewing prospects for future collaborations.

HISTORY AND BACKGROUND

Scholarly interest in social[1] relations between business establishments and their political consequences has a long history. Adam Smith's (1776 [1937]) concerns about collusion between entrepreneurs are an early precursor; however, the research traditions that are the subject of this review originated in the first decades of the twentieth century.

Interest in corporate behaviour and politics developed in reaction to a number of changes in capitalist economies. In its early stages capitalist production was dominated by family-controlled firms that were small relative to the size of the markets they operated in. Growth in the scale of production and the concomitant need to coordinate firms' complex and diverse activities created pressures leading to the creation of the modern corporate economy (Chandler, 1977). Five interrelated consequences accompanied these changes. First, large-scale production radically augmented firms' capital requirements and, thereby, their reliance on external sources of finance. Second, firms began producing on such scales that their output was a significant proportion of total supply. Third, the growth of joint stock led to the dilution of family ownership. Fourth, a corps of managers skilled in administration emerged who were not necessarily owners of the firms they ran. Fifth, explicit, bureaucratic mechanisms of coordination were substituted for market mechanisms within firms and across them through, for example, shared personnel on firms' boards of directors (interlocking directorates).

While these trends might appear to be primarily technical and economic, they attracted attention from political authorities and were perceived to have political consequences. In the United States the changes, especially inter-firm relations between nominal competitors, led to fears that the new large economic corporations would engage in monopolistic practices, such as price fixing. In response anti-trust laws were implemented, regulatory frameworks were developed, and, outside the United States, corporations in strategic industries were often nationalised.

Another response, which had a more profound impact on research traditions using network analyses, was formulated by a series of scholars who developed theories of finance capital and imperialism (Hobson, 1902; Hilferding, 1910; Lenin, 1916). For them, the changes in the economy, particularly the centralisation and concentration of finance needed to meet the investment needs of large-scale production, provided the basis for a powerful capitalist, ruling class. In the words of Lenin, 'Production becomes social, but appropriation remains private. The social means of production remain the private property of a few. The general framework of a formally recognised free competition remains, and oppression by a few monopolists of the rest of the population becomes a hundred times more intense, palpable and intolerable' (1916: 25). A few thousand capitalists, centred on banks, are able to use the new coordinated corporate order for their own private needs. One of the central political consequences is war between states in search of new territories for capital investment.

While not sharing Lenin's resolute Marxism, elite theorists (e.g. Mills, 1956; Domhoff, 1998) made similar points. C. Wright Mills argued that the growth of large-scale bureaucracies in modern societies had created conditions for the domination by a small elite. Mills departed from theorists of finance capital by adopting a Weberian, multidimensional view of power. The corporate elite is part of a broader integrated elite that is also drawn from the polity and the military. In spite of their differences about the distribution of power across elites and their view of modern society's developmental trends, theorists of finance capital and elite theorists agreed that corporate elites are few in number, well integrated, and powerful.

Of course, these claims were intensely disputed. Pluralist scholars argued that the integration of elites in general, and corporate elites in particular, had been assumed rather than demonstrated by elite and Marxist scholars (Rose, 1968). Although pluralists agreed economic power had migrated to a small number of individuals, they claimed modern societies have a number of countervailing forces (Galbraith, 1952). First, democratic control of the polity has provided an independent check on corporate power (Dahl, 1961). Second, corporate elites do not have a single unified set of interests – elite interests are as cross cutting as

they are reinforcing (Berg and Zald, 1978). Third, the separation of ownership and control (Berle and Means, 1932) has robbed capitalists of integrating social relations that would permit them to mobilise and take unified political action (Bell, 1960; Useem, 1984). The first two points are not amenable to examination by network methods; however, SNA has been deemed the most suitable method for examining whether corporations or directors (the issue of appropriate unit of analysis is discussed in the next section) have relations they can use to form a political community.

Details of specific network studies are presented later. For now it will suffice to provide a synoptic outline of the role of network methods and theories used in the power structure debate.

In response to pluralist critiques, elite and finance capital theorists collected and presented data bearing on capitalist social networks (Sweezy, 1953 [1939]; Aaronovitch, 1961; Kolko, 1962); however, they did so prior to the development of social network analytic measures and computational tools. Beginning in the 1970s a new set of scholars took advantage of developments in SNA and began mapping corporate networks (e.g. Levine, 1972; Carroll, 1982; Mizruchi, 1982; Scott and Griff, 1984; Scott, 1990; Carroll and Sapinski, this volume). They showed that (1) a wide variety of social relations link corporations, (2) most corporations are parts of connected components, and (3) there are central actors who could coordinate the actions of many others if they could garner authority from those relations (e.g. Mintz and Schwartz, 1985).

Difficulties remained. Although these studies confirmed the structure of corporate networks were consistent with the broad claims made by elite and finance capital theorists, weakness lay in their inferential frameworks. First, they lacked a probabilistic baseline. Knowledge of the features of random networks were either not known or were not diffused throughout the community of network scholars. It was unclear whether corporate networks' characteristics were signs of conscious design and coordination or whether more random processes generated them. Second, even if a network's characteristics were not random their political consequences were unapparent. Corporations might have the social resources permitting them to form a powerful political community, but there was no evidence that they could, or would, take advantage of them.

Judgement of this body of work is difficult. Any serious empirical researcher cannot help but admire the range of data collected and the ingenious measurement strategies deployed. The lack of an inferential framework, however, limits the trust one can place in their conclusions. A further problem with this research is that it is difficult to assess the political consequences of the network characteristics that have been identified.

Beginning in the 1980s a second generation of scholarship emerged that investigated the political consequences of corporate social networks. An early example was Useem's (1984) claims that there were a set of well-connected directors and corporations who are more likely, among other things, to make political donations or be active in think tanks. It was not, however, until three independent projects led by the American scholars Val Burris (1987), Dan Clawson and Alan Neustadtl (Clawson et al., 1986; Neustadtl and Clawson, 1988) and Mizruchi (1989, 1990, 1992) that network methodologies were systematically used to investigate corporate political behaviour. They exploited publicly available sources of data about contributions by American corporations to political campaigns, which had only recently become available because of changes in American election law. Their analytic concerns centred on the sources of unity and partisanship in corporate politics, which they studied in the context of historical debates about business's role in shifting American politics to the right in the 1980s.

As well as exploring political consequences, the studies innovated by focussing on dyadic and factional relations among politically active corporations. The structure of relations between politically active corporations displaced interest in the broader contours of national corporate networks. The dyadic, factional basis was an implicit consequence of accepting Dahl's (1958) arguments that unity is a necessary prerequisite of power. Corporations and their directors might have a great deal of potential collective power; however, if each pursues different aims or supports different candidates their collective power may never be actualised.

These studies made significant contributions to our knowledge about business politics; they developed inferential frameworks as well as creatively employing network methods. Perhaps most impressively, they treated the respective claims made on either side of the power structure debate as testable hypotheses. Their legacy is to have left a more nuanced picture of capitalist activity in capitalist economies.

Their achievements are many; however, their approach had certain limits. First, if one succumbs to Dahl's claims as these scholars more or less did, one can reasonably ignore the effects that many large, uncoordinated business contributions may have on a political system. This is a controversial decision. A principled line of criticism of capitalist societies has, after all, highlighted the distorting effects they can have on rational political discussion (Habermas, 1987). We are interested not only in meaningful but also in unintended

effects corporations have on political systems. At the very least, uncoordinated corporate political action can add random sources of error into political communication and deliberation. Second, their focus on politically active corporations and a dyadic framework hindered their ability to make statements about the entire network. Their research designs meant they could tell us nothing about the network sources of political inactivity or whether politically inactive corporations influence other firms' political activity. Inferences that earlier scholars had tried to make about the political consequences of national corporate structures were extremely difficult, given the preoccupation with politically active firms.

More recently, a new set of analytic concerns has attracted the scrutiny of scholars using network methodologies. Val Burris (1991, 2001, 2005; see also Bearden and Mintz, 1987) has broadened the focus of corporate political behaviour to include directors as well as corporations. This has enabled him to build links between the analysis of corporate political behaviour and research traditions that have focussed on elite individuals (e.g. Mills, 1956; Domhoff, 1998). Network methodologies developed to study corporations have been used to study elites. Other examples of papers examining the political consequences of director backgrounds and networks include Bond (2007), Harrigan (2007b) and Bond and colleagues (2006).

Bond (2004) has argued that recent research on American corporate behaviour has limited external validity. The focus on business unity is, to some extent, an artefact of American institutional relationships and the absence of an electorally viable American socialist or labour party. When powerful political forces threaten the existence of capitalist enterprise the field of corporate political choice is narrowed – the freedom of corporations to be disunited could be interpreted as evidence of American business dominance. For example, during the period of Labour-Conservative political competition for state power, the overwhelming majority of corporate political support has gone to the Conservative Party (see Pinto-Duschinsky, 1981; Linton, 1994; Ewing, 1987). These observations are consistent with Smith's (2000) finding that American businesses were most unified when in greatest peril.

As well as unity, mobilisation (measured as, for example, the proportion of corporations making a political donation) and intensity (measured as, for example, the size of donations) are important dimensions of corporate political behaviour. Shifting notice from unity has network implications – there is no reason to expect mobilisation to be influenced by the same network mechanisms as unity. A key analytic development in the emerging literature developing around mobilisation has been the widening of samples to include corporations/directors who are not politically active (Bond, 2004, 2007; Bond et al., 2006; see Harrigan, 2007a, b) for an example of research that simultaneously analyses partisanship and mobilisation). Giving all corporations within a defined population an opportunity to enter the sample has facilitated a shift away from dyadic relations between politically active corporations and brought it closer to earlier studies examining the structure of national corporate networks. Role positions in the corporate social structure *as well as* dyadic relations have been associated with mobilisation (Bond, 2007).

It is perhaps too early to judge the contribution of the latest wave of scholarship using network methodologies; however, some potential weaknesses stand out. First, social directories used to collect status information about directors are incomplete (only a subset of directors is included in them). This weakness is a prompt to empirical researchers to discover new data sources and for statistically minded social network researchers to outline the inferential consequences of missing data. Second, there are many outstanding questions about the role of selection and influence in these studies that would be more tractable if longitudinal and cross-national data were collected.

This brief review of social network studies of corporate politics demonstrates that there have been at least three analytic stages of network studies of corporate politics and growth in scientific knowledge and technique. Network methodologies have a firm and proven place in studying corporate politics. Analysts with diverse theoretical proclivities and investigating varied institutional environments have turned to SNA as a methodology and theoretical resource. In the next two sections we wish to give a slightly more formal assessment of the network methodologies and mechanisms emphasised in the literature.

NETWORK METHODOLOGY

In this section we highlight the general network analytic issues that have arisen in the study of corporate politics. We intend to guide researchers through some of the major challenges they face when translating theoretical claims about business behaviour into concrete research strategies.

Corporate networks

There are many data matrices that can be constructed to represent corporate networks. Most commonly,

we begin with two sets of actors: corporations and individuals affiliated to them. Overlapping affiliations can be used to construct inter-corporate and inter-individual networks. By far, the most studied inter-corporate networks have been based on interlocking directorates where the director of one corporation sits on the board of another; however, the framework we develop below is suitable to a wide range of different networks linking directors, corporations and other corporate stakeholders (e.g. networks could be constructed based on ownership; see Zeitlin, 1974).

The criterion most associated with selection into studies of business behaviour has been size. The sample is the n largest corporations in a national economy. These can be found in privately funded journalistic lists ranging from the Fortune 500 to the FTSE 500. By examining more primary sources, such as corporations' statutory reporting practices (annual reports), researchers can easily validate the lists' claims. Additional validation is granted to these lists, in many cases, because the number of actors they include exceeds theoretical expectations. For example, if we follow Lenin (1916), Mills (1956) or Baran and Sweezy (1966) we would not be surprised if the most nationally influential economic actors numbered in the tens or few hundreds – the lists should include every politically significant member of the business elite. A sample selection from large corporations, however, has loaded theoretical ramifications. The reasonableness of this assumption is an area deserving additional empirical and theoretical research. As well as the criterion of size, some studies limit themselves to politically active corporations or use a stratifying criterion, such as industry. Simple random samples of corporations taken from the universe of all corporations are absent from the literature.

Most generally, we study n corporations sampled from a larger universe of corporations. Directors are the most commonly studied corporate affiliates because they are assumed to be the ultimate political authority in corporations.[2] They approximate generally accepted descriptions of working capitalists. In the future, scholars could take a wider range of affiliates, ranging from owners through creditors to employees. The choice of affiliates is a theoretical decision.

We also study m individuals affiliated to n corporations. When we cross-tabulate corporations by affiliated individuals we have an $m \times n$ corporation by individual affiliation matrix **A** (Borgatti, this volume). Following Breiger (1974), if we post-multiply[3] **A** by its transpose,[4] $\mathbf{AA}^T$, we have an $m \times m$ corporation by corporation matrix, **B**. If we pre-multiply the matrix by its transpose we get an $n \times n$ individual by individual matrix, **C**. Although these matrices are related, they have distinct structural properties (see Bearden and Mintz, 1987). Networks of interlocking directorates are examples of **B** matrices (see Mizruchi, 1982; Scott and Griff, 1984; Bond, 2004).

Variations of these matrices can be created to reflect the multi-modal characteristics of corporate networks. Constructing additional matrices, **D,** linking either corporations, m, or individuals, n, to third actors, p, ranging from social clubs to political parties, can facilitate this. For example, Bond (2007) created a **D** ($n \times p$) individual by club matrix. He pre-multiplied this by an **A** ($m \times n$) corporation by director matrix, **AD,** giving an $m \times p$ matrix, **E.** Post-multiplying this matrix by its transpose, **EE^T,** he obtained a **B** ($m \times m$) matrix where cell entries are the products[5] of corporations' shared affiliations to clubs through their directors summed over all clubs.

Networks used in studies of corporate politics are not only constructed through affiliation matrices. They can be created by direct relations between firms or directors. For example, Mizruchi (1992) used inter-industry trade and market concentration to construct matrices of inter-corporate market constraint.

Many network measures have been used in studies of corporate politics. Researchers interested in detecting the political effects of dominant corporations ranging from a 'financial oligarchy' through 'interest groups' to an 'inner circle' have used measures of centrality to operationalise their concepts (Useem, 1984; Mintz and Schwartz, 1985). Measures of cohesion, including political homophily and clique analysis, have been used to detect particularistic or close-knit relationships between political factions (e.g. Bond, 2004; Clawson and Neustadtl, 1989). Finally researchers interested in mechanisms of social control producing mobilisation and unity in corporate politics have used measures of structural equivalence (Mizruchi, 1992; Bond, 2004). Structural equivalence has also been used as a basis for clustering corporations into social positions with typical role relations between them (Bond, 2007).

Corporate political behaviour

As we discussed earlier, network studies have treated political behaviour as the dependent variable that can be explained by network influences. Political behaviour is typically operationalised as mobilisation or unity.

In studies focussing on mobilisation the dependent variable is often treated as dichotomous, for example, whether a corporation does or does not make a donation to a political party (Bond, 2004, 2007). In studies that simultaneously examine mobilization and partisanship the dependent variable can be treated as polytomous, such as whether a corporation does not donate, makes ideological contributions, or hedges (Harrigan, 2007a).

In studies focussing on unity or partisanship the conceptualisation of the dependent variable displays the influence of network thinking. Unity researchers typically characterise similarity of political behaviour in dyadic terms. For example, Mizruchi constructed a similarity measure for all 1,596 dyads created by the 57 manufacturing corporations in his sample. For each dyad he calculated the following measure of similarity of political behaviour:

$$S_{ij} = n_{ij}/(n_i * n_j)^{1/2}$$

where n_{ij} is the total number of corporate donations that corporation i and corporation j make in common, n_i and n_j are the total numbers of donations each makes. Mizruchi then modelled the effects of dyadic social relations on the dyadic measure of political similarity. Su et al. (1995) created corporation by corporation data matrices where cell entries are dyadic measures of political similarity. Where they differed from Mizruchi is that they performed clique analyses (Alba, 1973) to cluster corporations into blocs depending on their similarity of political behaviour. They then attempted to explain membership of these groupings rather than dyadic relations directly.

Corporate attributes

Corporations' attributes are usually included in network studies of corporate politics as controls. They are there to avoid potential omitted variable biases, that is, biases created by variables that are simultaneously associated with the dependent political variable and the independent corporate network variable. For example, corporations in certain industries might independently be more likely to share a social relation and to take specific kinds of political behaviour – associations between social relations and political behaviour could be spurious when industry is controlled. Attributes are conceptualised either as properties of individuals or properties of dyads.

Statistical models

The attention devoted to studying the political consequences of corporations' social networks has inevitably led researchers to use statistical models in order to estimate the magnitude of the relationship between social factors and whether they are significantly different from a null model of no relationship. Depending on how political behaviour (the dependent variable) is measured, some variant of the generalised linear model is selected. Examples include least squares with dummy variables (LSDV) (Mizruchi, 1989), quadratic assignment procedure (QAP) regression, and logistic regression (Bond, 2004).

Because these projects use relational models, observations of both political behaviour and corporate networks are often not statistically independent. Unity researchers have paid most attention to this issue and incorporated corrections for lack of independence into their model. Harrigan (2007b) is one of the first to take advantage of statistical network models that are designed precisely to handle difficulties surrounding the lack of statistical independence in network observations.

The use of 'largeness' as a criterion for selecting corporations into samples raises sample selection issues (Berk, 1983; Breen, 1996; Heckman, 1979). Val Burris (2005) used Heckman selection models in an effort to control for sample selection but his is a lone example. Analysts may feel theoretically justified restricting their observations to large corporations but this choice has analytic consequences that should be accounted for. After all, are the rich (powerful) different from the poor (powerless) in any way other than having more money (power)? Systematic comparisons of differing sample plans are a promising area for future research.

NETWORK MECHANISMS

In this section we shift our attention from methodology to theory. We focus on three mechanisms that have been at the heart of network analyses of corporate politics: (1) centrality, (2) cohesion and (3) structural equivalence (Doreian et al., this volume; Hanneman and Riddle, this volume). While we discuss centrality independently the debates about cohesion and structural equivalence have become so entwined that we feel it makes sense to discuss them simultaneously; however, each of the measures has overlapping dimensions.

Centrality

The role of central actors in the corporate economy has been key to theories of business power. As we discussed, Marxist theories, such as

from Lenin (1916), and elite theories, such as from Mills (1956), lead us to expect powerful actors in modern corporate economies to be linked by many formal and informal ties.

Theorists of finance capital and bank control have given the most explicit predictions about the structure of national inter-corporate networks. Concentrations of financial power should lead to a few clusters of corporations centred on controlling banks. The key feature of the network is its centralisation, which reflects the extreme agglomeration of capital; however, the network is divided into separate cohesive groups united in their dependence on the same financial institutions, for example, interest groups (Sweezy, 1953 [1939]). The political importance of this structure is that it provides the organisational basis for a capitalist ruling class centred on a financial oligarchy.

An example of a sophisticated operationalisation of these ideas in network terms comes from Mintz and Schwartz (1981, 1983, 1985), who used data on interlocking directorates between large American corporations in the 1960s to test for structural configurations predicted by theories of bank control. Their theory had four elements. First, interlocking directorates were treated as indicators[6] of competition's absence – interlocked corporations do not compete. Instead, they indicated either cooperative or authoritative relations. Second, there should be a positive skew in corporations' degree centrality in the network of interlocking directorates with financial corporations being interlocked to the largest number. This reflects (a) corporations' dependence on capital, an inevitable concomitant of large-scale industrial production and (b) the concentration of finance capital in a few hands, a consequence of capitalist competition. Third, cohesive subgroups should be organised around financial corporations. Fourth, the presence of interlocks *within* subgroups reflects cooperation among firms dependent on the same financial institutions and their absence *between* reflects subgroup competition. The ratio of in-group to out-group interlocks measures levels of 'intra-group unity' relative to 'intergroup competition.'

The network analytic strategy adopted by Mintz and Schwartz (1981, 1983, 1985) to investigate these issues had two parts. First, theyconfirmed the centrality of financial corporations by using a weighted[7] centrality measure. Large financial corporations dominated the list of the 20 most central corporations. Second, they identified peaks and clusters of corporations around them. Peak analysis involves searching for corporations that are more central than all other corporations they are connected with – these corporations are called peaks. Once peaks are identified a corporation is considered part of a cluster centred on a peak if every other corporation it is linked to is more central than it is in the same cluster (i.e. linked to the same peak). Some special features of this way of defining clusters are worth note: a corporation does not need to be directly linked to a peak to be in a cluster defined by it (a concomitant of this is that corporations in the same cluster do not need to have a direct tie), a corporation cannot be in more than one cluster, and it is possible for some firms to be in none of the clusters.

Mintz and Schwartz found several peaks in the 1960s American corporate network but the clusters around them tended to be small. For example, in 1966 they found 10 'major' peaks, all commercial banks, but only 5 per cent of all corporations were members of a cluster. From these analyses, they concluded that while financial institutions are central and influential in the network the corporate network is not divided into discrete clusters around them. Mintz and Schwartz drew two conclusions from their findings: (1) the interest group formulation of finance capital theory does not accurately describe the network of interlocking directorates and (2) the lack of discrete, competing interest groups means 'that the trends toward unity outweigh the forces of division' (Mintz and Schwartz, 1983: 201).

Are these conclusions justified, or are they merely artefacts of their procedures?

Mintz and Schwartz, to their credit, outlined clear hypotheses about the relation between capital concentration and the structure of the interlocking directorate network, which were consistent with theorists of finance capital from Lenin (1916) to Sweezy (1953 [1939]). They also took effort to validate their findings by triangulating them with qualitative data from the business press that confirmed corporate unity. From a purely social network analytic perspective, however, inferential difficulties remain. How many peaks should we expect to find in networks with as many actors and as many ties as the American corporate network? How much clustering? Without the baseline of a random network it is difficult to judge whether the network features Mintz and Schwartz identified could arise entirely by chance or whether they represent systematic biases predicted by bank control or finance capital theorists.

Whereas Mintz and Schwartz and financial capital theorists used interlocking directorates primarily as indicators of capital flows or competition's absence, Michael Useem (1984) studied their role as a mechanism of political unity. He dismissed the idea that interlocks merely reflect financial dependencies. He based his rejection on his interview data with British and American directors who consistently denied interlocks

reflect dependence relations and on findings by Koenig et al. (1979), Ornstein (1980) and Palmer (1983) that broken interlocks are rarely replaced, which is inconsistent with their being indicators of inter-firm dependence. Instead, he argued that corporate interlocks were driven by an effort to gain general information about the broader corporate community.

Market pressures buffet directors and their corporations, giving them a short-sighted, technocratic and profit-driven focus. They are loath to involve themselves and their firms in political action unless it can be rationalised as having a direct positive effect on corporate profits. As business political activity has many collective action features (Olson, 1965; Bond, 2004), firms are likely to free-ride on others' political activity – firm-level rationality dominates community/class-level rationality. When directors sit on the boards of other corporations they become more sensitive to the challenges facing the corporate community and the mutual interests they share with other directors who are in the same class and situation. The heightened political consciousness of these multiple directors allows class-wide rationality to gain the upper hand over parochial firm-level concerns. Politically active multiple directors are termed the inner circle. Useem supported his contentions about multiple directorships by drawing on a wide range of examples, from donations to political parties to sitting on the boards of think tanks, where the most central directors and corporations are also the most active.

Useem's theories also made predictions about the quality of political activity by the inner circle. He argued that it would tend towards corporate liberalism (Weinstein, 1968), that is, it would be more compromising on some issues vital to business because its class-wide rationality would allow accommodation with labour and the state that are necessary for the long-term survival of the capitalist system.

Useem's theories about the effects of interlocks have received mixed support in the literature. Mizruchi (1989) and Burris (1987) found no effect of the number of direct interlocks on the similarity of American corporations' political behaviour. Clawson et al. (1986) found that highly interlocked corporations were most likely to follow pragmatic, firm, rational political-donation strategies. They argued that heavily interlocked firms had opportunities for defending class-wide political interests other than donations to ideological candidates. Firms with no interlocks had no other avenues to express class-wide political interests.

Bond (2004) found that central corporations in the British network of interlocking directorates were more likely to make donations to the

Conservative Party. The picture became more mixed when he partitioned interlocks depending on whether they were made by corporate executives, non-executives from outside the corporate community, or incidentally created between two firms when a director from a third firm sat on both their boards. Two key findings were that firms that 'sent' many directors were more likely to make donations and that corporations that 'received' ties were less likely to make donations unless they came from corporations that were donors themselves. He argued that these findings contradicted the idea that inner-circle positions influenced the political behaviour of firms and their directors. Instead, they were more consistent with 'influential', politically active corporations and directors selecting into multiple relations with other corporate actors. They then used their multiple ties to influence others to follow their political lead.

Centrality appears to be associated with political behaviour but not consistently. Disagreement remains about (1) whether firms with multiple directors are more likely to adopt a class-wide or firm-level perspective on politics; (2) whether firms central in corporate networks are politically influenced by their relations, or whether corporations with certain political preferences are likely to select into multiple relations; and (3) whether corporate interlocks have the same political effects in different national political systems.

Cohesion and structural equivalence

A central debate in social network theories has been the relative influence of cohesion and structural equivalence in creating social control. Protagonists in the debate define cohesion in dyadic terms as a direct relation between two actors and structural equivalence in triadic terms as the indirect, two-step relation actors have when they are tied to the same alter. At a macro level we study the systematic interaction between these, and potentially more removed, relations.

Three types of cohesion mechanisms can be discerned. Relations[8] between actors can alter (or not) the behaviour of either participant by (1) persuasion – ego agrees to agree/disagree with alter (e.g. Habermas, 1987); (2) influence – ego takes alter's behaviour as a role model (e.g. Friedkin, 1998), and (3) power, where ego's will dominates alter's will (e.g. Weber, 1947). These mechanisms have been theorised by social scientists from both within and without the social network community.

Two types of structural equivalence mechanisms can be discerned (compare with Burt, 1992).

Indirect, two-step relations can alter (or not) the behaviour of either participant by two, overlapping mechanisms: (1) competition – actors can compete for the set of resources controlled by a third actor and act similarly because they think that will be a key to unlocking the third's resources; and (2) third-party control – a third actor can exploit the forces for conformity in competition to ensure that two actors act in ways that satisfy her or his interests. These mechanisms have been most extensively theorised by social scientists using social network analytic concepts[9] or sociologists using reference group theory.

Both cohesion and structural equivalence mechanisms can contribute to dyadic covariance in individual behaviour in a network. Additional sources of observed covariance will arise from researcher and instrument fallibility, selection, and omitted variable biases. Each source is important but selection issues have posed the most pressing problems for social network analyses of corporate political behaviour. Similarity of behaviour by individuals in cohesive or structural equivalent relations might arise not because they are *influencing* each other but because they have similar characteristics that lead them independently to select into those relations. Two examples: a norm of homophily will lead actors to select into cohesive relations with others like them (Lazarsfeld and Merton, 1954), and actors' mutual interests in the resource controlled by a third will lead them to behave in similar ways (Burt, 1992; most basically, they will select into the same relation with a third actor).

In a series of papers and a monograph, Mizruchi (1989, 1990, 1992) argued strenuously for the importance of structural equivalence through indirect ties on corporate political behaviour in addition to cohesive relations. He claimed that we best understand the sources of dyadic similarity in political behaviour by embedding them in triadic social relations. He examined the sources of dyadic similarity of corporate political behaviour ranging from donations to the same political parties or candidates to testimony before congressional committees. Details of Mizruchi's sample and data analytic approach were discussed in the methodology section.

The analytic focus was on dyadic similarity because it is an expression of business solidarity. Mizruchi stressed that solidarity (i.e. similar behaviour) can have a basis either in direct cohesive relations or in structurally equivalent relations. Two corporations can make similar donations either because of direct cohesive relations between them or because they occupy structurally equivalent positions in the corporate network. An example of direct, cohesive relations encouraging political similarity would be if a corporation made a donation to a candidate, not because it supported the candidate but to curry favour with a vital supplier that did support him or her. An example of structural equivalence through indirect ties encouraging political similarity would be if two corporations made a donation to a candidate because they were linked to the same third corporation.

In the paper where he most explicitly elucidated the network mechanisms driving corporate political unity, Mizruchi (1990) highlighted two findings that consistently emerged from his research: (1) indirect interlocks (through financial institutions) have greater effects on dyadic similarity than direct interlocks, and (2) operating in the same industry has a greater effect on political similarity than the market constraint (defined as 'dependence of one industry[10] on another for sales and resources weighted by the concentration on the latter industry' [Mizruchi, 1989: 410, based on Burt, 1983b]).

These examples were selected because they demonstrated, according to Mizruchi, that structural equivalence mechanisms were playing as great, if not a greater, role in creating corporate unity than cohesion mechanisms. Mizruchi interpreted indirect interlocks effects and sharing primary industry as being examples of either third-party control or competition for resources held by a third actor. In both cases corporations 'adjust their behavior towards what they view as appropriate to their roles' (Mizruchi, 1990: 31).

Acceptance of Mizruchi's claims rests largely on the construct validity of his measures: are primary industry and indirect interlocks indicators of structural equivalence, cohesion or no network mechanism at all? Leaving aside the measurement issues involved in distinguishing structural equivalence and cohesion, that is, many actors that are in cohesive relations are also structurally equivalent (Burt, 1987), we believe that equally plausible, alternative interpretations of the variables exist.

We begin with the treatment of industry. First, we note that industry can be conceptualised as a shared attribute of corporations. The shared attribute does not imply any interaction (i.e. actors can have shared attributes and be in unconnected components). Features such as capital intensity or management structures may endogenously generate industrial political interests. We do not necessarily dispute Emirbayer and Goodwin's (1994) strong claims that most social concepts imply a relational ontology; however, if we are willing to accept that some influences on corporate political behaviour are more relational than others, then surely membership of the same primary industry is less obviously relational than other influences.

The same concerns that prompted Coleman's (1982) stinging criticism of interlocking directorate research are reflected in our scepticism about Mizruchi's structural equivalence interpretation of indirect interlocks. Coleman wrote:

The practice of industrial firms having executives of other firms or of financial institutions as members of boards of directors does not involve agency. These persons are board members in their capacity as persons, and their other positions are relevant only as they have acquired skills or knowledge from those positions. This points to a central difficulty of sociological studies of 'interlocking directorates' . . . Because the board member does not come as an agent but as a natural person, there is no interlock in the sense ordinarily meant. It is for this reason that such studies have never proved very useful for the study of the functioning of society. (Coleman 1982: 13)

When two corporations send an executive to the board of a third institution it creates an indirect tie between the corporations but a direct tie between the executives. In other words, the corporations are structurally equivalent but the executives are cohesively related. The two sides of the dual (Breiger, 1974) have different structural properties – different network mechanisms could be operating at the level of the individual or the corporation.

Figure 14.1 illustrates the differing consequences corporate interlocks have for directors and the corporations they are affiliated to. Corporations A and B have interlocked with Corporation C. They are structurally equivalent but they do not have a direct cohesive relation. Director 1 from Corporation A and Director 2 from Corporation B, however, do have a direct relation by virtue of sitting on the same board. Cohesion at the level of individual actors accompanies structural equivalence at the level of the organization. The question then arises whether the leading decision makers in corporations are acting as the agents of corporate political interests or of individual-level interests? Mizruchi implicitly assumes that political agency is rooted in organisational rather than class interests.

Three recent studies have highlighted the complexities these questions raise. Burris (2001, 2005) and Bond (2007) have studied the relations of directors and corporate-level interests. Burris (2001) found that American directors' patterns of political donations differed from the corporations they work for. He also found that individual-level characteristics of directors did not influence corporate political donations (although he does not display these findings). Bond (2007) found different

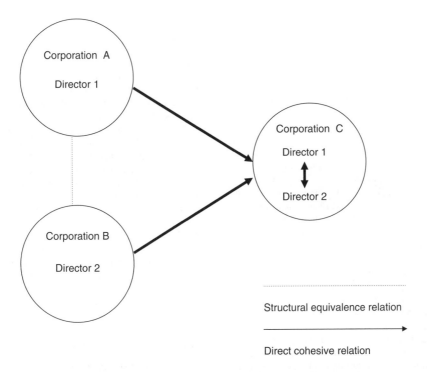

Figure 14.1　Structural equivalence between corporations and cohesion between directors

results in his study of political donations by large British corporations. Corporations' probabilities of making a donation to the Conservative Party were associated with their directors' educational backgrounds and social club affiliations. Further studies are required before assumptions can be safely made about the locus of political control in the large economic corporation.

Burris (2005) studied the effect of interlocking directorates on the similarity of directors' donations to candidates for president in primary elections. He found that direct, cohesive relationships between directors were associated with increased similarity in donation patterns. The magnitude of the coefficients in the models he estimated was identical for direct and indirect ties, and was significant even at six steps removed. Two lessons can be learnt from Burris's results. First, cohesive relations created by interlocking directorates could be mechanisms of political influences at the level of the individual if not the corporation. If directors were to use corporate political donations to further their interests, interlocking directorates could create cohesive political communities. Second, Burris's finding that political similarity is associated with ties as indirect as six steps implies that, if influence rather

than selection is producing the results, chains of structural equivalence or cohesion are driving political contagion or there are social mechanisms that operate at levels higher than the triad.

While Mizruchi's studies advanced the social network analytic study of corporate political behaviour his conclusions must remain tentative. The mutual conditioning of corporations' and their directors' political behaviour, and the effects of embedding dyads in broader corporate networks must be explored to validate (or not) his claims.

NEW DIRECTIONS

Social network studies of corporate politics have raised as many questions as they have answered. In what follows we list a number of possible directions the alliance can take in the future. We focus on topics that we think have greater network relevance. We do not, for example, discuss the need for cross-national studies because they do not have direct clear social network analytic consequences although we think they are key to understanding the nature and effects of corporate politics.

Moving beyond the power structure debate

The intellectual commitments of the antagonists in the power structure debate have tended to direct scholarly analysis of corporate politics towards a focus on unity and cohesion. We fear the focus on unity has limited the broader network analysis of corporate behaviour. First, it is unclear that a focus on unity is intellectually principled. For example, Marxist objections to capitalist society would not vanish if pluralist claims that the capitalist class is disunited and politically inefficacious were confirmed; they have a deeper basis rooted in the injustice, and historically stultifying effects, of exploitative relations between classes. Also, Marxist scholars such as Poulantzas (1973) have argued that the anarchic economic relations between capitalists will be mirrored in their political activity. Second, it limits our understanding of the political effects of corporate political action. Acceptance of the decisive importance of unity has meant neglect of mobilisation and intensity. If corporations are highly mobilised and devoting intense effort to achieving their political aims we think this can have significant effects on the political system. For example, even capitalists on different sides of the debate can crowd out other participants. If democracy has a deliberative element, intense, disunited corporate interventions can, at the very least, create a random error term that makes the political system less efficient. Third, the power structure debate has led to a systematic disregard of the effect that organised labour will have on the political behaviour of corporations. Has the American experience of having no electorally significant socialist party meant that scholars have focussed too much on searching for sources of opposition within business? Finally, the focus on unity has had research design implications for what is considered the appropriate network methodologies. It has encouraged a dyadic or triadic focus on cohesive and structural equivalence mechanisms. Examination of broader network effects such as centrality and the network characteristics of politically quiescent corporations have been neglected as a consequence.

Relations between the two sides of the duality: Directors and corporations

In the modern corporate order two sets of capitalist actors are important: corporations and their directors/owners. Until Burris's work (1991, 2001, 2005), these actors were largely treated separately (see Bearden and Mintz, 1987). Analysts of corporate politics studied corporations while elite theorists studied directors/owners. As we have pointed out at several points in this chapter, studying these two actors separately can present network analytic difficulties. Depending on the locus of political agency, the choice of unit of analysis will vary. This is important from a network perspective because the structural characteristics of the networks linking directors/owners on the one hand and corporations on the other will not necessarily coincide – as mentioned earlier, structural equivalence between corporations can imply cohesive relations between their directors. Inference about network mechanisms at one level of analysis can be misleading if political agency resides at another level. Social network analysts can make significant contributions to our understanding of corporate political behaviour by systematically studying the divergences between directors' and corporations' networks and the implications these have for corporate networks. Affiliation or two-mode networks could also be more usefully used in analyses of corporate politics.

Influence and selection

Network analysts face difficult identification problems. Are corporate actors' political predispositions and behaviour influenced by their relations in corporate networks, or are corporate actors with different political tendencies also likely to select into different kinds of social relations? The infeasibility of experimental design in research into corporate politics renders definitive answers to these questions impossible; however, some research designs will give more definitive answers than others. Researchers can mitigate the selection threat by collecting longitudinal data on corporate actors' relations with each other and their political behaviour. They can then, for example, detect whether directors' political activity changes as they develop more ties to the corporate community as predicted by inner circle theory. Recent developments in the statistical analysis of social networks have provided methods and computational tools for inferring the roles of influence and selection in longitudinal social networks (Snijders, 2001; Snijders and Steglich, this volume). Statistical SNA could lead to a renaissance in studies that examine whether corporate networks reflect capital concentration and ruling-class interaction. The problems of inference no longer appear so insoluble.

CONCLUSION

We have tried to outline the history, achievements, and problems of the alliances between social network analysts and scholars of corporate politics. We hope we have conveyed the diversity and scope of this research – it is, in our opinion, the area where SNA has made its greatest empirical contribution. Many intellectual challenges remain, which should attract both scholars interested in the balance of power in capitalist societies and scholars interested in modelling complex social structures as networks.

NOTES

1   As opposed to purely economic or market relations.

2   The extent to which directors' authority over political decisions is institutionalised varies with national electoral laws.

3   We mention pre/post-multiplication because the order in which matrices are multiplied affects their product. Matrix multiplication is not commutative.

4   The transpose of the matrix is simply when the rows and columns of the matrix are switched.

5   For example, if corporation A had two directors who were members of a social club and corporation B had three members the product would be six, reflecting six possible avenues of social interaction. The products are summed across all clubs to get the total number of possible avenues of social interaction in the social club network.

6   What is the meaning and/or function of an interlock between corporate directorates? This is a vexed question but one cannot stand on the sidelines if one thinks interlocking directorates are worth studying. Are they mini council halls where individual capitalists sit and discuss politics? Or are they areas where individuals from similar social backgrounds who have ended up in the same capitalist economic positions can sit with similar/different others? We are open-minded on these topics. We have our ideas about how directors should behave, but directors of large corporations act those roles out in observable sets of behaviours – because we are more interested in the behaviour of directors than we are in social scientists' ideas about what is best for them, our focus is on the former. Our guess is that interlocks have various meanings or functions. Social scientists judge whether they have these meanings or functions by examining their consequences and testing, within a probabilistic framework, whether those consequences are manifest in their observations. See Mizruchi, 1996, for a discussion of the meaning of interlocks.

7   Weighted by centrality of the corporations they are connected to, in other words, eigenvector centrality.

8   If we take Burris's (2005) stricture to study more and more distant relations (i.e. three-step, four-step, etc.) seriously then there are many more types of relation to study than cohesive and structural equivalence mechanisms. What mechanisms, if any, are influencing behaviour of individuals at greater than two steps of a relation?

9   One of the most important intellectual contributions is the systematic theorisation of relations that are not direct. The balance of direct and indirect relations in determining human behaviour is an unanswered question, but the answer to this question has potentially important consequences for the efficient allocation of intellectual resources between social network analytic and other types of social scientific perspectives.

10   Because input-output tables on business transactions are available at the industry level rather than firm level, constraint between industries is used as a proxy of constraint between individuals.

REFERENCES

Aaronovitch, S. (1961) *The Ruling Class. A Study of British Finance Capital*. London: Lawrence and Wishart.

Alba, R.D. (1973) 'A graph theoretic definition of a sociometric clique', *Journal of Mathematical Sociology*, 3: 113–26.

Baran, P.A. and Sweezy, P.M. (1966) *Monopoly Capital*. Harmondsworth: Penguin.

Bearden, J. and Mintz, B. (1987) 'The structure of class cohesion: The corporate network and its dual', in Mark S. Mizruchi and Michael Schwartz (eds), *Intercorporate Relations: The Structural Analysis of Business*. New York: Cambridge University Press. pp. 187–207.

Bell, D. (1960) *The End of Ideology*. New York: Collier.

Berg, I. and Zald, M. (1978) 'Business and society', *Annual Review of Sociology*, 4: 115–43.

Berk, R.A. (1983) 'An introduction to sample selection bias in sociological data', *American Sociological Review*, 48: 386–98.

Berle, A. and Means, G. (1932) *The Modern Corporation and Private Property*. New York: Harcourt Brace and World.

Bond, M. (2004) 'Social influences on corporate political donations in Britain', *British Journal of Sociology*, 55: 55–77.

Bond, M. (2007) 'Elite social relations and corporate political donations in Britain', *Political Studies*.

Bond, M., Glouharova, S. and Harrigan, N. (2006) *The Effects of Intercorporate Networks on Corporate Social and Political Behaviour*. Report to the Economic and Social Research Council (ESRC award ref. RES-000–22–0872).

Breen, R. (1996) *Regression Models: Censored, Sample Selected, or Truncated Data*. Thousand Oaks, CA: Sage.

Breiger, R.L. (1974) 'The duality of persons and groups', *Social Forces*, 53: 181–90.

Burris, V. (1987) 'The political partisanship of American business: A study of corporate political action committees', *American Sociological Review*, 52: 732–44.

Burris, V. (1991) 'Director interlocks and the political behavior of corporations and corporate elites', *Social Scientific Quarterly,* 72: 537–51.

Burris, V. (2001) 'The two faces of capital: Corporations and individual capitalists as political actors', *American Sociological Review,* 66: 361–81.

Burris, V. (2005) 'Interlocking directorates and political cohesion among corporate elites', *American Journal of Sociology,* 111: 249–83.

Burt, R.S. (1983a) 'Cohesion versus structural equivalence as a basis for network subgroups', in Ronald S. Burt, Michael J. Minor and Associates (eds), *Applied Network Analysis.* Beverly Hills: Sage. pp. 262–82.

Burt, R.S. (1983b) *Corporate Profits and Cooptation: Networks of Market Constraints and Directorate Ties in the American Economy.* New York: Academic Press.

Burt, R.S. (1987) 'Social contagion and innovation: Cohesion versus structural equivalence', *American Journal of Sociology,* 92: 1287–335.

Burt, R.S. (1992) *Structural Holes: The Social Structure of Competition.* Cambridge, MA: Cambridge University Press.

Carroll, W.K. (1982) 'The Canadian corporate elite: Financiers or finance capitalists?' *Studies in Political Economy,* 8: 89–114.

Chandler, A.D. (1977) *The Visible Hand: The Managerial Revolution in American Business.* Cambridge: Harvard University Press.

Clawson, D. and Neustadtl, A. (1989) 'Interlocks, PACs, and corporate conservatism', *American Journal of Sociology,* 94: 779–73.

Clawson, D., Neustadtl, A. and Bearden, J. (1986) 'The logic of business unity: Corporate contributions in the 1980 election', *American Sociological Review,* 51: 797–811.

Coleman, J.S. (1982) *The Asymmetric Society.* Syracuse, NY: Syracuse University Press.

Dahl, R.A. (1958) 'A critique of the ruling elite model', *American Political Science Review,* 52: 463–69.

Dahl, R.A. (1961) *Who Governs?* New Haven: Yale University Press.

Domhoff, G.W. (1998) *Who Rules America: Power and Politics in the Year 2000.* New York: McGraw Hill.

Emirbayer, M. and Goodwin, R. (1994) 'Manifesto for a relational sociology', *American Journal of Sociology.*

Ewing, K.D. (1987) *The Funding of Political Parties in Britain.* Cambridge: Cambridge University Press.

Friedkin, N. (1998) *A Structural Theory of Social Influence.* Cambridge: Cambridge University Press.

Galbraith, J.K. (1952) *American Capitalism.* Boston, MA: Transaction Press.

Habermas, J. (1987) *The Theory of Communicative Action, Vol II: The Critique of Functionalist Reason.* Cambridge: Polity Press.

Harrigan, N. (2007a) 'Political partisanship and corporate political donations in Australia', Unpublished manuscript. Australian National University.

Harrigan, N. (2007b) 'The inner circle revisited: A social selection model of the politics of interlocking directorates', unpublished manuscript. Australian National University.

Heckman, J.J. (1979) 'Sample selection bias as a specification error', *Econometrica,* 47: 153–61.

Hilferding, R. (1910) *Financial Capital.* London: Routledge Kegan Paul.

Hobson, A. (1902) *Imperialism: A Study.* London: James Pott and Company

Koenig, T., Gogel, R. and Sonquist, J. (1979) 'Models of the significance of interlocking corporate directorates', *American Journal of Economics and Sociology,* 103:173–86.

Kolko, G. (1962) *Wealth and Power in America.* New York: Frederick A. Praeger.

Lazarsfeld, P. and Merton, R.K. (1954) 'Friendship as social process: A substantive and methodological analysis', in Morroe Berger, Theodore Abel, and Charles Page (eds), *Freedom and Control in Modern Society.* New York: Van Nostrand. pp. 21–54.

Lenin, V.I. (1916) *Imperialism: The Highest Stage of Capitalism.* London: Martin Lawrence.

Levine, J. (1972) 'The Sphere of Influence' *American Sociological Review,* 37: 14–27.

Linton, M. (1994) *Money and Votes.* London: Institute for Public Policy Research.

Mills, C.W. (1956) *The Power Elite.* New York: Oxford University Press.

Mintz, B. and Schwartz, M. (1981) 'The structure of intercorporate unity in American business', *Social Problems,* 29: 87–103.

Mintz, B. and Schwartz, M. (1983) 'Financial interest groups and interlocking directorates', *Social Science History,* 7: 183–204.

Mintz, B. and Schwartz, M. (1985) *The Power Structure of American Business.* Chicago: University of Chicago Press.

Mizruchi, M.S. (1982) *The American Corporate Network, 1904–74.* Beverly Hills: Sage.

Mizruchi, M.S. (1989) 'Similarity of political behavior among large American corporations', *American Journal of Sociology,* 95: 401–24.

Mizruchi, M.S. (1990) 'Cohesion, structural equivalence, and similarity of behavior: An approach to the study of corporate political power', *Sociological Theory,* 8: 16–32.

Mizruchi, M.S. (1992) *The Structure of Corporate Political Action.* Cambridge, MA: Cambridge University Press.

Mizruchi, M.S. (1996) 'What do interlocks do? An analysis, critique, and assessment of research on interlocking directorates', *Annual Review of Sociology,* 22: 271–98.

Neustadtl, A. and Clawson, D. (1988) 'Corporate political groupings: Does ideology unify business political behaviour', *American Sociological Review,* 53: 172–90.

Olson, M. (1965) *The Logic of Collective Action.* Cambridge, MA: Harvard University Press.

Ornstein, M. (1980) 'Interlocking directorates in Canada: Evidence from replacement patterns', *Social Networks,* 4: 3–25.

Palmer, D. (1983) 'Broken ties: Interlocking directorates and intercorporate coordination', *Administrative Science Quarterly,* 28: 40–55.

Pinto-Duschinsky, M. (1981) *British Political Finance: 1830–1980.* Washington, DC: American Enterprise Institute.

Poulantzas, N. (1973) *Political Power and Social Classes.* London: New Left Books.

Rose, A. (1968) *The Power Structure: Political Process in American Life.* New York: Oxford University Press.

Scott, J. (ed.) (1990) *The Sociology of Elites, Vol III.* Aldershot: Edward Elgar.

Scott, J. and Griff, C. (1984) *Directors of Industry: The British Corporate Network: 1900–1976.* Cambridge: Polity Press.

Smith, A. (1776 [1937]) *An Inquiry into the Nature and Causes of the Wealth of Nations.* New York: Random House.

Smith, M.A. (2000) *American Business and Political Power.* Chicago: University of Chicago Press.

Snijders, T.A.B. (2001) 'The statistical evaluation of network dynamics', in M.E. Sobel and M.P. Becker (eds), *Sociological Methodology.* London: Basil Blackwell.

Su, T-t, Neustadtl, A. and Clawson, D. (1995) 'Business and the conservative shift: Corporate PAC contributions, 1976–1986', *Social Science Quarterly,* 76: 22–39.

Sweezy, P.M. (1953 [1939]). 'Interest groups in the American economy', in Paul M. Sweezy (ed.), *The Present as History.* New York: Monthly Review.

Useem, M. (1984) *The Inner Circle.* New York: Oxford University Press.

Weber, M. (1947) *The Theory of Social and Political Organization,* London: William Hodge.

Weinstein, J. (1968) *The Corporate Ideal in the Liberal State 1900–18.* Boston: Beacon.

Zeitlin, M. (1974) 'Corporate ownership and control: The large corporation and the capitalist class', *American Journal of Sociology,* 79: 1073–119.

15

Policy Networks

David Knoke

Je weniger die Leute davon wissen, wie Würste und Gesetze gemacht werden, desto besser schlafen sie. [The less people know about how sausages and laws are made, the better they sleep.]
—Chancellor Otto von Bismarck (1815–98)

Policy network analysis seeks to identify the important actors – governmental and nongovernmental organizations, interest groups, and persons – involved in policymaking institutions, to describe and explain the structure of their interactions during policymaking processes, and to explain and predict collective policy decisions and outcomes. To those ends, policy theorists and empirical researchers who apply network analytic perspectives have defined a multiplicity of concepts, principles, and propositions to explicate differential aspects of policy networks. Fundamental research objectives include showing how policy networks form, persist, and change over time. Social network theories of political influence and persuasion examine how relational ties among policy participants shape their political attitudes, preferences, and opinions. Other goals are to demonstrate the policy consequences of network structural relations for the actors contending and collaborating within specific public policy arenas. Comparative researchers explore the historical origins of national differences in network structural relations among state institutions and private interest groups, and their consequences for policy network dynamics and collective outcomes.

Probably the first explicit use of the term "policy network" appeared in an article by Peter Katzenstein (1976) comparing the foreign economic policies of France and the United States. Over the next three decades, the volume of theoretical and empirical work on both substantive policy networks and formal policymaking models expanded enormously, with scopes ranging from urban (e.g., Laumann and Pappi, 1976), to national (Schneider, 1992), to regional (Thomson et al., 2006), and to global levels of analysis (Witte et al., 2000). This chapter offers an overview of the history and current situation of policy network analysis; while it cannot be comprehensive and exhaustive, the chapter highlights crucial developments and controversies. The first section defines key concepts used by most policy network analysts. The second section summarizes the origins of policy network and policy domain ideas, while the third section describes more recent empirical research. The fourth section discusses the development of formal network models of collective decision making. The concluding section offers some suggestions for future directions in policy network analysis.

KEY POLICY NETWORK CONCEPTS

Like any social network, a ***policy network*** consists of a bounded set of actors and one or more sets of relations that connect these actors. Although policy network actors may be individual persons, at the national and international levels of analysis they are more typically formal organizations, such as political parties, legislatures, executive agencies, and interest group organizations. For example, Kenis and Schneider (1991) defined a policy network as a set of public and private corporate actors linked by communication ties for exchanging information, expertise, trust, and other political resources. The boundaries of a closely related concept, the *policy domain*, are socially constructed by the actors' mutual recognition that their preferences and actions on policy events must be taken into account by the other domain participants (Laumann and Knoke, 1987: 10). More formally, a policy domain is any subsystem "identified by specifying a substantively defined criterion of mutual relevance or common orientation among a set of consequential actors concerned with formulating, advocating, and selecting courses of action (i.e., policy options) that are intended to resolve the delimited substantive problems in question" (Knoke and Laumann, 1982: 256). Examples of policy domains include national defense, education, agriculture, welfare (Laumann and Knoke, 1987: 10), health, energy, and transportation (Burstein, 1991: 328). The twin concepts of policy network and policy domain can be reconciled by recognizing that a policy domain delineates a bounded system whose members are interconnected by multiple policy networks.

Social network theories assume that the primary unit of analysis is a social relation (a specific type of tie) connecting the members of a social system. The pattern of present and absent ties among a network's actors constitutes its social structure. Furthermore, "the perceptions, attitudes, and actions of organizational actors are shaped by the larger structural networks within which they are embedded, and in turn their behaviors can change these network structures" (Knoke, 2001: 63–64). These assumptions focus analysts' attention on the multiple types of interorganizational ties that may be important for explaining a policy domain's social structure, and for understanding the consequent actions at both the individual organizational level and for the policy domain as a whole. Knoke (2001: 65) argued that researchers should take into consideration five basic *types of interorganizational relations*, each of which may reveal a distinctive network structure: resource exchange, information transmission, power relations, boundary penetration, and sentimental attachments. Although resource exchanges in policy networks, such as money or personnel, are typically voluntary, sometimes governmental mandates – legislation or administrative regulations – impose and enforce interorganizational connections. Information transmission among organizations ranges from scientific and technical data to policy advice and opinions. Asymmetrical power relations rest less often on coercive force than on taken-for-granted beliefs

about the authority to issue commands and expect compliance (Weber's legitimate power). Public sector authorities usually possess greater power than private sector organizations to impose and enforce their interests on a domain. Boundary penetrations involve two or more actors coordinating their actions to achieve a common goal (Knoke, 2001: 65); classic illustrations are the lobbying coalitions discussed in the next paragraph. Finally, sentimental attachments refer to subjective, emotional affiliations that generate solidarity and mutual assistance among actors, for example, predispositions by labor unions to provide mutual political support.

A *lobbying coalition* involves consciously coordinated activity by two or more actors to influence a policy decision. Coalitions form around a specific *policy event*, a pending decision on a proposed legislative bill, regulatory order, or court case ruling. A coalition comprises an *action set* in which partners all hold the same policy preferences for an event, are connected through a communication network, and coordinate their lobbying and other policy-influencing activities (Knoke et al., 1996: 22). Although some organizations work alone in attempting to persuade legislators or regulators to choose proposed policies favorable to their interests, the chances of a successful outcome are usually greater when organizations pool their material and political resources into a joint policy campaign. An efficient division of labor among powerful coalition partners can enhance a group's political influence on a policy event outcome relative to a less-synchronized, opposing coalition with fewer resources. By combining their strengths and expertise, partners can deploy a wider variety of political influence tactics. For example, broad-based membership associations mobilize larger numbers of constituents to write letters and emails to their legislators. Organizations with well-staffed research operations present more compelling evidence during private meetings with governmental officials and in testimonies at public legislative or regulatory hearings. Lobbying is neither political bribery nor overt quid pro quo dealing (Browne, 1998). Rather, policy influence requires that a coalition present its most persuasive case to the ultimate decision-making body: Lobbyists give policymakers persuasive information, substantive technical analyses, proposed policy language, and politically accurate arguments about why they should support the coalition's preferred solution, instead of backing the opposition's so obviously inferior and indefensible policy alternative.

Lobbying coalitions are typically short-lived efforts to affect the outcome of a specific, narrowly defined policy event. After public officials render a decision, the coalition partners routinely disband to pursue their separate agenda items. Although some of those organizations may coalesce again around subsequent policy events, most coalitions involve distinctive constellations of participants, attracted by the substantive particulars affecting their interests. The aphorism "politics makes strange bedfellows" reflects an occasional occurrence of former enemies now working together on an event of mutual concern. For example, both liberals and conservatives opposed President Bush's warrantless wiretapping inside the United States as a serious erosion of Americans' civil liberties. However, most lobbying coalitions involve organizations that share similar preferences across a broad spectrum of interest, identity, or ideological concerns that guides their political calculations about policy stances. Broad and enduring cleavages often emerge within a policy domain; for example, business versus unions in labor policy, producers versus distributors in agricultural policy, and pharmaceutical companies versus consumers in health care policy (Heinz et al., 1993). Typically, only a subset of the organizations with general interests in a policy issue joins a coalition actively fighting to achieve a specific policy event outcome (Knoke, 2001: 351–56). Two fundamental research questions are: How best to describe and measure the network structure created by the overlapping participation of organizations in coalitions across multiple policy events? And how best to explain whether social cohesion and collective action by coalition participants leads to particular policy event outcomes? The next two sections review the initial efforts to answer these questions.

POLICY NETWORK AND DOMAIN RESEARCH

The extensive efforts to theorize and examine policy networks and policy domains can only be briefly summarized here (for more extensive overviews, see Knoke, 1998; Granados and Knoke, 2005; Robinson, 2006). The next three subsections discuss the origins of distinctive perspectives on policy networks in the United States, Britain, and Germany.

United States

A network approach to public policy analysis originated in a community power study, *New Directions in the Study of Community Elites,* by Edward O. Laumann and Franz Urban Pappi (1976). They demonstrated how multiple networks connecting the elites of a small German city facilitated and constrained their collective capacity to affect community policies. Replications of the approach in two middle-size Illinois cities revealed that organizations occupying central network positions were more influential in community affairs, more likely to mobilize for action in political controversies, and better able to achieve their preferred outcomes in public policy disputes (Laumann et al., 1978; Galaskiewicz, 1979). Laumann and Knoke's *The Organizational State* (1987) extended the network analysis of power structures to national policy domains conceptualized as multiplex networks among formal organizations, not elite persons. Their connections enable opposing interest organization coalitions to mobilize political resources in collective fights for influence over specific public policy decisions. A national power structure is revealed in patterns of multiplex networks of information, resources, reputations, and political support among organizations with partially overlapping and opposing policy interests. A comparison of U.S., German, and Japanese labor policy domains (Knoke et al., 1996) found that organizations that were more central in both the communication network (measured by policy information exchanges) and the support network (measured by resource exchanges) had higher reputations as especially influential players in labor policy. Centrality in both networks led to participation across numerous legislative events in six types of political influence activities, including coalitions with other domain organizations sharing the same policy preferences. In the United States and Germany, communication centrality had more impact than support centrality on organizational reputations and political activities, while the opposite pattern occurred in Japan (Knoke et al., 1996: 120). Most national labor policy fights were conducted by relatively small action sets, with labor unions and business associations making up the primary coalition leaders in all three nations. These factions usually took opposing positions on legislative bills and almost never collaborated, even on rare instances where they held the same policy outcome preferences.

United Kingdom

British scholars sought to identify the dimensions of national policy network structures according to their differentiated pluralist and corporatist features (Rhodes, 1985, 1990; Atkinson and Coleman, 1989, 1992; Jordan and Schubert, 1992). Beginning in the 1980s, as problems in such national policy domains as environment and health increased in complexity, British policymaking shifted away from entrenched subgovernments (i.e., policy domains at the national ministerial level) that tightly controlled consensual policy agendas. In their place, more fluid and unpredictable networks emerged in such policy domains as agriculture, civil nuclear power, youth employment, smoking, heart disease, sea defenses, and information technology (Richardson, 2000: 1009–11). British political scientists elaborated a *policy community* model of self-organizing groups drawing policy participants from government bureaucracies and associated pressure organizations (Wilks and Wright, 1987; Rhodes, 1990; Jordan, 1990). By the 1990s, rising intergovernmental management, new public management practices, and a "hollowed out" state sector had propelled networks into a persistent attribute of the British human services sector (Rhodes, 1996).

Marsh and Rhodes (1992) proposed a model of interest intermediation that emphasized the importance of structural relations among governmental ministries, pressure groups, and informal actors participating in the policy process. Their approach downplayed the significance of interpersonal relations and presented a static, unidirectional relation between policy networks and policy outcomes. Critics (Dowding, 1995, 2001; Raab, 2001) argued that the policy network approach lacked a theoretical basis and could not explain network transformation. In response, Marsh and Smith (2000) offered a model of dialectical change (and stability) involving three interactive effects among the policy network and the agents operating within it; the network and its social context; and the network and policy outcome. They applied the model's mutually causal and feedback relations to explain transformative changes in U.K. agricultural policy since the 1930s. For example, the National Farmers' Union preference for government price supports increased between 1930 and 1947 as it interacted with government officials and learned what demands it could make in shifting economic contexts. Marsh also applied the dialectical model to explain changes in U.K. policy on genetically modified (GM) food and crops, disclosing the power of "outsider" environmental groups in compelling GM foods to disappear from supermarket shelves (Toke and Marsh, 2003). More recently, Kisby (2007) advocated adding "programmatic beliefs" as antecedent ideational contexts in the Marsh dialectical model.

Germany

Germanic perspectives on policy networks are rooted in the American approach, through the collaboration of Franz Pappi and Edward Laumann (1973) on community power structure discussed above, and in Lehmbruch's (1984) analyses of corporatist politics in the Federal Republic of Germany (FRG) before reunification. Drawing from research on interlocking politics (Scharpf et al., 1976), Lehmbruch depicted the web of interorganizational networks as an important institutional constraint that stabilizes collective policy actions. In contrast to more centralized national states, such as France and the United Kingdom, the FRG resembled the U.S. federal system where states (*Länder*) retain important policy powers vis-à-vis the national government. Corporatist *concertation* in the FRG involved generalized exchanges among diverse interest organizations – private-sector organizations, state and federal agencies, and political parties – creating an interlocking system of autonomous, sectoral policy networks integrated under an overarching, noncentralized network (Lehmbruch, 1989). The economic policy network was oriented towards achieving national homogeneity, although regional policy networks apparently grew increasingly powerful. Bargaining and accommodation of interest groups took precedence over hierarchical centralization in the FRG. Lehmbruch's crucial insight – that institutions shape the specific forms and dynamics of policy networks – was largely overlooked by later researchers, who mostly investigated policy domains within a single governmental system.

In contrast to both American and British conceptualizations of policy networks as fundamental structures for intermediation between interest groups and governments, many German scholars tended to view them as a new form of governance. That is, policy networks are an alternative to both centralized authority hierarchies and deregulated markets for efficiently resolving policy conflicts between the state and its civil society (Börzel, 1998). The proliferation of policy networks, especially in supranational European Union policy domains, reflects several trends in state-society relations: increasing dispersion of resources among public and private organizations; elaboration of new policy domains demanding collective decisions; and overloaded governments that are dependent on the cooperation of private organizations, and therefore whose interests must be taken into account during policy formulation and implementation (Kenis and Schneider, 1991; Schneider, 1992). As structured interactions among interdependent but nonhierarchical organizations, policy networks facilitate their members' coordination of interests, the pooling and exchange of resources, and bargaining over policy proposals. In the absence of a central hierarchical authority that is capable of imposing its preferred policy solutions, cooperative policy blocks (based on communication, trust, support, resource exchange, and other interorganizational relations) constitute an informally institutionalized framework for conducting complex negotiations and reaching collective policy decisions (Marin and Mayntz, 1991; Mayntz, 1993; Benz, 1995). This analytic framework underlies the formal network decision models of European decision making discussed in another section below.

Volker Schneider's comparative research on the dangerous chemicals and telecommunications policy domains of Germany and the EU exemplified the Germanic conceptualization of policy networks as a distinct governance form (Schneider, 1986, 1992; Schneider et al., 1994). He found a variety of governance mechanisms – ranging from institutionalized formal advisory bodies to working committees to informal and secretive groups – for co-opting private-sector actors in the public policymaking process. A study of the 1990–94 privatization of former East German shipbuilding and steel conglomerates after German reunification revealed dense horizontal communication and medium hierarchical power networks as the emergent governance structure (Raab, 2002). Formal institutional rules, indicated by German constitutional provisions and interorganizational reporting requirements, were the dominant factors influencing network tie formation among interested public and private organizations and multilateral negotiations over privatizing or closing down the East German industrial properties.

RECENT POLICY NETWORK RESEARCH

The initial research on policy networks and domains failed to develop rigorous theories consisting of testable propositions about policy development and outcomes. They suffered from terminological imprecision and the proliferation of typologies, relying heavily on metaphor and description (Burstein, 1991; Dowding, 1995). At times, analysts seemed uncertain about whether to treat policy networks as primarily dependent or independent variables (Mikkelson, 2006: 18), that is, whether the primary objective was to explain the formation of policy networks or the consequences of network dynamics for collective action and policy outcomes. But those early efforts introduced a wealth of network concepts, principles, measures, and methods that invigorated the field and prepared the ground for subsequent advances. This section briefly examines recent examples of policy network research – in the United States, Europe, and non-Western

nations, and at the transnational level of analysis – that built on those foundations.

A fallow period followed the florescence of U.S. policy domain research in the 1980s, as the pioneering scholars turned their research attention elsewhere. However, the approach showed signs of revival as some political scientists examined old studies or extended policy domain research in new directions. For example, a reanalysis of Laumann and Knoke's health policy domain data showed that, as the domain's demand for policy information increased, interest organizations invested more time and resources in forging stronger communication ties to their trusted political allies rather than pursuing a broader acquaintance strategy (Carpenter et al., 2003). But strong ties tend to form within cliques, which fail to transmit novel information as quickly as interclique weak ties. Because of its inefficiency in distributing information when it is most in demand, the strong-tie strategy is vulnerable to network failure, the "tendency for a policy community to shatter into competing cliques that do not share information" (p. 433).

Other political scientists examined the relations between political institutions and policy networks. Local water-policy networks spawned local institutions that increased both enforcement and compliance with the federal Clean Water Act from 1994 to 2000, even in conservative areas that were prone to undermining those efforts (Scholz and Wang, 2006). Lubell (2007) found a strong relation between policy trust in the organizations involved in agricultural water policy and the policy-core beliefs of farmers in the Sacramento River watershed policy domain. At the national level, the policy coherence of 18 policy domains (measured by issue concentration, interest concentration, and policy targeting) was highest among domains with a dominant congressional committee or involvement of a lead federal agency (May et al., 2006). A comparative study of biotechnology policy domains found the United States bifurcated into distinct agricultural and food networks that shared key actors, while the Canadian domain split between a network to manage biotech promotion and another network focused on assessing environmental and health risks (Montpetit, 2005). One consequence of these national structural differences is a more permissive regulatory climate in the United States. Despite the encouraging evidence of continuing empirical research on U.S. policy domains, no one has proffered a comprehensive new theoretical framework for systematizing and stimulating further inquiry.

In contrast to the quiescent American scene, European research on policy networks proliferated in recent years, with extensions to new nations and to the supranational European Union.

This increased activity accompanied shifts to broader foci: from government to governance processes; from unitary central government to multilayered policymaking; from top-down hierarchies to bottoms-up bargaining; from national to both supra- and subnational levels of analysis; and from policy formation to policy implementation. A case study of constructing a new British hospital concluded that implementation networks in multilayered government undermined the democratic accountability of elected local officials (Greenaway et al., 2007). In contrast, an investigation of sustainable development in two local communities found broader participation when the state actively manipulated the network than when it withdrew from its central position (Hudson et al., 2007). A "lobbyism" paradigm for state-society relations emerged in Germany as selective lobbying supplanted institutionalized corporatist forms of interest advocacy (von Winter, 2004). Following reunification, a reorientation of federal and local authorities and an increasing number of interest groups induced structural changes in the German poverty policy network (von Winter, 2001). In other European countries, scholars investigated diverse policy networks, including French and Dutch urban policy (Le Gales, 2001; De Vries, 2008), Greek rural development (Papadopoulos and Liarikos, 2007), Swiss energy policy (Kriesi and Jegen, 2001), and Czech social welfare (Anderson, 2003).

Analysts of European Union policymaking emphasized the importance of policy networks, in such domains as higher education (Lavdas et al., 2006), genetically modified foods (Skogstad, 2003), and industrial regulation (Coen and Thatcher, 2008). A comparative study of three policy domains (European integration, agriculture, and immigration) in seven Western nations highlighted the heavy influence of the EU context and the conditional effects of domain-specific domestic power structures (Kriesi et al., 2006). Blockmodel analyses of the integration domain revealed distinctive coalitions and cleavages, implying that theories must aim "to understand the combined impact of country- and policy-specific contexts" (358). The next section discusses formal efforts to model bargaining and negotiation over legislative decision making among EU member-states.

Policy network analyses of non-Western nations are much rarer than projects conducted in advanced democratic societies. The few extant reports are largely descriptive efforts rather than theoretically guided investigations. Some recent instances include free-trade negotiations in Chile (Bull, 2008), water policy in Egypt and Ethiopia (Luzi et al., 2008), Mexican forestry policy (Paredes, 2008), and national development in South Korea and Taiwan (Kondoh, 2002). Clearly, substantial opportunities exist to expand cross-national research on policy domains.

Other scholars have taken tentative but promising steps toward identifying and mapping global or transnational policy networks (e.g., Witte et al., 2000; Benner et al., 2004). These networks involve relations among the important organizations that deal with a boundary-spanning policy issue; for example, global trade, plagues and pandemics, trafficking in illegal substances and endangered species, and climate change. The United Nations' complex of organizations and agencies make up one network with transnational reach in several policy domains (Reinicke and Deng, 2000). Numerous national governmental, private sector, and nongovernmental organizations (NGOs) also populate these policy networks. The key players in these power structures typically consist of international organizations and institutions possessing limited mandates and legitimate authority to set and enforce extra-territorial rules and standards (e.g., World Trade Organization, International Monetary Fund, Convention on International Trade in Endangered Species). Goldman (2007) described how the World Bank facilitated the creation of a transnational water-policy network, linking environmental and development NGOs with business firms. The consequence was a rapid privatization of water supplies in Africa, Asia, and Latin America under the control of a few multinational corporations. In contrast, transnational advocacy networks act as counterweights to corporation-dominated economic globalization. These loose-knit networks mobilize grassroots activists, social movements, and other civil society organizations across borders to pressure governments and business to change their policies and practices. Well-known instances include the Global Fund to fight AIDS/HIV, tuberculosis and malaria and the Campaign for Access to Essential Medicines (Kohlmorgen et al., 2007), human rights and election monitoring, and the anti-globalization protests at Seattle, Davos, and Genoa.

FORMAL NETWORK DECISION MODELS

An enduring theoretical challenge is to forsake generic metaphors and apply rigorous social network analysis principles to construct formal models of public policymaking. Formal models try to elucidate how binding decisions about proposed laws and regulations emerge within collective action systems – such as legislatures, courts, and regulatory agencies – through information exchanges, political resource pooling, coalitions, vote trading, and other dynamic political interactions. For example, log rolling (pork-barrel politics) involves one legislator agreeing to vote for another's bill in exchange for the second's vote supporting the first's favored bill. Or legislators may make concessions on the contents of a less important bill in exchange for others' support on issues of more central interest.

Formal network decision models, typically using matrix algebraic formulations, assume that the collective outcomes across a set of policy domain events, such as legislative bills, involve exchanges of resources controlled by policy actors with varied interests in particular event outcomes. The more powerful actors mobilize and deploy their political resources to affect the actions of the less powerful actors, making the latter dependent on the former, and thus increasing the powerful actors' capabilities to achieve their preferred policy outcomes. The following subsections discuss a variety of noteworthy efforts to construct formal models based on such assumptions. These models are impossible to describe adequately without resort to some simple matrix algebra notation.

Social influence models

These models, also called network effects or contagion models, show how network connections among actors mutually shape one another's beliefs and actions. The general hypothesis is that the greater the proximity of two actors in a network, the higher the probability that one actor's responses will be modified by the other's actions, which may occur without deliberate or consciously attempted influence (Marsden and Friedkin, 1994: 4). Friedkin (1984, 2004) proposed a deterministic, discrete-time linear process model in which each actor's attitude or preference is adjusted to the views of the other actors who have some influence over that actor (e.g., a direct network tie). All actors' opinions are simultaneously determined by the structural relations in the network. In formal matrix algebraic terms, where y is a vector of actors' attitudes at time t, and W is a matrix of network ties among the actors, the vector of attitudes at time $t+1$ is shown in Equation 15.1. Friedkin and Johnson (1990) generalized this model to include a matrix X of independent variables and a column vector b of their regression coefficients (shown in Equation 15.2).

$$y_{t+1} = Wy_t \qquad (15.1)$$
$$y_{t+1} = aWy_t + \beta Xb \qquad (15.2)$$

Several research studies yielded results consistent with the social network influence model's hypothesized effects. An example of the application of the social influence model in policy network research was Mark Mizruchi's (1989, 1990) demonstration that manufacturing corporations operating in the same primary industry tend to give financial contributions to the same political candidates. The behavioral similarity was even stronger to the extent that firms were located in related industries and were indirectly interlocked through shared banks and insurance companies.

Collective action models

James S. Coleman, in *The Mathematics of Collective Action* (1973), modeled legislative vote trading as an open market with perfect information about policy preferences that yields resulting prices (power) of actors over event outcomes. A legislator's power at market equilibrium is proportional to her control over valued resources for events (i.e., her votes on a set of bills) in which the other legislators have high interest. Power-driven actors seek to maximize their subjective expected utilities by exchanging votes, giving up their control of low-interest events in return for acquiring control over events having high interest to them. To illustrate this log-rolling process, if Senator A from a farming state has high interest in a price-support bill, while Senator B from a coastal state wants to pass a port-development bill, this dyad may mutually agree to vote for one another's event. In effect, each senator transfers control over the event of lesser interest for control over the event of greater importance. The Coleman model's simultaneous power equation solution for the entire legislature can be expressed in matrix algebra notation as the following, where P is a vector of legislators' equilibrium power, after all vote exchanges have taken place; X is a matrix of legislator interests in a set of legislative events (bills) to be decided by vote; and C is each legislator's control over each event (i.e., one vote per person on each bill).

$$P = PXC \qquad (15.3)$$

Network access models

Peter V. Marsden (1983) modified Coleman's market exchange model so that network relations could restrict actors' access to potential vote exchanges. In contrast to Coleman, whose market model allowed every legislator to trade votes with all others, Marsden assumed varying opportunities for dyadic vote trades. Compatibility of interests – based on trust, ideology, or party loyalty – might restrict the subset of actors among whom legislators prefer to log-roll their votes. The network access model's power equation (shown in Equation 15.4) differs from the Coleman model by including access matrix A, where $a_{ij} = 1$ if a vote exchange between actors i and j is possible, and $a_{ij} = 0$ if no exchange can occur. A is equivalent to the W matrix of network ties in social influence models. Marsden's simulations of his restricted network access model revealed (1) reduced levels of resource exchanges among actors; (2) power redistributed to actors in the most advantaged network positions; and (3) a possible shift to a more efficient system (i.e., higher aggregate interest satisfaction).

$$P = PAXC \qquad (15.4)$$

Dynamic policy models

Franz Pappi's institutional access models of network exchange were designed to explicate the underlying mechanisms by which interest groups influence the collective decision making of the organizational state. The approach distinguished *actors* (e.g., interest groups) from *agents* (e.g., public authorities with voting rights, such as legislatures) in national policy domains, with network structures built into the interest component (Pappi and Kappelhoff, 1984; Pappi, 1993; König, 1993; Pappi et al., 1995). An actor's power comes from its ability to gain access to effective agents, who are a subset of the network members (that is, agents can also be actors with their own interests in some event outcomes). Actors can gain control over policy events either by deploying their own policy information or by mobilizing the agents' information. The key equation in the mobilization version of the dynamic policy model is in Equation 15.5, where K* is the event-control matrix at equilibrium (L actors control the votes of K agents), and the W is the matrix of network ties. The alternative resource deployment version of the model operationalized actors' control as *confirmed* policy communication network, and measured *self-control* as the number of organizations not confirming the sender's information exchange offers (i.e., an indicator of independence in the system).

$$PXA = WK^* \qquad (15.5)$$

When Pappi and his colleagues applied the institutional access model to predict legislative outcomes in the U.S., German, and Japanese labor policy domain networks, they found that the information mobilization process fit more closely with American data, while the deployment process provided a better explanation of German policy decisions (Knoke et al., 1996: 184). Both models performed equally well for Japan, during the period when the Liberal Democratic Party had long dominated the Diet. The public authorities in all three countries, in both executive and legislative bodies, that also played the roles of agents were the most powerful actors. These organizations' power stemmed from their ability to maintain high levels of self-control over policy information sought by the other public- and private-sector actors.

Dynamic access models

In Frans Stokman's dynamic access models, collective decisions occur in a two-stage process where actors first mutually choose their preferred policies, then vote based on those derived preferences. More specifically, (1) each actor's policy event preferences are influenced by the preferences held by all the actors who have access to them through network ties; (2) then public officials cast their votes based on the set of policy preferences formed during the first stage where influence activities could occur (Stokman and Van den Bos, 1992; Stokman and Van Oosten, 1994; Stokman and Zeggelink, 1996). The dynamic access model's three key equations are shown in Equation 15.6, where C is control over events, R is actors' resources, and A is network access to other actors; X is actor interest in events and S is the salience of event decisions; V is voting power of the public officials and O is the predicted event outcomes.

$$C = RA \qquad X = XCS \qquad O = XV \qquad (15.6)$$

Stokman and Berveling (1998) compared predictions made by alternative versions of the dynamic access model to the actual outcomes of 10 Amsterdam policy decisions. The policy maximization model performed better than either the control maximization or the two-stage model. In the maximization version, policy-driven actors selectively agree to requests that they believe will mostly likely improve their own policy positions. Realizing that more distant powerful opponents aren't readily accessible, actors instead attempt to influence others who are most similar to themselves. That is, actors deliberately choose influence strategies that enhance the chances of success for their preferred policy positions but avoid having to change their preferences as they try to persuade others to support them (1998: 598).

Dynamic access models were most extensively applied to institutionalized political bargaining and negotiation over legislative decisions among the member states of the European Union (Bueno de Mesquita and Stokman, 1994; Thomson et al., 2006). Under the EU's governance rules, the executive European Commission (consisting of one commissioner from each of the 25 member-states) introduces a policy proposal either to the Council of the EU (a body of national ministers responsible for the policy area being addressed) or to both the Council and the European Parliament (EP, consisting of 785 members directly elected by the EU citizenry). After consultations and voting under a qualified majority system, which distributes votes among EU member-states roughly by their population sizes, the legislative bodies ultimately either adopt or reject the proposed policy (Thomson and Hosli, 2006: 12–19). Diverse interest groups may try to influence the policy proposal during the Commission's preparatory stage or during the decision-making stage by the Council and EP. The chapters in Thomson et al. (2006) apply various models of informal bargaining and formal decision-making procedures to 66 Commission proposals and 162 policy decisions from 1999 to 2001.

Most relevant to the policy network perspective are comparisons of three alternative two-stage models in which actors try to build winning coalitions by influencing others to support their policy positions (Arregui et al., 2006). Each model consists of an initial round of informal bargaining among actors holding different policy preferences, which may lead to some actors shifting positions over time, followed by a formal voting stage at which policies are adopted. The simple *compromise model* (Achen, 2006), which traces back to Thucydides' analysis of the balance of city-state power in the Peloponnesian War, treats governmental institutions as the key actors whose relative power determines policy outcomes. During informal bargaining, if actors' common policy interests are higher than their divergent preferences, some may change their positions on the basis of convincing information and persuasion. Then, using John Nash's solution to bargaining games, the policy decision can be predicted as a weighted average of actors' most-preferred policies, where weights are calculated as the product of actor power times policy salience. In the *challenge model* (Bueno de Mesquita, 2002), based on rational utility-maximizing decisions in noncooperative game theory, the actors experience a series of potentially hostile encounters during the informal bargaining stage. Coalitions try to compel other actors with divergent positions to change their policy preferences, using power dominance rather than persuasive

arguments, before a policy decision is formally adopted. The *position exchange model* (Arregui et al., 2006) assumes that actors may willingly change their initial preferences to support other positions at the final voting stage, because actors engage in mutually beneficial exchanges across pairs of policy decisions (that is, log-rolling).

Analysts initially found that the challenge model made the most accurate predictions of decision outcomes (Bueno de Mesquita and Stokman, 1994), based on only 16 policy issues. However, when the three models were applied to the much larger dataset of 162 EU policy decisions, overall the simple compromise model made the fewest errors in predicting policy adoptions, although not statistically fewer than the position exchange model (Arregui et al., 2006: 151). The position exchange model's predictions were most accurate for more polarized policy issues; the compromise model led to poor predictions for dichotomous issues; and the position exchange model fared best under co-decision procedures requiring both unanimity and qualified majority voting. Although each model captured some aspects of policymaking overlooked by the others, the authors' main conclusion was that the compromise model best explained EU legislative processes, where information and persuasion are central and members willingly compromise their positions to reach common solutions (Arregui et al., 2006: 152).

FUTURE DIRECTIONS FOR POLICY NETWORKS

Over the past three decades, policy network theory and research moved from a vague metaphor about the interconnectedness of political actors to the demonstration that formal network concepts, principles, and data analytic methods could yield important insights into network formation, structural configurations, collective actions, and policy outcomes. This concluding section offers my suggestions for some possible future directions.

Raab (2002: 581) presciently asked, "Where do policy networks come from?" and answered that macrostructures emerge from conscious micro-decisions about gaining access to resources. At present, researchers know far more about routine activities within established policy domains than about the origins, evolution, and transformation of policy networks. To explain how conditions in civil society generate new policy domains and interorganizational networks, analysts should painstakingly uncover the dynamic interplay between agency and structure through historical time. Knoke (2004) proposed a provisional framework for the sociopolitical construction of national policy domains. He argued that "focusing events" and innovations, exemplified by the 9/11 terror attacks and fiber-optic surveillance technologies, disrupt routine arrangements. The Internet is a particularly disruptive political force (Rethemeyer, 2007), generating new streams of political money and communication patterns. Policy entrepreneurs reframe policy issues as requiring either a major restructuring or the creation of a new domain with sufficient resources to deal with those disruptions. The eventual outcome is "a new institutional configuration of actors, programs, and procedures for conducting routine policymaking on the reframed substantive issues" (Knoke 2004: 93). To test this model, longitudinal data would have to be culled from archival documents.

As in most social network research, theoretical rigor in policy network analysis lags behind its increasingly sophisticated methods of data analysis (Carlsson, 2000; Raab and Kenis, 2007). Yet opportunities abound for developing new concepts, propositions, and theoretical frameworks. For example, political capital is the conceptual analogue of social capital, defined as an ego actor's access to the resources held by its alters (Knoke, 2009). Organizations acquire political capital through favor trading, such as unions contributing money and campaign workers to party politicians in exchange for sponsoring legislation (Hersch et al., 2008). Although political capital, with few exceptions (Siegel, 2008; Sørensen and Torfing, 2003), has rarely been explicitly studied from a social network perspective, it could be incorporated into formal network decision models. Another possible line of theory construction could assimilate insights from the advocacy coalition framework (ACF) approach to policy subsystems (Weible and Sabatier, 2007). Like policy network analysis, ACF emphasizes that participants coordinate with allies who share policy preferences and that policy brokers mediate conflicts between opposing sides. ACF offers three mechanisms to explain policy changes – external shocks, a "hurting stalemate," and accumulation of scientific/technical information. A third theory development option is to forge closer ties to neoinstitutionalism, particularly by identifying how formal governance rules constrain the capacity of informal networks to achieve collective decisions (Blom-Hansen, 1997; Klijn and Koppenjan, 2006).

The ultimate sign that political network research has intellectually matured will be the emergence of a distinctive theoretical explanation able to account fully for the origins, evolution, and policy outcomes of policy domains at every level of analysis. That theory should be capable of generating novel propositions and testing them with precisely measured network concepts and longitudinal data analytic methods. Although these desiderata seem utopian at present, the policy network field showed such impressive gains over the past three decades that a breakthrough may occur sooner than anyone could reasonably anticipate.

REFERENCES

Achen, C. (2006) 'Institutional realism and bargaining models', in Robert Thomson, Frans N. Stokman, Christopher H. Achen and Thomas König (eds), *The European Union Decides*. Cambridge, UK: Cambridge University Press. pp. 86–123.

Anderson, L.S. (2003) 'Constructing policy networks: Social assistance reform in the Czech Republic', *International Journal of Public Administration*, 26: 635–63.

Arregui, J., Stokman, F. and Thomson, R. (2006) 'Compromise, exchange and challenge in the EU', in Robert Thomson, Frans N. Stokman, Christopher H. Achen and Thomas König (eds), *The European Union Decides*. Cambridge, UK: Cambridge University Press. pp. 124–52.

Atkinson, M.M. and Coleman, W.D. (1989) 'Strong states and weak states: Sectoral policy networks in advanced capitalist economies', *British Journal of Political Science*, 19: 47–67.

Atkinson, M.M. and Coleman. W.D (1992) 'Policy networks, policy communities and the problems of governance', *Governance*, 5: 154–80.

Benner, T., Reinicke, W.H. and Witte, J.M. (2004) 'Multisectoral networks in global governance: Towards a pluralistic system of accountability', *Government and Opposition*, 39(2): 191–210.

Benz, A. (1995) 'Politiknetzwerke in der horizontalen Politikverflechtung', in Dorothea Jansen and Klaus Schubert (eds), *Netzwerke und Politikproduktion: Konzepte, Methoden, Perspektiven*. Marburg, Germany: Schüren. pp. 185–204.

Blom-Hansen, J. (1997) 'A new institutional perspective on policy networks', *Public Administration*, 75: 669–93.

Börzel, T.A. (1998) 'Organizing Babylon: On the different conceptions of policy networks', *Public Administration*, 76: 253–73.

Browne, W.P. (1998) *Groups, Interests, and U.S. Public Policy*. Washington: Georgetown University Press.

Bueno de Mesquita, B. (2002) *Predicting Politics*. Columbus, OH: Ohio State University Press.

Bueno de Mesquita, B. and Stokman, F. (eds) (1994) *European Community Decision Making: Models, Applications and Comparisons*. New Haven: Yale University Press.

Bull, B. (2008) 'Policy networks and business participation in free trade negotiations in Chile', *Journal of Latin American Studies*, 40(2): 195–224.

Burstein, P. (1991) 'Policy domains: Organization, culture, and policy outcomes', *Annual Review of Sociology*, 17: 327–50.

Carlsson, L. (2000) 'Policy networks as collective action', *Policy Studies Journal*, 28: 502–20.

Carpenter, D., Esterling, K. and Lazer, D. (2003) 'The strength of strong ties: A model of contact-making in policy networks with evidence from U.S. health politics', *Rationality and Society*, 15(4):411–40.

Coen, D. and Thatcher, M. (2008) 'Network governance and multi-level delegation: European networks of regulatory agencies', *Journal of Public Policy*, 28: 49–71.

Coleman, J.S. (1973) *The Mathematics of Collective Action.* Chicago: Aldine.

De Vries, M.S. (2008) 'Stability despite reforms: Structural asymmetries in Dutch local policy networks', *Local Government Studies*, 34: 221–43.

Dowding, K. (1995) 'Model or metaphor? A critical review of the network approach', *Political Studies*, 43: 136–58.

Dowding, K. (2001) 'There must be an end to confusion: Policy networks, intellectual fatigue, and the need for political science methods courses in British universities', *Political Studies*, 49(1): 89–105.

Friedkin, N.E. (1984) 'Structural cohesion and equivalence explanations of social homogeneity', *Sociological Methods and Research*, 12: 235–61.

Friedkin, N.E. (2004) 'Social cohesion', *Annual Review of Sociology*, 30: 409–25.

Friedkin, N.E. and Johnson, E.C. (1990) 'Social influence and opinions', *Journal of Mathematical Sociology*, 15: 193–205.

Galaskiewicz, J. (1979) *Exchange Networks and Community Politics.* Beverly Hills, CA: Sage.

Goldman, M. (2007) 'How "Water for All!" policy became hegemonic: The power of the World Bank and its transnational policy networks', *Geoforum*, 38: 786–800.

Granados, F.J. and Knoke, D. (2005) 'Organized interest groups and policy networks', in Thomas Janoski, Robert R. Alford, Alexander M. Hicks, and Mildred A. Schwartz (eds), *Handbook of Political Sociology: States, Civil Societies, and Globalization.* New York: Cambridge University Press. pp. 287–309.

Greenaway, J., Salter, B. and Hart, S. (2007) 'How policy networks can damage democratic health: A case study in the government of governance', *Public Administration*, 85(3): 717–38.

Heinz, J.P., Laumann, E.O., Nelson, R.L. and Salisbury, R.H. (1993) *The Hollow Core: Private Interests in National Policymaking.* Cambridge, MA: Harvard University Press.

Hersch, P., Netter, J.M. and Pope, C. (2008) 'Do campaign contributions and lobbying expenditures by firms create "political" capital?', *Atlantic Economic Journal*, 36: 395–405.

Hudson, J., Lowe, S., Oscroft, N. and Snell, C. (2007) 'Activating policy networks: A case study of local environmental policy-making in the United Kingdom', *Policy Studies*, 28: 55–70.

Jordan, G. (1990) 'Sub-government, policy communities and networks: Refilling the old bottles?' *Journal of Theoretical Politics*, 2(3): 319–38.

Jordan, G. and Schubert, K. (1992) 'A preliminary ordering of policy network labels', *European Journal of Political Research*, 21: 7–27.

Katzenstein, P. (1976) 'International relations and domestic structures: Foreign economic policies of advanced industrial states', *International Organization*, 30: 1–45.

Kenis, P. and Volker, S. (1991) 'Policy networks and policy analysis: Scrutinizing a new analytical toolbox', in Bernd Marin and Renate Mayntz (eds), *Policy Networks: Empirical Evidence and Theoretical Considerations.* Boulder/Frankfurt: Campus/Westview Press. pp. 25–62.

Kisby, B. (2007) 'Analysing policy networks: Towards an ideational approach', *Policy Studies*, 28: 71–90.

Klijn, E.-H. and Koppenjan, J.F.M. (2006) 'Institutional design: Changing institutional features of networks', *Public Management Review*, 8: 141–60.

Knoke, D. (1998) 'The organizational state: Origins and prospects', *Research in Political Sociology*, 8: 147–63.

Knoke, D. (2001) *Changing Organizations: Business Networks in the New Political Economy.* Boulder, CO: Westview.

Knoke, D. (2004) 'The sociopolitical construction of national policy domains', in Christian H.C.A. Henning and Christian Melbeck (eds), *Interdisziplinäre Sozialforschung: Theorie und empirische Anwendungen.* Frankfurt: Campus Verlag. 81–96.

Knoke, D. (2009) 'Playing well together: Creating corporate social capital in strategic alliance networks', *American Behavioral Scientist*, 52: 1690–708.

Knoke, D. and Laumann, E.O. (1982) 'The social structure of national policy domains: An exploration of some structural hypotheses', in Peter V. Marsden and Nan Lin (eds), *Social Structure and Network Analysis.* Beverly Hills: Sage. pp. 255–70.

Knoke, D., Pappi, F., J Broadbent, J. and Tsujinaka, Y. (1996) *Comparing Policy Networks: Labor Politics in the U.S., Germany and Japan.* New York: Cambridge University Press.

Kohlmorgen, L., Wolfgang, H. and Sonja, B. (2007) 'Networks and governance. Transnational networks as a basis for emancipatory politics in global society?', *Peripherie*, 27(105–6): 8–34.

Kondoh, H. (2002) 'Policy networks in South Korea and Taiwan during the democratic era', *Pacific Review*, 15(2): 225–44.

König, T. (1993) 'The impact of policy networks in a model of political decision making and public-private influence', *Journal für Sozialforschung*, 33: 343–67.

Kriesi, H. and Jegen, M. (2001). 'The Swiss energy policy elite: The actor constellation of a policy domain in transition', *European Journal of Political Research*, 39(2): 251–87.

Kriesi, H., Silke, A. and Margit, J. (2006) 'Comparative analysis of policy networks in Western Europe', *Journal of European Public Policy*, 13: 341–61.

Laumann, E.O., Galaskiewicz, J. and Marsden, P.V. (1978) 'Community structure as interorganizational linkages', *Annual Review of Sociology*, 4: 455–84.

Laumann, E.O. and Knoke, D. (1987) *The Organizational State: A Perspective on the Social Organization of National Energy and Health Policy Domains.* Madison: University of Wisconsin Press.

Laumann, E.O. and Pappi, F.U. (1976) *Networks of Collective Action: A Perspective on Community Influence Systems.* New York: Academic Press.

Lavdas, K.A., Papadakis, N.E. and Gidarakou, M. (2006) 'Policies and networks in the construction of the European higher education area', *Higher Education Management and Policy*, 18: 129–39.

Lehmbruch, G. (1984) 'Concertation and the structure of corporatist networks: Order and conflict in contemporary capitalism', in John H. Goldthorpe (ed.), *Order and Conflict in Contemporary Capitalism.* Oxford: Oxford University Press. pp. 60–80.

Le Gales, P. (2001) 'Urban governance and policy networks: On the urban political boundedness of policy networks: A French case study', *Public Administration*, 79: 167–84.

Lehmbruch, G. (1989) 'Institutional linkages and policy networks in the federal system of West Germany', *Publius*, 19(4): 221–35.

Lubell, M. (2007) 'Familiarity breeds trust: Collective action in a policy domain', *Journal of Politics*, 69(1): 237–50.

Luzi, S., Hamouda, M.A., Sigrist, F. and Tauchnitz, E. (2008) 'Water policy networks in Egypt and Ethiopia', *Journal of Environment and Development*, 17: 238–68.

Marin, B. and Mayntz, R. (eds) (1991) *Policy Networks: Empirical Evidence and Theoretical Considerations.* Boulder, CO: Westview Press.

Marsden, P.V. (1983) 'Restricted access in networks and models of power', *American Journal of Sociology*, 88: 686–717.

Marsden, P.V. and Friedkin, N.E. (1994) 'Network studies of social influence', in Stanley Wasserman and Joseph Galaskiewicz (eds), *Advances in Social Network Analysis: Research in the Social and Behavioral Sciences.* Thousand Oaks, CA: Sage. pp. 3–25.

Marsh, D. and Rhodes, R.A.W. (eds) (1992) *Policy Networks in British Government.* Oxford: Clarendon Press.

Marsh, D. and Smith, M. (2000) 'Understanding policy networks: Towards a dialectical approach', *Political Studies*, 48(4): 4–21.

May, P.J., Sapotichne, J. and Workman, S. (2006) 'Policy coherence and policy domains', *Policy Studies Journal*, 34(3): 381–403.

Mayntz, R. (1993) 'Modernization and the logic of interorganizational networks', *Knowledge and Policy*, 6: 3–16.

Mikkelsen, M. (2006) 'Policy network analysis as a strategic tool for the voluntary sector', *Policy Studies*, 27: 17–26.

Mizruchi, M.S. (1989) 'Similarity of behavior among large American corporations', *American Journal of Sociology*, 95: 401–24.

Mizruchi, M.S. (1990) 'Cohesion, structural equivalence, and similarity of behavior: An approach to the study of corporate political power', *Sociological Theory*, 8: 16–32.

Montpetit, E. (2005) 'A policy network explanation of biotechnology policy differences between the United States and Canada', *Journal of Public Policy*, 25(3): 339–66.

Papadopoulos, A.G. and Liarikos, C. (2007) 'Dissecting changing rural development policy networks: The case of Greece', *Environment and Planning C: Government and Policy*, 25: 291–313.

Pappi, F.U. (1993) 'Policy-Netze: Erschienungsform moderner Politiksteuerung oder methodischer Ansantz?' *Sonderheft 24 der Politischen Vierteljahresschrift*, pp. 84–94.

Pappi, F.U. and Kappelhoff, P. (1984) 'Abhängigkeit, Tausch und kollektive Entscheidung in einer Gemeindeelite', *Zeitschrift für Soziologie*, 13: 87–117.

Pappi, F.U., König, T. and Knoke, D. (1995) *Entscheidungsprozesse in der Arbeits- und Sozialpolitik. Der Zugang der Interessengruppen zum Regierungssystem über Politikfeldnetze: Ein deutsch-amerikanischer Vergleich.* Frankfurt/NewYork: Campus Verlag.

Paredes, S.V. (2008) 'Policy networks and organizational change in Mexican forestry policy', *Gestion y Politica Publica*, 17: 101–44.

Raab, C. (2001) 'Understanding policy networks: A comment on Marsh and Smith', *Political Studies*, 49: 551–56.

Raab, J. (2002) 'Where do policy networks come from?' *Journal of Public Administration Research and Theory* 12: 581–622.

Raab, J. and Kenis, P. (2007) 'Taking stock of policy networks: Do they matter?' in Frank Fischer, Gerald J. Miller and Mara S. Sidney (eds), *Handbook of Public Policy Analysis: Theory, Methods and Politics.* London: Taylor & Francis. pp. 187–200.

Reinicke, W.H. and Deng, F. (2000) *Critical choices: The United Nations, Networks, and the Future of Global Governance.* Ottawa, Canada: International Development Research Centre.

Rethemeyer, R.K. (2007) 'Policymaking in the age of Internet: Is the Internet tending to make policy networks more or less inclusive?' *Journal of Public Administration Research and Theory*, 17: 259–84.

Rhodes, R.A.W. (1985) 'Power dependence, policy communities and inter-governmental networks', *Public Administration Bulletin*, 49: 4–29.

Rhodes, R.A.W. (1990) 'Policy networks: A British perspective', *Journal of Theoretical Politics*, 2(3): 293–317.

Rhodes, R.A.W. (1996) 'The new governance: Governing without government', *Political Studies*, 44: 652–67.

Richardson, J.J. (2000) 'Government, interests groups and policy change', *Political Studies*, 48: 1006–25.

Robinson, S.E. (2006) 'A decade of treating networks seriously', *Policy Studies Journal*, 34: 589–98.

Scharpf, F., Reissert, B. and Schnabel, F. (1976) *Politikverflechtung: Theorie unde Empirie des kooperativen Föderalismus in der Bundesrepublik.* Kronberg, Germany: Scriptor Verlag.

Schneider, V. (1986) 'Exchange networks in the development of policy: Regulation of chemicals in the OECD, EEC, and the Federal Republic of Germany', *Journal Fur Sozialforschung*, 26: 383–416.

Schneider, V. (1992) 'The structure of policy networks: A comparison of the "chemicals control" and "telecommunications" policy domains in Germany', *European Journal of Political Research*, 21(1–2): 109–29.

Schneider, V., Dang-Nguyen, G. and Werle, R. (1994) 'Corporate actor networks in European policy-making: Harmonizing telecommunications policy', *Journal of Common Market Studies*, 32(4): 473–98.

Scholz, J.T. and Wang, C.-L. (2006) 'Cooptation or transformation? Local policy networks and federal regulatory enforcement', *American Journal of Political Science*, 50: 81–97.

Siegel, J. (2008) 'Contingent political capital and international alliances: Evidence from South Korea', *Administrative Science Quarterly*, 52: 621–66.

Skogstad, G. (2003) 'Legitimacy and/or policy effectiveness? Network governance and GMO regulation in the European Union', *Journal of European Public Policy*, 10: 321–38.

Sørensen, E. and Torfing, J. (2003) 'Network politics, political capital, and democracy', *International Journal of Public Administration*, 26: 609–34.

Stokman, F. and Berveling, J. (1998) 'Dynamic modeling of policy networks in Amsterdam', *Journal of Theoretical Politics*, 10: 577–601.

Stokman, F.N. and Van den Bos, J.M.M. (1992) 'A two-stage model of policymaking with an empirical test in the U.S. energy-policy domain', *Research in Politics and Society*, 4: 219–53.

Stokman, F.N. and Oosten, R.V. (1994) 'The exchange of voting positions: An objective-oriented model of policy networks', in Bruce Bueno de Mesquita and Frans Stokman (eds), *European Community Decision Making: Models, Applications and Comparisons*. New Haven, CT: Yale University Press. pp. 105–27.

Stokman, F.N. and Zeggelink, E.P.H. (1996) 'Is politics power or policy oriented? A comparative analysis of dynamic access models in policy', *Journal* of Mathematical *Sociology*, 21: 77–111.

Thomson, R. and Hosli, M.O. (2006) 'Explaining legislative decision-making in the European Union', in Robert Thomson, Frans N. Stokman, Christopher H. Achen and Thomas König (eds), *The European Union Decides*. Cambridge, UK: Cambridge University Press. pp. 1–24.

Thomson, R., Stokman, F.N., Achen, C.H. and König, T. (eds) (2006) *The European Union Decides*. Cambridge, UK: Cambridge University Press.

Toke, D. and Marsh, D. (2003) 'Policy networks and the GM crops issue: Assessing the utility of a dialectical model of policy networks', *Public Administration*, 81: 229–51.

von Winter, T. (2001) 'From corporatism to statism: Changes in the structure of the German poverty policy network', *Zeitschrift für Politikwissenschaft*, 11: 1573–608.

von Winter, T. (2004) 'From corporatism to lobbyism: A change of paradigm in the theory and analysis of advocacy', *Zeitschrift für Parlamentsfragen*, 35: 761–76.

Weible, C.M. and Sabatier, P.A. (2007) 'A guide to the advocacy coalition framework', in Frank Fischer, Gerald J. Miller and Mara S. Sidney (eds), *Handbook of Public Policy Analysis: Theory, Methods and Politics*. London: Taylor & Francis. pp. 123–36.

Wilks, S. and Wright, M. (eds) (1987) *Government-Industry Relations: West Europe, U.S. and Japan*. Oxford: Clarendon Press.

Witte, J.M., Reinicke, W.H. and Benner, T. (2000) 'Beyond multilateralism: Global public policy networks', *Internationale Politik und Gesellschaft*, 2: 176–88.

16

Social Movements and Collective Action

Mario Diani

This chapter examines the relation between network analytical approaches and collective action from two distinct angles.[1] First, it introduces the contribution of network analysis to the "collective action" dilemma proper, namely, how embeddedness in networks affects people's decisions to engage in collective action. Next, it looks at the emergence of collective actors as the result of coalitions and, more broadly, purposively built ties. Here, the focus is on fields, constituted by the interactions between a multiplicity of organizations and individuals. I conclude by identifying a few areas for future research.

While students of social movements and collective action are increasingly adopting network concepts and perspectives in their work, their use of formal network analytical tools is still limited. Accordingly, this chapter also covers studies that do not follow the classic quantitative approach but focus instead on qualitative observation (a strategy now largely represented even at the annual Sunbelt conferences). Instead, it looks far more sparingly at broader theoretical discussions of the role of networks in social processes (for relevant examples, see Emirbayer and Goodwin, 1994; Gilchrist, 2000; Livesay, 2002; Fine and Harrington, 2004).

SOCIAL NETWORKS AND COLLECTIVE ACTION

Individual effects

Network processes have always been relevant for analysts of political behavior (Zuckerman, 2005).

However, attention has become massive since the 1960s, when a new generation of scholar (often with an activist background) found themselves struggling with the inadequacy of previous accounts of collective action as driven by "personal pathology and social disorganization" (McAdam, 2003: 281). This prompted an intellectual movement that stressed how activism would normally be embedded in a rich texture of social relations.[2]

Several studies ensued, illustrating how involvement in extensive connections to people already active facilitated participation (Booth and Babchuk, 1969; Snow et al., 1980; Stark and Bainbridge, 1980; McAdam, 1986; Klandermans and Oegema, 1987; della Porta, 1988; Diani and Lodi, 1988; Opp, 1989; Opp and Gern, 1993; Oegema and Klandermans, 1994). Some suggested that networks mattered most for adhesion to groups that were somehow integrated in society, while adhesion to world-rejecting sects would be largely a matter for isolated individuals (Snow et al., 1980). For others, involvement in specific networks was most important for participation in demanding forms of activism, whether religious or political, whereas more individualistic, market-oriented, and/or less confrontational forms of behavior were more likely to occur without previous connections (Stark and Bainbridge, 1980; Diani and Lodi, 1988). Embeddedness in social networks not only mattered for recruitment, but it also discouraged leaving, and it supported continued participation (McPherson et al., 1992), with substantial bandwagon effects (Sandell, 1999).

Evidence on the important role of social networks in fostering participation has kept piling up to date (for a review, Crossley, 2007), with examples ranging from local communities in Romania (Vasi, 2004) and Mexico (Holzner, 2004) to university students' networks in the United Kingdom (Crossley, 2008), from peace (Nepstad, 2004) and civil rights activism (Lowe, 2007) to white power groups (Futrell and Simi, 2004). Most important, however, is the fact that over the years, questions such as "Which networks do explain what?" and "Under what conditions do specific networks become relevant?" have been constantly refined. Some have found previous activism to increase centrality in interpersonal networks, which in turn facilitated involvement in subsequent campaigns (e.g., Fernandez and McAdam, 1988, 1989). The form of prospective participants' ego-networks, that is, the distribution and density of the ties between the actors that one is connected to, also matters. The number of relevant others, who are already involved and densely connected, positively correlates with social incentives to join (Sandell and Stern, 1988). The impact of the context in which recruitment attempts take place has also been assessed. Specific political networks have been found to matter most where countercultural communities are weak (Kriesi, 1988: 58; McAdam and Fernandez, 1990). Where alternative communities are strong, more people are recruited through personal friendship networks or even through other channels, including self-applications. However, we can also find examples of the opposite situation, in which milieus with fewer protests see people mobilizing through contacts developed in contexts that are not directly associated with political protest. People may be embedded in settings, ranging from PTAs to sport clubs, that do not directly promote activism, but create opportunities for people with similar presuppositions to meet and eventually develop joint action (Ohlemacher, 1996). The workplace has also been found to exert a persistent positive effect on people's chances to mobilize (Dixon and Roscigno, 2003).

Increasingly, researchers have recognized that people are involved in multiple ties; while some may facilitate participation, others may discourage it. As such, neither embeddedness in organizational links nor strong ties to people already active necessarily predict activism. Lack of direct ties may be overcome if prospective participants are embedded in broader organizational networks, compatible with the campaign or organization they are considering to join (Kriesi, 1988; McAdam and Fernandez, 1990; McAdam and Paulsen, 1993). Similar mechanisms may also occur between people involved in religious congregations (Becker and Dhingra, 2001; Smilde, 2005).

Over the last few years, it has been increasingly argued that we ought to look for mechanisms rather than correlations, that is, we should clarify how networks really operate and what impact they have on participation. Kitts (2000) differentiated between *information, identity*, and *exchange* mechanisms. Along similar lines, McAdam (2003) identified four crucial mechanisms: recruitment attempts, identity-movement linkages, and positive and negative influence attempts. Passy (2001, 2003; see also Passy and Giugni, 2000) differentiated between *socialization, structural-connection*, and *decision-shaping* functions of networks. These functions take different forms depending on the traits of the organization promoting recruitment and its visibility in the public space.

Population effects

The analyses presented in the previous section treat network location mainly as an individual attribute, the impact of which is to be evaluated controlling for education, age, profession, or status. However, a structural account of participation requires analysts to look at how individual ties combine into more complex network patterns, to affect the proportion of people willing to contribute to a cause, or the intensity of participation in a certain population. These questions have been addressed through both formal modeling and empirical case studies. Marwell and Oliver (1993; Oliver and Marwell 2001) used formal models[3] to challenge Olson's (1963) well-known claim that only small groups can actually generate collective action. They emphasized the crucial role of a critical mass of people ("organizers"), prepared to face the costs of starting collective action, regardless of the size of the group taken as a whole. Their simulations also found a strong positive relationship between centralization of a group and its members' propensity to become involved in collective action (Marwell and Oliver 1993: 101–29), while the presence of *cliques* had apparently no effects. Kim and Bearman (1997) found that collective action occurs only if interest in specific issues and actors' network centrality are positively correlated.

Network heterogeneity also seems to matter. In highly heterogeneous networks, selective mobilization attempts, targeting specific subgroups of a population, are more effective than in homogeneous networks (Marwell and Oliver, 1993: 130–56). This line of argument is consistent with the more general point that recruitment strategies differ in how they balance the capacity to address a broad and diversified group of prospective participants (*reach*) with the capacity to mobilize with strong messages a more restricted yet more motivated constituency (*selectivity*; see Friedman and McAdam, 1992).

Explorations of collective action dynamics from this particular, systemic angle also address the broader question of why networks ultimately matter. Some stress that network ties enable people to calculate the impact of their actions (Kim and Bearman, 1997). Norms of fairness are also important in determining collective outcomes. The denser a network, the higher the levels of collective action, as people do not want to be perceived as free riders (Gould, 1993b). Rates of participation also increase much more steeply if those who started collective action in the first place are centrally located in the overall network (Gould, 1993b).

Gould (1991, 1993a, 1995) pioneered the empirical study of the relationship between collective performance and network variables. In a path-breaking project, he showed that levels of collective action by different Parisian neighborhoods in the Commune uprising of Spring 1871 were accounted for by organizational and informal relations between neighborhoods[4] as well as by nonrelational properties, such as levels of wealth in the neighborhood, percentage of resident salaried workers, and percentage of resident middle-class white-collar laborers.

Peter Hedström and his associates also stressed the link between territorial units and mobilization processes, yet with an emphasis on diffusion processes rather than levels of participation. They found that spatial proximity and the resulting increased likelihood of personal acquaintances to significantly influenced the spread of trade union and social democratic party organizations in Sweden from 1890 to 1940 (Hedström, 1994; Hedström et al., 2000; Sandell, 2001). Edling and Liljeros (2003) also referred to Swedish unions in their analysis of the diffusion of new organizational forms. Expanding this line of inquiry, Hedström et al. (2000) paid special attention to the role of specific activists ("socialist agitators") in creating a macro network between otherwise disjointed groups of actors and regions. The visit of an agitator made a difference along with the strength of ties between regions, given by geographical proximity, or the number of social democratic members in other districts. The presence of committed activists was also found crucial to the spread of civil rights activities in the 1960s American South (Andrews and Biggs, 2006).

Insisting on the classic distinction between strong and weak ties, Centola and Macy (2007) have suggested that weak ties may actually impede rather than facilitate complex contagion. What works at the individual level does not necessarily work at the collective level. In a rare application to empirical data, Biggs (2005) has shown strikes to expand following a power law distribution and a model he assimilates to the "forest fire," again pointing (as Centola and Macy, and of course Hedström et al., 2000) to spatial proximity as being a crucial element in diffusion processes.

Do networks really matter?

The empirical evidence demonstrating the role of networks in recruitment processes has been questioned from different angles. Some have defended the breakdown/malintegration argument, noting that it only refers to collective violence and disruptive behavior, not to the broader and less contentious forms of action that most collective action theorists include in their studies (Piven and Cloward, 1992: 308–9). Some recent studies actually stress the relevance of some of the mechanisms identified by breakdown theorists. McVeigh (2006) shows levels of involvement in activist groups of the left and the right in the United States to be significantly linked to indicators of problematic social integration, such as ethnic and religious heterogeneity or income inequality. Anheier (2003) showed the importance of "isolated members," that is, people who joined without previous ties to already active members, in the activities of the Nazi party. Or, Biggs (2006) showed that grievances mattered more than integration in church networks to account for individual participation in civil rights protests in the 1960s American South (see also Snow et al., 1980; Luker, 1984; Mullins, 1987).

The network thesis would also be largely tautological, given the spread of ties across groups and individuals (Piven and Cloward, 1992: 311). Even when network effects are discovered, findings are sometimes ambiguous (Oliver, 1984; Nepstad and Smith, 1999). Rather than highlighting exclusively those cases in which active people are involved in network ties, analysts should also look at those cases when networks are there, yet participation is not (e.g., see Klandermans and Oegema, 1987; Dixon and Roscigno, 2003).

The growing interest in collective action in countries with nondemocratic regimes has further questioned the role of networks in recruitment, as this is often dependent on public associational activities that are discouraged if not openly repressed in those settings. For example, Vala and O'Brien (2007) have looked at the recruitment in Protestant denominations in China. They have shown that under repressive circumstances networks count less for recruitment than is usually assumed, and networks are often the outcome of recruitment attempts rather than their precondition. Similar indications come from studies of Islamist activism in the Middle East (Bennani-Chraïbi and Fillieule, 2003; Pedahzur and Perliger, 2006) and in Central Asia (Collins, 2007). The role of networks is similarly ambiguous in contexts in which recruitment to a political organization may be coerced, as in the case of Central American guerrilla groups (Viterna, 2006).

Similar doubts have been raised in reference to organizational population dynamics. A study of the diffusion of civil rights campaigns in the American South in the spring of 1960 shows social networks played a limited role in diffusion processes, as core activists of movement organizations and news media turned out to be more important (Andrews and Biggs, 2006). A study of participation in mass rallies on highly emotional issues also had the same conclusion, suggesting that the media play a much greater role than social networks (Walgrave and Massens, 2000). Looking at survival rates of MADD chapters, Edwards and McCarthy (2004) found that, despite the importance of weak ties, stronger ties emerging from bloc recruitment mechanisms do not seem to contribute to organizational survival.

SOCIAL MOVEMENTS, COALITIONS, AND ORGANIZATIONAL FIELDS

Social movements as networks

Large-scale collective action has always been organized in network forms (see e.g., Ansell, 2001; Rosenthal et al., 1985, 1997), and the network nature of social movements has long been highlighted (Gerlach, 1971, 2001; Curtis and Zurcher, 1973). Recently, Diani (2003a; Diani and Bison, 2004) proposed a relational typology of forms of collective action that focuses on actors' different responses to issues of coordination and boundary definition. Social movements are collective actors in which coordination takes place through informal networks between formally independent actors, who all identify nonetheless – if with variable intensity – with a common cause. They are contrasted to coalitions, organizations, and communities that are driven by different logics of action (see also Jackson, 2006).

In many cases, network dynamics remain purely informal. For example, in the environmental justice movement of the 1990s, many grassroots groups preferred to coordinate through an informal networking strategy, rather than relying on the intermediation of the rigid environmental bureaucracies that had so far secured "ownership"

of those issues (Schlosberg, 2002: Chapter 5). Oftentimes, however, a hybrid model of "network organization" (Powell, 1990; Monge and Contractor, 2003) develops, combining elements of formality with those elements from a loose network structure. The "network organization" model is frequently found among organizations mobilizing on a transnational scale (e.g., Anheier and Themudo, 2002; Katz and Anheier, 2007; Smith, 2008).

Network organizational forms facilitate alliance building, which in turn has been found to increase the chances of success for interest organizations (Laumann and Knoke, 1987: 387; Knoke, 1990: 208); they also foster the diffusion of ideas and practices, and reduce the negative effects of failure in a certain organizational population (Gerlach, 1971). With the legitimation crisis experienced by political parties and other established forms of political representation since the 1980s, networks are also being regarded as a desirable, more legitimate, and democratic form of political organization (see Dumoulin, 2006; on networks and democratic theory, Hadenius, 2001: Chapter 3).

On the other hand, although loose network forms increase the resources available to social movement organizations, they also raise the danger of internal conflict, both between different organizational units and different ideological factions (Kleidman, 1993: 39–40; Brooks, 2004). Also for this reason, the lives of many network organizations tend to be shorter and less stable than that of more bureaucratic organizations (Anheier and Themudo, 2002: 192–93; Markham, 2005).

Types of ties

While traditionally applied to the study of individual recruitment and, more generally, individual behavior, the classic distinction between strong and weak ties has also been used in reference to organizational networks. Within civil society, weak ties seem to operate mostly as bridges between different organizational clusters, be they defined by reference to locality (e.g., Musso et al., 2006), issues (Baldassarri and Diani, 2007), or something else. While weak ties better connect civil society, their bridging functions usually do not go beyond information exchange or ad hoc coalition work. On the other hand, stronger bonding ties may facilitate collective action, but at the cost of reproducing inequalities within civil society (Musso et al., 2006) or encouraging the fragmentation of civil society in non- or little-communicating clusters (Baldassarri and Diani, 2007).

Strong ties have often been conceptualized as the overlap of organizational exchanges and the links provided by individual activists and their multiple memberships (for general applications of this principle: Simmel, 1908 [1955]; McPherson, 1983; Cornwell and Harrison, 2004). Looking at how individuals link organizations through their memberships generates useful insights on the structure of social movement milieus. Carroll and Ratner (1996) analyzed networks of multiple memberships in the social movement sector in Vancouver, relating different structural positions to different activists' frames and representations. In their study of the organizational affiliations of 202 leading feminists in New York State between 1840 and 1914, Rosenthal et al. (1985, 1997) provided one of the earliest and most systematic treatment of overlapping memberships as interorganizational links. Access to diachronic data enabled them to chart the transformation of networks through different historical periods. Looking at both local and nationwide organizational milieus, they were also able to address issues of core-periphery relations and division of labor in the women's organizational fields.

Most studies of the duality of individuals and groups focus on core activists and movement leaders. Schmitt-Beck (1989) has explored the connections between central figures in the German peace movement of the 1980s, and their ties to churches, trade unions, university, media, and other established social and political organizations. So have Schurman and Munro (2006), if in qualitative terms, in reference to mobilizations opposing genetic engineering in European agriculture. Alongside religious identity, cohesive networks have been found to play an important role in shaping expectations and ideological stances of leaders in American evangelicalism since the 1970s (Lindsay, 2008). From a historical sociology perspective, Hillmann (2008) has looked at political and mercantile elite networks in the English Civil War, while Han (2009) has explored the role of individual brokers, most notably Paul Revere, in the American revolution.

Some studies explicitly address the multiplicity of ties within movement networks. Diani (1995) differentiate between "visible" ties, consisting of exchanges between organizations, and "latent" ties, consisting of the connections created by activists' personal friendships and multiple memberships. Baldassarri and Diani (2007) reformulate the weak versus strong ties dichotomy in terms of "transactions," consisting only of resource exchanges, and "social bonds," that combines resource exchange and shared members (see also Lémieux, 1998). Studying the structure of the Korean environmental movement, Park (2008) explores how governance structures (that he identifies with member overlaps), knowledge structures (given by shared ideological elements between organizations) and affiliation structures (given by shared participation in events) operate in the same context.[5]

Movement structures: Segmentation and division of labor within movement networks

Social movement networks may actually take very different forms. Diani (2003a) has proposed a typology based on two fundamental dimensions: network centralization vs. decentralization, and network integration vs. segmentation. This generates four types of networks: "wheel/star" networks, highly centralized and integrated (see Diani, 1995, 2003b, and Figure 16.1); "policephalous" networks, consisting of sets of different clusters, with variable degrees of centralization, in which the average distance between nodes is higher than in the wheel/star model (see, for example, Phillips, 1991); "clique" networks, totally decentralized and highly integrated as all nodes are adjacent to each other (in reality, of course, we'll have most probably 2-clique networks, as nodes will be unlikely to be connected to all other nodes); and "segmented, decentralized" networks, consisting of different components, each in turn made of horizontal dyads or cliques (Diani, 2003a: 306–12). More recently, Baldassarri and Diani (2007) identified a "small-world" type of structure for local civil society networks, with dense clusters of interaction connected by rarer bridging ties and overall lower levels of hierarchy than one would find in random networks.

Looking at global network structures and in particular to centrality measures may also illuminate some aspects of leadership dynamics within social movements. While network studies of profit-oriented organizations have long established a relation between network centrality and influence (Brass and Burckhardt, 1993), it is more disputed whether this might also apply to networks of nonprofit, often protest-prone, organizations. An early influential account of social movements actually pointed at their nature as being policephalous (Gerlach, 1971), or even acephalous, networks (Gerlach, 2001). Brokerage roles, bridging otherwise noncommunicating milieus, seem particularly relevant for movements operating on the global scale (Smith, 2002, 2005, 2008). Other studies have stressed the relative centralization of movement networks. Phillips (1991: 779) showed that centrality, rather than resources, explained perception of efficacy among

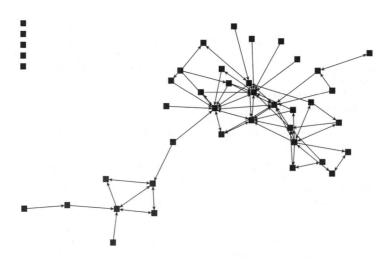

Figure 16.1 Structure of the Milanese environmental movement, mid-1980s

Canadian women's groups. Diani (2003b) found that high in-degree scores among Milanese environmental groups were accounted for by the social capital created by members' multiple memberships, while high brokerage scores depended more on organizational resources. However, looking at the issue from the perspective of Actor Network Theory, others (Routledge et al., 2007) found no correlation between resources and centrality.

But what does generate structural patterns? Movement networks emerge from discrete choices that independent actors make regarding their partners in alliances, their privileged sources of information, or, in the case of individuals, the organizations to join and the groups to be part of. Particular network forms are not, in fact, the result of deliberate planning but rather of provisional or contingent choices (Padgett and Ansell, 1993). What determines such choices — that is, the principles behind alliance building — has been the object of a lot of work recently (Rucht, 2004; van Dyke and McCammon, 2010), yet with minimal reference to SNA tools (see Ansell, 2003).

Practical considerations, related to differences in issue agendas and time and resource constraints, and mechanisms of path dependence undoubtedly play a significant role in shaping alliances. Despite the rhetoric on movement networks' volatility, there is substantial continuity in the choices of partners made at least by the most important and persistent organizations. For example, Shumate, et al. (2005) show that previous ties account for alliances between international NGOs active on the HIV crisis. Diani (1995: 152–62) found the same for the Milanese

environmental associations between the 1980s and 1990s.

Still, neither functional division of labor nor path dependencies enable us to make full sense of the structure of movement networks. We also need to look at homophily mechanisms, or, in other words, at what characteristics of actors, of their belief systems and identities, facilitate or hinder the building of ties. For example, the development of broad alliances on environmental, gender, or citizens' rights issues may be hampered by the strength of cultural differences — in turn based on race, class, or again gender — running within the communities that movements are supposed to mobilize (e.g., Lichterman, 1995; Croteau, 1995). How movement actors represent themselves, their adversaries, and what is at stake in the conflict in which they are involved can also have multiple effects on the selection of potential allies, regardless of the political system in which they operate (Diani, 1995; Lichterman, 1995; Lavalle et al., 2007).

Socio-demographic processes are often shaping network patterns. Let us think for instance of the varying salience of ethnic segregation. The chances for the development of pan-Asian collective action in the United States seem higher when American Asians as a whole are segregated from the rest of society; if segregation patterns apply unevenly between Asian subgroups, then the chances of pan-Asian collaboration diminish (Okamoto, 2003). Drastic changes of the socioeconomic system like those induced by neoliberal policies may also affect coalition building. For instance, chances for transnational networking may grow while opportunities for domestic collective action may be reduced (Bandy, 2004).

CONCLUSIONS

Over the last few years, network concepts have gained increasing attention in the study of social movements and collective action. The contribution of networks to individual recruitment in particular has been both widely explored and critically discussed (Diani, 2004); in contrast, despite a few exceptions (Phillips, 1991; Diani, 1995; Ansell, 2003; Diani and Bison, 2004; Mische, 2003, 2008; Park, 2008), applications of SNA tools to interorganizational processes have been relatively rare. As a conclusion, I try to identify a few issues that in my opinion deserve greater attention.

We need to take more seriously into consideration the spatial dimension of networks, which do not develop in a vacuum but are embedded in specific territories (Hägerstrand, 1967). Political and urban geographers have devoted substantial attention to collective action processes both at the local and the global levels. However, most of that work has been conducted without drawing upon SNA tools (Cumbers et al., 2008; Leitner et al., 2008; Routledge, 2003; Routledge et al., 2006, 2007, 2008; Nicholls, 2008, 2009), while additions to analytical works like Hedstrom et al.'s or Gould's have been far more rare.

We also need to pay more attention to time dynamics and network evolution. Like in the case of space, research covering long time spans is severely hampered by constraints on resources and, most important, data availability. To date, the most sophisticated attempt to adopt a diachronic perspective in the analysis of individual networks has been Ann Mische's (2003, 2008) exploration of Brazilian youth activist networks from the 1970s to the 1990s. Mische maps the evolution of networks over time through the multiple memberships of different activist cohorts. To this purpose she provides a pioneering application to collective action processes of Galois lattice techniques (Mische and Pattison, 2000), which enables her to combine information on individuals, organizations, and events. David Tindall (2002, 2004; Tindall et al., 2003) has provided another rare example of research by mapping the evolution of activist careers (in this case, British Columbia environmental activists) over time, drawing upon a three-stages panel study spanning three decades. A more economic approach than panel studies or life histories consists of using available survey data on individual memberships to map, using two-mode network principles and techniques

(Breiger, 1974; Borgatti and Everett, 1997), or the evolution over time of relations between different sectors of civil society (see, for example, Rosenthal et al., 1985, 1997; see also McPherson and Rotolo, 1996). Available surveys like the General Social Survey in the United States or the World Values Survey can be used (and sometimes have been used: Cornwell and Harrison, 2004) to this purpose.

As for organizational data, the major obstacle to diachronic research remains the difficulty of identifying valid sources of data to chart the evolution of interorganizational networks over time without depending on data about core members. Sometimes, media reports mentioning the involvement of specific organizations in protest events have been drawn upon to map relations between those organizations, again following a two-mode logic of analysis (Bearman and Everett, 1993; Rootes, 2003; Boudourides and Botetzagias, 2007). Archival data have also been dug up to map interactions between collaborating and conflicting actors in a variety of historical settings (Franzosi, 1999; Tilly and Wood, 2003).

We also have to pay far more attention to applications of SNA to the analysis of virtual networks. Over the last few years, a considerable debate has developed whether computer-mediated communication (CMC) is capable of creating new social ties or simply expanding and amplifying "real," "face-to-face" ties (on CMC and collective action, see, among others, Walgrave and Massens, 2000; Earl and Schussman, 2003; Tilly, 2004: 95–108; van de Donk et al., 2004; della Porta and Diani, 2006: 131–34). However, the available evidence using network analysis tools is still very rare, at least in the case of social movement studies. Among the few exceptions are studies of the links between websites of global justice organizations (van Aelst and Walgrave, 2004), and of organizations and activists mobilizing on global communication rights (Mueller et al., 2004; Padovani and Pavan, 2009; Pavan, 2011).

Finally, more theorizing and research must be put into the exploration of the link between context — in particular, its structural, cultural, and political features — and network structures. The relationship between context and social networks has only recently gained attention in SNA at large (Entwisle et al., 2007). In the case of social movement analysis, properties of the context, and in particular "political opportunities" (Tarrow, 1998; Meyer and Minkoff, 2004), are normally taken as explanations for individual or aggregate behavior. However, it may also be worth studying how they may shape interaction patterns. For example, Stevenson and Greenberg (2000) show that political opportunities affect actors' network strategies in policy networks. Cinalli and Füglister

(2008) claim that actors mobilizing on unemployment issues generate different coalitions in different European countries, depending on national peculiarities of collective action, in turn linked to dominant repertoires and styles of policy making. Carmin and Hicks (2002) look at the impact of transnational networks on domestic mobilization in former Socialist countries.

This logic might be extended to collective action proper, as the salience of traditional cleavages might affect levels of segmentation within movement networks and the overall distribution of alliance ties; likewise, the overall strength of protest cultures and repertoires could encourage certain alliances to the detriment of others. Some studies point in this direction. For example, environmental organizations in Italy in the 1980s mostly allied with actors on the same side of the major political cleavage, and a relatively integrated movement developed only when the salience of major cleavages was reduced (Diani, 1995). Two decades later, U.S. peace movement activists tended to join different sectors of the peace movement depending on their partisan loyalties (Heaney and Rojas, 2007); the networks generated in several European countries by peace campaigners through their multiple involvements also seemed to vary depending on the salience of pre-existing cleavages (Diani, 2009). Other studies, however, found no relation between cleavage salience and the structural properties of civil society networks (Baldassarri and Diani, 2007). Once again, more research is needed before we can develop more solid theoretical arguments on this important issue.

NOTES

1 Here I draw on and expand on previous treatments of the issue, most notably Diani (2003a, 2004) and della Porta and Diani (2006).

2 Pinard (1968); Bolton (1972); Oberschall (1973); Pickvance (1975); McCarthy and Zald (1977); Tilly (1978). See Diani (2004: 340–43) for a more detailed account of these early phases.

3 Other systematic attempts to apply formal modeling to the investigation of collective action dynamics include Macy's (1990, 1991, 1993) and Heckathorn's (1989, 1990, 1993, 1996), as well as, more recently, Oliver and Myers (2003) and Takacs et al. (2008). Although applications of formal theories to the analysis of concrete empirical cases are relatively rare (Gould, 2003), the works cited above have actually also inspired empirical research (see, for example, Brown and Boswell, 1995).

4 Network links between neighborhoods were measured as the number of residents of district *i*

enlisted in the battalion of district *j*, divided by the overall number of *i* residents enlisted anywhere else. Other indicators of linkages included rates of marriages between residents of different districts.

5 See also Molm and Cook (1995) on the role of different types of connections in coalition processes

REFERENCES

Andrews, K.T. and Biggs, M. (2006) 'The dynamics of protest diffusion: Movement organizations, social networks, and news media in the 1960 sit-ins', *American Sociological Review*, 71: 752–77.

Anheier, H. (2003) 'Movement development and organizational networks: The role of 'single members' in the German Nazi party, 1925–1930', in Mario Diani and Doug McAdam (eds), *Social Movements and Networks*. Oxford: Oxford University Press. pp. 49–74.

Anheier, H. and Themudo, N. (2002) 'Organizational forms of global civil society: Implications of going global', in Marlies Glasius, Mary Kaldor, and Helmut Ahheier (eds), *Global Civil Society 2002*. Oxford: Oxford University Press. pp. 191–216.

Ansell, C. (2001) *Schism and Solidarity in Social Movements. The Politics of Labour in the French Third Republic*. Cambridge: Cambridge University Press.

Ansell, C. (2003) 'Community embeddedness and collaborative governance in the San Francisco Bay Area environmental movement', in Mario Diani and Doug McAdam (eds), *Social Movements and Networks*. Oxford: Oxford University Press.

Baldassarri, D. and Diani, M. (2007) 'The integrative power of civic networks', *American Journal of Sociology*, 113: 735–80.

Bandy, J. (2004) 'Paradoxes of transnational civil societies under neoliberalism: The Coalition for Justice in the Maquiladoras', *Social Problems*, 51: 410–31.

Bearman, P. and Everett, K.D. (1993) 'The structure of social protest, 1961–1983', *Social Networks*, 15:171–200.

Becker, P.E. and Dhingra, P. (2001) 'Religious involvement and volunteering: Implications for civil society', *Sociology of Religion*, 62: 315–35.

Bennani-Chraïbi, M. and Fillieule, O. (eds) (2003) *Résistances et protestations dans les sociétés musulmanes*. Paris: Presses de Sciences Po.

Biggs, M. (2005) 'Strikes as forest fires: Chicago and Paris in the late nineteenth century', *American Journal of Sociology*, 110: 1684–1714.

Biggs, M. (2006) 'Who joined the sit-ins and why: Southern black students in the early 1960s', *Mobilization*, 11: 241–56.

Bolton, C.D. (1972) 'Alienation and action: A study of peace group members', *American Journal of Sociology*, 78: 537–61.

Booth, A. and Babchuk, N. (1969) 'Personal influence networks and voluntary association affiliation', *Sociological Inquiry*, 39: 179–88.

Borgatti, S.P. and Everett, M.G. (1997) 'Network analysis of 2-mode data', *Social Networks*, 19: 243–69.

Boudourides, M. and Botetzagias, I.A. (2007) 'Networks of protest on global issues in Greece 2002–2003', in Derrick Purdue (ed.), *Civil Societies and Social Movements*. London: Routledge. pp. 109–23.

Brass, D.J. and Burckhardt, M.E. (1993) 'Potential power and power use', *Academy of Management Journal*, 36: 441–70.

Breiger, R.L. (1974) 'The duality of persons and groups', *Social Forces*, 53: 181–90.

Brooks, C.D. (2004) 'Faction in movement: The impact of inclusivity on the anti-globalization movement', *Social Science Quarterly*, 85: 559–77.

Brown, C. and Boswell, T. (1995) 'Strikebreaking or solidarity in the Great Steel Strike of 1919: A split labor market, game-theoretic, and QCA analysis', *American Journal of Sociology*, 100: 1479–519.

Carmin, J. and Hicks, B. (2002) 'International triggering events, transnational networks, and the development of Czech and Polish environmental movements', *Mobilization*, 7: 305–24.

Carroll, W.K. and Ratner, R.S. (1996) 'Master framing and cross-movement networking in contemporary social movements', *Sociological Quarterly*, 37: 601–25.

Centola, D. and Macy, M. (2007) 'Complex contagions and the weakness of long ties', *American Journal of Sociology*, 113: 702–34.

Cinalli, M. and Füglister, K. (2008) 'Networks and political contention over unemployment: A comparison of Britain, Germany, and Switzerland', *Mobilization*, 13: 259–76.

Collins, K. (2007) 'Ideas, networks, and Islamist movements. Evidence from central Asia and the Caucasus', *World Politics*, 60: 64–96.

Cornwell, B. and Harrison, J.A. (2004) 'Union members and voluntary associations: Membership overlap as a case of organizational embeddedness', *American Sociological Review*, 69: 862–81.

Crossley, N. (2007) 'Social networks and extraparliamentary politics', *Sociology Compass*, 1: 222–37.

Crossley, N. (2008) 'Social networks and student activism: On the politicising effect of campus connections', *Sociological Review*, 56: 18–38.

Croteau, D. (1995) *Politics and the Class Divide. Working People and the Middle Class Left*. Philadelphia: Temple University Press.

Cumbers, A., Routledge, P. and Nativel, C. (2008) 'The entangled geographies of global justice networks', *Progress in Human Geography*, 32: 183–201.

Curtis, R.L. and Zurcher, L.A.Jr. (1973) 'Stable resources of protest movements: The multi-organizational field', *Social Forces*, 52: 53–61.

della Porta, D. (1988) 'Recruitment processes in clandestine political organizations: Italian left-wing terrorism', in Bert Klandermans, Hanspeter Kriesi, and Sidney Tarrow (eds), *From Structure to Action*. Greenwich: JAI Press. pp. 155–72.

della Porta, D. and Diani, M. (2006) *Social Movements*. Oxford: Blackwell.

Diani, M. (1995) *Green Networks. A Structural Analysis of the Italian Environmental Movement*. Edinburgh: Edinburgh University Press.

Diani, M. (2003a) 'Networks and social movements: A research programme', in Mario Diani and Doug McAdam (eds), *Social Movements and Networks*. Oxford: Oxford University Press. pp. 299–318.

Diani, M. (2003b) 'Leaders or brokers?', in Mario Diani and Doug McAdam (eds), *Social Movements and Networks*. Oxford: Oxford University Press. pp. 105–22.

Diani, M. (2004) 'Networks and participation', in David Snow, Sarah Soule, and Hanspeter Kriesi (eds), *The Blackwell Companion to Social Movements*. Oxford: Blackwell. pp. 339–59.

Diani, M. (2009) 'The structural bases of protest events. Multiple memberships and networks in the February 15th 2003 anti-war demonstrations', *Acta Sociologica*, 52: 63–83.

Diani, M. and Bison, I. (2004) 'Organizations, coalitions, and movements', *Theory and Society*, 33: 281–309.

Diani, M. and Lodi, G. (1988) 'Three in one: Currents in the Milan ecology movement', in Bert Klandermans, Hanspeter Kriesi, and Sidney Tarrow (eds), *From Structure to Action*. Greenwich, CT: JAI Press. pp. 103–24.

Dixon, M. and Roscigno, V.J. (2003) 'Status, networks, and social movement participation: The case of striking workers', *American Journal of Sociology*, 108: 1292–327.

Dumoulin, D. (2006) 'Usage comparé de la notion de reseau. Propositions d'analyse pour l'action collective', *Cahiers des Amériques Latines*, 51–52: 125–44.

Earl, J. and Schussman, A. (2003) 'The new site of activism: On-line organizations, movement entrepreneurs, and the changing location of social movement decision-making', *Research in Social Movements, Conflict and Change*, 24: 155–87.

Edling, C.R. and Liljeros, F. (2003) 'Spatial diffusion of social organizing: Modeling trade union growth in Sweden, 1890–1940', *Advances in Strategic Management: A Research Annual*, 20: 267–90.

Edwards, B. and McCarthy, J.D. (2004) 'Strategy matters: The contingent value of social capital in the survival of local social movement organizations', *Social Forces*, 83: 621–51.

Emirbayer, M. and Goodwin, J. (1994) 'Network analysis, culture, and the problem of agency', *American Journal of Sociology*, 99: 1411–54.

Entwisle, B., Faust, K., Rindfuss, R.R. and Kaneda, T. (2007) 'Networks and contexts: Variation in the structure of social ties', *American Journal of Sociology*, 112: 1495–533.

Fernandez, R. and McAdam, D. (1988) 'Social networks and social movements: Multiorganizational fields and recruitment to Mississippi freedom summer', *Sociological Forum*, 3: 357–82.

Fernandez, R. and McAdam, D. (1989) 'Multiorganizational fields and recruitment to social movements', in Bert Klandermans (ed.), *Organizing for Change*. Greenwich, CT: JAI Press. 315–44.

Fine, G.A. and Harrington, B. (2004) 'Tiny publics: Small groups and civil society', *Sociological Theory*, 22: 341–56.

Franzosi, R. (1999) 'The return of the actor. Interaction networks among social actors during periods of high mobilization (Italy, 1919–1922)', *Mobilization,* 4: 131–49.

Friedman, D. and McAdam, D. (1992) 'Collective identity and activism: Networks, choices, and the life of a social movement', in Aldon D. Morris and Carol Mueller (eds), *Frontiers in Social Movement Theory.* New Haven: Yale University Press. pp. 156–73.

Futrell, R. and Simi, P. (2004) 'Free spaces, collective identity, and the persistence of U.S. white power activism', *Social Problems,* 51: 16–42.

Gerlach, L. (1971) 'Movements of revolutionary change. Some structural characteristics', *American Behavioral Scientist,* 43: 813–36.

Gerlach, L. (2001) 'The structure of social movements: Environmental activism and its opponents', in John Arquilla and David Ronfeldt (eds), *Networks and Netwars: The Future of Terror, Crime, and Militancy.* Santa Monica, CA: Rand. 289–310.

Gilchrist, A. (2000) 'The well-connected community: Networking to the "edge of chaos"', *Community Development Journal,* 35: 264–75.

Gould, R.V. (1991) 'Multiple networks and mobilization in the Paris Commune, 1871', *American Sociological Review,* 56: 716–29.

Gould, R.V. (1993a) 'Trade cohesion, class unity, and urban insurrection: Artisanal activism in the French commune', *American Journal of Sociology,* 98: 721–54.

Gould, R.V. (1993b) 'Collective action and network structure', *American Sociological Review,* 58: 182–96.

Gould, R.V. (1995) *Insurgent Identities: Class, Community, and Protest in Paris from 1848 to the Commune.* Chicago: University of Chicago Press.

Gould, R.V. (2003) 'Why do networks matter? Rationalist and structuralist interpretations', in Mario Diani and Doug McAdam (eds), *Social Movements and Networks.* Oxford: Oxford University Press. pp. 233–57.

Hadenius, A. (2001) *Institutions and Democratic Citizenship.* Oxford: Oxford University Press.

Hägerstrand, T. (1967) *Innovation Diffusion as a Spatial Process.* Chicago: University of Chicago Press.

Han, S.-K. (2009) 'The other ride of Paul Revere: Brokerage role in the making of the American Revolution', *Mobilization,* 14: 143–62.

Heaney, M.T. and Rojas, F. (2007) 'Partisans, nonpartisans, and the antiwar movement in the United States', *American Politics Research,* 35: 431–64.

Heckathorn, D.D. (1989) 'Collective sanctions and the creation of prisoner's dilemma norms', *American Journal of Sociology,* 94: 535–62.

Heckathorn, D.D. (1990) 'Collective sanctions and compliance norms: A formal theory of group-mediated social control', *American Sociological Review,* 55: 366–84.

Heckathorn, D.D. (1993) 'Collective action and group heterogeneity: Voluntary provision versus selective incentives', *American Sociological Review,* 58: 329–50.

Heckathorn, D.D. (1996) 'The dynamics and dilemmas of collective action', *American Sociological Review,* 61: 250–77.

Hedström, P. (1994) 'Contagious collectivities: On the spatial diffusion of Swedish trade unions, 1890–1940', *American Journal of Sociology,* 99: 1157–79.

Hedström, P., Sandell, R. and Stern, C. (2000) 'Mesolevel networks and the diffusion of social movements: The case of the Swedish Social Democratic Party', *American Journal of Sociology,* 106: 145–72.

Hillmann, H. (2008) 'Mediation in multiple networks: Elite mobilization before the English Civil War', *American Sociological Review,* 73: 426–54.

Holzner, C. (2004) 'The end of clientelism? Strong and weak networks in a Mexican squatter movement', *Mobilization,* 9: 223–40.

Jackson, B.A. (2006) 'Groups, networks, or movements: A command-and-control-driven approach to classifying terrorist organizations and its application to Al Qaeda', *Studies in Conflict & Terrorism,* 29: 241–62.

Katz, H. and Anheier, H. (2007) 'Global connectedness: The structure of transnational NGO networks', in Marlies Glasius, Mary Kaldor, and Helmut Anheier (eds), *Global Civil Society 2005/2006.* London: Sage. pp. 240–65.

Kim, H. and Bearman, P.S. (1997) 'The structure and dynamics of movement participation', *American Sociological Review,* 62: 70–93.

Kitts, J. (2000) 'Mobilizing in black boxes: Social networks and SMO participation', *Mobilization,* 5: 241–57.

Klandermans, B. and Oegema, D. (1987) 'Potentials, networks, motivations, and barriers: Steps towards participation in social movements', *American Sociological Review,* 52: 519–31.

Kleidman, R. (1993) *Organizing for Peace: Neutrality, the Test Ban, and the Freeze.* Syracuse, NY: Syracuse University Press.

Knoke, D. (1990) *Organizing for Collective Action. The Political Economies of Associations.* New York: Aldine de Gruyter.

Kriesi, H. (1988) 'Local mobilization for the people's petition of the Dutch peace movement', in Bert Klandermans, Hanspeter Kriesi, and Sidney Tarrow (eds), *From Structure to Action.* Greenwich, CT: JAI Press. pp. 41–82.

Laumann, E.O. and Knoke, D. (1987) *The Organizational State. Social Choice in National Policy Domains.* Madison: University of Wisconsin Press.

Lavalle, A.G., Castello, G. and Bichir, R.M. (2007) 'Leading actors within civil society: Networks and centralities of civil organizations in Sao Paulo', *Dados-Revista De Ciencias Sociais,* 50: 465–98.

Leitner, H., Sheppard, E. and Sziarto, K.M. (2008) 'The spatialities of contentious politics', *Transactions of the Institute of British Geographers,* 33: 157–72.

Lémieux, V. (1998) *Les coalitions: liens, transactions e contról.* Paris: P.U.F.

Lichterman, P. (1995) 'Piecing together multicultural community: Cultural differences in community building among grass-roots environmentalists', *Social Problems,* 42: 513–34.

Lindsay, D.M. (2008) 'Evangelicals in the power elite: Elite cohesion advancing a movement', *American Sociological Review,* 73: 60–82.

Livesay, J. (2002) 'The duality of systems: Networks as media and outcomes of movement mobilization', *Current Perspectives in Social Theory*, 22: 185–222.

Lowe, M.R. (2007) 'An "oasis of freedom" in a "closed society": The development of Tougaloo College as a free space in Mississippi's Civil Rights Movement, 1960 to 1964', *Journal of Historical Sociology*, 20: 486–520.

Luker, K. (1984) *Abortion and the Politics of Motherhood*. Berkeley: University of California Press.

Macy, M.W. (1990) 'Learning-theory and the logic of critical mass', *American Sociological Review*, 55: 809–26.

Macy, M.W. (1991) 'Chains of cooperation: Threshold effects in collective action', *American Sociological Review*, 56: 730–47.

Macy, M.W. (1993) 'Backward-looking social-control', *American Sociological Review*, 58: 819–36.

Markham, W.T. (2005) 'Networking local environmental groups in Germany: The rise and fall of the Federal Alliance of Citizens' Initiatives for Environmental Protection (BBU)', *Environmental Politics*, 14: 667–85.

Marwell, G. and Oliver, P. (1993) *The Critical Mass in Collective Action*. Cambridge: Cambridge University Press.

McAdam, D. (1986) 'Recruitment to high risk activism: The case of freedom summer', *American Journal of Sociology*, 92: 64–90.

McAdam, D. and Fernandez, R. (1990) 'Microstructural bases of recruitment to social movements', in Louis Kriesberg (ed.), *Research in Social Movements, Conflict and Change. Vol.12*. Greenwich, CT: JAI Press. pp. 1–33.

McAdam, D. and Paulsen, R. (1993) 'Specifying the relationship between social ties and activism', *American Journal of Sociology*, 99: 640–67.

McAdam, D. (2003) 'Beyond structural analysis: Toward a more dynamic understanding of social movements', in Mario Diani and Doug McAdam (eds), *Social Movements and Networks*. Oxford: Oxford University Press. pp. 281–98.

McCarthy, J.D. and Zald, M.N. (1977) 'Resource mobilization and social movements: A partial theory', *American Journal of Sociology*, 82: 1212–41.

McPherson, M. (1983) 'An ecology of affiliation', *American Sociological Review*, 48: 519–32.

McPherson, M, Popielarz, P. and Drobnic, S. (1992) 'Social networks and organizational dynamics', *American Sociological Review*, 57: 153–70.

McPherson, M. and Rotolo, T. (1996) 'Testing a dynamic model of social composition: Diversity and change in voluntary groups', *American Sociological Review*, 61: 179–202.

McVeigh, R. (2006) 'Structural influences on activism and crime: Identifying the social structure of discontent', *American Journal of Sociology*, 112: 510–66.

Meyer, D. and Minkoff, D. (2004) 'Conceptualizing political opportunity', *Social Forces*, 82: 1457–92.

Mische, A. (2003) 'Cross-talk in movements: Reconceiving the culture-network link', in Mario Diani and Doug McAdam (eds), *Social Movements and Networks*. Oxford: Oxford University Press. pp. 258–80.

Mische, A. (2008) *Partisan Publics*. Princeton, NJ: Princeton University Press.

Mische, A. and Pattison, P. (2000) 'Composing a civic arena: Publics, projects, and social settings', *Poetics*, 27: 163–94.

Molm, L.D. and Cook, K.S. (1995) 'Social exchange and exchange networks', in Karen S. Cook, Gary A. Fine, and J.S. House (eds), *Sociological Perspectives on Social Psychology*. Stanford: Stanford University Press. pp. 209–35.

Monge, P.R. and Contractor, N.S. (2003) *Theories of Communication Networks*. Oxford: Oxford University Press.

Mueller, M., Pagé, C. and Kuerbis, B. (2004) 'Civil society and the shaping of communication-information policy: Four decades of advocacy', *Information Society*, 20: 169–85.

Mullins, P. (1987) 'Community and urban movements', *Sociological Review*, 35: 347–69.

Musso, J.A., Weare, C., Oztas, N. and Loges, W.E. (2006) 'Neighborhood governance reform and networks of community power in Los Angeles', *American Review of Public Administration*, 36: 79–97.

Nepstad, S.E. (2004) 'Persistent resistance: Commitment and community in the plowshares movement', *Social Problems*, 51: 43–60.

Nepstad, S.E. and Smith, C. (1999) 'Rethinking recruitment to high-risk/cost activism: The case of Nicaragua exchange', *Mobilization*, 4: 25–40.

Nicholls, W. (2008) 'The urban question revisited: The importance of cities for social movements', *International Journal of Urban and Regional Research*, 32: 841–59.

Nicholls, W. (2009) 'Place, networks, space: Theorising the geographies of social movements', *Transactions of the Institute of British Geographers*, 34: 78–93.

Oberschall, A. (1973) *Social Conflict and Social Movements*. Englewood Cliffs: Prentice-Hall.

Oegema, D. and Klandermans, B. (1994) 'Why social movement sympathizers don't participate: Erosion and nonconversion of support', *American Sociological Review*, 59: 703–22.

Ohlemacher, T. (1996) 'Bridging people and protest: Social relays of protest groups against low-flying military jets in West Germany', *Social Problems*, 43: 197–218.

Okamoto, D.G. (2003) 'Toward a theory of panethnicity: Explaining Asian American collective action', *American Sociological Review*, 68: 811–42.

Oliver, P. (1984) 'If you don't do it, nobody else will: Active and token contributors to collective action', *American Sociological Review*, 49: 601–10.

Oliver, P. and Marwell, G. (2001) 'Whatever happened *to* critical mass theory? A retrospective and assessment', *Sociological Theory*, 19: 292–311.

Oliver, P. and Myers, D. (2003) 'Networks, diffusion, and cycles of collective action', in Mario Diani and Doug McAdam (eds), *Social Movements and Networks*. Oxford: Oxford University Press. 173–204.

Olson, M. (1963) *The Logics of Collective Action*. Cambridge, MA: Harvard University Press.

Opp, K.-D. (1989) *The Rationality of Political Protest*. Boulder: Westview Press.

Opp, K.-D. and Gern, C. (1993) 'Dissident groups, personal networks, and spontaneous cooperation. The East German revolution of 1989', *American Sociological Review*, 58: 659–80.

Padgett, J.F. and Ansell, C.K. (1993) 'Robust action and the rise of the Medici, 1400–1434', *American Journal of Sociology*, 98: 1259–319.

Padovani, C. and Pavan, E. (2009) 'Fra reti tematiche e reti sociali. Un ritratto delle mobilitazioni sui diritti di comunicazione in Italia', *Quaderni di Sociologia*, p. 49.

Park, H.-S. (2008) 'Forming coalitions: A network-theoretic approach to the contemporary South Korean environmental movement', *Mobilization*, 13: 99–114.

Passy, F. (2001) 'Socializing, connecting, and the structural agency/gap. A specification of the impact of networks on participation in social movements', *Mobilization*, 6: 173–92.

Passy, F. (2003) 'Social networks matter. But how?', in Mario Diani and Doug McAdam (eds), *Social Movements and Networks*. Oxford: Oxford University Press. pp. 21–48.

Passy, F. and Giugni, M. (2000) 'Life-spheres, networks, and sustained participation in social movements. A phenomenological approach to political commitment', *Sociological Forum*, 15: 117–44.

Pavan, E. (2011) Networking Global Communication Governance. Lanham: Rowman & Littlefield.

Pedahzur, A. and Perliger, A. (2006) 'The changing nature of suicide attacks: A social network perspective', *Social Forces*, 84: 1987–2008.

Phillips, S.D. (1991) 'Meaning and structure in social movements. Mapping the network of national Canadian women's organizations', *Canadian Journal of Political Science*, 24: 755–82.

Pickvance, C. (1975) 'On the study of urban social movements', *Sociological Review*, 23: 29–49.

Pinard, M. (1968) 'Mass society and political movements: A new formulation', *American Journal of Sociology*, 73: 682–90.

Piven, F.F. and Cloward, R. (1992) 'Normalizing collective protest', in Aldon D. Morris and Carol Mueller (eds), *Frontiers in Social Movement Theory*. New Haven: Yale University Press. 301–25.

Powell, W.W. (1990) 'Neither markets nor hierarchy: Network forms of organization', *Research in Organizational Behavior*, 12: 295–336.

Rootes, C. (ed.) (2003) *Environmental Protest in Western Europe*. Oxford: Oxford University Press.

Rosenthal, N., Fingrutd, M., Ethier, M., Karant, R. and McDonald, D. (1985) 'Social movements and network analysis', *American Journal of Sociology*, 90: 1022–54.

Rosenthal, N., McDonald, D., Ethier, M., Fingrutd, M. and Karant, R. (1997) 'Structural tensions in the nineteenth century women's movement', *Mobilization*, 2: 21–46.

Routledge, P. (2003) 'Convergence space: Process geographies of grassroots globalization networks', *Transactions of the Institute of British Geographers*, 28: 333–49.

Routledge, P., Cumbers, A. and Nativel, C. (2007) 'Grassrooting network imaginaries: Relationality, power, and mutual solidarity in global justice networks', *Environment and Planning A*, 39: 2575–92.

Routledge, P., Cumbers, A. and Nativel, C. (2008) 'The entangled geographies of global justice networks', *Progress in Human Geography*, 32: 183–201.

Routledge, P., Nativel, C. and Cumbers, A. (2006) 'Entangled logics and grassroots imaginaries of global justice networks', *Environmental Politics*, 15: 839–59.

Rucht, D. (2004) 'Movement allies, adversaries, and third parties', in David Snow, Sarah Soule, and Hanspeter Kriesi (eds), *The Blackwell Companion to Social Movements*. Oxford: Blackwell. pp. 197–216.

Sandell, R. (1999) 'Organizational life aboard the moving bandwagons: A network analysis of dropouts from a Swedish temperance organization, 1896–1937', *Acta Sociologica*, 42: 3–15.

Sandell, R. (2001) 'Organizational growth and ecological constraints: The growth of social movements in Sweden, 1881 to 1940', *American Sociological Review*, 66: 672–93.

Sandell, R. and Stern, C. (1988) 'Group size and the logic of collective action: A network analysis of a Swedish temperance movement 1896–1937', *Rationality and Society*, 10: 327–45.

Schlosberg, D. (2002) *Environmental Justice and the New Pluralism*. Oxford: Oxford University Press.

Schmitt-Beck, R. (1989) 'Organizational interlocks between new social movements and traditional elite', *European Journal of Political Research*, 17: 583–98.

Schurman, R. and Munro, W. (2006) 'Ideas, thinkers, and social networks: The process of grievance construction in the anti-genetic engineering movement', *Theory and Society*, 35: 1–38.

Shumate, M., Fulk, J. and Monge, P. (2005) 'Predictors of the international HIV-AIDS INGO network over time', *Human Communication Research*, 31: 482–510.

Simmel, G. (1908 [1955]) 'The web of group affiliations', in *Conflict and the Web of Group Affiliations*. New York: Free Press.

Smilde, D. (2005) 'A qualitative comparative analysis of conversion to Venezuelan evangelicalism: How networks matter', *American Journal of Sociology*, 111: 757–96.

Smith, J. (2002) 'Bridging global divides? Strategic framing and solidarity in transnational social movement organizations', *International Sociology*, 17: 505–28.

Smith, J. (2005) 'Building bridges or building walls? Explaining regionalization among transnational social movement organizations', *Mobilization*, 10: 251–70.

Smith, J. (2008) *Social Movements for Global Democracy*. Baltimore, MD: John Hopkins University Press.

Snow, D.A., Zurcher, L.A. and Ekland-Olson, S. (1980) 'Social networks and social movements: A microstructural approach to differential recruitment', *American Sociological Review*, 45: 787–801.

Stark, R. and Bainbridge, W.S. (1980) 'Networks of faith: Interpersonal bonds and recruitment to cults and sects', *American Journal of Sociology*, 85: 1376–95.

Stevenson, W.B. and Greenberg, D. (2000) 'Agency and social networks: Strategies of action in a social structure of position, opposition, and opportunity', *Administrative Science Quarterly*, 45: 651–78.

Takacs, K., Janky, B. and Flache, A. (2008) 'Collective action and network change', *Social Networks*, 30: 177–89.

Tarrow, S. (1998) *Power in Movement*. Cambridge: Cambridge University Press.

Tilly, C. (1978) *From Mobilization to Revolution*. Reading, MA: Addison/Wesley.

Tilly, C. (2004) *Social Movements 1768–2004*. Boulder, CO: Paradigm.

Tilly, C. and Wood, L. (2003) 'Contentious connections in Great Britain, 1828–1834', in Mario Diani and Doug McAdam (eds), *Social Movements and Networks*. Oxford: Oxford University Press. pp. 147–70.

Tindall, D.B. (2002) 'Social networks, identification and participation in an environmental movement: Low-medium cost activism within the British Columbia Wilderness Preservation Movement', *Canadian Review of Sociology and Anthropology*, 39: 413–52.

Tindall, D.B. (2004) 'Social movement participation over time: An ego-network approach to micro-mobilization', *Sociological Focusm*, 37: 163–84.

Tindall, D.B., Davies, S. and Mauboules, C. (2003) 'Activism and conservation behavior in an environmental movement: The contradictory effects of gender', *Society & Natural Resources*, 16: 909–32.

Vala, C.T. and O'Brien, K.J. (2007) 'Attraction without networks: Recruiting strangers to unregistered Protestantism in China', *Mobilization*, 12: 79–94.

Van Aelst, P. and Walgraave, S. (2004) 'New media, new movements? The role of the Internet in shaping the "anti-globalization" movement', in Wim van de Donk, Brian Loader, Paul Nixon, and Dieter Rucht (eds), *Cyberprotest. New Media, Citizens and Social Movements*. London: Routledge. pp. 97–122.

van de Donk, E., Loader, B., Nixon, P. and Rucht, D. (eds) (2004) *Cyberspace Protest*. London: Routledge.

van Dyke, N. and McCammon, H. (ed.) (2010) *Social Movement Coalitions*. Minneapolis: University of Minnesota Press.

Vasi, I.B. (2004) 'The fist of the working class: The social movements of Jiu Valley miners in post-socialist Romania', *East European Politics and Societies*, 18: 132–57.

Vasi, I.B. (2006) 'Organizational environments, framing processes, and the diffusion of the program to address global climate change among local governments in the United States', *Sociological Forum*, 21: 439–66.

Viterna, J.S. (2006) 'Pulled, pushed, and persuaded: Explaining women's mobilization into the Salvadoran guerrilla army', *American Journal of Sociology*, 112: 1–45.

Walgrave, S. and Massens, J. (2000) 'The making of the White March: The mass media as mobilizing alternative to movement organizations', *Mobilization*, 5: 217–39.

Zuckerman, A.S. (ed.) (2005) *The Social Logics of Politics*. Philadelphia: Temple University Press.

17

Crime and Social Network Analysis

Peter J. Carrington

Applications of social network analysis in the study of crime fall mainly into three topic areas: the influence of the personal network on ego's delinquency or crime, the influence of neighborhood networks on crime in the neighborhood, and the organization of criminal groups and activities. Of course, the literature is not so neatly organized as this scheme suggests – even the boundaries of the relevant literature are fuzzy – but the following account is organized around these categories, while acknowledging the instances of work that straddle them, or lie only partly within them.

INFLUENCE OF PERSONAL NETWORKS ON DELINQUENCY AND CRIME

The most common use of social network analysis in criminology has been in analyses of the effects of personal networks on adolescents' delinquency (and, to a lesser extent, on adults' crime). Almost all of this research is based, explicitly or implicitly, on one or both of two theories of crime and delinquency: differential association theory and social control theory.

Differential association theory

According to this theory of delinquency, first formulated in 1939 by Edwin Sutherland (1939; Sutherland et al., 1992), criminal attitudes

and behavior are not innate, but are learned from "intimate personal groups." According to the sixth proposition of this theory, the likelihood that a child or adolescent will be delinquent is affected by the relative strength of criminal and anticriminal "definitions" (i.e., norms) among his or her close associates:

> 6. *A person becomes delinquent because of an excess of definitions favorable to violation of law over definitions unfavorable to violation of law.* This is the principle of differential association. It refers to both criminal and anticriminal associations and involves counteracting forces. (Sutherland et al., 1992: 89)

Later reformulations of differential association theory have resulted in the "social learning" theory (Burgess and Akers, 1966) and "peer influence" theory of delinquency (Warr, 1993, 2002): the latter claiming that "peer influence is the *principal proximate cause* of most criminal conduct" (Warr, 2002: 136; emphasis in the original).

Consistently strong empirical correlations between subjects' delinquency and that of their friends or "peer group," even in the presence of controls for other factors, has been interpreted as strong support for differential association theory (Shoemaker, 2005: 152; Warr, 2002: 76). However, the theory has been criticized on the grounds (among others) of the difficulty of measuring the relative strength of pro- and anticriminal definitions among ego's associates (Shoemaker, 2005: 151; see also "Measuring peers' delinquency" later).

Sutherland's seventh proposition offered some guidance on this issue:

7. *Differential associations may vary in frequency, duration, priority, and intensity.* (Sutherland et al., 1992: 89)

Luckenbill commented in 1992 on the measurement issue:

In a precise description of the criminal behavior of a person, these modalities would be rated in quantitative form and a mathematical ratio would be reached. A formula in this sense has not been developed, and the development of such a formula would be extremely difficult. (Sutherland et al., 1992: 89)

To anyone familiar with social network analysis, its potential usefulness in operationalizing the main concepts in differential association theory is obvious. The "intimate personal groups" in which criminal learning occurs are simply ego's personal network (Chua et al., this volume). Measuring the "frequency, duration, priority, and intensity" of associations is a staple of personal networks research (Hanneman and Riddle, this volume). Evaluating communication processes and the diffusion of information in networks are staples of social network research on communication and information diffusion (e.g., Monge and Contractor, 2003; Myers, 2000; Shih and Chang, 2009; Valente, 1995). Differential association theory can be seen as a specific instance of the more general network theory of social learning, that ego's attitudes and behavior are affected by the attitudes and behavior of the members of his or her personal network, and the effects are conditioned by the characteristics of the network. This would be consistent with Sutherland's own insistence that "the processes which result in systematic criminal behavior are fundamentally the same in form as the processes which result in systematic lawful behavior" (cited in Warr, 2002: 75).

Social control theory

Social control theory, first formulated by Hirschi (1969), proposes that the propensity for antisocial, deviant, or criminal behavior is innate but is normally restrained by internalized and external informal social control, due to bonding to social control agents such as parents, family, peers, school, and community – that is, to the social integration of the individual. Thus, delinquency and crime are a result of weak social bonds.

Social control theory has been interpreted in network terms to imply that delinquents tend to be social isolates, rejecting and being rejected by their peers (Ekland-Olson, 1983: 275–76) and other potential agents of informal social control, and conversely that nondelinquents tend to be well connected with such agents. This is in clear contrast with differential association theory, which characterizes both delinquents and nondelinquents as being embedded in peer and family networks but with differing normative balances. The contradictory implications of the two theories of delinquency have motivated social network research researchers to attempt to assess the level of empirical support for each theory.

Krohn's network theory of delinquency

Marvin Krohn's (1986) network theory represents an early attempt to apply social network analysis explicitly to the explanation of delinquency. Krohn's theory combines elements of social control and differential association theories of delinquency. According to this theory, the social cohesion of ego's personal network, as indicated by its multiplexity and density, affects both ego's social integration (as in social control theory) and the balance of influences of procriminal and anticriminal definitions in the network (as in differential association theory). At the macrostructural level, the delinquency rate of a community will be inversely related to the density and multiplexity of its social networks, which are affected by social structural characteristics of the community, such as population density, geographic mobility, and the social stratification system.

Krohn's theory treats attachment to parents, teachers, and other adults as an aspect of social bonding, and therefore as an element of social control theory, not of differential association theory. This distinction between adults and age peers is consistent with much of the subsequent research that tests or employs differential association theory, whether informed by social network analysis or not: the "intimate personal groups" within which the balance of procriminal and anticriminal definitions are measured are often assumed to be exclusively composed of the young person's age peers, or "friends," so that differential association theory is treated as being equivalent to peer influence theory (Warr, 2002: 73). Relationships with parents and family are taken as evidence of social bonding. However, Sutherland's formulation of differential association theory does not distinguish between adult agents of social control such as parents, and the young person's age peers (Sutherland et al., 1992: 89; Warr, 2002: 73). Differential association research that is more informed by social network analysis considers the influence of persons in *any* role vis-à-vis ego, using the type and strength of the tie, not generational equivalence, as the criterion of inclusion in the personal network.

Krohn's network theory of delinquency has received limited attention. Following Friday and Hage (1976), Krohn et al. (1988) found that multiplexity or role overlap in personal networks, including parents and friends, partly explained the cigarette smoking behavior of high school students in a Midwestern city: youth who participated jointly with their parents or friends in activities, such as homework, athletics, church, and membership in other organizations, were less likely to smoke cigarettes. Haynie (2001) found that personal network density is an important conditioner of the association between ego's and peers' delinquency: the relationship was stronger for egos with higher-density networks. Going beyond Krohn's theory, she found that ego's centrality and popularity also condition the relationship, but less so than network density: the relationship is stronger for egos with higher centrality and higher popularity.

Network composition

Most of the research that refers to social networks in relation to differential association or social control theory is concerned only with the *composition* of the peer network – the number or proportion of delinquent friends and (in some cases) of family members – and ignores its structural features (e.g., Capowich et al., 2001; Deptula and Cohen, 2004; Elliott and Menard, 1996; Giordano et al., 1993; Gutierrez-Lobos et al., 2001; Hanson and Scott, 1996; Laird et al., 1999; Lee, 2004; McCarthy and Hagan, 1995; Weerman and Bijleveld, 2007). In one of the more sophisticated attempts to measure the balance of criminal and anticriminal definitions in the peer network, Haynie (2002) found that it is the proportion of friends who are delinquent that is most strongly correlated with ego's delinquency, rather than the number of delinquent friends, the average level of delinquency of friends, or the total level of friends' delinquency. She also found that consensus (either pro- or antidelinquency) in the peer network was most strongly associated with ego's own behavior. Bruinsma (1992) is a rare example of differential association research that includes parents as possible sources of deviant definitions in ego's personal network. Using data on 1,096 Dutch

secondary school students and stepwise path analysis, he found that frequency of contact with deviant parents and with deviant peers both have positive influences on the respondent's formation of positive definitions of deviant behavior, which in turn increases the frequency of the respondent's criminal behavior; however, the impact of deviant friends was much greater. Lonardo et al. (2009) found that parents' and peers' deviance were associated with adolescents' deviance, but having a deviant romantic partner was especially influential.

Measuring peers' delinquency

Research on delinquent peers traditionally relied on the respondent's assessment of his or her peers' delinquency. This approach has been criticized for vulnerability to measurement error due to limitations on the respondents' ability to observe and remember their peers' delinquent attitudes and behavior, and also to bias arising from projection by respondents of their own attitudes and behavior onto their peers; thus inflating the crucial correlation between the delinquency of self and of peers (see Meldrum et al., 2009, for a review of this issue). Research comparing the size of the correlations obtained from respondents' reports and peers' own reports of their delinquency has found that the correlation is indeed considerably larger when respondents' reports are used. Weerman and Smeenk (2005: 518) interpret this finding to mean that the true correlation lies somewhere between the two estimates. This is an instance of the more general measurement problem in research on egocentric networks: that "proxy reports" provided by ego of alters' characteristics and behavior are of variable accuracy, depending on the type of information solicited (see Marsden, this volume, for a discussion).

Gender composition

A somewhat different approach to the relationship between peer network composition and ego's delinquency is to examine the gender composition of the peer network. The general idea is that female-dominated networks tend to provide "more social control, fewer opportunities and less motivation for offending and may therefore discourage crime," for both males and females, but especially for females (McCarthy et al., 2004). This suggests social control theory, but the effect of female-dominated networks may also be due to differential association, as females are much less criminal than males. Lacasse et al. (2003) found that the gender composition of adolescents' friendship networks affects the incidence of potentially offensive sexual behavior but not the subject's tolerance of such behavior. Haynie and Piquero

(2006) found that the relationship between the onset of puberty and violent victimization is moderated by the gender composition of boys' personal networks: the relationship is weaker for boys with a higher proportion of girls in their network. For girls, no moderating effect of network composition was found. In a sample of adult heroin injectors in Baltimore, Curry and Latkin (2003: 482) found that "for females but not males, a higher number of females in one's network was associated with a lower frequency of arrests." Lichtenstein (1997) found that in a small sample of Alabama women incarcerated for drug-related crimes, their personal networks comprised mainly male intimates, and the use of crack cocaine was attributed to the influence of these male intimates. Weerman and Bijleveld (2007) found that differences in the personal networks of non-, minor, and serious delinquents in a sample of Dutch high school students were mainly due to cross-gender friendships. Delinquent students appeared to be more popular than nondelinquents in cross-gender friendships (girls nominated delinquent boys more often, boys nominated delinquent girls more often), while non-, minor, and serious delinquents were on average not more or less popular among students from their own gender.

Types of ties

Houtzager and Baerveldt (1999) differentiated different types of ties among Dutch high school students. They found that a respondent's level of self-reported delinquency was not associated with the emotional closeness of peer relations, the occurrence of positive relations such as practical support, emotional support, friendship and intimate friendship, or with unpopularity. Using the same data, Baerveldt et al. (2004) analyzed 10 different types of ties and found no evidence that delinquents have poorer peer relationships, and evidence of a correlation between ego's level of delinquency and that of both weakly and strongly tied peers – implicitly suggesting support for differential association theory but not for social control theory. Weerman and Smeenk (2005) found that both "regular friends" and "best friends" in the networks of Dutch high school students affect ego's delinquency, with little difference in strength of effect.

Patacchini and Zenou (2008) analyzed data from the AddHealth survey within the framework of Granovetter's (1973) "strength of weak ties" theory. Granovetter proposed that the individuals to whom one is weakly tied are more likely to be sources of influence for change than those to whom one is more strongly tied. Strong ties, such as family and close friends, tend to know one another and therefore tend to form closed communication circles, in which the same information and attitudes are recycled. Furthermore, following the principle of homophily (McPherson et al., 2001; and see below, under "Gangs, groups and networks"), one's close friends tend to hold attitudes and opinions similar to one's own. In contrast, persons to whom one is weakly tied, such as acquaintances, school friends and colleagues, and more distant family members, are more likely to have attitudes that are less congruent with one's own and to belong to social circles that one is not a member of. Thus, weak ties are more likely to form "bridges" between otherwise unconnected social circles and consequently to be sources of new information and attitudes. In relation to delinquency, Granovetter's theory implies that the close friends of nondelinquents will also be nondelinquent, and it is the weak ties of nondelinquents who are more likely to be delinquent and therefore to exert a delinquent influence. Patacchini and Zenou (2008) found support for this hypothesis: the proportion of weak versus strong ties in the friendship network was found to have a positive impact on the onset of delinquency.

Structure: centrality, cohesiveness, and bridging

Baerveldt and Snijders (1994) found no support for hypotheses concerning the relationship between ego's delinquency and segmentation in the network. Baron and Tindall (1993) found that the strength of a gang member's delinquent attitudes was positively associated with his or her centrality (betweenness and geodesic closeness) in the gang, as well as to weak conventional bonds. Pearson and West's (2003) study of the adoption of "risky behaviors" (smoking and cannabis use) by students in a Scottish high school suggests that ego's position in the peer network ("as a group member, a group peripheral or a relative isolate") and the cohesiveness of the network both have positive effects on ego's influence on other members of the network. Lee (2004) used data from the National Household Survey on Drug Abuse to examine the network positions of marijuana users, nonusers, and sellers. Users tended to cluster in subgroups that were both more central and more cohesive than those of nonusers; sellers tended to be at the center of user groups. However, the centrality and cohesiveness of groups of users varied significantly across survey sampling units.[1]

Using a cross-sectional analysis of data from the first wave of the AddHealth survey, Schreck et al. (2004) found that centrality in dense delinquent peer networks was associated with higher risk for violent victimization, while centrality in dense conventional networks had the opposite effect. McGloin and Shermer (2009) used longitudinal analysis of data from the same survey to examine the roles of network density, Bonacich centrality, and ego's involvement with the peer network, as well as ego's self-control (Gottfredson and Hirschi, 1990) and other variables on ego's future delinquency. Concerning direct network effects, McGloin and Shermer found that network density reduces delinquency and that centrality and involvement increase it; the strength of the effect of centrality is positively related to the overall level of deviance in the peer network (2009: 53). Involvement with the peer network is inversely related to ego's self-control (2009: 59). Mangino (2009: 147) found that "African American boys who are a social bridge across two or more large but cohesive peer groups are less delinquent than are their counterparts who are members of a single peer group," and this is due to the enhanced prosocial influence of parents on these bridging children.

Peer influence versus selection

The strong and consistent correlation observed between adolescents' delinquency and that of their peers is susceptible of at least three interpretations: (1) differential association – that peers influence ego's delinquency; (2) selection (homophily), or the "birds of a feather [flock together]" theory – that individuals prefer to associate with people who are similar to them; or (3) neither, because the correlation is spurious. Researchers have used longitudinal social network analyses to assess the relative explanatory power of the influence and selection theories. The consensus is that the two processes reinforce each other through interaction (as Thornberry [1987] proposed), but the evidence on the relative contribution of each process to the correlation is mixed.

Structural equation modeling of a three-wave cross-lagged panel model of data from the National Youth Survey led Elliott and Menard (1996) to conclude that peer influence leading to delinquency tends to precede and be stronger than selection of delinquent peers. However, another cross-lagged panel model analysis of data from the same survey found that "the effect of delinquency on peer associations is larger than that of peer associations on delinquency" (Matsueda and Anderson, 1998). Brook et al. (2003) found that marijuana use at T1 in a sample of Colombian adolescents predicted having marijuana-using friends at T2 (i.e., selection).

Espelage et al. (2007) used $p*$ modeling (Robins, this volume) to study the microstructures in a seventh-grade friendship network and their relationships with bullying behavior; they found evidence of both homophily (selection) and peer influence.

From their analyses of a two-wave survey of Dutch high school students, Snijders and Baerveldt (2003) found that similarity in delinquency affects both tie formation and tie dissolution. This provides support for the selection hypothesis, but the study did not test the influence hypothesis. Using actor-oriented social network modeling ("SIENA" – see Snijders, this volume) with data on students in 16 Dutch high schools, Baerveldt et al. (2008) found that influence was a "universal" process, found in all 16 schools; whereas selection operated in only four schools. The strength of selection depended on network differences between the schools. The authors suggested that the networks with significant selection were dominated by a small number of lifetime persistent delinquents. From a longitudinal analysis of a sample of Swedish adolescents, employing SIENA, Burk et al. (2007, 2008) concluded that both selection and peer influence play roles in the co-evolution of early adolescent friendship networks, but the role of peer influence is stronger.

Using data from the AddHealth survey, Haynie and Osgood (2005: 1109) found that "the normative influence of peers on delinquency is more limited than indicated by most previous studies, [and] normative influence is not increased by being more closely attached to friends or spending more time with them." They also found support for the *opportunity theory* of Osgood et al. (1996), which derives from Cohen and Felson's (1979) routine activity theory: that having delinquent friends provides more opportunities for delinquent behavior, regardless of their normative influence. Using data from the same survey, McGloin (2009) found support for a version of peer influence theory modified by balance theory: an imbalance at T1 between ego's and the best friend's level of delinquency predicts a change in ego's delinquency in the direction of the best friend's level at T2. Using SIENA to analyze data on middle-school students in Oregon, Light and Dishion (2007) tested the "confluence hypothesis": that rejection by peers leads to the formation of cliques of high-risk youth, who then reinforce one another's deviant propensities. Thus, peer rejection leads to selection of deviant peers, who influence ego's own delinquency. They found strong support for the first part of the hypothesized causal chain – that rejected youth form cliques – but only weak support for peer influence within these cliques.

Diffusion in peer networks

Kirke (1990, 1995, 2006) studied the diffusion of illicit drug use in the networks of teenagers' strong peer ties. She concluded that drug use is diffused through strong ties from users to nonusers, who then become users and potential sources of new diffusion to additional nonusers; thus, "a cycle of drug diffusion occurs in which, under specified social conditions, the structure influences individual action and individual action influences the structure" (1990: Abstract). Korobow et al. (2007) analyzed an agent-based simulation model of tax (non-) compliance incorporating social networks and found that individuals with limited knowledge of their immediate network neighbors' payoffs are more likely to be compliant than those who can factor knowledge of neighbor payoffs into their decisions.

Desistance

Personal networks have also been implicated in desistance from delinquency, crime, or drug abuse. Gainey et al. (1995) studied the personal networks of a sample of heavy cocaine users who were seeking treatment. They found that the sample had "stable and supportive conventional bonds (1995: 27) and their closest emotional ties were to nonusers. However, they were significantly more likely to have certain types of functional ties, such as lending or borrowing things or money, with users. Gainey et al. speculated that the nature of cocaine users' social networks may partly explain the decision to seek treatment. Sommers et al. (1994) found that forming new personal networks was part of the process of "getting out of the life" of female long-term street offenders. The supportiveness of the personal network was also found by Shivy et al. (2007) to be a factor influencing successful re-entry into the workforce of ex-offenders. Zhang (1998) advocates the inclusion of data on social networks in evaluation of the effectiveness of boot-camp treatments for delinquents.

There is a sizeable literature on the role of personal networks in the success of substance abuse treatment programs. The consensus finding of these studies is that the composition of the personal network – primarily the number or proportion of deviant peers – and its emotional supportiveness, especially the quality of ties with family members, have a substantial impact on the likelihood of treatment success (e.g., Griffith et al., 1998; Knight and Simpson, 1996; Skeem et al., 2009; Sung et al., 2004; Wild et al., 2006).

Reverse or complex causality

Some research has examined the effect that delinquency and crime have on ego's personal network, or the mediating role of personal networks in three-variable causal schemes. Following up earlier research results suggesting that one's occupation may affect the quality of one's personal network, Romans et al. (2001) found no differences in network quality between the networks of a convenience sample of female sex workers and those of two large community samples of age-matched women in New Zealand. Kandel and Davies (1991) found that illicit drug use led to strong bonds among young adult males but not among females. Moss et al. (2003) found that the children of drug-dependent fathers are more likely to have deviant peers from preadolescence through mid-adolescence, and speculated that these deviant affiliations may lead to the children's own antisocial behavior. Van der Poel and van de Mheen (2006) found that crack use by a sample of 16- to 24-year-olds accelerated a process of marginalization that had begun before their drug abuse. With crack use, their personal networks shrank and the proportion of crack users in them increased. Schroeder et al. (2007) found that changes in the personal network, especially partner criminality, partly mediate the effect of illicit drug use on future offending. Bernburg et al. (2006) found that deviant peer affiliations mediate the impact of juvenile justice intervention on future delinquency.

Conclusion

The differential association and social control theories of crime and delinquency both invoke the immediate micro-level social environment of the individual to explain his or her behavior. Social network analysis has been used to operationalize, or model, this environment as a *personal network*. Variations in the attributes of the personal network, such as its composition, types of ties, and structural features, have been used to explain variations in ego's delinquency or crime and to assess the competing claims of the social control and differential association theories. Much work remains to be done on measuring the relevant attributes of personal networks and on establishing causal pathways.

NEIGHBORHOOD NETWORKS

Social network analysis has also been applied to the explanation of crime at the level of the neighborhood. It has long been observed that crime rates are higher in disadvantaged and heterogeneous neighborhoods. One explanation for this phenomenon proposes that crime is caused by social disorganization, or the breakdown of informal social control, in the neighborhood, which in turn is caused by socioeconomic disadvantage, ethnic heterogeneity, and residential mobility (Shoemaker, 2005). While this explanation is usually treated as a theory in itself, it can also be seen as a neighborhood-level version of the social control theory of individual criminality. A competing explanation proposes that delinquent and criminal peer influences are stronger in disadvantaged neighborhoods; this is differential association theory but at the neighborhood level.

Social disorganization theory

The precise meaning of the mediating concept of "social disorganization" was left unspecified for a long time after the theory was first proposed by Shaw et al. (1929). Sampson (1987) argued that social disorganization is a weakening of social bonds within the community, consequently a weakening of *informal social control*. Certain structural conditions in the neighborhood, such as concentrated disadvantage, ethnic heterogeneity, and residential mobility, impair the community's ability to informally regulate behavior in the neighborhood to conform to its shared values – resulting in an increased level of crime, whether committed by residents or by outsiders (Sampson, 2006a: 49–50). Thus, social disorganization theory is a form of social control theory, but at the level of the neighborhood rather than the individual. Sampson (2004a, 2004b; Sampson et al., 1997: 918) later introduced the concept of *collective efficacy*: "defined as social cohesion among neighbors combined with their willingness to intervene on behalf of the common good." Sampson (1987: 110) and Leighton (1988: 365) suggested that this cohesion among neighbors might rest on social networks among residents of the community, and Sampson (2006b: 151–153) emphasized the role of the weak ties that are said to characterize neighborly relations in the modern city. Sampson's conceptualization of social disorganization as impaired collective efficacy is a "contextual" and "situational" view, not an individual-developmental one: ". . . whereas collective efficacy predicts the event-based rate of violence in a neighborhood, it does not necessarily predict rates of offending by neighborhood youth" (2006a: 50).

In a similar vein, Clear (2008) introduced neighborhood social networks as the intervening variable in the effect of high incarceration rates on high crime rates: high rates of incarceration of parent-aged men, concentrated in certain neighborhoods, can damage local social networks (and other prosocial neighborhood institutions), and this in turn leads to lower collective efficacy and higher community crime rates. Other researchers (e.g., Galster and Killen, 1995; Galster and Mikelsons, 1995; Kennedy et al., 1998) have also found links between neighborhood structural conditions, social networks, and crime but have relied on the concepts of social cohesion and social capital. According to Sampson (2006a: 37; see also Sampson, 2003), while social networks contribute to social cohesion, this in itself is insufficient to capture the concept of collective efficacy, which includes the additional elements of "mutual trust and shared expectations."

Differential social organization theory

Other research has found that the relationship between neighborhood networks and the neighborhood crime rate is not always the straightforward negative one implied by social control or collective efficacy theory (e.g., Friedman et al., 2007; Gayne, 2004; Triplett et al., 2003; Warner and Rountree, 1997). Pattillo (1998) showed that in a black, middle-class community in Chicago, the dense social networks attributable to home ownership and residential stability were criminogenic as well as protective. These dense networks of kin, friends, and neighbors facilitated informal social control of neighborhood youth, consistent (but inversely) with social disorganization theory, but also facilitated the integration of local criminals and their criminogenic influence. This finding suggests support also for differential association and peer influence theories but at the level of the neighborhood: some types of neighborhoods are differentially likely to foster an excess of procriminal over anticriminal definitions via their criminogenic networks of deviant adolescents and adults.

Matsueda (2006) theorized the varying composition, structure, and prosocial versus antisocial effects of neighborhood social networks in terms of Sutherland's (1939) little-known theory of differential social organization – the "sociological counterpart to his social psychological theory of differential association" (Matsueda 2006: 3):

Society has become organized in such a way that a premium has been placed both on perpetrating crime and on refraining from crime. An individual may now be a member of a group organized for crime and at the same time be a member of a group organized against crime. (Sutherland et al., 1992: 105–6)

In other words, differential social organization at the neighborhood level leads to differential association at the individual level.

Consistent with this theory, Browning et al. (2004) found that social networks in Chicago neighborhoods characterized by a high level of social organization and a high level of crime play a dual role: promotion of prosocial collective efficacy but also provision of social capital to offenders. James et al. (2004) analyzed data from semi-structured interviews with a random sample of 24 women in the American CASAWORKS substance abuse program and found that residence in poor neighborhoods exposed women to local law-breaking and substance-abusing networks, while at the same time limiting their access to supportive, prosocial networks. Harding (2009) compared the age composition of adolescent boys' social networks and their criminogenic influence in neighborhoods with varying levels of disadvantage. He found that the boys in more disadvantaged neighborhoods were more likely to spend most of their time with older males and that this resulted in "cross-cohort socialization" into crime.

Conclusion

The social disorganization and differential social organization theories that explain the rates of crime and delinquency in neighborhoods can be seen as the neighborhood-level analogues of the social control and differential association theories of individual crime and delinquency. Social network analysis has been used to model neighborhood networks, and variations in the attributes of neighborhood networks have been used to explain variations in their rates of crime and delinquency.

In Sutherland's differential social organization theory, structural aspects of the neighborhood such as disadvantage, heterogeneity, and residential mobility, are exogenous variables that affect the balance of antisocial and prosocial influences in neighborhood networks, which in turn affect neighborhood crime rates. This theory and associated research can therefore be subsumed under the influence of personal networks on individual criminality, and social network research in this tradition generally analyzes the characteristics of personal networks of potential delinquents and criminals, as outcomes of exogenous structural conditions.

But social disorganization theory, in its modern version as Sampson's collective efficacy theory, is radically different. Collective efficacy theory and research sees neighborhood networks as *networks of (prosocial) residents*, which vary, according to exogenous structural conditions, in their efficacy in exerting informal social control of crime and delinquency in the neighborhood – whether due to locals or to outsiders. In this theory, the social control that reduces neighborhood crime is exerted not through the personal networks of potential delinquents or criminals but through the personal networks of prosocial residents, who are seen as putative social control agents. The implication for collective efficacy research using social network analysis is that it is not the attributes of the personal networks of potential delinquents and criminals that explain neighborhood crime but the attributes of the whole network existing among the residents of the neighborhood, particularly its cohesion and its capacity for the mobilization of collective action.

A major conceptual difficulty in collective efficacy theory, as some of the cited research suggests, is that the population of the neighborhood cannot be divided so neatly into potential delinquents and criminals, and prosocial residents who are potential social control agents; many, if not most, residents fall into both categories, as each individual experiences some balance of prosocial and antisocial definitions. Furthermore, the whole network of the neighborhood contains ties not only among the supposedly prosocial residents, but also among the supposedly antisocial residents who are potential delinquents or criminals, and finally, between members of these nonmutually exclusive groupings. As Sweetser (1942: 533) put it,

. . . that many boys in the most delinquent areas fail to absorb the delinquent "tradition" and remain law-abiding is thus possible if the culture of the delinquency area be conceived in terms of the spatial interpenetration of a delinquent and a law-abiding tradition, perpetuated by differential acquaintance and association among neighbors.

A methodological difficulty of research on neighborhood networks is that it is extremely difficult to collect data on the attributes of, and ties among, the population of the whole neighborhood. In practice, this research has relied on the personal networks of samples of residents. However, inference from sampled personal networks to whole networks is by no means straightforward (Frank, this volume). More research is needed that addresses these conceptual and methodological issues.

CRIMINAL NETWORKS

Social network analysis is also used to model the social organization of crime. Network models are employed in this literature to provide static and dynamic representations of criminal groups and criminal activities. This research tends to be exploratory and descriptive rather than theory-testing, although two theoretical issues underlie much of it:

1   What intra- and inter-organizational network structures emerge in response to various task-related and environmental contingencies?
2   What are the performance-related consequences of the adoption of various intra- and inter-organizational network structures? (Here, "performance" refers mainly to indicators of organizational success, such as profitability, longevity, etc.)

These are also two of the fundamental questions in the sociology of organizations (e.g., Aldrich, 1979; Handel, 2003; Perrow, 1986) and of industrial organization studies (e.g., Pepall et al., 2008; Williamson, 1975), and social network analysis is used in the study of criminal networks in ways that parallel its applications in those disciplines (e.g., Burt, 1983, 1992, 2000; Carrington, 1981; Cross and Parker, 2004; Kilduff and Krackhardt, 2008; White, 1981, 2002).

Waring (2002: 43) has argued that the nature of criminal activity makes it best conceptualized as a network form of organization, rather than other forms, such as the hierarchy or market, and that criminal activity is therefore subsumed within a broader class of activities organized as networks, including policy coalitions, joint ventures, movie projects, friendships, and business, political, and community elites. Felson (2009) identified four levels of criminal cooperation, ranging from "primordial clusters" to "an extended patrimonial system."

A key difference between network research on criminal networks and on peer influence and neighborhood networks is that, in principle, criminal networks include only people who are already involved in criminal activity, so the research questions involve not the etiology of crime, but its organization and the causes and consequences thereof. Also, in contrast to peer network studies, criminal network analyses are usually of whole networks rather than of personal or egocentric networks: that is, the networks are generally not conceptually centered on individuals, but comprise entire criminal groups, however defined. (However, these "whole networks" are often assembled from egocentric network data arising from police investigations [Renée van der Hulst, personal communication].)

Gangs, groups, and networks

Studies reviewed in this section mainly deal with applications of social network analysis to criminal groups that have fewer members than those studied under the rubric of "organized crime," and commit more localized and relatively unsophisticated "street crime." Many of these studies concern "youth gangs" or "delinquent groups," which are further distinguished from organized crime not only by the age of the members but also by the presumed motives for participation: primarily instrumental in the case of organized crime, but a mix of instrumental and expressive motives in the case of youth gangs.

Analysis of sociograms and sociomatrices (Hanneman and Riddle, this volume), recording subjects' friends or companions (and co-offenders), has a long history in the study of criminal organization: indeed, it was Moreno's invention of this technique to study the social structure of incarcerated offenders at Sing Sing prison (1932) and the Hudson School for Girls (1934) that is identified by many historians as the birth of social network analysis (e.g., Freeman, 2004: 7). However, Moreno's invention of sociometry is predated by Shaw and McKay's (1931: 200–221) use of a two-mode incidence matrix (Borgatti and Halgin, this volume) to study co-offending cliques.[2] Spaulding (1948) reviewed the early development of the use of the concepts and methods of social network analysis to study "cliques, gangs, and networks."

Do gangs exist?

Social network analysis has been used to address a central question in the literature on delinquent and criminal groups and gangs: Do they really exist? Or are so-called gangs really just spontaneous, temporary, and opportunistic loosely knit, shifting alliances of unorganized individuals? There is a striking parallel to the question (see below) of the degree of "organization" of so-called organized crime groups. Network analyses of putative gang members have generally found that they – like so-called organized crime groups – exhibit local clustering within larger loosely knit networks, that is, small groups with two to a dozen or so members, with varying degrees of connection to other such groups (Daly, 2005; Fleisher, 2002; Hood and Sparks, 1970; Klein and Crawford, 1967; McGloin, 2005; Reiss, 1988; Sarnecki, 1990, 2001, 2009; Short and Strodtbeck, 1965; Spergel, 1990: 203–4;

Warr, 1996, 2002: 39; Whyte, 1943). These findings motivate the use of local clustering (clique) analysis to identify delinquent groups within larger networks (e.g., Cadwallader and Cairns, 2002; Clarke-McLean, 1996; Sarnecki, 2001).

A different way of asking whether criminal groups are really groups is to analyze the temporal stability of their composition, that is, their membership. Warr, for example, writes of ". . . the extreme instability of [the membership of] most delinquent groups . . . all groups are . . . so short-lived that it may make little sense to even speak of delinquent *groups* at all . . ." (1996: 33; emphasis in the original). Other research on delinquent groups has reached similar, though not always so extreme, conclusions (Sarnecki, 1990, 2001; van Mastrigt, 2008; Warr, 1996). On the other hand, Clarke-McLean (1996) found "reasonably stable" networks among a sample of 92 incarcerated youth – perhaps because they were incarcerated.

Homophily

Network research on delinquent groups has generally found evidence of homophily (McPherson et al., 2001) in relation to age, place of residence, and criminal experience (Clarke-McLean, 1996; Daly, 2005; Sarnecki, 2001). There is strong gender homophily (Clarke-McLean, 1996), but it is weaker for female offenders (Daly, 2005; Fleisher, 2002; Sarnecki, 2001, 2004; Warr, 1996). Carrington (2002) used a probabilistic model and Canadian co-offending data to show that the lower level of homophily among female offenders is explained by the offender sex ratio, and it does not imply any preference (see also van Mastrigt, 2008). Other research on mixed-sex delinquent groups has found evidence of recruitment of girls by older males and of male influence over, and exploitation of, females (Fleisher and Krienert, 2004; but cf. Pettersson, 2005), as well as gendered criminal roles in the group (Mullins and Wright, 2003; Waring, 1993). There is racial or ethnic homophily in delinquent groups in the United States (Clarke-McLean, 1996; Daly, 2005) and, in a more complex way, in Sweden (Pettersson, 2003; Sarnecki, 2001).

Structure

Waring (1993) used data from presentence reports for white-collar criminals sentenced in U.S. federal courts during the 1980s to study the structures of white-collar co-offending networks. She constructed 377 co-offending networks involving 747 sample members, focusing on networks that had either of two configurations: the complete (sub-)network, or clique, in which all members are directly connected to one another; and the star

(sub-)network, in which a central member is connected to all other members, none of whom are connected to one another. Within these two structural types, she also distinguished networks by their size and role differentiation. She used qualitative analysis to explore why networks take on these forms and to look at the consequences of these structures for the activities of network members. In a simulation study, Calvó-Armengol and Zenou (2004) found that Nash equilibria for delinquent competition and cooperation are determined by the structure of links in the criminal network.

Morselli and Tremblay (2004) showed that nonredundancy in ego's criminal contacts affects his or her criminal success, measuring nonredundancy by the "effective size" of the egocentric criminal network (Burt, 1992). McGloin and Piquero (2010) showed that redundancy, measured by the density of ties in the egocentric criminal network, is positively associated with crime type specialization in ego's co-offenses.

Individual centrality – and its inverse, peripherality – has been used as an indicator of the extent of ego's embeddedness in a criminal group (Sarnecki, 2001, 2004). Central members tend to be the most criminally experienced and active (Sarnecki, 1990, 2001), to have the most criminal attitudes (Baron and Tindall, 1993), and to be at most risk of violent victimization (Schreck et al., 2004). Females tend to be less central than males (Sarnecki, 2004). Using data from the AddHealth Survey and Nash equilibrium analysis, Calvó-Armengol et al. found that an adolescent's Bonacich centrality in a network of delinquents "is a key determinant of her level of [delinquent] activity" (2005: 1).

McGloin (2005: 625–26) suggested that gang suppression efforts concentrate on members who are "cut-points" – that is, individuals who constitute the only connections between two individuals or groups and are therefore ideally placed as "contagion agents" for a "deterrence message." However, the effectiveness of such "key player" interdiction strategies (Borgatti, 2006) is called into question by empirical research discussed below (Milward and Raab, 2006; Morselli and Petit, 2007), suggesting the adaptability of criminal networks in the face of threats, and by simulations that treat network structure as endogenous (Easton and Karaivanov, 2009).

Intergang networks

Papachristos (2009) studied the "social structure of gang homicide" by analyzing the social network formed by gang-related homicides in Chicago in 1994. The 66 gangs whose members were involved in the homicides as perpetrators or victims were defined as the nodes of the network, and the homicides themselves defined the directed ties from the gang of the perpetrator to the gang of the victim. Longitudinal analyses supported the hypothesis of contagion (diffusion) of homicidal behavior. Structural analyses confirmed that homicides were influenced by, and in turn affected, the nature of members' gang affiliations and the dominance structure of intergang relations.

Organized crime

The distinction between organized crime and criminal gangs and groups is not clear-cut, but it points to differences in scale, reach, type of criminal activity, and motivation. The following review of network analyses of organized crime is necessarily selective; additional references are available in two recent literature reviews (Morselli, 2009b; von Lampe, 2009).

Early research in the United States on the organization of the Mafia used a formal organization or hierarchical model, epitomized by the reports in the 1950s and 1960s of the Kefauver and McClellan Committees of the U.S. Senate (Albanese, 2007: 105–6; Cressey, 1969). However, lack of fit with data on many criminal organizations and activities led to dissatisfaction with this model as being overly structured. On the other hand, the economic enterprise model (Reuter, 1983), which conceptualizes criminal businesses and markets as operating according to the same principles of economic rationality as legal business enterprises, has also been criticized for its inadequacy (Liddick, 1999) – as it has in the analysis of legal business activity (Powell, 1990; White, 1981, 2002; Williamson, 1975).

Some early research (e.g., Albini, 1971; Ianni, 1974; Ianni and Reuss-Ianni, 1972; Lupsha, 1983) suggested a network model, in which no particular structure is assumed *a priori*, but rather the social organization of the group is derived "bottom-up" (von Lampe, 2009: 94) from the observed configurations and qualities of connections and transactions among the actors, and the attributes of the actors. While network analysis makes no prior assumptions about structure, a preference for the "network model" of organized crime implies rejection of both the formal organization model and the economic model: the former having too much structure, the latter too little (Waring, 2002: 33). Thus, in the network model, criminal groups and activities are seen as "a system of loosely structured [profit-oriented] relationships" (Albini, 1971, cited in Albanese, 2007: 110). However, adoption of network analysis *methods* does not necessarily imply adoption of the net-

work *model*: for example, Natarajan (2000) used network analysis to study the organization of a cocaine trafficking group and found that it did fit the classic "corporate" type of organization.

On the other hand, in a study of wiretapped conversations among 294 members of a heroin-dealing network in New York City, combining network concepts and measures, such as cohesiveness (density), subgroups (cliques), and individuals' power (centrality), with several other forms of analysis, Natarajan (2006) concluded that this population did not form a unitary organization or "conspiracy" but was a "loosely structured network . . ., with little or no hierarchy" (189). However, while this network had little "formal organization," it did not lack what might be called "network organization": there were elements of local clustering and stratification of centrality. Similar conclusions are reached by several other recent studies of smuggling and trafficking, such as Kenney's (2007) analysis of the Colombian drug trade, Heber's (2009a) analysis of drug traffickers in Stockholm, Desroches's (2005) study of drug trafficking in Canada, Xia's (2008) review of organizational structures in Chinese organized crime, and several studies of human smuggling and trafficking (Kleemans, 2009; Lehti and Aromaa, 2006; Soudijn and Kleemans, 2009; Surtees, 2008; Zhang, 2008; Zhang and Gaylord, 1996).

Social capital

Two recurrent themes in the literature on organized crime are the related problems of trust and of access to resources. Criminal enterprise requires the cooperation and coordination of multiple actors, sometimes very distant from one another geographically, but criminal actors lack recourse to conventional legal procedures for enforcement of agreements. Thus, the issue of trust is especially salient in criminal enterprise, and social relations support trust, whether they are preexisting (e.g., family, ethnicity, friendship) or have developed in the course of criminal collaboration (Bruinsma and Bernasco, 2004; Felson, 2009; Granovetter, 1985: 492; Kleemans, 2007; Kleemans and de Poot, 2008; Kleemans and van de Bunt, 1999; Morselli, 2003, 2005; Tremblay, 1993; von Lampe and Johansen, 2004; von Lampe, 2009; Waring, 2002: 38–39; but cf. van de Bunt, 2008). Another theme is the need for connections – with suppliers, customers, and sources of funding and expertise (Morselli, 2005). Kleemans and his colleagues define the "social opportunity structure" as "social ties providing access to profitable criminal opportunities" (Kleemans and de Poot, 2008: 75) and emphasize that access to such opportunities is limited and distributed unequally over the population and over the life course (van Koppen et al., 2010). Their "social opportunity structure" is very similar to the concept of social capital. For example, Lin (2001: 19) defines social capital as "investment in social relations with expected returns in the marketplace," or alternatively, "a social asset by virtue of actors' connections and access to resources in the network or group of which they are members." Thus, Bouchard and Nguyen (2010) contrasted the payoff from the *social capital* of a sample of young cannabis cultivators, defined as "who you know – connections" or "resources in social networks," with the payoff from *criminal capital*, defined as "what you know – talent" or "[criminal] education, training, experience" (the equivalent of *human capital* in the noncriminological literature). McCarthy and Hagan (1995; Hagan, 1997; Hagan and McCarthy, 1998) linked the notions of "who" and "what" one knows by defining criminal capital as the criminal knowledge and skill that are derived from embeddedness in criminal networks.

Structure

Bruinsma and Bernasco (2004) found differences in cohesiveness (density), multiplexity, and clustering in the structures of networks operating in the Netherlands and involved in international trafficking in heroin, women, and stolen cars. Networks of heroin trafficking – a high-risk activity – were characterized by dense, multiplex ties in a single cluster. Ties among those involved in the trafficking of women and stolen cars were less dense, tended to be uniplex and instrumental, and each network had two or more clusters, connected in a chain by intermediate individuals or clusters. They concluded that these differences "appear to be related to the legal and financial risks . . . and . . . the [consequent] required level of trust" (2004: 79). Canter (2004) used partial-order scalogram analysis to compare the organization of 29 British drug-dealing, property-crime, or hooligan networks, along six dimensions of network structure. He identified three types of groups – ad hoc, oligarchies, and organized criminals – that differed on two dominant axes related to group size and leadership centrality. There was only a weak relationship between the tripartite typologies of criminal activities and of organizational structures. Heber (2009b) identified two central roles in the Swedish black market in construction labor: "fixers" and "network entrepreneurs," and described the characteristics of the networks of each. McNally and Alston (2006) used intelligence data on the associations and communications of members of three Canadian

outlaw motorcycle gangs to assess structural "weaknesses and vulnerabilities" in these groups by identifying core, peripheral, and cut-point members, and estimating overall gang cohesion and communication flow paths, based on measures of density, centrality, clustering, and bridging.

Morselli (2003, 2005) used the concept of structural holes (Burt, 1992; Hanneman and Riddle, this volume) to analyze the careers of two organized criminals, in an instance of criminal network analysis that uses personal networks rather than whole networks. In a combined crime-script and network analysis, Morselli and Roy (2008) used two measures of brokerage (Burt, 2005) – *betweenness centrality* (Hanneman and Riddle, this volume), and *brokerage leverage* (Gould and Fernandez, 1989) – to analyze two Canadian "ringing networks" involved in the sale of stolen vehicles. Morselli (2009a) used degree centrality and betweenness centrality (brokerage) to study the organization of the criminal activities of the Hells Angels motorcycle club in the province of Quebec – in particular to test the hypothesis that they exhibited the tightly structured hierarchical organization of the traditional organized crime paradigm. The results indicated that the organization of criminal activities was more complex and nuanced.

Implications for interdiction

Extending the work of Calvó-Armengol and colleagues (above), Easton and Karaivanov (2009) identified "optimal criminal networks" by finding Nash equilibria for simulated networks whose size and structure were allowed to vary (i.e., were endogenous) according to individuals' decisions concerning their level of criminal activity *and* their links to others in the network, taking into account crime-reduction efforts of the authorities. They concluded that models that assume fixed (i.e., exogenous) criminal network size and structure can produce misleading results; for example, the policy of "taking out" the key player (Borgatti, 2006) may not reduce crime, because criminals may reconfigure their network in response. Milward and Raab (2006: 333) concluded from their review of research on the responses of Al Qaeda and of Colombian cocaine traffickers to efforts by control agents to suppress them that the resilience of "dark networks" lies in their ability to "rebalance differentiation and integration mechanisms in their internal structure." Morselli and Petit (2007) reached a similar conclusion from their analysis of the reaction of a drug importation network in Montreal, Canada, to law enforcement targeting.

Methodological and programmatic work

A substantial part of the literature on criminal networks, or more generally "dark networks,"[3] consists of methodological and programmatic papers that advocate the adoption of the "network model" or the use of social network analysis to study organized crime or that explain how to do network analysis, sometimes with illustrative case studies. Classic examples are Davis (1981), Ianni and Reuss-Ianni (1990), and Sparrow (1991a, 1991b). More recent examples include McIllwain (1999), Coles (2001), Chattoe and Hamill (2005), McAndrew (2000), Robins (2009), and van der Hulst (2009). Many recent programmatic contributions present new analytic methods or software for criminal network analysis (e.g., Borgatti, 2006; Carley et al., 2002; Chen, 2002; Hadjidj et al., 2009; Hu et al., 2009; Huang, 2005; Kaza et al., 2009; Marshall et al., 2008; Oatley, 2006; Oatley et al., 2005; Oatley et al., 2008; Rhodes and Keefe, 2007; Schwartz and Rouselle, 2009; Smith and King, 2002; Stovin and Davies, 2008; Tsvetovat and Carley, 2007; Tutzauer, 2007; Xu and Chen, 2003, 2005a, 2005b; Xu et al., 2004).

Conclusion

Much of the social network research on criminal networks is exploratory and descriptive, and it seeks to give a (literally) graphic account of the structure of the networks being studied. Some research goes beyond description and explores the causes or consequences of compositional and morphological variations in criminal networks. Researchers on organized crime networks, whose members are presumed to be predominantly rational-instrumental in their behavior, have explored both task-related and environmental determinants of network attributes and also the outcomes of these attributes in terms of organizational success. Research on criminal networks has also investigated the implications of network attributes for interdiction strategies.

As van der Hulst (this volume) has pointed out in relation to network analyses of terrorism, researchers on criminal networks tend, with a few exceptions, to fall into two distinct classes, each operating under severe constraints. Academic researchers have expertise in criminological theory and research but tend to lack "domain expertise" and access to good data. Operational (crime) analysts have domain expertise and access to classified data but tend to lack the motive or training to do research on criminological issues – or may be prevented by secrecy considerations from publishing their research. More generally, accurate and comprehensive data on "dark networks" are, as the term implies, inherently difficult to obtain. The empirical research cited in this section is a testament to the ingenuity and assiduousness of the authors. Perhaps the gradual diffusion of knowledge of the value of social network analysis in the study of criminal groups will result in better access for criminologists to classified data.

DISCUSSION

The use of social network analysis in criminology is in its infancy. The great majority of so-called network studies of crime and delinquency consider only the composition, or characteristics, of the members or of the networks, and not of the structure of their relationships. Most analyses of network structures are impressionistic, relying on visual examination of sociograms, rather than being computational. Even the computational analyses tend to limit themselves to the simplest network concepts and indices, such as density and centrality. Few criminologists appreciate the usefulness of social network analysis in modeling criminological concepts and propositions, or are trained in network methods, or use network analysis software. Suitable data are difficult to obtain or to generate.

Nevertheless, a small number of criminologists are knowledgeable in the concepts and methods of social network analysis, and some have shown great ingenuity in finding or generating suitable data. They have produced a number of sophisticated and powerful criminological network analyses over the past decade. Much more needs to be done, particularly in training in social network analysis and access to data. The recent publication of the first pedagogical article on social network analysis to appear in a criminological journal (McGloin and Kirk, 2010) may be a harbinger of future developments.

NOTES

This chapter has benefited greatly from discussions at the 7th Blankensee-Colloquium, Human Capital and Social Capital in Criminal Networks, Berlin, 2008, and from bibliographic suggestions and comments on a previous draft by Sean Bergin, Martin Bouchard, Reagan Daly, Edward Kleemans, Chris Lewis, Carlo Morselli, Lynn Vincentnathan, Renée van der Hulst, Klaus von Lampe, and Frank Weerman. Preparation of this chapter was supported by a grant from the Social Sciences and Humanities Research Council of Canada.

1 For explanations of these and other network concepts, please see the chapters in this volume by Hanneman and Riddle.

2 Frank and Carrington (2007; Frank, 2001) also used a two-mode incidence matrix and a probabilistic model to estimate the "dark figures" in estimates of co-offending and individual criminal activity based on official data.

3 "Dark networks" include both criminal and terrorist networks, which are sometimes not distinct. I have included sources on "dark networks" in this chapter if they are particularly germane to the study of organized crime; for a review of the literature on social network analysis of terrorist networks, please see the chapter by van der Hulst in this volume.

REFERENCES

Albanese, J.S. (2007) *Organized Crime in Our Times*. 5th ed. Newark, NJ: LexisNexis.

Albini, J.L. (1971) *The American Mafia: Genesis of a Legend*. New York: Irvington.

Aldrich, H. (1979) *Organizations and Environments*. Englewood Cliffs, NJ: Prentice-Hall.

Baerveldt, C. and Snijders, T.A.B. (1994) 'Influences on and from the segmentation of networks: Hypotheses and tests'. *Social Networks*, 16(3): 213–32.

Baerveldt, C., Van Rossem, R., Vermande, M. and Weerman, F. (2004) 'Students' delinquency and correlates with strong and weaker ties: A study of students' networks in Dutch high schools'. *Connections*, 26(1): 11–28.

Baerveldt, C., Voelker, B. and Van Rossem, R. (2008) 'Revisiting selection and influence: An inquiry into the friendship networks of high school students and their association with delinquency'. *Canadian Journal of Criminology and Criminal Justice*, 50(5): 559–87.

Baron, S.W. and Tindall, D.B. (1993) 'Network structure and delinquent attitudes within a juvenile gang'. *Social Networks*, 15(3): 255–73.

Bernburg, J.G., Krohn, M.D. and Rivera, C.J. (2006) 'Official labeling, criminal embeddedness, and subsequent delinquency: A longitudinal test of labeling theory'. *Journal of Research in Crime and Delinquency*, 43(1): 67–88.

Borgatti, S. (2006) 'Identifying sets of key players in a social network'. *Computational & Mathematical Organization Theory*, 12(1): 21–34.

Bouchard, M. and Nguyen, H. (2010) 'Is it who you know, or how many that counts? Criminal networks and cost avoidance in a sample of young offenders'. *Justice Quarterly*, 27: 130–58.

Brook, J.S., Brook, D.W., Rosen, Z. and Rabbitt, C.R. (2003) 'Earlier marijuana use and later problem behavior in Colombian youths'. *Journal of the American Academy of Child and Adolescent Psychiatry*, 42(4): 485–92.

Browning, C.R., Feinberg, S.L. and Dietz, R.D. (2004) 'The paradox of social organization: Networks, collective efficacy, and violent crime in urban neighborhoods'. *Social Forces*, 83(2): 503–34.

Bruinsma, G.J.N. (1992) 'Differential association theory reconsidered: An extension and its empirical test'. *Journal of Quantitative Criminology*, 8: 29–49.

Bruinsma, G.J.N. and Bernasco, W. (2004) 'Criminal groups and transnational illegal markets: A more detailed examination on the basis of Social Network Theory'. *Crime Law and Social Change*, 41(1): 79–94.

Burgess, R.L. and Akers, R.L. (1966) 'A differential association-reinforcement theory of criminal behavior'. *Social Problems*, 14: 128–47.

Burk, W.J., Kerr, M. and Stattin, H. (2008) 'The co-evolution of early adolescent friendship networks, school involvement, and delinquent behaviors'. *Revue Française de Sociologie*, 49(3): 499–522.

Burk, W.J., Steglich, C.E.G. and Snijders, T.A.B. (2007) 'Beyond dyadic interdependence: Actor-oriented models for co-evolving social networks and individual behaviors'. *International Journal of Behavioral Development*, 31(4): 397–404.

Burt, R.S. (1983) *Corporate Profits and Cooptation*. New York: Academic Press.

Burt, R.S. (1992) *Structural Holes: The Social Structure of Competition*. Cambridge, MA: Harvard University Press.

Burt, R.S. (2000) 'The network structure of social capital', in Robert I. Sutton and Barry M. Staw (eds), *Research in Organizational Behavior*. Greenwich, CT: JAI Press.

Burt, R.S. (2005) *Brokerage and Closure: An Introduction to Social Capital*. Oxford: Oxford University Press.

Cadwallader, T.W. and Cairns, R.B. (2002) 'Developmental influences and gang awareness among African-American inner city youth'. *Social Development*, 11(2): 245–65.

Calvó-Armengol, A., Patacchini, E. and Zenou, Y. (2005) *Peer Effects and Social Networks in Education and Crime*. Working Paper. Vol. 645. Stockholm: Research Institute of Industrial Economics.

Calvó-Armengol, A. and Zenou, Y. (2004) 'Social networks and crime decisions: The role of social structure in facilitating delinquent behavior'. *International Economic Review*, 45(3): 939–58.

Canter, D. (2004) 'A partial order scalogram analysis of criminal network structures'. *Behaviormetrika*, 31(2): 131–52.

Capowich, G.E., Mazerolle, P. and Piquero, A. (2001) 'General strain theory, situational anger, and social networks: An assessment of conditioning influences'. *Journal of Criminal Justice*, 29(5): 445–61.

Carley, K.M., Lee, J.-S.L. and Krackhardt, D. (2002) 'Destabilizing networks'. *Connections*, 24(3): 79–92.

Carrington, P.J. (1981) 'Horizontal co-optation through corporate interlocks'. Doctoral dissertation, University of Toronto.

Carrington, P.J. (2002) 'Sex homogeneity in co-offending groups', in J. Hagberg (ed.), *Contributions to Social Network Analysis, Information Theory and Other Topics in Statistics. A Festschrift in Honour of Ove Frank*. Stockholm: Stockholm University. pp. 101–16.

Chattoe, E. and Hamill, H. (2005) 'It's not who you know – it's what you know about people you don't know that counts: Extending the analysis of crime groups as social networks'. *British Journal of Criminology,* 45(6): 860–76.

Chen, H.C. (2002) 'From digital library to digital government: A case study in crime data mapping and mining'. Digital Libraries: People, Knowledge, and Technology, Proceedings. *Lecture Notes in Computer Science,* vol. 2555. Berlin: Springer-Verlag.

Clarke-McLean, J.G. (1996) 'Social networks among incarcerated juvenile offenders'. *Social Development,* 5(2): 203–17.

Clear, T.R. (2008) 'The effects of high imprisonment rates on communities', in Michael Tonry (ed.), *Crime and Justice: A Review of Research,* vol. 37. Chicago: University of Chicago Press. pp. 97–132.

Cohen, L.E. and Felson, M. (1979) 'Social Change and Crime Rate Trends: A Routine Activity Approach'. *American Sociological Review,* 44: 588–608.

Coles, N. (2001) 'It's not what you know – it's who you know that counts. Analysing serious crime groups as social networks'. *British Journal of Criminology,* 41(4): 580–94.

Cressey, D.R. (1969) *Theft of the Nation.* New York: Harper Row.

Cross, R.L. and Parker, A. (2004) *The Hidden Power of Social Networks: Understanding How Work Really Gets Done in Organizations.* Cambridge, MA: Harvard Business Press.

Curry, A.D. and Latkin, C.A. (2003) 'Gender differences in street economy and social network correlates of arrest among heroin injectors in Baltimore, Maryland'. *Journal of Urban Health,* 80: 482–93.

Daly, R.M. (2005) 'Delinquent networks in Philadelphia: The structure of co-offending among juveniles'. Ph.D. thesis, University of Pennsylvania.

Davis, R.H. (1981) 'Social network analysis: An aid in conspiracy investigations'. *FBI Law Enforcement Bulletin,* 50(12): 11–19.

Deptula, D.P. and Cohen, R. (2004) 'Aggressive, rejected, and delinquent children and adolescents: A comparison of their friendships'. *Aggression and Violent Behavior* 9(1): 75–104.

Desroches, F.J. (2005) *The Crime That Pays: Drug Trafficking and Organized Crime in Canada.* Toronto: Canadian Scholars' Press.

Easton, S.T. and Karaivanov, A.K. (2009) 'Understanding optimal criminal networks'. *Global Crime,* 10(1): 41–65.

Ekland-Olson, S. (1983) 'Deviance, social control and social networks'. *Research in Law, Deviance and Social Control,* 4: 271–99.

Elliott, D.S. and Menard, S. (1996) 'Delinquent friends and delinquent behavior: Temporal and developmental patterns', in J. D. Hawkins (ed.), *Delinquency and Crime: Current Theories.* Cambridge: Cambridge University Press. pp. 28–67.

Espelage, D.L., Green, H.D., Jr. and Wasserman, S. (2007) 'Statistical analysis of friendship patterns and bullying behaviors among youth'. *New Directions for Child and Adolescent Development,* 118: 61–75.

Felson, M. (2009) 'The natural history of extended co-offending'. *Trends in Organized Crime,* 12(2): 159–65.

Fleisher, M.S. (2002) 'Doing field research on diverse gangs: Interpreting youth gangs as social networks', in C. Ronald Huff (ed.), *Gangs in America.* Thousand Oaks, CA: Sage. pp. 199–217.

Fleisher, M.S. and Krienert, J.L. (2004) 'Life-course events, social networks, and the emergence of violence among female gang members'. *Journal of Community Psychology,* 32: 607–22.

Frank, O. (2001) 'Statistical estimation of co-offending youth networks'. *Social Networks,* 23(3): 203–14.

Frank, O. and Carrington, P.J. (2007) 'Estimation of offending and co-offending using available data with model support'. *Journal of Mathematical Sociology,* 31(1): 1–46.

Freeman, L.C. (2004) *The Development of Social Network Analysis.* Vancouver, BC: Empirical Press.

Friday, P.C. and Hage, J. (1976) 'Youth crime in postindustrial societies: An integrated perspective'. *Criminology,* 14: 347–68.

Friedman, S.R., Mateu-Gelabert, P., Curtis, R., Maslow, C., Bolyard, M., Sandoval, M. and Flom, P.L. (2007) 'Social capital or networks, negotiations, and norms? A neighborhood case study'. *American Journal of Preventive Medicine,* 32(6): S160–S170.

Gainey, R.R., Peterson, P.L., Wells, E.A., Hawkins, J.D. and Catalano, R.F. (1995) 'The social networks of cocaine users seeking treatment'. *Addiction Research,* 3: 17–32.

Galster, G.C. and Killen, S.P. (1995) 'The geography of metropolitan opportunity: A reconnaissance and conceptual-framework'. *Housing Policy Debate,* 6(1): 7–43.

Galster, G.C. and Mikelsons, M. (1995) 'The geography of metropolitan opportunity: A case-study of neighborhood conditions confronting youth in Washington, DC'. *Housing Policy Debate,* 6(1): 73–102.

Gayne, M.K. (2004) 'Illicit wigmaking in eighteenth-century Paris'. *Eighteenth-Century Studies,* 38(1): 119–37.

Giordano, P.C., Cernkovich, S.A. and Demaris, A. (1993) 'The family and peer relations of black-adolescents'. *Journal of Marriage and the Family,* 55(2): 277–87.

Gottfredson, M.R. and Hirschi, T. (1990) *A General Theory of Crime.* Stanford, CA: Stanford University Press.

Gould, R.V. and Fernandez, R.M. (1989) 'Structures of mediation: A formal approach to brokerage in transaction networks', in Clifford C. Clogg (ed.), *Sociological Methodology.* Vol. 19. Oxford: Basil Blackwell. pp. 89–126.

Granovetter, M. (1973) 'Strength of weak ties'. *American Journal of Sociology,* 78(6): 1360–80.

Granovetter, M. (1985) 'Economic action and social structure: The problem of embeddedness'. *American Journal of Sociology,* 91: 481–510.

Griffith, J.D., Knight, D.K., Joe, G.W. and Simpson, D.D. (1998) 'Implications of family and peer relations for treatment engagement and follow-up outcomes: An integrative model'. *Psychology of Addictive Behaviors,* 12(2): 113–26.

Gutierrez-Lobos, K., Eher, R., Grunhut, C., Bankier, B., Schmidl-Mohl, B., Fruhwald, S. and Semler, B. (2001) 'Violent sex offenders lack male social support'.

International Journal of Offender Therapy and Comparative Criminology, 45(1): 70–82.

Hadjidj, R., Debbabi, M., Lounis, H., Iqbal, F., Szporer, A. and Benredjem, D. (2009) 'Towards an integrated email forensic analysis framework'. *Digital Investigation,* 5(3–4): 124–37.

Hagan, J. (1997) 'Crime and capitalization: Toward a developmental theory of street crime in America', in Terence P. Thornberry (ed.), *Developmental Theories of Crime and Delinquency.* Vol. 7 of *Advances in Criminological Theory.* New Brunswick, NJ: Transaction. pp. 287–308.

Hagan, J. and McCarthy, B. (1998) *Mean Streets: Youth Crime and Homelessness.* Cambridge, UK: Cambridge University Press.

Handel, M.J. (ed.) (2003) *Sociology of Organizations: Classic, Contemporary and Critical Readings.* Thousand Oaks, CA: Sage.

Hanson, R.K. and Scott, H. (1996) 'Social networks of sexual offenders'. *Psychology Crime and Law,* 2(4): 249–58.

Harding, D.J. (2009) 'Violence, older peers, and the socialization of adolescent boys in disadvantaged neighborhoods'. *American Sociological Review,* 74(3): 445–64.

Haynie, D.L. (2001) 'Delinquent peers revisited: Does network structure matter?' *American Journal of Sociology,* 106(4): 1013–57.

Haynie, D.L. (2002) 'Friendship networks and delinquency: The relative nature of peer delinquency'. *Journal of Quantitative Criminology,* 18(2): 99–134.

Haynie, D.L. and Osgood, D.W. (2005) 'Reconsidering peers and delinquency: How do peers matter?' *Social Forces,* 84(2): 1109–30.

Haynie, D.L. and Piquero, A.R. (2006) 'Pubertal development and physical victimization in adolescence'. *Journal of Research in Crime and Delinquency,* 43(1): 3–35.

Heber, A. (2009a) 'The networks of drug offenders'. *Trends in Organized Crime,* 12(1): 1–20.

Heber, A. (2009b) 'Networks of organised black market labour in the building trade'. *Trends in Organized Crime,* 12(2): 122–44.

Hirschi, T. (1969) *Causes of Delinquency.* Berkeley: University of California Press.

Hood, R. and Sparks, R. (1970) *Key Issues in Criminology.* New York: McGraw-Hill.

Houtzager, B. and Baerveldt, C. (1999) 'Just like normal: A social network study of the relation between petty crime and the intimacy of adolescent friendships'. *Social Behavior and Personality,* 27(2): 177–92.

Hu, D., Kaza, S. and Chen, H. (2009) 'Identifying significant facilitators of dark network evolution'. *Journal of the American Society for Information Science and Technology,* 60(4): 655–65.

Huang, C.Y. (2005) 'File sharing as a form of music consumption'. *International Journal of Electronic Commerce,* 9(4): 37–55.

Ianni, F.A.J. (1974) *Black Mafia: Ethnic Succession in Organized Crime.* New York: Simon and Schuster.

Ianni, F.A.J. and Reuss-Ianni, E. (1972) *A Family Business.* New York: Russell Sage Foundation.

Ianni, F.A.J. and Reuss-Ianni, E. (1990) 'Network analysis', in Paul P. Andrews, Jr. and Marilyn B. Peterson (eds), *Criminal Intelligence Analysis.* Loomis, CA: Palmer Enterprises. pp. 67–84.

James, S.E., Johnson, J. and Raghavan, C. (2004) '"I couldn't go anywhere" – Contextualizing violence and drug abuse: A social network study'. *Violence against Women,* 10(9): 991–1014.

Kandel, D. and Davies, M. (1991) 'Friendship networks, intimacy, and illicit drug-use in young adulthood: A comparison of 2 competing theories'. *Criminology,* 29(3): 441–469.

Kaza, S., Xu, J., Marshall, B. and Chen, H. (2009) 'Topological analysis of criminal activity networks: Enhancing transportation security'. *IEEE Transactions on Intelligent Transportation Systems,* 10(1): 83–91.

Kennedy, B.P., Kawachi, I. and Brainerd, E. (1998) 'The role of social capital in the Russian mortality crisis'. *World Development,* 26(11): 2029–43.

Kenney, M. (2007) 'The architecture of drug trafficking: Network forms of organisation in the Colombian cocaine trade'. *Global Crime,* 8(3): 233–59.

Kilduff, M. and Krackhardt, D. (2008) *Interpersonal Networks in Organizations: Cognition, Personality, Dynamics, and Culture.* Cambridge, UK: Cambridge University Press.

Kirke, D.M. (1990) 'Teenage drug abuse: An individualistic and structural analysis'. Ph.D. thesis, University College, Dublin.

Kirke, D.M. (1995) 'Teenage peer networks in the community as sources of social problems: A sociological perspective', in T.S. Brugha (ed.), *Social Support and Psychiatric Disorder: Research Findings and Guidelines for Clinical Practice.* Cambridge: Cambridge University Press.

Kirke, D.M. (2006) *Teenagers and Substance Use.* New York: Palgrave-Macmillan.

Kleemans, E.R. (2007) 'Organized crime, transit crime, and racketeering. Crime and justice in the Netherlands', in Michael Tonry and Catrien Bijleveld (eds), *Crime and Justice: A Review of Research,* vol. 35. Chicago: University of Chicago Press. pp. 163–215.

Kleemans, E.R. (2009) 'Human smuggling and human trafficking', in Michael Tonry (ed.), *The Oxford Handbook of Crime and Public Policy.* Oxford: Oxford University Press.

Kleemans, E.R. and van de Bunt, H.G. (1999) 'Social embeddedness of organized crime', *Transnational Organized Crime,* 5(1): 19–36.

Kleemans, E.R. and de Poot, C.J. (2008) 'Criminal careers in organized crime and social opportunity structure'. *European Journal of Criminology,* 5(1): 69–98.

Klein, M.W. and Crawford, L.Y. (1967) 'Groups, gangs, and cohesiveness'. *Journal of Research in Crime and Delinquency,* 4(1): 63–75.

Knight, D.K. and Simpson, D.D. (1996) 'Influences of family and friends on client progress during drug abuse treatment'. *Journal of Substance Abuse,* 8(4): 417–29.

Korobow, A., Johnson, C. and Axtell, R. (2007) 'An agent-based model of tax compliance with social networks'. *National Tax Journal,* 60: 589–610.

Krohn, M.D. (1986) 'The web of conformity: A network approach to the explanation of delinquent behavior'. *Social Problems,* 33(6): S81–S93.

Krohn, M.D., Massey, J.L. and Zielinski, M. (1988) 'Role overlap, network multiplexity, and adolescent deviant-behavior'. *Social Psychology Quarterly,* 51(4): 346–356.

Lacasse, A., Purdy, K.T. and Mendelson, M.J. (2003) 'The mixed company they keep: Potentially offensive sexual behaviours among adolescents'. *International Journal of Behavioral Development,* 27(6): 532–40.

Laird, R.D., Pettit, G.S., Dodge, K.A. and Bates, J.E. (1999) 'Best friendships, group relationships, and antisocial behavior in early adolescence'. *Journal of Early Adolescence,* 19: 413–37.

Lee, J.S. (2004) 'Generating networks of illegal drug users using large samples of partial ego-network data'. Intelligence and Security Informatics, Proceedings. *Lecture Notes in Computer Science,* vol. 3073. Berlin: Springer-Verlag.

Lehti, M. and Aromaa, K. (2006) 'Trafficking for sexual exploitation', in Michael Tonry (ed.), *Crime and Justice: A Review of Research,* 34: 133–227.

Leighton, B. (1988) 'The community concept in criminology – Toward a social network approach'. *Journal of Research in Crime and Delinquency,* 25(4): 351–74.

Lichtenstein, B. (1997) 'Women and crack-cocaine use: A study of social networks and HIV risk in an Alabama jail sample'. *Addiction Research,* 5(4): 279–96.

Liddick, D. (1999) 'The enterprise "model" of organized crime: Assessing theoretical propositions'. *Justice Quarterly,* 16(2): 403–30.

Light, J.M. and Dishion, T.J. (2007) 'Early adolescent antisocial behavior and peer rejection: A dynamic test of a developmental process'. *New Directions for Child and Adolescent Development,* 118: 77–89.

Lin, N. (2001) *Social Capital.* Cambridge, UK: Cambridge University Press.

Lonardo, R.A., Giordano, P.C., Longmore, M.A. and Manning, W.D. (2009) 'Parents, friends, and romantic partners: Enmeshment in deviant networks and adolescent delinquency involvement'. *Journal of Youth and Adolescence,* 38(3): 367–83.

Lupsha, P. (1983) 'Networks versus networking: Analysis of an organized crime group', in G. Waldo (ed.), *Career Criminals.* Beverly Hills, CA: Sage. pp. 59–87.

Mangino, W. (2009) 'The downside of social closure: Brokerage, parental influence, and delinquency among African American boys'. *Sociology of Education,* 82(2): 147–72.

Marshall, B., Chen, H. and Kaza, S. (2008) 'Using importance flooding to identify interesting networks of criminal activity'. *Journal of the American Society for Information Science and Technology,* 59(13): 2099–114.

Matsueda, R.L. (2006) 'Differential social organization, collective action, and crime'. *Crime Law and Social Change,* 46: 3–33.

Matsueda, R.L. and Anderson, K. (1998) 'The dynamics of delinquent peers and delinquent behavior'. *Criminology,* 36(2): 269–308.

McAndrew, D. (2000) 'The structural analysis of criminal networks', in David Canter and Laurence Alison (eds), *The Social Psychology of Crime: Groups, Teams and Networks,* vol. III. Aldershot, UK: Ashgate. pp. 51–94.

McCarthy, B., Felmlee, D. and Hagan, J. (2004) 'Girl friends are better: Gender, friends, and crime among school and street youth'. *Criminology,* 42(4): 805–35.

McCarthy, B. and Hagan, J. (1995) 'Getting into street crime: The structure and process of criminal embedded-ness'. *Social Science Research,* 24(1): 63–95.

McGloin, J.M. (2005) 'Policy and intervention considerations of a network analysis of street gangs'. *Criminology and Public Policy,* 4(3): 607–36.

McGloin, J.M. (2009) 'Delinquency balance: Revisiting peer influence'. *Criminology,* 47(2): 439–77.

McGloin, J.M. and Kirk, D.S. (2010) 'An overview of social network analysis'. *Journal of Criminal Justice Education,* 21: 169–81.

McGloin, J.M. and Piquero, A.R. (2010) 'On the relationship between co-offending network redundancy and offending versatility'. *Journal of Research in Crime and Delinquency,* 47: 63–90.

McGloin, J.M. and Shermer, L.O.N. (2009) 'Self-control and deviant peer network structure'. *Journal of Research in Crime and Delinquency,* 46(1): 35–72.

McIllwain, J.S. (1999) 'Organized crime: A social network approach'. *Crime Law and Social Change,* 32(4): 301–23.

McNally, D. and Alston, J. (2006) 'Use of social network analysis (SNA) in the examination of an outlaw motorcycle gang'. *Journal of Gang Research,* 13(3): 1–25.

McPherson, M., Smith-Lovin, L. and Cook, J.M. (2001) 'Birds of a feather: Homophily in social networks'. *Annual Review of Sociology,* 27: 415–44.

Meldrum, R.C., Young, J.T.N. and Weerman, F.M. (2009) 'Reconsidering the effect of self-control and delinquent peers: Implications of measurement for theoretical significance'. *Journal of Research in Crime and Delinquency,* 46: 353–76.

Milward, H.B. and Raab, J. (2006) 'Dark networks as organizational problems: Elements of a theory'. *International Public Management Journal,* 9(3): 333–60.

Monge, P.R. and Contractor, N. (2003) *Theories of Communication Networks.* New York: Oxford University Press.

Moreno, J.L. (1932) *Application of the Group Method to Classification.* New York: National Committee on Prisons and Prison Labor.

Moreno, J.L. (1934) *Who Shall Survive?* Washington, DC: Nervous and Mental Disease Publishing Company.

Morselli, C. (2003) 'Career opportunities and network-based privileges in the Cosa Nostra'. *Crime Law and Social Change,* 39(4): 383–418.

Morselli, C. (2005) *Contacts, Opportunities, and Criminal Enterprise.* Toronto: University of Toronto Press.

Morselli, C. (2009a) 'Hells Angels in springtime'. *Trends in Organized Crime,* 12(2): 145–58.

Morselli, C. (2009b) *Inside Criminal Networks.* New York: Springer.

Morselli, C. and Petit, K. (2007) 'Law-enforcement disruption of a drug importation network'. *Global Crime*, 8(2): 109–30.

Morselli, C. and Roy, J. (2008) 'Brokerage qualifications in ringing operations'. *Criminology*, 46(1): 71–98.

Morselli, C. and Tremblay, P. (2004) 'Criminal achievement, offender networks and the benefits of low self-control'. *Criminology*, 42(3): 773–804.

Moss, H.B., Lynch, K.G. and Hardie, T.L. (2003) 'Affiliation with deviant peers among children of substance dependent fathers from pre-adolescence into adolescence: Associations with problem behaviors'. *Drug and Alcohol Dependence*, 71: 117–25.

Mullins, C.W. and Wright, R. (2003) 'Gender, social networks, and residential burglary'. *Criminology*, 41(3): 813–39.

Myers, D.J. (2000) 'The diffusion of collective violence: Infectiousness, susceptibility, and mass media networks'. *American Journal of Sociology*, 106: 173–208.

Natarajan, M. (2000) 'Understanding the structure of a drug trafficking organization: A conversational analysis'. *Crime Prevention Studies*, 11: 273–98.

Natarajan, M. (2006) 'Understanding the structure of a large heroin distribution network: A quantitative analysis of qualitative data'. *Journal of Quantitative Criminology*, 22(2): 171–92.

Oatley, G. (2006) 'Decision support systems for police: Lessons from the application of data mining techniques to "soft" forensic evidence'. *Artificial Intelligence and Law*, 14: 35–100.

Oatley, G.C., Belem, B., Fernandes, K., Hoggarth, E., Holland, B., Lewis, C., Meier, P., Morgan, K., Santhanam, J. and Squires, P. (2008) 'The gang gun crime problem: Solutions from social network theory, epidemiology, cellular automata, Bayesian networks and spatial statistics'. *Computational Forensics*. New York: Springer.

Oatley, G., Zeleznikow, J., Leary, R. and Ewart, B. (2005) 'From links to meaning: A burglary data case study'. *Knowledge-based Intelligent Information and Engineering Systems, Part 4, Proceedings. Lecture Notes in Artificial Intelligence*, vol. 3684. Berlin: Springer-Verlag.

Osgood, D.W., Wilson, J.K., O'Malley, P.M., Bachman, J.G. and Johnston, L.D. (1996) 'Routine activities and individual deviant behavior'. *American Sociological Review*, 61: 635–55.

Papachristos, A.V. (2009) 'Murder by structure: Dominance relations and the social structure of gang homicide'. *American Journal of Sociology*, 115(1): 74–128.

Patacchini, E. and Zenou, Y. (2008) 'The strength of weak ties in crime'. *European Economic Review*, 52(2): 209–36.

Pattillo, M.E. (1998) 'Sweet mothers and gangbangers: Managing crime in a black middle-class neighborhood'. *Social Forces*, 76(3): 747–74.

Pearson, M. and West, P. (2003) 'Drifting smoke rings: Social network analysis and Markov processes in a longitudinal study of friendship groups and risk-taking'. *Connections*, 25(2): 59–76.

Pepall, L., Richards, D. and Norman, G. (eds) (2008) *Industrial Organization: Contemporary Theory and Empirical Applications*. 4th ed. Malden, MA: Blackwell.

Perrow, C. (1986) *Complex Organizations: A Critical Essay*. 3rd ed. New York: McGraw-Hill.

Pettersson, T. (2003) 'Ethnicity and violent crime: The ethnic structure of networks of youths suspected of violent offences in Stockholm'. *Journal of Scandinavian Studies in Criminology and Crime Prevention*, 4(2): 143–61.

Pettersson, T. (2005) 'Gendering delinquent networks. A gendered analysis of violent crimes and the structure of boys' and girls' co-offending networks'. *Young Nordic Journal of Youth Research*, 13(3): 247–67.

Powell, W. (1990) 'Neither hierarchies nor markets', in Barry Shaw and L. L. Cummings (eds), *Research in Organizational Behavior*, vol. 12. Greenwich, CT: JAI Press. pp. 295–336.

Reiss, A.J., Jr. (1988) 'Co-offending and criminal careers', in Michael Tonry and Norval Morris (eds), *Crime and Justice: A Review of Research*. 10: 117–70.

Reuter, P. (1983) *Disorganized Crime: The Economics of the Visible Hand*. Cambridge, MA: MIT Press.

Rhodes, C.J. and Keefe, E.M.J. (2007) 'Social network topology: A Bayesian approach'. *Journal of the Operational Research Society*, 58(12): 1605–11.

Robins, G. (2009) 'Understanding individual behaviors within covert networks: The interplay of individual qualities, psychological predispositions, and network effects'. *Trends in Organized Crime*, 12(2): 166–87.

Romans, S.E., Potter, K., Martin, J. and Herbison, P. (2001) 'The mental and physical health of female sex workers: A comparative study'. *Australian and New Zealand Journal of Psychiatry*, 35(1): 75–80.

Sampson, R.J. (1987) 'Communities and crime', in Michael R. Gottfredson and Travis Hirschi (eds), *Positive Criminology*. Beverly Hills, CA: Sage. pp. 91–114.

Sampson, R.J. (2003) 'The neighborhood context of well-being'. *Perspectives in Biology and Medicine*, 46(3): S53–S64.

Sampson, R.J. (2004a) 'Networks and neighbourhoods: The implications of connectivity for thinking about crime in the modern city', in Helen McCarthy, Paul Miller and Paul Skidmore (eds), *Network Logic: Who Governs in an Interconnected World?* London, UK: Demos. 157–66.

Sampson, R.J. (2004b) 'Neighbourhood and community: Collective efficacy and community safety'. *New Economy*, 11: 106–13.

Sampson, R.J. (2006a) 'How does community context matter? Social mechanisms and the explanation of crime rates', in Per-Olof Wikström and Robert J. Sampson (eds), *The Explanation of Crime: Context, Mechanisms, and Development*. Cambridge, UK: Cambridge University Press. pp. 31–60.

Sampson, R.J. (2006b) 'Collective efficacy theory: Lessons learned and directions for future inquiry', in Francis T. Cullen, John Paul Wright and Kristie R. Blevins (eds), *Taking Stock: The Status of Criminological Theory*, vol. 15. New Brunswick, NJ: Transaction. pp. 149–67.

Sampson, R.J., Raudenbush, S.W. and Earls, F. (1997) 'Neighborhoods and violent crime: A multilevel study of collective efficacy'. *Science*, 277(5328): 918–24.

Sarnecki, J. (1990) 'Delinquent networks in Sweden'. *Journal of Quantitative Criminology*, 6(1): 31–50.

Sarnecki, J. (2001) *Delinquent Networks: Youth Co-offending in Stockholm*. Cambridge: Cambridge University Press.

Sarnecki, J. (2004) 'Girls and boys in delinquent networks'. *International Annals of Criminology*, 42: 29–57.

Sarnecki, J. (2009) 'Delinquent networks: youth co-offending', in Hans Joachim Schneider (ed.), *Internationales Handbuch der Kriminologie*, vol. 2. Berlin: Walter de Gruyter. pp. 995–1023.

Schreck, C.J., Fisher, Bonnie S. and Miller, J.M. (2004) 'The social context of violent victimization: A study of the delinquent peer effect'. *Justice Quarterly*, 21: 23–47.

Schroeder, R.D., Giordano, P.C. and Cernkovich, S.A. (2007) 'Drug use and desistance processes'. *Criminology*, 45(1): 191–222.

Schwartz, D.M. and Rouselle, T. (2009) 'Using social network analysis to target criminal networks'. *Trends in Organized Crime*, 12(2): 188–207.

Shaw, C.R. and McKay, H.D. (1931) *Social Factors in Juvenile Delinquency. Report on the Causes of Crime*, vol. II. Washington, DC: National Commission on Law Observance and Enforcement.

Shaw, C.R., Zorbaugh, F.M., McKay, H.D. and Cottrell, L.S. (1929) *Delinquency Areas*. Chicago: University of Chicago Press.

Shih, H.-Y. and Chang, T.-L.S. (2009) 'International diffusion of embodied and disembodied technology: A network analysis approach'. *Technological Forecasting and Social Change*, 76: 821–34.

Shivy, V.A., Wu, J.J., Moon, A.E., Mann, Shay C., Holland, J.G. and Eacho, C. (2007) 'Ex-offenders reentering the workforce'. *Journal of Counseling Psychology*, 54(4): 466–73.

Shoemaker, D.J. (2005) *Theories of Delinquency*. 5th ed. New York: Oxford University Press.

Short, J.F., Jr. and Strodtbeck, F.L. (1965) *Group Process and Gang Delinquency*. Chicago, IL: University of Chicago Press.

Skeem, J., Louden, J.E., Manchak, S., Vidal, S. and Haddad, E. (2009) 'Social networks and social control of probationers with co-occurring mental and substance abuse problems'. *Law and Human Behavior*, 33(2): 122–35.

Smith, M.N. and King, P.J.H. (2002) 'Incrementally visualising criminal networks'. Proceedings of the Sixth International Conference on Information Visualisation, 2002.

Snijders, T.A.B. and Baerveldt, C. (2003) 'A multilevel network study of the effects of delinquent behavior on friendship evolution'. *Journal of Mathematical Sociology*, 27(2–3): 123–51.

Sommers, I., Baskin, D.R. and Fagan, J. (1994) 'Getting out of the life: Crime desistance by female street offenders'. *Deviant Behavior*, 15(2): 125–49.

Soudijn, M.R.J. and Kleemans, E.R. (2009) 'Chinese organized crime and situational context: Comparing human smuggling and synthetic drugs trafficking'. *Crime, Law and Social Change*, 52: 457–74.

Sparrow, M.K. (1991a) 'The application of network analysis to criminal intelligence: An assessment of the prospects'. *Social Networks*, 13(3): 251–74.

Sparrow, M.K. (1991b) 'Network vulnerabilities and strategic intelligence in law enforcement'. *International Journal of Intelligence and CounterIntelligence*, 5(3): 255–74.

Spaulding, C.B. (1948) 'Cliques, gangs and networks'. *Sociology and Social Research*, 32: 928–37.

Spergel, I.A. (1990) 'Youth gangs: Continuity and change', in Michael Tonry and Norval Morris (eds), *Crime and Justice: A Review of Research*, vol. 12. Chicago: University of Chicago Press. pp. 171–275.

Stovin, G. and Davies, C. (2008) 'Beyond the network: A crime science approach to organized crime'. *Policing*, 2(4): 497–505.

Sung, H.E., Belenko, S., Feng, L. and Tabachnick, C. (2004) 'Predicting treatment noncompliance clients: A theoretical and among criminal justice-mandated empirical exploration'. *Journal of Substance Abuse Treatment*, 26(1): 315–28.

Surtees, R. (2008) 'Traffickers and trafficking in Southern and Eastern Europe: Considering the other side of human trafficking'. *European Journal of Criminology*, 5(1): 39–68.

Sutherland, E.H. (1939) *Principles of Criminology*. 3rd ed. Philadelphia, PA: Lippincott.

Sutherland, E.H., Cressey, D.R. and Luckenbill, D.F. (1992) *Principles of Criminology*. 11th ed. Dix Hills, NY: General Hall.

Sweetser, F.L., Jr. (1942) 'A new emphasis for neighborhood research'. *American Sociological Review*, 7: 525–33.

Thornberry, T.P. (1987) 'Toward an interactional theory of delinquency'. *Criminology*, 25(4): 863–91.

Tremblay, P. (1993) 'Searching for suitable co-offenders', in Ronald V. Clarke and Marcus Felson (eds), *Routine Activity and Rational Choice. Advances in Criminological Theory*. 5: 17–36.

Triplett, R.A., Gainey, R.R. and Sun, I.Y. (2003) 'Institutional strength, social control and neighborhood crime rates'. *Theoretical Criminology*, 7(4): 439–67.

Tsvetovat, M. and Carley, K. (2007) 'On effectiveness of wiretap programs in mapping social networks'. *Computational and Mathematical Organization Theory*, 13(1): 63–87.

Tutzauer, F. (2007) 'Entropy as a measure of centrality in networks characterized by path-transfer flow'. *Social Networks*, 29: 249–65.

Valente, T.W. (1995) *Network Models of the Diffusion of Innovations*. Cresskill, NJ: Hampton Press.

van de Bunt, H. (2008) 'A case study on the misuse of hawala banking'. *International Journal of Social Economics*, 35(9): 691–702.

van der Hulst, R.C. (2009) 'Introduction to Social Network Analysis (SNA) as an investigative tool'. *Trends in Organized Crime*, 12(1): 101–21.

van der Poel, A. and van de Mheen, D. (2006) 'Young people using crack and the process of marginalization'. *Drugs-Education Prevention and Policy*, 13(1): 45–59.

van Koppen, M.V., de Poot, C.J., Kleemans, E.R. and Nieuwbeerta, P. (2010) 'Criminal trajectories in organized crime'. *British Journal of Criminology*, 50: 102–23.

van Mastrigt, S.B. (2008) 'Co-offending: Relationships withage, gender and crime type'. Ph.D. thesis, University of Cambridge.

von Lampe, K. (2009) 'Human capital and social capital in criminal networks: Introduction to the special issue on the 7th Blankensee Colloquium'. *Trends in Organized Crime,* 12(2): 93–100.

von Lampe, K. and Johansen, P.O. (2004) 'Organized crime and trust: On the conceptualization and empirical relevance of trust in the context of criminal networks'. *Global Crime,* 6: 159–84.

Waring, E.J. (1993) 'Co-offending in white-collar crime: A network approach'. Ph.D. thesis, Yale University.

Waring, E.J. (2002) 'Co-offending as a network form of social organization', in Elin J. Waring and David Weisburd (eds), *Crime and Social Organization*, vol. 10. New Brunswick, NJ: Transaction. pp. 31–47.

Warner, B.D. and Rountree, P.W. (1997) 'Local social ties in a community and crime model: Questioning the systemic nature of informal social control'. *Social Problems,* 44(4): 520–36.

Warr, M. (1993) 'Age, peers, and delinquency'. *Criminology,* 31(1): 17–40.

Warr, M. (1996) 'Organization and instigation in delinquent groups'. *Criminology,* 34(1): 11–37.

Warr, M. (2002) *Companions in Crime: The Social Aspects of Criminal Conduct.* Cambridge, UK: Cambridge University Press.

Weerman, F.M. and Bijleveld, C. (2007) 'Birds of different feathers: School networks of serious delinquent, minor delinquent and non-delinquent boys and girls'. *European Journal of Criminology,* 4(4): 357–83.

Weerman, F.M. and Smeenk, W.H. (2005) 'Peer similarity in delinquency for different types of friends: A comparison using two measurement methods'. *Criminology,* 43(2): 499–523.

White, H.C. (1981) 'Where do markets come from?' *American Journal of Sociology,* 87: 517–47.

White, H.C. (2002) *Markets from Networks: Socioeconomic Models of Production.* Princeton, NJ: Princeton University Press.

Whyte, W.F. (1943) *Street Corner Society.* Chicago: University of Chicago Press.

Wild, T.C., Cunningham, J.A. and Ryan, R.M. (2006) 'Social pressure, coercion, and client engagement at treatment entry: A self-determination theory perspective'. *Addictive Behaviors,* 31(10): 1858–72.

Williamson, O.E. (1975) *Markets and Hierarchies: Analysis and Antitrust Implications.* New York: Macmillan.

Xia, M. (2008) 'Organizational formations of organized crime in China: Perspectives from the state, markets, and networks'. *Journal of Contemporary China,* 17(54): 1–23.

Xu, J. and Chen, H.C. (2003) 'Untangling criminal networks: A case study'. Intelligence and Security Informatics, Proceedings. *Lecture Notes in Computer Science*, vol. 2665. Berlin: Springer-Verlag.

Xu, J. and Chen, H.C. (2005a) 'Criminal network analysis and visualization'. *Communications of the ACM,* 48(6): 100–107.

Xu, J. and Chen, H.C. (2005b) 'CrimeNet explorer: A framework for criminal network knowledge discovery'. *ACM Transactions on Information Systems,* 23(2): 201–26.

Xu, J., Marshall, B., Kaza, S. and Chen, H.C. (2004) 'Analyzing and visualizing criminal network dynamics: A case study'. Intelligence and Security Informatics, Proceedings. *Lecture Notes in Computer Science*, vol. 3073. Berlin: Springer-Verlag.

Zhang, S.X. (1998) 'In search of hopeful glimpses: A critique of research strategies in current boot camp evaluations'. *Crime & Delinquency,* 44(2): 314–34.

Zhang, S.X. (2008) *Chinese Human Smuggling Organizations. Families, Social Networks and Cultural Imperatives.* Stanford, CA: Stanford University Press.

Zhang, S.X. and Gaylord, M.S. (1996) 'Bound for the Golden Mountain: The social organization of Chinese alien smuggling'. *Crime Law and Social Change,* 25: 1–16.

18

Terrorist Networks: The Threat of Connectivity

Renée C. van der Hulst

Extremism and terrorism are ever evolving problems in our society. Terror is used as a weapon to achieve goals and, not surprisingly, the associated opportunity structures often reside in socially embedded networks. It has become top priority all over the world to make every effort to prevent future terrorist attacks. To further this cause, the systematic analysis of (terrorist) networks, the associated relational structures and exchange of resources (e.g. information, skills, money or weapons) are assumed to provide key leads. Contrary to most social networks that are the objects of study in this field, however, the networks associated with terrorism are inherently covert. This calls for a sophisticated array of research methods and tools to improve our ability to detect, prevent, and respond to terrorist events. The objective of this chapter is to review the international literature of terrorism research for applications of social network analysis (SNA). What do we know and where is it heading? This chapter illustrates how the network paradigm is applied to the terrorism domain, evaluates the state of the art of research, critically reflects on the developments and explores some future directions.

IN THE NAME OF GOD

Although an internationally agreed-upon definition of terrorism is currently still lacking, most definitions emphasise that terrorist acts involve violent and aggressive methods, deliberately exploited to create fear in order to further political or ideological objectives. The 'fourth generation' of terrorists threatening our society today, for example, is motivated by fundamental interpretations of a religious identity. Most recently at the forefront is the stream of violent attacks under the umbrella of Islam as a religion (Rapoport, 2003). In the early twenty-first century the world is faced with horrific acts of terror, justified by the 'holy battle of jihad', that have ravaged places all over the world and killed thousands of innocent people. Who doesn't remember the airplanes that were hijacked and crashed in the United States on September 11, 2001 (9/11), or the bombings that took place in Bali (Indonesia, 2002), Casablanca (Morocco, 2003), Madrid (Spain, 2004), London (United Kingdom, 2005) and most recently Mumbai (India, 2008) to name a few. Ever since the tragedy of 9/11 the battle against terrorist crimes has intensified and has become the top priority all over the world.

The focus in this chapter is to study terrorism from a social networks point of view. A social network is defined as a collection of actors (e.g. persons, groups, organisations) and relations between actors (connections, activities) (Wasserman and Faust, 1994). With the exigency to gain a better understanding of the rise and functioning of terrorist networks (including associated radical or extremist movements), the need for advanced methods, information technologies and analytical tools increased accordingly. As early as two decades ago, Sparrow (1991b: 251) emphasised that law enforcement and intelligence agencies were quite behind and 'relatively unsophisticated in their use of analytic tools and concepts', in particular with regard to the academic discipline of SNA. Although SNA has been an approved research method in many disciplines (e.g. in sociology, business management, biology), it was only after 9/11 that the method gained serious interest for applications in the intelligence and security domain. Major research programmes were launched, generated by abundant funding, and academics from various disciplines joined efforts to tackle the global security problem by way of advanced information technologies and analysis tools. In particular the recent influx of physicists, biologists, computer scientists, artificial intelligence researchers, engineers and military operations researchers resulted in an increased emphasis on examining very large networks (e.g. the Internet), network dynamics, and their resilience to attacks (Carley, 2003; Stohl and Stohl, 2007). Despite these developments, most of the work in this area is still in its infancy. In the following section we will evaluate the general line of thought around networks as it evolved over the last decade within the domain of counterterrorism.

THE DISCOVERY OF STRUCTURE

Most processes of radicalisation, indoctrination, attitude formation, terrorist plots, and collective action rise, evolve and develop in relation to others (Borum and Gelles, 2005; Dean, 2007; Ressler, 2006; Sageman, 2004, 2008). Based on this, the systematic analysis of relational structures is a 'sine qua non' to a more thorough understanding of terrorist behaviour (Koschade, 2006; Schwartz and Rouselle, 2008; Stohl and Stohl, 2007). Although the importance of social networks in relation to terrorism is frequently emphasised, studies on terrorism have predominantly focussed on individual (i.e. micro-level) and the socio-, cultural- or political (i.e. macro-level) conditions associated with terrorism. Despite the fact that more and more people from various disciplines have entered the network arena, systematic and empirical social network studies of terrorism remain extremely scarce[1] (according to the academic literature). Either lacking the analytical skills or the appropriate data and domain expertise, much of what we find in the literature on terrorist networks is theoretical discourse. Moreover, different views of terrorist networks appear to compete for validation whereas they are in fact complementary to each other. The following sections outline two streams of thinking: one focuses on the global threat and the other focuses on the local threat of terrorism.

The global threat of terrorism

A popular idea among mainstream terrorism experts nowadays is that globalisation prompted organisations to change their traditional (hierarchical) modus operandi into decentralised, self-governing project teams in order to work more efficiently (Arquilla and Ronfeldt, 2001). The idea of decentralised systems and semi-autonomous project teams has circulated in business management ever since the 1980s and 1990s (see Borgatti and Foster, 2003; Rothenberg, 2001). The tendency for terrorist organisations to be organised and regarded as networks (i.e. cellular structures rather than hierarchies), however, is relatively new. In particular the scale-free 'hub-and-spoke' structures appear to meet with general approval to characterise terrorist organisations previously assumed to operate hierarchically (Barabási and Albert, 1999; Watts, 1999; Zanini and Edwards, 2001; Qin et al., 2005).

Hub-and-spoke networks are efficiently organised structures of connected cells that are resilient to disruption. There is no fixed arrangement of human resources among cells but they are likely to entail structurally equivalent roles (e.g. ideological leaders, strategic leaders, resource concentrators and specialised experts) (Tsvetovat and Carley, 2005). Operational knowledge and communication among cells is kept to a minimum based on a 'need-to-know' principle. Actors, ties, and cells are all redundant in the sense that information, materials and other resources have alternative routes to travel through the network (i.e. the loss of one actor or cell is easily replaced by taking over operational activities by another). The cell leaders however, are most likely to be senior members, are often part of multiple cells and are more knowledgeable than other members (Carley et al., 2001).

The majority of actors in these networks have limited links and communicate or exchange resources through a limited number of highly connected actors. These highly connected actors, also referred to as hubs, reduce the chain of command (i.e. lower the average path length) between any two nodes in the network (e.g. leaders and followers). In essence, they coordinate activities in the absence of a central control hierarchy. Since the network as a whole still remains sparse, terrorist plots may remain inconspicuous because of their low density, and the impact of random disruptions is likely to be limited because the network lacks central leadership. The elimination of the hubs, on the other hand, can cause major disruptions to the network even if the hubs are not the actual leaders.

It is generally assumed that due to their increasing dispersed and scale-free cellular characteristics, groups or movements such as Al Qaeda have become less vulnerable to detection or disruption. Although scale-free networks are popular among intelligence analysts, Tsvetovat and Carley (2007: 76) argued that they do not fit well with reality as it is not just the hubs but also local dense cells that continue to provide connectivity when hubs are removed (i.e. the networks are resilient because they also exhibit small-world properties) (see Milgram, 1967; Watts, 1999). Tsvetovat and Carley (2005) refer in this respect to the safety net of 'sleeper links': non-operational ties from one cell to the other cell (e.g. family ties) that are mainly used for coordinating actions and are rarely activated. Within cells, only few members would have such links.

Local threats from within

The global rise of terrorist organisations, such as Al Qaeda, is partly sustained by their ability to appeal to Muslims all over the world, irrespective of their nationality (Rothenberg, 2001; Tsvetovat and Carley, 2005). As conglomerates, terrorist organisations do not necessarily have to coordinate activities. Individual actors and groups, irrespective of where they are, are free to operate 'on behalf' of the global jihad (or organisation). Indeed, many terrorist conspiracies in Western Europe are self-organised and develop locally and are decentralised. Garfinkel (2003) referred to 'leaderless resistance' to delineate the threat of a new generation of small, dispersed clandestine networks and cells (not limited to religiously motivated terrorism) that lack a formal hierarchical command structure. Later on, Sageman (2008) used the term leaderless jihad to catch the idea of dispersed cellular Islamist terrorist structures of self-organised, home-grown wannabes.

Inspired by the globalisation of terror, local networks radicalise with their members willing to exploit equivalent, and sometimes fatal, acts of violence (e.g. the killing of the Dutch filmmaker Theo van Gogh in Amsterdam in 2004). Perpetrators become inspired to commit violent acts by what they read and see rather than being recruited by a terrorist organisation and receiving orders to commit crimes and violent terrorist acts (Sageman, 2004). Tsvetovat and Carley (2007) characterise these networks as relatively small cells (6 to 10 actors) that are well manageable based on their size. Within cells, group members are like-minded, share strong religious or ideological bonds, are in close physical proximity to each other (e.g. share living arrangements), and are able to substitute for each other (i.e. they are structurally equivalent) (Sparrow, 1991b).

The small and self-organised groups lack a formalised and central coordination system. Actors often gain access through the Internet[2] to span different geographic boundaries, share information, reinforce ideology, and coordinate activities to achieve mutual goals (e.g. recruit, motivate and mobilise young members, conduct illegal activities, and solicit funding) (Chen, 2006; Coates, 1996). They operate leaderlessly by way of their shared ideology or religion, with the network being governed by strong, informal, and trusted relationships rather than by hierarchical organisational structures. Still, locally connected conspiracies may actively search for links to global terrorist organisations on their own initiative (i.e. bottom-up in addition to top-down recruitment). Moreover, although decentralised in its operations, terrorist cells may turn out to be semi-autonomous and receive peripheral support through funding or direction (Borum and Gelles, 2005; Rothenberg, 2001).

A continuum of clandestine networks

All in all, the debate around terrorist networks is characterized by a growing awareness of the 'need' for decentralised structures, but it is not a matter of rigorous categories: terrorist networks come in many different forms that are not mutually exclusive. Governance structures can vary from hierarchical to decentralised systems, and the scope of activities can be either local (i.e. relating to a particular area or region) or global (i.e. involving the entire world). Moreover, both governance and the scope of activities can change over time. The Al Qaeda network of Osama bin Laden, for example, has evolved from a hierarchical military local movement of mujahedin (fighting the Russian occupation in Afghanistan) to a global ideological movement and infrastructure that supports a variety of self-organising actors (Borum and Gelles, 2005: 470).

It is not just the misspecification of network boundaries (Stohl and Stohl, 2007: 108) but also the lack of differentiation between terrorist networks that may compromise the usefulness of the social network metaphor for combating terrorism. After all, different networks have different implications in terms of intelligence strategies and counterterrorism policies. To overcome this problem, we propose a continuum of clandestine networks that explicitly distinguishes between governance structures (horizontal axis: decentralised v hierarchical) and the scope of activities (vertical axis: local v global), where terrorist networks can be plotted as 'coordinates' on the continuum. The two-dimensional 'radar' spheres

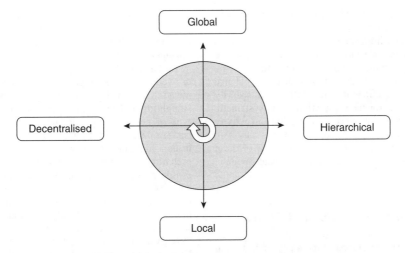

Figure 18.1   The two-dimensional 'radar' spheres of clandestine networks

(TDRS) of terrorist or any clandestine networks is presented in Figure 18.1.

Balancing needs through structure: The efficiency/security trade-off

The TDRS coordinate in and of themselves do not necessarily characterise network structure. It is very likely, however, that clandestine networks who find themselves in a particular sphere share identical features and regularities (or profiles) in their social structures. The thing is that social networks are not disorganised but develop and evolve based on socio-dynamic and psychological processes (e.g. *opportunity* structures, *selection* preferences, and social *influence*). So far, network research on terrorism tends to neglect combining the explanatory mechanisms related to analytical metrics (that are in essence based on such theories), whereas such processes may well be contingent to different types of governance structures or the scope of terrorist activities.

According to homophily theory (see McPherson et al., 2001), for example, people are more likely to initiate contact with other people who share similar characteristics (e.g. religion, nationality, background) and who are in close social or spatial proximity to them (e.g. within training camps, mosques). Moreover, the importance of trust is one of the main reasons why terrorists recruit mainly among their own nationalities, families, friends and religious circles (sometimes characterised by strong, historical or social bonds)[3] (Krebs, 2001; Sageman, 2004; Tsvetovat and Carley, 2005, 2007; Qin et al., 2005). Likewise, people are also more likely to be influenced by their close friends and associates, which is considered the main reason why actors' beliefs, social norms, attitudes, and behaviours become more homogeneous in dense networks over time (Borgatti and Foster, 2003; Friedkin and Johnsen, 1999). In particular strong transitive ties (i.e. the tendency of friends of friends to become friends) may reinforce an actor's willingness to participate in costly, risky or controversial behaviour (Centola and Macy, 2007).

Such dense, cohesive affiliation networks are generally characterised by high redundancy, trust and social support (Lin et al., 2001). Loosely connected brokerage networks, on the other hand, are characterised by structural holes, non-redundancy and more competitive information benefits (see Burt, 1992, 2005; Granovetter, 1973). Indeed, both types of structures have different functional implications in terms of operational efficiency and secrecy (Erickson, 1981; Kadushin, 2002; Krebs, 2001; Morselli et al., 2007; Rothenberg, 2001; Stohl and Stohl, 2007). Dense cohesive networks facilitate coordination within the group, increase group compliance, are less likely to be infiltrated by outsiders, and are difficult to destabilize. The trusted ties promote security within but are vulnerable upon detection since it takes only one actor to release critical information about many others (Xu et al., 2004). Brokerage, on the other hand, promotes the dissemination of new information and resources across groups or social circles, which creates benefits and change. Although at higher risk for betrayal and infiltration, such loosely connected networks may be more difficult to trace and are able to respond more flexibly to change. Clandestine networks somehow need to balance between the efficiency, flexibility and security requirements for their operations. The systematic analysis of affiliation, communication and activity patterns in radical or terrorist networks may help to understand and predict the behaviour of these social systems and to identify their weak spots.

THE STUDY OF SOCIAL STRUCTURES

For decades, traditional link analysis has been used in the law enforcement and intelligence domains to visually map clandestine structures (Harper and Harris, 1975; Klerks, 2001; Schroeder et al., 2003). Social network analysis (SNA) adds to this that structural patterns are modelled mathematically, providing a variety of quantified metrics of network activity, positions, power, dependency and social roles (Wasserman and Faust, 1994). Sparrow (1991a, 1991b) was about the first to emphasise the importance of network analysis to (criminal) intelligence. Other scholars have endorsed this view and postulate SNA as a sophisticated array of tools that can help unravel clandestine networks and improve the ability to detect, prevent, and respond to terrorist events (Asal and Rethemeyer, 2006; Carley et al., 2001, 2007; Chen, 2006; Koschade, 2006; Reid et al., 2004; Ressler, 2006; Van der Hulst, 2009a).

Typical actors of importance

One of the most frequently reported metrics in social network research is actor centrality (Bonacich, 1972; Burt, 1992; Freeman, 1979). Actor centrality is used as a measure relative importance to infer social control. Terrorists may be of influence in a network or plot, for example, because they are active players connected to many people (i.e. degree centrality), because they are able to quickly access or diffuse information and resources to and from the network (i.e. closeness centrality), because they can bring people together and control the flows of communication and resources between otherwise disparate parts of the network (i.e. betweenness or max-flow centrality), or because their neighbours are well positioned (i.e. eigenvector centrality). In particular actors who frequently broker connections are in powerful positions: they can control the flow of communication, propagate new information, and play important roles to coordinate terrorist attacks (e.g. by supplying chemicals, weapons, forged documents or other resources).

Researchers have to be cautious, however, not to overestimate the importance of centrality. The meaning attached to this measure may not be straightforward and can be contingent upon the type of network (e.g. hierarchical or decentralised) or data (Carley et al., 2001). Moreover, key leaders and suicide terrorists (i.e. 'sleeper cells' preparing for action) may prefer to keep a low profile and operate in the periphery of a larger network. To keep connected to the main body of the network they may be relying on liaisons (e.g. high central actors) and only coordinate actions when necessary (see Chen, 2006; Krebs, 2001; Tsvetovat and Carley, 2007). Adding to this, Borgatti (2006) argued that traditional measures such as centrality (or even cutpoints and cutsets) do not provide optimal solutions in certain problem scenarios. For counterterrorism purposes, for example, one may want to target an optimal *set* of actors and not actors who would be optimal targets if isolated individually based on their centrality ranks. Moreover, he argues, there is a difference between maximal disruption or fragmentation of a network by neutralizing actors (i.e. key player negative) and maximal diffusion or gathering of information for preventive or intelligence purposes (i.e. key player positive).

Ideally, the qualities associated with actors (e.g. their abilities), ties (e.g. their nature or duration) and resources (e.g. uniqueness) should be taken into account in studying terrorist networks (Sparrow, 1991b; Tsvetovat and Carley, 2007). Borgatti (2006) emphasised the need to incorporate actor attributes into the key player metrics to make fragmentation (or information) dependent on both network position and particular traits of the involved actors. Building on the key player problem, Schwartz and Rouselle (2008) proposed two core concepts for the analysis of covert networks: (1) network capital (NC) for optimised fragmentation, and (2) intelligence worth (IW) for optimised information gathering. Both measures are based on actors' centrality and the propensity to share resources, while additionally taking into account the actual resources of actors (for NC), and the actual information gaps and tie strength between actors (for IW).

Typical tasks, roles, and resources of importance

Although meant to come by surprise, terrorist attacks are far from random and generally require careful planning, preparation and coordinated

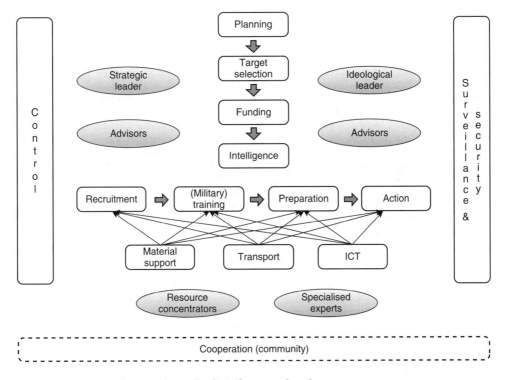

Figure 18.2   Script of key tasks and roles of a terrorist plot

effort of multiple, interrelated actors. Identifying the elementary (sequence of) segments of a terrorist plot (e.g. key tasks, roles, and activities), and associating these patterns to perpetrators will allow a more thorough understanding of logistics, opportunity structures, and terrorist strategies (cf. Cornish and Clarke, 2002). Figure 18.2 illustrates a hypothetical scenario of a terrorist plot from planning, to recruitment, to facilitating activities, to the actual operation.

The rectangles in Figure 18.2 represent tasks and are distinguished in a 'plan' and 'do' segment (see also Rothenberg, 2001: 37 who distinguishes between these two categories of people). The ellipses represent essential roles as distinguished by Tsvetovat and Carley (2007: 68)[4]: 'ideological (often charismatic) and strategic leaders', 'advisors', 'resource concentrators' and 'specialised experts'. If the systematic analysis of terrorist cells or networks could be associated to such key tasks and roles (including demographical, sociopsychological, cultural and contextual factors), this may offer rich clues about the functioning of actors and groups. Most studies that report on terrorist networks, however, do not even distinguish between different types of relationships, let alone focus on the various processes involved in a terrorist plot. The meta-matrix, proposed by Carley and associates, is considered as an exception. Carley et al. (2001) argued that if centrality measures are used as a lead to disrupt networks (e.g. to limit information flows or general task performance) or to identify emergent leaders (e.g. actors close to the original leader in terms of task, knowledge and resource networks), multiple networks should be considered simultaneously (see also Moon and Carley, 2007). The meta-matrix serves as a good example and combines information from multiple classification systems (e.g. actors along with their knowledge, attributes, resources, tasks or events, group membership, roles, actions and locations).

Dynamic network analysis

By and large, one of the major drawbacks of SNA is that it treats networks as static systems whereas they are fluid and subject to change. Three clusters of methods are distinguished to examine dynamic networks: descriptive, mathematical and simulation studies (Borgatti and Foster, 2003).

The least sophisticated way is to compare network properties over time in a descriptive manner. More sophisticated are mathematical studies, such as exponential random graph or p* models (see Robins, this volume), that allow the testing of hypotheses. These studies estimate model parameters from data and evaluate how well these parameters fit with observed data (see also Snijders et al., 2010). Agent-based simulation studies, finally, model actors as strategic rational decision-makers (referred to as agents) who act to maximise utility. Agents can learn from prior events and the choices of multiple agents determine how the network evolves (Tsvetovat and Carley, 2007). Only recently, the development of more advanced statistical tools and computational techniques has increased the interest in SNA applications from the law enforcement and intelligence domains (Carley, 2004; Stohl and Stohl, 2007).[5] Certainly, information on the research efforts from the intelligence domain is not likely to be made public. So what do we really know about the structural properties of terrorist networks?

WHAT DO WE KNOW?

There are essentially two kinds of researchers who study terrorist networks: operational analysts with domain expertise (i.e. investigators on the job), and scientific researchers with the expertise to model behaviour (i.e. academics) (Ressler, 2006; Schroeder et al., 2003). Both deal with unavoidable collection biases. In the former category investigations start with a prime suspect and little by little the ego-network of a suspect is mapped inside-out. The drawback of this method, known as snowball sampling, is that it is biased towards highly connected actors, which may lead to wrong perceptions of the core-periphery structure of a network (DSTL, 2004). The latter category is biased mostly because they lack access to restricted data and integrated datasets (Reid et al., 2004). As a result, research on terrorist networks relies to a great extent on open data sources, such as archival data that provide information of terror incidents (e.g. court documents, indictments, testimonies) or media reports (Baker and Faulkner, 1993; Krebs, 2001; Sageman, 2004). However, these sources are likely to be incomplete if not wrong, and most scientists lack the required domain expertise to interpret their results. This is probably one of the reasons why systematic and empirical studies of terrorist networks, at least those that are *publicly* available, are extremely scarce.

Domain experts are increasingly aware of the importance of networks, and compelling books

have demonstrated this (e.g. Arquilla and Ronfeldt, 2001; Sageman, 2004, 2008). In the absence of actual network metrics, however, most of the work remains limited to the discussion of social networks as a paradigm, some theoretical arguments, or basic qualitative analysis. The same goes for the academic network literature, where the majority of papers is essentially descriptive (but limited) or outline the potential value of SNA to study clandestine networks. The actual number of empirical studies (at least those that are publicly available) remains sparse and few studies actually test hypotheses (Contractor and Monge, 2004). Critical of this development, Asal and Rethemeyer (2006: 68) described the domain as much *theory building with little empirical verification*. In fact, SNA research in the domain of terrorism is overwhelmingly concentrated on the development of advanced algorithms and integrated software systems.[6] Evaluating what is state of the art, Ressler (2006) emphasised quite keenly that other than the work of Carley and associates (CASOS, Carnegie Mellon University) the complex modelling of terrorist networks is rather limited. Without the pretension of being exhaustive we will review some fundamental research findings known from the international literature.

Empirical analysis

Applications of social network analysis in the counterterrorism domain appear to still be in its infancy, but the topic raises a lot of interest (if not adrenaline) from researchers along with the need for advanced methodological development. Some studies that are found in the academic literature are more exploratory, somewhat speculative and less sophisticated in their analysis than others. Most of the work relies heavily on publicly available sources, such as media reports, and varies in scope. Based on the co-occurrence of names of terrorist organisations or cross-links of Web sites on the Internet, for example, network metrics are used to identify key ideological groupings or clusters of hate groups and activist organisations (Basu, 2005; Chen, 2006; Garfinkel, 2003). Memon et al. (2008) used publicly available data of the train bombings in Madrid (2004) and on the London tube (2005) to explore and illustrate how critical actors from online sources such as the Internet can be detected. According to Jordán (2008), a social network analysis of maps of the London underground suggested that the bombings in 2005 may have been chosen to cause maximal damage to the transport system as a critical infrastructure (i.e. by blocking the shortest pathways).

Other analyses are more typical to descriptive case studies. Based on secondary analysis, for example, the four major terrorist groups of the Global Salafi Jihad (GSJ) (N = 364) (as identified by Sageman, 2004) were all found to be scale-free networks (Chen, 2006; Qin et al., 2005). The few high-degree and between-central actors were positively identified by domain experts as the GSJ leaders of the four geographical 'clumps', and block-modelling analysis identified coordinators between Osama bin Laden and these four clumps. In addition to the GSJ leaders, the immediate associates and coordinators of the leaders (i.e. the 'lieutenants') were also high between central. Interestingly, 65 per cent of the ties among leaders were characterised as strong and trusted (e.g. family, friends) as opposed to only 38 per cent of the ties among leaders and followers. The importance of weak ties was also emphasised by Rodríguez (2004), who explored the social network underlying the Madrid bombings.

A sophisticated analysis was performed on the Jemaah Islamiyah terrorist network responsible for the Bali bombings (October 2002) by Koschade (2006). Compared to findings about the 9/11 hijackers (N = 19, density 16 per cent) (Krebs 2001, 2002 – see following section), the Jemaah Islamiyah network was much more cohesive (N = 17, density 43 per cent).[7] Two dense clusters were involved with activities that required considerable coordination: the bomb construction team (plan A) and a support team to be called on for assistance when necessary (plan B). Both the field and the logistic commanders (i.e. Samudra and Idris) were by far the most central actors of the network (measured by standardised degree, betweenness, and closeness centrality). Overall, the network was quite centralised around the bombing operation, with the support team and two support actors being kept relatively isolated from the core.

A secondary analysis of the Dutch Hofstad network (Van der Hulst, 2009b) identified the core of the network (N = 13) to be highly cohesive. All actors who made an assault on people's lives (or prepared for action) – as well as the Syrian fugitive and alleged ideological leader of the group, Al Issa – were highly central in terms of degree, closeness, betweenness and eigenvector and flow betweenness. Most central were the actors involved in recruitment and propaganda activities. Advisers and facilitators who were involved in criminal activities were operating on the periphery of the network. Interestingly, actors who were central in all centrality metrics except for brokering (i.e. betweenness or flow betweenness) were sympathisers and provided services to the core (e.g. housing). The reverse, actors who were brokers but who were *not* central in the other

centrality metrics, provided the network with access to valuable and unique resources (e.g. state secrets, document forgery, international training camps, and links to another terrorist cell). One of the women (i.e. the wife of one of the core members) stood out as well as being in a position to play an important brokering function in the network.

The 9/11 hijacking plot

Probably the most cited analysis, however, is the one by Krebs (2001, 2002) who became renowned for being the first to examine the 9/11 hijacking network using SNA metrics based on information gathered from open sources (newspapers). This section provides a comprehensive summary of the main results. The four airplanes that crashed in the United States on September 11, 2001 involved 19 hijackers who were linked to Al Qaeda. They were highly connected through trusted prior contacts, had probably bonded after completing a training camp in Afghanistan, and had shared living arrangements, P.O. boxes, credit cards and phone numbers. Some attended the same college, flight school or training camp, and some were tied by kinship (Jonas and Harper, 2006). To remain secret, however, the strong ties between members of disparate cells were rarely active once the hijackers were in the United States (Krebs, 2001: 49).

The core network (N = 19, k = 54) had a density of 16%, a clustering coefficient of 0.41, and an average path length of 4.75. When dormant cross-ties were taken into account (i.e. temporary sleeper links to coordinate activities) (k = 66), the average path length dropped from 4.75 to 2.79. Krebs used datasets of different size: one of the 'entire plot' (N = 63) and a smaller segment of the core of the operation (i.e. hijackers and their direct associates) (N = 37). The average actor centrality and group centralisation for both networks are presented in Table 18.1.

Table 18.1 Average actor centrality and group centralisation of the 9/11 plot

	Bigger plot	Core of operation
	(N = 63)	(N = 37)
Degree centrality	0.081	0.128
Betweenness centrality	0.032	0.046
Closeness centrality	0.352	0.393
Degree centralisation	0.289	0.306
Betweenness centralisation	0.565	0.296
Closeness centralisation	0.482	0.372

Source: From Krebs (2001, 2002)

Table 18.2 Centrality metrics of 9/11 hijackers, direct and indirect associates

(ID) Actor centrality	Degree (rank)		Betweenness (rank)		Closeness (rank)	
	N = 63	N = 37	N = 63	N = 37	N = 63	N = 37
33 - Mohammed Atta[a]	0.361	0.417	0.588	0.318	0.587	0.571
	(1)	(1)	(1)	(2)	(1)	(1)
40 - Marwan Al-Shehhi[a]	0.295	0.389	0.088	0.158	0.466	0.500
	(2)	(2)	(7)	(4)	(2)	(4)
46 - Hani Hanjour[a]	0.213	0.278	0.126	0.227	0.445	0.507
	(3)	(3,4,5)	(5)	(3)	(3)	(3)
55 - Nawaf Alhazmi	0.180	0.278	0.154	0.334	0.442	0.537
	(4,5)	(3,4,5)	(4)	(1)	(4)	(2)
21 - Essid S.B. Khemais	0.180	–	0.252	–	0.433	–
	(4,5)		(2)		(7)	
15 - Zacarias Moussaoui	0.131	0.056	0.232	0.000	0.436	0.371
	(13)	(34)	(3)	(36)	(5,6)	(22)
25 - Ramzi bin Al-Shibh	0.164	0.222	0.048	0.010	0.436	0.414
	(6,7)	(6)	(9)	(19)	(5,6)	(12)
41 - Ziad Jarrah[a]	0.164	0.278	0.017	0.076	0.424	0.480
	(6,7)	(3,4,5)	(17)	(8)	(9)	(5)

The metrics are based on the top five central actors for the core (N = 37) and the bigger plot (N = 63). The relative rankings in centrality are between brackets.
[a]Identified as a pilot of one of the hijacked airplanes.
Source: From Krebs (2001, 2002)

Although the reported analyses did not include standardised measures (which makes it difficult to compare between groups) the findings suggest that, on average, *actors* in the core were more central than in the bigger plot. Interestingly, the bigger plot was more dominated by a single few actors in terms of coordination (i.e. closeness centrality) and connecting segregated parts of the network (i.e. betweenness centrality). A summary of actor centralities (with relative rankings between brackets) is presented in Table 18.2.

Both analyses consistently identified three of the four pilots (Mohammed Atta, Marwan Al-Shehhi and Hani Hanjour) and Nawaf Alhazmi (senior operative and considered second-in-command to Mohammed Atta) in the top five of key central actors. Mohammed Atta seems to be even more between central in the bigger, perhaps planning, plot than in the core of the operation. The centrality of other actors also varied with network size. Ziad Jarrah (the fourth pilot), for example, was more central in the core but less so in the bigger plot. The reverse holds for Essid Sami Ben Khemais, Ramzi bin Al-Shibh and Zacarias Moussaoui, who were quite central in the bigger plot but far from central to the core of the operation. Interestingly, Moussaoui and Bin Al-Shibh appeared to coordinate activities and broker connections in the bigger plot only,

with Bin Al-Shibh was an active player in both the bigger plot and the core operation. These findings are consistent with publicly available sources that state that Bin Al-Shibh and Moussaoui intended to take part in the 9/11 plot as pilots. Bin Al-Shibh, however, failed to obtain a visa to enter the United States and continued to facilitate between the 9/11 operatives and Al Qaeda leaders in Afghanistan and Pakistan. Moussaoui was arrested three weeks prior to the attacks. Essid S.B. Khemais is believed to have supervised a regional network of Al Qaeda operations in Europe (Global Security).[8]

Over the years, various other studies of the 9/11 network appeared and were based on some variant of the Krebs dataset. Some added network metrics that were not presented in earlier work; others explored new algorithms and illustrated results (for matters of convenience, the analyses are not reported) (Brams et al., 2006; Latora and Marchiori, 2004; Shaikh et al., 2007; Qin et al., 2005). The majority of studies, however, serve exploratory purposes or illustrations and do not elaborate much about the results. Some are even incomplete and focus on visualisations without full reports of the network metrics. Moreover, different criteria (not reported) are used for boundary specification. Broadly speaking, most findings are quite consistent with the ones reported by Krebs (2001). The problem with most studies is, however, that the data used in the analysis are based on media reports that are not complete, and the results cannot be tested for their validity or reliability. The study of Qin et al. (2005) appears an exception with analysis based on more profound qualitative data material of Sageman (2004). Their analysis of the first order 9/11 network identified Osama bin Laden as the most influential actor (i.e. in terms of betweenness centrality) and Ayman Al-Zawahiri – bin Laden's chief deputy within the Al Qaeda movement – as the most active (i.e. in terms of degree centrality). Although the analysis results seem to identify key members of the terrorist plot, media attention may have been selective towards the pilots and Al Qaeda leaders. On the other hand, be this as it may, parts of the analyses support information about actors in such a way that it may offer good starting points and leads to further investigation. After all, intelligence will not only provide investigative leads but also 'squeeze' more out of information that is readily available but would otherwise be overlooked. Nevertheless, one needs to be reminded that SNA can never change the quality of data that serves as input to the analysis.

Practice-based simulation experiments

All 19 hijackers later appeared to be within two steps of Al Qaeda members who had been targeted by the CIA well over a year before the 9/11 attacks occurred (Dryer, 2006). Given that hindsight examining (with known perpetrators, modus operandi, and targets) is relatively easy, Jonas and Harper (2006) questioned whether the mere use of innovative technology would have been able to prevent the 9/11 attacks. To what extent can SNA actually be used to detect hidden structures, improve on intelligence strategies or signal change that can serve as an early warning system? We briefly discuss some studies.

Identify missing links
One of the main problems to combat terrorism is that actors may not be discovered even though they are in fact key players of a terrorist plot. Moreover, for social network analytical purposes, incomplete data can cause undesirable bias. The identification of missing actors and links is therefore a major challenge to overcome. Research methods are being developed to effectively discover core relevant actors (Maeno and Ohsawa, 2009). In an impressive study by Rhodes and Keefe (2007), for example, a Bayesian statistical inference approach reached a prediction accuracy

of 64 per cent to infer network topology and predict terrorist links. Based on these findings the authors emphasise that the inference of network topology can assist in strategic and tactical decision making (e.g. to prioritise intelligence and deploy assets).

Effective intelligence strategies
Tsvetovat and Carley (2007) performed simulation experiments to evaluate the effectiveness of intelligent wiretapping strategies (e.g. based on metrics of degree and betweenness centrality). The goal was to optimise the breadth *and* accuracy of network identification at the lowest possible costs in terms of intelligence resources. SNA-based sampling turned out to be more effective than snowball or random sampling, with the best outcomes generated when combined with the content of communications (e.g. central in cognitive demand and knowledge exclusivity).

Signal change
More recently, McCulloh and Carley (2008) presented an interesting study that combined SNA with statistical process control charts to detect significant changes in communication networks as an alert system to possible signals of threat. The technique successfully signalled network change in communication links between Al Qaeda members (1988–2004), with the initial root of the tragic events of 9/11 being traced back to 1997 (i.e. the reunification of Al Qaeda leader Osama bin Laden, and Ayman Al Zawahiri, leader of Egyptian Islamic Jihad).[9]

Methodological issues

Specific methodological problems have been emphasised extensively in the academic literature. These relate, for example, to data access, data quality (e.g. open sources), the validity of results, boundary specification, inevitable missing data, correlated measures, network changes, statistical assumptions and scaling in relation to network size (Carley, 2004; Reid et al., 2004; Sparrow, 1991b; Stohl and Stohl, 2007; Van der Hulst, 2009a). The boundary specification problem may be of particular concern when studying clandestine networks. Whereas the decisions of what constitutes a network link and who should be included in the network under investigation depend on the research aims of the investigator (see also Scott, 2000: 54), it remains difficult to distinguish significant terrorist connections and activities from casual connections to ignorant acquaintances or sympathisers.

What's more, imperfect and missing data affect analytical outcomes (although this is inherent to any analysis of clandestine networks since they operate covertly and underground). It's important that researchers are aware of these consequences and differentiate in their results, since some measures are more robust to incomplete data than others. Centrality measures, for example, are quite robust in random networks under small amounts of random error (e.g. 10 per cent or less) (Borgatti et al., 2006).[10] The problem becomes more serious, however, if data are not randomly missing but result from systematic errors in data collection (e.g. missing peripheral actors) (Borgatti et al., 2006). The good news is that recent studies have shown that it is possible to estimate networks from just parts of it (Rhodes and Keefe, 2007). Nevertheless, more research is needed to model networks with parameters that are robust in the face of missing data (Carley, 2004), to estimate the effects under various types of missing data (Butts, 2000), and to develop tools to identify areas where important data may be missing (Rhodes and Keefe, 2007).

CRITICAL REFLECTION AND FUTURE DIRECTIONS

A critical review of the state of the art today shows that SNA appears to be a promising field in the fight against terrorism. However, its application is still in its infancy and its toolbox should not be considered as a panacea (Carley et al., 2001). Moreover, the SNA community should be aware of the downside of proliferation since there are a whole lot of studies that appear to play fast and loose with academic standards. The influx of academics from different disciplines is considered to be a necessary requirement for advanced methodological tools (in particular for counterterrorism purposes). There's a looming risk, however, for SNA to become overlooked and swallowed as a mere trick of knowledge discovery, data mining and mass surveillance. Whereas SNA may be useful in retrieving information from huge volumes of data, the discipline is much more than that and the link to social theory and sciences should not be dismissed. In the following sections we address four critical issues to explore and encourage new directions of research that will move the field beyond its current limits: (1) the need for more detailed definitions and differentiation of networks, (2) more empirical network studies, (3) integrated theory and hypothesis testing, and (4) maximised exploitation of available network tools.

Detail and differentiation

First of all, a lot of unnecessary confusion that stems from the literature is the lack of differentiation between terrorist networks (e.g. their governance and scope). Failing to make this distinction limits the development of a practicable topology and counterterrorism strategies that warrant such precision. Another lost opportunity reflected in many studies is the failure to accumulate rich data by way of differentiating between distinctive properties of ties, activities and resources in the data. Data are often insufficiently explored and exploited, limiting a 'dynamic and coherent theory of social action' (Stohl and Stohl, 2007: 102). Stohl and Stohl (2007), for example, stressed the importance to distinguish between uniplex ties (e.g. a shared ideology reinforced by the Internet) and multiplex ties (e.g. actors sharing not just an ideology but also ethnical, kinship or friendship ties). Other relevant distinctions may be the duration of ties, their role categories (formal, informal or both), resources (instrumental, expressive or both), channels of communication (e.g. phone calls, emails, Web sites, face-to-face meetings) and the variety of activities in relation to structure (e.g. travel records, money transfers) (Carley et al., 2004; Krebs, 2001; Van der Hulst, 2004, 2009a).

Also remarkably limited attention is paid to the association of structure with actual roles (e.g. leadership, experts, facilitators), demographic attributes (e.g. age, sex, family status, nationality, ethnicity, education, occupation, working status), psychological attributes (e.g. personality, attitudes, values, religious background), knowledge attributes (e.g. type of education, type of occupation, religion, expertise), even behavioural attributes (e.g. activities, criminal records) and geography. Although labour-intensive, the strength of the SNA method comes with such details, and the formation, evolvement and consequences of social structures may be contingent upon these properties (Burt, 1997; Contractor and Monge, 2004; Robins, 2009; Van der Hulst, 2004, 2009a).

Empirical studies

Second, a lot of work in the realm of SNA and terrorism has been focussed on the development of advanced methods and software. Empirical network studies, however, are quite rare and concentrate for the main part on Islamic terrorism. There is a strong need for more empirical case studies to evaluate and complement these findings in order to develop a topology of static and dynamic network properties. These studies should explicitly consider the preliminary stages of terrorism (e.g. radicalisation, recruitment), other groups and related phenomena (e.g. animal rights, environmental activists, cyber terrorism, network dynamics of youth, the role of women in terrorist networks) and incorporate work from other fields or disciplines (e.g. social movements) (cf. Macy et al., 2004; Wiktorowicz, 2001; Zanini and Edwards, 2001). A particular area of interest that has been neglected so far is the cross-links between terrorism and organised crime. We know that crime has become a critical source of terrorist funding, but it remains unclear to what extent activities are actually joined efforts, on what basis actors decide to cooperate, and whether these cross-links should be considered to pose a 'new threat' or offer 'new opportunities' to counter them (e.g. infiltration) (Makarenko, 2004; Shelley and Picarelli, 2005; Stohl, 2008). Finally, of course, future research is needed to evaluate the effectiveness of SNA-based counterterrorism strategies and interventions (cf. Lum et al., 2006).

Integrated theory and hypothesis testing

Third, an alarming trend observed in the literature is the lack of theory-driven research and the apparently thoughtless applications of descriptive network measures. To improve our understanding of terrorist networks (and be able to provide actionable knowledge in terms of prevention), future network studies should build on explanatory mechanisms related to social, cultural and social psychological theories (e.g. attitudes, norms, status, identity) (Contractor and Monge 2004; Koschade, 2006; Ressler, 2006; Robins and Kashima, 2008; Steglich et al., 2010; Stohl and Stohl, 2007). For valid interpretations of network analyses and the development of automated information retrieval and data manipulation, domain experts may be consulted to help identify behavioural risk indicators and associated parameters.

Analytical exploitation

Fourth, the analytical possibilities of SNA are extensive but they are not fully exploited (Asal and Rethemeyer, 2006). Powerful tools and metrics other than centrality, for example, tend to be overlooked whereas they can add useful (perhaps even better) insights. Although hypotheses can be tested at different levels (e.g. actors, ties, subgroups, the network as a whole, or an interplay of variables) (Borgatti and Foster, 2003; Reid et al., 2004; Wasserman and Faust, 1994),

most studies do not even bother to distinguish between these levels. Insofar as network metrics are used, the most obvious ones (e.g. centrality) appear to be applied without deliberate thinking about what metrics best apply to a particular situation or research problem. This lack of creativity, simply choosing metrics because others do so, may cause an abundance of misapplications.

Part of the criticism addressed here probably stems from the shift of focus from small-scale to large-scale networks (such as the Internet). Issues such as sampling, missing data, variable distributions, modelling change, visualisation techniques, theory-driven computational algorithms, metrics or statistics will remain ongoing methodological challenges in the future (Carley, 2004; McCulloh and Carley, 2008; Reid et al., 2004). Moreover, we expect the trend for collaborative and multidisciplinary research to increase even further (e.g. to develop software systems for automated collection, manipulation, and identification of networks from huge volumes and variable types of data). In fact, scholarly disciplines from information technology, knowledge management, data mining and social network analysis are likely to merge in this domain. However, given that the thriving force behind terrorism is still behaviourally motivated and characterised by human factors (both locally and globally), it may be wise to regain this balance for research purposes and get 'the sociology' back in.

IN SUM

To conclude, although interest is rising, the application of SNA to the study of terrorism is still in its infancy. Methodologically and technically, however, progress has been achieved over recent years. The time is ripe for academics and for security and intelligence agencies to fully exploit new opportunities in SNA research. More than in other areas of network research, it is not unlikely for this domain to transform into a practice-based, multidisciplinary field of cross-disciplinary collaborations between computer scientists, system developers, social scientists and domain experts. Bridging this gap will allow us to:

- Improve our understanding of complex and covert networks (e.g. identify patterns of activity, roles, governing mechanisms);
- Identify and uncover clandestine networks (e.g. core members, overlap between subgroups, missing links);
- Issue more timely and critical warnings of terrorist plots (e.g. through intelligence platforms); and

- Develop more effective counterterrorism and control strategies (e.g. identify vulnerabilities and seek out optimal intelligence, infiltration and destabilisation strategies).

New theoretical paradigms may push innovative progress even further, which at the same time may warrant caution for the discipline to become a mere infusion of technology at the expense of pure substance. We trust this to be a critical warning to all researchers investigating terrorism to keep an eye on the balance between theory, research, practice and technology.

NOTES

1   Many studies concentrate on the process of knowledge management and technological solutions to facilitate conditions *prior* to the analysis (e.g. efficient data collection, automated filtering processes, data mining, information fusion). Because data mining and knowledge management are not equivalent to social network analysis these subjects are beyond the scope of this chapter.

2   Arquilla and Ronfeldt (2001) used the term *netwar* (after Zanini, 1999) to refer to conspirators who, in the absence of a formal enemy, heavily rely on information and communication technology (ICT).

3   Note that strong ties may appear as weak ties if these 'dormant linkages' are activated only when necessary (Krebs, 2001).

4   With kind permission from Springer Science+Business Media: *Computational & Mathematical Organization Theory*, 'On effectiveness of wiretap programs in mapping social networks', vol. 13, 2007, p. 68, M. Tsvetovat & K.M. Carley.

5   Carley et al. (2007), for example, created an integrated toolbox (DNA) that combines features of automated extraction, link analysis (visualisation), statistical analysis and multiagent dynamic modelling (simulation).

6   Some scholars in computer science and engineering, such as Chen and associates (the Artificial Intelligence Lab, University of Arizona), concentrate on automated analysis and dark web mining.

7   For further comparion: the overall network density of the Revolutionary Organisation November 17 (N = 22) was 27 per cent (Rhodes and Keefe, 2007), of the complete network of the Madrid bombings (N = 74) 9 per cent (Rodríguez, 2004), and of the complete network (N = 67) and the core (N = 13) of the Hofstad network in the Netherlands 24 per cent and 62 per cent, respectively (Van der Hulst, 2009b).

8   GlobalSecurity.org is an online database that provides comprehensive information and reference materials (e.g. profiles of terrorist suspects) from various sources worldwide in the areas of defense, intelligence and homeland security.

9   McCulloh and Carley (2008) emphasise that the results should be interpreted with care because findings were not validated. Moreover, the change detection method can only be applied to normally distributed network measures (which may imply that it cannot be used for networks smaller than 30 nodes) and after a period of dynamic equilibrium (to estimate parameters).

10   Borgatti et al. (2006) estimate the correlation between true and observed centrality (in random networks) to be still 0.90 if 5 per cent of network ties are randomly missing.

REFERENCES

Arquilla, J. and Ronfeldt, D. (2001) *Networks and Netwars: The Future of Terror, Crime and Militancy.* Washington DC: Rand.

Asal, V. and Rethemeyer, R.K. (2006) 'Researching terrorist networks', *Journal of Security Education,* 1(4): 65–74.

Baker, W.E. and Faulkner, R. (1993) 'The social organization of conspiracy: Illegal networks in the heavy electronical equipment industry', *American Sociological Review,* 58(6): 837–60.

Barabási, A.-L. and Albert, R. (1999) 'Emergence of scaling in random networks', *Science,* 286: 509–12.

Basu, A. (2005) 'Social network analysis of terrorist organizations in India', at the 2006 Conference of the North American Association for Computational Social and Organizational Science.

Bonacich, P. (1972) 'Factoring and weighting approaches to status scores and clique identification', *Journal of Mathematical Sociology,* 2: 113–20.

Borgatti, S. (2006) 'Identifying sets of key players in a network', *Computational and Mathematical Organization Theory,* 12(1): 21–34.

Borgatti, S., Carley, K.M. and Krackhardt, D. (2006) 'On the robustness of centrality measures under conditions of imperfect data', *Social Networks,* 28(2): 124–36.

Borgatti, S.P. and Foster, P.C. (2003) 'The network paradigm in organizational research: A review and topology', *Journal of Management,* 29(6): 991–1013.

Borum, R. and Gelles, M. (2005) 'Al-Qaeda's operational evolution: Behavioral and organizational perspectives', *Behavioral Sciences and the Law,* 23: 467–83.

Brams, S.J., Mutlu, H. and Ramirez, S.L. (2006) 'Influence in terrorist networks: From undirected to directed graphs', *Studies in Conflict and Terrorism,* 29(7): 703–18.

Burt, R.S. (1992) *Structural Holes: The Social Structures of Competition.* Cambridge, MA: Harvard University Press.

Burt, R.S. (1997) 'The contingent value of social capital', *Administrative Science Quarterly,* 42(2): 339–65.

Burt, R.S. (2005) *Brokerage and Closure: An Introduction to Social Capital.* Oxford: Oxford University Press.

Butts, C. (2000) *Network Inference, Error, and Informant (In) Accuracy: A Bayesian Approach.* Pittsburgh, PA: Carnegie Mellon University.

Carley, K.M. (2003) 'Dynamic network analysis', in R. Breiger, K. Carley and P. Pattison (eds.), *Dynamic Social Network Modeling and Analysis: Workshop Summary and Papers.* Washington, DC: National Academy Press. pp. 133–45.

Carley, K.M. (2004) 'Linking capabilities to needs', in R. Breiger, K. Carley and P. Pattison (eds.), *Dynamic Social Network Modeling and Analysis: Workshop Summary and Papers.* Washington, DC: National Academy Press. pp. 324–44.

Carley, K.M., Diesner, J., Reminga, J. and Tsvetovat, M. (2004) *An Integrated Approach to the Collection and Analysis of Network Data.* Pittsburgh, PA: Carnegie Mellon University.

Carley, K.M., Diesner, J., Reminga, J. and Tsvetovat, M. (2007) 'Toward an interoperable dynamic network analysis toolkit', *Decision Support Systems,* 43: 1324–47.

Carley, K.M., Lee, J.-S. and Krackhardt, D. (2001) 'Destabilizing networks', *Connections,* 24(3): 79–92.

Centola, D. and Macy, M. (2007) 'Complex contagions and the weakness of long ties', *American Journal of Sociology,* 113: 702–34.

Chen, H. (2006) *Intelligence and Security Informatics for International Security: Information Sharing and Data Mining.* New York: Springer.

Coates, J.F. (1996) 'A thriving future for terrorism', *Technological Forecasting and Social Change,* 51: 295–99.

Contractor, N.S. and Monge, P.R. (2004) 'Using multi-theoretical multi-level (MTML) models to study adversarial networks', in R. Breiger, K. Carley, and P. Pattison (eds.), *Dynamic Social Network Modeling and Analysis: Workshop Summary and Papers.* Washington, DC: National Academy Press. pp. 324–44.

Cornish, D.B. and Clarke, R.V. (2002) 'Analyzing organized crimes', in A. Piquero and S.G. Tibbetts (eds.), *Rational Choice and Criminal Behavior.* New York: Garland. pp. 41–62.

Dean, G. (2007) 'Criminal profiling in a terrorism context', in R.N. Kocsis (ed.), *Criminal Profiling: International Theory, Research, and Practice.* Totowa, NJ: Humana Press. pp. 169–88.

Dryer, A. (2006) 'How the NSA does social network analysis', *Washington Post.*

DSTL (2004) *Network Methods as a Tool for Defence Analysis.* London: UK Defence Science and Technology Laboratory.

Erickson, B.H. (1981) 'Secret societies and social structure', *Social Forces,* 60(1): 188–210.

Freeman, L.C. (1979) 'Centrality in social networks, I: Conceptual clarification', *Social Networks,* 1(3): 215–39.

Friedkin, N.E. and Johnsen, E.C. (1999) 'Social influence networks and opinion change', *Advances in Group Processes,* 16: 1–29.

Garfinkel, S.L. (2003) 'Leaderless resistance today', *First Monday,* 8(3). www.firstmonday.org.

Granovetter, M.S. (1973) 'The strength of weak ties', *American Journal of Sociology,* 78: 1360–80.

Harper, W.R. and Harris, D.H. (1975) 'The application of link analysis to police intelligence', *Human Factors,* 17(2): 157–64.

Jonas, J. and Harper, J. (2006) 'Effective counterterrorism and the limited role of predictive data mining', *Policy Analysis,* 584: 1–12. Washington, DC: Cato Institute.

Jordán, F. (2008) 'Predicting target selection by terrorists: A network analysis of the 2005 London underground attacks', *International Journal of Critical Infrastructures,* 4(1/2): 206–14.

Kadushin, C. (2002) 'The motivational foundation of social networks', *Social Networks,* 24: 77–91.

Klerks, P. (2001) 'The network paradigm applied to criminal organisations', *Connections,* 24(3): 53–65.

Koschade, S. (2006) 'A social network analysis of Jemaah Islamiyah: The applications to counterterrorism and intelligence', *Studies in Conflict and Terrorism,* 29: 559–75.

Krebs, V.E. (2001) 'Mapping networks or terrorist cells', *Connections,* 24(3): 43–52.

Krebs, V.E. (2002) 'Uncloaking terrorist networks', *First Monday,* 7(4). www.firstmonday.org/issues/issue7_4/krebs.

Latora, V. and Marchiori, M. (2004) 'How science of complex networks can help in developing strategy against terrorism', *Chaos, Solitions and Fractals,* 20: 69–75.

Lin, N., Cook, K. and Burt, R.S. (2001) *Social Capital: Theory and Research.* New York: Aldine de Gruyter.

Lum, C., Kennedy, L.W. and Sherley, A. (2006) 'Are counter-terrorism strategies effective? The results of the Campbell systematic review on counter-terrorism evaluation research', *Journal of Experimental Criminology,* 2: 489–516.

Macy, M.W., Kitts, J.A., Flache, A. and Benard, S. (2004) 'Polarization in dynamic networks: A Hopfield model of emergent structure', in R. Breiger, K. Carley and P. Pattison (eds.), *Dynamic Social Network Modeling and Analysis: Workshop Summary and Papers.* Washington, DC: National Academy Press. pp. 162–73.

Maeno, Y. and Ohsawa, Y. (2009) 'Analyzing covert social network foundation behind terrorism disaster', *International Journal of Services Sciences,* 2(2): 125–41.

Makarenko, T. (2004) 'The crime-terror continuum: Tracing the interplay between transnational organised crime and terrorism', *Global Crime,* 6(1): 129–45.

McCulloh, I.A. and Carley, K.M. (2008) *Social Network Change Detection.* CASOS technical report CMU-ISR-08–116. Pittsburgh, PA: Carnegie Mellon University.

McPherson, M., Smith-Lovin, L. and Cook, J.M. (2001) 'Birds of a feather: Homophily in social networks', *Annual Review of Sociology,* 27: 415–44.

Memon, N., Larsen, H.L., Hicks, D.L. and Harkiolakis, N. (2008) 'Detecting hidden hierarchy in terrorist networks: Some case studies', in C.C. Yang et al. (eds.), *Intelligence and Security Informatics—LNCS 5075.* Berlin: Springer-Verlag. pp. 477–89.

Milgram, S. (1967) 'The small world problem', *Psychology Today,* 2(1): 60–67.

Moon, I.-C. and Carley, K.M. (2007) 'Modeling and simulation of terrorist networks in social and geospatial dimensions', *IEEE Intelligent Systems, special issue on Social Computing,* 22: 40–49.

Morselli, C., Giguère, C. and Petit, K. (2007) 'The efficiency/ security trade-off in criminal networks', *Social Networks*, 29: 143–53.

Qin, J., Xu, J.J., Hu, D., Sageman, M. and Chen, H. (2005) 'Analyzing terrorist networks: A case study of the Global Salafi Jihad network', in P. Kantor et al. (eds.), *Intelligence and Security Informatics—LNCS 3495*. Berlin: Springer-Verlag. pp. 287–304.

Rapoport, D. (2003) 'The four waves of rebel terror and September 11', in C. Kegley (ed.), *The New Global Terrorism*. New Jersey, NJ: Prentice Hall. pp. 36–51.

Reid, E., Qin, J., Chung, W., Xu, J., Zhou, Y., Schumaker, R., Sageman, M. and Chen, H. (2004) 'Terrorism knowledge discovery project: A knowledge discovery approach to addressing the threats of terrorism'. Working paper.

Ressler, S. (2006) 'Social network analysis as an approach to combat terrorism: Past, present, and future research', *Homeland Security Affairs*, 2(2). www.hsaj.org/pages/volume2/issue2/pdfs/2.2.8.pdf.

Rhodes, C.J. and Keefe, E.M.J. (2007) 'Social network topology: A Bayesian approach', *Journal of the Operational Research Society*, 58: 1605–11.

Robins, G. (2009) 'Understanding individual behaviors within covert networks: The interplay of individual qualities, psychological predispositions, and network effects', *Trends in Organized Crime*, 12(2): 166–87.

Robins, G. and Kashima, Y. (2008) 'Social psychology and social networks: Individuals and social systems', *Asian Journal of Social Psychology*, 11: 1–12.

Rodríguez, J.A. (2004). 'The March 11th terrorist network: In its weakness lies its strength', Paper presented at the VIII Congreso Español de Sociología, Alicante.

Rothenberg, R. (2001) 'From whole cloth: Making up the terrorist network', *Connections*, 24(3): 36–42.

Sageman, M. (2004) *Understanding Terror Networks*. Philadelphia: University of Pennsylvania Press.

Sageman, M. (2008) *Leaderless Jihad: Terror Networks in the Twenty-First Century*. Philadelphia: University of Pennsylvania Press.

Schroeder, J., Xu, J. and Chen, H. (2003) 'CrimeLink Explorer: Using domain knowledge to facilitate automated crime association analysis', *Lecture Notes and Computer Science*, 2665: 168–80.

Schwartz, D.M. and Rouselle, T. (2008) 'Targeting criminal networks: Using social network analysis to develop enforcement and intelligence priorities', *IALEIA Journal*, 18(1): 18–44.

Scott, J. (2000) *Social Network Analysis*. London: Sage.

Shaikh, M.A., Wang, J, Yang, Z. and Song, Y. (2007) 'Graph structural mining in terrorist networks', in R. Alhaij et al. (eds.), *Advanced Data Mining and Applications—LNAI 4632*. Berlin: Springer-Verlag. pp. 570–77.

Shelley, L.I. and Picarelli, J.T. (2005) 'Methods and motives: Exploring links between transnational organized crime and international terrorism', *Trends in Organized Crime*, 9(2): 52–67.

Snijders, T.A.B., Steglich, C.E.G. and Van de Bunt, G.G. (2010) 'Introduction to stochastic actor-based models for network dynamics', *Social Networks*, 32: 44–60.

Sparrow, M.K. (1991a) 'Network vulnerabilities and strategic intelligence in law enforcement', *Journal of Intelligence and Counterintelligence*, 5(3): 255–74.

Sparrow, M.K. (1991b) 'The application of network analysis to criminal intelligence: An assessment of the prospects', *Social Networks*, 13: 251–74.

Steglich, C., Snijders, T.A.B. and Pearson, M. (2010) 'Dynamic networks and behavior: Separating selection from influence', *Sociological Methodology*, 40: 329–93.

Stohl, C. and Stohl, M. (2007). 'Networks of terror: Theoretical assumptions and pragmatic consequences', *Communication Theory*, 17: 93–124.

Stohl, M. (2008) 'Networks, terrorists and criminals: The implications for community policing', *Crime, Law and Social Change*, 50: 59–72.

Tsvetovat, M. and Carley, K.M. (2005) 'Structural knowledge and success of anti-terrorist activity: The downside of structural equivalence', *Journal of Social Structure* 6. www.casos.cs.cmu.edu/publications/papers/.

Tsvetovat, M. and Carley, K.M. (2007) 'On effectiveness of wiretap programs in mapping social networks', *Computational and Mathematical Organization Theory*, 13: 63–87.

Van der Hulst, R.C. (2004) 'Gender differences in workplace authority: An empirical study on social networks'. Thesis, Groningen: Groningen University.

Van der Hulst, R.C. (2009a) 'Introduction to Social Network Analysis (SNA) as an investigative tool', *Trends in Organized Crime*,12(2): 101–21.

Van der Hulst, R.C. (2009b) 'Terroristische netwerken en intelligence: Een sociale netwerkanalyse van de Hofstadgroep [Terrorist networks and intelligence: A social network analysis of the Dutch Hofstad network]', *Tijdschrift voor Veiligheid*, 8(2): 8–27.

Wasserman, S. and Faust, K. (1994) *Social Network Analysis: Methods and Applications*. Cambridge: Cambridge University Press.

Watts, D.J. (1999) 'Networks, dynamics and the small world phenomenon', *American Journal of Sociology*, 105(2): 493–527.

Wiktorowicz, Q. (2001) 'The new global threat: Transnational salafis and jihad', *Middle East Policy*, 8(4): 18–38.

Xu, J., Marshall, B., Kaza, S. and Chen, H.C. (2004) 'Analyzing and visualizing criminal network dynamics: A case study', in H. Chen et al. (eds.), *Intelligence and Security Informatics – LNCS 3073*. Berlin: Springer-Verlag. pp. 359–77.

Zanini, M. (1999) 'Middle Eastern terrorism and netwar', *Studies in Conflict and Terrorism*, 22(3): 247–56.

Zanini, M. and Edwards, S.J.A. (2001) 'The networking of terror in the information age', in J. Arquilla and D. Ronfeldt (eds.), *Networks and Netwars: The Future of Terror, Crime and Militancy*. Washington, DC: Rand. 29–60.

19

Scientific and Scholarly Networks

Howard D. White

INTRODUCTION

In Randall Collins's (1998) authoritative phrase, scientific and scholarly networks are "coalitions in the mind." Key ties in them are of two sorts. They may be social, involving direct interactions among living persons such as coauthors or other colleagues. Or they may be cultural, involving persons known only through reading, which induces ties beyond the boundaries of personal acquaintanceship. Both social and cultural ties, moreover, can appear in the same network. Citation networks, for example, are frequently "sociocultural," in that scholars may routinely cite and be cited with living or dead acquaintances, living or dead contemporaries they have never met, and dead non-contemporaries they could not possibly have met. Contrast that with exclusively social networks, such as those consisting of sexual partners or drug users who share needles.

As a matter of course, scientists and scholars must not only read but write; their eminence grows with publication output and peer recognition of its value. In writing, furthermore, they must link their texts with earlier ones by using appropriate terminology and references to precedent work. These practices define learned literatures – bodies of writings with specialized vocabularies and explicit cross-textual links. Scientific and scholarly networks (S&SNs) are thereby uniquely grounded in literatures. Even studies of personal communication in such networks – who emailed whom and how frequently, who shared data, and the like – generally support an ultimate interest in the *authors* associated in a given literature. Readers especially want to know who is linked to whom and how closely, because that can reveal both intellectual and social structures within a specialty or discipline.

If not available from transaction logs, data on authors as persons must be gathered through labor-intensive interviews and surveys, since their social interactions go largely unrecorded. In contrast, data on their connections in literatures – in texts – are available in existing bibliographic databases, whose records can be mined with relative ease. Hence, many studies of S&SNs are bibliometric in nature. They reveal patterns of, for example, coauthorship, cocitation, or co-term relationships; the latter are noun phrases that co-occur in the titles, indexing, abstracts, or full texts of publications. (A network of author names can be converted into a network of co-terms and vice versa; see, for example, Lievrouw et al., 1987). As units of analysis in network studies, the names of publishing scientists or scholars thus have an unusual ambiguity. On the one hand, they can be understood as referring to *persons*, realized in the flesh as interviewees. On the other, they can be understood as referring to *bylines*, realized in a database as bibliographic types with countable tokens. (The string "Barry Wellman," for example, may refer to a Toronto-based professor or to words appearing across the title-pages of his books and articles.) Either usage – person or byline – may appear in a study without involving the other. But this ambiguity can also be exploited in the same study: social variables on persons can be put in a matrix with bibliometric variables on the same persons as bylines, and relationships can be sought between them. Moreover, if the individuals in a network can be ranked and compared on a variable, this necessarily makes for the superlatives – highest-lowest, most-least, best-worst – that pique human interest. (Bibliometric rankings not tied to networks may be even more provocative, but they will not be treated in any depth here.[1])

THE EIES FILE

Superlative positions are particularly noticeable when network data are visualized. As an illustration, consider a well-known data file on how 32 geographically dispersed social scientists used the Electronic Information Exchange System (EIES) in the pre-Internet days of 1978. Funded by a grant from the National Science Foundation, EIES allowed these researchers to send then-novel email and newsgroup messages to each other by dedicated computers (Freeman and Freeman, 1980). The 32 were themselves specialists in social networks research and now became linked nodes in their own emergent structure. The variables in the file include the number of messages between each pair of researchers, their disciplines, and their citation counts for 1978 from the Social Sciences Citation Index, which is a rough gauge of their eminence as authors.

The EIES matrices are distributed as specimen data with UCINet, a leading analytical software package, and can be visualized with its built-in NetDraw. Figure 19.1 displays one result, an interplay of social and bibliometric variables. The nodes represent the 32 (unidentified) researchers, with node shapes coding their disciplines. The nodes are also sized proportionately to the researchers' citation counts for 1978, which are added as labels. Links have been pruned to represent only flows of at least 25 messages between pairs. Message volume is represented by link widths, and so the thinnest represent flows of about 25; the thickest, about 560. Arrow heads indicate direction of flow; if links are one-headed, only the target person received 25 or more messages from the other pair member; if two-headed, both persons did. The higher value for the pair determines thickness.

The EIES network plainly has a core of highly interactive researchers. The person at the center with 19 citations – call him "19" – has ties at the ≥ 25 level with all but three other group members. This same central person is connected by dense message traffic with an inner ring of seven others having (clockwise from lower left) 17, 18, 12, 15, 1, 9, 3, and 0 citations. Several of these latter

persons exchange messages heavily with others as well. These eight are the group's superlative communicators.

However, the visualization reveals an interesting split. The eight persons with the highest citation counts, the group's superlative scholars, are all on the lower *periphery* of the network. On the basis of their one-year counts, from 46 to 170, these worthies are all more eminent than the persons in the core. Yet they are linked to only one or two core researchers, and their message volume is comparatively low. Furthermore, the three most eminent citees, those with counts of 56, 64, and 170, are all *recipients* of messages from "19" at the center. They did not send him or anyone else enough messages to meet the ≥ 25 threshold. (For example, the most highly cited EIES member, "170" at lower right, sent a total of four messages to "19" and five each to two other members during the entire study.) Other high-ranked citees in the lower periphery, those with counts of 54, 46, and 31, also received more messages than they sent.

The split characterizes, then, a core of less established, possibly younger researchers who used the EIES technology vigorously, and a peripheral group of more established, possibly older researchers who were much cooler toward it. (Did the latter regard newfangled email as a distraction from more serious writing?) This non-meeting of minds and tastes is not explained by disciplinary affiliation. While there are other identifiable subgroups in the network (persons with middling citation and message counts; persons with few or no citations and few EIES partners), the possible social and psychological differences between the less eminent "enthusiasts" and the more eminent "lurkers" remain provocative 30 years after the 1978 experiment.

SOCIAL TIES

Almost all studies of S&SNs are historical, based on time-bound relationships of real (if sometimes unidentified) individuals or their publications. The exception would be studies that simulate the dynamics and properties of such networks by computer (e.g., Barabási et al., 2002; Börner et al., 2004) and even these are validated against historical data. Granted the base in history, however, the styles of research on S&SNs differ sharply, depending on whether one approaches networks abstractly, at a level in which individual authors are hidden in summary measures, or concretely, at a level in which they and their works are discussed in rich detail. The physicists Mark Newman and Albert-László Barabási usually take

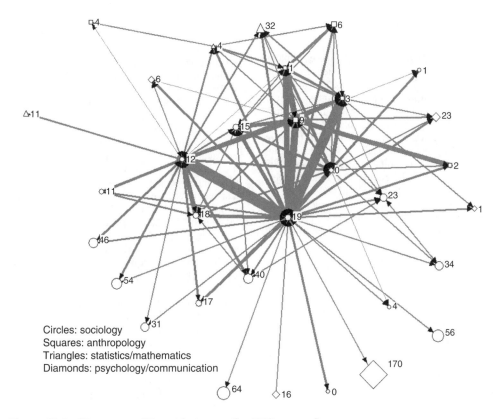

Figure 19.1 Messages ≥ 25 sent between the EIES researchers

the first approach; the sociologist Randall Collins, the second. In between are studies that derive the communication, collaboration, or citation patterns of named authors from numeric matrices.

Remarks on some pairwise social ties in author matrices follow. The authors are presumed to be living, although recent decedents could also appear. The examples of ties from the literature are meant simply to be typical; they do not to exhaust the possibilities.

Degree of acquaintanceship

As described in Wasserman and Faust's textbook (1994: 62–63), the variables in the EIES file also included self-reported degrees of acquaintanceship between each pair of researchers in January and September 1978. As one would expect, the scale (slightly paraphrased here) was ordinal: 0, Do not know; 1, Have heard of but not met; 2, Have met; 3, Am a friend of; 4, Am a close personal friend of. An obvious hypothesis to test

is the effect of the EIES postings on degree of acquaintanceship as of September, given the January baseline. This was done in Freeman and Freeman (1980).

Modes of communication

White et al. (2004a) described communication modes among 16 members of Globenet, a pseudonym for a small multinational organization devoted to multidisciplinary research in human development. The Globenetters met informally in small groups and also formally three times a year. The 16 were asked how frequently they used specific modes with one another – face-to-face conversation, telephone, paper/post, email, and fax – and whether communications were scholarly or nonscholarly. Except for email, the list is like one in Lievrouw et al. (1987). Nowadays, one would expect email to dominate in any dispersed academic group, but the other modes still occur and must be presented in questionnaires.

Type of collaboration

There are many kinds of collaboration besides coauthorships (Sonnenwald, 2007, has examples), and they may or may not be acknowledged in print (Cronin, 1995, Cronin et al., 2003). Obviously they will vary from field to field. Some researchers, for instance, give software or machine-readable data to others (McCain, 2000), and some exchange physical materials, such as fruit flies in *Drosophila* genetics (McCain, 1991). The categories of Globenetters' collaborations used in White et al. (2004a) include reading each other's papers and discussing each other's ideas. These are varieties of the "trusted assessor" role noted in Mullins (1973: 18–19) and Chubin (1976). According to Laudel (2002), coauthorship credit in bylines results from divisions of *creative* labor among peers. Acknowledgements, a lesser credit, go to peers who simply consult as trusted assessors, provide access to equipment, transmit know-how, or stimulate ideas.

A noteworthy collaboration between non-peers is the mentor-pupil relationship. For the field of library and information science, this relationship is quantified and visualized on an interesting website called MPACT (Marchionini et al., 2006). Collins (1998) observes that mentor-pupil ties are almost invariably integral to the close-knit structure of S&SNs. His book includes many diagrams of intellectual lineages in which such ties are shown for world-class figures. For example, his transgenerational diagram of "Young Hegelians and Religious/Political Radicals, 1835–1900" (p. 766) shows that the German philosopher Friedrich Schelling taught Søren Kierkegaard, Friedrich Engels, Mikhail Bakunin, and Jacob Burckhardt. Burckhardt in turn taught Friedrich Nietzsche. By publishing research on scientific or scholarly problems in creative reaction to the work of others, intellectuals build up what Collins terms "cultural capital." Over time, the perceived novelty and importance of their ideas earn them varying degrees of recognition (through, for example, citation or commentary). It is advantageous for pupils to have mentors whose cultural capital they can share, and no less advantageous for mentors to have pupils who can extend their lines of thought. Renown and resources depend on individuals' positions in networks, where being the focus of attention or not translates into positions of relative centrality and peripherality.

Coauthorships

Quantitative studies of networks of all kinds have grown rapidly in the past two decades, prompted not least by fascination with graph-theoretic models of the Internet and the Web (Newman et al., 2006). Coauthorship networks are among those frequently studied, both within library and information science and beyond it. However, influential theorists from other disciplines such as Newman and Barabási do not write about this form of collaboration primarily as historians. They are interested in the structural and evolutionary properties of very large networks regardless of what, or whom, the nodes represent. Hence, they will analyze structures in websites or electrical grids as readily as people. If they do sometimes write about people, it is because the necessary data are already computerized, solid, and vast, with scores or hundreds of thousands of names linked in bibliographic records.

A famous precedent sketched by Newman and explored at length by de Castro and Grossman (1999) is the network of persons who coauthored papers with the Hungarian mathematician Paul Erdös (1913–1996). He was hugely prolific, and, in wry homage, friends have assigned an Erdös number of 1 to his more than 500 immediate coauthors, an Erdös number of 2 to those who coauthored papers with the 1s, and so on. According to Wikipedia, "Some have estimated that 90% of the world's active mathematicians have an Erdös number smaller than 8 . . . ." Grossman (2007) discusses this phenomenon on the Web, with downloadable raw data; for visualizations, see Batagelj and Mrvar (2000).

Other visualizations of coauthorship that may interest present readers include one in Otte and Rousseau (2002) of 57 social network researchers (many well-known, such as Barry Wellman, Lin Freeman, Patrick Doreian, Stanley Wasserman) and a larger one of 630 network scientists in Börner (2007). The latter gives hyperlinks to color enlargements of its coauthorship maps on the Web.

Conflicts between authors

Collins (1998: 1) starts his book with the sentence, "Intellectual life is first of all conflict and disagreement." He argues that scientists and scholars vie for attention and recognition either by enhancing an existing body of thought or by attacking it from a rival viewpoint. The tie between Bakunin and Karl Marx in his diagram "Young Hegelians and Religious/Political Radicals, 1835–1900" is one of mutual opposition. Marx is also shown as attacking Max Stirner, and Stirner as attacking G. W. F. Hegel, his former teacher. The novelists Ivan Turgenev and Fyodor Dostoyevsky are shown to be at odds with the "Russian nihilists"–Nikolai Chernyshevsky, Dimitri Pisarev, and Sergey Nechaiev. The conflicts

Collins notes are not based on his systematic assessment of each pair of authors in an "intellectual hostility" matrix; he simply codes salient oppositions from his reading. But such a matrix could be formed. In our own day, countless intellectuals both obscure and famous have clashed (e.g., Stephen Jay Gould and Steven Pinker).

Conflicts and competition may of course occur between subdisciplinary groups as well as individuals. Throughout his book Collins asserts that, at any given time, fields are structured by three to six groups competing for "attention space": "What I refer to as the law of small numbers proposes that there is always a small number of rival positions at the forefront of intellectual creativity; there is no single inner chamber, but there are rarely more than half a dozen" (Collins, 1998: 42). We will see an example of opposed groups later in a cocited author map of science studies.

A note on invisible colleges

This 17th-century term was repurposed by Derek J. de Solla Price (1961) and later examined at book length by the sociologist Diana Crane (1972). Originally it referred to a group of amateurs in natural philosophy – a kind of forerunner to the Royal Society – who met periodically in London to discuss ideas on the science and technology of the day. In Price's 20th-century usage, it refers to in-groups of researchers who work in different locales but who intercommunicate intensively because of their common interests in subject specialties (cf. Zuccala, 2006).

Price saw modern invisible colleges emerging as vehicles for quick transmission of scientific news. He guessed that up to 100 scientists could efficiently trade messages by word of mouth or informal letters as a corrective to slow-paced journal publication. Whatever their numbers, his invisible colleges comprise living researchers who exhibit all the social ties mentioned previously in this section. Members convene meetings; talk to and write other members; battle over claims and theories; exchange drafts, preprints, and reprints of their articles for critical scrutiny; and routinely enter into various forms of collaboration, including coauthorships. This last practice is adaptive because it speeds up productivity and allows more authors to gain credit for publications.

Building on Price, Crane (1970, 1972) saw invisible colleges as developing core-and-periphery structures on several levels (White and McCain, 1989: 130). Socially, the ties in them are very unequally distributed, with a few core people ("stars") defined by many more communicative or productive activities than peripheral people (as was manifest in the indegrees and outdegrees

of the EIES group). Bibliometrically, the works published in invisible colleges are concentrated in relatively few core journals, with the remainder scattered over many more peripheral journals; also, the indexing of these publications involves relatively few core terms that are used again and again, while many peripheral terms are used with decreasing frequency. Cognitively, members of invisible colleges must strike a balance between cores and peripheries as they seek information (cf. Sandstrom, 2001). If they look only to the cores – that is, read and talk to the same insiders, cite only personal acquaintances and themselves, retrieve publications already known, search on familiar indexing terms and in familiar journals – they risk research that is inbred and redundant. If they look only to the peripheries – that is, consult people at the edge of (or beyond) their specialties, expand their vocabularies for document retrieval, browse widely for novel items, read to push the limits of interdisciplinarity – they risk research that is eccentric and noncumulative. Invisible colleges grow as subject specialties over time, Crane implied, when individual members avoid either of these extremes.

CITATION TIES

Author intercitation

One way to find the inner and outer rings of specialties is to analyze intercitation – the record of who has cited whom within a fixed set of authors. Such data start with the author names in identical order on the rows and columns of a matrix. (The same structure appears in the EIES matrix of senders and receivers of email.) Each row name designates a possible citer of other members of the set (a sender). Each column name designates the same person as a possible citee of the other members (a receiver). From citation indexes, counts of "outcitations" sent and "incitations" received are placed in the off-diagonal cells, as in Figure 19.2. Cells on the diagonal can be left blank or filled with self-citations. The resulting matrix is asymmetric, since, for example, author A and author B need not cite each other equally.

	A	B	C
A	-	3	2
B	5	-	0
C	9	4	-

Figure 19.2 Intercitation matrix

Figure 19.2, which excludes self-citations, shows that author A has received the most citations from others, 14, while author C has sent the most, 13. Theoretically, A may be regarded as an intellectual leader (influencing the group's ideas), whereas C is more of an organizational leader (binding the group together). These two roles, discussed in Mullins (1973), appeared clearly among the Globenetters in White et al. (2004a).

Figure 19.3 displays an unpublished network from a study of communication patterns in a national organization for multidisciplinary water research (Dimitrova et al., 2007). Made with NetDraw, it reveals how 12 academics have cited each other the years. The data were obtained in 2007 from Scisearch and Social Scisearch combined. To preserve anonymity, real names have been masked by disciplinary identifications. As in Figure 19.1, two-headed arrows represent mutual citation, whereas one-headed arrows represent citation that went unreciprocated. Intercitation counts ranged from 1 (thinnest links) to 31 (from

Biologist 1 to Ecologist 2). While 31 is the largest single flow of outcitation, the author receiving incitations from the most other authors – five – is Ecologist 3. His citations from others total 30, suggesting that he is something of an intellectual influence among these scientists. The subnetwork of Ecologists and Biologists is central to the group; the others are peripheral, especially the two linked Economists and the isolate Geographer.

Author cocitation

As noted earlier, intercitation ties may and often do – but need not – coincide with social ties among the living. The same is true of cocitation ties. However, the sources of intercitation and cocitation are quite different. Intercitation occurs only among authors in a predesignated set (whether formally organized or not). Cocitation is *studied* for authors in a predesignated set, but those doing the cociting are authors in general, an open-ended

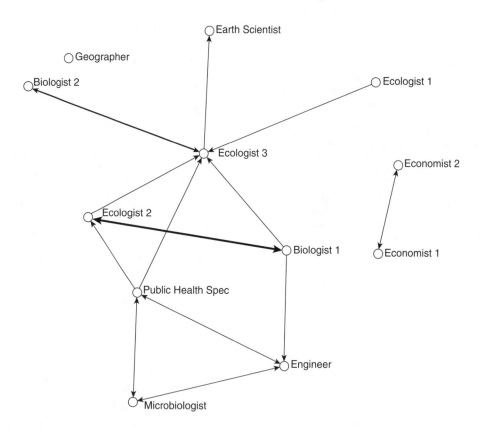

Figure 19.3   Intercitation map of 12 water researchers

group possibly running into the thousands. Author cocitation analysis thus reveals the "citers' consensus" about a field. It is especially useful for identifying major authors and grouping them into specialties – for example, researchers on terrorism as seen in Reid and Chen (2005).

Two authors are cocited when any of their works appear in the references of another work by anyone (White and McCain, 1989). Every time works by the two authors co-occur in an additional list of references, their cocitation count goes up by one. It is the cociting works themselves that are counted, and not the number of works by either author that are cocited in reference lists. Author cocitation networks are created from matrices of such counts.

The first studies of cocitation involved scientific *articles* as the linked nodes. Cocited *authors* as nodes are simply aggregations of cited articles or other publications. Thus, an "author" in this sense is a collection of bylines – an *oeuvre* – not a person. But, to repeat, data on *oeuvres* and on their authors as persons can be combined in the same matrix for analysis.

As seen in Figure 19.4, cocitation is symmetric: A's count with B equals B's with A. Any two authors whatever may be substituted for A and B; for instance, White (2000) cocites Eugene Garfield, the father of citation analysis, with Walt Whitman. But if such pairings are not widely picked up by others (as Garfield-Whitman has not been), they have only idiosyncratic meanings. It is the *repeated* cocitation of a pair of authors over time that implies some important tie between them.

Small (1978) advanced the idea that scientific articles may be repeatedly cited because they serve as convenient shorthand for specific concepts: a chemist simply invokes, say, "Cromer and Weber, 1965" rather than explaining the concept of "atomic scattering factors." So, too, a highly cocited author pair may come to imply a fairly stable meaning over time. The most common reason for cocitation is probably perceived similarity of topic (or sometimes of method). Cocited author pairings tend to narrow the range of topics that two author names might imply singly. For example, Derek J. de Solla Price was a polymath who made major contributions to the history of

science, the history of technology, the sociology of scientific communication, and bibliometrics. But when he and Diana Crane are cited together (as they are in 416 articles in Social Scisearch at this writing), the topic their joint names symbolize is most likely to be "invisible colleges." When either Price or Crane is cited separately, that topic is of course not necessarily implied.

It frequently happens that highly cocited authors are "on the same side" intellectually; they may even have written works together. But cocitation can also reflect conflicts or oppositions of the sort Collins displays. In an early paper on cocited author networks, McCain (1983) mapped macroeconomists and found that the nodes for James Tobin and Milton Friedman were algorithmically placed in close proximity. This is not because the two are soulmates, but because citers have so often joined them as symbols of warring schools of thought. A textbook quoted by McCain (p. 289) calls Tobin "the outspoken arch-opponent of Milton Friedman's analysis of monetary problems and of his opposition to activist government intervention." Sandstrom and White (2007) likewise assembled the authors most highly cocited with the anthropologist Marvin Harris for a chapter in a book on his intellectual legacy. The top three were Clifford Geertz, Marshall Sahlins, and Claude Levi-Strauss, all of whom Harris has severely criticized (with Sahlins returning the favor).

Figure 19.5 illustrates some cocited author relations. It is an "ego-centered" map of late 20th-century science studies that was created with the multifaceted Derek J. de Solla Price as seed. The map shows him (bottom center) and the 24 other authors most frequently cited with him in Arts and Humanities Citation Index (AHCI) during 1988–1997.[2] Names have the terse "surname-hyphen-initials" format of the AHCI database; Price becomes "Price-DJD." The numbers on the links are the cocitation counts for each author pair. The structure displayed is a Pathfinder Network (PFNET), whose algorithm examines the cocitation count for every pair of authors in the matrix and then draws links reflecting only the *highest* (or tied highest) counts between author pairs. Thus Garfield's highest count in these data is with Price, but Price's and Crane's are with the sociologist Robert K. Merton. All other ties are pruned away, even though most author pairs in the matrix have counts greater than zero, and Price has nonzero counts with everyone.

Given the names and barebones cocitation links of Figure 19.5, a knowledgeable interpreter can discern a "coalition in the mind" – one involving different generations, multidisciplinarity, personal ties, and conflicts, as Collins would predict

	A	B	C
A	-	22	7
B	22	-	0
C	7	0	-

Figure 19.4   Cocitation matrix

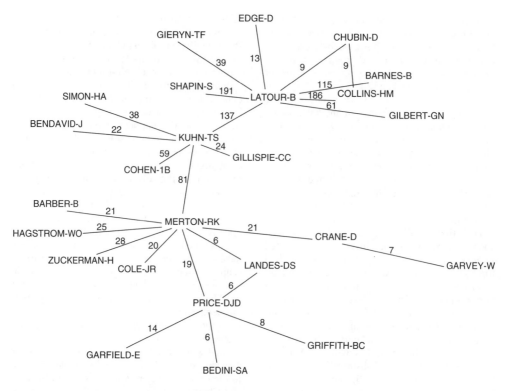

Figure 19.5   PFNET of Derek J. de Solla Price and 24 authors cocited with him

(see also the map in White and McCain, 2000). The map does not capture the latest generation of leaders in science studies, but rather two previous ones. Some of the authors in it are dead (e.g., Price died at 61 in 1983; Merton at 92 in 2003), and the living are very senior in their fields. Specialties represented include bibliometrics (Garfield, Griffith, Simon), the sociology of science (Merton and the group around him; Ben-David, Gieryn, Chubin), the history of science (Kuhn, Gillispie, Cohen, Shapin), the history of technology, notably of scientific instruments (Bedini, Landes), and the sociology of scientific knowledge (Latour, Edge, Barnes, H. M. Collins, Gilbert). Social ties include husband-wife (Merton-Zuckerman) mentor-pupil (e.g., Merton-Cole, Price-Crane), acquaintances (e.g., Gieryn-Latour), close personal friends (e.g., Price-Griffith), and coauthors (e.g., Zuckerman-Cole, Garvey-Griffith).

Because of the way author cocitation works, Figure 5 automatically captures two schools of thought that began competing for attention space in the 1970s – American sociology of science centered on Merton and constructivist accounts of science centered on Bruno Latour.[3] The map also picks up individual authors who have engaged in controversies (e.g., Latour vs. H. M. Collins; Griffith vs. Edge). Price was much closer intellectually to Merton than to Latour, which is why relatively few constructivists appear in his top 24 cocitees. (To some degree, this opposition is maintained in two journals, *Scientometrics*, which is Pricean and relatively Mertonian, and *Social Studies of Science*, which is constructivist.) It is fitting that the two opposed schools are joined in the map through Thomas S. Kuhn, a supremely equivocal figure. Distinguishing Mertonians and anti-Mertonians (broadly, constructivists), Doty et al. (1991: 26) comment: ". . . the work of Thomas Kuhn, especially *The Structure of Scientific Revolutions* (1970) with its emphasis on the cognitive aspects of science, has usually been placed on the anti-Mertonian side. The identification of Kuhn as an anti-Mertonian, however, is clearly wrong-headed: both Merton and Kuhn expressed admiration for the other's work and disappointment in those who insisted on their incompatibility.... "

Author cocitation maps stimulate one to look for such guidance in interpreting linkages. It is especially interesting to have authors comment on cocitation networks centered on them, as does the population geneticist Montgomery Slatkin in White et al. (2004b).

Historiographs

These are descent-chains of scientific or scholarly publications ordered by year. They resemble genealogies, in the sense of earlier writings that give rise to later writings like a series of "begats." They also somewhat resemble Collins's diagrams of interpersonal relationships. Although their unit of analysis is individual publications (and not *oeuvres* or persons), they can corroborate intellectual influences on scientists and scholars as persons, including self-influence. The example in Figure 19.6, to be discussed shortly, is taken from the literature on "small world" networks and includes two authors already mentioned, Barabási and Newman.

The first major historiograph appeared in Garfield et al. (1964). That technical report drew its inspiration from Isaac Asimov's *The Genetic Code*, a popular history of genetics from its 19th century origins to the work on the structure of DNA by Watson and Crick and their immediate successors in the 1950s. Garfield and his coauthors wanted to know the extent to which the lines of influence claimed by Asimov could also be traced through citation chains, then newly available in the database that became the Science Citation Index. They indeed found overlaps between Asimov's account and the citation record. They also found some connections missed by Asimov that would have enriched his history.

As the founder of the Institute for Scientific Information (now Thomson Reuters) and the databases offered through the Web of Science, Garfield has had a lifelong interest in citation-based historiography. In recent years he and a team of programmers have developed HistCite, a tool for analyzing citation-linked literatures downloaded from the Web of Science (Garfield et al., 2003). HistCite can, for example, array the linked publications in chronological order, rank them by citation counts, show the differing productivity of the authors, journals, and organizations that contributed them, and create historiographs of

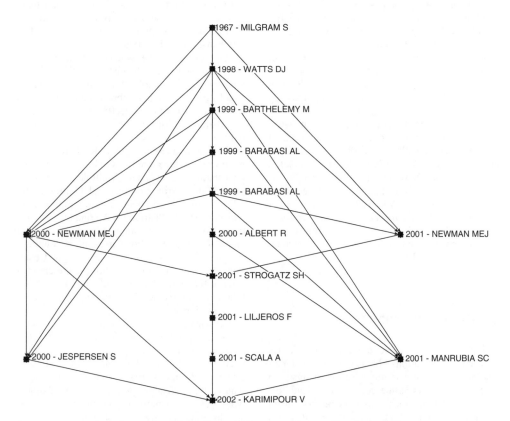

Figure 19.6   Historiograph of "small-world" papers descending from Milgram

publications that meet a certain threshold of citedness. HistCite is now a commercial product, but Garfield provides free access on the Web to many data sets formatted for historiographic analysis.

Figure 19.6 renders a small subset of one of the HistCite data sets – a bibliography of publications through 2002 that cite Stanley Milgram's "Small World Problem" (the famous 1967 article that gave rise to the idea of "six degrees of separation"). The data, which are available in Batagelj and Mrvar (2006), have been specially formatted for Pajek, a free software package for visualizing large matrices. (The Pajek download site can be reached from the page just referenced.) A genealogical macro included with Pajek (All Before–All After) makes well-structured diagrams from HistCite input, like the one in Figure 19.6. (HistCite's more tangled plot of some of the same "small world" papers is reproduced in Garfield, 2004: 132 and Börner, 2007: 816).

For clarity of presentation, Pajek commands have been used to limit the diagram to 14 articles out of 396. All but the most recent four at bottom had sizeable citation counts, ranging from 365 for Watts [with Strogatz] to 33 for Liljeros [with others]. Milgram's count is 148. The arrows, all pointing downward, reflect the relation "cited by." As a nice feature of the Pajek algorithm, the central chain from Watts to Karimipour automatically consists of articles that cite all or almost all of the articles above them. However, Figure 19.6 suggests not the complete history of Milgram's "Small World Problem" — note the long time-gap between it and the next article — but the explosion of interest that occurred when network modeling was taken over by mathematical sophisticates, mostly from physics. Milgram published in *Psychology Today*. Thirty years later, successors like Newman, Barabási, Douglas J. Watts, Steven H. Strogatz, and Réka Albert were publishing in *Science, Nature, Physica A, Physical Review E*, and the *Proceedings of the National Academy of Sciences*. (They were also reinventing some of Price's work in the process; see Newman et al., 2006: 17–18.)

COAUTHORSHIP STUDIES

Although widely understood, the coauthor tie has different implications in different academic disciplines. These variations cause analysts to study such factors as the conventions of author-ordering in bylines, the number of coauthors listed on a given publication, the number of times authors have published together, and the different kinds of publications they produce (e.g., Börner, 2007).

A fair number of quantitative studies of S&SNs report the size and density of coauthor clusters in disciplines or specialties (e.g., Börner et al., 2005), along with standard measures of author centrality (e.g., degree, betweenness, closeness) and average number of links between authors (e.g., Otte and Rousseau, 2002, Liu et al., 2005). Also seen are studies that examine the growth trends of coauthorships within and across disciplines and across nations (e.g., Ding et al., 1999, Yoshikane and Kageura, 2004). A third kind of study seeks variables correlated with coauthorship, such as disciplinary and social ties, institutional affiliations, and academic rank (e.g., Rodriguez and Pepe, 2008).

Because contemporary science involves costly projects with many participants, all of whom want recognition for their efforts, team-authored papers are now commonplace. Beaver (2004) gives evidence of one payoff: scientific papers with multiple authors are cited more frequently and for longer periods, on average, than single-authored papers, even when both kinds appear in high-impact journals. He concludes that collaboration with peers (not students) increases epistemic authority. This would not invariably be true, of course; most disciplines have classics by lone intellects. But the trends show collaborative authorship on the rise, whether the fields are big (e.g., biomedicine, chemistry, mathematics in Glänzel, 2002; sociology in Moody, 2004) or small (e.g., Australian library and information science in Willard et al., 2008). Moreover, teams increasingly consist of scientists from different nations.

Bordons and Gomez (2000) and Cronin (2001) review issues of authorial credit when multiple contributors are involved. "Multiple authorship in publication," write Bordons and Gomez (2000: 201), "raises the probem of how credit for the papers should be distributed. Among the solutions proposed we can mention that of giving total credit to the first author (first author counting), assigning full credit to every author (total counting) or giving an equal fraction of the credit to each of the authors (fractional counting).*** The total counting method is most frequently used in collaboration studies."

But what now counts as "authorship" and what do author positions on title pages mean? This matters because considerations of credit affect what the nodes and links in network displays represent. To traditionalists, an author is someone who writes publishable prose, and in collaborative work the person most responsible for the prose should automatically be first author. But some research groups dilute "authorship" by adding honorific names to bylines (e.g., directors of laboratories where the research is conducted). Others put the head of the research team first in the byline sequence, regardless of who contributed most to the paper, or put the main author of the paper last. Another variation is to list multiple authors alphabetically, which again obscures relative merit.

The Web of Science databases now distinguish between first and secondary authors when crediting citations in coauthorships. (Only first authors used to be credited.) Frandsen and Nicolaisen (2008) show that, in information science, where many researchers are savvy about Web of Science conventions, first author position usually goes to the principal writer (the one to whom correspondence should be directed), but in economics, where many researchers are bibliometrically innocent, names in author teams are often simply alphabetized. Consequently, while multiple authorships grew in both fields during 1978–2007, alphabetization of names increased in economics but decreased in information science.

Analysts of collaborative networks in science also encounter papers with coauthor counts that far exceed historical norms. Cronin (2001) calls this phenomenon "hyperauthorship" and notes its prevalence in parts of biomedicine and especially in experimental high-energy physics, where papers with more than 100 (and even more than 1,000) authors can be found. What is the meaning of "total counting" when 100 authors each get full credit for a single paper, or of "fractional counting" when each gets one one-hundredth of it? Who, either way, is intellectually accountable for the paper? More to the point here, how does one study collaborative networks when "authorship" has become a concept wholly vague and diffuse?

The answer is that collaborative networks are summed up by statistics that gloss over such concerns. Influential work by Newman (2001, 2004a, 2004b) offers a template of key measures (see also Börner et al., 2004). Using various bibliographic databases, Newman assembled data on author collaborations in biomedicine, various specialties of physics, amd computer science during 1995 through1999. In Newman (2004b) he added data on collaborations in mathematics from 1940 through *ca.* 2003. He thus is able to report total papers and total authors, average papers per author and authors per paper, and average collaborators per author (among other things). "Authors typically wrote about four papers in the five year period covered by this study," he observes (Newman, 2001: 406). "The average paper had about three authors. Notable exceptions are in theoretical high-energy physics and computer

science in which smaller collaborations are the norm (average two people), and the SPIRES high-energy physics database with an average of 9 authors per paper." His most striking statistic is average collaborators per author: about four in computer science and theoretical high energy physics, about 15 in biomedicine and astrophysics, and *173* for experimental (as opposed to theoretical) high-energy physics in the SPIRES data. He shows that papers and collaborators per author are well fit by power laws with exponential cutoffs (the truncation perhaps an artifact of the five-year window of analysis).

All Newman's networks, moreover, exhibit a so-called giant component, defined as "a large group of individuals who are all connected to one another by paths of intermediate acquaintances" (Newman, 2001: 407). In several fields these components comprise roughly 80 to 90 percent of scientists under study. The scientists *least* connected are the theoretical high-energy physicists (71 percent) and the computer scientists (57 percent). Newman found that, in fact, scientists are typically within six links of each other, even in a large field like biomedicine – another instance of the legendary six degrees of separation. (In Newman, 2004a, he *names* the best connected scientists in three fields, which is unusual for network analysts from physics.) Furthermore, working with the clustering coefficient *C* (Watts and Strogatz, 1998), he finds "a very strong clustering effect in the scientific community: two scientists typically have a 30 percent or greater probability of collaborating if they have both collaborated with another third scientist" (Newman, 2001: 408). Evidently science requires high levels of interpersonal linkage. The humanities, which still include many scholars who publish alone, would presumably be much more fragmented.

Barabási et al. (2002) continued this line of research by showing how networks of collaborative scientists evolve. By analyzing coauthorship data from mathematics and neuroscience at one-year intervals over the period 1991–1998, they show that Newman's measures are time-dependent. Among their conclusions are that (1) links attached to author-nodes follow power-law (also known as scale-free) distributions, with relatively few highly connected nodes and a long tail of increasingly less-connected nodes; (2) paths of links between nodes are relatively short and decrease over time, which is characteristic of "small world" as opposed to randomly-generated networks; and (3) the relative size of the "giant component" increases over time. The mode by which networks grow is called "preferential attachment." That is, new nodes ". . . link with higher probability to those nodes that already have a larger number of links . . ." (Barabási et al., 2002: 599). More specifically, new authors are likelier to write papers with people already rich in coauthors, a form of cultural capital. (Price called the same phenomenon "cumulative advantage," often translated as "the rich get richer.") The other mode of evolution is that authors already in the network join to form new coauthorships, again according to preferential attachment. This latter mode adds a greater fraction of new links to the network than links created by new authors (Barabási et al., 2002: 613).

THE TRUE GLUE

What binds scientific and scholarly networks together? At the most basic level, it is what members can competently write about – *what* they know, rather than *whom*. People with complementary substantive talents will often have personal relationships, ranging from hostility to friendship to loving intimacy. Given the specialization of learned interests, it is not surprising when those who share them find occasions in their lives to meet. But, in research, social and affective ties are secondary to intellectual relevance. Disciplines and specialties exist to bring people with mutually relevant interests together. At the same time, they exist to remind the living of the continuing relevance of authors now dead.

Various articles suggest the importance of what may broadly be called intellectual ties. Rodriguez and Pepe (2008), for example, studied the U.S.-based Center for Embedded Networked Sensing and used four different algorithms to detect structural communities among its multidisciplinary, multi-institutional teams of coauthors. Characteristics on which communities might be based were academic department, university affiliation, country of origin, and academic position. For the 291 coauthors in the sample, all four algorithms showed that common academic department is by far the strongest characteristic, with university affiliation also significant. This suggests that perceived intellectual ties are reinforced by physical proximity. But of course proximity means little in coauthorship without the requisite knowledge and interests on both sides.

Moody (2004) provides another example of the importance of mutually relevant knowledge. Drawing mainly on data from *Sociological Abstracts*, he presents a complex multivariate analysis of coauthorship in 36 topical areas over the period 1963–1999. Here, only two major findings will be quoted. With regard to *participation* in the coauthorship network, "There is a clear

effect of specialty on the likelihood of having coauthored. Authors who write in historical, qualitative, radical and interpretive specialties are less likely to coauthor than those writing in more positivist and quantitative specialties" (Moody, 2004: 224). For predicting the degree of *embeddedness* in the coauthorship network – the number of other authors to whom a collaborator is directly or indirectly linked – specialty is less important than the ability to upgrade a research team's methodological sophistication. "Coauthorship," says Moody (2004: 235) "is not evenly distributed across sociological work. As predicted by others, coauthorship is more likely in specialties that admit to an easier division of labor. Research method seems particularly important, showing that quantitative work is more likely to be coauthored than non-quantitative work."

A third example involves coauthorship, cocitation, and intercitation. As noted above, White et al. (2004a) analyzed pairwise data for the 16 members of Globenet, the goal being to discover whether any of a range of social and communication variables predicted intercitation in, first, their journal articles over a period of more than two decades and, second, in a summative 1999 book to which all Globenetters contributed. Considered separately, nine variables turned out to be correlated with intercitation in articles. Social ties were (1) knowing a person before Globenet was formed, (2) being friends with a person, and (3) having sought a person's advice. Intellectual ties were (4) cocitation count, (5) being in the same discipline, and (6) having read a person's work. Ties that combined the social with the intellectual were (7) having collaborated with a person, (8) being an editor of the 1999 book, or (9) coauthoring a chapter in the book.

However, when the nine were entered into a regression to predict intercitation in articles, a single variable wiped out all the others: the cocitation count for each pair of Globenetters. In other words, a cocitation count, which represents how citers in general view any pair of authors, was the best predictor of how any two authors viewed each other. This is not to say that ties such as friendship, advice-seeking, and collaboration are unreal or unimportant. It is to say that the main force driving citation over time, and subsuming other ties, is perceived similarity of topic and method. This is what repeated cocitation captures.

By contrast, intercitation in the book did not vary with cocitation patterns at all. Rather, it varied principally with being one of the book's editors or coauthors. But even these are not purely social relations; they are grounded, once more, in ties that are intellectual and content-laden. As we saw in Rodriguez and Pepe (2008) and Moody

(2004), such ties are the "true glue" binding coauthors. The same point is made about citation in White et al. (2004a: 112):

> . . . social ties are neither *necessary* for citation (one may cite authors without knowing them) nor *sufficient* for citation (knowing authors is not reason enough to cite them). Nor is there a clear temporal arrow in the matter: citing may or may not lead to meeting, and meeting may or may not lead to citing. So any attempt to explain citation primarily in terms of acquaintanceship fails. For a better explanation of why people cite, one must look to intellectual factors, such as commonality of discipline, subject matter, research methods, and perspective (e.g., theoretical versus empirical, quantitative versus qualitative.)

Thus, coauthor networks and citation networks have a unified interpretation in the sense that both derive from perceptions of intellectual relevance.

This interpretation justifies their study in an analytical framework that combines papers published (productivity) with citations received (impact) to show the relative success of collaborations. To take a last example, Börner et al. (2005) have devised impact weights for coauthored papers that reflect the citations shared by each author team. When the data are visualized, with authors as nodes, links representing coauthorships, and thickness of links representing the summed citations received, it is apparent how various authors are connected and which teams have had the greatest impact. This is important because increasing coauthorship in many fields presages, according to Börner et al. (2005: 66), "a more interdisciplinary, globally connected science as opposed to science driven by single experts." Börner's metaphor for this is "the emerging global brain." Any single instance of it would be, quite fittingly, one of Collins's "coalitions in the mind."

NOTES

1   Such rankings generally reflect authorial productivity (measured by publication counts) or authorial impact (measured by citation counts), or some combination thereof. The h-index and the g-index, explained in Wikipedia and in many papers on the Web, have gained currency as ways of comparing the productivity and impact of individual scientists. These indicators are still controversial (and various refinements have been proposed), but even more controversial are measures that permit the productivity and impact of research units, such as academic departments, to be ranked. The latter measures are contested because policy-makers may use them to determine levels of funding for the units – something many researchers want to leave to peer review. (These researchers tend to mistrust bibliometric data, often justifiably.) At the same time, peer review in large-scale research evaluations has become laborious to the point of breakdown, thereby inviting bibliometric rankings as a more cost-effective and efficient replacement. A large and fast-growing literature addresses this controversy. Hicks (2009) surveys outcomes from America, Britain, and Australia and links them to a good introductory bibliography.

2   The 10-year subset of AHCI was given by its publisher, Thomson Reuters, to Drexel University for research purposes. To obtain the map, Price's name is entered into AuthorWeb, network visualization software developed at Drexel. Price and his 24 highest cocitees are retrieved in rank order of their cocitation counts with him. The software then retrieves the cocitation counts of all 24 with each other and forms a matrix with (25 x 24) / 2 = 300 unique author pairs. The PFNET algorithm is one of three in AuthorWeb that can operate on this matrix.

3   These counts for authors in science studies are taken from a decade of *humanities* journals in which social constructivists like Latour loom large. Were the data from journals covered by the Social Sciences Citation Index during the same decade, counts for all pairs would be higher, and those of the constructivists would not dominate as here. Also, in this Price-based matrix, Gieryn's and Chubin's works are most highly cocited with Latour's, but they are not members of his school. Further data would bring Randall Collins into this map; for example, he studied and coauthored articles with Joseph Ben-David.

REFERENCES

Barabási, A. L., Jeong, H., Néda, Z., Ravasz, E., Schubert, A. and Vicsek, T. (2002) 'Evolution of the social network of scientific collaborations', *Physica A*, 311: 590–614.

Batagelj, V. and Mrvar, A. (2000) 'Some analyses of Erdös collaboration graph', *Social Networks*, 22: 173–86.

Batagelj, V. and Mrvar, A. (2006) 'Citation networks', http://vlado.fmf.uni-lj.si/pub/networks/data/cite/default.htm (accessed May 2009).

Beaver. D. deB. (2004) 'Does collaborative research have greater epistemic authority?' *Scientometrics*, 60(3): 399–408.

Bordons, M. and Gomez, I. (2000) 'Collaboration networks in science'. In Blaise Cronin and Helen B. Atkins (eds), *The Web of Knowledge; A Festschrift in Honor of Eugene Garfield*. Medford NJ: Information Today. pp. 197–213.

Börner, K. (2007) 'Making sense of mankind's scholarly knowledge and expertise: Collecting, interlinking, and organizing what we know and different approaches to mapping (network) science'. *Environment and Planning B: Planning and Design,* 34: 808–25.

Börner, K., Dall'Asta, L., Ke, W. and Vespignani, A. (2005) 'Studying the emerging global brain: Analyzing and visualizing the impact of co-authorship teams'. *Complexity,* 10(4): 57–67.

Börner, K., Maru, J.T. and Goldstone, R.L. (2004) 'The simultaneous evolution of author and paper networks'. *Proceedings of the National Academy of Sciences,* 101(Supp 1): 5266–73.

Chubin, D.E. (1976) 'The conceptualization of scientific specialties.' *Sociological Quarterly,* 17(4): 448–76.

Collins, R. (1998) *The Sociology of Philosophies: A Global Theory of Intellectual Change.* Cambridge MA and London: Belknap Press of Harvard University Press.

Crane, D. (1970) 'The nature of scientific communication and influence'. *International Social Science Journal,* 22(1): 28–41.

Crane, D. (1972) *Invisible Colleges: Diffusion of Knowledge in Scientific Communities.* Chicago: University of Chicago Press.

Cronin, B. (1995) *The Scholar's Courtesy: The Role of Acknowledgements in the Primary Communication Process.* London: Taylor Graham.

Cronin, B. (2001) 'Hyperauthorship: A postmodern perversion or evidence of a structural shift in scholarly communication practices?' *Journal of the American Society for Information Science and Technology,* 52(7): 558–69.

Cronin, B., Shaw, D. and Barre, K.L. (2003) 'A cast of thousands: Coauthorship and subauthorship collaboration in the 20th century as manifested in the scholarly journal literature of psychology and philosophy'. *Journal of the American Society for Information Science and Technology,* 54(9): 855–71.

de Castro, R. and Grossman, J.W. (1999) Famous trails to Paul Erdös. *Mathematical Intelligencer,* 21(3): 51–63.

Ding, Y., Foo, S. and Chowdhury G. (1999) 'A bibliometric analysis of collaboration in the field of information retrieval'. *International Information and Library Research,* 30: 367–76.

Dimitrova, D., Koku, E., Wellman, B. and White, H. (2007) *Network Mapping Study (Final Report): Prepared for the Canadian Water Network.* Accessed December 2010.

Doty, P., Bishop, A.P. and McClure, C.R. (1991) 'Scientific norms and the use of electronic research networks'. *Proceedings of the 54th Annual Meeting of the American Society for Information Science,* 28: 24–38.

Frandsen, T.F. and J Nicolaisen, J. (2008) 'Reactive tendencies of bibliometric indicators: Alphabetization of authorship in economics and information science'. *Proceedings of the 71st Annual Meeting of the American Society for Information Science and Technology,* 45: unpaginated CDROM.

Freeman, L. and Freeman, S. (1980) 'A semi-invisible college: Structural effects on a social network group.' In M. M. Henderson and M. J. MacNoughton (eds), *Electronic Communication: Technology and Impacts.* (AAAS Selected Symposium Series, No. 52.) New York: Westview Press. pp. 77–85.

Garfield, E. (2004) 'Historiographic mapping of knowledge domains literature'. *Journal of Information Science,* 30(2): 119–45.

Garfield, E., Pudovkin, A. I. and Istomin V. S. (2003) 'Why do we need algorithmic historiography?' *Journal of the American Society for Information Science and Technology,* 54(5): 400–412.

Garfield, E., Sher, I.H. and Torpie, R.J. (1964) *The Use of Citation Data in Writing the History of Science.* Philadelphia: Institute for Scientific Information. http://www.garfield. library.upenn.edu/papers/useofcitdatawritinghistofsci.pdf (accessed May 2009).

Glänzel, W. (2002) 'Coauthorship patterns and trends in the sciences: A bibliometric study with implications for data-base indexing and search strategies – 1980–1998'. *Library Trends,* 50(3): 461–73.

Grossman, J.W. (2007) 'The Erdös Number Project'. http:// www4.oakland.edu/enp/ (accessed May 2009).

Hicks, D. (2009) 'Evolving regimes of multi-university research evaluation'. *Higher Education,* 57(4): 393–404.

Kuhn, T.S. (1970) *The Structure of Scientific Revolutions.* 2nd. ed. Chicago: University of Chicago Press.

Laudel, G. (2002) 'Collaboration and reward. What do we measure by co-authorships?' *Research Evaluation,* 11(1): 3–15.

Lievrouw, L.A., Rogers, E.M., Lowe, C.U. and Nadel, E. (1987) 'Triangulation as a research strategy for identifying invisible colleges among biomedical scientists'. *Social Networks,* 9: 217–48.

Liu, X., Bollen, J., Nelson, M.L. and Sompel, H.V.D. (2005) 'Co-authorship networks in the digital library research community'. *Information Processing and Management,* 41: 1462–80.

Marchionini, G., Solomon, P., Davis, C. and Russell, T. (2006) 'Information and library science MPACT: A preliminary analysis'. *Library and Information Science Research,* 28: 480–500. The visualizations are at http://ils.unc.edu/mpact (accessed May 2009).

McCain, K.W. (1983) 'The author co-citation structure of macroeconomics'. *Scientometrics,* 5: 277–89.

McCain, K.W. (1991) 'Communication, competition, and secrecy; The production and dissemination of research-related information in genetics.' *Science Technology and Human Values,* 16(4): 491–516.

McCain, K.W. (2000) 'Sharing digitized research-related information on the World Wide Web.' *Journal of the American Society for Information Science,* 51(14): 1321–27.

Milgram, S. (1967) 'The small world problem'. *Psychology Today,* 1(1): 60–67.

Moody, J. (2004) 'The structure of a social science collabora-tion network: Disciplinary cohesion from 1963 to 1999'. *American Sociological Review,* 69(2): 213–38.

Mullins, N.C. (1973) *Theories and Theory Groups in Contemporary American Sociology.* New York: Harper and Row.

Newman, M.E.J. (2001) 'The structure of scientific collaboration networks'. *Proceedings of the National Academy of Sciences*, 98: 404–9.

Newman, M.E.J. (2004a) 'Who is the best connected scientist? A study of scientific coauthorship networks'. In E. Ben-Naim, H. Frauenfelder, Z. Toroczkai (eds), *Complex Networks*. Berlin: Springer. pp. 337–70.

Newman, M.E.J. (2004b) 'Coauthorship networks and patterns of scientific collaboration'. *Proceedings of the National Academy of Sciences*, 101(Supp 1): 5200–5205.

Newman, M., Barabási, A.-L. and Watts, D.J. (eds) (2006) *The Structure and Dynamics of Networks*. Princeton: Princeton University Press.

Otte, E. and Rousseau, R. (2002) 'Social network analysis: A powerful strategy, also for the information sciences'. *Journal of Information Science*, 28(6): 443–55.

Price, D. de.S. (1961) *Science since Babylon*. New Haven and London: Yale University Press. (Enlarged edition, 1975.)

Reid, E. and Chen, H. (2005) 'Mapping the contemporary terrorism research domain: Researchers, publications, and institutions analysis'. In P. Kantor et al. (eds), *Lecture Notes on Computer Science*, 3495: 322–39.

Rodriguez, M.A. and Pepe, A. (2008) 'On the relationship between the structural and socioacademic communities of a coauthorship network'. *Journal of Informetrics*, 2: 195–201.

Sandstrom, P.E. (2001) 'Scholarly communication as a socioecological system'. *Scientometrics*, 51(3): 573–605.

Sandstrom, P.E. and White, H.D. (2007) 'The impact of cultural materialism; A bibliometric analysis of the writings of Marvin Harris'. In Lawrence A. Kuznar and Stephen K. Sanderson (eds), *Studying Societies and Cultures; Marvin Harris's Cultural Materialism and Its Legacy*. Boulder CO and London: Paradigm Press. pp. 20–55.

Small, H.G. (1978) 'Cited documents as concept symbols'. *Social Studies of Science*, 8(3): 327–40.

Sonnenwald, D.H. (2007) 'Scientific collaboration'. *Annual Review of Information Science and Technology*, 41: 643–81.

Wasserman, S. and Faust, K. (1994) *Social Network Analysis; Methods and Applications*. Cambridge, UK: Cambridge University Press.

Watts, D.J. and Strogatz, S.H. (1998) 'Collective dynamics of "small-world" networks'. *Nature*, 393: 440–42.

White, H.D. (2000) 'Toward ego-centered citation analysis'. In Blaise Cronin and Helen Barsky Atkins (eds), *The Web of Knowledge: A Festschrift in Honor of Eugene Garfield*. Medford NJ: Information Today. pp. 475–96.

White, H.D. and McCain, K.W. (1989) 'Bibliometrics'. *Annual Review of Information Science and Technology*, 24: 119–86.

White, H.D. and McCain, K.W. (2000) 'In memory of Belver C. Griffith'. *Journal of the American Society for Information Science*, 51(10): 959–62.

White, H.D., Wellman, B. and Nazer, N. (2004a) 'Does citation reflect social structure? Longitudinal evidence from the "Globenet" interdisciplinary research group'. *Journal of the American Society for Information Science and Technology*, 55: 111–26.

White, H.D., Lin, X., Buzydlowski, J. and Chen, C. (2004b) 'User-controlled mapping of significant literatures'. *Proceedings of the National Academy of Sciences*, 101(Supp 1): 5297–302.

Willard, P., Kennan, M.A., Wilson, C.S. and White, H.D. (2008) 'Publication by Australian LIS academics: A preliminary investigation'. *Australian Academic and Research Libraries*, 39(2): 65–78.

Yoshikane, F. and Kageura, K. (2004) 'Comparative analysis of coauthorship networks of different domains: The growth and change of networks'. *Scientometrics*, 60(3): 433–44.

Zuccala, A. (2006) 'Modeling the invisible college'. *Journal of the American Society for Information Science and Technology*, 57(2): 152–68.

20

Cultural Networks

Paul DiMaggio

Forty years ago, this chapter's title might have seemed oxymoronic. Early network analysis was rooted in social psychology (sociometry) or in a radical structuralism (blockmodeling) that viewed culture as a fog obscuring social reality, rather than as a legitimate analytic category (Freeman, 2004; White et al., 1976).[1] For their part, cultural analysts either defined culture so broadly that it encompassed all patterned behavior and symbol systems (anthropologists) or so abstractly that it resisted empirical research (Parsonsian sociologists). Even communications scholars who used network analysis to understand information flows largely avoided questions of meaning central to the study of culture (Rogers, 1962).

Things have changed. Developments in both social network analysis (SNA) and the study of culture have brought these fields closer together. As Breiger (2004) has noted, White's embrace of cultural analysis in *Identity and Control* (1992a), the connectionist turn in cognitive science (Strauss and Quinn, 1997), and developments in cultural sociology and anthropology (e.g., Fuhse, 2009) have contributed to this trend. Moreover, the rise of the Internet has made it easier to conceive of culture as a kind of network (Castells, 2000; Turner, 2006), while generating vast amounts of textual data amenable to SNA.

I hope to convince the reader that *network analysis is the natural methodological framework for empirically developing insights from leading theoretical approaches to cultural analysis*. For the most influential analytic approaches to culture, relationality is central to understanding how cultural systems operate (Emirbayer and Goodwin,

1994; Mische, this volume). Although few students of culture employ formal network-analytic methods, their theories lead them to the edge of SNA, where exemplary studies bring the two fields ever closer.

Social-scientific work on culture has three analytic foci: *formally organized systems that produce and distribute cultural products*; *expressive symbols that facilitate the production of individual and group identities and intergroup boundaries*; and *the symbolic organization of meaning*. Relational theories are central to each of these topics.

Cultural production systems. Research on the arts has converged on the analysis of art worlds (Becker, 1982), fields (Bourdieu, 1983), and production systems (Peterson and Anand, 2004; Caves, 2002). Becker (1974) argues that collaborative networks ("artworlds") produce art and that these, rather than individual "artists," are the proper objects of social-scientific analysis. Bourdieu depicts artists and other creative workers (scientists, preachers, chefs) as constrained by their positions in fields (*champs*), readily reconceived as networks, that influence returns to different aesthetic strategies. The production of culture approach, developed in research on media industries (Peterson and Berger, 1971), studies how networks of collaborating organizations guide the flow of symbolic goods from creators through gatekeepers to publics. The economics variant (Caves, 2002) contrasts systems that internalize production in firms to those (increasingly prevalent) that organize production through social networks and short-term projects. Although foundational papers in each tradition used the term "network" only casually, recent studies have employed SNA to realize the potential of formative ideas. Work on science (White, this volume) has formalized the foundational imagery of the "invisible college" (Crane, 1972) in analogous ways. Research in this area focuses on single-mode networks of relations among culture producers and on dual-mode networks linking producers to gatekeepers.

Culture, identity, and boundaries. Students of culture examine ways in which expressive symbols, tastes, and styles constitute and signal identities and define social boundaries (Lamont and Molnár, 2002). This approach descends from Weber's argument that status groups develop distinctive cultures useful for claiming honor, identifying in-group members, and maintaining solidarity (Weber, 1946 [1925]); and from Durkheim's (1933 [1893]) contention that complex societies require new forms of cultural cohesion based on occupational differentiation and on diffusion of ideas and symbols through exchange networks (i.e., *organic* vs. *mechanical* solidarity). Shared culture facilitates the construction and persistence of social networks through two mechanisms. First, visible symbols permit persons to recognize others with whom they share a status or identity (Goffman, 1951); second, shared knowledge, tastes, and styles produce bonding by facilitating and by enhancing emotional rewards derived from conversational exchange (Collins, 2004; Erickson, 2004). It follows that relations between persons and cultural symbols are characterized by duality, such that shared tastes or interests constitute social groups and shared publics constitute genres or subcultures (DiMaggio, 1987; Breiger, 2000). This perspective lends itself to the use of two-mode networks (Borgatti, this volume) to depict ties between persons (or organizations) and cultural products, symbols, or beliefs.

Meaning through relations. The Swiss linguist Ferdinand de Saussure (1977 [1916]), argued that linguistic meaning emerges from relations among words and phonemes. The Russian semiotician Mikhail Bakhtin extended the principle to longer textual elements, and beyond texts to other symbol systems (1986). Because interpretive work on culture views meaning as reflecting the *relationship between words or symbols* rather than the fixed content of each, network analysis of relations among cultural objects is a natural way to address the problem of meaning (Mohr, 1998). More recently, students of mental models (Carley and Palmquist, 1992) and narrativity (Franzosi, 1998) have advanced a relational understanding of culture and cognition consistent with the view that "in addition to social networks, institutional life is organized around cultural networks, relational structures that link meanings, values, stories and rhetorics" (Mohr and White, 2008). Such an approach lends itself to the use of single-mode networks of co-occurrence relations among such cultural elements as words, tropes, attitudes, symbols, or tastes.

This chapter reviews network studies in these three areas *seriatim*. I define "network analysis" liberally, including some studies that generate relationality matrices suitable for conventional network methods but that produce results with nonnetwork scaling and clustering methods. I favor studies depicting systems as networks over those using spatial methods; and focus on empirical work, neglecting research that uses computational network models to contribute to theories of cultural change. I avoid two relevant topics – sociology of science and research on diffusion and contagion – to which other chapters are devoted.

CULTURAL PRODUCTION SYSTEMS

Much social-scientific work on culture examines settings – industries, professions, organizations, informal work groups – in which cultural products are produced. By "cultural product," I refer to discrete and apprehensible human creations – songs, paintings, newspaper articles, meals, sermons, laws, poems, scientific papers, garments – associated with institutionalized fields of cultural production. Such cultural products are produced in and by networks of collaborating firms and persons.

Early examples of this approach – White and White's study of the origins of impressionism (1965), Bourdieu's study of photographers (Bourdieu et al., 1965), Becker's analyses of the visual and performing arts (1974), Peterson and Berger's (1971) and Hirsch's (1972) work on cultural industry systems – used network imagery rather than network methods, but formal work followed quickly.

Perhaps the earliest such study was Kadushin's examination of the U.S. intellectual elite (1974). Kadushin identified several critical characteristics common to many cultural production networks, including circularity (high levels of mutual awareness and attention); unclear boundaries; opacity to outsiders; limited roles for formal institutions, which serve as interaction *foci* but do not claim long-term, complete commitments from creative workers; dense cores and sparse peripheries, without formal leadership structures; and chronic resource uncertainty and ambiguity of prestige, both leading to active exchange of information and evaluations.

Four approaches have dominated recent network analyses of creative fields: Bourdieu's theory of competition; theories of efficient boundaries; research on small worlds; and analyses of structural mechanisms that induce creative or financial success. SNA has also addressed the chronic challenge of sampling artist populations, which can rarely be identified through standard means.

ANALYZING FIELDS

Bourdieu (1983) views fields as sites of strategic competition between actors with varying degrees of cultural capital (ease and familiarity with prestigious forms of culture) and economic resources. (He identified social capital [ego networks] as a third resource, but failed to develop this insight empirically [1986].) To simplify considerably, Bourdieu contends that the volume and composition (i.e, relative proportion) of economic and cultural capital that actors possess influence the social relations they can form, which, in turn, shape expected returns from alternative creative strategies.

Anheier and Gerhards's (1991; Anheier et al., 1995) study of literary authors in Cologne, Germany, unites Bourdieuian analysis with SNA. The researchers collected data on friendship, awareness, assistance, and reference-group ties, using blockmodels to describe the field's structure and correspondence analysis (Bourdieu's favored technique) to map network position onto attitudes, membership, literary genres, and professional success. The network was sparse, with dense connections limited to a small elite, and it was vertically bifurcated between producers of literary and vernacular fiction.

In an innovative study, DeNooy (2002) produced an affiliation network of 18 Dutch and Flemish literary magazines and 249 authors who published in them from 1970 to 1981, and used Markov Monte Carlo estimation procedures to explore relationships between authors' and magazines' prestige. Unsurprisingly, prestigious authors flowed to prestigious magazines. More tellingly, the flow was predicted not by static popularity but by a dynamic prestige measure, intended to operationalize Bourdieu's (1983) ideas about the dual constitution of locations in the literary field, that tracked recent movements between magazines.

Several other studies explore Bourdieu's insight that genre classifications are homologous to social distinctions. DeNooy (2003b) links Bourdieu's argument to White's theory of catnets in a study of relations among 40 Dutch literary authors and critics. DeNooy argues that networks, themselves shaped by authors' social origins, constitute literary genres that double as author identities, which in turn influence social and aesthetic hierarchies. DeNooy's approach is novel in that he uses balance theory and triad censuses to understand microstructures that generate hierarchy. Giuffre (2001) also draws on field theory to analyze relationships between networks (New York photographers sharing gallery representation during the 1980s) and genre classifications. The most successful photographers sustained structural *and* aesthetic ambiguity, bridging positions in the network and defying critical efforts to label their styles. Kirschbaum and Vasconcelos (2007) explore relationships between social networks and genre classifications in a study of Brazilian *tropicália* music, which they portray as emerging out of the accretion of collaboration ties among artists previously recording in structurally distant genres.

ORGANIZING CULTURAL MARKETS

Much work on cultural industries suggests that coordination by contract or the use of ad hoc project teams are more efficient ways to allocate talent than through formal organization when each product is unique and markets are uncertain (Peterson and Berger, 1971; Caves, 2002). Network analysts have begun to contribute to this literature.

In an exemplary study of the organization of live popular music in the Boston area, Foster and colleagues (2006) analyze linkages between performance venues and two kinds of bands – "cover" bands (which reproduce tunes by prominent recording artists) and "indie" bands (which create and perform original material). The authors combine several kinds of data: a band-by-club network based on more than 10,000 performances, interviews with club booking staff, advice networks among booking agents, and classification of bands by expert informants. They find that the cover-band segment is characterized by close ties among club managers, but weak club-artist ties, whereas the indie sector is dominated by club-focused patron-client nets, a difference they attribute to greater market uncertainty in the latter.

Giuffre (1999) employs blockmodeling and optimal-matching sequence analysis to explore how networks shaped careers of New York photographers between 1981 and 1992. She depicts careers as a two-mode game wherein both photographers *and* galleries try to move up by forming ties to increasingly prestigious counterparts. Thus, photographers' prestige is subject to choices that other photographers make to join or leave the galleries with which each is associated. Another study of artist-gallery networks (Boari and Corrado, 2007) contends that endemic uncertainty led contemporary artists to invest heavily in identifying and occupying structural holes, producing a system with marked small-world properties.

SMALL-WORLD STUDIES

In his analysis of the Internet Movie Database (IMDB; www.imdb.com) actor-by-film network (transformed to an actor-collaboration net), Watts (1999) first observed that artistic networks (among others) display small-world properties: a coincidence of high levels of local clustering and very low average path distances (both compared to random nets). His example engendered an explosion of descriptive studies of collaboration networks, all reporting that their fields are "small worlds" (e.g., Gleiser and Danon [2003] on early jazz musicians; Jacobson and Sandler [2008] on musicians' Myspace friends; DeLima e Silva et al. [2004] on Brazilian popular musicians).

The challenge in such studies, which is only sometimes met, is to connect structural analysis of fields as small worlds to substantive questions worth engaging – for example, by using comparative methods or linking structural properties to field performance. An exemplar of the former approach (Park et al., 2006; Teitelbaum et al., 2008) compares two "networks" of musical recording artists – an actual network of recording collaboration and a similarity matrix based on expert judgments about the same bands' styles. Although both networks exhibit standard small-world properties, the similarity network maps neatly onto genres, whereas the collaboration network is an amalgam of geographic clusters, center-spoke structures around major bands, and diffuse collaborations. The authors use innovative visualization methods to demonstrate that increased cross-genre collaboration has reduced the coincidence of partitions based on stylistic similarity and those based on collaboration over time.

Uzzi's study of Broadway musicals (2008; Uzzi and Spiro, 2005) is an exemplar of research on how small-world properties affect system performance. Uzzi examines the network of key artistic team members and producers involved in 523 original musical productions mounted between 1945 and 1989 (where edges connect participants who worked together on a production). He finds stability over that period in degree distributions, path lengths, and assortativity, despite substantial institutional change and much volatility in the clustering coefficient. Good times on Broadway were characterized by moderate clustering, whereas both high *and* low coefficients were associated with financial *and* critical downturns. These results, Uzzi argues, suggest that low and high clustering produce different forms of stagnation, whereas moderate clustering optimizes cross-fertilization.

HOW NETWORKS SHAPE CREATIVITY AND SUCCESS

Uzzi's work is unusual in its focus on system properties. But research on the relationship between social networks and success in cultural fields dates back to Merton's essay, "The Matthew Effect in Science" (1968), and to the Whites' study of the Impressionist movement (1965).

Collins's (1989, 1998, 2000) conflict theory of intellectual change, illustrated by his magisterial study of the social organization of philosophical schools over more than two millennia, and developed further in a comparative study (Collins and Guillen, 2009) of philosophers and architects, offers a valuable framework. Collins makes several claims about networks that drive intellectual movements. First, intellectual and creative progress is characterized by strong positive network externalities, causing temporal and spatial concentration of significant movements. Second, the most eminent thinkers are densely connected to well-known peers. Third, reputational contagion ("halo" or "Matthew" effects) lifts all boats in an ascendant school (i.e., a densely connected cluster of culture producers who share an identity). Fourth, movement leaders create new ties to extend their influence outward (and not to extract rents by occupying structural holes). Fifth, schools tend toward schism through generational conflict. Sixth, systems have a carrying capacity of three to six active schools at any one time. Finally, institutional change often unleashes rapid network elaboration and an explosion of creativity. Crossley (2009) emphasizes similar themes in his analysis of networks that produced Britain's punk music scene: the indispensability of a critical mass of strong reciprocal ties, positive network externalities, resource pooling, reputational contagion, and identity as a collective good.

Burt (2004) offers a valuable approach to understanding the relationship between individual-level network location and creativity. He argues that unique occupancy of brokerage positions ("structural holes") exposes occupants to a broad range of ideas. Such boundary-spanners, in turn, generate *more* ideas, and the ideas they generate are better received than those of their less cosmopolitan counterparts. Although Burt's evidence comes from research on an electronics company, the argument readily generalizes to artistic creativity.

Much research analyzes how network position affects individual or team success, and much of this work focuses on the film industry. Films are produced by ad hoc creative teams, generating comparatively dense and rapidly evolving collaboration networks. Faulkner and Anderson (1987) first documented the prevalence of status homophily in team development and the association between team status and box-office revenues. The availability of IMDB data has stimulated this literature, which typically depicts networks in which creative workers are nodes, participation in the same film project creates an edge, and edges decay over time. Notable examples include Esparza and Rossman's study (2006) of the impact of ties to Academy members and team-member performance on an actor's risk of receiving an Oscar nomination; Cattani and Ferriani's (2008) study of the impact of individual and team centrality on award nominations and financial success; and Sorenson and Waguespack's study of repeat contracting between production teams and film distributors (2006).

Other work focuses on musical innovations in jazz. Kirschbaum and Vasconcelos (2006) use musician/recording affiliation matrices from 1930 to 1969 to trace the emergence of Swing, Bop, and other genres. Innovation develops on the network's periphery, with innovators moving to the core as new styles gain recognition. Grandadam (2008) explores the collaboration network induced by the Blue Note record label, demonstrating that the label's efforts to boost new artists by giving them established sidemen increased network integration and facilitated the emergence of new genres.

USING NETWORK THEORY TO FIND ARTISTS

It is difficult to study artists' communities systematically because artists are often hard to find: independent contractors who find work through informal contacts join few formal organizations, rarely advertise, and only rise to public attention if they become relatively successful. Conventional solutions to this problem – ethnography, studying artists tied to identifiable institutions, or relying on lists of union members or grant winners – introduce different forms of selection bias. In a

groundbreaking paper that offers a better solution, Heckathorn and Jeffri (2001) use respondent-driven sampling (RDS), a method of highly controlled respondent referrals developed to study such hidden populations as HIV-positive drug users, to identify populations of jazz musicians in four U.S. cities. McPherson (2001) describes the applicability of another network-based method, hypernetwork sampling, to locating artists through sample surveys in populations too large to be accessed by RDS.

CULTURE, IDENTITY, AND BOUNDARIES

Any cultural analysis must take into account identities: how identities (of people and things) emerge, how they are sustained, and under what conditions they become salient. Cultural analysis must also take into account the way that actors employ classification schemes to categorize one another (Lamont and Molnár, 2002). In worlds organized around groups (moieties, clans, villages, castes, classes-for-themselves) identities and boundaries are relatively unproblematic. In worlds organized around fluid, open-ended, functionally differentiated networks, social identity and intergroup boundaries are more complex, context-dependent, and ambiguous (Castells, 1997; Tilly, 1998). Network analysts have provided four powerful ideas (and methods to go with them) for understanding these processes.

Fundamental ideas: duality, catnets, network switching, and homology between structural and cultural diversity

The first of these four ideas is *duality* (Breiger, 1974) – the recognition that each mode in a two-mode network constitutes the identity of the other. Initially, duality referred to the mutual constitution of groups (defined by persons who join them) and persons (defined by the intersection of group affiliations). But we may also think of cultural entities as constituted by and constituting the actors who share them. We see this most easily in language: in a linguistically diverse community, analysis of a two-mode network representing utterances as a set of ties between speakers and the words they employ would quickly partition speakers into language groups (and, with the right algorithm, identify bilinguals) and would partition word sets into languages (perhaps identifying loan words as well). By analogy, one might use actor-by-artwork nets (with links of like and dislike) to identify genres and taste groups; actor-by-consumer-good nets (with ties representing possession) to identify subcultures; and actor-by-proposition nets (with ties of belief and disbelief) to identify thought communities and belief systems.

A second critical idea is that shared identities serve as shortcuts in network formation, raising the probability that two persons will form a positive tie. Harrison White (2008 [1965]) captured this insight in his early work on catnets – the intersection of networks and social categories. Subsequent empirical work confirmed White's insight, indicating that persons meeting one another for the first time establish footing by identifying common ties (shared friends) or shared categorical identities (Erickson, 1975). Extending White's insight from named roles to categories of shared culture (tastes, beliefs, communication styles) provides further leverage in understanding patterns of network formation.

A third important concept is *network switching* (Mische and White, 1998). Traditional views of culture as coherent, stable, and grounded in values rendered cultural theory powerless to explain such ubiquitous phenomena as people's ability to hold apparently inconsistent beliefs, rare but earth-shaking events like political revolutions and genocides, or large-scale shifts in social attitudes like religious revivals. More recently, scholars in sociology and anthropology have reconceived culture as a repertoire of loosely coupled representations, fluid and variably shared within social groups (Swidler, 1986; Hannerz, 1996). Parallel work in cognitive psychology has demonstrated the schematic basis of culture, the domain-specificity of schema, and the role of social context in triggering alternative constructions of social reality (D'Andrade, 1995; DiMaggio, 1997). White (1995; Mische and White, 1998) drew on research on linguistic code-switching to highlight the role of networks as contexts that trigger particular identities, representations, value orientations, and the cultural symbols associated with them. Movement across social networks shifts attention across social domains (e.g., work, family, politics, community), evoking distinctive schematic structures associated with each. White (1992a) coined the term *netdoms* to refer to networks specific to a particular domain.

A final idea is that *the diversity of culture is homologous to the diversity of social networks* (DiMaggio, 1987; Erickson, 2001). This insight formalizes traditional ideas about cosmopolitanism (Merton, 1949). People with diverse social networks have the most diverse cultural repertoires as well because diverse networks enable people to learn more culture and because dyads with diverse repertoires are more likely to find common interests or identities that facilitate the creation of ties. Erickson (1996) demonstrated this relationship empirically in her classic study of participants in the Ontario private security industry (see also Lizardo, 2006).

Duality and cultural analysis

The notion of duality has informed studies of social-welfare agencies in Progressive America, the changing healthcare system in the twentieth-century United States, pornography in Denmark, and curricular and program change in U.S. universities. Much of this work also draws on the notion of "institutional logic" (Friedland and Alford, 1991), conceived as a set of rules that links particular practices to particular identities.

John Mohr pioneered the application of duality to cultural analysis in a remarkable set of papers employing data from New York City social service directories from the late nineteenth and early twentieth centuries, coded as a three-mode network of organizations by groups receiving assistance by services offered (Mohr, 1994; Mohr and Duquenne, 1997; Mohr and Guerra-Pearson, 2010). Mohr studied the evolution of the social-service domain from an institutional logic based on private charity to one rooted in professionalism and social progressivism. This transformation entailed changes in prevailing beliefs about salient group identities, about problems associated with such groups, and about appropriate treatments for such problems. Mohr's use of SNA to study this transformation grew out of the insight that classes of organizations, clients, problems, and treatments were mutually constitutive.

In a similar manner, Ruef (1999) used thousands of texts on the healthcare system to construct a matrix of organization type by descriptor. Subjected to multidimensional scaling, these data illuminated the discursive construction of the healthcare field, enabling him to map the transformation of health care in the late twentieth century. Jensen (2006) coded as ties shared visual and textual elements in Danish film posters to identify the gradual emergence of a comedy-soft-porn genre after sexually explicit films were legalized in the late 1960s. Rawlings and Bourgeois (2004) explored the internal differentiation of agricultural education, analyzing nets constituted by over-time data on the availability of 117 degree programs (e.g., dairy technology, rural sociology, agricultural bacteriology) at 65 agricultural schools between 1890 and 1940.

The conventional method for analyzing duality in person-group networks is structural-equivalence analysis, which enables the analyst simultaneously to identify and assign cases to structural positions in each of two populations. Although students of person-by-culture networks employ this method (Breiger and Mohr, 2004), they also use other approaches such as correspondence analysis and Galois lattices. Breiger (2000) uses correspondence analysis to identify blocks of Supreme Court justices based on their interest in and control over decisions in several areas of law (see also DeNooy, 2003a). Mohr and Duquenne (1997) employ Galois lattices to depict the mutual constitution of social groups and treatment modalities in Progressive-era New York. Mohr and colleagues (2004; see also Mohr and Lee, 2000), drawing on University of California documents, use Galois lattices to analyze the mutual constitution of student categories (especially ethnic labels) and university services (e.g., summer programs and mentoring) as the system adapted to a ban on affirmative-action programs.

NETWORKS, CONTEXTS, AND IDENTITIES

If, as White (1992b: 210) puts it, "actual human beings take shape as ensembles of identities," a central challenge for social science is to understand how social relations evoke particular identities in particular places at particular times. Relevant research began and flourished in the field of sociolinguistics but has expanded to other fields.[2]

Code-switching: How networks shape talk and how language marks network domains

Basil Bernstein and John Gumperz initiated fundamental work on the relationship between language and social networks in the 1960s. Bernstein (1971), drawing on Durkheim, demonstrated, first, that persons with more complex social networks (i.e., less closure and multiplexity) used more formal speech forms and more abstract concepts ("elaborated code") than persons with simpler, more densely connected, nets; and, second, that persons more often use elaborated code when speaking in public settings and with acquaintances than when conversing in private with intimates. Gumperz (1982) described "code-switching" based on his research on

bilinguals, which revealed, first, that bilinguals use different languages and speech forms when speaking to persons in different parts of their social networks; and, second, that speakers switch among speech forms *within conversations* in order to *reference* different parts of their social worlds.

This tradition has developed in several directions. One is toward more sophisticated network measures: Milroy and Margrain (1980) developed a measure of social network density and multiplexity that significantly predicted the extent to which working-class Belfast residents used traditional working-class speech forms (see Villena-Ponsada, 2005, for similar results in Spain). Others have focused on how listeners' identities influence language use: Gal (1979), employing data from dyads of residents of a Hungarian town on the Austrian border, demonstrated that the status of speakers' conversational partners was a stronger predictor of speakers' language use than the status of the speakers themselves. Other research has emphasized the way in which references to context *within* conversations induce code-switching: Gal's Hungarian respondents were more likely to use German words when discussing formal topics; Labov (1972) found that African-American young people adopted standard American English for discussing solemn topics; and Wei (1994) reported that bilingual Chinese in the United Kingdom marked disagreements with parents and grandparents by switching to English in mid-conversation.

From code-switching to culture-switching

As White (1995) has argued, one can view work on language as a paradigm for research on culture more broadly, with conversational topics, expressed tastes or other opinions, or interactional styles serving as privileged indicators. Research suggests that conversational topics, like linguistic codes, can mark identities and provide coherence to networks. In a study of community-college counseling encounters, Fred Erickson (1975) found that unacquainted dyads began conversations by trying to establish membership in the same network through common kin, friends, or acquaintances or, failing that, to find shared avocational interests. Consistent with this, Erickson (1996) reported that the breadth of conversational topics in which subjects engaged, and their range of local cultural knowledge increased with the diversity of their social networks. Using Erickson's network-diversity measure, Harshaw and Tindall (2005) predict the complexity of personal identities and the range of values respondents place on forest resources. Bearman and Parigi (2004) demonstrate a correspondence between topic and role relationship: Americans talk with their spouses about kids and money, with their friends about religion and community affairs, and with everyone about news and politics.

Networks shape conversational norms as well as topics and codes. Gibson's (2005) innovative study of social relationships and conversational shifts demonstrates the influence of social ties on conversational roles. For example, superiors claim turns and respond when addressed less than subordinates, friends reinforce one another's interventions, and subordinates redirect attention to their superiors. Interactional styles (e.g., modes of address) also reflect actors' efforts to upgrade their networks, as McLean (1998) argues in his analysis of job-seekers' letters in Renaissance Florence. At the meso level, Eliasoph and Lichterman (2003) find that persons in different relational settings (e.g., taverns *vs.* community meetings) enforce varying expectations about conversation topics and styles (e.g., joking, or earnestness).

Several researchers have developed social network implications of Weber's and Bourdieu's theories of culture's role in establishing and maintaining group boundaries. In such work, aesthetic taste plays a similar role to language in marking identity and facilitating the development of new ties; and network structure, in turn, influences the breadth and nature of persons' tastes. Lizardo (2006), using the General Social Survey, reports a positive association between the size of people's networks and the number of activities in which they participate. A model in which tastes predict ties fits better than the reverse. Moreover, consistent with the contention that high culture differentiates and popular culture provides cohesion, Lizardo finds that a high-culture taste pattern is associated with more strong ties, whereas engagement in popular culture is associated with larger weak-tie nets. In a study of college students' ego networks and cultural participation, Kane (2004) reports that personal-network density is associated with interest in sports, that ego-net heterogeneity is associated with taste for high culture, and that these associations are stronger for women than for men. Yair (1995) constructs a network cross-national alliances, based on votes for candidates in the Eurovision Song Contest.

Consumption patterns also reflect structure in networks. Schweitzer (1993) used lattice models to reveal the dual ordering of persons and goods in communities in the developing world. Schummer (2005) analyzed co-purchase networks (derived from person-by-book-purchase matrices) to identify distinct patterns of interest in and understanding of nanotechnology. (Some book buyers appeared to associate nano with science, and others with science fiction.)

Identities from third parties

Identities may be chosen or imposed. An innovative study of industry boundaries (Kennedy, 2005) uses longitudinal analysis of two co-occurrence matrices – one of the names of workstation firms used in articles in the business press, and one on peer references in press releases by these same firms – to demonstrate that the companies' own definitions of industry boundaries follow rather than precede boundaries emergent from media narratives. Kennedy argues that these media narratives, rather than direct experience, are the source of executives' understandings of "both the meaning of market categories and the structure of competitive rivalry and their positions in it."

Networks and political identities

Bearman's (1993) study of the elite patronage and ideological change in the century preceding the British Civil Wars combines blockmodels of multiple relations among elites with analysis of ideology. The author argues that the elite's embrace of Puritanism appeared as traditional social structure fell into crisis and that religious faith served to bridge local networks, creating a rhetoric that united gentry with many different grevances under a common banner.

Mische's (2007) ambitious analysis of Brazilian activist groups in the 1990s combines the study of switching dynamics with analysis of duality. The author focuses on actors who linked different sectors of the social movement that effected the impeachment and removal from office of Brazil's president in 1992. Such boundary-spanners manipulated different identities and forms of discourse to produce successful intergroup collaborations. Mische and Pattison (2000) use Galois lattices to analyze a three-mode network consisting of movement organizations, political causes, and political events. They demonstrated that Brazil's SMOs shifted from single-issue strategies to collaboration across multiple issues. In so doing, they produced an efficacious movement integrated by the voluntary suppression of controversial positions (much as Bearman's local elites used religion to elide difference). Mische's work challenges us to reconceptualize "networks as multiple, cross-cutting sets of relations sustained by conversational dynamics, shared story-lines and shifting definitions of social settings" (2003: 258) – not just to explore the relationship *of* networks *to* cultural phenomena, but to view networks themselves as cultural formations.

CULTURE AND BOUNDARIES ON-LINE

Most of the work described in this section focuses on networks of face-to-face interaction. We know little about how the dynamics of identity and social-boundary enactment on-line. But the relative ease of harvesting large-scale network data on-line makes the topic irresistible, and the ability of such research to address core social-science problems is significant.

Adamic and Adar's (2003) exemplary study of links between personal home pages at Stanford and MIT presents a method that could address a chronic problem for students of cultural boundaries: identifying which tastes, interests, or competencies have the greatest impact on the formation of networks. The authors identify shared interests that raise the probability of links, and of the emergence of community, more than others: at Stanford, pearl tea (an identity marker for members of one sorority), technology systems, and infectious diseases (a research interest) were highly salient, whereas at MIT, references to fraternities, neuroscience, and an Hispanic Union group were strong predictors. At both Stanford and MIT personal homepage links were associated with shared outlinks to sites related to science and to ethnic identity; at MIT, but not at Stanford, religious sites (Campus Crusade for Christ, a Pagan student group) were also salient. The paper offers a model for how SNA can convert chronic theoretical disputes in the study of culture into productive empirical research programs.

NETWORKS OF MEANING

Nothing is more central to the study of culture than the interpretation of meaning, yet nothing is more difficult. In the humanities and anthropology, interpretation is often a matter of virtuoso performance. Interpretive accountability, however, requires replicable procedures for representing meaning. Of available approaches, SNA best captures the foundational insight that meaning emerges from relations among cultural elements rather than inhering in the elements themselves. Although there are still relatively few examples,

researchers have taken promising steps in applying SNA to the study of meaning, in general, and of narrativity (a central theme in the study of culture), specifically. As a rule, studies that focus on meaning employ two-mode networks to graph the co-occurrence of terms in some set of texts (e.g., newspaper articles, reference books, interview transcripts, or opinion surveys), whereas studies of narrativity analyze single-mode data associated through some form of temporal ordering.

Extracting meaning from networks of cultural elements

Earlier I described Mohr's research as a dualistic approach to revealing salient identities. Yet it is also a means of producing networks from texts in order to recreate shared meaning. Mohr and Neely (2009) use structural-equivalence methods to identify institutional logics in the practices of carceral institutions in late-nineteenth-century New York. Rendering operational ideas from Foucault (1977), the authors treat relational patterns between social identities (rows) and treatments applied to persons with these identities (columns) as describing a semiotic code.

Such codes can define frames (combinations of symbols, examples, and arguments that evoke particular understandings of a social issue) as well as identities. Vedres and Csigo (2002) studied frames employed in economic-policy discourse during a key period in Hungary's postsocialist transition. The authors blockmodel a matrix of statements by speech acts to identify "frames" (that is, structural positions characterized by frequent use of some statements and avoidance of others) and then analyze discursive strategies by exploring the sequencing of frame combinations over brief periods of public controversy.

Yeung (2005) uses Galois lattices to compare the meaning of relationships reported by members of 49 urban communes, based on associations among trait attributions that commune members made to one another in a survey and the ways dyad members characterized their ties. Terms like "love" and "charisma," he demonstrates, take on different meanings (i.e., are associated with different attributions to both personalities and relationships) in different communes. Yeung explains how differences in community structure generate these cultural differences.

DiMaggio and colleagues (2007, 2008) developed a network-analytic approach to attitude-survey data in order to address schematic heterogeneity among respondents. Central to the approach is the insight that similar answers may mean different things depending on the other responses to which they are linked. The method represents mental models graphically after partitioning respondents into subsets based on a relational similarity matrix. The key to the method (which was implemented algorithmically by Amir Goldberg [2011]) is a proximity measure based on relations between responses to pairs of items (i.e., patterns of shared relevance) rather than responses to individual items (i.e., patterns of shared opinion). Using this approach to analyze Americans' attitudes toward science, religion, and the occult, DiMaggio et al. (2008) find that only half of the U.S. public perceive science and religion as mutually antagonistic, with other subsets viewing science and religion as mutually supportive (and opposed to less legitimate forms of belief), orthogonal, or jointly suspect.

Earlier I noted the centrality of code-switching to work on culture and identity. The analogous switching mechanism for meaning in texts is *multivocality* (containing many voices or meanings). Multivocal elements, by inviting diverse readings, may appeal to heterogeneous readerships and become switches for semantic segmentation among multiple interpretive communities (Bakhtin, 1986). In a pioneering study, Carolan (2008) analyzes readership overlap among often-downloaded articles from a leading educational research journal. In contrast to studies based on co-citation nets, he finds a single giant component, at the center of which is a set of articles notable for multivocality. By bringing in readers from varying communities, he argues, the articles in the multivocal core "maintain ecological control over how readership flows across the network" (70).

Kathleen Carley has developed empirical approaches to representing mental models as networks of concepts (Carley and Palmquist, 1992) derived from analysis of texts. Carley builds bridges between work in cognitive science and sociology of culture to develop a structural theory of meaning. Her models are syntactic (i.e., classifying textual elements by their structural relation to one another) as well as semantic. The investigator extracts concepts from a set of texts (e.g., utterances collected through fieldwork, novels, or chains of synonyms in a thesaurus), defines a set of relations among them, explores the relations among concepts present in the texts, and represents these relations as a graph. Carley and collaborators have applied this method to analyzing Americans' maps of "drama" and "comedy," changing depictions of robots in science fiction novels, children's story recall (Carley, 1994), and the development of the organizational culture research field (Hill and Carley, 1999).

Anjewierden and colleagues (2004) take a similar approach on-line, using network methods to ask if bloggers who use the same phrases understand their meanings in the same way. The authors identify a set of terms (proper names and topics) and produce a network for each of several blogs, with terms as nodes and ties representing co-occurrence, expressed as conditional probabilities. The software permits users to produce graphical representations of concept networks from each blogger's corpus, as well as to compare networks of different bloggers.

Narrative networks

The notion of narrativity is central to much cultural research. Indeed, White (1992a) contends that narratives constitute social life by making action interpretable. Because narratives are sequential and because they often generate multiple forks, graphic representation is natural. Moreover, the tendency for narratives within a speech community to become conventionalized, so that similar tropes or sequences appear within different narratives, renders SNA a natural way to explore similarity (DeNooy, 2001) and intertextuality (Kristeva, 1980). Specific elements of narrative theory – for example, the distinction between ancillary statements and kernels (statements so central to the narrative that their removal undermines the stability of the narrative network) – reinforces the resonance between narrativity and SNA (Franzosi, 1998).

Bearman and Stovel (2000) analyze a set of essays prepared by German Nazis for an essay contest in 1934. The narratives describe how the authors became Nazis. They were rich in detail, so that the number of links between events was sufficient to construct meaningfully dense networks. Focusing on a single narrative, the authors combine SNA and content analysis to identify relationships among, and the relative importance of, macro events, local events, and thought processes (recognition, realization, and so on) in the authors' conversion to Nazism.

Smith (2007) likewise uses SNA to explore "how meaning emerges from the structure of relations among narrative elements" (p. 24). The author analyzes life-history narratives from Istrians, residents of a contested region containing both ethnic Croats and ethnic Italians that was partitioned between Italy and Yugoslavia after World War II. She compares narratives from current residents of Italian and Croatian Istria to those of immigrants in an Istrian neighborhood in New York. Whereas in Europe, the stories of Italians and Croats vary dramatically, in New York, where Istrians of both types share churches and other institutions, narratives omit contentious elements. Links among story components are expressed as ties and aggregated to graphic representations of typical story types by ethnic group and place of residence.

The application of SNA to problems of meaning is less well developed than are network approaches to creative communities, group boundaries, or identity formation, and the enterprise faces distinct challenges. Analysis of natural language is challenging for well-known reasons (homonyms, divergent spellings, synonyms, variously punctuated compound words, and so on), but computer scientists are making progress on these technical issues (e.g., Anjewierden and Efimova, 2006; on visualization, DeJordy et al., 2007). In addition, however, investigators face a range of *non*technical choices about the kind of information to collect (e.g., should proper nouns be tagged for valuation or treated identically regardless of evaluative content? should textual elements be classified [e.g., as actor, action, or object of action?]). They also face choices about how to interpret co-occurrence ties (e.g., does co-occurrence imply mutual relevance, shared approval, functional interdependence, or something else?). Researchers who employ SNA to study narrative contend with especially daunting challenges: time is central to narrative but difficult to represent in matrix form, and narrative networks are often very sparse. Yet researchers have made advances and research objectives often dictate the right answer to methodological dilemmas. Most important, such work, properly conducted, can bring scientific rigor to acts of interpretation and, in so doing, bring problems of meaning back to the center of cultural analysis.

CONCLUSION

I have contended in this chapter that social network analysis (SNA) is the natural way to refine and explore empirically several central ideas in the study of culture: that cultural products are produced by networks of collaborating creative professionals and organizations rather than by individual geniuses; that group and individual identity emerges from relations among persons and between persons and many kinds of culture; and that meaning itself emerges from relations among symbols or other elements of texts, broadly defined. To be sure, not all cultural processes are sustained or mediated through social networks; constitutive understandings embedded in physical arrangements or transmitted by media may operate at least somewhat independently. But by and large, a relational understanding of culture demands relational analytic methods.

As we have seen, a large body of scientific work has developed out of efforts to give concrete expression to relational theories of culture. Longstanding habits of mind – the reluctance of many students of culture, in the social sciences as well as the humanities, to employ formal methods and the radical structuralism explicit in formative contributions to modern SNA – stood in the way of these developments. It is no accident that well over half of the books and papers cited in this chapter have been published (if at all) in the twenty-first century. But however long in coming, the movement has reached critical mass, and social network analysis will play an increasingly important role in research on culture in years to come.

ACKNOWLEDGMENTS

I am grateful to Stephanie Schacht for assistance in identifying and digesting materials reviewed in this chapter and to Ron Breiger, Peter Carrington, and Amir Goldberg for helpful comments.

NOTES

1   In early, long unpublished, work, White wrote of the need to introduce "cultural elements into our very definitions of the elementary terms of social structure." Shared meanings, he argued, make ties interpretable and define network boundaries: "there must be a common culture to define a type of relation sharply and clearly, if there is to be a net" (2008 [1965], 2, 3). Although the acuity of White's insight that local cultures provide schemata that shape members' perception of networks was soon confirmed experimentally (Killworth and Bernard, 1976), early blockmodeling work bracketed culture (Santoro, 2008).

2   A separate research tradition has identified what appears to be an increasing salience of cultural factors, including educational background (Smits, 2003) and religious faith (Sherkat, 2004), to marital selection, an especially important network link. Such research has not employed social network data, however.

REFERENCES

Adamic, L. and Eytan, A. (2003) 'Friends and neighbors on the Web', *Social Networks*, 25: 211–30.

Anheier, H.K. and Gerhards, J. (1991) 'Literary myths and social structure', *Social Forces*, 69(3): 811–30.

Anheier, H.K., Gerhards, J. and Romo, F.P. (1995) 'Forms of capital and social structure in cultural fields: Exploring Bourdieu's social topography', *American Journal of Sociology*, 100(4): 859–903.

Anjewierden, A., Brussee, R. and Efimova, L. (2004) 'Shared conceptualizations in weblogs', Manuscript, https://doc.telin.nl/dsweb/Get/Document-43470/Shared_conceptualisations_in_weblogs.pdf (accessed January 5, 2009).

Anjewierden, A. and Efimova, L. (2006) 'Understanding weblog communities through digital traces: A framework, a tool and an example', in Robert Meersman, Zahir Tari, and Pilar Herrero (eds), *On the Move to Meaningful Internet Systems*. Lecture Notes in Computer Science, Volume 4277. New York: Springer. pp. 279–89.

Bakhtin, M.M. (1986) *Speech Genres and Other Late Essays*. Edited by Caryl Emerson and Michael Holquist. Translated by Vern McGee. Austin: University of Texas Press.

Bearman, P. (1993) *Relations into Rhetorics: Local Elite Social Structure in Norfolk, England: 1540–1640*. New Brunswick, NJ: Rutgers University Press.

Bearman, P. and Parigi, P. (2004) 'Cloning headless frogs and other important matters: Conversation topics and network structure', *Social Forces*, 83(2): 535–57.

Bearman, P. and Stovel, S. (2000) 'Becoming a Nazi: A model for narrative networks', *Poetics*, 27: 69–90.

Becker, H.S. (1974) 'Art as collective action', *American Sociological Review*, 39(6): 767–76.

Becker, H.S. (1982) *Art Worlds*. Chicago: University of Chicago Press.

Bernstein, B. (1971) *Class, Codes and Control, Volume 1: Theoretical Studies Towards a Sociology of Language*. Boston: Routledge & Kegan Paul.

Boari, C. and Corrado, R. (2007) 'Network and egocentric uncertainty: Relationships among art galleries in the contemporary art system', paper presented at the 23rd EGOS Colloquium, http://papers.ssrn.com/sol3/papers.cfm?abstract_id=1013270 (accessed January 5, 2009).

Bourdieu, P. (1983) 'The field of cultural production, or the economic world reversed', *Poetics*, 12(4–5): 311–56.

Bourdieu, P., Boltanski, L., Castel, R. and Chamboredon, J-C. (1965) *Un art moyen: Essai sur les usages sociaux de la photographie*. Paris: Editions de Minuit.

Breiger, R.L. (1974) 'The duality of persons and groups', *Social Forces*, 53: 181–90.

Breiger, R.L. (2000) 'A tool kit for practice theory', *Poetics*, 27: 91–115.

Breiger, R.L. (2004) 'The analysis of social networks', in Melissa Hardy and Alan Brymann (eds), *Handbook of Data Analysis*. London: Sage. pp. 505–26.

Breiger, R.L. and Mohr, J.M. (2004) 'Institutional logics from the aggregation of organizational networks: Operational procedures for the analysis of counted data', *Computational and Mathematical Organization Theory*, 10: 17–43.

Burt, R.L. (2004) 'Structural holes and good ideas', *American Journal of Sociology*, 110(2): 349–99.

Carley, K.M. (1994) 'Extracting culture through textual analysis', *Poetics*, 22: 291–312.

Carley, K.M. and Palmquist, M. (1992) 'Extracting, representing, and analyzing mental models,' *Social Forces*, 70(3): 601–36.

Carolan, B.V. (2008) 'The structure of educational research: The role of multivocality in promoting cohesion in an article interlock network', *Social Networks*, 30: 69–82.

Castells, M. (1997) *The Power of Identity*, vol. 2 in *The Information Age: Economy, Society, Culture*. New York: Blackwell.

Castells, M. (2000) 'Materials for an exploratory theory of the network society', *Journal of Sociology*, 51(1): 5–21.

Cattani, G. and Ferriani, S. (2008) 'A core/periphery perspective on individual creative performance: Social networks and cinematic achievements in the Hollywood film industry', *Organization Science*, 19(6): 824–44.

Caves, R. (2002) *Creative Industries: Contracts between Art and Commerce*. Cambridge: Harvard University Press.

Collins, R. (1989) 'Toward a theory of intellectual change: The social causes of philosophies', *Science, Technology and Human Values*, 14(2): 107–40.

Collins, R. (1998) *The Sociology of Philosophies: A Global Theory of Intellectual Change*. Cambridge: Harvard University Press.

Collins, R. (2000) 'The sociology of philosophies: A précis', *Philosophy of the Social Sciences*, 30(2): 157–201.

Collins, R. (2004) *Interaction Ritual Chains*. Princeton: Princeton University Press.

Collins, R. and Guillen, M. (2009) 'Mutual halo effects in cultural production networks: Eminence and success among modernist architects', working paper, Wharton School, University of Pennsylvania.

Crane, D. (1972) *Invisible Colleges: Diffusion of Knowledge in Scientific Communities*. Chicago: University of Chicago Press.

Crossley, N. (2009) 'The man whose web expanded: Network dynamics in Manchester's post/punk music scene 1976–1980', *Poetics*, 37: 24–49.

D'Andrade, R. (1995) *The Development of Cognitive Anthropology*. New York: Cambridge University Press.

DeJordy, R., Borgatti, S.P., Roussin, C. and Halgin, D.S. (2007) 'Visualizing proximity data', *Field Methods*, 19: 239–63.

DeLima e Silva, D., Soares, M.M., Henriques, M.V.C., M.T. Schivani Alves, S.G. de Aguiar, Carvalho, T.P.D., Corso, G. and Lucena, L.S. (2004) 'The complex network of the Brazilian popular music', *Physica A*, 332: 559–65.

DeNooy, W. (2001) 'Stories and social structure: A structural perspective on literature in society', in Dick Schram and Gerard Steen (eds), *The Psychology and Sociology of Literature: In Honor of Elrud Ibsch*. Amsterdam: J. Benjamins. pp. 359–77.

DeNooy, W. (2002) 'The dynamics of artistic prestige', *Poetics*, 30(3): 147–67.

DeNooy, W. (2003a) 'Fields and networks: Correspondence analysis and social network analysis in the framework of field theory', *Poetics*, 31: 305–27.

DeNooy, W. (2003b) 'Artistic classifications as collective representations', paper presented at the 6th conference of the European Sociological Association, http://home.medewerker.uva.nl/w.denooy/bestanden/ESA2003.pdf (accessed January 5, 2009).

DiMaggio, P. (1987) 'Classification in art', *American Sociological Review*, 52 (4): 440–55.

DiMaggio, P. (1997) 'Culture and cognition', *Annual Review of Sociology*, 23: 263–87.

DiMaggio, P., Goldberg, A. and Shepherd, H. (2008) 'Science vs. religion? A new look at an old opposition using data on public attitudes in the U.S.', paper presented at the Annual Meeting of the American Sociological Association, Boston.

DiMaggio, P., Shepherd, H. and Goldberg, A. (2007) 'Can exploring schematic heterogeneity in attitude data help us adjudicate debates about white Americans' racial attitudes?' paper presented at the annual meeting of the American Sociological Association, New York.

Durkheim, E. (1933 [1893]) *The Division of Labor in Society*. Translated by George Simpson. New York: Free Press.

Eliasoph, N. and Lichterman, P. (2003) 'Culture in interaction', *American Journal of Sociology*, 108(4): 735–94.

Emirbayer, M. and Goodwin, J. (1994) 'Network analysis, culture, and the problem of agency', *American Journal of Sociology*, 99(6): 1411–54.

Erickson, B.H. (1996) 'Culture, class and connections', *American Journal of Sociology*, 102(1): 217–51.

Erickson, B.H. (2001) 'Networks and linkages: Cultural aspects', in N.J. Smelser and P.B. Baltes (eds), *International Encyclopedia of the Social & Behavioral Sciences*. Amsterdam: Elsevier. pp. 10505–9.

Erickson, F. (1975) 'Gatekeeping and the melting pot', *Harvard Educational Review*, 45(1): 44–70.

Erickson, F. (2004) *Talk and Social Theory*. Cambridge, UK: Polity.

Esparza, N. and Rossman, G. (2006) 'I'd like to thank the Academy: Complementary productivity and social networks', working paper CCPR-035–06, California Center for Population Research, University of California, Los Angeles.

Faulkner, R.R. and Anderson, A.B. (1987) 'Short-term projects and emergent careers: Evidence from Hollywood', *American Journal of Sociology*, 92(4): 879–909.

Foster, P., Borgatti, S. and Jones, C. (2006) 'The contingent value of embeddedness: Gatekeeper search and decision making in a local culture market', paper presented at the Organizations and Markets Workshop, Graduate School of Business, University of Chicago, http://www.chicagogsb.edu/research/workshops/orgs-markets/docs/Foster-LocalMarkets.pdf (accessed January 5, 2009).

Foucault, M. (1977) *Discipline and Punish*. New York: Pantheon.

Franzosi, R. (1998) 'Narrative analysis – or why (and how) sociologists should be interested in narrative', *Annual Review of Sociology*, 24: 517–54.

Freeman, L.C. (2004) *The Development of Social Network Analysis: A Study in the Sociology of Science*. Vancouver, BC: Empirical Press.

Friedland, R. and Alford, R. (1991), 'Bringing society back in: Symbols, practices, and institutional contradictions', in Walter W. Powell and Paul DiMaggio (eds), *The New Institutionalism in Organizational Analysis*. Chicago: University of Chicago Press. pp. 232–63.

Fuhse, J.A. (2009) 'The meaning structure of social networks', *Sociological Theory*, 27(1): 51–73.

Gal, S. (1979) *Language Shift: Social Determinants of Linguistic Change in Bilingual Austria*. New York: Academic Press.

Gibson, D. (2005) 'Taking turns and talking ties: Networks and conversational interaction', *American Journal of Sociology*, 110(6): 1561–97.

Giuffre, K. (1999) 'Sandpiles of opportunity: Success in the art world', *Social Forces*, 77(3): 815–32.

Giuffre, K. (2001) 'Mental maps: Social networks and the language of critical reviews', *Sociological Inquiry*, 71(3): 381–93.

Gleiser, P.M. and Danon, L. (2003) 'Community structure in jazz', *Advances in Complex Systems*, 6(4): 565–73, arXiv: cond-mat/0307434v2 [cond-mat.dis-nn].

Goffman, I. (1951) 'Symbols of class status', *British Journal of Sociology*, 2 (4): 294–304.

Goldberg, A. (2011) 'Mapping shared understandings using Relational Class Analysis: The case of the cultural omnivore reexamined', *American Journal of Sociology* 116(5) (in press).

Grandadam, D. (2008) 'Evolving networks and the finest in jazz', paper presented at the Creative Industries and Intellectual Property Conference, May 22–23, 2008, London, http://www.dime-eu.org/working-papers/wp14/41 (accessed March 18, 2009).

Gumperz, J.J. (1982) *Discourse Strategies*. New York: Cambridge University Press.

Hannerz, U. (1996) *Transnational Connections: Culture, People, Places*. New York: Routledge.

Harshaw, H.W. and Tindall, D.B. (2005) 'Social structure, identities and values: A network approach to understanding people's relationships to forests', *Journal of Leisure Research*, 37(4): 426–49.

Heckathorn, D.D. and Jeffri, J. (2001) 'Finding the beat: Using respondent-driven sampling to study jazz musicians', *Poetics*, 28: 307–29.

Hill, V. and Carley, K.M. (1999) 'An approach to identifying consensus in a subfield: The case of organizational culture', *Poetics*, 27:1–30.

Hirsch, P.M. (1972) 'Processing fads and fashions: An organization set approach to cultural industry systems', *American Journal of Sociology*, 77(4): 639–59.

Jacobson, K. and Sandler, M. (2008) 'Musically meaningful or just noise? An analysis of on-line artist networks'. *Proceedings of the CMMR* http://doc.gold.ac.uk/~map01bf/papers/kjacobson_cmmr2008.pdf.

Jensen, M. (2006) 'Legitimizing illegitimacy: Identity spaces and markets for illegitimate products', manuscript, University of Michigan, http://www.chicagogsb.edu/research/workshops/orgs-markets/docs/jensen-legitimacy.pdf (accessed January 5, 2009).

Kadushin, C. (1974) *The American Intellectual Elite*. Boston: Little, Brown.

Kane, D. (2004) 'A network approach to the puzzle of women's cultural participation', *Poetics*, 32: 105–27.

Kennedy, M.T. (2005) 'Behind the one-way mirror: Refraction in the construction of product market categories', *Poetics*, 33: 201–26.

Killworth, P.D. and Bernard, H.R. (1976) 'Informant accuracy in social network data', *Human Organization*, 35(3): 269–86.

Kirschbaum, C. and Vasconcelos, F. (2006) 'Jazz: Structural changes and identity creation in cultural movements', in Martin Kornberger and Siegfried Gudergan (eds), *Only Connect: Neat Words, Networks and Identities*. Malmo, Sweden: Liber, Copenhagen Business School. pp. 230–56.

Kirschbaum, C. and Vasconcelos, F. (2007) 'Tropicália: Strategic maneuvers in networks of musicians', *RAE. Revista de Administração de Empresas*, 47: 10–26, http://www.rae.com.br/rae/index.cfm?FuseAction=Artigo&ID=3453&Secao=ARTIGOS&Volume=47&numero=3&Ano=2007.

Kristeva, J. (1980) *Desire in Language: A Semiotic Approach to Literature and Art*. New York: Columbia University Press.

Labov, W. (1972) *Sociolinguistic Patterns*. Philadelphia: University of Pennsylvania Press.

Lamont, M. and Molnár, V. (2002) 'The study of boundaries in the social sciences', *Annual Review of Sociology*, 28: 167–95.

Lizardo, O. (2006) 'How cultural tastes shape personal networks', *American Sociological Review*, 71: 778–807.

McLean, P.D. (1998) 'A frame analysis of favor seeking in the Renaissance: Agency, networks, and political culture', *American Journal of Sociology*, 104(1): 51–91.

McPherson, M. (2001) 'Sampling strategies for the arts: A hypernetwork approach', *Poetics*, 28: 291–306.

Merton, R.K. (1949) 'Patterns of influence: Local and cosmopolitan influentials', in Paul F. Lazarsfeld (ed.), *Communication Research, 1948–49*. New York: Duell, Sloan & Pearce. pp. 441–74.

Merton, R.K. (1968) 'The Matthew Effect in Science', *Science*, 159(3810): 56–63.

Milroy, L. and Margrain, S. (1980) 'Language loyalty and social network', *Language and Society*, 9(1): 43–70.

Mische, A. (2003) 'Cross-talk in movements', in Mario Diani and Doug McAdam (eds), *Social Movements and Networks: Relational Approaches to Collective Action*, New York: Oxford University Press. pp. 258–80.

Mische, A. (2007) *Partisan Publics: Communication and Contention Across Brazilian Youth Activist Networks*. Princeton: Princeton University Press.

Mische, A. and Pattison, P. (2000) 'Composing a civic arena: Publics, projects and social settings', *Poetics*, 27: 163–94.

Mische, A. and White, H. (1998) 'Between conversation and situation: Public switching dynamics across network domains,' *Social Research*, 65(3): 695–724.

Mohr, J. (1994) 'Soldiers, mothers, tramps and others: Discourse roles in the 1907 New York City charity directory', *Poetics*, 22: 327–57.

Mohr, J. (1998) 'Measuring meaning structures', *Annual Review of Sociology*, 24: 345–70.

Mohr, J.W., Bourgeois, M. and Duquenne, V. (2004) 'The logic of opportunity: A formal analysis of the University of California's outreach and diversity discourse', Center for Studies in Higher Education working paper CSHE-9–04, University of California.

Mohr, J.W. and Duquenne, V. (1997) 'The duality of culture and practice: Poverty relief in New York City, 1888–1917', *Theory and Society*, 26(2/3): 305–56.

Mohr, J.W. and Guerra-Pearson, F. (2010) 'The duality of niche and form: The differentiation of institutional space in New York City, 1888–1917', in Greta Hsu, Ozgecan Kocak, & Giacomo Negro (eds), *Categories in Markets: Origins and Evolution, Research in the Sociology of Organizations*, 31: 321–68.

Mohr, J.W. and Lee, H.K. (2000) 'From affirmative action to outreach: Discourse shifts at the University of California', *Poetics*, 28: 47–71.

Mohr, J.W. and Neely, B. (2009) 'Modeling Foucault: Dualities of power in organizational fields', in Renate Meyer, Kerstin Sahlin-Andersson, Marc Ventresca & Peter Walgenbach (eds), *Ideology and Organizational Institutionalism, Research in the Sociology of Organizations*, 27: 203–56.

Mohr, J.W. and White, H.C. (2008) 'How to model an institution', *Theory and Society*, 37: 485–512.

Park, J., Celma, O., Koppenberger, M., Cano, P. and Buldú, J.M. (2006) 'The social network of contemporary popular musicians', *Physics and Society* arXiv:physics/0609229v1 [physics.soc-ph].

Peterson, R.A. and Anand, N. (2004) 'The production of culture perspective', *Annual Review of Sociology*, 30: 311–34.

Peterson, R.A. and Berger, D. (1971) 'Entrepreneurship in organizations: Evidence from the popular music industry', *Administrative Science Quarterly*, 16(1): 97–106.

Rawlings, C.M. and Bourgeois, M.D. (2004) 'The complexity of institutional niches: Credentials and organizational differentiation in a field of U.S. higher education', *Poetics*, 32: 411–37.

Rogers, E.M. (1962) *Diffusion of Innovation*. New York: The Free Press.

Ruef, M. (1999) 'Social ontology and the dynamics of organizational forms: Creating market actors in the healthcare field, 1966–94'. *Social Forces*, 77: 1403–32.

Santoro, M. (2008) 'Framing notes: An introduction to "Catnets"', *Sociologica*, http://www.sociologica.mulino.it/doi/10.2383/26574.

Saussure, F. de (1977 [1916]) *Course in General Lingustics*. Translated by W. Baskin. Glasgow: Fontana/Collins.

Schummer, J. (2005) 'Reading nano: The public interest in nanotechnology as reflected in purchase patterns of books', *Public Understanding of Science*, 14: 163–83.

Schweizer, T. (1993) 'The dual ordering of actors and possessions', *Current Anthropology*, 34(4): 469–83.

Sherkat, D.E. (2004) 'Religious intermarriage in the United States: Trends, patterns and predictors', *Social Science Research*, 33: 606–25.

Smith, T. (2007) 'Narrative boundaries and the dynamics of ethnic conflict and conciliation', *Poetics*, 35: 22–46.

Smits, J. (2003) 'Social closure among the higher educated: Trends in educational homogamy in 55 countries', *Social Science Research*, 32: 251–77.

Sorenson, O. and Waguespack, D.M. (2006) 'Social structure and exchange: Self-confirming dynamics in Hollywood', *Administrative Science Quarterly*, 51(4): 560–89.

Strauss, C. and Quinn, N. (1997) *A Cognitive Theory of Cultural Meaning.* Cambridge: Cambridge University Press.

Swidler, A. (1986) 'Culture in action: Symbols and strategies', *American Sociological Review,* 51(2): 273–86.

Teitelbaum, T., Balenzuela, P., Cano, P. and Buldú, J.M. (2008) 'Community structures and role detection in music networks', *Chaos* 18, doi: 10.1063/1.2988285.

Tilly, C. (1998), *Durable Inequality.* Berkeley: University of California Press.

Turner, F. (2006) *From Counterculture to Cyberculture: Stewart Brand, the Whole Earth Network, and the Rise of Digital Utopianism.* Chicago: University of Chicago Press.

Uzzi, B. (2008) 'A social network's changing statistical properties and the quality of human innovation', *Journal of Physics A: Mathematical and Theoretical,* 41, doi:10.1088/1751–8113/41/22/224023.

Uzzi, B. and Spiro, J. (2005) 'Collaboration and creativity: The small world problem', *American Journal of Sociology,* 111(2): 447–504.

Vedres, B. and Csigo, P. (2002) 'Negotiating the end of transition: A network approach to local action in political discourse dynamics, Hungary 1997', Institute for Social and Economic Research and Policy, Columbia University, working paper, http://www.iserp.columbia.edu/research/working_papers/downloads/2002_06.pdf (accessed January 5, 2009).

Villena-Ponsoda, J.A. (2005) 'How similar are people who speak alike?: An interpretive way of using social networks in social dialectology research', in Peter Auer, Frans Hinskens, and Paul Kerswill (eds), *Dialect Change: Convergence and Divergence in European Languages.* Cambridge: Cambridge University Press. pp. 303–34.

Watts, D.J. (1999) 'Networks, dynamics and the small world phenomenon', *American Journal of Sociology,* 105(2): 493–527.

Weber, M. (1946 [1925]) 'Class, status and party', in Hans Gerth and C. Wright Mills (eds. and trans.), *From Max Weber: Essays in Sociology.* New York: Oxford University Press. pp. 180–95.

Wei, L. (1994) *Three Generations, Two Languages, One Family: Language Choice and Language Shift in a Chinese Community in Britain.* Clevedon, UK: Multilingual Matters.

White, H.C. (1992a [2nd ed. 2008]) *Identity and Control.* Princeton: Princeton University Press.

White, H.C. (1992b) 'Social grammar from culture: Reply to Steven Brint', *Sociological Theory,* 10(2): 209–13.

White, H.C. (1995) 'Network Switchings and Bayesian Forks', *Social Research,* 62: 1035–62.

White, H.C. (2008) 'Notes on the constituents of social structure – Soc. Rel. 10 – Spring '65', *Sociologica,* http://www.sociologica.mulino.it/doi/10.2383/26575.

White, H.C., Boorman, S.A. and Breiger, R.L. (1976) 'Social structure from multiple networks (part 1): Blockmodels of roles and positions', *American Journal of Sociology,* 81(4): 730–80.

White, H.C. and White, C. (1965) *Canvasses and Careers: Institutional Change in the French Painting World.* Chicago: University of Chicago Press.

Yair, G. (1995) '"Unite Unite Europe": The political and cultural structures of Europe as reflected in the Eurovision song contest', *Social Networks,* 17: 147–61.

Yeung, K.-T. (2005) 'What does love mean? Exploring network culture in two network settings', *Social Forces,* 84(1): 391–420.

21

Social Networks, Geography and Neighbourhood Effects

Ron Johnston and Charles Pattie

The United States, according to Bishop (2008: 5), has over recent years developed a 'stark geographical pattern of political belief, one that has grown more distinct in presidential elections since 1976. . . . [It] has been sorting itself, sifting at the most microscopic levels of society, as people have packed children, CDs, and the family hound and moved'. When moving, he argues, people deploy a range of criteria in selecting their new home at the neighbourhood scale, and this includes making 'choices about who their neighbors will be and who will share their new lives'. Such choices, he contends, have major political impacts. Thus at the county scale, whereas in 1976 less than one-quarter of all Americans lived in places in which one of the candidates for the presidency won by a landslide, by 2004 the proportion was more than one-half. The country has become spatially more polarised politically because in their migration patterns 'people were creating new, more homogeneous relations' (6).

Those homogeneous neighbourhoods then become self-perpetuating societal divisions. Again, as Bishop (2008: 6) expresses it, 'The like-minded neighbourhood supported the like-minded church, and both confirmed the image and beliefs of the tribe that lived and worshipped there'. Other local institutions – schools, formal clubs and associations and so forth – sustain and enhance these processes, as do informal interactions with neighbours. A greater homogeneity of ways of living was shaping a greater spatial polarisation of political beliefs and voting patterns.

Such political/electoral polarisation is not unique to the United States. In the United Kingdom,

Curtice and Steed (1982) noted a growing spatial polarisation of the electorate – which later studies have confirmed at a variety of scales (Johnston and Pattie, 2006). Like Bishop, too, they associated this – at least in part – with selective migration, although later studies found little evidence that this made a substantial contribution to the polarisation (McMahon et al., 1992; Denver and Halfacree, 1992). To others, a much more important influence has been the operation of contextual or neighbourhood effects. Following on from the seminal work of Butler and Stokes (1969: 182), which concluded that 'once a partisan tendency becomes dominant in a local area processes of opinion formation will draw additional support to the party that is dominant', Miller (1977, 1978) argued that 'contact is a condition for consensus' (1977: 48) so that contact, including within neighbourhoods, would generate polarisation:

> Social contacts are structured by family, choice of friends, social characteristics and locality. If party appeals to group interest or group attitudes evoke any differential political responses, the patterns of contact between individuals will tend to increase the political consensus within high-contact groups.

Indeed, he found that locality was a better predictor of how people voted than their social characteristics because 'people who talk together vote together' (Miller, 1977: 65). Others have argued similarly, Andersen and Heath (2002: 126), for example, contending that we would expect to find tendencies towards class voting to be reinforced among voters who regularly associate with others from the same social class. On the other hand, we would expect to find the tendency towards class voting to be undermined among voters who frequently interact with people from other social classes since the interaction will tend to move them towards agreement with members of other social classes. Simply put, the more that people interact with members of other social classes, the weaker we expect class voting to be.

Many studies using aggregate (ecological) data have come up with findings that are consistent with this hypothesis – basically that there is a greater spatial polarisation of voting for a given party than there is of the social groups who tend to support that party (e.g. there is greater polarisation in voting for the British Labour party than there is of people in the social classes – basically blue-collar workers – among whom that party derives its greatest support). But almost all of these provide circumstantial evidence only of the neighbourhood effect; the patterns are consistent with that effect, but the processes are unobserved.

Underpinning the argument for the neighbourhood effect is the following series of propositions.

1 Locational decisions involve a considerable degree of social selection, whereby people choose to live in areas – especially residential neighbourhoods – where people like themselves dominate.
2 The neighbourhood social networks that people join are thus dominated by people like themselves, not only in their socio-economic, -demographic, and other characteristics but also in their ideologies, attitudes, and behaviour. Such interaction sustains and may even enhance their own attitudes and behaviour; living among people who think and act like you merely reinforces your own tendencies and makes it even more likely that you will think and act accordingly.
3 Nevertheless, for a variety of reasons few local areas are socially and behaviourally homogeneous and most will contain some people from different social backgrounds than the majority. Some social contacts within the neighbourhood are thus likely to expose people to attitudes and behaviours different from their own. Those in the majority locally will have less exposure to such 'deviant' tendencies than will those in the minority to the majority's norms so it is much more likely that the minority will be converted to the majority view – 'conversion by

conversation' – than vice versa. The result will be the observed polarisation.

These propositions in turn rest on a series of assumptions. For the present purposes the most important of these is that much social interaction takes place in localised social networks involving neighbours. Such social networks are extremely unlikely to be isolated – many members will have links to either or both of other, nonlocal networks (based on workplaces or family/kin, for example) and separate networks in adjacent neighbourhoods: such external links are continual sources of new information to the importing networks, providing stimuli to which they respond, in some cases altering their attitudes and behaviour as a consequence. The local social network is thus structure within which information (almost invariably interpreted information) flows – with the consequences just discussed. But relatively little is known about such flows: they are assumed to be there because observed patterns of behaviour are consistent with models and hypotheses that assume their existence.

Such arguments apply to a much wider set of attitudes and behaviours than those associated with electoral decision making. Just as political information and attitudes flows through such networks so, too, does a wide range of other material that is linked to other types of behaviour – such as the adoption of innovations, as argued by Mark (1998) with regard to musical preferences. Furthermore, such networks are also identified as the major conduits for other flows – of infectious diseases, for example. Again, aggregate patterns are consistent with such models but in many cases the underlying processes – the actual flows along the network links – are not revealed, with some exceptions (e.g. in Rothenberg et al.'s 2005 study of the spread of HIV in Colorado Springs, CO; they found that geographical distance between the homes of individuals was not 'fully explanatory' but nevertheless 'geography distance may be an integral part of some network configurations that can foster the transmission of disease'[511]; see also Rothenberg, 2007).[1]

In reviewing the literature on the link between local social networks, information spread, and attitudes/behaviour, therefore, we have to combine works that directly address the hypotheses identified here – that social networks are geographically concentrated and that flows through those networks influence attitudes and behaviour – with a wider set that identifies patterns consistent with those hypotheses but that does not reveal the ongoing processes. In undertaking that task, much of our attention focuses on political attitudes and voting behaviour as one example of such processes and patterns, highlighting evidence from both types of study.

ON THE SPATIALITY OF SOCIAL NETWORKS

A core argument in much social science over many decades has been a major difference between rural and urban areas in the nature of social interaction there. In Tönnies's well-known dichotomy, the former were characterised by gemeinschaft – or community – whereas the latter were characterised by gesellschaft – or association. The assumption, for it was little more than that, was that rural areas – including relatively small settlements – were based on intense patterns of social contact whereas urban areas were characterised by much diverser and more transient contact patterns, with relatively few intense relationships, reflecting the fragmentation of such places (as with the spatial separation of home and workplace). Empirical research challenged this dichotomy, however, by identifying both communities as exemplifying gemeinschaft within urban areas (especially, though not exclusively, working-class residential areas and enclaves comprising minority immigrant communities) whereas, on the other hand, many 'urban' patterns of living were spreading into rural areas, leading to the breakdown of many of the well-established communities there.

The importance of social networks is stressed by Tilly (1992: 2):

> It is through personal networks that society is structured and the individuals integrated into society. . . . [D]aily life proceeds through personal ties: workers recruit in-laws and cousins for jobs on a new construction site; parents choose their children's pediatricians on the basis of personal recommendation; and investors get tips from their tennis partners. . . . The interactions among the abstract parts of society – "the family", "the economy", and so on – usually turn out to be personal dealings between real individuals who know one another, turn out to be operations of personal networks. . . . All through life, the facts, fictions, and arguments we hear from kin and friends are the ones that influence our actions most. Reciprocally, most people affect their society only through personal influences on those around them. Those personal ties are also our greatest motives for action: to protect relatives, impress friends, gain the respect of colleagues, and simply enjoy companionship.

If, therefore, we want, in Tilly's words, to 'protect relatives, impress friends, gain the respect of colleagues, and simply enjoy companionship' then we must interact with individuals – usually, though not necessarily (academics can win the respect of their colleagues through the written word alone), through face-to-face contact. Because – as geographers

have stressed for more than half a century, since a pioneer established that the geographical field was a 'discipline in distance' (Watson, 1955; Johnston, 2003) – most encounters, especially our frequent encounters with kin, colleagues, and friends, are spatially constrained, not least because of the time, cost, and effort involved in overcoming the friction of distance (Hägerstrand, 1982). Both the establishment and the maintenance of such social contacts are spatially constrained; social worlds are geographically structured.

These contentions were substantially exemplified in a study of the social networks of people living in a variety of Californian places as reported by Tilly (1982). Most respondents had each had a social network of 15–19 identified individuals; the largest group within those networks was composed of kin (over 40 per cent of all those named), with work colleagues and neighbours each making up a further 10 per cent. Nonkin, nonwork associate neighbours did not dominate such networks, therefore, but were a significant component of people's contact circles. But local people – who could be in two or even all three of those categories – were a major component of the average social network: they were some 16 persons, of whom five lived within 5 minutes' drive of a respondent's home and a further six between a 5- to 60-minute drive away; the final five lived even more distant. And although there were differences between type of settlement (semirural, town, metropolitan, regional core – the latter basically San Francisco and Oakland) in the number of local (within a 5-minute drive) kin named, there were few differences in the number of nonkin; respondents in each type of place had the same number (averaging 3.6) members of their social network living within a 5-minute drive from their home (i.e. neighbours), although those living in the metropolitan area and its core named more people living further away (i.e. they had both larger and spatially more dispersed social networks than their rural counterparts). Overall, however, Tilly (1982: 162) found that people living in small towns were more involved with their fellow residents than those living in larger settlements and that 'urbanites [especially high-income urbanites] substitute more distant relations for the foregone local ones' (1982: 167).

When the nature of interpersonal contacts is taken into account, Tilly (1982: 174–75) found that the percentage that were with near-neighbours varied considerably. The activities considered ranged from the sociable (visiting and having dinner together) through discussing a hobby, discussing personal issues, obtaining advice on important matters, and lending money and

> as one moves from exchanges for which distance is crucial to ones for which it is a marginal cost,

from contacts requiring frequent physical presence to ones calling for occasional interactions possibly by telephone or mail, and from casual matters to critical matters, the advantage of close associates declines. For sociable interactions, distant associates were much less often cited than nearby ones. For discussion of hobbies, which often involves engaging in the hobby together, nearby associates were again more commonly cited, though not as much more. Physical presence promotes discussing personal matters, but it is not essential and the advantage of local associates is marginal. Giving advice on important decisions and lending money in an emergency can easily be done occasionally and at a distance, and there is no advantage to proximity.

If, therefore, much of the information flowing through social networks that is linked to a range of attitudes and behaviours associated, for example, with politics and voting – much of which may be unstructured and unplanned – then neighbourhood circles are likely to be important.

This conclusion is sustained by Huckfeldt's (1988) study of neighbourhood contexts among a sample in Detroit. The respondents' networks were very much structured by social class, and across all classes around 40 per cent had a majority of their friends drawn from their local neighbourhood (within a 10-minute drive) and less than one-third had no friends locally. The local social context was an important influence on friendship choice, however; people living in areas where class x is dominant are more likely to have one or more friends drawn from that class, whatever their own class may be. In line with the earlier argument on neighbourhood effects, therefore, people in a minority in an area are likely to be exposed to the majority view there. And this is likely to have the hypothesised effects with regard to political attitudes. Huckfeldt (1996: 50) found that working-class respondents in a Buffalo, New York, study were much more likely to identify with the Democratic party if they lived in strongly than weakly working-class neighbourhoods (0.60 as against 0.48), whereas the reverse was the case with nonworking-class individuals (0.49 as against 0.37). The differences between neighbourhood types were as large as those between classes within neighbourhood types – which is consistent with Miller's argument. Furthermore, members of the middle class (according to their occupation, etc.) who identified with the working class were much more likely to identify as Democrats the more working-class friends they had and the more working-class the neighbourhood in which they lived. And the differences according to context extended well beyond political affiliation: friendship selection, ethnic loyalties, and residential

satisfaction were also linked to neighbourhood social characteristics – and these are influenced by both structured, primary-group, and unstructured (casual) interactions within the local milieu.

These data were derived from surveys that pre-date widespread use of the Internet and mobile phones, which many argue have changed the nature of conversation networks; proximity is no longer as important in sustaining contacts and delivering information. Thus, for example, Wellman has identified three types of community – lost, saved, and liberated – which differ, among other characteristics, on the importance of face-to-face and phone contact, which they contrast with a number of other typologies (see Wellman and Potter, 1999). Surveys of Toronto residents in the 1960s showed that although 'people who live near each other continue [as in traditional gemeinschaft communities] to have more frequent contact' (64), nevertheless proximity in this case is a relative concept; most of the networks involving nonkin friends were metropolitanwide in their spatial range rather than just the respondents' immediate neighbourhoods. Only 13 per cent of their most intimate relationships were with people living in the same neighbourhood (Wellman, 1979, 1996).

Wellman's data allow exploration of whether distance was an important constraint on social interaction prior to the Internet's creation, and they provide a baseline against which later studies can be assessed. Analysis of a 1978 survey shows not only the expected distance-decay pattern in the intensity of social interaction with both kin and nonkin intimates, but also that there was a marked decrease in the frequency of face-to-face contacts if the distance between the two individuals' addresses was more than five miles (Mok et al., 2007) although none of the East York respondents had most of their active social ties with individuals living within one mile's walking distance of their homes (Wellman et al., 1988); telephone contact only starts to decline beyond a distance of 100 miles. A 2005 survey of residents in the same area allowed a comparison with those findings. It showed that, as in 1978, face-to-face contact declined above a distance of 5 miles between the two individuals' homes, and phone contact at about 100 miles, but email contact was only slightly sensitive to distance. There is thus a continuing pattern of face-to-face contact being local and phone contact being regionally structured, but the new, Internet-enabled form of communication is largely unconstrained by distance (Mok et al., 2008). Social networks have not been transformed as much as extended, therefore, and the relative importance of local as against regional and distant contacts depends on whether they are kin or nonkin, intimates or not, since the intensity of contact varies by group, as well as by income (Carrasco et al., 2008a, b). In a parallel study of movers to a wired suburb, Hampton and Wellman (2001) found that those who did not realise the potential of the Internet experienced a decline in their social contacts after the move, whereas those who did experienced no change – but this included contacts with their neighbours as well as with more distant others; Hampton and Wellman thus concluded that although for some the move reduced both contact with and support from friends and relatives, for those who used the Internet being wired fostered contact and support both near and far in what Wellman (1999) describes as a more 'loosely-coupled world'.

As cyberspace becomes more important and localised, intense communities decline in their significance and we move into a situation that Wellman (2001: 3) and others term glocalization:

> Except in situations of ethnic or racial segregation, contemporary Western communities are usually loosely-bound, sparsely-knit, ramifying networks of specialized ties. Rather than being full members of one solidary neighbourhood or kinship group, community has become "glocalized". Contemporary urbanites juggle limited memberships in multiple, specialized, far-flung, interest-based network communities as they deal with shifting amorphous networks of kin, neighbours, friends, workmates, and organizational ties. Only a minority of network members are directly connected with each other. Most friends and relatives live in different neighbourhoods; many live in different metropolitan areas. At work, people often work *with* distant others and not those sitting near them. People usually obtain support, sociability, information and a sense of belonging from those who do not live in the same neighbourhood.

INFORMATION FLOW THROUGH NETWORKS AND NEIGHBOURHOOD EFFECTS

Whatever their spatial dimensions, social networks are communication conduits whereby people exchange information, which may be entirely factual or involve value judgements. Those flows, it is argued, can influence people's beliefs, attitudes, and behaviour, so that knowing who speaks to whom and about what can be crucial in exploring who thinks and does what. In political contexts, for example, this can include discussions about a variety of electoral matters – such as parties' policies, governments' performance, and individual

politicians' leadership credentials. In turn, such material may influence how people vote at elections. The study of social networks in operation can thus enable investigations of political action and advance understanding of election outcomes. Further if, as argued above, there is a clear spatial configuration to many social networks, especially those based on face-to-face interaction, then the result of such information flows through locally focused networks should be realised in clear patterns of political behaviour, as argued above.

Following this argument, the logical research design is to study the processes leading to the patterns, using the results of investigations of the flow of electorally relevant information through local networks to account for observed voting patterns. Relatively little research has adopted this format, however, for a variety of reasons – many of them associated with the cost of such intensive research strategies. Thus, as exemplified here, the outcomes have been of two types: the identification of voting patterns, which are consistent with the concept of a neighbourhood effect, leading to inferences that these have been generated by local residents discussing relevant issues; and the study of people's decision making in the context of their conversations, which if they show that these lead to some people changing their minds regarding how they vote can imply that the outcome will be consistent with neighbourhood effects. The two clearly should be integrated, but few studies have done so, hence the organisation of the following sections.

Local social context and neighbourhood effects

As discussed above, if conversations, especially conversations with individuals having opposing views on political issues and who to vote for in an election, stimulate people to reconsider their own positions, then in any social network with a majority of the population supporting one view/candidate/party and the remainder supporting another, the weight of opinion encountered is more likely to lead adherents of a majority view to switch to the minority than vice versa. The outcome would be that the majority view within the network would dominate to a greater degree than could be predicted from knowledge of the individuals' personal characteristics (e.g. whether they would vote Conservative or Labour at British general elections). And if those conversation networks are spatially constrained, then the political complexion of areas should be more polarised than their social composition implies – as suggested by Cox (1969) in a seminal paper.

This argument has been the foundation for a large number of ecological studies using aggregate areal data at a wide variety of scales. In many of these the independent variables, representing the local context, are predominantly socio-economic and demographic data taken from censuses and the dependent variables are election results. Many of them – especially in the United Kingdom where there is a paucity of voting data at other than the Parliamentary constituency scale, where the average constituency contains some 70,000 electors – are at much larger spatial scales than local neighbourhoods within which much social interaction is assumed to occur. Nevertheless, if such large-scale analyses find the polarised patterns associated with the neighbourhood effect this can be taken as circumstantial evidence sustaining that argument. If, say, the Labour party in a dominantly working-class British Parliamentary constituency has a greater share of the votes cast than predicted from its class composition (as is generally the case: Johnston et al., 1988), this could indicate that (a) more neighbourhoods in the constituency have predominantly working-class than nonworking-class populations and (b) that therefore a pro-Labour neighbourhood effect will dominate across the constituency.

Such circumstantial evidence – of which there is a great deal (as reviewed in Johnston and Pattie, 2006; see Cho and Rudolph, 2008) – has increasingly been sustained by other evidence that has merged survey data on individuals' voting behaviour with census data on their local contexts. (An early example was Harrop et al., 1992.) Such work has been extended recently with studies using contextual data on what have been termed 'bespoke neighbourhoods' in which instead of locating each survey respondent in a relatively large census area – such as an electoral ward in the United Kingdom – very small-area census data are used to identify the characteristics of the immediate area around each respondent's home. These have found clear patterns, circumstantially even stronger, entirely consistent with the neighbourhood effect; voters from any class background were more likely to vote for a party the larger the proportion of the local population that was drawn from that party's 'natural' class supporters (McAllister et al., 2001). Furthermore, this relationship was found at a variety of spatial scales for the bespoke neighbourhoods: the greater the intensity of local support for a particular party, the greater the polarisation of voting towards it (Johnston et al., 2001, 2005a, 2007). And later work showed that patterns consistent with the neighbourhood effect were much stronger among respondents, the higher their levels of local social capital and interaction with their neighbours (Johnston et al., 2005b).

Social interaction is not the only process that can generate voting patterns consistent with the neighbourhood effect, however. Many people's voting decisions are based on their evaluations of government policy, especially economic policy. They will reward governments that have delivered economic prosperity by voting for their return to power but will punish them by voting for an opposition party (especially one that seems likely to govern well) if they have not. Such calculi operate at a variety of scales: the individual level ('Have I prospered over the last year?'; 'Do I think my income/quality of living will improve over the next year?'); the national level ('Has the national economy improved recently?'; 'Will it during the immediate future?'); and the regional/local level ('Have things improved locally recently?'; 'Will they continue to do so?'). And calculi can refer to a range of government policies – on aspects of the welfare state, for example (Johnston and Pattie, 2001a, 2001b). Context is important in these calculi, too: indeed, studies using the bespoke neighbourhood approach found that people who were economically optimistic about their own financial situation were less likely to vote for the government to be returned to office if they lived in relatively deprived areas than they were if they lived in places where their neighbours were also prospering (Johnston et al., 2000). Context, it seems, stimulated altruistic behaviour.

Another geographically variable influence on voting decisions is party campaigning, much of which is spatially focused to ensure that a party's supporters turn out in those constituencies where their participation is most needed – in particular, the marginal seats that could be won or lost depending on who abstains. As such activity has become increasingly targeted by a range of advertising and other strategies aimed at contacting and mobilising individual voters (and hoping that they will mobilise others through their social networks) – with clear impacts, especially with regard to the intensity of campaigns mounted by opposition candidates/parties (Pattie and Johnston, 2008b). The outcome of such geographically focused campaigns is likely to be a pattern of voting consistent with that generated by the classic neighbourhood effect – which could mean that social interaction is an irrelevant influence. However, analyses incorporating both economic voting and party campaign intensity into the bespoke neighbourhood approach have shown that all three are complementary: parties perform better in areas where they have stimulated prosperity, where they have campaigned most intensively, and where the local social network is likely to be favourably inclined towards them (Johnston et al., 2007). In sum, therefore, there is a very substantial body of research findings that is entirely consistent with the neighbourhood effect hypothesis and implies that information flowing through social networks influences voting decisions – but that evidence is overwhelmingly circumstantial only.

Conversion through conversation

Discussion between citizens lies at the heart of most theories of democracy. For democracy to function there has to be scope for diversity of opinion, free expression of those opinions, and resolution of differences and conflicts. Political conversations provide one means for spreading salient information, opinion, and argument through an electorate, and they can enable individuals to determine their positions on the relevant issues and/or personalities by testing their views against those of others. A celebrated two-step flow model of political communication, for instance, argues that local 'opinion leaders' pick up political information from the media and then in their turn pass this information on to others in their communities with whom they are in contact (Katz and Lazarsfeld, 1955). Individuals' social networks might be dominated by others who largely share their own views, prejudices, and values, but they may encounter others with very different views from their own. Conversations with others are likely to reinforce one's own beliefs in the former case, whereas in the latter they may well cause individuals to question their opinions – especially if they are not strongly committed to any position, candidate, or party and hold minority views within the conversation network. Other things being equal, therefore, such holders of minority views may change their minds and agree with the network's majority. Evidence supports this argument; the more supporters of a particular party an individual talks to, the more likely they are to switch their vote to that party if they previously either voted for an alternative or abstained (Huckfeldt and Sprague, 1995; Pattie and Johnston, 2000, 2001).

Involvement in relevant conversations could also encourage political participation (Putnam, 2000), with information on how to take part and providing indirect confirmation that one's associates are likely to participate, hence enhancing the impact of social norms – although those already likely to participate may, as a result of their commitment, be more likely to discuss politics with others than those not intending to participate. Studies confirm that those with extensive conversation networks participate more than those with limited networks, particularly if conversations are focused on politics (Leighley, 1990; McClurg, 2003, 2006a, 2006b).

The content of conversations is likely to be at least as important as their prevalence. It is one thing to be surrounded by individuals who all confirm the correctness of one's own opinions, and some may seek to achieve this, by their choice of networks (Finifter's 1974 study of American car-plant workers demonstrated that individuals who held a minority view – supporting the Republicans in a predominantly Democrat-voting environment – not only were more likely to form friendships with like-minded people at work but were also less likely than their Democrat-supporting workmates to discuss politics outside the workplace). It is potentially quite another thing to be faced with widespread disagreement. Most individuals will encounter at least some disagreement within their discussion networks, however, and few can insulate themselves from heterogeneous opinions; pressures towards homogeneity of opinion within networks notwithstanding, disagreement is an endemic feature of conversation (Huckfeldt et al., 2004). And, of course, some disagreement is essential for influence to occur (McPhee, 1963). Where people agree entirely, they cannot persuade.

The impact of disagreement within networks on participation has proved controversial. Classic pluralist accounts of democracy suggest that where differences of opinion exist, people and/or groups will be mobilised to represent the various views expressed, thereby acting as a mobilising force (Dahl, 1989). But psychological models suggest that as individuals are conflict-averse they will try to avoid conflict, whether by acquiescence or by silence (Festinger, 1957; Ulbig and Funk, 1999). In line with that position some have shown that countervailing opinions in discussion networks can discourage participation, in part by increasing uncertainty among citizens (Mutz, 2002a, 2002b; Mutz and Mondak, 2006; Pattie and Johnston, 2008a). McClurg (2006a), on the other hand, reports that the impact of disagreement is modified by context, in particular by whether an individual is part of a local political majority or minority. His results suggest that political participation by individuals who share the majority view in their local context is unaffected by exposure to disagreement in their discussion networks but those in the local minority become less likely to participate as their exposure to disagreement increases: disagreement disincentivises participation by those in the local minority.

Individuals are more likely to participate if they feel their discussants are politically sophisticated and less likely to do so if they feel discussants lack expertise (McClurg, 2006b).

Putting it all together

What much of the literature reviewed above lacks is an integration of the two main approaches to studying neighbourhood effects – information flow through social networks, and spatially polarised aggregate voting patterns. Our conclusions are very strong in providing support for the argument that locally focused social interaction does influence people's voting decisions in ways that are very likely to generate polarised patterns, but the evidence is not conclusive.

A few people have sought to remedy this – largely through very small-scale studies of selected locales (e.g. Fitton, 1973) or by deploying sample data in which contact with neighbours was surveyed (Curtice, 1995). By far the most important of such studies, however, have been the large sample surveys conducted by Huckfeldt and his collaborators, which have studied social networks in their spatial settings. The original, seminal work (Huckfeldt and Sprague, 1995) used a survey of the residents of South Bend, Indiana, who were interviewed on three occasions before and after the 1984 U.S. presidential election and who provided information about those with whom they discussed political issues (subdivided into spouses, other kin, and nonkin). These and other data on the individual were integrated with data on the neighbourhoods in which they lived; one-third of the nominated discussants lived in the respondents' home neighbourhoods and 40 per cent worked at the same location. (Only 6 per cent were both workmates and neighbourhood co-residents.) The impact of discussants' political choices was greatest when the respondent's nominated main discussant was a spouse; with the immediate household, the main discussant's influence was greatest when the respondent correctly identified that person's own political preferences (in 1984, whether or not he or she supported Reagan or Mondale).

Huckfeldt and Sprague's (1995: 189) conclusion that 'vote preferences are socially structured, not only by the characteristics of the voter, but also by the characteristics and preferences of others with whom the voter discusses politics' was extended by incorporating further variables to represent the political characteristics of their respondents' neighbourhood socio-political milieux but also the apparent intensity of the election campaign there. They found that contact with voters in a neighbourhood influenced not only those connected but also others in the locality, with the contact thus acting as 'a catalyst that sets into motion a series of events' (255) because 'people know their neighbour's politics, and one reason they know is party organization aimed at informing them' (p. 254). Thus, the proportion of a neighbourhood's respondents (their sample was spatially clustered to allow this to be estimated)

who supported a particular party was strongly related to whether an individual living there also identified with that party, whatever her or his individual characteristics. Not everybody is converted to the local majority view, of course; later studies showed that disagreement with one's main discussant is sometimes sustained through interaction, not diminished – especially if that disagreement is inconsistent with the general tenor of opinion within an individual's network (Huckfeldt et al., 2002). And, of course, reaction to the local milieu depends upon the nature of that awareness: Baybeck and McClurg (2005) found that a substantial majority of the South Bend respondents could accurately represent the characteristics of their home neighbourhood – and then, as they put it, 'When a neighbourhood's majority becomes obvious, even opposing voters seem capable of figuring that out' (p. 509).

Although the early Huckfeldt studies integrated social networks and neighbourhood contexts much more firmly than almost all other analysts, nevertheless the network geographies were to a considerable extent inferred. Later work in two cities took the work further, however, by using post-coded information on the respondents' and their main discussants' homes to establish the degree of spatial dispersion of those networks. As anticipated from other work on the geography of social interaction reviewed earlier, the networks were not intensely localised: for kin (excluding spouses) only 23 per cent lived within 1 km. of the respondent's home and the average distance between the two locations was 6.4 km.; for nonkin, the percentage was only 15 and the mean distance 8.4 km – nevertheless over half of this group lived within 15 minutes' driving time of the respondent's home (Baybeck and Huckfeldt, 2002a). The more dispersed the network, however, the less intense were the discussions taking place within it. Information is spread more widely through the more dispersed networks, across a wider range of neighbourhood contexts – even though they do not necessarily connect individuals who are socially and politically more diverse than is the case with the spatially more clustered networks, the neighbourhoods act as the 'bridges between socially and politically diverse locales' (p. 273), or what Granovetter (1973) terms the 'weak ties' that introduce (perhaps dissonant) information to otherwise separate networks and locales, even though two individuals so connected are less likely to converge in their opinions over an election campaign than are two similar individuals who are members of spatially higher density networks, among whom contact is also more frequent (Baybeck and Huckfeldt, 2002b). Spatially dispersed networks, it seems, create a politically homogeneous overlay on a politically diverse urban area – a conclusion that is now being explored with experimental data (e.g. Ahn et al., 2007).[2]

NOTES

1. The type of relationship that was involved in the disease spread would also be important. Contact with prostitutes was less likely to be structured with neighbourhood networks, for example.

2. See the special issue on social networks in PS: Political Science and Politics, 44(1), 2011.

REFERENCES

Ahn, T.K., Huckfeldt, R. and Ryan, J.B. (2007) 'Networks, groups, and contextual constraints on political communication'. Available at http://faculty.psdomain.ucdavis.edu/rhuckfeldt. Last accessed 14 February 2011.

Andersen, R. and Heath, A.F. (2002) 'Class matters: The persisting effects of contextual social class on individual voting in Britain', 1964–97. *European Sociological Review*, 18: 125–38.

Baybeck, B. and Huckfeldt, R. (2002a) 'Spatially dispersed ties among interdependent citizens; connecting individuals and aggregates'. *Political Analysis*, 10: 261–75.

Baybeck, B. and Huckfeldt, R. (2002b) 'Urban contexts, spatially dispersed networks and the diffusion of political information'. *Political Geography*, 21: 195–210.

Baybeck, B. and McClurg, S.D. (2005) 'What do they know and how do they know it? An examination of citizen awareness of context'. *American Politics Research*, 33: 492–520.

Bishop, B. (2008) *The Big Sort: Why the Clustering of Like-Minded America Is Tearing Us Apart*. Boston: Houghton Mifflin.

Butler, D. and Stokes, D. (1969) *Political Change in Britain: Forces Shaping Electoral Choice*. London: Macmillan.

Carrasco, J.-A., Miller, E.J. and Wellman, B. (2008a) 'How far and with whom do people socialize? Empirical evidence about the distance between social network members'. *Transportation Research Record: Journal of the Transportation Research Board*, 2076: 114–22.

Carrasco, J.-A., Hogan, B., Wellman, B. and Miller, E.J. (2008b) 'Agency in social activity interactions: The role of social networks in time and space'. *Tijdschrift voor Economische en Sociale Geografie* 99: 562–83.

Cho, W.K.T. and Rudolph, T.J. (2008) 'Emanating political participation: Untangling the spatial structure behind participation'. *British Journal of Political Science*, 38: 273–89.

Cox, K.R. (1969) 'The voting decision in spatial context'. *Progress in Geography*, 1: 83–117.

Curtice, J. (1995) 'Is talking over the garden fence of political import?' In M. Eagles (ed.), *Spatial and Contextual Models in Political Research*. London: Taylor and Francis. pp. 195–209.

Curtice, J. and Steed, M. (1982) 'Electoral choice and the production of government: The changing operation of the electoral system in the United Kingdom since 1955'. *British Journal of Political Science*, 12: 249–98.

Dahl, R. (1989) *Democracy and Its Critics*. New Haven: Yale University Press.

Denver, D.T. and Halfacree, K. (1992) 'Inter-constituency migration and turnout at the British general election of 1983'. *British Journal of Political Science*, 22: 248–54.

Festinger, L. (1957) *A Theory of Cognitive Dissonance*. Palo Alto: Stanford University Press.

Finifter, A. (1974) 'The friendship group as a protective environment for political deviants'. *American Political Science Review*, 68: 607–25.

Fitton, M. (1973) 'Neighbourhood and voting: A sociometric explanation'. *British Journal of Political Science*, 3: 445–72.

Granovetter, M. (1973) 'The strength of weak ties'. *American Journal of Sociology*, 78: 1360–80.

Hägerstrand, T. (1982) 'Diorama, path and project'. *Tijdschrift voor Economische en Sociale Geografie*, 73: 323–39.

Hampton, K. and Wellman, B. (2001) 'Long distance community in the network society: Contact and support beyond Netville'. *American Behavioral Scientist*, 45: 476–95.

Harrop, M., Heath, A. and Openshaw, S. (1992) 'Does neighbourhood influence voting behaviour—and why?' In I. Crewe, P. Norris, D. Denver and D. Broughton (eds), *British Elections and Parties Yearbook 1*. Hemel Hempstead: Harvester Wheatsheaf. pp. 103–20.

Huckfeldt, R.R. (1988) 'Social contexts, social networks, and urban neighborhoods: Environmental constraints on friendship choice'. *American Journal of Sociology*, 89: 651–69.

Huckfeldt, R.R. (1996) *Politics in Context: Assimilation and Conflict in Urban Neighborhoods*. New York: Agathon Press.

Huckfeldt, R., Johnson, P.E. and Sprague, J. (2002) 'Political environments, political dynamics, and the survival of disagreement'. *Journal of Politics*, 64: 1–21.

Huckfeldt, R., Johnson, P.E. and Sprague, J. (2004) *Political Disagreement: The Survival of Diverse Opinions within Communication Networks*. Cambridge: Cambridge University Press.

Johnston, R.J. (2003) 'Order in space: Geography as a discipline in distance'. In R.J. Johnston and M. Williams (eds.), *A Century of British Geography*. Oxford: Oxford University Press for the British Academy. pp. 303–46.

Johnston, R.J., Dorling, D.F.L., Tunstall, H., Rossiter, D.J., McAllister, I. and Pattie, C.J. (2000) 'Locating the altruistic voter: Context, egocentric voting and support for the Conservative party at the 1997 general election in England and Wales'. *Environment and Planning A*, 32: 673–94.

Johnston, R.J., Jones, K., Propper, C. and Burgess, S. (2007) 'Region, local context, and voting at the 1997 general election in England'. *American Journal of Political Science*, 51: 640–54.

Johnston, R.J. and Pattie, C.J. (2001a) 'Dimensions of retrospective voting: Economic performance, public service standards and Conservative party support at the 1997 British general election'. *Party Politics*, 5: 39–54.

Johnston, R.J. and Pattie, C.J. (2001b) 'It's the economy, stupid—but which economy'? Geographical scales, retrospective economic evaluations and voting at the British 1997 general election'. *Regional Studies*, 35: 309–19.

Johnston, R.J. and Pattie, C.J. (2006) *Putting Voters in Their Place: Geography and Elections in Great Britain*. Oxford: Oxford University Press.

Johnston, R.J., Pattie, C.J. and Allsopp, J.G. (1988) *A Nation Dividing? The Electoral Map of Great Britain 1979–1987*. London: Longman.

Johnston, R.J., Pattie, C.J., Dorling, D.F.L., McAllister, I., Tunstall, H. and Rossiter, D.J. (2001) 'Housing tenure, local context, scale and voting in England and Wales', 1997. *Electoral Studies*, 20: 195–216.

Johnston, R.J., Propper, C., Burgess, S., Sarker, R., Bolster, A. and Jones, K. (2005a) 'Spatial scale and the neighbourhood effect: Multinomial models of voting at two recent British general elections'. *British Journal of Political Science*, 35: 487–514.

Johnston, R.J., Propper, C., Jones, K., Sarker, R., Bolster, A. and Burgess, S. (2005b) 'Neighbourhood social capital and neighbourhood effects'. *Environment and Planning A*, 37: 1443–57.

Katz, E. and Lazarsfeld, P.F. (1955) *Personal Influence: The Part Played by People in the Flow of Mass Communications*. Glencoe, IL: Free Press.

Leighley, J.E. (1990) 'Social interaction and contextual influences on political participation'. *American Politics Quarterly*, 18: 459–75.

Mark, N. (1998) 'Birds of a feather sing together'. *Social Forces*, 77: 453–85.

McAllister, I., Johnston, R.J., Pattie, C.J., Tunstall, H., Dorling, D.F.L. and Rossiter, D.J. (2001) 'Class dealignment and the neighbourhood effect: Miller revisited'. *British Journal of Political Science*, 31: 41–59.

McClurg, S.D. (2003) 'Social networks and political participation'. *Political Research Quarterly*, 56: 448–64.

McClurg, S.D. (2006a) 'Political disagreement in context: The conditional effect of neighborhood context, disagreement and political talk on electoral participation'. *Political Behavior*, 28: 349–66.

McClurg, S.D. (2006b) 'The electoral relevance of political talk: Examining disagreement and expertise effects in social networks on political participation'. *American Journal of Political Science*, 50: 737–54.

McMahon, D., Heath, A.F., Harrop, M. and Curtice, J. (1992) 'The electoral consequences of north-south migration'. *British Journal of Political Science*, 22: 419–43.

McPhee, W.N. (1963) *Formal Theories of Mass Behavior*. New York: The Free Press of Glencoe.

Miller, W.L. (1977) *Electoral Dynamics in Britain since 1918*. London: Macmillan.

Miller, W.L. (1978) 'Social class and party choice in England: A new analysis'. *British Journal of Political Science*, 8: 259–84.

Mok, D., Wellman, B. and Basu, R. (2007) 'Did distance matter before the internet? Interpersonal contact and support in the 1970s'. *Social Networks*, 29: 430–61.

Mok, D., Wellman, B. and Carrasco, J.-A. (2008) 'Does distance matter in the age of the internet?' Available at http://homes.chass.utoronto.ca/~wellman/publications/ Last accessed 14 February 2011.

Mutz, D. (2002a) 'The consequences of cross-cutting networks for political participation'. *American Journal of Political Science*, 46: 838–55.

Mutz, D. (2002b) 'Cross-cutting social networks: Testing democratic theory in practice'. *American Political Science Review*, 96: 111–26.

Mutz, D. and Mondak, J. (2006) 'The workplace as a context for cross-cutting political discourse'. *The Journal of Politics*, 68: 140–55.

Pattie, C.J. and Johnston, R.J. (2000) 'People who talk together vote together: An exploration of contextual effects in Great Britain'. *Annals of the Association of American Geographers*, 90: 41–66.

Pattie, C.J. and Johnston, R.J. (2001) 'Talk as a political context: Conversation and electoral change in British elections'. *Electoral Studies*, 20: 17–40.

Pattie, C.J. and Johnston, R.J. (2008a) 'It's good to talk: Talk, disagreement and tolerance'. *British Journal of Political Science*, 38: 677–98.

Pattie, C.J. and Johnston, R.J. (2008b) 'Still talking but is anybody listening? The changing face of constituency campaigning in Britain, 1997–2005'. *Party Politics*, 14.

Potterat, J.J. et al. (2002) 'Sexual network structure as an indicator of epidemic phase'. *Sexually Transmitted Infections*, 78: 152–58.

Putnam, R. D. (2000) *Bowling Alone*. New York: Simon and Schuster.

Rothenberg, R. (2007) 'Maintenance of endemicity in urban environments: A hypothesis linking risk, network structure and geography'. *Sexually Transmitted Infections*, 83: 10–15.

Rothenberg, R., et al. (2005) 'Social and geographic distance in HIV risk'. *Sexually Transmitted Disease*, 32: 506–12.

Tilly, C. (1982) *To Dwell among Friends: Personal Networks in Town and City*. Chicago: University of Chicago Press.

Ulbig, S.G. and Funk, C.L. (1999) 'Conflict avoidance and political participation'. *Political Behavior*, 21: 265–82.

Watson, J.W. (1955) 'Geography: A discipline in distance. *Scottish Geographical Magazine*, 71: 1–13.

Wellman, B. (1979) 'The community question: The intimate networks of East Yorkers'. *American Journal of Sociology*, 84: 1201–31.

Wellman, B. (1996) 'Are personal communities local? A Dumptarian reconsideration?' *Social Networks*, 18: 347–54.

Wellman, B. (1999) 'From little boxes to loosely-bound networks: The privatization and domestication of community', in J. Abu-Lughod (ed.), *Sociology for the Twenty-First Century: Continuities and Cutting-Edges*. Chicago: University of Chicago Press. pp. 94–114.

Wellman, B. (2001) *The Persistence and Transformation of Community: From Neighbourhood Groups to Social Networks. Report to the Law Commission of Canada*. Toronto: Wellman Associates.

Wellman, B., Carrington, P. and Hall, A. (1988) 'Networks as personal communities'. In B. Wellman and S.D. Berkowitz (eds.), *Social Structures: A Network Approach*. Cambridge: Cambridge University Press. pp. 130–84.

Wellman, B. and Potter, S. (1999) 'The elements of personal communities'. In B. Wellman (ed.), *Networks in the Global Village*. Boulder, CO: Westview Press. pp. 49–82.

22

A Multiple-Network Analysis of the World System of Nations, 1995–1999

Edward L. Kick, Laura A. McKinney,
Steve McDonald, and Andrew Jorgenson

INTRODUCTION

In this chapter we address the theoretical and empirical foundations of network approaches in macrosociological studies of the world system, we offer multiple-network findings to address the structure of the modern world system and nations' positions in it. With these results, we replicate the pioneering global network findings of Snyder and Kick (1979). Their effort still enjoys considerable currency in the literature (see Mahutga, 2006), but they use network data from the early 1960s that are now a dated representation of the modern world system.

Network analyses such as ours are relatively new in the study of macrosociology. Empirical analysis of social networks truly "arrived" in sociology only in the last three decades (Granovetter, 1973; White et al., 1976; Wellman, 1983), and applications of network analysis to the study of the world system began with Snyder and Kick (1979). However, their work, as well as our present treatment, remains indebted to historical and contemporary theories of the effects of network dynamics on a range of national development outcomes. For instance, the modernization and world-system/dependency perspectives that Snyder and Kick test owe much of their theorization to classical treatments of the societal-level networks that prompt national economic development.

A brief summary of this legacy is warranted here and in our concluding remarks. Consider, for instance, Comte's ([1842] 1854) pioneering work, which centered on a rapidly industrializing Europe and the networks of societal-level changes that led the most "primitive" societies to their modern forms. As well, Spencer (1887), Tönnies (1887), and Durkheim ([1893] 1964: 236–60) emphasized the movement from simple and undifferentiated forms of societal linkages (gemeinschaft; mechanical solidarity) to more complex and interdependent forms (gesellschaft; organic solidarity), which broadened the societal division of labor. Weber (1921 [1978]), in addition, addressed linkages across national boundaries when he wrote about the role of the spread of Western cultural values in the expansion of capitalism and modern societal forms.

These classical approaches follow themes articulated in the network thinking of earlier writers, such as Adam Smith (1776 [1977]), in *Wealth of Nations*. Smith advocated that nations exploit their "comparative advantage" in the international system by engaging in networks of trade that maximize their economic well-being. The comparative advantage of Western European countries was obvious to those nineteenth-century sociologists who theorized about the economic and noneconomic dynamics that brought the Western world to the fore in the global system. Their emphases are apparent, as well, in the contemporary modernization and world-system/dependency approaches to global structure and national well-being that drove the network analysis of Snyder and Kick (1979) and which prompt our replication of their work.

Contemporary articulations

Snyder and Kick test themes taken from contemporary "modernization" theory, which uses classical networking constructs such as "differentiation" and "integration," in arguing that the global exchanges that bring Western technology and value systems to developing countries can spur change by removing traditional obstacles to national development (Parsons, 1966; Eisenstadt, 1974). Others also follow Weber and argue that links to Western social institutions introduce new values such as the Protestant ethic, which can help poor nations grow their economies and compete in the global division of labor (Inkeles and Smith, 1974; Rostow, 1960).

Snyder and Kick also emphasize that modernization approaches in macrosociology have been challenged by Marxian-inspired dependency and world-system perspectives on the global system and national well-being. Economists of Latin American dependency such as Prebisch (1962) challenge the view that "westernization" creates evolutionary progress in Third World societies. They propose instead that the international division of labor is controlled by rich countries and the linkages that bring westernization also bring unequal exchanges that engender underdevelopment in poorer societies (Frank, 1966; Cardoso, 1970; Cardoso and Faletto, 1979; Evans, 1979).

World-system theory focuses upon a worldwide system of networks that emerged in the middle to late 1400s (Wallerstein, 1974), in which investments and expansive trade networks greatly favored the most powerful or "core" nations. Core advantages have come at the expense of a "periphery" (e.g., Africa), due to the exploitive nature of these global relationships of exchange (Armer et al., 1989). "Semiperipheral" countries are a heterogenous and widespread tier of countries that benefit relative to the periphery from these global arrangements but, due to similar dynamics, continue to fall further behind the core, in relative terms. This makes it difficult for peripheral or semiperipheral countries to attain the advanced societal characteristics of Western European nations, as had been idealized by many nineteenth-century sociologists.

World-system arguments and network studies of them dominate our treatment, just as they were central to Snyder and Kick's effort. Throughout our replication we recognize that the network applications we develop rest ultimately on classical foundations. The network metaphor, whether expressly labeled as such or not, is central to centuries of thought on national development.

GLOBAL STRUCTURE AND KEY NETWORKS

Overview of global-system arguments

The global system, just like all social systems (Emerson, 1962; Homans, 1961; Blau, 1964; Cook et al., 1983), reflects the structure and processes of exchange among its constituent units. The global-system units we focus upon theoretically and empirically are nation-states, although multinational corporations and global cities (Sassen, 1998) are central to the modern world economy, too. We agree with Sklair (1999) that the ascendancy of globalizing forces is not so powerful that the existence of the nation-state is in serious doubt, and we conclude that a continuing emphasis on the international system is warranted.

We focus on the work of world-system and dependency theorists, who to some extent disagree over the relative importance of a range of mechanisms of "value transfer" in the world system (Chase-Dunn and Rubinson, 1977; Arrighi and Drangel, 1986). For present purposes we emphasize the important role of global trade and the fact that the commodity exports of periphery nations typically are concentrated in primary products, including agricultural goods. In contrast to the more favorable outcomes theorized by Adam Smith and the progress anticipated by modernization approaches, global trade networks help to ensure that as periphery nations follow their "comparative advantage" they will in comparative terms continue to be technologically and educationally disadvantaged, with substantial segments of their labor forces engaged only in the least advanced production activities. Economic stagnation and a lack of mobility in the world system are a consequence of the structure of peripheral societies' participation in the global trade network (Kentor, 1998). The opposite is true for the core nations that head the global hierarchy. In relative terms, they benefit greatly from these structural arrangements in which they trade capital-intensive, high-end goods and services with the periphery and semiperiphery.

Semiperipheral nations, including much of the Middle East, Latin America, Asia, and part of

Africa, share the global network characteristics of both the core and periphery (Terlouw, 1993; Arrighi and Drangel, 1986: 12). The "buffering" position of the semiperiphery stems from its networks of trade, which include their export of finished goods, high-demand resources, and the products of industrialization to dependent peripheral nations, coupled with their trade subservience to the technically advanced core (World Bank, 2008). Global trade networks structure the relatively rapid industrializations of the semiperiphery, compared to the periphery, which are accompanied by transitions in national institutions and human well-being. Consequently, much of the semiperiphery reflects the evolutionary change theorized in the classical macrosociology theories and modernization treatments identified earlier. This is true, even though it has also led to some alarming environmental outcomes in semiperipheral countries (see, e.g., Burns et al., 1994; McKinney et al., 2009).

Critical issues in conceptualizing the world system

Economic and noneconomic linkages

With the primary themes of world-system theory established, we focus upon key issues in conceptualizing that system. We follow Snyder and Kick's logic in emphasizing that, aside from economic linkages, fundamental roles in the world system are played by cultural networks (Snyder and Kick, 1979; Ramirez and Boli, 1987; Meyer et al., 1997) and political-military networks (Snyder and Kick, 1979; Szymanski, 1981; Giddens, 1985; Mann, 1988; Chase-Dunn, 1989). The roles of noneconomic linkages in globalization are increasingly acknowledged in their own right as direct effects on societies, but also due to their deep interpenetration with other linkages having comparable impacts (see Galtung, 1971; Sklair, 1999).

Because this view about the importance of noneconomic forces to world-system approaches is contested in some studies (Delacroix and Ragin, 1981; Nemeth and Smith, 1985), we offer a few illustrations. Consider, for instance, that by the sale of conventional armaments the United States is provided access to "police" and control much of the world system that is geographically remote from it (e.g., most recently, the Middle East) (see Albrecht et al., 1974; Mann, 1986). As well, Beckfield (2008) emphasizes that intergovernmental organizations (IGOs) exert a powerful impact on national policies and international trade, as core states employ IGOs and an emerging world polity to oversee an

international order that benefits them relative to the semiperiphery and periphery (Meyer et al., 1997; Schofer and Meyer, 2005; True and Minstrom, 2001; Hafner-Burton and Tsutsui, 2005).

We argue, too, that power-dependence relations in other social systems (groups, organizations, societies) seldom hinge on mechanisms of economic exchange only, and in the interests of general social science theory an approach to social-system structure that explicitly recognizes its many dimensions is appropriate. Based on this logic, Snyder and Kick and the present treatment rely upon multiple networks of international linkages that are economic and noneconomic in nature.

Network relationships and national attributes

Also a necessary preliminary to our study, we point to a tendency to mistrust country classifications derived from global, multiple-network results, such as those we subsequently present. For instance, Bollen (1983) questions Snyder and Kick's (1979) country classifications for three of the 118 countries analyzed, because these countries are "outlier" cases in his regression analysis of political democracy.

A concern with "classification error" and the use of other national attributes to re-classify nations as a remedy is understandable but questionable. A number of theorists have noted the inability of attribute-based "substantialist" inquiry to account for the relational characteristics of social actors and historical processes (e.g., Granovetter, 1985; Emirbayer, 1997). Further, and more concretely, world-system theory is a structural theory based on the analysis of linkages among global units (especially nations) and the consequences of these linkages for them (Wallerstein, 1974; Chirot, 1985). Unit attributes may be a result of the structure but it is inappropriate to use attributes to identify the components of that structure (i.e., the "positions" of nations in the system). When taken to its logical conclusion, the classification or reclassification of countries' world-system positions based on the attribute or outcome measures used to test the theory essentially renders the world-system perspective true by definition. Based on this logic, Snyder and Kick and the present study use multiple network analyses of international linkages to identify world-system structure and nations' positions in it, and we invite replications that use network methodologies to address the veracity of our results.

Other network relationships and international attributes

Some studies claim that indicators such as invest-ment dependence, trade concentration, and so on, measure "position" or "control" in the world system (Rubinson, 1976; Delacroix and Ragin, 1978; Kentor, 1981). However, these are continu-ous variables that stratify nations on given criteria. They do not *represent* position any more than an individual's income or education measures his or her (discrete) class position (Wright and Perrone, 1977; see also White and Breiger, 1975: 68). Missed are the institutional locus of transnational flows; for example, the value of trade of a given peripheral nation does not identify whether tran-snational capital flows originate entirely, partly, or negligibly from, say, the core or other types of nations. The differential effect of those origins is theoretically plausible and is a central component of world-system theorization. The multiple-network approach, in contrast, is a superior meth-odology for measuring such flows, and this logic is our justification for the methodologies used here and by Snyder and Kick. That said, we now briefly review the empirical literature in sociology that employs the multiple-network approach to world-system structure.

Empirical articulations of world-system structure and national consequences

A number of scholars have used social network analysis to examine the structure of the core/periphery hierarchy and to evaluate hypotheses concerning the relational structure of the modern world system and its impact on national character-istics.[1] As Lloyd et al. (forthcoming) suggest, most of these studies are nested within two gen-eral approaches to the identification of the world system's structure that vary with respect to the forms of relational data employed. One approach, which explicitly focuses on economic exchanges, distinguishes between trade relationships for par-ticular forms of commodities. The other general approach, which follows in the footsteps of Snyder and Kick (1979), combines noneconomic and economic data to study the relational structure of the world system. In the following paragraphs we briefly summarize key contributions to each of these approaches.[2]

The first approach largely begins with Breiger (1981), who utilizes a structural equivalence crite-rion with the CONCOR program to analyze trade relationships. He focuses on the trade of raw materials, agricultural products, manufactured goods, and energy resources. However, Breiger restricts his analyses to wealthy OECD nations. Even with the restricted dataset, he finds core/periphery relationships between nations, suggest-ing power differences between economically developed nations. What is more, his analytic strategy is very similar to that of Snyder and Kick (1979), as both studies identify blockgroups on the basis of structural equivalence (i.e., identical relations among countries).

Also using CONCOR, Nemeth and Smith (1985) attempt to differentiate periphery, semipe-riphery, and core relations based on patterns of trade in commodities between nations. Their find-ings reveal a core, a strong semiperiphery, a weak semiperiphery, and a periphery. Following the identification of the four distinct categories, regression analyses suggest that the core nations have higher levels of wealth and lower child mor-tality rates than nations in the weak semiperiphery and periphery, and higher wealth generation and energy consumption than all noncore nations.

Largely drawing from Nemeth and Smith (1985), Smith and White (1992) employ the meas-ure of regular equivalence and also conduct an analysis of mobility in the world system. Through the use of regular equivalence (which groups actors based on their ties to similar others), Smith and White (1992) analyze trade data and identify five world-system zones: core, strong semiperi-phery, weak semiperiphery, strong periphery, and weak periphery. Their analysis of world-sys-tem mobility indicates that from 1965 to 1980, upward mobility was more common than down-ward mobility. However, causal explanations for these mobility patterns were left for future investigations.

More recently, Mahutga (2006) utilizes an analytic strategy similar to that of Smith and White (1992) to assess changes in the structure of the world economy from 1965 to 2000. Through the analysis of trade data for different commodity types, Mahutga finds that core/periphery patterns of interaction remained relatively intact through-out the 35-year period, that commodity exchanges across the zones of the world system remained unequal, and that a small number of nations experienced notable upward mobility in the interstate system.

The second approach, which builds on the original analyses conducted by Snyder and Kick (1979), involves the analyses of various forms of relational data. Surprisingly, this body of sociological inquiry is much smaller than the approach that focuses explicitly on international trade relationships. In fact, we identify only two additional studies that make noteworthy contribu-tions to this approach. First, in a follow-up to Snyder and Kick (1979), Kick and Davis (2001) employ a structural equivalence analysis, which confirms that the core consists of the Western industrial nations. These nations dominate the world system in political, military, transportation, communication, sociocultural, *and* economic networks. Second, Van Rossem (1996) utilizes relational data on the presence of foreign troops, diplomatic exchange, imports, and exports. To "test the world-systems paradigm as a general theory of development" (Van Rossem, 1996: 508), Van Rossem employs a role equivalency measure based on the triad census. In the analyses he also attempts to determine if the core/periphery hierarchy is best treated as continuous or categorical. Regarding the structure of the world system, Van Rossem's (1996) results are relatively consistent with Snyder and Kick (1979) and Kick and Davis (2001). However, he stresses that "coreness" in the world system is more continuous than categorical, and his world-system position measurements do not appear to be directly related to economic development, which greatly contrasts with Snyder and Kick's earlier (1979) panel analyses.

Our network methodology for analyzing the world system

Data

We operationally define world-system structure according to four types of international networks (trade; arms transfers; IGOs; and embassies) for the 1995–99 period. The four networks were first represented by separate adjacency matrices, with each instance of a "tie" from one member to another coded "1" in the appropriate cell, and the absence of a "tie" coded "0." Our blockmodel analyses are based on 166 nations for which data were available for all networks. Our coding procedures utilized a series of years (1995–99) that minimize idiosyncratic characteristics of a single year, capture the modern era, and permit researchers to examine time-ordered reciprocities between the modern global structure and the attributes of nations.

Trade
Trade data are taken from the International Monetary Fund (IMF, 2000). The IMF only records annual transactions totaling $1 million or more, so $1 million for any year in the time period from 1995 to 1999 becomes the threshold for coding a tie in the trade matrix.

Armament Transfers
The Stockholm International Peace Research Institute (SIPRI, 2007) presents transfers of conventional weaponry, including aircraft, naval vessels, missiles, and armored fighting vehicles (downloaded from the SIPRI Web site). A binary coding scheme was used, with "1" representing arms transfers from an exporting country to the recipient nation for 1995–99 inclusive.

IGOs
The data on IGOs reflect shared affiliations. The data were converted from two-mode data (country-to-organization relations) to one-mode data (country-to-country relations). This conversion created a nondirected matrix with cell contents representing the number of affiliations shared across countries. To match the other three binary network relations matrices, the values in the matrix were dichotomized, with values that exceeded the mean set to one and all other values set to zero. We tested multiple cutpoints for this conversion but settled on the mean value because it resulted in a matrix with sufficient variability for the blockmodeling analysis and ultimately produced a similar set of blocked results as the valued data. Beckfield (2008) was kind enough to share his IGO data with us.

Embassies
Data for the embassies matrix are taken from the list of representations in foreign countries (Anzinger, 2002). This source provides for each "sender" nation a list of "recipient" countries in which an embassy headquarters exists. For each "sender" country we coded a 1 if that country sent foreign representation (i.e., an embassy) to another "host" nation, and 0 otherwise.

The matrices vary in their densities, with the trade and IGO data being the most dense (44 and 41 percent densities, respectively) and the embassies and arms transfer data the least (7 and 2 percent, respectively). Each individual matrix was joined (or stacked) into a single file and analyzed simultaneously.[3] The four networks together capture the substantively important dimensions of transnational interaction discussed above and permit a reasonable replication of Snyder and Kick (1979).

ANALYSES

We used the CONCOR program in UCINET (Borgatti et al., 2002). CONCOR (Breiger et al., 1975; White et al., 1976) identifies blockgroups on the basis of structural equivalence, which determines the extent to which actors display identical relationships with other actors. While others (e.g., Mahutga, 2006) have argued that structural equivalence provides an overly stringent criterion for identifying positioning in the world system, we employ this technique in order to replicate the methodological choices of Snyder and Kick.

Specifically, CONCOR splits the initial network matrix into two structurally distinct groups and then splits each of the two resulting groups into two more groups, and so on. The process of block splitting continues until a single actor occupies a block group or all actors in the block group have identical network relations. However, UCINET allows researchers to determine how many partitions to make. We base partitioning decisions on the goals of maximizing block group homogeneity and making comparisons with the partitions reported by Snyder and Kick.

To identify potential "outliers," we compute individual country densities with the rest of the system (total send-and-receive ties for each country divided by all possible ties) and compare this with the densities across the system for their respective block groups. Thus, we use degree centrality as a criterion to test for validity in block groups, and we report outlying countries below.

FINDINGS

Table 22.1 shows our listing of ten blocks, presented across from Snyder and Kick's (1979) findings. Table 22.2 presents the densities of ties within and between each of the blocks of nations, calculated separately for each of the four types of tie (i.e., operator-specific densities), and also the mean over all four relations. Figure 22.1 depicts the magnitude of densities with bolder lines reflecting greater ties.

The clusterings presented in Table 22.1 are ordered in a rough hierarchy in anticipation of the information on densities reported in Table 22.2. Before moving to the density data and relevant evidence for these preliminary impressions, we highlight a few of the most obvious cases of "outliers." In block 4, Albania is noted as an outlying country, with an overall density score that is considerably lower than that of the block mean (individual country coefficients are available upon request). This is understandable based on its well-known international linkage characteristics. In the same block Russia is a prominent outlier, and so is Ukraine in block 6, the most prominent global players from the former Soviet Union. Outlying cases are to be expected, given the stringent combinatorial rules that attend structural equivalence modeling (see Mahutga, 2006).

The densities presented in Table 22.2 (see also Figure 22.1, created using NetDraw – see Borgatti et al., 2002) suggest that for all relations taken together ("All") what we call the "center core" block is more extensively linked with all the rest of the system than are any of the other blocks.

This nodal block clearly forms the "core of the core" of the world system, although the density of block 1's ties to the other blocks tends to trail off as we move from this center. Blocks 2 and 3 are tied to the rest of the system in ways that rather closely resemble this centermost block. When taken together, and with a few exceptions, blocks 1, 2, and 3 reproduce much of the "core" in Snyder and Kick's study. The exceptions compose a set of nations with the least prima facie validity to us, such as India, Indonesia, Malaysia, Pakistan, the Philippines, Thailand, and possibly even China, despite its recognizable ascendancy in the system in recent times. We note that when we partitioned this block further, these "hangers-on" to core standing split off from the Western European nations and the center core.

The densities of linkages fall off for succeeding blocks, starting with the Eastern European cluster, consisting of a heterogeneous grouping of what might be conceded to be "upper semiperipheral" countries. Block 4 is more weakly tied to the rest of the system than is the core of blocks 1–3, even though it is more strongly tied than the remaining blocks. Thereafter, the Southeast Asian/Middle East, Former Soviet, Middle East, and South American blocks form more of a traditional semiperiphery of the system. We make this designation because they are rather extensively tied throughout the system when compared with the remaining two blocks (9, 10), although less expansively connected than blocks 1–4.

The Africa block (9) and a cluster of predominantly South Pacific and Middle Eastern nations occupy the periphery of the world system. Densities show some dependencies in blocks 9 and 10 upon the core, but an even greater decoupling from the bulk of the global social system than is true for blocks 1–8.

Table 22.2's densities of overall ties suggest a structure for the global system that very roughly parallels world-system arguments and the results presented by Snyder and Kick. The gradual decline in ties moving from core to periphery in the system appears to support more "continuous" interpretations of the world-system hierarchy, rather than purely "discrete" interpretations that rely on dichotomous (core/periphery) or trichotomous (core/semiperiphery/periphery) articulations (see Chase-Dunn, 1989; Van Rossem, 1996).

In the trade densities matrix, with few exceptions, all blocks remain very closely tied in exports and imports to the most central core block. The other two seemingly core blocks also reproduce this role overall in the global economy structure. Pending further analyses, two semiperipheries appear to be in evidence in the trade matrix in

Table 22.1 Blockmodel country lists from current study and from Snyder and Kick (1979)

Results for 1995–1999	Results for Circa 1960–65
Block 1 (Center Core Block) – France, Germany, Italy, Netherlands, United Kingdom, United States	**Block C (Core)** – Australia, Austria, Belgium, Canada, Denmark, France, Greece, Italy, Japan, Luxembourg, Netherlands, Norway, Portugal, South Africa, Spain, Sweden, Switzerland, United Kingdom, United States, West Germany, Yugoslavia
Block 2 (Western European Block) – Austria, Belgium-Luxembourg, Brazil, Denmark, Finland, Greece, Ireland, Israel, Norway, Poland, Portugal, Spain, Sweden, Switzerland, Turkey	**Block D (Semiperiphery)** – Bulgaria, Cuba, Cyprus, East Germany, Hungary, Iran, Iraq, Ireland, Israel, Jordan, Kenya, Lebanon, Romania, Turkey, USSR
Block 3 (Asian Block) – Australia, Canada, China, India, Indonesia, Japan, Malaysia, Pakistan, Philippines, South Africa, South Korea, Thailand	**Block D´ (Semiperiphery)** – Burma, Ceylon, Finland, India, Malaysia, Pakistan, Philippines, Saudi Arabia, Taiwan
	Block C´ (Semiperiphery) – Argentina, Peru, South Korea, Uruguay, Venezuela
Block 4 (Eastern European Block) –Albania*, Bulgaria, Croatia, Czech Republic, Hungary, Malta, New Zealand, Romania, Russia*, Slovak Republic, Slovenia	**Block F (Periphery)** – Cambodia, China, Czechoslovakia, Jamaica, Iceland, Laos, Malta, Mongolian Republic, Nepal, New Zealand, Poland, Thailand, Trinidad and Tobago
Block 5 (Southeast Asian/Middle East Block) – Afghanistan, Bahrain, Cameroon, Kuwait, Myanmar, Nepal, North Korea, Oman, Saudi Arabia, Singapore*, United Arab Emirates, Vietnam	**Block F´ (Periphery)** – Afghanistan, Albania, Indonesia, Kuwait, North Korea, South Vietnam, Syria
Block 6 (Former Soviet Block) – Armenia, Azerbaijan, Belarus, Bosnia and Herzegovina, Estonia, Georgia, Iceland, Kazakhstan, Kyrgyz Republic, Latvia, Lithuania, Macedonia, Moldova, Ukraine**, Uzbekistan, Turkmenistan, Yugoslavia	**Block E (Periphery)** – Bolivia, Brazil, Chile, Colombia, Ecuador, North Vietnam, Panama, Paraguay
Block 7 (Middle East Block) – Bangladesh, Cyprus, Egypt, Iran, Jordan, Lebanon, Morocco, Sri Lanka, Syrian Arab Republic, Tunisia	**Block E´ (Periphery)** – Costa Rica, Dominican Republic, El Salvador, Guatemala, Haiti, Honduras, Mexico, Nicaragua
Block 8 (South American Block) – Algeria, Argentina, Bahamas, Barbados*, Bolivia, Cape Verde, Chile, Colombia, Costa Rica, Cote d'Ivoire, Cuba, Dominican Republic, Ecuador, El Salvador, Guatemala, Guyana, Haiti, Honduras, Jamaica, Kenya, Mexico, Nicaragua, Nigeria, Panama, Paraguay, Peru, Suriname*, Trinidad and Tobago, Uruguay, Venezuela	**Block A (Periphery)** – Algeria, Burundi, Chad, Congo, Ethiopia, Libya, Malagasy Republic, Morrocco, Rwanda, Somalia, Sudan, Tunisia, Uganda, United Arab Republic, Yemen
Block 9 (African Block) – Angola, Benin, Botswana, Burkina Faso, Burundi, Cambodia, Central African Rep., Chad, Comoros*, Congo, Djibouti, Equatorial Guinea*, Ethiopia, Gabon, Gambia, Ghana*, Guinea, Guinea-Bissau, Lesotho, Liberia, Libya, Madagascar, Malawi, Mali, Mauritania, Mauritius, Mozambique, Namibia, Niger, Rwanda, Senegal*, Sierra Leone, Somalia, Sudan*, Swaziland, Tanzania*, Togo, Uganda, Zambia, Zimbabwe	**Block B (Periphery)** – Cameroun, Central African Republic, Dahomey, Gabon, Ghana, Ivory Coast, Liberia, Mali, Mauritania, Niger, Nigeria, Republic of Guinea, Senegal, Sierra Leone, Togo, Upper Volta
Block 10 (South Pacific/Middle East Block) – Bhutan, Brunei Darussalam, Eritrea, Fiji, Iraq, Laos, Mongolia, Papua New Guinea, Qatar, Solomon Islands, Tajikistan, Tuvalu, Yemen	

*outlier (±.1); **outlier (±.15), block means are in parens.

Table 22.2 Block densities

	Center Core	Western Europe	Asian	Eastern Europe	SE Asian/ME	Former Soviet	Middle East	South America	African	South Pacific/ME
All										
1. Center Core	.917	.906	.917	.739	.517	.517	.742	.651	.458	.295
2. Western Europe	.700	.606	.615	.537	.289	.376	.498	.466	.309	.145
3. Asian	.705	.610	.663	.495	.393	.211	.527	.467	.346	.250
4. Eastern Europe	.606	.527	.506	.487	.182	.303	.407	.279	.123	.079
5. SE Asian/ME	.372	.250	.382	.114	.186	.059	.277	.076	.081	.074
6. Former Soviet	.456	.346	.199	.293	.070	.217	.150	.061	.028	.033
7. Middle East	.571	.460	.513	.371	.279	.111	.470	.239	.204	.115
8. South America	.571	.431	.428	.240	.072	.036	.254	.375	.113	.018
9. African	.388	.247	.291	.091	.055	.012	.184	.108	.231	.013
10. South Pacific/ME	.228	.081	.192	.040	.070	.008	.100	.014	.012	.029
Trade										
1. Center Core	1.000	1.000	1.000	1.000	.986	.990	.967	.994	1.000	.808
2. Western Europe	.956	.948	.972	.952	.872	.945	.933	.920	.778	.554
3. Asian	.986	.978	.970	.902	.896	.750	.933	.858	.777	.679
4. Eastern Europe	1.000	.939	.909	.864	.621	.738	.818	.536	.311	.259
5. SE Asian/ME	.972	.811	.896	.447	.576	.230	.717	.258	.273	.186
6. Former Soviet	.951	.824	.657	.679	.260	.636	.482	.218	.087	.113
7. Middle East	.917	.840	.925	.782	.733	.359	.889	.290	.317	.269
8. South America	.972	.762	.714	.409	.242	.122	.357	.501	.114	.033
9. African	.842	.533	.563	.227	.171	.047	.230	.095	.121	.017
10. South Pacific/ME	.718	.297	.500	.140	.179	.018	.208	.018	.012	.064

Arms

	1	2	3	4	5	6	7	8	9	10
1. Center Core	.667	.711	.792	.258	.431	.108	.317	.244	.067	.141
2. Western Europe	.100	.095	.111	.048	.044	.047	.040	.044	.010	.021
3. Asian	.111	.028	.091	.030	.063	.005	.050	.022	.029	.032
4. Eastern Europe	.030	.030	.076	.064	.076	.064	.100	.045	.045	.028
5. SE Asian/ME	.014	.017	.028	.000	.008	.005	.017	.000	.002	.006
6. Former Soviet	.000	.004	.039	.021	.015	.011	.047	.008	.025	.005
7. Middle East	.000	.000	.008	.000	.000	.012	.022	.007	.000	.000
8. South America	.000	.000	.000	.000	.000	.000	.000	.006	.001	.000
9. African	.000	.000	.000	.000	.000	.000	.002	.000	.001	.002
10. South Pacific/ME	.000	.005	.000	.000	.000	.005	.000	.000	.002	.000

Embassies

	1	2	3	4	5	6	7	8	9	10
1. Center Core	1.000	.911	.875	.712	.458	.461	.717	.444	.271	.167
2. Western Europe	.744	.381	.378	.152	.089	.043	.073	.044	.022	.000
3. Asian	.722	.433	.591	.182	.153	.044	.150	.128	.019	.058
4. Eastern Europe	.409	.145	.174	.055	.023	.005	.018	.015	.002	.014
5. SE Asian/ME	.306	.022	.146	.000	.008	.000	.025	.006	.000	.006
6. Former Soviet	.363	.090	.054	.064	.005	.037	.006	.002	.000	.005
7. Middle East	.400	.053	.142	.009	.033	.006	.011	.013	.002	.000
8. South America	.389	.104	.139	.033	.008	.004	.010	.033	.001	.000
9. African	.217	.028	.044	.005	.000	.000	.005	.000	.001	.000
10. South Pacific/ME	.128	.015	.038	.007	.006	.000	.000	.000	.002	.000

Table 22.2 Cont.

IGOs	Center Core	Western Europe	Asian	Eastern Europe	SE Asian/ME	Former Soviet	Middle East	South America	African	South Pacific/ME
1. Center Core	1.000	1.000	1.000	.985	.194	.510	.967	.922	.492	.064
2. Western Europe	1.000	1.000	1.000	.994	.150	.467	.947	.856	.427	.005
3. Asian	1.000	1.000	1.000	.864	.458	.044	.975	.858	.558	.231
4. Eastern Europe	.985	.994	.864	.964	.008	.406	.691	.518	.132	.014
5. SE Asian/ME	.194	.150	.458	.008	.152	.000	.350	.039	.050	.096
6. Former Soviet	.510	.467	.044	.406	.000	.184	.065	.016	.000	.009
7. Middle East	.967	.947	.975	.691	.350	.065	.956	.647	.498	.192
8. South America	.922	.856	.858	.518	.039	.016	.647	.961	.335	.038
9. African	.492	.427	.558	.132	.050	.000	.498	.335	.801	.031
10. South Pacific/ME	.064	.005	.231	.014	.096	.009	.192	.038	.031	.051

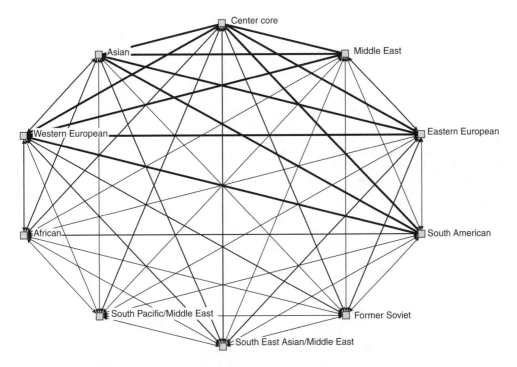

Figure 22.1   Circle graph of density relations between blocks

blocks 4 and 5, and blocks 6–8, respectively, and the sharpest degree of de-coupling again is visible with peripheral blocks 9 and 10.

Arms transfers show significantly different arrangements. Only the center core links to much of the core and semiperiphery of the system. The relative absence of arms export ties from block 1 to the former Soviet block is interpretable on the basis of the continuation of "cold war politics." Arms exports for the rest of the world system are trivial or simply do not exist. Although the Eastern European block is somewhat more prominent than others, no clear division of an "upper" and "lower" semiperiphery is evident. Most apparent is a center core/noncore structuration, with a few select, central core gatekeepers at the helm.

Embassy memberships replicate the nodal position of the center core, but again secondarily of the Western European and Asian core – block 3's density profile approximates that of the Western European core. Across the semiperipheral clusters homogeneity in generic structure relative to the core is evident, and the relative de-coupling of blocks 9 and 10 again is evident.

IGO relational data display a relatively denser set of international ties. The center core is relatively more dominant than others, but blocks 2 and 3 approximate one another in the breadth of their

ties followed by blocks 4, 7, and 8, then 5, 6, and 9. Block 10 again occupies an essentially de-coupled, peripheral role. The thick regional ties reflected in the diagonal add an interesting nuance to Beckfield's (2008) recent emphasis on global, as opposed to regional, political and cultural norms. A tendency toward universal norms may be indicated in the breadth of center core and European ties in the system, but the persistence of regional dynamics is evident as well.

A comparison of network structure, country classifications, and inferences here and in Snyder and Kick (1979) is instructive. With some exceptions, both studies identify what best may be described as a "loose" core/semiperiphery/ periphery structure that reflects a centuries-long consistency in global structure, despite changes in hegemons and some vertical mobility, either ascendancy or decline, in the system.

Parallels in the *core* blocks (C in Snyder and Kick; center core, Western European, and some of the Asian blocks here) across the two treatments are evident. The identification of a set of most central core nations refines the results Snyder and Kick present, although had they iterated their block C, similar partitions likely would have surfaced. The present study finds evidence for the "coreness" of a newer set of the very large Asian countries, which for the most part dominate the global population period and are certainly to be viewed as "emerging," relative to their positions in 1960–65, the era of data for the Snyder and Kick study. This consistency is less true for the clusters of countries outside the world system's core, although we find a true periphery of African countries that squares with Snyder and Kick's periphery blocks A and B. We also identify another periphery block (10) that includes a number of countries not analyzed by Snyder and Kick. Events surrounding Iraq's position in the system during the 1995–99 period of isolation versus 1960–65 suggest a rather clear interpretation of why it has "moved" to peripheral standing in our replication.

Snyder and Kick identify several other peripheral clusters (E, E´, F, and F´) comprised of Central and South American countries, and Asian countries, that we feel for the most part are better classified in the lower semiperiphery today. The rest of our semiperiphery contains roughly the same countries designated as such by Snyder and Kick (blocks C´, D and D´). In recent years, the ascendancy of a number of formerly peripheral or near-peripheral countries (Brazil, China) is striking (see Evans, 1995; Smith and White, 1992; Sklair, 1999). It is also true that a number of world-system studies identify an expansive and heterogeneous semiperiphery (Wallerstein, 1974; Terlouw, 1993; Arrighi and Drangel, 1986). Their clustering of African, South and Central American, Pacific, and Asian nations in the semiperiphery roughly parallels the classifications presented here.

Graphical interpretation

To graphically represent network linkages in a simpler way, we applied NetDraw (Borgatti et al., 2002) to dichotomize block densities. Blocks are considered to be linked if their density scores exceed the mean block density score (.313). These relationships were graphed using the spring embedding graph theoretic, which locates nodes based on relative geodesic distances (see Figure 22.2). As before, ties with higher density scores are thicker. Furthermore, the nodes are sized on the basis of their betweenness centrality scores, which measures the extent to which actors are positioned on paths with the shortest tie length between other actors (Knoke and Yang, 2008). The center core block clearly stands out in this regard, as it is directly and rather strongly connected to the other block groups.

Overall, Figure 22.2 shows a world system that is almost entirely connected, as anticipated by world-system theorizations. The exceptions are the peripheral blocks (African; South Pacific), which are in many ways structural isolates from the rest of the system. Within the connected graph

component, the center and European core (blocks 1 and 2) clearly are the most broadly and intensively connected actors in the system. As well, this is relatively true for the large and ascending Asian countries and the prominent "ex-colonies" of Great Britain (block 3). The more semiperipheral blockgroups (4–8) are directly and rather strongly connected with the core blocks, but less so with each other.

The representations in Figure 22.2 do not display the extensiveness of global connections that are shown in Figure 22.1, and they do not fully reflect the density coefficients or the related interpretations we made above. Nevertheless, the representations in Figure 22.2 have their own appeal in terms of simplicity, while offering a number of conclusions that mesh with our more complex visual representations in the form of density scores.

CONCLUSIONS AND IMPLICATIONS

Our introductory remarks noted that Adam Smith (1776) argued for the principle of comparative advantage. His articulation centers on a world division of labor in which countries export the commodities that, by gift of nature or labor, they are able to market for maximal profit. He recognized this as a mechanism for national advance, although it by no means guarantees parity between nations. Indeed, the converse may be true. Nineteenth-century sociologists adopted the organic metaphor Smith and others developed and applied in examining the networks endogenous to nations and their impacts on national trajectories. More contemporary modernization theorists accepted these network themes as a focal point in their theorizations about the global system, viewing the westernization of the world as foundational for the advance of nations relative to their earlier circumstances. Modern dependency and world-system applications contest these interpretations and focus on how internation links serve to ensure the progress of richer core societies at the relative, though perhaps not absolute, expense of more dependent nations.

Our findings address these network themes and although space limitations prevent us from tying our results to national development characteristics, they do set the stage for subsequent examinations of the impacts of global structure on national development in the contemporary world. Essentially we offer an alternative to Snyder and Kick's earlier study, which set a foundation for the short- and longer-run effects of world-system structure circa the early 1960s. Our results for the

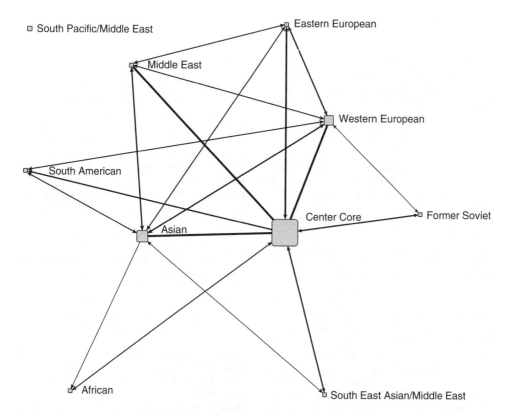

Figure 22.2   Network graph with spring embedding of density relations between blocks

current period show the axes of the westernization of the world addressed in classical treatments in macrosociology, as well as contemporary world-system/ dependency and modernization approaches. Thus, our network analyses allow for the testing of longstanding theoretical streams, including foundational principles about comparative advantage, the "evolutionary" progress of nations outside the developed world as compared with Western European countries, the role of westernization in prompting or limiting national development throughout the world, and the ascension of alternative global powers (e.g., the "Asian block").

The data employed here reflect modern regional and global reconfigurations and introduce some new, theoretically justifiable operators that resemble those employed by Snyder and Kick. We might anticipate that this alone would lead to notable variations in results between the present effort and their earlier study and with other primarily economic approaches to world-system structure. However, our treatment of world structuration and the positionality of nations in it shows there are significant parallels between our findings and those from prior treatments.

Our results roughly conform with the core/ semiperiphery/periphery structure identified by the pioneers of world-system theory (Wallerstein, 1974) and in early empirical applications (Snyder and Kick, 1979). Nevertheless, at a more specific empirical level, we find multiple cores, which agrees with Breiger's (1981) network analysis of OECD trade relations. As well, our findings identify what might be viewed as a dual or upper (blocks 5–6) and lower-tiered (blocks 7–8) semiperiphery, which is initially argued in Delacroix and Ragin (1981) and shown in Nemeth and Smith's (1985) and Smith and White's (1992) network analyses of international trade. Mahutga's (2006) finding of continuity in a core/periphery trade structure across the period 1965 to 2000 also is confirmed in the present analysis (see also Snyder and Kick, 1979; Kick, 1987; Kick and Davis, 2001).

When taken as a whole, we think our results suggest it is appropriate to apply ideal-typical categories such as "core," "semicore," "upper semiperiphery" and "lower semiperiphery," and "periphery" to the structure of the contemporary world system. However, our results are suggestive of another alternative, the characterization of the system as a hierarchy that can be measured by a continuous metric of power and dependency instead of more discrete types. More concretely, cell densities overall, and for both economic and noneconomic operators when taken together (except for military transfers), suggest the possible explanatory power of cluster-based rankings on a 1–10 scale, with the scores reflecting the relative power/dependency of nations in the system. This strategy may not align squarely with Wallerstein's (1974) tripartite articulations of the world system, or Frank's (1966) earlier "North-South" approach. Nonetheless, it squares with more recent formulations that advocate for continuous gradations as appropriate measures of nations' positions in the world system (Chase-Dunn, 1989; Kentor, 2000).

Kentor (2000: 26) argues that "a reformulation of the problem of (whether) position in the core/periphery hierarchy is a continuum or discrete strata (zones) should be empirically determined rather than assumed on an a priori basis." We agree with him on this point, and with his view that despite the utility of using ideal-typical approaches for analyzing certain substantive issues, in the case of the world system and its effects the complexity is much greater than a three-tiered, or two-tiered, hierarchy can effectively capture. Further, these nuances are best understood by a power/dependency approach that expressly acknowledges and empirically treats the multiple, and sometimes combined, avenues for global power offered by economic, military, political, and cultural opportunities.

We view multiple-network approaches based on economic and noneconomic ties as the optimal way to address the structural configuration of the world (social) system, if not the world economy. There is a rough parity in generic results using economic versus noneconomic ties, but a fruitful direction for subsequent research would be a more theoretically driven project linking the position of nations in *each* network type to relevant domestic outcomes and antecedents. For instance, cultural or military centrality may be viewed as an optimal route for global power or ascendancy for some nations (India, Israel).

Our results should prove useful to studies linking world-system structure and block membership to the international and domestic characteristics of nations. The continuing replications and use of the original Snyder and Kick findings are evidence of its durability, but our present findings extend to a far larger and more current world system than was analyzed before. Thus, it may be helpful in addressing the central questions of classical and contemporary macrosociology as they apply to the modern era.

Apart from these substantive issues there are some important implications from this study with respect to methodology. CONCOR produced a set of theoretically and empirically defensible blocks, but one might consider employing alternative modeling strategies. Wasserman and Faust (1994) have criticized the way that CONCOR partitions data into an even number of blockgroups, which can potentially lead to a degree of arbitrariness in the results. Here we use CONCOR to more closely approximate the original blockmodeling analysis of 30 years prior, but future research should consider a comparison of the results derived from these distinct approaches (e.g., Burt, 1990; Batagelj et al., 1991; Lloyd et al., forthcoming).

Moreover, while the present effort was driven by a replication of Snyder and Kick's pioneering study, future research might also consider developing world-system blocks on the basis of different forms of network equivalence. Structural equivalence sets a strict criterion for the identification of equivalent actors – identical links to others – but some have suggested that regular equivalence may be more appropriate, since this blocks together countries based on ties to similarly positioned actors rather than identical actors (Lloyd et al., forthcoming). Future studies might also do blocking based on other forms of equivalence as well, including automorphic equivalence (Knoke and Yang, 2008). Researchers should carefully consider both the theoretical and empirical implications of utilizing different forms of equivalence.

In the future, researchers should also consider employing a more deductive approach to analyzing the structure of the world system and its consequences. The generalized blockmodeling approach available in Pajek is particularly appropriate for hypothesis testing (Doreian et al., 2005). Using this technique, one could (1) test whether various block densities meet a prior theoretical criterion for a core/semiperiphery/periphery structure or (2) assess stability and change in the structure of the world system. Each of these innovations would aid in describing and explaining the structure of the world system and its impact on a range of national outcomes, such as economic development, environmental degradation, and many other important national characteristics.

We invite a range of replications based on these suggestions and others. As well, we advocate a closer inspection of the block memberships advanced in network studies of the world system – in effect, a meta-analysis of networkers' conclusions. Part of that analysis might be the use of different schemas in predicting a variety of national characteristics, ranging from economic development and inequality to population and environmental transitions.

ACKNOWLEDGEMENT

We wish to thank SAGE's anonymous referees and the editors for their helpful criticisms although we bear sole responsibility for this paper's content.

NOTES

1 Related bodies of inquiry beyond the scope of the current discussion involve using network analysis to study the global city system (e.g., Alderson and Beckfield, 2004; Smith and Timberlake, 2001), the structure of the world polity (e.g., Beckfield, 2008), and global interlocking directorates (e.g., Kentor and Jang, 2004).

2 For a more detailed summary of these bodies of literature, see Lloyd et al. (forthcoming).

3 We also blocked the data by combining the matrices into a single matrix by summing the cell values across all relations. Both strategies produced findings reflective of the same hierarchical structure for the system. They produced near-identical block memberships, except for nations in the "middle tiers" of the global hierarchy. In the end, we utilized the standard stacking procedure because it retains the greatest amount of information and replicates previous analyses.

REFERENCES

Alderson, A.S. and Beckfield J. (2004) *Power and Position in the World City System.*

Anzinger, G. (2002) 'Governments on the WWW: Representations in foreign countries'. http://www.gksoft.com/govt/en/representations.html (accessed May 31, 2008).

Armer, M., Jeong, I. et al. (1989) 'The contributions of schooling to economic growth in East Asia: Japan, Korea, and Taiwan'. *American Sociological Association Proceedings Paper.*

Arrighi, G. and Drangel J. (1986) 'The stratification of the world-economy: An exploration of the semi-peripheral zone'. *Review*, 10(1): 9–74.

Batagelj, V., Doreian, P., et al. (1991) *An Optimizational Approach to Regular Equivalence.* 11th Annual Sunbelt Social Network Conference, Tampa, Florida.

Beckfield, J. (2008) 'The dual world polity: Fragmentation and integration in the network of intergovernmental organizations'. *Social Problems*, 55(3): 419–42.

Blau, P.M. (1964) *Exchange and Power in Social Life.* New York: John Wiley.

Bollen, K. (1983) 'Orld system position, dependency, and democracy—the cross-national evidence'. *American Sociological Review*, 48(4): 468–79.

Borgatti, S.P. and Everett, M.G. (1992) 'Notions of position in social network analysis'. *Sociological Methodology*, 22: 1–35.

Borgatti, S., Everett, M., et al. (2002) *UCINET.* Harvard Analytic Technologies.

Breiger, R. (1981) 'Structures of economic interdependence among nations'. In *Continuities in Structural Inquiry.* London: Sage. pp. 353–79.

Breiger, R.L., Boorman, S.A. et al. (1975) 'Algorithm for clustering relational data with applications to social network analysis and comparison with multidimensional-scaling'. *Journal of Mathematical Psychology*, 12(3): 328–83.

Burns, T.J., Kick, E.L. et al. (1994) 'Demography, develeopmentand deforestation in a world-system perspective'. *International Journal of Comparative Sociology*, 35(3–4): 221–39.

Burt, R.S. (1990) 'Detecting role equivalence'. *Social Networks*, 12(1): 83–97.

Burt, R.S. (1992) *Structural Holes.* Cambridge, MA: Harvard University Press.

Cardoso, F.H. (1970) 'Structural and institutional impediments to development'. *Revista Mexicana de Sociologia*, 32(6): 1461–82.

Cardoso, F.H. and Faletto, E. (1979) *Dependency and Development in Latin America.* Berkeley: University of California Press.

Chase-Dunn, C. (1989) *Global Formation: Structures of the Global Economy.* Cambridge, MA: Basil Blackwell.

Chase-Dunn, C. and Rubinson, R. (1977) 'Toward a structural perspective on the world system'. *Politics and Society* 7(4): 453–76.

Chirot, D. (1985) 'The rise of the west'. *American Sociological Review*, 50(2): 181–95.

Comte, A. ([1842] 1854) *The Positive Philosophy of Auguste Comte.* New York: D. Appleton.

Cook, K.S., Emerson, R.M., et al. (1983) 'The distribution of power in exchange networks—theory and experimental results'. *American Journal of Sociology*, 89(2): 275–305.

Delacroix, J. and Ragin, C.C. (1978) 'Modernizing institutions, mobilization, and 3rd-world development—cross-national-study'. *American Journal of Sociology*, 84(1): 123–50.

Delacroix, J. and Ragin, C.C. (1981) 'Structural blockage—a cross-national-study of economic dependency, state efficacy, and underdevelopment'. *American Journal of Sociology*, 86(6): 1311–47.

Doreian, P., Batagelj, V. and Ferligoj, A. (2005) 'Positional analyses of sociometric data'. In P. Carrington, J. Scott and S. Wasserman (eds), *Models and Methods in Social Network Analysis.* New York: Cambridge University Press. pp. 77–97.

Durkheim, E. ([1893] 1964) *The Division of Labor in Society.* Glencoe, IL: The Free Press.

Eisenstadt, S.N. (1974) 'Studies of modernization and sociological theory'. *History and Theory*, 13(3): 225–52.

Emerson, R. (1962) 'Power-dependence relations'. *American Sociological Review*, 27(1): 31–41.

Emirbayer, M. (1997) 'Manifesto for a relational sociology'. *American Journal of Sociology*, 103(2): 281–317.

Evans, P. (1979) *Dependent Development: The Alliance of Multinational, State, and Local Capital in Brazil*. Princeton, NJ: Princeton University Press.

Frank, A.G. (1966) 'The development of underdevelopment'. *Monthly Review*, 18: 17–31.

Galtung, J. (1971) 'Structural theory of imperialism'. *Journal of Peace Research*, 8(2): 81–117.

Giddens, A. (1985) *The Nation-State and Violence*. Berkeley: University of California Press.

Granovetter, M. (1973) 'Strength of weak ties'. *American Journal of Sociology*, 78(6): 1360–80.

Hafner-Burton, E.M. and Tsutsui, K. (2005) 'Human rights in a globalizing world: The paradox of empty promises'. *American Journal of Sociology*, 110(5): 1373–411.

Homans, G. (1961) *Social Behavior*. New York: Harcourt, Brace and World.

IMF (2000) *Direction of Trade Statistics*. Washington, DC: International Monetary Fund.

Inkeles, A. and Smith, D.H. (1974) *Becoming Modern: Individual Change in Six Developing Countries*. Cambridge, MA: Harvard University Press.

Kentor, J. (1981) 'Structural determinants of peripheral urbanization—the effects of international dependence'. *American Sociological Review*, 46(2): 201–11.

Kentor, J. (1998) 'The long-term effects of foreign investment dependence on economic growth, 1940–1990'. *American Journal of Sociology*, 103(4): 1024–46.

Kentor, J. (2000) *Capital and Coercion*. London: Taylor and Francis Group—The Garland Publishing, Inc.

Kentor, J. and Jang, Y.S. (2004) 'Yes, there is a (growing) transnational business community—A study of global interlocking directorates 1983–98'. *International Sociology*, 19(3): 355–68.

Kick, E.L. (1987) 'World-system structure, national development, and the prospects for a socialist world order'. In T. Boswell and A. Bergesen (eds), *America's Changing Role in the World System*. New York: Praeger. pp. 127–55.

Kick, E.L. and Davis, B.L. (2001) 'World-system structure and change—An analysis of global networks and economic growth across two time periods'. *American Behavioral Scientist*, 44(10): 1561–78.

Knoke, D. and Yang, S. (2008) *Social Network Analysis*, Thousand Oaks, CA: Sage.

Lloyd, P., Mahutga, M.C. and Leeuw, J.D. (Forthcoming) 'Looking back and forging ahead: Thirty years of social network research on the world-system'.

Mahutga, M.C. (2006) 'The persistence of structural inequality? A network analysis of international trade, 1965–2000'. *Social Forces*, 84(4): 1863–89.

Mann, M. (1986) *The Sources of Social Power*. Cambridge, MA: Cambridge University Press.

Mann, M. (1988) *States, War and Capitalism*. Oxford: Blackwell.

McKinney, L.A., Fulkerson, G.M., et al. (2009) 'Investigating the correlates of biodiversity loss: A cross-national quantitative analysis of threatened bird species'. *Human Ecology Review*, 16(1): 103–13.

Meyer, J.W., Boli, J. et al. (1997) 'World society and the nation-state'. *American Journal of Sociology*, 103(1): 144–81.

Meyer, J. W., Hannan, M.T., et al. (1979) 'National economic development, 1950–1970: Social and political factors'. In J. W. M. a. M. T. Hannan (eds), *National Development and the World System: Educational, Economic, and Political Change 1950–1970*. Chicago: University of Chicago Press. pp. 85–116.

Nemeth, R.J. and Smith, D.A. (1985) 'International trade and world system structure: A multiple network analysis'. *Review*, 8: 517–60.

Parsons, T. (1966) 'Religion in a modern pluralistic society'. *Review of Religious Research*, 7(3): 125–46.

Prebisch, R. (1962) 'The economic development of Latin America and its principal problems'. *Economic Bulletin for Latin America*, 7(February 1962): 1–22.

Ramirez, F. and J. Boli. (1987) 'The political construction of mass schooling: European origins and worldwide institutionalization'. *Sociology of Education*, 60: 2–17.

Robinson, W.I. (2004) *A Theory of Global Capitalism: Production, Class and State in a Transnational World*. Cambridge, MA: Cambridge University Press.

Rostow, W.W. (1960) *The Stages of Economic Growth: A Non-communist Manifesto*. Cambridge, MA: Harvard University Press.

Rubinson, R. (1976) 'World-economy and distribution of income within states—cross-national-study'. *American Sociological Review*, 41(4): 638–59.

Sassen, S. (1998) *Globalization and Its Discontents*. New York: New Press.

Schofer, E. and Meyer, J.W. (2005) 'The worldwide expansion of higher education in the twentieth century'. *American Sociological Review*, 70(6): 898–920.

SIPRI (2007) 'Arms transfers database'. Stockholm International Peace Research Institute. http://armstrade.sipri.org/arms_trade/values.php (accessed June 31, 2008).

Sklair, L. (1999) *The Transnational Capitalist Class*. Oxford: Blackwell.

Smith, A. (1776 [1977]) *An Inquiry into the Nature and Causes of the Wealth of Nations*. Chicago: University of Chicago Press.

Smith, D.A. and Timberlake, M.F. (2001) 'World city networks and hierarchies, 1977–1997—An empirical analysis of global air travel links'. *American Behavioral Scientist*, 44(10): 1656–78.

Smith, D.A. and White, D.R. (1992) 'Structure and dynamics of the global economy—network analysis of international-trade 1965–1980'. *Social Forces*, 70(4): 857–93.

Snyder, D. and Kick, E.L. (1979) 'Structural position in the world system and economic-growth, 1955–1970—multiple-network analysis of transnational internations'. *American Journal of Sociology*, 84(5): 1096–26.

Spencer, H. (1887) *The Factors of Organic Evolution*. London: Williams and Norgate.

Szymanski, A. (1981) *The Logic of Imperialism.* New York: Praeger.

Terlouw, C. P. (1993) 'The elusive semiperiphery—a critical-examination of the concept semiperiphery'. *International Journal of Comparative Sociology,* 34(1–2): 87–102.

Tönnies, F. (1887) *Gemeinschaft and Gesellschaft.* Leipzig: Fues's Verlag.

True, J. and M. Minstrom. (2001) 'Transnational networks and policy diffusion: The case of gender'. *International Studies Quarterly,* 45: 27–57.

Van Rossem, R. (1996) 'The world system paradigm as general theory of development: A cross-national test'. *American Sociological Review,* 61(3): 508–27.

Wallerstein, I. (1974) *The Modern World System: Capitalist Agriculture and the Origins of the European World-Economy in the Sixteenth Century.* New York: Academic Press.

Wasserman, S. and K. Faust. (1994) *Social Network Analysis: Methods and Applications.* Cambridge, MA: Cambridge University Press.

Weber, M. ([1921] 1978) *Economy and Society.* Berkeley: University of California Press.

Wellman, B. (1983) 'Network analysis: Some basic principles'. *Sociological Theory,* 1: 155–200.

White, H.C., Boorman, S.A. and Breiger, R.L. (1976) 'Social-structure from multiple networks. 1. Blockmodels of roles and positions'. *American Journal of Sociology,* 81(4): 730–80.

White, H.C. and Breiger, R.L. (1975) 'Pattern across networks'. *Society,* 12(5): 68–73.

World Bank (2008) *World Development Indicators.* CD-ROM.

Wright, E.O. and Perrone, L. (1977) 'Marist class categories and income inequality'. *American Sociological Review,* 42(1): 32–55.

Concepts and Methods

23

A Brief Introduction to Analyzing Social Network Data

Robert A. Hanneman and Mark Riddle

INTRODUCTION

Social network analysts use two kinds of tools from mathematics to represent information about patterns of ties among social actors: graphs and matrices. In this chapter, we'll provide a very quick sketch about how social networks can be represented with these tools and we will discuss some of the things that these representations let us see more clearly. We'll extend our look at the "toolkit" of social network analysts by looking at how they approach some of the most commonly asked questions about the texture of whole networks and the ways that individuals are embedded in them.

There is a lot more to these topics than we will cover here. The visual representation of social networks as graphs is discussed in depth in the chapter by Lothar Krempel in this volume. Mathematics has whole subfields devoted to "graph theory" and to "matrix algebra." Social scientists have borrowed just a few things that they find helpful for describing and analyzing patterns of social relations. Representing data as matrices is the basis for manipulating data and calculating the measures we discuss in the next chapter. The chapter by Pip Pattison (this volume) shows some advanced applications.

By the time you've worked through this chapter and the next, we hope that you will have an introductory understanding of the most commonly used formal representations of social networks and some of the most commonly used basic descriptive indexes. This is only an introduction; longer and more complete presentations are available in Wasserman and Faust (1994), John Scott (2000), and our own online text (Hanneman and Riddle, 2005) (this chapter and the following chapter are cut-down and edited versions).

Working with network data and calculating measures of their properties is almost always done with software. We will present a number of examples using the UCINET package (Borgatti et al., 2002), because we are most familiar with it. There are, however, a number of excellent software tools that you will want to review (see Huisman and van Duijn, this volume) when you want to try your hand.

USING GRAPHS TO REPRESENT SOCIAL RELATIONS

A good drawing of a graph can immediately suggest some of the most important features of overall network structure. Are all the nodes connected? Are there many or few ties among the actors? Are there subgroups or local "clusters" of actors that are tied to one another but not to other groups? Are there some actors with many ties, and some with few?

A good drawing can also indicate how a particular "ego" (node) is "embedded" in (connected to) its "neighborhood" (the actors that are connected to ego, and their connections to one another). By looking at "ego" and the "ego network," we can get a sense of the structural constraints and opportunities that an actor faces;

we may be better able to understand the role that an actor plays in a social structure.

Graphs representing networks are composed of nodes (the individual actors) and relations. Either arcs (one-directional arrows) or edges (lines without arrow heads) represent which actors are tied to which others, for asymmetric and symmetric relations, respectively. Figure 23.1 shows an example of information sharing among 10 organizations as studied by Knoke and Wood (1981). (The original versions, in color, of the images in this chapter can be seen at http://faculty.ucr.edu/~hanneman/chapter_23_figures.htm.)

Figure 23.1 is a "directed graph." That is, it provides information that is asymmetric and not necessarily reciprocated. In this example, each node represents an organization, and each relation represents whether or not it provides information to each other organization (if a relation has the value of zero, it is not graphed).

Looking at the "big picture", we note that the "texture" of the network is uneven. All but one organization is connected to others, but overall the density of connections isn't very high. There is a good bit of variability in how connected the organizations are. There seems to be qualitative

variation, with different organizations serving as "sources," "receivers," and "transmitters."

Individual organizations are "embedded" in the network in quite different ways. The Educ organization has multiple alternative sources of information from different regions of the network but does not serve as a source of information for others. The WRO (welfare rights organization) is isolated; the UWAY (United Way) seems to be "central."

Graphs can be more or less informative and can highlight or obscure features. Krempel (this volume) provides an extended treatment of visualization. But let us identify a few key features of graphs that can be helpful for getting started.

Graphing node and relation attributes

Using colors and shapes are useful ways of conveying information about what "type" of actor each node is. Institutional theory might suggest that information exchange among organizations of the same type would be more common than information exchange between organizations of

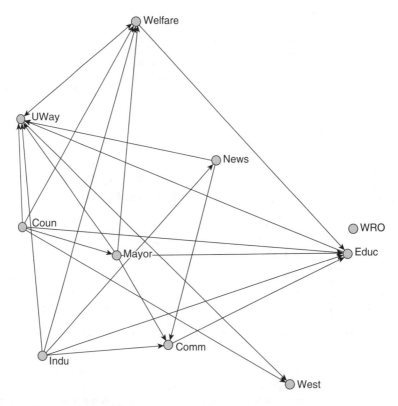

Figure 23.1   Directed graph of information ties (Knoke bureaucracies)

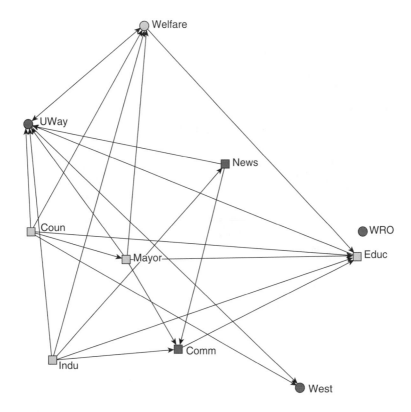

Figure 23.2   Knoke information network with government/nongovernment (solid) and generalist/specialist (shaded) indicated

different types. Some of the organizations here are governmental (Welfare, Coun, Educ, Mayor, Indu); some are nongovernmental (UWay, News, WRO, Comm, West). Ecological theory of organizations suggests that a division between organizations that are "generalists" (e.g., perform a variety of functions and operate in several different fields) and organizations that are "specialists" (e.g., work only in social welfare) might affect information-sharing patterns.

A visual inspection of the Figure 23.2 with the two attributes highlighted by node color and shape is much more informative about the hypotheses of differential rates of connection among black and lightly shaded (red and blue, respectively, in our online version) and among circles and squares. It doesn't look like this diagram is very supportive of either of our hypotheses.

Nodes may differ quantitatively as well as qualitatively. In a graph of trade flows in the world system of nationally bounded economies, for example, it might be useful to make each node's size proportional to its GDP. The quantities that distinguish nodes may also be based on measures that describe their relational positions in a

network; for example, nodes might be shown with sizes proportional to the number of ties each actor has. Figure 23.3 combines the quantitative and qualitative, using color and size to indicate features describing how each node is embedded in the network.

Figure 23.3 shows four subgroups, which are shaded differently to identify which nodes are members of which "K-core" (a K-core is one approach to identifying coherent subgroups in a graph, discussed in the next chapter). In addition, the sizes of the nodes in each K-core are proportional to the sizes of the K-core. The largest group contains government members (Mayor, County Government, Board of Education), as well as the main public (Welfare) and private (United Way) welfare agencies. A second group, colored in solid black, groups together the newspaper, chamber of commerce, and industrial development agency. Substantively, this actually makes some sense!

The relations among the actors can also have "attributes." It can be very helpful to use color and size to indicate difference of kind and amount among the relations. Where the ties among actors have been measured as a value, the magnitude of

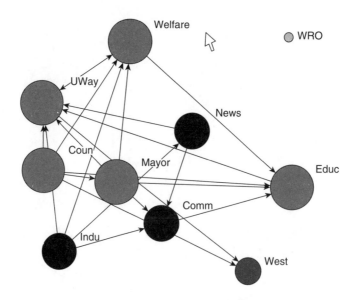

Figure 23.3   Knoke information exchange network with K-cores

the tie can be suggested by using thicker lines to represent stronger ties. Dashed lines, or lines of different colors, can be used to indicate different kinds of relations among actors, allowing multiplex data (data with more than one kind of relation) to be displayed in a single graph.

closeness of points indicates similarity (by some definition, and there are many alternative definitions) of nodes. The X and Y axes may also suggest patterns to be explored. Note that the public nodes tend to be grouped to the lower right, and that the private organizations are not very clustered.

Node location

Most graphs of networks are drawn in a two-dimensional "X-Y axis" space (Mage and some other packages allow three-dimensional rendering and rotation). Where a node or a relation is drawn in the space is essentially arbitrary — the full information about the network is contained in its list of nodes and relations. Figure 23.4 shows exactly the same network (Knoke's money flow network) that has been rendered in several different ways.

The first drawing locates the nodes randomly, the second drawing uses a "circle," and the third locates points according to its scores on a two-dimensional nonmetric scaling of the similarity of the node's tie profiles. It may be helpful to create graphs (based on the random graph) that group certain cases close together, or create clusters so that we can see differences in the patterns of ties within and between groups. Circle graphs highlight which nodes are highly connected and which are less so. Drawings that indicate scaling or clustering of network data, like the third one, may be particularly illustrative. In this drawing, the

Ego networks (neighborhoods)

A very useful way of understanding complicated network graphs is to see how they arise from the local connections of individual actors. The network formed by selecting a node, including all actors that are connected to that node, and all the connections among those other actors is called the "ego network" or (one-step) neighborhood of an actor ("neighborhoods" can also be found for two or more degrees of distance from ego).

To visualize the way in which individual nodes are embedded in the whole network, drawings of their ego networks are often very helpful. One of the basic insights of the social network perspective is that actors' attributes and behaviors are shaped by those with whom they have direct relations, and actors may act to re-shape these constraints. Graphing individuals' local networks and comparing them (e.g., are the ego neighborhoods of all government actors bigger than nongovernment actors? Which actors have neighborhoods that are composed mostly of actors of the same type?) can give great insight into similarities and differences among actors.

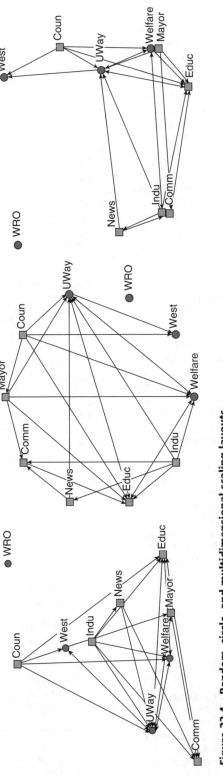

Figure 23.4   Random, circle, and multidimensional scaling layouts

A lot of the work that we do with social networks is primarily descriptive or exploratory, rather than confirmatory hypothesis testing. For small networks, visual inspection of graphs can give a feel of the overall "texture" of the social structure and can suggest how individuals are "embedded" in the larger structure. All of the numerical indices that we will discuss in the next chapter are really just efforts to attach numbers to features that we naturally "see" in graphs. Working with drawings can be a lot of fun, and it is a bit of an outlet for one's creative side. A well-constructed graphic can also be far more effective for sharing your insights than any number of words. Large networks can be difficult to study visually, however. Formal description of the properties of networks and testing hypotheses about them require that we convert our graphs to numbers.

USING MATRICES TO REPRESENT SOCIAL RELATIONS

Graphs are very useful ways of presenting information about social networks. But when there are many actors or many kinds of relations, they can become so visually complicated that it is very difficult to see patterns. It is also possible to represent information about social networks in the form of matrices. We'll briefly review some of the most commonly used matrix representations of social network data. The language of matrices and matrix operations is important if you are going to work with network data. You don't have to do the math (that's why we have computers), but the mathematical concepts provide an efficient way to think about data handling and analysis.

A *matrix* is nothing more than an array (or list) of data (usually named with a bold letter). We might call a list of the 10 organizations names in the Knoke bureaucracy study **A**. Each *element* (organization name) can be *indexed* by its place in the list (name 1, name 2, etc.). There are a several types of matrices that are used, often in combination, in social network analysis.

Vectors

Matrices can have a single dimension (e.g., a list of names). Matrices with one dimension are called *vectors*; *row vectors* are "horizontal" lists of elements, and *column vectors* are "vertical" lists of elements. Row or column vectors are most commonly used in social network analysis to present information about the attributes of nodes.

Consider the list of the Knoke organizations and a dummy coding of whether they are governmental (1) or not (0) in Figure 23.5.

Figure 23.5 actually has two column vectors: organization ID and coding of government or not (the row and column labels 1–10 and 1G were added by UCINET). This makes the data array a ten-by-two (number of rows by number of columns) rectangular matrix. Rectangular matrices are simply "lists of lists" (either horizontally or vertically).

Most network data sets include arrays of variables that describe the attributes of the nodes. These attributes can be purely qualitative (e.g., the name of the organization), or nominal, ordinal, or interval (e.g., number of employees). Each variable can be stored in a single vector, or the vectors can be gathered into a rectangular array like in the example in Figure 23.5. These attribute data sets look very much like conventional social science data: rows representing cases, each coded with columns representing variables.

Arrays like Figure 23.5 are used to provide information about each node. We may code this information from our independent observations, as in the example. Each node might also be described by a variable that is based on its relational properties, such as its number of ties to other nodes, or its "betweenness centrality." A very common use of attribute vectors in social network analysis is to indicate the "group" to which a case belongs. There is a special name for these kinds of codes: partitions. Partitions (like the codes of zero or one in Figure 23.5) can be used to select subsets of cases, rearrange the data, and compute summary measures (e.g., what is

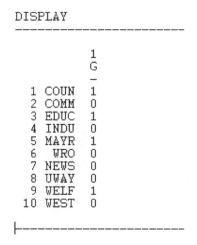

Figure 23.5   Attribute vector for Knoke bureaucracies data

the relative density of ties among government organizations relative to their average densities of ties to nongovernmental organizations?).

Square matrices

In formal mathematics, a network is defined as a collection of nodes and relations. Generally, vectors or rectangular collections of vectors are used to describe the attributes of the nodes. Square matrices of two dimensions, in which both rows and columns contain lists of the same nodes, are used to describe the relations or connections between each pair of actors. Consider the example in Figure 23.6.

```
Matrix #1: KNOKI

                                    1|
       1 2 3 4 5 6 7 8 9 0
       C C E I M W N U W W
      - - - - - - - - - -
 1     0 1 0 0 1 0 1 0 1 0
 2     1 0 1 1 1 0 1 1 1 0
 3     0 1 0 1 1 1 1 0 0 1
 4     1 1 0 0 1 0 1 0 0 0
 5     1 1 1 1 0 0 1 1 1 1
 6     0 0 1 0 0 0 1 0 1 0
 7     0 1 0 1 1 0 0 0 0 0
 8     1 1 0 1 1 0 1 0 1 0
 9     0 1 0 0 1 0 1 0 0 0
10     1 1 1 0 1 0 1 0 0 0
```

```
Matrix #2: KNOKM

                                    1
       1 2 3 4 5 6 7 8 9 0
       C C E I M W N U W W
      - - - - - - - - - -
 1     0 0 1 0 1 0 0 1 1 1
 2     0 0 1 0 0 0 0 0 0 0
 3     0 0 0 0 0 0 0 1 0 0
 4     0 1 1 0 0 0 1 1 1 0
 5     0 1 1 0 0 0 0 1 1 0
 6     0 0 0 0 0 0 0 0 0 0
 7     0 1 0 0 0 0 0 1 0 0
 8     0 0 0 0 0 0 0 0 1 1
 9     0 0 1 0 0 0 0 1 0 0
10     0 0 0 0 0 0 0 0 0 0
```

Figure 23.6   Adjacency matrices of information and money ties among Knoke's bureaucracies

The simplest and most common matrix to show relations is binary. That is, if a tie is present, a one is entered in a cell; if there is no tie, a zero is entered. This kind of a matrix is the starting point for almost all network analysis and is called an "adjacency matrix" because it represents who is "next to" (adjacent) to whom in the social space mapped by the relations that we have measured. Figure 23.6 shows two such adjacency matrices.

A matrix may be symmetric or asymmetric. By convention, in a directed (i.e., asymmetric) matrix, the sender of a tie is the row and the target of the tie is the column. Let's look at a simple example. In Figure 23.6, we see that organization 1 sends information to organization 2 (i.e., the entry in cell 1, 2 = 1), and this relation is reciprocated (i.e., the entry in cell 2, 1 =1). Organization 1 also sends information to organization 7, but this tie is not reciprocated. Asymmetric ties are not necessarily reciprocated, though they may be. A symmetric matrix represents "bonded ties" or "co-membership" or any kind of social relation in which, if A is tied to B, B must logically be tied to A (which is the case in most institutionalized or role relations).

Each node-by-node square matrix represents a map of a particular relation between all pairs of actors in the network. If there are multiple relations, as in Figure 23.6, these are represented as a third dimension (or slice or stack). The quantity in each cell of the matrix represents the strength of the tie between two actors (in symmetric data) or the quantity directed from the node on the row to the node on the column. The strength of relations can be measured as a nominal dichotomy or adjacency (as in our example), or at higher levels. A more in-depth discussion of data types is provided by Peter Marsden (this volume).

In representing social network data as matrices, the question always arises: what do I do with the elements of the matrix where $i = j$? That is, for example, does organization 1 "send information" to itself? This part of the matrix is called the *main diagonal*. Sometimes the value of the main diagonal is meaningless, and it is ignored (and left blank or filled with zeros or ones). Sometimes, however, the main diagonal can be very important and can take on meaningful values.

Multiplex matrices

Many social network analysis measures focus on structures defined by patterns in a single kind of relationship among actors: friendship, kinship, economic exchange, warfare, and so on. Social relations among actors, however, are usually more complex, in that actors are connected in multiple ways simultaneously. In face-to-face groups of persons, the actors may have emotional connections, exchange relations, kinship ties, and other connections all at the same time. Organizations exchange personnel, money, and information and can form groups and alliances. Relations among nation-states are characterized by numerous forms of cultural, economic, and political exchange.

Multiplex data consist of a series of matrices (or "slices"), each of which is a square matrix describing a single type of tie among all pairs of actors. The various relations may be symmetric or asymmetric and may be scored at different levels of measurement. The two matrices shown in Figure 23.6 are two slices of the Knoke bureaucracies data, showing information sending/receiving and money sending/receiving relations among the 10 organizations.

One may apply all the tools of network analysis to each matrix in multiplex data, separately. For example, is there greater network centralization in the flow of money than there is in the flow of information among organizations? But we may also wish to combine the information on multiple relations among the same actors. There are two general approaches: reduction and combination. The reduction approach seeks to combine information about multiple relations among the same set of actors into a single relation that indexes the *quantity* of ties. The combination approach also seeks to create a single index of the multiplex relations, but attempts to represent the *quality* of ties, resulting in a qualitative typology. Role algebras (see Pattison, this volume) are a particularly important approach to qualitative reduction of multiplex data.

A special type of multiplex data arises when we obtain multiple reports or views about the same social structure. This type of cognitive social structure data maps the ties among pairs of actors in each slice and has a slice for each perceiver. One may wish to use matrix operations to combine the multiple cognitive maps (e.g., averaging, minimum value, maximum value, etc.), or one may wish to find groups of perceivers who have more or less similar views of the social structure.

Affiliation (two-mode) matrices

A central focus of sociological analysis is the embedding of individuals in larger structures (e.g., families, organizations, communities, networks, identity categories). These larger structures are often seen as arising from the agency of individuals. Social network analysis may be used to map and study the relations within and between

multiple levels of analysis: individuals affiliate with groups and organizations; organizations are linked in community ecology by their overlapping memberships.

Any array of relational data that maps the connections between two different sets of actors is said to be "two-mode." In sociological analysis, it is common for one mode to be individual actors and for the other mode to be sets of events, organizations, or identity categories. These types of data are called affiliation networks because they map the membership of connections, or affiliations, of actors with structures. Borgatti and Halgin (this volume) provide an in-depth treatment of the analysis of two-mode data.

It is not uncommon to translate two-mode data into a series of one-mode matrices. For example, one might transform a matrix that displays which persons were members of which voluntary organizations in a community into a matrix showing how many times each pair of persons happened to be co-members. One can transform the same data into a one-mode matrix that shows how many times each pair of organizations was connected by overlapping memberships. Asymmetric one-mode data can also be viewed as two-mode data in which the same actors are the lists for the two modes.

Image matrices and hyper-graphs

Relational matrices that show which actors are connected to which others are of great descriptive and practical use. Often, though, our interest is in more abstract categories and relations among them. For example, it is interesting to note that the United States imports many relatively low-tech manufactured goods from China, and it sells many high-tech and brand-name goods in return. To a world-systems analyst, however, this relation is simply one example of a larger class of equivalent relationships involving core and semiperipheral nations. Ferligoj et al. (this volume) provide an introduction to methods of identifying and working with "equivalence classes."

Once classes and their member nodes have been identified, we can represent ties among them with graphs. These hyper-graphs have classes as nodes, and edges or arcs as defined by the equivalence relation. Such graphs can greatly reduce the difficulty in visualizing networks with large numbers of nodes and can provide great analytic insight.

The information in a hyper-graph can also be represented in matrix form. The original rows and columns of the actor-by-actor relation matrix are re-arranged (permuted) to group the actors in the same class together. This re-arranged matrix is made up of "blocks" that map relations of members of a class to one another (in the diagonal blocks) and all the relations of the actors in one class to all those in another class in off-diagonal blocks.

The blocked and permuted matrix is then often reduced to a new class-by-class matrix by summarizing the information within each block. Sometimes, the average density of ties, or the average value of tie strength, is used to summarize the blocked matrix. Frequently, some cut-off value is chosen (often the average value of ties for the entire network) and blocks are assigned a value of 1 if ties exceed the cut-off or 0 if they fall below the cutoff. This type of zero-one matrix, with groups or equivalence classes as nodes, is called the "image" matrix. Thoughtfully constructed image matrices can greatly simplify complex patterns among large numbers of actors (and, of course, badly constructed matrices can obscure them).

Dynamic networks

Increasing attention is being given to the dynamics of networks, with particular attention to understanding how the embedding of actors in a particular place in a network at one time may effect change in their attributes or behavior and how the attributes and behaviors of actors at one point in time may shape the pattern of ties that are built and dissolved over time. Snijders (this volume) discusses approaches to studying network dynamics; many of the statistical models for the analysis of network data discussed in the chapters by van Duijn and Huisman and by Robins (this volume) are specifically aimed at the analysis of change.

A dynamic network can be represented as a series of matrix cross-sections, and it is often the case that dynamic data are observed this way. This approach results in a multiplex matrix in which one dimension (usually the slice) is defined by "time." Alternatively, we may have information on the exact times at which events began and ceased (e.g., when actors joined the network and departed, when ties were formed or dissolved). Data of these types are becoming increasingly common with the use of digital instruments for network data collection (e.g., computer server logs, video recordings). Generally, such dynamic data are stored as lists of events (the network analysis package Pajek has a number of data formats and algorithms specifically designed for dynamic data), and programming is used to build matrices for analysis from them.

CONCLUSION

Once a pattern of social relations or ties among a set of actors has been represented in a formal way (via a graph or matrix), we can define some important ideas about social structure in quite precise ways using mathematics for the definitions. In the next chapter we will examine some of the most commonly used approaches to describing the "texture" of whole networks and the positions of individual nodes in them.

REFERENCES

Borgatti, S.P., Everett, M.G. and Freeman, L.C. (2002) *UCINET for Windows: Software for Social Network Analysis*. Harvard, MA: Analytic Technologies.

Hanneman, R. and Riddle, M. (2005) *An Introduction to Social Network Methods*. http://faculty.ucr.edu/~hanneman/nettext.

Knoke, D. and Kuklinski, J.H. (1982) *Network Analysis*. Beverly Hills, CA: Sage.

Knoke, D. and Wood, J. (1981) *Organized for Action: Commitment in Voluntary Associations*. New Brunswick, NJ: Rutgers University Press.

Scott, J. (2000) *Social Network Analysis: A Handbook*. 2nd ed. London: Sage.

Wasserman, S. and Faust, K. (1994) *Social Network Analysis: Methods and Applications*. Cambridge: Cambridge University Press.

24

Concepts and Measures for Basic Network Analysis

Robert A. Hanneman and Mark Riddle

NETWORKS AND ACTORS

The social network perspective emphasizes multiple levels of analysis: differences among actors are traced to the constraints and opportunities that arise from how they are embedded in networks; the structure and behavior of networks are grounded in and enacted by local interactions among actors.

In this chapter we will examine basic concepts and measures used in formal social network analysis. Despite the simplicity of the ideas, there are good theoretical reasons (and considerable empirical evidence) to believe that these basic properties of social networks have very important consequences for both individuals and the larger social structures of which they are parts.

There are many ways that one could organize this survey, and we will only be able to provide an introduction. For more extended treatments, the reader may wish to consult John Scott's *Social Network Analysis* (2000), Stanley Wasserman and Katherine Faust's *Social Network Analysis: Methods and Applications* (1994), David Knoke and Song Yang's *Network Analysis* (2008), and our own text (Hanneman and Riddle, 2005).

In the first half of this chapter we will focus on the network as a whole; this sort of "top-down" perspective enables us to see and measure aspects of whole social structures (e.g., families, groups, communities, markets, polities) that may be predictive of their dynamics. For example, networks where a high percentage of all possible ties among actors are actually present (high "density") are often more prone to rapid "information cascades"

than graphs with low density (Watts, 2003). Network analysts have developed a considerable number of measures to describe the "texture" of the "social fabric." At the broadest level, the concern is with the solidarity and robustness of the whole structure and with the presence of – and relations among – substructures.

In the second half of this chapter we will shift our perspective to the "bottom up." We will focus on some concepts and measures that provide insight into the ways that individuals are embedded in networks. For example, it is often the case that actors who have many others in their "neighborhood" (i.e., "alters" to whom "ego" has a direct connection) are more influential but sometimes also more constrained than those who have fewer connections. We will examine a number of related approaches that identify different aspects of the "ego network" of actors as potential sources of opportunity and constraint (Wellman et al., 1988).

Throughout this chapter we'll illustrate the concepts and measures discussed with output from the analysis of a small, binary, directed graph. These analyses are performed with UCINET (Borgatti et al., 2002), but there are many excellent software packages that provide similar tools (see, particularly, Huisman and van Duijin, this volume).

Our illustrations will examine the flow of information among 10 formal organizations concerned with social welfare issues in one midwestern U.S. city (Knoke and Wood, 1981). Without reading further, take just a moment to examine the graph of this network in Figure 24.1.

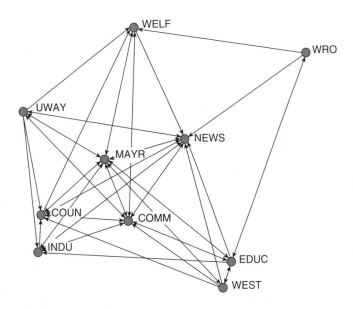

Figure 24.1   Knoke information exchange

The formal methods that we will be discussing in this chapter are really just ways of indexing features readily seen in the graph. From the "top down," we can see, for example, that there are a limited number of actors here (size), and all of them are connected (a single component). Not every possible connection is present (density), and there are thin spots (structural holes) in the fabric. There are some sets of organizations where everyone exchanges information with everyone (cliques), and these cliques are connected by overlapping membership (bridges).

Looking at the same graph from the "bottom up," there appear to be some differences among the actors in how connected they are; compare the newspaper to the welfare rights advocacy organization. If you look closely, you can see that some actors' connections are likely to be reciprocated (that is, if A shares information with B, B also shares information with A), while other actors are more likely to be senders than receivers of information. As a result of the variation in how connected individuals are, and whether the ties are reciprocated, some actors may be quite "central" and others less so. Actors may have "equivalent" positions in the network, which constitute "types" or "roles."

Social network analysts and graph theorists have developed a large number of formal algorithms to index these kinds of features about whole networks and about the positions of individuals within them. The remainder of this chapter is a quick tour of some of the most commonly used approaches.

THE WHOLE NETWORK

Since networks are defined by their actors and the connections among them, it is useful to begin our description by examining these very simple properties. Small groups differ from large groups in many important ways; indeed, population size figures largely in much sociological analysis (Finsveen and van Oorschot, 2008; Totterdell et al., 2008). The extent to which actors are connected may be a key indicator of the "cohesion" (Burris, 2005; Fominaya, 2007; Moody and White, 2003; Sanders and Nauta, 2004), "solidarity," "moral density," and "complexity" of the social organization (Crossley, 2008; Schnegg, 2007; Urry, 2006).

Size and density

The size of a network is often very important. Imagine a group of 12 students in a seminar. It would not be difficult for each of the students to know each of the others fairly well and to build up exchange relationships (e.g., sharing reading notes). Now imagine a large lecture class of 300 students. It would be extremely difficult for any student to know all of the others, and it would be virtually impossible for there to be a single face-to-face network for exchanging reading notes. Size is critical for the structure of social relations because of the limited resources and capacities that each actor has for building and maintaining ties.

Our example network has 10 actors. The size of a network is indexed simply by counting the number of nodes.

In any network there are $(k * k-1)$ unique ordered pairs of actors (i.e., AB is different from BA, and self-ties are ignored), where k is the number of actors. You may wish to verify this for yourself with some small networks. So, in our network of 10 actors, with directed data, there are 90 logically possible relationships. If we had undirected (i.e., symmetric) ties, the number would be 45, since the relationship AB would be the same as BA. The number of logically possible relationships then grows exponentially as the number of actors increases linearly. It follows from this that the range of logically possible social structures increases (or, by one definition, "complexity" increases) exponentially with size.

The density of a binary network is simply the proportion of all possible ties that are actually present. For a valued network, density is defined as the sum of the ties divided by the number of possible ties (i.e., the ratio of all tie strength that is actually present to the number of possible ties). The density of a network may give us insights into such phenomena as the speed at which information diffuses among the nodes and the extent to which actors have high levels of social capital and/or social constraint.

In our example data, we see that there are 10 nodes; therefore, there are 90 possible connections. Of these, 49 are actually present. The network density then is .5444.

Connections

Size and density give us the overall sense of the range of possible social structures that could be present in a population, but what really matters is the pattern or "texture" of these connections. There are many widely used indexes that summarize various aspects of the structure of connections in a graph.

Reachability

An actor is "reachable" by another if there is a set of connections by which we can trace from the source to the target actor, regardless of how many others fall between them. If the data are asymmetric or directed, it is possible that actor A can reach actor B, but that actor B cannot reach actor A. With symmetric or undirected data, of course, each pair of actors either is or is not reachable to one another. If some actors in a network cannot reach others, there is potential for a division of the network. Or it may indicate that the population we

are studying is really composed of more than one subpopulation. In the Knoke information exchange data set, it turns out that all actors are reachable by all others. A message or signal originating anywhere in the network could potentially be received by all other nodes.

Connectivity

Even though one actor may be able to reach another, the connection may not be a strong one. If there are many different pathways that connect two actors, they have high "connectivity" in the sense that there are multiple ways for a signal to reach from one to the other (Burris, 2005; Crossley, 2008; Finsveen and van Oorschot, 2008; Fominaya, 2007; Haythornthwaite, 2005; Hermann, 2008; Kien, 2008; Kratke and Brandt, 2009). The measure "connectivity" counts the number of nodes that would have to be removed in order to make one actor unreachable by another. Figure 24.2 shows the point connectivity for the flow of information among the 10 Knoke organizations.

The result demonstrates the tenuousness of organization 6's (the welfare rights organization) connection as both a source (row) or receiver (column) of information. To get its message to most other actors, organization 6 has only one alternative; should a single organization refuse to pass along information, organization 6 would receive none at all! Point connectivity can be a useful measure to get at notions of dependency and vulnerability.

Distance

The properties of the network that we have examined so far primarily deal with adjacencies, or the

	1 C	2 C	3 E	4 I	5 M	6 W	7 N	8 U	9 W	10 W
1	5	5	3	4	5	1	6	4	4	3
2	5	8	3	5	8	1	6	5	3	4
3	3	3	4	4	3	1	4	3	3	3
4	5	5	3	5	5	1	5	4	3	4
5	5	8	3	5	8	1	6	5	3	5
6	1	1	1	1	1	1	2	1	2	1
7	5	6	3	5	6	1	6	4	2	3
8	5	5	3	5	5	1	5	5	4	4
9	3	3	3	3	3	1	3	3	3	3
10	4	5	3	4	5	1	4	4	3	5

Figure 24.2 Point connectivity of Knoke information exchange

direct connections from one actor to the next. But the way that people are embedded in networks is more complex than this. Two persons, call them A and B, might each have five friends. But suppose that none of person A's friends have any friends except A. Person B's five friends, in contrast, each have five friends. The information available to B, and B's potential for influence is far greater than A's. That is, sometimes being a "friend of a friend" may be quite consequential.

To capture this aspect of how individuals are embedded in networks, one common approach is to examine the distance between actors. If two actors are adjacent, the distance between them is one (that is, it takes one step for a signal to go from the source to the receiver). If A tells B, and B tells C (and A does not tell C), then actors A and C are at a distance of two. The distances among actors in a network may be an important macro-characteristic of the network as a whole. Where distances are great, it may take a long time for information to diffuse across a population. It may also be that some actors are quite unaware of and not influenced by others; even if they are technically reachable, the costs may be too high to conduct exchanges.

The most commonly used definition of the distance between two actors in a network is *geodesic distance*. For binary data, the geodesic distance is the number of relations in the shortest possible pathway from one actor to another. The geodesic distance from one actor to another that is not reachable is usually treated as infinite, or equal to the largest observed distance in the graph. Valued data are often dichotomized in order to calculate the geodesic distance.

For valued networks, there are several alternative approaches to defining distances. Where we have measures of the strengths of ties (e.g., the dollar volume of trade between two nations), the "nearness (the opposite of distance)" between two actors is often defined as the strength of the weakest path between them. If A sends 6 units to B, and B sends 4 units to C, the "strength" of the path from A to C (assuming A to B to C is the shortest path) is 4. Where we have a measure of the cost of making a connection (as in an "opportunity cost" or "transaction cost" analysis), the "distance" between two actors is defined as the sum of the costs along the shortest pathway. Where we have a measure of the probability that a link will be used, the "distance" between two actors is defined as the product along the pathway (as in path analysis in statistics).

Indices of nearness or distance may also be weighted in various ways. For example, we might imagine that the value or potency of a signal decays exponentially, rather than linearly, as it passes through more and more intervening nodes between two actors.

In our example, we are using simple directed adjacencies, and the results (Figure 24.3) are quite straightforward.

Because the network is moderately dense, the geodesic distances are generally small. This suggests that information may travel pretty quickly in this network.

For each actor, that actor's largest geodesic distance is called its *eccentricity*, a measure of how far an actor is from the furthest other. For the network as a whole, the *diameter* is defined as the largest eccentricity. The mean (or median) geodesic distance and the standard deviation in geodesic distances may be used to summarize overall distance and the heterogeneity of distances in a network.

The use of geodesic paths to examine properties of the distances between individuals and for the whole network often makes a great deal of sense. There may be other cases, however, for which the distance between two actors and the connectedness of the graph as a whole is best thought of as involving all connections, not just the most efficient ones. For example, if I start a rumor, it will pass through a network by all pathways, not just the most efficient ones. How much credence another person gives my rumor may depend on how many times they hear it from different sources, and not merely how soon they hear it (Frank, 1996; Gallie, 2009; Gurrieri, 2008; Lai and Wong, 2002; Rycroft, 2007). For uses of distance like this, we need to take into account all of the connections among actors.

One approach to measuring how connected two actors are is to ask how many different actors in

```
Geodesic Distances

                                          1
          1  2  3  4  5  6  7  8  9  0
          C  C  E  I  M  W  N  U  W  W
          -- -- -- -- -- -- -- -- -- --
     1    0  1  2  2  1  3  1  2  1  2
     2    1  0  1  1  1  2  1  1  1  2
     3    2  1  0  1  1  1  1  2  2  1
     4    1  1  2  0  1  3  1  2  2  2
     5    1  1  1  1  0  2  1  1  1  1
     6    3  2  1  2  2  0  1  3  1  2
     7    2  1  2  1  1  3  0  2  2  2
     8    1  1  2  1  1  3  1  0  1  2
     9    2  1  2  2  1  3  1  2  0  2
    10    1  1  1  2  1  2  1  2  2  0
```

Figure 24.3 Geodesic distances for Knoke information exchange

the neighborhood of a source lie on pathways to a target. If I need to get a message to you, and there is only one other person to whom I can send this for retransmission, my connection is weak, even if the person I send it to may have many ways of reaching you. If, on the other hand, there are four people to whom I can send my message, each of whom has one or more ways of retransmitting my message to you, then my connection is stronger. The "flow" approach suggests that the strength of my tie to you is no stronger than the weakest link in the chain of connections, where weakness means a lack of alternatives. For our directed information flow data, the results of UCINET's count of maximum flow are shown in Figure 24.4.

You should verify for yourself that, for example, there are four alternative routes in flows from actor 1 to actor 2, but five such points in the flow from actor 2 to actor 1. The higher the number of flows from one actor to another, the greater the likelihood that communication will occur, and the less "vulnerable" the connection. Note that actors 6, 7, and 9 are relatively disadvantaged. In particular, actor 6 has only one way of obtaining information from all other actors (the column vector of flows to actor 6).

Reciprocity

The smallest "social structure" represented in a graph is a "dyad," the relation between two actors. With symmetric dyadic data, two actors are either connected or they are not. Density tells us pretty much all there is to know. If we are considering a directed relation, there are three kinds of dyads (no tie, a single tie, or ties in both directions).

The extent to which a population is characterized by "reciprocated" ties may tell us about the degree of cohesion in populations. Some theorists feel that there is an equilibrium tendency toward dyadic relationships to be either null or reciprocated and that asymmetric ties may be unstable. A network that has a predominance of null or reciprocated ties over asymmetric connections may be a more "equal" or "stable" network than one with a predominance of asymmetric connections (which might be more of a hierarchy).

There are several different approaches to indexing the degree of reciprocity in a population. Consider the very simple network shown in Figure 24.5. Actors A and B have reciprocated ties, actors B and C have a nonreciprocated tie, and actors A and C have no tie.

What is the prevalence of reciprocity in this network? One approach is to focus on dyads, and ask which pairs have a reciprocated tie between them. This would yield one such tie for three possible pairs (AB, AC, BC), or a reciprocity rate of .333. More commonly, analysts are concerned with the ratio of the number of pairs with a reciprocated tie relative to the number of pairs with any tie. In large populations, most actors are linked directly to relatively few other actors, and it may be more sensible to focus on the degree of reciprocity among pairs that have any ties between them. In our simple example, this would yield one reciprocated pair divided by two tied pairs, or a reciprocity rate of .500. In the Knoke information tie network, the proportion of all dyads having a tie that has a reciprocated tie is .5313. This is neither "high" nor "low" in itself but does seem to suggest a considerable degree of institutionalized horizontal connection within this

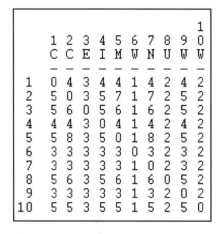

Figure 24.4   UCINET "maximum flow" for Knoke information network

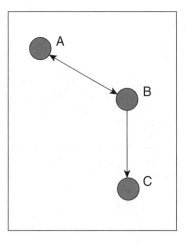

Figure 24.5   Definitions of reciprocity

organizational population. One may also focus on relations, rather than on dyads, by asking what the proportion is of all relations in the graph as part of reciprocated relations. For our example data, this approach yields a result of .6939. That is, of all the relations in the graph, 69% are parts of reciprocated ties.

Transitivity

The smallest social structure that has the true character of a "society" is the triad, any "triple" {A, B, C} of actors. Such a structure "embeds" dyadic relations in a structure where "other" is present along with "ego" and "alter." In (directed) triads, we can see the emergence of tendencies toward equilibrium and consistency of social structures ("institutionalization"), as well as features such as balance and transitivity. Triads are also the simplest structures in which we can see the emergence of hierarchy.

With undirected data, there are four possible types of triadic relations (no ties, one tie, two ties, or all three ties). Counts of the relative prevalence of these four types of relations across all possible triples (that is, a "triad census") can give a good sense of the extent to which a population is characterized by "isolation," "couples only," "structural holes" (i.e., where one actor is connected to two others who are not connected to each other), or "clusters."

With directed data, there are actually 16 possible types of relations among three actors, including relationships that exhibit hierarchy, equality, and the formation of exclusive groups (e.g., where two actors connect and exclude the third). Thus, small-group researchers suggest that all of the really fundamental forms of social relationships can be observed in triads. Because of this interest, we may wish to conduct a "triad census" for each actor and for the network as a whole.

Of the 16 possible types of directed triads, six involve zero, one, or two relations, and can't display transitivity because there are not enough ties to do so. One type with three relations (AB, BC, CB) does not have any ordered triples (AB, BC) and hence can't display transitivity. In three more types of triads, there are ordered triples (AB, BC) but the relation between A and C is not transitive. The remaining types of triads display varying degrees of transitivity.

Figure 24.6 displays the results of one type of transitivity analysis of the Knoke information data.

With 10 nodes, there are 720 triads. However, only 146 have enough ties to display transitivity. That is, there are 146 cases where, if AB and BC are present, then AC is also present. There are a number of different ways in which we could try to norm this count so that it becomes more meaningful. One approach is to divide the number of transitive triads by the total number of triads of all kinds (720). This shows that 20.28 percent of all triads are transitive. Perhaps more meaningful is to norm the number of transitive triads by the number of cases where a single link could complete the triad. That is, norm the number of {AB, BC, AC} triads by the number of {AB, BC, anything} triads. Seen in this way, about two-thirds or all relations that could easily be transitive actually are.

Clustering

Most of the time, most people interact with a fairly small set of others, many of whom know one another. The extent of local "clustering" in populations can be quite informative about the texture of everyday life. Watts (1999) and many others have noted that in large, real-world networks (of all kinds of things) there is often a structural pattern that seems somewhat paradoxical.

On one hand, in many large networks (like, for example, the Internet), the average geodesic distance between any two nodes is relatively short (Field et al., 2006; Hampton and Wellman, 1999). The "six degrees" of distance phenomenon is an

```
TRANSITIVITY
--------------------------------------------------------------------------------

Type of transitivity:          ADJACENCY
Input dataset:                 C:\Program Files\Ucinet 6\DataFiles\KNOKBUR

Relation: KNOKI
----------------

Number of non-vacuous transitive ordered triples: 146
Number of triples of all kinds: 720
Number of triples in which i-->j and j-->k: 217

Percentage of all ordered triples: 20.28%
Transitivity: % of ordered triples in which i-->j and j-->k that are transitive: 67.28%
```

Figure 24.6   Transitivity results for Knoke information network

example of this. So, most of the nodes in even very large networks may be fairly close to one another. The average distance between pairs of actors in large empirical networks is often much shorter than in random graphs of the same size.

On the other hand, most actors live in local neighborhoods where most others are also connected to one another. That is, in most large networks, a very large proportion of the total number of ties are highly "clustered" into local neighborhoods. That is, the density in local neighborhoods of large graphs tends to be much higher than we would expect for a random graph of the same size.

Most of the people we know may also know one another, which gives the impression that we live in a very narrow social world. Yet, at the same time, we can be at quite short distances to vast numbers of people whom we don't know at all. The "small-world" phenomena – a combination of short average path lengths over the entire graph, coupled with a strong degree of "clique-like" local neighborhoods – seems to have evolved independently in many large networks.

We've already discussed one part of this phenomenon. The average geodesic distance between all actors in a graph gets at the idea of how close actors are together. The other part of the phenomenon is the tendency toward dense local neighborhoods, or what is now thought of as "clustering."

One common way of measuring the extent to which a graph displays clustering is to examine the local neighborhood of an actor (that is, all the actors who are directly connected to ego), and to calculate the density in this neighborhood (leaving out ego). After doing this for all actors in the whole network, we can characterize the degree of clustering as an average of all the neighborhoods in the whole graph.

Figure 24.7 shows the clustering of the Knoke information network.

Two alternative measures are presented. The "overall" graph clustering coefficient is simply the average of the densities of the neighborhoods of all of the actors. The "weighted" version gives weight to the neighborhood densities proportional to their size; that is, actors with larger neighborhoods get more weight in computing the

average density. Since larger graphs are generally (but not necessarily) less dense than smaller ones, the weighted average neighborhood density (or clustering coefficient) is usually less than the unweighted version. In our example, we see that all of the actors are surrounded by local neighborhoods that are fairly dense; our organizations can be seen as embedded in dense local neighborhoods to a fairly high degree. Lest we overinterpret, we must remember that the overall density of the entire graph in this population is rather high (.54). So, the density of local neighborhoods is not really much higher than the density of the whole graph. In assessing the degree of clustering, it is usually wise to compare the clustering coefficient to the overall density.

Connections among groups

In addition to dyads, triads, and local clustering, the texture of connections in a network can be affected by "categorical social units" or "subpopulations" defined either by shared attributes or contexts. Persons of the same gender may be more likely to form friendship ties; persons who attend the same school are more likely to be acquainted. The extent to which these subpopulations are open or closed (i.e., the extent to which most individuals have most of their ties within the boundaries of these groups) may be a telling dimension of social structure.

Block density

In an organizational community, we might suppose that there may be competition (expressed as information hoarding) between organizations of the same type, and cooperation between organizations of different, complementary types. We have used an attribute or partition to divide the cases in Knoke information exchange data into three subpopulations (governmental agencies, nongovernmental generalists, and welfare specialists) so that we can see the amount of connection within and between groups. We can then examine the patterns of ties within and between "blocks" of nodes of the same type. Consider the results in Figure 24.8.

```
Input dataset:                C:\Program Files\Ucinet 6
Relation: KNOKI
----------------
Overall graph clustering coefficient: 0.607
Weighted Overall graph clustering coefficient: 0.599
```

Figure 24.7   Clustering coefficient of Knoke information network

```
Column
Block Old Code        Members:
----- --------        --------
  1         1         COUN EDUC MAYR
  2         2         COMM INDU NEWS
  3         3         WRO UWAY WELF WEST


Relation: KNOKI

                                   1
        1 3 5   2 4 7   6 8 9 0
        C E M   C I N   W U W W
      --------------------------------
 1  |      1 | 1   1 |     1      |
 3  |      1 | 1 1 1 | 1       1  |
 5  | 1 1    | 1 1 1 |   1 1 1    |
    --------------------------------
 2  | 1 1 1 |   1 1 | 1 1        |
 4  | 1   1 | 1   1 |            |
 7  |     1 | 1 1   |            |
    --------------------------------
 6  |   1   |   1   |     1      |
 8  | 1   1 | 1 1 1 |     1      |
 9  |     1 | 1   1 |            |
10  | 1 1 1 | 1   1 |            |
    --------------------------------



Density / average value within blocks

              1       2       3
              1       2       3
            ------- ------- -------
  1 1     0.6667  0.8889  0.5000
  2 2     0.6667  1.0000  0.1667
  3 3     0.5833  0.6667  0.1667


Standard Deviations within blocks

              1       2       3
              1       2       3
            ------- ------- -------
  1 1     0.4714  0.3143  0.5000|
  2 2     0.4714  0.0000  0.3727
  3 3     0.4930  0.4714  0.3727
```

Figure 24.8 Block density of three subpopulations in Knoke information network

The density in the 1,1 block is .6667. That is, of the six possible directed ties among actors 1, 3, and 5, four are actually present (ignoring the diagonal, which is the most common approach). We can see that the three subpopulations appear to have some differences. Governmental generalists (block 1) have quite dense in- and out-ties to one another, and to the other populations; nongovernment generalists (block 2) have out-ties among themselves and with block 1 and have high

densities of in-ties with all three subpopulations. The welfare specialists have high density of information sending to the other two blocks (but not within their block), and receive more input from governmental than from nongovernmental organizations.

The extent to which these simple characterizations of blocks characterize all the individuals within those blocks – essentially the validity of the blocking – can be assessed by looking at the standard deviations within the partitions. The standard deviations measure the lack of homogeneity within the partition, or the extent to which the actors vary.

Group-external and group-internal ties

Krackhardt and Stern (1988) developed a very simple and useful measure of group embedding based on comparing the numbers of ties within groups to those between groups. The E-I (external–internal) index takes the number of ties of group members to outsiders, subtracts the number of ties to other group members, and divides by the total number of ties. The resulting index ranges from –1 (all ties are internal to the group) to +1 (all ties are external to the group). Since this measure is concerned with any connection between members, the directions of ties are ignored (i.e., either an out-tie or an in-tie constitutes a tie between two actors).

The E-I index can be applied at three levels: the entire population, each group, and each individual. That is, the network as a whole (all the groups) can be characterized in terms of the boundedness and closure of its subpopulations. We can also examine variation across the groups in their degree of closure; each individual can be seen as more or less embedded in its group.

To assess whether a given E-I index value is significantly different than what would be expected by random mixing (i.e., no preference for within- or without-group ties by group members), a permutation test can be performed. A large number of trials are run in which the blocking of groups is maintained, and the overall density of ties is maintained, but the actual ties are randomly distributed. A sampling distribution of the numbers of internal and external ties under the assumption that ties are randomly distributed is calculated and used to assess the frequency with which the observed result would occur by sampling from a population in which ties were randomly distributed. Results for the blocked Knoke data are shown as Figure 24.9.

The observed block densities are presented first. Since any tie (in or out) is regarded as a tie, the densities in this example are quite high. The densities off the main diagonal (out-group ties) appear to be slightly more prevalent than the densities on the main diagonal (in-group ties).

Next, we see the numbers of internal ties (14, or 22 percent) and external ties (50, or 78 percent) that yield a raw (not rescaled) E-I index of +.563. That is, this graph displays a preponderance of external over internal ties. Also shown are the maximum possible numbers of internal and external ties given the group sizes and density. Note that, due to these constraints, the result of a

preponderance of external ties is not unexpected: under a random distribution, the E-I index would be expected to have a value of .467, which is not very much different from the observed value.

We see that, given the group sizes and density of the graph, the maximum possible value of the index (1.0) and its minimum value (+.25) are both positive. If we re-scale the observed value of the E-I index (.563) to fall into this range, we obtain a re-scaled index value of –.167. This suggests that, given the demographic constraints and overall density, there is a very modest tendency toward group closure.

The last portion of the results gives the values of the permutation-based sampling distribution. Most important here is the standard deviation of the sampling distribution of the index, or its standard error (.078). This suggests that the value of the raw index is expected to vary by this much from trial to trial (on the average) just by chance. Given this result, we can compare the observed value in our sample (.563) to the expected value (.467) relative to the standard error. The observed difference of about .10 could occur fairly frequently just by sampling variability ($p = .203$). Most analysts would not reject the null hypothesis that the deviation from randomness was not "significant." That is, we cannot be confident that the observed mild bias toward group closure is not random variation.

Substructures

One of the most common interests of structural analysts is in the "substructures" that may be present in a network. The dyads, triads, and ego-centered neighborhoods that we examined earlier can all be thought of as substructures. In this section, we'll consider some approaches to identifying larger groupings.

Many of the approaches to understanding the structure of a network emphasize how dense connections are built up from simpler dyads and triads to more extended dense clusters, such as "cliques." This view of social structure focuses attention on how solidarity and connection of large social structures can be built up out of small and tight components, a sort of "bottom up" approach. Network analysts have developed a number of useful definitions and algorithms that identify how larger structures are compounded from smaller ones: cliques, N-cliques, N-clans, K-plexes, and K-cores all look at networks this way.

We can also look for substructure from the "top down." Looking at the whole network, we can think of substructures as areas of the graph that

```
Density matrix

                1        2        3
                1        2        3
              _____    _____    _____
  1 1       0.667    1.000    0.667
  2 2       1.000    1.000    0.667
  3 3       0.667    0.667    0.333

64 ties.

Whole Network Results

                   1         2         3         4
                 Freq      Pct    Possib   Densit
               _____    _____   _____   _____
  1 Internal   14.000     0.219   24.000    0.583
  2 External   50.000     0.781   66.000    0.758
  3      E-I   36.000     0.563   42.000    0.467


Max possible external ties:  66.000
Max possible internal ties:  24.000

E-I Index:  0.563
Expected value for E-I index is:  0.467

Max possible E-I given density & group sizes:  1.000
Min possible E-I given density & group sizes:  0.250

Re-scaled E-I index:  -0.167


Permutation Test
Number of iterations = 5000

                   1        2        3        4        5         6         7
                 Obs      Min      Avg      Max      SD  P >= Ob  P <= Ob
               _____  _____  _____  _____  _____  _____  _____
  1 Internal    0.219    0.625    0.733    0.844    0.039    1.000    0.000
  2 External    0.781    0.156    0.267    0.375    0.039    0.000    1.000
  3      E-I    0.563    0.250    0.467    0.688    0.078    0.203    0.953
```

Figure 24.9   E-I index output for the Knoke information network

seem to be locally dense but are separated, to some degree, from the rest of the graph. This idea has been applied in a number of ways: components, blocks/cutpoints, K-cores, Lambda sets and bridges, factions, and f-groups will be discussed here. It is important to note (Moody and White, 2003), that bottom-up and top-down approaches to substructures in graphs often do not identify the same groupings. The choice of method should be informed by the researcher's definition of a meaningful substructure for the purposes of analysis.

The idea that some regions of a graph may be less connected to the whole than others may lead to insights into lines of cleavage and division. Weaker parts in the "social fabric" also create opportunities for brokerage and less

constrained action. So the numbers and sizes of regions, and their "connection topology" may be consequential for predicting both the opportunities and constraints facing groups and actors, as well as for predicting the evolution of the graph itself.

Most computer algorithms for locating substructures operate on binary symmetric data. We will use the Knoke information exchange data for most of the illustrations that follow. Where algorithms allow it, the directed form of the data will be used. Where symmetric data are called for, we will analyze "strong ties." That is, we will symmetrize the data by insisting that ties must be reciprocated in order to count (i.e., a tie only exists if xy and yx are both present). The reciprocity-symmetric data matrix and graph are shown in Figure 24.10.

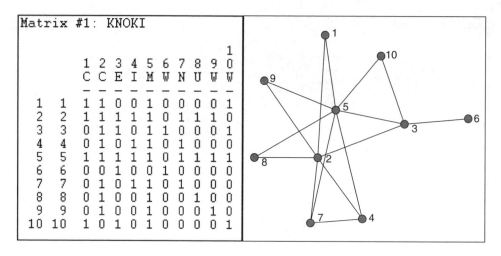

```
Matrix #1: KNOKI

                              1
          1 2 3 4 5 6 7 8 9 0
          C C E I M W N U W W
          - - - - - - - - - -
 1   1    1 1 0 0 1 0 0 0 0 1
 2   2    1 1 1 1 1 0 1 1 1 0
 3   3    0 1 1 0 1 1 0 0 0 1
 4   4    0 1 0 1 1 0 1 0 0 0
 5   5    1 1 1 1 1 0 1 1 1 1
 6   6    0 0 1 0 0 1 0 0 0 0
 7   7    0 1 0 1 1 0 1 0 0 0
 8   8    0 1 0 0 1 0 0 1 0 0
 9   9    0 1 0 0 1 0 0 0 1 0
10  10    1 0 1 0 1 0 0 0 0 1
```

Figure 24.10   Reciprocated relations in the Knoke information network

Bottom-up approaches: Clique, clan, plex, core, and f-group

In a sense, all networks are composed of groups (or subgraphs). When two actors have a tie, they form a "group." One approach to thinking about the group structure of a network begins with this most basic group and seeks to see how far this kind of close relationship can be extended. This is a useful way of thinking, because sometimes more complex social structures evolve, or emerge, from very simple ones.

Cliques are the (maximal) subgraphs of nodes that have all possible ties present among themselves. That is, a clique is the largest possible collection of nodes (more than two) in which all actors are directly connected to all others. Figure 24.11 shows part of the UCINET analysis of cliques in our symmetrized data.

There are seven maximally complete subgraphs present in these data. The largest one is composed of 4 of the 10 actors (2, 4, 5, and 7), and all of the other smaller cliques share some overlap with some part of the largest clique. The second panel shows how "adjacent" each actor (row) is to each clique (column). Actor 1, for example, is adjacent to two-thirds of the members of clique 5. There is a very high degree of common membership in these data.

We can look at the extent to which the cliques overlap with one another, as measured by the numbers of members in common, as in Figure 24.12.

A cluster analysis of the closeness of the cliques shows that cliques 6 and 7 are (a little) separate from the other cliques. That is, there is a tendency toward one larger "clique of cliques" and one smaller one.

N-cliques

The strict clique definition (maximally connected subgraph) may be too strong for many purposes. It insists that every member of a subgroup should have a direct tie with each and every other member. One alternative is to define an actor as a member of a clique if they are connected to every other member of the group at some distance greater than one. Usually, a path distance of two is used. This corresponds to being "a friend of a friend." This approach to defining substructures is called an N-clique, where *n* stands for the maximum length of paths to all other members (Figure 24.13).

The cliques that we saw before have been made more inclusive by the relaxed definition of group membership. The first N-clique includes everyone but actor 6. The second is more restricted, and includes 6 (WRO), along with two elements of the core. With larger and fewer subgroups, the mayor (5) no longer appears to be quite so critical. With the more relaxed definition, there is now an "inner circle" of actors that are members of both larger groupings. This can be seen in the co-membership matrix and by clustering.

In some cases, N-cliques can be found that have a property that is undesirable for many purposes: it is possible for members of N-cliques to be connected by actors who are not, themselves, members of the clique. For most sociological applications, this is quite troublesome. To overcome this problem, some analysts have suggested a related grouping, the N-clan. Members of the "clan" are all connected at a distance *n* (or less), and all intermediate actors must also be members of the clan.

The K-plex is an alternative way of relaxing the requirement for clique membership (where

```
7 cliques found.

    1:   COMM INDU MAYR NEWS
    2:   COMM EDUC MAYR
    3:   COUN COMM MAYR
    4:   COMM MAYR UWAY
    5:   COMM MAYR WELF
    6:   COUN MAYR WEST
    7:   EDUC MAYR WEST

Clique Proximities: Prop. of clique members adjacen

              1     2     3     4     5     6     7
            ----- ----- ----- ----- ----- ----- -----
  1  1     0.500 0.667 1.000 0.667 0.667 1.000 0.667
  2  2     1.000 1.000 1.000 1.000 1.000 0.667 0.667
  3  3     0.500 1.000 0.667 0.667 0.667 0.667 1.000
  4  4     1.000 0.667 0.667 0.667 0.667 0.333 0.333
  5  5     1.000 1.000 1.000 1.000 1.000 1.000 1.000
  6  6     0.000 0.333 0.000 0.000 0.000 0.000 0.333
  7  7     1.000 0.667 0.667 0.667 0.667 0.333 0.333
  8  8     0.500 0.667 0.667 1.000 0.667 0.333 0.333
  9  9     0.500 0.667 0.667 0.667 1.000 0.333 0.333
 10 10     0.250 0.667 0.667 0.333 0.333 1.000 1.000
```

Figure 24.11 Cliques in the reciprocity-symmetric Knoke information network

members form a maximally complete subgraph). It allows actors to be members of a clique if they have ties to all but k other members. For example, if A has ties with B and C, but not D; while both B and C have ties with D, all four actors could still be in a clique under the K-plex approach, as in Figure 24.14.

This approach says that a node is a member of a clique of size n if it has direct ties to $n–k$ members of that clique. In Figure 24.15, we have

allowed k to be equal to 2 but insisted that each K-plex should include at least four members.

The K-plex method of defining cliques tends to find "overlapping social circles" when compared to the maximal or N-clique method. The K-plex approach to defining substructures makes a good deal of sense for many problems. It requires that members of a group have ties to (most) other group members and that a tie by way of nonclique intermediaries (which are permissible in the

```
Clique-by-Clique Actor Co-membership matrix

       1 2 3 4 5 6 7
       - - - - - - -
  1    4 2 2 2 2 1 1
  2    2 3 2 2 2 1 2
  3    2 2 3 2 2 2 1
  4    2 2 2 3 2 1 1
  5    2 2 2 2 3 1 1
  6    1 1 2 1 1 3 2
  7    1 2 1 1 1 2 3

HIERARCHICAL CLUSTERING OF OVERLAP MATRIX

Level    1 2 3 4 5 6 7
-----    - - - - - - -
2.000    XXXXXXXXX XXX
1.072    XXXXXXXXXXXXX
```

Figure 24.12 Clique overlap in the reciprocity-symmetric Knoke information network

```
2 2-cliques found.

    1:   COUN COMM EDUC INDU MAYR NEWS UWAY WELF WEST
    2:   COMM EDUC MAYR WRO WEST


                                  1
             1 2 3 4 5 6 7 8 9 0
             C C E I M W N U W W
             - - - - - - - - - -
    1  1     1 1 1 1 1 0 1 1 1 1
    2  2     1 2 2 1 2 1 1 1 1 2
    3  3     1 2 2 1 2 1 1 1 1 2
    4  4     1 1 1 1 1 0 1 1 1 1
    5  5     1 2 2 1 2 1 1 1 1 2
    6  6     0 1 1 0 1 1 0 0 0 1
    7  7     1 1 1 1 1 0 1 1 1 1
    8  8     1 1 1 1 1 0 1 1 1 1
    9  9     1 1 1 1 1 0 1 1 1 1
   10 10     1 2 2 1 2 1 1 1 1 2

HIERARCHICAL CLUSTERING OF OVERLAP MATRIX

             C I N U W   M E C W
             O N E W E   W A D O E
             U D W A L   R Y U M S
             N U S Y F   O R C M T

                                  1
  Level     1 4 7 8 9 6 5 3 2 0
  -----     - - - - - - - - - -
  2.000     . . . . . . XXXXXXX
  1.000     XXXXXXXXX XXXXXXXXX
  0.833     XXXXXXXXXXXXXXXXXXX
```

Figure 24.13   N-cliques of reciprocity-symmetric Knoke information network (N = 2)

N-clique approach) does not qualify a node for membership. The picture of group structure that emerges from K-plex approaches can be rather different from that of N-clique analysis.

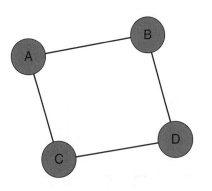

Figure 24.14   Illustration of a K-plex (K = 2)

K-cores are a variation on K-plexes that may be particularly helpful with larger numbers of actors. The K-core approach allows actors to join the group if they are connected to k members, regardless of how many other members they may not be connected to. The K-core definition is intuitively appealing for some applications. If an actor has ties to a sufficient number of members of a group, they may feel tied to that group even if they don't know many (or even most) members. It may be that identity depends on connection, rather than on immersion in a subgroup.

Top-down approaches: Component, cutpoint, block, and faction

The approaches we've examined to this point start with the dyad, and extend this kind of tight structure outward. Overall structure of the network is seen as "emerging" from overlaps and

```
15 k-plexes found.

    1:   COUN COMM EDUC MAYR WEST
    2:   COUN COMM INDU MAYR
    3:   COUN COMM MAYR NEWS
    4:   COUN COMM MAYR UWAY
    5:   COUN COMM MAYR WELF
    6:   COMM EDUC INDU MAYR
    7:   COMM EDUC MAYR NEWS
    8:   COMM EDUC MAYR UWAY
    9:   COMM EDUC MAYR WELF
   10:   COMM INDU MAYR NEWS
   11:   COMM INDU MAYR UWAY
   12:   COMM INDU MAYR WELF
   13:   COMM MAYR NEWS UWAY
   14:   COMM MAYR NEWS WELF
   15:   COMM MAYR UWAY WELF


           1  2  3  4  5  6  7  8  9 10
           CO CO ED IN MA WR NE UW WE WE
           -- -- -- -- -- -- -- -- -- --
    1  1    5  5  1  1  5  0  1  1  1  1
    2  2    5 15  5  5 15  0  5  5  5  1
    3  3    1  5  5  1  5  0  1  1  1  1
    4  4    1  5  1  5  5  0  1  1  1  0
    5  5    5 15  5  5 15  0  5  5  5  1
    6  6    0  0  0  0  0  0  0  0  0  0
    7  7    1  5  1  1  5  0  5  1  1  0
    8  8    1  5  1  1  5  0  1  5  1  0
    9  9    1  5  1  1  5  0  1  1  5  0
   10 10    1  1  1  0  1  0  0  0  0  1

HIERARCHICAL CLUSTERING OF OVERLAP MATRIX

              I E C M C N U W W
            W N D O A O E W E E
            R D U U Y M W A L S
            O U C N R M S Y F T

                              1
   Level    6 4 3 1 5 2 7 8 9 0
   ------   - - - - - - - - - -
   15.000   . . . . XXX . . . .
    5.000   . . . XXXXX . . . .
    4.000   . . XXXXXXX . . . .
    3.400   . XXXXXXXXX . . . .
    3.000   . XXXXXXXXXX . . .
    1.909   . XXXXXXXXXXXXX . .
    1.420   . XXXXXXXXXXXXXXX .
    0.082   . XXXXXXXXXXXXXXXXX
    0.000   XXXXXXXXXXXXXXXXXXX
```

Figure 24.15   K-plex groups in Knoke reciprocity-symmetric information network

couplings of smaller components. Alternatively, one might start with the entire network and identify "substructures" as parts that are locally denser or thinner than the field as a whole. Places where the social fabric is more thinly woven may define lines of division or cleavage in the network and can point to how it might be decomposed into smaller units. This top-down perspective leads us to think of dynamics that operate at the level of group selection and to focus on the constraints under which actors construct networks.

There are numerous ways that one might define the divisions and "weak spots" in a network. Below are some of the most common approaches.

Components of a graph are subgraphs that are connected within – but disconnected between – subgraphs. If a graph contains one or more "isolates," these actors are components. More interesting components are those that divide the network into separate parts with each having several actors. For directed graphs we can define two different kinds of components. A weak component is a set of nodes that is connected, regardless of the direction of ties. A strong component requires that there be a directed path from A to B in order for the two to be in the same component.

Because the Knoke information network has a single component, it isn't very interesting as an example. Let's look instead at the network of large donors to California political campaigns, where the strength of the relation between two actors is defined by the number of times that they contributed on the same side of an issue (Figure 24.16).

If we set a very high cut-off value of 13 issues in common to define membership in the same component, then our graph has only nonisolate components (made up of the Democratic Party and the School Employees union). Progressively lower cut-offs produce multiple, separate components until we reach a value of seven issues in common. At this point, the nonisolated nodes all become connected into a single component.

Blocks and cutpoints (bi-components) are an alternative approach to finding the key "weak" spots in the graph. If a node were removed, would the structure become divided into unconnected parts? If there are such nodes, they are called "cutpoints." One can imagine that such cutpoints may be particularly important actors. The divisions into which cutpoints divide a graph are called blocks (not the same usage of the term as in "blockmodels" or "block images"). Another name for a block is a "bi-component." We apply the bi-component idea to the Knoke data in Figure 24.17.

Two blocks are identified, with EDUC a member of both. This means that if EDUC (node 3) were removed, the WRO would become isolated.

Moody and White (2003) provide new algorithms for identifying nested cut-sets, and make a strong case for the close correspondence of their approach to graph substructure to the concept of "structural cohesion." Their approach identifies hierarchies of nested cohesive groups and is particularly sensitive to identifying the robustness of groups in the face of the removal of individual nodes, and the identification of K-components (maximal K-connected subgraphs).

Lambda sets and bridges are alternative approaches to the issue of connectivity. Here we ask if there are certain *connections* (rather than nodes) in the graph that, if removed, would result in a disconnected structure. In our example, the only relationship that qualifies is that between EDUC and WRO. The Lambda set approach ranks each of the relationships in the network in terms of importance by evaluating how much of the flow among actors in the net goes through each link. It then identifies sets of relationships, which, if disconnected, would most greatly disrupt the flow among all of the actors. The math and computation is rather extreme, though the idea is fairly simple. We apply this to our Knoke data in Figure 24.18.

This approach identifies the 2 to 5 (MAYR to COMM) linkage as the most important one in the graph: it carries a great deal of traffic, and the graph would be most disrupted if it were removed.

M. E. J. Newman (2006) has advanced the closely related idea of "modularity" as an approach to identifying substructures in graphs. In Newman's approach, substructures are defined by having more ties within, and fewer ties between, groups than would be expected on the basis of the degrees of the nodes. This is an important advance on earlier approaches, which seek to minimize the number of bridging ties between groups but do not take account of group size or node degree.

Factions: Imagine a society in which each person was closely tied to all others in their own subpopulation (i.e., all subpopulations are cliques), and there are no connections at all between subpopulations (i.e., each subpopulation is a component). Most real populations do not look like this, but the "ideal type" of complete connection within and complete disconnection between subgroups is a useful reference point for assessing the degree of "factionalization" in a population.

If we took all the members of each "faction" in this ideal-typical society and put their rows and columns together in an adjacency matrix (i.e., permuted the matrix so all members of the same group occupied adjacent rows and columns), we would see a distinctive pattern of "1-blocks" and "0-blocks." All connections among actors within a faction would be present; all connections between actors in different factions would be absent. With valued data, the average tie strength within a block would be high; the average tie strength between blocks would be low.

We applied this idea to the Knoke data. After running several alternative numbers of blocks, we settled on four as meaningful for our purposes. This result is shown in Figure 24.19.

The "final number of errors" can be used as a measure of the "goodness of fit" of the "blocking"

```
HIERARCHICAL COMPONENTS

                    F
                    E
                    D                   S                   G
                    E                   T                   R
                    R                   A                   A
                    A           S       T       B           N
                    T   S D E   E       E       U           I
                    I   C E R           E       I H         T
            P       O   H M V   E       M R D W E   J D     S
            I T N   O O I   E   D W     I     O O   T E
            E E _ O C C     P E I L     C     H O   E P
    P R A O L R E   L E N E O   D G T   N A   H T
    A R C F _ A _   O D G T     S O   N A   H T
    M E H _ E T E   Y _ _ T     T B   _ L E E I
    _ _ E T M I M   E H I _     _ _ I   T D L N M
    O O R E P C P   E A N P C R         I
    M M S A L _ L A S S D A H U R   W F _ I D
    I I _ C O P O F _ T _ C E C E I A I B _ R
    D D A H Y A Y S A I A K V T I N L S R B A
    Y Y S E E R E C S N S A R I N T T H O I P
    A A S R E T E M S G S R O O E E O E A N E
    R R N S S Y S E N S N D N N R L N R D G R

                5 3 2 2 7 5 1 4 9 7 9 4 7 2 5 9 2
Value       1 2 3 5 7 3 9 4 3 9 7 6 8 9 3 6 1 8 0 6 4
--------    - - - - - - - - - - - - - - - - - - - - -
13.000      . . . . . XXX . . . . . . . . . . . . . . .
12.000      . . XXX XXX . . . . . . . . . . . . . . . .
11.000      . . XXX XXX . . . . XXX . . . . . . . . . . .
10.000      . . XXXXXXXXXXX . . . XXX . . . . . . . . . .
 9.000      . . XXXXXXXXXXXXX . XXXXX . . . . . . . . . .
 8.000      . . XXXXXXXXXXXXX XXXXXXXXX . . . . . . . . .
 7.000      . . XXXXXXXXXXXXXXXXXXXXXXXXXXXXX . . . . . .
 6.000      . . XXXXXXXXXXXXXXXXXXXXXXXXXXXXXXXXXX . . .
 5.000      . . XXXXXXXXXXXXXXXXXXXXXXXXXXXXXXXXXXXXX .
 4.000      . . XXXXXXXXXXXXXXXXXXXXXXXXXXXXXXXXXXXXXXXX
 3.000      . . XXXXXXXXXXXXXXXXXXXXXXXXXXXXXXXXXXXXXXXX
 2.000      . . XXXXXXXXXXXXXXXXXXXXXXXXXXXXXXXXXXXXXXXX
 1.000      XXXXXXXXXXXXXXXXXXXXXXXXXXXXXXXXXXXXXXXXXXXX
 0.000      XXXXXXXXXXXXXXXXXXXXXXXXXXXXXXXXXXXXXXXXXXXX
-1.000      XXXXXXXXXXXXXXXXXXXXXXXXXXXXXXXXXXXXXXXXXXXX
-2.000      XXXXXXXXXXXXXXXXXXXXXXXXXXXXXXXXXXXXXXXXXXXX
```

Figure 24.16 Weak component hierarchy for California political donors

of the matrix. This count (27) is the sum of the number of zeros within factions (where all the ties are supposed to be present in the ideal type) plus the number of ones in the nondiagonal blocks (ties between members of different factions, which are supposed to be absent in the ideal type). Since there are 49 total ties in our data, being wrong 27 times is not a terribly good fit. It is, however, the best we can do with four "factions." The four

factions are identified, and we note that two of them are individuals (10, 9), and one is a dyad (3, 6).

The "blocked" or "grouped" adjacency matrix shows a picture of the solution. We can see that there is quite a lot of density "off the main diagonal" where there shouldn't be any. The final panel of the results reports the "block densities" as the number of ties that are present in blocks as proportions of all possible ties.

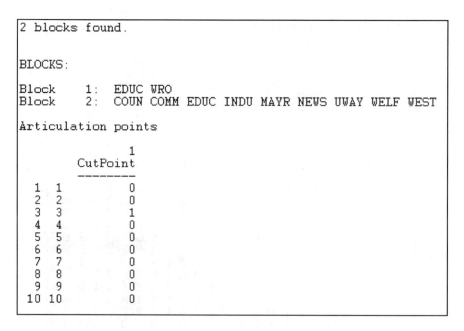

```
2 blocks found.

BLOCKS:

Block     1:   EDUC WRO
Block     2:   COUN COMM EDUC INDU MAYR NEWS UWAY WELF WEST

Articulation points

                       1
            CutPoint
            ---------
    1   1         0
    2   2         0
    3   3         1
    4   4         0
    5   5         0
    6   6         0
    7   7         0
    8   8         0
    9   9         0
   10  10         0
```

Figure 24.17   Cutpoints and blocks in the Knoke information network

Core-periphery and other blockmodels extend the idea of factions to identify groups or "types" (or, technically, equivalence classes) of cases based on their patterns of ties (Boyd et al., 2006; Clark, 2008; Raval and Kral, 2004). Patterns of core and periphery are often found in sociological data; in this blockmodel, there are many ties among members of the core, few ties among members of the periphery, and some ties (definitions vary) between core and periphery members. Grouping cases into types based on similarity of their positions or roles in the graph has proven to be one of the most important approaches to identifying substructures in social structures. Ferligoj et al. (this volume) cover this topic in depth.

```
LAMBDA SETS

HIERARCHICAL LAMBDA SET PARTITIONS

          U W C E I M C N W
          W W E O D N A O E E
          R A L U U D Y M W S
          O Y F N C U R M S T

                                    1
Lambda    6 8 9 1 3 4 5 2 7 0
------    - - - - - - - - - -
    7     . . . . . . XXX . .
    3     . . . XXXXXXXXXXXXX
    2     . XXXXXXXXXXXXXXXXX
    1     XXXXXXXXXXXXXXXXXXX
```

Figure 24.18   Lambda sets in the Knoke information network

THE "EMBEDDED" INDIVIDUAL: EGO NETWORKS

The approaches to exploring networks that we've examined so far tend to be views from the "top down." That is, they focus attention on the whole network's structure, texture, and substructures. For many problems, it can be useful to view social networks from the "bottom up," focusing attention on individuals and their connections. Describing and indexing the variation across individuals in the way they are embedded in "local" social structures is the goal of the analysis of *ego networks*. We need some definitions.

"Ego" is an individual "focal" node. A complete network has as many egos as it has nodes. However, our data may also consist of one or many ego networks that are not connected to one another. Egos can be persons, groups, organizations, or whole societies.

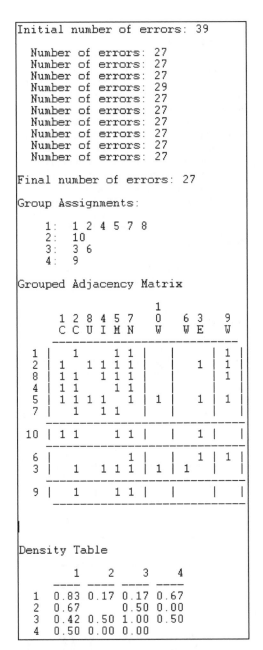

Figure 24.19   Four-faction solution for the directed Knoke information network

A one-step neighborhood consists of ego and all nodes to whom ego has a direct connection. Importantly, the neighborhood also includes all of the ties among all of the actors to whom ego has a connection. Neighborhoods of greater path length than one are rarely used in social network analysis. When we use the term "neighborhood" here, we mean the one-step neighborhood. The N-step neighborhood expands the definition of the size of ego's neighborhood by including all nodes to whom ego has a connection at a path length of N or less, and all the connections among all of these actors.

In and out, and other kinds of neighborhoods

Most of the analyses of ego networks use simple graphs (i.e., graphs that are symmetric and show only the presence or absence of connections, but not their direction). If we are working with a directed graph, it is possible to define different kinds of ego-neighborhoods. An *out neighborhood* would include all the actors to whom ties are directed *from* ego. An *in neighborhood* would include all the actors who send ties directly to ego. It is also possible to define a neighborhood of only those actors with whom ego has reciprocated ties. These are just a few of the ways of defining ego neighborhoods; there isn't a single "right" way for every research question.

Strong and weak tie neighborhoods

Most analyses of ego networks use binary data (actors are connected or they aren't), which makes defining the ego neighborhood fairly straightforward. If we have measured the strength of the relation between two actors or its valence (positive or negative), however, we need to make choices about the definition of "neighbor." With ties that are measured as strengths or probabilities, a reasonable approach is to define a cut-off value (or, better, explore several reasonable alternatives). When ties are characterized as positive or negative, the most common approach is to analyze the positive tie neighborhood and the negative tie neighborhood separately.

Ego network data commonly arise in two ways: surveys may be used to collect information on ego networks. We can ask each research subject to identify all of the actors to whom they have a connection, and to report to us (as an informant) the links among these other actors. Alternatively, we could use a snowball method: first ask ego to identify others to whom ego has a tie, then ask each of those identified about their ties to additional others. With each stage, the size of the network increases, until all members of the component originally sampled have been included.

Data collected in this way cannot directly inform us about the overall embeddedness of the networks in a population, but it can tell us about the prevalence of various kinds of ego networks in even very large populations. This kind of investigation results in a data structure that is composed of a collection of networks. As the actors in each network are likely to be different, the networks need to be treated as separate actor-by-actor matrices stored as different data sets.

The second major way in which ego network data arise is by "extracting" them from regular complete network data. This is the approach that we will take in our example. Rather than treating the Knoke information exchange network as a single network, we will treat it at 10 ego networks (which happen to be connected and overlapping). One might, for example, extract all the ego networks from a full network where ego was male and compare their structures to all the ego networks where ego was female. When you create a sample of ego networks by extracting them from a single full network, you need to remember that these are not independent samples from a population, and normal statistical sampling assumptions don't apply.

Connections

There are quite a few characteristics of the ego-neighborhoods that may be of interest. Figure 24.20 displays a collection of many of the most commonly used measures of the texture of ego's neighborhood. In this example, we are looking at the one-step out neighborhood of each of the 10 egos in the Knoke information

exchange data. That is, each ego's neighborhood is defined by those actors to whom ego sends information. A parallel analysis of in neighborhoods might also be of interest.

Some measures of the structure of ego networks are parallel to those for complete networks. Many others, though, reflect the particular interests of "bottom-up" analysis, and describe ego's opportunities and constraints due to how they are embedded in their local structure of connections.

The size of an ego network is the number of nodes that are one-step neighbors of ego, plus ego itself. Actor 5 has the largest ego network; actors 6, 7, and 9 have the smallest networks. The number of directed ties is the number of connections among all the nodes in the ego network. Among the four actors in ego 1's network, there are 11 ties. The number of ordered pairs is the number of possible directed ties in each ego network. In node 1's network there are four actors, so there are 4*3 possible directed ties. The density is the number of actual ties divided by the number of pairs (i.e., possible ties). Note that actors 7 and 9 live in neighborhoods where all actors send information to all other actors; they are embedded in very dense local structures. The welfare rights organization (node 6) lives in a small world where the members are not tightly connected. This kind of difference in the constraints and opportunities facing actors in their local neighborhoods may be very consequential, as we shall see in examining "structural holes" below.

The average geodesic distance is the mean of the shortest path lengths among all connected pairs in the ego network. Where everyone is directly connected to everyone (e.g., nodes 7 and 9), this

```
Density Measures

        1      2      3      4      5      6      7      8      9     10     11     12     13     14
     Size   Ties  Pairs Densit AvgDis Diamet nWeakC pWeakC 2StepR ReachE Broker nBroke EgoBet nEgoBe
     -----  -----  -----  -----  -----  -----  -----  -----  -----  -----  -----  -----  -----  -----
 1    4.00  11.00  12.00  91.67   1.08   2.00   1.00  25.00 100.00  29.03   0.50   0.04   0.00   0.00
 2    7.00  24.00  42.00  57.14   1.43   2.00   1.00  14.29 100.00  18.75   9.00   0.21   8.17  19.44
 3    6.00  17.00  30.00  56.67                 1.00  16.67 100.00  23.08   6.50   0.22   8.25  27.50
 4    4.00  11.00  12.00  91.67   1.08   2.00   1.00  25.00 100.00  28.13   0.50   0.04   0.33   2.78
 5    8.00  29.00  56.00  51.79   1.57   3.00   1.00  12.50 100.00  16.98  13.50   0.24  14.67  26.19
 6    3.00   2.00   6.00  33.33                 1.00  33.33 100.00  42.86   2.00   0.33   1.00  16.67
 7    3.00   6.00   6.00 100.00   1.00   1.00   1.00  33.33  88.89  36.36   0.00   0.00   0.00   0.00
 8    6.00  24.00  30.00  80.00   1.20   2.00   1.00  16.67 100.00  20.45   3.00   0.10   0.00   0.00
 9    3.00   6.00   6.00 100.00   1.00   1.00   1.00  33.33 100.00  36.00   0.00   0.00   0.00   0.00
10    5.00  16.00  20.00  80.00   1.20   2.00   1.00  20.00 100.00  23.68   2.00   0.10   0.33   1.67

 1.  Size. Size of ego network.
 2.  Ties. Number of directed ties.
 3.  Pairs. Number of ordered pairs.
 4.  Density. Ties divided by Pairs.
 5.  AvgDist. Average geodesic distance.
 6.  Diameter. Longest distance in egonet.
 7.  nWeakComp. Number of weak components.
 8.  pWeakComp. NWeakComp divided by Size.
 9.  2StepReach. # of nodes within 2 links of ego.
10.  ReachEffic. 2StepReach divided Size.
11.  Broker. # of pairs not directly connected.
12.  Normalized Broker. Broker divided by number of pairs.
13.  Ego Betweenness. Betweenness of ego in own network.
14.  Normalized Ego Betweenness. Betweenness of ego in own network.
```

Figure 24.20 Ego network connections for Knoke information out neighborhoods

distance is one. In our example, the largest average path length for connected neighbors is for actor 5 (average distances among members of the neighborhood is 1.57). The diameter of an ego network is the length of the longest path between connected actors (just as it is for any network). The idea of a network diameter is to index the span or extensiveness of the network: how far apart are the two furthest actors? In the current example, they are not very far apart in the ego networks of most actors.

The size, density, and distances in an ego neighborhood are very much parallel to the same ideas for whole networks. In addition to these fairly basic and reasonably straightforward measures, ego network analysts have developed a number of approaches to understanding the role that ego plays in connecting the neighborhood and to understanding ego's positional advantage and disadvantage.

One interesting feature is the extent to which ego's neighborhood consists of separate components of factions. To what extent does ego play a critical role in connecting others? A weak component is the largest number of actors who are connected, disregarding the direction of the ties (a strong component pays attention to the direction of the ties for directed data). In Figure 24.21, if ego (E) was connected to A and B (who are connected to one another), and ego is connected to C and D (who are connected to one another), but A and B are not connected in any way to C and D (except by way of everyone being connected to ego) then there would be two "weak components" in ego's neighborhood.

In our example, there are no such cases – each ego is embedded in a single component neighborhood. That is, there are no cases where ego is the only connection between otherwise disjointed sets of actors. The likelihood that there would be more than one weak component in ego's neighborhood would be a function of neighborhood size if connections were random. So, to get a sense of whether ego's role in connecting components is

"unexpected" given the size of the network, it is useful to normalize the count of components by size. In our example, since there are no cases of multiple components, this is a pretty meaningless exercise.

The two-step reach goes beyond ego's one-step neighborhood to report the percentage of all actors in the whole network that are within two directed steps of ego. In our example, only node 7 cannot get a message to all other actors within "friend-of-a-friend" distance. The reach efficiency (two-step reach divided by size) norms the two-step reach by dividing it by size. The idea here is, how much (nonredundant) secondary contact do I get for each unit of primary contact? If reach efficiency is high, then I am getting a lot of "bang for my buck" in reaching a wider network for each unit of effort invested in maintaining a primary contact. On the other hand, if I share many contacts with my neighbors, I have low efficiency.

Ego may be the "go-between" for pairs of other actors. In an ego network, ego is connected to every other actor (by definition). If these others are not connected directly to one another, ego may be a "broker" if ego falls on the paths between the others. One item of interest is simply how much potential for brokerage there is for each actor (how many times pairs of neighbors in ego's network are not directly connected). In our example, actor 5, who is connected to almost everyone, is in a position to broker many connections. Normalized brokerage (brokerage divided by number of pairs) assesses the extent to which ego's role is that of a broker. One can be in a brokering position a number of times, but this is a small percentage of the total possible connections in a network (e.g., the network is large). Given the large size of actor 5's network, the relative frequency with which actor 5 plays the broker role is not so exceptional.

Betweenness is an aspect of the larger concept of "centrality." In an ego network, ego is "between" two other actors if ego lies on the shortest directed path from one to the other. The ego betweenness measure indexes the percentage of all geodesic paths from neighbor to neighbor that pass through ego. Normalized betweenness compares the actual betweenness of ego to the maximum possible betweenness in neighborhood of the size and connectivity of ego's. The "maximum" value for betweenness would be achieved where ego is the center of a "star" network; that is, no neighbors communicate directly with one another, and all directed communications between pairs of neighbors go through ego.

The ideas of brokerage and betweenness are slightly differing ways of indexing just how central or powerful ego is within its own neighborhood. This aspect of how an actor's embedding

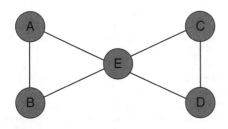

Figure 24.21 Illustration of a graph with two weak components in the neighborhood of actor E

may provide it with strategic advantage has received a great deal of attention. The next two sections, on structural holes and brokerage elaborate on ways of looking at positional opportunity and constraint of individual actors.

Structural holes

Ronald Burt (1992) coined and popularized the term "structural holes" to refer to some very important aspects of positional advantage and disadvantage of individuals that result from how they are embedded in neighborhoods. Burt's formalization of these ideas, and his development of a number of measures (including the computer program *Structure*, which provides these measures and other tools), has facilitated a great deal of further thinking about how and why the ways that an actor is connected affect their constraints and opportunities, and hence their behavior.

The basic idea is simple, as good ideas often are. Imagine a network of three actors (A, B, and C), in which each is connected to each of the others. Suppose that actor A wanted to influence or exchange with another actor. Assume that both B and C may have some interest in interacting or exchanging, as well. Actor A will not be in a strong bargaining position in this network, because both of A's potential exchange partners (B and C) have alternatives to treating with A; they could isolate A and then exchange only with one another.

Now imagine that we open a "structural hole" between actors B and C. That is, a relation or tie is "absent" such that B and C cannot exchange (perhaps they are not aware of one another, or there are very high transaction costs involved in forming a tie). In this situation, actor A has an advantaged position because he or she has two alternative exchange partners; actors B and C have only one choice, if they choose to (or must) enter into an exchange. Ego A now has power with respect to two dependent alters and is not constrained by the threat of being excluded from an exchange opportunity.

Burt developed a number of measures related to structural holes that can be computed on both valued and binary data. The normal practice in sociological research has been to use binary (a relation is present or not). Interpretation of the measures becomes quite difficult with valued data. The structural holes measures may be computed for either directed or undirected data – and the interpretation, of course, depends on which is used. Here, we've used the directed binary data. Figure 24.22 shows UCINET output for a "structural holes" analysis of the neighborhoods of each of our 10 egos.

Dyadic redundancy means that ego's tie to an alter is "redundant." If A is tied to both B and C, and B is tied to C, A's tie to B is redundant, because A can influence B by way of C. The dyadic redundancy measure calculates, for each actor in ego's neighborhood, how many of the other actors in the neighborhood are also tied to a given alter. The larger the proportion of others in the neighborhood who are tied to a given "alter," the more "redundant" is ego's direct tie. In the example, we see that actor 1's (COUN) tie to actor 2 (COMM) is largely redundant, as 72% of ego's other neighbors also have ties with COMM. Actors that display high dyadic redundancy are actors who are embedded in local neighborhoods where there are few structural holes.

Dyadic constraint is a measure that indexes the extent to which the relationship between ego and each alter in ego's neighborhood "constrains" ego. A full description is given in Burt's 1992 monograph, and the construction of the measure is somewhat complex. At the core though, A is constrained by its relationship with B to the extent that A does not have many alternatives (has few other ties except that to B), and A's other alternatives are also tied to B. If A has few alternatives to exchanging with B, and if those alternative exchange partners are also tied to B, then B is likely to constrain A's behavior. In our example, constraint measures are not very large, as most actors have several ties. COMM and MAYR are, however, exerting constraint over a number of others and are not very constrained by them. This situation arises because COMM and MAYR have considerable numbers of ties, and many of the actors to whom they are tied do not have many independent sources of information.

The effective size of the network (EffSize) is the number of alters that ego has, minus the average number of ties that each alter has to other alters. Suppose that A has ties to three other actors. Suppose that none of these three has ties to any of the others. The effective size of ego's network is three. Alternatively, suppose that A has ties to three others and that all of the others are tied to one another. A's network size is three, but the ties are "redundant" because A can reach all three neighbors by reaching any one of them. The average degree of the others in this case is two (each alter is tied to two other alters). So, the effective size of the network is its actual size (three), reduced by its redundancy (two), to yield an efficient size of one.

The efficiency (Efficie) norms the effective size of ego's network by its actual size; that is, it measures the proportion of ego's ties to its neighborhood that are "nonredundant." The effective size of ego's network may tell us something about ego's total impact; efficiency tells us how much

```
Dyadic redundancy

           1     2     3     4     5     6     7     8     9    10
         COUN  COMM  EDUC  INDU  MAYR  WRO  NEWS  UWAY  WELF  WEST
         ----  ----  ----  ----  ----  ----  ----  ----  ----  ----
   1     0.00  0.72  0.00  0.61  0.78  0.00  0.72  0.61  0.56  0.39
   2     0.43  0.00  0.33  0.47  0.87  0.00  0.57  0.40  0.33  0.40
   3     0.00  0.50  0.00  0.50  0.60  0.05  0.70  0.00  0.00  0.35
   4     0.61  0.78  0.56  0.00  0.78  0.00  0.61  0.61  0.00  0.00
   5     0.44  0.81  0.38  0.44  0.00  0.00  0.56  0.38  0.31  0.31
   6     0.00  0.00  0.13  0.00  0.00  0.00  0.38  0.00  0.13  0.00
   7     0.54  0.71  0.58  0.46  0.75  0.13  0.00  0.50  0.46  0.38
   8     0.69  0.75  0.00  0.69  0.75  0.00  0.75  0.00  0.63  0.00
   9     0.63  0.63  0.00  0.00  0.63  0.06  0.69  0.63  0.00  0.00
  10     0.50  0.86  0.50  0.00  0.71  0.00  0.64  0.00  0.00  0.00


Dyadic Constraint

           1     2     3     4     5     6     7     8     9    10
         COUN  COMM  EDUC  INDU  MAYR  WRO  NEWS  UWAY  WELF  WEST
         ----  ----  ----  ----  ----  ----  ----  ----  ----  ----
   1     0.00  0.13  0.00  0.04  0.15  0.00  0.06  0.04  0.04  0.03
   2     0.05  0.00  0.04  0.05  0.11  0.00  0.06  0.04  0.04  0.02
   3     0.00  0.09  0.00  0.03  0.10  0.04  0.06  0.00  0.00  0.06
   4     0.04  0.13  0.03  0.00  0.13  0.00  0.10  0.04  0.00  0.00
   5     0.05  0.09  0.04  0.04  0.00  0.00  0.06  0.04  0.03  0.03
   6     0.00  0.00  0.27  0.00  0.00  0.00  0.11  0.00  0.07  0.00
   7     0.03  0.10  0.04  0.06  0.11  0.01  0.00  0.03  0.03  0.02
   8     0.05  0.15  0.00  0.05  0.15  0.00  0.06  0.00  0.05  0.00
   9     0.05  0.13  0.00  0.00  0.13  0.02  0.06  0.05  0.00  0.00
  10     0.04  0.08  0.12  0.00  0.17  0.00  0.06  0.00  0.00  0.00


Structural Hole Measures

             1        2        3        4
         EffSize  Efficie  Constra  Hierarc
         -------  -------  -------  -------
   1      2.611    0.373    0.481    0.103
   2      4.200    0.525    0.401    0.052
   3      3.300    0.550    0.386    0.044
   4      2.056    0.343    0.479    0.082
   5      4.375    0.547    0.387    0.032
   6      2.375    0.792    0.454    0.139
   7      4.500    0.500    0.424    0.097
   8      1.750    0.292    0.514    0.079
   9      2.750    0.458    0.436    0.101
  10      1.786    0.357    0.486    0.072
```

Figure 24.22   Structural holes analysis for Knoke information exchange ego networks

impact ego is getting for each unit invested in using ties. An actor can be effective without being efficient, and an actor can be efficient without being effective.

The constraint (Constra) is a summary measure of the extent to which ego's connections are to others who are connected to one another. If ego's potential trading partners all have one another as potential trading partners, ego is highly constrained. If ego's partners do not have other alternatives in the neighborhood, they cannot constrain ego's behavior. The logic is pretty simple, but the measure itself is not (see Burt's 1992 book). The idea of constraint is an important one because it points out that actors who have many ties to others may actually lose freedom of action rather than gain it, depending on the relationships among the other actors. This is the same basic insight as Bonacich's analysis of the difference between influence and power.

The hierarchy is another quite complex measure that describes the nature of the constraint on ego. If the total constraint on ego is concentrated in a single other actor, the hierarchy measure will have a higher value; if the constraint arises from multiple actors in ego's neighborhood, hierarchy will have a lower value. The hierarchy measure does not assess the degree of constraint directly but, given some level of constraint on ego, it measures an important property of dependency: inequality in the distribution of constraints on ego across the alters in its neighborhood.

Brokerage among groups

The extent to which ego is "between" alters is the focus of brokerage, betweenness, and structural holes analyses; it is a major theme in the analysis of ego networks. Gould and Fernandez (1989) extended these ideas in an interesting way by taking into account the possibility that egos and alters might also be affiliated with social groups.

Suppose that ego's network is composed of both men and women (or any qualitative difference). We might be interested in the extent to which ego is "between" men and women in the network, rather than simply whether ego has high betweenness, overall. Gould and Fernandez's "brokerage" notions examine ego's relations with its neighborhood from the perspective of ego acting as an agent in relations among groups (or categories).

To examine the brokerage roles played by a given actor, we find every instance where that actor lies on the directed path between two others. So each actor may have many opportunities to act as a "broker." For each one of the instances where ego is a broker, we examine which *kinds* of actors are involved. That is, what are the group memberships of each of the three actors? There are five possible combinations.

If ego falls on a directed path between two members of the same category as themselves (e.g., a woman falling between two other women in a path), ego is called a coordinator. If ego falls on the path between two members of a group of which they are not a part (e.g., a man falling on a path from one woman to another), the members are called consultants. If ego falls on the path from a member of another group to a member of its own group (e.g., ego, a man, falls on a path from a woman to another man), the ego is called a gatekeeper. If ego falls on the path from another member of its own group to a member of another group, ego is a representative. Lastly, if ego falls on a path from a member of one group to another but is not a member of either of those groups, ego is a liaison.

As an example, we've taken the Knoke information exchange network and have classified each of the organizations as either a general government organization (group 1), a private nonwelfare organization (group 2), or an organizational specialist (group 3).

Figure 24.23 shows the results of a basic analysis of brokerage roles for each of the 10 egos in the Knoke directed information network.

The actors have been grouped together into "partitions" for presentation; actors 1, 3, and 5, for example, are the general government organizations group. Each row counts the raw number of times that each actor plays each of the five roles in the whole graph. While we have analyzed the entire graph here, the analysis could be restricted to the one-step neighborhood of each ego. Two actors (5 and 2) are the main sources of interconnection among the three organizational populations. Organizations in the third population (6, 8, 9, 10), the welfare specialists, have overall low

	1 Coordinat	2 Gatekeepe	3 Represent	4 Consultan	5 Liaison	6 Total
1	0	0	0	1	1	2
3	0	1	1	2	5	9
5	2	6	5	5	9	27
2	0	3	7	5	6	21
4	0	0	1	1	0	2
7	0	5	0	0	1	6
6	0	1	0	0	0	1
8	0	0	0	0	0	0
9	0	0	2	0	0	2
10	0	0	0	1	0	1

Figure 24.23 Brokerage role scores for the Knoke information network

rates of brokerage. Organizations in the first population (1, 3, 5), the government organizations, seem to be more heavily involved as liaisons than as other roles. Organizations in the second population (2, 4, 7), nongovernmental generalists, play more diverse roles. Overall, there is very little coordination within each of the populations.

Centrality

Network analysts often describe the way that an actor is embedded in a relational network as imposing constraints on the actor and as offering the actor opportunities (Granovetter, 1982). Actors that face fewer constraints, and have more opportunities than others, are in favorable structural positions. Having a favored position means that an actor may extract better bargains in exchanges, have greater influence, and may be a focus for deference and attention from those in less favored positions.

The question of what we mean by having a "favored position," "more opportunities," or "fewer constraints" has no single correct and final answer. As we have seen above, having structural holes in one's neighborhood may confer advantage; being in a position to act as a broker between substructures may also provide a structurally favorable position.

The most widely used approach to understanding the structural sources of individuals' advantage and disadvantage relative to their neighbors is that of "centrality." The core idea is very simple: actors who are more "central" to social structures are more likely to be influential or powerful (but possibly also more constrained). But the simple idea of being central turns out to not be so simple. Consider the situation of actor A in the three simple networks in Figure 24.24.

A moment's inspection suggests that actor A has a highly favored structural position in the star network (upper right). The star network shows a neighborhood of maximum inequality: A is central, and everyone else is equally peripheral. In the circle network (upper left), all actors in the neighborhood are in equivalent positions, and A is no more or less central than anyone else. In the line network at bottom, A would seem to be marginalized, and the overall distribution of advantage in the neighborhood is between the two extremes of the star and circle.

But what are the sources of the advantage or disadvantage of the egos in the figures above? The centrality of an ego relative to its alters has been approached in three major ways by network analysts. One approach focuses on the actor's degree. Actors who have more ties, that is, a higher degree (or ties to the "right" others), may be advantaged. Degree-based approaches to centrality are closely connected to the notion of "social capital." A second approach, based on closeness, argues that egos who can "reach" more alters with less effort have an advantaged position. A third major approach suggests that egos who bridge gaps *between* alters have an advantage.

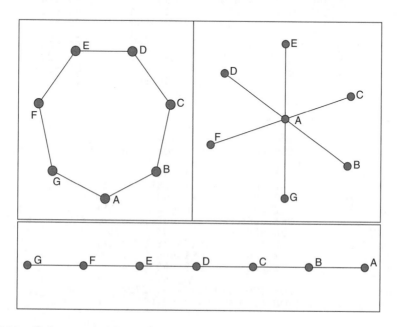

Figure 24.24   Circle, star, and line networks

Degree centrality: Connectedness

In undirected data, egos differ from one another only in how many connections they have. With directed data, however, it can be important to distinguish centrality based on in-degree from centrality based on out-degree. If an actor receives many ties, they are often said to be prominent, or to have high prestige. That is, many other actors seek direct ties to them, and this may indicate their importance. Actors who have unusually high out-degrees are actors who are able to exchange with many others or to make many others aware of their views. Actors who display high out-degree centrality are often said to be influential actors.

Linton Freeman (1979) developed basic measures of the centrality of actors based on their degree. Figure 24.25 shows the out-degree and in-degree centrality of each of the egos in the Knoke information network.

Actors 5 and 2 have the greatest out-degrees and might be regarded as the most influential (though it might matter to whom they are sending information; this measure does not take that into account). Actors 5 and 2 are joined by 7 (the newspaper) when we examine in-degree.

Other organizations might share information with these three in an effort to exert influence. This could be seen as an act of deference, or a recognition that the positions of actors 5, 2, and 7 might be worth trying to influence. If we were interested in comparing influence in networks of different sizes or densities, it might be useful to "standardize" the measures of in- and out-degrees. In the last two columns of the first panel, all the degree counts have been expressed as percentages of the number of actors in the network, less one (ego).

If we are analyzing the egos in a complete network (as we are here) instead of separate ego neighborhoods (as we would if we had collected information about the ego network of a sample of individuals from some population) we can also examine the distribution of ego centralities to learn more about the population as a whole. In Figure 24.22, we see that, on average, actors have a degree of 4.9, which is quite high given that there are only nine other actors. The range of in-degree is slightly larger (minimum and maximum) than that of out-degree, and there is more variability across the actors in in-degree than out-degree (based on their standard deviations and variances).

	1 OutDegree	2 InDegree	3 NrmOutDeg	4 NrmInDeg
1	4.000	5.000	44.444	55.556
2	7.000	8.000	77.778	88.889
3	6.000	4.000	66.667	44.444
4	4.000	5.000	44.444	55.556
5	8.000	8.000	88.889	88.889
6	3.000	1.000	33.333	11.111
7	3.000	9.000	33.333	100.000
8	6.000	2.000	66.667	22.222
9	3.000	5.000	33.333	55.556
10	5.000	2.000	55.556	22.222

DESCRIPTIVE STATISTICS

		1 OutDegree	2 InDegree	3 NrmOutDeg	4 NrmInDeg
1	Mean	4.900	4.900	54.444	54.444
2	Std Dev	1.700	2.625	18.889	29.165
3	Sum	49.000	49.000	544.444	544.444
4	Variance	2.890	6.890	356.790	850.617
5	SSQ	269.000	309.000	33209.875	38148.148
6	MCSSQ	28.900	68.900	3567.901	8506.173
7	Euc Norm	16.401	17.578	182.236	195.316
8	Minimum	3.000	1.000	33.333	11.111
9	Maximum	8.000	9.000	88.889	100.000

Network Centralization (Outdegree) = 38.272%
Network Centralization (Indegree) = 50.617%

Figure 24.25 Degree centrality of egos in the Knoke information network

The range and variability of degree (and other network properties) can be quite important, because they describe whether the population is homogeneous or heterogeneous in structural positions. Finally, Freeman's graph centralization measures describe the population as a whole, the macro level. The graph centralization measure expresses the degree of inequality or variance in our network as a percentage of that of a perfect star network of the same size. In the current case, the out-degree graph centralization is 51% and the in-degree graph centralization is 38% of these theoretical maximums. We would arrive at the conclusion that there is a substantial amount of concentration or centralization in this whole network. That is, the power of individual actors varies rather substantially, and this means that, overall, positional advantages are rather unequally distributed in this network.

Degree centrality: Influence and power

Phillip Bonacich (1987) proposed a modification of the degree centrality approach. Suppose that Bill and Fred each have five close friends. Bill's friends, however, happen to be pretty isolated folks and don't have many other friends, save Bill. In contrast, Fred's friends each have lots of friends, who have lots of friends, and so on. Who is more central? One argument would be that Fred is likely to be more influential because he can quickly reach a lot of other actors, but if the actors that one is connected to are themselves well connected, they are not highly dependent on you. Bonacich argued that being connected to others who are connected makes an actor influential but not powerful. Somewhat ironically, being connected to others that are not well connected makes one powerful, because these other actors are dependent on you, whereas well-connected actors are not.

Let's examine the Bonacich influence and power positions of the egos in our information exchange data. The Bonacich influence or power indexes are calculated by using an attenuation factor (beta) or weight to show whether the index increases with the degree of those to whom ego is connected (influence) or decreases with the degree of those to whom ego is connected (power). The results for our information exchange network are shown in Figures 24.26 and 24.27.

If we look at the absolute value of the index scores, we see a familiar story. Actors 5 and 2 are clearly the most central. This is because they have high degree, and because they are connected to each other and to other actors with high degree. Actors 8 and 10 also appear to have high centrality by this measure; this is a new result. In this case, it is because the actors are connected to all of the

```
Actor Power

                        1
                     Power
                   ------------
   1               -2.732
   2               -3.938
   3               -3.235
   4               -2.855
   5               -4.428
   6               -1.167
   7               -2.610
   8               -3.526
   9               -2.488
  10               -3.472


STATISTICS

                                1
                             Power
                          ------------
   1        Mean            -3.045
   2     Std Dev             0.856
   3         Sum           -30.452
   4    Variance            0.732
   5         SSQ           100.056
   6       MCSSQ             7.321
   7    Euc Norm           10.003
   8     Minimum            -4.428
   9     Maximum            -1.167
```

Figure 24.26   Bonacich influence in the Knoke network (beta = + .50)

other actors with high degree. Actors 8 and 10 don't have extraordinary numbers of connections, but they have "the right connections."

Let's take a look at the power side of the index, which is calculated by the same algorithm, but gives negative weights to connections with well-connected others and positive weights for connections to weakly connected others.

Not surprisingly, these results are very different from many of the others we've examined. Egos 2 and 6 are distinguished because their ties are mostly ties to alters with high degree, making actors 2 and 6 "weak" by having powerful neighbors. Egos 3, 7, and 9 have more ties to alters who have few ties, making them "strong" by virtue of having weak neighbors.

Closeness centrality

Degree centrality measures might be criticized because they take into account only an actor's immediate ties, or the ties of the actor's neighbors, rather than indirect ties to all others. One actor might be tied to a large number of others, but

```
Actor Power

                        1
                     Power
                    ---------
      1              4.667
      2             -9.333
      3             12.667
      4              6.000
      5             -8.000
      6            -11.333
      7              8.667
      8              1.333
      9              7.333
     10              0.667


STATISTICS

                                  1
                               Power
                              ---------
      1      Mean               1.267
      2      Std Dev            7.828
      3         Sum            12.667
      4    Variance           61.284
      5         SSQ           628.888
      6       MCSSQ           612.843
      7    Euc Norm           25.078
      8     Minimum          -11.333
      9     Maximum           12.667
```

Figure 24.27   Bonacich power in the Knoke information network (beta = − .50)

those others might be relatively disconnected from the network as a whole. In a case like this, the actor could be quite central but only in a local neighborhood. Of course, if the only data we have available are for the one- or two-step neighborhoods of egos, this is the best we can do. If we have full network data, however, there are a number of influence centrality measures available that are based on overall closeness of each ego to all others in the graph (see Hanneman and Riddle, 2005, Chapter 10). Closeness measures such as the geodesic path distance, eigenvector centrality, reach centrality, Hubbell, Katz, Taylor, and Stephenson and Zelen all extend the influence centrality idea to larger networks (or the full graph).

Betweenness centrality

Suppose that I want to influence you by sending you information, or I want to make a deal to exchange some resources, but in order to talk to you, I must go through one or more intermediaries. This gives the people who lie "between" me and others power with respect to me. To the extent that I can use multiple pathways to reach others,

however, my dependency on any one intermediary is reduced (Cook et al., 1983).

The extent to which connections between alters in a neighborhood depend on ego can vary. In a star network, ego mediates all connections; in a clique, each alter can reach each other without ego's help. The extent of ego's "betweenness" can be an important dimension of relative power.

For networks with binary relations, Freeman (1979) created some measures of the centrality of individual actors based on their geodesic path betweenness, as well as overall graph centralization. Freeman et al. (1991) extended the basic approach to deal with all paths between actors.

With binary data, betweenness centrality views an actor as being in a favored position to the extent that the actor falls on the geodesic paths between other pairs of actors in the network. That is, the more people depend on me to make connections with other people, the more power I have. If, however, two actors are connected by more than one geodesic path, and I am not on all of them, I lose some power. If we add up, for each actor, the proportion of times that they are "between" alters we get a measure of ego "betweenness" centrality. We can norm this measure by expressing it as a percentage of the maximum possible betweenness that an actor could have. The results for the Knoke information network are shown in Figure 24.28.

These results in Figure 24.28 are based on treating the whole network as the neighborhood of each actor. Betweenness, though, could be calculated on each ego's *n*-step neighborhood. We see here that ego 5 is most central and that there is a clear "inner circle" (egos 5, 2, and 3). There is considerable variation in the betweenness of the egos (mean of 4.8, with a standard deviation of 6.2, which yields a coefficient of variation of 130).

Another way to think about betweenness is to ask which *relations* are most central, rather than which *actors*. Freeman's definition can be easily applied: a relation is *between* to the extent that it is part of the geodesic path between pairs of actors. Using this idea, we can calculate a measure of the extent to which each relation in a binary graph is *between*.

Suppose that two actors want to have a relationship, but the geodesic path between them is blocked by a reluctant broker. If there exists another pathway, the two actors are likely to use it, even if it is longer and "less efficient." In general, actors may use all of the pathways connecting them, rather than just geodesic paths. The flow betweenness (Freeman et al., 1991) approach to centrality expands the notion of betweenness centrality. It assumes that actors will use all pathways that connect them, in proportion to the length of

	1 Betweenness	2 nBetweenness
5	17.833	24.769
2	12.333	17.130
3	11.694	16.242
7	2.750	3.819
9	1.222	1.698
4	0.806	1.119
1	0.667	0.926
10	0.361	0.502
6	0.333	0.463
8	0.000	0.000

DESCRIPTIVE STATISTICS FOR EACH MEASURE

		1 Betweenness	2 nBetweenness
1	Mean	4.800	6.667
2	Std Dev	6.220	8.639
3	Sum	48.000	66.667
4	Variance	38.689	74.632
5	SSQ	617.290	1190.760
6	MCSSQ	386.890	746.316
7	Euc Norm	24.845	34.507
8	Minimum	0.000	0.000
9	Maximum	17.833	24.769

Network Centralization Index = 20.11%

Figure 24.28   Freeman betweenness for Knoke information network

those pathways. Betweenness is measured by the proportion of the entire flow between two actors (that is, through all of the pathways connecting them) that occurs on paths of which a given actor is a part. For each actor, then, the measure adds up how involved an actor is in all of the flows between all other pairs of actors (the amount of computation with more than a couple actors can be pretty intimidating!). Because the magnitude of this index number would be expected to increase with the sheer size of the network and with network density, it is useful to standardize it by calculating the flow betweenness of each actor in ratio to the total flow betweenness that does not involve the actor. Figure 24.29 shows the flow betweenness of each ego in the information network.

By this more complete measure of betweenness centrality, actors 2 and 5 are clearly the most important mediators. Actor 3, who was fairly important when we considered only geodesic flows, appears to be rather less important. While the overall picture does not change a great deal, the elaborated definition of betweenness does give us a somewhat different impression of who is most central in this network.

CONCLUSION

The social network analysis approach to social science emphasizes the relations between actors as being equally important (or perhaps more important) than the attributes of actors. The social network analysis approach also strongly emphasizes the interactions between individuals and their social context. Individuals make and enact social structure by their agency, but the choices they make are strongly conditioned by their locations in the texture of the larger social fabric in which they are embedded.

In this chapter, we've examined some of the most widely used concepts and measures found in quantitative approaches to basic social network analysis. At the core of the often bewildering complexity of specific approaches are a few basic

```
              1            2
          FlowBet      nFlowBet
        ------------  ------------
  1        3.854        5.352
  2       20.783       28.866
  3       16.954       23.547
  4        4.220        5.861
  5       25.876       35.939
  6        1.500        2.083
  7        8.401       11.668
  8        2.954        4.102
  9        4.054        5.630
 10        4.092        5.683


Network Centralization Index = 25.629%


DESCRIPTIVE STATISTICS FOR EACH MEASURE

                      1            2
                  FlowBet      nFlowBet
                ------------  ------------
  1   Mean          9.269       12.873
  2   Std Dev       8.230       11.430
  3   Sum          92.687      128.732
  4   Variance     67.725      130.642
  5   SSQ        1536.335     2963.609
  6   MCSSQ       677.249     1306.421
  7   Euc Norm     39.196       54.439
  8   Minimum       1.500        2.083
  9   Maximum      25.876       35.939
```

Figure 24.29 Flow betweenness centrality for Knoke information network

ideas about social structures. Size, density, connection, distance, substructures (including groups and equivalence classes), and their interconnections are the common themes that emerge as major structural properties of social structures, whether global or local. As social network analysts have demonstrated again and again, these ideas, though simple, are powerful, and they help to provide insight into the behavior of both whole social structures and the individuals that form and enact them.

REFERENCES

Bonacich, P. (1987) 'Power and centrality: A family of measures', *American Journal of Sociology* 92: 1170–82.

Borgatti, S.P., Everett, M.G. and Freeman, L.C. (2002) *UCINET for Windows: Software for Social Network Analysis*. Harvard, MA: Analytic Technologies.

Boyd, J.P., Fitzgerald, W.J. and Beck, R.J. (2006) 'Computing core/periphery structures and permutation tests for social relations data', *Social Networks* 28: 165–78.

Burris, V. (2005) 'Interlocking directorates and political cohesion among corporate elites', *American Journal of Sociology* 111: 249–83.

Burt, R.S. (1992) *Structural Holes: The Social Structure of Competition*. Cambridge: Harvard University Press.

Clark, R. (2008) 'Dependency, network integration, and development', *Sociological Perspectives* 51: 629–48.

Cook, K.S., Emerson, R.M., Gillmore, M.R. and Yamagishi, T. (1983) 'The distribution of power in exchange networks: Theory and experimental results', *American Journal of Sociology* 89: 275–305.

Crossley, N. (2008) 'Small-world networks, complex systems and sociology', *Sociology* 42: 261–77.

Field, S., Frank, K.A., Schiller, K., Riegle-Crumb, C. and Muller, C. (2006) 'Identifying positions from affiliation networks: Preserving the duality of people and events', *Social Networks* 28: 97–123.

Finsveen, E. and Wim van Oorschot. (2008) 'Access to resources in networks: A theoretical and empirical critique of networks as a proxy for social capital', *Acta Sociologica* 51: 293–307.

Fominaya, C.F. (2007) 'The role of humour in the process of collective identity formation in autonomous social movement groups in contemporary Madrid', *International Review of Social History* 52: 243–58.

Frank, K.A. (1996) 'Mapping interactions within and between cohesive subgroups', *Social Networks* 18: 93–119.

Freeman L.C. (1979) 'Centrality in social networks: Conceptual clarification', *Social Networks* 1: 215–39.

Freeman L.C., Borgatti S.P. and White, D.R. (1991) 'Centrality in valued graphs: A measure of betweenness based on network flow', *Social Networks* 13: 141–54.

Gallie, E.-P. (2009) 'Is geographical proximity necessary for knowledge spillovers within a cooperative technological network? The case of the French biotechnology sector', *Regional Studies* 43: 33–42.

Gould, J., and Fernandez, J. (1989) 'Structures of mediation: A formal approach to brokerage in transaction networks', *Sociological Methodology.* 89–126.

Granovetter, M.S. (1982) 'Alienation reconsidered: The strength of weak ties', *Connections* 5: 4–16.

Gurrieri, A. Rosa. (2008) 'Knowledge network dissemination in a family-firm sector', *The Journal of Socio-Economics* 37: 2380–89.

Hampton, K.N. and Wellman, B. (1999) 'Netville online and offline: Observing and surveying a wired suburb', *American Behavioral Scientist* 43: 475–92.

Hanneman, R. and Riddle, M. (2005) *Introduction to Social Network Methods.* Riverside, CA: University of California.

Haythornthwaite, C. (2005) 'Social networks and Internet connectivity effects', *Information, Communication & Society* 8: 125–47.

Hermann, R.J. (2008) 'National security challenges and competition: US defense and space R&D in a strategic context', *Technology in Society* 30: 371–81.

Knoke, D. and Yang, S. (2008) *Network Analysis.* 2nd ed. Thousand Oaks, CA: Sage.

Knoke, D. and Wood, J. (1981) *Organized for Action: Commitment in Voluntary Associations.* New Brunswick, NJ: Rutgers University Press.

Kien, G. (2008) 'Beijing, 2006: International connectivity the way it is supposed to be', *Qualitative Inquiry* 14: 1264–71.

Krackhardt, D. and Stern, R.N. (1988) 'Informal networks and organizational crises: An experimental simulation', *Social Psychology Quarterly* 51(2): 123–40.

Kratke, S. and Brandt, A. (2009) 'Knowledge networks as a regional development resource: A network analysis of the interlinks between Scientific Institutions and regional firms in the metropolitan region of Hanover, Germany', *European Planning Studies* 17: 43–63.

Lai, G. and Wong, O. (2002) 'The tie effect on information dissemination: The spread of a commercial rumor in Hong Kong', *Social Networks* 24: 49–75.

Moody, J. and White, D.R. (2003) 'Structural cohesion and embeddedness: A hierarchical concept of social groups', *American Sociological Review* 68: 103–27.

Newman, M.E.J. (2006) 'Modularity and community structure in networks', *Proceedings of the National Academy of Sciences [PNAS]* 103(23): 8577–82. www.pnas.org/cgi/doi/10.1073/pnas.0601602103.

Raval, V.V. and Kral, M.J. (2004) 'Core versus periphery: Dynamics of personhood over the life-course for a Gujarati Hindu woman', *Culture & Psychology* 10: 162–94.

Rycroft, R.W. (2007) 'Does cooperation absorb complexity? Innovation networks and the speed and spread of complex technological innovation', *Technological Forecasting and Social Change* 74: 565–78.

Sanders, K. and Nauta, A. (2004) 'Social cohesiveness and absenteeism: The relationship between characteristics of employees and short-term absenteeism within an organization', *Small Group Research* 35: 724–41.

Schnegg, M. (2007) 'Blurred edges, open boundaries: The long-term development of a peasant community in rural Mexico', *Journal of Anthropological Research* 63: 5–32.

Scott, J. (2000) *Social Network Analysis: A Handbook.* 2nd ed. Thousand Oaks, CA: Sage.

Totterdell, P., Holman, D. and Hukin, A. (2008) 'Social networkers: Measuring and examining individual differences in propensity to connect with others', *Social Networks* 30: 283–96.

Urry, J. (2006) 'Complexity', *Theory, Culture & Society* 23: 111–15.

Wasserman, S. and Faust, K. (1994) *Social Network Analysis: Methods and Applications.* Cambridge: Cambridge University Press.

Watts, D.J. (1999) *Small Worlds: The Dynamics of Networks between Order and Randomness.* Princeton, N.J.: Princeton University Press.

Watts, D.J. (2003) *Six Degrees: The Science of a Connected Age.* New York: W.W. Norton.

Wellman, B., Carrington, P.J. and Hall, A. (1988) 'Networks as personal communities', in Barry Wellman and S.D. Berkowitz (eds), *Social Structures: A Network Approach.* Cambridge: Cambridge University Press.

25

Survey Methods for Network Data

Peter V. Marsden

INTRODUCTION

Surveys and questionnaires are widely used to assemble data on connections among persons or other social actors. Such methods have a long heritage: researchers used them to study interpersonal relationships among children as early as the 1920s (Freeman, 2004). In the twenty-first century, archival measures of linkages and transactions based on administrative records or computer-mediated communication systems have become much more abundant and accessible. Surveys nonetheless remain a vital source of network data for the many situations in which such records do not exist or do not include information about the relationships of interest, or in which direct observation, diaries, and other methods of collecting network data are impractical.

This chapter reviews basic issues in conducting network surveys, beginning with the common forms that survey network data take, approaches to defining the boundaries of the study population, and methods of selecting subjects/respondents. It then discusses instruments for data collection in both whole-network and egocentric designs, illustrating different approaches with empirical studies. Next, it reviews some cognitive considerations to keep in mind when developing and administering network surveys. The chapter closes by reviewing some research into the quality of network data obtained using survey methods and by highlighting special issues of human subject protection that can arise in the course of conducting network surveys.

TEMPLATES FOR NETWORK DATA

Two principal types of network surveys focus on different, though related, objects of measurement: "whole" and "egocentric" networks. *Whole-network* studies seek to measure the structure of some bounded social group by collecting data on one or more types of relationships that link the units or actors within the group. *Egocentric network* studies have the more limited objective of describing local social environments by measuring the relationships in the vicinity of one or more focal units or actors. Whole-network studies subsume egocentric ones, in a sense: whole-network data include an egocentric network for each actor.[1]

Most often, surveys to measure whole networks collect *one-mode* network data on relationships among elements of a single set of units or actors – such as friendships among students in a school, or collaborative ties linking employees in an organization. Sometimes, however, they measure *two-mode* networks based on relationships among elements in two distinct sets; examples include school networks consisting of student memberships in groups such as extracurricular clubs or athletic teams, and organizational networks defined by employee assignments to committees or project teams.

Many design variations arise within these broad study templates. The minimal design measures only a single type of relationship, such as friendship or advising, on a single occasion. Extensions include designs that measure relationships among a set of actors on multiple occasions and designs that measure multiple types of ties (e.g., friendship, advising, and collaboration) at a single time point. Most studies supplement network data with information on attributes of units/actors, attributes of dyadic ties, or both. Studies that measure networks for two or more groups may also include group-level attributes.

DEFINING AND SAMPLING THE STUDY POPULATION

Defining the target population to be described and constructing a sampling frame that enumerates (or otherwise provides access to) it are early decisions in conducting social surveys. For network studies, these decisions about the population of elements and linkages to be measured are known as the "boundary specification problem" (Laumann et al., 1989).

Whole-network studies

For some whole-network studies, formal or positional criteria offer relatively self-evident definitions of inclusion within the group of interest. Examples include employment by a physician practice (Keating et al., 2007), assignment to a school classroom (Hansell, 1984), and residence in a district (Kirke, 1996).

Delineating boundaries can be more challenging for groups that are not formally defined, such as "regulars" at a beach (Freeman and Webster, 1994), policy domains (Laumann and Knoke, 1987), or social services delivery systems (Doreian and Woodard, 1992). Positional criteria can help to identify some actors in such populations. Observing (or referring to records documenting) participation in some set of relevant events also can be useful. For example, Laumann and Knoke's (1987) study identified some organizational participants in the U.S. health and energy policy domains based on appearances before relevant congressional committees, filing of *amicus curiae* briefs with appellate courts, and registration of lobbyists, among other criteria. Asking knowledgeable informants to nominate participants on a reputational basis (prior to data collection) can supplement positional and event-based approaches to boundary specification.

Social relationships themselves can also indicate inclusion in a population, while their absence can signal group boundaries; Laumann et al. (1989) term this a "relational" strategy for boundary specification. For example, a Colorado Springs study of persons engaged in high-risk behaviors (Klovdahl et al., 1994) enrolled partners of prostitutes and injecting drug users in its study population. Studies of service delivery systems could begin with some core agencies, later adding others to which they refer clients (Doreian and Woodard, 1992). Relational criteria are often used to add actors to the study population during the course of fieldwork, on the basis of ties to or nominations made by early respondents. Positional, event-based, reputational and relational criteria can be used together to identify populations for network studies; a study might begin with a list of actors included on a positional basis, and then supplement it using event-based or reputational criteria before fieldwork begins.

The process of boundary specification often results in a complete listing or roster of the study population. This can be an important aid to whole-network data collection.

Egocentric network studies

When egocentric network studies are conducted as part of representative sample surveys (e.g., Marsden, 1987), boundary specification follows the definition of the target population for those surveys. A second boundary-determination problem for egocentric studies has to do with delimiting the set of "alter" actors within any given respondent's egocentric network. In practice, "name generators" used in eliciting egocentric network data (see below) often serve this purpose.

Network sampling

In contrast to many social science surveys, network surveys only sometimes draw samples. Whole-network studies very often attempt to collect data on relationships among all actors in a population, for example, because they seek measures of relational properties (Lazarsfeld and Menzel, 1980) for all elements. When data collection uses survey methods, this is realistic only for populations of small to moderate size. Egocentric network data are often obtained within sample surveys, relying on their sampling methods to select a representative set of focal actors.

Some structural properties of whole networks may be estimated by sampling from networks. Samples may be drawn by selecting units or actors, or by selecting relationships. Sampling actors is usually a practical choice for surveys, since they assemble data by contacting actors.

Frank (1981) describes several network sampling schemes. One approach draws a probability sample of actors (e.g., by using a simple-random or Bernoulli scheme), and then observes only those relationships within the subset of sampled actors. Another draws a probability sample of actors and then observes all relationships incident to those actors.[2] Networks may also be sampled by link-tracing methods that begin with a probability sample of actors, elicit their contacts, and subsequently sample the contacts (e.g., Liebow et al., 1995). Such link-tracing may then be repeated one or more times to yield sampled "random walks" containing three or more linked actors.[3]

Different inferences about network properties are available from different sampling designs, so one must consider carefully what properties of a network are to be estimated when designing a network sampling scheme. The literature on network sampling (Frank, this volume) should be consulted at this stage.

INSTRUMENTS FOR MEASURING NETWORKS

This section introduces approaches commonly used in standardized questionnaires and interviews to obtain data on social relationships, beginning with methods for measuring whole networks. It then turns to techniques for measuring egocentric networks, concentrating on "name generator" instruments that yield the most extensive network data. Last, the section introduces some shorter instruments: global survey items and multiple-item instruments that measure one or more specific egocentric network properties but do not elicit reports about specific actor-to-actor relationships.

Instruments for whole-network data

Measuring whole networks requires information sufficient to assign a value to the relationship a_{ij} between each (ordered) pair of actors i and j, $i \neq j$, within a network. We concentrate here on instruments for one-mode networks.

The sociometric test

Surveys to assess whole networks usually administer some variant of the sociometric test developed by Moreno (1953). The basic technique asks each person i within a network to identify the "alters" (j) with whom he or she has – or would like to have – a given type of relationship, yielding a value of a_{ij} based on i's "choice" or

"non-choice" of j. Originally developed to measure preferences to associate with (or to avoid) others, the sociometric test generalizes to measuring "actually existing" relationships (e.g., communication, friendship, support). Likewise, it can be readily adapted to measuring two-mode networks by asking respondents to report group memberships or other affiliations of interest. Sociometric items have been administered in most survey modes, especially in-person interviews and self-administered questionnaires. Many contemporary applications use computer-assisted modes, which can simplify presentation of questions and data processing.

Studies use varying criteria – guided by the substantive questions they pose – to elicit sociometric choices. Some examples of such questions appear in Table 25.1. Keating et al. (2007) surveyed primary care physicians about their influential conversations about women's health issues. Singleton and Asher (1977) questioned third-grade students about who they like to play with and (separately) who they like to work with. Espelage et al. (2007) asked seventh-graders to name others whom they "hang out with most often" at school. Laumann and Knoke (1987) asked informants representing organizations in the U.S. energy policy domain to indicate other organizations in the domain with which their organization "regularly and routinely discusses national energy policy matters." Many studies elicit two or more types of contact; Brass (1985), for example, asked employees at a newspaper publishing company about workflow ties, work-related communication, and close friendships.

Many surveys that administer sociometric items supply a roster of possible alters in the network for respondents to consult when naming associates. Examples of studies that use such recognition techniques include Hansell's (1984) study of fifth- and sixth-grade classrooms, Lazega's (2001) study of attorneys in a law firm, and Provan et al.'s (2009) study of agencies serving the severely mentally ill in an Arizona county. Other versions ask respondents to freely recall their ties from memory, as in Coleman's (1961) study of networks within high schools, Brass's (1985) study of a newspaper publishing company, or Burt's (2004) study of supply chain managers.

Rosters simplify the reporting task by reminding respondents of the eligible alters within the network. Using rosters limits measurement error due to the forgetting of associates documented by Brewer (2000). Sudman's (1985) experiments demonstrated that recognition methods yield larger networks (see also Hlebec and Ferligoj, 2002). Reviewing and considering all names on a large roster can be a cumbersome, tedious task for

Table 25.1 Examples of whole-network measurement tasks

A. Single-criterion recognition question (Keating et al., 2007)

Please circle the number of conversations that you have had with each of the following [clinic name] primary care physicians in the last six months that have influenced your thinking about women's health issues.

[followed by alphabetized list of physicians and response categories '0', '1–3' and '≥4']

B. Multiple-criterion recognition questions (Singleton and Asher, 1977)

How much do you like to play with this person at school?

How much do you like to work with this person at school?

[presented within roster listing students in a class alphabetically; responses were numbers 1–5 accompanied by faces ranging from frowning to smiling]

C. Free-recall question (Coleman, 1961)

What fellows here in school do you go around with most often? *(Give both first and last names)*

[from boys' version of questionnaire; girls received a questionnaire with slightly different wording]

D. Cognitive social structure task (Casciaro et al., 1999)

By putting an X in the cells of the following matrix, please indicate whether you think the people listed in each row consider the people listed in each column as personal friends. For example, if you think that Ms. J (row 9) considers Mr. N (column N) as a friend, place an 'X' in the corresponding cell '9N.'

[followed by square matrix listing persons, with solid shading in diagonal (self-relation) cells]

E. Social-cognitive mapping task [free recall] (Cairns et al., 1985)

Now tell me about your class: Are there some people who hang around together a lot? Who are they? Are there some people who don't hang around with a particular group? Who are they?

respondents, however. Care with names of alters is warranted, using either approach: recall methods must ensure that citations of alters known by different names (e.g., nicknames, titles, spelling variations) are correctly matched, while rosters used to aid recognition must use the names by which persons are actually known.

Some early guidelines for sociometric measurement recommended that respondents be permitted to make an unlimited number of choices (Lindzey and Borgatta, 1954), but others suggested a limit of three or four citations (Northway, 1952). Network surveys using such limits include Coleman et al.'s (1966) study of physicians and Laumann and Pappi's (1976) study of community leaders. Limits have practical advantages in survey administration: they simplify and specify a sociometric task for respondents, thereby reducing burden. Measurement error considerations also arise, however. Imposing limits can induce both false negatives (if a respondent's actual number of associates exceeds the limit) and false positives (if respondents are encouraged to cite additional alters in order to reach the limit). Bias is thereby produced in many basic network structure statistics including the degree distribution(s), network summaries such as the dyad and triad censuses (Holland and Leinhardt, 1973), and others.

Sociometric items measure relationships using diverse sets of response categories and formats. Binary measurement is very common: respondents may indicate those alters with whom they have a given type of contact by listing them,

marking them on a roster or checklist, or making a separate "yes/no" response about each one. The latter "forced-choice" format is more time-consuming but may encourage deeper processing and more thoughtful answers (Smyth et al., 2006). Many studies request ordinal assessments: Keating et al.'s (2007) study of physicians used a three-category frequency scale (0, 1–3, or 4+ conversations); Fernandez (1991) measured respect relationships in a public finance agency using a five-point scale ("very little" to "very much"); and Johnson and Orbach (2002) asked political actors to rate their interactions with one another on an 11-point scale. In some studies of elementary school students or adolescents (Singleton and Asher, 1977; Hansell, 1984), icons supplement ordinal response categories: a face with a broad smile indicates that the respondent likes an alter "a lot," for example.

Cognitive social structure task

Typical sociometric items ask respondents to report only on relationships in which they are directly involved. A cognitive social structure (CSS) design (Krackhardt, 1987) measures respondent perceptions of a whole network, by using respondents as informants about social ties between alters as well as their own relationships. Such data may be collected via separate questions about the outgoing ties of each actor (e.g., "Who would X go to for advice at work?") as in Krackhardt (1987), or by asking informant actors to fill out a matrix grid (Casciaro et al., 1999; see Table 25.1D). Either way, a CSS task poses substantial demands on respondent time and memory, especially for networks of even moderate size.

A CSS task yields multiple assessments $\{a_{ij}^{(k)}\}$ of each directed tie, where $a_{ij}^{(k)}$ is the perception of ordered pair (i,j) by the kth informant. Krackhardt (1987) suggests several ways of combining these assessments to obtain a single measure for each relationship a_{ij} in a whole network. Setting $a_{ij} = a_{ij}^{(i)}$ – that is, treating each informant as the authority on her or his outgoing ties – yields a "locally aggregated structure" essentially equivalent to the data obtained via a typical sociometric item. An alternative "consensus structure" uses the average assessment $\frac{1}{K}\sum_k a_{ij}^{(k)}$ (where K is the total number of assessments), or a binary measure of a_{ij} based on whether the average assessment exceeds some threshold.

Socio-cognitive mapping and pile sorts

A procedure known as socio-cognitive mapping (SCM; Cairns et al., 1985) produces a form of cognitive social structure data that entails much lower respondent burden. It elicits respondent perceptions of cliques or clusters. Primarily used in measuring networks among children and adolescents, the SCM task asks respondents to report sets of people who "hang around together a lot" via free recall (see Table 25.1E). The pile-sort task used by Freeman and Webster (1994) to measure perceived networks resembles the SCM procedure but uses recognition methods. It provides each respondent with a randomized deck of cards containing the names of the actors in a network, asking that the respondent sort them into mutually exclusive piles including subsets of actors who are close to one another or who interact frequently.

Using either the SCM instrument or the pile-sort method, each respondent's reports yield a binary matrix with entries indicating whether the informant placed a given person in a certain subgroup. These matrices may be combined into a consensus perception of relationships in the whole network. Values can then be assigned to a_{ij} as a function of the number of informants who placed two actors together in a subgroup.

Name generator instruments for egocentric networks

Suites of survey questions called "name generator" instruments elicit data on the individual dyadic relationships and "alter" actors in a focal actor's neighborhood. They are so-called because such instruments begin by administering one or more *name generator* questions that elicit a roster of the alters within a respondent's egocentric network, thereby establishing its boundaries. Name generators are much like sociometric items, but they almost always depend on respondent recall, because rosters of eligible alters are typically not available in egocentric network studies. Surveys that use name generator instruments ordinarily treat respondents as informants who provide data about the entire egocentric network surrounding them; they generally do not survey or interview the alters themselves. *Name interpreter* questions follow the name generator(s), asking about attributes of particular alters or relationships. Such instruments can require considerable administration time when alters or name interpreters are numerous. Analysts later combine responses to name generators and name interpreters to measure a wide variety of egocentric network properties.

Like sociometric items, name generator questions must specify a particular type of relationship. Common criteria are role relations (e.g., friends, neighbors), aspects of relational form (e.g., closeness or frequency of contact), or specific types of resource transfer or exchange. Criteria of the latter type, which elicit alters using a specific relational content, are especially common. Among these is the widely used "discuss important matters" name generator (Panel A, Table 25.2) first administered in the 1985 General Social Survey (GSS) to elicit alters in a respondent's "core" network (Marsden, 1987). Other studies use name generators tailored to their topical content; for example, Huckfeldt and Sprague (1995) asked respondents for names of alters whom they "talked with most about the events of the past election year."

To facilitate the subsequent administration of name interpreters, name generators usually ask respondents to identify alters by first name only; egocentric designs do not need to match alter and respondent names. A name generator may be followed by one or more probes that prompt a respondent for additional alters. Marin (2004) demonstrates that using several such probes can increase egocentric network size substantially, as respondents add previously forgotten alters. Probes should be used judiciously, however, especially with behaviorally nonspecific name generators that respondents must define for themselves. Respondents may understand extensive probing as an indication that they are expected to cite more alters than they have already named, leading them to alter their definition of the name generator's relational content.

Some name generator instruments incorporate visual interfaces to assist respondents. Kahn and

Table 25.2 Examples of name generators

A   Single Name Generator (from 1985 and 2004 General Social Surveys [GSSs]; Davis et al., 2007)

> From time to time, most people discuss important matters with other people. Looking back over the last six months, who are the people with whom you discussed matters important to you? Just tell me their first names or initials.

> IF LESS THAN FIVE NAMES MENTIONED, PROBE: Anyone else?

B   Multiple Name Generator (Kogovšek et al., 2002: 14)

> 1   From time to time, people borrow something from other people, for instance, a piece of equipment,or ask for help with small jobs in or around the house. Who are the people you usually ask for this kind of help?

> 2   From time to time, people ask other people for advice when a major change occurs in their life, for instance, a job change or a serious accident. Who are the people you usually ask for advice when such a major change occurs in your life?

> 3   From time to time, people socialize with other people, for instance, they visit each other, go together on a trip or to a dinner. Who are the people with whom you usually do these things?

> 4   From time to time, people discuss important personal matters with other people, for instance if they quarrel with someone close to them, when they have problems at work, or other similar situations. Who are the people with whom you discuss personal matters that are important to you?

> 5   Suppose you find yourself in a situation, when you would need a large sum of money, but do not have it yourself at the moment, for instance, five average monthly wages (approximately 500,000 tolars). Whom would you ask to lend you the money (a person, not an institution such as a bank)?

Antonucci (1980), for example, elicited social support networks by asking respondents to place alters within concentric circles surrounding them. McCarty and Govindaramanujam (2006) propose a dynamic visual interface in which respondents place alters in relation to one another, thereby simplifying the collection of name interpreter data.

Two or more name generators may be used to delimit an egocentric network. Fischer (1982a), for example, elicited social support networks using nine name generators; van der Poel (1993) recommends sets of three and five name generators for measuring personal support networks. The multiple-generator social support instrument in section B of Table 25.2 includes name generators for minor instrumental aid, advice, socializing, confiding about personal matters and major instrumental aid. Studies using multiple name generators should be mindful of possible order effects on the number of alters given in response to particular questions (Pustejovsky and Spillane, 2009).

As in whole-network measurement, some name generator instruments ask respondents to name a specific number of alters. Laumann (1973) asked for three "best friends," for example, while Huckfeldt and Sprague (1995) asked for three political discussants, and Wellman (1979) elicited six persons to whom a respondent felt closest. The "important matters" name generator (Table 25.2) does not limit the number of alters but probes for more only when a respondent names fewer than five. Many other studies (e.g., Fischer, 1982a) impose no limitations on the number of alters.

After name generators ascertain the boundaries of a respondent's egocentric network, follow-up name interpreter questions ask for information about its form and content. Because of the name interpreters, egocentric network data collection poses more demands on respondents than do whole-network instruments.

Three common types of name interpreter items are exemplified in Table 25.3. The first section contains questions requesting proxy reports about attributes of the alters in a network, such as race/ethnicity or age. The second section has questions about properties of ego-alter ties such as emotional closeness, conflict/discomfort, duration of acquaintance, or frequency of contact. Such name interpreters may ask whether a tie includes a particular strand of content of special interest to a study. For example, the National Social Life, Health and Aging Project (NSHAP) asked about the likelihood that respondents would discuss health with each alter (Cornwell et al., 2009), while a 1984 South Bend, Indiana, election study asked about the frequency of discussing politics with alters (Huckfeldt and Sprague, 1995). Finally, name interpreters may ask about relationships among the alters themselves (the third section of Table 25.3), in order to measure egocentric network density and other aspects of egocentric network structure.

Instruments may organize name interpreter questions in "alter-wise" blocks consisting of all questions about each alter, or "question-wise" blocks that ask a given item about all alters (Vehovar et al., 2008). Question-wise blocking

Table 25.3 Examples of name interpreters

A   Name Interpreters for Alter Characteristics (from 1985 and 2004 GSSs; Davis et al., 2007)

    1   Is (NAME) Asian, Black, Hispanic, White, or something else?

       ASK FOR EACH NAME

    2   How old is (NAME)?

       PROBE: Your best guess.

       ASK FOR EACH NAME

B   Name Interpreters for Properties of Ego-Alter Ties (Kogovšek et al., 2002: 14–15)

    1   How close do you feel to this person? Please describe how close you feel on a scale from 1 to 5, where 1 means not close and 5 means very close.

    2   How often does this person upset you?

    [Responses are often, sometimes, rarely, never]

C   Name Interpreters for Egocentric Network Structure (from 1985 and 2004 GSSs; Davis et al., 2007)

    Please think about the relations between the people you just mentioned. Some of them may be total strangers in that they wouldn't recognize one another if they bumped into each other on the street. Others may be especially close, as close or closer to each other as they are to you.

    First, think about (NAME 1) and (NAME 2).

    A   Are (NAME 1) and (NAME 2) total strangers?

       IF YES, PROCEED TO NEXT PAIR

    B   Are they especially close?

       PROBE: As close or closer to each other as they are to you

REPEAT FOR EACH PAIR OF NAMES

(e.g., the first section of Table 25.3) asks respondents to answer several consecutive questions having identical response alternatives, a "battery" format shown to elicit less reliable survey data (Alwin, 2007). Vehovar et al. (2008), however, found question-wise presentation to be superior on several data-quality grounds, with notably lower dropout and item nonresponse rates. Because respondents know the number of alters they cited but not the number of name interpreters in a questionnaire, the alter-wise format allows them to better anticipate the length of the name-interpreter task. Alter-wise presentation (e.g., the second section of Table 25.3) took less administration time in the Vehovar et al. (2008) study, perhaps because respondents can access different pieces of information about a given alter more rapidly in this format (Kogovšek et al., 2002).

Whether administered alter-wise or question-wise, answering name interpreter items is repetitive and time-consuming, especially if respondents have large egocentric networks. Some studies therefore ask name interpreters about subsets of the alters elicited. Data for a subset of alters may be sufficient if a study seeks to measure properties of a respondent's egocentric network, as opposed to individual respondent-alter dyads. For example, White and Watkins (2000) elicited only up to four alters with whom respondents "chatted" because their respondents found the name interpreters tedious. The GSS name generator instrument (Burt, 1984) asks name interpreters about only the first five alters cited (few respondents name more than five, however). Fischer (1982a) asked some name interpreter questions about a subset of alters, those named first in response to five different name generators. Because respondents tend to name their closer ties sooner (Burt, 1986), selecting alters based on citation order is apt to measure name interpreter data for stronger ties. McCarty et al. (2007) and Marin and Hampton (2007) suggest sampling alters at random. The number of alters required to measure a given egocentric network property with adequate reliability depends on the homogeneity of alter characteristics within respondents (Marsden, 1993; McCarty et al., 2007).

Name generator instruments have been administered as part of face-to-face interviews as in the GSS (Marsden, 1987), telephone interviews (e.g., Kogovšek, 2006), mail questionnaires (e.g., Marin and Hampton, 2007), and Web-based instruments (e.g., Vehovar et al., 2008). Name generator instruments entail some complexity: at a minimum, names of alters must be inventoried and organized appropriately for the administration of name interpreters. Instruments that use more than one name generator must eliminate redundant names before presenting name interpreters, and those that administer name interpreters for a subset of alters must use a consistent protocol to select the subset. Well-trained interviewers can assist respondents in avoiding organizational and navigation errors in these processes, but computer-assisted instruments – either self- or interviewer-administered – have special appeal in this setting (Gerich and Lehner, 2006).

To the extent that respondents view the survey content as sensitive, self-administration of name generator instruments can enhance data quality, if it promotes higher levels of disclosure (Gerich and Lerner, 2006). Self-administration also avoids the interviewer differences in responses to name generators documented by van Tilburg (1998) and Marsden (2003). Respondents may, however, err when answering self-administered instruments, for example, by entering references to plural alters or groups (e.g., "my parents") or other replies that do not name specific alters (e.g., "don't want to respond") in response to name generators (Lozar Manfreda et al., 2004). Moreover, interviewer presence may provide motivation and encourage respondents to be attentive. Matzat and Snijders (2010) report mode comparisons that raise concern that respondents may be prone to satisficing when answering Web-based name generator instruments in private. In any event, the visual design of self-administered instruments warrants care: respondents may take the amount of space left after a name generator question as an indication of the number of alters they are expected to name, for example (Lozar Manfreda et al., 2004; Vehovar et al., 2008).

Analysts use data from name generator instruments to construct indices that measure many different egocentric network properties (e.g., Marsden, 1987). For respondent i, the most basic of these is egocentric network size (n_i), the number of alters elicited by the name generator(s). Name interpreter data on relationships among alters can be used to construct measures of local density, for example, $d_i = \dfrac{2\sum_{j=2}^{n_i}\sum_{k=1}^{j-1} r_{jk}^{(i)}}{n_i(n_i-1)}$, where $r_{jk}^{(i)}$ measures the strength of the tie between alters j and k in respondent i's egocentric network. Measures of network composition can be based on name interpreter data about alters, for example, the mean level of an attribute $c_i = \dfrac{\sum_{j=1}^{n_i} x_j^{(i)}}{n_i}$ (where $x_j^{(i)}$ is an attribute value for alter j in i's network) or the proportion of alters in i's network who have a given value of an attribute. Likewise, network heterogeneity measures can be based on the variability of alter characteristics, for example, the standard deviation $s_i = \sqrt{\dfrac{\sum_{j=1}^{n_i}(x_j^{(i)} - c_i)^2}{n_i - 1}}$ or alternatives suitable for categorical measurements. Versions of indices in Burt's (1992) "structural hole" suite and many other egocentric network measures also can be constructed using data from name generator instruments.

Global questions about egocentric network properties

Numerous single-item survey measures ask respondents to provide summary assessments of some egocentric network property – most often their level or volume of informal social contact. They do not yield data on specific actor-to-actor ties. Table 25.4 provides some examples. The first item there asks about the frequency with which a respondent socializes with a particular type of alter (friends outside the neighborhood), while the second asks about the size of the respondent's network of "close friends." The third item asks that a respondent estimate his or her total daily number of direct social contacts, while the fourth asks for an ordinal assessment of friendship network density. The fifth item measures the presence of a confidant.

Global items like these are simple to administer within sample surveys. Their formats resemble those of other common survey questions. They are efficient, requiring comparatively little interview time. Some display construct validity in that they have robust statistical associations with measures of other phenomena of interest, such as individual well-being.

Multiple-item instruments

Position generator
A position generator instrument (Lin et al., 2001) measures a respondent's relationships to particular *types* of alters. It does not elicit ties to particular individuals. Developed within a social capital framework, this instrument usually assesses ties to occupational positions that vary in socioeconomic standing, presuming that alters that have more prestigious occupations offer access to more valuable social resources. This measurement strategy also could be used to assess ties to other types of social locations, such as ethnic or religious groups.

The position generator illustrated in Table 25.5 asks respondents to indicate whether or not they have a specified type of contact (here, kinship,

Table 25.4 Examples of single-item measures of egocentric social network properties

A. Frequency of Socializing with Friends (from 1974-2008 GSSs; Davis et al., 2007)

   Would you use this card and tell me which answer comes closest to how often you do the following things . . .

   Spend a social evening with friends who live outside the neighborhood

   [Responses on card: Almost every day, Once or twice a week, Several times a month, About once a month, Several times a year, About once a year, Never]

B. Friendship Network Size (from 1998 GSS; Davis et al., 2007)

   Do you have any good friends that you feel close to?

   IF YES: About how many good friends do you have?

C. Typical Daily Social Contact (Fu, 2005: 173)

   On an average, about how many people do you have contact with in a typical day, including all those who you say hello, chat, talk, or discuss matters with, whether you do it face-to-face, by telephone, by mail or on the internet and whether you personally know the person or not? Please give your estimate and select one from the following categories that best matches your estimate: (1) 0–4 persons, (2) 5–9 persons, (3) 10–19 persons, (4) 20–49 persons, (5) 50–99 persons, (6) over 100 persons

D. Friendship Network Density (from 1985 GSS; Davis et al., 2007)

   Some people have friends who mostly know one another. Other people have friends who don't know one another. Would you say that all of your friends know one another, most of your friends know one another, only a few of your friends know one another, or none of your friends know one another?

F. Availability of a Confidant (Lowenthal and Haven, 1968)

   Is there anyone in particular you confide in or talk to about yourself or your problems?

Table 25.5 Example of position generator

Among your relatives, friends, or acquaintances, are there people who have the following jobs?

   a. High school teacher

   b. Electrician

   c. Owner of small factory/firm

   d. Nurse

   (etc.)

FOR EACH JOB FOR WHICH RESPONDENT ANSWERS 'YES', ASK:

What is his/her relationship to you?

   1. Relative

   2. Friend

   3. Acquaintance

[IF RESPONDENT KNOWS MORE THAN ONE CONTACT WHO HOLDS A GIVEN JOB, ASK ABOUT THE FIRST CONTACT WHO COMES TO MIND]

Source: Lin et al. (2001: 77)

friendship, or acquaintance) with anyone in a particular socioeconomic location. Follow-up questions ask respondents who have contact with particular locations to indicate whether the relationship is strong (kinship, friendship) or weak (acquaintanceship). Other follow-ups can be added.

Responses to a position generator are usually combined into summary measures of the composition and range of the respondent's egocentric network. Three widely used summary measures are *extensity*, *upper reachability*, and *range* (Lin et al., 2001). Let x_{ij} be an indicator variable telling whether respondent i has contact with position j, and p_j be the prestige of position j. Then the extensity of respondent i's network – the number of locations contacted – can be measured as $\sum_{j=1}^{J} x_{ij}$, where J is the total number of positions included in the instrument. The upper reachability

i's network is defined as the highest-prestige location accessed, $\max_j(x_{ij}p_j)$. Finally, the range of a respondent's network is the difference between the highest-prestige and lowest-prestige positions found in the respondent's network, $\max_j(x_{ij}p_j) - \min_{j|x_{ij}=1}(x_{ij}p_j)$. Other summary measures for position-generator data can be developed via sophisticated multivariate methods (van der Gaag et al., 2008).

The position generator is a relatively efficient instrument, requiring less interview time than the name generator instruments described above. A major decision in developing a position generator concerns the set of positions presented to respondents. Positions presented should cover the range of variation along dimensions underlying the locations of interest in a study (e.g., prestige or socioeconomic standing, in the case of occupational locations) and should be relatively common positions within the population of interest. Position generator instruments require that respondents be able to inventory their contacts of a given type, to assess whether one or more of them is with someone who occupies a specific position (e.g., bank teller). Such instruments become more demanding of respondents as the number of positions and the number of follow-up questions per position increase. In 19 surveys including position generators reported in Lin and Erickson (2008), the number of positions ranged from 6 to 40 with a median of 17. These applications involved face-to-face, telephone, and mail administration.

Resource generator

The resource generator (Van der Gaag and Snijders, 2005) assesses access to social resources directly by asking respondents if they have personal contact with anyone who possesses certain assets or capabilities. Like position generators, resource generators do not measure individual ties. Table 25.6 presents some example resource generator items. If a respondent has at least one contact who controls a given resource, the instrument probes for the strength of the strongest linkage to it.

Like the position generator, the resource generator does not enumerate alters individually or measure network structure: it focuses on resource-related network composition. It requires less administration time than a typical name generator instrument. Van der Gaag and Snijders (2005) use latent trait analysis to develop measures of aspects of social capital based on resource generator data.

Social support scales

A vast literature on social support includes numerous instruments that elicit reports about the support perceived to be available or the support actually received (Wills and Shinar, 2000). Some measures take the form of name generator instruments that associate support with individual alters (e.g., the second section of Table 25.2). Others ask about whether a respondent has access to anyone who could provide a given type of

Table 25.6 Example of resource generator

Do you know anyone who . . .

    a.   Can repair a car, bike, etc.?

    b.   Is handy repairing household equipment?

    c.   Knows a lot about governmental regulations?

    d.   Can give a good reference when you are applying for a job?

    (etc.)

[Note: the definition of 'knowing' a person is that the respondent would know the person's name if he or she were to encounter the person by accident on the street and that both parties could initiate conversation with the other.]

FOR EACH ITEM TO WHICH RESPONDENT ANSWERS 'YES', ASK:

What is his/her relationship to you?

    1.   Family member

    2.   Friend

    3.   Acquaintance

[IF RESPONDENT KNOWS MORE THAN ONE CONTACT FOR A GIVEN ITEM, CODE STRONGEST RELATIONSHIP ONLY, I.E., FAMILY MEMBER IN PREFERENCE TO FRIEND, FRIEND IN PREFERENCE TO ACQUAINTANCE]

Source: Van der Gaag and Snijders (2005: 12)

support, a format like that of the resource generator; see, for example, Cohen and Hoberman's (1983) Interpersonal Support Evaluation List. Still other social support instruments pose separate questions about forms of support available from classes of alters, such as family, friends, and coworkers (e.g., Turner and Marino, 1994).

COGNITIVE CONSIDERATIONS FOR NETWORK SURVEYS

Recent thinking about how respondents answer survey questions stresses a four-stage cognitive model: comprehending a question, retrieving relevant information from memory, integrating the information retrieved (perhaps adding other considerations) to develop a judgment about an answer, and providing a response within the format given in the survey instrument (Tourangeau et al., 2000). This section discusses some research that bears on these processes for questions about other persons and a respondent's relationships to them.

Sociometric questions may be misunderstood – or understood in varying ways – when they ask about diffuse, behaviorally nonspecific relationships. One ground cited by advocates of using "specific exchanges" (e.g., confiding, socializing) rather than affective (e.g., closeness) or role-relation (e.g., friends, neighbors) criteria to word name generators is that respondents are apt to answer exchange questions more consistently (McAllister and Fischer, 1978). Some research nonetheless examines variations in interpretation assigned to the widely used "important matters" name generator. Bailey and Marsden (1999) debriefed respondents using cognitive interviewing, finding that some took it to be asking for close or frequent contacts and that most regarded "important matters" as those having to do with family or personal life. They suggested that interview context might influence a respondent's definition of important matters: politics was more apt to be part of this when a series of survey items with political content preceded the name generator; see also Bearman and Parigi (2004). Cornwell et al. (2009) placed their name generator instrument at the beginning of the NSHAP interview to avoid such context effects. Bearman and Parigi (2004) asked respondents to report the important matter they had most recently discussed, finding that matters involving money and household finance were mentioned most frequently. A fifth of their respondents were "silent," claiming that they had not discussed anything important with anyone during the preceding six months.

"Friend" is among the more common role-relation criteria used in sociometric questions. Studies using a variety of methods document wide contextual variability – notably by gender and class – in definitions and behaviors associated with "friendship," however (Adams and Allan, 1998). Fischer (1982b) explored how a sample of Californians identified "friends," finding considerable ambiguity: they used it rather unspecifically to cover ties having no other label – often long-duration, same-age, nonfamily contacts with whom they socialize.

Sociometric questions relying on free recall call attention to the way in which respondents organize their memories for persons, which shapes the accessibility of information at the retrieval stage. Studies of person memory may also suggest ways of wording questions or probing answers to encourage accurate reporting of associates. Brewer (1995) conducted several studies revealing that social structural factors organize memories for persons. Subjects recalling those enrolled in their graduate program, for example, tended to give names in clusters corresponding to entering cohorts. More generally, recall of persons corresponds to their perceived social proximity (Brewer et al., 2005): alters perceived to interact frequently tend to be remembered close together.

Other research by Brewer (2000) documents pervasive forgetting of associates in free recall tasks; this appears to be more severe for weaker ties. Bell et al. (2007) reported greater forgetting for less specific relationships ("friends" compared with sex or drug use partners), for less salient ties (drug use versus sexual partners), and longer reference periods. The above-mentioned research on memory organization suggests that administering probes and reminders to call a respondent's attention to relevant contexts, or to contacts proximate to those already named, may reduce forgetting. Brewer (2000) also suggests that instruments should include several name generators to provide respondents with additional opportunities to name alters.

When developing name interpreter items that ask respondents to make proxy reports about characteristics of alters, researchers should be mindful of differences between memories for self and others (Sudman et al., 1994). People learn data about others via observation or communication rather than experience. Memories about others may be less elaborate and accessible and less organized into summary judgments than those about oneself. Respondents may need to estimate rather than retrieve data about others, and they often do so by anchoring a proxy report on their own attitude or behavior (Sudman et al., 1996). An advantage of proxy reports is that social desirability pressures may be weaker for reports about others than those about respondents themselves.

Apart from memory structures for persons are memories for relationships among them. Freeman (1992) shows that people tend to impose transitivity on relationships, recalling that others are connected when in fact they are not. This is consistent with Brewer's conclusion that group affiliations organize person memories; nuances of within-group dyadic relationships may not be encoded precisely, however.

It is not difficult to develop social network items that make considerable demands on respondent cognitive capacity. Consider global items like those shown in Table 25.4. The second item on "close friends" requires that respondents first define both "friend" and "close," and then enumerate or estimate their number of such contacts. Perhaps as a result, some comparisons between responses to global items and network data assembled using other instruments suggest that global questions have limited reliability. Sudman (1985) showed that global estimates of network size exhibit considerable response variance by comparison to more time-consuming network measurements based on recognition or free recall. The "ersatz" network density item (section D in Table 25.4) makes, if anything, even stronger demands on memory and judgment. Burt (1987) shows that answers to it are only weakly associated with a local density measure constructed using data from a name generator instrument.

The judgment tasks involved in answering name interpreter questions about individual alters and relationships are simpler than those posed by global items, though much more numerous. Judgment tasks involved in answering items like those posed in position generator or resource generator instruments can be simplified by asking – as the examples in Tables 25.5 and 25.6 do – whether *anyone* in an egocentric network has the attribute or resource in question, rather than *how many* alters have it.

Once a respondent reaches a judgment, she or he must format it to conform with the response categories offered by a survey question. When possible, instruments should avoid presenting response categories involving "vague quantifiers" (Bradburn and Miles, 1979), such as "rarely," "often," or "some," in favor of numerical reports or responses that involve widely understood units of measurement (e.g., "daily" or "at least monthly"). While respondents may experience difficulty in reaching precise judgments within the latter frameworks, using such categories reduces measurement errors stemming from variation across respondents in classifying judgments into vaguely quantified categories. Alwin (2007) concludes that the reliability of reports about past behavior is lower when items use vague quantifiers.

DATA QUALITY

Numerous sources can produce errors of measurement in survey data about social networks. For example, errors in self-reported data about relationships can arise because of respondent memory limitations, or because respondents seek to present themselves favorably when answering – incorrectly claiming ties to certain alters, while omitting contacts with others. Researchers may pose questions that correspond imperfectly with the concepts they seek to measure, or respondents may interpret them differently than intended. Different interviewers may administer survey items (such as name generators) in varying ways that contribute errors.

Some therefore view survey network data with skepticism. Survey designs lend themselves, however, to obtaining the repeated measures that systematic investigations of measurement quality require. Numerous studies examine aspects of data quality for survey-based social network measures. Many of these offer convincing evidence that survey responses can reliably and validly reflect underlying social network phenomena. Such studies, however, assess quality using different standards (e.g., validity, reliability, item nonresponse), focus on different objects of measurement (e.g., dyadic ties, characteristics of alters, egocentric network properties), examine substantively different network ties, and measure quality using different indices and metrics. As for survey data more generally (Alwin, 2007), quality assessments for network data are population-specific, and the findings of any given investigation are therefore suggestive rather than definitive.

Available data quality studies do not yield a single or unambiguous verdict about the quality of survey measures of networks. Some measurements appear highly valid and reliable, while others are less so. We call attention here to some influential lines of work in this area but do not attempt either to exhaustively cover or to synthesize all relevant methodological research; for further discussion, see Marsden (1990, 2005). We first discuss studies that assess data quality for measures of respondent-alter relationships (sociometric items and name generators). Subsequently, we cover research that examines name interpreter items and measures of network composition.

Accuracy and validity studies for relational items

Important and influential "informant accuracy" studies summarized in Bernard et al. (BKS; 1981) examined the accuracy or validity of reported communication ties in whole networks. These studies compared reports about relationships based on sociometric items with "gold standard" measurements of behavior obtained using diaries or logs or systematic observation. Across several small populations surveyed using varying measurement methods (e.g., rankings versus ratings), the survey reports and the "behavioral" measurements of communication exhibited moderate agreement, at most. These findings posed serious questions about the quality of "cognitive" reports on social ties obtained using surveys, although we note in passing that diaries and observations of behavior also may include measurement errors. A similarly designed classroom study (Gest et al., 2003) drew more encouraging conclusions about the quality of survey data obtained using the SCM.

The BKS studies stimulated numerous reanalyses and follow-up studies. Kashy and Kenny (1990) dissected the overall correspondence between survey reports and behavioral data into two "individual" components involving actor-level tendencies to communicate with others and a "dyadic" component involving their tendencies to communicate with *particular* others. Their data analyses revealed a relatively close actor-level correspondence between survey citations received and overall observed interaction levels, and moderate dyadic-level correlations. Survey citations made and observed interaction levels corresponded quite poorly, however, a conclusion later echoed by Feld and Carter's (2002) finding of "expansiveness bias" – wide actor-level variation in reports about outgoing relationships – in survey network data. These studies indicate that survey data may measure some network properties more validly than others.

A separate line of work by Freeman and Romney (1987; see also Freeman et al., 1987) argued that measurement errors in survey reports of past social interactions are not random but instead tend to be biased toward long-term patterns. These studies obtained two-mode survey data in which respondents reported whether others had been present at a recent meeting. Analyses then compared those reports to attendance records – both for the particular meeting in question and for a series of meetings held over a longer period of time. They found that persons falsely reported as being present at the meeting in question were apt to attend most meetings; those incorrectly reported as missing the recent meeting tended to be infrequent attenders over the longer run. These findings suggest that survey respondents can report stable patterns of social interaction validly, but are less capable of recalling time-specific episodes with precision. This resonates

with more general findings about the cognitive challenges respondents face when answering survey questions asking them to report event dates (Tourangeau et al., 2000: Chapter 4).

Reliability of relational items

Many other studies compare two or more survey measurements of the same datum, thereby assessing the reliability of instruments. One approach examines the reciprocation of citations, reasoning that a conceptually undirected relationship should be reported by both actors involved in it. Marsden (1990) inventoried several studies of reciprocation, finding rates that ranged widely, with some indication that reciprocity is higher for closer ties. In some more recent studies, Feld and Carter (2002) reported a reciprocation rate of about 58 percent for college students who were questioned about who they spent time with, while White and Watkins (2000) reported reciprocation of only 20 percent for reports about informal family planning discussions ("chats") by rural Kenyan women. For a high-risk population (sex workers, intravenous drug users, and their sexual partners) adams and Moody (2007) reported much higher reciprocation levels: 85 percent for sexual relationships, 72 percent for drug-sharing, and 79 percent for "social" ties. These rates fell only slightly when calculations took timing into account, counting reported citations as reciprocated only when they referred to overlapping time intervals. Gest et al. (2003) indicate that observed interaction is higher in reciprocated dyads, thereby offering some evidence that reciprocated citations may have higher validity.

In the data studied by adams and Moody (2007), respondents also made CSS-like reports about contacts of their contacts. Reports about relationships among contacts of contacts were corroborated relatively often by self-reports from participants in those relationships, though at rates lower than the above-cited reciprocation levels. In particular, observer reports were less often consistent with self-reports about sexual relationships, which ordinarily take place in settings not open to observation by others.

Test-retest studies compare two or more measurements made using the same instrument on different occasions. Test-retest correlations reflect some combination of stability in the phenomenon under study and reliability in a measuring instrument, so they are not unambiguous indicators of data quality. For survey network data, test-retest assessments can be made at different levels. Some studies examine the percentage of stability/turnover in citations of individual alters. For example, Morgan et al. (1997) showed that about 55 percent of the alters elicited by a name generator were named again after two-month periods. In White and Watkins's (2000) study covering a two-year interval, respondents re-named only 18 percent of the partners with whom they first reported "chatting" about family planning. Bignami-Van Assche (2005) gives an even lower figure (about 10 percent) for similar reports in Malawi that were separated by a three-year interval. Less than 30 percent of alters were elicited on both of two occasions separated by a much shorter period (about 10 days). Alters having close ties to a respondent appear much more apt to be reported repeatedly across occasions than those having weaker relationships. For reviews of other evidence on the repeated citation of alters across waves of panel studies, see Marsden (1990) and Brewer (2000).

Instruments may measure properties of respondents' egocentric networks reliably across occasions of measurement despite substantial turnover in the individual alters that respondents name, if actor-level measures of network form and composition remain stable. In one study, Morgan et al. (1997) obtained repeated measures of egocentric network size and the percent of family members in a respondent's egocentric network over two-month intervals, reporting between-wave correlations above 0.6. In another, Bignami-Van Assche's (2005) name generators elicited similar numbers of alters when readministered after a short time interval, though respondents often did not name the same specific alters.

Several data quality studies estimate the reliability of survey network measures using a multitrait-multimethod (MTMM) approach. Such studies repeatedly measure several relationships using different methods and are thereby able to assess both the reliability of measurements and the extent to which reliable variance is attributable to differences in methods. For eight whole-network classroom studies, Ferligoj and Hlebec (1999) reported relatively high reliability levels (above 0.85) for four social support measures. Their measures of emotional and informational support were somewhat more reliable than those of informational support and companionship. While measures using binary response scales appeared somewhat less reliable than those involving ordinal scales, method-related variance in true scores was only modest (see also Hlebec and Ferligoj, 2002).

Name interpreter data: proxy reporting and network composition measures

Responses to name interpreters provide the content for most egocentric network measures constructed using data elicited by name generator instruments. Relevant data quality studies examine responses to name interpreters at the alter level, and they assess indices and scales based on those data.

Proxy reporting

When they answer name interpreters about alter characteristics, survey respondents make "proxy" reports about alters. The survey research literature includes numerous studies examining the quality of such reports (e.g., Moore, 1988), mostly for respondents reporting about their spouses or other household members. Alwin (2007) assessed the reliability of spousal proxy reports about socioeconomic status, finding them to be relatively reliable – though less so than self-reports. Sudman et al. (1994) reason that the quality of proxy reports should rise with respondent-alter interaction.

Many studies of proxy reports obtain self-reports directly from alters, and then compare them with an original respondent's proxy report. If we regard the alter as the authority on his or her characteristics, such a design estimates the validity of the proxy measure. Some social network studies use such designs to assess the quality of proxy reports about friends or other nonhousehold alters. A common finding is that respondents can report observable data about alters – age, sex, household possessions, number of children – reasonably well; proxy answers about less observable features such as political party affiliation or contraceptive use are of lower quality (Laumann, 1969; White and Watkins, 2000), and often biased toward the proxy respondent's own value on such measures. See Marsden (1990) for further discussion.

Reliability of network composition measures

As noted earlier, many measures that describe egocentric networks are within-respondent means of data obtained via name interpreter items; for example, egocentric network density can be expressed as the mean strength of tie between pairs of alters in a respondent's network. Marsden (1993) assesses the reliability of such measures using methods from generalizability theory. Their reliability rises with the number and homogeneity of measures on different alters. Many – but not all – such properties can be reliably measured using name generator instruments that elicit five or fewer alters.

Some other studies estimate the reliability of such measures using MTMM designs. Kogovšek and Ferligoj (2005), for example, report reliability coefficients above 0.8 for average frequency of contact with, and average closeness to, alters in an egocentric network. They found that measures with behavioral rather than emotional content are more reliable. In interviewer-administered modes, "alter-wise" presentation of name interpreters yielded more reliable measures than did "question-wise" presentation (Kogovšek et al., 2002; Kogovšek and Ferligoj, 2005). The question-wise approach appears to be more reliable in the Internet mode, however (Coromina and Coenders, 2006; Vehovar et al., 2008). Kogovšek and Ferligoj (2002) find that the reliability of composition measures is higher for "core" networks composed of strong ties than for "extended" ones that also include weaker relationships.

Another set of MTMM studies exploits the hierarchical structure of data from name generator instruments, in which observations on alters are nested within respondents. This allows estimation of reliability coefficients for alters within respondents and for between-respondent differences. Coromina and Coenders (2006) report reliability coefficients above 0.8 at both levels for advice, collaboration, information exchange, and socializing among members of research groups. Reports about collaboration were most reliable, those about socializing least so. Coromina et al. (2004) report similar findings for common measures of tie strength, such as closeness and frequency of contact.

HUMAN SUBJECT PROTECTIONS AND NETWORK SURVEYS

Surveys that collect data on social networks must comply with all laws, regulations, and norms that govern the conduct of survey research. Among these are obtaining voluntary, informed consent from respondents, minimizing risks to them, and protecting their confidentiality after data are assembled (see Citro, 2010) when disseminating research reports or archiving data sets. Special vigilance is warranted when such surveys ask respondents for information about their relationships involving sensitive behaviors such as sexual activity or drug use. See Klovdahl (2005) and Woodhouse et al. (1995) for discussion of steps that may be taken under such circumstances.

Network surveys often collect information about third parties – the alters or associates connected to respondents. Some regard such third parties as research participants, contending that researchers must locate and seek informed consent from them as "secondary subjects,"

though this view is debated (see Klovdahl, 2005; Morris, 2004: 3). Without question, however, researchers are obligated to protect secondary subjects against harms arising from disclosure of research data and to ensure that any risks to them are minimal and outweighed by potential research benefits. Woodhouse et al. (1995) suggest that investigators may have more extensive responsibilities to such third parties, should the research discover that they are at risk because of the behavior of primary subjects.

CONCLUSION

Survey methods are, and seem apt to remain, a leading approach to collecting social network data. Like other research methods, they have drawbacks. Assembling survey data can be both expensive and time-consuming, especially for large samples or populations. Much methodological research examines possible measurement errors in survey network data, but they can also include error attributable to factors such as nonresponse or interviewer differences.

All research data include errors, however, and such legitimate concerns about the survey approach should not blind us to its strengths, many of which have to do with its flexibility. Researchers control the definition of network boundaries when they conduct surveys. Survey methods can elicit all strands of relationships, not only those recorded within a specific medium such as electronic mail. Survey researchers can measure the aspects of relationships that are of conceptual interest in a study – rather than (for example) relying on those tracked by a record-keeping system – thereby improving validity. Survey data are collected under relatively standardized conditions. Surveys often require only modest time commitments from participants, by comparison with the demands made by some alternative methods such as diaries.

Looking forward, we can anticipate continued attention to assessing and reducing different forms of error in survey data. As well, investigations that seek to develop more efficient instruments and innovations in modes of collecting survey data seem likely. Internet surveys offer many prospective gains – including substantial cost and time savings, respondent convenience, and the possibility of using new and different visual interfaces. These innovative methods may, however, hold consequences for data quality, investigation of which has only begun for survey data about social networks.

ACKNOWLEDGMENTS

For helpful comments, I am grateful to Peter Carrington, Anuška Ferligoj, and Sameer Srivastava.

NOTES

1   This view of the relationship between whole-network and egocentric data assumes, however, that the egocentric networks for all focal actors of interest lie within whatever boundary is established for the corresponding whole network. In practice, many egocentric studies are conducted in large, open populations where this assumption may be untenable.

2   Obtaining egocentric network data on respondents in conventional sample surveys resembles this design.

3   We omit discussion of network sampling methods such as respondent-driven sampling (Heckathorn, 1997), which use social connections among elements of rare or hidden populations to draw samples of actors in those populations, rather than to sample whole or partial networks per se.

REFERENCES

Adams, J. and Moody, J. (2007) 'To tell the truth: Measuring concordance in multiply reported network data', *Social Networks*, 29 (1): 44–58.

Adams, R.G. and Allan, G. (eds) (1998) *Placing Friendship in Context*. New York: Cambridge University Press.

Alwin, D.F. (2007) *Margins of Error: A Study in the Reliability of Survey Measurement*. Hoboken, NJ: Wiley Interscience.

Bailey, S. and Marsden, P.V. (1999) 'Interpretation and interview context: Examining the General Social Survey name generator using cognitive methods', *Social Networks*, 21(3): 287–309.

Bearman, P. and Parigi, P. (2004) 'Cloning headless frogs and other important matters: Conversation topics and network structure', *Social Forces*, 83(2): 535–57.

Bell, D.C., Belli-McQueen, B. and Haider, A. (2007) 'Partner naming and forgetting: Recall of network members', *Social Networks*, 29(2): 279–99.

Bernard, H.R., Killworth, P.D. and Sailer, L. (1981) 'Summary of research on informant accuracy in social network data, and on the reverse small world problem', *Connections*, 4(summer): 11–25.

Bignami-Van Assche, S. (2005) 'Network stability in longitudinal data: A case study from rural Malawi', *Social Networks*, 27(3): 231–47.

Bradburn, N.M. and Miles, C. (1979) 'Vague quantifiers', *Public Opinion Quarterly*, 43(1): 92–101.

Brass, D.J. (1985) 'Men's and women's networks: A study of interaction patterns and influence in an organization', *Academy of Management Journal*, 28(2): 327–43.

Brewer, D.D. (1995) 'The social structural basis of the organization of persons in memory', *Human Nature*, 6(4): 379–403.

Brewer, D.D. (2000) 'Forgetting in the recall-based elicitation of personal and social networks', *Social Networks*, 22(1): 29–43.

Brewer, D.D., Rinaldi, G., Mogoutov, A. and Valente, T.W. (2005) 'A Quantitative review of associative patterns in the recall of persons', *Journal of Social Structure* 6. http://www.cmu.edu/joss/.

Burt, R.S. (1984) 'Network items and the General Social Survey', *Social Networks*, 6(4): 293–339.

Burt, R.S. (1986) 'A note on sociometric order in the General Social Survey network data', *Social Networks*, 8(2): 149–74.

Burt, R.S. (1987) 'A note on the General Social Survey's ersatz network density item', *Social Networks*, 9(1): 75–85.

Burt, R.S. (1992) *Structural Holes: The Social Structure of Competition*. Cambridge, MA: Harvard University Press.

Burt, R.S. (2004) 'Structural holes and good ideas', *American Journal of Sociology*, 110(2): 349–99.

Cairns, R.B., Perrin, J.E. and Cairns, B.D. (1985) 'Social structure and social cognition in early adolescence: Affiliative patterns', *Journal of Early Adolescence*, 5(3): 339–55.

Casciaro, T., Carley, K.M. and Krackhardt, D. (1999) 'Positive affectivity and accuracy in social network perception', *Motivation and Emotion*, 23(4): 285–306.

Citro, C.F. (2010) 'Legal and human subjects considerations in surveys', in Peter V. Marsden and James D. Wright (eds.), *Handbook of Survey Research*. 2nd ed. Bingley, UK: Emerald Group Publishing. pp. 59–79.

Cohen, S. and Hoberman, H.M. (1983) 'Positive events and social supports as buffers of life change stress', *Journal of Applied Social Psychology*, 13(2): 99–125.

Coleman, J.S. (1961) *The Adolescent Society: The Social Life of the Teenager and Its Impact on Education*. New York: Free Press.

Coleman, J.S., Katz, E. and Menzel, H. (1966) *Medical Innovation: A Diffusion Study*. Indianapolis: Bobbs-Merrill.

Cornwell, B.L., Schumm, P., Laumann, E.O. and Graber, J. (2009) 'Social networks in the NSHAP study: Rationale, measurement, and preliminary findings', *Journal of Gerontology: Social Sciences*, 64B (S1): i47–i55.

Coromina, L. and Coenders, G. (2006) 'Reliability and validity of egocentered network data collected via Web: A meta-analysis of multilevel multitrait multimethod studies', *Social Networks*, 28(3): 209–31.

Coromina, L., Coenders, G. and Kogovšek, T. (2004) 'Multilevel multitrait multimethod model: Application to the measurement of egocentered social networks', *Metodološki zvezki*, 1(2): 323–49.

Davis, J.A., Smith, T.W. and Marsden, P.V. (2007) *General Social Surveys: Cumulative Codebook: 1972–2006*. Chicago: NORC.

Doreian, P. and Woodard, K.L. (1992) 'Fixed-list versus snowball selection of social networks', *Social Science Research*, 21(2): 216–33.

Espelage, D.L., Green, H.D.Jr. and Wasserman, S. (2007) 'Statistical analysis of friendship patterns and bullying behaviors among youth', in Philip C. Rodkin and Laura D. Hanish (eds), *Social Network Analysis and Children's Peer Relationships.* San Francisco: Jossey-Bass. pp. 61–75.

Feld, S.L. and Carter, W.C. (2002) 'Detecting measurement bias in respondent reports of personal networks', *Social Networks,* 24(4): 365–83.

Ferligoj, A. and Hlebec, V. (1999) 'Evaluation of social network measurement instruments', *Social Networks,* 21(2): 111–30.

Fernandez, R.M. (1991) 'Structural bases of leadership in intraorganizational networks', *Social Psychology Quarterly,* 54(1): 36–52.

Fischer, C.S. (1982a) *To Dwell Among Friends: Personal Networks in Town and City.* Chicago: University of Chicago Press.

Fischer, C.S. (1982b) 'What do we mean by "friend": An inductive study', *Social Networks,* 3(4): 287–306.

Frank, O. (1981) 'A survey of statistical methods for graph analysis', in Samuel Leinhardt (ed.), *Sociological Methodology 1981.* San Francisco: Jossey-Bass. pp. 110–55.

Freeman, L.C. (1992) 'Filling in the blanks: A theory of cognitive categories and the structure of social affiliation', *Social Psychology Quarterly,* 55(2): 118–27.

Freeman, L.C. (2004) *The Development of Social Network Analysis: A Study in the Sociology of Science.* Vancouver, BC: Empirical Press.

Freeman, L.C., Romney, A.K. and Freeman, S.C. (1987) 'Cognitive structure and informant accuracy', *American Anthropologist,* 89(2): 311–25.

Freeman, L.C. and Romney, A.K. (1987) 'Words, deeds and social structure: A preliminary study of the reliability of informants', *Human Organization,* 46(4): 330–34.

Freeman, L.C. and Webster, C.M. (1994) 'Interpersonal proximity in social and cognitive space', *Social Cognition,* 12(3): 223–47.

Fu, Y.-C. (2005) 'Measuring personal networks with daily contacts: A single-item survey question and the contact diary', *Social Networks,* 27(3): 169–86.

Gerich, J. and Lerner, R. (2006) 'Collection of ego-centered network data with computer-assisted interviews', *Methodology,* 2(1): 7–15.

Gest, S.D., Farmer, T.W., Cairns, B.D. and Xie, H. (2003) 'Identifying children's peer social networks in school classrooms: Links between peer reports and observed interactions', *Social Development,* 12(4): 513–529.

Hansell, S. (1984) 'Cooperative groups, weak ties, and the integration of peer friendships', *Social Psychology Quarterly,* 47(4): 316–28.

Heckathorn, D.D. (1997) 'Respondent-driven sampling: A new approach to the study of hidden populations', *Social Problems,* 44(2): 174–99.

Hlebec, V. and Ferligoj, A. (2002) 'Reliability of social network measurement instruments', *Field Methods,* 14(3): 288–306.

Holland, P.W. and Leinhardt, S. (1973) 'The structural implications of measurement error in sociometry', *Journal of Mathematical Sociology,* 3(1): 85–111.

Huckfeldt, R. and Sprague, J. (1995) *Citizens, Politics, and Social Communication: Information and Influence in an Election Campaign.* New York: Cambridge University Press.

Johnson, J.C. and Orbach, M.K. (2002) 'Perceiving the political landscape: Ego biases in cognitive political networks', *Social Networks,* 24(3): 291–310.

Kahn, R.L. and Antonucci, T.C. (1980) 'Convoys over the life course: Attachment, roles and social support', in Paul B. Baltes and Orville G. Brim (eds), *Life Span Development and Behavior,* vol. 3. San Diego: Academic Press. pp. 253–86.

Kashy, D.A. and Kenny, D.A. (1990) 'Do you know whom you were with a week ago Friday? A re-analysis of the Bernard, Killworth, and Sailer studies', *Social Psychology, Quarterly,* 53(1): 55–61.

Keating, N.L., Ayanian, J.Z., Cleary, P.D. and Marsden, P.V. (2007) 'Factors affecting influential discussions among physicians: A social network analysis of a primary care practice', *Journal of General Internal Medicine,* 22(6): 794–98.

Kirke, D.M. (1996) 'Collecting peer data and delineating peer networks in a complete network', *Social Networks,* 18(4): 333–46.

Klovdahl, A.S. (2005) 'Social network research and human subjects protection: Towards more effective infectious disease control', *Social Networks,* 27(2): 119–37.

Klovdahl, A.S., Potterat, J.J., Woodhouse, D.E., Muth, J.B., Muth, S.Q. and Darrow, W.W. (1994) 'Social networks and infectious disease: The Colorado Springs study', *Social Science and Medicine,* 38(1): 79–88.

Kogovšek, T. (2006) 'Reliability and validity of measuring social support networks by Web and telephone', *Metodološki zvezki,* 3(2): 239–52.

Kogovšek, T. and Ferligoj, A. (2002) 'The quality of measurement of personal support networks', *Quality and Quantity,* 38(5): 517–32.

Kogovšek, T. and Ferligoj, A. (2005) 'Effects on reliability and validity of egocentered network measurements', *Social Networks,* 27(3): 205–29.

Kogovšek, T. Ferligoj, A., Coenders, G. and Saris, W.E. (2002) 'Estimating the reliability and validity of personal support measures: Full information ML estimation with planned incomplete data', *Social Networks,* 24(1): 1–20.

Krackhardt, D. (1987) 'Cognitive social structures', *Social Networks,* 9(2): 109–34.

Laumann, E.O. (1969) 'Friends of urban men: An assessment of accuracy in reporting their socioeconomic attributes, mutual choice, and attitude agreement', *Sociometry,* 32(1): 54–69.

Laumann, E.O. (1973) *Bonds of Pluralism: The Form and Substance of Urban Social Networks.* New York: Wiley Interscience.

Laumann, E.O. and Knoke, D. (1987) *The Organizational State: Social Choice in National Policy Domains.* Madison: University of Wisconsin Press.

Laumann, E.O., Marsden, P.V. and Prensky, D. (1989) 'The boundary specification problem in network analysis', in Linton C. Freeman, Douglas R. White, and A. Kimball Romney (eds), *Research Methods in Social Network*

Analysis. Fairfax, VA: George Mason University Press. pp. 61–87.

Laumann, E.O. and Pappi, F.U. (1976) *Networks of Collective Action: A Perspective on Community Influence Systems*. New York: Academic Press.

Lazarsfeld, P.F. and Menzel, H. (1980) 'On the relation between individual and collective properties', in Amitai Etzioni and Edward W. Lehman (eds), *A Sociological Reader on Complex Organizations*. 3rd ed. New York: Holt, Rinehart and Winston. pp. 508–21.

Lazega, E. (2001) *The Collegial Phenomenon: The Social Mechanisms of Cooperation Among Peers in a Corporate Law Partnership*. New York: Oxford University Press.

Liebow, E., McGrady, G., Branch, K., Vera, M., Klovdahl, A., Lovely, R., Mueller, C. and Mann, E. (1995) 'Eliciting social network data and ecological model-building: Focus on choice of name generators and administration of random-walk study procedures', *Social Networks*, 17(3–4): 257–72.

Lin, N. and Erickson, B.H. (2008) *Social Capital: An International Research Program*. New York: Oxford University Press.

Lin, N., Fu, Y.-C. and Hsung, R.-M. (2001) 'The position generator: Measurement techniques for investigations of social capital', in Nan Lin, Karen Cook, and Ronald S. Burt (eds), *Social Capital: Theory and Research*. New York: Aldine de Gruyter. pp. 57–81.

Lindzey, G. and Borgatta, E.F. (1954) 'Sociometric measurement', in Gardner Lindzey (ed.), *Handbook of Social Sychology*. Vol. 1. Reading, MA: Addison Wesley. pp. 405–48.

Lowenthal, M.F. and Haven, C. (1968) 'Interaction and adaptation: Intimacy as a critical variable', *American Sociological Review*, 33(1): 20–30.

Lozar Manfreda, K., Vehovar, V. and Hlebec, V. (2004) 'Collecting ego-centred network data via the Web', *Metodološki zvezki*, 1(2): 295–321.

Marin, A. (2004) 'Are respondents more likely to list alters with certain characteristics? Implications for name generator data', *Social Networks*, 26(4): 289–307.

Marin, A. and Hampton, K.N. (2007) 'Simplifying the personal network name generator: Alternatives to traditional multiple and single name generators', *Field Methods*, 19(2): 163–93.

Marsden, P.V. (1987) 'Core discussion networks of Americans', *American Sociological Review*, 52(1): 122–31.

Marsden, P.V. (1990) 'Network data and measurement', *Annual Review of Sociology*, 16: 435–63.

Marsden, P.V. (1993) 'The reliability of network density and composition measures', *Social Networks*, 15(4): 399–421.

Marsden, P.V. (2003) 'Interviewer effects in measuring network size using a single name generator', *Social Networks*, 25(1): 1–16.

Marsden, P.V. (2005) 'Recent developments in network measurement', in Peter J. Carrington, John Scott, and Stanley Wasserman (eds), *Models and Methods in Social Network Analysis*. New York: Cambridge University Press. pp. 8–30.

Matzat, U. and Snijders, C. (2010) 'Does the online collection of ego-centered network data reduce data quality?' *Social Networks*, 32(2): 105–11.

McAllister, L. and Fischer, C.S. (1978) 'A procedure for surveying personal networks', *Sociological Methods and Research*, 7(2): 131–48.

McCarty, C. and Govindaramanujam, S. (2006) 'A modified elicitation of personal networks using dynamic visualization', *Connections*, 26(2): 61–69.

McCarty, C., Killworth, P.D. and Rennell, J. (2007) 'Impact of methods for reducing respondent burden on personal network structural measures', *Social Networks*, 29(2): 300–315.

Moore, J.C. (1988) 'Self-proxy response status and survey response quality: A review of the literature', *Journal of Official Statistics*, 4(2): 155–72.

Moreno, J.L. (1953) *Who Shall Survive? Foundations of Sociometry, Group Psychotherapy, and Sociodrama*. Beacon, NY: Beacon House.

Morgan, D.L., Neal, M.B. and Carder, P. (1997) 'The stability of core and peripheral networks over time', *Social Networks*, 19(1): 9–25.

Morris, M. (ed.) (2004) *Network Epidemiology: A Handbook for Survey Design and Data Collection*. New York: Oxford University Press.

Northway, M.L. (1952) *A Primer of Sociometry*. Toronto: University of Toronto Press.

Provan, K.G., Huang, K. and Milward, H.B. (2009) 'The evolution of structural embeddedness and organizational social outcomes in a centrally governed health and human services network', *Journal of Public Administration Research and Theory*, 19(4): 873–93.

Pustejovsky, J.E. and Spillane, J.P. (2009) 'Question-order effects in social network name generators', *Social Networks*, 31(4): 221–29.

Singleton, L.C. and Asher, S.R. (1977) 'Peer preferences and social interaction among third-grade children in an integrated school district', *Journal of Educational Psychology*, 69(4): 330–36.

Smyth, J.D., Dillman, D.A., Christian, L.M. and Stern, M.J. (2006) 'Comparing check-all and forced-choice formats in Web surveys', *Public Opinion Quarterly*, 70(1): 66–77.

Sudman, S. (1985) 'Experiments in the measurement of the size of social networks', *Social Networks*, 7(2): 127–51.

Sudman, S., Bickart, B., Blair, J. and Menon, G. (1994) 'The effect of participation level on reports of behavior and attitudes by proxy reporters', in Norbert Schwarz and Seymour Sudman (eds), *Autobiographical Memory and the Validity of Retrospective Reports*. New York: Springer-Verlag. pp. 251–65.

Sudman, S., Bradburn, N.M. and Schwarz, N. (1996) *Thinking About Answers: The Application of Cognitive Processes to Survey Methodology*. San Francisco: Jossey-Bass.

Tourangeau, R., Rips, L.J. and Rasinski, K. (2000) *The Psychology of Survey Response*. New York: Cambridge University Press.

Turner, R.J. and Marino, F. (1994) 'Social support and social structure: A descriptive epidemiology', *Journal of Health and Social Behavior*, 35(3): 193–212.

Van der Gaag, M. and Snijders, T.A.B. (2005) 'The resource generator: Social capital quantification with concrete items', *Social Networks*, 27(1): 1–29.

Van der Gaag, M., Snijders, T.A.B. and Flap, H. (2008) 'Position generator measures and their relationship to other social capital measures', in Nan Lin and Bonnie H. Erickson (eds), *Social Capital: An International Research Program*. New York: Oxford University Press. pp. 28–48.

Van der Poel, M.G.M. (1993) 'Delineating personal support networks', *Social Networks*, 15(1): 49–70.

Van Tilburg, T. (1998) 'Interviewer effects in the measurement of personal network size', *Sociological Methods and Research*, 26(3): 300–328.

Vehovar, V., Lozar Manfreda, K., Koren, G. and Hlebec, V. (2008) 'Measuring ego-centered social networks on the Web', *Social Networks*, 30(3): 213–22.

Wellman, B. (1979) 'The community question: The intimate networks of East Yorkers', *American Journal of Sociology*, 84(5): 1201–31.

White, K. and Watkins, S.C. (2000) 'Accuracy, stability, and reciprocity in informal conversational networks in rural Kenya', *Social Networks*, 22(4): 337–55.

Wills, T.A. and Shinar, O. (2000) 'Measuring perceived and received social support', in Sheldon Cohen, Lynn G. Underwood, and Benjamin H. Gottlieb (eds), *Social Support Measurement and Intervention*. New York: Oxford University Press. pp. 86–135.

Woodhouse, D.E., Potterat, J.J., Rothenberg, R.B., Darrow, W.W., Klovdahl, A.S. and Muth, S.Q. (1995) 'Ethical and legal issues in social network research: The real and the ideal', in Richard H. Needle, Susan L. Coyle, Sander G. Genser, and Robert T. Trotter (eds), *Social Networks, Drug Abuse, and HIV Transmission*. Rockville, MD: National Institute on Drug Abuse. pp. 131–43.

26

Survey Sampling in Networks

Ove Frank

INTRODUCTION

Network structures appear in many different areas: social relations between individuals, economic transactions, spread of infections, behavioural patterns among children, co-offending activities of offenders, links between Internet sites and so forth. Data collected in an investigation of a particular network are normally confined to only partial information about the network. Special statistical methodology is being developed both for modelling networks, for planning and designing network investigations, and for analysing network data and drawing appropriate conclusions. The role of survey sampling in this connection is the topic of the present chapter.

Survey sampling in ordinary populations developed largely in the 1930s from a need to improve the quality of opinion polls and make more reliable predictions of election results. By using probabilistic sampling designs the sampling variation could be quantified and a technical meaning could be given to such concepts as likelihood of different values on an unknown population quantity and confidence attached to error estimates of sample quantities. It became possible to calculate the effects of larger sample sizes and weight desired levels of confidence against sampling costs. The investigator should stratify the population according to factors of importance and implement a controlled probabilistic sampling design. Modern methods of survey design in ordinary populations are described by Särndal et al. (1992), Cassel et al. (1993), Thompson (1997) and Mukhopadhyay (2001).

Interest in surveys of populations with a relational structure started in the 1960s when social scientists could combine mathematical tools from graph theory with efficient numerical algorithms and new calculation possibilities made available by the rapid development of computer technology. Sampling in graphs was independently studied in early articles by Goodman (1961), Proctor (1967), Stephan (1969), Frank (1969), Capobianco (1970) and Sirken (1970) and in two monographs by Bloemena (1964) and Frank (1971). Later Granovetter (1976) and Morgan and Rytina (1977) also saw the need for network sampling, and many methodological results on network surveys and estimation were published in the 1970s. Further references are given in Frank (1977, 1980, 1981, 1987) and Proctor (1979).

Graph theory is an old combinatorial branch of mathematics. The theory of random graphs is an expanding vivid area of modern graph theory, which was initiated by Erdös and Renyi (1959, 1960). There are many books on graphs and random graphs. Some advanced mathematical books are by Bollobas (2001), Diestel (2005) and Janson et al. (2000). The literature on random graphs is mainly devoted to asymptotic results for large graphs. The simple structure of a Bernoulli graph on n vertices with an edge probability $p = p(n)$ depending on n exhibits surprisingly many intrinsic asymptotic results. Random graphs with a specified degree distribution are the objects of much contemporary research. The World Wide Web as described by Bonato (2008) contributes to an interest in models for very large graphs.

The next two sections define basic concepts in survey sampling and introduce network structures of attributive and relational data. In particular, the distinction between local and global network properties is pointed out because it is fundamental for the possibility to draw inference from network sample data. Inference for global properties requires that sample data are supplemented by a network model. A review of some statistical network models serves the purpose of introducing various statistics that are useful in network analysis. This rather comprehensive preparation is followed by presentations of various network sampling designs and demonstrations of statistical estimation based on available sample data. The focus is on principles for constructing estimators with different kinds of data. Special emphasis is given to snowball and walk sampling designs, which are discussed in separate sections.

SURVEY SAMPLING

Data and samples

A common data structure consists of n independent observations $x_1, \ldots, x_n$ on a univariate or multivariate variable that takes values in some range space R. The space R can be finite or infinite. The standard model assumption is to consider the observations as realisations of n independent identically distributed (i.i.d.) random variables. The relative frequencies of observations in different regions of R or at different values in R can be used as estimates of probabilities assigned to regions or values in R. However, the interpretation of these probabilities might be problematic if the observations are selected with different probabilities at different population units. Such selection would imply that the observed relative frequencies are not reflecting the relative frequencies in the population of values from which the observations are sampled. This is the concern of survey sampling theory, and it is of special importance in network surveys in which there might be compelling reasons to believe that selection probabilities vary for the units sampled.

Survey sampling is often designed so that the selection probabilities vary in convenient ways. Sometimes the design is not controlled by the investigator but is rather an effect of the observation process. In such cases, probabilistic modelling of the observation process might be appropriate. Network surveys can benefit from both controlled and modelled sampling designs as will be illustrated in this chapter.

Sampling designs in finite populations

Let U be a finite population of N observational units, and let x be a variable defined on U with values in R. The subset of units with $x(u) = r$ is denoted by U_r and its size by N_r for values r in R. The relative frequencies $P_r = N_r/N$ of different values among the population units define the population distribution $(P_r)_R = (P_r : r \in R)$.

Sample units $u_1, \ldots, u_n$ selected with equal probabilities and with replacement from U provide sample values $x_1, \ldots, x_n$ that are i.i.d. observations on a random variable with probability distribution equal to the population distribution. If n_r is the number of observations with $x_i = x(u_i) = r$ for $i = 1, \ldots, n$, then $(n_r)_R = (n_r : r \in R)$ is multinomially distributed with parameters n and $(P_r)_R$. It follows that n_r/n is an unbiased estimator of P_r for r in R.

If the sample units are selected with equal probabilities and without replacement, $(n_r)_R$ is hypergeometrically distributed with parameters n and $(N_r)_R$. Again n_r/n is an unbiased estimator of P_r for r in R.

If the sample units are selected with probabilities $(p_u)_U$ and with replacement, then $(n_r)_R$ is multinomially distributed with parameters n and $(p(U_r))_R$ where $p(U_r)$ is the sum of the probabilities p_u for u in U_r. Now n_r/n is an unbiased estimator of $p(U_r)$, and this probability is generally not equal to the population frequency P_r. In fact, $p(U_r) = P_r$ if and only if the average selection probability among the N_r units in U_r is $1/N$. Such a case is the uniform selection distribution considered above, which has $p_u = 1/N$ for all u in U. Other selection distributions with $p(U_r) = P_r$ cannot be designed when N_r is unknown.

If we assume that the range space R consists of positive real numbers and that units are selected with probabilities that are proportional to their values on the x-variable, say $p_u = cr$ for some constant c and for u in U_r, then $p(U_r) = crN_r$. Since these probabilities sum to 1 it follows that $c = 1/\Sigma_r rN_r$. Now the ratio between the expected values

$$E(n_r/r) = ncN_r$$

and

$$E\Sigma_r(n_r/r) = ncN$$

is equal to the relative population frequency P_r so that the ratio

$$(n_r/r)/\Sigma_r(n_r/r)$$

can be used for estimating P_r for r in R. This estimator is asymptotically unbiased for large populations. The estimator can also be expressed as

$$(n_r/r)/\Sigma_r(n_r/r) = hn_r/rn$$

where

$$h = n/\Sigma_r(n_r/r) = n/\Sigma_i(1/x_i)$$

is the harmonic mean of the observations. This illustrates that when the sampling design is not simple uniform random sampling, the relative sample frequencies n_r/n have to be adjusted to provide estimators of the relative population frequencies. The adjustment factor in this case is h/r. We also notice that the population mean value

$$\Sigma_u x(u)/N = \Sigma_r r P_r$$

is estimated by

$$\Sigma_r(rhn_r/rn) = h,$$

which is just the harmonic mean value of the sample observations. This value is generally smaller than the arithmetic mean value $\Sigma_i x_i/n$ of the observations. By using the harmonic mean we compensate for selection that is biased towards large values of the variable.

When the sample units are selected with probabilities $(p_u)_U$ and with replacement, the same unit u can be drawn several times. Let $(m_u)_U$ be the multiplicities

$$m_u = \Sigma_i I(u_i = u)$$

for u in U. It follows that $(m_u)_U$ is multinomially distributed with parameters n and $(p_u)_U$. The sample frequencies

$$n_r = \Sigma_u m_u I(u \in U_r)$$

for r in R are also multinomially distributed with parameters n and $p(U_r)$ for r in R as noted above. If we let $S_u = I(m_u > 0)$ indicate whether unit u is included in the sample, the numbers of distinct sample units in U_r and U are given by

$$d_r = \Sigma_u S_u I(u \in U_r)$$

and $d = \Sigma_r d_r$. The indicators S_u are dependent Bernoulli variables with

$$ES_u = 1 - (1-p_u)^n$$

and

$$Cov(S_u, S_v) = (1-p_u-p_v)^n - (1-p_u)^n(1-p_v)^n \text{ for } u \neq v.$$

Using the sample multiplicities and the sample inclusion indicators, two unbiased estimators of the population frequency N_r are given by

$$N_r' = \Sigma_u [m_u I(u \in U_r)/Em_u]$$
$$= \Sigma_u [m_u I(u \in U_r)/np_u]$$

and

$$N_r'' = \Sigma_u [S_u I(u \in U_r)/ES_u]$$
$$= \Sigma_u [S_u I(u \in U_r)/(1-(1-p_u)^n)]$$

Even if N is known it might be preferable to use $N' = \Sigma_r N_r'$ and $N'' = \Sigma_r N_r''$ to estimate P_r by N_r'/N' and N_r''/N''. In particular, uniform sampling with $p_u = 1/N$ for u in U implies that $N_r' = Nn_r/n$ and

$$N_r'' = d_r/[1-(1-1/N)^n].$$

Therefore $N_r'/N' = n_r/n$ and N_r''/N'' can be used as unbiased estimators and $N_r''/N'' = d_r/d$ as an asymptotically unbiased estimator of the relative population frequency P_r for r in R. Generally estimators based on distinct units are preferable to those involving multiplicities.

Super-populations

When the population values $x(u)$ for u in U are considered as fixed and appropriately summarized by the population distribution $(P_r)_R$, inference uncertainty is entirely due to sampling variation. Measurement errors, nonresponse, and other sources of uncertainty have to be modelled. In the survey sampling literature the so-called super-population modelling is a tool that allows for uncertainty in the population values. The population values $x(u)$ are modelled as realisations of i.i.d. random variables over data range space R with a theoretical probability distribution that is specified by some unknown multivariate parameter θ. The focus for inference could then be shifted from the realized population distribution to the super-population described by θ, which is assumed to have generated the population values. There is also an intermediate approach that is called model-assisted inference. Without actually assuming more than that the super-population is a rough model of the population and without focusing on θ, the model is only used for deducing presumptively interesting summary measures of the population. Design-based inference on such measures could then contribute to improved population knowledge.

NETWORKS

Graphs and networks

Graphs used in social network analysis may have variables defined on vertices or edges. The values can be categorical or numerical. Vertex variables can specify properties of the individuals, as in conventional social data analysis. A graph with a categorical vertex variable is sometimes described by a vertex-coloured graph. A graph with variables defined on the edges is called a valued graph. For instance, edge variables can specify strength or intensity of contacts between individuals.

When there are several variables defined on the vertices and edges of a graph, and the focus of interest is on interrelationships between the variables, one often speaks of the valued graph as a network. Large networks with many vertices and complicated structure are of interest in numerous applications. Statistical inference on various properties of the network is then normally based on partial knowledge obtained from sample information collected in the network. The network provides possibilities to vary sampling designs by selecting sample units and observation units in many different ways. Structural and compositional properties of the network might also imply that observations made in the network are obtained by selection procedures that are not controlled by the investigator. The tools of survey sampling theory with controlled sampling designs and model-based or model-assisted estimators can be adapted to network surveys.

Local versus global network properties

Consider a finite population network with N units taken as the vertices in the network. There are N vertex values $x(u)$ in a range space R_1, and $N(N-1)$ edge values $y(u,v)$ in a range space R_2 for $u \neq v$. The frequency distributions of the vertex and edge values describe the composition of the network but are not sufficient to give an appropriate description of its structural properties. Various summary measures of structural properties are given by the dyad counts specifying how the $N(N-1)/2$ unordered pairs of vertices are distributed in $R_1^2 R_2^2$, and by the triad counts specifying how the $N(N-1)(N-2)/6$ unordered triples of vertices are distributed in $R_1^3 R_2^6$. Counts of higher order include star counts specifying how the k-stars are distributed in $R_1 R_2^{2k}$ or in $R_1^{k+1} R_2^{2k}$ for $k = 1, 2, \ldots$. Such counts describe local properties of the network that are informative of part of its structure like symmetry, transitivity, and isolation.

Global properties like connectivity, distance, and clustering are not captured by counts of local properties. Therefore, a probabilistic modelling complement to a probabilistic sampling design is often indispensable in order to gain information about special global network properties.

Generally, the population network can be seen as a data point in the range space

$$R = R_1^N R_2^{N(N-1)}$$

and a general random network corresponds to a probability distribution over R. A meaningful specification has to substantially reduce the dimensionality or the degrees of freedom of that distribution. Needless to say, such modelling must contain a multivariate parameter θ, capturing properties of interest. The network model specified by θ generates the vertex and edge values of the network as realisations of random variables. Thus, a super-population network is a random network with dependence between its vertex and edge values reflecting as much as possible of what is known about the population network. This is in contrast to the super-population approach in ordinary survey sampling where population values are generated by i.i.d. random variables. Network modelling can be considered as an extension of time series modelling that could apply to a network consisting of a single chain or path. Stochastic lattices and random fields are examples of random structures that are of interest in network modelling.

Network models

The combination of probabilistic sampling designs with probabilistic population models is sometimes useful even if the model is rather coarse and does not capture more than some rough structural tendencies in the network. The benefit of the model is that it might suggest essential network statistics that could serve as important population parameters and be estimated by design-based methods. The models might also be useful as "base-line" models for testing specific properties of the network.

Random directed graphs with independent dyads and categorical vertex and edge variables are used as models for different kinds of social structure. Holland and Leinhardt (1970, 1975, 1981) and Frank (1981) are early methodological papers. The textbook by Wasserman and Faust (1994) provides many references. Wellman et al. (1991) is an application of survey sampling with a latent categorical vertex variable. Applications often need exploratory variable selection methods to choose appropriate vertex and edge variables for the dyad statistics. A cluster analysis technique for dyad selection is used by Frank et al. (1985b) and Frank et al. (1985a). General formulae for nonisomorphic dyads and triads when there are categorical vertex and edge variables are given by Frank (1988). Blockmodels are investigated by Snijders and Nowicki (1997) and Nowicki and Snijders (2001).

Markov graphs were introduced by Frank and Strauss (1986). Further work on Markov graphs is given by Robins (1998) and Robins and Pattison (2005). Generalisations to exponential models with arbitrary structural statistics are treated in many recent papers. Some references are Wasserman and Pattison (1996), Pattison and Wasserman (1998), Wasserman and Robins (2005), and Snijders et al. (2006). An important estimation technique for exponential models is described by Snijders (2002). Further references on current trends in statistical network surveys can also be found in theses by Corander (2000), Hagberg (2003), Jansson (1997), Karlberg (1997), Koskinen (2004), Schweinberger (2007), Spreen (1999), Tallberg (2003), and in several contributions to the edited volumes by Brandes and Erlebach (2005), Carrington et al. (2005), Hagberg (2002), and Meyers (2009).

Network statistics

The classical Bernoulli graph is a model that captures only the edge density of the graph by its single parameter p. A blockmodel variant that uses different edge probabilities within and between K blocks of vertices assumes that there is a K-categorical vertex variable affecting the occurrence of edges. This leads to a model with $K(K + 1)/2$ parameters conditional on the vertex variables. If the vertex values are generated as independent outcomes of a K-categorical random variable, $K - 1$ more parameters are added to the model. The Bernoulli blockmodel has $K(K + 1)$ sufficient statistics given by the dyad counts. The appropriateness of the Bernoulli blockmodel can be judged by comparing the $2K(K + 1)(2K + 1)/3$ triad counts with their estimated expected values according to the dyad counts.

For a directed graph a simple model has i.i.d. dyads, and the dyad probabilities are estimated by the relative dyad counts. Using these estimates we can compare the triad counts with their estimated expected values and judge the usefulness of the homogeneous dyad independence model. If the fit is poor, an alternative might be a nonhomogeneous dyad independence model, which allows vertex-specific parameters. A directed

K-categorical blockmodel with independent dyads has $(2K + 1)K$ nonisomorphic dyads and $(3K + 1)K/2$ degrees of freedom. Sufficient statistics are given by the corresponding dyad counts.

Dyad independence in blockmodels has been studied in many different varieties. The vertex variable could be treated as having known or unknown fixed values. The values could also be considered as the outcomes of i.i.d. vertex variables specified by a common probability distribution on the K categories, thereby adding $K - 1$ degrees of freedom to the model. The K-categorical blockmodel has

$$4K(8K^2 + 3K + 1)/3$$

triad counts that can be compared with their estimated expected counts obtained by using the dyad counts. Goodness of fit can be judged after agglomeration of counts corresponding to expected frequencies that are too small.

An alternative nonhomogeneous dyad independence model reflecting local network structure assumes that the dyad probabilities depend on effects for in-degree, out-degree, and local mutuality at its incident vertices. This leads to a structural dyad independence model with $3N - 1$ degrees of freedom and sufficient statistics given by the in-degrees, out-degrees, and number of two-cycles at each vertex. This is the same number of degrees of freedom as in the blockmodel with K around $(2N)^{1/2}$. The classic Holland-Leinhardt model is a further simplification of this structural dyad independence model that assumes that the local mutuality effects are the same for all vertices. This leads to a model with $2N$ degrees of freedom and sufficient statistics given by the total number of two-cycles (mutual edges) and the in-degree and out-degree at each vertex. The Holland-Leinhardt model has the same number of degrees of freedom as a blockmodel with K around $(4N/3)^{1/2}$.

Markov models for undirected graphs have sufficient statistics given by the number of edges, the numbers of m-stars for $m = 2, \ldots, N - 1$, and the number of triangles. An equivalent set of sufficient statistics is obtained by replacing the edge and star counts by the degree distribution. Thus, the degree distribution and the triangle count are sufficient statistics under homogeneity and Markov dependence. It is interesting to note that if we confine the statistics for the degree distribution to its mean and variance, this is equivalent to keeping the counts of edges, two-stars, and triangles only and putting all the parameters for three-stars and larger stars equal to zero. Equivalently, the four triad counts are sufficient statistics in this case.

Markov models for homogeneous directed graphs have sufficient statistics given by counts of edges, mutual edges and various types of triangles and stars. An equivalent set of sufficient statistics is the triangle counts and the trivariate degree distribution that counts vertices according to their numbers of in-edges, out-edges, and mutual edges. A natural simplification restricts the statistics to means, variances and covariances of the trivariate degree distribution. These nine statistics together with the seven triangle counts yield a model with 16 degrees of freedom that seems not to have received the attention it deserves. The triangle counts and the moments of the trivariate degree distribution are all population totals that are easily estimated from sample data by design-based estimators as demonstrated in the following section.

In general exponential models the sufficient statistics are chosen to reflect those structural properties in the network that seem important to control. Thus the properties are not derived from a specified dependence structure in the adjacency matrix. Therefore the sufficient statistics can be adjusted to any available structural statistics. Much research has been devoted to numerical methods for handling estimation and testing for general exponential models.

NETWORK SAMPLING DESIGNS AND DATA

General overview

There are many different designs for data collection in a network. The sampling units can be vertices, pairs of vertices, edges, walks, stars or other subgraphs, and the data observed can be vertex and edge values related to the sampling units in different ways.

If we take the sampling units to be vertices, then a common data set consists of observations on vertex values and edge values in the subgraph induced by the vertex sample. Another data structure consists of edge values for all edges that are incident to any of the sampled vertices. Such data on an induced subgraph and on incident stars generated by a vertex sample are considered in this section. Different vertex sampling designs and estimation methods are treated. Other designs using several sampling stages in the network are walk sampling and snowball sampling. Such designs and data collected from them are considered in separate sections later in this chapter. Specific design possibilities are encountered for walks and snowballs, and they are

illustrated with examples. Various estimation principles that could be convenient for long walks and multiwave snowballs are also discussed. It should be noted that the estimation methods for general vertex sampling designs discussed in this section also apply to walk sampling and snowball sampling.

Vertex sampling

Let V be a finite vertex set of N vertices, and let $(u_1, \ldots, u_n)$ be a sample sequence of vertices selected from V according to a specified probabilistic design. Let S be the set of distinct vertices contained in the sample sequence. Inclusion probabilities according to the sampling design are denoted by

$$P(v \in S) = \pi(v),\ P(u \in S\ \&\ v \in S) = \pi(u, v), \ldots$$

and so forth for vertices $u, v, \ldots$ in V. In particular, $\pi(v, v) = \pi(v)$. If the sequence $(u_1, \ldots, u_n)$ is drawn uniformly at random without replacement

$$\pi(v) = n/N \quad \text{and} \quad \pi(u, v) = n(n - 1)/N(N - 1)$$

for $u \neq v$. If the sequence is drawn with replacement and with probability p_v for $v \in V$, where $\Sigma_v p_v = 1$, the inclusion probabilities are

$$\pi(u) = 1 - (1 - p_u)^n \text{ and } \pi(u, v) = 1 - (1 - p_u)^n$$
$$- (1 - p_v)^n + (1 - p_u - p_v)^n$$

for $u \neq v$. In particular, uniform random sampling with replacement has inclusion probabilities

$$\pi(u) = 1 - (1 - 1/N)^n \quad \text{and} \quad \pi(u, v)$$
$$= 1 - 2\ (1 - 1/N)^n + (1 - 2/N)^n$$

for $u \neq v$. The two uniform sampling designs are examples of homogeneous designs that have inclusion probabilities of any k distinct vertices $v_1, \ldots, v_k$ depending on their number k only,

$$\pi(v_1, \ldots, v_k) = \pi_k$$

for $k = 1, 2, \ldots$. A third example of a homogeneous design is Bernoulli(p) sampling. According to this design the units in V are independently selected for S with a common probability p. The three homogeneous designs mentioned have

$$\pi_k = n^{(k)}/N^{(k)} \qquad \text{(without replacement)}$$
$$\pi_k = \Sigma_{j=0,\ldots,k}\ (-1)^j\ (k^{(j)}/j!)(1 - j/N)^n$$
$$\qquad \text{(with replacement)}$$
$$\pi_k = p^k \qquad \text{(Bernoulli)}$$

for $K = 1, 2, \ldots$. A general Bernoulli design is also of interest. For each vertex v it is independently decided whether v is selected for S with a specified probability $\pi(v)$ strictly between 0 and 1. Thus

$$\pi(u, v) = \pi(u)\pi(v)$$

for $u \neq v$, and so forth for several distinct vertices.

Data on an induced subgraph and estimation of totals

Assume that the data obtained from the vertex sample S consist of the vertex and edge values in the subgraph induced by S. Thus, x_u for u in S and y_{uv} for distinct u and v in S are observed. The population has vertex value total

$$T_1 = \Sigma_u x_u$$

and edge value total

$$T_2 = \Sigma\Sigma_{u \neq v} y_{uv}.$$

In order to estimate these population totals it is convenient to consider a general total

$$Z = \Sigma_u \Sigma_v z_{uv}$$

where the N^2 terms are random variables with expected values

$$Ez_{uv} = \mu_{uv}$$

and covariances

$$Cov(z_{uv}, z_{u'v'}) = \sigma_{uvu'v'}.$$

To handle the N^4 terms in

$$VarZ = \Sigma\Sigma\Sigma\Sigma\sigma_{uvu'v'}$$

the sequences in V^4 are separated into four classes $C_1, \ldots, C_4$ where C_k consists of sequences (u, v, u', v') with k distinct vertices for $k = 1, \ldots, 4$. The sequences in C_2 are further separated into seven classes corresponding to (u,u,u,v), (u,u,v,u), (u,v,u,u), (v,u,u,u), (u,u,v,v), (u,v,u,v), (u,v,v,u) for distinct u and v, and the sequences in C_3 are further separated into six classes corresponding to (u,u,v,w), (u,v,u,w), (u,v,w,u), (v,u,u,w), (v,u,w,u), (v,w,u,u) for distinct u, v, and w. It follows that C_1 has N sequences, C_2 has $7N^{(2)}$ sequences, C_3 has $6N^{(3)}$ sequences, and C_4 has $N^{(4)}$ sequences.

Unbiased estimators of T_1 and T_2 are given by

$$T_1' = \Sigma_v [x_v S_v/\pi(v)]$$

and

$$T_2' = \Sigma\Sigma_{u \neq v} [y_{uv} S_u S_v/\pi(u,v)],$$

where $S_v = I(v \in S)$ are indicator variables. Define

$$z_{uv} = y_{uv} S_u S_v/\pi(u,v)$$

for $u \neq v$ and

$$z_{vv} = x_v S_v/\pi(v).$$

It follows that

$$Z = T_1' + T_2'$$

and

$$VarZ = VarT_1' + VarT_2' + 2Cov(T_1', T_2'),$$

where $VarZ$ is a sum of 15 sub-sums corresponding to the classes C_k and their subclasses. Writing out all sub-sums we get

$$VarT_1' = \Sigma_v x_v^2[1 - \pi(v)]/\pi(v) + \Sigma\Sigma_{u \neq v} x_u x_v \\ [\pi(u,v) - \pi(u)\pi(v)]/\pi(u)\pi(v),$$

$$VarT_2' = \Sigma\Sigma_{u \neq v} y_{uv}(y_{uv} + y_{vu})[1 - \pi(u,v)]/\pi(u,v) + \\ \Sigma\Sigma\Sigma_{\neq} (y_{uv} + y_{vu})(y_{uw} + y_{wu})[\pi(u,v,w) \\ - \pi(u,v)\pi(u,w)]/\pi(u,v)\pi(u,w) + \\ \Sigma\Sigma\Sigma\Sigma_{\neq} y_{uv}y_{u'v'}[\pi(u,v,u',v') - \pi(u,v) \\ \pi(u',v')]/\pi(u,v)\pi(u',v'),$$

$$Cov(T_1', T_2') = \Sigma\Sigma_{u \neq v} x_u(y_{uv} + y_{vu})[1 - \pi(u)]/\pi(u) + \\ \Sigma\Sigma\Sigma_{\neq} x_u y_{vw}[\pi(u,v,w) - \pi(u) \\ \pi(v,w)]/\pi(u) \pi(v,w).$$

In particular, for homogenous sampling designs the formulae simplify to

$$VarT_1' = \Sigma_v x_v^2(1 - \pi_1)/\pi_1 + \Sigma\Sigma_{u \neq v} x_u x_v (\pi_2 - \pi_1^2)/\pi_1^2,$$

$$VarT_2' = \Sigma\Sigma_{u \neq v} y_{uv}(y_{uv} + y_{vu})(1 - \pi_2)/\pi_2 + \\ \Sigma\Sigma\Sigma_{\neq} (y_{uv} + y_{vu})(y_{uw} + y_{wu})(\pi_3 - \pi_2^2)/\pi_2^2 \\ + \Sigma\Sigma\Sigma\Sigma_{\neq} y_{uv}y_{u'v'}(\pi_4 - \pi_2^2)/\pi_2^2,$$

$$Cov(T_1', T_2') = \Sigma\Sigma_{u \neq v} x_u(y_{uv} + y_{vu})(1 - \pi_1)/\pi_1 \\ + \Sigma\Sigma\Sigma_{\neq} x_u y_{vw}(\pi_3 - \pi_1\pi_2)/\pi_1\pi_2.$$

Both for a general sampling design and for a homogeneous design the variances and covariances depend on further population quantities than just T_1 and T_2. In order to estimate those we notice that they are all totals over V, $V^{(2)}$, $V^{(3)}$ or $V^{(4)}$ and can therefore be estimated in a similar way as the totals T_1 and T_2. In general, totals over $V^{(k)}$ are estimated by totals over $S^{(k)}$ with the terms modified by dividing them with the appropriate inclusion probabilities. In the homogeneous case this is simply π_k. For instance, $Cov(T_1',T_2')$ has an unbiased estimator

$$[Cov(T_1',T_2')]' =$$
$$\Sigma\Sigma_{u \neq v} x_u(y_{uv} + y_{vu})S_uS_v[1 - \pi(u)]/\pi(u)\pi(u,v) +$$
$$\Sigma\Sigma\Sigma_{\neq} x_u y_{vw} S_u S_v S_w[\pi(u,v,w) - \pi(u)\pi(v,w)]/$$
$$\pi(u)\,\pi(v,w)\pi(u,v,w),$$

which in the homogeneous case simplifies to

$$[Cov(T_1', T_2')]' = \Sigma\Sigma_{u \neq v} x_u(y_{uv} + y_{vu})S_uS_v(1 - \pi_1)/$$
$$\pi_1\pi_2 + \Sigma\Sigma\Sigma_{\neq} x_u y_{vw} S_u S_v S_w (\pi_3 - \pi_1\pi_2)/\pi_1\pi_2\pi_3.$$

Arbitrary population counts, like dyad counts, triad counts, as well as more general totals of subgraph values, can be handled by this estimation technique.

Estimation of degree distributions

An undirected graph on the population $V = \{1, \ldots, N\}$ is given by its adjacency matrix $y = (y_{uv})$ with $y_{uv} = y_{vu}$ and $y_{vv} = 0$ for u and v in V. The degrees are $y_u = \Sigma_v y_{uv}$ and the degree distribution is given by

$$N_k = \Sigma_u I(y_u = k)$$

for $k = 0, \ldots, N - 1$. Let

$$M_k = \Sigma_{j = 0, \ldots, N - 1} j^k N_j = \Sigma_u y_u^k$$

be the kth moment of the degree distribution for $k = 1, 2, \ldots$. In particular, the first two moments are

$$M_1 = \Sigma_u y_u = \Sigma\Sigma\, y_{uv}$$

and

$$M_2 = \Sigma_u y_u^2 = \Sigma\Sigma\Sigma\, y_{uv} y_{uw},$$

and the mean and variance of the degree distribution are given by

$$\mu = M_1/N$$

and

$$\sigma^2 = M_2/N - M_1^2/N^2$$

Consider a probabilistic sampling design with vertex sample S and sample inclusion indicators $S_u = I(u \in S)$. The inclusion probabilities are

$$E\,S_u = \pi(u),\; E\,S_uS_v = \pi(u,v),\; \text{etc.}$$

Assume that data obtained consist of the subgraph induced by S. The degree within S of a

vertex u in S is given by $\Sigma_v y_{uv}S_v$ and the degree distribution within S is given by

$$n_k = \Sigma_u S_u\, I(\Sigma_v\, y_{uv}S_v = k)$$

for $k = 0, \ldots, n - 1$, where $n = \Sigma_u S_u$ is the size of S. Let

$$m_k = \Sigma_j j^k n_j = \Sigma_u S_u(\Sigma_v y_{uv}S_v)^k$$

be the kth moment of the degree distribution within S. In particular, the first two sample moments are

$$m_1 = \Sigma_u S_u(\Sigma_v y_{uv}S_v) = \Sigma_u\Sigma_v y_{uv}S_uS_v$$

and

$$m_2 = \Sigma_u S_u(\Sigma_v y_{uv}S_v)^2 = \Sigma_u\Sigma_v\Sigma_w y_{uv}y_{uw}S_uS_vS_w.$$

In order to estimate the population moments

$$M_1 = \Sigma_u y_u = \Sigma\Sigma\, y_{uv}$$

and

$$M_2 = \Sigma_u y_u^2 = \Sigma\Sigma\Sigma\, y_{uv}y_{uw} = M_1 + \Sigma\Sigma\Sigma_{v \neq w} y_{uv}y_{uw},$$

the general technique for estimating totals yields the unbiased estimators

$$M_1' = \Sigma\Sigma\, y_{uv}S_uS_v/\pi(u,v)$$

and

$$M_2' = \Sigma\Sigma\Sigma\, y_{uv}y_{uw}S_uS_vS_w/\pi(u,v,w)$$
$$= M_1' + \Sigma\Sigma\Sigma_{v \neq w} y_{uv}y_{uw}S_uS_vS_w/\pi(u,v,w).$$

For homogeneous sampling designs the estimators simplify to

$$M_1' = \Sigma\Sigma\, y_{uv}S_uS_v/\pi_2 = m_1/\pi_2$$

and

$$M_2' = M_1' + \Sigma\Sigma\Sigma_{v \neq w} y_{uv}y_{uw}S_uS_vS_w/\pi_3$$
$$= m_1/\pi_2 + (m_2 - m_1)/\pi_3.$$

The same technique provides unbiased or asymptotically unbiased estimators of M_1^2, μ, and σ^2, as well as unbiased or asymptotically unbiased estimators of their variances. For instance, with homogeneous sampling designs, the mean and variance of the degree distribution are estimated by

$$\mu' = m_1/N\pi_2$$

and

$$(\sigma^2)' = [m_1/\pi_2 + (m_2 - m_1)/\pi_3]/N - [2m_1/\pi_2$$
$$+ 4(m_2 - m_1)/\pi_3 + (m_1^2 + 2m_1 - 4m_2)/\pi_4]/N^2.$$

An unbiased estimator of N is given by $N' = n/\pi_1$, and an unbiased estimator of N^2 is given by $(N^2)' = n(n-1)/\pi_2 + n/\pi_1$.

Let us now consider the estimation of the different population frequencies N_k of vertices of degree k for $k = 0, \ldots, N-1$. The degree distribution within the sample is available to estimate the degree distribution in the population. Consider a sample obtained by uniform random sampling without replacement. The sample degree $\Sigma_v y_{uv} S_v$ has a conditional hypergeometric distribution with parameters $(n-1, k, N-1)$ if $S_u = 1$ and $y_u = k$. The hypergeometric probabilities are defined by

$$h(j; n-1, k, N-1) = \binom{k}{j}\binom{N-1-k}{n-1-j} \Big/ \binom{N-1}{n-1}$$

and they satisfy

$$h(j; n-1, k, N-1) = h(j; k, n-1, N-1)$$

for $j = 0, \ldots, \min(k, n-1)$. It follows that the frequency n_j of sample vertices with sample degree j has the expected value

$$E\, n_j = \Sigma_{k=j, \ldots, N-1}\, (n/N)N_k h(j; n-1, k, N-1)$$

for $j = 0, \ldots, k$. This is a linear equation system that is underdetermined unless we impose further restrictions. It should be natural to assume that $N_k = 0$ for $k \geq n$, which means that the sample size is larger than the maximum degree in the population. This leads to a triangular equation system, which can be solved to give N_k/N as linear functions of $E\, n_j/n$ for $j = k, \ldots, n-1$ and $k = 0, \ldots, n-1$. By substituting n_j for $E\, n_j$ in these solutions we get unbiased estimators N_k' for N_k. They can be formally expressed as

$$N_k'/N = \Sigma_{j=k, \ldots, n-1}\, (n_j/n)\, h(k; j, N-1, n-1)$$

for $k = 0, \ldots, n-1$.

Now assume that the sample S is selected according to a Bernoulli(p) design. Conditional on $S_u = 1$ and $y_u = k$, the sample degree is binomial(k, p), and it follows that

$$E\, n_j = \Sigma_{k=j, \ldots, n-1}\, pN_k\, b(j; k, p)$$

for $j = 0, \ldots, n-1$, where

$$b(j; k, p) = (k^{(j)}/j!)p^j(1-p)^{k-j}.$$

By assuming $N_k = 0$ for $k \geq n$ a triangular equation system is obtained that can be solved for N_k in terms of $E\, n_j$ for $j = k, \ldots, n-1$ and $k = 0, \ldots, n-1$. Substituting n_j for $E\, n_j$, the estimators of N_k are formally given by

$$N_k' = \Sigma_{j=k, \ldots, n-1}\, (n_j/p)\, b(k; j, 1/p)$$

for $k = 0, \ldots, n-1$.

Data on stars obtained from a vertex sample

Assume that the data obtained from the vertex sample S consist of the vertex values x_u for u in S and the edge values y_{uv} for u in S and v in V. As before $y_{vv} = 0$. Thus, the edge values of the stars centred at the sampled vertices are observed together with the vertex values at the star centres only. The vertex value total T_1 of the population can be estimated exactly as in the case with induced subgraph data treated before. For the edge value total T_2 of the population, better estimates can now be obtained because more edge data are available.

Let $y_u = \Sigma_v y_{uv}$ so that $T_2 = \Sigma_u y_u$. Thus, the formulae for estimators, variances, and variance estimators can be copied from those for T_1 with vertex values x_u replaced by vertex degrees y_u. The covariance between the two estimators T_1' and T_2' can be handled by the same technique. We find that

$$Cov(T_1', T_2') = \Sigma\Sigma\, x_u y_v[\pi(u, v) - \pi(u)\pi(v)]/\pi(u)$$
$$\pi(v) = \Sigma_v x_v y_v[1 - \pi(v)]/\pi(v) + \Sigma\Sigma_{\neq} x_u y_v$$
$$[\pi(u, v) - \pi(u)\pi(v)]/\pi(u)\pi(v),$$

and an unbiased covariance estimator is given by

$$[Cov(T_1', T_2')]' = \Sigma_v x_v y_v S_v[1 - \pi(v)]/\pi(v)^2$$
$$+ \Sigma\Sigma_{\neq} x_u y_v S_u S_v[\pi(u,v) - \pi(u)\pi(v)]/\pi(u)\pi(v)$$
$$\pi(u, v).$$

For a homogeneous sampling design the formulae simplify to

$$Cov(T_1', T_2') = \Sigma_v x_v y_v(1 - \pi_1)/\pi_1 + \Sigma\Sigma_{\neq}$$
$$x_u y_v(\pi_2 - \pi_1^2)/\pi_1^2$$

for the covariance and

$$[Cov(T_1', T_2')]' = \Sigma_v x_v y_v S_v(1 - \pi_1)/\pi_1^2 + \Sigma\Sigma_{\neq}$$
$$x_u y_v S_u S_v(\pi_2 - \pi_1^2)/\pi_1^2\pi_2$$

for the covariance estimator.

Degree distributions can be estimated from star data simply by summing inverted inclusion probabilities for all star centres of degree k to get an unbiased estimator of N_k:

$$N_k' = \Sigma_u S_u I(y_u = k)/\pi(u).$$

SNOWBALL SAMPLING

Background

Statistical problems for snowball sampling are considered by Frank (1977, 1979) and Thompson and Frank (2000). Frank and Snijders (1994) use snowball sampling to estimate the size of a hidden population. Sudman and Kalton (1986) and Salganik and Heckathorn (2004) discuss hidden population surveys and respondent-driven sampling. Thompson (2006) treats walk sampling. Network surveys might lack a clear distinction between design-based and model-based statistical inference. However, inclusion probabilities and other tools from survey sampling can be useful even though they need to be estimated. An illustration of this is given by Frank and Carrington (2007) in a study of criminal co-offenders, which shows the power of network survey methods for handling dark figures in statistics on offenders and offences.

Basic definitions and results

Snowball sampling proceeds by successively joining so-called sample waves to the current snowball sample. An initial sample S_0 of vertices is first selected from $V = \{1, \ldots, N\}$ according to an arbitrary sampling design. The first wave W_1 is selected according to a probability sampling design over the class of subsets of the nonsampled vertices that are adjacent after the initial sample. Thus, W_1 is a subset of

$$(V - S_0) \cap A(S_0) = \{v \in V: S_{0v} = 0 \ \& \ \max_u S_{0u} y_{uv} = 1\}$$

where $S_{0v} = I(v \in S_0)$ for v in V. The union of the initial sample and the first wave is the one-wave snowball $S_1 = S_0 U W_1$. Generally, the kth wave W_k is selected according to a probability sampling design over the class of subsets of the nonsampled vertices that are adjacent after the last wave. Thus, W_k is a subset of

$$(V - S_{k-1}) \cap A(W_{k-1}) = \{v \in V: S_{k-1, v} = 0 \ \& \ \max_u W_{k-1, u} y_{uv} = 1\}$$

for $k = 1, 2, \ldots$ with $S_0 = W_0$. Indicator variables are denoted $S_{kv} = I(v \in S_k)$ and $W_{kv} = I(v \in W_k)$ for v

in V and $k = 1, 2, \ldots$. The k-wave snowball is given by the union $S_k = S_{k-1} U W_k$ for $k = 1, 2, \ldots$. The waves are disjoint and satisfy

$$W_k = S_k - S_{k-1},$$

and

$$S_k = W_0 U \ldots U W_k$$

for $k = 1, 2, \ldots$. If all vertices adjacent after W_k have already been sampled in earlier waves, the snowballing stops at stage k and S_k is called a saturated snowball. The snowballing process is then said to have reached an absorbing state. The snowballing process $(S_k: k = 0, 1, \ldots)$ evolves as a stochastic process with a two-step memory. The probability distribution of S_k conditional on $(S_0, \ldots, S_{k-1})$ depends on S_{k-1} and $W_{k-1} = S_{k-1} - S_{k-2}$, that is on S_{k-1} and S_{k-2} only, for $k = 2, 3, \ldots$. Because any two among the three sets S_k, W_{k+1}, S_{k+1} suffice to determine all three, an alternative and equivalent way to look at the snowballing process is to consider the kth state of the process to consist of the pair (S_k, W_k) of the current snowball and its last wave. The snowballing process $[(S_k, W_k): k = 1, 2, \ldots]$ is a Markov chain with transition probabilities

$$P(S_{k+1}, W_{k+1} \mid S_k, W_k) = P(W_{k+1} \mid S_k, W_k)$$

for $S_{k+1} = S_k U W_{k+1}$. The Markov chain is assumed to be time-homogeneous so that the transition probabilities do not depend on the stage parameter k. This means that the wave W_{k+1} is selected according to a design that conditional on (S_k, W_k) depends on y_{uv} for u in W_k and v in $V - S_k$ but not on k. If we denote the set of relevant adjacency indicators by

$$y_k = y(W_k, V - S_k) = \{(u, v, y_{uv}): u \in W_k \ \& \ v \in V - S_k\}$$

it follows that the transition probabilities can be written

$$P(W_{k+1} \mid S_k, W_k) = P(W_{k+1} \mid y_k)$$

and the marginal distribution of the k-wave snowball equals

$$P(S_k) = \Sigma \ldots \Sigma P(W_0)P(W_1 \mid y_0) \ldots P(W_k \mid y_{k-1})$$

where the summation is over all disjoint waves $W_0, \ldots, W_k$ with union S_k. The initial sample $S_0 = W_0$ and each new wave needs to contain at least one vertex so that S_k contains at least $k + 1$ vertices. If S_k contains more vertices, the sum contains one term for each possible distribution of these vertices among the waves. Usually we do not need to determine the selection probabilities for the snowballs but only their low-order inclusion probabilities. The probability of inclusion of vertex v in S_k equals

$$E\,S_{kv} = E\,W_{0v} + \ldots + E\,W_{kv}$$

since the waves are disjoint, and inclusions in different waves are mutually exclusive events. We shall return to the determination of inclusion probabilities for snowball samples after the introduction of a convenient snowballing process in the next section.

Designing recruitments

A convenient model for snowball sampling is a general Bernoulli design for independent recruitments of new vertices. At each new sampled vertex u the vertices v adjacent after u are independently recruited for the next wave with a probability p_{uv}, where $0 < p_{uv} < 1$ if $y_{uv} = 1$, and $p_{uv} = 0$ of $y_{uv} = 0$. A simple example is $p_{uv} = p y_{uv}$ with $0 < p < 1$, but these basic recruitment probabilities should preferably be modelled as some function of latent or observable vertex properties. For instance, it might be possible to set up $p_{uv} = f(a_u, b_v)$ where a_u and b_v are categorical vertex variables with K_1 recruitment activity levels and K_2 recruitment attraction levels, respectively. Thus, each vertex belongs to one of at most K_1K_2 categories and the activity of u and the attraction of v determines the recruitment probability if $y_{uv} = 1$. With such a model there are at most K_1K_2 basic recruitment parameters.

According to a general Bernoulli design for the recruitments, it follows that the transition probabilities for the snowballing process are given by

$$P(W_{k+1} \mid S_k, W_k) = P(W_{k+1} \mid y_k) = p(W_k, W_{k+1})$$
$$q(W_k, V - S_{k+1})$$

where

$$p(A, B) = \prod_{v \in B} p(A, v) = \prod_{v \in B} [1 - q(A, v)]$$

is the probability that every vertex in B is recruited by at least one vertex in A, and

$$q(A, B) = \prod_{v \in B} q(A, v) = \prod_{u \in A, v \in B} q_{uv}$$

is the probability that no vertex in B is recruited by any vertex in A, for arbitrary subsets A and B of V. Here $q_{uv} = 1 - y_{uv}p_{uv}$ and p_{uv} are the

recruitment parameters that could be specified by at most K_1K_2 basic parameters as above.

In order to determine the selection probabilities of the k-wave snowball S_k extensive numerical calculation is required. However, usually it is sufficient to determine inclusion probabilities of low order to set up estimators and their variance estimators. The inclusion probabilities of the initial sample and of the first and second waves can suffice to set up simple estimators, which can be extended by Rao-Blackwellisation to new estimators based on all available snowball data. Rao-Blackwellisation, however, is also a computer-intensive endeavour.

Inclusion probabilities

Assume that the initial sample S_0 has inclusion probabilities $\pi_{0v} > 0$ for v in V and that the recruitments are made by general Bernoulli designs for the waves as described above. Let sample, wave, and recruitment indicators be denoted by

$$S_{kv} = I(v \in S_k), \quad W_{kv} = I(v \in W_k)$$
$$\text{and} \quad z_{uv} = I(u \text{ recruits } v)$$

To find the inclusion probabilities

$$E\,S_{kv} = \pi_{kv}, \quad E\,W_{kv} = \pi_{kv} - \pi_{k-1,v}$$
$$\text{and} \quad E\,S_{kv}S_{kw} = \pi_{kvw}$$

for $k = 1, 2, \ldots$ consider the following relation, which explains that v is included in S_{k+1} if it is either included in S_k or recruited by at least one vertex in the last wave W_k:

$$S_{k+1,v} = S_{kv} + (1 - S_{kv}) \max_u W_{ku} z_{uv}$$

Conditionally on (S_k, W_k), the indicators $S_{k+1,v}$ are independent for different v in V and their expected values are equal to

$$E(S_{k+1,v} \mid S_k, W_k) = S_{kv} + (1 - S_{kv})p(W_k, v)$$

where, as before,

$$p(W_k, v) = 1 - q(W_k, v) = 1 - \prod_u(1 - W_{ku}p_{uv})$$

It follows that the first and second order inclusion probabilities are given by

$$\pi_{k+1,v} = 1 - E[(1 - S_{kv})q(W_k, v)]$$

and, for distinct v and w,

$$\pi_{k+1,vw} = \pi_{k+1,v} + \pi_{k+1,w} - 1 + E[(1 - S_{kv})(1 - S_{kw})q(W_k, v)q(W_k, w)].$$

Using a first order approximation

$$(1 - S_{kv})q(W_k, v) = 1 - S_{kv} - \Sigma_u W_{ku} p_{uv}$$

in these equations leads to the following approximations for the inclusion probabilities

$$\pi_{k+1, v} = \pi_{kv} + \Sigma_u(\pi_{ku} - \pi_{k-1, u})p_{uv}$$

and

$$\pi_{k+1, vw} = \pi_{k+1, v} - \pi_{kv} + \pi_{k+1, w} - \pi_{kw}$$
$$+ \pi_{kvw} - \Sigma_u(\pi_{ku} - \pi_{k-1, u})(1 - q_{uv}q_{uw})$$

for $k = 1, 2, \ldots$ and distinct v and w. The initial values needed for these recursions are given by the inclusion probabilities π_{0v} and $\pi_{0vw} = \pi_{0v} \pi_{0w}$ of the initial sample and the exact values of the inclusion probabilities

$$\pi_{1v} = 1 - \prod_u(1 - \pi_{0u} p_{uv})$$

and

$$\pi_{1vw} = \pi_{1v} + \pi_{1w} - 1 + \prod_u[1 - \pi_{0u}(1 - q_{uv}q_{uw})]$$

of the one-wave snowball. Here, $p_{vv} = 1$ for v in V.

WALK SAMPLING

Basic definitions and results

A special case of snowball sampling that selects only one further vertex at each selection stage is called walk sampling. It is convenient if many one-unit waves can be selected instead of a few larger waves. Walk sampling provides benefits in terms of simplified analysis and more versatile design possibilities. Recent investigations of the World Wide Web and in particular its page ranks have used walk sampling. Walk sampling seems to have potential for social network analysis carried out in large data banks or on the Internet.

Consider a random walk sampling on vertex set $V = \{1, \ldots, N\}$ in a graph with adjacency matrix (y_{uv}). The sample sequence $(u_1, u_2, \ldots)$ is successively selected according to a time-homogeneous Markov chain with transition probabilities

$$P(u_{k+1} = v \mid u_k = u) = P_{uv},$$

where P_{uv} is independent of the stage parameter k, $\Sigma_v P_{uv} = 1$ for u in V, and $P_{uv} = 0$ if and only if $y_{uv} = 0$. The initial vertex u_1 can be arbitrarily selected but if it is possible it is preferable to select it according to the stationary distribution $(p_v)_V$ that satisfies $p_v = \Sigma_u p_u P_{uv}$ for v in V and $\Sigma_v p_v = 1$.

The Markov chain should be irreducible and aperiodic. This means for undirected graphs that the graph should be connected and contain at least one cycle of length one or three. For directed graphs, strong connectedness is required and all cycles must not have lengths that are multiples of a common factor two or larger. An irreducible and aperiodic time-homogeneous Markov chain has a unique limiting distribution

$$P(u_n = v \mid u_1 = u)$$

for increasing n that is independent of u and positive for all v in V. The limiting distribution is equal to the stationary distribution $(p_v)_V$.

If the graph is undirected and transitions are made with equal probabilities to all adjacent vertices, then

$$P_{uv} = y_{uv}/y_u$$

where $y_u = \Sigma_v y_{uv}$ is the degree of vertex u. It follows that the stationary distribution is equal to

$$p_v = y_v / \Sigma_u y_u$$

for $v = 1, \ldots, N$. Thus, a uniform distribution for the transitions implies that the limiting distribution is proportional to the degrees.

If the first sampled vertex u_1 is selected according to the stationary distribution, it follows that the marginal distribution of any vertex u_k in the sample sequence also equals the stationary distribution. With an arbitrary fixed initial vertex u_1 or an initial vertex selected according to a distribution different from the stationary distribution, the distribution of u_n asymptotically approaches the stationary distribution as the sample size n increases. According to ergodic theory, it also follows that the empirical distribution of the sample sequence $(u_1, \ldots, u_n)$ converges to the stationary distribution as n tends to infinity. More precisely, if

$$m_v = \Sigma_i I(u_i = v)$$

is the multiplicity of vertex v in the sample sequence, then $(m_1/n, \ldots, m_N/n)$ converges in distribution to the limiting distribution $(p_1, \ldots, p_N)$ given by the stationary distribution.

The stationary distribution is useful for the scaling of estimators of vertex value totals and edge value totals. For instance, a vertex value total $T_1 = \Sigma_v x_v$ has an estimator

$$T_1' = \Sigma_i \Sigma_v (x_v/p_v) I(u_i = v)$$

that is unbiased if the initial vertex is selected according to the stationary distribution. Otherwise it is asymptotically unbiased. Similarly, an edge value total $T_2 = \Sigma\Sigma_{\neq} \, y_{uv}$ has an estimator

$$T_2' = \Sigma_{i=1,\ldots,n-1} \Sigma\Sigma_{\neq} \, (y_{uv}/p_u P_{uv}) \, I(u_i = u \ \& \ u_{i+1} = v).$$

The sample sequence $(u_1, \ldots, u_n)$ obtained from a random walk sample can sometimes be reduced to the set S of distinct vertices in the sequence. It is required that repeated vertices in the sample sequence can be identified. For instance, data collected for $u_i = v$ should comprise the identity of v. An estimator of T_1 based on S can be given as

$$T_1'' = \Sigma_{v \in S} \, [x_v/\pi(v)],$$

where the inclusion probability $\pi(v) = P(m_v > 0)$ is the probability that vertex v is included in the sample sequence. To estimate an edge value total T_2 from data based on S, we need inclusion probabilities

$$\pi(u,v) = P(m_u > 0 \ \& \ m_v > 0).$$

Unless the walk sample sequence is very short, it might be difficult to calculate the inclusion probabilities. For long walk sample sequences, it is preferable to keep the sample sequence with multiplicities and use the limiting stationary distribution to adjust sample data.

Designing the limiting distribution

The stationary limiting distribution is fundamental for drawing inference from random walk samples. Therefore, it is important that it is possible to design the walk sampling to obtain any preassigned limiting distribution. This is achieved by modifying the transition probabilities $P = (P_{uv})$ determined by the population graph.

In order to obtain an arbitrary specified limiting distribution $q = (q_1, \ldots, q_N)$, the transitions according to P cannot be applied without a special checking by the investigator. Trial transitions according to P should be accepted or rejected. To specify a rule for accepting a transition from u to v, we consider new transition probabilities $Q = (Q_{uv})$, satisfying a reversibility condition

$$q_u Q_{uv} = q_v Q_{vu}$$

for all u and v in V. The stationary distribution according to Q is given by q since by reversibility

$$\Sigma_u q_u Q_{uv} = \Sigma_u q_v Q_{vu} = q_v$$

for v in V. If Q is defined by

$$Q_{uv} = \min(P_{uv}, q_v P_{vu}/q_u)$$

for $u \neq v$, and

$$Q_{uu} = 1 - \Sigma_{v \neq u} \, Q_{uv},$$

it follows that Q satisfies the reversibility condition. In fact,

$$q_u Q_{uv} = \min(q_u P_{uv}, q_v P_{vu}) = q_v Q_{vu}$$

for $u \neq v$.

If the walk at stage k is in position $u_k = u$, the next transition is determined in two steps. First, a transition trial according to P is made. It would be to v with probability P_{uv} but in a second step it is accepted with a probability Q_{uv}/P_{uv} and rejected with a probability $1 - Q_{uv}/P_{uv}$. Thus, after the second step the transition either goes to v with probability Q_{uv} or is forced to stay at u for another transition trial according to P. The investigator has to be able to decide whether to accept or reject a transition. Therefore, the acceptance probability

$$Q_{uv}/P_{uv} = \min(1, \, q_v P_{vu}/q_u P_{uv})$$

must be known, and it must be judged whether the probability P_{vu} of a return to u from the next suggested position v is smaller than $q_u P_{uv}/q_v$.

As an illustration of this procedure, we consider a directed graph with out-degrees $a_u = \Sigma_v y_{uv}$ and equal transition probabilities

$$P_{uv} = y_{uv}/a_u$$

for all vertices adjacent after u. It might be difficult to find the stationary distribution. Assume that it is desired to adjust the transition probabilities so that its stationary distribution has probabilities proportional to the out-degrees:

$$q_u = a_u/(a_1 + \ldots + a_N).$$

According to the formula above, the modified transition probabilities should be equal to

$$Q_{uv} = \min(y_{uv}/a_u, \, q_v y_{vu}/a_v q_u) = y_{uv} y_{vu}/a_u$$

for $u \neq v$. This means that a transition from u to v is accepted if and only if there are mutual edges between u and v. The investigator must be able to verify mutuality.

As another example, assume that the desired stationary distribution should have probabilities proportional to in-degrees $b_u = \Sigma_v y_{vu}$. With

$$q_u = b_u/(b_1 + \ldots + b_N)$$

it follows that the transition probabilities should be modified for $u \neq v$ to

$$Q_{uv} = \min(y_{uv}/a_u, q_v y_{vu}/a_v q_u) = (y_{uv} y_{vu}/a_u)$$
$$\min(1, r_v/r_u),$$

where $r_u = b_u/a_u$ is the in-degree to out-degree ratio of vertex u in V. This means that a transition from u to v is accepted to mutual contacts with a probability $\min(1, r_v/r_u)$. A vertex v with mutual edges to u is always accepted if it has $r_v \geq r_u$; otherwise, it is accepted with probability r_v/r_u. Now the investigator needs to be able to verify mutuality and to calculate the ratio r_u at the sampled vertices. For instance, the investigator might observe both in- and out-degrees at the sampled vertices.

Finally, consider how a uniform limiting distribution $q_v = 1/N$ for v in V can be obtained. The transition probabilities should be equal to

$$Q_{uv} = \min(P_{uv}, P_{vu}) = (y_{uv} y_{vu}/a_u) \min(1, a_u/a_v)$$

for $u \neq v$. Again only transitions to mutual contacts are allowed. Those v with an out-degree smaller than that of u are always accepted. Others are accepted with probability a_u/a_v. The investigator should be able to verify mutuality and observe out-degrees at the sampled vertices.

REFERENCES

Bloemena, A.R. (1964) *Sampling from a Graph*. Amsterdam: Mathematical Centre Tracts.

Bollobas, B. (2001) *Random Graphs*. Cambridge: Cambridge University Press.

Bonato, A. (2008) *A Course on the Web Graph*. Providence, RI: American Mathematical Society.

Brandes, U. and Erlebach, T. (eds) (2005) *Network Analysis*. Berlin: Springer Verlag.

Capobianco, M. (1970) 'Statistical inference in finite populations having structure', *Transactions of the New York Academy of Science*, 32: 401–13.

Carrington, P.J., Scott, J. and Wasserman, S. (eds) (2005) *Models and Methods in Social Network Analysis*. Cambridge: Cambridge University Press.

Cassel, C.M., Särndal, C.E. and Wretman, J. (1993) *Foundations of Inference in Survey Sampling*. Malabar, FL: Krieger Publ. Comp.

Corander, J. (2000) 'On Bayesian graphical model determination'. PhD dissertation, Stockholm University, Stockholm.

Diestel, R. (2005) *Graph Theory*. New York: Springer Verlag.

Erdös, P. and Renyi, A. (1959) 'On random graphs. I', *Publicationes Mathematicae Debrecen*, 6: 290–97.

Erdös, P. and Renyi, A. (1960) 'On the evolution of random graphs', *Publ. Math. Inst. Hungar. Acad. Sci.*, 5: 17–61.

Frank, O. (1969) 'Structure inference and stochastic graphs', *Swedish Research Institute of National Defence FOA-Reports*, 3(6): 1–10.

Frank, O. (1971) 'Statistical inference in graphs', PhD dissertation, Stockholm University, Stockholm.

Frank, O. (1977) 'Survey sampling in graphs', *Journal of Statistical Planning and Inference*, 1: 235–64.

Frank, O. (1979) 'Estimation of population totals by use of snowball samples', in P. Holland and S. Leinhardt (eds), *Perspectives on Social Network Research*. New York: Academic Press. pp. 319–47.

Frank, O. (1980) 'Estimation of the number of vertices of different degrees in a graph', *Journal of Statistical Planning and Inference*, 4: 45–50.

Frank, O. (1981) 'A survey of statistical methods for graph analysis', in S. Leinhardt (ed.), *Sociological Methodology – 1981*. San Francisco: Jossey-Bass. pp. 110–55.

Frank, O. (1987) 'Random sampling and social networks – a survey of various approaches', *Mathematique, Informatique et Sciences Humaines*, 26(104): 19–33.

Frank, O. (1988) 'Triad count statistics', *Discrete Mathematics*, 72: 141–49.

Frank, O. and Carrington, P.C. (2007) 'Estimation of offending and co-offending using available data with model support', *Journal of Mathematical Sociology*, 31: 1–46.

Frank, O., Hallinan, M. and Nowicki, K. (1985a) 'Clustering of dyad distributions as a tool in network modelling', *Journal of Mathematical Sociology*, 11: 47–64.

Frank, O., Komanska, H. and Widaman, K. (1985b) 'Cluster analysis of dyad distributions in networks', *Journal of Classification*, 2: 219–38.

Frank, O. and Snijders, T. (1994) 'Estimating the size of hidden populations using snowball sampling', *Journal of Official Statistics*, 10: 53–67.

Frank, O. and Strauss, D. (1986) 'Markov graphs', *Journal of the American Statistical Association*, 81: 832–42.

Goodman, L.A. (1961) 'Snowball sampling', *Annals of Mathematical Statistics*, 32: 148–70.

Granovetter, M. (1976) 'Network sampling: Some first steps', *American Journal of Sociology*, 81: 1287–303.

Hagberg, J. (ed.) (2002) *Contributions to Social Network Analysis, Information Theory and Other Topics in Statistics. A Festschrift in Honour of Ove Frank on the Occasion of His 65th Birthday*. Stockholm: Dept. of Statistics, Stockholm University.

Hagberg, J. (2003) 'On degree variance in random graphs', PhD dissertation, Stockholm University, Stockholm.

Holland, P.W. and Leinhardt, S. (1970) 'A method for detecting structure in sociometric data', *American Journal of Sociology*, 76: 492–513.

Holland, P.W. and Leinhardt, S. (1975) 'Local structure in social networks', in D. Heise (ed.), *Sociological Methodology*. San Francisco: Jossey-Bass. pp. 1–45.

Holland, P.W. and Leinhardt, S. (1981) 'An exponential family of probability distributions for directed graphs', *Journal of the American Statistical Association*, 76: 33–65.

Janson, S., Luczak, T. and Rucinski, A. (2000) *Random Graphs*. New York: Wiley.

Jansson, I. (1997) 'On statistical modelling of social networks', PhD dissertation, Stockholm University, Stockholm.

Karlberg, M. (1997) 'Triad count estimation and transitivity testing in graphs and digraphs', PhD dissertation, Stockholm University, Stockholm.

Koskinen, J. (2004) 'Essays on Bayesian inference for social networks', PhD dissertation, Stockholm University, Stockholm.

Meyers, R. (ed.) (2009) *Encyclopaedia of Complexity and Systems Science*. New York: Springer Verlag.

Morgan, D.L. and Rytina, S. (1977) 'Comment on "Network sampling: Some first steps, by M Granovetter"', *American Journal of Sociology*, 83: 722–27.

Mukhopadhyay, P. (2001) *Topics in Survey Sampling*. New York: Springer Verlag.

Nowicki, K. and Snijders, T.A.B. (2001) 'Estimation and prediction for stochastic blockstructures', *Journal of the American Statistical Association*, 96: 1077–87.

Pattison, P. and Wasserman, S. (1998) 'Logit models and logistic regressions for social networks. II: Multivariate relations', *British Journal of Mathematical and Statistical Psychology*, 52: 169–93.

Proctor, C.H. (1967) 'The variance of an estimate of linkage density from a simple random sample of graph nodes', *Proceedings of the Social Statistics Section of the American Statistical Association*, 342–43.

Proctor, C.H. (1979) 'Graph sampling compared to conventional sampling', in P.W. Holland and S. Leinhardt (eds), *Perspective on Social Network Research*. New York: Academic Press. pp. 301–18.

Robins, G.L. (1998) 'Personal attitudes in inter-personal contexts: Statistical models for individual characteristics and social relationships', PhD dissertation, University of Melbourne, Melbourne.

Robins, G.L. and Pattison, P. (2005) 'Interdependencies and social processes: Dependence graphs and generalized dependence structures', in P.J. Carrington, J. Scott and S. Wasserman (eds), *Models and Methods in Social Network Analysis*. Cambridge: Cambridge University Press. pp. 192–214.

Salganik, M.J. and Heckathorn, D.D. (2004) 'Sampling and estimation in hidden populations using respondent-driven sampling', *Sociological Methodology*, 34: 193–239.

Särndal, C.E., Swensson, B. and Wretman, J. (1992) *Model Assisted Survey Sampling*. New York: Springer Verlag.

Schweinberger, M. (2007) 'Statistical methods for studying the evolution of networks and behaviour', PhD dissertation, University of Groningen, Groningen.

Sirken, M.G. (1970) 'Household surveys with multiplicity', *Journal of the American Statistical Association*, 63: 257–66.

Snijders, T.A.B. (2002) 'Markov chain Monte Carlo estimation of exponential random graph models', *Journal of Social Structure*, 3(2).

Snijders, T.A.B. and Nowicki, K. (1997) 'Estimation and prediction of stochastic blockmodels for graphs with latent block structure', *Journal of Classification*, 14: 75–100.

Snijders, T.A.B., Pattison, P., Robins, G.L. and Handcock, M. (2006) 'New specifications for exponential random graph models', *Sociological Methodology*, 36(1): 99–153.

Spreen, M. (1999) 'Sampling personal network structures: Statistical inference in Ego-graphs', PhD dissertation, University of Groningen, Groningen.

Stephan, F.F. (1969) 'Three extensions of sample survey technique', in N.L. Johnson and H. Smith Jr. (eds), *New Developments in Survey Sampling*. New York: Wiley.

Sudman, S. and Kalton, G. (1986) 'New developments in the sampling of special populations', *Annual Review of Sociology*, 12: 401–29.

Tallberg, C. (2003) 'Bayesian and other statistical approaches for analyzing network block-structures', PhD dissertation, Stockholm University, Stockholm.

Thompson, M.E. (1997) *Theory of Sample Surveys*. London: Chapman & Hall.

Thompson, S.K. (2006) 'Targeted random walk designs', *Survey Methodology*, 32: 11–24.

Thompson, S. and Frank, O. (2000) 'Model-based estimation with link-tracing sampling designs', *Survey Methodology*, 26: 87–98.

Wasserman, S. and Faust, K. (1994) *Social Network Analysis*. Cambridge: Cambridge University Press.

Wasserman, S. and Pattison, P. (1996) 'Logit models and logistic regressions for social networks. I: An introduction to Markov random graphs and p*', *Psychometrika*, 60: 401–26.

Wasserman, S. and Robins, G.L. (2005) 'An introduction to random graphs, dependence graphs, and p*', in P.J. Carrington, J. Scott and S. Wasserman (eds), *Models and Methods in Social Network Analysis*. Cambridge: Cambridge University Press. pp 148–61.

Wellman, B., Frank, O., Espinoza, V., Lundquist, S. and Wilson, C. (1991) 'Integrating individual, relational and structural analysis', *Social Networks*, 13: 223–49.

27

Qualitative Approaches

Betina Hollstein

INTRODUCTION

From the outset, network research has made use of qualitative data, less structured approaches to data collection, and interpretive methods in describing and analyzing social networks. In the 1950s and 1960s, British social anthropologists conducted ethnographic community studies on class structures in small Norwegian island parishes (Barnes, 1954), networks in Central African towns (Mitchell, 1969), and also personal networks in their own country (Bott, 1957). Roethlisberger and Dickson's (1939) seminal study of the Western Electric Company, a pathbreaking contribution to organization research, adopted an explorative, interpretive, and inductive approach geared toward openness and responsiveness for what was happening in the work teams under study. Besides experiments, they mostly relied on participant observation at the workplace and nondirective interviewing. The concepts developed in these studies became important points of reference in network research, for instance, density (Mitchell, 1969), cliques and clusters (Barnes, 1969), or the distinction between formal and informal organization (Roethlisberger and Dickson, 1939).

The potential benefits of a qualitative approach in network research, however, are not just limited to the opportunities for exploring and developing new concepts. Qualitative approaches to data collection and analysis are powerful tools, which can enrich the study of social networks in substantial ways. Among other things, qualitative research methods offer special tools for addressing challenges faced in network research, namely to explicate the problem of agency, linkages between network structure and network actors, as well as questions relating to the constitution and dynamics of social networks. The most fruitful results are achieved when qualitative methods, more standardized methods used to describe network structures, as well as quantitative methods are employed in concert.

The following chapter gives an overview of qualitative approaches and methods used in studying social networks. It gives a systematic account of the contributions of qualitative methods to social network research, illustrating them with empirical studies from a variety of research fields.

First, however, we must determine more precisely what we mean when speaking of qualitative research and qualitative data.

QUALITATIVE APPROACHES TO SOCIAL REALITY: THE SEARCH FOR MEANING

When we speak of qualitative methods, we are referring to a heterogeneous research landscape, which, due to this variety, is difficult to comprehensively account for. Among them are different forms of observation, interviewing techniques with low levels of standardization (such as open-ended, unstructured interviews, partially or semistructured interviews, guided or narrative interviews), and the collection of documents or archival data. At the same time, a host of methods are used for analysis, which rest on various theoretical assumptions and methodological positions. Among them are symbolic interactionism, sociology of knowledge, phenomenology, ethnomethodology, and constructivism to name but a few major approaches. Yet, in spite of their differences, those approaches all share some common ground, as advocates of the "interpretive paradigm" agree on certain ideas about the nature of social reality (Hollstein and Ullrich, 2003). First, social reality is not simply given but *constructed*. Recall the well-known Thomas theorem, "If men define situations as real, they are real in their consequences." Second, social reality is shaped by social meaning. Social reality is always a *meaningful* reality and, by representing meaning, refers to a context of action in which actors (deliberately) organize action. Third, social reality always depends on a certain *point of view* or perspective and is therefore tied to social location. And last, since social reality is negotiated, it is always *dynamic*: social reality is a process. In these aspects, one can recognize a common basis of such different methodological positions as symbolic interactionism, ethnomethodology, or phenomenology.[1]

Interpretive approaches view these aspects of social reality to be of such key importance that they make up an area of social research in its own right that also requires an appropriate methodology of its own. The defining feature of qualitative methods is the pivotal role assigned the *understanding of meaning (Sinn-Verstehen)*. Qualitative research aims to systematically reconstruct such meaning or, in other words, involves what in German has been coined a *methodically controlled understanding of the other*. Qualitative approaches emphasize that making sense of action and meaning (verbal utterances are also speech acts) always involves understanding the other. In this respect, they adopt a stance akin to everyday communication, which also fundamentally relies on interpretation and understanding (*first-order constructs*) and in this regard is not categorically different from the process of understanding as applied by the researcher (*second-order constructs*). As opposed to the objects of research, however, the researcher has the privilege of being in a position to reflect upon and reconstruct the situation without facing demands to act and being forced to do so under the time constraints imposed by the situation. Differences between qualitative approaches emerge depending on the conception of "meaning" one adopts and/or the kind of "meaning" that is supposed to be analyzed. For example, phenomenology is concerned with actors' subjective perspectives. In contrast, objective hermeneutics aims at reconstructing latent

(unconscious) meaning and the inner logic of interaction systems (Oevermann et al., 1979; cf. Titscher et al., 2000). Finally, ethnomethodology is not interested in the thematic content of meaning (instead, it focuses on the "how" of action, actors' sense-making practices, and the formal rules of communication).

Given the objective of understanding meaning, the two most important aspects for analysis can be derived: first of all, if something has a "meaning," it is understood that such meaning does not exist apart from a context, that is, from a specific frame of reference. This is the basic idea of *contextuality*: one can only understand the meaning of an action and/or an act of expression with reference to the context of this action or expression. For example, in a biographical interview the frame of reference (context) would be the entire life history. Second, an approach along the lines of a *methodically controlled understanding of the other* demands the researcher be open to the subject matter and acknowledge that any *previous understanding* of the topic in question is only *preliminary*: that which is not yet recognized, cannot yet be defined. This does not suggest handling preconceptions about the subject matter in a naïve fashion, for instance, by simply denying the preconceptions' existence. Rather, an explorative and inductive approach systematically geared toward maintaining openness must start with an explication of one's own preconceptions and commonsense knowledge on the matter of concern. This should occur while at the same time remaining responsive to the new and unexpected – that is, open toward the object of research (Hopf, 1979).

Certain methodological principles for data collection and analysis follow from the objective of understanding meaning.[2] *Open* procedures are required in collecting data (i.e., in particular, less structured interviews and observation methods or use of documents already available), and data analysis calls for use of *interpretive* methods. Applying openness in data collection, above all else, means to design the instrument employed for this purpose in a way that it can cover as broad a data stream as possible. We must take care not to exclude certain data beforehand by the design of our research instruments (i.e., by phrasing questions in very general terms, thus avoiding suggestive questions, and allowing interviewees to elaborate their own frame of relevance and symbol systems when giving answers). The context of meaning should thus be allowed to unfold in as undistorted a form as possible. Accordingly, any act of expression (be it action, a verbal utterance, or a written text) that allows inferences about the context of action, system of meaning, and frame of reference related to the instance of expression in question is considered *qualitative data*.

Overall, as one zeroes in on the object of research, a qualitative approach does so in an open mindset and gradually, inductive and by way of iteration. There are different ways to ensure validity and methodically control the fact that researchers are bound by their perspectives. For example, theoretical sampling and comparative analyses, like in grounded theory (Glaser and Strauss, 1967), interpretation and discussion of the material in groups of researchers, as well as the explication and representation of the steps of analyses. Of course, such a stepwise, gradual approach to the subject matter does not allow raising claims of representativity. Instead, when making statements that go beyond the sample, detailed theoretical justification has to be provided on the basis of the concrete results and procedure. This implies careful consideration of the selectivity of the cases investigated as well as the sampling criteria applied.

The discussion so far has sought to argue the case that qualitative methods are especially well suited for certain kinds of research questions and objects of research (Hopf, 1979). In formal respect, new or marginal phenomena fall into this category or are phenomena that have not yet been studied. In terms of content, we must distinguish between interpretations, relevances, and complex interpretation systems as well as between structured social entities and interaction systems. The latter are made of loose systems of interaction (such as conversations or consultations), group and clique relationships, as well as industrial, state, and other types of organizations (Hopf, 1979).

CONTRIBUTIONS OF QUALITATIVE APPROACHES TO NETWORK STUDIES

Now that we have determined the nature of qualitative methodology let us turn to possible applications in network research. There are essentially six areas most suitable for qualitative research: exploration of networks, network practices, network orientations and assessments, network effects, network dynamics, and the validation of network data. These are the areas where a qualitative approach can hence be expected to yield the most promising results. They will be exemplified drawing on empirical case studies from different fields of network research.

Exploration of networks

First of all, there is the classical field for applying qualitative procedures: issues that one knows little

about because they are either entirely new or have yet to be studied. In such cases, qualitative studies are employed to explore new or yet unexplored forms of networks, integration patterns, and network practices, which are then followed up by quantitative, hypothesis-testing forms of investigation at a later time. This can involve exploring egocentric networks of certain people or groups of people, for instance, networks of "corner boys" in slums (Whyte, 1955), networks of migrants (Wong and Salaff, 1998; Schütze, 2006), or junior researchers commuting between continents in pursuit of their academic careers (Scheibelhofer, 2009). Networks of organizations can be the objects of such exploration as well, for instance, the effectiveness of community mental health networks (Provan and Milward, 1995) or the networks in which firms are embedded (Uzzi, 1997). Finally, entire networks are also explored: networks in small villages (Barnes, 1954), in towns (Mitchell, 1969), social movements (Broadbent, 2003; Mische, 2003, 2008), or transnational issue networks, their actors, their knowledge practices, and networking activities (Riles, 2000).

In many cases, such exploration is only the first – preparatory – stage leading up to the main study, which then follows a quantitative design, for instance, when policy networks or networks of research collaborators are initially assessed for important topics, events, actors, and types of collaboration (Franke and Wald, 2006; Baumgarten and Lahusen, 2006). The methods of choice in those cases are typically document research and expert interviews. Thorough preliminary studies of a qualitative nature and pretests are in order especially in quantitative, standardized research on entire networks. Since such studies typically require expending huge efforts on data collection, detailed knowledge of the field under study is an important precondition for research to yield rich results (Baumgarten and Lahusen, 2006).

Network practices

The concrete acts, practices, interactions, and communication patterns in light of the respective contexts in which they occur – thus what actors actually do and how they network are other ways to apply qualitative approaches. What kinds of exchange patterns characterize the network ties of immigrants (Menjivar, 2000; Dominguez and Watkins, 2003) or the ties between entrepreneurial firms (Uzzi, 1997)? What do cooperation and interaction patterns in innovation networks (Franke and Wald, 2006; Gluesing et al., forthcoming) look like? What cultural practices are involved in the "art of networking" among the nobility during the time of the Italian Renaissance (McLean, 1998), or what are the main conversational mechanisms in Brazilian youth organizations (Mische, 2003, 2008)?

In investigating network practices, traditional social anthropological methods are most valuable. The methods used are mostly observational techniques and in-depth interviewing, for instance, for the study of class structures in small Norwegian island parishes (Barnes, 1954) or in investigating gossip in Central African social networks (Epstein, 1969). The Chicago School and the Birmingham Centre for Contemporary Cultural Studies applied ethnographic approaches in research on their own society, especially in studies on the cultural practices of fringe groups and subcultures, for instance, as in William Foote Whyte's (1955) classic study of the *Street Corner Society* in an Italian slum. Furthermore, ethnographic approaches, observation techniques, and open-ended interviews are also used in research on collaboration and innovation networks, new patterns of work, newly emerging roles, and new meaning within global networking organizations (Gluesing et al., forthcoming). Ethnographic research also played a key role in observing the modes of discourse, communication patterns, and conversational dynamics that Ann Mische, an advocate of relational sociology, studied in Brazilian social movements (2003, 2008).

Sometimes documents are the main source of information in uncovering cultural practices of networking: for instance, in his study on the art of networking in the Italian Renaissance, Paul McLean (1998) analyzed several hundreds of private letters through which Florentines sought favors from one another. Based on an interactionist approach to the presentation of self and political culture, he analyzed the strategies reflected in these writings that members of this society employed in constructing network ties with patrons and in building their own careers. "Network work" can also be approached by reconstructing types of actors. This, for example, is how Engelbrecht (2006) examined the dynamics of knowledge in religious networks in a phenomenological analysis. Based on in-depth interviews with key members of religious communities, he differentiates two forms of contact (bridges) among religious networks, the type he coins "diplomat" and the type referred to as "traveler." While the diplomat mainly acts as a mediator, translator, and innovator in the dialogue of the religions, the traveler is characterized by spiritual learning that transcends the traditional demarcation lines drawn by religious groups and traditions.

Network orientations and assessments

Qualitative procedures are particularly suitable for collecting data on actor interpretations, individual systems of relevance, and orientations of action. This aspect gains relevance in network research concerned with actors' perceptions and assessments of the relationships and networks of which they are a part. Research falling into this category may address, for instance, how people locate themselves in their social networks, people's sense of belonging, or feelings of loneliness, as in studies on patterns of integration and network strategies of migrants (Wong and Salaff, 1998; Schütze, 2006), commuters (Scheibelhofer, 2009), members of social movements (Höfer et al., 2006), or the elderly (Schütze and Lang, 1996; Hollstein, 2002). These studies are preoccupied with individual perceptions, meanings, orientations, and strategies involved in personal networks. Sometimes only certain relationships are subjected to qualitative analysis, for instance, different meanings of friendship (Pahl and Spencer, 2004). Other studies specifically examine certain aspects of relationships, for instance, which ties play a role in parenthood decisions (Keim et al., forthcoming), the significance of emotional closeness (Hollstein, 2002), or what people mean when they state in the U.S. General Social Survey that they consult others in "important matters" (Bearman and Parigi, 2004). Individual perceptions and assessments, however, not only play a role in personal, egocentric networks but also in networks within and between organizations. Research concerned with the functioning and evaluation of research and innovation networks (Franke and Wald, 2006) or the assessment of the effectiveness of mental health systems (Provan and Milward, 1995) belongs in this category. In these cases, the respondents are approached as experts of their field of action. Their perception of their environment (context of action) is shaped by their specific social position. They define problems and objectives, assign relevance, and pursue strategies accordingly.

Typically, unstructured or semistructured interviews and open-ended questions are used for data collection, allowing interviewees to freely respond in accordance with their own systems of relevance to the greatest possible extent. Of course, perceptions, systems of relevance, and attributions of meaning can also be assessed by employing standardized methods of data collection and formal methods of analysis (Krackhardt, 1987; Carley, 1984, 1997). Nevertheless, an open, inductive approach is in order in any research of a more exploratory nature as well as in cases where individual meanings or systems of relevance can be expected to vary considerably among respondents or where there is reason to suspect considerable disparity between respondents' perspectives and the system of relevance assumed by the researcher (Hollstein, 2001; Franke and Wald, 2006).

Whereas the previous uses are primarily of a descriptive nature, qualitative approaches can also be of explanatory value: they can help to uncover how networks actually matter (i.e., the effects of networks) and how networks evolve and change over time. Here, open, less structured procedures of data collection and interpretive approaches in data analysis are in order in cases where we expect *context* and *actor strategies* to play a crucial role in determining network impact or network composition and network dynamics (Provan and Milward, 1995; Mische, 2003; Franke and Wald, 2006).

How networks matter

Qualitative approaches not only give insight into how networks work (i.e., the practices of networking), but they can also contribute to a better understanding of how networks matter and – in combination with quantitative approaches – of what mechanisms and conditions figure in when producing certain network outcomes. Sandra Susan Smith (2005), for instance, examined job-finding assistance and strategies of activating social capital among the black urban poor. The in-depth interviews show that people who have job-relevant information and some leverage in this respect are very reluctant to provide job-finding assistance for the time and emotional energy it involves and, in some cases, the risk it may pose to one's own reputation. Other research has employed qualitative interviews and participant observation in the study of assistance practices among poor immigrants (Menjivar, 2000; Dominguez and Watkins, 2003), the impact of personal networks on decisions to emigrate (Wong and Salaff, 1998), and on decisions affecting fertility (Bernardi, 2003; Bernardi et al., 2007), as well as for the analysis of connections between network position and conversion (Smilde, 2005). Qualitative interviewing and participant observation are also used in organization research, for instance, to account for success or failure of research or innovation networks (Franke and Wald, 2006) or to identify conditions for the effectiveness of mental health systems (Provan and Milward, 1995). The members of organizations are considered as experts on the networks of which they are part. Accordingly, they are interviewed about their perceptions and assessments of

problems (e.g., why cooperation between research teams failed) and about specific contexts and strategies of action (e.g., framework conditions and patterns of interpretation in the fields of nanotechnology, astrophysics, and microeconomics; Franke and Wald, 2006). Drawing on ethnographic fieldwork in entrepreneurial firms, Brian Uzzi (1997) identifies characteristics of embedded interfirm relationships (trust, fine-grained information transfer, and joint problem-solving arrangements) and explicates the mechanisms by which embeddedness shapes organizational and economic outcomes. It is worth noting that the studies that go beyond *thick descriptions* (Geertz, 1973) to explain the impact of networks in terms of *Verstehen* are always comparative studies. Generalization of findings and the formulation of theoretical models that are grounded in data (Glaser and Strauss, 1967) are achieved by systematically comparing cases and taking different contexts of action into consideration (e.g., Provan and Milward, 1995; Franke and Wald, 2006), as well as by careful analysis of (on first glance) contradictory observations (e.g., Provan and Milward, 1995; Mische, 2003).

Understanding network dynamics

Apart from the question of how networks function, issues related to the formative conditions, dynamic processes, and change of networks pose the greatest theoretical and methodological challenges for network research (cf. Jansen, 1999; Snijders, this volume). This concerns not only fluctuation or change in networks over time but also fluctuation and change in networks in physical space (e.g., migrant networks). Qualitative social research provides unique means for understanding (in the sense of *Verstehen*) network change: since so far little is still known about the emergence and change of networks, qualitative research frequently serves for purposes of network exploration. Actor orientations and strategies are a first source of important insights into network formation and change. However, since network dynamics always involve at least two actors, analysis of concrete interaction and network practices are key to understanding the dynamic side of network development. For example, Uzzi's (1997) in-depth interviews with managers of entrepreneurial firms reveal how embedded ties are formed. *Embedded ties* are distinct from so-called *arm's-length ties* in that the former are defined by special bonds of trust entailing specific competitive advantages. Embedded ties are products of third-party referral networks and already existing personal networks;

in forging such ties, so-called *go-betweens* (persons acting as links between previously unconnected actors) play an important mediating role (Uzzi, 1997). In cases where research on network dynamics also seeks to understand connections between network orientations and actual network changes, longitudinal data on concrete networks, changes in those networks, actor orientations, and shifts in such orientations are most suited. The studies on migrant acculturation by Menjivar (2000) and Schütze (2006) or on socialization and social integration of young adults by Bidart and Lavenu (2005) are examples for such research. An interpretive analysis of network change can also be based on document analysis, as in Crossley's study (2008) of the changing music scene in Manchester. If the inquiry is concerned with the influence of concrete social interaction and actor practices on network dynamics, observation over lengthy periods of time can be expected to deliver the best data basis for this purpose. Gluesing et al.'s study (forthcoming) of innovation networks in global teams or Ann Mische's studies (2003, 2008) of Brazilian youth movements are cases in point. Based on participant observation and semistructured interviews, Mische reconstructs different conversational mechanisms (identity qualifying, temporal cuing, generality shifting, and multiple targeting), each of which has a different impact on network building and network mobilization depending on institutional setting (Mische, 2003, 2008).

Validation of network data and field access

Besides the applications just mentioned, it can be worthwhile to complement data from standardized surveys with qualitative data even in studies that rely exclusively on the formal procedures of social network analysis in analyzing network data. There are several advantages in doing so. First of all, combining data in this way can serve as a strategy for validating network data. For instance, in their study of network effectiveness of community mental health systems, Provan and Milward (1995) employed three qualitative strategies to enhance validity of the data and validity of the results: in-depth meetings with members of the organizations in focus to review questionnaire items and responses to ensure that respondents were interpreting them as the researcher had intended; follow-up by telephone and additional interviewing to collect missing data and to check data that appeared to be inaccurate after comparing questionnaire responses with field notes; and, finally, after data were initially analyzed, to

discuss findings with organization members ("reality check") to ensure that major conclusions were consistent with members' understandings of system operations (Provan and Milward, 1995). Second, a systematic, standardized survey to identify alters and the content of relationships, designed to enable comparison, involves considerable time and effort (Marsden, this volume). For this reason, standardized studies on whole networks mostly limit themselves to assessing only a few contact and relationship variables and asking only about more general relationship patterns. Thus, in research on heterogeneous groups of actors (such as in policy networks) or multiplex relationships, use of open-ended, less structured methods of collecting data on certain aspects of network structures can prove to be more effective than sole reliance on standardized procedures. In such cases, open-ended questions aiming at respondents' systems of relevance and meaning may be more appropriate for capturing the multidimensional nature of these networks (Baumgarten and Lahusen, 2006; Franke and Wald, 2006). Third, the "soft" approach employed in qualitative interviewing sometimes may be the best (or only) way of obtaining information from certain populations. The advantage of less structured interviews is that in contrast to standardized questionnaires they to a greater extent resemble "normal communication." Moreover, they can easily be adapted to the respective interviewee and the demands of the situation at hand. This can be crucial for being able to obtain network information from some populations at all, for instance, because they are greatly pressed for time (e.g., politicians), their activities are illegal (e.g., the mafia, drug addicts), or they are in danger (e.g., human rights activists under authoritarian regimes). Network data involve sensitive and sometimes even delicate data. This is more likely to be the case when such data concern not only ego's networks but also relationships among alters.

QUALITATIVE STRATEGIES FOR DATA COLLECTION AND DATA ANALYSIS

As demonstrated above, research on social networks uses different kinds of qualitative data and a range of different modes of data collection: observation techniques, various forms of interviewing and open-ended questions, as well as collecting all kinds of documents and archival material. Different interpretive methods are used in data analysis. Theoretical and methodological points of reference are symbolic interactionism

(Fine and Kleinman, 1983; Lazega, 1997; McLean, 1998) and pragmatism (Franke and Wald, 2006), relational sociology (Mische, 2008), phenomenology, sociology of knowledge (Engelbrecht, 2006), and actor-network theory (cf. Mützel, 2009; Knox et al., 2006). Because the qualitative methods employed for data collection and data analysis in network research are essentially the same as the methodology otherwise used in qualitative social research, the following section will be limited to providing a cursory overview of qualitative research strategies as they are put to use in social network analysis. For details on individual methods, the reader may consult the respective literature (e.g., Miles and Huberman, 1984; Denzin and Lincoln, 2005; Bryman and Burgess, 1999; Bernard 1994, 2000).

Data collection

Several aspects need to be considered in choosing the method of data collection. First of all, it needs to be clarified what aspects of social relations will be studied and how relations and networks are to be theoretically conceptualized (Marsden, 1990). A key question in this respect is whether the research will be concerned with actually existing relations (e.g., network practices) or with actors' perceptions of such relations (e.g., network orientations and assessments). This distinction is consequential, inter alia, for issues concerning network effects: "Accurate knowledge of actually existing ties is arguably important to the study, for example, of certain diffusion processes . . . while perceived ties might be more appropriate for studying social influence on attitudes or opinions" (Marsden, 1990: 437). The focus can also be directed at concrete interaction *between* actors when network dynamics are being studied. Besides, such an approach also lends itself to research aimed at describing strategies and network orientations at the level of *individual* actors (e.g., McLean, 1998). The decision to use observation data or to rely on actor self-reports (in interviews or in written ego documents) will depend on whether actual behavior or strategies of action and perceptions of relations are at the center of attention.

Explorative research often adopts a *holistic, ethnographic approach* marked by utmost openness toward its subject matter and aimed at achieving as comprehensive as possible an understanding of the phenomenon in question. Here, as much data as possible are collected from multiple sources to shed light on the phenomenon from different angles: observation data, documents, interviews, diaries, and questionnaires. Some network studies begin with an exploratory phase

in which all available data are compiled and significant actors, relationships, and modes of communication are identified. This is especially pertinent in studies concerned with whole networks in order to be able to determine network boundaries (cf. Marsden, 2005), which is a particularly challenging task in the case of flux networks, such as social movements (Diani and McAdam, 2003) or transnational NGO networks (Riles, 2000). Initially approaching the field in this holistic, ethnographic manner is generally useful when network research is concerned with unfamiliar social worlds (e.g., other cultures) that the researcher has to first become acquainted with, for instance, in case of organizations (Provan and Milward, 1995; Uzzi, 1997; Gluesing et al., forthcoming), migrant communities (Menjivar, 2000; Dominguez and Watkins, 2003), or comparative cultural analyses (Lonkila and Salmi, 2005). Furthermore, such a multisource approach, drawing on different types and sources of data (e.g., combining participant observation and interviewing), represents a strategy for validating data (e.g., Provan and Milward, 1995; Uzzi, 1997; Gluesing et al., forthcoming).

Of course, the choice of method also involves pragmatic considerations, particularly concerning available time and funding: observation, for instance, is very time-consuming. Archival data, on the other hand, often have the advantage of being easily accessible and thus economical. And sometimes there is actually little scope for choice of method because only certain data are available, as in McLean's study of favor-seeking letters from Florentine nobility during the Renaissance (1998). This situation forces the researcher to carefully consider what kinds of questions and what aspects of networks can be tackled in view of the available data. Accordingly, McLean (1998) in his analysis of letters concentrates on strategies of self-presentation and how actors sought to mobilize social capital through writing letters. In general, utmost attention must be paid to the conditions under which data originated. The conditions of origin are the ultimate measure in gauging whether certain data lend themselves to answering a specific question and thus can be considered valid (cf. Marsden, 2005).

Observations

Observation methods belong to the ethnographer's traditional toolkit. In the early days of network research, they found most prominent use in social anthropological studies (e.g., Mitchell, 1969; Epstein, 1969). Today, observation methods are employed in research on social movements (Mische, 2008; Broadbent, 2003), organizations (Provan and Milward, 1995; Uzzi, 1997;

Gibson, 2005; Häussling, 2006; Gluesing et al., forthcoming), and ethnic communities (Dominguez and Watkins, 2003; Menjivar, 2000; Smilde, 2005). Only rarely does observation data serve as a main data source, as in Gibson's (2005) investigation of the conversation practices of managers or Häussling's study of interaction and network formation in school classes (2010). For the most part, observation is used to complement other data. On the one hand, it serves to access the field (actors, content of relationships, forms of interaction). For instance, in social movement research, meetings and gatherings of various groups are attended in order to identify conversation practices, topics, and significant actors (Broadbent, 2003; Mische, 2008). Some researchers shadow actors, as did Gluesing et al. (forthcoming), who escorted the members of the innovation team under study over a number of days to find out who they met, how often, for how long, and what topics they talked about. On the other hand, observation data play an important role in complementing and checking data from other sources (e.g., Provan and Milward, 1995; Uzzi, 1997). In this vein, Gluesing et al. (forthcoming) analyzed thousands of emails (documents) and also face-to-face encounters (observed) in their study, revealing national differences in email usage. Observation data are considered to be particularly reliable[3] when actual behavior (that is, the content of relationships and modes of communication) is the main concern (cf. Marsden, 1990, 2005). Of course, there can be great variation in the quality of observation data. For instance, much depends on the window of observation selected (time-sampling; Kashy and Kenny, 1990; cf. Marsden, 2005). To be sure, repeated observation over extended periods of time is an appropriate strategy for ensuring good data quality (e.g., Menjivar, 2000; Dominguez and Watkins, 2003; Mische, 2008; Gluesing et al., forthcoming). Yet it is also very time-consuming. Careful attention must further be paid to the number and training of research staff involved in observation, the choice of recording devices (video, audio), placement of recording devices, as well as the mode of transcription.

Interviews

Open-ended interviewing of some kind is employed in almost all of the qualitative studies discussed in this overview: in-depth-interviews (e.g., Wong and Salaff, 1998; Menjivar, 2000; Broadbent, 2003; Smith, 2005; Gluesing et al., forthcoming), narrative interviews (e.g., Hollstein, 2002), focused, thematic, or problem-centered interviews (e.g., Lonkila and Salmi, 2005; Bernardi et al., 2007; Scheibelhofer, 2008), but also single,

open-ended questions as part of standardized surveys (e.g., Bearman and Parigi, 2004). Qualitative interviews are typically used to complement other data, particularly observation data, in research on actual behavior (network practices; see above, e.g., Uzzi, 1997; Gluesing et al., forthcoming). They are the first choice in studying actors' networking strategies, network orientations, and assessments (thus, the individual significance attached to and perception of relationships and networks). This includes studies of integration into personal networks (Höfer et al., 2006; Schütze, 2006), the impact of networks on life course decisions (Lonkila and Salmi, 2005; Bernardi et al., 2007), or the assessment of networking strategies and network success among and between networks of organizations (Provan and Milward, 1995; Uzzi, 1997; Franke and Wald, 2006). In addition, open-ended interviews are a useful way of becoming familiar with the field under study (exploration) and for accessing certain populations (politicians, criminals; see above). An open-ended approach in inquiring about significant relationships and relationship content can also be in order for economical reasons, for instance, when a standardized survey would be too time-consuming due to the multiplexity of relationships or contents (Franke and Wald, 2006; Baumgarten and Lahusen, 2006). Franke and Wald (2006) argue that, as a rule of thumb, questions should be designed as open-ended: the more open-ended that questions are, the less one knows about a phenomenon, and the more important individual actors' strategies and systems of relevance are, and the greater impact context factors can be assumed to have.

In case of self-reports, we must bear in mind that utterances (as a matter of perspective) are always bound to social location. This can be the particular focus of research, as is the case in research concerned with the individual perception of integration into personal networks. However, in cases when actors are approached as experts on specific behavior (e.g., routines, other actors, or relations in organizations), the socially biased nature of individual perception must be reckoned with in the choice of interview partners and the interpretation of statements. For example, persons who occupy central positions in networks are more knowledgeable about network events compared to persons on the fringes (Krackhardt, 1990). The greater the proximity between persons the more accurate are their statements concerning the other (Bondonio, 1998). Research has produced an array of findings on factors affecting the accuracy of self-reports; the work in the wake of studies by Bernard et al. (1981) are especially noteworthy in this respect (cf. the overviews provided in Johnson, 1994; Marsden, 2005; this volume).

Finally, it must be noted that even the most open and unstructured interviews are typically combined with some form of standardized inquiry, especially for obtaining information via name generators and name interpreters (Hanneman and Riddle, Marsden, this volume; e.g., Franke and Wald, 2006; Bernardi et al., 2007). Such method triangulation ensures the comparability of data (across cases as well as between certain aspects of an individual case). At the same time, it allows making substantive statements about the structure of networks that go beyond a merely metaphorical reference to the term "network" (cf. Johnson, 1994). Network charts are another useful tool for collecting qualitative data, for instance, on egocentric networks (cf. Straus, 2002; McCarty et al., 2007; Hogan et al., 2007). Kahn and Antonucci's concentric circles (1980) are a good example of such an instrument. Due to its semi-standardized design, the instrument also supports the comparability of cases. Furthermore, the graphical representation of networks functions as a cognitive aid in describing relationships. It keeps track of the relationships discussed in the interview. In qualitative interviews, geared toward approaching as close as possible the systems of relevance and action orientations of interviewees, mapping networks is a well-suited means of facilitating the discussion of relationships while it provides a strong stimulus for the production of narratives (e.g., Hollstein, 2002; Bernardi et al., 2007).

Documents and archival data

In addition to qualitative data obtained through observation and interviewing, various kinds of documents can also be put to use in network-related inquiry: archival data, newspaper articles, biographies, letters, emails, blogs, etc. The main advantage of this type of data is that it is mostly easily accessible and available at low cost. In recent years, data offered by computer-mediated systems have gained increasing importance in network research. Because of the large volume, such data are usually subjected to computerized, more strongly standardized, and formalized methods of data mining (see below; on archival records, see Batagelj et al., this volume). In these cases, documents are mostly the primary data sources. Studies based on interpretive methods of analysis, on the other hand, generally draw on documents only for complementary information. For instance, newspaper articles, books, archival material are used in research on political parties and social movements (e.g., Broadbent, 2003; Mische, 2008) or company documents and company portrayals in company case studies (e.g. Gluesing et al., forthcoming). Of course,

documents are the key source of data in historical studies. Examples for network research of this type are McLean's work on network practices of Florentine nobility based on analysis of favor-seeking letters (1998) or Crossley's (2008) study of the changing music scene in 1970s Manchester based on musicians' biographies and autobiographies, as well as on online resources. Documents represent data "not created expressly for social research" (Marsden, 2005: 24). This to an even greater extent demands giving close thought to the conditions under which the data originated with an eye to the respective research question (see above). Data interpretation requires giving consideration to such aspects as motives, purpose, and mode of data production, the specific demands posed by the medium, and initiating parties and the intended audience.

Data analysis

In principle, qualitative data can be analyzed using interpretive as well as formal (quantitative) methods of analysis. The majority of qualitative studies referred to in this chapter employ grounded theory as the method of choice (e.g., Lonkila and Salmi, 2005; Bernardi et al., 2007), often in conjunction with ethnographic descriptions (e.g., Provan and Milward, 1995; Uzzi, 1997; Menjivar, 2000, Broadbent, 2003; Dominguez and Watkins, 2003, Gluesing et al., forthcoming). Yet it needs to be emphasized that, depending on research focus and methodological orientation[4] (interactionist, structuralist, pragmatic, or oriented by sociology of knowledge), a range of interpretive methods may qualify as candidates well suited for the analysis of network practices, network orientations, and network assessments. Methods of analysis are frame analysis (e.g., McLean, 1998), conversation analysis (e.g., Mische, 2003), various types of interaction analyses (e.g., Häussling, 2006), narrative analysis (e.g., Uzzi, 1997; Hollstein, 2002), as well as analytical procedures based on sociology of knowledge or phenomenology (e.g., Engelbrecht, 2006).

However, qualitative data can also be analyzed using quantitative or other methods of a more formal nature. Methods of this type applied to qualitative data are, for instance, methods designed to analyze texts (transcripts, documents) for formal structures, such as quantitative content analysis (Franzosi, 2008), semantic network analysis (Carley, 1984, 1997), network analysis of narratives (e.g., Bearman and Stovel, 2000; Smith, 2007), or Galois lattice analysis (e.g., Yeung, 2005; Mische, 2008). Those methods of analysis are to a greater degree standardized, are less interpretive, and in this sense can reduce data complexity. For this reason, they have clear advantages when the task is handling large volumes of data (cf. Bagatelj et al., this volume), as increasingly is the case in the wake of easier access to large quantities of data via the Internet as well as ongoing advances in software development (cf. Huisman and van Duijn, this volume).

This is not the place to discuss the various methods in detail. Instead, some final considerations will be devoted to the general strategies pursued in analyzing qualitative data as observed in the qualitative studies touched upon so far. They can be distinguished by the generalizability of their findings and the claims they can make as to the scope of explanation. There is some agreement that systematically combining qualitative with quantitative data and data on network structures (so-called mixed method designs) enhances the explanatory power of analysis.

Thick descriptions and typologies

A common strategy of analyzing qualitative data is to give a detailed account of individual cases by way of "thick descriptions" (Geertz, 1973) that are geared toward tracing how actions or events unfold and the impact they have in order to make them comprehensible (*Verstehen*) and in this way to explain them. Understanding the individual case is the objective and, as such, an "end in itself," as exemplified by Riles's study on knowledge practices and networking activities in transnational issue networks (2000). In another strategy, analysis proceeds by systematic comparison and abstraction aimed at developing typologies that capture the range of possible variation that can be expected in a certain field of action. An example is the typology of "traveler" and "diplomat" developed by Engelbrecht (2006) to account for the different modes of bridging the gap between different religious communities.

Developing models and theories

Typologies based on descriptions leave questions unanswered pertaining to the conditions under which the respective types emerge and the impact they have. Generalization of findings and formulation of theoretical models grounded in data (Glaser and Strauss, 1967) require using the respective data for systematically comparing cases and contrasting patterns of action and the conditions surrounding them (e.g., Provan and Milward, 1995; Franke and Wald, 2006) as well as systematic and careful analysis of (on first glance) contradictory findings and outliers (e.g., Provan and Milward, 1995; Mische, 2003). This also involves careful consideration of sample composition and the selection of cases (cf. Frank, this volume).

The surplus of mixed method designs

Mixed method designs open an array of opportunities for data analysis (cf. Tashakkori and Teddlie, 2003; Axinn and Pearce, 2006; Bryman, 2006; Creswell and Plano, 2007). In network research, this refers, first, to research designs that employ both qualitative data as well as standardized data used to describe formal properties of networks, such as network size, measures of density, centrality, and so on. This specific mode of *data triangulation* (Denzin, 1970) is a key element in network research in order to make substantive statements about actual networks that range beyond using the term "network" merely in a metaphorical sense (Johnson, 1994). Relating data in this way also has theoretical implications: since qualitative data comes closer to individual actors, their systems of relevance (compared to relational data on relationship and network structures), incorporating qualitative and structural data provides a way of linking theoretical perspectives that either focus on structure or agency (Hollstein, 2001; Häussling, 2006). Advocates of a relational sociology have been arguing to that effect since the early 1990s (White, 1992; Emirbayer and Goodwin, 1994; Mizruchi, 1994). We can thus expect empirical studies along such lines to also yield theoretically inspiring insights.

Moreover, mixed method designs can enhance the explanatory power and generalizability of statements. This is the case if, secondly, qualitative and quantitative *strategies of analysis* are combined *as well* ("method-triangulation"; Denzin, 1970). Combining qualitative and quantitative analyses can take very different shapes depending on the research in question. Quantitative analyses can provide a general framework for selecting specific cases for qualitative analysis (e.g., typical cases, outlier) and for determining their significance (in terms of quantity, distribution, relevance, etc.) (*mapping*; e.g., White, 1961; McLean, 1998; Wong and Salaff, 1998; Hollstein, 2002). In this way, McLean (1998) maps networking strategies of Florentine nobility by using multidimensional scaling techniques. Quantitative analyses not only allow more precisely assessing the extent to which certain patterns of action are spread among a certain population. They also help gaining a more complete picture of the conditions (institutional settings) under which such patterns have effects (Mische, 2003, 2008). By means of in-depth interviews about assistance practices among the black urban poor, Smith (2005), for example, brings to the fore why people having job-relevant information are reluctant to pass such knowledge on to others. She then employs quantitative survey data to check for circumstances (strength of ties, socioeconomic status of neighborhood) that make providing assistance more or less likely. In other research, quantitative and qualitative approaches are used simultaneously and are more strongly integrated (e.g., Häussling, 2006; Bernardi et al., 2007; Gluesing et al., forthcoming), for instance, by applying formal procedures like cross-site display (Miles and Huberman, 1984; adopted for network research by Uzzi, 1997) or qualitative comparative analysis (Ragin, 1987; applied in network research by Smilde, 2005).

I believe to have demonstrated that qualitative approaches have important contributions to make to social network research. Their definite strengths lie with exploring networks, validating network data, describing network practices, performing network orientations and assessments, and providing insight into network impacts and dynamics. Combining qualitative and quantitative data and analyses promises to yield the most fruitful results.

NOTES

For helpful comments on an earlier draft, I am grateful to Janet Salaff, Stephan Elkins, Laura Bernardi, and Werner Rammert.

1 Although these approaches share the same basic assumptions, they focus on different aspects in detail. For example, some focus more on the process of action and the construction of reality (like ethnomethodology). Other approaches are more concerned with the results of the construction processes, that is, the "structures of meaning" (like objective hermeneutics; cf. Titscher et al., 2000).

2 For details on qualitative approaches and individual methods, see, for example, the overviews in Miles and Huberman (1984), Denzin and Lincoln (2005), Bryman and Burgess (1999), and Bernard (1994, 2000).

3 In particular, see the seminal studies by Bernard et al. on informant accuracy (1981). For details about the important debates initiated by these studies, see Johnson (1994); Marsden (1990, 2005, this volume).

4 Acts of expression can be analyzed for different layers of meaning, for instance, with regard to an intended or deliberate meaning but also for latent meaning. Depending on the level of meaning targeted by an analysis, either more phenomenological approaches (which focus on actor perspectives) or methods relying on a more in-depth, structural hermeneutical analysis (like objective hermeneutics,

which focuses on the latent, unconscious aspects of meaning and the logic of action; Oevermann et al., 1979, cf. Titscher et al., 2000) are employed.

REFERENCES

Axinn, W.G. and Pearce, L.D. (2006) *Mixed Method Data Collection*. Cambridge: Cambridge University Press.

Barnes, J.A. (1954) 'Class and committees in a Norwegian island parish', *Human Relations*, 7: 39–58.

Barnes, J.A. (1969) 'Networks and political process', in J. Clyde Mitchell (ed.), *Social Networks in Urban Situations. Analyses of Personal Relationships in Central African Towns*. Manchester: Manchester University Press. pp. 51–77.

Baumgarten, B. and Lahusen, C. (2006) 'Politiknetzwerke – Vorteile und Grundzüge einer qualitativen Analysestrategie', in Betina Hollstein and Straus, Florian (eds), *Qualitative Netzwerkanalyse. Konzepte, Methoden, Anwendungen*. Wiesbaden: VS Verlag für Sozialwissenschaften. pp. 177–199.

Bearman, P.S. and Parigi, P. (2004) 'Cloning headless frogs and other important matters: Conversation topics and network structure', *Social Forces,* 83(2): 535–57.

Bearman, P.S. and Stovel, K. (2000) 'Becoming a Nazi: A model for narrative networks', *Poetics,* 27(2–3): 69–90.

Bernard, H.R. (1994) *Research Methods in Anthropology: Qualitative and Quantitative Approaches*. Thousand Oaks, CA: Sage.

Bernard, H.R. (2000) *Social Research Methods: Qualitative and Quantitative Approaches*. 2nd ed. Thousand Oaks, CA: Sage.

Bernard, H.R., Killworth, P. and Sailer, L. (1981) 'Summary of research on informant accuracy in network data and on the reverse small world problem', *Connections,* 4(2): 11–25.

Bernardi, L. (2003) 'Channels of social influence on reproduction', *Population Research and Policy Review,* 22: 527–55.

Bernardi, L., Keim, S. and von der Lippe, H. (2007) 'Social influence on fertility. A comparative mixed methods study in Eastern and Western Germany', *Journal of Mixed Methods Research,* 1(1): 23–47.

Bidart, C. and Lavenu, P. (2005) 'Evolutions of personal networks and life events', *Social Networks,* 27(4): 359–376.

Bondonio, D. (1998) 'Predictors of accuracy in perceiving informal social networks', *Social Networks,* 20: 301–30.

Bott, E. (1957) *Family and Social Network*. London: Tavistock.

Broadbent, J. (2003) 'Movement in context: Thick networks and Japanese environmental protest', in Mario Diani and McAdam, Doug (eds), *Social Movements and Networks. Relational Approaches to Collective Action*. Oxford: Oxford University Press. pp. 204–29.

Bryman, A. (ed.) (2006) *Mixed Methods Set*. 4 vols. London: Sage.

Bryman, A. and Burgess, R.G. (eds) (1999) *Qualitative Research*. 4 vols. London: Sage.

Carley, K. (1984) 'Extracting culture through textual analysis', *Poetics,* 22(4): 291–312.

Carley, K. (1997) 'Network text analysis: The network position of concepts', in Carl W. Roberts (ed.), *Text Analysis for the Social Sciences: Methods for Drawing Statistical Inferences from Texts and Transcripts*. Mahwah, NJ: Lawrence Erlbaum. pp. 79–100.

Creswell, J.W. and Plano, V.L. (2007) *Designing and Conducting Mixed Methods Research*. Thousand Oaks: Sage.

Crossley, N. (2008) 'The man whose web expanded: Network dynamics in Manchester's post/punk music scene 1976–1980', *Poetics*, 37(1): 24–49.

Denzin, N.K. and Lincoln, Y.S. (eds) (2005) *The SAGE Handbook of Qualitative Research*. 3rd ed. Thousand Oaks, CA: Sage.

Denzin, N.K. (1970) *The Research Act*. Chicago: Aldine.

Diani, M. and McAdam, D. (eds) (2003) *Social Movements and Networks. Relational Approaches to Collective Action*. Oxford: Oxford University Press.

Dominguez, S. and Watkins, C. (2003) 'Creating networks for survival and mobility: Social capital among African-American and Latin American low-income mothers', *Social Problems*, 50(1): 111–35.

Emirbayer, M. and Goodwin, J. (1994) 'Network analysis, culture, and the problem of agency', *American Journal of Sociology*, 99(6), 1411–54.

Engelbrecht, M. (2006) 'Netzwerke religiöser Menschen – Die Dynamik von Wissensbeständen und Netzwerken religiöser Traditionen zwischen kollektiver Selbstabgrenzung und individueller Wahl', in Betina Hollstein and Florian Straus (eds), *Qualitative Netzwerkanalyse. Konzepte, Methoden, Anwendungen*. Wiesbaden: VS Verlag für Sozialwissenschaften. pp. 243–67.

Epstein, A.L. (1969) 'Gossip, norms and social network', in J. Clyde Mitchell (ed.), *Social Networks in Urban Situations. Analyses of Personal Relationships in Central African Towns*. Manchester: Manchester University Press. pp. 117–28.

Fine, G.A., and Kleinman, S. (1983) 'Network and meaning: An interactionist approach to structure', *Symbolic Interaction*, 6: 97–110.

Foote Whyte, W. (1955) *Street Corner Society The Social Structure of an Italian Slum*. Chicago: University of Chicago Press.

Franke, K. and Wald, A. (2006) 'Möglichkeiten der Triangulation quantitativer und qualitativer Methoden in der Netzwerkanalyse', in Betina Hollstein and Straus, Florian (eds), *Qualitative Netzwerkanalyse. Konzepte, Methoden, Anwendungen*. Wiesbaden: VS Verlag für Sozialwissenschaften. pp. 153–77.

Franzosi, R. (ed.) (2008) *Content Analysis*. 4 vols. Beverly Hills, CA: Sage.

Geertz, C. (1973) *The Interpretation of Cultures*. New York: Basic Books.

Gibson, D.R. (2005) 'Taking turns and talking ties. Network structure and conversational sequences', *American Journal of Sociology*, 110(6): 1561–97.

Glaser, B.G. and Strauss, A.L. (1967) *The Discovery of Grounded Theory. Strategies for Qualitative Research*. Chicago: Aldine.

Gluesing, J., Riopelle, K. and Danowski, J.A. (forthcoming) 'Innovation networks in global organizations: Understanding network practices and dynamics by mixing ethnography and information technology data', in Silvia Dominguez and Betina Hollstein (eds), *Mixed-Methods in Studying Social Networks*.

Häussling, R. (2006) 'Interaktionen in Organisationen. Ein Vierebenenkonzept des Methodologischen Relationalismus und dessen empirische Anwendung'. Karlsruhe: Universität Karlsruhe.

Häussling, R. (2010) 'Allocation to Social Positions in Class: Interactions and Relationships in First Grade School Classes and Their Consequences', *Current Sociology*, 58(1): 119–138.

Höfer, R., Keupp, H. and Straus, F. (2006) 'Prozesse sozialer Verortung in Szenen und Organisationen – Ein netzwerko-rientierter Blick auf traditionale und reflexiv moderne Engagementformen', in Betina Hollstein and Florian Straus (eds), *Qualitative Netzwerkanalyse. Konzepte, Methoden, Anwendungen*. Wiesbaden: VS Verlag für Sozialwissenschaften. pp. 267–95.

Hogan, B., Carrasco, J.A. and Wellman, B. (2007) 'Visualizing personal networks: Working with participant-aided socio-grams', *Field Methods*, 19(2): 116–44.

Hollstein, B. (2001) *Grenzen sozialer Integration. Zur Konzeption informeller Beziehungen und Netzwerke*. Opladen: Leske + Budrich.

Hollstein, B. (2002) *Soziale Netzwerke nach der Verwitwung. Eine Rekonstruktion der Veränderungen informeller Beziehungen*. Opladen: Leske + Budrich.

Hollstein, B. and Ullrich, C.G. (2003) 'Einheit trotz Vielfalt? Zum konstitutiven Kern qualitativer Sozialforschung', *Soziologie. Forum der Deutschen Gesellschaft für Soziologie*. pp. 29–44.

Hopf, C. (1979) 'Soziologie und qualitative Sozialforschung', in Christel Hopf and Elmar Weingarten (eds), *Qualitative Sozialforschung*. Stuttgart: Klett-Cotta. pp. 11–41.

Jansen, D. (1999) *Einführung in die Netzwerkanalyse*. Opladen: Leske + Budrich.

Johnson, J.C. (1994) 'Anthropological contributions to the study of social networks: A review', in Stanley Wasserman and Joseph Galaskiewicz (eds), *Advances in Social Network Analysis*. Thousand Oaks: Sage. pp. 113–51.

Kahn, R.L. and Antonucci, T.C. (1980) 'Convoys over the life course: Attachment, roles, and social support', in Paul B. Baltes and Olim G. Brim (eds), *Life-span Development and Behavior*. New York: Academic Press. pp. 383–405.

Kashy, D.A. and Kenny, D.A. (1990) 'Do you know whom you were with a week ago Friday? A re-analysis of the Bernard, Killworth, and Sailer Studies', in *Social Psychology Quarterly*, 53: 55–61.

Keim, S., Klärner, A. and Bernardi, L. (forthcoming) 'Qualifying social influence on fertility intentions: Composition, structure, and meaning of fertility-relevant social networks in western Germany', *Current Sociology*.

Knox, H., Savage, M. and Harvey, P. (2006) 'Social networks and the study of social relations: Networks as method, metaphor and form', *Economy and Society*, 35(1): 113–40.

Krackhardt, D. (1987) 'Cognitive social structure', *Social Networks*, 9(2): 109–34.

Krackhardt, D. (1990) 'Assessing the political landscape: Structure, cognition, and power in organizations', in *Administrative Science Quarterly*, 35: 432–69.

Lazega, E. (1997) 'Network analysis and qualitative research: A method of contextualisation', in Gale Miller and Dingwall, Robert (eds), *Context and Method in Qualitative Research*. London: Sage. pp. 119–38.

Lonkila, M. and Salmi, A.-M. (2005) 'The Russian work collective and migration', *European-Asia Studies*, 57(5): 681–703.

Marsden, P.V. (1990) 'Network data and measurement', *Annual Review of Sociology*, 16: 433–63.

Marsden, P.V. (2005) 'Recent developments in network measurements', in Peter J. Carrington, John Scott, and Stanley Wasserman (eds), *Models and Methods in Social Network Analysis*. Cambridge: Cambridge University Press. pp. 8–31.

McCarty, C., Molina, J.L., Aguilar, C. and Roth, L. (2007) 'A comparison of social network mapping and personal network visualization', *Field Methods*, 19(2): 145–62.

McLean, P.D. (1998) 'A frame analysis of favour seeking in the Renaissance: Agency, networks, and political culture', *American Journal of Sociology*, 104(1): 51–91.

Menjívar, C. (2000) *Fragmented Ties: Salvadoran Immigrant Networks in America*. Berkeley: University of California Press.

Miles, M. and Huberman, M. (1984) *Qualitative Data Analysis*. Newbury Park, CA: Sage.

Mische, A. (2003) 'Cross-talk in movements: Rethinking the culture-network link', in Mario Diani and Doug McAdam (eds), *Social Movements and Networks: Relational Approaches to Collective Action*. New York: Oxford University Press. pp. 258–80.

Mische, A. (2008) *Partisan Publics. Communication and Contention across Brazilian Youth Activist Networks*. Princeton: Princeton University Press.

Mitchell, J.C. (ed) (1969) *Social Networks in Urban Situations. Analyses of Personal Relationships in Central African Towns*. Manchester: Manchester University Press.

Mizruchi, M.S. (1994) 'Social network analysis: Recent achievements and current controversies', *Acta Sociologica*, 37: 329–43.

Mützel, S. (2009) 'Networks as culturally constituted processes: A comparison of relational sociology and actor-network-theory', *Current Sociology*, 57 (6): 871–887.

Oevermann, U., Allert, T., Konau, E. and Krambeck, J. (1979) 'Die Methodologie einer "objektiven Hermeneutik" und ihre allgemeine forschungslogische Bedeutung in den Sozialwissenschaften', in Hans-Georg Soeffner (ed.), *Interpretative Verfahren in den Sozial- und Textwissenschaften*. Stuttgart: Enke. pp. 352–434.

Pahl, R. and Spencer, L. (2004) 'Personal communities: Not simply families of "fate" or "choice"', *Current Sociology*, 52(2): 192–221.

Provan, K.G. and Milward, H.B. (1995) 'A preliminary theory of interorganizational network effectiveness: A comparative study of four mental health systems', *Administrative Science Quarterly*, 40(1): 1–33.

Ragin, C.C. (1987) *The Comparative Method. Moving beyond Qualitative and Quantitative Strategies*. Berkeley: University of California Press.

Riles, A. (2000) *The Network Inside Out*. Ann Arbor: University of Michigan Press.

Roethlisberger, F.J. and Dickson, W.J. (1939) *Management and the Worker*. Cambridge, MA: Harvard University Press.

Scheibelhofer, E. (2008) 'Combining narration-based interviews with topical interviews: Methodological reflections on research practices', *International Journal of Social Research Methodology*, 11(5): 403–16.

Scheibelhofer, E. (2009) 'Understanding European Emigration in the Context of Modernization Processes: Contemporary Migration Biographies and Reflexive Modernity', *Current Sociology*, 57 (1): 5–25.

Schütze, Y. (2006) 'Quantitative und Qualitative Veränderungen in den sozialen Netzwerken junger Migranten – Eine Langzeitstudie', in Betina Hollstein and Florian Straus (eds), *Qualitative Netzwerkanalyse. Konzepte, Methoden, Anwendungen*. Wiesbaden: VS Verlag für Sozialwissenschaften. pp. 295–311.

Schütze, Y. and Lang, F.R. (1996) 'Integration in family, kinship and friendship networks', in Heidrun Mollenkopf (ed.), *Elderly People in Industrialized Societies*. Berlin: Sigma. pp. 25–40.

Smilde, D. (2005) 'A qualitative comparative analysis of conversion to Venezuelan evangelicalism: How networks matter', *American Journal of Sociology*, 111(3): 757–796.

Smith, S.S. (2005) '"Don't put my name on it": Social capital activation and job-finding assistance among the black urban poor', *American Journal of Sociology*, 111(1): 1–57.

Smith, T. (2007) 'Narrative boundaries and the dynamics of ethnic conflict and conciliation', *Poetics*, 35: 22–46.

Straus, F. (2002) *Netzwerkanalysen*. Wiesbaden: Dt. Univ.-Verlag.

Tashakkori, A. and Teddlie, C. (eds) (2003) *Handbook of Mixed Methods in Social and Behavioral Research*. Thousand Oaks, CA: Sage.

Titscher, S., Meyer, M., Wodak, R. and Vetter, E. (2000) *Methods of Text and Discourse Analysis, in Search of Meaning*. London: Sage.

Uzzi, B. (1997) 'Social structure and competition in interfirm networks: The paradox of embeddedness', *Administrative Science Quarterly*, 42(1): 35–67.

White, H.C. (1961) 'Management conflict and sociometric structure', *American Journal of Sociology*, 67(2): 185–99.

White, H.C. (1992) *Identity and Control*. Princeton: Princeton University Press.

Wong, S.-L. and Salaff, J.W. (1998) 'Network capital: Emigration from Hong Kong', *British Journal of Sociology*, 49(3): 358–74.

Yeung, K.-T. (2005) 'What does love mean? Exploring network culture in two network settings', *Social Forces*, 84(1): 391–420.

28

Analyzing Affiliation Networks

Stephen P. Borgatti and Daniel S. Halgin

In social network analysis, the term "affiliations" usually refers to membership or participation data, such as when we have data on which actors have participated in which events. Often, the assumption is that co-membership in groups or events is an indicator of an underlying social tie. For example, Davis et al. (1941) used data provided by the society pages of a local newspaper to uncover distinct social circles among a set of society women. Similarly, Domhoff (1967) and others have used co-membership in corporate boards to search for social elites (e.g., Allen, 1974; Carroll et al., 1982; Galaskiewicz, 1985; Westphal and Khanna 2003). Alternatively, we can see co-participation as providing opportunities for social ties to develop, which in turn provide opportunities for things like ideas to flow between actors. For example, Davis (1991; Davis and Greve, 1997) studied the diffusion of corporate practices such as poison pills and golden parachutes. He found evidence that poison pills diffuse through chains of interlocking directorates, where board members who sit on multiple boards serve as conduits of strategic information between the different firms. An important advantage of affiliation data, especially in the case studying elites, is that affiliations are often observable from a distance (e.g., government records, newspaper reports), without requiring access to the actors.

In this chapter, we focus on issues involving the analysis of affiliation data, as opposed to the collection or the theoretical interpretation of affiliation data.

BASIC CONCEPTS AND TERMINOLOGY

Affiliation data consist of a set of binary relationships between members of two sets of items. For example, the well-known dataset collected by Davis et al. (1941) recorded which women attended which social events in a small southern town. Thus, there are two sets of items, women and events, and there is a binary relation that connects them, namely the "attended" relation. Figure 28.1 gives the Davis et al. (henceforth, DGG) data matrix in its original form. The rows correspond to the women and the columns are the events they attended.

In general, the kinds of binary relations we consider affiliations are limited to part/whole relations such as "is a member of" or "is a participant in" or "has" (in the sense of having a trait). Examples of affiliation data that have found their way into the social science literature include corporate board memberships (e.g., Mizruchi, 1983, 1992, 1996; Carroll et al., 1982; Davis, 1991; Lester and Canella, 2006; Robins and Alexander, 2004; Westphal, 1998), attendance at events (e.g., Davis et al., 1941; Faust et al., 2002), membership in clubs (e.g., McPherson, 1982; McPherson and Smith-Lovin, 1986, 1987), participation in online groups (Allatta, 2003, 2005), authorship of articles (e.g., Gmür, 2006; Lazer et al., 2009; Newman et al., 2001), membership in production teams (Uzzi and Spiro, 2005), and even course-taking patterns of high school students (e.g., Field et al., 2006). In addition, affiliation data are well known outside the social sciences, as in the

	E1	E2	E3	E4	E5	E6	E7	E8	E9	E10	E11	E12	E13	E14
EVELYN	1	1	1	1	1	1	0	1	1	0	0	0	0	0
LAURA	1	1	1	0	1	1	1	1	0	0	0	0	0	0
THERESA	0	1	1	1	1	1	1	1	1	0	0	0	0	0
BRENDA	1	0	1	1	1	1	1	1	0	0	0	0	0	0
CHARLOTTE	0	0	1	1	1	0	1	0	0	0	0	0	0	0
FRANCES	0	0	1	0	1	1	0	1	0	0	0	0	0	0
ELEANOR	0	0	0	0	1	1	1	1	0	0	0	0	0	0
PEARL	0	0	0	0	0	1	0	1	1	0	0	0	0	0
RUTH	0	0	0	0	1	0	1	1	1	0	0	0	0	0
VERNE	0	0	0	0	0	0	1	1	1	0	0	1	0	0
MYRNA	0	0	0	0	0	0	0	1	1	1	0	1	0	0
KATHERINE	0	0	0	0	0	0	0	1	1	1	0	1	1	1
SYLVIA	0	0	0	0	0	0	1	1	1	1	0	1	1	1
NORA	0	0	0	0	0	1	1	0	1	1	1	1	1	1
HELEN	0	0	0	0	0	0	1	1	0	1	1	1	0	0
DOROTHY	0	0	0	0	0	0	0	1	1	0	0	0	0	0
OLIVIA	0	0	0	0	0	0	0	0	1	0	1	0	0	0
FLORA	0	0	0	0	0	0	0	0	1	0	1	0	0	0

Figure 28.1   DGG women-by-events matrix

species-by-trait matrices of numerical taxonomy (Sokal and Sneath, 1973).

We can represent affiliations as mathematical graphs (Harary, 1969) in which nodes correspond to entities (such as women and events) and lines correspond to ties of affiliation among the entities. Figure 28.2 provides a representation of the DGG data. Affiliation graphs are distinctive in having the property of bipartiteness, which means that the graph's nodes can be partitioned into two classes, so that all ties occur only between classes and never within classes. We see in Figure 28.2 that there are only lines between women and the events that they attended. While all affiliation graphs are bipartite, in our view the reverse is not necessarily true. In empirical network data, graphs can be bipartite by chance alone, perhaps because of sampling error. What makes affiliation graphs different is that the two node sets are different kinds of entities, and the lack of ties within sets is by design, not happenstance. Formally, we define an affiliation graph as a bipartite graph $G(V_1,V_2,E)$, in which V_1 and V_2 are sets of nodes corresponding to different classes of entities, and E is an affiliation relation that maps the elements of V_1 to V_2. The relation is typically conceived as a set of unordered pairs in which one element of each pair belongs to V_1 and the other belongs to V_2. In contexts where we discuss multiple graphs, we use the notation $V_1(G)$ to indicate the V_1 node set in graph G, and E(H) to refer to the ties in graph H.

Affiliation graphs or networks are often called "two-mode graphs." The terminology of "modes" refers to the number of different kinds of entities referenced in the rows and columns of a matrix. A one-mode matrix is square, and its rows and columns refer to the same set of entities—a single mode. An example, drawn from the famous Hawthorne studies (Roethlisberger and Dickson, 1939), is shown in Figure 28.3.[1]

In contrast, a two-mode matrix is rectangular, and the rows and columns refer to two different sets of entities—two modes. For example, Figure 28.4 shows a two-mode, n-by-m person-by-group *incidence* matrix that is also based on the Hawthorne data. An incidence matrix has rows corresponding to nodes and columns corresponding to n-ary edges (also called hyperedges) that connect sets of nodes. In this case, the matrix indicates each individual's membership in each of five different groups.[2] The matrix clearly represents affiliations, and indeed all affiliation graphs can be represented as two-mode matrices, where the two modes correspond to the affiliation graph's two node sets.

It is important to note that while affiliation graphs can be represented by two-mode matrices, not all two-mode matrices are considered affiliation graphs. For example, a standard sociological case-by-variables matrix (e.g., person-by-demographics) might be seen as two-mode but would not normally be called an affiliation. "Affiliation" is reserved for the case when the data consist of

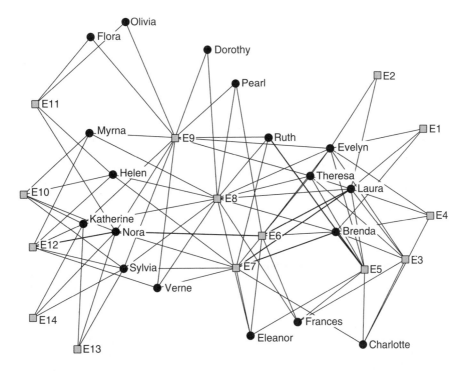

Figure 28.2 DGG women-by-events graph

	I1	I3	W1	W2	W3	W4	W5	W6	W7	W8	W9	S1	S2	S4
I1	0	0	0	0	1	0	0	0	0	0	0	0	0	0
I3	0	0	0	0	0	0	0	0	0	0	0	0	0	0
W1	0	0	0	0	1	1	0	0	0	0	0	1	0	0
W2	0	0	0	0	0	0	0	0	0	0	0	0	0	0
W3	1	0	1	0	0	1	0	0	0	0	0	1	0	0
W4	0	0	1	0	1	0	0	0	0	0	0	1	0	0
W5	0	0	0	0	0	0	0	0	0	0	0	0	0	0
W6	0	0	0	0	0	0	0	0	0	0	0	0	0	0
W7	0	0	0	0	0	0	0	0	0	1	1	1	0	0
W8	0	0	0	0	0	0	0	0	1	0	1	0	0	1
W9	0	0	0	0	0	0	0	0	1	1	0	0	0	1
S1	0	0	1	0	1	1	0	0	1	0	0	0	0	0
S2	0	0	0	0	0	0	0	0	0	0	0	0	0	0
S4	0	0	0	0	0	0	0	0	0	1	1	0	0	0

Figure 28.3 One-mode person-by-person positive relationship matrix

	Gr1	Gr 2	Gr 3	Gr4	Gr 5
I1	1	0	0	0	0
I3	0	0	0	0	0
W1	1	1	1	0	0
W2	1	1	0	0	0
W3	1	1	1	0	0
W4	1	1	1	0	0
W5	0	0	1	0	0
W6	0	0	0	1	0
W7	0	0	0	1	1
W8	0	0	0	1	1
W9	0	0	0	1	1
S1	0	1	1	0	0
S2	0	0	0	0	0
S4	0	0	0	0	1

Figure 28.4 Two-mode person-by-group matrix

some kind of participation or membership, as in people in events, projects, or groups.[3] In this chapter we focus on affiliation data, but the techniques we discuss apply to two-mode data in general.

CO-AFFILIATION

In some cases, the purpose of collecting affiliation data is not to understand the pattern of ties between the two sets but to understand the pattern of ties within one of the sets. It would seem perverse, in that case, to collect affiliation data, since by definition affiliation data do not include ties among members of either set. However, given affiliation data, we can in fact construct some kind of tie among members of a node set simply by defining *co-affiliation* (e.g., attendance at the same events, membership on the same corporate board) as a tie. For example, for the DGG dataset, we can construct a woman-by-woman matrix S in which s_{ij} gives the number of events that woman i and woman j attended together (see Figure 28.5). If we like, we can then dichotomize so that there is a tie between two women if and only if they co-attended at least some number of events. Thus, affiliation data give rise to co-affiliation data, which constitute a kind of tie among nodes within a set.

One justification for relying on co-affiliation is the idea that co-affiliation provides the conditions for the development of social ties of various kinds. For example, the more often people attend the same events, the more likely it is they will interact and develop some kind of relationship. Feld (1981) suggests that individuals whose activities are organized around the same focus (e.g., voluntary organization, workplaces, hangouts, family, etc.) frequently become interpersonally connected over time. Physical proximity (which is simply co-affiliation with respect to spatial coordinates) is also clearly a major factor in enabling and, in the breach, preventing interaction (Allen, 1977). Another justification is almost the reverse of the first, namely that common affiliations can be the consequence of having a tie. For example, married couples attend a great number of events

	EVE	LAU	THE	BRE	CHA	FRA	ELE	PEA	RUT	VER	MYR	KAT	SYL	NOR	HEL	DOR	OLI	FLO
EVELYN	8	6	7	6	3	4	3	3	3	2	2	2	2	1	2	1	1	1
LAURA	6	7	6	6	3	4	4	2	3	2	1	1	2	2	2	1	0	0
THERESA	7	6	8	6	4	4	4	3	4	3	2	2	3	3	2	2	1	1
BRENDA	6	6	6	7	4	4	4	2	3	2	1	1	2	2	2	1	0	0
CHARLOTTE	3	3	4	4	4	2	2	0	2	1	0	0	1	1	1	0	0	0
FRANCES	4	4	4	4	2	4	3	2	2	1	1	1	1	1	1	1	0	0
ELEANOR	3	4	4	4	2	3	4	2	3	2	1	1	2	2	2	1	0	0
PEARL	3	2	3	2	0	2	2	3	2	2	2	2	2	1	2	1	1	1
RUTH	3	3	4	3	2	2	3	2	4	3	2	2	3	2	2	2	1	1
VERNE	2	2	3	2	1	1	2	2	3	4	3	3	4	3	3	2	1	1
MYRNA	2	1	2	1	0	1	1	2	2	3	4	4	4	3	3	2	1	1
KATHERINE	2	1	2	1	0	1	1	2	2	3	4	6	6	5	3	2	1	1
SYLVIA	2	2	3	2	1	1	2	2	3	4	4	6	7	6	4	2	1	1
NORA	2	2	3	2	1	1	2	2	2	3	3	5	6	8	4	1	2	2
HELEN	1	2	2	2	1	1	2	1	2	3	3	3	4	4	5	1	1	1
DOROTHY	2	1	2	1	0	1	1	2	2	2	2	2	2	1	1	2	1	1
OLIVIA	1	0	1	0	0	0	0	1	1	1	1	1	1	2	1	1	2	2
FLORA	1	0	1	0	0	0	0	1	1	1	1	1	1	2	1	1	2	2

Figure 28.5 DGG woman-by-woman matrix of overlaps across events

together and belong to a great number of groups together, and indeed they may come to share a great number of activities, interests, and beliefs. Thus, co-affiliation can be viewed as an observable manifestation of a social relation that is perhaps unobservable directly (such as feelings).

If either of these justifications is valid, then we may collect affiliation data simply because it is more convenient than collecting direct ties among a set of nodes. For example, if we are interested in studying relationships among celebrities, we could try to interview them about their ties with other celebrities, but this could be quite difficult to arrange. It would be easier to simply read celebrity news and record who has attended what Hollywood social event or who has worked on what project.

In deciding whether to use affiliation data as a proxy for social relations, it is useful to think about the conditions under which any of these justifications is likely to prove valid. One consideration is the size of affiliation events. For example, suppose we have a person-by-club matrix indicating who is a member of which club. If the clubs are small (like a board of directors), then our justifications seem, well, justifiable. But if the clubs are large (on the order of thousands of members), co-membership may indicate very little about the social tie between a given pair of members. Two people can be members of all the same (large) clubs or attend all the same (large) events, and yet they may not even be aware of each other's existence and never even meet.

It should also be noted that in adopting co-affiliations as a proxy for social ties, we confound the concept of social proximity with that of social similarity, which in other contexts are treated as competing alternatives (Burt, 1987; Friedkin, 1984). To see that co-affiliations are similarity data, consider the woman-by-woman co-affiliation network in Figure 28.5, constructed from the original two-mode woman-by-event attendance data. For each pair of women, we look at their respective rows in X, and count the number of times that they have 1s in the same places. This is simply an unnormalized measure of similarity of rows. In effect, for any pair of women we construct a simple 2-by-2 contingency table as shown in Figure 28.6 that shows the relationship between their pair of rows.

The quantity a gives the number of times that the pair of women co-attended an event. The quantity $a + b$ gives the total number of events that woman i attended, and $a + c$ gives the corresponding value for woman j. The quantity n is simply the number of events—the number of columns in matrix X. A simple way to bound a between 0 and 1 and promote comparability across datasets is to simply divide a by n, as shown in Equation 28.1.

$$a^* = \frac{a}{n} \tag{28.1}$$

Bounding a by the maximum possible score introduces the notion of other normalizations that take into account characteristics of the women, such as the number of events they attended. For example, if woman i and woman j attend three events in common, and woman k and woman l do as well, we would likely regard the two pairs as equally close. But if we knew that i and j each only attended 3 events, whereas k and l each attended 14 events, we would be more likely to conclude that the 100 percent overlap between i and j signals greater closeness than the 21 percent overlap between k and l.

Therefore, if we wanted to normalize the quantity a for the number of events that each woman attended, we might divide a by the minimum of $a + b$ and $a + c$, as shown in Equation 28.2. The resulting coefficient runs between 0 and 1, where 1 indicates the maximum possible overlap given the number of events attended by i and j. This approach takes into account that the number of overlaps between two women cannot exceed the number of events that either attended.

$$a_{ij}^* = \frac{a}{Min(a+b, a+c)} \tag{28.2}$$

Another well-known approach to normalizing a is provided by the Jaccard coefficient, which is described in Equation 28.3. It gives the number of events attended in common as a proportion of events that are "attendable," as determined by the fact that at least one of the two women attended the event.

$$a_{ij}^* = \frac{a}{a+b+c} \tag{28.3}$$

Alternatively, we could take $a + d$ as a raw measure of social closeness. By including d, we effectively argue that choosing not to attend a

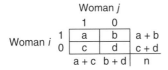

Figure 28.6 Contingency table

given event is as much of a statement of social allegiance as attending an event. A well-known normalization of $a + d$ is given by Equation 28.4, which is equal to the simple Pearson correlation between rows i and j of matrix X.

$$r_{ij} = \frac{\frac{1}{m}\sum_k x_{ik}x_{jk} - u_i u_j}{s_i s_j} \qquad (28.4)$$

Another approach, devised specifically for affiliation data, is provided by Bonacich (1972), who proposes normalizing the co-occurrence matrix according to Equation 28.5. Effectively, this measure gives the extent to which the overlap observed between i and j exceeds the amount of overlap we would expect by chance, given the number of events that i and j each attended.

$$a_{ij}^* = \frac{a - \sqrt{adbc}}{ad - bc}, \quad \text{for} \quad ad \neq bc \qquad (28.5)$$

All of these normalizations essentially shift the nature of co-affiliation data from frequencies of co-occurrences to tendencies or revealed preferences to co-occur. If we interpret frequencies of co-occurrences as giving the number of opportunities for interaction or flow of information or goods, then the raw, unnormalized measures

are the appropriate indices for measuring co-affiliation. In contrast, if the reason for studying affiliations is that co-affiliations reveal otherwise unseen relationships between people (e.g., sociometric preferences), the normalized measures are the most appropriate, as they essentially give us the tendency or preference for a pair of actors to co-occur while controlling for nuisance variables such as the number of times an actor was observed. The normalized measures tell us how often two actors are co-attending relative to the number of times they could have.

Consider the following hypothetical research project. Say that we are interested in analyzing connections between a group of 13 individuals based on their memberships in different social clubs (16 of them). Because we are interested in understanding relationships between the 13 individuals we convert the affiliation data (person-by-social club) into co-affiliations (person-by-person). We construct both a raw unnormalized co-affiliation matrix and a normalized co-affiliation matrix. Figure 28.7 is a graphical representation of the raw co-affiliation network using a standard graph layout algorithm. Individuals are labeled a through m. A line connecting two individuals indicates that they are members of at least two of the same social clubs. Node size varies by the number of social clubs that each individual is a member of; thus the larger the node, the more socially active the individual. Figure 28.8 is a depiction of Jaccard coefficients for each pair of individuals, such that a line connecting two individuals

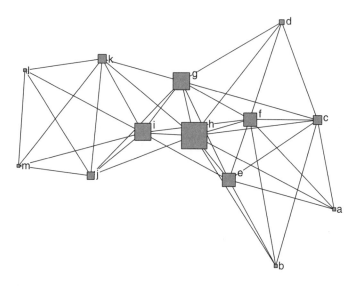

Figure 28.7   Co-membership in two or more social clubs. Node size is based on the number of social clubs that each individual is a member of

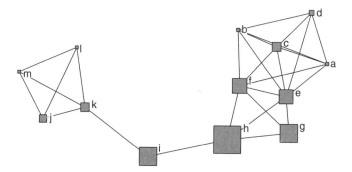

Figure 28.8   Spring embedding of Jaccard coefficients. An edge is shown if $c_{ij} > 0.38$. Node size is based on the number of social clubs that each individual is a member of

indicates that their social club membership profiles are correlated at greater than 0.38.

The raw co-affiliation network (presented in Figure 28.7) can be described as a core-periphery structure in that there is a set of core individuals who are members of multiple social clubs (persons *e, f, g, h, i*) and are surrounded by a collection of less connected individuals. We see that there are opportunities for interaction between many of the 13 individuals. However, the high social activity of the core individuals places them in the middle of the graph, which tends to obscure any subgrouping structure. Now consider the Jaccard similarity network (presented in Figure 28.8). This graph effectively highlights that there are two groupings of individuals with different membership profiles. The graph also effectively reveals the bridging role of individual *i*, which was not at all discernable when visualizing unnormalized co-occurrences among the individuals (see Figure 28.7).

Another kind of normalization worth mentioning has to do with the size of the events (or social clubs) that the individuals are affiliated with. If, in analyzing co-affiliation data, we are taking the point of view that greater co-affiliation creates more opportunities for social ties to develop, then when measuring person-to-person co-affiliations, we would probably want to take into account the relative sizes of different events. In the DGG data, for example, if two women co-attend an event that included just five people in total, it would seem that the likelihood of being aware of each other, of meeting, and indeed of changing their relationship is reasonably high. We would want to give that event a lot of weight. On the other hand if the same women co-attend an event in which thousands are present (such as a concert), we might want to weight that very little. An obvious approach, then, is to weight events inversely by

their size. Thus, referring back to Figure 28.6, the quantity *n* becomes the sum of weights of all events, and the quantity *a* is the sum of weights of the events that were co-attended by *i* and *j*. The measures described by Equations 28.1 to 28.4 can then be computed without modification.

Table 28.1 summarizes which normalization approaches are appropriate given one's attitude toward the nature of the co-affiliation data. For convenience, it is assumed that the two-mode affiliation data are actor-by-event and that we are interested in constructing the actor-by-actor co-affiliation matrix. As such, we refer to the actors/rows as "variables" and the events/columns as "cases." Therefore, the first kind of normalization discussed above can be referred to as "variable normalization" and the second as "case normalization."

Analysis of co-affiliation

Having constructed a co-affiliation matrix, we would typically want to analyze the data using all the tools of social network analysis—as with any other kind of tie. For the most part, this is unproblematic, aside from the caveats already voiced. The main issue we typically encounter is that the

Table 28.1 Appropriate normalizations by view of data

Co-affiliation as opportunity	Co-affiliation as indicator
• No normalization (simple overlap counts) • Case normalization (e.g., weighting inversely by event sizes)	• Variable normalization (e.g., Jaccard or Pearson correlations)

co-affiliation matrix is valued and many network-analytic techniques assume binary data – particularly those techniques with graph-theoretic roots. In those cases, the data will need to be dichotomized. Since the level of dichotomization is arbitrary, the normal procedure is to dichotomize at different levels and obtain measures for networks constructed with different thresholds for what is considered a tie. In other cases, there will be no need for dichotomization. For example, eigenvector centrality (Bonacich, 1972) and beta centrality (Bonacich, 1987, 2007) are quite happy to accept valued data, particularly when the values are "positive" in the sense that larger values can be interpreted as enhancing flows or coordination. Other centrality measures need to be modified to work with valued data. In general, measures based on lengths of paths, such as betweenness and closeness centrality, can easily be modified to handle valued data, provided the data can be sensibly transformed into distances or costs (Brandes, 2001). For example, the number of events co-attended by two women can be subtracted from the number of events in total and then submitted to a valued betweenness analysis.

Another possible difficulty with co-affiliation data is that, being similarity metrics, they tend to have certain mathematical properties that social network data may not. For example, most similarity metrics are symmetric so that $s(u,v) = s(v,u)$. We can construct nonsymmetric similarity measures, but these are rarely used and none of the ones we consider above are nonsymmetric. Similarity matrices such as Pearson correlation matrices have numerous other properties as well, such as being positive semi-definite (e.g., all eigenvalues are nonnegative). The main consequence is that the norms or baseline expectations for network measures on co-affiliation data should not be based on norms or expectations developed for sociometric data in general (cf. Wang et al., 2009).

At this point, we leave the discussion of co-affiliation data and focus entirely on visualizing and analyzing affiliation graphs directly without converting to co-affiliations.

DIRECT VISUALIZATION OF AFFILIATION GRAPHS

Affiliation graphs are typically visualized using the same graph layout algorithms used for ordinary graphs. In principle, certain algorithms, such as spring embedders or multidimensional scaling of path distances, should be less than optimal when applied to bipartite graphs because these algorithms place nodes in space such that distances between them are loosely proportional to the path distances that separate them. Since nodes belonging to the same node set are necessarily a minimum of two links apart, we might expect some difficulty in detecting grouping in bipartite graphs. In practice, however, this is not a problem and ordinary graph layout algorithms work well on bipartite graphs.

The only adjustment that we typically have to make for affiliation data is to visually distinguish the two node sets, such as by using different colors and shapes for node symbols of different sets. For example, Figure 28.2 shows a visualization of the DGG dataset using the spring embedding procedure in NetDraw (Borgatti, 2002). Women are represented by circles, and events are represented by squares. In the figure, we can see a group of women on the far right together with a group of events (E1 through E5) that only they attend. On the left, one can see another group of women who also have their exclusive events (E10 through E14). In the middle of the figure are four events (E6 through E9) that are attended by both groups of women. The figure also makes clear that Olivia and Flora are a bit separate from the rest of the network and are structurally similar because they attended exactly the same events.

Another approach is to use a two-mode multivariate analysis technique such as correspondence analysis to locate nodes. Correspondence analysis delivers a map in which points corresponding to both the n rows and m columns of an n-by-m two-mode matrix are represented in a joint space. Computationally, correspondence analysis consists of a double-normalization of the data matrix to reduce the influence of variation in the row and column sums, followed by a singular value decomposition. The result is that, in the case of a woman-by-event matrix, two women will be placed near each other to the extent that they have similar event profiles, controlling for the sizes of the events, and two events will be near each other if they tend to have similar attendee profiles, controlling for the overall participation rates of the attendees. In the case of the DGG dataset, correspondence analysis gives the diagram shown in Figure 28.9. As a general rule, the advantage of correspondence representations is that, in principle, the map distances are meaningful and can be related precisely back to the input data. This is not the case with most graph layout algorithms, as they respond to multiple criteria such as avoiding the placement of nodes directly on top of each other or keeping line lengths approximately equal. The disadvantage of correspondence analysis layouts is that they can be less readable. For example, in Figure 28.9, Olivia is obscured by Flora, and the (accurate) portrayal of exactly how

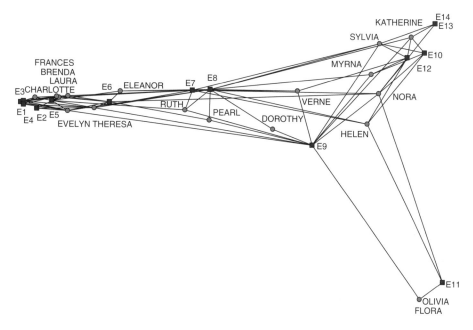

Figure 28.9   Correspondence analysis of two-mode DGG matrix

different Flora, Olivia, and Event 11 are from the rest makes the majority of the display very hard to read.

Direct analysis of affiliation graphs

There are several different approaches to analyzing affiliation data without converting to co-affiliations. Because affiliation graphs are graphs, an obvious approach is to simply use all the standard algorithms and techniques in the network analysis toolkit that apply to graphs in general. In doing this, we either effectively assume that the special nature of affiliation graphs will not affect the techniques, or we can pretend that ties within node sets could have occurred and just didn't. This approach works for a small class of methods, but by no means for all. A case where it does not work is measuring transitivity: calculating transitivity fails because transitive triples are impossible in bipartite graphs (all ties are between node sets, which means that if $a \rightarrow b$ and $b \rightarrow c$ then a and c must be members of the same class, and therefore cannot be tied, making transitivity impossible).

An alternative approach is to develop new metrics and algorithms specifically designed for the bipartite case (affiliation graphs), taking into account the fact that the observed network is not just bipartite by happenstance but is by design – similar to the concept of structural zeros in log-linear modeling. This sounds like a great deal more work, but in practice it is often possible to adjust metrics designed for general graphs by simply applying an appropriate post hoc normalization. This is the strategy we shall take in applying centrality metrics to affiliation data. In other cases, a wholly different approach must be constructed. For example, for the case of measuring transitivity, we might redefine transitivity in terms of quadruples, such that a quad is called transitive if $a \rightarrow b$, $b \rightarrow c$, $c \rightarrow d$, and $a \rightarrow d$.

Centrality

As discussed elsewhere in this book (cf. Hanneman and Riddle's chapter), centrality refers to a family of properties of node positions. A number of centrality concepts have been developed, together with their associated measures (Borgatti and Everett, 2006). In this section, we consider the measurement of four well-known centrality concepts.

Degree

In ordinary graphs, degree centrality, d_i, is defined as the number of ties incident upon a node i. In the affiliation case, of course, the degree of a node is the number of ties it has with members of the other node set. So in the DGG data, for women, it is the number of events they attended, and for events, it is the number of women who attended. If we represent affiliations as a bipartite graph, we can compute degree centrality as usual and obtain perfectly interpretable values, at least with respect to the raw counts. However, it is usual to normalize centrality measures by dividing by the maximum value possible in a graph of that size. For ordinary graphs, this value is $n - 1$, where n is the number of nodes in the graph. However, for affiliation graphs, this is not quite right because a node cannot have ties to its own node set, and so the value of $n - 1$ cannot be attained.[4] The maximum degree is always the size of the other node set. In the DGG dataset, the maximum possible degree for a woman is the number of events (14), and the maximum possible degree for an event is the total number of women (18). Therefore, to normalize degree centrality in the case of affiliation data, we must apply two separate normalizations depending on which node set a node belongs to, as shown in Equation 28.6.

$$d_i^* = \frac{d_i}{n_2}, \text{ for } i \in V_1$$
$$d_j^* = \frac{d_j}{n_1}, \text{ for } j \in V_2$$

(28.6)

The key benefit of normalizing degree centrality in this way is that we can not only assess the relative centrality of two women or two events but also whether a given woman is more central than a given event. Without such normalization, nodes with equal propensities to have ties could only have equal degrees if the node sets were the same sizes. However, while normalization handles the mathematical issues of comparability, the substantive interpretation of a woman's centrality relative to an event's is still an issue, and depends on the details of the research setting. For example, it may be that the events are open to all, and ties in the affiliation graph reflect only a woman's agency in choosing which events to attend. In this case, if a woman has greater degree than a given event, we might say that her gregariousness is greater than the event's attractiveness, although this implies that the degree centrality measurement does not measure the same thing for women as for events, which runs counter to the basic idea in the direct analysis of affiliation graphs. On the other hand, the events might be by invitation only, in which case both women and events have a kind of agency. In general, centrality measures in this context have the most straightforward interpretations

when the affiliations result from some kind of bilateral matching process, such as speed dating.

Closeness

In ordinary graphs, closeness centrality, c_i, refers to the sum of geodesic distances from node i to all $n - 1$ others in the network. As such, it is an inverse measure of centrality in which greater centrality is indicated by a lower score. The lowest score possible occurs when the node has a tie to every other node, in which case the sum of distances to all others is $n - 1$. To normalize closeness centrality, we usually divide the raw score into $n - 1$, which simultaneously reverses the measure so that high scores indicate greater centrality.[5]

As with degree centrality, raw closeness can be calculated in affiliation graphs using the same algorithms we use for any graph. But, also like degree centrality, we must do something different to normalize closeness in the affiliation case. In affiliation graphs, the closest that a node can be to all others is $n_2 + 2(n_1 - 1)$, which is distance 1 from all nodes in the other node set and distance 2 from all other nodes in its own set. Therefore, to normalize (and simultaneously reverse) closeness in the bipartite case, we divide the raw closeness of a node in V_1 into $n_2 + 2(n_1 - 1)$ and the raw closeness of a node in V_2 into $n_1 + 2(n_2 - 1)$, as shown in Equation 28.7 in which c_i represents raw closeness centrality, and n_1 and n_2 represent the number of nodes in each node set.

$$c_i^* = \frac{n_2 + 2(n_1 - 1)}{c_i}, \text{ for } i \in V_1$$
$$c_j^* = \frac{n_1 + 2(n_2 - 1)}{c_j}, \text{ for } j \in V_2$$

(28.7)

Using the DGG dataset for illustration, we can see that the maximum number of nodes that can be distance 1 from a woman is 14 (since there are 14 events), and the maximum number of nodes that can be distance 2 from any of the 18 women is 17 (since there are 18 women). Thus, the theoretical minimum value of closeness centrality for a woman is $14 + 2*(18 - 1)$, and the theoretical minimum value for an event is $18 + 2*(14 - 1)$.

Betweenness

In any graph, betweenness centrality, b_i, refers to the "share" of shortest paths in a network that pass through a node i, as given by Equation 28.8.

$$b_k = \frac{1}{2} \sum_{i \neq k}^{n} \sum_{j \neq k, i}^{n} \frac{g_{ikj}}{g_{ij}}$$

(28.8)

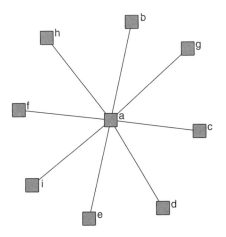

Figure 28.10   Star-shaped network

To normalize betweenness, we divide by the maximum possible value, which in the case of an ordinary graph is achieved by the center of a star-shaped network, as shown in Figure 28.10.

In the bipartite case, unless one node set contains just one node, an affiliation graph cannot attain that level of centralization. As a result, the maximum possible betweenness for any node in a bipartite graph is limited by the relative size of the two node sets, as given by Equation 28.9. To normalize betweenness, we simply divide b_i by either b_{v1max} or b_{v2max} (see Equation 28.9), depending on whether node i belongs to node set V_1 or V_2.

$$b_{V_1 \, max} = \frac{1}{2}[n_2^{\,2}(s+1)^2 + n_2(s+1)(2t-s-1)$$
$$- t(2s-t+3)]$$
$$s = (n_1 - 1) \, \text{div} \, n_2, \, t = (n_1 - 1) \, \text{mod} \, n_2$$

$$b_{V_2 \, max} = \frac{1}{2}[n_1^{\,2}(p+1)^2 + n_1(p+1)(2r-p-1)$$
$$- r(2p-r+3)]$$
$$p = (n_2 - 1) \, \text{div} \, n_1, \, r = (n_2 - 1) \, \text{mod} \, n_1$$

$$(28.9)$$

Eigenvector
Eigenvector centrality, e_i, is defined as the principal eigenvector of the adjacency matrix of a graph (Bonacich, 1972), as defined by Equation 28.10. In eigenvector centrality, a node's score is proportional to the sum of the scores of its neighbors. In a bipartite graph such as the one created by DGG, this means a woman's centrality will be proportional to the sum of centralities of the events she attends, and similarly the centrality of an event will be proportional to the sum of

centralities of the women who attend it. As a result, eigenvector centrality applied to the adjacency matrix of an affiliation graph is conceptually and mathematically identical to singular value decomposition (Eckhardt and Young, 1936) of the two-mode incidence matrix.[6] In addition, both of these are equivalent to an eigenvector analysis of the simple co-affiliation matrix.

$$e_i = \lambda \sum_j a_{ij} e_j \qquad (28.10)$$

where λ is the principal eigenvalue of A.

Empirical illustration of centrality measures

As an illustration, Figure 28.11 presents normalized centrality scores for all four types of centrality discussed above for the DGG bipartite graph presented in Figure 28.2. Note that three events (E8, E9, and E7) are more central than any of the women on all of the measures except for normalized degree centrality. It is also worth highlighting that E7 has 10 ties while Nora has only 8, but Nora has a slightly higher normalized degree centrality because there are fewer events than women, so here 8 represents a greater percentage of the possible ties.

COHESIVE SUBGROUPS

Cohesive subgroups refer to dense areas in a network that typically have more ties within a group than with the rest of the network. Affiliation data pose special problems for cohesive subgroup analysis because the area around any given node can never be very dense since none of a node's "friends" can be friends with each other. As a result, some traditional graph-theoretic methods of finding subgroups need to be modified for the bipartite case.

One of the most fundamental subgroup concepts is that of a clique (Luce and Perry, 1949). A clique is defined as a maximally complete subgraph, which means that every member of the clique has a tie to every other (a property known as completeness), and there is no other node that could be added to the subgraph's set of vertices without violating the completeness requirement (this is the property of maximality). Cliques of large size are rare in ordinary graphs, and they are impossible in bipartite graphs. As a result, applying ordinary clique algorithms to affiliation graphs is not useful.

One solution is to use the N-clique concept, which is a relaxation of the clique idea. In an N-clique, we do not require each member of the clique to have a direct tie with every other, but

Node	No. of ties	Normalized degree	Normalized closeness	Normalized betweenness	Normalized eigenvector
E8	14	0.78	0.85	0.24	0.51
E9	12	0.67	0.79	0.23	0.38
E7	10	0.56	0.73	0.13	0.38
Nora	8	0.57	0.80	0.11	0.26
Evelyn	8	0.57	0.80	0.10	0.33
Theresa	8	0.57	0.80	0.09	0.37
E6	8	0.44	0.69	0.07	0.33
Sylvia	7	0.50	0.77	0.07	0.28
Laura	7	0.50	0.73	0.05	0.31
Brenda	7	0.50	0.73	0.05	0.31
Katherine	6	0.43	0.73	0.05	0.22
E5	8	0.44	0.59	0.04	0.32
Helen	5	0.36	0.73	0.04	0.20
E3	6	0.33	0.56	0.02	0.25
Ruth	4	0.29	0.71	0.02	0.24
Verne	4	0.29	0.71	0.02	0.22
E12	6	0.33	0.56	0.02	0.20
Myrna	4	0.29	0.69	0.02	0.19
E11	4	0.22	0.54	0.02	0.09
Eleanor	4	0.29	0.67	0.01	0.23
Frances	4	0.29	0.67	0.01	0.21
Pearl	3	0.21	0.67	0.01	0.18
E4	4	0.22	0.54	0.01	0.18
Charlotte	4	0.29	0.60	0.01	0.17
E10	5	0.28	0.55	0.01	0.17
Olivia	2	0.14	0.59	0.01	0.07
Flora	2	0.14	0.59	0.01	0.07
E2	3	0.17	0.52	0.00	0.15
E1	3	0.17	0.52	0.00	0.14
Dorothy	2	0.14	0.65	0.00	0.13
E13	3	0.17	0.52	0.00	0.11
E14	3	0.17	0.52	0.00	0.11

Figure 28.11   Normalized centrality scores for the DGG affiliation graph

instead that the member be no more than distance n from every other. Choosing $n = 2$ gives us subgroups in which all pairs of members are within two links of each other. Applied to an ordinary graph, this yields subgroups that are "looser" than ordinary cliques, meaning that they are less than 100 percent dense. However, when applied to an affiliation graph, a two-clique can be regarded as complete, since all possible ties are present, due to the constraints of bipartite graphs. For this reason, Borgatti and Everett (1997) give two-cliques in affiliation graphs a name of their own, the *bi-clique*. Effectively, a bi-clique is to affiliation graphs what a clique is to ordinary graphs.

Because bi-cliques can be numerous and overlapping, it is often useful to perform a secondary analysis by constructing a node-by-clique matrix and by correlating the profiles of each node across bi-cliques so that nodes that are members of many of the same bi-cliques will be given a high correlation. This correlation matrix can then be treated as a valued adjacency matrix and visualized using standard graph layout algorithms. Figure 28.12 shows the result of such an analysis. The results are striking in the way they differentiate between two groups of women tied to two distinct groups of events. In addition, the diagram clearly shows the separation of Flora and Olivia, and the bridging position of Ruth.

Structural equivalence

Structural equivalence refers to the extent that pairs of nodes have ties to the same third parties. In affiliation graphs such as the DGG dataset,

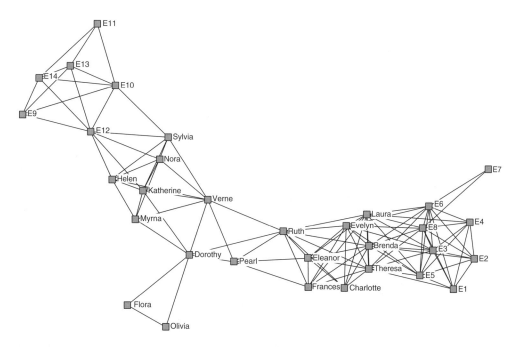

Figure 28.12   A tie indicates that the correlation between two nodes is greater than 0.60

actors are structurally equivalent to the extent that they attend the same events, and events are structurally equivalent to the extent that they are attended by the same actors. Strictly speaking, in affiliation graphs there can be no equivalence between nodes of different node sets, because they cannot have any nodes in common. As a result, structural equivalence analyses of affiliation graphs are virtually identical to analyses of the actor-by-actor and event-by-event co-affiliation matrices. For example, a standard approach to measuring structural equivalence in ordinary graphs is to correlate the rows (and columns) of the adjacency matrix, and then do a hierarchical cluster analysis of the correlation matrix to identify blocks of approximately equivalent nodes. If we take this approach to the $(n + m)$ by $(n + m)$ adjacency matrix of an affiliation graph, we are virtually guaranteed to find the two modes of the affiliations dataset as the dominant partition in the hierarchical clustering. The next partition will then split one of the two node sets, and so on. In the end, the results are essentially the same as if we had simply clustered each of the co-affiliation matrices separately.

An alternative approach to structural equivalence is blockmodeling (White et al., 1976). In ordinary graphs, blockmodeling refers to partitioning the rows and columns of the adjacency matrix in order for those corresponding to nearly

equivalent nodes to be placed in the same classes, as shown in Figure 28.13. Partitioning the rows and columns based on structural equivalence has the effect of partitioning the cells of the adjacency matrix into matrix blocks that have a characteristic pattern of homogeneity: either all of the cells in the block are 1s (called 1-blocks), or they all 0s (called 0-blocks). The job of a blockmodeling algorithm is to find a partitioning of the rows and columns that makes each matrix block as homogeneous as possible (Borgatti and Everett, 1992).

	A1	A2	A3	B1	B2	B3	B4	C1	C2	C3
A1	0	0	0	1	1	1	1	0	0	0
A2	0	0	0	1	1	1	1	0	0	0
A3	0	0	0	1	1	1	1	0	0	0
B1	1	1	1	0	0	0	0	1	1	1
B2	1	1	1	0	0	0	0	1	1	1
B3	1	1	1	0	0	0	0	1	1	1
B4	1	1	1	0	0	0	0	1	1	1
C1	1	1	1	1	1	1	1	0	0	0
C2	1	1	1	1	1	1	1	0	0	0
C3	1	1	1	1	1	1	1	0	0	0

Figure 28.13   Structural equivalence blockmodeling in an ordinary adjacency matrix

Applying this approach directly to affiliation graphs would mean partitioning the rows and columns of the $(n + m)$-by-$(n + m)$ bipartite adjacency matrix B. This can be done, but the bipartite structure imposes certain constraints. For example, matrix blocks involving within-mode ties (e.g., woman-to-woman, event-to-event) are necessarily 0-blocks. In addition, the best two-class partition will almost certainly be the mode partition (except in trivial cases), and in general, all other partitions will be refinements of the mode partition (i.e., they will be nested hierarchically within the mode partition).

A more elegant (and computationally efficient) approach is to work directly from the two-mode incidence matrix X (Borgatti and Everett, 1992). To do this, we redefine the concept of a blockmodel to refer to not one but two independent partitions: one for the rows and one for the columns. We then apply an algorithm to find the pair of partitions that yields the most homogeneous matrix blocks. In other words, a structural equivalence blockmodeling of the two-mode incidence matrix is one in which row nodes are in the same class if they have similar rows, and column nodes are in the same class if they have similar columns. An example involving four classes of rows and three classes of columns is shown in Figure 28.14.

REGULAR EQUIVALENCE

In ordinary graphs, the idea of regular equivalence is that a pair of equivalent nodes is connected not necessarily to the same nodes (as in structural equivalence) but to equivalent nodes (White and Reitz, 1983). In other words if nodes u and v are perfectly regularly equivalent, then if u has a friend p, we can expect v to have a friend q who is equivalent to p. In blockmodeling terms, this translates to a partitioning of the rows and columns of the adjacency matrix such that the resulting matrix blocks are either 0-blocks, or a special kind of 1-block in which every row and column in the matrix block has at least one 1.

In the case of structural equivalence, it was possible to apply the concept to the adjacency matrix of an affiliation graph, making it possible to use existing algorithms/programs to compute it. In the case of regular equivalence, there is a complication. Regular equivalence defines a lattice of partitions that all have the regularity property (Borgatti, 1989; Borgatti and Everett, 1989). Most standard regular equivalence algorithms deliver the maximum regular equivalence. Unfortunately, in undirected data, which is normally the case with affiliation graphs, the maximum regular equivalence is always trivial, placing all nodes in the same class. There are ways of handling this, but a better approach is to redefine regular equivalence for two-mode incidence matrices, as developed by Borgatti and Everett (1992). As they did with structural equivalence, Borgatti and Everett (1992) redefine the concept of a blockmodel to refer to not one but two independent partitions: one for the rows and one for the columns. Regular equivalence implies that we can section the matrix into rectangular blocks such that each block is a 0-block or a regular 1-block. For example, if the affiliation graph indicates which consumers visit which restaurants, the two-mode regular blockmodel shown in Figure 28.15 identifies four different types of consumers that visit three kinds of restaurants. Consumers of the same type do not necessarily visit the same restaurants, but they do visit the same kinds of restaurants. Thus all

	E1	E2	E3	F1	F2	F3	F4	G1	G2	G3
A1	1	1	1	1	1	1	1	0	0	0
A2	1	1	1	1	1	1	1	0	0	0
A3	1	1	1	1	1	1	1	0	0	0
B1	1	1	1	0	0	0	0	0	0	0
B2	1	1	1	0	0	0	0	0	0	0
B3	1	1	1	0	0	0	0	0	0	0
B4	1	1	1	0	0	0	0	0	0	0
C1	0	0	0	1	1	1	1	0	0	0
C2	0	0	0	1	1	1	1	0	0	0
C3	0	0	0	1	1	1	1	0	0	0
D1	0	0	0	1	1	1	1	1	1	1
D2	0	0	0	1	1	1	1	1	1	1

Figure 28.14 Two-mode structural equivalence blockmodel

	R1	R2	R3	R4	R5	R6	R7	R8	R9	R10
C1	1	0	1	0	1	1	0	0	0	0
C2	0	0	1	0	0	1	0	0	0	0
C3	0	1	0	1	1	0	1	0	0	0
C4	1	0	0	0	0	0	0	0	1	1
C5	1	0	1	0	0	0	0	1	1	0
C6	0	1	0	0	0	0	0	0	1	1
C7	0	1	1	0	0	0	0	1	0	1
C8	0	0	0	0	1	1	0	0	0	0
C9	0	0	0	0	0	1	0	0	0	0
C10	0	0	0	1	1	0	1	0	0	0
C11	1	0	1	1	0	1	0	0	1	1
C12	0	1	0	0	1	0	1	1	0	1

Figure 28.15 A two-mode regular equivalence blockmodel

consumers in the first class visit the first two kinds of restaurants, while all consumers in the second class visit only the first and third kinds of restaurants.

TWO-MODE RELATIONAL ALGEBRAS

In social network analysis, the term "relational algebra" is typically used very loosely to refer to the composition of relations. For example, if we measure both friendship and "teacher of" relations among a set of nodes, we can construct new, compound relations that link the actors, such as "friend of a teacher of" or "teacher of a friend of," as well as "friend of a friend" and "teacher of a teacher of." If the relations are represented as adjacency matrices, the composition relation can be equated to Boolean matrix multiplication[7] of the adjacency matrices, so that if F represents the friendship relation and T represents the teacher of relation, then the Boolean matrix product FT represents the "friend of a teacher of" relation. Since the result of a composition is just another relation, we can construct compositions of compositions, yielding a long string of Boolean matrix products. For example, the string FTT'F' gives a relation in which, if u is tied to v via this relation, it indicates that v is liked by a student of someone who is the teacher of a friend of u. (Note that the transpose T'is used to represent the inverse relation "is taught by.")

Relational composition is also possible with affiliation data, provided the incidence matrices are conformable. For example, suppose we have a binary person-by-organization matrix M, indicating which persons are members of which organizations. Suppose we also have an organization-by-event matrix S, which indicates which organizations were sponsors of which events. Finally, suppose we have a person-by-event matrix (A), indicating which person attended which event. The product MS is a new matrix in which $MS(u,v) > 0$ indicates that person u belongs to at least one organization that sponsored event v. In a given research setting, we might use MS to explain matrix A—that is, test the hypothesis that people are more likely to attend events that are sponsored by their organizations.

Relational algebras can incorporate a mix of affiliation and ordinary networks. For example, if we also had a matrix F, indicating which persons were friends with which others, we could generate compositions such as FMS, in which $FMS(u,v) > 0$ indicates that a person u has a friend who is a member of an organization that sponsors an event v. Krackhardt and Carley (1998) use compositions of this type in their PCANS model, which relates persons, tasks, and resources to each other, including person-to-person communications and task-to-task dependencies. For example if matrix A indicates which person is assigned to which task, and matrix P indicates which task precedes another, then the product AP relates each person u to each task v, indicating whether person u has a task that precedes task v. The triple product APA' relates each person u to each person v, indicating whether person u has a task that precedes a task that person v does—that is, it indicates whether person v is dependent on person u to get work done.

CONCLUSION

In this chapter we provide an introduction to the analysis of affiliation data. Two basic approaches are discussed: a conversion approach and a direct approach. The conversion approach consists of analyzing co-affiliations or similarities among elements of one node set with respect to their profiles across the other node set. The similarities are then treated as ties among the nodes. Co-affiliations are frequently analyzed to identify opportunities for interaction (e.g., the flow of goods or information) or unseen relationships between people (e.g., sociometric preferences). The direct approach consists of analyzing both node sets simultaneously, treating the elements of each on an equal footing. As discussed, the direct approach often requires the use of new metrics and algorithms specifically designed for bipartite graphs.

Our survey has focused on analysis, and within that, measurement of network concepts such as centrality, cohesive subgroups, structural equivalence, and regular equivalence. In doing so, we have ignored statistical modeling, such as the nascent field of exponential random graph models for affiliation data (see Robins's chapter in this volume for a more detailed discussion).

We close with suggestions for future analyses of affiliation data. One element that is underexplored in affiliation work is the temporal dimension. There are two important ways in which time can be brought into affiliation analysis. First, there is the case of affiliation graphs changing over time. We can conceptualize this as a series of person-by-organization matrices representing different slices of time, or a single three-mode affiliation network in which each tie links together a person, an organization, and a time period. Many of the direct analysis techniques discussed in this chapter can be generalized to this three-mode case (Borgatti and Everett, 1992).

The other important case is in the analysis of two-mode person-by-event data, where the events are ordered by time. For example, if we study Hollywood film projects, we typically have a data matrix that is actor by film, and the films are ordered by release date (or start date, etc.). If we are interested in how actors' previous collaboration ties affect the quality of a film project they are jointly engaged in, we need to construct the collaboration network continuously over time, since we would not want to predict film success based on collaborations that occur after the film was produced. Social network analysis programs such as UCINET (Borgatti et al., 2002) are just beginning to include tools for these kinds of analyses.

Another example of time-ordered affiliation data occurs in the study of career trajectories. Taking the three-mode approach we can examine how actors' co-location (in terms of both organization and time) ties affect their future careers. Or we can look at how individuals flow from organization to organization along directed paths. Here, the organizations can be ordered in time differently for each individual, although a key research question is whether an underlying ordering of the organizations (such as status) creates consistency in individual career moves.

NOTES

1 The node labels indicate whether the individual is an inspector (I), a worker (W), or a supervisor (S).

2 The groups were constructed by the present authors for illustrative purposes, based on a clique analysis.

3 This is not to imply that the data must be binary as we could have data in which persons have a degree of membership or participation in various groups or events.

4 Except for nodes that are in the only members of their special case where one vertex set contains just one node set.

5 Of course, this is a nonlinear transformation, unlike all other centrality normalizations. To maintain consistency we could instead divide raw closeness by its maximum and simply remember that it is a reverse measure.

6 In addition, singular value decomposition yields the measures of hubs and authorities proposed by Kleinberg (1999). Therefore, in affiliation data, eigenvector centrality and hubs and authorities are identical concepts, which is not true in ordinary graphs.

7 Boolean multiplication is simply ordinary matrix multiplication in which the resulting matrix is dichotomized so that any value greater than 0 is assigned a 1.

REFERENCES

Allatta, J.T. (2003) 'Structural analysis of communities of practice: An investigation of job title, location, and management intention', in M. Huysman, E. Wenger, and V. Wulf (eds), *Communities and Technologies*. Amsterdam: Kluwer Academic Publishers. pp. 23–42.

Allatta, J.T. (2005) *Worker Collaboration and Communities of Practice*. Ph.D. dissertation, University of Pennsylvania.

Allen, M. (1974) 'The structure of interorganizational elite cooptation: Interlocking corporate directorates', *American Sociological Review*, 39(3): 393–406.

Allen, T. (1977) *Managing the Flow of Technology*. Cambridge, MA: MIT Press.

Bonacich, P. (1972) 'Factoring and weighting approaches to status scores and clique identification', *Journal of Mathematical Sociology*, 2: 112–20.

Bonacich, P. (1987) 'Power and centrality: A family of measures', *American Journal of Sociology*, 92: 1170–82.

Bonacich, P. (2007) 'Some unique properties of eigenvector centrality', *Social Networks*, 29(4): 555–64.

Borgatti, S.P. (1989) *Regular Equivalence in Graphs, Hypergraphs, and Matrices*. University of California, Irvine.

Borgatti, S.P. (2002) *NetDraw: Graph Visualization Software*. Harvard: Analytic Technologies

Borgatti, S.P. and Everett, M.G. (1989) 'The class of all regular equivalences: Algebraic structure and computation', *Social Networks*, 11: 65–88.

Borgatti, S.P. and Everett, M.G. (1992) 'Regular blockmodels of multiway, multimode matrices', *Social Networks*, 14: 91–120.

Borgatti, S.P. and Everett, M.G. (1997) 'Network analysis of 2-mode data', *Social Networks*, 19(3): 243–69.

Borgatti, S.P. and Everett, M.G. (2006) 'A graph-theoretic framework for classifying centrality measures', *Social Networks*, 28(4): 466–84.

Borgatti, S.P., Everett, M.G. and Freeman, L.C. (2002) *UCINET for Windows: Software for Social Network Analysis*. Harvard, MA: Analytic Technologies.

Brandes, U. (2001) 'A faster algorithm for betweenness centrality', *Journal of Mathematical Sociology*, 25(2): 163–77.

Burt, R. (1987) 'Social contagion and Innovation: Cohesion versus structural equivalence', *American Journal of Sociology*, 92(6): 1287–335.

Carroll, W.K., Fox, J. and Ornstein, M.D. (1982) 'The network of directorate interlocks among the largest Canadian firms', *Canadian Review of Sociology and Anthropology*, pp. 245–68.

Davis, G. (1991) 'Agents without principles? The spread of the poison pill through the intercorporate network', *Administrative Science Quarterly*, 36(4): 583–613.

Davis, G. and Greve, H. (1997) 'Corporate elite networks and governance changes in the 1980s', *American Journal of Sociology*, 103(1): 1–37.

Davis, A., Gardner, B. and Gardner, R. (1941) *Deep South.* Chicago: University of Chicago Press.

Domhoff, W. (1967) *Who Rules America?* Englewood Cliffs, NJ: Prentice-Hall.

Eckhardt, C. and Young, G. (1936) 'The approximation of one matrix by another of lower rank', *Psychometrika,* 1: 211–18.

Faust, K. Willber, K, Rowlee, D. and Skvoretz, J. (2002) 'Scaling and statistical models for affiliation networks: Patterns of participation among Soviet politicians during the Brezhnev era', *Social Networks,* 24: 231–59.

Feld, S. (1981) 'The focused organization of social ties', *American Journal of Sociology,* 86: 1015–35.

Field, S., Frank, K., Schiller, K., Riegle-Crumb, C. and Muller, C. (2006) 'Identifying positions from affiliation networks: Preserving the duality of people and events', *Social Networks,* 28(2): 97–186.

Friedkin, N. (1984) 'Structural cohesion and equivalence explanations of social homogeneity', *Sociological Methods and Research,* 12: 235–61.

Galaskiewicz, J. (1985) *Social Organization of an Urban Grants Economy.* New York: Academic Press.

Gmür, M. (2006) 'Co-citation analysis and the search for invisible colleges: A methodological evaluation', *Scientometrics,* 57(1): 27–57.

Harary, F. (1969) *Graph Theory.* Reading, MA: Addison-Wesley.

Kleinberg, J. (1999) 'Authoritative sources in a hyperlinked environment', *Journal of the ACM,* 46(5): 604–32.

Krackhardt, D. and Carley, K.M. (1998) 'A PCANS model of structure in organization', in *Proceedings of the 1998 International Symposium on Command and Control Research and Technology.* Monterey, CA. pp. 113–19.

Lazer, D., Mergel, I. and Friedman, A. (2009) 'Co-Citation of Prominent Social Network Articles in Sociology Journals: The Evolving Canon', *Connections,* 29(1): 43–64.

Lester, R. and Cannella, A. (2006) 'Interorganizational familiness: How family firms use interlocking directorates to build community-level social capital', *Entrepreneurship: Theory & Practice,* 30(6): 755–75.

Luce, R. and Perry, A. (1949) 'A method of matrix analysis of group structure', *Psychometrika,* 14(2): 95–116.

McPherson, J.M. (1982) 'Hypernetwork sampling: Duality and differentiation among voluntary organizations', *Social Networks,* 3: 225–49.

McPherson, J.M. and Smith-Lovin, L. (1986) 'Sex segregation in voluntary associations', *American Sociological Review,* 51(1): 61–79.

McPherson, J.M. and Smith-Lovin, L. (1987) 'Homophily in voluntary organizations: Status distance and the composition of face-to-face groups', *American Sociological Review,* 52(3): 370–79.

Mizruchi M. (1983) 'Who controls whom? An examination of the relation between management and boards of directors in large American corporations', *Academy of Management Review,* 8: 426–35.

Mizruchi, M. (1992) *The Structure of Corporate Political Action: Interfirm Relations and Their Consequences.* Cambridge, MA: Harvard University Press.

Mizruchi, M. (1996) 'What do interlocks do? An analysis, critique, and assessment of research on interlocking directorates', *Annual Review of Sociology,* 22: 217–98.

Newman, M. Strogatz, H. and Watts, D. (2001) 'Random graphs with arbitrary degree distributions and their applications', *Physical Review* E., 64: 1–17.

Robins, G. and Alexander, M. (2004) 'Small worlds among interlocking directors: Network structure and distance in bipartite graphs', *Computational & Mathematical Organization Theory,* 10(1): 69–94.

Roethlisberger F. and Dickson, W. (1939) *Management and the Worker.* Cambridge: Cambridge University Press.

Sokal, R. and Sneath, P. (1973) *Numerical Taxonomy.* San Francisco: W.H. Freeman.

Uzzi, B. and Spiro, J. (2005) 'Collaboration and creativity: The small world problem', *American Journal of Sociology,* 111(2): 447–504.

Wang, P., Sharpe, K., Robins, G. and Pattison, P. (2009) 'Exponential random graph (p*) models for affiliation networks', *Social Networks,* 31(1): 12–25.

Westphal J.D. and Khanna, P. (2003) 'Keeping directors in line: Social distancing as a control mechanism in the corporate elite', *Administrative Science Quarterly,* 48(3): 361–98.

Westphal, J.D. (1998) 'Board games: How CEOs adapt to increases in structural board independence from management', *Administrative Science Quarterly,* 43: 511–37.

White, H.C., Boorman, S.A. and Breiger, R.L. (1976) 'Social structure from multiple networks, I: Blockmodels of roles and positions', *American Journal of Sociology,* 81: 730–80.

White, D. and Reitz, K. (1983) 'Graph and semigroup homomorphisms on networks of relations', *Social Networks,* 5: 193–224.

29

Positions and Roles

Anuška Ferligoj, Patrick Doreian, and
Vladimir Batagelj

We start our chapter with a discussion of social systems composed of positions and roles. This is followed by a set of methods for identifying positions and roles and for delineating social network structures. We finish by listing some important open problems that require solutions, so that we can better understand the structure and operation of role systems.

INTRODUCTION

The paired concepts of positions and roles are staples among social science terms. Intuitively, the idea of a position is a location in some social structure and a role has a set of expected behaviors corresponding to the location (e.g., Faust and Wasserman, 1992). Given a family as a social system, a parent is a location and the parental role includes appropriate behaviors for rearing children. The child is another position that carries age-graded expectations of appropriate conduct by children toward their parents. Expectations of parents and children are coupled into a system of roles. Similarly, in an organization there are locations in some structure – stereotypically, a hierarchy – and roles are coupled to these locations. Expectations include rules for how superiors and subordinates behave in relation to each other inside their organization. Roles are defined for all levels and positions in the hierarchy and form a coupled system of expectations. Of course, this simple description identifies an

idealized form for which there can be many variations. Key empirical issues involve delineating positions in social systems, identifying roles that correspond to these positions, the nature of, and extent to which, these roles exist, and examining how both role systems and social structures change over time.

Social network analysis provides a set of tools that includes ways of mapping social structures in ways that help identify positions and roles. When used for studying social structures over time, these tools help analysts understand how social structures and role systems change over time. If there are only simple descriptions of networks over time, this activity can be called studying network dynamics. However, if we are able to identify process rules that generate the observed changes over time, then we are examining the evolution of social structures over time. While both network dynamics and network evolution have their place in studying positions and roles, characterizing evolution is both more demanding and more important for constructing cumulative knowledge and understanding of roles and positions.

Social networks

A simple social network consists of a set of units, called social actors, with a single relation defined over them. For example, the units could be children and the relation defined as "plays with." For a family, the units are parents and children, and one relationship is "controls" for parents acting toward their children. A more complex network has multiple relations. For the children on a playground, the relations studied could be "plays with" and "likes." An even more complicated network has multiple relations and multiple levels. For a family, the levels are for parents and for children and the relationships studied could include "controls," "loves (and/or hates)," "respects," and "confides." Additional levels could include multiple generations. In formal organizations with hierarchies, units can be individuals occupying locations at multiple levels with the relations "reports," "seeks work-related help," "provides work-related help," and "socializes at breaks."

Units in a social network can also include groups, organizations, and nations as well as the individuals in these larger and more extensive units. If the groups are gangs, the relations between them include alliance ties and enemy ties. For organizations, relations can include sending goods or people between organizations, sharing information, or forming alliances. For nations, the relations can include exports, imports, providing aid, belonging to military alliances, and waging war. Networks can also be made up of objects that have no obvious action identity as actors in the sense of individuals, groups, organizations, or nations. An example is the set of scientific documents for one or more scientific fields. These units include books, articles, and research reports. One relation defined over these objects is citation. Each scientific document contains references to earlier relevant work and the relational ties are citations of earlier documents by later documents. Patents form a similar set of units where the citations are governed by legal requirements to acknowledge prior inventions and their patents. For scientific articles, depending on the field, there are differing volumes of solo authored publications and joint productions by two or more scientists. For the latter, co-authorship is a relation defined over authors of documents and this can be coupled to citation networks to create a network database with networks involving quite different units. Ties in networks often have values capturing dimension such as intensity, frequency, or volume depending on the relation considered. In general, data sets can be created with both very large networks and multiple types of units. Regardless of the complexity of a network, the notions of positions and roles can be considered for them. Obviously, the way this is done depends on the size and complexity of the networks considered. But it can be done, and the approach known as generalized blockmodeling provides the tools for establishing positions and roles and thereby delineating social structures in a very general way. For the ease of exposition, most of our discussion is focused on simple networks but the tools can be used for any degree of network complexity.

BLOCKMODELING

One publication changed dramatically the way network analysts viewed the delineation and examination of social structure (as network structure). Lorrain and White (1971) introduced the concept of structural equivalence (defined below) as a way of operationalizing both position and role. In doing so, they set the foundations for studying rigorously empirical social structure and examining role systems. This led to the creation of blockmodeling. Based on their insights, Breiger et al. (1975) presented a practical algorithm for establishing positions in a network. It was based on a particular way of operationalizing structural equivalence. Burt (1976) provided an alternative operationalization and with it a different algorithm. Sailer (1978) provided another way of thinking about blockmodeling. This was later formalized by White and Reitz (1983) with the introduction of regular equivalence as a formal generalization of structural equivalence. In 1992, the flagship journal of the field, Social Networks, devoted a special issue to blockmodeling featuring a variety of approaches that had been created since the early statements that helped define the field. This helped create the conditions for the emergence of generalized blockmodeling as a systematic statement of the approach and secured the foundations of blockmodeling (Doreian et al., 2005). In the following, we do not discuss the details of the various algorithms used for establishing blockmodels. Instead, we focus attention on the core ideas. Our discussion of blockmodeling distinguishes classic blockmodeling and generalized blockmodeling. In doing so, we put the formal/mathematical foundations to one side. The cited documents informing our discussion provide the technical and formal details behind the nonmathematical statement provided here.

Classic blockmodeling

Some terms are used to provide a way of describing networks precisely. Actors are represented by *vertices* and social ties between them are represented by *lines*. A shorthand way of labeling a network is $N = (V, R)$, where V represents the set of vertices and R is a label for the relation. Networks with one relation can be viewed as simple networks. For representing networks with multiple relations, this notation extends naturally to $N = (V, R_1, R_2, . . ., R_r)$ for a set of r relations. The ideas discussed below apply to all networks and, for ease of exposition, we use simple networks.

Some relations are inherently symmetric, for example, co-authoring a scientific paper. For such relations, a line representing a symmetric tie is called an *edge*. Other social relations are inherently asymmetric. For example, "parent of" is a relation represented by a line that goes from the parent to a child. A child can never be a parent of their parent(s). For networks with only asymmetric ties, the lines are called *arcs*. Some relations are defined with an inherent direction but contain symmetric edges. Liking provides an example with an obvious direction, but if one person likes another and the sentiment is reciprocated then, for such a pair, there is a symmetric tie (edge) between them. Other liking ties need not be reciprocated and there is an arc from one person to another. Such networks contain both arcs and edges. The distinction between arcs and edges needs to be included when thinking about positions and roles.

When two actors are *structurally equivalent* they are connected in exactly the same way to other actors in the network. A formal definition can be found in Doreian et al. (2005: 172). In essence, they are structurally identical. A set of structurally equivalent actors is called a *position*. If the network has only sets of structurally equivalent actors then it is fully consistent with structural equivalence. This means the set of vertices, V, can be partitioned into a set of k clusters, $\{C_1, C_2, ..., C_k\}$ so that the vertices in a cluster C_i are structurally identical. In this sense, given this definition of equivalence, there are k positions in the network (representing a social structure). This provides a precise definition and operationalization of the term "position" as a cluster. Given two positions, C_i and C_j, the set of ties from all actors in C_i to all actors in C_j forms a *block*. Given k positions there are k^2 blocks and the whole structure is represented by these blocks. There are k blocks where the ties are within positions and these are called *diagonal blocks*. There are $k(k–1)$ *off-diagonal blocks* containing ties between positions. If there are n actors in the network and if n is much larger than k, then the large network is represented by the *blockmodel image* where there are only positions and blocks. Put differently, the original network is modeled by the sets of positions and blocks – hence, the term blockmodel. White et al. (1976) argue that the representation of a network as a blockmodel image describes a role structure precisely with a clear formulation of positions and roles. This also allows the study of these role structures as relational algebras.

Most empirical networks are not described perfectly by the blockmodel just described. Pairs of actors are more likely to be "almost structurally equivalent" in the sense that their ties are with almost the same other actors. These differences, if small in number, are assumed to not matter that much empirically, which permits the retention of the idea of representing an observed network as a blockmodel. This raises the issue of empirically determining the positions and blocks. While there are many ways of doing this we confine our attention to those used most frequently. Two of these methods hinge on ways of representing the extent to which pairs of actors are structurally equivalent. Breiger et al. (1975) provided an algorithm based on having correlations represent the notion of "almost structurally equivalent." The *location* of an actor in a network is the vector of ties (both present and absent) involving an actor. For an undirected graph, the row (or column) is the location. For a directed graph, both the row and the column of ties for an actor represent the actor's location. If two actors are structurally equivalent, the correlation of their locations will be 1. Two actors are "almost structurally equivalent" if the correlation of their positions is "close enough to 1." The algorithm proposed by Breiger et al. (1975) iteratively uses correlations of locations to identify positions and, therefore, blocks.

Burt (1976) proposed an alternative way of operationalizing "almost structurally equivalent" by using the Euclidean distances between locations. If two actors are structurally equivalent, then the Euclidean distance between their locations is 0. "Almost structurally equivalent" became "the Euclidean distance is close enough to 0." The matrix of locations is turned into a matrix of distances, which is then subjected to a standard clustering method. Doreian et al. (2005) describe algorithms of the sort suggested by Burt and Breiger et al. as "indirect methods" because the network data are converted into (dis)similarities that are then clustered. There are three broad problems with these approaches: (i) there are many ways of constructing dis(similarities) and not all of them are compatible with structural equivalence; (ii) there are thousands of clustering algorithms and choosing one of them seems arbitrary, and (iii) the methods can be used only in an inductive fashion. The third is due to the fact that clustering diagrams or dendrograms are examined in order to discern the clusters that are then labeled positions. There is no upfront conceptualization beyond the idea of structural equivalence being applicable and analysts tend to accept what is returned by the joining of a clustering algorithm with a measure of (dis)similarity. These problems led Batagelj et al. (1992a) to pursue an approach they called a "direct approach" to blockmodeling. This was formalized further into "generalized blockmodeling" (Doreian et al., 1994, 2005) as a general method for partitioning networks into positions and blocks. Their analyses suggest that the direct approach produces better fitting partitions based on equivalence concepts than the indirect approach. Even so, the indirect approach remains useful and can be used more effectively for larger networks than the direct approach (described below) can handle.

Generalized blockmodeling

Generalized blockmodeling (Batagelj, 1997; Batagelj et al., 1992a, 1992b; Doreian et al., 1994, 2005), as a direct approach to network data, rests on some simple ideas. First, rather than think about structural equivalence as being approximated by a measure of (dis)similarity, it is more useful to think about what are the kinds of blocks that are consistent with structural equivalence. They are few in number: (i) diagonal blocks can have only two forms and (ii) off-diagonal blocks also have just two forms consistent with structural equivalence. The off-diagonal ideal or permitted blocks have only 0s in them or only 1s in them. They are, respectively, called *complete blocks* and *null blocks*. This captures exactly the idea of pairs of actors in different positions being connected in the same way to other actors. The same logic applies to diagonal blocks but the diagonal permitted blocks look slightly different. One permitted diagonal block has 1s everywhere except on the diagonal, which has only 0s. The other permitted form has 0s everywhere and 1s on the diagonal. The second block type of these two is rare empirically. We use the terms "complete blocks" and "null blocks" to describe both diagonal and off-diagonal blocks.

The direct approach sets up comparisons of an ideal blockmodel based on structural equivalence (which can have complete and null blocks anywhere) and an empirical blockmodel with the same number of positions and blocks. In general, the empirical blockmodel approximates an ideal blockmodel. Differences between ideal and empirical blockmodels are easy to construct conceptually. Wherever a 1 appears in a null block there is one type of inconsistency, and wherever there is a 0 in a complete block there is another type of inconsistency. All we have to do is count the inconsistencies and seek an empirical partition that makes the number of inconsistencies as small as possible. To do this, a clustering problem is formulated with a *criterion function* that represents the sum of all of the inconsistencies from all of the blocks. The clustering problem is the

following one: in the set of all possible partitions into k clusters we search for the best partition according to the selected criterion function. The two types of inconsistencies can be weighted differently if one type of inconsistency is deemed more important than the other. If null blocks are thought to be important parts of a network structure then the presence of 1s in them can be penalized heavily so that blocks identified as null blocks contain no 1s.

Solving the clustering problem is not easy. While it sounds useful to compare all possible ideal blocks with all possible empirical blocks this can be done only for very small networks. So some heuristic is needed. The one used in solving the generalized blockmodeling problem is a relocation algorithm that makes local comparisons of possible ideal and empirical partitions. Some number (k) of partitions is chosen and the network is partitioned randomly into k provisional positions. The *neighborhood* for such a partition is made up of other partitions that can be reached by either of the two types of changes. One is simply to move a vertex from one provisional position to another position. The second is to exchange a pair of vertices between two provisional positions. For each change, the criterion function can be calculated before and after the change. If the criterion function does not decline, then the new partition is discarded. But if it does decline we move to the new partition and repeat the changes (moving a vertex or exchanging a pair of vertices between positions) from the new partition. If a change lowers the criterion function, we move again to the new partition and continue until no further reduction is possible. Because this is a local optimization method, this is repeated many times to maximize the likelihood of reaching a globally best (optimal) partition rather than only a locally best (local) partition.

White and Reitz (1983) generalized the idea of structural equivalence to regular equivalence. Two actors are *regularly equivalent* if they are connected in equivalent ways to equivalent others. (A formal definition can be found in Doreian et al., 2005: 173.) This somewhat mysterious definition is best illustrated by a formal hierarchy with multiple levels that reach down to the same extent in each division. A partition based on regular equivalence will identify each of the levels as a position and captures the idea of position roles nicely. Subordinates (in a position) are expected to behave in the same way with their superordinates (bosses) while bosses are expected to behave in the same way toward their subordinates. Structural equivalence does not lead to this kind of partition. White and Reitz (1983) proved that regular equivalence is a proper generalization of structural equivalence. This equivalence was included in generalized blockmodeling through a theorem that regular equivalence permits only two block types: null blocks and blocks that have at least one 1 in every row and column of the block. Such blocks are called *1-covered blocks*. (The proper generalization is shown with the complete block of structural equivalence being a very special case of a 1-covered block.) Again, a criterion function expressing inconsistencies between ideal and empirical blocks for regular equivalence can be constructed and the local optimization method described above can be used.

The underlying strategy of the generalized blockmodel is simple to describe and involves turning a definition of a type of equivalence into a set of permitted block types. Structural equivalence permits only null and complete blocks. Regular equivalence permits only null blocks and 1-covered blocks. The link between a type of equivalence and its permitted blocks is driven by theorems establishing the permitted blocks for an equivalence type. A natural avenue for expanding the types of equivalences for establishing new types of blockmodels is to expand the permitted block types. One set of expanded block types can be found in Doreian et al. (2005: Chapter 7). These new types included row-regular blocks (each row is 1-covered) and column-regular blocks (each column is 1-covered). These were used to partition baboon-grooming networks at two points in time where neither structural equivalence nor regular equivalence were useful. This general strategy of expanding block types, and hence types of blockmodels, permits an indefinite expansion of blockmodeling into different substantive domains where the new block types can be more general and more useful than relying only on structural or regular equivalence. Davis and Leinhardt (1972) explored the structure of small-group networks and suggested there was a tendency toward the formation of ranked-cluster systems. Based on these ideas, Doreian et al. (2000, 2005: Chapter 11) present a "ranked-cluster" blockmodel to study the structure of children's networks and the marriage system for nobility in Ragusa (now known as Dubrovnik) in the eighteenth and nineteenth centuries.

There are some important and useful results from using generalized blockmodeling. First, by setting up a clustering problem with a criterion function that is fully compatible with a type of blockmodel, the criterion function becomes an explicit measure of fit for the blockmodel. Of course, different criterion functions are defined for different types of blockmodels and each is tailored to the type of blockmodel used. This implies that the values of the criterion function cannot be used to compare the fits of different types of blockmodels. The logic of the approach is

to formulate models and then fit them to the data by using an appropriate criterion function that is compatible with the blockmodel type. Each blockmodel stands or falls on its own to fit the data. Brusco and Steinley (2006, 2007) present results based on different optimization approaches that suggest the (relocation) heuristic used in generalized blockmodeling usually does return optimal partitions for small networks.

Second, much can be done within the rubric of "formulating models and fitting them." Thus far, we have described an inductive approach to blockmodeling: all that matters is the statement of equivalence, usually structural or regular. Then some clustering algorithm is used to find positions and blocks. The notions of null, complete, and 1-covered blocks are all left implicit and can appear anywhere in the blockmodel returned by an algorithm. Yet, we often know more about a network than the applicability of a particular type of equivalence. The more we know, or think we know, about a network, the more we can "prespecify" a blockmodel. We may know not only the permitted block types but also where some of them are in a blockmodel. (Indeed, we might know where all of them appear in a blockmodel.) If we have some knowledge – which can be simply empirical or it could have a theoretical foundation – it is useful to prespecify a blockmodel that uses this knowledge. When this is done, generalized blockmodeling is used deductively.

A theoretical driven example of deductive blockmodeling is found with structural balance theory (Heider, 1946; as formalized by Cartwright and Harary, 1956). If a signed network is balanced, then the partition structure is known from a pair of structure theorems that state, depending exactly on how balance is defined, that the actors in the network can be partitioned into two positions (Cartwright and Harary, 1956) or into two or more positions (Davis, 1967) such that all of the positive ties are within positions and all of the negative ties are between positions. Doreian and Mrvar (1996) noted that this implies a particular blockmodel structure with two types of blocks. *Positive blocks* contain only positive or null ties and *negative blocks* contain only negative or null ties. The implied blockmodel has positive blocks on the diagonal and negative blocks off the diagonal. Doreian and Mrvar proposed a way of partitioning signed networks that are as close as possible to a partition expected for exact structural balance. The criterion function they proposed counts two types of inconsistencies: positive ties in negative blocks and negative ties in positive blocks. These inconsistencies can be weighted differently if desired. The relocation algorithm described earlier is used to solve this clustering problem and is now an integral part of the generalized blockmodeling approach.

Another element of knowledge is that some actors belong together in a position or that some pairs of actors will belong to different positions. This kind of knowledge is expressed in the form of constraints on which positions actors can be placed within. The extreme level of knowledge is that we know the structure of the blockmodel image and the positions to which all actors belong and this would be expressed in a *completely prespecified blockmodel*. More likely, prespecification, if possible, will be partial. Examples of some prespecified blockmodels are found in Doreian et al. (2005: 233–46). Of course, without the knowledge for prespecifying a blockmodel, the inductive use of blockmodeling is the preferred option.

Nuskesser and Sawitzki (2005) also present a formal overview of blockmodeling based on the conception of a position and link blockmodeling to a wider variety of network representations and methods.

SOME RECENT EXTENSIONS TO GENERALIZED BLOCKMODELING

We provide here some examples of ideas and analyses that can be viewed as extending generalized blockmodeling ideas in different ways that hold promise.

Two-mode and three-mode network arrays

Borgatti and Everett (1992), in a special double issue of *Social Networks* devoted to blockmodeling approaches, suggested applying blockmodeling ideas to multinetwork arrays and provided a way of doing so. This moved the approach beyond analyzing one-mode networks. This extension can also be formulated as a generalized blockmodeling problem where the network is defined by several sets of units and ties between them. Doreian et al. (2004, 2005) did this for blockmodeling two-mode networks. The examples they used included the classic Deep South data set and Supreme Court voting for a single term. More recently, Batagelj et al. (2006) applied these ideas to three-way network data. In addition to analyzing network data with three distinct types of social objects, they considered two special cases. One allowed that the two of the modes were the same in a three-way array and the second always has the same mode in the three-way array.

Krackhardt's (1987) office data were used to illustrate the approach. Each of the 22 actors in the network provided their image of the one-mode relational data for the office. When these 22 perceptions are coupled, a full three-way array is created. Even this special case poses severe computational problems for the direct approach that have not been solved. Instead, Batagelj et al. (2007) proposed a dissimilarity measure for structural equivalence for all three cases and adopted an indirect approach. To do this they expressed structural equivalence as an interchangeability condition across modes for three-way networks. This allowed the construction of a compatible dissimilarity measure. Ward's clustering method was used to obtain the three-dimensional partitioning via hierarchical clustering.

Roffilli and Lomi (2006) proposed a quite different approach to blockmodeling two-mode networks. It is based on a family of learning algorithms called Support Vector Machines (SVM). The analytical framework provided by SVM provides a flexible statistical environment for solving many classification tasks while reframing regression and density estimation problems. They also used the Deep South data and compared their results with other partitions of these data obtained by employing different methods. Their method acts as a data-independent preprocessing step and they were able to reduce the complexity of clustering problems. This reduction in complexity enabled the use of simpler clustering methods.

Valued networks

Doreian et al. (2005) confined their attention to binary networks where the ties are simply present or absent. Given the increased collection of valued network data, this is a clear limitation. This makes extending generalized blockmodeling to a valued network a necessary and important development. This task was picked up initially by Batagelj and Ferligoj (2000) and later by Žiberna (2007). Žiberna proposed three approaches to generalized blockmodeling for valued network data by assuming that the values of the ties are measured on at least an interval scale.

The first approach proposed by Žiberna (2007) is straightforward generalized blockmodeling of binary networks to valued blockmodeling. He uses a threshold parameter, and ties are assessed in relation to the value of the threshold (without binarizing the network). Patterns within blocks, as signatures of block types, are still examined to identify block types. One problem that emerges is that two blocks with the same pattern of ties but with different values for the ties that are present cannot be distinguished. This implies that such differences in tie values cannot be used to locate optimal partitions. This problem led Žiberna (2008) to consider a second approach that he called homogeneity blockmodeling. In this approach the inconsistency of an empirical block, compared with a corresponding ideal block, is measured by variability of values within a block. Ideally, all of the values inside a block are the same. This is fully consistent with the founding idea of blocks being composed of identical ties. (Instead of seeing if ties are present with a value of 1, the homogeneity partitioning establishes blocks with minimum variation in the values of the ties within the blocks.) While this approach helps identify blocks with values that are as homogeneous as possible where ties need to be present, it runs into another problem. For binary blockmodeling there is a clear distinction between null blocks and other block types. Yet a null block is homogeneous (with a value of 0) and cannot be readily distinguished as a special distinctive block type under homogeneity blockmodeling. As a result, while homogeneity blockmodeling is well suited for distinguishing empirical blocks based on tie values and finding partitions based on such differences, it is less suited for distinguishing empirical blocks based on block types and finding partitions based on such distinctions. This led Žiberna to consider implicit blockmodeling of valued networks.

Implicit blockmodeling can distinguish empirical blocks based on tie values and block types. However, it is heavily influenced by the values of block maxima and often classifies blocks differently than would be desired. As a result, the partitions that it finds are heavily influenced by the classification of blocks and can lead to unsatisfactory partitions. This is especially problematic if block maximum normalization is also used. The partitions that it produces can be improved, but this improvement comes at the price of one of the main advantages of implicit blockmodeling, which is its ability to distinguish between the null block type and other block types.

While the three approaches to blockmodeling valued relations proposed by Žiberna, all have problems that are best viewed as important first steps toward establishing better solutions to this class of network partitioning problems. They were proposed, in part, as a response to some results Žiberna obtained while examining an obvious strategy for blockmodeling a valued network. This is to select some threshold and use it to binarize the network: ties at, or above, the threshold are coded 1 while ties below the threshold are set to 0. The binarized networks were then treated with the approach advocated by Doreian et al. (2005).

Žiberna suggests binarization is a poor first step of a general strategy because the established partitions can be unstable and produce different blockmodels depending on the threshold selected. It follows that using one of the three types of generalized blockmodeling of valued networks proposed by Žiberna is preferable to using binary blockmodeling whenever we have networks measured on an interval scale. Generalized blockmodeling of valued networks produces better partitions and fewer equally well-fitting partitions because it measures the block inconsistencies more precisely. The problems encountered reflect the brute fact that moving from binary networks to valued networks moves us to a difficult set of partitioning problems.

We note that for structural equivalence, the indirect approach is available because similarities like correlations and dissimilarities like Euclidean distances can be computed for valued network data as long as they are compatible with structural equivalence. This is not the case for regular equivalence where we still do not have a widely accepted way of computing the extent to which vertices in networks are regularly equivalent.

Nordlund (2007) also tackled the problem of partitioning valued networks in terms of regular equivalence and his argument is consistent with Žiberna: applying techniques appropriate for binary networks directly to valued networks is problematic. He proposed a formal heuristic for viewing ties as regular based on their linkages given the role set of actors. He combined this idea with measures for block criteria fulfillment to establish reduced graphs where methods were more sensitive to patterns of ties rather than their strengths.

Weber and Denk (2007) proposed an approach for valued blockmodeling for input-output relations viewed as networks. Flows between industrial or economic sectors, as an aggregation of flows between businesses, are clearly valued. And the flows that go into national input-output tables can be analyzed also at a "lower" level with businesses as the units. Regardless of whether data for these flows express the volume of goods and services flowing or their monetary values, it is foolish to even think of these data as being binary. So if blockmodeling is contemplated, it has to deal with valued data whose values can vary greatly. Given that goods and services flow between units, it is natural to think of these data as two-mode data with the rows as transmitters (exporters) and the columns as receivers (importers). Doreian et al. (2005: 265–69) did exactly this for journal-to-journal citation networks. For business-to-business transaction patterns, businesses can remain a part of a trading network or leave while other businesses can join the trading flows. Studying such economic networks includes evaluating businesses, characterizing the overall structure of these networks, and clustering both units and relations. It is possible to identify gaps, both in the form of missing actors and missing ties, in these networks. Additionally, the flows are not simply between pairs of units because indirect flows are important and merit attention. While indirect paths of varying length have been considered by network analysts thinking of what flows from one unit to another and then on to a third unit in social networks is much harder to conceptualize than for economic flow networks.

Stochastic blockmodeling

The generalized blockmodeling approach, as described above, is explicitly deterministic. A criterion function expressing the core of a clustering problem is minimized to determine the "best" partition(s) given the criterion function. An alternative strategy is to adopt a probabilistic approach and treat the underlying processes in a stochastic fashion. Mirroring structural equivalence as an underlying conception, two actors are stochastically equivalent if they have the same probability distribution of their ties to other units (Holland et al., 1983; Wasserman and Anderson, 1987, Anderson et al., 1992). Using probabilities for ties established from the data, positions are populated with stochastically equivalent units.

Nowicki and Snijders (2001) developed a Bayesian approach for stochastic blockmodeling where the units are dyads. The ties can have categorical values and the parameters of their model are estimated by a Markov chain Monte Carlo ("MCMC") procedure. Two features of their approach are noteworthy for this discussion: (1) missing data can be handled and (2) given the network data, some vertices may be unclassifiable into a position. Most discussions of blockmodeling quietly ignore the problems of missing data, which can have serious implications (see below). The idea of there being some units not belonging to positions was first noted by Burt (1976) in the form of a "residual cluster" and this, too, has been ignored in generalized blockmodeling.

Airoldi et al. (2007a, 2007b) introduced a family of stochastic blockmodels that combine features of mixed-membership models and blockmodels for relational data in a hierarchical Bayesian framework. They proposed a nested variance inference scheme for this class of models, which is necessary to successfully perform fast approximate posterior inference. Handcock et al. (2007) proposed a new model with latent positions under which the probability of a tie between two units depends on the distance between them in an unobserved Euclidean "social space," and the locations of units in the latent social space arise from a mixture of distributions, each corresponding to a cluster. Handcock et al. proposed two estimation methods: a two-stage maximum likelihood method and a fully Bayesian method that uses MCMC sampling. They also proposed a Bayesian way of determining the number of clusters that are present by using approximate conditional Bayes factors.

Generalized blockmodeling of signed networks

As noted above, structural balance theory implies a distinctive blockmodel structure for signed social networks. Yet structural balance as a process, or a set of processes, is not the only force creating signed social relations between human actors. It is quite possible that there are some actors that are universally liked (or liked by most members of a group), despite the presence of the kind of divisions predicted by structural balance theory. If this is present then, there will be positive blocks off the main diagonal of an image matrix. From the perspective of conflict resolution, when social groups are completely split into mutually hostile subgroups, with positive ties only within these groups, this is not a good situation because there are no actors in locations to mediate conflicts between these subgroups. Mediators would have positive ties to members of at least two of the mutually hostile subgroups. But were there to be one or more mediators between a pair of opposed subgroups this would also imply positive blocks off the image matrix's main diagonal. Finally, there are groups where there are some mutually hostile individuals and their presence would imply a negative block on the main diagonal of the image matrix. Structural balance, with its signature blockmodel structure, would bury all of these features into inconsistencies with structural balance. If these other processes left traces in the structure of a group, they could not be identified using structural balance.

To deal with these problems, Doreian and Mrvar (2009) relaxed the specification of structural balance by allowing positive and negative blocks to appear anywhere in a blockmodel. They retained the same criterion function as used for structural balance and called this relaxed structural balance. They proved that this is a proper generalization of structural balance and applied this revised version of balance to some of the classical signed social network data sets and obtained blockmodels with better fits to the data.

The original Heiderian balance theory had two types of relations. One type was social relations between people and the other took the form of "unit formation" relations between people and social objects (like values and beliefs). The generalization provided by Cartwright and Harary (1956) buried this distinction and used only signed relations. In effect, the unit formation relations were discarded. While the formalization changed dramatically the study of signed social relations in groups and permitted great progress, something was lost. Mrvar and Doreian (2009) formalized the idea of unit relations as signed two-mode networks and extended the relaxed balance partitioning algorithm to partition-signed two-mode data. The primary empirical example featured the voting patterns of Supreme Court justices for one term.

Partitioning large or complex networks

A complementary way to generalized blockmodeling for large networks was proposed by Hsieh and Magee (2008), who presented another algorithm for decomposing a social network into an optimal number of structurally equivalent classes. The k-means method is used to determine the best decomposition of the social network for various numbers of positions. This best number of positions is determined by minimizing the intra-position variance of similarity subject to the constraint that the improvement in going to more subgroups is better than partitioning a random network would achieve. They also describe a decomposability metric that assesses how closely the derived decomposition approaches an ideal network having only structurally equivalent classes.

Reichardt and White (2007) presented a framework for blockmodeling the functional classes of agents within a complex network. They derived a different measure for the fit compared to one used by Batagelj, Doreian, and Ferligoj of a network to any given blockmodel. Their method can handle both two-mode and one-mode data, and directed and undirected as well as valued networks, and allows for different types of links to be dealt with simultaneously. They applied their approach to a world trading network and were able to establish the roles played by countries as occupants of positions in world trading.

Wang and Lai (2008) picked up the problem of detecting positions and hence blockmodels in a complex network. Using the mixture models and the exploratory analysis presented by Newman and Leicht (2007), they developed an algorithm

that is applicable to a network with any degree distribution for the vertices in the network. The language of "finding communities" in a network can be seen as a variant of identifying positions in networks but with some differences. In general, clusters of similar components are not necessarily identical with the communities in a community network; thus partitioning a network into clusters of similar components provides additional information of the network structure. Their proposed algorithm can be used for community detection when the clusters and the communities overlap. By introducing a parameter that controls the involved effects of the heterogeneity, they investigated how the cluster structure can be coupled with the heterogeneity characteristics. They show how a group partition can evolve into a community partition in some situations when the involved heterogeneity effects are tuned. Their algorithm can be extended to valued networks.

Recently, two approaches were proposed for blending blockmodeling with graph theoretical constraints. At the Dagstuhl Seminar 08191 in May 2008, a group of participants (Batagelj et al., 2008) started developing a general framework for graph decompositions. Kemp and Tenenbaum (2008) also proposed an approach based on graph grammars.

OPEN GENERALIZED BLOCKMODELING PROBLEMS

There are a wide variety of open problems to merit attention. Some of them are general in the sense that they are relevant for all generalized blockmodeling problems. Doreian (2006) provided a partial characterization of these general problems. Other open problems pertain to specific applications. To some extent, this classification is arbitrary and we do not imply that the general problems are more important for the future of generalized blockmodeling. Both contain problems where their solutions will constitute advances for using generalized blockmodeling to identify positions and roles. We first discuss some specific open problems before moving on to consider some general open problems.

Open specific generalized blockmodeling problems

Regular equivalence
One of the vexing problems with regular equivalence is that while it has a conceptual superiority to structural equivalence as a definition

of role, it seems to be less successful empirically. As noted earlier, there is no compatible measure of the extent to which two locations are regularly equivalent, and this handicaps the indirect approach to blockmodeling networks in terms of regular equivalence. From the vantage point of generalized blockmodeling, there are two large issues. One is that so many blocks are consistent with the permitted 1-covered block type. They range from the one block of structural equivalence to blocks with just one 1 in each row and column. This is a wide range of variation to include within a single definition of regular equivalence. One consequence is that many equally well-fitting blockmodels for a given number of positions can be identified in a given network under regular equivalence without nonarbitrary ways of selecting one of them. The second stems from the deep result of Borgatti and Everett (1989) that each network has a lattice of regularly equivalent partitions. Sometimes these lattices are trivial but in most cases they are not. This raises an obvious question for generalized blockmodeling. Given multiple exact partitions of a network that are consistent with regular equivalence, which is the most appropriate for an ideal blockmodel when trying to establish an empirical blockmodel based on regular equivalence? A formal approach to role structures based on regular equivalence is provided by Lerner (2005).

Partitioning signed networks

A general criticism of the use of the relocation algorithm in the direct blockmodeling approach is that there is no guarantee that the use of the method provides the optimal solutions or yields all of the equally well-fitting partitions for a particular network. Brusco et al. (2010) provide convincing evidence that for "small problems" (where the number of vertices is less than 30 to 35) the relocation method does return all of the optimal partitions of a signed one-mode network. This was done through the comparison of the performance of the relocation method with a branch and bound algorithm that is guaranteed to return all of the optimal partitions. However, while the relocation algorithm can handle much larger signed networks, the branch and bound method cannot. So the guarantee cannot be extended to larger networks. Also, the two algorithms are not identical in terms of the difficulties they encounter with different network features such as size, density of ties, and the relative proportions of positive and negative ties. Brusco et al. (2010) advocate using both algorithms, rather than relying on only one, whenever this is possible. And the idea of a guarantee, at this time, has not been extended to signed two-mode

networks. Potential applications of two-mode signed partitioning of two-mode networks include, in addition to Supreme Court voting patterns, U.S. congressional voting, voting in other deliberative bodies, and voting at the United Nations. For all of these potential examples, the networks are large and very dense. There is a clear need for establishing sound ways of partitioning these large networks.

The general method proposed for partitioning signed networks (Doreian and Mrvar, 1996, 2009; Mrvar and Doreian, 2009) allows for the differential weighting of positive inconsistencies in negative blocks and negative inconsistencies in positive blocks. However, the differential weighting has not been explored in any detail and the implications of using this differential weighting needs to be mapped for empirical networks. When one sign predominates, it may be necessary to weight the two types of inconsistencies differentially. The best ways of doing this are not known. It seems that potential null blocks in signed networks also have relevance and need to be specified. General ways of doing this in a principled fashion are not known and establishing such methods forms another open problem.

Open General Problems for Blockmodeling

Boundary problems

The blockmodeling approach is avowedly positional because the location of an actor is defined as the pattern of ties to and from all other locations in the network. This implies that identifying the boundary of a network correctly is very important. Laumann et al. (1983) pointed to "the boundary problem" as important for network analysis in general. However, its importance for positional approaches to the analysis of network structure is particularly acute. We simply do not know the implications of an incorrect identification of a network boundary for generalized blockmodeling beyond the intuition that the approach is highly vulnerable to identifying the boundary incorrectly. Establishing some bounds of the sensitivity to identified blockmodels (as positions and roles) is an important open problem.

Measurement errors

We also have a limited understanding of the vulnerability of both generalized and classic blockmodeling to measurement errors. This problem takes two forms. One is that data can be missing and that often, perhaps too often, a tie that is recorded as a null tie is really a case of missing data. The other is that, while some value for a tie is recorded, the actual value recorded may be of the wrong magnitude. The presence of the first type of measurement error can affect seriously the blockmodeling of both binary and valued networks and the presence of the second is most acute for blockmodeling valued networks. Obtaining a better understanding of the vulnerability of establishing blockmodels to errors of measurement is an important open problem. There are proposals for imputing values for missing data (e.g., Huisman, 2009) and we may need to assess the impact of imputation methods for missing data on delineated blockmodels or roles and positions. There are two broad ways of making these assessments. One is through controlled simulations where variations in (fictitious) recorded data are generated and the impacts on blockmodeling results are assessed. The other is to start with real data and introduce controlled amounts of measurement error and examine the results (Doreian, 2006).

Assessing fits of blockmodels

In making comparisons between partitions, based on either structural or regular equivalence, using direct and indirect blockmodeling approaches, Doreian et al. (1994) showed that the minimized values of the criterion functions for the indirect approach were never lower than those obtained via the direct approach. And, in many cases, the values of the criterion functions for partitions obtained when using the indirect approach were much higher than for the direct approach. However, their argument is partially circular as their methods are designed to minimize criterion functions that are defined for a particular equivalence. There may be alternative and better criterion functions than the ones they considered. The analyses of Reichardt and White (2007) reopen this issue, for they use a different criterion function for a particular definition of equivalence than the corresponding one used by Doreian et al. (1994, 2005). Establishing better criterion functions for many types of blockmodels remains an important open issue.

The value of the minimized criterion function for structural equivalence for empirical networks can be quite large. When the value of the minimized criterion function is zero, or close to zero, it is clear that the delineated blockmodel fits. While the criterion function has been minimized, a high value of the criterion function often stems from the stringency of it counting all discrepancies with null blocks or complete blocks in

empirical networks. There is no obvious guarantee that, with a "high" value of the criterion function a delineated partition "really" is consistent with the idea of structural equivalence. Establishing better bounds is an important open problem and insights may well come from fitting blockmodels based on stochastic equivalence of the sort suggested by Nowicki and Snijders (2001). An impression about the nature and quality of obtained partitions can be gained also from where the value of their criterion functions lie in the distribution of values of criterion function obtained using the Monte Carlo method.

Blockmodeling large networks

For generalized blockmodeling, using the direct approach, the predominant methods are based on local optimization algorithms. However, the current versions of the algorithms can handle networks having some hundreds of units. Even for networks of this limited size we do not know if they will return all of the optimal partitions. And their use is impossible for larger networks. To make progress we need to formulate blockmodels that can be fitted for large networks and develop faster algorithms, or we need more effective heuristics. Indirect approaches appear to be much more useful for large networks, yet their applicability is for a very restricted range of equivalence types. In the main, structural equivalence – while very restricted – is the only viable option for partitioning large networks as a whole. However, various forms of preprocessing of large networks generates reduced networks that can be analyzed further with regard to positions and roles. Those based on different connectivity decompositions – for example, weak components, strong components, graph condensation, symmetric-acyclic decomposition, bi-connected components – can be determined very efficiently.

Numbers of positions

Determining the number of positions is a difficult problem for generalized blockmodeling even when the networks are not large. The methods proposed by Handcock et al. (2007) and by Reichardt and White (2007) both include a way of establishing the number of positions empirically from the data. This seems important as a general feature to be included in blockmodeling. Yet the most useful way of establishing the number of positions for a blockmodel may rest on a sound understanding of the substantive processes driving network tie formation and the generated network structures in given empirical contexts.

For example, friendship formation in a school system seems most constrained or driven by the classes and levels into which students are distributed. The best guess for the number of positions, most likely, is the number of grades in the school system.

Dynamic blockmodels

The origins of blockmodeling are located in attempts to analyze and understand the operation of role systems. Blockmodeling was established as an effective way of doing this because of its ability to identify positions and roles. As such, it became a useful empirical method for partitioning social networks. Over time, this meant that it could be used for partitioning any network, even networks where there appeared to be no obvious connection to role systems. Yet the notions of positions and roles acquired a generalized form that led to establishing well-defined positions, roles, and role structures in many networks. If there is an attempt to understand how networks, as role structures, form and change, there is a deep problem requiring a solution.

The presumption underlying most attempts to delineate network structures using blockmodeling ideas is that the "surface networks" we observe are the manifestation, or indicators, of an underlying "more fundamental structure" of the network. Blockmodeling, regardless of the specific forms used, allow us to identify this fundamental structure. And we can do this at various points over time. If the structure remains the same over the observation period this is useful knowledge. And if it changes over time then it is possible to create a sequence of blockmodels that capture the fundamental structure as it changes. This, too, will be useful knowledge but the sequence of blockmodels fitted at successive time points is only a sequence of descriptions. If a social structure as a network really is changing then it is the fundamental structure that is changing, with the observed changes being indicators of the underlying fundamental change. If these changes are not just random events, then we need to account for them. When a system is evolving over time, most likely, there will be coherent process rules driving these changes. Mere descriptions of the changes involved, even if couched in terms of blockmodels, seem insufficient. We need to understand the processes generating structural change and this implies understanding how blockmodels, as representations of positions and role systems, evolve. This is the biggest open problem for generalized blockmodeling and understanding the operation of role systems.

REFERENCES

Airoldi, E.M., Blei, D.M., Fienberg, S.E. and Xing E.P. (2007a) 'Combining stochastic block models and mixed membership for statistical network analysis', in *Lecture Notes in Computer Science*. Heidelberg: Springer. pp. 57–74.

Airoldi, E.M., Blei, D.M., Fienberg, S.E. and Xing, E.P. (2007b) *Mixed Membership Stochastic Blockmodels*. Department of Statistics, Carnegie Mellon University.

Anderson, C.J., Wasserman, S. and Faust, K. (1992) 'Building stochastic blockmodels', *Social Networks*, 14: 137–61.

Batagelj, V. (1997) 'Notes on blockmodeling', *Social Networks*, 19: 143–55.

Batagelj, V., Brandenburg, F.J., Didimo W., Liotta, G. and Patrignani, M. (2008) 'Working group report – X-graphs of Y-graphs and their representations'. Dagstuhl seminar 08191, May 4–9, 2008. http://drops.dagstuhl.de/portals/index.php?semnr=08191.

Batagelj, V. and Ferligoj, A. (2000) 'Clustering relational data', in W. Gaul, O. Opitz, and M. Schader (eds), *Data Analysis*. Heidelberg: Springer. pp. 3–15.

Batagelj, V., Doreian, P. and Ferligoj, A. (1992b) 'An optimization approach to regular equivalence', *Social Networks*, 14: 63–90.

Batagelj, V., Ferligoj, A. and Doreian, P. (1992a) 'Direct and indirect methods for structural equivalence', *Social Networks*, 14: 121–35.

Batagelj, V., Ferligoj, A. and Doreian, P. (2007) 'Blockmodeling of 3-way networks', in P. Brito, G. Cucumel, P. Bertrand, and F. de Carvalho (eds), *Selected Contributions in Data Analysis and Classification*. Heidelberg: Springer. 151–59.

Borgatti, S.P. and Everett, M.G. (1989) 'The class of all regular equivalences: Algebraic structure and computation', *Social Networks*, 21: 183–88.

Borgatti, S.P. and Everett, M.G. (1992) 'Regular blockmodels of multiway multimode matrices', *Social Network*, 14: 91–120.

Breiger, R.L., Boorman, S.A. and Arabie, P. (1975) 'An algorithm for clustering relational data with applications for social network analysis and comparison to multidimensional scaling', *Journal of Mathematical Psychology*, 12: 328–83.

Brusco, M. J. and Steinley, D. (2006) 'Inducing a blockmodel structure on two-mode data using seriation procedures', *Journal of Mathematical Psychology*, 50: 468–77.

Brusco, M. J. and Steinley, D. (2007) 'An evaluation of a variable-neighborhood search method for blockmodeling of two-mode binary matrices based on structural equivalence', *Journal of Mathematical Psychology*, 51: 325–38.

Brusco, M., Doreian, P., Mrvar, A. and Steinley, D. (2011) 'Two algorithms for relaxed structural balance partitioning: Linking theory, models and data to understand social network phenomena', *Sociological Methods and Research*, 40: 57–87.

Burt, R.S. (1976) 'Positions in networks', *Social Forces*, 93–122.

Cartwright, D. and Harary, F. (1956) 'Structural balance: A generalization of Heider's theory', *Psychological Review*, 63: 277–92.

Davis, J.A. (1967) 'Clustering and structural balance in graphs', *Human Relations*, 20: 181–87.

Davis, J.A. and Leinhardt, S. (1972) 'The structure of positive interpersonal relations in small groups', in J. Berger, M. Zelditch Jr. and B. Anderson (eds), *Sociological Theories in Progress, Volume 2*. Boston: Houghton Mifflin. pp. 218–51.

Doreian, P. (2006) 'Some open problems sets for generalized blockmodeling', in H.-H. Bock, V. Batagelj, A. Ferligoj and A. Žiberna (eds), *Data Science and Classification*. Heidelberg: Springer. pp. 119–30.

Doreian, P., Batagelj, V. and Ferligoj, A. (1994) 'Partitioning networks based on generalized concepts of equivalence', *Journal of Mathematical Sociology*, 19: 1–27.

Doreian, P., Batagelj, V. and Ferligoj, A. (2000) 'Symmetric-acyclic decomposition of networks', *Journal of Classification*, 17: 3–28.

Doreian, P., Batagelj, V. and Ferligoj, A. (2004) 'Generalized blockmodeling of two-mode network data', *Social Networks*, 26: 29–53.

Doreian, P., Batagelj, V. and Ferligoj, A. (2005) *Generalized Blockmodeling*. New York: Cambridge University Press.

Doreian, P. and Mrvar, A. (1996) 'A partitioning approach to structural balance', *Social Networks*, 18: 149–168.

Doreian, P. and Mrvar, A. (2009) 'Partitioning signed networks', *Social Networks*, 18: 149–68.

Faust, K. and Wasserman, S. (1992) 'Blockmodels: Interpretation and evaluation', *Social Networks* 14: 5–61.

Handcock, M.S., Raftery, A.E. and Tantrum, J.M. (2007) 'Model-based clustering for social networks', *Journal of the Royal Statistical Society: Series A*, 170: 301–54.

Heider, F. (1946) 'Attitudes and cognitive organization,' *Journal of Psychology*, 21: 107–12.

Holland, P.W., Laskey, K.B. and Leinhardt, S. (1983) 'Stochastic blockmodels: Some first steps', *Social Networks*, 5: 109–37.

Hsieh, M.-H. and Magee C.L. (2008) 'An algorithm and metric for network decomposition from similarity matrices: Application to positional analysis', *Social Networks*, 30: 146–58.

Huisman, M. (2009) 'Imputation of missing network data: Some simple procedures', *Journal of Social Structure*, 10:1.

Kemp, C. and Tenenbaum, J.B. (2008) 'The discovery of structural form', *Proceedings of the National Academy of Sciences USA*, 105(31): 10687–92.

Krackhardt, D. (1987) 'Cognitive social structures', *Social Networks*, 9: 109–34.

Laumann, E.O., Marsden, P.V. and Prensky, D. (1983) 'The boundary specification problem in network analysis', in R.S. Burt and M.J. Minor (eds), *Applied Network Analysis: A Methodological Introduction*. Beverly Hills, CA: Sage. pp. 18–34.

Lerner, J. (2005) 'Role assignments', in Brandes and Erlebach (eds), *Network Analysis: Methodological Foundations*. Heidelberg: Springer. pp. 216–52.

Lorrain, F., and White, H.C. (1971) 'Structural equivalence of individuals in social networks', *Journal of Mathematical Sociology*, 1: 49–80.

Mrvar, A. and Doreian, P. (2009) 'Partitioning signed two-mode data', *Journal of Mathematical Sociology*, 33: 196–221.

Newman, M.E.J. and Leicht, E.A. (2007) 'Mixture models and exploratory data analysis in networks', *Proceedings of the National Academy of Sciences USA*, 104: 9564–69.

Nordlund, C. (2007) 'Identifying regular blocks in valued networks: A heuristic applied to the St. Marks carbon flow data, and international trade in cereal products', *Social Networks*, 29: 59–69.

Nowicki, K. and Snijders, T.A.B. (2001) 'Estimation and prediction for stochastic block structures', *Journal of the American Statistical Association*, 96: 1077–87.

Nuskesser, M. and Sawitzki, D. (2005) 'Blockmodels', in U. Brandes and Erlebach (eds), *Network Analysis: Methodological Foundations*. Heidelberg: Springer. pp. 253–92.

Reichardt, J. and White, D.R. (2007) 'Role models for complex networks', *The European Physical Journal B – Condensed Matter and Complex Systems*, 60: 217–24.

Roffilli, M. and Lomi, A. (2006) 'Identifying and classifying social groups: A machine learning blockmodeling', in H.-H. Bock V. Batagelj, A. Ferligoj, and A. Žiberna (eds), *Data Science and Classification*. Heidelberg: Springer. pp. 149–57.

Sailer, L.D. (1978) 'Structural equivalence: Meaning and definition, computation and application', *Social Networks*, 1: 73–90.

Wang, J. and Lai, C.-H. (2008) 'Detecting groups of similar components in complex networks', *New Journal of Physics*, 10: 1–26.

Wasserman, S. and Anderson, C.J. (1987) 'Stochastic a posteriori blockmodels: Construction and assessment', *Social Networks*, 9: 1–36.

Weber, M. and Denk, M. (2007) 'Valued blockmodeling for input-output applications', a paper presented at the Workshop on Blockmodeling, Faculty of Social Sciences, Ljubljana.

White, D.R. and Reitz, K.P. (1983) 'Graph and semigroup homomorphisms on networks of relations', *Social Networks*, 5: 193–234.

White, H.C., Boorman, S.A. and Breiger, R.L. (1976) 'Social structure from multiple networks, I Blockmodels of roles and positions', *American Journal of Sociology*, 81: 730–79.

Žiberna, A. (2007) 'Generalized blockmodeling of valued networks', *Social Networks*, 29: 105–26.

Žiberna, A. (2008) 'Direct and indirect approaches to blockmodeling of valued networks in terms of regular equivalence', *Journal of Mathematical Sociology*, 32: 57–84.

Žiberna, A. (2009) 'Evaluation of direct and indirect blockmodeling of regular equivalence in valued networks by simulations', *Metodološki zvezki*, 6: 99–134.

30

Relation Algebras and Social Networks

Philippa Pattison

INTRODUCTION

Algebraic approaches have played an important historical role in formulating conceptions of structure and structural change in networks. In this chapter, I outline some of the algebraic constructions that have informed an understanding of structure in social networks and argue that these constructions make what are termed *relation algebras* a natural framework for algebraic network analysis. I describe a number of ways in which this algebraic characterisation of networks may be useful for network analysis and discuss some contemporary challenges for which it is likely to be particularly well suited.

Why are algebraic models of interest?

Social networks are generally construed as discrete entities, describing a pattern of social relations among a particular set of actors at a particular moment in time. Each time we observe one or more social networks for a set of actors, we see a particular instantiation of one of many possible relational patterns, and it is often of interest to understand what kinds of structural regularities characterise that particular pattern. Structural regularities are likely to occur as the result of a potentially small number of common though unobserved social processes driving the formation of network ties. The form of these regularities provides a useful empirical guide to the nature of

the unobserved social processes from which they emerge. In addition, structural regularities may point to the likelihood of common consequences for the actors involved; as a result, their identification may afford potential predictive power. Examples of such regularities abound in the networks literature and include such features as *tie reciprocity* – the tendency for mutual directed ties to occur (e.g. as the result of a reciprocity process); *structural* or *regular equivalence* – the tendency for some actors to be related in the same way to the same or similar alters (perhaps through a process of social role differentiation); *clustering* – the tendency for dense subgraphs to occur in a network (e.g. as the result of tie closure processes); the presence of *network hubs* – the tendency for high degree nodes to occur (possibly as the result of an underlying heterogeneity among nodes, or as the result of an endogenous attraction process); and the presence of *cycles* – the tendency for closed paths to occur in a network (possibly as the result of a generalised exchange process).

Algebraic constructions are of particular interest in this context because they provide a language for expressing regularities in social forms, and hence they provide an important part of the process of their identifcation. In the next section, a collection of specific algebraic constructions are described, and these are then used as the basis for defining a *relation algebra*. In the following sections, several applications of this algebraic characterisation are outlined. The chapter concludes with a discussion of future challenges and prospects.

History of algebraic approaches

Algebraic approaches to understanding relational network structures are often traced to earlier work on the analysis of kinship systems, where structural regularities were argued to be associated with the use of certain distinctive relational and classificatory terms (e.g. Boyd, 1969; Boyd et al., 1972; White, 1963).

White foreshadowed as early as 1963 the potential application of these algebraic approaches to a much broader and more contemporary array of social relationships. Nadel (1957) appealed to an abstract set-theoretic formulation in an attempt to develop a formal account of interlocking role structures within social systems. In a now well-known paper, White, Boorman and Breiger (1971) presented the concept of *structural equivalence* of two actors in a social system as a potent analytical concept, giving rise to the concept of a *blockmodel*, an assignment of actors to social positions and a description of the social relations among those positions. In a less well-known companion paper, Boorman and White (1976) developed a representation of role structures embedded in social networks in terms of algebraic semigroups. An important connection between these two papers resides in the observation that the semigroup of a set of relations for a given set of actors is identical to the semigroup of its associated blockmodel (Lorrain and White, 1971). These papers spawned a series of important generalisations and a deepening understanding of the relationship between partitions among actors in a collection of social networks and the algebraic structure of those networks (Borgatti et al., 1989; Boyd et al., 1972; Kim and Roush, 1984; Pattison, 1982, 1993; White and Reitz, 1983; Winship, 1988).

Further work extended the set of algebraic tools available for analysing these algebraic representations (Pattison and Bartlett, 1982; Pattison, 1982; Boyd, 1990). Algebraic representations were also generalised to accommodate a richer array of potential relational contexts (Breiger and Pattison, 1986; Mandel, 1983; Pattison, 1989; Winship and Mandel, 1983; Wu, 1983) as well as additional relational information (Pattison, 1993). In addition, a number of methods for extracting structural regularities from potentially stochastic network observations began to be developed; I discuss these approaches further below.

RELATION ALGEBRAS FOR SOCIAL NETWORKS

A social network can be conceptualised as a set of social linkages or *ties* among members of a set of social actors. Some ties, such as 'seeks advice from' are regarded as *directed*, so that the tie from actor l to actor k is distinguished from the tie from actor k to actor l, whereas others, such as 'exchange information' may be regarded as *nondirected*, with no distinction between the tie from k to l and the tie from l to k. In the former case, the tie is regarded as a property of the ordered pair (k, l) of actors; in the latter, the tie is a property of the unordered pair $\{k, l\}$. We also regard the ties as *labelled*, and we distinguish ties with different labels: a tie with the label 'is a friend of', for example, is regarded as distinct from a tie with the label 'seeks advice from'. Formally, we denote the set of *actors* among whom linkages are defined as $N = \{1, 2, \ldots, n\}$ and the set of relation *labels* for the ties as $K = \{1, 2, \ldots, r\}$. If there is a tie with label m from actor k to actor l, we write $X_m(k, l) = 1$; if there is no such tie, we set $X_m(k, l) = 0$. In cases where only one type of tie label is of interest (i.e. $r = 1$), we can omit the subscript m since there is no ambiguity in the label for the relation.

For each relation label m, we can regard the set of ties with label m in terms of three equivalent representations.

First, X_m is a *binary relation* on N. A binary relation on the set N is simply a set of ordered pairs of members of N. Any binary relation X_m is a subset of the set $N \times N$ of all possible ordered pairs of members of N; in other words, $X_m \subseteq N \times N$.

Second, the ties with label m may be construed as a *directed graph* if X_m is directed, or simply a *graph* if X_m is nondirected. The *node set* of the graph or directed graph G_m is the set N. If the relation X_m is directed, the *arc set* $E_m = \{(k, l): X_m(k, l) = 1\}$, whereas if X_m is nondirected, the *edge set* $E_m = \{(k, l): X_m(k, l) = 1 \text{ and } k < l\}$. A *graph drawing* assigns a *point* or *node* to each actor in the node set and an edge or arc is drawn from the point assigned to actor k to the point assigned to actor l if $X_m(k, l) = 1$. By convention, edges are drawn as lines and arcs are drawn as arrows.

Third, X_m may be regarded as an $n \times n$ binary array recording the presence or absence of a tie with label m between each pair of actors; X_m is referred to as the *adjacency matrix* for the directed graph G_m. The matrix has a 1 in the cell (k, l) if $X_m(k, l) = 1$; otherwise, the entry in cell (k, l) is 0. In the case that the relation with label m is nondirected, then $X_m(k, l) = 1$ if and only if $X_m(l, k) = 1$ and thus X_m is a symmetric matrix. In many contexts, we exclude consideration of self-ties of the form $X_m(k, k)$ in the set of observed relations, so that there are no loops in the graph or the directed graph corresponding to each relation, and the entries on the diagonal of its adjacency matrix are regarded as structural zeros.

Table 30.1 Three representations of a directed network relation on a node set N = {A,B,C,D,E,F}

Directed graph	Matrix	Relation
	0 1 1 0 0 0 1 0 0 1 0 0 0 0 0 1 0 1 0 0 0 0 1 1 0 1 0 1 0 1 0 0 0 1 1 0	{(A,B), (A,C), (B,A), (B,D), (C,D), (C,F), (D,E), (D,F), (E,B), (E,D), (E,F), (F,D), (F,E)}

For convenience, however, we set $X_m(k, k) = 0$ and we allow nonzero values in certain relations derived from the observed relations below. Table 30.1 illustrates the three representational forms in the directed case.

Algebraic operations

In describing relationships among actors, we typically make use of a variety of algebraic operations even though we may generally be unaware of these algebraic underpinnings. We consider a number of such operations in turn.

Converse

The asymmetry in many directed relations is well recognised in our language for describing them. For example, if actor k 'reports to' actor l, then we recognise actor l as 'the boss of' actor k. We can regard the relation 'is the boss of' as the converse of the relation 'reports to': we define the *converse*

relation Y' of a relation Y to be the relation for which $Y'(k, l) = 1$ if and only if $Y(l, k) = 1$; otherwise, $Y'(k, l) = 0$. For example, the converse of the relation shown in Table 30.2a appears in Table 30.2c. Many role terms reflect the importance of converse relations in everyday dialogue about social relations; for example, a parent and child stand in converse relations to one another, as do a teacher and student, a leader and follower, an advisor and advisee and so on.

Complement

We also recognise the absence of relationships in many instances; for example, we may be aware that one actor 'is not acquainted with' another, or that one actor 'does not seek advice from' another. The absence of ties with a particular label can be captured by the complement of the relation: we define the *complement* Y^- of a relation Y to be the relation for which $Y^-(k, l) = 1 - Y(k, l)$. (Where *self-ties* are disallowed, we could choose to disallow them in the complement Y^- as well;

Table 30.2 Relational operations on two relations

(a) Y_1	(b) Y_2	(c) Y_1' (converse)	(d) Y_1^- (complement)
0 1 1 0 0 0	0 1 0 0 0 1	0 1 0 0 0 0	1 0 0 1 1 1
1 0 0 1 1 0	1 0 0 0 0 1	1 0 0 0 0 0	0 1 1 0 0 1
0 0 0 1 0 1	0 0 0 0 0 1	1 0 0 0 0 0	1 1 1 0 1 0
0 0 0 0 1 1	0 0 0 0 1 1	0 1 1 0 1 1	1 1 1 1 0 0
0 0 0 1 0 1	0 0 0 1 0 1	0 1 0 1 0 1	1 1 1 0 1 0
0 0 0 1 1 0	0 0 0 1 1 0	0 0 1 1 1 0	1 1 1 0 0 1

(e) $Y_1 \cap Y_2$ (intersection)	(f) $Y_1 \cup Y_2$ (union)	(g) $Y_1 \circ Y_2$ (composition)	(h) Y_1^* (star)
0 1 0 0 0 0	0 1 1 0 0 1	1 0 0 0 0 1	1 1 1 1 1 1
1 0 0 0 0 0	1 0 0 1 1 1	0 1 0 0 1 1	1 1 1 1 1 1
0 0 0 0 0 1	0 0 0 1 0 1	0 0 0 1 1 1	0 0 1 1 1 1
0 0 0 0 1 1	0 0 0 0 1 1	0 0 0 1 1 1	0 0 0 1 1 1
0 0 0 1 0 1	0 0 0 1 0 1	0 0 0 1 1 1	0 0 0 1 1 1
0 0 0 1 1 0	0 0 0 1 1 0	0 0 0 1 1 1	0 0 0 1 1 1

however, we do not make that choice here and instead we set $Y^-(k, k) = 1$ if $Y(k, k) = 0$.) The complement of the relation in Table 30.2a is shown in Table 30.2d. Role descriptors may also reflect complementary relations; for example, a *stranger* is a person who is not in an acquaintance relation.

Intersection

In some cases, ties with distinct labels link a particular pair of actors; in this case, we often refer to the tie as *multiplex* and contrast it with the case where only a single or *uniplex* tie links the actors. The presence of multiple ties can be expressed in terms of intersections among relations. We define the intersection $Y \cap Z$ of two relations Y and Z to be the relation for which $Y \cap Z(k, l) = 1$ if and only if $Y(k, l) = 1$ *and* $Z(k, l) = 1$; otherwise, $Y \cap Z(k, l) = 0$. Table 30.2e shows the intersection of the relations in Table 30.2a and Table 30.2b. Everyday referents may invoke intersection; for example, we may refer to a *friend from work* as a person to whom we have both friendship and co-worker relations.

The intersection operation also allows us to represent partial ordering among relations in a very natural way. We can define a partial ordering among relations as follows: for two binary relations Y and Z, let $Y \le Z$ if and only if $Z(k, l) = 1$ implies $Y(k, l) = 1$ for any ordered pair (k, l) of actors. In other words, $Y \le Z$ if the set of ordered pairs connected in Y is a subset of the set of ordered pairs connected in Z. It can readily be seen that:

$$Y \le Z \quad \text{is equivalent to} \quad Y \cap Z = Y.$$

Union

It may also be of interest to describe the presence of any of a number of distinct types of relations among actors, and for this the union operation is useful. We define the *union* $Y \cup Z$ of two relations Y and Z to be the relation for which $Y \cup Z(k, l) = 1$ if and only if $Y(k, l) = 1$ *or* $Z(k, l) = 1$; otherwise $Y \cup Z(k, l) = 0$. Table 30.2f shows the union of relations in Tables 30.2a and 30.2b. Common role descriptors may also refer to the union of relations; for example, a *relative* is a person to whom we stand in one of many possible kinship relations.

As for the intersection, there is a natural expression for the partial ordering of relations in terms of the union operation; in this case:

$$Y \le Z \quad \text{is equivalent to} \quad Y \cup Z = Z,$$

which, as noted above, is also equivalent to $Y \cap Z = Y$. We also use the fact below that the union and intersection relations are related through complementation, that is,

$$Y \cap Z = (Y^- \cup Z^-)^-$$

and

$$Y \cup Z = (Y^- \cap Z^-)^-.$$

As a result, we can construct the intersection operation from the union operation, and vice versa, provided that the complement operation is available for use.

Composition

A particularly important operation on relations allows us to trace sequences of ties of various types across a network: for example, we may refer to 'my friend's friend' or the 'friend of my friend'. In this case, 'is the friend of my friend' may be regarded as a compound relation, arising as the composition of 'is a friend of' and 'is a friend of'. For example, if actor l is the friend of actor k, and actor h is the friend of actor l, then actor h is the friend of a friend of actor k. In some cases, such as 'is the sister of my parent' or 'is the parent of my parent', specific composite relation labels such as 'is the aunt of' and 'is the grandparent of' have emerged to describe the compound relation; in other cases, we use the compound form in everyday language.

We can define composition more formally in the following terms. The composition $Y \circ Z$ of two relations Y and Z is the relation with ordered pairs $\{(k, h): \{(k, l) \in Y$ and $\{(l, h) \in Z$ for some actor $l \in N\}$. Of course, we may form compound relations among compound relations, giving rise to more complex forms such as 'is the friend of my friend of my friend' or 'is the brother of the wife of my boss'.

The composition operation also has natural expression in graph-theoretical and binary matrix terms. From a graph-theoretical perspective, we can think of each composite relation $Y \circ Z$ as a set of all *walks* with the label YZ among actors in N: actor k is connected to actor l by a *walk with label* YZ if there is some actor h such that k is connected to h by a Y tie and h is connected to l by a Z tie (e.g. see Pattison, 1993). If Y and Z are themselves compound relations, we can define walks making up more than two ties. The binary matrix of the composite relation $Y \circ Z$ is the *Boolean product* of the binary matrices corresponding to the relations Y and Z; in other words,

$$Y \circ Z(k, l) = [Y(k, 1) \cap Z(1, l)] \cup [Y(k, 2) \cap Z(2, l)]$$
$$\cup \ldots \cup [Y(k, n) \cap Z(n, l)]$$

The composition of the relation in Table 30.2a with the relation in Table 30.2b is shown in Table 30.2g.

Of the five relational operations just defined, converse and complement are *unary* operations since they transform *one* relation into another, whereas intersection, union and composition are *binary* operations, transforming a *pair* of relations into another relation.

Special relations

We also define three particular relations with important properties:

- The *null* relation O is the relation with no ties: $O(k, l) = 0$ for all pairs k, l of actors;
- The *universal* relation $U = O^-$ is the complement of O and is the relation with all possible ties: $U(k, l) = 1$ for all pairs k, l of actors; and
- The *identity* relation I is the relation with self-ties only: $I(k, l) = 1$ if $k = l$, and $I(k, l) = 0$ if $k \neq l$, for all k, l.

These special relations are also termed *nullary* relations.

Star

Finally, we define the unary star operation for a relation Y:

$$Y^* = I \cup Y \cup Y^\circ Y \cup Y^\circ Y^\circ Y \cup \ldots$$

The star operation adds self-ties to the ties in Y as well as the sets of all ordered pairs who are connected by some composite of Y ties. It is the *reflexive and transitive closure* of the relation Y, that is, as the least relation that contains Y and is both *reflexive* ($Y^* \supseteq I$) and *transitive* ($Y^* \circ Y^* \subseteq Y^*$). An ordered pair (k, l) is included in Y^* if k is identical to l or if there is some path of Y ties from k to l. Thus the star operation yields the reachability pattern for the relation Y, since it includes pairs (k, l) of actors in which either k is the same as l or l can be reached from k by a sequence of Y ties. The application of the star operation to the network in Table 30.2a yields the network in Table 30.2h.

Are other operations of value?

Arguably the list of operations just described is sufficient to describe many patterns and regularities of interest in networks. White (1992) made a strong case for including at least the converse, intersection and composition operations in any attempt to discriminate among social structural forms; we have here added complementation to

this basic set, hence bringing in the derivative operations of union and star as well. Complementation allows us to talk about absent relationships as well as those that are present, and many authors have highlighted the absence of relationships in their discussions of significant relational patterns, including White et al. (1971) in descriptions of blockmodel patterns, Granovetter (1973) on patterns characterizing strong and weak ties, Freeman (1979) on patterns characterizing various forms of centrality in networks, and Burt (1992, 2005) on patterns characterizing structural holes and certain forms of social capital. The union operation adds the capacity to create aggregate relational categories from more elemental relationship terms; examples include 'relative' from various kin term descriptors, or 'social contact' from terms such as 'acquaintance', 'friend', 'relative', 'neighbour' and 'co-worker'. The star operation adds the valuable capacity to distinguish ordered pairs of network actors for which a basic connectivity condition holds, or not.

Relation algebras

For a given set N of actors, imagine the collection R_N of all possible binary relations on N. If N comprises n actors, then R_N has $2^{n \times n}$ elements, since each of the $n \times n$ ordered pairs of actors in N may have a tie or not. Using $Y, Z, W, \ldots$ to refer to various relations in R_N, we may consider the application of the various operations just defined to members of R_N and we can see that the operations yield other members of R_N. Indeed, the set of relations R_N and the set of operations $F = \{', ^-, \cup, \circ\}$ (or, equivalently, $F = \{', ^-, \cap, \cup, \circ\}$) give rise to an algebra termed a *relation algebra* (e.g. Birkhoff, 1967; Tarski, 1941).

More generally, we can consider algebras of the form $[A, F]$, where A is a set of relations, $F = \{', ^-, \cup, \circ\}$ is a set of operations, and A is *closed* under F: that is, for any relations $Y, Z \in A$, the relations $Y', Y^-, Y \cap Z, Y \cup Z$, and $Y^\circ Z$ are also members of the set A. We can then describe a relation algebra $[A, \{', ^-, \cup, \circ\}]$ as an algebra whose operations satisfy a number of rules, or axioms. The axioms for a relation algebra have been set out in various forms by Alfred Tarski and his collaborators, following foundational work in the calculus of relations by Augustus de Morgan, Charles Sanders Peirce and Ernst Schröder.

Specifically, $[A, \{', ^-, \cup, \circ\}]$ is a *relation algebra* if the following axioms hold for all $Y, Z, W, \ldots \in A$ (e.g. see Birkhoff, 1967; Givant, 2006; Maddux, 1991):

[RA1] $Y \cup Z = Z \cup Y$
[RA2] $Y \cup (Z \cup W) = (Y \cup Z) \cup W$

[RA3] $(Y^-\cup Z)^- \cup (Y^-\cup Z^-)^- = Y$
[RA4] $(Y^\circ Z)^\circ W = Y^\circ(Z^\circ W)$
[RA5] $Y^\circ I = Y$
[RA6] $(Y')' = Y$
[RA7] $(Y^\circ Z)' = (Z')^\circ(Y')$
[RA8] $(Y\cup Z)' = Y'\cup Z'$
[RA9] $(Y\cup Z)^\circ W = (Y^\circ W)\cup(Z^\circ W)$
[RA10] $(Y'^\circ(Y^\circ W)^-)\cup W^- = W^-$

It may be noted that the operations $\cap$ and $*$ have been omitted from the list of operations in F since they can readily be defined in terms of union and complementation, as noted above. Many of these axioms are familiar from other algebras. For example, RA1 refers to the *commutativity* of the union operation; RA2 and RA4 refer to the *associativity* of the union and composition operations, respectively; RA8 and RA9 refer to the *distributivity* of the converse and composition operations, respectively, over union; and RA5 establishes the special relation I as an *identity* for the composition operation.

Subsets of these axioms also describe other algebraic forms. For example, axioms RA1 to RA3 establish that $[A, \{^-,\cup\}]$ is a *Boolean algebra* under the union and complementation operations. Axioms RA4 and RA5 establish that $[A, \{^\circ\}]$ is a *monoid with identity* I under composition; moreover, in conjunction with RA4 and RA5, axioms RA6 and RA7 establish that $[A, \{',^\circ\}]$ is a monoid with identity in which the converse operation is an *involution* with respect to composition.

Axiom RA10 is due to Tarski (1941), but other equivalent axiomatisations are possible, as, for example, Maddux (1991) explains. Pratt (1990), for example, showed that the equations for a Boolean monoid together with:

[RAT] $((Z^-{}^\circ Y')^- {}^\circ Y)\cup Z = Z\cap(Y'^\circ(Y^\circ Z)^-)^-$

provide a complete equational axiomatisation for relation algebras.

Relation algebra with transitive closure

If the set $F = \{',^-,\cup,^\circ,*\}$ also includes the unary star operation, $[A, F]$ is termed a *relation algebra with transitive closure* (e.g. Pratt, 1990), also satisfying all of the axioms RA1 to RA10 above. In addition, star is defined by:

[S1] $I \leq Y^*$
[S2] $Y^\circ Y^* \leq Y^*$

and

[S3] $(Y^*)^\circ Z \leq Z \cup (Y^*)^\circ((Y^\circ Z)\cap Z^-).$

Although Y^* is necessarily included in any relation algebra containing I and Y, the potential importance of the operation makes it a valuable addition, particularly where partial algebras are under consideration (see below).

RA(N) and RAT(N)

In the case in which A comprises the set R_N of all binary relations on a set N, we write $RA(N) = [R_N, \{',^-,\cup,^\circ\}]$ and $RAT(N) = [R_N,\{',^-,\cup,^\circ,*\}]$.

The relation algebra generated by an observed set of relations

In empirical contexts we are not necessarily interested in all possible relations on a set of actors. Rather, we are likely to have observed a small subset A_{obs} of specific relations on N, each with a different label, such as 'works with' and 'seeks advice from'. It is helpful to define A to be the *closure* of A_{obs} under the set $F = \{',^-,\cup,^\circ\}$ or $\{',^-,\cup,^\circ,*\}$ of operations; in other words, A is the smallest set of relations that contains A_{obs} and is closed under F (that is, any operation in F applied to any relation or pair of relations – as appropriate – in A yields an element in A). The algebra $[A, F]$ is then the algebra *generated by* A_{obs} under F and $[A, F]$ is a relational algebra if $F = \{',^-,\cup,^\circ\}$ and a relational algebra with transitive closure if $F = \{',^-,\cup,^\circ,*\}$. Suppose, for example, that we have observed relations of work collaboration (Y_1) and advice-seeking (Y_2) among members of a professional firm. In this case, the observed set of *generator* relations is $A_{obs} = \{Y_1,Y_2\}$ and relations in A can be obtained by successive application of operations in F.

For example, initial application of all operations in $F = \{',^-,\cup,^\circ,*\}$ to relations in $A_1 = A_{obs}$ yields $A_2 = \{Y_1', Y_2', Y_1^-, Y_2^-, Y_1\cup Y_1, Y_1\cup Y_2, Y_2\cup Y_1, Y_2\cup Y_2, Y_1^\circ Y_1, Y_1^\circ Y_2, Y_2^\circ Y_1, Y_2^\circ Y_2, Y_1*, Y_2*\}$. Some of these relations in A_2 will be distinct from those in A_{obs} whereas others will be identical, either because of the axioms RA1 to RA10 that govern the operations or because of the particular patterns of ties in the relations involved. For example, we know from RA1 that $Y_1\cup Y_2 = Y_2\cup Y_1$ no matter what specific pairs are linked by Y_1 and Y_2, whereas it may happen to be true that $Y_1^\circ Y_2$ is equal to Y_1 for a specific pair of relations, Y_1 and Y_2. We can consider each relation in A_2 in turn, removing it from A_2 if it is equal to some element in A_1 or an earlier relation in A_2, recording such equalities as *equations* of the algebra. We then apply operations in F to the distinct set of relations in $A_1 \cup A_2$ to obtain a set A_3 of additional distinct relations and additional equations, and we continue this process until no new distinct relations are generated. We will then have constructed the *algebra* $[A, F]$ = generated by A_{obs} and F. The equations generated in the process of algebra construction represent structural regularities characteristic of relations in the generator set.

A GENERALISED AXIOM OF QUALITY

The construction just described relies on a generalised version of what Boorman and White (1976) termed the *Axiom of Quality*: 'Regard as equal any pair of relations comprising exactly the same set of ordered pairs and refer to the equality as an equation in the relation algebra generated by the generator set A_{obs}'.

Application of the generalised Axiom of Quality leads to equations in the relation algebra (or relation algebra with transitive closure). With such equations, many important features of network relations can be expressed. For example:

- The relation Y is *symmetric* if $Y = Y'$
- The relation Y is *reflexive* if $Y \cap I = I$
- The relation Y is *transitive* if $Y°Y \cap Y = Y°Y$
- The relation Y is an *equivalence relation* if $Y = Y'$, $Y \cap I = I$ and $Y°Y \cap Y = Y°Y$
- The relation Y is a *permutation relation* if $Y°Y' \cap Y'°Y = I$
- The relation Y is a *quasi-order* if $Y \cap I = I$ and $Y°Y \cap Y = Y°Y$
- The relation Y is *antisymmetric* if $Y \cap Y' \cap I = Y \cap Y'$
- The relation Y is a *partial order* if $Y \cap Y' \cap I = Y \cap Y'$, $Y \cap I = I$, and $Y°Y \cap Y = Y°Y$
- The relation Y is *strongly connected* if $Y^* = U$
- The relation Y is *weakly connected* if $(Y \cup Y')^* = U$

APPLICATIONS OF RELATION ALGEBRAS AND RELATION ALGEBRAS WITH TRANSITIVE CLOSURE

Four distinct ways of utilising the algebraic constructions just described have emerged in the literature. I briefly discuss each of these approaches in turn.

Construction and analysis of the full algebra

For small networks, it is feasible to analyse the full relation algebra generated by one or more

network relations. Boorman and White (1976) proposed applying such an approach to a block-model constructed from one or more relations, and thus of developing a more exact understanding of relational patterns at the level of relations among *social positions* in the network, represented by blocks in a blockmodel, rather than at the level of individual actors. A number of examples of this approach can be found in the literature (for example, Mullins et al., 1977; Breiger and Pattison, 1978). Pattison (1993) used this approach to develop an extended capacity for structural analysis in the case of partially ordered semigroups built from blockmodels; Pattison (2009) generalised this structural analytic approach to quite general algebraic forms and hence also to relation algebras.

Comparing relation algebras

One particular application of this approach deserves special mention as it provides the means to make comparisons of structural regularities across relation networks on distinct actor sets. An important construction is a *structure-preserving* mapping or *homomorphism* from the relation algebra associated with a set of relations on one actor set to the relation algebra associated with a simiar set of relations on a second actor set. We assume a set of relations $A_{obs} = \{Y_1, Y_2, \ldots, Y_k\}$ on an actor set N as well as a set of relations $B_{obs} = \{W_1, W_2, \ldots, W_k\}$ on a second actor set M. We assume that the relation Y_j is comparable to the relation W_j; indeed, in most cases we will assume that they are described by identical relational terms.

A *homomorphism* from an algebra $[A, F]$ generated by a set of relations $A_{obs} = \{Y_1, Y_2, \ldots, Y_k\}$ on a set N onto an algebra $[B, F]$ generated by a set of relations $B_{obs} = \{W_1, W_2, \ldots, W_k\}$ on a set M is a mapping $\varphi: S \to T$ such that, for all $Y, Z \in A$:

$$\varphi(Y') = \varphi(Y)', \ \varphi(Y^-) = \varphi(Y)^- \ \text{and} \ \varphi(Y^*) = \varphi(Y)^*;$$

and

$$\varphi(Y \cup Z) = \varphi(Y) \cup \varphi(Z) \ \text{and} \ \varphi(Y°Z) = \varphi(Y) °\varphi(Z).$$

The algebra $[B, F]$ is termed a (*homomorphic*) *image* of $[A, F]$, and we write $B = \varphi(A)$. Each homomorphism φ from $[A, F]$ onto $[B, F]$ has a corresponding equivalence relation π on A termed a *congruence relation* in which $(Y, Z) \in \pi$ if and only if $\varphi(Y) = \varphi(Z)$.

If $[B, F]$ is a *homomorphic image* of $[A, F]$, then its algebra has all of the equations of $[A, F]$, plus some additional ones. It may therefore be regarded as an 'abstraction' of $[A, F]$ in the sense that it makes fewer relational distinctions than $[A, F]$.

Of course, relation algebras are strictly comparable in this sense only if one is a *homomorphic image* of the other. Nonetheless, we might regard them as 'similar' if they share many homomorphic images. In the context of semigroup algebras (or monoids), Boorman and White proposed that the largest shared homomorphic image (the so-called *joint homomorphic image*) is a useful construction for comparing network algebras. Bonacich (1980; also Bonacich and McConaghy, 1979; McConaghy, 1981), on the other hand, argued that the smallest semigroup algebra containing each of two network semigroups (the so-called *common structure semigroup*) was a more appropriate representative of common semigroup structure. As Pattison and Breiger argued, both of these constructions are useful though for different purposes. The joint homomorphic image provides a representation of shared homomorphic images whereas the common structure semigroup provides a representation of shared equations.

Linking homomorphisms of a relation algebra to network blockmodels

A second important strategy for understanding structural regularities is to determine the conditions under which network homomorphisms induce homomorphisms of the network semigroup. A *network homomorphism* from a multiple network $\{Y_1, Y_2, \ldots, Y_r\}$ on actor set N to a multiple network $\{W_1, W_2, \ldots, W_r\}$ on actor set M is a mapping ψ from N onto M such that (a) $Y_m(k, l) = 1$ implies $W_m(\psi(k), \psi(l)) = 1$, for any k, l, m; and (b) $W_m(i, j) = 1$ for some i, j implies that $Y_m(k, l) = 1$, for some k, l such that $\psi(k) = I$ and $\psi(l) = j$. The network on M is termed the *image* of the network on N under the mapping ψ.

The mapping ψ satisfies the *structural equivalence* condition if for any m, and for any $k, l \in N$, $\psi(k) = \psi(l)$ if and only if:

- $Y_m(k, j) = 1$ iff $Y_m(l, j) = 1$ for any $j \in N$; and
- $Y_m(j, k) = 1$ iff $Y_m(j, l) = 1$ for any $j \in N$.

If two multiple networks are related by a network homomorphism satisfying the structural equivalence condition, then their semigroups are isomorphic and they can be said to possess the *same* relational structure (Lorrain, 1975; Lorrain and White, 1971).

The more general question of the conditions under which a homomorphism between two networks induces a homomorphism between their semigroups has been addressed by Kim and Roush (1984).

A network homomorphism ψ satisfies Kim and Roush's *condition G_i* if the following holds for any pair of equivalence classes ρ_1 and ρ_2 on N

induced by the mapping ψ (so that $k, l \in \rho_h$ for some h if $\psi(k) = \psi(l)$). Let the number of elements in ρ_1 and ρ_2 be n_1 and n_2, respectively. Let D be any subset of ρ_1 of i elements or, if $i > n_1$, let $D = \rho_1$. Then, for any $m = 1, 2, \ldots, r$, the set $\{l: l \in \rho_2$ and $Y_m(k, l) = 1$ for some $k \in D\}$ has at least $\min(i, n_2)$ elements. The condition G_1 is also known as the *outdegree condition* and G_n is also termed the *indegree condition*. A network homomorphism that satisfies both G_1 and G_n is termed *regular*.

Kim and Roush demonstrated that if ψ is a network homomorphism from one multiple network onto another that satisfies the condition G_i, then there is a homomorphism mapping the semigroup of the first onto the semigroup of the second.

A more general condition combines the condition G_i with what Pattison (1982) termed the *central representatives condition*. Let ψ be a network homomorphism. Then ψ satisfies the condition G_{im} if, for each class ρ of elements of N induced by ψ,

- there exists a *central subset C* of ρ such that for any X_m
  - $Y_m(k, l) = 1$ for some $k \in \rho$ implies $Y_m(k^*, l)$ $= 1$ for some $k^* \in C$, and
  - $Y_m(l, k) = 1$ for some $k \in \rho$ implies $Y_m(l, k^*)$ $= 1$ for some $k^* \in C$; and
- if C^* denotes the union of central subsets C, then the central subsets C satisfy Kim and Roush's condition G_i on the network defined on C^*.

If each central subset C comprises a single actor, then the condition is equivalent to Pattison's central representatives condition, while if each central subset C comprises the whole of the equivalence class on N induced by ψ, it is equivalent to the condition G_i. Kim and Roush (1984) showed that if one network can be mapped onto another by a network homomorphism satisfying the condition G_{im}, then there is a homomorphism from the semigroup of the first to the semigroup of the second. The condition G_{im} is the most general condition known that guarantees the existence of such a homomorphism.

The constructions just described are readily defined for relation algebras and relation algebras with transitive closure. The joint homomorphic image of two algebras $[A, F]$ and $[B, F]$ is simply the algebra with the greatest number of distinct relations that is a homomorphic image of both $[A, F]$ and $[B, F]$. The joint relational algebra of $[A, F]$ and $[B, F]$, on the other hand, is the relational algebra with the fewest number of distinct relations that contains both $[A, F]$ and $[B, F]$ as a homomoprhic image. It is straightforward to show that the joint relational structure of $[A, F]$ and $[B, F]$ is the relation algebra $[C, F]$ generated by $C_{obs} = \{V_1, V_2, \ldots, V_k\}$ defined on the disjoint union of the sets N and M; specifically, V_j in C is a relation constructed as the disjoint union of Y_j on N and W_j on M.

Limitations of exact structural analyses

More generally, while an exact analytical approach is arguably very useful when the blockmodel(s) that provide(s) the starting point for analysis (is) are the faithful representation of underlying network relations among actors, it is clearly less satisfying when the blockmodel(s) omit(s) some potentially important structural regularities. This is an important qualification, since it is almost certainly rare that a blockmodel can be claimed to provide a faithful representation. Hence, it has proved valuable to supplement the exact algebraic analytical approaches just described with several other approaches to be described below.

Construction and analysis of a partial algebra

In empirical contexts, $[A,F]$ may contain a very large number of distinct elements. Mandel (1983) and Pattison and Wasserman (1995; also Pattison, 1986; Pattison et al., 2000) developed an approach for working with partial algebras making up subsets of full algebras that are obtained when restrictions are placed on the number of times that operations in F are applied. A summary of this body of work is presented in Pattison (2009).

More specifically, define the *partial algebra* $[A,F]_k$ *of rank* k to comprise the set of relations $A_{obs} \cup A_2 \cup \ldots \cup A_k$ generated by application of no more than $k-1$ operations in F as well as the relations in A_{obs} themselves. The algebra is termed *partial* because it is not closed: that is, the application of one or more operations to elements of $[A, F]_k$ may yield an element that is not contained in the set $A_{obs} \cup A_2 \cup \ldots \cup A_k$; in this case, the outcome of the operation is regarded as undefined and is denoted by an asterisk. Despite its lack of closure, however, the algebra will satisy all of the axioms of the relation algebra $[R_N, F]$ *whenever all relations relevant to an axiom are defined*. In addition, applying the Generalised Axiom of Quality to the partial algebra $[A,F]_k$ yields the set of all distinct relations in $A_{obs} \cup A_2 \cup \ldots \cup A_k$ and all equations involving relations generated by application of no more than $k-1$ operations in F. Thus, partial algebras may be used to identify relational regularities among relations that arise from the

application of no more than a fixed number of operations, and can have the advantage of restricting attention to derived relations that are likely to be more salient for actors in the network, as Mandel (1983) originally proposed. For examples of the application of this approach, see Pattison (1993, 2009) and Pattison and Wasserman (1995).

This approach has several appealing features. First, it is applicable to observed networks of relations among actors, avoiding the need for a preliminary aggregation of actors into blocks. Second, by restricting the value of k to a relatively small value such as 2 or 3, we restrict attention to derived relations that are arguably accessible to actors in their appraisals of their relational contexts and in their reasoning about the relational consequences of action. We may be aware, for example, of the friends of our friends, but we are less likely to be fully cognizant of the friends of the friends of our friends. Keeping k small in the construction of a partial algebra restricts analysis to those relations of which network members are potentially aware and hence identifies what we may think of as *local* regularities.

One potential disadvantage of this approach, though, is that it assumes that relational ties are deterministic and observed without error. No allowance is made for variability or error. This may be a tenuous assumption, and several important developments described below have attempted to utilise algebraic constructions while also recognising the likely presence of network tie variability.

Development of approximate algebraic representations through statistical identification of equations

The full and partial algebras just described provide exact and detailed representations of structural relationships among observed relations. The algebraic constructions on which they depend assume fixed relationships, measured accurately. The next approach that we discuss relaxes the requirement that ties be regarded as fixed rather than as variable.

In this approach, the Generalised Axiom of Quality introduced earlier is replaced by an *Approximate Axiom of Quality*: 'Regard as equal any pair of relations for which there is "sufficient evidence" of equality and regard the equality as an equation in the relation algebra generated by the generator set A_{obs}'. Such an approach can lead to a theoretically guided and structurally focussed form of exploratory data analysis for multiple networks. Theoretical guidance comes from the choice of operations in the set F, while structural focus resides in the algebra or partial algebra to which the approach gives rise.

In the context of specific algebraic constructions, Pattison and Wasserman (1995) and Pattison et al. (2000) further proposed to generate approximate equations among elements of $[A,F]_k$ by statistically evaluating evidence for relational equations. They proposed that one of a number of possible random multigraph distributions could be adopted to systematically assess evidence for both the *statistical significance* and *degree* of overlap among all pairs of relations in $A_{obs} \cup A_2 \cup \ldots \cup A_k$ for some value of k. They developed a software package PACNET to perform the required statistical calculations and to generate all of the derived equations implied by application of the axioms to a set of approximate equations identified by PACNET. PACNET is currently restricted to the operations $\{',^\circ\}$, though the complement and star of each empirical generator relation as well as their intersections and unions can readily be computed and added to the generator set if desired.

PACNET implements one statistical procedure for assessing the level of equality of two relations and a second procedure for assessing an ordering relation between them. For relation algebras, the statistical assessment of equality is pertinent. Two relations are judged to be approximately equal if a statistical test of association between the two relations meets predetermined thresholds for significance and effect size. The relevant statistical tests are constructed by regarding the observed networks as members of some conditional uniform random multigraph distribution on the given actor set. Pattison et al. (2000) discuss the important considerations that affect choice of a particular conditional uniform random multigraph distribution as appropriate for the statistical assessment.

Pairs of relations found to be approximately equal by the process just described can be equated as the Approximate Axiom of Quality allows. Pattison et al. (2000) describe how to ensure that a closed partial algebra emerges from this construction, and they illustrate application of the approach, including the use of several different conditional uniform random multigraph distributions in one setting.

The advantage of this approach is that it combines a distinctive statistical tradition for network analysis based on random graph distributions with an algebraic perspective, and hence allows statistical assessment of those many structural properties of relations that can be expressed in algebraic form, including those listed earlier.

This statistical tradition began with the analysis of the property of reciprocity (Moreno and Jennings, 1938) and includes both the analysis of the triad structure of a network including the assessment of transitivity (e.g. Holland and Leinhardt, 1970,

1978) and application of the quadratic assignment procedure to assess the association between two networks (e.g. Hubert and Arabie, 1989).

Relational configurations in statistical models for social networks

The final potential application of relation algebras is to the development of stochastic models for social networks.

A logical next step in the development of approaches that construe network ties as variables is to develop a *parametric* model for the ensemble of tie variables for a given set N of nodes, or actors. In this approach, each potential tie for an (ordered) pair of actors is considered as a variable and a model is developed for the array of tie variables describing relations among actors in N (Holland and Leinhardt, 1981; Frank and Strauss, 1986; Wasserman and Pattison, 1996). As Frank and Strauss (1986) explain, a general formulation of this approach yields the so-called *exponential random graph models*, of the form:

$$\Pr(\mathbf{Y}) = \exp(\Sigma_A \gamma_A z_A(\mathbf{Y}))/\kappa$$

where:

- A is a subset of tie variables (defining a potential network *configuration*);
- γ_A is a model parameter associated with the configuration A (to be estimated) and is nonzero only if the subset A is a clique in the dependence graph D;
- $z_A(\mathbf{Y}) = \Pi_{Y_{ij} \in A} Y_{ij}$ is the sufficient statistic corresponding to the parameter γ_A, and indicates whether or not all tie variables in the configuration A have values of 1 in the network $\mathbf{Y}$; and
- κ is a normalizing quantity.

The associated *dependence graph* D codifies expected dependencies among tie variables and has as nodes the set of tie variables among nodes in N. Two tie variables are joined by an edge in D if they are assumed to be conditionally dependent, given the values of all other tie variables.

The link between this stochastic formulation of a network model and equations in a relation algebra is that the latter equations give rise to expected graph configurations and hence may be associated with the designated effects of a stochastic model. For example, suppose there is a tendency for any partner's partner in a network to also be a partner (that is, there is a tendency for the equation $Y^\circ Y = Y$ to hold). A stochastic formulation of this equation implies an otherwise unpredictably large number of transitive triples (i,j,k) in which $Y(i,j) = 1 = Y(i,k) = Y(k,j)$.

This link between algebraic and stochastic formulations of network regularities are exemplified by what are termed *degenerate* forms of exponential random graph models for networks (Robins et al., 2005). Since an exponential random graph model defines a probability distribution on the set of all networks on a node set N as a function of some parameter vector, for any parameter vector, a subset of networks has what can be defined as minimum 'energy'. These minimum-energy networks can be seen as highly constrained or 'frozen' structural forms associated with the stochastic model. The structure of these forms will often warrant algebraic analysis; in addition, we can understand the nonfrozen models as stochastic generalisations of these structural forms.

PROSPECTS AND CHALLENGES

The characterisation of networks in terms of relation algebras is a compelling one because of the very natural connection between the operations defining a relation algebra and our everyday conceptualisations of derivative network relations. In addition, the four applications of these ideas that we have just described make clear the considerable flexibility of application. Nonetheless, some significant further work remains. Not only do the links between stochastic and deterministic formulations need further elaboration, but there are also some important generalisations to be developed. Arguably, the most important of these is the development of models for time-dependent relation variables (Moody, 2002; Pattison et al., 2008), since the capacity to reflect the impact of temporal constraints on relational operations is vital to understanding the consequences of network relations for the fundamental social processes that underpin them.

REFERENCES

Birkhoff, G. (1967) *Lattice Theory*. 3rd ed. Providence, RI: American Mathematical Society.

Bonacich, P. (1980) 'The "common structure semigroup", a replacement for the Boorman and White "joint reduction", *American Journal of Sociology*, 86: 159–66.

Bonacich, P. and McConaghy, M. (1979) 'The algebra of blockmodeling', in K.F. Schuesler (ed.), *Sociological Methodology 1980*. San Francisco: Jossey-Bass. pp. 489–532.

Boorman, S.A. and White, H.C. (1976) 'Social structures from multiple networks. II. Role structures', *American Journal of Sociology*, 81: 1384–446.

Borgatti, S. P., Boyd, J. P. and Everitt, M. G. (1989) 'Iterated roles – mathematics and application', *Social Networks*, 11: 159–72.

Boyd, J. P. (1969) 'The algebra of group kinship', *Journal of Mathematical Psychology*, 6: 139–67.

Boyd, J. P. (1990) *Social Semigroups: A Unified Theory of Scaling and Blockmodelling as Applied to Social Networks*. Fairfax, VA: George Mason University Press.

Boyd, J. P., Haehl, J. H. and Sailer, L. D. (1972) 'Kinship systems and inverse semigroups', *Journal of Mathematical Sociology*, 2: 37–61.

Breiger, R.L. and Pattison, P.E. (1978) 'The joint role structure of two communities' elites', *Sociological Methods and Research*, 7: 213–26.

Breiger, R.L. and Pattison, P.E. (1986) 'Cumulated social roles: The duality of persons and their algebras', *Social Networks*, 8: 215–56.

Burt, R.S. (1992) *Structural Holes: The Social Structure of Competition*. Cambridge, MA: Harvard University Press.

Burt, R.S. (2005) *Brokerage and Closure: An Introduction to Social Capital*. Oxford: Oxford University Press.

Frank, O. and Strauss, D. (1986) 'Markov graphs', *Journal of the American Statistical Association*, 81: 832–42.

Freeman, L.C. (1979) 'Centrality in social networks: Conceptual clarification', *Social Networks*, 1: 215–39.

Givant, S. (2006) 'Calculus of relations as a foundation of mathematics', *Journal of Automated Reasoning*, 37: 277–322.

Granovetter, M. (1973) 'The strength of weak ties', *American Journal of Sociology*, 78: 1360–80.

Holland, P.W. and Leinhardt, S. (1970) 'A method for detecting structure in sociometric data', *American Journal of Sociology*, 76: 492–513.

Holland, P.W. and Leinhardt, S. (1978) 'An omnibus test for social structure using triads', *Sociological Methods and Research*, 7: 227–55.

Holland, P.W. and Leinhardt, S. (1981) 'An exponential family of probability distributions for directed graphs', *Journal of the American Statistical Association*, 76: 33–50.

Homans, G. (1951) *The Human Group*. London: Routledge and Kegan Paul.

Hubert, L.J. and Arabie, P. (1989) 'Combinatorial data analysis: Confirmatory comparisons between sets of matrices', *Applied Stochastic Models and Data Analysis*, 5: 273–325.

Kim, K.H. and Roush, F.W. (1984) 'Group relationships and homomorphisms of Boolean matrix semigroups', *Journal of Mathematical Psychology*, 28: 448–52.

Lorrain, F. (1975) *Reseaux sociaux et classifications sociales*. Paris: Hermann.

Lorrain, F. and White, H.C. (1971) 'Structural equivalence of individuals in social networks', *Journal of Mathematical Sociology*, 1: 49–80.

Luce, R.D. (1956) 'A note on Boolean matrix theory', *Proceedings of the American Mathematical Society*, 3: 382–88.

Maddux, R.D. (1991) 'The origin of relation algebras in the development and axiomatization of the calculus of relations', *Studia Logica*, 50: 421–55.

Mandel, M. (1983) 'Local roles and social networks', *American Sociological Review*, 48: 376–86.

McConaghy, M. (1981) 'The common role structure: Improved blockmodelling methods applied to two communities' elites', *Sociological Methods and Research*, 9: 267–85.

Moreno, J.L. and Jennings, H.H. (1938) 'Statistics of social configurations', *Sociometry*, 1: 342–74.

Moody, J. (2002) 'The importance of relationship timing for diffusion', *Social Forces*, 81: 25–56.

Mullins, N., Hargens, L., Hecht, P. and Kick, E. (1977) 'The group structure of cocitation clusters: A comparative study', *American Sociological Review*, 42: 552–62.

Nadel, S.F. (1957) *The Theory of Social Structure*. Melbourne: Melbourne University Press.

Pattison, P.E. (1982) 'The analysis of semigroups of multirelational systems', *Journal of Mathematical Psychology*, 25: 87–118.

Pattison, P.E. (1989) 'Mathematical models for local social networks', in J. Keats, R. Taft, R. Heath and S. Lovibond (eds), *Mathematical and Theoretical Systems*. Amsterdam: North Holland.

Pattison, P.E. (1993) *Algebraic Models for Social Networks*. New York: Cambridge University Press.

Pattison, P.E. (2009) 'Algebraic models for social networks', in R. Myers (ed.), *Encyclopaedia of Complexity and System Science*. Berlin: Springer.

Pattison, P.E. and Bartlett, W.K. (1982) 'A factorization procedure for finite algebras', *Journal of Mathematical Psychology*, 25: 51–81.

Pattison, P.E., Robins, G.L. and Koskinen, J. (2008) 'Algebraic foundations for dynamic relation algebras: Preliminary steps', Sunbelt International Conference on Social Networks, San Diego.

Pattison, P.E. and Wasserman, S. (1995) 'Constructing algebraic models for local social networks using statistical methods', *Journal of Mathematical Psychology*, 39: 57–72.

Pattison, P., Wasserman, S., Robins, G. and Kanfer, A. (2000) 'Statistical evaluation of algebraic constraints for social networks', *Journal of Mathematical Psychology*, 44: 536–68.

Pratt, V. (1990) 'Dynamic algebras as a well-behaved fragment of relation algebras', Proceedings of Algebra and Computer Science, Ames, Iowa, June 2–4, 1988. Lecture Notes in Computer Science series.

Robins, G., Pattison, P. and Woolcock, J. (2005) 'Small and other worlds: Global network structures from local processes', *American Journal of Sociology*, 110: 894–936.

Tarski, A. (1941) 'On the calculus of relations', *Journal of Symbolic Logic*, 6: 73–89.

Wasserman, S. and Pattison, P. (1996) 'Logit models and logistic regressions for social networks, I. An introduction to Markov graphs and p^*', *Psychometrika*, 61: 401–25.

White, D.R. and Reitz, K.P. (1983) 'Graph and semigroup homomorphisms on networks of relations', *Social Networks*, 5: 193–234.

White, H.C. (1963) *An Anatomy of Kinship*. Englewood Cliffs, NJ: Prentice-Hall.

White, H.C. (1992) *Identity and Control*. Chicago: University of Chicago Press.

White, H.C., Boorman, S.A. and Breiger, R.L. (1971) 'Social structure from multiple networks: I. Blockmodels of roles and positions', *American Journal of Sociology*, 81: 730–80.

Winship, C. (1988) 'Thoughts about roles and relations: An old manuscript revisited', *Social Networks*, 10: 209–31.

Winship, C. and Mandel, M. (1983) 'Roles and positions: A critique and extension of the blockmodelling approach', in S. Leinhardt (ed.), *Sociological Methodology 1983–1984*. San Francisco: Jossey-Bass. pp. 314–44.

Wu, L. (1983) 'Local blockmodel algebras for analyzing social networks', in S. Leinhardt (ed.), *Sociological Methodology 1983–1984*. San Francisco: Jossey-Bass. pp. 272–313.

31

Statistical Models for Ties and Actors

Marijtje A.J. van Duijn and Mark Huisman

INTRODUCTION

Can we predict friendship between researchers if we know how many email interactions they have? Do researchers on a conference prefer to get acquainted with colleagues from the same research area or do they interact instead with colleagues who have a high citation index? Could it be that email contact, homophily, and scientific status are all important to explain friendship or acquaint-anceship, and if so, which of these effects is strongest? Can we distinguish different groups of researchers based on how well they know each other, and if so, is this grouping related to a research field or scientific status?

To answer these types of questions we need statistical models that can deal with the combination of network data and individual actor and/or dyadic attributes. They are presented in this chapter. The statistical models are categorized by the type of research question they can handle. Two streams of analysis are distinguished: the first are relationship-level models, modeling the ties between actors, and the other are actor-level models with an emphasis on differences between or grouping of actors.

The first three questions stated above can be answered with models that explain or predict the occurrence or value of ties in the network, using additional information on the relationships or actors if available. The last question is addressed using stochastic a posteriori block models that categorize or group actors based on their ties to each other, again using additional covariate infor-mation if available. The principle of stochastic

blockmodels is to identify (groups of) stochasti-cally equivalent actors, that is, actors who have the same probability distribution of ties to the other actors.[1]

The two different modeling approaches can be viewed as analyses of the same data (a social rela-tional system according to Wasserman and Faust [1994: 89]) with a different emphasis. In the models for ties, the focal variable is formed by the relationship, expressed as a tie variable or pair of tie variables in a dyad whose outcome is observed and may be explained by attributes. In the models for actors, the focal variable is the group membership of the actors, expressed as a latent (unobserved) actor variable, whose value may be derived from the observed ties between actors and additional actor and dyadic characteristics.

The models presented here can be viewed as a sequel to the two earlier chapters by Hanneman and Riddle (this volume) that described the basic concepts of the analysis of egocentric networks and of complete network data, including some of their statistical properties used for testing simple hypotheses. Other introductions to statistical net-work models can be found in Wasserman and Faust (1994) and Scott (2000). The exponential random graph models treated by Robins (this volume) have the same goal as the models for ties in this chapter but model the complete network using statistics to represent more complex depend-ence structures than the dyadic dependence that is handled by most of the models presented in this chapter. The stochastic actor-oriented or actor-based models for longitudinal network data in the chapter by Snijders (this volume) are aimed at explaining changes in the observed networks and in the observed actor characteristics. O'Malley and Marsden (2008) present a broad overview of social network analysis with illustrations of exponential random graph models and individual outcome regression models. Goldenberg et al. (2009) review an even wider range of statistical models for social network analysis.

The methods and models are presented in a nontechnical manner, avoiding the use of formulas. Our aim is to convey the main objective of a model and relate it to the research question it can answer. Moreover, we try to compare and link models that, although their definition or assumptions may differ, answer similar questions. We use the EIES data (Freeman and Freeman, 1979) and various software programs to illustrate the methods and models presented in this chapter.[2]

DESCRIPTION OF THE EIES DATA

The EIES data (Freeman and Freeman, 1979, taken from Wasserman and Faust, 1994, Appendix B, Tables 8–11) contain two observations of an acquaintanceship network. Acquaintanceship is a directed valued network, measured on a five-point scale ranging from (0) "don't know the other" to (4) "close personal friend." Complete network data are available for 32 out of 50 researchers participating in a study carried out in 1978, which investigated the influence of electronic communication using the Electronic Information Exchange System (EIES). Participants were able to use the then novel technology to send each other email. The number of messages were recorded over the eight-month period that the experiment lasted and can thus be regarded as a directed valued network. The acquaintanceship network was determined at the beginning (time 1) and at the end of the study (time 2). In addition to the acquaintanceship and communication relations, actor attributes are available: The number of citations of the researchers, which we consider as a scientific status measure, and their primary disciplinary affiliation (research field). Four categories are distinguished: sociology, anthropology, mathematics/statistics, and a rest category "other" discipline. Because of the skewedness of the number of messages and the number of citations, the square roots of these (sometimes large) numbers were used in the analyses. Two more sociomatrices were constructed: the first by taking the difference in status, to express the status hierarchy between the researchers, and the second by taking the absolute difference in status, measuring their distance.[3] Moreover, a (symmetric adjacency) matrix was created to indicate the similarity or homophily of the researchers with respect to their research field (including "other").

The data are summarized in Table 31.1. For most social network analyses the acquaintanceship network(s) had to be dichotomized, which we chose to indicate friendship: categories 3 and 4 ("friend" or "close personal friend") versus "did not know," "had heard of but not met," and "had met" the other, categories 0–2. Measures are calculated on the complete network ($n = 32$), and on subnetworks defined by research field. The summary statistics were calculated with the programs StOCNET (Boer et al., 2006) and NetMiner 3 (Cyram, 2009).

For the acquaintance network the mean weighted (column and row) sum of the ties is 42.4 at the first time point, which increases to 52.1 at the second time point. The incoming tie sum has a larger standard deviation than the outgoing tie sum. Note that the acquaintance ties are valued (0–4), making the numbers somewhat hard to interpret. Therefore, the degree distributions of the dichotomized acquaintance network ($0 \rightarrow 0$ and $>0 \rightarrow 1$) are presented in Figure 31.1. Both indegree and outdegree distributions at the two time points are slightly left skewed. At time 1, the average number of ties is 20.3 (out of 31 possible relations; not reported in table), indicating that the mean value of these 20.3 relations is about 2.1 ("had met the other"). At time 2, the average number of ties has increased to 23.7, making the mean value slightly larger, 2.2. The acquaintance networks of the smaller groups of anthropologists and the statisticians/mathematicians have on average the strongest relations: at time 1 the mean values are 2.7 and 2.5, respectively, and at time 2 the mean values are 2.8 and 2.35 (numbers not presented in Table 31.1).

The friendship network has mean degrees of 4.8 and 6.4 at times 1 and 2, respectively, with densities 0.15 and 0.21. The increase in the number of friends is largest in the sociologist network, whereas in the other fields the mean degrees stay more or less the same. Thus, friendships between actors of different fields were established. The subnetworks of the anthropologists and statisticians/mathematicians have the highest densities (at both time points). All (sub)networks have become slightly denser at the second time point, with more mutual relations, except the (small) network of the statisticians/mathematicians, which did not change. The statisticians/mathematicians have the highest reciprocity score, 1, because there is one mutual dyad and two null dyads in this group of three. At the second time point, all (sub)networks have reciprocity scores of 0.59 or higher, showing that friendship nominations are often reciprocated. Transitivity only increased

Table 31.1 Description of the EIES network attribute data obtained with StOCNET and NetMiner

	Research field				
	Socio.	Anthro.	St/Ma.	Other	Total
n	17	6	3	6	32
Acquaintance 1					
Mean sum	28.88	12.50	3.67	4.33	42.44
SD column sum[1]	8.64	2.59	2.31	2.25	17.36
SD row sum[2]	6.98	3.15	1.53	3.08	13.29
Acquaintance 2					
Mean sum	31.76	13.17	4.67	5.00	52.09
SD column sum[1]	8.09	3.65	2.31	2.19	16.39
SD row sum[2]	7.92	2.32	0.58	3.52	14.33
Friendship 1					
Mean degree	3.53	2.50	0.67	0.17	4.78
SD indegree	2.15	1.38	0.47	0.37	3.47
SD outdegree	2.52	1.38	0.47	0.37	3.53
Density	0.22	0.50	0.33	0.03	0.15
Reciprocity[3]	0.67	0.53	1.00	0.00	0.56
Transitivity[4]	0.44	0.50	–	–	0.38
Friendship 2					
Mean degree	4.82	2.67	0.67	0.50	6.38
SD indegree	2.73	1.80	0.47	0.50	4.78
SD outdegree	3.00	0.94	0.47	0.50	3.82
Density	0.30	0.53	0.33	0.10	0.21
Reciprocity[3]	0.66	0.63	1.00	0.67	0.59
Transitivity[4]	0.44	0.50	–	0.00	0.40
Citations (square root)					
Mean	4.61	1.93	3.66	4.22	3.95
SD	2.27	0.72	1.85	4.68	2.75
Range	0.0–8.0	1.0–3.0	2.0–5.7	1.0–13.0	0.0–13.0
Messages sent (square root)					
Mean[5]	2.10	2.88	1.28	1.87	2.13
SD	2.47	2.06	0.90	1.81	2.15
Range	0.1–9.0	0.2–5.3	0.3–2.1	0.2–5.2	0.1–8.9
Messages received (square root)					
Mean[5]	2.06	2.85	1.76	1.79	2.13
SD	1.69	1.39	0.73	1.44	1.51
Range	0.8–7.1	1.1–4.3	0.9–2.3	0.8–4.6	0.8–7.1

[1] The sample standard deviation of the n column sums.

[2] The sample standard deviation of the n row sums.

[3] $R = 2M/(2M + A)$, with M the number of mutual ties and A the number of asymmetric ties.

[4] The proportion of the triplets with two ties present that are transitive.

[5] The mean number of messages to/from all other actors (within and between groups).

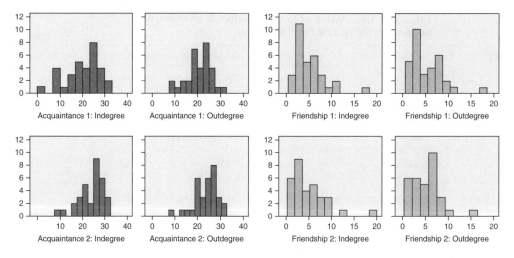

Figure 31.1   Degree distributions of the dichotomized acquaintanceship and friendship network at both time points

slightly in the total network and remained unchanged for the networks of sociologists and of anthropologists. It is not defined for the small group of statisticians/mathematicians at both time points and at time 1 for the group of "other" researchers.

For citations, messages sent, and messages received, the mean score, standard deviation, and range are reported in Table 31.1. The fields of sociologists and "other" contain actors with the highest number of citations and the highest variation in number of citations. The anthropologists have the smallest number of citations, but on average the highest number of messages sent and received. Interestingly, the statisticians/mathematicians received more messages than they sent, where for the other fields the numbers are almost the same.

The friendship network at time 2 is depicted in Figure 31.2. The graph was made using the layout option group by categorical attribute in NetDraw (Borgatti, 2002) to show the ties within and between the different fields. In the upper left corner the largest group of 17 sociologists (represented by circles) is positioned. Their status (depicted by the node size) varies from small to medium, approximately. The researcher with the largest number of citations belongs to the group of six researchers with an "other" research field (reflected in the large standard deviation of the number of citations in Table 31.1). This group is much less dense (with only one mutual and one asymmetric dyad) than the groups with specific disciplines. This is visually most clear in the comparison with the group of the same size in the lower right corner, consisting of six anthropologists with relatively low status. The small group in the lower left corner are the three

statisticians/mathematicians of whom one is connected mainly with the group of sociologists, the second mainly to the anthropologists, and the third, with the highest number of citations, has about the same number of ties to all three other groups.

MODELING TIES

An interesting research question for the EIES data concerns the impact of the communication during the experiment as measured by the number of messages sent on the acquaintanceship at time 2, taking into account the research area and status of the researchers, and possibly also their acquaintanceship at time 1. Such a question implies modeling one complete network (acquaintanceship at time 2) using covariate network information (communication, hierarchy, distance, acquaintanceship at time 1) as well as actor attributes (status, research field).

Several types of statistical models for (complete) network data are available. They differ in measurement level of the tie variable (dichotomous or continuous) on the one hand and the statistical modeling tradition on the other hand.

The section starts with QAP (Quadratic Assignment Procedure). This method is based on regression models and permutation tests for continuous tie variables (see Dekker et al., 2007 for an overview of its development). Next, the Social Relations Model (SRM) is explained. The SRM was first proposed by Kenny and La Voie (1984) and is rooted in an ANOVA-tradition. It has been used in many applications in social psychology

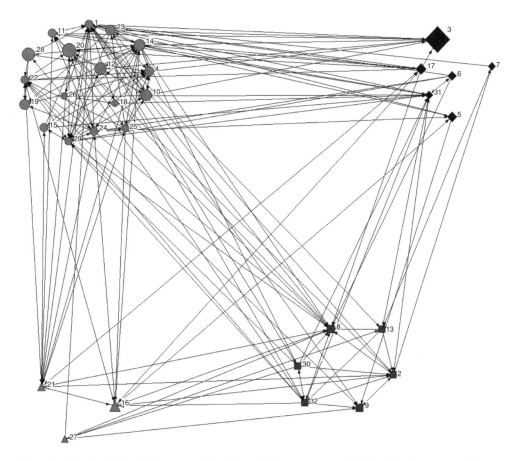

Figure 31.2   EIES friendship network at time 2. The actors are distinguished by research field (node shape and color) and by number of citations (node size). The graph was made with NetDraw

and other fields (see Kenny et al., 2006 for a more detailed account). An important extension is the random effects or multilevel model version of the SRM proposed by Snijders and Kenny (1999, see also Snijders and Bosker, 1999, Chapter 11.3.3). QAP and SRM assume continuous tie variables (or at least a relation with a sufficient number of values).

Based on loglinear modeling, Holland and Leinhardt (1981) proposed the p_1 model for the analysis of binary complete network data. The p_2 model (Van Duijn et al., 2004) combines this tradition with a random effects approach borrowed from the SRM, including actor and dyadic attributes. A different extension of the p_1 model is the so-called $p*$ model or exponential random graph model (Wasserman and Pattison, 1996; Snijders et al., 2006; Robins et al., 2007). This model is not treated in this chapter but is the topic of the chapter by Robins (this volume). The final

model shared under the models for ties is the bilinear model developed by Hoff (2005). The bilinear model resembles the SRM and p_2 in its way of incorporating dyadic and actor covariates, with random and correlated sender and receiver effects. It is more than dyadic, however, because it incorporates additional parameters to capture third-order dependence (such as transitivity and balance) between the actors. The extra parameters define a (latent) space in which the actors are positioned relative to each other. The bilinear model is related to the latent cluster model (Handcock et al., 2007) presented later in this chapter.

QAP

When investigating the association between two (or more) network matrices one has to take into account the dependence inherent in the data due to

Table 31.2 QAP correlations for the EIES complete network data obtained with UCINET based on 5000 permutations (*p*-values in parentheses; QAP correlations of square-root transformed variables below the diagonal)

		1	2	3	4	5
1	Network time 1	–	0.800 (<0.0001)	0.214 (0.001)	−0.039 (0.153)	0.001 (0.490)
2	Network time 2	–	–	0.355 (<0.0001)	−0.043 (0.114)	−0.076 (0.215)
3	Communication	0.250 (<0.0001)	0.431 (<0.0001)	0.888 (<0.0001)	−0.020 (0.170)	−0.157 (0.001)
4	Hierarchy	−0.070 (0.031)	−0.060 (0.039)	−0.045 (0.077)	0.928 (<0.0001)	0.000 (1.000)
5	Distance	−0.126 (0.067)	−0.180 (0.021)	−0.189 (0.009)	0.000 (1.000)	0.905 (<0.0001)

the fact that actors send and receive multiple ties. Thus, the observed outcomes of the tie variable are not independent. One could use OLS correlation and regression models to estimate the association, implicitly assuming independence over and within dyads. This approach results in incorrect tests of the correlation and regression coefficients (due to underestimation of the standard errors). The quadratic assignment procedure (QAP), applied to social networks by Hubert (1987) and Krackhardt (1987), tests the null hypothesis of no correlation between two matrices, Y and X, by repeatedly permuting the order of the rows (and columns) of one of the matrices, Y, while keeping X intact. The resulting sample of product-moment correlations of the permuted Y and X after vectorization provides the distribution of the correlation coefficient under the null hypothesis to which the observed correlation can be compared. When the association between two matrices is investigated while controlling for a third matrix Z, a more complex procedure is needed because of the dependence between X and Z, comparable to multicollinearity in multiple regression (MR). Several MR-QAP procedures have been proposed, of which the residual permutation methods are found to perform best (Dekker et al., 2007). In these approaches the residuals of either the regression of Y on Z or X on Z obtained in a first step in the analysis are permuted and included in the regression equation in the second step to compute the association between Y and X controlling for Z. The latter approach is the Double-Semi-Partialing approach used in the application.

Application to acquaintance network

The QAP and MR-QAP methods are implemented in UCINET (Borgatti et al., 2002), and SNA (Butts, 2008). As a first step, correlations are computed between the five available social networks with continuous tie variables. These are presented in Table 31.2.

The QAP correlations between the EIES networks are highest for the strength of acquaintanceship at time 1 and time 2 (0.80) and with the number of messages sent between the researchers stronger at time 2 than at time 1, even more so when the square-root transformed variable is used. The correlations of the absolute difference between actors in number of citations (distance) and the difference measure (hierarchy) with acquaintanceship at both time points are all negative, weak and only significant for the square root transformed variables, except for distance and acquaintance time 1.

The expected negative effect of distance reflects that researchers far apart in status are less well acquainted; the negative effect of hierarchy indicates the asymmetric phenomenon that researchers tend to rate the intensity of acquaintanceship higher with others who are "higher in rank" in terms of the number of citations than vice versa, which may be called a status effect or aspiration effect. There is some evidence of a weak relation between communication and distance, as researchers at a smaller distance tend to communicate more ($r = −0.16$ and $−0.19$ for the transformed variables). The correlations between the explanatory variables and their square-root transformed version are quite high, as expected.

In Table 31.3, the results of an MR-QAP analysis are given with the acquaintanceship at time 2 as outcome variable. We start with hierarchy and distance as explanatory variables to decide which of the two effects of citations is stronger: hierarchy or distance. Next, the effect of the messages sent is added to the model (Model 2 in Table 31.3). The results are computed using MR-QAP with the residual permutation method

Table 31.3 MR-QAP analyses results for the EIES acquaintanceship data at time 2 obtained with UCINET based on 2000 permutations (*p*-values in parentheses)

	Model 1	Model 2	Model 3
Intercept	1.866	1.458	0.576
	–	–	–
Communication		0.175	0.102
		(0.001)	(0.001)
Hierarchy	−0.017	−0.012	0.000
	(0.041)	(0.103)	(0.454)
Distance	−0.060	−0.047	−0.019
	(0.028)	(0.080)	(0.079)
Network time 1			0.735
			(0.001)
R^2 (adjusted)	0.035	0.196	0.698
	(0.012)	(<0.0001)	(<0.0001)

proposed by Dekker et al. (2007), called "Double Dekker Semi-Partialling" in UCINET (based on the 2000 permutations and the *t*-statistic). No *p*-value for the intercept is reported. The QAP and MR-QAP procedures are also available in the R package sna and take slightly longer to produce (almost) identical results.

Model 1 in Table 31.3 shows that distance has a stronger effect on acquaintanceship than hierarchy. When communication (i.e., the square root of the number of messages sent) is added to the model, the effects of distance and hierarchy are reduced and not significant anymore. The effect of communication is strong, as is also shown by a large increase in (adjusted) R^2, the proportion of variance explained in the analysis. Adding the degree of acquaintanceship at time 1 as explanatory variable to the model increases the amount of explained variance even more. The parameter value of communication is smaller while still significant. The effect of hierarchy is gone, apparently completely absorbed in or represented by the acquaintanceship at the start of the experiment. Thus, evidence is found for a positive impact of communication on acquaintanceship.

Social Relations Model (SRM)

The Social Relations Model (SRM; Kenny and La Voie, 1984) assigns the variance observed in dyadic relations Y_{ij} to parts attributable to senders of the relations, to their receivers, and to their interaction. This definition makes it clear that the model was originally formulated as an ANOVA model (Kenny and La Voie, 1984). It was later

reformulated as a random effects or multilevel model (Snijders and Kenny, 1999) incorporating explanatory dyadic covariates and using actor characteristics to further model (random) sender and receiver effects. Note that the dyadic and actor covariates can be categorical or continuous. The SRM can be regarded as a cross-nested multilevel (regression) model where dyads are nested within actors, who for each of the directed relations act as sender or receiver (Snijders and Bosker, 1999, Chapter 11).[4]

The SRM requires continuous dyadic outcomes in order to make the assumption of a normal error distribution of the residuals at tie-level and at actor-level. The dependence between the two roles of each actor is represented by the covariance between the *random* sender and receiver effects. The random effects and their (co)variances can be viewed as measures of (unexplained) actor sociability. In multilevel terminology, the regression parameters for the actor and dyadic covariates are *fixed* effects. The SRM does not require complete network data and is easily extended to the situation of multiple (independent) networks by adding an extra level (see, for example, Gerlsma et al., 1997). The SRM for observations of independent dyads (networks with only two actors) is known as the Actor Partner Interdependence Model (APIM) developed by Cook and Kenny (2005); see also the textbook on dyadic data analysis by Kenny et al. (2006).

Application to acquaintance network

The SRM is estimated with MLwiN (Rasbash et al., 2005), using a macro written by Tom Snijders, available from his Web site (http://stat.gamma. rug.nl/). Note that the model can be estimated with any software that allows specification of random effects model with a complex variance structure (see David Kenny's Web site, http:// davidakenny.net/srm/srm.htm, for more specific information about software for estimating the SRM). The SRM is applied to the EIES acquaintanceship data in four models presented in Table 31.4. The first one is a so-called null or empty model. This model serves as a baseline model, to obtain information on the overall mean strength of acquaintanceship, while taking into account individual differences between the researchers acting as both senders and receivers of ties through the sender and receiver variances. Moreover, an estimate of within-dyad reciprocity is obtained, in the form of the covariance (or correlation) between the residuals of the directed ties. An estimate of the tie variance is also available, which can be viewed as a measure of the within-actor variability of the acquaintanceship intensity.

These parameters are present in all subsequent models. Next, an SRM is estimated with exactly the same effects as the first MR-QAP model, hierarchy, and distance, dyadic covariates based on the actor covariate status (the square root of the number of their citations). As a third model, separate sender and receiver effects of status are used instead of the dyadic hierarchy effect to demonstrate the properties of the SRM. The dyadic communication effect and homophily effect of research field are added as well. In the fourth and final model, the first measurement of the acquaintanceship network is added, to judge the strength of the previously present effects and for comparison with the MR-QAP results. The models are compared by deviance tests. Although the deviance serves to assess improvement of the model after adding (or deleting) covariates, it does not provide a direct measure of the variance explained by the model. Because these models are *nested*, the usual procedures of model comparison apply.

Table 31.4 SRM analyses results for the EIES acquaintanceship data at time 2 obtained with MLwiN (standard errors in parentheses)

	Model 0	Model 1	Model 2	Model 3
Intercept	1.680	2.109	1.059	0.661
	(0.17)	(0.19)	(0.22)	(0.012)
Communication			0.120	0.0655
			(0.014)	(0.00091)
Hierarchy		−0.0150		
		(0.0098)		
Distance		−0.142	−0.123	−0.0365
		(0.022)	(0.020)	(0.012)
Network time 1				0.690
				(0.021)
Same field			0.331	−0.0362
			(0.084)	(0.050)
Sender status			0.0655	0.00654
			(0.026)	(0.015)
Receiver status			0.0929	0.00830
			(0.026)	(0.014)
Sender variance	0.198	0.234	0.128	0.0366
	(0.057)	(0.065)	(0.038)	(0.012)
Receiver variance	0.264	0.266	0.124	0.0301
	(0.073)	(0.073)	(0.037)	(0.010)
Sender/Receiver	0.193	0.215	0.0842	0.0206
covariance	(0.059)	(0.063)	(0.031)	(0.0087)
Residual tie variance	0.869	0.809	0.717	0.328
	(0.047)	(0.043)	(0.037)	(0.015)
Reciprocity	0.531	0.471	0.370	0.0534
within-dyad covariance	(0.047)	(0.043)	(0.037)	(0.015)
Deviance	2563.7	2521.6	2437.2	1769.1

Model 0 in Table 31.4 shows that the overall average strength of acquaintanceship is 1.68, a little left from the middle of the 0–4 scale. The actor receiver variance is somewhat larger than the sender variance, corresponding to what is found in Table 31.1. The covariance of the random sender and receiver effects is equal to 0.19, implying a high correlation of 0.84 (0.19/ $\sqrt{(0.20 \cdot 0.26)}$) between them. This means that an actor with a positive sender effect (i.e., who has a higher than average mean strength of outgoing acquaintanceships) tends to also have a higher than average mean strength of received acquaintanceship ratings (a positive receiver effect). Note that this model describes the overall structure in the network, without using any of the covariate information. The residual tie variance is much larger than the actor variances. The overall reciprocity in the network is high, with a correlation of 0.61(0.53/0.87) between the two directed ties.

Like in the MR-QAP analysis, the effect of distance is stronger than that of hierarchy, as is evident from the small and nonsignificant effect of hierarchy in Model 1. The model is a clear improvement over the empty model with a difference in deviance of 42.1 (2563.7 − 2521.6), which is significant at the .001 level with two degrees of freedom (due to adding two parameters). The reduced total variance leads to a lower residual tie variance and slightly higher sender and receiver variances (a phenomenon well known in multilevel analysis, cf. Snijders and Bosker, 1999: 100). The correlation between sender and receiver effects and the unexplained reciprocity are approximately the same as in Model 0 (0.86 and 0.58, respectively).

In Model 2 both actor variances and residual tie variances are reduced after adding sender and receiver covariates of status, communication, and field homophily. The parameters pertaining to these effects are all significant, as is assessed by a t-test (or approximate z-test) dividing the parameter estimate by its standard error. A value larger than 2 is a rough indication of significance at the 5 percent level. After adding acquaintance at time 1 in Model 3, the covariate effects are greatly reduced, and all parameter estimates except communication and distance are no longer significant. The variances are reduced by more than half, with an unexplained reciprocity of only 0.16(0.05/0.33). The correlation between random sender and receiver effects remains strong at 0.62 $(0.02/\sqrt{(0.03 \cdot 0.04)})$.

An interpretation of these changes is that much of the acquaintance network at time 2 can be explained by its state at time 1. Especially the effects of field similarity and (sender and receiver) status are captured by the network at time 1,

which makes sense, and to a lesser extent the effect of distance. The amount of communication, however, adds to the explanation of the acquaintanceship at time 2. This seems very much in line with the purpose of the study and could be interpreted as a success of the experiment with computer communication.

The p_1 and p_2 model

In a separate development, statistical models for dichotomous relations (in a directed graph) were proposed that distinguish the four possible outcomes of a dyad: one null (0,0), one mutual (1,1), and two asymmetric (0,1) and (1,0) dyadic states. Holland and Leinhardt (1981) proposed the first so-called p_1 model. It can be considered as the loglinear pendant of the Kenny and La Voie (1984) ANOVA SRM, distinguishing the sender and receiver roles of all n actors. The model contains $2n$ actor parameters in addition to a density and reciprocity parameter representing the overall propensity to engage in any relationship (no matter the direction) and a mutual relationship, respectively.

Similar to the Snijders and Kenny (1999) SRM, the p_1 model was extended with random sender and receiver effects to the so-called p_2 model (Lazega and Van Duijn, 1997). The model provides the possibility to include (actor) sender and receiver effects as well as dyadic covariates for density and reciprocity effects. In the p_2 model, the four outcomes of a dyad for binary relations are modeled explicitly (comparable to polytomous logistic regression) with the null dyad (0,0) as the reference category. It has correlated random sender and receiver effects (like in the SRM). Its density parameter represents the log-odds of a directed tie (vs. no tie), regardless of the outcome of the other tie in the dyad. The reciprocity parameter represents the interaction effect of the increase in log-odds of a mutual dyad in comparison to the sum of the two log-odds of the asymmetric dyads.

Unlike the p_1 model, which can be estimated easily using straightforward methods for loglinear or generalized linear models, the IGLS estimation first proposed by Van Duijn et al. (2004) for the p_2 model was improved by using Markov Chain Monte Carlo methods (Zijlstra et al., 2009). They used a Bayesian model formulation in the tradition of Wong (1987), which was extended to categorical covariates by Wang and Wong (1987) and Gill and Swartz (2004). The p_2 model can also be estimated for multiple (independent) networks (Zijlstra et al., 2006) and multiple relations (Zijlstra, 2008).

Application to friendship network

We turn our attention to the binary friendship network, to demonstrate the p_1 and p_2 models. The p_2 model is estimated using the P2 module in StOCNET. The results are presented in Table 31.5. The p_1 estimates were obtained with UCINET and only reported in the text. After estimating the p_1 model, four p_2 models are fitted to the EIES friendship data, starting with the null model. The next model is comparable to SRM Model 2 in Table 31.4, estimating the effect of communication, distance, and status. The third model shows the specific feature of the p_2 model to include covariates for the reciprocity parameter. In the fourth model this model is extended with the (density) effect of friendship at the start of the experiment.

The analysis of the EIES data with the p_1 model results in a negative estimate of the density (–3.34). This implies that the probability of a tie is much smaller than 0.50 (corresponding to the observed overall density of 0.21). The reciprocity parameter is positive (4.33), slightly larger in absolute value than the density parameter. These values reflect that the occurrence of a mutual dyad is somewhat more likely than one of the asymmetric dyadic outcomes (corresponding to the observed number of 60 mutual dyads, which is more than half the number of asymmetric dyads, 82). The 32 individual estimates for sender and receiver effects are summarized by their variances and covariances 1.74, 2.23, and –1.26, respectively (the latter implying a correlation of –0.64).

The p_2 null model (Model 0 in Table 31.5) shows, as expected, a negative density parameter estimate and positive reciprocity parameter. The receiver variance is, again, higher than the sender variance and the covariance (and correlation) negative. Different than for the SRM, this correla-

Table 31.5 p1 and p2 analyses results for the EIES friendship data at time 2 obtained with StOCNET (standard errors in parentheses)

	p_1	p_2			
	Model	*Model 0*	*Model 1*	*Model 2*	*Model 3*
Density	–3.34	–3.01	–4.67	–4.12	–5.22
		(0.27)	(0.50)	(0.53)	(0.76)
Communication			0.426	0.424	0.484
			(0.061)	(0.067)	(0.078)
Distance			–0.224	–0.365	–0.340
			(0.055)	(0.084)	(0.121)
Same field			0.717	0.736	0.677
			(0.20)	(0.20)	(0.34)
Network time 1					6.59
					(0.62)
Reciprocity	4.33	3.82	3.30	2.43	0.839
		(0.45)	(0.48)	(0.60)	(0.71)
Distance				0.364	0.519
				(0.16)	(0.21)
Sender status			0.171	0.155	0.108
			(0.12)	(0.13)	(0.14)
Receiver status			0.0962	0.0851	0.0251
			(0.077)	(0.087)	(0.10)
Sender variance	1.74[1]	1.06	3.40	3.49	2.97
		(0.40)	(1.20)	(1.29)	(1.34)
Receiver variance	2.23[2]	1.46	0.730	0.740	0.731
		(0.52)	(0.35)	(0.34)	(0.48)
Sender/ Receiver covariance	–1.26[3]	–0.829	–1.15	–1.18	–0.901
		(0.40)	(0.51)	(0.55)	(0.55)
Deviance (approx.)		663.7	531.2	526.8	258.5

[1] Based on the variance of the *n* estimated sender parameters.
[2] Based on the variance of the *n* estimated receiver parameters.
[3] Based on the covariance of the *n* pairs of sender and receiver parameters.

tion cannot be linked to the observed correlation between in- and outdegree, because of the inclusion of the reciprocity parameter in the model. Finally, a deviance value is reported, that due to the nonlinearity of the model is only approximate (cf. random effects logistic regression). No formal tests for model comparison can be based on the deviance (see Zijlstra et al., 2005).

Model 1 in Table 31.5 is analogous to SRM Model 2 in Table 31.4 and has the same substantive interpretation with positive effects of communication and field similarity and a negative effect of distance on friendship. The actor status effects, however, are too small to be significant. (Direct comparison of the regression parameters to the previous model is difficult, because they tend to increase in size with more variables in the model. This is a well-known phenomenon in logistic regression with random effects, see, for example, Snijders and Bosker [1999].) Note that the sender variance has increased as well. This is best interpreted in comparison to the receiver variance. Apparently the network effects included in the model explain more of the differences between the friendship ties received than those sent. A similar pattern, although not quite as strong, was also observed in the SRM analysis.

In Model 2, the typical p_2 feature of reciprocity covariates is demonstrated, by including distance in the model, not only for density but also for reciprocity. An interesting positive effect of distance for reciprocity is found, which can be interpreted in combination with the negative effect of distance for density. The negative effect of distance on density implies that the overall probability of a friendship tie is smaller for researchers with a larger status difference. The reciprocity distance parameter is an interaction effect, implying that the negative effect of distance on density is reduced in mutual dyads by the positive effect of density on reciprocity, thus making mutual and asymmetric ties approximately equally likely for dyads with the same distance between actors.

Finally, the friendship network at time 1 is added to the model.[5] Model 3 shows that this covariate has by far the largest influence, and like in the SRM analysis, the effects of field similarity and distance are reduced (although not for reciprocity), whereas the effect of communication remains relatively strong.

The bilinear model

Hoff's (2005) bilinear model builds on the earlier presented dyadic models, by incorporating dyadic and actor covariate effects. The model goes beyond dyadic dependence, because it includes additional parameters to capture specific forms of third-order dependence, defined as balance or clusterability. This can be understood as looking for further structure in the residuals of the model. The residuals are defined as a function of latent actor characteristics, forming a distance or space. Thus, a more complex dependence structure is modeled than in the SRM or p_2 model, although not as complete or complex as in the Exponential Random Graph Models. The bilinear model is set up as a Bayesian Generalized Linear Model, accommodating normal, Poisson and binomial tie distributions, and is estimated using MCMC methods. The dimensionality of the latent space is to be decided on by the researcher, with the help of (Bayesian) fit statistics. If the dimensions of the latent space are chosen equal to zero, the bilinear model with a normal distribution for the ties amounts to the Social Relations Model. For dichotomous ties there is no equivalence with the p_2 model because the bilinear model does not include a reciprocity parameter in the fixed (mean) part of the model. Bayesian model summary and selection tools are available to decide whether the model fits the data satisfactorily.

Application to acquaintance network

The bilinear model is not part of the statnet suite in R (Handcock et al., 2003), but for its estimation R source code is available at Peter Hoff's Web site (http://www.stat.washington.edu/hoff/Code/GBME/). The bilinear model presented here is used for illustration and is not intended to be presented as the best fitting model to the EIES data. A model is fitted with parameters equal to those of Models 2 of the SRM model and p_1 model, that is, including the effect of communication, distance, and field similarity, as well as sender and receiver effects of status but without the acquaintanceship network at time 1 (as this explains so much of the acquaintanceship at time 2). Further, the latent space is chosen to be two-dimensional to facilitate graphical representation obtained after a Procrustes rotation.[6]

Comparing the model results of the bilinear model, presented in Table 31.6 to those of the Social Relations Model (Model 2 in Table 31.4 and also obtained with the bilinear model setting the number of latent space dimensions equal to 0), it becomes clear that the effects of the covariates are considerably reduced, notably the effects of field homophily, distance and sender status, and, to a lesser extent, of receiver status. The sender and receiver variances are practically the same, but the residual tie variance has

Table 31.6 Bilinear model analysis results for the EIES acquaintanceship data at time 2 obtained with StOCNET (standard errors in parentheses)

Density	1.14	(0.25)
Communication	0.107	(0.014)
Distance	−0.0496	(0.026)
Same field	0.175	(0.089)
Sender status	0.0363	(0.028)
Receiver status	0.0650	(0.030)
Sender variance	0.117	(0.039)
Receiver variance	0.136	(0.045)
Sender/Receiver covariance	0.0880	(0.036)
Residual tie variance	0.544	(0.029)
Within-dyad covariance	0.363	(0.041)
Latent dimension 1 variance	0.317	(0.10)
Latent dimension 1 variance	0.312	(0.094)

gone down. The variances of the two latent dimensions are in size between the sender and receiver variances and the residual tie variance, and (compared to the SRM) picking up some of the residual variance.

Our interpretation of the results is that, since the latent space serves to capture third order dependence, some of these structural effects were hidden in field similarity and distance. This seems plausible for effects like transitivity and balance on acquaintanceship, which may well work through colleagues in the same field or with a similar status. Interesting is that the (truly) dyadic effect of communication is only slightly reduced. Figure 31.3 depicts the position of the actors in the latent space. The symbols represent the locations of the actors, obtained as posterior mode from the MCMC runs. The tiny dots are the realizations obtained in all runs of the MCMC sampler, and they give an indication of the spread of nodal locations and of the overlap between nodes. Actors who are located close together have many ties to

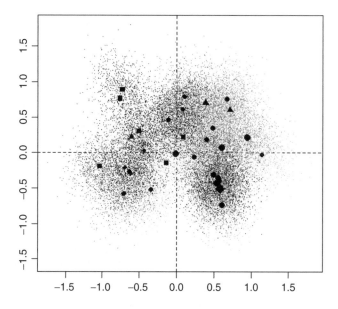

Figure 31.3   Bilinear model results for the EIES friendship network at time 2

each other and/or a similar pattern of ties to others (Hoff, 2005). Some grouping seems to be present; the grouping of actors will be further investigated in the next section, after the summary of the results obtained with the tie models.

Summary and discussion of the tie models

Four different models with increasing complexity were discussed and illustrated in this section. With the MR-QAP model, we were able to identify a sizable influence of communication on the EIES acquaintanceship network at time 2, also (be it less strong) after controlling for the relations at time 1.

All other models are more geared toward social network data in the sense that they specifically model dyadic dependence. In addition to the dyadic effect of communication, the analyses with these models showed a symmetric dyadic effect of status (distance), also after controlling for the first measurement of the network (not computed for the bilinear model). If the distance between actors is large, both tie values reported are lower, on average. The individual status effects were stronger in the SRM and bilinear model (with only a significant receiver effect) than in the p_2 model. Because the p_2 model models "friendship" (defined as dichotomized acquaintanceship), this difference might be interpreted substantively as that acquaintanceship is more sensitive to individual status than friendship. Such an interpretation is tentative because an alternative explanation could be lack of power due to the dichotomous tie variable (as indicated by the larger standard errors for all parameters in the p_2 model).

The interpretation of the random effects included in the models may seem difficult at first but is informative. The most important information in the SRM and bilinear model is captured by the reciprocity effect, reporting the association between the two ties in the dyad. The sender and receiver variances can be interpreted relative to each other, so for the EIES data it was found that researchers differ more from each other in reporting ties than in receiving ties. The positive covariance implies that researchers who report more than average tie values also tend to receive such values, which could be interpreted as a general sociability effect. Reciprocity is treated as a fixed effect in the p_2 model and also showed the expected positive effect. The results of the bilinear model with a two-dimensional latent space showed that the effects obtained with the other models were probably somewhat inflated due to the presence of third-order effects.

INVESTIGATING GROUPS OF ACTORS

In this section we take a different perspective on the social relational system. Instead of focusing on the relation(s), trying to explain the observed social network using dyadic and/or actor characteristics, we now turn to the actors. For the EIES data this amounts to how we can categorize the researchers best, based on the individual covariates available or on the acquaintance relations and the communication network. Before we proceed with presenting some stochastic a posteriori block models, we mention other methods and models with the aim to compare actors across known groups (for instance, according to research field) or to explain or predict an actor outcome variable using the network ties and possibly actor and dyadic covariates (for instance, scientific status using the acquaintanceship or friendship network and field).

Comparing groups of actors

The use of well-known methods like t-tests and ANOVA for the comparison of actors and their network characteristics suffers from the incorrect assumption of independence of observations (see, e.g., Hanneman and Riddle, 2005: Chapter 18). It is easy to summarize relational data to the actor level (although the choice for summary statistics may be overwhelming), but the resulting "actor" data are dependent by definition. As for correlations, a solution is to use permutation-based methods (cf. QAP), which are implemented in UCINET for t-tests, ANOVA and regression with actor outcomes. In the case of the EIES researchers it would be natural to compare the researchers by their disciplinary affiliation.

To investigate the influence of relations on actor characteristics, contagion models were proposed by, for example, Doreian (1980), Burt (1987), Friedkin (1998) and Leenders (2002). In these models the outcome variable is an actor characteristic, where the dependence between actors is represented by including (some form of) the social network in the regression equation. A contagion model is thus a kind of spatial regression model (cf. Ord, 1975; Anselin, 1988), modeling autoregression or (network) autocorrelation or both. Contagion models can be estimated using software for spatial regression or sna (Butts, 2008). See O'Malley and Marsden (2008) for a good overview and application of these models. We do not illustrate these models here for the reason that continuous time models are available in which contagion can be distinguished from selection effects (cf. Steglich et al., 2010).

Identifying groups of actors

The aim of a stochastic blockmodel analysis is the identification of groups (or positions) of actors. As in latent class analysis, one of the questions in such an analysis is to determine how many groups are needed to distinguish the set of actors sufficiently, with the immediate next question whether the group assignment is consistent with the researcher's expectation or can be understood given other quantitative (or qualitative) information. In some stochastic blockmodels additional information on the positions of the actors is obtained, to be used for a graphical representation. Note that the bilinear model presented in the previous section also had this feature. Early examples of stochastic blockmodels can be found in Anderson and Wasserman (1992), who group the sender and receiver parameters of the p_1 model.

In the remainder of this section we present four stochastic blockmodels, which will be indicated by the name of the software in which they are implemented. The first stochastic blockmodel, BLOCKS, was proposed by Nowicki and Snijders (2001) for (valued) social network data. This model follows an earlier model for (binary) network data to assign actors to (latent) groups (Snijders and Nowicki, 1997). Tallberg (2005) proposed an extension of the model by further modeling the group probabilities using covariate information (not illustrated here because no software is readily available). The next model presented is the stochastic block model proposed by Frank (1995), KliqueFinder. In addition to a group assignment, a graphical display of the positions of the actors is obtained. A somewhat different approach is the third model, proposed by Schweinberger and Snijders (2003) and based on the ultrametric distances between actors involving triads of actors and resulting in hierarchically clustered groups. As a final model the latent cluster models of Handcock et al. (2007), latentnet, are presented, in which dyadic and actor covariate information is incorporated. These models are related to the models presented by Hoff et al. (2002), Shortreed et al. (2006), and Krivitsky et al. (2009).

Blocks

The stochastic a posteriori model proposed by Nowicki and Snijders (2001) defines groups of stochastic equivalent actors, having the same probability of dyadic outcomes with actors in their own group and the same probability of dyadic outcomes with actors in other groups. It is based on the assumption of dyad independence in the observed social network, conditional on the latent (unknown) group membership of the actors (their so-called colors). Together with a color distribution defining a priori probabilities for each color (similar to latent class analysis), the joint distribution of dyadic outcome and color is obtained. Parameter estimates of the a posteriori probabilities for each color (per actor) are obtained using MCMC estimation, which is implemented in BLOCKS. Note that this model only uses the observed (binary) network and no covariate information.

Each actor is assigned to the color with the highest posterior probability for that actor. To determine the number of groups, two fit statistics pertaining to the extra information (I_y) and clarity (H_x) of the obtained actor positions are available. For both measures, values close to zero are preferred. The statistics are compared across models with a (predetermined) different number of groups to obtain the best solution.

Application to friendship data

BLOCKS was run on the EIES friendship data in an exploratory approach to obtain solutions for models with two to six classes. It turned out that none of the group assignments could be classified as very informative or clear. We focused on the solutions for three to five groups (colors). BLOCKS has the option to discard stepwise the "worst" fitting actors in order to obtain a network with a reduced number of actors who are more easily assigned to groups such that the probability of within-group ties is higher than between-group ties. Using the stepwise approach, only four groups remained in the five-group solution. We therefore chose four as the desired number of groups. For reasons of comparability with the other stochastic block models we did not want to leave out actors of the network (although it can be an attractive feature to identify "ungroupable" actors), and therefore we used the option to re-assign actors to groups. The algorithm gives the three or four best-fitting actors, that is, actors who are unambiguously assigned to different groups. The first three actors all had different research fields and we chose this as a starting configuration for the four-group solution. The obtained group assignment is depicted in Figure 31.4 and Table 31.7. For this solution, the values $H_x = 0.27$ and $I_y = 0.70$ were obtained, indicating that the solution is not particularly informative, which is at least partly due to our choice to assign all actors to a group.

Table 31.7 and Figure 31.4 show that the groups indicate no association with the research field as there are researchers from different disciplines (depicted by the shapes of their nodes

Table 31.7 BLOCKS four-group solution for the EIES friendship data at time 2 (excerpt from output obtained with StOCNET; slightly adapted to distinguish groups (Grp: A–D), actors (Id), and research fields (Fld: Sociology, Anthropology, Statistics/Mathematics, and Other)

```
                    Group And Actor Id
              |AAA|BBBBBBBBBBBB|CCCCCCCCCCC|DDDDD|
              | |          |         | |
              |  3|   1111112222|   1112233|12222|
   Grp  Id  Fld|181|3450256790138|26791386702|42459|
  -------------+---+------------+-----------+-----+
    A    1   S |A22|3.33.3.3..333|23322222332|3.3.2|
    A    8   A |2A.|......33..3..|33..23..332|3.333|
    A   31   O |2.A|.....2.......|22..2223.32|3...2|
  -------------+---+------------+-----------+-----+
    B    3   O |4..|B4..4..3...2.|....4......|2....|
    B    4   S |...|3B.2.3..2..33|...........|33.33|
    B    5   O |4..|..B...3......|....4......|3.3..|
    B   10   S |4..|.2.B2....2.2.|...........|...32|
    B   12   S |...|3..2B...4....|...........|3...3|
    B   15   S |4.2|.4...B....3..|...........|2...2|
    B   16  SM |.4.|..4...B3..2..|..........3|2233.|
    B   17   O |44.|4.....4B.42..|....4......|24...|
    B   19   S |...|.2......B..33|...........|32...|
    B   20   S |...|...23..3.B4..|...........|22222|
    B   21  SM |44.|.....422.3B..|.4...4.....|3232.|
    B   23   S |4..|24.2....4..B.|...........|2..34|
    B   28   S |4..|.4......4...B|...........|343..|
  -------------+---+------------+-----------+-----+
    C    2   A |242|.........3..|C..243...22|.....|
    C    6   O |442|............|.C.........|.4.4|
    C    7   O |4..|............|..C..2.....|.....|
    C    9   A |2..|..3.........|2..C....2.2|.3...|
    C   11   S |222|3.....3..3..|3...C.....2|.3..|
    C   13   A |242|............|4.2..C..2.4|.....|
    C   18   S |2.2|............|.....C3....|...|
    C   26   S |2.4|............|.....4C....|...|
    C   27  SM |44.|............|...2.2..C3.|.....|
    C   30   A |444|............|2.......4C4|3...4|
    C   32   A |222|.....4......|2..223...3C|.4..4|
  -------------+---+------------+-----------+-----+
    D   14   S |444|244.422242424|.........4.|D2222|
    D   22   S |...|.4....23222.3|...4......3|2D232|
    D   24   S |44.|..4...4..24.4|.3..4......|22D22|
    D   25   S |.4.|.4.4..4..224.|...........|242D.|
    D   29   S |242|.4.242...2.3.|.3.......33|222.D|
```

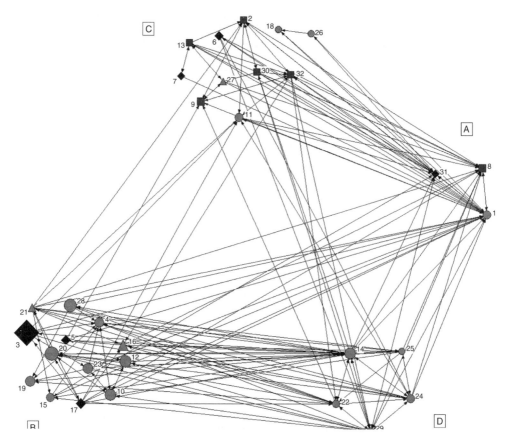

Figure 31.4   EIES friendship network at time 2. The actors are assigned to four different groups (distinguished by location) and are distinguished by research eld (node shape and color; same as in Figure 31.2) and by number of citations (node size). The program NetDraw is used to draw the group solution obtained with BLOCKS

in the graph) in all groups except for group D, positioned in the lower righthand corner. There are many ties among the groups, especially between the groups B and D on the lower side of the picture. The picture, however, seems to show a hierarchy in citation status among the groups: the largest group, B (bottom left), contains the researchers with high citation status, followed by the smaller group, D positioned bottom right, consisting of five sociologists. The second largest group, C (top left), and the small group, A (top right), consist of the researchers with different fields with the lowest status, where the researchers in group C have a lower status than those in group A. Some more precise information can be derived from Table 31.7. It represents the adjacency matrix, as available in the output of BLOCKS, slightly adapted by replacing the original 1s

(indicating a null relation) by dots and adding the information on the actors' fields. The 2s indicate mutual relations, the 3s and 4s asymmetric relations, from column to row and vice versa, respectively. Group A (top right in Figure 31. 4) has mutual relations within the group and mainly sends relations to the other groups (in view of the many 3s in the rows of group A), with also a good deal of mutual relations with group C (top left in Figure 31.4), the group with a slightly lower status. Group B (bottom left in Figure 31.4) is the largest, with the highest status, and exhibits all forms of dyadic relations within the group (with many null dyads), and only sends some ties to the first group and even fewer to the third group but receives a lot of ties (some reciprocal) to the fourth group. Group C is large and like group B has relatively few ties within the group. It has hardly any ties with groups B and D and more ties (some reciprocal) with group A. Finally, group D is quite dense and its actors send ties to especially groups A and B (some reciprocal) but have hardly any ties with researchers in group C. The many ties with group B are well visible in Figure 31.4. In terms of hierarchy defined as receiving many choices by other groups, the order of the groups is A, C, B, D.

KliqueFinder

The procedure implemented in KliqueFinder (Frank, 1995, 1996, 2009) is based on a p_1-like model[7] extended with a categorical actor covariate (group), in the form of a group similarity (homophily) effect on the density. The underlying idea is that of cohesion: Actors in the same group should have a higher probability to interact with each other than with actors from other groups. Just like in BLOCKS no other information is necessary than one observed social network. Unlike BLOCKS, KliqueFinder makes no distinction between the direction of ties.

The model was developed before MCMC estimation became more common and is estimated with an algorithm called iterative partitioning. The actors are preassigned to a group, starting with a clique of three actors, and this assignment is changed iteratively until no further improvement of the objective function is possible. The objective function is usually defined to maximize the probabilities of in-group ties, but some other, related, definitions are also available. Preassignment of actors to different groups is optional. A graphical representation of the groups and the actors within them is obtained using MDS on distances between actors and groups defined by the amount of interaction between them.

Application to friendship data

The EIES friendship data were analyzed with KliqueFinder. This resulted in five groups, depicted in Figure 31.5. It is clear that the five groups do not correspond to the four research fields distinguished in the EIES data. A possible interpretation is a hierarchy of actors according to status but with a different result than the BLOCKS solution with four groups. The upper group (B in Table 31.8) consists of researchers with a relatively low number of citations and is far away from the middle two groups (A and E) containing most actors. Of these middle groups, only three or four (in the lower-middle group E) have a higher status. The two overlapping lower groups (C and D) consist of fewer actors. These actors have the

highest status and are all sociologists except for the most-cited researcher from an "other" discipline but are further apart within the groups. Figure 31.6, obtained with UCINET, confirms this view of the KliqueFinder solution and gives some more information on the middle groups (bottom left and top right), which have a high density and also many relations with each other. Finally, the adjacency matrix representation in Table 31.8 (slightly adapted from the KliqueFinder output to indicate the original research fields) shows the high density within the five groups, where the 1s indicate either asymmetric or mutual relations and the dots no relation.

ULTRAS

The model proposed by Schweinberger and Snijders (2003) to find groups (or settings as they call it) is based on the assumption that there is an unknown distance between the actors in the network that governs the probability of ties between them, leading to a nested grouping of the actors. The distance (or proximity) is measured by an ultrametric (latent) space defined for pairs of actors, relative to their distance to third actors, and implies a transitive structure. The larger the distance between actors, the lower their probability of a tie. The nested grouping leads to regions with higher density like a geographic map with contour lines (see Schweinberger and Snijders, 2003: Figure 2). The ULTRAS model requires a symmetric matrix and can deal with dichotomous, count, or continuous tie variables, using, respectively, a Bernoulli, Poisson, or normal distribution for the tie probabilities, intensities, or strengths. It is estimated using Maximum Likelihood or Bayesian methods.

Application to the symmetrized friendship data

The "ultrametric" model is implemented in the STOCNET module ULTRAS. The results for the EIES friendship data are based on a standard setup with three runs of 10,000 iterations of the MCMC sampler. The first step is to decide how many levels are needed in the grouping of the actors. Running the module for 2 to 9 levels, it was found that four levels sufficed in the sense that solutions with five or more levels had all very small probabilities of ties between actors at a distance of five or more. We did not run extensive checks for convergence or model fit. The solution is presented in Figure 31.7, not as a map but in the form of an adjacency matrix, consisting of several "blocks" or "settings," where the last simply comprises the

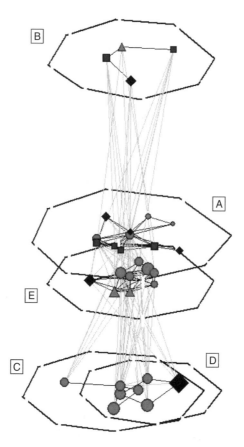

Figure 31.5 EIES friendship network at time 2. The actors are assigned to five different groups (distinguished by location) and are distinguished by research eld (node shape and color; same as in Figure 31.2) and by number of citations (node size). The program NetDraw is used to draw the graph obtained with KliqueFinder

whole network, with a very low overall probability (approximately 0.001) of a tie between actors not belonging to a further nesting (here, none of the actors). The lower right block consisting of actors 7 through 12 (as ordered by ULTRAS, see Figure 31.7) has a probability of 0.05 of a tie, whereas within the upper left block (actors 4 through 20) this probability has increased to 0.20. This division roughly corresponds to the two largest groups in the BLOCKS solution. Within these two settings a large number of groups are nested, many of which contain only pairs of actors. The highest density is found in the darker blocks, with a tie probability of 0.70. The largest block of actors this close together is the second block in the adjacency matrix (consisting of actors 8 through 25), which shows some resemblance with

the fifth group of the KliqueFinder solution (see Table 31.8).

Latentnet

The latent position cluster model proposed by Handcock et al. (2007) is based on a different concept of latent space, which was previously discussed for Hoff's (2005) bilinear model. The latent space model proposed by Hoff et al. (2002) does not have the feature of assigning group positions to actors. It was extended to the latent position cluster model by assuming unknown group (latent cluster) membership of the actors on the dimension(s) in the latent space. Actor and dyadic covariates can be included in the model as

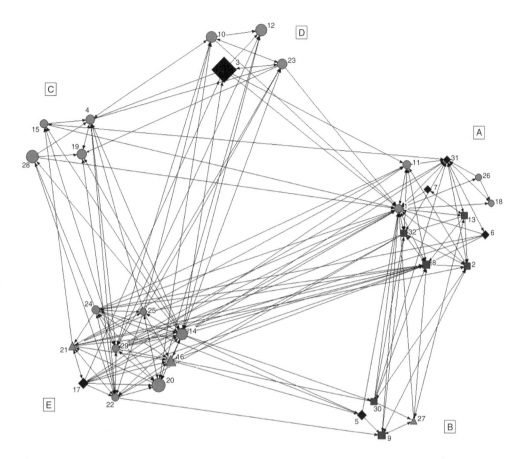

Figure 31.6   EIES friendship network at time 2. The actors are assigned to five different groups (distinguished by location) and are distinguished by research eld (node shape and color; same as in Figure 31.2) and by number of citations (node size). The program NetDraw is used to draw the group solution obtained with KliqueFinder

well, which makes the model more elaborate than the previously presented stochastic a posteriori blockmodels. The model is estimated with advanced Bayesian (MCMC) techniques and has several options for the definition of distance on which graphical representation is based (see Shortreed et al., 2006). Various statistics are available to make the sometimes difficult choice on the optimal number of latent clusters (as in the BLOCKS model), and the number of dimensions of the latent space. The model was extended with random sender and receiver effects (comparable to the bilinear model) by Krivitsky et al. (2009).

Application to friendship data

The EIES friendship data are analyzed using the R package latentnet (see Krivitsky and Handcock,

2008) with the same covariates as in the bilinear model. Again, we did not search for a best-fitting model but compared the four and five latent cluster solutions, including the dyadic covariates for communication, distance, and field homophily. The four latent cluster solution was to be preferred according to the Bayesian Information Criterion. The regression parameters (not shown in a table) revealed that the effect of communication was strongest, but interestingly, there was also a significant effect of field similarity, whereas the effect of distance was small and insignificant. (Recall that in the bilinear model with random sender and receiver effects both field similarity and distance did not reach significance.) The graphical representation of the solution in Figure 31.8 shows large overlap in the four clusters and a lot of variation around the cores of

Table 31.8 KliqueFinder five-group (Grp: A–E) solution for the EIES friendship data at time 2. Actors (Id) and Research fields (Fld: Sociology, Anthropology, Statistics/Mathematics, and Other) are distinguished

```
N               Group And Actor Id
32              |AAAAAAAAAAA|BBBB|CCCC|DDDD|EEEEEEEEE|
                |           |    |    |    |         |
                |  1313   2 1| 2 3| 112|112 |122221221|
 Grp  Fld Id|81118227663|9750|4958|2033|612094457|
------------+-----------+----+----+----+---------+
  1A   A    8|A11..1.....|....|....|....|.........|
  1A   S    1|1A11111.1.1|1...|....|....|....1....|
  1A   S   11|11A1.1.....|....|....|....|.........|
  1A   O   31|.11A111..11|....|..1.|....|....1....|
  1A   S   18|.1.1A......|....|....|....|.........|
  1A   A   32|1111.A1....|1...|....|....|1.1.1....|
  1A   A    2|1111.1A....|1..1|....|....|.........|
  1A   O    7|.1.....A..1|....|....|....|.........|
  1A   S   26|.1.11...A..|....|....|....|.........|
  1A   O    6|11.1.....A.|....|....|....|....1.1..|
  1A   A   13|11.1.111..A|.1..|....|....|.........|
------------+-----------+----+----+----+---------+
  2B   A    9|.1...11....|B1..|....|....|.........|
  2B   SM  27|11........1|1B..|....|....|.........|
  2B   O    5|.1.........|1.B.|....|....|.........|
  2B   A   30|11.1.11....|.1.B|....|....|....1....|
------------+-----------+----+----+----+---------+
  3C   S    4|...........|....|C1..|.1..|.........|
  3C   S   19|...........|....|1C..|....|.1.....|
  3C   S   15|.1.1.......|....|1.C.|....|....11...|
  3C   S   28|.1.........|....|11.C|....|..1.....|
------------+-----------+----+----+----+---------+
  4D   S   12|...........|....|....|D1..|...1.....|
  4D   S   10|.1.........|....|1...|1D1.|...11....|
  4D   S   23|.1.........|....|11..|.1D1|....11...|
  4D   O    3|.11........|....|1...|1.1D|.....1...|
------------+-----------+----+----+----+---------+
  5E   SM  16|1..........|...1.|....|....|E11..1...|
  5E   SM  21|111...1....|....|..1.|....|1E1....11|
  5E   S   22|..........|1...|11..|....|11E1111..|
  5E   S   20|..........|....|....|.1..|.11E1111.|
  5E   S   29|11.1......|....|1.1.|11..|..11E11..|
  5E   S   14|11.1......|..11|1111|1.11|11111E111|
  5E   S   24|111.......|..1.|...1|....|111111E1.|
  5E   S   25|1.........|....|1...|.11.|1111.11E.|
  5E   O   17|111.......|....|....|...1|1111.1..E|
```

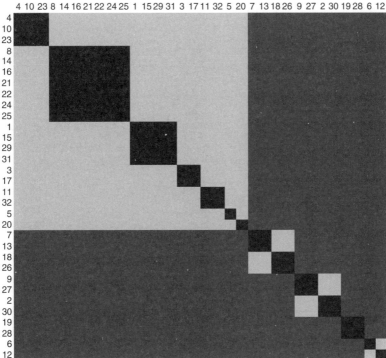

Figure 31.7   Block structure obtained with ULTRAS for the symmetrized EIES friendship network at time 2

the clusters. A general positive association between the positions on the two dimensions is visible. The resemblance with the BLOCKS solution is larger than with the KliqueFinder solution.

Summary

Four different stochastic a posteriori block models were presented. Although they have the same goal, finding a (good) classification of the actors in a network, their properties are very different. The first three models do not use covariate information and aim to find groups consisting of stochastic equivalent actors, which in the case of KliqueFinder is defined simply as having an as high as possible probability of within-group ties (and therefore lower between-group ties). This is also one of the assumptions in ULTRAS, whose definition of distance leads to a classification of actors in nested groups. In BLOCKS the definition of stochastic equivalence is more general and

extended to all possible dyadic outcomes (four in the case of binary data). The concept of stochastic equivalence is not as clearly defined in the latent position cluster model, because group membership is defined on the latent space dimensions (possibly while taking into account covariate effects on the probability of a tie). The interpretation of these dimensions is not always easy or immediately clear. ULTRAS is conceptually related to latentnet but employs a different definition of latent space and distance.

Given the different definitions of stochastic equivalence it is not surprising that rather different solutions are found. KliqueFinder gave a five-group solution with high within-group density (see Figures 31.5 and 31.6) which seemed to be somewhat related to the scientific status of the actors and not so much to research field, although scientific status is related to field as the sociologists have the highest number of citations (cf. Table 31.1). For the four-group solution found by BLOCKS, a weak relation with scientific status

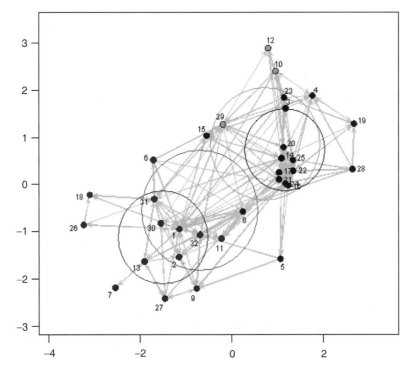

Figure 31.8   Latent position and latent cluster graph obtained with latentnet for the EIES friendship network at time 2

was suggested as well. The nested group structure obtained with ULTRAS could be roughly related to both earlier solutions but contained many more smaller groups. The analysis with latentnet indicated that a solution with four groups was to be preferred over a five-group solution, although from the overlap between clusters a solution with fewer clusters might have been better. The assignment of actors to groups (not precisely shown here) resembled the group assignment by BLOCKS and is therefore also weakly related to scientific status of the actors. Interestingly, no significant effect of scientific status (through dyadic distance) was found. A possible interpretation is that distance does not directly influence the (dyadic) probability of a tie but is present in the latent dimensions that capture third-order dependence.

CONCLUDING REMARKS

Although we did not find an answer to all of the questions posed in the introduction of this chapter, the models and methods presented gave a lot of insight into the structure of the EIES data and the association between the networks and covariates. Some tentative answers are that communication is an important explanatory variable for the observed acquaintanceship at time 2 for the EIES researchers. This could be regarded as a proof of the success of the experiment that led to the data. Status effects are less clear, and the influence of working in the same area on the relationship seems to depend to some extent on the model applied. Whether and how the actors could be assigned to different groups has not become very clear, as the methods presented gave different solutions. If anything, the grouping seems related to scientific status, not to research area.

The difference in (ease of) interpretation underlines the differences between the two classes of stochastic models we discussed. Modeling the ties using dyadic and actor covariate information is relatively straightforward because the focus is on the explanatory power of the covariates and less on unexplained differences between actors. In the models for finding groups of actors, there seems to be a need to interpret the groups a posteriori using additional (covariate) information as well.

The latent space models with covariates form in this sense an interesting hybrid class of models with the possibility of using covariate information and finding groups, although this does not solve the problem of interpreting the latent space dimension(s), capturing a form of triadic dependence. The random effects in the models for ties can be regarded as latent variables as well, forming a two-dimensional latent space of (unexplained) sender and receiver effects related to the actors. Such an interpretation is easier and more straightforward than the interpretation of the latent space defined by the bilinear model and latent space models. Even if no further interpretation can be obtained, it is expected that modeling network dependence explicitly improves the estimates of the covariate parameters.

All models and methods presented can be estimated with (more or less readily) available software. The development of the R packages for social network analysis have made it almost easy to apply the complex latent position cluster models. The interpretation of social network data, however, remains not very easy. It requires the expertise of applied researchers, who, just like the EIES researchers, may want to have colleagues with statistical expertise in their network.

ACKNOWLEDGMENTS

The authors would like to thank Christian Steglich, Tom Snijders, and Peter Carrington for helpful comments, and Ken Frank for advice on the use of KliqueFinder.

NOTES

1 The principles of blockmodeling are laid out by Doreian et al. (this volume); see also De Nooy et al. (2005) and Wasserman and Faust (1994, Chapter 10).

2 Although the availability of software is discussed to some extent, a more complete overview of software for network analysis can be found in Huisman and van Duijn's chapter (this volume). Full-color versions of the figures are available on http://www.gmw.rug.nl/~huisman/sna/figures.html.

3 This is just a simple and straightforward way to express status differences among the researchers and is here mainly used for illustration. We have not investigated other definitions and cannot claim that this would be the best or most meaningful way to operationalize status. The square-root transformation is preferred over the log-transformation, another commonly used transformation of right-skewed data,

because it preserves the 0 and 1, both frequently occurring as citation numbers.

4 A straightforward multilevel model is obtained for egocentric data, where (ties to) alters are nested in egos, under the assumption of nonoverlapping ego networks, leading to a simple distinction of within-ego and between-ego variance (see also Van Duijn et al., 1999).

5 Note that it would have been possible to use the acquaintanceship network instead of the binary friendship network, because the network is used as a covariate.

6 The results are based on a sample of 1,000 draws from a sample of 50,000 from the posterior distribution of the parameters, taking every 50th draw, after a burn-in of 50,000.

7 Note that the p_1 model and its early extensions with categorical actor variables are also considered stochastic blockmodels (with groups defined a priori) because in these models the actors belonging to the same group are stochastically equivalent.

REFERENCES

Anderson, C.J. and Wasserman, S. (1992) 'Building stochastic blockmodels', *Social Networks*, 14(1–2): 137–61.

Anselin, L. (1988) *Spatial Econometrics: Methods and Models*. Dordrecht, Netherlands: Kluwer Academic.

Boer, P., Huisman, M., Snijders, T.A.B., Steglich, C.E.G., Wichers, L.H.Y. and Zeggelink, E.P.H. (2006) *StOCNET: An Open Software System for the Advanced Statistical Analysis of Social Networks*. Version 1.8. Groningen: ICS, University of Groningen/SciencePlus.

Borgatti, S.P. (2002) *NetDraw: Graph Visualization Software*. Harvard: Analytic Technologies.

Borgatti, S.P., Everett, M.G. and Freeman, L.C. (2002) *UCINET 6 for Windows: Software for Social Network Analysis*. Harvard, MA: Analytic Technologies.

Burt, R.S. (1987) 'Social contagion and innovation: Cohesion versus structural equivalence', *American Journal of Sociology*, 92(6): 1287–335.

Butts, C.T. (2008) 'Social network analysis with sna', *Journal of Statistical Software*, 24(6): 30.

Cook, W.L. and Kenny, D.A. (2005) 'The actor-partner interdependence model: A model of bidirectional effects in developmental studies', *International Journal of Behavioral Development*, 29(2): 101–9.

Cyram (2009) *Cyram NetMiner 3*. Seoul: Cyram Co., Ltd.

Dekker, D., Krackhardt, D. and Snijders, T.A.B. (2007) 'Sensitivity of MRQAP tests to collinearity and autocorrelation conditions', *Psychometrika*, 72(4): 563–81.

De Nooy, W., Mrvar, A. and Batagelj, V. (2005) *Exploratory Social Network Analysis with Pajek*. Cambridge: Cambridge University Press.

Doreian, P. (1980) 'Linear models with spatially distributed data.' *Sociological Methods and Research*, 9(1): 29–60.

Frank, K.A. (1995) 'Identifying cohesive subgroups', *Social Networks,* 17(1): 27–56.

Frank, K.A. (1996) 'Mapping interactions within and between cohesive subgroups', *Social Networks,* 18(2): 93–119.

Frank, K. (2009) *KliqueFinder for Windows.* Version 0.11. East Lansing: Michigan State University.

Freeman, S.C. and Freeman L.C. (1979) 'The networks network: A study of the impact of a new communications medium on sociometric structure', *Social Science Research Reports 46.* Irvine: University of California.

Friedkin, N.E. (1998) *A Structural Theory of Social Influence.* Cambridge: Cambridge University Press.

Gerlsma, C., Snijders, T.A.B., van Duijn, M.A.J. and Emmelkamp, P.M.G. (1997) 'Parenting and psychopathology: Differences in family members perceptions of parental rearing styles', *Personality and Individual Differences,* 23(2): 271–82.

Gill, P.S. and Swartz, T.B. (2004) 'Bayesian analysis of directed graphs data with applications to social networks', *Journal of the Royal Statistical Society. Series C (Applied Statistics),* 53(2): 249–60.

Goldenberg, A., Zheng, A.X., Fienberg, S.E. and Airoldi, E.M. (2009) 'A survey of statistical network models', *Foundations and Trends in Machine Learning,* 2(2): 129–233.

Handcock, M.S., Hunter, D.R., Butts, C.T., Goodreau, S.M., Krivitsky , P.N. and Morris, M. (2003) *Statnet: Software Tools for the Statistical Modeling of Network Data.* Version 2.1-1.31.

Handcock, M.A., Raftery, A.E. and Tantrum, J.M. (2007) 'Model-based clustering for social networks. With discussion', *Journal of the Royal Statistical Society A,* 170(2): 301–54.

Hanneman, R.A. and Riddle, M. (2005) *Introduction to Social Network Methods.* Riverside: University of California. http://faculty.ucr.edu/~hanneman/.

Hoff, P.D. (2005) 'Bilinear mixed-effects models for dyadic data', *Journal of the American Statistical Association,* 100(469): 286–95.

Hoff, P.D., Raftery, A.E. and Handcock, M.S. (2002) 'Latent space approaches to social network analysis', *Journal of the American Statistical Association,* 97(460): 1090–98.

Holland, P.W. and Leinhardt, S. (1981) 'An exponential family of probability distributions for directed graphs', *Journal of the American Statistical Association,* 76(373): 33–50.

Hubert, L.J. (1987) *Assignment Methods in Combinatorial Data Analysis.* New York: Marcel Dekker.

Kenny, D.A., Kashy, D.A. and Cook, W.L. (2006) *Dyadic Data Analysis.* New York: Guilford.

Kenny, D.A. and La Voie, L. (1984) 'The social relations model', in L. Berkowitz (ed.), *Advances in Experimental Social Psychology,* Vol. 18. New York: Academic Press. pp. 141–82.

Krackhardt, D. (1987) 'QAP partialling as a test of spuriousness', *Social Networks,* 9(2): 171–86.

Krivitsky, P.N. and Handcock, M.S. (2008) 'Fitting latent cluster models for networks with latentnet', *Journal of Statistical Software,* 24(5): 1–23.

Krivitsky, P.N., Handcock, M.S., Raftery, A.E. and Hoff, P.D. (2009) 'Representing degree distributions, clustering, and homophily in social networks with latent cluster random effects models', *Social Networks* 31(3): 204–13.

Lazega, E. and van Duijn, M.A.J. (1997) 'Formal structure and exchanges of advice in a law firm: A logistic regression model for dyadic network data', *Social Networks,* 19(4): 375–97.

Leenders, R.Th.A.J. (2002) 'Modeling social influence through network autocorrelation: Constructing the weight matrix', *Social Networks,* 24(1): 21–47.

Nowicki, K. and Snijders, T.A.B. (2001) 'Estimation and prediction for stochastic blockstructures', *Journal of the American Statistical Association,* 96(455): 1077–87.

O'Malley, A.J. and Marsden, P.V. (2008) 'The analysis of social networks', *Health Services and Outcomes Research Methodology,* 8(4): 222–69.

Ord, K. (1975) 'Estimation methods for models of spatial interaction', *Journal of the American Statistical Association,* 70(349): 120–26.

Rasbash, J., Charlton, C., Browne, W.J., Healy, M. and Cameron, B. (2005) *MLwiN Version 2.02.* Bristol: Centre for Multilevel Modelling, University of Bristol.

Robins, G.L., Snijders, T.A.B., Wang, P., Handcock, M.S. and Pattison, P. (2007) 'Recent developments in exponential random graph (p_ p*) models for social networks', *Social Networks,* 29(2): 192–215.

Schweinberger, M. and Snijders, T.A.B. (2003) 'Settings in social networks: A measurement model', *Sociological Methodology,* 33(1): 307–41.

Scott, J. (2000) *Social Network Analysis: A Handbook.* London: Sage.

Shortreed, S., Handcock, M.S. and Hoff, P.D. (2006) 'Positional estimation within a latent space model for networks', *Methodology,* 2(1): 24–33.

Snijders, T.A.B. and Bosker, R.J. (1999) *Multilevel Analysis: An Introduction to Basic and Advanced Multilevel Modeling.* London: Sage.

Snijders, T.A.B. and Kenny, D.A. (1999) 'The social relations model for family data: A multilevel approach', *Personal Relationships,* 6(4): 471–86.

Snijders, T.A.B. and Nowicki, K. (1997) 'Estimation and prediction for stochastic blockmodels for graphs with latent block structure', *Journal of Classification,* 14(1): 75–100.

Snijders, T.A.B., Pattison, P.E., Robins, G.L. and Handcock, M.S. (2006) 'New specifications for exponential random graph models', *Sociological Methodology,* 36(1): 99–153.

Steglich, C., Snijders, T.A.B. and Pearson, M. (2010) 'Dynamic networks and behavior: Separating selection from influence', *Sociological Methodology,* 40(1): 329–393.

Tallberg, C. (2005) 'A Bayesian approach to modeling stochastic blockstructures with covariates', *Journal of Mathematical Sociology,* 29(1): 1–23.

Van Duijn, M.A.J., Snijders, T.A.B. and Zijlstra, B.J.H. (2004) 'p_2: A random effects model with covariates for indirected graphs', *Statistica Neerlandica,* 58(2): 234–54.

Van Duijn, M.A.J., van Busschbach, J.T. and Snijders, T.A.B. (1999) 'Multilevel analysis of personal networks as dependent variables', *Social Networks,* 21(2): 187–209.

Wang, Y.J. and Wong, G.Y. (1987) 'Stochastic blockmodels for directed graphs', *Journal of the American Statistical Association,* 82(397): 8–19.

Wasserman, S. and Faust, K. (1994) *Social Network Analysis: Methods and Applications.* Cambridge: Cambridge University Press.

Wasserman, S. and Pattison, P. (1996) 'Logit models and logistic regression for social networks: I. An introduction to Markov graphs and p*', *Psychometrika,* 61(3): 401–25.

Wong, G.Y. (1987) 'Bayesian models for directed graphs', *Journal of the American Statistical Association,* 82(397): 140–48.

Zijlstra, B.J.H. (2008) 'Random effects models for directed graphs with covariates'. Unpublished Ph.D. thesis, University of Groningen, The Netherlands.

Zijlstra, B.J.H., van Duijn, M.A.J. and Snijders, T.A.B. (2005) 'Model selection in random effects models for directed graphs using approximated Bayes factor', *Statistica Neerlandica,* 59(1): 107–18.

Zijlstra, B.J.H., van Duijn, Marijtje A.J., and Snijders, Tom A.B. (2006) 'The multilevel p_2 model: A random effects model for the analysis of multiple social networks', *Methodology* 2(1): 42–47.

Zijlstra, B.J.H., van Duijn, M.A.J. and Snijders, T.A.B. (2009) 'MCMC estimation of the p_2 network regression model with crossed random effects', *British Journal of Mathematical and Statistical Psychology,* 62(1): 143–66.

32

Exponential Random Graph Models for Social Networks

Garry Robins

INTRODUCTION

Humans constantly monitor and respond to their social environment. We seek advantage from the opportunities the social environment presents, to adapt our behaviors in response to social constraints imposed on us, and to change our social worlds to maximize those opportunities and minimize those constraints. This incessant flow of social process implies that social networks are not fixed structures that are predetermined and singular. Rather, they are changeable, evolving not towards a single optimal point – for there is no single optimal point of social structure – but towards a *range* of varying networks, each broadly consistent with one another but instantiated at different points in time. This constant change does not imply that social networks are random and unpredictable. They are built by social processes that are ongoing and multiple, and they result in the presence of observable network substructures. Each network presents with a "structural signature" that embodies certain self-organizing principles. For a given network, the stability of these principles arises from the constancy of general social behaviors that we as humans have evolved, combined with the more specific norms, localized cultures, and other particular features of the social contexts within which we operate, features that do not change rapidly. But these organizing principles can and do vary locally to a greater or lesser extent, so they are not deterministic and do not have an optimum. Social processes are variable; social networks are stochastic entities; network properties need to be assessed statistically.

How can a researcher, confronted by only a single network observation, infer particular organizing principles for that network? In what sense can we detect a structural signature? Even when data are impeccably collected under the very best of conditions, a single network observation is no more than a solitary instance from an ongoing stream of change. Yet because of the relative constancy of network organizing principles, a single network observation captures the accumulation of social processes, like an archaeological trace. Stable organizing principles will result in patterns of network ties that can be observed in the data, even when data are from a single instance in time. These patterns of network ties are indeed the structural signature of the network and provide evidence from which we may infer something of the social processes that build the network.

So we look for patterns in the network. Yet it is not sufficient to inspect the data for one pattern at a time, because structures build on one another. For instance, a triangle contains three network ties, so it follows that if the network has many ties we will see more triangles simply by chance. The question then is, *given* the density of the network, do we see more triangles than expected? If so, perhaps we need to postulate a specific social process that could lead to triangles (e.g., network closure – see below). If not, we have no need for a triangulation mechanism, as density alone – the propensity for individuals within the network to form network ties – is a sufficient and parsimonious explanation.

Exponential random graph models (ERGMs) – sometimes called p^* models – are a family of statistical models for social networks that permit inference about prominent patterns in the data, given the presence of other network structures. In a loose sense, they enable network pattern recognition. There are several classes of ERGMs, some with a long tradition in social network analysis. Holland and Leinhardt's (1981) p_1 model can be seen as an early dyadic independent version. Frank and Strauss (1986) proposed Markov random graph models, further elaborated by Wasserman and Pattison (1996). Robins, Pattison et al. (2007) provide an introductory review of these earlier developments. Recent work has focused on new improvements to model specifications, as described below. There will be more model development in the future, but the underlying impetus will continue to be the search for a parsimonious description of the small network patterns – termed *configurations*[1] – that can be seen as the building blocks of the network.

Each different class of ERGM involves different assumptions of dependence among network ties. These are the theoretical ground for different models, not just technical decisions. Through a dependence assumption, a researcher makes claims about the type, extent, and accumulation of patterning that builds the network. Dependence is crucial. Independence of observations – the fundament of general linear model statistical techniques – cannot simply be presupposed. The presence of some ties will encourage other ties to come into existence, to be maintained, or to be destroyed. The dependence assumption is thereby a theory about the basis of tie-formation processes. The network's self-organizing principles represent the way that ties lead to other ties (or their absence). The observable configurations of ties then constitute the network's structural signature.

The focus on network ties is important: attention is on pairs of actors and the possible relationships between them. This is a major difference from other areas of social science where the unit of analysis is typically the individual. This is not to say that features of individuals need be excluded. They can be important explanations of how ties come into existence and need to be incorporated into models in ways described below. But in this chapter, we concentrate on methods for understanding endogenous network tie formation, using exogenous node attribute information to assist.

THE GENERAL FORM OF AN EXPONENTIAL RANDOM GRAPH MODEL

The intent of this chapter is to provide a relatively intuitive introduction to exponential random graph models. However, a modicum of mathematical notation and technical terminology is required. A social network comprises a set of n actors and a set of network ties among those actors. For every pair i and j of actors in the network, let $X_{ij} = 1$ if there is a network tie from actor i to actor j, and $X_{ij} = 0$ if there is no such tie. X_{ij} is then a binary random variable, and we denote $\mathbf{X}$ as the matrix of all such variables (with empty cells X_{ii} on the diagonal, since actors are assumed not to have ties with themselves). Let x_{ij} be the observed value of the variable X_{ij} and $\mathbf{x}$ the matrix of observed ties (i.e., the observed network). $\mathbf{X}$ may be *directed* (so that X_{ij} is distinguished from X_{ji}) or *undirected*.

For a given set of n actors, an ERGM models an observed network $\mathbf{x}$ by assigning a probability to every network of n actors, based on network configurations that are hypothesized through the dependence hypothesis. The form of the model is:

$$\Pr(\mathbf{X} = \mathbf{x}) = (1/\kappa) \exp\{\Sigma_A \, \eta_A g_A(\mathbf{x})\} \quad (32.1)$$

where:

the summation is over all configuration types A;

η_A is a parameter corresponding to configuration type A;

$g_A(\mathbf{x})$ is the *network statistic* for A and is a count of the number of configurations A observed in $\mathbf{x}$ (although recent work has extended the statistic beyond a simple count);

κ normalizes (1) to be a proper probability distribution.

For readers not keen on mathematical formulations, equation 32.1 essentially tells us that the probability of a network $\mathbf{x}$ depends on the configurations A, that is, small network patterns such as triangles or reciprocated ties. These configurations can be chosen by the researcher but at a deeper level can be derived from theories of dependence among ties, as presented below. Given a set of configurations, the probability of $\mathbf{x}$ depends on how many configurations are actually observed in $\mathbf{x}$ (the statistics $g_A(\mathbf{x})$), weighted by how important those patterns are (the parameters η_A). In simple terms, if a configuration is important, and there are many observed in $\mathbf{x}$, then the model says the probability of $\mathbf{x}$ will be larger. (In that sense, the summation inside the exponential is equivalent to a regression.) Equation 32.1 implies that there is a probability distribution of all possible networks with n nodes, with each possible network having a distinct probability.

If we have a single network observation $\mathbf{x}$, our goal is to find a set of parameter values that best represents our network, and then to interpret the results in terms of the patterns that are important in $\mathbf{x}$.

Before considering how we do this, it is worth noting that a tractable model has to impose some level of *homogeneity* to limit the number of parameters. Typically this means that there is one parameter for one type of configuration: for instance, one parameter for triangles in the network, rather than one for every single possible triangle in the network. The idea is that a single process of triangulation can be inferred across the entire network, with local variations subsumed as statistical noise. Of course, this is an assumption that may or may not be correct, as evidenced by how well the model fits the data.

Parameters

From where do we get parameter values η_A that represent the importance of different configurations in our model? For a given network dataset **x**, we seek to *estimate* parameter values using the following approach. The model assumes that **x** is a single network from the distribution of networks given by equation 32.1, for which we do not know parameter values η_A. In reality, **x** could conceivably come from a distribution of networks in which it is very unusual, but we have no grounds to suppose that. Rather **x** is *most likely* to come from a distribution in which it is typical. Accordingly, we seek parameter values that produce a distribution of graphs in which **x** is most typical. These parameter values are called *maximum likelihood estimates*. Actual procedures for maximum likelihood estimation are discussed below. Of course, there is no guarantee that a set of maximum likelihood estimates exists: it may be, for instance, that the configurations chosen for our model are not adequate to represent the data. But a well-specified model for the data will have sensible maximum likelihood estimates.

When a parameter estimate is large and positive, we infer that the configuration occurs more frequently than expected by chance, given the other effects in the model. For instance, suppose we fit a model to a directed network using two parameters: an *arc* parameter that represents the baseline propensity to form ties and a *reciprocity* parameter that represents the presence of reciprocated arcs within dyads. A large and positive reciprocity estimate indicates a distinct process of reciprocation over and above the baseline propensity to form arcs (i.e., the network density). On the other hand, a large but negative parameter estimate indicates a tendency against such configurations. In this way, the set of parameter estimates indicate the structural signature of the network, enabling us to make inferences about the self-organizing network processes that are operating.

NETWORK BUILDING BLOCKS FOR UNDIRECTED GRAPHS

We begin by describing the various configurations relevant to different families of ERGMs for undirected networks. There are currently three important classes of models, each based on a different dependence hypothesis.

Bernoulli graph models

The simplest dependence hypothesis is of no dependence at all among the tie variables. This assumption results in the Bernoulli random graph model (also known as simple random graph, or Erdös-Renyi, models [Erdös and Renyi, 1959], where the only applicable configuration is that of a single edge [Figure 32.1a]). This model simply proposes that pairs of individuals have a propensity to form ties with a given probability p. The resulting distribution exhibits networks of varying density with a mean of p. The probability of any graph **x** in this distribution can be described as:

$$\Pr(\mathbf{X} = \mathbf{x}) = (1/\kappa) \exp\{\theta\, L(\mathbf{x})\} \qquad (32.2)$$

where θ is an edge or density parameter and $L(\mathbf{x})$ is the number of edges in the graph **x**. The maximum likelihood estimate of θ turns out to be log $\{p/(1-p)\}$, where p is the density of **x**.

The Bernoulli assumption is inadequate for most social networks because social relationships are typically intertwined in ways that are not independent. In particular, a Bernoulli graph model does not represent well the way in which social networks tend to *cluster* into denser regions of network ties. The most basic form that a clustering process can take is triangulation, where three actors, if they are connected through a two-path, tend to form a clique (for three nodes, a triangle). In social network theory, this frequently observed configuration represents a process known as *network closure*. With independent ties, a Bernoulli model has no mechanism (other than chance) whereby a two-path can lead to network closure. Another common feature of real social network data is a skewed degree distribution whereby a small number of nodes have high degree, while many nodes have low degree. This skew cannot be adequately captured using a Bernoulli graph model, which tends to produce symmetric degree distributions. Nevertheless, the Bernoulli model can be a useful baseline and has important properties that are well studied (e.g., Bollobás, 1985).

Markov random graph models

Frank and Strauss (1986) proposed the more realistic dependence assumption that tie variables might be conditionally dependent if they shared an actor. The resulting models were called *Markov random graph models*. Under Markov dependence, tie variables X_{ij} and X_{ik} are conditionally dependent because they both involve actor i, whereas X_{ij} and X_{rs} with no nodes in common are conditionally independent.[2]

It can be shown that configurations for a Markov random graph model comprise those where every edge is connected to every other edge in the configuration. A little thought convinces that, apart from the simple edge (Figure 32.1a), possible configurations are those with star-like structures (with all edges centered on one actor – Figure 32.1b – with the number of edges k termed a *k-star*) and the triangle (Figure 32.1c). Markov dependence then results in models that have a capacity to handle variation in the number of degrees (through the star parameters) and the tendency for network closure (through the triangle parameter).

Of course, for the sake of parsimony we do not have to include parameters for all the star configurations in the model, any more than we have to include every higher order interaction in a standard regression. So, following equation 32.1, a simplified model including edge, 2-star, 3-star, and triangle parameters would take the following form:

$$Pr(\mathbf{X} = \mathbf{x}) = (1/\kappa) \exp(\theta\, L(\mathbf{x}) + \\ \sigma_2\, S_2(\mathbf{x}) + \sigma_3\, S_3(\mathbf{x}) + \tau\, T(\mathbf{x})) \quad (32.3)$$

where, as for Bernoulli graphs, θ is an edge or density parameter, and $L(\mathbf{x})$ the number of edges in $\mathbf{x}$; σ_2 and σ_3 are parameters for 2- and 3-stars, respectively, and $S_2(\mathbf{x})$ and $S_3(\mathbf{x})$ are the numbers of 2- and 3-stars in $\mathbf{x}$; τ is a triangle parameter, and $T(\mathbf{x})$ is a count of the number of triangles in $\mathbf{x}$.

The four-parameter model in equation 32.3 suggests the network is built up from intertwining processes: a baseline propensity to form ties; (nonlinear) tendencies for nodes to have differing numbers of partners, depending on the star parameters; and a tendency for network closure. For instance, if the 2-star parameter is positive and the 3-star parameter is negative, actors seek multiple partners but with a ceiling effect. Some level of

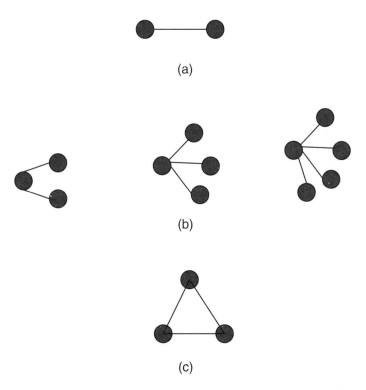

(a)

(b)

(c)

Figure 32.1 Configurations for Markov random graph model for undirected graphs (a) edge; (b) 2-star, 3-star, 4-star (higher-order star configurations may also be included); (c) triangles

network activity is desired but too much is costly (Robins et al., 2005).

For several years, Markov random graph models were the ERGM mainstay. Wasserman and Pattison (1986) elaborated them as p^* models, with extensions to multivariate (Pattison and Wasserman, 1999) and valued networks (Robins et al., 1999). However, with more sophisticated estimation and simulation procedures, it became apparent that Markov random graph models were frequently not adequate to model real data. Despite the hopes that they could handle skewed degree distributions and areas of triangulation, these models faced difficulties when there were serious heterogeneities in the data, as is often the case for real social networks. There were two steps that needed to be taken: first, a more complex representation of triangulation was required (single triangles were insufficient to describe the tendencies for denser regions of the network), and a method to permit greater heterogeneities in degrees and clustering.

Social circuit models

Snijders et al. (2006) proposed new specifications for ERGMs to be used in addition to Markov parameters. These were intended to overcome the deficiencies of Markov models and were based on a novel dependence assumption. Pattison and Robins (2002) had argued that dependence between tie variables might arise because of the presence of other network edges: *partial conditional dependence.* Snijders et al. proposed a version of partial conditional dependence termed *social circuit dependence* (Robins, Snijders et al., 2007b).

Under the social circuit assumption, two tie variables not sharing a node may be still conditionally dependent, provided other edges exist in the observed network. In particular, there need to be at least two observed network ties such that if the two original tie variables are also present, a four-cycle is created. So, for instance, tie variables X_{kl} and X_{rs} become conditionally dependent when $X_{rk} = X_{ls} = 1$ in the observed network. Although this assumption may seem complex, the argument is relatively straightforward and similar ideas go back at least to Coleman (1988). Suppose Rochelle and Ken have a friendship, and also Liam and Sally, so that $X_{rk} = X_{ls} = 1$. If Ken knows Liam, the chances of Sally coming to know Rochelle increase: that is, X_{rs} is contingent on the state of X_{kl} – and vice versa – so that the two variables are dependent. There are two important points. First, this argument simply does not work unless $X_{rk} = X_{ls} = 1$, so that the dependence *emerges* from

network observations. Second, the argument is independent of triangulation, so there is no requirement that Ken also need have a tie to Sally (although that could be the case). The point is more apparent with a relationship less generic than simple "knowing." Suppose that the relationship is some form of professional collaboration, so that $X_{rk} = X_{ls} = 1$, which means that Liam and Sally collaborate on one project, and Rochelle and Ken on another. Then, a little thought will show that it is quite possible that collaboration in the form of a four-cycle could emerge across four different projects, without any triangulation.

Nevertheless, it is equally apparent that triangulated collaboration is possible, and perhaps even likely, so Snijders et al. (2006) proposed that Markov dependence be retained in models, with social circuit dependence an additional refinement. Snijders et al. then showed that a number of new configurations would be possible. While Markov star structures (Figure 32.1) continue to be important elements, new configurations reflecting both triangulated and nontriangulated cycles were consistent with the dependence assumption. *Multiple triangulation* configurations, termed *k-triangles* (in analogue to *k*-stars), were now possible: a *k*-triangle has an edge between two nodes i and j (the *base* of the *k*-triangle), with multiple triangles involving k *shared partners* of i and j built on a common base (Figure 32.2). Additional configurations representing short-range *multiple connectivity* were based on two-paths between nodes i and j (irrespective of whether they were tied or not). These configurations were termed *k-2paths* (Figure 32.2).

These novel configurations were the first step proposed by Snijders et al. (2006). The second step involved a further extension to model homogeneity, where higher order parameters were assumed to have a relationship to lower order parameters, in such a way that the effects of higher order parameters were attenuated so as not to dominate. They proposed that *k*-star, *k*-triangle, and *k*-2path parameters could each be incorporated into one degree-based parameter, one triangulation parameter, and one connectivity parameter, respectively. The specific proposal was an *alternating parameter* form. For the star parameters the alternating form was $\sigma_k = -(1/\lambda)\,\sigma_{k-1}$, where σ_k is the parameter for a *k*-star and λ is an attenuation factor, with analogous versions for the *k*-triangle and *k*-2path parameters. Snijders et al. (2006) showed that for the star parameters this step explicitly models the degree distribution but puts more weight on the numbers of nodes with lower degrees, with weights decreasing geometrically as the degrees increase (see also Hunter, 2007; Hunter and Handcock, 2006). The upshot is that

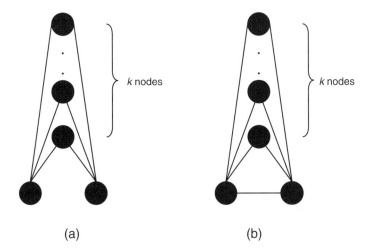

Figure 32.2 Some configurations for social circuit model for undirected graphs (a) _k_-2path; (b) _k_-triangle

heterogeneities in the form of very high degree nodes can be better tolerated by the model. Similarly, the _k_-triangle parameter models (with a geometric attenuation) the distribution of shared partners across all pairs of tied nodes. This parameter is much better than the Markov triangle parameter at dealing with regions of the network with high triangulation. The attenuation factor can be set at a given value ($\lambda = 2$ has been widely used – Robins et al., 2007 a,b) but can also be specified as a parameter and an optimal value estimated (Hunter 2007; Hunter and Handcock, 2006).

SOME TECHNICAL ISSUES

Simulation

By choosing a model specification and setting parameter values, it is possible to simulate exponential random graph models using standard statistical algorithms (e.g., Metropolis-Hastings algorithms) to produce a distribution of graphs, from which a sample of graphs can be taken (Handcock, 2002, 2003; Hunter and Handcock, 2006; Robins et al., 2005; Snijders, 2002; Strauss, 1986). The properties of the sampled graphs can be examined, including properties that do not relate directly to model configurations. For instance, it is possible to examine the typical degree distribution, geodesic distribution, level of clustering, and so on. This procedure permits understanding of the properties of exponential random graph models with different parameters.

For instance, for 30-node networks, consider three different models:

1 Bernoulli model (equation 2), with $\theta = -2$
2 Markov model (equation 3), with $\theta = -2$, $\sigma_2 = 1$, $\sigma_3 = -0.5$, $\tau = 0$
3 Markov model (equation 3), with $\theta = -2$, $\sigma_2 = 1$, $\sigma_3 = -0.5$, $\tau = 1$

The first model is a simple random graph model, whereas the second imposes constraints on the degree distribution, notably, a propensity for nodes to exhibit some variability in degrees (the positive 2-star parameter) but with a tendency against nodes having high degrees (the negative 3-star parameter). The third model includes the star effects of the second model but also includes a positive triangulation parameter.

By simulating this model with 500,000 iterations, and taking a sample of 1,000 graphs we examine the propensity for triangulation for each model. Figure 32.3 gives histograms of the number of triangles for each sample, as well as an example graph from each simulation. It can be seen that the number of triangles is considerably greater for model 3, a result that is not surprising given that we have explicitly included a positive triangulation effect in that model.

Estimation

For observed network data, simulation can be used in algorithms to estimate parameter values. Strauss and Ikeda (1990) originally suggested

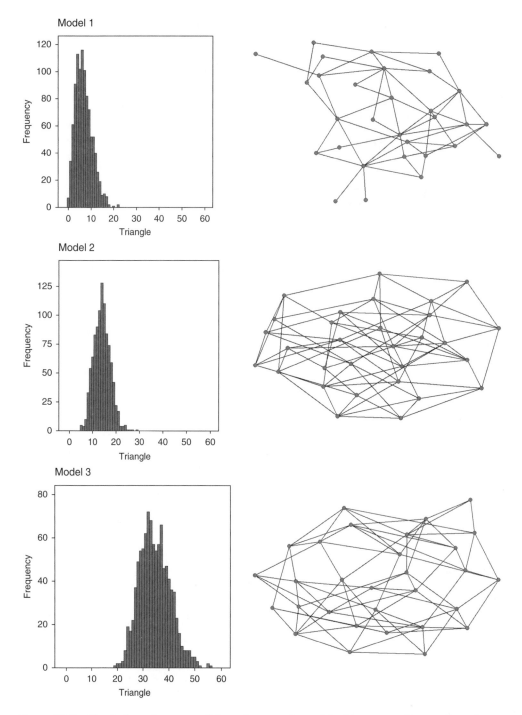

Figure 32.3   Simulation of exponential random graph models: histograms for number of triangles for samples of 1,000 graphs for three models on 30 nodes, together with an example graph from each simulation

pseudo-likelihood estimation based on logistic regression, a procedure approximate at best and in some cases quite misleading (Van Duijn et al., 2009). Monte Carlo Markov chain maximum likelihood estimation (MCMCMLE) is a more principled approach. There is a variety of possible methods but they share a common conceptual basis. Approximate parameter estimates are obtained as a starting point, and then the model is simulated and the means of the distributions of model statistics compared with the observed data. The trial parameter estimates are then adjusted to attempt to get closer to the means. Once the means are sufficiently close to the observed data, the estimation has *converged* and the final parameter estimates approximate the maximum likelihood values. Approximate standard errors for the parameter estimates can also be obtained, enabling inference about whether a parameter is important in the model. Snijders (2002) and Hunter and Handcock (2006) discuss different methods within this general approach. Robins, Snijders et al. (2007b) review publicly available software that can estimate these models (see also Handcock et al., 2008).

Diagnostic goodness of fit

With convergent parameter estimates, we can investigate how well the model reproduces the data using simulation, including aspects of the data not explicitly modeled. Suppose for instance that the graph in the bottom righthand corner of Figure 32.3 (from model 3 with the positive triangle parameter) is the observed social network. The data have 32 triangles, whereas the sample of Bernoulli graphs (model 1) has a mean of 6.8 triangles, with a standard deviation of 3.7. So the Bernoulli model does not convincingly reproduce this number of triangles, in that a network with 32 triangles is highly unlikely for a Bernoulli model with $\theta = -2$ (as can be seen from the histogram at the top lefthand corner of the figure). Rather than relying on visual inspection, the observed graph with 32 triangles, assuming it came from the Bernoulli model, has a *t*-statistic of nearly 7 in the distribution of triangles from the Bernoulli model. Using the heuristic rule that observations are unlikely if they have a *t*-ratio with an absolute value larger than 2, the distribution of triangles for this Bernoulli model does not seem a plausible representation of triangulation in the data.

Such a procedure gives an indication of which aspects of the observed data a model can plausibly reproduce and which it cannot. Graphical inspection can also be conducted to decide qualitatively

how well a model is consistent with the degree distribution, the geodesic distribution, and other global features of the data (Hunter et al., 2008). This heuristic procedure amounts to a diagnostic goodness of fit examination of a model.

Model degeneracy, nonconvergence, and multiple regions

The previous paragraphs have supposed that it is possible to obtain a convergent set of parameter estimates. Sometimes this is not so for a given model applied to a given network. A related problem arises when a set of parameter values implies two or more regions of graphs, resulting in a bimodal or multimodal distribution of edges. Often these two regions feature the uninteresting possibilities of the (near) empty and the complete graph. In cases like these, the model will be a poor representation of the data, and the models are described as *near degenerate* (Handcock, 2002, 2003). It is beyond the scope of this chapter to discuss these issues in depth but interested readers can refer to a number of authors who investigate details (e.g., Burda et al., 2004; Häggström and Jonasson, 1999; Handcock, 2002, 2003; Jonasson, 1999; Park and Newman, 2004; Robins, Pattison et al., 2005; Robins et al., 2007; Snijders, 2002; Snijders et al., 2006). Suffice to say that, on the whole, Markov models are much more likely than social circuit models to exhibit degeneracy, multiple regions, and nonconvergence (Robins, Snijders et al., 2007b). If parameter estimation does not converge, if the model is degenerate and there is evidence of multiple regions, then the model is not adequate for the data. A different model specification is required.

EXAMPLE FOR UNDIRECTED GRAPHS

Figure 32.4 presents a simple undirected network of acquaintanceship among 20 people. The results of fitting Markov and social circuit models are presented in Table 32.1, including parameter estimates and standard errors, as well as convergence statistics. The convergence statistic is a *t*-ratio that reports how close statistics from the observed data are to the mean statistics from the distribution of graphs implied by the model. It is calculated in exactly the same way as for the heuristic goodness of fit discussed above. Good convergence is then indicated by a convergence statistic that is very small. An absolute value less than 0.1 is evidence for successful convergence (Snijders et al., 2006;

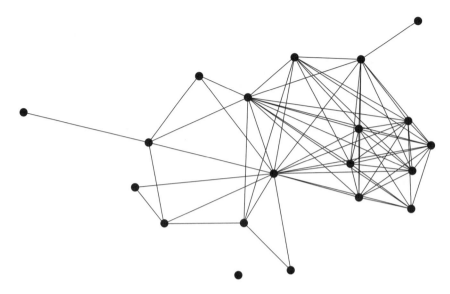

Figure 32.4   An undirected acquaintanceship network

Table 32.1 Parameter estimates, standard errors, and convergence statistics for two models for the network in Figure 32.4.

Parameter	Estimate	Standard error	Convergence
Markov model			
Edge	−2.165*	0.716	−0.046
2-star	0.108	0.100	−0.038
3-star	−0.044*	0.012	−0.032
Triangle	0.733*	0.104	−0.022
Social circuit model			
Edge	−2.232	1.270	−0.015
Popularity/Activity (*k*-stars)	−0.165	0.476	−0.015
Multiple triangulation (*k*-triangles)	1.355*	0.535	−0.016
Multiple connectivity (*k*-2paths)	−0.252*	0.088	−0.025

*indicate estimates that are more than twice the standard error in absolute value; model fitted with pnet.

Robins, Snijders et al., 2007b). We can see from the table that both models converged well.

However, good convergence does not necessarily imply that the models avoid the problem of multiple regions of graphs. Following simulations from the parameter estimates, Figure 32.5 shows distributions of the number of edges and the number of 2-stars (just as examples – we could have used other model statistics to illustrate the same point). The figure shows bimodal distributions for the Markov model but not for the social circuit model. The observed network has 68 edges and 583 2-stars, which can be seen to be in the regions of the distributions between the two

modes for the Markov model (as they must be if the model has converged – 68 edges and 583 2-stars are very close to the means of each distribution, respectively, consistent with the convergence statistics in Table 32.1). In other words, although the observed network is in the center of the two distributions as required by the estimation procedure, it is not "typical" of the networks implied by the model, with more networks having either lower or higher density (and lower and higher numbers of 2-stars). Accordingly, the Markov model is not a good representation of the data. As can be seen from panels (c) and (d) of Figure 32.5, the same problem does not arise for

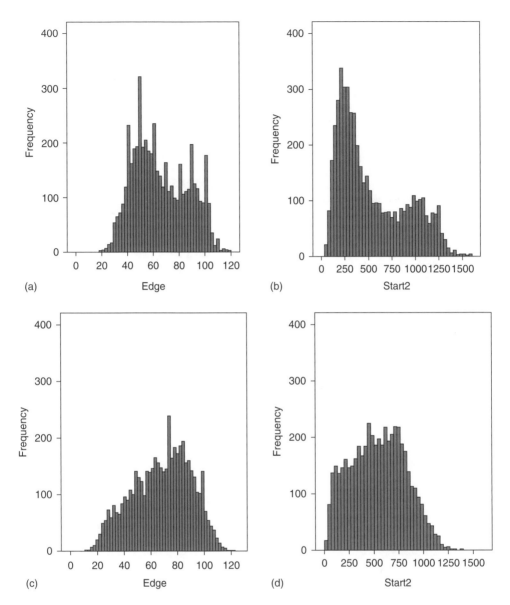

Figure 32.5   Simulation results for models from Table 32.1: histograms for (a) number of edges for Markov model; (b) number of 2-stars for Markov model; (c) number of edges for social circuit model; (d) number of 2-stars for social circuit model

the social circuit model, so the social circuit model is to be preferred.

The interpretation of the social circuit model is relatively straightforward. Important reliable effects in the model are asterisked in the table (indicating a parameter estimate in absolute value more than twice the standard error). Although not asterisked because of a large standard error (and so we cannot be entirely sure that the parameter is reliably different from zero), the negative edge parameter suggests that edges are uncommon, unless they are part of the higher order configurations represented in the model. The popularity/ activity effect (corresponding to the alternating k-star configurations) is small, suggesting that there are no particular high-degree actors in this network, unless they are involved in triangulation or multiple connectivity effects. In other words, there is no need to invoke a degree-based explanation for this network. The strongly positive triangulation effect indicates that a number of actors have formed a denser core of multiple triangles. The negative connectivity effect indicates a tendency against multiple 2-paths unless those are implicated in triangles. This suggests that triangulation occurs through the formation of k-triangle bases, rather than edges: that is, that sharing a number of network partners tends to encourage a direct tie. To use a more network-theoretic explanation, structural holes tend to lead to network closure when those holes are bridged by several others.

To see how well this model reproduces the network, we can simulate to investigate goodness of fit t-ratios for nonmodeled effects. For instance, the t-ratios for Markov 2-stars, 3-stars, and triangles are 0.15, 0.34, and 0.78. For effects that are not directly parameterized, we assess a t-statistic with an absolute value greater than two as a poorly fitted effect. So we can say that the model is plausible for the Markov configurations (perhaps not surprising given that k-star and k-triangle effects are in the model). However, the model does not do such a good job in reproducing other effects. For instance, t-ratios for the standard deviation and the skewness of the degree distribution are 2.1 and

1.1, respectively, so the model implies a degree distribution that is somewhat more spread out than is seen in the data. The global clustering coefficient[3] has a t-statistic of 3.5, indicating that, although the model does reproduce the number of triangles well, it underestimates the number of 2-stars that are implicated in triangles. The model suggests strong clustering effects, but they are even stronger in the actual data.

EXTENSIONS FOR DIRECTED GRAPHS

When dealing with directed networks, possible configurations become more complex. Wasserman and Pattison (1996) described Markov configurations for directed networks. The most common Markov configurations are depicted in Figure 32.6. Snijders et al. (2006) originally provided a limited range of directed social circuit configurations, again using the alternating parameter forms. Robins et al. (2009) proposed an extended range of social circuit configurations, including those set out in Figure 32.7.

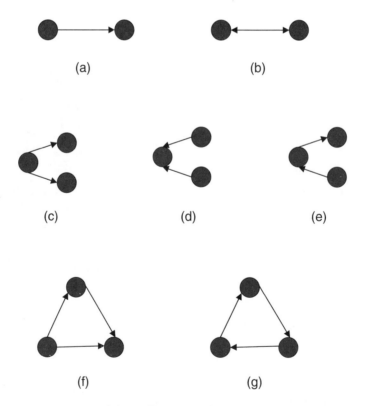

(a)

(b)

(c)

(d)

(e)

(f)

(g)

Figure 32.6   Some common Markov configurations for directed graphs. (a) Arc (b) reciprocated arc, (c) 2-outstar, (d) 2-instar, (e) 2-path, (f) transitive triad , and (g) cyclic triad

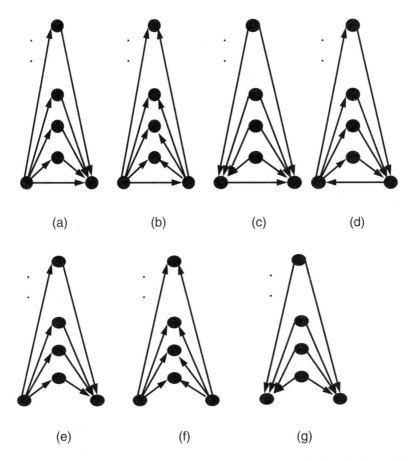

Figure 32.7 Closure and connectivity configurations for directed social circuit models: (a) path closure (AT-T); (b) activity closure (AT-U); (c) popularity closure (AT-D); (d) cyclic closure (AT-C); (e) multiple two-paths (A2P-T); (f) shared activity (A2P-U); and (g) shared popularity (A2P-D)

Robins et al. (2009) provided theoretical interpretations of the parameters associated with these closure configurations. The *path closure* parameter (Figure 32.7a), with associated statistic AT-T (for *alternating k-triangle-transitive*), represents transitive path closure. A nonclosed two-path can also represent a structural hole with connections from actors i to j through partners k, so the path closure parameter expresses tendencies for structural holes to close when there are multiple two-paths between i and j. The *activity closure* parameter (Figure 32.7b), with statistic AT-U (where U stands for "up"), represents what Robins et al. called a form of *structural homophily*, whereby actors who make similar choices of others form a tie. This is structural homophily based on shared choices or shared network activity. On the other hand, the *popularity closure* parameter, with statistic AT-D (Figure 32.7c – D

indicates "down") is a structural homophily effect based on shared popularity. The *cyclic closure* parameter, with statistic AT-C (Figure 32.7d – C for "cyclic") represents closure in the form of nontransitive (i.e., nonhierarchical) cycles. Robins et al. argue that these can be thought of as a generalized exchange version of structural hole closure.

The multiple connectivity configurations (*multiple 2paths, shared activity, shared popularity* – Figure 32.7e–g) are lower order to the closure configurations. When counterpart parameters for closure and connectivity are both in the model, inferences can be made about whether a closure effect arises because of the formation of the base or of the side of the k-triangle. The interpretations in the previous paragraph assume that the base arises because of the multiple connections between two actors. A pattern of a positive closure parameter and a negative connectivity parameter would suggest that multiple connections are relatively unlikely unless they occur in closed form. This would be consistent with an argument that multiple connectivity configurations are likely to lead to closure at the base.

In addition to the closure and connectivity configurations in Figure 32.7, Robins et al. proposed parameters for the following effects:

- *density* and *reciprocity*, as in Markov models (Figure 32.6a, b);
- *activity spread* and *popularity spread*, with associated statistics of alternating *k*-outstars and alternating *k*-instars, as originally proposed by Snijders et al.; these parameters control for the outdegree and indegree distribution, respectively;
- *sources* (number of nodes with zero indegree), *sinks* (number of nodes with zero outdegree), *isolates* (number of isolated nodes);
- a *generalized transitivity* effect combining with equal strengths the path closure, activity closure, and popularity closure effects into the one parameter; a counterpart *generalized connectivity* parameter is also possible.

ACTOR ATTRIBUTES

Individual-level variables may also contribute to the formation of social relationships. Individual-level variables may be incorporated into ERGMs in a variety of ways, but here we present some simple dyadic *social selection* parameters (Robins, Elliott et al., 2001). Social selection processes occur when network relationships are formed as a result of node attributes. For instance, *homophily* is a process whereby individuals who are similar to one another form a relationship (McPherson et al., 2001).

Assuming social selection processes, we are interested in modeling the network **x** not just in terms of the network-based configurations described above but also in terms of a vector of attributes **y** that represent a measure on the nodes. Instead of equation 32.1, we then have a slightly more complex form:

$$\Pr(\mathbf{X} = \mathbf{x} \mid \mathbf{Y} = \mathbf{y}) = (1/\kappa) \exp\{\Sigma_A \, \eta_A g_A(\mathbf{x}) + \Sigma_B \, \eta_B g_B(\mathbf{x}, \mathbf{y})\} \qquad (32.4)$$

where η_B is a set of parameters relating to selection effects, and $g_B(\mathbf{x}, \mathbf{y})$ are statistics that are essentially counts of configurations that involve both attributes and network ties. In this chapter, we consider attribute variables **Y** that are either binary or continuous measures. Information about a binary attribute (with values 0 or 1) can be incorporated into visual representations of network configurations by coloring the nodes, whereas information about a continuous attribute can be incorporated using node size. For directed networks, and for each type of measure, five dyadic configurations that may be incorporated into a model (32.4) are presented in Figure 32.8.

Interpretations are straightforward. A large positive parameter estimate for configuration 32.8a provides evidence that individuals who have an attribute score of 1 (i.e., who "have" the attribute) are more active in the network (often called a *sender effect* because the "sender" of the tie has the attribute); whereas in contrast configuration 32.8b refers attribute-based popularity effect, or *receiver effect*, relating to whether people with the attribute tend to be more popular by receiving more ties. Configuration 32.8c represents a homophily effect whereby people who share the attribute are more likely to be tied. Configurations 32.8d and 32.8e are reciprocal-tie counterparts for activity/popularity and for homophily. Configurations 32.8f to 32.8j are analogous versions for continuous attribute measures.

More complex configurations with attributed nodes involving stars and triangles could also be incorporated into models (e.g., Robins, Elliott et al., 2001). The choice of parameters will be dependent on the research issue under consideration. For instance, sometimes reciprocity may not be of particular relevance to the attribute under study, so that reciprocated activity and homophily may be excluded from models in the interests of parsimony. It is usually important to include activity and popularity parameters as attribute-based main effects. Strongly positive activity and popularity parameters alone are evidence for a form of homophily since individuals with the attribute both send and receive more arcs, and hence the probability of an arc from a person with the attribute to another person with the attribute is enhanced. What we cannot ascertain, though, from these two parameters alone is whether there are distinct homophily effects over and above activity and popularity.

Example for directed networks

As an empirical example of fitting models including attributes, we fit the Krackhardt Hi-tech managers (directed) advice network (Krackhardt, 1987), including a binary attribute indicating position (1= "more senior," 0 = "less senior") and a continuous attribute for age in years. We fitted

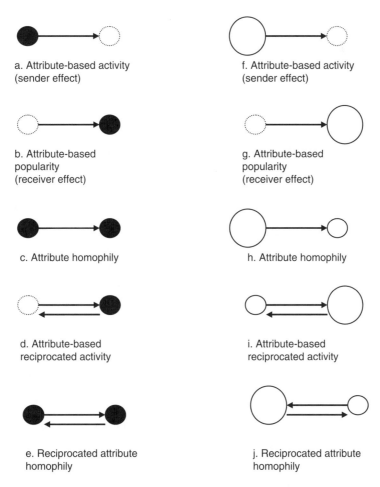

Figure 32.8   Configurations including attribute variables (binary attributes in left column; quantitative in right column. Dotted border indicates a node irrespective of attribute value; a black node indicates binary attribute value of one; the size of node for quantitative attributes indicates value of the attribute measure)

four models: the first with only network effects, the second with network effects and position, the third with network effects and age, and the fourth with network effects, position, and age. We fitted sender, receiver, and homophily parameters for attribute effects (as there was little reciprocity in the network – see below – the reciprocated versions of these parameters were excluded). After some experimentation with different triangulation configurations (Figure 32.7), we settled on a model with only the path closure and two-path connectivity parameters. Parameter estimates and standard errors are presented in Table 32.2. (Convergence statistics are not presented in the table, but all were under 0.1 in absolute value.)

From the first column of Table 32.2, we see reliable effects for path closure (positive) and multiple two-paths (negative), a pattern that indicates a tendency for structural hole closure, which is more pronounced as the number of actors who bridge the hole increase. Reciprocity is close to zero, so advice seems quite hierarchical. There is no pronounced effect of activity spread, so there is no tendency for any actors to seek advice from many others. Although we cannot be assured of the reliability of the effects represented by the positive density and negative popularity parameter estimates because of large standard errors, this pattern of estimates suggests that there is a readiness to seek advice (positive density), constrained by a tendency for no one actor to be

Table 32.2 Parameter estimates (standard errors in brackets) for four models for the Krackhardt advice network, with position and age attributes: model 1—network structural effects; model 2—network structural effects plus position; model 3—network structural effects plus age; model 4—network structural effects plus position and age (model fitted with pnet)[5]

	Structural	+ position	+ age	+position +age
Arc	3.64 (2.20)	6.09 (2.12)*	3.19(2.34)	7.17 (2.46)*
Reciprocity	0.14(0.25)	0.24 (0.30)	0.09 (0.27)	0.19 (0.31)
Activity spread	−0.64 (0.51)	0.39 (0.53)	−0.74 (0.47)	0.34 (0.56)
Popularity spread	−1.94 (1.01)	−4.11(1.05)*	−1.71(0.99)	−4.39 (1.18)*
Path closure	0.85 (0.24)*	0.62 (0.25)*	0.83(0.23)*	0.55 (0.26)
Multiple two–paths	−0.36 (0.03)*	−0.33 (0.03)*	−0.37(0.03)*	−0.33 (0.04)
Sender position		0.02(0.22)		0.02 (0.24)
Receiver position		1.03 (0.28)*		1.03 (0.29)*
Homophily position		1.11 (0.74)		1.27 (0.81)
Sender age			0.01 (0.01)	0.005 (0.01)
Receiver age			0.01(0.01)	−0.003 (0.01)
Homophily age			0.03(0.01)*	0.03 (0.01)*

*indicate estimates that are more than twice the standard error in absolute value; model fitted with pnet.

a pronounced source of advice (negative popularity). To the extent that any of these managers is a popular source of advice, this happens within triadic configurations involving path closure. If anything, the evidence here suggests that, given the various effects in the model, this is an antipreferential attachment network. Responsibility for advice is spread rather evenly among the managers: there are few obvious organizational bottlenecks here.

Including the attributes adds to the interpretation. Model 2 includes position effects. More senior managers receive more advice ties, and once this is controlled for, the positive density/negative popularity parameters become stronger (in opposite directions). So among more junior managers, advice responsibilities are spread even more equally than among senior managers. Again, reliability is uncertain because of a large standard error, but there is a suggestion here of homophily among senior managers. Model 3 includes age effects and we see a reliable effect for age homophily. Model 4 includes both position and age effects. Interpretations do not change from previous findings. This is not a trivial result and indicates that age and position effects are relatively independent in this network. If, for instance, advice tended to be sought from senior managers who were older, it is possible that age and position could have been somewhat confounded and that when both were included in the model, one set of parameters may have ceased to be important. This is not the case here.

FURTHER EXTENSIONS AND FUTURE DIRECTIONS

The form of equation 32.1 is quite general and is not restricted to a single binary network. In principle, ERGMs can be applied to any form of relational data, although there are often important and complex decisions to be made about the exact parameterization that is most suitable for actual datasets. It is beyond the scope of this article to go into full detail on possible extensions, but interested readers can consult the relevant literature in the following areas:

- Bipartite networks: Markov models were originally proposed by Skvoretz and Faust (1999), with Agneessens et al. (2004) adding node-level effects. Recently, Wang et al. (2009) updated model specification with social circuit-type dependence assumptions.
- Valued networks: There has not been much recent work on valued networks. Robins et al. (1999) provided a Markov parameterization.
- Multivariate networks: Human social life implicates many different types of networks that can operate simultaneously and be associated with one another. For instance, in an organization there may be interest in how trust and communication networks intersect and relate to one another. Multivariate ERGMs permit inferences about structural processes both within and between networks. Pattison and Wasserman (1999) first set out Markov models of this type.

Further interesting extensions were provided by Koehly and Pattison (2005), including extensions to cognitive social structures (Krackhardt, 1987). There has been some important applied work in organizations using these approaches (Lazega and Pattison, 1999; Lomi and Pattison, 2006; Rank et al., 2010). A straightforward approach to incorporating social circuit effects into a bipartite model is to include within-network effects using standard social circuit parameters and then include dyadic multiplex tie association parameters between networks (although more complex across network effects are possible).

- Social influence models: Rather than modeling network ties conditional on a fixed set of attributes, it is possible to model a set of (changeable) attributes conditional on a fixed network within an ERGM-type framework. Such a model represents a social influence or social contagion process. Robins, Pattison, and Elliott (2001b) first described this approach: more recent work includes that of Daraganova et al. (2007).

- There is some interesting early work on models for missing network data and on related issues such as snowball sampling of networks. If brought to full fruition, these developments have considerable potential to enhance the scope of ERGMs in application. See Handcock and Gile (2010) and Koskinen et al. (2010).

CONCLUSIONS

Since the Wasserman and Pattison paper in 1996, there has been greatly increased interest in exponential random graph models. Due to some important and innovative technical work in recent years, these models are now much better understood and new social circuit specifications have dramatically enhanced their applicability for real data. This does not mean, however, that issues of model specification have been finalized or that current models are capable of dealing with all network data. It is harder to obtain convergence for models for directed networks and for larger networks. The computational requirements for estimation imply that modeling large networks is difficult and currently is not feasible for very large networks. Snowball sampling could assist with this situation, but techniques still need to be developed fully. As we move to the modeling of larger networks it is quite possible that additional parameters will be required to capture dependencies.

Work is proceeding on all of these fronts. Given the rapid advances of the last few years, we may expect further developments lie ahead.

NOTES

1 This follows terminology first used by Moreno and Jennings (1938), rather than the more recent network motifs of Milo et al. (2002).

2 Conditional independence – conditional on all other tie variables – is what is important here, because tie variable X_{ij} does affect X_{rs} under Markov dependence, as it is dependent on X_{ir} which in turn is dependent on X_{rs}. But once the values of "intervening" tie variables such as X_{ir} are controlled, X_{ij} has no further effect on X_{rs}. In other words, there is no direct effect between X_{ij} and X_{rs}.

3 The clustering coefficient is thrice the number of triangles divided by the number of 2-stars. It is an index between 0 and 1 that measures the propensity for 2-stars in the network to "close" into triangles. The factor of three (applicable to undirected networks) is because every undirected triangle contains three 2-stars.

4 This labeling of the figure to indicate the direction of the arcs (in this case "Up") is consistent with the usage of Holland and Leinhardt (1970) in labeling the triad census.

5 Regular users of pnet will realize that homophily on continuous attributes is evidenced by a negative parameter estimate, given an absolute difference effect (but not for binary attributes). Here, the sign of the continuous attribute difference effect has been changed for simplicity. So in Table 32.2 a positive parameter estimate indicates homophily (not heterophily) for both binary and continuous attribute measures.

REFERENCES

Agneessens, F., Roose, H. and Waege, H. (2004) 'Choices of theatre events: p* model for affiliation networks with attributes', *Metodološki zvezki*, 1:419–39.

Bollobás, B. (1985) *Random Graphs*. London: Academic Press.

Burda, Z., Jurkiewicz, J. and Kryzwicki, A. (2004) 'Network transitivity and matrix models', *Physical Review E*, 69: 026106.

Coleman, J.S. (1988) 'Social capital in the creation of human capital', *American Journal of Sociology*, S95–S120.

Daraganova, G., Pattison, P., Robins, G. and Wang, P. (2007) *Social Influence Models*. 8th Asia-Pacific Complex Systems Conference, Queensland, Australia.

Erdös, P. and Renyi, A. (1959) 'On random graphs. I', *Publicationes Mathematicae*, (Debrecen) 6: 290–97.

Frank, O. and Strauss, D. (1986) 'Markov graphs', *Journal of the American Statistical Association*, 81: 832–42.

Häggström, O. and Jonasson, J. (1999) 'Phase transition in the random triangle model', *Journal of Applied Probability*, 36: 1101–15.

Handcock, M. (2002) 'Statistical models for social networks: Degeneracy and inference', in R. Breiger, K. Carley and P. Pattison (eds), *Dynamic Social Network Modeling and Analysis*. Washington, DC: National Academies Press. pp. 229–40.

Handcock, M. (2003) *Assessing Degeneracy in Statistical Models of Social Networks*. Center for Statistics and the Social Sciences, Working Paper no. 39, University of Washington.

Handcock, M. and Gile, K. (2010) 'Modeling networks from sampled data', *Annals of Applied Statistics*, 4: 5–25.

Handcock, M., Hunter, D., Butts, C., Goodreau, S. and Morris, M. (2008) 'Statnet: Software tools for the representation, visualization, analysis and simulation of network data', *Journal of Statistical Software*, 24(1).

Holland, P. and Leinhardt, S. (1970) 'A method for detecting structure in sociometric data', *American Journal of Sociology*, 70: 492–513.

Holland, P. and Leinhardt, S. (1981) 'An exponential family of probability distributions for directed graphs (with discussion)', *Journal of the American Statistical Association*, 76: 33–65.

Hunter, D. (2007) 'Curved exponential family models for social networks', *Social Networks*, 29: 216–30.

Hunter, D., Goodreau, S. and Handcock, M. (2008) 'Goodness of fit of social network models', *Journal of the American Statistical Association*, 103: 248–58.

Hunter, D. and Handcock, M. (2006) 'Inference in curved exponential families for networks', *Journal of Computational and Graphical Statistics*, 15: 565–83.

Jonasson, J. (1999) 'The random triangle model', *Journal of Applied Probability*, 36: 852–67.

Koehly, L.M. and Pattison, P.E. (2005) 'Random graph models for social networks: Multiple relations or multiple raters', in P. J. Carrington, J. Scott, and S. Wasserman (eds), *Models and Methods in Social Network Analysis*. New York: Cambridge University Press. pp. 162–91.

Koskinen, J., Robins, G. and Pattison, P. (2010) 'Analysing exponential random graph (p*) models with missing data using Bayesian data augmentation', *Statistical Methodology*, 7: 366–384.

Krackhardt, D. (1987) 'Cognitive social structures', *Social Networks*, 9: 104–34.

Lazega, E. and Pattison, P. (1999) 'Multiplexity, generalized exchange and cooperation in organizations', *Social Networks*, 21: 67–90.

Lomi, A. and Pattison, P. (2006) 'Manufacturing relations: An empirical study of the organization of production across multiple networks', *Organization Science*, 17: 313–32.

McPherson, M., Smith-Lovin, L. and Cook, J. (2001) 'Birds of a feather: Homophily in social networks', *Annual Review of Sociology*, 27: 415–44.

Milo, R., Shen-Orr, S., Itzkovitz, S., Kashtan, N., Chkovskii, D. and Alon, U. (2002) 'Network motifs: Simple building blocks of complex networks,' *Science*, 298: 824–27.

Moreno, J. and Jennings, H. (1938) 'Statistics of social configurations', *Sociometry*, 1: 342–74.

Park, J. and Newman, M. (2004) 'Solution of the 2-star model of a network', *Physical Review E*, 70: 066146.

Pattison, P. and Robins, G. (2002) 'Neighbourhood based models for social networks', *Sociological Methodology*, 32: 301–37.

Pattison, P. and Wasserman, S. (1999) 'Logit models and logistic regressions for social networks, II. Multivariate relations', *British Journal of Mathematical and Statistical Psychology*, 52: 169–94.

Rank, O., Robins, G. and Pattison, P. (2010) 'Structural logic of intra-organizational networks', *Organization Science*. 21: 745–64.

Robins, G., Elliott, P. and Pattison, P. (2001a) 'Network models for social selection processes', *Social Networks*, 23: 1–30.

Robins, G., Pattison, P. and Elliott, P. (2001b) 'Network models for social influence processes', *Psychometrika*, 66: 161–90.

Robins, G., Pattison, P., Kalish, Y. and Lusher, D. (2007) 'An introduction to exponential random graph (p*) models for social networks', *Social Networks*, 29: 173–91.

Robins, G., Pattison, P. and Wang, P. (2009) 'Closure, connectivity and degrees: New specifications for exponential random graph (p*) models for directed social networks', *Social Networks*, 31:105–17.

Robins, G., Pattison, P. and Wasserman, S. (1999) 'Logit models and logistic regressions for social networks, III. Valued relations', *Psychometrika*, 64: 371–94.

Robins, G., Pattison, P. and Woolcock, J. (2005) 'Social networks and small worlds', *American Journal of Sociology*, 110: 894–936.

Robins, G.L., Snijders, T.A.B., Wang, P., Handcock, M. and Pattison, P. (2007) 'Recent developments in exponential random graph (p*) models for social networks', *Social Networks* 29: 192–215.

Skvoretz, J. and Faust, K. (1999) 'Logit models for affiliation networks', *Sociological Methodology*, 29: 253–80.

Strauss, D. (1986) 'On a general class of models for interaction', *SIAM Review*, 28: 513–27.

Strauss, D. and Ikeda, M. (1990) 'Pseudo-likelihood estimation for social networks', *Journal of the American Statistical Association*, 85: 204–12.

Snijders, T.A.B. (2002) 'Markov chain Monte Carlo estimation of exponential random graph models', *Journal of Social Structure*, 3: 2.

Snijders, T.A.B., Pattison, P., Robins, G. and Handcock, M. (2006) 'New specifications for exponential random graph models', *Sociological Methodology*, 36: 99–153.

Van Duijn, M., Gile, K. and Handcock, M. (2009) 'A framework for comparison of maximum pseudo likelihood and maximum likelihood estimation of exponential family random graph models', *Social Networks*, 31: 52–62.

Wang, P., Sharpe, K., Pattison, P. and Robins, G. (2009) 'Exponential random graph (p*) models for affiliation networks', *Social Networks*, 31: 12–25.

Wasserman, S. and Pattison, P. (1996) 'Logit models and logistic regressions for social networks: I. An introduction to Markov graphs and p*', *Psychometrika*, 61: 401–25.

33

Network Dynamics

Tom A.B. Snijders

A DYNAMIC APPROACH TO NETWORK ANALYSIS

Dynamic ideas have been pursued in much of social network analysis. Network dynamics is important for domains ranging from friendship networks (e.g., Pearson and West, 2003; Burk et al., 2007) to, for example, interorganizational networks (see the review articles by Borgatti and Foster, 2003; Brass et al., 2004). However, formal models of analysis, both in the tradition of discrete mathematics and in the tradition of statistical inference, have for a long time focused mainly on single (i.e., cross-sectional) methods of analysis.

Some history: empirical research

Important early longitudinal network studies were those by Nordlie (1958) and Newcomb (1961), who studied friendships in a college fraternity based on the empirical data collected; Coleman's (1961) Adolescent Society study with friendship data in 10 schools and 9,702 individuals; Kapferer's (1972) study of observed interactions in a tailor shop in Zambia (then Northern Rhodesia) over 10 months, in a period of industrial conflict; Sampson's (1969) Ph.D. dissertation on the developments of the relations in a group of 18 monks in a monastery; and the study by Hallinan with seven waves (see Hallinan, 1974, 1979; Sørensen and Hallinan, 1976). However, attention before about 1990 was mostly on single observations of networks. Of the 20 data sets distributed with the UCINET package (Borgatti et al., 1998), only three provide longitudinal data: Kapferer's Taylor Shop, Newcomb's Fraternity, and Sampson's Monastery. The leading textbook on social network analysis, by Wasserman and Faust (1994), has a section of half a page on dynamic and longitudinal network models. The limited amount of attention paid to explicit longitudinal treatment of social network analysis may be understood from the difficulties of collecting network data, which are multiplied when a researcher wishes to collect them longitudinally, and from the difficulties in explicitly modeling the dynamics of social networks.

Starting in the 1980s, network panel data started to be collected more widely. Panel data are data collections where the researchers collected data on a given group of social actors at two or more consecutive moments, called the "panel waves". Examples are Bauman's study of friendship networks in five schools, collected in the course of a study focusing on dynamics of cigarette smoking (Bauman et al., 1984), with 954 complete questionnaires in a two-wave study; and the Teenage Friends and Lifestyle Study in Scotland with three waves (West and Sweeting, 1995; Michell and Amos, 1997; Pearson and West, 2003). The currently most well-known study probably is the Add Health study in the United States with three waves (Harris et al., 2003; Udry, 2003). Christakis and Fowler (2007) discovered interesting network data in the Framingham Heart Study, a longitudinal study not originally intended to contain a network component. Official records and directories also have been used as sources of longitudinal network data. Some examples of such studies are Gulati and Gargiulo (2000), Powell et al. (2005), and the review by Hagedoorn (2002).

Some history: statistical models

A probabilistic model for network dynamics requires to specify the simultaneous probability distribution of ¶←$X(t)$ ♣←$t\psi$ ←$T\Diamond$ where t is the time parameter, which assumes values in a set T of time points, and $X(t)$ is the network at time t. In probability theory, this is called a stochastic process, where the outcome space is a space of networks. It will be convenient to think of the network as a directed graph (digraph), although depending on the situation at hand it might be a different structure – for example, undirected, a valued network, and so on. For a directed graph, the network $X(t)$ is composed of directed tie variables $X_{ij}(t)$ indicating by the value 1 that there exists an arc $i \to j$ at time t, and by 0 that no such tie exists. In all cases we assume that there are no self-loops, that is, always $X_{ii}(t) = 0$. We shall focus on situations where the node set is fixed and denoted by $\{1, ..., n\}$. Thus, the network is comprised of n actors. This is usually meaningful for network panel data, if we allow some flexibility for nodes representing actors who entered after the start of data collection or left before the end. It should be noted that there are models also for growing networks, with nodes entering the network, often with the additional assumption that ties do not change once they are established, and the network change is determined by the links created by the newly created nodes. This is a classical approach in the mathematical theory of random graphs (e.g., Bollobás, 1985).

Dynamic network models have to represent the feedback processes that are characteristic of networks. As examples, consider some of the processes of tie creation that are traditional in social network analysis: reciprocation (Moreno, 1934), transitive closure (Rapoport, 1953a, 1953b; Davis, 1970), and the Matthew effect ("unto him that hath is given and unto him that hath not is taken away, even that which he hath"; Merton, 1963; de Solla Price, 1965, 1976; called "preferential attachment" by Barabási and Albert, 1999). If at some moment t the tie $i \to j$ does not exist, then at some later moment it might be created by reciprocation if currently there is a tie $j \to i$; it might be created by transitive closure if there are two ties arranged in a two-path $i \to h \to j$ – that is, there currently is an indirect connection from i to j; and it might be created by the Matthew effect if there are many other actors h for which there is a tie $h \to j$ – that is, currently, actor j is highly popular in the sense of having a high in-degree. These examples illustrate that statistical models for network dynamics have to express dependence between ties as well as dependence across time.

Dependence across time

For modeling dependence across time, the great majority of published models seem to have used some variation of the Markov property. Loosely defined, this is a property, defined for stochastic processes, which expresses that the future depends on the past via the present. A more formal definition (although still slightly incomplete) is that, for time points $t_1 < t_2 < t_3$, $X(t_3)$, conditional on $X(t_2)$, is independent of $X(t_1)$. The earliest proposed models postulated that, if the panel data are $X(t_1)$, $X(t_2)$, ... $X(t_n)$, then these n consecutive observations constitute a Markov process. This was assumed, for example, by Katz and Proctor (1959), Wasserman (1987), Wasserman and Iacobucci (1988), and Robins and Pattison (2001). Since the observations are finite in number, this is called a discrete-time Markov process.

However, the feedback processes mentioned above may be assumed to operate, unobserved, between the observations. For example, in a group in which the Matthew effect operates, if at time t_1 some node i has a low in-degree and at the next observation t_2 it has a very high in-degree then it is likely that this has come about by the gradual accumulation of ties directed toward i; the first of these may have been chance occurrences, but once the in-degree was relatively high, it became a self-reinforcing process. Such a model presupposes that there were changes occurring between the observation moments t_1 and t_2. The most elegant and mathematically tractable way of modeling this is to postulate a continuous-time Markov process $\{X(t) \mid t_1 \leq t \leq t_m\}$, in other words to let the set of time points of the process T be the entire interval $[t_1, t_m]$, while still sticking to the panel design for the observed networks: thus, it is postulated that the process of network change goes on, unobserved, between the moments of data collection. This was proposed by Sørensen and Hallinan (1976) and Holland and Leinhardt (1977). These authors also proposed that in this change process, at any instance of time t no more than one tie variable $X_{ij}(t)$ can change. This decomposes the change process into its smallest possible constituents and rules out coordination in the form of the simultaneous creation of a set of ties, as in mutual love at first sight or the spontaneous creation of a group of friends. This is a reasonable requirement that greatly reduces the complexity of modeling. The model of Sørensen and Hallinan (1976) focused on the dynamics of the triad census (Holland and Leinhardt, 1975) and had the set of vectors defining the outcomes of the triad census as the outcome space. This model was incomplete, however, as it did not elaborate the dependence between the triads in a network. A similar but simpler model was presented by Hallinan (1979), focusing on the dyad census. General models representing the dynamics of networks as continuous-time Markov processes where ties change one by one were proposed by Holland and Leinhardt (1977). They did not, however, elaborate ways to specify the dependence of ties in the network.

Dependence across ties

The Markov chain model of Katz and Proctor (1959) assumed independent tie variables that could change according to a Markov chain at each next observation. Independence of ties is, of course, no more than a straw-man assumption as it goes against basic ideas of social network analysis. A first relaxation of this assumption is to postulate independence of dyads, or pairs of tie variables of the type $(X_{ij}(t), X_{ji}(t))$. Such an assumption was made, for longitudinal models, by Wasserman (1977, 1979, and other publications), Hallinan (1979), and Leenders (1995 and other publications) for continuous-time Markov processes; and Wasserman (1987) and Wasserman and Iacobucci (1988) for discrete-time Markov processes.

The assumption of independent dyads breaks apart the stochastic process into $n(n-1)/2$ independent subprocesses. This helps for tractability, but of the three basic component processes mentioned above as examples – reciprocity, tranitivity, and the Matthew effect – it represents only reciprocity. Wasserman (1980) proposed the so-called popularity model, which may be said to represent the Matthew effect but without the reciprocity process. In that model the rows of the random adjacency matrix $(X_{ij}(t))$ are independent, which again gives a simplification of the model to make it tractable.

Stochastic models that allow triadic and other higher-order dependencies were proposed for data in the form of rankings – as in the Newcomb-Nordlie data by Snijders (1996), and for data in the form of digraphs by Snijders and Van Duijn (1997) and Snijders (2001). The latter model is described in detail later in this chapter.

Scale-free networks

De Solla Price (1976), Barabási and Albert (1999), and Dorogovtsev et al. (2000) proposed models where new nodes are added to an existing network and each new node links to m existing nodes with probabilities that depend linearly on the degrees of the existing nodes. This leads to so-called scale-free networks where the distribution of degrees has a power distribution. For most types of networks between human individuals, this does not seem realistic because various constraints will limit the frequency of occurrence of very high degrees.

STOCHASTIC MODELS FOR NETWORK DYNAMICS

One of the reasons why stochastic models for network dynamics did not take off before the 1990s is that the dependence structures that characterize networks are so complicated that plausible models for network dynamics can be implemented only (at least, so it seems in the current state of knowledge) as computer simulation models, like in agent-based models, and do not permit the exact calculations that were used in data analysis in the precomputer era.

In this section we first present tie-based dynamic models, then actor-based models. The former are simpler; the latter are closer to most theories in social science. Both should be regarded as process models, which can be defined by probabilistic rules that give a representation of how the network might have evolved from one observation to the next. Technically speaking, all models presented are Markov processes on the space of digraphs. These are continuous-time models, which means that time increases gradually in an infinitesimal fashion, and now and then, at random moments, a change takes place. To keep the model relatively simple, the assumption is followed, which first was made by Holland and Leinhardt (1977), that at any given moment ("in any split second") only one tie can change. This decomposes the dynamics of the network in the smallest possible steps. It assumes away the possibility of simultaneous coordination by actors: actors are dependent because they react to each other (cf. Zeggelink, 1994), not because they coordinate.

Tie-based models

The simplest approach to construct dynamic network models with quite general dependence structures is by formulating a model where a random pair (i, j) is chosen and with some probability it is decided to change the value of tie variable X_{ij}: create a new tie (change the value 0 to 1) or terminate an existing tie (change 1 to 0).

The probability of change can depend on various function of the network, thus representing the combination of several "mechanisms," theories, constraints, and so forth. Technically this is based on the combination of ideas about exponential random graph models with ideas about Markov processes and Gibbs sampling. Let us first consider an example with four components of the theory, or mechanisms, driving the network dynamics: the tendency to a given average degree, toward reciprocation, transitivity, and the Matthew effect. The Matthew effect is interpreted here as self-reinforcing popularity, contributing to the dispersion of the in-degrees. All of these are understood as stochastic, not deterministic, tendencies. These four components will be reflected by the following network statistics:

$$L(X) = \sum_{ij} X_{ij} \qquad \text{number of ties (33.1)}$$

$$M(X) = \sum_{ij} X_{ij} X_{ji} \qquad \text{number of reciprocal dyads (33.2)}$$

$$T(X) = (1/6) \sum_{ij} X_{ij} X_{jh} X_{ih} \qquad \text{number of transitive triplets (33.3)}$$

$$V_{in}(X) = (1/n)\sum_{j} (X_{+i} - X_{+.})^2 \qquad \text{in-degree variance (33.4)}$$

where

$$X_{+i} = \sum_{j} X_{ji} \qquad \text{in-degree of i (33.5)}$$

$$X_{+.} = (1/n) \sum_{i} X_{+i} \qquad \text{average degree (33.6)}$$

If the network dynamics has a tendency to favor changes that increase the value of these four statistics, respectively, then this will steer the network process into a direction, respectively, of higher density, more reciprocity, stronger transitivity, or larger in-degree (popularity) differences. This can be achieved by a model in the following way. First, let us rewrite the in-degree variance $V_{in}(X)$ as follows:

$$
\begin{aligned}
V_{in}(X) &= (1/n)\sum_{i} X_{+i}^2 - \bar{X}_{+.}^2 \\
&= (1/n)\sum_{i} X_{+i}(X_{+i} -1) + \bar{X}_{+.} - \bar{X}_{+.}^2 \\
&= (1/n)S_2(X) - \bar{X}_{+.}(\bar{X}_{+.} -1)
\end{aligned}
$$

where $S_2(X)$ is the number of two-in-stars in the digraph X, that is, the number of configurations i, j, k with $j \to i$; $k \to i$ and $j \neq k$. This shows that, for a fixed average degree $X^{+.}$, having a large in-degree variance $V_{in}(X)$ is just the same as having a large number of two-in-stars $S_2(X)$. We shall henceforth be working with two-in-stars instead of the in-degree variance to express the Matthew effect.

For allowing differential strengths for the tendency toward the four theoretical components, define the linear combination

$$f(x; \beta) = \beta_1 L(x) + \beta_2 M(x) + \beta_3 T(x)$$
$$+ \beta_4 S_2(x) \qquad (33.7)$$

where the values of the parameters β_k determine the strength of these four tendencies, and x is an arbitrary digraph. A change process for networks now will be defined, which operates by changing ("toggling") single tie variables $X_{ij}(t)$ and that favors changes in the statistics L, M, T, and S_2, depending on the values of the coefficients β_k. This is achieved by the following algorithm, which shows how to transform the current graph $X(t)$ to the next graph, and when this change occurs.

Algorithm 1. Tie-based network dynamics.

For digraphs x, define $x^{(ij+)}$ and $x^{(ij-)}$ as the graphs that are identical to x in all tie variables except those for the ordered pair (i, j), and for which $x^{(ij+)}$ does have a tie $i \to j$, while $x^{(ij-)}$ does not have this tie. In other words, $x_{ij}^{(ij+)} = 1$ and $x_{ij}^{(ij-)} = 0$.

1. *Choose a random pair (i, j) with equal probabilities, given that $i \neq j$.*
2. *Define x = X(t).*
3. *Define*

$$P_{ij} = \frac{\exp(f(x^{(ij+)}); \beta)}{\exp(f(x^{(ij+)}); \beta) + \exp(f(x^{(ij-)}); \beta)}$$

*With probability π_{ij}, choose the next network to be $x^{(ij+)}$;
with probability $1 - \pi_{ij}$, choose the next network to be $x^{(ij-)}$.*

4. *Increment the time variable t by the amount Δt, being a random variable with the exponential distribution with parameter ρ.*

This is a model for network dynamics closely related to the exponential random graph model developed by Frank and Strauss (1986), Frank (1991), and Wasserman and Pattison (1996). To elucidate the link to this model, the basic issue is that (33.8) is the conditional probability for the existence of the tie $i \to j$, given that we know the entire network x except whether this particular tie exists, under the exponential random graph distribution defined by the probability function

$$P\{X = x\} = \frac{\exp(f(x; \beta))}{C} \qquad (33.9)$$

where C is the normalizing constant

$$C = \sum_{x} \exp(f(x; \beta))$$

the summation extending over all digraphs x. Thus, the dynamic algorithm above selects whether or not the tie $i \rightarrow j$ exists using the conditional probability of this tie under model (33.9), the condition being the total network configuration outside of the existence of this tie. From general theorems about Markov processes, or more specifically about Gibbs sampling (Geman and Geman, 1983), it follows that when this algorithm is repeated indefinitely, the distribution of $X(t)$ (where repeating indefinitely means that t tends to infinity) tends to the distribution with probability function (33.9). This dynamic algorithm is one of the standard algorithms to obtain random draws from this model (see Snijders, 2002; Robins et al., 2005).

By choosing the parameters β_k in (33.7), one can choose different models with different strength of the tendencies toward density, reciprocation, transitivity, and self-reinforcing popularity. For example, for $\beta_2 = \beta_3 = \beta_4 = 0$ one obtains a random ("Erdös–Rényi," "Bernoulli") graph. For $\beta_3 = \beta_4 = 0$ this is a special case of the reciprocity model of Wasserman (1977, 1979), with independent dyads. This independence between dyads is broken when $\beta_3 \neq 0$ or $\beta_4 \neq 0$. For $\beta_2 = \beta_3 = 0$, one obtains the popularity model of Wasserman (1977, 1980). The possibility of having positive values of β_3 as well as β_4, allows us to have a model that expresses a tendency towards transitivity as well as the Matthew effect.

Actor-based models

One of the challenges of network analysis is to incorporate agency in a network model. This was formulated forcefully by Emirbayer and Goodwin (1994) – who likewise stressed the importance of culture, which has to be left aside in this chapter. A natural way to combine agency and structure in a statistical model is to use a model for network dynamics where changes of ties are initiated by actors. Such a model can be a good vehicle for expressing and testing social science theories in which the actors have a central role (cf. Udehn, 2002; Hedström, 2005). Actor-based models were proposed by Snijders (1996) for ranked network data and by Snijders and van Duijn (1997) for binary network data. Here, the presentation of Snijders (2001) will be followed. A tutorial introduction to these models, also including practical advice on how to employ and specify them, is given by Snijders et al. (2010).

The actor-based nature of the model means that the model is formulated as if the actors have control over their outgoing ties – under constraints

that in the continuous-time representation ties are changed only one at a time, and that the probabilities of changes take into account the total current network configuration. The model specification employs the so-called rate function $\lambda_i(x;\alpha)$, depending on actors i and the current network state x, which indicates the frequency per unit of time with which actor i gets the opportunity to change an outgoing tie; and the objective function $f_i(x;\beta)$, which can be interpreted as a measure of how attractive the network state x is for actor i. Formulated more neutrally, the objective function is such that, when making a change, actors have a higher probability to move toward networks x for which the objective function $f_i(x;\beta)$ is higher. The statistical parameters α and β are used to reflect the strengths of the various different components included in the rate and objective functions. (For extensions of this model without antisymmetry between creating a new tie and terminating an existing tie, see the discussion in the mentioned literature about gratification or endowment functions.)

The algorithm is formulated in terms of probability distributions only, but it can be interpreted as representing actors embedded in a network, being each others' changing environment (cf. Zeggelink, 1994), who make changes in their outgoing ties each at a rate $\lambda_i(x; \alpha)$ (which could be constant, but which will be changing if the rate function is a nonconstant function of x) so as to optimize the value of the objective function that will obtain after their change is made, given that random disturbances are added to the objective function. This may be called myopic stochastic optimization of the objective function and is often used in game-theoretical models of network formation (e.g., Bala and Goyal, 2000).

Algorithm 2. Actor-based network dynamics.

For digraphs x, define $x^{(ij\pm)}$ as the graph that is identical to x in all tie variables except those for the ordered pair (i, j), and for which the tie variable X_{ij} in $x^{(ij\pm)}$ is just the opposite of this tie variable in x, in the sense that $x_{ij}^{(ij\pm)} = 1 - x_{ij}$.

Define $x^{(ii\pm)} = x$ (as a convenient formal definition without ulterior meaning).

1. *Define $x = X(t)$.*
2. *For $i \in \{1, \ldots, n\}$, define*

$$\tau_i = \frac{\lambda_i(x;\alpha)}{\sum_{h=1}^{n} \lambda_h(x;\alpha)} \tag{33.10}$$

Choose actor i with probability τ_i.

3. For $j \in \{1, ..., n\}$, define

$$\pi_{ij} = \frac{\exp(f_i(x^{(ij\pm)};\beta))}{\sum_{h=1}^{n} \exp(f_i(x^{(ih\pm)};\beta))} \qquad (33.11)$$

With probability π_{ij}, choose the next network to be $x(ij\pm)$.

4. Increment the time variable t by the amount Δt, being a random variable with the exponential distribution with parameter $\sum_{h=1}^{n} \lambda_h(x;\alpha)$.

The properties of the exponential function imply that equation (12) can be rewritten as

$$\pi_{ij} = \frac{\exp(f_i(x^{(ij\pm)};\beta) - f_i(x;\beta))}{\sum_{h=1}^{n} \exp(f_i(x^{(ih\pm)};\beta) - f_i(x;\beta))} \qquad (33.12)$$

that is, the probability of a given change depends monotonically on the increase in objective function that would be generated by this change. This shows that an actor i for whom the current state x of the network is near the optimum of the objective function $f_i(x;\beta)$, is rather likely to make no change, because the probability π_{ii} of choosing to keep the current state $x^{(ii\pm)} = x$ as the next network then is relatively high.

Model specification

In the tie-based as well as in the actor-based model, the researcher has to specify the function $f(x;\beta)$ or $f_i(x;\beta)$, respectively, to specify the model (and in the actor-based model also the rates of change $\lambda_i(x;\alpha)$). This choice should be based on knowledge of the subject matter, theoretical considerations, and the hypotheses to be investigated. We discuss here only the actor-based case.

Like in generalized linear modeling, a convenient class of functions is offered by linear combinations

$$f_i = \sum_k \beta_k s_{ki}(x) \qquad (33.13)$$

where the $s_{ki}(x)$ are functions of the network, as seen from the point of view of actor i – in many cases, functions of the personal network of i. An analogue of (33.7), but now defined for the actor-based model, is

$$f_i(x;\beta) = \beta_1 \sum_j x_{ij} + \beta_2 \sum_j x_{ij} x_{ji}$$
$$+ \beta_3 \sum_{j,h} x_{ij} x_{jh} x_{ih} + \beta_4 \sum x_{ij} x_{hj} \qquad (33.14)$$

Just like the four terms in (33.7), but now seen from the point of view of actor i, these four statistics represent, respectively, the number of ties, number of reciprocated ties, number of transitive triplets $\{i \rightarrow j \rightarrow h, i \rightarrow h\}$, and the added

in-degrees $\sum_h x_{hj}$ of the actors j toward whom i has an outgoing tie. The tie-based model with specification (33.7) and the actor-based model with specification (33.14) define very similar but nevertheless different probability distributions for the network dynamics; the choice between the tie-based and actor-based specifications will have to be based on theoretical preferences or on empirical fit if any differences in fit can be discerned.

This model specification just serves here as an example of how these models can be used to represent, by the four parameters β_1 to β_4, tendencies toward a given value for the mean degree, toward reciprocity, transitive closure, and preference for already popular actors. It should be noted that these four statistics are highly correlated, which implies that although the parameters β_2, β_3, and β_4 can be used to test the respective tendencies, these parameters all collaborate in their implications for the probability distributions of the statistics that could be calculated from the network. In practically all cases it will be desirable to control for the average degree, and testing hypotheses about β_1 does not seem very meaningful in general.

Many other statistics of the personal network of actor i may be used as the $s_{ki}(x)$ in expression (33.13) for the objective function. Such statistics are called *effects*. Since the actor has control only over the outgoing tie variables, what is important here is how the effects depend on the outgoing tie variables x_{ij}; effects depending only on incoming tie variables have no consequence on the conditional probability (33.11). An ample discussion of many statistics that could be included to reflect various theoretically interesting network tendencies and that can be helpful to give a good representation of the dependencies between tie variables is given by Snijders et al. (2010). The following is an incomplete outline.

1. Two fundamental statistics are

   (a) the outdegree $\sum_j x_{ij}$, of which the parameter – such as β_1 in example (33.14) – can be used to fit the level and tendency of the average degree; most other statistics will be correlated with the average degree, which implies that the precise value of this parameter will depend strongly also on the other parameters; and

   (b) the reciprocated degree defined as $\sum_j$ implies $x_{ij} x_{ji}$ the number of reciprocal ties in which actor i is involved, and also included in (33.14); in almost all directed social networks reciprocity is a basic tendency, and including this effect will allow a good representation of the tendency toward reciprocation.

2. The local structure of networks is determined by triads, that is, subgraphs on three nodes (Holland and Leinhardt, 1975). The main dependencies between ties in triads are captured by

 (a) transitivity: the tendency that "friends of friends become, or stay, friends," expressed by the number of transitive triplets in the personal network, $\sum_{j,h} x_{ij}\, x_{jh}\, x_{ih}$, included as the third term in (33.14); and
 (b) three-cycles: the tendency to form closed cycles $i \rightarrow j \rightarrow h \rightarrow i$, measured by $\sum_{j,h} x_{ij}\, x_{jh}\, x_{hi}$. This can represent generalized exchange (Bearman, 1997); however, it is more frequent to observe that this effect has a negative sign, meaning that three-cycles tend to be avoided (Davis, 1970), a sign of local hierarchy.

3. In- and out-degrees are fundamental aspects of individual network position, and creation or termination of ties can be more or less likely depending on the degrees of the actors involved. This is expressed by degree-related effects. The basic degree effects are

 (a) in-degree popularity, indicating the extent to which those with currently high in-degrees are more popular as receivers of new ties – which is just the Matthew effect mentioned above and the fourth term in (33.14);
 (b) out-degree activity, indicating whether those with currently high out-degrees have a greater tendency to create rather than terminate ties; and analogously
 (c) out-degree popularity and
 (d) in-degree activity.

 Also higher-order degree effects such as degree-based assortativity may be included, which express a stronger or weaker tendency to form and maintain ties depending on the combination of the degrees of both.

4. In addition to these effects based on the network structure itself, it is important to include statistics depending on attributes of the actors – their demographic characteristics, indicators of resources, etc. A given actor variable can be included as an ego effect, reflecting the effect of this variable on the propensity to send ties, and as an alter effect, reflecting the effect on the propensity to receive ties. In addition, the combination of sender and receiver usually is important, such as their similarity on salient attributes, reflecting tendencies toward homophily (McPherson et al., 2001).

5. It is also possible to include attributes of pairs of actors – which may be their relatedness in a different network. Such dyadic covariates can express, for example, meeting opportunities, costs, and benefits of the dyadic tie, etc.

STATISTICAL INFERENCE FOR ACTOR-BASED MODELS

Varying the parameters α and β can yield very different network dynamics, and for a given longitudinal network data set the question is how to determine these parameter values to achieve a good fit between model and data. This is the usual question of statistical inference. A technical difficulty here is that no easily computable measure exists for the fit between the model and the data, like the sum of squares in the analysis of variance, and the properties of the model can be assessed in practice only by computer simulation. Indeed the actor-based model can be seen as an agent-based computational model (cf. Macy and Willer, 2002) that is meant to mimic the way in which the network evolves.

Estimation

For parameter estimation in actor-based models, three methods have been proposed in the literature. In the Method of Moments (Snijders and van Duijn, 1997; Snijders, 2001), a set of statistics of the longitudinal network data set is suitably chosen, one for each estimated parameter, and the parameters are determined so that for these statistics there is a perfect fit between observed values and the expected values in the population of all simulations from this model: the expected values should be equal to the observed values. This can in practice be achieved only approximately, by a stochastic approximation algorithm, with some randomness in the results due to the limited number of simulations actually conducted.

Bayesian procedures were proposed by Koskinen and Snijders (2007) and Schweinberger (2007). The Bayesian method postulates a probability distribution of the parameters that represents prior beliefs or prior ignorance, and then calculates or approximates the so-called posterior distribution of the parameters. The latter is the conditional distribution of the parameters given the data that were observed, and it represents how the prior beliefs have been transformed by the empirical observations. Third, an algorithm to approximate the Maximum Likelihood estimator was developed by Snijders et al. (2010). This algorithm is based on simulating the likely continuous-time process that might have led from one panel wave observation to the next, and then approximating the parameters using an appropriate method of averaging.

For data sets that are not too small, and if the model holds to a good approximation, these three methods will yield similar estimation results.

Testing

Connected to the Method of Moments and the Maximum Likelihood method as estimation methods, there are procedures for testing statistical hypotheses about the parameters, following the general principles for constructing statistical tests (see, for example, Cox and Hinkley, 1974). Often the most straightforward way is to use the parameter estimates and their standard errors. For testing a null hypothesis such as

$$H_0 : \beta_k = 0$$

the test statistic, then, is the ratio of the estimate to the standard error,

$$t = \frac{\hat{\beta}_k}{\text{s.e.}(\hat{\beta}_k)} \qquad (33.15)$$

This can be tested in a standard normal reference distribution. This may be called a *t*-test, as it is based on a *t*-ratio. Multiparameter tests can be derived in an analogous fashion. For estimates obtained by the method of moments such tests may be called Wald-type tests, for Maximum Likelihood estimates Wald tests.

There is a different way of hypothesis testing that does not require that the tested parameter is estimated. This is the general principle of Rao's efficient score test. For the method of moments a special adaptation is required, which yields the score-type test as developed by Schweinberger (2008). There is a special practical advantage to score or score-type tests for these models, because the Monte Carlo algorithms for parameter estimation may fail to converge in cases when the model is relatively complicated given the amount of information in the data; the score principle then can provide a test even if one does not have a parameter estimate.

Associated with Maximum Likelihood estimation is the likelihood ratio test. An algorithm is presented in Snijders et al. (2010).

The algorithms currently available for Method of Moments are much less time-consuming than those for Maximum Likelihood estimation and testing. However, this is an area of active development, and the computational efficiency of the available algorithms may change.

DYNAMICS OF NETWORKS AND BEHAVIOR

What makes networks important often are the individual behavior and other individual outcomes that are in some way related to the network

embeddedness of the actors (see, for example, Granovetter, 1973; Burt, 1992; and Lin et al., 2001). Such individual characteristics, however, will also play a role in the explanation of the network dynamics. Thus we encounter the situation where the network and the behavior – a term that we use here as a shorthand for the relevant changeable characteristics of the actors, which also could be attitudes, performance, and so on – both can be considered as dependent variables, changing interdependently. It is assumed here that the behavior variables are ordinal discrete variables, with values 1, 2, and so forth, up to some maximum value, for instance, several levels of alcohol consumption, or several levels of political attitudes on a left-right scale; a binary variable is a special case. The dependence of the network dynamics on network and behavior jointly will be called the social selection process, and the dependence of the behavior dynamics on network and behavior will be called the social influence process (An, this volume).

Both social influence and social selection can lead to similarity between tied actors, which is descriptively called network autocorrelation (Doreian, 1989; Leenders, 1997). Whether this network autocorrelation is caused mainly by influence or mainly by selection can be an important question. This is demonstrated by Ennett and Bauman (1994) for smoking and by Haynie (2001) and Carrington (this volume) for delinquent behavior.

Actor-based models

To answer such questions, it can be helpful to employ process models that represent the interdependent evolution of the tie variables as well as the actors' behavior variables. Here actor-based models are especially natural; such models were specified in Snijders et al. (2007) and in Steglich et al. (2010). They assume that the outgoing ties of an actor, as well as the behavior of the actor, are under this actor's control, subject to various restrictions.

The process model assumes that at random moments, either a network tie or a behavior variable can be changed. The actors have rate functions and objective functions for the network and the behavior separately. That networks and behavior are governed potentially by different processes can be argued, for example, by regarding network choice and behavior choice as being determined by different decision frames (Lindenberg, 2001).

Decomposing the changes in the smallest possible steps here means that at one given ("infinitesimal") moment in time, the possibilities for an actor to change his or her behavioral variable are limited to moving one category up or down on the ordered scale.

We denote the behavior of actor i at time t by $Z_i(t)$, collected in the vector $Z(t)$. It now is assumed that the change probabilities of the network will depend on the current state of the network as well as the behavior; and the change probabilities of the behavior will depend on the current state of the behavior as well as the network. The objective function for actor i for the network is denoted $f_i^X(x,z;\beta)$, and for the behavior $f_i^Z(x,z;\beta)$. Similarly to the objective function for the network, the objective function for behavior is such that changes toward higher values of the objective function are more likely than changes toward lower values. The rate function for actor i for network change is denoted $\lambda_i^X(x,z;\alpha)$, and for behavior change $\lambda_i^Z(x,z;\alpha)$.

Algorithm 3. Actor-based dynamics of network and behavior.

For the network, the same definitions are used as in the algorithm for actor-based network dynamics. For the behavior, for any actor i and a potential increment d, define $z^{(i+d)}$ as the vector of behaviors, which is identical to z in all coordinates except that d is added to the i'th coordinate: $z_i^{(i+d)} = z_i + d$.

1. *Define $x = X(t)$, $z = Z(t)$.*
2. *Calculate the ratio*

$$\phi_X = \frac{\sum_{h=1}^n \lambda_h^X(x,z;\alpha)}{\sum_{h=1}^n \left(\lambda_h^X(x,z;\alpha) + \lambda_h^Z(x,z;\alpha)\right)} \quad (33.16)$$

With probability φ_X, go to item 3 to make a network step; else (with probability $1-\varphi_X$), go to item 5 to make a behavior step.

3. *For $i \in \{1,\dots,n\}$, define*

$$\tau_i^X = \frac{\lambda_i^X(x,z;\alpha)}{\sum_{h=1}^n \lambda_h^X(x,z;\alpha)} \quad (33.17)$$

Choose actor i with probability τ_i^X.

4. *For $j \in \{1,\dots,n\}$, define*

$$\pi_{ij}^X = \frac{\exp(f_i^X(x^{(ij\pm)},z;\beta))}{\sum_{h=1}^n \exp(f_i^X(x^{(ih\pm)},z;\beta))} \quad (33.18)$$

With probability π_{ij}^X choose the next network to be $x^{(ij\pm)}$.
Go to step 7.

5. *For $i \in \{1,\dots,n\}$, define*

$$\tau_i^Z = \frac{\lambda_i^Z(x,z;\alpha)}{\sum_{h=1}^n \lambda_h^Z(x,z;\alpha)} \quad (33.19)$$

Choose actor i with probability τ_i^Z.

6. *For $d \in \{-1, 0, 1\}$, if $z_i + d$ is in the permitted range of Z, define*

$$\pi_{id}^Z = \frac{\exp(f_i^Z(x,z^{(i+d)};\beta))}{\sum_{k=-1}^1 \exp(f_i^Z(x,z^{i+k};\beta))} \quad (33.20)$$

Values d for which $z_i + d$ would be outside of the permitted range are not included in the denominator.
With probability π_{id}^Z, choose the next behavior vector to be $z^{(i+d)}$.
Go to step 7.

7. *Increment the time variable t by the amount Δt, being a random variable with the exponential distribution with parameter $\sum_{h=1}^n \left(\lambda_h^X(x;\alpha) + \lambda_h^Z(x;\alpha)\right)$.*

The choice $d = 0$ means that actor i has the opportunity to change her or his behavior but refrains from doing so. The probability of this will be higher, accordingly as the value of the objective function of the current state, $f_i^Z(x,z;\beta)$ is higher compared to the value of the neighboring states $f_i^Z(x,z^{(i+d)};\beta)$ for $d = -1, +1$.

Model specification

For the behavior also, the most convenient expression for the objective function is a linear combination

$$f_i^Z(x,z;\beta) = \sum_k \beta_k^Z s_{ki}^Z(x,z), \quad (33.21)$$

where the $s_{ki}^Z(x,z)$ are functions of the behavior and other characteristics of actor i, but may depend also on the personal network, the behavior of those to whom i is tied, and so on. In studies of selection and influence, the behavior-dependent selection part is modeled by the specification of the model for network dynamics, for example, by a term expressing the preference (homophily) for ties to others who are similar on the behavioral variable Z.

The network-dependent influence part is modeled by appropriate terms in the objective function for behavior. A basic example of a specification for this function is

$$f_i^Z(x,z;\beta) = \beta_1^Z z_i + \beta_2^Z z_i^2 + \beta_3^Z z_i \left(\frac{\sum_j x_{ij} z_j}{\sum_j x_{ij}}\right) \quad (33.22)$$

The first two terms represent a quadratic preference function for the behavior Z. If preferences are unimodal, then the coefficient of the quadratic term, β_2^Z, is negative. For addictive behaviors, however, this coefficient can be positive. The third term indicates that the "value" for actor i of behavior z_i depends on the average behavior of those to whom i has an outgoing tie.

EXAMPLES

Because of space constraints, this chapter does not contain an elaborate empirical example. The mentioned methodological articles that further explain the actor-based model for network dynamics can be consulted for some examples. Other published examples of network dynamics (ordered by the age of the population of actors) include Schaefer et al. (2010) about the effects of reciprocity, transitivity, and popularity in friendship dynamics between preschool children; Selfhout et al. (2010) about the way in which friendship dynamics of adolescents depend on personality characteristics; van Duijn et al. (2003) about the effects of visible and nonvisible attributes on dynamics of friendship between university students; and Checkley and Steglich (2007) about how the mobility of managers affects interfirm ties.

Examples of the joint dynamics of networks and behavior have been published only recently, because of the recency of the model. Some of these examples are the following.

Burk et al. (2007) present a study on influence and selection processes in the dynamics of friendship and delinquent behavior of adolescents. Steglich et al. (2010) studied the co-evolution of friendship and smoking as well as drinking behavior in a secondary school cohort. Mercken et al. (2009) studied influence and selection processes in smoking initiation among adolescents in a large-scale study with networks in 70 schools in 6 countries. The study by De Klepper et al. (2010) is set in a naval academy and studies the mutual dependence in the evolution of friendships and military discipline.

THE SIENA PROGRAM

The actor-based model for network dynamics as well as the model for dynamics of networks and behavior are implemented in the SIENA ("Simulation Investigation for Empirical Network Analysis") program. Initially a standalone program with a user interface through the program StOCNET, since 2009 it is a package within the

statistical system R (R Development Core Team, 2009), called RSiena. The R system and its packages are freeware, running on Windows, Mac, and Unix/Linux systems. An extensive and frequently updated manual is available (Ripley and Snijders, 2010). This manual gives detailed instructions for installing and working with RSiena.

A first requirement is to install R, the package RSiena, and a few auxiliary packages, as described in the RSiena manual. If desired, RSiena can be operated apparently without any knowledge of R, by means of a graphical user interface; after the installation, it is then not necessary to operate R. Once the installation is done, RSiena can be run in two ways:

1. Run R, load the package RSiena and the auxiliary packages, and run the graphical user interface for RSiena from within R by the command siena01Gui(). This offers the basic functionality of RSiena, with the possibility to integrate the use of RSiena with the use of any other R packages. It has the advantage that no knowledge of the commands of RSiena is required.
2. Run R, load the package RSiena and the auxiliary packages, and run RSiena by using its R commands. This is the best option for users fully conversant with RSiena.

As basic literature, the best combination is to use Snijders et al. (2010) as a tutorial for the methodology, and Ripley and Snijders (2010) (or more recent versions) for the requirements on data formats and the operation of the software.

OUTLOOK AND DISCUSSION

Statistical methods for social network analysis that represent network dependencies in a satisfactory way have been available only since recent years. The methods presented here for analyzing network evolution, and for the co-evolution of networks and behavior, allow researchers to test competing as well as complementary theories about dynamics elating to networks. More reflection now is needed from a theoretical as well as methodological viewpoint to combine the statistical approach with the network approach. The network approach is rich in structural and positional analysis. The statistical approach, by contrast, has a tradition of parsimony, which often limits model specification for hypothesis testing to the choice of tested variables together with a few control variables. Much research in the statistical approach is purely individualistic, ignoring the importance of distinguishing multiple types of unit of analysis and where hypotheses are uniquely formulated without further ado in the scheme of "*X* leads to *Y*, when controlling for *A*". Convincing gatekeepers such as reviewers and editors of journals of the importance of a network approach, where theories and statistical models are more complex, can be difficult.

Two major limitations of the purely individualistic approach can be mentioned here. In the first place, most network research is observational rather than experimental, which means that methods of analysis must incorporate adequate control for competing hypotheses or theories, and a good specification of statistical dependencies between observed variables is essential to obtain reliable conclusions. In network phenomena, endogenous (also called self-referential, emergent, self-organizing, feedback) processes are essential, and these lead to dependencies between variables rather than effects of some measured variable *X* on a dependent variable *Y*. The failure to specify such dependencies appropriately will lead to hypothesis tests with inadequate control for competing theories.

Second, network dependencies can be a treasure grove of interesting theories and hypotheses, and the infusion of network approaches into theoretical thinking and statistical hypothesis testing, along theoretical lines such as Hedström's (2005) analytical sociology, can lead to better explanations of empirical phenomena and to improved interventions in domains such as public health. A similar kind of progress has started earlier in contextual analysis by multilevel modeling, where the analytical use of several types of unit of analysis is now generally accepted to be fruitful and even necessary, although not yet generally practiced; examples are Sampson et al. (2002) and O'Campo (2003).

Such theoretical-methodological advances will be easier when further progress in statistical modeling for network dynamics will have been made along three lines: models for richer data structures, less restrictive models, and richer statistical procedures. With respect to data structures, when remaining within the confines of network panel designs, one can think of extending this type of modeling to data types such as valued networks, multivariate networks, and nondirected networks. Developments should not be limited to panel designs, however. In studies of networks between organizations, sometimes the observation moments are spaced so tightly that it is reasonable to make the approximation that the preceding observation of the network state is used to directly predict the next observation in a network autoregressive model, as done by Leenders (1997) and Gulati and Gargiulo (1999); sometimes the observations even provide a continuous record of tie creation,

although not always of tie termination, such as in Hagedoorn (2002). Second, with respect to models, it will be worthwhile to develop models that are non-Markovian, for example, models with latent variables or more general hidden Markov models (Cappé et al., 2005). The models presented here assume implicitly that actors have full knowledge of the network, and to model larger networks in a plausible way it will be helpful to develop models that do not assume complete information. Third, statistical procedures have to be developed further. Algorithms should be improved and their mathematical properties investigated. In addition, procedures for assessing goodness of fit should be developed and the robustness of parameter estimators and tests for misspecification should be studied. Together with the software implementation, this implies a considerable amount of methodological work.

REFERENCES

Barabási, A.L. and Albert, R. (1999) 'Emergence of scaling in random networks', *Science*, 286: 509–12.

Bala, V. and Goyal, S. (2000) 'A noncooperative model of network formation', *Econometrica*, 68: 1181–229.

Borgatti, S.P. and Foster, P.C. (2003) 'The network paradigm in organizational research: A review and typology', *Journal of Management*, 29: 991–1013.

Brass, D.J., Galaskiewicz, J., Greve, H.R. and Tsai, W. (2004) 'Taking stock of networks and organizations: a multilevel perspective', *Academy of Management Journal*, 47: 795–817.

Bauman, K.E., Fisher, L.A., Bryan, E.S. and Chenoweth, R.L. (1984) 'Antecedents, subjective expected utility, and behavior: A study of adolescent cigarette smoking', *Addictive Behaviors*, 9: 121–36.

Bearman, P.S. (1997) 'Generalized exchange', *American Journal of Sociology*, 102: 1383–415.

Bollobás, B. (1985) *Random Graphs*. London: Academic Press.

Borgatti, S., Everett, M.G. and Freeman, L.C. (1998) *UCINET V, Reference Manual*. Columbia, SC: Analytic Technologies.

Burk, W.J., Steglich, C.E.G. and Snijders, T.A.B. (2007) 'Beyond dyadic interdependence: Actor-oriented models for co-evolving social networks and individual behaviors', *International Journal of Behavioral Development*, 31: 397–404.

Burt, R.S. (1992) *Structural Holes*. Cambridge, MA: Harvard University Press.

Cappé, O., Moulines, E. and Rydén, T. (2005) *Inference in Hidden Markov Models*. New York: Springer.

Checkley, M. and Steglich, C.E.G. (2007) 'Partners in power: Job mobility and dynamic deal-making', *European Management Review*, 4: 161–71.

Christakis, N.A. and Fowler, J.H. (2007) 'The spread of obesity in a large social network over 32 years', *New England Journal of Medicine* 357: 370–379.

Coleman, J.S. (1961) *The Adolescent Society.* New York: Free Press of Glencoe.

Cox, D.R. and Hinkley, D.V. (1974) *Theoretical Statistics.* London: Chapman & Hall.

Davis, J.A. (1970) 'Clustering and hierarchy in interpersonal relations: Testing two graph theoretical models on 742 sociomatrices', *American Sociological Review,* 35: 843–52.

De Klepper, M., Sleebos, E., van de Bunt, G. and Agneessens, F. (2010) 'Similarity in friendship networks: Selection or influence? The effect of constraining contexts and non-visible individual attributes', *Social Networks,* 32: 82–90.

de Solla Price, D. (1965) 'Networks of scientific papers', *Science,* 149: 510–15.

de Solla Price, D. (1976) 'A general theory of bibliometric and other advantage processes', *Journal of the American Society for Information Science,* 27: 292–306.

Doreian, P. (1989) 'Network autocorrelation models: Problems and prospects', in D.A. Griffith (ed.), *Spatial Statistics: Past, Present, Future.* Ann Arbor: Michigan Document Services.

Dorogovtsev, S.N., Mendes, J.F.F. and Samukhin, A.N. (2000) 'Structure of growing networks with preferential linking', *Physical Review Letters,* 85: 4633–36.

Emirbayer, M. and Goodwin, J. (1994) 'Network analysis, culture, and the problem of agency', *American Journal of Sociology,* 99: 1411–54.

Ennett, S.T. and Bauman, K.E. (1994) 'The contribution of influence and selection to adolescent peer group homogeneity: The case of adolescent cigarette smoking', *Journal of Personality and Social Psychology,* 67: 653–63.

Frank, O. (1991) 'Statistical analysis of change in networks', *Statistica Neerlandica,* 45: 283–93.

Frank, O. and Strauss, D. (1986) 'Markov graphs', *Journal of the American Statistical Association* 81: 832–42.

Geman, S. and Geman, D. (1983) 'Stochastic relaxation, Gibbs distributions, and the Bayesian restoration of images', *IEEE Transactions on Pattern Analysis and Machine Intelligence,* 6: 721–41.

Granovetter, M.S. (1973) 'The strength of weak ties', *American Journal of Sociology,* 78: 1360–80.

Gulati, R. and Gargiulo, M. (1999) 'Where do interorganizational networks come from?', *American Journal of Sociology,* 104: 1439–93.

Hagedoorn, J. (2002) 'Inter-firm R&D partnerships: an overview of major trends and patterns since 1960', *Research Policy,* 31: 477–92.

Hallinan, M.T. (1974) *The Structure of Positive Sentiment.* New York: Elsevier.

Hallinan, M.T. (1979) 'The process of friendship formation', *Social Networks,* 1: 193–210.

Harris, K.M., Florey, F., Tabor, J., Bearman, P.S., Jones, J. and Udry, J.R. (2003) 'The national longitudinal study of adolescent health: Research design'. Technical report, University of North Carolina. http://www.cpc.unc.edu/projects/addhealth/design/.

Haynie, D.L. (2001) 'Delinquent peers revisited: Does network structure matter?' *American Journal of Sociology,* 106: 1013–57.

Hedström, P. (2005) *Dissecting the Social: On the Principles of Analytical Sociology.* Cambridge: Cambridge University Press.

Holland, P.W. and Leinhardt, S. (1975) 'Local structure in social networks', *Sociological Methodology – 1976,* pp.1–45.

Holland, P.W. and Leinhardt, S. (1977) 'A dynamic model for social networks', *Journal of Mathematical Sociology,* 5: 5–20.

Kapferer, B. (1972) *Strategy and Transaction in an African Factory.* Manchester: Manchester University Press.

Katz, L. and Proctor, C.H. (1959) 'The configuration of interpersonal relations in a group as a time-dependent stochastic process', *Psychometrika,* 24: 317–27.

Koskinen, J.H. and Snijders, T.A.B. (2007) 'Bayesian inference for dynamic network data', *Journal of Statistical Planning and Inference,* 13: 3930–38.

Leenders, R.T.A.J. (1995) 'Models for network dynamics: A Markovian framework', *Journal of Mathematical Sociology,* 20: 1–21.

Leenders, R.T.A.J. (1997) 'Longitudinal behavior of network structure and actor attributes: Modeling interdependence of contagion and selection', in P. Doreian and F.N. Stokman (eds), *Evolution of Social Networks.* New York: Gordon and Breach.

Lin, N., Cook, K. and Burt, R.S. (eds) (2001) *Social Capital: Theory and Research.* New York: Aldine de Gruyter.

Lindenberg, S. (2001) 'Social rationality versus rational egoism', in J. Turner (ed.), *Handbook of Sociological Theory.* New York: Kluwer/Plenum. pp. 635–68.

Macy, M.W. and Willer, R. (2002) 'From factors to actors: Computational sociology and agent-based modelling', *Annual Review of Sociology* 28: 143–66.

McPherson, M., Lynn, S.-L. and James M.C. (2001) 'Birds of a feather: Homophily in social networks', *Annual Review of Sociology,* 27: 415–44.

Mercken, L., Snijders, T.A.B., Steglich, C. and de Vries, H. (2009) 'Dynamics of adolescent friendship networks and smoking behavior: Social network analyses in six European countries', *Social Science and Medicine,* 69: 1506–14.

Merton, R. (1963) 'The Matthew effect in science', *Science,* 159(3810): 56–63.

Michell, L. and A. Amos, (1997) 'Girls, pecking order and smoking', *Social Science and Medicine,* 44: 1861–69.

Newcomb, T.M. (1961) *The Acquaintance Process.* New York: Holt, Rinehart and Winston.

Nordlie, P.G. (1958) 'A longitudinal study of interpersonal attraction in a natural group setting', PhD thesis, University of Michigan.

O'Campo, P. (2003) 'Invited commentary: Advancing theory and methods for multilevel models of residential neighborhoods and health', *American Journal of Epidemiology,* 157: 9–13.

Pearson, M. and West, P. (2003) 'Drifting smoke rings: Social network analysis and Markov processes in a longitudinal study of friendship groups and risk-taking', *Connections,* 25(2): 59–76.

Powell, Walter W., White, Douglas R., Koput, Kenneth W. and Owen-Smith, Jason. (2005) 'Network dynamics and field evolution: The growth of interorganizational collaboration in the life sciences', *American Journal of Sociology,* 110: 1132–205.

R Development Core Team (2009) *R: A Language and Environment for Statistical Computing.* R Foundation for Statistical Computing, Vienna, Austria. http://www.R-project.org.

Rapoport, A. (1953a) 'Spread of information through a population with socio-structural bias: I. Assumption of transitivity', *Bulletin of Mathematical Biophysics,* 15: 523–33.

Rapoport, A. (1953b) 'Spread of information through a population with socio-structural bias: II. Various models with partial transitivity', *Bulletin of Mathematical Biophysics,* 15: 535–46.

Ripley, R. and Snijders, T.A.B. (2010) *Manual for SIENA version 4.0.* Oxford: University of Oxford, Department of Statistics, http://www.stats.ox.ac.uk/siena/.

Robins, G. and Pattison, P. (2001) 'Random graph models for temporal processes in social networks', *Journal of Mathematical Sociology,* 25: 5–41.

Robins, G.L., Woolcock, J., and Pattison, P. (2005) 'Small and other worlds: Global network structures from local processes', *American Journal of Sociology* 110: 894–936.

Sampson, R. J., Morenoff, J.D. and Gannon-Rowley, T. (2002) 'Assessing "neighborhood effects": Social processes and new directions in research', *Annual Review of Sociology* 28: 443–78.

Sampson, S.F. (1969) 'Crisis in a cloister', Ph.D. dissertation, Cornell University.

Schaefer, D.R., Light, J.M., Fabes, R.A., Hanish, L.D. and Martin, C.L. (2010) 'Fundamental principles of network formation among preschool children', *Social Networks* 32: 61–71.

Schweinberger, M. (2007) 'Statistical methods for studying the evolution of networks and behavior', Ph.D. dissertation, University of Groningen.

Schweinberger, M. (2008) 'Statistical modeling of network dynamics given panel data: Goodness-of-fit tests'. Submitted for publication.

Selfhout, M., Burk, W., Branje, S., Denissen, J.J.A., Van Aken, M.A.G. and Meeus, W. (2010) 'Emerging late adolescent friendship networks and big five personality traits: A dynamic social network perspective', *Journal of Personality,* 78: 509–38.

Snijders, T.A.B. (1996) 'Stochastic actor-oriented dynamic network analysis', *Journal of Mathematical Sociology,* 21: 149–72.

Snijders, T.A.B. (2001) 'The statistical evaluation of social network dynamics', *Sociological Methodology – 2001,* 361–95.

Snijders, T.A.B. (2002) 'Markov chain Monte Carlo estimation of exponential random graph models', *Journal of Social Structure,* 3: 2.

Snijders, T.A.B. (2005) 'Models for longitudinal network data', in P.J. Carrington, J. Scott, and S. Wasserman (eds), *Models and Methods in Social Network Analysis.* New York: Cambridge University Press.

Snijders, T.A.B., Koskinen, J.H. and Schweinberger, M. (2010) 'Maximum likelihood estimation for social network dynamics', *Annals of Applied Statistics,* 4: 567–588.

Snijders, T.A.B., Pattison, P., Robins, G.L., Handock, M. (2006) 'New specifications for exponential random graph models', *Sociological Methodology – 2006,* 99–153.

Snijders, T.A.B., Steglich, C.E.G. and Schweinberger, M. (2007) 'Modeling the co-evolution of networks and behavior', in Kees van Montfort, Han Oud and Albert Satorra (eds), *Longitudinal Models in the Behavioral and Related Sciences.* Mahwah, NJ: Lawrence Erlbaum. pp. 41–71.

Snijders, T.A.B., van de Bunt, G.G. and Steglich, C.E.G. (2010) 'Introduction to stochastic actor-based models for network dynamics', *Social Networks,* 32: 44–60.

Snijders, T.A.B., and van Duijn, M.A.J., 'Simulation for statistical inference in dynamic network models'. In: R. Conte, R. Hegselmann, and P. Terna, (eds) *Simulating Social Phenomena.* Lecture Notes in Economics and Mathematical Systems, 456. Berlin: Springer, 1997, pp. 493–512.

Sørensen, A. B. and Hallinan, M.T. (1976) 'A stochastic model for change in group structure', *Social Science Research,* 5: 43–61.

Steglich, C.E.G., Snijders, T.A.B. and Pearson, M. (2010) 'Dynamic networks and behavior: Separating selection from influence', *Sociological Methodology – 2010,* pp. 329–393.

Udehn, L. (2002) 'The changing face of methodological individualism', *Annual Review of Sociology,* 8: 479–507.

Udry, J.R. (2003) 'The national longitudinal study of adolescent health (add health), Waves I & II, 1994–1996; Wave III, 2001–2002', technical report, Carolina Population Center, University of North Carolina at Chapel Hill.

van Duijn, M.A.J., Zeggelink, E.P.H., Huisman, M., Stokman, F.N. and Wasseur, F.W. (2003) 'Evolution of sociology freshmen into a friendship network', *Journal of Mathematical Sociology,* 27: 153–91.

Wasserman, S. (1977) 'Stochastic models for directed graphs', Ph.D. dissertation, University of Harvard, Dept. of Statistics.

Wasserman, S. (1979) 'A stochastic model for directed graphs with transition rates determined by reciprocity', *Sociological Methodology – 1980,* pp. 392–412.

Wasserman, S. (1980) 'Analyzing social networks as stochastic processes', *Journal of the American Statistical Association,* 75: 280–94.

Wasserman, S. (1987) 'The conformity of two sociometric relations', *Psychometrika,* 53: 261–82.

Wasserman, S. and K. Faust. (1994) *Social Network Analysis: Methods and Applications.* New York: Cambridge University Press.

Wasserman, S. and D. Iacobucci. (1988) 'Sequential social network data', *Psychometrika,* 53: 261–82.

Wasserman, S. and Pattison, P.E. (1996) 'Logit models and logistic regression for social networks: I. An introduction to Markov graphs and p*', *Psychometrika,* 61: 401–25.

West, P. and Sweeting, H. (1995) 'Background rationale and design of the West of Scotland 11–16 Study', Working Paper No. 52. Glasgow: MRC Medical Sociology Unit Glasgow.

Zeggelink, E.P.H. (1994) 'Dynamics of structure: An individual oriented approach', *Social Networks,* 16: 295–333.

34

Models and Methods to Identify Peer Effects

Weihua (Edward) An

INTRODUCTION

There have been numerous studies on peer effects. But inadequate attention has been paid to making valid causal inference about peer effects, either due to intellectual negligence or methodological limitations. This paper will review recent advances in statistical modeling and inference on peer effects and point out some directions for future research in this area. In sociology, the literature on methodological issues in studying peer effects can be traced back at least to the classic paper written by Duncan et al. (1968). Other notable studies and reviews include Kandel (1978), Marsden and Friedkin (1993), Doreian (2001), Carrington et al. (2005), Valente (2005), Mouw (2006), O'Malley and Marsden (2008), Smith and Christakis (2008), and so forth. There also exist some very good reviews on this topic in economics, including Manski (1993, 2000, and 2010), Brock and Durlauf (2001a), Blume and Durlauf (2005), Soetevent (2006), Hartmann et al. (2008), Jackson (2008) and Moffitt (forthcoming); in political science, including Fowler, Heaney et al. (2009); and in physics and statistics, including Albert and Barabási (2002), Newman (2003), Goldenberg et al. (2009), and Kolaczyk (2009).

Generally speaking, methodological studies of peer effects can be divided into two different approaches. One is about mathematical modeling of peer effects, like Jackson (2008, esp. Chapter 8), which mainly studies the long run behaviors or equilibria of the social interactions of peer groups. The other is about statistical identification and estimation of peer effects. This review will mostly focus on the second approach, especially

the identification issues. In addition, this review differs from the above ones in two aspects. First, it is interdisciplinary, drawing on literature not only from sociology but also from economics, political science, statistics, etc. Second, it uses the potential outcomes framework etc. to unify and elaborate the critiques and emphasizes the conditions in which peer effects can be attributed as causal.

What peer effects are and why they are important

In the literature, there is no consensus on exactly what "peers" mean. They can refer to friends, roommates, classmates, colleagues, neighbors, co-offenders, inmates, even firms making same products or providing same services or operating in same neighborhoods, and so forth, depending on the context. To facilitate elaboration, I will use "peer" and "friend" interchangeably in the following text unless it is explicitly specified otherwise. Although sometimes people nominate their spouses or siblings as their best friends, in general, researchers tend not to view social contacts connected through marriage or kinship as peers. Even so, it can still be very hard in practice to clearly define peership. Take "friends" as an example: different subjects may have very different definitions of what friends mean. A general approach to dealing with this kind of ambiguity is to provide an explicit name generator, like "Whom do you usually discuss important affairs with?" But what constitute important affairs are likely to differ across subjects and discussing important affairs is neither the only nor the central element of friendship. Regardless of these conceptualization issues, there are at least eight ways we can categorize peer effects, which may help us better understand the subtleties and varieties of peer effects.

1 Exogenous vs. endogenous peer effects. The difference between exogenous and endogenous peer effects mainly lies in the ultimate cause of peer effects. The former usually refers to the spillover effects of some exogenous policy intervention on subjects who are not originally targeted by the intervention but are connected to the original target population of the intervention. For example in Figure 34.1, there is an exogenous intervention (e.g., a smoking prevention or cessation program) that is aimed to change subject j's attitude and behavior regarding smoking, Y_j. Peer effects in this case refer to the spillover or contagion effects of subject j's attitudinal or behavioral change in smoking due to the intervention on his or her friend subject i's attitude and behavior regarding smoking. In contrast, endogenous peer effects come directly from peers. Still using Figure 34.1 to illustrate, endogenous peer effects refer to situations in which subject j directly influences subject i without being affected by any external intervention first. In reality, it could be very difficult to completely separate endogenous peer effects from exogenous ones, as many of the endogenous peer effects could originally be generated by external forces unobservable to researchers.

2 Positive vs. negative peer effects. By desirability, peer effects can be viewed either as positive or negative. For example, peers who smoke cigarettes are usually considered to have negative effects on their contacts while students who study hard may have a positive influence on their classmates.

3 Active vs. passive peer effects. Active peer effects come from connections that a person can explicitly recognize while passive peer effects come from peers that a subject does not have an explicit tie with. Friends' effects are examples of the former. Transmission of infectious diseases or market competition can serve as examples of the latter.

4 Contemporaneous vs. lagged peer effects. The effects due to peers' contemporaneous influence are called contemporaneous peer effects while the effects due to peers' previous influence are called lagged peer effects. Social interactions in a study group generate contemporaneous peer effects while diffusions of infectious diseases represent lagged peer effects.

5 Group vs. individual peer effects. Peer effects can be either based on the group or the individual. Sometimes people are more likely to be influenced by their peer groups while other times only by their best friends or other types of individual social ties. Peer effects within a study group can be an example for the former while obesity, smoking, or monopolistic competition can be examples for the latter.

6 Unidirectional vs. bidirectional peer effects. Unidirectional peer effects occur when peer effects flow only one way, from one subject to another, but not the other way around. Bidirectional peer effects happen that peers influence each other and the peer effects flow reciprocally.

7 Symmetric vs. asymmetric peer effects. The effect a subject has on his or her peer is the same as the effects that this peer has on the subject him/herself, they are called symmetric peer effects. When the two effects are not equal, they are called asymmetric peer effects. For example, religious persons are may have stronger effects in converting their contacts into religions than the effects their contacts have in pulling them out of religions. Similar are the peer effects between smokers and nonsmokers.

8 Peer effects on preference, behavior, or outcome. In terms of the content of peer influence, peer effects can be operate on preference, behavior, outcome, or any combination of them.

The important role played by peer effects in mediating social economic outcomes have been repeatedly documented in the literature. Researchers have shown that peers matter on diffusion of innovations (Coleman et al., 1957) and technology adoption (Oster and Thornton, 2009), job seeking and status attainment (Granovetter, 1973, 1974; Williams, 1981; Fernandez and Weinberg, 1997; Lin, 1999; Fernandez et al., 2000), widening of socioeconomic inequality (Finneran and Kelly, 2003; Calvo-Armengol and Jackson, 2004, 2007; Salganik et al., 2006), social spreading of obesity (Christakis and Fowler, 2007; Trogdon et al., 2008; Halliday and Kwak, 2009; Carrell et al., 2010), autism (Liu et al., 2010), cigarette smoking (Ennett and Baumann, 1993; Maxwell, 2002; Christakis and Fowler, 2008), criminal or delinquent behaviors (Baerveldt et al., 2008; Carrington, this volume), and sexually transmitted diseases (Laumann and Youm, 1999;

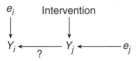

Figure 34.1 Exogenous peer effects from to Y_j to Y_i

Bearman et al., 2004), flow of mass communication (Katz and Lazarsfeld, 2005), mobilization of social movements and civic participation (Diani and McAdam, 2003; Lim, 2009), patterns of migrations (Garip, 2008) and energy consumption (Ayres et al., 2009), conformity of political opinions (Lazer et al., 2008), spillover of workers' productivity (Moretti, 2004; Greenstone et al., 2008; Mas and Moretti, 2009), and so on.

Understanding peer effects through the lens of social network analysis has important implications for public policies. We can either change or utilize the social network structures of peer groups to improve policy effectiveness. Take the seating arrangement in a classroom, for an example. If students with high GPAs have larger positive peer effects on students with low GPAs than on students with high GPAs, then students with high GPAs should be seated with students with low GPAs to maximize the average student GPA. Certainly, the seat arrangement also depends on the objectives of the education and the incentives of the teachers. Maybe the teachers do not care about the average GPA but the number of students who have GPAs above a certain threshold. If that is the case, students with high GPAs probably should be seated together. Take smoking prevention for another example. We can choose the popular subjects, for example, those who receive the most friendship nominations in a peer group, as opinion leaders to lead smoking prevention programs and accelerate the diffusion of positive information, attitudes and behaviors regarding smoking (Valente and Davis, 1999).

Understanding peer effects using DAGs and counterfactuals

An important issue in studying peer effects is how to identify the observed correlations among peers' attitudes, behaviors, or outcomes as causal. Directed acyclic graphs (DAGs) (Pearl, 2000) provide a very intuitive conceptual tool to present causal paths and can be deployed here to show the causal paths of peer effects. For simplicity, suppose we have data on some outcome of interest (Y) and attributes (X) of a group of subjects and we are interested in whether subjects' outcomes are affected by their peers' outcomes. We can use the following DAG to present the hypothetical causal paths of such endogenous peer effects.

In Figure 34.2, we assume that subject i has nominated j as his or her peer and are interested in if Y_j has any effects on Y_i. We assume that each subject's outcome Y is affected not only by their own covariates, X_i, but also by the covariates of their connected peers, X_j. e_i and e_j are just idiosyncratic error terms. This is an extremely simplified

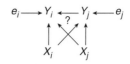

Figure 34.2 The causal paths of endogenous peer effects from Y_j to Y_i

version of peer(s) effects. If we have perfect measurement on all the relevant variables and the diagram accurately characterizes how peer effects work in reality, the causal effects from Y_j to Y_i are certainly identifiable, as all the backdoor paths are essentially blocked. But there are several issues to be solved before we can make such an optimistic claim.

The first issue is what we mean by "causal effects". There has been a tremendous amount of philosophical discussion on this, from Aristotle to Hume, to Lewis, and so on (Zalta, 2008). Among them, Donald Rubin's counterfactual model or potential outcomes framework (1974) is increasingly popular and more relevant here. Below is a simple introduction to it. See Morgan and Winship (2007) and Pearl (2009) for more comprehensive reviews.

Suppose there is a binary treatment D and outcome Y that we are interested in. Let $Y_i(1)$ denote the potential outcome for unit i under treatment while $Y_i(0)$ is its potential outcome under control. Then the individual treatment effect is defined as the difference between the two potential outcomes, that is, $\tau_i = Y_i(1) - Y_i(0)$. However, since we can observe only one of the potential outcomes for each unit, τ_i is not directly identifiable. To identify each individual treatment effect, τ_i, we need to impute the missing potential outcome for each unit, for example, by matching on covariates or propensity scores, and so on. Below I will use the potential outcomes framework to examine the various difficulties in identifying peer effects.

Ambiguity of the treatment

If we are studying the peer effects of some exogenous policy intervention, then the treatment is well defined, which is the designed policy intervention. But if we are interested in endogenous peer effects, then the treatment is conceptually ambiguous. To fix ideas, let's suppose we are studying the effects of a hypothetical person's best friend's smoking status on his or her own smoking status. What is the treatment in this case? Is it the pure fact that this person's friend is or is not a smoker, or the number of cigarettes smoked per day by the friend, or both? In addition, what is the counterfactual in this case? Is it that this person has no friends at all, or that this person does not know this particular friend, or that this person knows this friend but he or she is not a smoker? In practice, peer effects are usually estimated using dyadic data, which implicitly assumes that the estimated peer effects only apply to populations who have friends but not to those who do not have friends. From this perspective, it can be argued that peer effects are conditional effects, conditioning on the fact that there is at least one friend for the subjects of interest. Hence, in the above example, the counterfactual for a person whose best friend is a smoker would be that this person's best friend is not a smoker. If we are going to use matching methods to estimate peer effects, we would have to adopt a double-matching algorithm, namely, both the person of focus and his/her friend need to be matched with another pair of people who share similar characteristics with the original pair of people respectively, except that the counterfactual friend is not a smoker. In general, careful thoughts are needed to define the counterfactual clearly in any specific study.

Violation of ignorability

A very important condition for the use of potential outcomes framework to analyze causal effects in observational studies is conditional ignorability, meaning that conditional on covariates, potential outcomes are independent of treatment. It is very likely that the conditional ignorability does not hold when studying peer effects, for two reasons. One is because of selection bias or homophily. Namely, subjects tend to be friends with other subjects who are similar to them, which may lead assignment of treatment to depend on potential outcomes. For example, overweight people may tend to be friends with other overweight people, corrupt officials tend to befriend other corrupt officials, and so on. Hence, it is not your overweight or corrupt friends who make you overweight or corrupt, but you select people who are overweight or corrupt to be friends from the beginning. Without taking such a selection into account, estimates of peer effects will certainly be biased, often upwardly. The other reason that the

conditional ignorability may not hold is due to confounding, meaning other factors correlated with the outcomes of both the subject and his or her peers, be they biological or contextual, are omitted from the model. For example, it might be the poor neighborhood that a person and his friend both reside in that leads both of them to be obese or overweight. Not taking into account this neighborhood alike factors in the analysis will lead to omitted variable bias in the estimated peer effects. Below is a diagram showing the causal paths of peer effects with an omitted variable U. Without control for U, the backdoor path between Y_j and Y_i will be left open.

Violation of STUVA

A fundamental assumption of potential outcomes framework is the stable treatment unit value assumption (STUVA), which says that a subject's treatment status should not affect another subject's outcome. There are two features of peer effects that clearly violate such an assumption – one is simultaneity and the other is transitivity. Simultaneity means that Y_i also affects Y_j at the same time Y_j is affecting Y_i. Simultaneity causes ordinary least squares (OLS) estimates of peer effects to be both biased and inconsistent. Transitivity means subject k is a common friend of both subject j and subject i, and Y_k affects both Y_j and Y_i. It also allows Y_i and Y_j to react to Y_k. In some sense, transitivity can be viewed as a special type of simultaneity. Below is a diagram showing peer effects with simultaneity and transitivity.

Special techniques have to be employed to address the simultaneity and transitivity problem. For example, we can check for simultaneity using the Hausman test. If simultaneity does exist and the parameters governing peer effects are not underidentified, either indirect least squares (ILS) or two stage least squares (2SLS) estimators can be applied to estimate the peer effects. See Chapters 18–20 of Gujarati (2002) for an introduction to the simultaneity problem. As to the transitivity problem, a sort of system of equations method seems necessary. Further work needs to be done in this area.

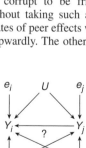

Figure 34.3   Peer effects with omitted variable *U*

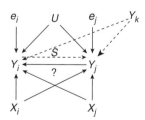

Figure 34.4   Peer effects with omitted variable, simultaneity, and transitivity

The second large issue in modeling and estimating peer effects originates from the static view of network and behavior. We usually assume that social networks and social behaviors embedded in them are fixed. But in many cases, both networks and behaviors keep evolving and we need to model the co-evolution of the networks and behaviors in order to separate peer selection from peer influence and obtain precise estimates of peer effects. There have been only a few studies taking this approach. I will review them more thoroughly below.

The third issue in identifying peer effects comes from missing data and measurement error. They can arise from a variety of reasons. For example, people may forget some of their social ties being inquired, there might be coding errors in the data (e.g., because of duplicated names), or a social network is constructed only using a convenience sample in which subjects are not appropriately sampled and their links are not fully traced, and so forth.

In summary, some of the biggest problems in studying peer effects arise from (1) unclear definition of peer effects; (2) ambiguity of treatment; (3) violation of ignorability either due to selection or confounding; (4) violation of STUVA either due to simultaneity or transitivity; (5) static view of networks and behaviors; and (6) missing data and measurement error.

The first two problems are more at a conceptual level and have been addressed above. I will provide more thorough review on the rest four issues in the following sections. More specifically, in section 2, I will review the literature on why and how people form peer networks. This will help us better understand the mechanisms of how peer effects work out and the importance to separate peer selection from peer influence in order to obtain valid casual estimates of peer effects. In section 3, I will review some of the popular models and methods that were developed recently to identify peer effects. This is the central part of this review. Section 4 will focus on missing data and measurement error in social networks and review their consequences on the estimations and inference of peer effects. Lastly, I will summarize and discuss some breakthroughs in studying peer effects that are tangible in the near future.

WHY AND HOW PEER NETWORKS ARE FORMED

Choice, chance, and gene

To fix ideas, I will use the friendship network as an example to illustrate why and how peer networks are formed. In the literature, three factors

have been considered as important in friendship formation. To put it simply, they are choice, chance, and gene. Choice means subjects have certain preference and the autonomy to choose whom they want to affiliate with. The underlining assumption is that friendship formation is based on utilitarian consideration. Unsurprisingly, many economists take this point of view and treat friendship as an instrument to obtain material or emotional benefits. For example, Jackson and Wolinsky (1996: 44) assumed that "self-interested individuals choose to form new links or to sever existing links." For another example, Bala and Goyal (2000: 1181) argued that "social networks are formed by individual decisions that trade off the costs of forming and maintaining links against the potential rewards from doing so. We suppose that a link with another agent allows access, in part and in due course, to the benefits available to the latter via his own links." Similar utilitarian argument can be found in Christakis et al. (2010) and Ellison (2010) as well. See Demange and Wooders (2005) for more papers on economic view of group formation. The utilitarian view of friendship formation leads to predictions of particular networks which usually consist of only simple architectures like the wheel and the star (Bala and Goyal, 2000).

Another important factor in friendship formation is chance. By chance I do not mean "randomness" but the structure governing the opportunities for people to meet or know each other. According to Zeng and Xie (2008: 4), opportunity structure refers to "the influence of all factors other than preference on choice" and it can include population composition and organizational structure and activities. Obviously, it is very difficult to operationalize and measure opportunity structure accurately. The basic point is that the likelihood for any pair of subjects to form a friendship is not only determined by their preference and choice, but also by the possibility and the number of times that they can meet and interact. In this sense, researchers like Zeng and Xie recognize and emphasize that choices of friends are bounded by the opportunity structure. The following studies present some of the empirical evidence supporting the important role played by opportunity structure. For example, Abu-Ghazzeh (1999: 41) showed that "opportunities to walk around a small group of houses or to sit in small, confined spaces, by contrast, were significantly related to social interaction and friendship formation." For another example, Carrington (2002) demonstrated that the observed amount of sex homogeneity among co-offenders, particularly among males, to a large extent can be attributed to the relatively small number of females involved in crime, rather than signifying a preference for sex homophily. Lastly, Marmaros, and Sacerdote (2004: 1) presented that "two randomly chosen white students interact three times more often than do a black student and a white student. However, placing the black and white student in the same freshman dorm increases their frequency of interaction by a factor of three."

Many scholars acknowledge that the above two factors may work together in generating social networks. For example, Jackson and Rogers (2007: 1) showed that social networks generated through the combination of both random and local search process "results in a spectrum of features exhibited by large social networks." Currarini et al. (forthcoming: 1) showed that empirical social networks "can be generated by biases in preferences and biases in meetings."

Whatever the specific driving force is underneath, social networks present a large degree of homophily regarding to many sociodemographic, behavioral, and intrapersonal characteristics (McPherson et al., 2001: 415). Homophily due to selection on the outcomes will bias the estimates of peer effects if not accounted for properly. For example, Arala et al. (2009) found that previous methods overestimated peer influence in product adoption decisions by three to seven folds and that homophily explained more than 50 percent of the perceived behavioral contagion in a global instant messaging network of 27.4 million users.

According to some recent studies, genes also played some part in producing the correlations of friends' behaviors and some features of their social networks. Fowler et al. (2007) found a significant genetic influence on adolescent friends' alcohol use (about 30%) and significant correlations between the genetic influences on friends' alcohol use and adolescents' own use and their problem use of alcohol. Fowler, Dawesa et al. (2009) showed that at least three social network attributes including in-degree, transitivity, and centrality, were inheritable and could be attributed to genetic factors. Also see Madden et al. (2002) for a similar study using twins or siblings pairs to assess the respective contributions of peer selection and peer influence to the correlations of peer behaviors.

One limitation of the above studies is that they neglect the social opportunities produced and delimited by the structures of the social networks and their roles in friendship formation. Random graph models are invented partly to address this problem.

Random graph models

For brevity, I will review only three classic random graph models here. Readers are encouraged to read other related models like stochastic blockmodels (Holland et al., 1983; Wang and Wong, 1987) and latent space model (Hoff et al., 2002).

Assuming dyadic independence, Holland and Leinhardt (1981) developed the p1 model for friendship formation. Given two randomly chosen subjects i and j, there are four possible relationships between them: (1) there is no tie between them; (2) there is a tie from i to j; (3) there is a tie from j to i; and (4) there is a mutual tie between i and j. The probabilities of these four types of ties are assumed to be given as follows.

$$\ln(P_{00}) = k_{ij} \tag{34.1}$$

$$\ln(P_{10}) = k_{ij} + a_i + \beta_j + \mu \tag{34.2}$$

$$\ln(P_{01}) = k_{ij} + a_j + \beta_i + \mu \tag{34.3}$$

$$\ln(P_{11}) = k_{ij} + a_i + \beta_j + a_j + \beta_i + 2\mu + \rho_{ij} \tag{34.4}$$

where k_{ij} is a normalizing constant, ensuring probabilities summarized to one, a the sender effect (or "a productivity parameter"), β the receiver effect (or "an attractiveness parameter"), μ a base rate of tie formation or a density parameter, and ρ the reciprocity effect ("force of reciprocation"). For identification reason, it is assumed that ρ_{ij} is same across all ties, designated as ρ. Then the log likelihood function for observing a network w can be written as

$$\ln P_1(w) \propto \mu L(w) + \sum_i^N a_i w_{i+}$$
$$+ \sum_j^N \beta_j w_{+j} + \rho M(w) \tag{34.5}$$

with the constraint that $a_+ = \beta_+ = 0$. $L(w)$ is the number of ties in the network, w_{i+} the number of outgoing ties, w_{+j} the number of incoming ties, and $M(w)$ the number of mutual ties. Maximum Likelihood method can be used to estimate the parameters.

As a random effects version of the p1 model, the p2 model was developed to account for the dependence between ties sharing a same subject and the effects of covariates on tie formation (Van Duijn et al., 2004). The model setup is the same as in the p1 model except for the following:

$$a_i = X_{1i}\gamma_1 + a \tag{34.6}$$

$$\beta_i = X_{2i}\gamma_2 + \beta \tag{34.7}$$

$$\mu_{ij} = \mu + Z_{1ij}\lambda_1 \tag{34.8}$$

$$\rho_{ij} = \rho + Z_{2ij}\lambda_2 \tag{34.9}$$

where a and β are random variables drawn from a multivariate distribution with mean zero, and Z's are attributes measured at dyadic level. The estimation is usually done by generalized least squares or by Markov Chain Monte Carlo (MCMC) methods.

p* model can contain more complicated forms of dependence between network structures. The literature on p* model has been growing dramatically in the past few years. Some of the notable papers include Wasserman and Robins (2005), Snijders et al. (2006), Goodreau (2007), Robins, Pattison et al. (2007), Robins, Snijders et al. (2007), and Robins (this volume), to name only a few. In the p* model, the probability of observing any social network is assumed to take the following form:

$$\ln P(W = w|\theta) \propto \sum_k \theta_k S_k(w) \qquad (34.10)$$

S_k can be any network statistics of interest, for example, the number of reciprocal ties, the number of triangles, and so on. Note that p1 model is actually a special form of p* model, both belonging to exponential random graph models (ERGMs). Pseudo-likelihood methods or MCMC methods are generally used to estimate the parameters in p* models.

To conclude this section, we can see that peer networks are not formed randomly. On the one hand, people are free to choose their friends. On the other hand, their freedom to choose friends is constrained by their biological predisposition and whom they can meet in the physical or social environment in which they are embedded. Taking into account the process of friendship formation is very crucial for addressing the selection problem in estimating peer effects.

MODELS AND METHODS TO IDENTIFY PEER EFFECTS

Now let's look at how selection, confounding, and simultaneity problems are handled in specific models. Depending on the data structure, these models can be roughly divided into four groups: static models, dynamic models, experiments and natural experiments, and simulation studies.

Static models

There are generally two types of static models for studying peer effects, depending on the feature of the dependent variables. The linear-in-means models is suitable for modeling continuous outcomes while the binary model aims at dealing with binary outcomes.

Linear-in-means model

The linear-in-means model is very popular in economics (Manski, 1993; Weinberg, 2007; Graham and Hahn, 2009; Bramoullé et al., 2009). It assumes that a subject's outcome is determined by not only his or her own covariates but also the respective mean values of the covariates and outcomes of his or her peer group. Without loss of generality, we can assume there are only two subjects in any peer group. Their outcomes are modeled by the following equations:

$$Y_i = a_1 X_i + a_2 X_j + \beta Y_j + e_i \qquad (34.11)$$

$$Y_j = a_1 X_j + a_2 X_i + \beta Y_i + e_j \qquad (34.12)$$

First note that the above simultaneous equations cannot be estimated using OLS, because the Y's in the regressors are correlated with the error terms. If we write out the reduced form of the above two equations, we can see that

$$Y_i = \frac{\alpha_1 + \beta \alpha_2}{1 - \beta^2} X_i + \frac{\alpha_2 + \beta \alpha_1}{1 - \beta^2} X_j + (be_j + e_i) \qquad (34.13)$$

Basically what we try to do using the reduced form of equation is to regress the outcomes on all the exogenous covariates and use the estimated coefficients to recover the original parameter values. Since there are only two exogenous covariates but three parameters (a_1, a_2, and β) to be estimated, the above simultaneous equations are not identified without further assumptions. One assumption, which is reasonable in some cases, is that there is an exogenous variable included in one equation but excluded in the other equation. For example, we can think of a_2 is equal to zero in equation (34.11). If this is the case, then (34.11) is identifiable and indirect least squares (ILS) will provide an estimate of the coefficient of peer effects, β. If there are more than one such exogenous variable, the model will be overidentified. In that case, two-stage least squares (2SLS) can be used to estimate the peer effects. Another approach is to use instrumental variables (IVs) for Y_i and Y_j in the regressors so that their correlations with the error terms are blocked. For example, we can use lagged Y's as instruments for Y's in the regressors, but this requires dynamic data. Bramoullé et al. (2009) proposed using the outcomes of intransitive and indirect contacts as IVs to identify peer effects. For example, according to Bramoullé et al. (2009), suppose there is an intransitive triad in which subject i is affected by j and j is affected by k, but i is not affected by k, then k's outcome can be used as an instrumental variable for j's outcome to identify the effects of j on i. Bramoullé et al. (2009) also extended the above technique to deal with situations in which fixed network effects are present. See Chapter 15 of Greene (2002) and Chapters 10–11 of Wooldridge (2002) for more discussions on the general techniques to address the simultaneity problem. If transitivity exists, namely, some of the peer groups overlap with one another, either the method proposed by Bramoullé et al. (2009) or some other methods based on system of equations have to be employed to estimate peer effects. This needs further investigation.

Binary outcome model

If the outcomes of interest are measured as binary, a logit or probit model is usually adopted to model peer effects (Brock and Durlauf, 2001a and 2001b; Bulte and Lilien, 2001; Sorensen, 2006; Krauth, 2009). Below shows the logit model:

$$\text{logit}[P(Y_i = 1)] = \ln\left[\frac{P(Y_i = 1)}{P(Y_i = 0)}\right]$$
$$= \alpha_1 X_i + \alpha_2 X_i + \beta Y_i \qquad (34.14)$$

$$\text{logit}[P(Y_j = 1)] = \ln\left[\frac{P(Y_j = 1)}{P(Y_j = 0)}\right]$$
$$= \alpha_1 X_j + \alpha_2 X_i + \beta Y_i \qquad (34.15)$$

The likelihood function can be written as

$$L(Y \mid X, \alpha_1, \alpha_2, \beta) = \prod_{i=1}^{n}\left[\frac{1}{1+e^{-(\alpha_1 X_i + \alpha_2 X_j + \beta Y_j)}}\right]^{y_i}$$
$$\left[\frac{1}{1+e^{(\alpha_1 X_i + \alpha_2 X_j + \beta Y_j)}}\right]^{1-y_i} \qquad (34.16)$$

According to Brock and Durlauf (2001b), the nonlinearity between predictors and outcomes solves the simultaneity problem and facilitate the identification of peer effects.

One challenge to the static models is that there may be omitted variable bias. In other words, the estimated peer effects may be due to common environment factors rather than peer influence. For example, Bulte and Lilien (2001) showed that when pharmaceuticals' marking efforts were controlled for, the social contagion of physician prescription, originally attributed to peer influence by Coleman et al. (1957), disappeared.

Other static methods to identify peer effects include variance decomposition (Glaeser et al., 1996), comparison of group and individual level of regression coefficients (Glaeser et al., 2002), Rosenbaum's nonparametric methods (2007), strategies based on group size variations (Davezies et al., 2009; Lee, 2009), and so on.

Dynamic models

Dynamic network data are very useful to solve or mitigate the selection and confounding problems. Besides the models being reviewed below, some other useful techniques suitable for analyzing dynamic network data include event history analysis (e.g., Liu et al., 2010), the dynamic matched sample estimation framework (Aral et al., 2009), and so forth.

Dynamic logit model

Christakis and Fowler (2007 and 2008) and Fowler and Christakis (2009a) applied dynamic logit models to analyze peer effects on obesity, smoking and happiness, respectively. The outcomes are assumed to be generated according to the following model:

$$\text{logit}[P(Y_{it} = 1)] = \alpha_1 X_{it} + \gamma Y_{it-1} + \beta_1 Y_{jt}$$
$$+ \beta_2 Y_{jt-1} + e_{it} \qquad (34.17)$$
$$\text{logit}[P(Y_{jt} = 1)] = \alpha_1 X_{jt} + \gamma Y_{jt-1} + \beta_1 Y_{it}$$
$$+ \beta_2 Y_{it-1} + e_{jt} \qquad (34.18)$$

According to Christakis and Fowler (2007: 373), they used "generalized estimating equations to account for multiple observations of the same ego across examinations and across ego-alter," and "assumed an independent working correlation structure for the clusters. . . . The use of a time-lagged dependent variable (lagged to the previous examination) eliminated serial correlation in the errors (evaluated with a Lagrange multiplier test) and also substantially controlled for the egos genetic endowment and any intrinsic, stable predisposition to obesity. The use of a lagged independent variable for an alter weight status controlled for homophily."

Cohen-Colea and Fletcherb (2008) raised some critiques of the dynamic logit model used in Christakis and Fowler (2007), claiming that it may overestimate peer influence by ignoring contextual effects. Regardless of the model specification issue, some recent research finds that the magnitudes of peer influence may vary by health behaviors or outcomes. For example, VanderWeele (2010) finds that the contagion effects for obesity and smoking are reasonably robust to possible homophily or contextual effects while those for happiness are less so.

Fixed effects model

Fixed effects can be used to explicitly account for some part of the omitted variable bias and selection bias (e.g., Nanda and Sorensen, 2008; Mas and Moretti, 2009). For example, suppose there is a variable measuring the common environmental factor for subject i and j, U_{ij}, and there is another variable measuring the propensity for subject i and j to form a tie, S_{ij}. We can use G to represent the time-invariant variables like race, gender, or even genes. Then a dynamic linear peer effects model can be written as:

$$Y_{it} = \alpha_1 X_{it} + \alpha_2 X_{jt} + \beta Y_{jt} + \theta_1 U_{ijt}$$
$$+ \theta_2 S_{ijt} + \theta_3 G_i + e_{it} \qquad (34.19)$$

Using a first-difference estimator by subtracting both sides of the above equation by previous values, we will get

$$\Delta Y_{it} = \alpha_1 \Delta X_{it} + \alpha_2 \Delta X_{jt} + \beta \Delta Y_{jt}$$
$$+ \theta_1 \Delta U_{ijt} + \theta_2 \Delta S_{ijt} + \Delta e_{it} \qquad (34.20)$$

The effects of time-invariant variables are dropped out. If we assume both U_{ijt} and S_{ijt} do not change over time, their effects will be dropped out as well and the above equation can be simplified to

$$\Delta Y_{it} = \alpha_1 \Delta X_{it} + \alpha_2 \Delta X_{jt} + \beta \Delta Y_{jt} + \Delta e_{it} \qquad (34.21)$$

If U_{ijt} and S_{ijt} do change over time and cannot be observed or measured directly, there are generally two ways to solve the problem. One is to use proxy variables to measure the two change variables. For example, ΔU_{ijt}, representing environmental changes, can be approximated by the average change in the outcomes of the neighbors of subjects i and j. It is difficult to find proxy variables for ΔS_{ijt}. So a model for friendship formation is needed to predict the propensity for any pair of subjects to form friendship. For example, we can use the random graph models covered in the previous section to model friendship formation and plug into the outcome model the predicted probabilities of friendship formation to account for friendship selection. The other way is to use IVs. Since it is difficult to come up with any IVs for ΔS_{ijt}, this approach is more suitable to address the unobserved ΔU_{ijt} problem. For example, we can use the outcome of subject j's siblings who do not live in the same neighborhood as does subject j, to instrument for subject j's outcome. In many cases, it is reasonable to assume that siblings' outcomes are correlated and there are no direct effects of subject j's siblings' outcomes on subject i's outcome and so the IVs are valid in this sense. Of course, if there are good measures for environmental changes, we should directly include them into the model. But in practice measures of the environmental changes may not be available, comprehensive, or accurate. So the above approaches may still be useful in many cases.

In addition, we can include lagged outcome variables on the right side of equation 34.19 to account for any inertia between successive outcomes. Arellano and Bond (1991) proposed a method to estimate this type of dynamic panel data model.

Stochastic actor-oriented model

The stochastic actor-oriented model was developed by Snijders (2001 and 2005) and also presented in Snijders et al. (2009), Steglich et al. (2010), Snijders (this volume), and so on, to model peer network formation and peer influence (i.e., behavioral changes) jointly. It assumes changes in peer networks and behaviors follow two separate continuous Markov processes. The frequencies of the two types of changes are determined by two rate functions, one for each: λ_N for network and λ_B for behavior. The waiting time for any change is assumed to follow an exponential distribution, $P(T > t) = e^{-(\lambda_N + \lambda_B)}t$. Potentially, the λ's can vary across subjects, by incorporating subjects' covariates and network positions into the rate functions. Subjects make both types of changes according to two objective functions, which are assumed to be a linear summation of the effects of network structures and behavioral features.

$$f_i^N(w, w', z) = \sum_k \beta_k^N S_k^N(i, w, w', z), \qquad (34.22)$$

$$f_i^B(w, w', z) = \sum_k \beta_k^B S_k^B(i, w, w', z, z') \qquad (34.23)$$

w and w' represent the network statistics of subject i and his or her peers, respectively and z and z' the covariates (including behavioral measures) of subject i and his or her peers respectively. Thus, this model combines both the random network model with the behavioral model, and so allows us to separate peer selection from peer influence. One drawback of this model is that it is too complicated to allow for closed-form estimation of the parameters. Usually stochastic simulation techniques like MCMC are needed to estimate the parameters. Koskinen (2004) and Koskinen and Snijders (2007) have extended the stochastic actor-oriented model using Bayesian methods. Another limitation of this model is that it assumes at any given time, there can only be one change happening in a social network, which might not be realistic in some cases. For example, in faction politics, the rupture between leaders of members of the two factions may lead to massive dissolving of ties between the members of the two factions at the same time. Similar examples can be found in international politics, in social events where people make multiple friends at the same time, etc.

Experiments and natural experiments

If we say the above models and methods try to address the various problems in estimating peer effects in the data analysis process, experiments and natural experiments are used to solve some of those problems in the data generation process. Broadly speaking, there are two types of experiments. One is randomly assigning policy treatment to subjects. This type of experiment is not particularly concerned with estimating peer effects. Instead, it provides an estimate of the total policy effects including peer effects. To separate peer effects, special experimental designs are necessary. For example, a partial population design can be used for estimating peer effects under control (PEC), in which treatment is applied to only partial members of each of the treatment groups. The difference between the average outcome of the untreated units in the treatment groups and the average outcome of the control units in the control groups can be viewed as an estimate of PEC. To estimate peer effects under treatment (PET), a group-based treatment design is needed in which treatment is assigned to two groups, with participants in one group being random individuals with no connections between one another while participants in the other group with internal connections among them, for examples, a group of friends or colleagues. The difference between the average outcome of the former participants and that of the latter participants will provide an estimate of PET.

The other type of experiment is randomly assigning friends to subjects. This aims at eliminating the selection problem, but note that it does not necessarily eliminate the confounding problem. For example, in many colleges roommates are randomly assigned. Suppose there is a positive correlation of the academic performance of the roommates. Because the roommates are randomly assigned, we know such a correlation cannot be attributed to the fact that the students select others whose academic performance is similar to them to be their roommates. But this does not eliminate the possibility that part of the correlation may be due to a roommates' common teaching fellow, common living environment, and so on. Special care has to be taken to mitigate the effects of the common environmental factors in order to obtain good estimates of peer effects.

There have been many studies using the first type of experiment. Here are a few examples for studying PEC. Duflo and Saez (2003) recruited a random sample of employees in a number of departments in a university to attend a retirement plan information fair by promising a monetary reward for attendance. They found that "the experiment multiplied by more than five the

attendance rate of these treated individuals (relative to controls), and tripled that of untreated individuals within departments where some individuals were treated" (Duflo and Saez, 2003: 815). They also found that the retirement plan enrollment five and eleven months after the fair was significantly higher in departments where some employees were treated than in departments where none was treated." For another example, Cipollone and Rosolia (2007) provided evidence on the social interaction effects of the schooling achievement of young men on those of young women. The authors found that an exemption from compulsory military service was granted to a few cohorts of males living in southern Italy as a result of an earthquake in 1980, and showed that the exemption increased boys' high school graduation rates by more than 2 percentage points and that at the same time the graduation rates of girls in the same cohorts increased by about 2 percentage points. Since in Italy women are not subject to military draft, they attributed the change in their schooling achievements to the schooling behavior of the exempt males (Cipollone and Rosolia, 2007: 948).

As examples for studying PET, Wing and Jeffrey (1999) showed that in a weight loss program, participants recruited with friends had a higher treatment completion rate and greater weight loss than those who were recruited to participate in the program alone; Falk and Ichino (2006) provided experimental evidence showing that subjects working as a pair had higher productivity than those working alone; and Babcock and Hartman (2010) found that students who had been incentivized to exercise increased gym usage more if they had more treated friends.

Examples for the second type of experiment are abundant. Sacerdote (2001) found that among freshman year roommates and dormmates who were randomly assigned at Dartmouth College, peers had an impact on grade point average and on decisions to join social groups such as fraternities. Kremer and Levy (2003) examined students at a large state university who were randomly assigned roommates through a lottery system and found that on average, males assigned to roommates who had reported drinking in the year prior to entering college had one quarter-point lower GPA than those assigned to non-drinking roommates. Using a dataset in which students were exogenously assigned to peer groups, Carrell et al. (2009) were able to find much larger academic peer effects than in previous studies Boisjoly et al. (2006: 2) presented that "white students at a large state university who were randomly assigned African-American roommates in their first year are more likely to endorse affirmative action and view a diverse student body as essential for a high-quality education." Camargo et al (2010: 1) also documented that "randomly assigned roommates of different races are as likely to become friends as randomly assigned roommates of the same race," and "in the long-run, white students who are randomly assigned black roommates have a significantly larger proportion of black friends than white students who are randomly assigned white roommates." Rao et al. (2007) found that at a large private university where undergraduates were randomly assigned to residential halls, a student becames up to 8.3 percentage points more likely to get immunized if an additional 10 percent of his or her friends received flu shots. Carrell et al. (2010) reported that when individuals were randomly assigned to peer groups, there were statistically significant peer effects on fitness outcomes and such effects were caused primarily by friends who were the least fit. Another interesting study is conducted by Cook et al. (2007) who showed that sixth grade students attending middle schools were much more likely to be cited for discipline problems than those attending elementary schools. The authors explained that this was possibly because the sixth graders attending middle schools were exposed to older peers and relatively loose supervision. In a recent experiment on trust games conducted by Fowler and Christakis (2009b: 1), "subjects were randomly assigned to a sequence of different groups." They showed that "focal individuals ('egos') are influenced by fellow group members ('alters') in future interactions with others. Furthermore, this influence persists for multiple periods and spreads up to three degrees of separation (from person to person to person)."

Admittedly, there are also some studies that reported only modest or marginal peer effects. For example, Angrist and Lang (2004) found that a school integration program sending minority students from Boston schools to more affluent suburban schools did not significantly affect the scores of white students and only modestly decreased the scores of the minority third graders, both in the host districts. Another study done by Imberman et al. (2009) suggested that the influx of evacuated students because of Hurricanes Katrina and Rita moderately reduced elementary math test scores in the receiving schools in Houston, whereas Katrina evacuees benefited from the relocation, experiencing a .15 standard deviation improvement in scores (Sacerdote, 2008). Jackson (2010: 1) indicated that within-school increases in peer achievement improved outcomes only at high-achievement schools. See Boozer and Cacciola (2001), Boruch (2005), Carrell et al. (2008), Ammermueller and Pischke (2009), and Duflo et al. (2009) for more experimental studies on educational peer effects.

It should be noted that peer effects are often connected to neighborhood effects. In general, we can say peer effects reflect the impact of the social environment of a neighborhood. In this sense, recent studies using experiments (e.g., Moving to Opportunity) to detect neighborhood effects are informative to studying peer effects (Kling et al., 2007; Clampet-Lundquist and Massey, 2008; Ludwig et al., 2008; Sampson, 2008). Three comments are in order on these studies. First, if there are no neighborhood effects there might not be peer effects either, as peer effects are often nested in neighborhood effects. Second, some measures need to be taken to account for the selection bias when participants of the experiments can move into different neighborhoods. If by neighborhood effects we mean "the consequences of living in a certain type of neighborhood," then we should fix the assignment of neighborhood. For example, we can move subjects from a disadvantaged neighborhood to an advantaged neighborhood and do not allow them to move afterwards to other types of neighbourhoods, especially to disadvantaged ones. Otherwise, if we allow individuals to freely choose the neighborhoods they want to reside in, the resulting estimates of the neighborhood effects will be biased. Third, a more interesting question is why subjects from disadvantaged neighborhoods tend to move to other disadvantaged neighborhoods. As Sampson (2008) pointed out, selection bias is a fundamental social process that is worth studying in itself. Is this due to personal preference, stocks of social capital in different neighborhoods, or segregative policies and actions in the receiving neighborhoods? Similarly, if we are studying peer effects on smoking, we need to ask why smokers tend to be friends with other smokers and where such homophily comes from, and so on. Answers to these questions are very crucial for us to better understand and correctly estimate both neighborhood effects and peer effects.

Simulation studies

Simulations enable researchers to manipulate the features of social networks and policy treatments at their will and so provide them with a flexible tool to model and identify peer effects and to evaluate model performance, etc. Here are some notable studies using simulations to study peer effects. Christakis and Fowler (2007) argued that the directionality of social ties could be used as an identification strategy for distinguishing peer influence from other social correlation effects. They showed that mutual friends influence each other the most and people who are nominated by others as friends have influence on the nominators while the nominators have no influence on the nominees. Anagnostopoulos et al. (2008) reformulated this as the edge-reversal test, arguing that, "Since other forms of social correlation (other than social influence) are only based on the fact that two friends often share common characteristics or are affected by the same external variables and are independent of which of these two individuals has named the other as a friend, we intuitively expect reversing the edges not to change our estimate of the social correlation significantly. On the other hand, social influence spreads in the direction specified by the edges of the graph, and hence reversing the edges should intuitively change the estimate of the correlation" (2008: 11). However, the simulations he conducted indicated that the edge-reversal test might not be so effective as expected. One reason for this, I conjecture, is that even though the edge-reversal test could possibly eliminate the bias due to contextual effects, it does not necessarily exclude selection bias. It might be that the nominees just tend to have a smaller variation in outcomes of interest. For example, people who are fitter may be more likely to be nominated as friends. In the simplest OLS framework, when you use these friends' weight as predictors of the nominators' weight, it is likely to see significance. But in the reverse regression setting where you use the nominators' weight to predict the nominees' weight, due to the larger variation in the nominators' weight, it is likely you do not obtain significance.

In addition, this might happen because of random sampling errors. The nominees are usually just a small subset of the subjects in a social network who are repeatedly nominated by others as friends or social contacts. Even if the nominees are randomly chosen from the total subjects, the variation in the nominees' outcomes is likely to be smaller than the variation in the nominators' outcomes due to the repetition of nominations while the variance of the variation in the nominees' outcomes is likely to be larger than the variance of the variation in the nominators' outcomes from trial to trial. Hence, any observed directional peer effects may just be a result of sampling error.

Anagnostopoulos et al. (2008) brought up another type of innovative test of peer effects in dynamic network data: the shuffle test. In brief, they showed that if social influence does not play a role, the estimates of peer effects will be close to each other whether the timing of peers' actions are shuffled or not while in contrast, if social influence indeed plays a role, the estimates of peer effects will generally be different when the timing of peers' actions are shuffled.

Bahr et al. (2009) provided an interesting example of using simulations to study social contagion of obesity. The authors showed that "individuals with similar BMIs will cluster together into groups, and if left unchecked, current social forces will drive these groups toward increasing obesity. . . . The popular strategy for dieting with friends is shown to be an ineffective long-term weight loss strategy, whereas dieting with friends of friends can be somewhat more effective by forcing a shift in cluster boundaries . . . simulations also show that interventions targeting well-connected and/or normal-weight individuals at the edges of a cluster may quickly halt the spread of obesity" (Bahr et al., 2009: 723). See Fu (2011) for another interesting simulation study on the imitation dynamics of vaccination behaviors on social networks.

MISSING DATA AND MEASUREMENT ERROR

So far we have been assuming that there are neither missing data nor measurement error in the observed social networks. But, in reality, missing data and measurement error are quite prevalent in social network data. First, missing data can arise from several scenarios (Handcock and Gile, 2007). Here are some examples:

1   Nonrandom sampling of subjects. A typical example for this is that social network data is collected using only a convenience sample in which subjects and their contacts are not properly sampled.
2   Missing links. Subjects may not want to release any information about their contacts or just forget to nominate some of their friends. So when there is no tie between subjects, we may not be able to distinguish if there is really not a relationship between them or the relationship is missing in the data collection process.
3   Not fully traced links. For example, in a fixed-choice design, subjects are asked to nominate only a fixed number of contacts. As a result, subjects with more than the fixed number of contacts will underreport their real number of contacts. This problem may also come from the fact that the boundary of the social network being studied is not clearly defined. For example, what we mean by friendship, peer group, and neighborhoods are not always clearly or consistently understood by researchers and respondents.
4   Absence or attrition of subjects. These may occur when subjects or their contacts are dropped out

of a study, due to their absence at the survey time, moving or death, and so on.

5 Missing covariates. Some covariates like income and education may not be readily available when the social network data are collected.

Similarly, measurement error in social network data can arise because of several reasons. First, it might be that what friendship means is different to each respondent—do we allow respondents to cite themselves, their spouses, or relatives as their best friends? Second, although unlikely but still possible, people may misreport their contacts. For example, if you ask middle school students to nominate their close friends, many of them may over-report the number of close friends they have, because of implicit social competition for popularity. In addition, it is well known that due to the sensitivity issue, some of the covariates like income, sexual activities, political orientation, psychological measures, and so on, tend to be reported with a lot of measurement error. Last, inaccurate data input can generate another source of measurement error. For example, people with same names might bring about errors in data input, etc.

Missing data and measurement error may have severe consequences on social network analysis of peer effects. Brewer and Webster (1999: 361) noticed that "on average, residents forgot 20 per cent of their friends. Forgetting also influenced the measurement of some social network structural properties, such as density, number of cliques, centralization, and individuals' centralities." Ghani et al. (1998: 2079) found that when there were missing data, "substantial systematic biases are introduced. The direction and magnitude of these biases suggest that, by ignoring them, the risk for the establishment and persistence of infection in a population may be underestimated." Robins et al. (2004: 257) distinguished "ties between respondents from ties that link respondents to non-respondents", and found that "if we assume that the non-respondents are missing at random, . . . treating a sizable proportion of nodes as non-respondents may still result in estimates, and inferences about structural effects, consistent with those for the entire network. . . . If, on the other hand, the principal research focus is on the respondent-only structure, with non-respondents clearly not missing at random, . . . values of parameter estimates may not be directly comparable to those for models that exclude non-respondents." Kossinets (2006: 247) showed that "network boundary specification and fixed choice designs can dramatically alter estimates of network-level statistics. The observed clustering and assortativity coefficients are overestimated via

omission of affiliations or fixed choice thereof, and underestimated via actor non-response, which results in inflated measurement error."

There have been some attempts to address the problems due to missing data and measurement error. Butts (2003: 103) developed a family of hierarchical Bayesian models to allow for "the simultaneous inference of informant accuracy and social structure in the presence of measurement error and missing data." Handcock and Gile (2007) developed inferences for social networks with missing data based on information from adaptive network mechanisms. Koskinen et al. (2008: 2) discussed "various aspects of fitting exponential family random graph models to networks with missing data and present a Bayesian data augmentation algorithm for the purpose of estimation."

A general procedure to deal with missing data (and potentially measurement error as well) in social network analysis has been laid out by Butts (2003: 105), which is worth repeating here. "(1) Determining the extent of error in existing data. (2) Determining the mechanisms by which error is produced. (3) Finding means of collecting higher quality data. (4) Minimizing and accounting for the uncertainty associated with missing data in network analyses."

SUMMARY AND FUTURE DIRECTIONS

This chapter reviewed the literature on models and methods to identify peer effects. Below is a summary of what we can learn from the literature. Bear in mind this summary only provides a general outline to handle the problems in studying peer effects. There must be ad hoc considerations and solutions to the problems in any specific research.

(1) Explicitly define the concept of peers and the boundary of the peer group. (2) Clearly discuss the content, meaning, and directionality of the peer effects. (3) If possible, try to use dynamic data analysis techniques (e.g., fixed effects models) to model the co-evolution of network and behavior and to control for confounding and selection. (4) Use statistical techniques like instrumental variables, 2SLS, or system of equations to account for simultaneity or transitivity. (5) Adjust for missing data and measurement error through imputation, etc.

Despite the significant progress that has been made in the last decade in modeling and analyzing peer effects, there are certain areas that need further investigation and the study of which may generate fruitful results.

1 Experiments. Given the complexity and difficulty in analyzing peer effects using observational data, experiments like those with the partial population design should be applied more often to surpass some of the barriers and to obtain better estimates of peer effects.
2 Front door mechanisms. More research needs to be done to identify and describe the specific mechanisms by which peer effects operate. For example, suppose we are interested in the social spreading of obesity. The potential front door mechanisms may include that friends tend to share similar norms or standards on what constitute a normal weight, that friends tend to eat similar food, that friends tend to do group exercises together, and so on. If we can operationalize some of these mechanisms and obtain measures on the variables involved, we can study the specific mechanisms by which peers affect each other (e.g., Anderson, 2009; de la Haye et al., 2009). In addition, qualitative studies (e.g., Michell and West, 1996; Stewart-Knox et al., 2005) based on interviews and focus groups can serve for that purpose as well.
3 Model network formation and peer effects jointly. On the one hand, those continuous Markov process models need to be refined to account for more nuanced processes of peer network formation and peer influence, for example, by properly distinguishing social contagion, social influence, and social learning from each other (Young, 2009). On the other hand, new models and methods, simpler to communicate and compute while still with good approximations to the real world, need to be developed (e.g., Merckena et al., 2009). Given the similarities between spatial models and network models, some techniques developed in spatial analysis may be applicable to social network analysis as well (e.g., O'Malley and Marsden, 2008; Lee, 2009).
4 Computation with large social networks. With large social network data becoming increasingly available and models becoming more complicated, there must be new and better solutions to reduce the mounting computational cost in social network analysis. One possible solution is to use partial samples of social network data to estimate and infer peer effects. The other is more of a brute force approach, just inventing faster computational methods such as parallel computing. Both network sampling and computing for analysis of large social network data demand further research.

Last, I want to close this review with a quote from *The Analects of Confucius* (adopted from the English version by Legge, 2004), which perfectly accords with one of the main purposes of this review and may shed some light on the dynamics of the peer influence process: "When we see men of worth, we should think of equalling them; when we see men of a contrary character, we should turn inwards and examine ourselves."

NOTE

The author wants to thank Professor Nicholas Christakis, Christopher Winship, Filiz Garip and Peter Carrington for their helpful comments and suggestions. Sincere thanks also go to relevant participants of the American Sociological Association Methodology Section Conference at University of Illinois at Urban-Champaign (04/03, 2010), the Health and Social Structure Workshop at the Department of Health Care Policy of Harvard Medical School (06/24, 2010), the SunBelt XXX of International Network for Social Network Analysis at Riva del Garda, Italy (07/04, 2010), the International Sociological Association World Congress in Gothenburg, Sweden (07/12, 2010) and the 105th American Sociological Association Meeting in Atlanta, Georgia, USA (08/15, 2010).

REFERENCES

Abu-Ghazzeh, T.M. (1999) 'Housing layout, social interaction, and the place of contact in Inabu-Nuseir, Jordan'. *Journal of Environmental Psychology,* 19: 41–73.

Albert, R. and Barabási, A.-L. (2002) 'Statistical mechanics of complex networks'. *Reviews of Modern Physics,* 74(1): 47–97.

Ammermueller, A. and Pischke, J.-S. (2009) 'Peer effects in European primary schools: Evidence from the progress in international reading literacy study'. *Journal of Labor Economics,* 27(3): 315–48.

Anagnostopoulos, A., Kumar, R. and Mahdian, M. (2008) 'Influence and correlation in social networks'. In *Proceedings of the 14th ACM SIGKDD International Conference on Knowledge Discovery and Data Mining.* New York: ACM, pp. 7–15.

Anderson, L.B. (2009) 'The trend in obesity: The effect of social norms on perceived weight and weight goal'. *Working paper,* http://www2.binghamton.edu/economics/graduate/documents/prospectus-by-l-anderson.pdf.

Angrist, J.D. and Lang, K. (2004) 'Does school integration generate peer effects? Evidence from Boston's Metco program'. *American Economic Review,* 94(5): 1613–34.

Aral, S., Muchnika, L. and Sundararajana, A. (2009) 'Distinguishing influence-based contagion from homophily-driven diffusion in dynamic networks'. *PNAS,* 106(51): 21544–49.

Arellano, M. and Bond, S. (1991) 'Some Tests of Specification for Panel Data: Monte Carlo Evidence and an Application to Employment Equations'. *The Review of Economic Studies*, 58(2): 277–297.

Ayres, I., Raseman, S. and Shih, A. (2009) 'Evidence from two large field experiments that peer comparison feedback can reduce residential energy usage'. *NBER Working Paper* No. 15386, http://www.nber.org/papers/w15386.pdf

Babcock, P.S. and Hartman, J.L. (2010) 'Networks and Workouts: Treatment Size and Status Specific Peer Effects in a Randomized Field Experiment'. *NBER Working Paper* No. 16581, http://www.nber.org/papers/w16581.pdf

Baerveldt, C., Volker, B. and Rossem, R.V. (2008) 'Revisiting selection and influence: An inquiry into the friendship networks of high school students and their association with delinquency'. *Canadian Journal of Criminology and Criminal Justice*, 50(5): 559–87.

Bahr, D.B., Browning, R.C., Wyatt, H.R. and Hill, J.O. (2009) 'Exploiting social networks to mitigate the obesity epidemic'. *Obesity*, 17(4): 723–28.

Bala, V. and Goyal, S. (2000) 'A noncooperative model of network formation'. *Econometrica*, 68(5): 1181–229.

Bearman, P.S., Moody, J. and Stovel, K. (2004) 'Chains of affection: The structure of adolescent romantic and sexual networks'. *American Journal of Sociology*, 110: 33–91.

Blume, L. and Durlauf, S.N. (2005) 'Identifying social interactions: A review'. http://www.ssc.wisc.edu/econ/archive/wp2005–12.pdf.

Boisjoly, J., Duncan, G.J., Kremer, M., Levy, D.M. and Eccles, J. (2006) 'Empathy or antipathy? The impact of diversity'. *American Economic Review*, 96(5): 1890–905.

Boozer, M.A. and Cacciola, S.E. (2001) 'Inside the 'bBlack box' of Project Star: Estimation of peer effects using experimental data'. Yale Economic Growth Center Discussion Paper No. 832, http://www.econ.yale.edu/growth_pdf/cdp832.pdf.

Boruch, R.F. (ed.). (2005) *Place-Based Trials: Experimental Tests of Public Policy*. Thousand Oaks, CA: Sage.

Bramoullé, Y., Djebbari, H. and Fortin, B. (2009) 'Identification of peer effects through social networks'. *Journal of Econometrics*, 150(1): 41–55.

Brewer, D. and Webster, C. (1999) 'Forgetting of friends and its effects on measuring friendship networks'. *Social Networks*, 21: 361–73.

Brock, W.A. and Durlauf, S.N. (2001a) 'Interactions-based models'. Chapter 54 of *Handbook of Econometrics V*, edited by J.J. Heckman and E. Leamer. Elsevier Science.

Brock, W.A. and Durlauf, S.N. (2001b) 'Discrete choice with social interactions'. *The Review of Economic Studies*, 68(2): 235–60.

Bulte, C.V. d. and Lilien, G.L. (2001) 'Medical innovation revisited: Social contagion versus marketing effort'. *American Journal of Sociology*, 106(5): 1409–35.

Butts, C. (2003) 'Network inference, error, and informant (in) accuracy: A Bayesian approach'. *Social Networks*, 25: 103–40.

Calvo-Armengol, A. and Jackson, M. (2004) 'The effects of social networks on employment and inequality'. *American Economic Review*, 94 (3): 426–54.

Calvo-Armengol, A. and Jackson, M. (2007) 'Networks in labor markets: Wage and employment dynamics and inequality'. *Journal of Economic Theory*, 132: 27–46.

Camargo, B., Stinebrickner, R. and Stinebrickner, T.R. (2010) 'Interracial Friendships in College'. *NBER Working Paper* No. 15970, http://www.nber.org/papers/w15970.pdf

Carrell, S.E., Fullerton, R.L. and West, J.E. (2009) 'Does your cohort matter? Measuring peer effects in college achievement'. *Journal of Labor Economics*, 27(3): 439–64.

Carrell, S.E., Hoekstra, M. and West, J.E. (2010) 'Is poor fitness contagious? Evidence from randomly assigned friends'. *NBER Working Paper* No. 16518, http://www.nber.org/papers/w16518.pdf.

Carrell, S.E., Malmstrom, F.V. and West, James E. (2008) 'Peer effects in academic cheating'. *Journal of Human Resources*, 43(1): 173–207.

Carrington, P.J. (2002) 'Sex homogeneity in co-offending groups', in J. Hagberg (ed.), *Contributions to Social Network Analysis, Information Theory and Other Topics in Statistics: A Festschrift in Honour of Ove Frank*. Stockholm: Stockholm University. pp. 101–16.

Carrington, P.J., Scott, J. and Wasserman, S. (eds) (2005) *Models and Methods in Social Network Analysis*. New York: Cambridge University Press.

Christakis, Nicholas A., and Fowler, James H. (2007) 'The spread of obesity in a large social network over 32 years'. *New England Journal of Medicine* 357(4): 370–79.

Christakis, N.A. and Fowler, J.H. (2008) 'The collective dynamics of smoking in a large social network'. *New England Journal of Medicine*, 358(21): 2249–58.

Christakis, N.A., Fowler, J.H., Imbens, G.W. and Kalyanaraman, K. (2010) 'An empirical model for strategic network formation'. *NBER Working Paper* No. 16039, http://www.nber.org/papers/w16039.pdf

Cipollone, P. and Rosolia, A. (2007) 'Social interactions in high school: Lessons from an earthquake'. *The American Economic Review*, 97(3): 948–65.

Clampet-Lundquist, S. and Massey, D.S. (2008) 'Neighborhood effects on economic self-sufficiency: A reconsideration of the moving to opportunity experiment'. *American Journal of Sociology*, 114(1): 107–43.

Cohen-Colea, E. and Fletcherb, J.M. (2008) 'Is obesity contagious? Social networks vs. environmental factors in the obesity epidemic'. *Journal of Health Economics*, 27: 1382–1387.

Coleman, J., Katz, E. and Menzel, H. (1957) 'The diffusion of an innovation among physicians'. *Sociometry*, 20: 253–70.

Cook, P.J., MacCoun, R., Muschkin, C. and Vigdor, J. (2007) 'Should sixth grade be in elementary or middle school? An analysis of school configuration and student behavior'. *NBER Working Paper* No. w12471, http://www.nber.org/papers/w12471.pdf.

Currarini, S., Jackson, M. and Pin, P. (forthcoming) 'An economic model of friendship: Homophily, minorities and segregation'. *Econometrica*.

Davezies, Laurent, D"Haultfoeuille, Xavier Fougre, Deni. (2009) 'Identification of peer effects using group size variation'. *Econometrics Journal*, 12: 397C413.

Demange, G. and Wooders, M. (2005) *Group Formation in Economics: Networks, Clubs, and Coalitions*. New York: Cambridge University Press.

Diani, M. and McAdam, Doug. (eds) (2003) *Social Movements and Networks: Relational Approaches to Collective Action*. New York: Oxford University Press.

Doreian, Pa. (2001) 'Causality in social network analysis'. *Sociological Methods & Research* 30(1): 81–114.

Duflo, E., Dupas, P. and Kremer, M. (2009) 'Peer effects, teacher incentives, and the impact of tracking: Evidence from a randomized evaluation in Kenya'. *NBER Working Paper* No. 14475, http://www.nber.org/papers/w14475.pdf.

Duflo, E. and Saez, E. (2003) 'The role of information and social interactions in retirement plan decisions: Evidence from a randomized experiment'. *The Quarterly Journal of Economics*, 118(3): 815–42.

Van Duijn, M., Snijders, T. and Zijlstra, B. (2004) 'p2: A random effects model with covariates for directed graphs'. *Statistica Neerlandica*, 58: 234–54.

Duncan, O.D., Haller, A.O. and Portes, A. (1968) 'Peer influences on aspirations: A reinterpretation'. *American Journal of Sociology*, 74(2): 119–37.

Ellison, G., Glaeser, E.L. and Kerr, W.R. (2010) 'What causes industry agglomeration? Evidence from coagglomeration patterns'. *American Economic Review*, 100: 1195–1213.

Ennett, S.T. and Baumann, K.E. (1993) 'Peer group structure and adolescent cigarette smoking: A social network analysis'. *Journal of Health and Social Behavior*, 34: 226–36.

Falk, A. and Ichino, A. (2006) 'Clean evidence on peer effects'. *Journal of Labor Economics*, 24(1): 39–57.

Fernandez, R.M., Castilla, E.J. and Moore, P. (2000) 'Social capital at work: Networks and employment at a phone center'. *American Journal of Sociology*, 105(5): 1288–356.

Fernandez, R.M. and Weinberg, N. (1997) 'Sifting and sorting: Personal contacts and hiring in a retail bank'. *American Sociological Review*, 62(6): 883–902.

Finneran, Lisa, and Kelly, Morgan (2003) 'Social networks and inequality'. *Journal of Urban Economics* 53: 282–99.

Fowler, J.H. and Christakis, N.A. (2009a) 'Dynamic spread of happiness in a large social network: Longitudinal analysis over 20 years in the Framingham heart study', *British Medical Journal* 337(42): 2338–47.

Fowler, J.H. and Christakis, N.A. (2009b) 'Cooperative behaviour cascades in human social networks'. http://www.citebase.org/abstract?id=oai:arXiv.org:0908.3497.

Fowler, J., Dawesa, C. and Christakis, N. (2009) 'Model of genetic variation in human social networks'. *Proceedings of the National Academy of Sciences of the USA*, 106(6): 1720–24.

Fowler, J.H., Heaney, M.T., Nickerson, D.W., Padgett, J.F. and Sinclair, Betsy (2009) 'Causality in political networks'. *Political Networks Paper Archive Working Papers*, Southern Illinois University Carbondale, http://opensiuc.lib.siu.edu/cgi/viewcontent.cgi?article=1034&context=pn_wp.

Fowler, T., Shelton, K., Lifford, K., Rice1, F., McBride, A., Nikolov, I., Neale, M.C., Harold, G., Thapar, A. and van den Bree, M.B.M. (2007) 'Genetic and environmental influences on the relationship between peer alcohol use and own alcohol use in adolescents'. *Addiction*, 102: 894–903.

Fu, F., Rosenbloom, D.I., Wang, L. and Nowak, M.A. (2011) 'Imitation dynamics of vaccination behaviour on social networks'. *Proceedings of Royal Society B*, 278 (1702): 42–49.

Garip, F. (2008) 'Social capital and migration: How do similar resources lead to divergent outcomes?', *Demography*, 45(3): 591–617.

Ghani, A.C., Donnelly, C.A. and Garnett, G.P. (1998) 'Sampling biases and missing data in explorations of sexual partner networks for the spread of sexually transmitted diseases'. *Statistics in Medicine*, 17(18): 2079–97.

Glaeser, E.L., Sacerdote, B.I. and Scheinkman, J.A. (1996) 'Crime and social interactions'. *Quarterly Journal of Economics*, 111(2): 507–48.

Glaeser, E.L., Sacerdote, B.I. and Scheinkman, J.A. (2002) 'The social multiplier'. *NBER Working Paper* 9153, http://www.nber.org/papers/w9153.pdf.

Goldenberg, A., Zheng, A.X., Fieberg, S.E., and Airoldi, E.M. (2009) 'A survey of statistical network models'. *Foundations and Trends in Machine Learning*.

Goodreau, S. (2007) 'Advances in exponential random graph (p*) models applied to a large social network'. *Social Networks*, 29: 231–48.

Graham, B.S. and Hahn, J. (2009) 'Identification and estimation of the linear-in-means model of social interactions'. *Economics Letters*, 88(1): 1–6.

Granovetter, Mark S. (1973) 'The strength of weak ties'. *American Journal of Sociology* 78(6): 1360–80.

Granovetter, M.S. (1974) *Getting a Job: A Study of Contacts and Careers*. Chicago: University of Chicago Press.

Greene, W.H. (2002) *Econometric Analysis*. 5th ed. Prentice Hall.

Greenstone, M., Hornbeck, R. and Moretti, E. (2008) 'Identifying agglomeration spillovers: Evidence from million dollar plants'. *NBER Working Paper* 13833, http://www.nber.org/papers/w13833.pdf.

Gujarati, D. (2002) *Basic Econometrics*. 4th ed. McGraw-Hill/Irwin.

Halliday, T.J. and Kwak, S. (2009) 'Weight gain in adolescents and their peers'. *Economics and Human Biology*, 7: 181–90.

Handcock, M. and Gile, K. (2007) 'Modeling social networks with sampled or missing data'. *Working Paper* No. 75, Center for Statistics and the Social Sciences, University of Washington, http://www.csss.washington.edu/Papers/wp75.pdf.

Hartmann, W.R., Manchanda, P., Nair, H., Bothner, M., Dodds, P., Godes, D., Hosanagar, K. and Tucker, C. (2008) 'Modeling social interactions: Identification, empirical methods and policy implications'. *Marketing Letters*, 19: 287–304.

de la Haye, K., Robins, G., Mohrd, P. and Wilsone, C. (2009) 'Obesity-related behaviors in adolescent friendship networks'. *Social Networks*.

Hoff, P.D., Raftery, A.E. and Handcock, M.S. (2002) 'Latent space approaches to social network analysis'. *Journal of the American Statistical Association*, 97: 1090–98.

Holland, P.W., Laskey, K.B. and Leinhardt, S. (1983) 'Stochastic blockmodels: First steps'. *Social Networks,* 5(2): 109–37.

Holland, P.W. and Leinhardt, S. (1981) 'An exponential family of probability distributions for directed graphs (with discussion)'. *Journal of the American Statistical Association,* 76: 33–65.

Imberman, S, Kugler, A.D. and Sacerdote, B. (2009) 'Katrina's children: Evidence on the structure of peer effects from Hurricane evacuees'. *NBER Working Paper* No. 15291, http://papers.nber.org/papers/w15291.pdf.

Jackson, C.K. (2010) 'Peer Quality or Input Quality?: Evidence from Trinidad and Tobago'. *NBER Working Paper* No. 16598, http://www.nber.org/papers/w16598.pdf

Jackson, M.O. (2008) *Social and Economic Networks.* Princeton: Princeton University Press.

Jackson, M.O. and Rogers, B.W. (2007) 'Meeting strangers and friends of friends: How random are socially generated networks?' *American Economic Review,* http://citeseerx.ist.psu.edu/viewdoc/download?doi=10.1.1.84.8381&rep=rep1&type=pdf.

Jackson, M.O. and Wolinsky, A. (1996) 'A strategic model of social and economic networks'. *Journal of Economic Theory,* 71: 44–74.

Kandel, D.B. (1978) 'Homophily, selection, and socialization in adolescent friendships'. *American Journal of Sociology,* 84(2): 427–36.

Katz, E. and Lazarsfeld, P.F. (2005) *Personal Influence: The Part Played by People in the Flow of Mass Communications.* New Brunswick, NJ: Transaction.

Kling, J.R., Liebman, J.B. and Katz, L.F. (2007) 'Experimental analysis of neighborhood effects'. *Econometrica,* 75(1): 83–119.

Kolaczyk, E. (2009) *Statistical Analysis of Network Data.* Springer.

Koskinen, J. (2004) 'Bayesian inference for longitudinal social networks'. Research Report 2004:4, Department of Statistics, Stockholm University, http://gauss.stat.su.se/site/pdfer/RR2004_4.pdf.

Koskinen, J.H., Robins, G.L. and Pattison, P.E. (2008) 'Analysing exponential random graph (p-star) models with missing data using Bayesian data augmentation'. MelNet Social Networks Laboratory Technical Report 08–04, Department of Psychology, School of Behavioural Science, University of Melbourne, Australia, http://www.sna.unimelb.edu.au/publications/MelNet_Techreport_08_04.pdf.

Koskinen, J. and Snijders, T. (2007) 'Bayesian inference for dynamic social network data.' *Journal of Statistical Planning and Inference,* 137: 3930–38.

Kossinets, G. (2006) 'Effects of missing data in social networks'. *Social Networks* 28: 247–68.

Krauth, B.V. (2009) 'Simulation-based estimation of peer effects'. *Journal of Econometrics,* 1: 243–71.

Kremer, M. and Levy, D.M. (2003) 'Peer effects and alcohol use among college students'. *Working Paper,* http://www.povertyactionlab.org/papers/12_Kremer_Peer_Effects_and_Alcohol_Use.pdf.

Laumann, E.O. and Youm, Y. (1999) 'Racial/ethnic group differences in the prevalence of sexually transmitted diseases in the United States: A network explanation'. *Sexually Transmitted Diseases,* 26(5): 250–61.

Lazer, D., Rubineau, B., Katz, N., Chetkovich, C. and Neblo, M.A. (2008) 'Networks and political attitudes: Structure, influence, and co-evolution'. *Harvard Kennedy School Faculty Research Working Paper Series* RWP08-044, http://web.hks.harvard.edu/publications/getFile.aspx?Id=310

Lee, L.-f. (2009) 'Identification and estimation of spatial econometric models with group interactions, contextual factors and fixed effects'. *Journal of Econometrics,* 140(2): 333–74.

Legge, J. (Trans.) (2004) *The Analects of Confucius,* http://ebooks.adelaide.edu.au/c/confucius/c748a/part4.html.

Lim, C. (2009) 'Mobilizing on the margin: How does interpersonal recruitment affect citizen participation in politics?' *Social Science Research.*

Lin, N. (1999) 'Social networks and status attainment'. *Annual Review of Sociology,* 25: 467–87.

Liu, K.-Y., King, M. and Bearman, P.S. (2010) 'Social influence and the autism epidemic'. *American Journal of Sociology,* 115(5): 1387–1434.

Ludwig, J., Liebman, J.B., Kling, J.R., Duncan, G.J., Katz, L.F., Kessler, R.C. and Sanbonmatsu, L. (2008) 'What can we learn about neighborhood effects from the moving to opportunity experiment?', *American Journal of Sociology,* 114(1): 144–88.

Madden, Pamela A. F., Bucholz, Kathleen K., Todorov, Alexandre A., Grant, Julia D., and Heath, Andrew C. (2002) 'The assessment of peer selection and peer environmental influences on behavior using pairs of siblings or twins'. *Twin Research,* 5(1): 38–43.

Manski, C.F. (1993) 'Identification of endogenous social effects: The reflection problem'. *Review of Economic Studies,* 60: 531–42.

Manski, C.F. (2000) 'Economic analysis of social interactions'. *NBER Working Paper* No. 7580, http://papers.nber.org/papers/w7580.pdf.

Manski, C.F. (2010) 'Identification of treatment response with social interactions'. *Working Paper,* http://faculty.wcas.northwestern.edu/~cfm754/treatment_with_interactions.pdf.

Marmaros, D. and Sacerdote, B. (2004) 'How do friendships form?' *NBER Working Paper* 11530, http://www.nber.org/papers/w11530.pdf.

Marsden, P.V. and Friedkin, N.E. (1993) 'Network studies of social influence'. *Sociological Methods Research,* (22): 127–51.

Mas, A. and Moretti, E. (2009) 'Peers at work'. *American Economic Review,* 99(1): 112–45.

Maxwell, K.A. (2002) 'Friends: The role of peer influence across adolescent risk behaviors'. *Journal of Youth and Adolescence,* 31(4): 267–77.

McPherson, M., Smith-Lovin, L. and Cook, J.M. (2001) 'Birds of a feather: Homophily in social networks'. *Annual Review of Sociology,* 27: 415–44.

Merckena, L., Candela, M., Willemsd, P. and de Vries, H. (2009) 'Social influence and selection effects in the context of smoking behavior: Changes during early and mid adolescence'. *Health Psychology,* 28(1): 73–82.

Michell, L., and West, P. (1996) 'Peer pressure to smoke: The meaning depends on the method'. *Health Education Research,* 11(1): 39–49.

Moffitt, R.A. (forthcoming) 'Policy interventions, low-level equilibria, and social interactions'. In Steven Durlauf and Peyton Young (eds), *Social Dynamics.* MIT Press.

Moretti, E. (2004) 'Workers' education, spillovers and productivity: Evidence from plant-level production functions'. *American Economic Review,* 94(3): 656–90.

Morgan, S.L. and Winship, C. (2007) *Counterfactuals and Causal Inference: Methods and Principles for Social Research.* New York: Cambridge University Press.

Mouw, T. (2006) 'Estimating the Causal Effects of Social Capital: A Review of Recent Research'. *Annual Review of Sociology,* 32: 79–102.

Newman, M.E.J. (2003) 'The structure and function of complex networks'. *SIAM Review,* 45: 167–256.

Nanda, R. and Sorensen, J.B. (2008) 'Peer effects and entrepreneurship'. *Harvard Business School Working Paper,* pp. 08–051, http://papers.ssrn.com/sol3/papers.cfm?abstract_id=1084874.

O'Malley, J.A. and Marsden, P.V. (2008) 'The analysis of social networks'. *Health Services and Outcomes Research Methodology,* 8(4): 222–69.

Oster, E. and Thornton, R. (2009) 'Determinants of Technology Adoption: Private Value and Peer Effects in Menstrual Cup Take-Up'. *NBER Working Paper* No. 14828, http://www.nber.org/papers/w14828.pdf.

Pearl, J. (2000) *Causality: Models, Reasoning, and Inference.* New York: Cambridge University Press.

Pearl, J. (2009) 'Causal inference in statistics: An overview'. *Statistics Surveys,* 3: 96–146.

Rao, N., Mobius, Markus M. and Rosenblat, T. (2007) 'Social networks and vaccination decisions'. *FRB of Boston Working Paper* No. 07–12, http://papers.ssrn.com/sol3/papers.cfm?abstract_id=1073143.

Robins, G., Pattison, P., Kalish, Y. and Lusher, D. (2007) 'An introduction to exponential random graph (p*) models for social networks'. *Social Networks,* 29: 173–91.

Robins, G., Pattison, P. and Woolcock, J. (2004) 'Missing data in networks: Exponential random graph (p*) models for networks with non-respondents'. *Social Networks,* 26: 257–83.

Robins, G., Snijders, T. Wang, P., Handcock, M. and Pattison, P. (2007) 'Recent developments in exponential random graph (p*) models for social networks'. *Social Networks,* 29: 192–215.

Rosenbaum, P.R. (2007) 'Interference between units in randomized experiments'. *Journal of the American Statistical Association,* 102(477): 191–200.

Sacerdote, B. (2001) 'Peer effects with random assignment: Results for Dartmouth roommates'. *Quarterly Journal of Economics,* 116: 681–704.

Sacerdote, B. (2008) 'When the saints come marching in: Effects of Hurricanes Katrina and Rita on student evacuees'. *NBER Working Paper* No. 14385, http://www.nber.org/papers/w14385.pdf.

Salganik, M.J., Dodds, P.S. and Watts, D.J. (2006) 'Experimental study of inequality and unpredictability in an artificial cultural market'. *Science,* 311: 854–56.

Sampson, R.J. (2008) 'Moving to inequality: Neighborhood effects and experiments meet social structure'. *American Journal of Sociology* 114(1): 189–231.

Smith, K.P. and Christakis, N.A. (2008) 'Social networks and health'. *Annual Review of Sociology,* 34: 405–29.

Snijders, T.A.B. (2001) 'The statistical evaluation of social network dynamics'. In M. Sobel and M. Becker (eds), *Sociological Methodology.* Boston: Basil Blackwell. 361–95.

Snijders, T.A.B. (2005) 'Models for longitudinal network data'. In Peter Carrington, John Scott, and Stanley Wasserman (eds), *Models and Methods in Social Network Analysis.* New York: Cambridge University Press. Chapter 11.

Snijders, T.A.B., van de Buntz, G.G. and SteglichIn, C.E.G. (2009) 'Introduction to stochastic actor-based models for network dynamics'. Draft article for special issue of *Social Networks on Dynamics of Social Networks,* http://www.stats.ox.ac.uk/~snijders/SnijdersSteglichVdBunt2009.pdf.

Snijders, T.A.B., Pattison, P., Robins, G. and Handcock, M. (2006) 'New specifications for exponential random graph models'. *Sociological Methodology,* 36: 99–153.

Soetevent, A.R. (2006) 'Empirics of the identification of social interactions: An evaluation of the approaches and their results'. *Journal of Economic Surveys,* 20(2): 193–228.

Sorensen, A.T. (2006) 'Social learning and health plan choices'. *RAND Journal of Economics,* 37(4): 929–45.

Steglich, C., Snijders, T. and Pearson, M. (2010) 'Dynamic networks and behavior: Separating selection from influence'. *Sociological Methodology,* http://www.stats.ox.ac.uk/~snijders/siena/SteglichSnijdersPearson2009.pdf.

Stewart-Knox, B.J., Sittlington, J., Rugkasa, J., Harrisson, S., Treacy, M. and Abaunza, P.S. (2005) 'Smoking and peer groups: Results from a longitudinal qualitative study of young people in Northern Ireland'. *British Journal of Social Psychology,* 44: 397–414.

Trogdon, J.G., Nonnemaker, J. and Pais, J. (2008) 'Peer effects in adolescent overweight'. *Journal of Health Economics,* 27: 1388–99.

Valente, T.W. (2005) 'Network models and methods for studying the diffusion of innovations'. In Peter Carrington, John Scott, and Stanley Wasserman (eds) *Models and Methods in Social Network Analysis.* New York: Cambridge University Press. pp. 98–116.

Valente, T.W. and Davis, R.L. (1999) 'Accelerating the diffusion of innovations using opinion leaders'. *The ANNALS of the American Academy of Political and Social Science,* 566: 55–67.

VanderWeele, T.J. (2010) 'Sensitivity analysis for contagion effects in social networks', Unpublished Manuscript.

Wang, Y.J. and Wong, G.Y. (1987) 'Stochastic blockmodels for directed graphs'. *Journal of the American Statistical Association,* 82(397): 8–19.

Wasserman, S. and Robins, G. (2005) 'An introduction to random graphs, dependence graphs, and p*'. In Peter Carrington, John Scott, and Stanley Wasserman (eds), *Models and Methods in Social Network Analysis.* New York: Cambridge University Press. Chapter 8.

Weinberg, B.A. (2007) 'Social interactions with endogenous associations'. *NBER Working Paper* No. 13038, http://www.nber.org/papers/w13038.pdf.

Williams, R.A. (1981) 'Peer influence vs. peer selection: An attempted separation'. *CDE Working Paper* 81–20, http://www.ssc.wisc.edu/cde/cdewp/8120.pdf.

Wing, R.R. and Jeffery, R.W. (1999) 'Benefits of Recruiting Participants With Friends and Increasing Social Support for Weight Loss and Maintenance'. *Journal of Consulting and Clinical Psychology,* 67(I): 132–138.

Wooldridge, J. (2002) *Econometric Analysis of Cross Section and Panel Data.* Cambridge: MIT Press.

Young, H. P. (2009) 'Innovation diffusion in heterogeneous populations: Contagion, social influence, and social learning'. *American Economic Review,* 99(5): 1899–924.

Zalta, E.N. (2008) *The Stanford Encyclopedia of Philosophy.* The Metaphysics Research Lab Center for the Study of Language and Information, Stanford University, http://plato.stanford.edu/. Especially the entries on 'Aristotle on Causality', 'David Hume', 'Causal Processes' amd 'Counterfactual Theories of Causation'.

Zeng, Z. and Xie, Y. (2008) 'A preference-opportunity-choice framework with applications to intergroup friendship'. *American Journal of Sociology,* 114(3): 615–48.

35

Kinship Network Analysis

Klaus Hamberger, Michael Houseman, and Douglas R. White

KINSHIP IN A NETWORK PERSPECTIVE

Kinship, like language, is a structure, not a substance.[1] The distinctive features of kinship networks reside less in how their constitutive ties – be they biological, jural, ritual, symbolic, or whatever – are defined and established than in the way these ties are organized. Kinship network theory is thus not just another "application" of general network theoretic methods to a particular social domain but a specific branch of social network theory in itself, defined by its own axioms and described by its own theorems.

Kinship networks are characterized by the interplay of three fundamental principles: filiation, marriage, and gender. We ordinarily represent *filiation* by a set of arcs (*descent arcs*) that are directed from parents to children, and *marriage* by a set of undirected edges (*marriage edges*) between spouses (for alternative representations of kinship networks without edges, see below). Kinship networks thus are mixed graphs, containing both arcs and edges. *Gender* is usually taken into account by a partitioning of the vertex set (the *gender partition*), usually into two or three disjoint classes (male, female, and possibly unknown sex).

The characteristic features of kinship networks can be described in terms of cyclicity. While kinship networks do not contain *oriented cycles* (nobody can be his or her own descendant[2]), they may contain *cycles* (where arc direction does not matter): people may marry persons with whom they are already linked by kinship or affinity. Now, such cyclic configurations occur not just randomly but in ways that are informative about the self-organizing behavior of the network. Some kinds of relatives hardly ever marry, while other kinds of kinship ties between spouses may be overrepresented. Marriage rules and prohibitions, but also residential organization, social morphology, and so forth, affect the relative frequencies of different types of cycles in a kinship network. Analyzing the distribution of cycles therefore is the key to kinship network classification and interpretation.

Paths and cycles in kinship networks

Kinship network theory thus rests on a theory of cyclic configurations. We call a *path* an alternating sequence of vertices and lines (edges or arcs of whatever direction), where every vertex is incident with the lines that precede and follow it in the sequence, and all vertices are distinct. If, by contrast, the first and the last vertices are identical (all others being distinct), we obtain a *cycle*. A path is said to be *closed* by a line connecting its first and last vertices, so that adding that line turns the path into a cycle. A path or cycle is called *oriented* if all lines are arcs oriented in the same direction.[3] A *weakly acyclic* network is one that contains no oriented cycles and an *acyclic* network contains no cycles whatsoever.

Alternatively to their definition as (open or closed) *sequences* of vertices and lines, paths and cycles are also often defined as the *graphs* made up of these vertices and lines (in this perspective, a cycle is a connected graph where every vertex has degree 2, a path a connected graph where two vertices have degree 1, and all others degree 2). There is, however, a crucial difference between the two concepts. If we define a path as a sequence, the starting point matters. A path ABC is distinguished from its inverse CBA, or to take a kinship example, the path "father's wife's daughter" (FWD) is distinguished from its inverse, "mother's husband's son" (MHS). If, by contrast, we define a path as a graph, ABC and CBA are only two different notations for one and the same mathematical object – for the kinship case, this means that FWD and MHS are two different ways to express the same kinship chain.

The ambiguity is less severe in the case of cycles, where, by convention, graph theorists treat starting and ending points as irrelevant: the sequences ABCA and BACB are considered identical. Nevertheless, in kinship network analysis we often need to distinguish them. In an ego-centric perspective, marrying one's "father's wife's daughter" (FWD) is different from marrying one's "son's wife's mother" (SWM). By contrast, in a socio-centric perspective – as it is required if, for example, we want to count all cycles of a given type in a kinship network – we have to treat FWD and SWM marriages as two different aspects of one and the same configuration. In other words, we should define paths and cycles as *sequences* when adopting an *ego-centric* view and as *graphs* when adopting a *socio-centric* view. In order to avoid any ambiguity, we shall reserve the terms "path" and "cycle" to sequences and use the terms "chain" and "circuit" when we speak of the corresponding graphs.[4] A *chain* is thus a graph made up by the vertices and lines of a single path, and a *circuit* is a graph made up by the vertices and lines of a single cycle (alternative definitions in terms of degrees and connectedness are given below).

- A *path* is an alternating sequence of vertices and lines (arcs or edges), where each vertex is incident to the preceding and the succeeding line, the vertices preceding and succeeding a line are its endpoints, and all vertices are distinct.
- A *cycle* is a sequence of vertices and lines sharing the properties of a path, except that the first and the last vertex are identical (all other vertices being distinct).
- A path or cycle is called *oriented* if all its lines are arcs oriented in the same direction.

- A *weakly acyclic* graph is one that contains no oriented cycles and an *acyclic* graph contains no cycles whatsoever.
- A *chain* is a graph whose vertices and arcs form a single path (alternatively, it may be defined as a connected graph where two vertices have degree 1 and all others have degree 2).
- A *circuit* is a graph whose vertices and arcs form a single cycle (alternatively, it may be defined as a connected graph where every vertex has degree 2).
- The first and the last vertices of a path are called *endpoints.* Any line connecting the endpoints of a path is said to *close* it; the line's addition to the path transforms the latter into a cycle.

Armed with these basic concepts, we can now describe kinship networks entirely in structural terms, without making statements regarding the nature of the relations involved. Characterizing kinship networks by weakly acyclic filiation, acyclic gendered descent, nonoccurrence of certain types of circuits, and so on is not equivalent to stating that no one can be engendered by his or her own offspring, that it takes a man and a woman to produce children, or that self-organization is brought about by incest prohibitions that prevent people in certain kinship relations from having sex with each other. Filiation does not necessarily involve a biological tie, procreation is not the only basis for parenthood, and marriage prohibitions are not defined everywhere in terms of sexual relations. Kinship network structures may have biological explanations, but these are culturally determined, variable from one society to another, and far from universal.

Biology is the privileged model for kinship inasmuch as it affords a universally intelligible code for expressing the latter's fundamental relations: procreation as a model for filiation, sex as a model for marriage, and so forth. However, being a model for a relationship does not mean being the essence of this relationship. There are many social networks that are clearly kinship networks, both according to structural criteria and in the minds of those concerned, but where filiation, marriage, and gender cannot be defined exclusively in reference

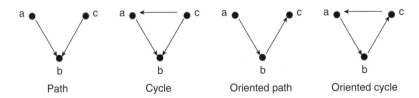

Figure 35.1 Paths and cycles in kinship networks

to biological givens. Kinship is a type of *social structure*, and if people all over the world have chosen to express its basic relations in a biological idiom, there are numerous cases where these relations are defined independently of, and sometimes even in opposition to, biological relationships. Defining kinship in network terms recognizes this fact.

NETWORK REPRESENTATIONS OF KINSHIP

Ore-graph representation

What we have described in our introductory statement is the most conventional representation of a kinship network, where vertices represent individuals, arcs represent filial ties, and edges represent marriages. Such networks are called *Ore-graphs*.[5] If not specified otherwise, kinship networks are treated in this article as Ore-graphs. Their characteristic feature is that they are weakly acyclic.[6] As a consequence, kinship networks contain a directed generational hierarchy.

Gender in Ore-graphs is represented by a partition of the vertex set. This gender partition gives rise to an analogous partition of arcs, according to the gender of the vertex from which they originate. The subgraph produced by arcs originating from parental vertices of the same gender can be termed a *descent graph*. Cycles in descent graphs are ruled out as soon as we impose the condition of *unique descent*, that is, filial arcs for only one parent of each gender: one father and one mother. Under this condition, descent graphs are acyclic, and their connected components are *trees* (the well-known unilinear descent trees of "lineages"). This condition is closely related to the condition of heterosexual marriage, according to which a marriage edge can only link vertices from a different gender. We speak of a *standard kinship network* if these two conditions – unique descent and heterosexual marriage – are satisfied. This allows for the possibility of nonstandard kinship networks, which, because they admit multiple descent[7] and homosexual marriage, require a more complex analysis. In this chapter, we will restrict ourselves to discussing standard kinship networks.

In many cases, marriage is the correlate, sometimes even the condition or equivalent of having children in common. It is therefore useful to distinguish, as a particular category of standard kinship networks, those networks that meet the condition of married co-parents: a standard kinship network will be called *canonical* if the presence of descent arcs from two parent vertices

to the same child vertex necessarily implies the existence of a marriage edge between the parent vertices.

A *kinship network* is a mixed graph G(V, E, A, ~), where V is a set of vertices, called *individual* vertices, E is a set of edges, called *marriage* edges, A is a set of arcs (directed from parents to children), called *descent* arcs, and ~ is an equivalence relation on V partitioning it into n disjoint classes V_i ($i = 1, …, n$), called *genders* (usually $n = 2$ for {male,female}), with the following property:

1 the network is weakly acyclic

The *descent graph* for the ith gender is the subgraph of a kinship network produced by all descent arcs springing from individuals of gender i. They are called *agnatic* for male gender and *uterine* for female gender.

A kinship network is *regular* if

2 [unique descent] no vertex in a subgraph G(V, A_i) (the descent graph for the ith gender) has indegree higher than 1 (which rules out cycles in descent graphs), where A_i is the subset of arcs with origin in V_i. Descent graphs of regular kinship networks are acyclic.

A regular kinship network is *standard* if

3 [heterosexual marriage] the subgraphs G(V_i, E) are empty.

A standard kinship network is *canonical* if

4 [married co-parents] any two vertices that are arc-adjacent to the same vertex[8] are edge-adjacent to each other.

Every kinship network G(V, E, A, ~) is *partially ordered* on V, as is any weakly acyclic graph. This is the *generational* partial order relation. In addition, a kinship network may be *ordered* on V by assigning an arbitrary unique identity number to each individual (this is important for computation issues, but also for data storage in general, see below).

Two individuals linked by a descent arc are called *parent* and *child* with respect to each other. Two individuals linked by an oriented path of descent arcs are called *ascendant* and *descendant* with respect to each other. Two individuals linked by a marriage edge are called the *spouses* of each other. Two individuals are called *co-parents* if they are parents of the same child (arc-adjacent to the same vertex), *siblings* if they are children of the same parent (arc-adjacent from the same vertex), and *co-spouses* if they are spouses

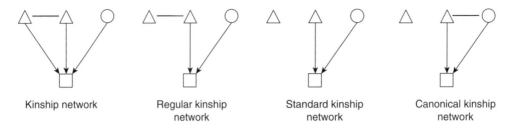

| Kinship network | Regular kinship network | Standard kinship network | Canonical kinship network |

Figure 35.2 Types of kinship networks

of the same spouse (edge-adjacent to the same vertex).

We can reformulate conditions (1)–(4) as follows:

1 In a kinship network, no individual can be his or her own ascendant or descendant.
2 In a regular kinship network, no individual has more than one parent of each gender.
3 In a standard kinship network, parents are regular and spouses are always of different gender.
4 In a canonical kinship network, spouses are standard and all co-parents are spouses.

Simple digraph representations

There are a variety of ways of representing standard kinship networks as digraphs. In addition to an Ore-graph, two of these, P-graphs (White and Jorion, 1992; Harary and White, 2001, also see White, this volume) and bipartite P-graphs (proposed by White, implemented by Batagelj and Mrvar, 2004), are represented in Figure 35.3 where letters indicate individuals (a married couple, wife A and husband B, who have a daughter C and a son D).[9] These are all isomorphic once arc-labels for P-graphs are included.

P-graphs

P-graphs[10] represent couples as vertices and individuals as individually and gender-labeled lines. As these individuals are at once born of one couple and may become partners in another, the arcs that represent them run from the couple formed by an individual and his or her spouse to the couple formed by his or her parents. Unmarried individuals are treated like couples.

P-graphs have the advantages of incorporating fewer lines and vertices, allowing marriage cycles to be more easily detected. An individual who marries several times is represented by several lines that are numbered with individual identity numbers (IDs) or can be given names. The way to distinguish two lines representing the same individual from those representing two same-gender full siblings is by either the line IDs or vectors for individual male or female IDs for each vertex. Apart from these two differences, P-graphs share the structural properties of Ore-graphs, such as weak acyclicity and generational partial ordering.

Bipartite P-graphs

Bipartite P-graphs are two-mode networks where individuals and couples are represented by

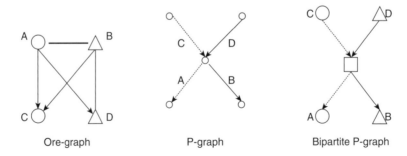

| Ore-graph | P-graph | Bipartite P-graph |

Figure 35.3 Graph representations of kinship networks

vertices. There are therefore no marriage edges, but there are arcs that run from individuals to couples and from couples to individuals.

Bipartite P-graphs are weakly acyclic and, because marriages are represented by vertices, it is possible to represent sibling relations even if the siblings' parents are unknown. In addition, marriages can be easily partitioned, for example, according to marriage dates.

KINSHIP PATHS, KINSHIP RELATIONS, AND MATRIMONIAL CIRCUITS

Kinship paths and relations

The most general definition of a kinship relation relies on the existence of a path linking one individual to another in a kinship network. If we abstract from the individual identity of vertices, kinship paths can be characterized by generic properties such as the *gender* of vertices and the *direction* of lines. This abstract form of a kinship path is an *elementary kinship relation*. Elementary kinship relations thus can be considered as abstract kinship paths (where vertex identity does not matter as long as vertex gender, line direction, and vertex-line incidence are preserved). Whatever property we may state of a path without reference to individual vertices, we may consider as a property of the corresponding elementary kinship relation.

We shall call a *simple* kinship relation one that connects Ego and Alter by a single line. By contrast, we shall call a relation *compound* if it connects Ego and Alter by several consecutive lines. Compound relations can be defined by the composition of simple relations. For instance, "father" is a simple kinship relation, while "mother's father" is a compound one.

Elementary kinship relations are defined by a complete specification of the gender and the direction pattern of a single kinship path connecting Ego and Alter. *Complex* kinship relations are obtained by combining elementary relations by means of one or more logical operations ("and," "or," "not," etc.). If the logical connective is "or," we obtain a *disjunctive* (or "classificatory") relation (e.g., "uterine sibling" is defined as "mother's son *or* mother's daughter"). If the connective is "and," we obtain a *conjunctive* (or "multiple") relation (e.g., "full brother" is defined as "mother's son *and* father's son"). If the connective is "not," we obtain a *residual* relation (e.g., "nonagnatic kin").

Finally, we call a kinship relation *mixed* if properties of vertices and lines other than gender

and direction enter into its definition; for example, the definition of "widow" requires a supplementary partition of vertices (alive vs. dead), the definition of "elder brother" makes reference to a partial order relation defined on filial arcs, and so forth.

- A *kinship path* is a path in a kinship network. The first vertex of a kinship path is called *Ego*; the last one is *Alter*.
- The *direction* of a line in a kinship path is 0 ("horizontal") if it is a marriage edge, −1 ("descending") if it is an arc directed to the successor, and +1 ("ascending") if it is inversely directed.
- Two kinship paths are *isomorphic* if there is a bijection between them that preserves the gender of vertices and the sequence and direction of lines.
- An *elementary kinship relation* corresponds to a maximal set of isomorphic paths in a kinship network. Any of these paths *represents* the kinship relation. Any invariant property of these paths – beginning with the gender and direction sequence – can be considered as a property of the elementary relation.
- A *complex kinship relation* is any relation that can be obtained by logical junction of several elementary kinship relations.

The notation of kinship paths and relations

The conventional notation of kinship relations uses capital letters for indicating direction and the gender of Alter (the gender of Ego must be indicated by additional signs such as ♂ [male Ego] or ♀ [female Ego] placed before the initial letter): ascending arcs are F(ather) and M(other), descending arcs are S(on) and D(aughter), marriage edges are H(usband) and W(ife), plus supplementary letters for B(rother) and Z (sister) relations. Examples of this are MBD (mother's brother's daughter, a matrilateral cross-cousin), ZH (sister's husband, a brother in-law), and FWS (father's wife's son, a stepbrother).

This conventional notation, a simple abbreviation of English kinship terminology, has the advantage of being easy to learn and to apply, but it is hardly the best tool for analysis. It may even obscure the structural similarities and the distinctive properties of kinship relations.

In this respect it can be contrasted with the alternative, positional notation developed by Barry (2004). Here, a kinship relation is represented by a sequence of letters specifying vertex labels (gender) and diacritical signs, which indicate the presence of a marriage edge (the point or full stop ".") and the apical position of a vertex (the parentheses "()"). All letters not separated by a point represent vertices connected by arcs, vertices in "apical" position (i.e., vertices that are not a neighbor's children) are put into parentheses and, by convention, all arcs to the left of an apical vertex have ascending direction, all arcs to its right have descending direction, and the marriage point implies change of direction.

Consider, for example, the kinship path linking a male Ego (1) to a female Alter (5) who is Ego's paternal sister's husband's daughter (Figure 35.4). In positional notation, this relation is written as 1 (2) 3 . (4) 5, where 2 is Ego's and 3's father, 4 is Ego's sister's husband and 5 is the latter's daughter.

By abstracting the concrete identity of the individuals concerned (represented by their number) and retaining their gender only (H for male and F for female[11]), one obtains the kinship relation in question: H(H)F.(H)F.[12] See Table 35.1 for an example of how standard and positional notations are used.

The principle of positional notation also applies to P-graphs. In P-graph notation, with labels for arcs rather than for vertices, the ZHD relation of Figure 35.4 is written HfH.hf, where H and F (solid and dotted lines) give the parents of a male and a female, respectively,[13] relation inverses h=H[-1], f=F[-1] give sons and daughters, and marriages are thus written fH and hF, respectively. The full stop "." in H.h identifies the same individual in a different couple – a distinction that is necessary to clarify that 5 is the child of 4 but not of 3.

Positional notation has a number of important advantages. It incorporates the gender of Ego as well as that of Alter, and it provides a clear representation of the structural properties of kinship relations, which is not radically changed by symmetry transformations. Thus, for example, a man who marries his HF()HF is his wife's FH()FH (in P-graph version: HFhf and FHfh), whereas in conventional notation, a man who marries his MBD is his wife's FZS. Allowing for a homogeneous representation of kinship paths (with individual numbers), of kinship relations (with gender letters), and of kinship relation classes (with gender variables), positional notation may be used not only as a means of notation but also as a classificatory or programming tool.

The classification of kinship relations

In order to compare kinship relations, and to analyze the ways they combine so as to give rise to particular network structures, these relations may be classified according to different criteria. We restrict ourselves here to some basic definitions (for a more extensive treatment, see Hamberger and Daillant, 2008 and Hamberger forthcoming).

A kinship relation is *linear* if it is oriented (we speak of "oriented" paths but of "linear" relations).

Any linear kinship relation can be represented by a *characteristic number* λ

$$\lambda = \sum_{i=0}^{\kappa} (1 + \sigma_i) . 2^i$$

where κ is the degree of the relation (see note 15) and σ_i is the gender number (0 = male, 1 = female) of the ith individual in ascending direction (starting with Ego $i=0$), for example, $\lambda = 1$ for male Ego, $\lambda = 3$ for F/S, $\lambda = 5$ for M/S, $\lambda = 7$ for FF/SS, $\lambda = 13$ for MM/DS, and so on.[14] Characteristic numbers impose an order on all linear kinship relations.

A kinship relation is *canonical* if it contains no linking children positions (i.e., if the kinship path does not pass through parental triads as defined below).

A canonical kinship relation is *consanguineous* if it contains no marriage edge.

A *consanguineous component* of a kinship network is a maximal set of individuals linked to each other by consanguineous paths (an individual

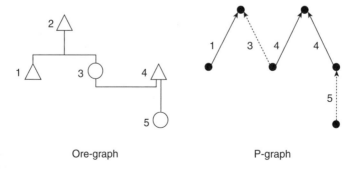

Ore-graph   P-graph

Figure 35.4 A kinship relation in Ore-graph and P-graph representation

Table 35.1 Matrimonial census

111 marriages (2.06%) involving 211 (1.41%) individuals (105 men, 106 women) in 114 circuits of 37 different types (average frequency 3.08) of order 1 and depth 3

ID	Standard	Positional	P-Graph	Marriages	Circuits	% Circuits
1	FBD	HH()HF	HHhf	3	3	2.63
2	FZD	HH()FF	HHff	5	5	4.39
3	FFSD	HH(H)HF	HHH.hhf	4	4	3.51
4	FFDD	HH(H)FF	HHH.hff	10	10	8.77
5	MBD	HF()HF	HFhf	9	9	7.89
6	MZD	HF()FF	HFff	2	2	1.75
7	MFSD	HF(H)HF	HFH.hhf	13	13	11.4
8	MFDD	HF(H)FF	HFH.hff	2	2	1.75
...						

372 marriages (6.89%) involving 667 (4.47%) individuals (339 men, 328 women) in 267 circuits of 152 different types (average frequency 1.76) of order 2 and depth 2

ID	Standard	Positional	P-Graph	Marriages	Circuits	% Circuits
46	FWFSD	H(H).F(H)HF	HH.hfH.hhf	6	3	1.12
47	FWFDD	H(H).F(H)FF	HH.hFH.hff	2	1	0.37
48	FWFFSD	H(H).FH(H)HF	HH.hFHH.hhf	2	1	0.37
49	MHBD	H(F).H()HF	HF.fHhf	2	1	0.37
50	BW	H().H.(F)	HhF	20	10	3.75
51	BWMD	H().H.F(F)F	HhFF.ff	2	1	0.37
...						

62 marriages (1.15%) involving 112 (0.75%) individuals (53 men, 59 women) in 23 circuits of 16 different types (average frequency 1.44) of order 3 and depth 1

ID	Standard	Positional	P-Graph	Marriages	Circuits	% Circuits
190	FWBWZ	H(H).F()H.F()F	HH.hFhFf	6	2	8.7
191	FWZHD	H(H).F()F.(H)F	HH.hFfH.hf	6	2	8.7
192	FWFSWFD	H(H).F(H)H.F(H)F	HH.hFH.hhFH.hf	3	1	4.35
193	FWFDHD	H(H).F(H)F.(H)F	HH.hFH.hfH.hf	6	2	8.7
194	BWBWFD	H()H.F()H.F(H)F	HhFhFH.hf	3	1	4.35
...						

without consanguineous kin constitutes a consanguineous component in itself).

The *length* of a kinship relation is the number of arcs and edges it contains. The *depth* of a kinship relation is the length of the longest linear kinship relation it contains. The *order* of a kinship relation is the number of consanguineous components it contains.[15] The kinship relation represented by the path in Figure 35.4, for example, has a length of 4, a depth of 2, and an order of 2.

Matrimonial circuits

The concept of a matrimonial circuit

Real-world kinship networks grow in two ways. On the one hand, new individuals are born, generally being assigned a father and a mother from birth. In other words, a new vertex emerges together with two arcs linking it to its parents, who are, at the moment of birth, the individual's only direct neighbors in the network. If we assume that the parents are already linked by a marriage edge (i.e., we are dealing with a canonical kinship network), the emergence of a new child vertex does not create a chain between individuals who are not already linked by a shorter chain. Its impact on global structure may thus be said to be marginal: it enlarges the network but does not alter its connectivity.

On the other hand, kinship networks also grow by marriage, that is, by the creation of new edges between two vertices, each of which can already be linked to a neighborhood of other vertices by several different lines going in all directions. The new marriage edge creates new connections between all these neighbors. In this way, marriage changes social structure. But at the same time, the way in which social structure would be changed by a potential marriage influences the marriage choice itself, be it explicitly (through marriage rules and incest prohibitions), implicitly (by virtue of preferences or strategies), directly (by taking into account kinship ties between potential spouses), or indirectly (by taking into account other factors that are in turn correlated with kinship). The probability of two potential partners becoming a couple thus depends upon the nature of the kinship chains between them. Now, the most direct way to study this dependency is to look for those kinship chains that actually connect marriage partners – in other words, to look for circuits.

It should be clear from the preceding remarks that we are not interested in just any type of circuit, but in those circuits that contain at least one marriage edge. However, this restriction is not enough. Every triangle formed by a couple and their child – a *parental triangle* – is a circuit containing a marriage edge, and yet the couple's relation to their common child is hardly a condition of marriage that we wish to consider. More generally, we want to exclude all circuits containing parents together with their children – *parental triads*. We can therefore define the types of circuits of interest to us as those that contain at least one marriage edge and no parental triads. But in fact, the second condition implies the first: as descent is weakly acyclic, the only way to form a circuit in a kinship network without passing through a parental triad is to pass through a marriage edge. We thus arrive at a simple definition of a *matrimonial circuit*:

A *parental triad* is a graph formed by three vertices and arcs pointing from two of them to the third (i.e., by parents and their child). If the parents are joined by a marriage edge, the resulting circuit constitutes a *parental triangle*.

A *matrimonial circuit* is a circuit that does not contain a parental triad. Alternatively, it can be defined as a connected subgraph where every vertex has degree 2 but no vertex has arc-indegree 2. Because of the weak acyclicity of descent (condition 1 in the definition of kinship networks), this definition implies that a matrimonial circuit necessarily contains at least one marriage edge. In P-graph representation (where marriages are vertices and not edges), every circuit is a matrimonial circuit.

Any maximal connected consanguineous chain within a circuit is called an *arch* of the circuit.

A *matrimonial path* is a kinship path that passes through all vertices of a matrimonial circuit as well as through all of its lines except the *closing* marriage edge, which links the first and the last vertex of the path. For a matrimonial circuit containing n marriage edges, there are $2n$ different matrimonial paths.

If the kinship network is ordered (e.g., by arbitrary identity numbers), there is a unique rule of selecting, for any matrimonial circuit, a *characteristic path*: it is the matrimonial path that has the lowest possible Ego and (if there are two such paths) the lowest possible Alter.

A *matrimonial circuit type* is a class of isomorphic matrimonial circuits. Any matrimonial circuit type can be represented as a complex kinship relation formed by a marriage relation and another elementary kinship relation. We can define a unique rule for selecting, among these relations, the *characteristic relation* of a matrimonial circuit type: for example, the relation that begins with the longest sequence of ascending arcs and (if there are several sequences of equal length) with the lowest characteristic number.

Circuit inclusion and rings

Matrimonial circuits have been defined in a most general manner as circuits that do not pass through parental triads. However, there may be situations where we might want to reduce our analysis to only some of these circuits – namely, those that have no "shortcut" linking two of its vertices. Consider, for example, a marriage with the daughter of the maternal uncle's wife (MBWD). Now, if this woman is at the same time the maternal uncle's daughter (MBD), many anthropologists would consider it improper to count her as an MBWD and would want to distinguish such marriages from marriages with "true" MBWDs (stepdaughters rather than daughters of maternal uncles). There is no a priori answer to the question of whether or not to count circuits that contain "shortcuts" of this kind. The choice depends both on the ethnographical context[16] and on the type of circuit in question.[17] In either case, it is useful to distinguish circuits that contain shortcuts from circuits without shortcuts that link their vertices. The latter are called *rings* (White, 2004).[18]

We say that a circuit A *includes* another circuit B if all vertices of the circuit B form part of the circuit A. This may also be stated by saying that B forms part of the subgraph *induced* by the vertices of A, that is, the graph constituted by these vertices and *all* of the lines that connect them in the global network (if a circuit A contains all the vertices of circuit B, the subgraph induced by these vertices also includes the lines of B). An *induced circuit* or *ring* can thus be defined as a circuit that is its own induced subgraph.[19]

The subgraph of a graph G *induced* by a vertex set V is the maximal subgraph of G having V as its vertex set (see Harary, 1969: 11). The subgraph induced by a circuit in the kinship network G is the subgraph of G induced by the vertices of the circuit. We also call it briefly the induced subgraph of the circuit.

A circuit A *includes* a circuit B if every vertex of B is also a vertex of A (i.e., if B lies in the induced subgraph of A).

An *induced circuit* or *ring* is a circuit that does not include any other circuit (i.e., a circuit that is its own induced subgraph). Alternatively, it can be defined as a circuit such that no two vertices of the circuit are connected by a line that is not itself part of the circuit.

Circuit intersection and composition

The definition of an induced circuit (or ring) rules out circuits whose vertices are connected by extra *lines*. It does not, however, exclude circuits whose vertices are connected by extra *chains* (consisting of more than one line). Consider, for example, Figure 35.5, in which a man marries his MMBDD, while his own mother is his father's FFZD.[20]

The chains 1-8-9-5 and 2-8-9-5 "shorten" the outer circuit 1-2-3-4-5-6-7-1 (of type MMBDD), forming two inner rings of type FFZD: 8-9-5-5-4-3-2-8 and 1-8-9-5-6-7-1. But note that the outer circuit also constitutes a ring: as the vertices 8 and 9 do not belong to it, neither of the inner rings is *included* in it.[21] However, it *intersects* with the two inner rings in the sense that it has one or more lines in common with them (for a further discussion of circuit intersection, see below). Moreover, the entire outer ring can be *composed* from the two inner rings and the parental triangle 1-2-8-1 by taking their union and deleting all lines that form part of more than one circuit (an operation called *circuit union*). A circuit that in this manner can be entirely decomposed into circuits shorter

than itself is called *reducible*; if it cannot, it is called *irreducible*. By definition, every irreducible circuit is also a ring.

It should be stressed that reducible circuits are not necessarily sociologically less relevant than irreducible circuits. If a Fulani man, for instance, marries an FFBSD who is at the same time an MBD (due to an FBD marriage between the husband's parents), the apparent cross-cousin marriage MBD may simply be a by-product of successive parallel-cousin marriages (FBD and FFBSD): it is then the longer and not the shorter ring that matters for marriage decisions. Nor does the formation of a reducible circuit presuppose the previous formation of some irreducible circuit (see note 17).

The study of irreducible matrimonial circuits is closely related to the idea of a *cycle basis* in general graph theory. A cycle basis for a graph is a minimal set of circuits from which *all* circuits of a graph can be composed by a circuit union. Different sets of circuits can constitute a cycle basis. However, the number of circuits in the basis (also called the *circuit rank* or *cyclomatic number* of the graph) is invariant: we can compute it from the numbers of its arcs, edges, and components by means of a simple formula (see below). In order to find a cycle basis for a kinship network, it is reasonable to concentrate on irreducible circuits. Note, however, that the cycle basis may well be smaller than the set of irreducible circuits: if a man marries three sisters, we have three irreducible circuits, but the circuit rank is only two (as two circuits are sufficient to compose the third).

Two circuits *intersect* if they have lines in common. They *intersect matrimonially* if they have marriage edges in common.

The *union* of two circuits is the graph that has the union of their line (vertex) set as its line (vertex) set. The *circuit union* of two intersecting circuits consists in taking their union and deleting the lines they have in common.

A circuit is *irreducible* if it cannot be composed by a circuit union from a set of circuits that are all shorter than itself.

A *cycle basis* of a graph is a minimal set of circuits whose union contains all the circuits of the graph.

The *cyclomatic number* or *circuit rank* of a graph is the number of circuits constituting its cycle basis (which is equivalent to the number of lines one has to remove from a graph to make it acyclic). For a graph with e lines, v vertices, and c components, it is calculated as

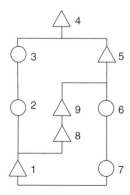

Figure 35.5 Circuit intersection and composition

$$\gamma = e - v + c$$

Counting circuits: The matrimonial census

A matrimonial census provides an exhaustive list of all matrimonial circuits of specified properties in a given kinship network, and it counts the occurrences of every distinct circuit type (which may or may not be aggregated into broader classes).

A circuit search usually has to be restricted to a limited set of circuit types. Even if the total number of circuits in a finite network is not infinite, it is usually so high that an unbounded search exceeds the capacities of the most advanced personal computers. For exploratory analysis, it is recommended to restrict matrimonial circuit search by criteria that are as neutral as possible, such as maximal order and depth of circuits. Do not just count first-cousin marriages in order to decide whether you are dealing with "generalized exchange," "arab marriage," and so on – a look at higher degree consanguineous marriages, and at marriages between affines, may change the entire picture! Kinship structures constitute a whole and can only be understood if one considers them as such; they cannot be characterized by the frequency of this or that circuit type but only by the relative proportions and the interdependency of these frequencies. A matrimonial census must therefore be comprehensive in order to provide the basis for further analysis and interpretation, even if subsequent circuit searches may be more restricted and refined. It is clear that, even for small networks, such a task cannot be accomplished without computer support.

Circuit searches can be undertaken on the entire network or restricted to certain subsets of vertices. This restriction does not imply that *all* vertices of the matrimonial circuit have to belong to the subset (if, for example, we are interested in consanguineous marriages concluded between people born after 1800, we, of course, allow consanguineous chains to pass through ancestors born before 1800). Subsets may be defined according to "exogenous" criteria recorded for the individuals in the network (dates of birth, death, or marriage, residence, occupation, etc.) but also according to "endogenous" criteria deriving from the kinship network itself (e.g., sibling group size, number of known ascendants, number of spouses, etc.). Such restrictions are not only convenient for comparative analysis and tests of representativity, but they may also be helpful in determining the optimal network to work with (see below).

Table 35.1 presents excerpts from a matrimonial circuit census produced by the software Puck (*infra*) of a kinship network collected among the Watchi of Togo,[22] restricted to circuits of order

1 and depth 3, circuits of order 2 and depth 2, and circuits of order 3 and depth 1.

NETWORK REPRESENTATIONS OF CIRCUIT STRUCTURES

The set of matrimonial circuits thus obtained can in turn be studied with genuine network-analytic tools.

One of these tools is to construct the network that the circuits compose; this gives us a *subnetwork* of the original kinship network. A second tool consists of constructing the network of the structural relations between the circuits themselves; this gives us a *second order network* in which the circuits represent the vertices and their structural interrelations are represented by lines.

In the following section, we shall discuss one network of the first type, the matrimonial network, and one of the second type, the circuit intersection network.

Networks derived from circuit sets: The matrimonial network

A *matrimonial network* is a subgraph of a kinship network resulting from the union of a set of matrimonial circuits, as, for instance, the circuits found by the matrimonial census in Table 35.1. Note that this is not equivalent to the subgraph *induced* by this set: for an arc or edge to be in the subgraph, it is not enough that each of its endpoints is in some circuit – the arc or edge must itself be part of a circuit. The matrimonial network derived from a set of matrimonial circuits found in a kinship network is thus simply the network composed of these circuits. It consists, in other words, of the matrimonially "interesting" regions of the original kinship network. The components of the matrimonial network (which we call *matrimonial components*) are connected subnetworks of matrimonial circuits, which may be studied from various perspectives. On the one hand, we may suppose that the frequent occurrence of particular matrimonial patterns is correlated with other properties of the network region concerned (e.g., social class, geographical region, or historical period); we may then apply several partitions to the network in order to evaluate the degree to which partition clusters correspond to matrimonial components. On the other hand, we may interpret the density of circuits as an effect of self-reinforcing social mechanisms (behavior transmission, imitation, or the presence of rules) or as a simple network effect (circuits combining to compose other circuits) that we did not consider when defining the criteria for our initial circuit search.

The concept of a matrimonial network is also meaningful in and of itself, independent of any particular circuit set. Even in cases where it is not possible to precisely identify all matrimonial circuits (without limits of size) that may exist in a kinship network, it is possible to determine which part of the network is composed of matrimonial circuits (of whatever length). The result – the largest possible matrimonial network – is the *nucleus* of the kinship network, the union of all existing circuits in the network (see Grange and Houseman, 2008).

The concept of the nucleus can be more strictly delineated by introducing the concept of a *matrimonial bicomponent*, that is, a maximal subgraph in which every two vertices form part of a matrimonial circuit (note that this is a stricter condition than that of simply forming part of a circuit, as is required for the more general notion of a bicomponent). The nucleus is simply the union of all matrimonial bicomponents.[23]

As a result, matrimonial *components* (consisting only of circuits) are closely related to matrimonial *bicomponents*: both are line-biconnected (two distinct line series link each vertex to every other), but matrimonial bicomponents have the additional feature of being vertex-biconnected as well (the two interconnecting line series never run through the same vertex).

In the kinship network represented in Figure 35.6, for example, the shaded individuals and their interconnections within the bold boundaries constitute the nucleus, which is composed of two matrimonial components (A and B) and three matrimonial bicomponents (1, 2, and 3), two of which overlap (one individual is included in both 1 and 2).

Given a set of circuits R in a kinship network K, the *matrimonial network* derived from R is the subgraph of K resulting from the union of the circuits of R. In other words, it is a subgraph in which every line belongs to some matrimonial circuit of R. The components of a matrimonial network are called the *matrimonial components* of K with respect to R. Matrimonial components are line-biconnected but not necessarily vertex-biconnected.

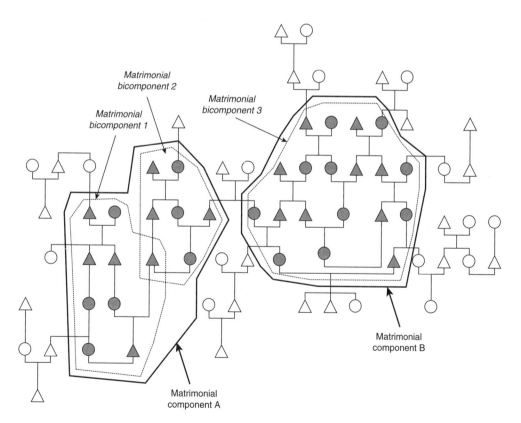

Figure 35.6 Matrimonial components and bicomponents

A *matrimonial bicomponent* is a subgraph of K in which every pair of vertices (no matter how distant) belongs to a matrimonial circuit (hence no pair of vertices can be separated by removal of a single intermediary vertex). In P-graph representation, every bicomponent is a matrimonial bicomponent.

The *nucleus* of a kinship network is the network resulting from the union of all matrimonial circuits in K. The nucleus is equivalent to the union of all matrimonial bicomponents of the kinship network. The largest of these matrimonial bicomponents constitutes the *kernel* of the kinship network.

Networks of circuits: The circuit intersection network

Circuit graphs are tools for analyzing the interdependence of matrimonial circuits. A simple example is the *circuit intersection network*, where circuit interdependence is measured by the frequency of shared marriage edges.

It is often the case that a given marriage forms part of two or several matrimonial circuits. Such overdetermination poses problems of sociological interpretation: if a man has married a woman who is at the same time his father's sister's daughter, his maternal aunt, and his sister-in-law, should we say that he married his cousin, his aunt, or his sister-in-law? And how shall we interpret such a situation if, for instance, it is considered to be very good to marry one's cousin but bad to marry one's aunt? Under such circumstances, it is clearly insufficient to simply count the frequency of maternal aunts that are spouses and affirm the presence of a high number of "bad" marriages, without considering the fraction of such aunts who are at the same time cousins and thus represent "good" spouses. But there is a further reason for wanting to determine the frequencies of circuit intersection: if a father's sister's daughter is at the same time a maternal aunt, such a configuration mathematically implies that the husband's father has married his sister's daughter. We shall therefore necessarily find a high number of niece marriages in our network, and if we did not yet search for them, such a finding will prompt us to do so.

Circuit intersection networks are an easy and intuitive way to approach these questions. In these networks, vertices represent circuit types, the size (or vector value) of vertices represents circuit frequencies, and the values of the lines connecting two vertices represent the number of marriages that are simultaneously part of a circuit of the two corresponding types.

The *matrimonial intersection* of two circuit types A and B is the set of all marriage edges belonging simultaneously to a circuit of type A and to a circuit of type B.

The *circuit intersection network* corresponding to a set of circuit types T is a valued graph G, such that

1 each vertex of G corresponds to a circuit type of T, and the value (size) of the vertex is proportional to the frequency of the corresponding circuit type

2 each edge between two vertices corresponds to a nonempty matrimonial intersection of the corresponding circuit types, and the weights of the edges correspond to the sizes of the intersections.

ALLIANCE NETWORKS

All matrimonial structures hitherto discussed have been defined in terms of filial and marriage relations between individuals. But kinship also has to do with relations between *groups* derived from relations between individuals. One convenient tool of analyzing these relations is the *alliance network*.

The *alliance network* corresponding to a given kinship network (real or simulated) is a network composed of vertices representing *groups* of individuals and arcs representing *marriage frequencies* between the groups, where the value of an arc from A to B indicates the number of marriages of a woman of A with a man of B. One can think of alliance networks as resulting from "shrinking" the kinship network with respect to some partition, after having transformed marriage edges into arcs that point in the husband's direction, that is, from the group of "wife-givers" to the group of "wife-takers." The clusters of the partition are those collectivities related by the marriages between their respective members. The partition used may be exogenous to kinship (e.g., if we are dealing with residential units, professional categories, or social classes), but it may also be derived from the kinship network itself. Thus, for example, clusters may represent the components of the agnatic or uterine subnetwork, that is, "lineages" within the kinship network.

Alliance networks no longer have the particularities of kinship networks. They are simple valued digraphs. Circuits in alliance networks may be called *connubial circuits* in order to distinguish them from matrimonial circuits in kinship networks, and the connubial circuit structure of an alliance network can be represented by its matrix (the *alliance matrix*). In exogamous systems, the alliance matrix will have only zero values in its diagonal; in a perfect system of balanced bilateral marriage alliances (designated by Lévi-Strauss [1949 (1967)] as "restricted exchange") it will be symmetric; in a system having a single directed Hamiltonian cycle ("generalized exchange"), it will be asymmetric and contain only one nonzero value in each line and column. Note, however, that real-world alliance structures are not as clear-cut. On the one hand, several circuit patterns may be superimposed, such that, for example, the resulting cumulative pattern may appear symmetrical even if partial patterns are asymmetric. On the other hand, the structure of alliance networks is highly sensitive to the definition of wife-giving and wife-taking groups, connubial circuit structures being in general not continuous with respect to changes in the level of group aggregation. Thus, what may appear to be endogamous unions on one level may be exogamous on another, with combinations of endogamy and balanced exchange on one level giving rise to asymmetrical patterns on another (for an example, see Gabail and Kyburz, 2008).

The *alliance network* corresponding to a partitioned kinship network K is a digraph G where

1   each vertex of G corresponds to a partition cluster of K
2   each arc between two vertices of G corresponding to two clusters A and B corresponds to the existence of a marriage of a woman of A with a man of B, and the weight of the arcs corresponds to the number of such marriages.

A *connubial circuit* is a circuit in an alliance network.

APPLICATION ISSUES

Data collection and saving

Orientations of data collection
Of course, the way kinship data collection is oriented depends largely on what one wants to find. However, in order to minimize biases and to allow the data to be used by others, there are some criteria that every corpus of kinship data should fulfill, regardless of the specific purpose of the collection:

- Document the dates and informant(s) for every part of the data set; this is not only useful for checking possible errors and biases but may be an interesting datum in itself, for instance, to appraise genealogical memory.
- Document missing data; indicate if the spouses and children you have noted for a given individual are, according to your knowledge, complete.
- In case of contradictory data, keep records regarding alternative items of information (and their origin) and on the reasons for your choices.
- Try to avoid biases from the start by always following both male *and* female lines; do not record only those kinship ties that are easily given but make an effort to search those that are missing, even if this may be costly in the case of an extensive matrimonial area.
- If you are interested in the kinship relations between two individuals, do not be content to ask how they are related but try to establish their entire pedigrees within given bounds – you will surely find quite a number of additional ties your informants did not mention spontaneously!
- Try to determine the relative order of births and marriages (in particular in the case of polygamy), even if absolute dates are not available. In interpreting marriages with affines or overlapping matrimonial circuits, this may turn out to be very important.
- Keep an account of the research method used and specify the purpose for which the corpus (or part of the corpus) is established.

Storing data without a computer
Data are not only a result but also a means of data collection. They should be easily accessible in order to guide your research and to cross-check informant answers. When dealing with archives, this is often fairly simple: you can take a computer with you. But in many fieldwork situations this is not possible. However, noting kinship "by hand" can be extremely fast and efficient, if some basic principles are observed.

- Always use a compact medium, such as a notebook. Do not use filesheets or loose papers. You cannot easily use them during interviews, and there is a high risk of losing some of them.
- Separate graphics and text. A good method is to use a notebook with the left page for drawing genealogies, the right page for listing the individuals and their properties, and numbers for identifying these individuals (if numbers get large, it is recommended to use, in addition, initial letters to prevent identification problems in case of numbering errors).
- Attribute an identity number to each individual and never attribute that number to another individual. If you have "duplicates," make a link from the redundant to the original number but

do not re-assign it. Gaps in the series of numbers do not cause any damage, but ambiguities in identity numbers cause much damage and are extremely difficult to detect.

- Do not use identity numbers as codes. Identity numbers serve to identify individuals and nothing else (except, perhaps, to recall the order in which you have entered them and to document the history of your corpus). If you want to convey information on individuals' gender, clan affiliation, residence, and so on, do not use identity numbers for that purpose.
- Never forget to make copies and store them in different places. This holds for all data, but especially for kinship data, due to the network properties of kinship: one lost notebook may render all other notebooks useless.

Data interpretation

It is necessary to know the biases, gaps, and limits of a genealogical corpus. In some cases, this may lead one to conclude that certain analyses simply cannot reasonably be made. For instance, it makes little sense to search for consanguineous marriage circuits in a corpus with very shallow genealogies. Here, as in all cases, knowledge of the basic qualities of the corpus is essential for interpreting the findings.

In particular it is important to keep in mind that kinship networks are virtually infinite. Every corpus is necessarily only a part of a larger whole, and incomplete both with regard to individuals and with regard to the links that connect them. Choices pertaining to the delimitation and composition of genealogical corpuses arise not only during fieldwork but also prior to analysis as a means of reducing the collected data to a meaningful core.

Choosing bases and boundaries

The usefulness of exogenous reductions bringing sociological, geographical, and demographical criteria into play is fairly self-evident. However, the value of endogenous reductions based on structural features of the network itself is perhaps less so, and depends on what one is trying to show. For example, one cannot first eliminate all unmarried individuals if one later wants to compare matrimonial circuit frequencies with those of kinship relations (e.g., White, 1999). This applies not only to endogenous reductions but also to endogenous augmentations of the network, such as the creation of fictive individuals in order to preserve information on full siblingship in those cases where one or both parents are unknown.

A related problem concerns the delimitation of the network to be used for analytic purposes. To begin with, it is important that results relating to unconnected components of the matrimonial network not be combined indiscriminately, as each component represents an autonomous matrimonial universe whose patterning may not obey the same rules. This also applies, to a lesser degree, to matrimonial bicomponents. However, even when analysis is limited to the largest matrimonial bicomponent (kernel) of the kinship network, additional restrictions are often necessary. Because bicomponents contain matrimonial circuits of any length, depth, and order, including those that incorporate very distant ties whose sociological relevance is questionable, it is helpful to confine analysis to subnetworks formed by matrimonial circuits of a certain maximal depth or order. It is not always easy to determine the optimal criteria for such restricted matrimonial networks, choices being largely guided by two contrary principles. On the one hand, the resulting subnetwork should be as large as possible so as to be sufficiently representative of the wider kinship network from which it is drawn. On the other hand, in order to avoid redundancies and to keep the number of circuits and circuit types at manageable proportions, it is essential that the latter be kept to a minimum.

Determining representativity and significance

Once a delimited data set has been chosen and first results obtained, another difficulty arises: to what extent do the regularities observed in the corpus provide information on the organization of the real social network? This, of course, is a general problem in network analysis; however, because issues of incompleteness are so omnipresent in genealogical research, questions regarding the representativity of kinship networks are particularly pressing.

One central question concerns the extent to which a corpus's boundaries correspond to endogenously definable subnetworks of the real kinship network. Another, related question concerns the over- and underrepresentation of persons belonging to certain kinship categories. These issues apply not only to the individuals (vertices) that make up the corpus, but to the relations (lines) between them. Kinship networks are often biased in that they favor some types of relations over others (agnatic over uterine relations, for example, for a population with patrilocal residence). It might be possible to adjust one's findings so as to eliminate such biases. However, these biases may themselves be a function of matrimonial behavior: kinship ties that form part of matrimonial circuits may be more easily remembered than others.

The stronger this correlation between network structure and collective memory, the more difficult it is to do away with the biases concerned.

The problem of network biases is directly related to issues of significance: are the observed regularities indicative of a behavioral pattern, or are they simply due to chance? In order to treat this question by means of a comparison with random kinship networks, it is necessary to simulate a network that not only reproduces the demographic features of the concerned population but also the biases of the corpus itself. Because of this, random permutation (see White, 1999; White, this volume) or explicit simulation of the data collection process (virtual fieldwork) may prove more useful than conventional demographic simulation.

Interpretation of results

If "interesting" regularities appear in analysis for which the known norms and institutions of the society do not provide a straightforward account, one is immediately tempted to take them as indicators of some hidden norm or institution. The most important thing in kinship data analysis is to resist this temptation. Before formulating a sociological hypothesis, one must always check the following:

- First, does the "interesting" structural feature simply reflect a bias of the corpus? (e.g., high incidences of patrilateral marriages in a corpus where uterine genealogies are shallow).
- Second, is the structural feature, if it does not correspond to any known rule, the result of a *combination* of known rules? (e.g., in a society where uterine nieces are preferred spouses and maternal aunts are avoided, patrilateral cross-cousins have a greater chance of being at the same time maternal aunts and therefore avoided, even if no rule states that they should be avoided as such).
- Finally, remember that a sociological hypothesis is not validated by the simple fact that *no other* interpretation can account for the structural feature observed. Sociological hypotheses often can be validated only in the field.

Resources

A wide variety of commercial software (Brother's Keeper, Family Tree Maker, Legacy, Kith and Kin, etc.) and noncommercial programs (Personal Ancestral File, Gramps, etc.) exist for entering, storing, and outputting genealogical data. Some of them are particularly flexible and are used extensively by social scientists: Généatique is used by many French historians; Alliance Project, developed by S. Sugito and S. Kubota in Japan (Sugito, 2004), is widely used by Australian anthropologists; Kinship Editor, written by M. Fischer, a key element of the European Kinship and Social Security (KASS) project, allows both for systematic data collection and the modeling of kinship phenomena such as terminological usage. There are also additional software tools developed by demographers or historians for managing records and calculating demographic and other variables on the basis of empirical genealogical data (e.g., CASOAR [Hainsworth and Bardet, 1981]). None of these programs, however, allow for an in-depth analysis of kinship networks as such.

Such analyses may be undertaken using general purpose social network analysis tools. Perhaps the software most used in this way is the network analysis and visualization program Pajek, developed by V. Batagelj and A. Mrvar (de Nooy et al., 2005; Batagelj and Mrvar, 2004, 2008; Mrvar and Batagelj, 2004). A number of kinship-centered macros have been developed for Pajek by the authors and by others (e.g., Tip4Pajek pack by K. Hamberger).

Finally, certain programs have been specifically developed for the analysis of kinship networks (including matrimonial circuit censuses). First attempts, such as Gen-Par by Selz (1987; see also Héritier, 1974) and Pgraph by White (1997; White et al., 1999), have since given way to more flexible and easier-to-use software such as Genos by Barry (2004) and, more recently, Puck by Hamberger et al. (2009).

An open depository of kinship networks from historical and anthropological sources, controlled by a scientific board, is hosted at the site of the *kinsources* project (http://kinsource.net).

NOTES

1 We are grateful to Isabelle Daillant and Vladimir Batagelj as well as to the editors Peter Carrington and John Scott for helpful comments and discussions.

2 We are talking of individuals and not of classes. An individual may well belong to one's parent's parent's marriage class, as in Australian alternating generation models.

3 In digraphs, the notions "path" and "cycle" are often restricted to oriented paths and cycles, whereas the terms "semipath" and "semicycle" are used if arcs are not consistently oriented. Because we are talking of mixed graphs (containing edges as well as arcs), we use "path" and "cycle" as the general terms (as in the case of undirected graphs) and

specify them as "oriented" if all of their lines are arcs pointing in the same direction.

4 The terms "chain" and "circuit" are equivalent to "path graph" and "cycle graph" in graph-theoretic literature. Note, however, that these terms are also sometimes used with a different meaning, namely, as synonyms for "walk" (open and closed, respectively).

5 Named after the Scandinavian mathematician Oystein Ore (1960). The representation of marriages by edges has been introduced by the computer program Pajek (see Batagelj and Mrvar, 2008).

6 Note that the weakly acyclic property of kinship networks holds for remarriage cycles because a cycle consisting entirely of edges is not an oriented cycle.

7 Kinship networks that incorporate adoptive, godparent, or co-genitor relations often have to allow for the possibility of more than one parent of a given gender (multiple descent).

8 A vertex x is arc-adjacent *to* another vertex y if the arc goes from x to y. It is arc-adjacent *from* y if the arc goes from y to x.

9 The upper and lower vertices of the P-graph and bipartite P-graph are reversed in Figure 35.3 compared to the Ore-graph. This is because their arrows run in reverse, from children to parents, usually as a unique function mapping a child to a unique parental couple. The inverse of this function gives the relation of parents to children.

10 The "P" stands for *parenté* (French for "kinship").

11 From the French *homme* (man) and *femme* (woman).

12 This positional notation may also be used, within limits, to represent complex kinship relations, by leaving the parentheses empty (or by putting two letters in it) if the relation entails kinship paths that pass through apical ancestors of both genders. For instance, the MBD (mother's brother's daughter) relation is represented as HF()HF, the ZH (sister's husband) relation as H()F.H.

13 Original P-graph notation (White and Jorion, 1992) used letters G and F (from the French *garçon* (boy) and *fille* (girl). In its present version, P-graph notation uses the same letters as positional Ore-graph notation (but applies them to lines while Ore-graph notation applies them to vertices).

14 This is a variant of the ahnentafel genealogical numbering system.

15 In the case of consanguineous kinship relations, length is also called roman (or civil) degree, whereas depth is also called german (or canonic) degree (these terms derive from the history of European kinship). In the case of linear kinship relations, roman and german degrees are identical, and we can simply speak of its degree.

16 For example, in the case of a Dravidian kinship network from southern India, where cross-cousin marriages may be considered as redoublings of

alliance relations rather than as consanguineous marriages (Dumont, [1953] 1975), counting all MBWDs, whether they are or are not also MBDs, would make good sense.

17 For instance, if two brothers marry two sisters, one brother dies, and the remaining brother marries the widow, the fact that the longer circuit (of type BWZ) includes two shorter ones (of types BW and WZ) does not in the least make it sociologically less relevant: the BWZ marriage clearly precedes the BW (and WZ) marriage (we are grateful to Isabelle Daillant for this example).

18 The distinction between circuits and rings (induced circuits) is a rather recent one. Much of what has been said regarding matrimonial rings in Hamberger et al. (2004) refers to matrimonial circuits in general, while *rings* in White (2004) refers to induced circuits.

19 Note, however, that this restriction may not mean the same thing in P-graph and in Ore-graph representation. The subgraph induced by the vertices of a circuit changes meaning according to whether vertices are defined as individuals (Ore-graph) or as marriages (P-graph). For instance, a marriage with an MMBDD who is at the same time an MBD constitutes a ring in Ore-graph but not in P-graph representation. If the context is not clear, one should therefore speak of Ore-rings and P-rings to avoid ambiguities.

20 This example holds in a P-graph as well as in Ore-graph representation: in both cases, the outer circuit is a ring. In general, Ore-rings are not always P-rings (see note 19).

21 This is equally true in P-graph representation, where the two individuals 8 and 9 are represented by two lines forming an extra chain between the vertices (representing marriages) of the outer circuit.

22 See http://kinsource.net/kinsrc/bin/view/KinSources/Watchi.

23 Every line of a matrimonial bicomponent is by definition in some matrimonial circuit. On the other hand, every matrimonial circuit is either a matrimonial bicomponent in itself or forms part of some larger matrimonial bicomponent. The concept of the nucleus is a restriction of the definition of the *core* by White and Jorion (1996; cf. Houseman and White, 1996) as the union of all matrimonial bicomponents *and* their single-link connections (equating with 2-core as defined by Seidman, 1983). Neither is necessarily connected.

REFERENCES

Barry, L. (2004) 'Historique et spécificités techniques du programme Genos', *École Collecte et traitement des données de parenté*, http://llacan.vjf.cnrs.fr/SousSites/EcoleDonnees/extras/Genos.pdf.

Batagelj, V. and Mrvar, A. (2004) 'Analysing large genealogical networks with Pajek', paper presented at Sources et Resources pour les Sciences Sociales, Paris, EHESS, December 9–11, 2004, http://vlado.fmf.uni-lj.si/pub/networks/doc/seminar/Geneo04.pdf.

Batagelj, V. and Mrvar, A. (2008) 'Analysis of kinship relations with Pajek', Social Science Computer Review, 26(2): 224–46, http://ssc.sagepub.com/cgi/content/abstract/26/2/224.

Dumont, L. ([1953] 1975) 'Le vocabulaire de parenté dravidien comme expression du mariage', in Dravidien et Kariera, l'alliance de mariage dans l'Inde du Sud et en Australie. Paris/La Haye: Mouton. pp. 85–100 and 145–46.

Gabail, L. and Kyburz, O. (2008) 'Hurons chez les Touregs', Annales de Démographie Historique, 116:197–232.

Grange, C. and Houseman, M. (2008) 'Objets d'analyse pour l'étude des réseaux de parenté', Annales de Démographie Historique, 116: 105–44.

Hainsworth, M. and Bardet, J.-P. (1981) 'Logiciel C.A.S.O.A.R.: Calculs et analyses sur ordinateur appliqués aux reconstitutions', Cahier des Annales de Démographie Historique, 1: 1–175.

Hamberger, K. (forthcoming) 'Matrimonial circuits in kinship networks: Calculation, enumeration and census', Social Networks.

Hamberger, K. and Daillant, I. (2008) 'L'analyse de réseaux de parenté: concepts et outils', Annales de Démographie Historique 116: 13–52.

Hamberger, K., Houseman, M., Daillant, I., White, D.R. and Barry, L. (2004) 'Matrimonial ring structures', Mathématiques et Sciences humaines, 168 (Les réseaux sociaux, ed. Alain Degenne), pp. 83–119.

Hamberger, K., Houseman, M. and Grange, C. (2009) 'La parenté radiographiée: Un nouveau logiciel pour l'analyse des réseaux matrimoniaux', L'Homme, 189: 107–137.

Harary, F. (1969) Graph Theory. Reading, MA: Addison-Wesley.

Harary, F. and White, D.R. (2001) 'P-systems: A structural model for kinship studies', Connections 24(2): 35–46.

Héritier, F. (1974) 'Systèmes Omaha de parenté et alliance. Etude sur ordinateur du fonctionnement réel d'une société africaine', in P.A. Ballonoff (ed.), Genealogical Mathematics. Paris-La Haye: Mouton.

Houseman, M. and White, D.R. (1996) 'Structures réticulaires de la pratique matrimoniale', L'Homme, 36(139): 59–85.

Lévi-Strauss, C. ([1949] 1967) Les structures élémentaires de la parenté. 2nd ed. Paris/La Haye: Mouton.

Mrvar, A. and Batagelj, V. (2004) 'Relinking marriages in genealogies', Metodološki zvezki – Advances in Methodology and Statistics (Ljubljana), 1: 407–18, http://mrvar.fdv.uni-lj.si/pub/mz/mz1.1/mrvar.pdf.

de Nooy, W., Mrvar, A. and Batagelj, V. (2005) Exploratory Social Network Analysis with Pajek. New York: Cambridge University Press.

Ore, O. (1960) 'Sex in graphs', Proceedings of the American Mathematical Society, 11: 533–39.

Seidman, S.B. (1983) 'Network structure and minimum degree', Social Networks, 5: 269–87.

Selz, M. (1987) 'Parenté et Informatique', Mathématiques et Sciences Humaines, 97: 57–66.

Sugito, S. (2004) 'Possibility of genealogical study in population study', Journal of Population Studies, 34: 23–29 (in Japanese).

White, D.R. (1997) 'Structural endogamy and the Graphe de Parenté', Mathématiques et sciences humaines, 137: 107–25.

White, D.R. (1999) 'Controlled simulation of marriage systems', Journal of Artificial Societies and Social Simulation, 2(3), http://www.soc.surrey.ac.uk/JASSS/2/3/5.html.

White, D.R. (2004) 'Ring cohesion in marriage and social networks', Mathématiques et sciences humaines, 168(4): 59–82.

White, D.R., Batagelj, V. and Mrvar, A. (1999) 'Analyzing large kinship and marriage networks with Pgraph and Pajek', Social Science Computer Review, 17(3): 245–74.

White, D.R. and Jorion, P. (1992) 'Representing and computing kinship: A new approach', Current Anthropology, 33(4): 454–62.

White, D.R. and Jorion, P. (1996) 'Kinship networks and discrete structure theory: Applications and implications', Social Networks, 18: 267–314.

Software

Alliance Project: http://study.hs.sugiyama-u.ac.jp/e/

Brother's Keeper: http://www.bkwin.org/

Family Tree Maker: http://www.familytreemaker.com/

Généatique: http://www.cdip.com/

Gramps: http://gramps-project.org/wiki/index.php?title=Main_Page

Kinship Editor: http://era.anthropology.ac.uk/Kinship/

Kith and Kin: http://www.spansoft.org/

Legacy: http://www.legacyfamilytree.com/

Pajek: http://pajek.imfm.si/doku.php

Personal Ancestral File: http://www.familysearch.org/eng/paf/

Pgraph: http://eclectic.ss.uci.edu/~drwhite/pgraph/pgraph.html

Puck: http://kintip.net/

Tip4Pajek: http://kintip.net/, http://intersci.ss.uci.edu/wiki/

36

Large-Scale Network Analysis

Vladimir Batagelj

INTRODUCTION

The interest in analysis of large networks started to rise in the mid-1990s as a result of the development of personal computers (with color graphics, larger working memories and disks, and the Internet) and the availability of large data sets from which large networks could be derived.

In computer science the problems, for which algorithms of polynomial (time) complexity exist, are considered easy or tractable. The main observation when dealing with large data sets (millions of data elements) is that already algorithms with quadratic complexity are too slow. In the analysis of large data sets we are limited to concepts for which fast, *subquadratic* algorithms exist.

Several algorithms were developed in the twentieth century in graph theory and related fields: different kinds of connectivity, minimum spanning tree, shortest paths, maximal flow, Pathfinder, CPM (Critical Path Method), topological sort, planarity testing, and so forth (Knuth, 1993; Ahuja et al., 1993; Cormen et al., 2001; Brandes and Erlebach, 2005).

The second observation about large networks is that they are usually *sparse*. Often there is an upper bound on capacity of "regular" units (actors) to link to other units. In sociology such a bound is known as *Dunbar's number* (Hill and Dunbar, 2002). It represents a cognitive limit to the number of people with whom one can maintain stable social relationships. Usually it is approximated

by 150. The studies by Bernard, Killworth et al. gave a limit around 290 for social networks (McCarty et al., 2001).

BASIC NOTIONS

A network is based on a nonempty set of vertices (units, actors, nodes) V. Pairs of vertices can be linked by lines (links, ties) determining the set of lines L. Lines can be either directed, called *arcs*, or undirected, called *edges*. For vertices u, v ∈ V and line p ∈ L we write:

- p(u : v): the line p links vertices u and v; u and v are *endpoints* of line p;
- p(u, v): the line p leads from vertex u to vertex v; if p is an arc, u is its *initial* and v is its *terminal* vertex (endpoint).

A line with both its endpoints being equal is called a *loop*.

The number of vertices is usually denoted by n = |V|, and the number of lines is shown by m = |L|.

The number of lines that have the vertex u ∈ V as their endpoint is called the *degree* of the vertex u and is denoted by deg(u). The *maximum degree* is denoted by $\Delta = \max\{\deg(v): v \in V\}$. The number of lines that lead into vertex u ∈ V is called the *indegree* of the vertex u and is denoted by indeg(u). The number of lines that lead out from vertex u ∈ V is called the *outdegree* of the vertex u and is denoted by outdeg(u).

The set of vertices V and set of lines L form a *graph* G = (V, L). It describes the structure of a network. In a network N = (V, L, P, W) additional *properties* P of vertices or *weights* W on lines are often known. Network N′ = (V′, L′, P′, W′) is a *subnetwork* of network N if V′ ⊆ V, L′ ⊆ L, P′ ⊆ P, W′ ⊆ W, and all endpoints of lines from L′ belong to V′. N′ is a *spanning subnetwork* of N if V′ = V.

A sequence of vertices and lines $v_0, p_1, v_1, p_2, v_2, p_3, \ldots, v_{k-1}, p_k, v_k$, where $p_i(v_{i-1}, v_i)$, for i = 1, 2, …, k, is called a *walk* from v_0 to v_k of *length* k. If only $p_i(v_{i-1} : v_i)$ holds, for i = 1, 2, …, k, it is called a *semi-walk* from v_0 to v_k. Note that the reversed sequence determines a *semi-walk* from v_k to v_0. A walk with all its vertices different is a *path*. A walk is *closed* if its initial vertex v_0 and its terminal vertex v_k are equal. A closed walk with all internal vertices different is a *cycle*. A network is *acyclic* if it does not contain any cycle. For acyclic networks some very efficient algorithms exist.

Vertices u and v are *(weakly) connected* if there is a semi-walk from u to v; and they are *strongly connected* if there is a walk from u to v and a walk from v to u. Weak and strong connectivities are both equivalence relations on the set of vertices.

Vertices u and v are *biconnected* if they lie on the same cycle. The biconnectivities determines an equivalence relation on the set of lines.

A connected network is vertex/line *k-connected* if we have to remove at least k vertices/lines to disconnect it or to reduce it to a one-vertex network. In a k-vertex/line-connected network, each pair of vertices is connected with k vertex/line disjoint paths.

Let U be a finite *set of units*. Its nonempty subset C is called a *cluster*; ∅ ⊆ C ⊆ U; and a set of clusters **C** = {C_1, C_2, …, C_k} is called a *clustering*. Generally, the clusters of the clustering **C** need not be pairwise disjoint; yet the clustering theory and practice mainly deal with clusterings that are the partitions of U ($\cup_i C_i = U$ and $i \neq j \Rightarrow C_i \cap C_j = \emptyset$). Each partition determines an equivalence relation on U, and vice versa. We denote the set of all partitions of U into k clusters by $\prod_k(U)$.

Clustering **C** is a *hierarchy* if $C_i \cap C_j \in \{\emptyset, C_i, C_j\}$, in words, two clusters from the hierarchy are either disjoint or one is contained in the other. Hierarchy **C** is *complete* if $\cup$ **C** = U and is *basic* if for all v ∈ $\cup$ **C** also {v} ∈ **C**.

There are some special types of networks:

- In a *two-mode* network the set of vertices is a union of two disjoint subsets V_1 and V_2 and every line has one endpoint in the set V_1 and the other endpoint in the set V_2.

- In a *multirelational* network the set of lines is a union of disjoint subsets $L_1, L_2, \ldots, L_s$.
- In a *temporal* network each vertex and line has additional information attached, which is about the time points intervals in which it is active (present).

APPROACHES

The details of large data sets cannot be grasped in their totality. The standard approach to get an overall view about a given (large) data set is to determine its different (statistical) characteristics and use them in analyses:

- Searching for (cor)relations between measured variables and structural variables. A classic example is Pitts's (1978) analysis of the trade network on medieval Russian rivers.
- In the 1970s and 1980s detailed research was done on describing networks on the basis of their triadic spectrum (Holland and Leinhardt, 1981; Batagelj and Mrvar, 2001).
- In the second half of the 1990s a characterization of networks based on their degree (and other) distributions was imported from physics. This approach is best known as "scale-free networks" (Watts and Strogatz, 1998; Albert and Barabási, 2002; Newman, 2003; Newman et al., 2006; Dorogovtsev and Mendes, 2003; Li et al., 2005).
- Probabilistic models of network evolution (Frank and Strauss, 1986; Robins et al., 2007).

In this chapter we will not deal further with statistical approaches (see also Kolaczyk, 2009). We shall discuss in details the other approach that tries to uncover the overall structure of network, identify important elements and parts of networks, and analyze the position of a selected element or group of elements in the network.

The structure of large networks can be revealed by partitioning them into smaller parts that are easier to handle. These parts can be either extracted and analyzed separately or shrunk into a smaller structure describing connections among parts.

NETWORK DECOMPOSITIONS

The basic decomposition of graphs is to (weakly) connected components: the partition of vertices (and links). The weak connectivity identifies the connected parts of the network. Most of the problems on networks can be solved by first solving them for each weak component and afterward combining the obtained solutions into a solution for the network. A fast O(m) algorithm exists for determining weak components (Cormen et al., 2001: 499–501).

The decomposition into biconnected components provides us with an additional internal structure of connected components. It is very important in the analysis of genealogies: in the p-graph of a genealogy the nontrivial (having at least two vertices) weak biconnected components correspond exactly to the relinking marriages. The biconnected components can be determined in O(m) time (Cormen et al., 2001: 558–59).

For directed graphs the fundamental decomposition results can be found in Harary et al. (1965). If in a directed graph we shrink every strong component into a vertex, we obtain an acyclic graph. For generalizations of this result to symmetric connectivity, see Doreian et al. (2000) and for short cycle connectivity, see Batagelj and Zaveršnik (2007). The strong components can be determined in O(n+m) time (Cormen et al., 2001: 552–56).

In real-life large directed networks, such as Web networks, a large strong component usually exists. With respect to this strong component the set of vertices of the corresponding weak component can be decomposed to: strong, incoming, outgoing, bypassing, and tendrillic – the *bow tie* decomposition (Kleinberg et al., 1999).

In the 1970s and 1980s Matula (1977) studied different types of connectivities in graphs and structures they induce. In most cases the algorithms are too demanding to be used on larger graphs. A recent overview of connectivity algorithms was made by Esfahanian (2008).

Efficient algorithms were developed also for modular decomposition (Habib and Paul, 2009; Papadopoulos and Voglis, 2006) and split decomposition (Joeris et al., 2009).

SKELETONS

An approach to get insight into the structures of large network is also to reduce a large network to its *skeleton* by removing less important lines and vertices. Two such methods for weighted networks are the minimum spanning tree and Pathfinder algorithms. Both methods preserve connectivity.

The minimum spanning tree in connected weighted network $N = (V, L, w)$, $w > 0$ is its subnetwork $T = (V, L_T, w)$ such that its value $w(T) = \sum\{w(e) : e \in L_T\}$ is minimal over all connected spanning subnetworks of N. There exists

an O(m + n.log n) algorithm for determining MST (Cormen et al., 2001: 561–79).

The Pathfinder algorithm was proposed in the 1980s (Schvaneveldt, 1990; Schvaneveldt et al., 1988, 1989) for simplification of weighted networks. It removes from the network all lines that do not satisfy the triangle inequality – if a shorter path exists that can connect a line's endpoints then the line is removed.

The original matrix-based Pathfinder algorithm has the complexity $O(qn^3)$, with q being the neighborhood size parameter. Therefore, it can be applied only to relatively small (up to some hundred vertices) networks. Interest for Pathfinder transformation was renewed around the year 2000 by Chen (1998).

The first improvement based on fast power computation was proposed by Guerrero-Bote et al. (2006) and reduced complexity to $O(n^3 \log q)$. When $q \geq n - 1$, the Pathfinder network can be determined by Fletcher's (1980) algorithm over the Pathfinder semiring. This improvement was proposed by Quirin et al. (2008b) and reduces complexity to $O(n^3)$. Additional improvement can be made for undirected networks in the case of $q \geq n - 1$ and $r = \infty$. In this case the Pathfinder network is the union of all minimal spanning trees of N. It can be obtained using an adapted version of Kruskal's minimal spanning tree algorithm as described in Quirin et al. (2008a). The complexity of this algorithm is $O(m.\log n)$. For sparse networks generally there is still some space for improvements – for each vertex we have to compute only the values of the shortest paths to all their neighbors (Batagelj and Vavpetič, 2010). This algorithm can be applied on sparse networks with hundreds of thousands of vertices.

A kind of skeleton is also a core. Among different notions that were introduced in graph theory to describe a dense group (Wasserman and Faust, 1994) only k-cores can also be efficiently determined. The notion of a core was introduced by Seidman (1983).

In graph $G = (V, L)$ a subgraph $H_k = (C, L \mid C)$ induced by the set C is a *k-core* or a *core of order k* if for all $v \in C$: $\deg_H(v) \geq k$, and H_k is the maximum subgraph with this property. The core of maximum order is also called the *main* core. The *core number* of vertex v is the highest order of a core that contains this vertex. The cores are nested: $i < j \Rightarrow H_j \subseteq H_i$ and are not necessarily connected subgraphs. An efficient, O(m), algorithm for determining the core's decomposition exists (Batagelj et al., 1999; Batagelj and Zaveršnik, 2003).

The notion of the core can be generalized to networks (V, L, p), where p is a vertex property function. It was shown that for the local monotone vertex property functions the corresponding cores can be determined in $O(m \cdot \max(\Delta, \log n))$ time (Batagelj and Zaveršnik, 2002).

Using cores, we can identify the densest parts of a graph (Alvarez-Hamelin et al., 2005, 2009). For revealing the internal structure of the main core we can use standard clustering procedures on dissimilarities between vertices or blockmodeling. Cores can be used also to localize and speed up the search for some computationally more demanding substructures.

MEASURES OF IMPORTANCE

The usual approach to identify important elements (vertices or lines) in a network is to express our intuitive notion of importance with an appropriate *measure* (property or weight) of *importance* of elements. This measure can be either measured when collecting the network data (e.g., frequency of interactions) or computed from them. It is very important that it is congruent with our goal (Roberts, 1976: 473–502). Using it we identify the important elements by identifying a selected number of elements with the largest values. Many such measures of importance were proposed.

Very popular properties of vertices are: *degree* – direct contacts of vertex in network; *betweenness* – control over communications in network (Anthonisse, 1971; Freeman, 1979; Brandes, 2001); *closeness* – overall communication centrality (Sabidussi, 1966); *eigenvector centrality* (Bonacich, 1987); *hubs and authorities* – two eigenvector-based importance measures (user, provider) for directed networks (Kleinberg, 1998); and *clustering coefficient* – local density (Watts and Strogatz, 1998).

There are also several popular weights of lines: *Jaccard's coefficient* – the relative overlap of endpoints neighborhoods, *cosine similarity*, and *edge betweenness* (Melançon and Sallaberry, 2008). Lines that belong to locally dense parts of networks also belong to several short semicycles called 3-rings and 4-rings (Ahmed et al., 2007; Batagelj and Zaveršnik, 2007; Schank and Wagner, 2005; Latapy, 2008).

In acyclic networks (genealogies, citations) an indicator of importance of an element is the number of different paths from some initial vertex, $indeg(v) = 0$, to some terminal vertex, $outdeg(v) = 0$, which contain the element (Hummon and Doreian, 1990; Batagelj, 2003). The CPM (Critical Path Method) from operations research can be used for their analysis.

CUTS AND ISLANDS

Suppose that in our network we are able to express the importance of each vertex by its property p, or the importance of each line by its weight w.

From a network $N = (V, L, p)$ we can get for a *threshold* t a subnetwork $N(t) = (V_t, L_t, w)$, where

$$V_t = \{v \in V : p(v) \geq t\} \text{ and}$$
$$L_t = \{e(u,v) \in L : u, v \in V_t\}$$

– a *vertex cut* at level t.

Similarly, from a network $N = (V, L, w)$ we can get for a threshold t a subnetwork $N(t) = (V_t, L_t, w)$, where

$$L_t = \{e \in L : w(e) \geq t\} \text{ and}$$
$$V_t = \{v \in V : deg_{N(t)}(v) > 0\}$$

– a *line cut* at level t.

From vertex/line cut $N(t)$ we can get a clustering $\mathbf{C}(t)$ with connected components as clusters. For different thresholds these clusterings form a hierarchy.

There are some problems with the cuts approach: we have to select an appropriate threshold value t, and the components in the obtained cut can be too large or too small. These problems were partially resolved by introducing *islands*.

A *vertex island* of size [k, K] is a weakly connected subnetwork of size in the interval [k, K], where vertices inside the island have larger values of the property p than their neighbors outside the island.

A *line island* of size [k, K] is a weakly connected subnetwork of size in the interval [k, K], where arcs linking vertices of the island to their neighbors outside the island have weights w lower than are the values of arcs of a spanning tree inside the island.

Very efficient, $O(\max(n.\log n, m))$ for vertex islands and $O(m.\log n)$ for line islands, algorithms exist for determining the islands hierarchy (Zaveršnik and Batagelj, 2004).

Cuts and islands are very general and efficient approaches to determine the important subnetworks in a given network as connected subnetworks (clusters) with stronger internal cohesion relatively to its neighbors. To use them we only have to express the goals of our analysis with a related property of the vertices or weight of the lines. An important property of islands is that they identify locally important subnetworks on different levels. Therefore, they can detect also emerging groups.

PATTERNS

If a selected *pattern* or fragment (also called *motif*, Milo et al., 2002), determined by a given small graph, does not occur frequently in a sparse network the straightforward backtracking algorithm applied for pattern searching finds all appearances of the pattern very fast even in the case of very large networks (Batagelj, 1989; Batagelj and Mrvar, 1997).

Pattern searching was successfully applied to searching for patterns of atoms in molecula (carbon rings) and searching for relinking marriages in genealogies (Batagelj and Mrvar, 2008).

CLUSTERING AND BLOCKMODELING

The *clustering problem* (Φ, P) can be expressed as follows:

Determine the clustering $C^* \in \Phi$ for which
$P(C^*) = \min \{P(C): C \in \Phi\}$.

where C is a clustering, Φ is a non-empty set of *feasible clusterings*, and P: $\Phi \rightarrow \mathbb{R}_0^+$ is a *criterion function*. Because in a graph G = (V, L) we have two kinds of objects – vertices and links – we can speak about *clustering of vertices* and *clustering of links*. Usually, we deal with clustering of vertices.

Because the set of units U is finite, the set of feasible clusterings is also finite. Therefore, the set Min(Φ, P) of all solutions of the problem (optimal clusterings) is not empty. We denote the value of the criterion function for an optimal clustering by min(Φ, P). In theory the set Min(Φ, P) can be determined by the complete search. Unfortunately, the number of feasible clusterings grows very fast with n = |U|. For example, card(Π_k) = S(n, k), where S(n, k) is the Stirling number of the second kind. For this reason the complete search algorithm is only of theoretical interest – up to 15 to 20 units. Although there are some special clustering problems of polynomial complexity it seems that they are mainly NP-hard (Brücker, 1978; Garey and Johnson, 1979).

Joining the individual units into a cluster C we make a certain "error," we create certain "tension" among them – we denote this quantity by p(C). The *criterion function* P(C) combines these "partial/ local errors" into a "global error" P(C) = $\oplus\{p(C): C \in C\}$, where $\oplus$ denotes operations such as + or max.

In standard clustering methods, the "cluster error" function p(C) is usually based on an appropriate dissimilarity between vertices.

The usual approach is to define a vector description [v] = [t_1, t_2, ..., t_m] of each vertex $v \in V$, and then use some standard dissimilarity δ on $\mathbb{R}^m$ to compare these vectors d(u, v) = $\delta([u], [v])$.

For some "nonstandard" such descriptions, see Moody (2001) and Harel and Koren (2001).

When clustering the vertices according to their properties we can consider the network structure also as a relational constraint – the obtained clusters should induce connected subnetworks of selected types (Ferligoj and Batagelj, 1983; Batagelj and Ferligoj, 2000). Recently we developed an efficient hierarchical clustering algorithm for large networks (Batagelj et al., 2010). To obtain an efficient algorithm for large networks we compute the dissimilarities between units (vertices of network) only for endpoints of existing links (of constraining relation), define the dissimilarities between clusters based only on the dissimilarities of the corresponding links, and derive the update relations. We also show that for selected dissimilarities between clusters, the Bruynooghe (1977) *reducibility* property holds. This allows us to speed up the hierarchical clustering procedure by using the reciprocal nearest neighbors approach (Murtagh, 1985).

Clustering of networks is an important topic also in other disciplines such as numerical mathematics and bioinformatics (Karypis and Kumar, 1999; Demmel, 1996). Physicists prefer the term "community detection." A recent detailed overview of results was prepared by Fortunato (2010).

Not all clustering problems can be expressed by a simple criterion function. In some applications a *general* criterion function of the form

$$P(C) = \oplus\{q(C_1,C_2): (C_1,C_2) \in C \times C\},$$
$$q(C_1,C_2) \geq 0$$

is needed. We shall use it in blockmodeling. The goal of *blockmodeling* is to reduce a large, potentially incoherent network to a smaller comprehensible structure that can be interpreted more readily.

A clustering C partitions also the lines L into *blocks* L(C_i, C_j) = {e(u, v) ∈ L : u ∈ C_i ∧ v ∈ C_j}. Each such block consists of vertices belonging to clusters C_i and C_j and all lines leading from cluster C_i to cluster C_j. If i = j, a block L(C_i, C_i) is called a *diagonal* block.

A *blockmodel* consists of structures obtained by identifying all units from the same cluster of the clustering C. For an exact definition of a blockmodel we have to be precise also about which blocks produce an arc in the *reduced* or *image* network and which do not, of what *type* is it, and what its *value* is. The set of allowed types determines the type of the equivalence (for details, see Doreian et al., 2005; Batagelj and Ferligoj, 2000; Žiberna, 2007).

The obtained optimization problem can be solved by local optimization. Also, blockmodeling problems are NP-hard (Roberts and Sheng, 2001). Efficient approximative blockmodeling algorithms for large networks are still to be developed.

TWO-MODE NETWORKS

A two-mode network $N = (V_1, V_2, L, w)$ can be represented by a matrix $A = [a_{uv}]_{V_1 \times V_2}$, where $a_{uv} = w(u, v)$ if $(u, v) \in L$, and $a_{uv} = 0$ otherwise.

Let $N_1 = (V_1, V_2, L_1, w_1)$ and $N_2 = (V_2, V_3, L_2, w_2)$ be two compatible (the second set of vertices of N_1 is the same as the first set of vertices of N_2) networks. Then we can multiply the corresponding matrices in the standard way. The network $N_3 = (V_1, V_3, L_3, w_3)$ determined by the product matrix is called a *product network* of networks N_1 and N_2. A problem with network product is that the product of two sparse networks needs not be sparse itself. Fortunately, in many important cases the sparsity can be guaranteed. For example in genealogies we can use the network multiplication to compute from basic kinship relations (parent, gender, and marriage) all other kinship relations: brother, uncle, grandmother, and so on (Batagelj and Mrvar, 2008).

Two-mode networks appear in many applications (e.g., papers, authors; people, events; board members, companies). Essentially we can transform any table units × properties into corresponding two-mode networks (units, property$_i$), where the vertices in the second set are (intervals of) values of property$_i$. Since the transpose of network (units, property$_i$) is compatible with the network (units, property$_j$), we can, using the network product, compute the derived network (property$_i$, property$_j$).

A traditional approach to analysis of two-mode networks is to multiply the network with its transpose and then analyze the obtained one-mode network.

There also are some direct methods for analyzing two-mode networks. The Kleinberg (1998) hubs and authorities can be straightforwardly extended to two-mode networks. To adapt the notion of cores for two-mode networks we define a (p, q)-core as the maximal subset (V'_1, V'_2), such that in the induced subnetwork each vertex from V'_1 has degree at least p and each vertex from V'_2 has degree at least q. A very efficient algorithm exists for determining (p, q)-cores. For determining dense parts in a two-mode network we compute the 4-rings weights (there is no 3-ring) and afterward apply the islands algorithm on them (Ahmed et al., 2007).

VISUALIZATION

Visualization of a network is an important tool for exploring its structure but also for communicating the obtained results of analyses (Freeman, 2000). Unfortunately, we get clear pictures only for smaller sparser networks. Therefore, we often visualize only selected important parts of the network or its blockmodel.

For not too large, denser networks quite informative visualizations can be obtained using matrix representation with an appropriate ordering of vertices (Batagelj et al., 1999; Henry and Fekete, 2006). The ordering is usually determined by clustering or blockmodeling.

In the graph drawing community several algorithms for visualization of large networks were proposed (Hu, 2005; Hachul and Jünger 2007; Brandes and Pich, 2009) that reveal the overall network structure if it exists.

Pajek

Most of the described procedures are implemented in the Pajek program for analysis and visualization of large networks (de Nooy et al., 2005; Batagelj and Mrvar, 2003). It is freely available, for noncommercial use, at http://pajek.imfm.si.

REFERENCES

Ahmed, A., Batagelj, V., Fu, X., Hong, S-H., Merrick, D. and Mrvar, A. (2007) 'Visualisation and analysis of the Internet Movie Database', Proceedings of the Asia-Pacific Symposium on Visualisation. New York: IEEE. pp. 17–24.

Ahuja, R.K., Magnanti, T.L. and Orlin, J.B. (1993) *Network Flows: Theory, Algorithms, and Applications.* New Jersey: Prentice-Hall.

Albert, R. and Barabási, A.-L. (2002) 'Statistical mechanics of complex networks', *Reviews of Modern Physics, 74:* 47–97.

Alvarez-Hamelin, J.I., Dall'Asta, L., Barrat, A. and Vespignani, A. (2005) 'k-core decomposition: A tool for the visualization of large scale networks', arXiv: cs.NI/0504107.

Alvarez-Hamelin, J.I., Gastón, B.M. and Busch, J.R. (2009) 'Understanding edge-connectivity in the Internet through core-decomposition', arXiv: cs.DM/0912.1424v1.

Anthonisse, J.M. (1971) 'The rush in a directed graph', Technical Report BN 9/71, Stichting Mathematisch Centrum, Amsterdam.

Batagelj, V. (1989) 'Similarity measures between structured objects', in A. Graovac (ed.), Proceedings of International Course and Conference on the Interfaces between Mathematics, Chemistry and Computer Science, Dubrovnik, 20–25 June 1988, Vol. 63. Amsterdam: Elsevier. pp. 25–40.

Batagelj, V. (2003) 'Efficient algorithms for citation network analysis', arXiv: cs/0309023.

Batagelj, V. and Ferligoj, A. (2000) 'Clustering relational data', in W. Gaul, O. Opitz, and M. Schader (eds), *Data Analysis*. Berlin: Springer. pp. 3–15.

Batagelj, V., Ferligoj, A. and Mrvar, A. (2010) 'Hierarchical clustering with relational constraints of large data sets', paper presented at IFCS'09, Dresden.

Batagelj, V. and Mrvar, A. (1997) 'Pajek 0.14: Fragments, June 15, 1997', http://pajek.imfm.si/doku.php?id=history.

Batagelj, V. and Mrvar, A. (2001) 'A subquadratic triad census algorithm for large sparse networks with small maximum degree', *Social Networks*, 23: 237–43.

Batagelj, V. and Mrvar, A. (2003) 'Pajek – Analysis and visualization of large networks', in M. Jünger and P. Mutzel (eds), *Graph Drawing Software*. Berlin: Springer. pp. 77–103.

Batagelj V. and Mrvar A. (2008) 'Analysis of kinship relations with Pajek', *Social Science Computer Review – SSCORE*, 26(2): 224–46.

Batagelj, V., Mrvar, A. and Zaveršnik, M. (1999) 'Partitioning approach to visualization of large graphs', in Jan Kratochvíl (ed.), Proceedings of 7th International Symposium on Graph Drawing, September 15–19, 1999, Štiřín Castle, Czech Republic. Berlin: Springer. pp. 90–97.

Batagelj, V. and Vavpetič, A. (2010) 'Fast Pathfinder algorithm for large sparse networks', submitted paper.

Batagelj, V. and Zaveršnik, M. (2002) 'Generalized cores', arXiv: cs.DS/0202039.

Batagelj, V. and Zaveršnik, M. (2003) 'An O(m) algorithm for cores decomposition of networks', arXiv: cs/0310049.

Batagelj, V. and Zaveršnik, M. (2007) 'Short cycle connectivity', *Discrete Mathematics*, 307(3–5): 310–18.

Bonacich, P. (1987) 'Power and centrality: A family of measures', *The American Journal of Sociology*, 92(5): 1170–82.

Brandes, U. (2001) 'A faster algorithm for betweenness centrality', *Journal of Mathematical Sociology*, 25(2): 163–77.

Brandes, U. and Erlebach, T. (eds) (2005) *Network Analysis: Methodological Foundations*. Berlin: Springer.

Brandes, U. and Pich, C. (2009) 'An experimental study on distance-based graph drawing', in Proceedings of the 16th International Symposium on Graph Drawing. Berlin: Springer. pp. 218–29.

Brücker, P. (1978) 'On the complexity of clustering problems', in R. Henn, B. Korte, and W. Oettli (eds), Optimization and Operations Research, Proceedings, Bonn 1977, Vol. 157. Berlin: Springer.

Bruynooghe, M. (1977) 'Méthodes nouvelles en classification automatique des données taxinomiques nombreuses', *Statistique et Analyse des Données*, 3: 24–42.

Chen, C. (1998) 'Generalised similarity analysis and Pathfinder network scaling', *Interacting with Computers*, 10(2): 107–28.

Cormen, T.H., Leiserson, C.E., Rivest, R.L. and Stein, C. (2001) *Introduction to Algorithms*. Cambridge, MA: MIT Press.

Demmel, J. (1996) 'U.C. Berkeley CS267: Applications of parallel computers/graph partitioning, part 1 and part 2', http://www.eecs.berkeley.edu/demmel/cs267/.

de Nooy, W., Mrvar, A. and Batagelj, V. (2005) *Exploratory Social Network Analysis with Pajek*. New York: Cambridge University Press.

Doreian, P., Batagelj, V. and Ferligoj, A. (2000) 'Symmetric-acyclic decompositions of networks', *Journal of Classification*, 17(1): 3–28.

Doreian, P., Batagelj, V. and Ferligoj, A. (2005) *Generalized Blockmodeling*. New York: Cambridge University Press.

Dorogovtsev, S.N. and Mendes, J.F.F. (2003) *Evolution of Networks: From Biological Nets to the Internet and WWW*. New York: Oxford University Press.

Esfahanian, A-H. (2008) 'On the evolution of graph connectivity algorithms', in Robin Wilson and Lowell Beineke (eds), *Selected Topics in Graph Theory*. New York: Cambridge University Press.

Ferligoj, A. and Batagelj, V. (1983) 'Some types of clustering with relational constraints', *Psychometrika*, 48(4): 541–52.

Fletcher, J.G. (1980) 'A more general algorithm for computing closed semiring costs between vertices of a directed graph', *CACM*, pp. 350–51.

Fortunato, S. (2010) 'Community detection in graphs', *Physics Reports*, 486: 75–174; also arXiv: 0906.0612.

Frank, O. and Strauss, D. (1986) 'Markov graphs', *Journal of the American Statistical Association*, 81: 832–42.

Freeman, L.C. (1979) 'Centrality in social networks: A conceptual clarification', *Social Networks*, 1: 211–13.

Freeman, L.C. (2000) 'Visualizing social networks', *Journal of Social Structure*, 1(1).

Garey, M.R. and Johnson, D.S. (1979) *Computers and Intractability*. San Francisco: Freeman.

Guerrero-Bote, V.P., Zapico-Alonso, F., Espinosa-Calvo, M.E., Crisóstomo, R.G. and de Moya-Anegón, F. (2006) 'Binary Pathfinder: An improvement to the Pathfinder algorithm', *Information Processing and Management*, 42(6): 1484–90.

Habib, M. and Paul, C. (2009) 'A survey on algorithmic aspects of modular decomposition', arXiv: cs. DM/0912.1457v2, 8 Dec 2009.

Hachul, S. and Jünger, M. (2007) 'Large-graph layout algorithms at work: An experimental study', *JGAA*, 11(2): 345–69.

Harary, F., Norman, R.Z. and Cartwright, D. (1965) *Structural Models: An Introduction to the Theory of Directed Graphs*. New York: John Wiley.

Harel, D. and Koren, J. (2001) 'On clustering using random walks', in LNCS 2245. Berlin: Springer-Verlag. pp. 18–41.

Henry, N. and Fekete, J.D. (2006) 'MatrixExplorer: A dual-representation system to explore social networks', *IEEE Transactions on Visualization and Computer Graphics*, 12(5): 677–84.

Hill, R.A. and Dunbar, R.I.M. (2002) 'Social network size in humans', *Human Nature*, 14(1): 53–72.

Holland, P.W. and Leinhardt, S. (1981) 'An exponential family of probability distributions for directed graphs', *Journal of the American Statistical Association*, 76(373): 33–50.

Hu, Y.F. (2005) 'Efficient and high quality force-directed graph drawing', *Mathematica Journal*, 10: 37–71.

Hummon, N.P. and Doreian, P. (1990) 'Computational methods for social network analysis', *Social Networks*, 12: 273–88.

Joeris, B.L., Lundberg, S. and McConnell, R.M. (2009) 'O(m log n) split decomposition of strongly-connected graphs', in Proceedings Graph Theory, Computational Intelligence and Thought, Haifa, September 2008, LNCS 5420. Berlin: Springer. pp. 158–71.

Karypis, G. and Kumar, V. (1999) 'A fast and high quality multilevel scheme for partitioning irregular graphs', *SIAM Journal on Scientific Computing*, 20(1): 359–92.

Kleinberg, J. (1998) 'Authoritative sources in a hyperlinked environment', Proceedings of the 9th ACM-SIAM Symposium on Discrete Algorithms.

Kleinberg, J., Kumar, R., Raghavan, P., Rajagopalan, S. and Tomkins, A. (1999) 'The Web as a graph: Measurements, models and methods', in Proceedings of the 5th International Computing and Combinatorics Conference, pp. 1–17

Knuth, D.E. (1993) *The Stanford GraphBase: A Platform for Combinatorial Computing*. New York: ACM Press.

Kolaczyk, E.D. (2009) *Statistical Analysis of Network Data: Methods and Models*. Springer Series in Statistics. Berlin: Springer.

Latapy, M. (2008) 'Main-memory triangle computations for very large (sparse (power-law) graphs', *Theoretical Computer Science*, 407(1–3): 458–73.

Li, L., Alderson, D., Tanaka, R., Doyle, J.C. and Willinger, W. (2005) 'Towards a theory of scale-free graphs: Definition, properties, and implications', arXiv: cond-mat/0501169.

Matula, D.W. (1977) 'Graph theoretic techniques for cluster analysis algorithms', in J. Van Ryzin (ed.), *Classification and Clustering*. New York: Academic Press. pp. 95–127.

McCarty, C., Killworth, P.D., Bernard, H.R. and Johnsen, E.C. (2001) 'Comparing two methods for estimating network size', *Human Organization*, 60(1): 28–39.

Melançon, G. and Sallaberry, A. (2008) 'Edge metrics for visual graph analytics: A comparative study', in 12th International Conference on Information Visualisation, IV. 610–15.

Milo, R., Shen-Orr, S., Itzkovitz, S., Kashtan, N., Chklovskii, D. and Alon, U. (2002) 'Network motifs: Simple building blocks of complex networks', *Science*, 298(5594): 824–27.

Moody, J. (2001) 'Peer influence groups: Identifying dense clusters in large networks', *Social Networks*, 23: 261–83.

Murtagh, F. (1985) 'Multidimensional clustering algorithms', Compstat lectures, 4. Vienna: Physica-Verlag.

Newman, M.E.J. (2003) 'The structure and function of complex networks', *SIAM Review*, 45: 167–256.

Newman, M.E.J., Barabási, A-L. and Watts, D. (2006) *The Structure and Dynamics of Networks*. Princeton Studies in Complexity. Princeton, NJ: Princeton University Press.

Papadopoulos, C. and Voglis, C. (2006) 'Drawing graphs using modular decomposition', in LNCS (GD'05) 3842. Berlin: Springer. pp. 343–54.

Pitts, F.R. (1978) 'The medieval river trade network of Russia revisited', *Social Networks*, 1: 285–92.

Quirin, A., Cordón, O., Guerrero-Bote, V.P., Vargas-Quesada, B. and Moya-Anegón, F. (2008a) 'A quick MST-based algorithm to obtain Pathfinder networks (∞, n−1)', *Journal of the American Society for Information Science and Technology*, 59(12): 1912–24.

Quirin, A., Cordón, O., Santamaria, J., Vargas-Quesada, B. and Moya-Anegón, F. (2008b) 'A new variant of the Pathfinder algorithm to generate large visual science maps in cubic time', *Information Processing and Management: An International Journal Archive*, 44(4): 1611–23.

Roberts, F.S. (1976) *Discrete Mathematical Models*. Englewood Cliffs, NJ: Prentice-Hall.

Roberts, F.S. and Sheng, L. (2001) 'How hard is it to determine if a graph has a 2-role assignment?' *Networks*, 37(2): 67–73.

Robins, G.L., Snijders, T.A.B., Wang, P., Handcock, M. and Pattison, P.E. (2007) 'Recent developments in exponential random graph (p*) models for social networks', *Social Networks*, 29(2): 192–215.

Sabidussi, G. (1966) 'The centrality index of a graph', *Psychometrika*, 31(4): 581–603.

Schank, T., and Wagner, D. (2005) 'Finding, counting and listing all triangles in large graphs, an experimental study', in Workshop on Experimental and Efficient Algorithms (WEA). LNCS 3503. Berlin: Springer, pp. 606–9.

Schvaneveldt, R.W. (ed.) (1990) *Pathfinder Associative Networks: Studies in Knowledge Organization*. Norwood, NJ: Ablex.

Schvaneveldt, R.W., Dearholt, D.W. and Durso, F.T. (1988) 'Graph theoretic foundations of Pathfinder networks', *Computers & Mathematics with Applications*, 15(4): 337–45.

Schvaneveldt, R.W., Durso, F.T. and Dearholt, D.W. (1989) 'Network structures in proximity data', in G. Bower (ed.), *The Psychology of Learning and Motivation: Advances in Research and Theory*, Vol. 24. New York: Academic Press. pp. 249–84.

Seidman, S.B. (1983) 'Network Structure and Minimum Degree', *Social Networks*, 5: 269–87.

Wasserman, S. and Faust, K. (1994) *Social Network Analysis: Methods and Applications*. Cambridge: Cambridge University Press.

Watts, D.J. and Strogatz, S. (1998) 'Collective dynamics of 'small-world' networks', *Nature*, 393: 440–42.

Zaveršnik, M. and Batagelj, V. (2004) 'Islands', slides from Sunbelt XXIV, Portorož, Slovenia, 12–16 May 2004. http://vlado.fmf.uni-lj.si/pub/networks/doc/sunbelt/islands.pdf

Žiberna, A. (2007) 'Generalized blockmodeling of valued networks', *Social Networks*, 29: 105–26.

37

Network Visualization

Lothar Krempel

INTRODUCTION

With the spread of the network paradigm to many disciplines from sociology and ethnology to computer science, biology, physics, and economics, many computer programs have become available that allow networks to be represented visually. While graphical representations of network data are easier to produce than ever before, the quick dissemination of these new technologies has not unlocked their potential as of yet. The knowledge of how to improve visual representations requires a much more active understanding of these new exploratory tools.

This chapter seeks to contribute to a more general understanding of visualization technologies. The aim is to set out some of the basic principles of network visualization and to disseminate knowledge about how the efficiency of network visualizations can be enhanced. How and why visualizations have the potential to supplement the numerical analysis of networks with a more exploratory approach needs to be better understood.

Collecting network data was for a long time cumbersome – even for small networks. The Internet has changed all this. Today, vast amounts of information have become available and allow us to analyze the interplay of thousands or even millions of individuals, technical units, or semantic units, linked into large systems.

Progress in network research has been driven by several developments that have eased access to ever larger network data in recent decades. Besides the tremendous increase in computing power

and database technologies, the development of efficient algorithms has become a technological driver in the last 20 years. While matrix algebra was the formal language that allowed many concepts of social network analysis to be formalized previously (Wasserman and Faust, 1994), it is not well suited to programming computers today, because large networks are typically sparse (Brandes and Erlebacher, 2005). All this allows us to analyze huge networks and large amounts of data that can hardly be overseen in numerical form. These days, the analysis of network data is typically accompanied with visualizations, which allow us to view the overall system easily.

While computers became available after the 1950s, the early computing technology deployed was especially suited to numerical computations. Graphical display devices were expensive, and the computing power was limited. Low-resolution graphical devices for small computers did not appear before the mid-1980s, and color output devices were not available before the early 1990s. Today, graphical depictions provide the means to examine networks of some thousands of nodes visually, which is not possible for numerical data.

Advances in the field are driven by different communities: the *social networks community* is often motivated by substantive and methodological questions, the *mathematical Graph Drawing Community* studies all sorts of mappings to 2D and 3D space under various constraints,[1] and the *information visualization community* is especially concerned with interfaces that enable us to gain additional insights into network data. A fourth group is the *statistical graphics community* (Wilkinson 2005, 2008; Chen et al., 2008), which actively strives to integrate many of the new visual options to enhance more traditional statistical diagrams. Motivated by the fascination of dynamic systems and the possibilities of digital visualization, artists, too, have turned their attention to the analysis and depiction of data flows and network topologies (Ars Electronica, 1994).

NETWORKS AS MATHEMATICAL GRAPHS

Networks are composed of *nodes* that are *linked* to each other. Nodes are entities of the real world: individuals, organizations, nations, and technical or logical instances that are connected by links. See Figure 37.1.[2]

Links can be of various kinds: contact, friendship, control, command, exchange, investment, trade, or information. Links can also describe co-occurrences, co-authorships, citations, and much more.

The formal definition of a *mathematical graph* describes observations as a set of *nodes* that are linked by *relations*. The links (pairs of nodes) are a subset of all possible pairs, the Cartesian product of the node set.

Links can be *undirected* or *directed*. If links in a network have different strengths, the graph is deemed to be *valued*. When *nodes* are connected by different types of *links*, it is a *multigraph*.

Graphs connecting two *distinct sets* of nodes are referred to as *bipartite* or *two-mode* graphs (Borgatti and Everett, 1997).

Especially rich graphs describe the interrelations of numerous concepts. Network text analysis (NTA), which seeks to represent the content of natural language by formal graph grammars (Diesner and Carley, 2004a, b), results in rich relational data sets that describe relations among *n different sets of nodes*. Graphs that represent text through various instances, such as *actors, places, resources, institutions*, and so on, are *n-mode graphs*.

MAPPING NETWORKS

The most important task in mapping networks is to determine the 2D or 3D locations of the nodes from the links of a graph. Such a *layout* encodes certain features of a network that maintain as much information as possible relating to the embeddedness of the nodes.

While higher dimensional spatial representations have greater degrees of freedom, a factor that allows them to disentangle more of the complexities of a network in the image space, intuitive navigation interfaces are needed to explore such orderings in greater detail. Additional transformations are also needed to explore 3D representations through a 2D window by perspective projections.

Some mappings of network data result in landscapes in which proximity in the image corresponds to the strength of the observed linkages. *Entities* linked up in networks are typically represented as points or rings, and *linkages* are represented as straight lines between the nodes. In contrast to geographical maps, proximity in networks is defined by functional references: who is strongly connected to whom, or who is connected

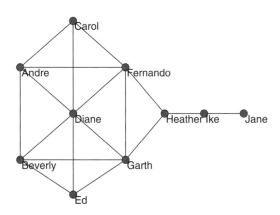

Figure 37.1 A schematic network drawing

in the same way to whom. Proximity in ordered social networks describes *spheres of influence*, *potential scopes of action*, and *contexts of entities that are mutually significant*. Their significance varies with the type of relationship (i.e., friendship, contact, communication, cooperation, exchange, commerce, transference of information, energy flows, or food chains).

Assigning nodes to coordinates in planar space was for a long time performed by trial and error. Today, we employ algorithms that are capable of moving connected nodes close to each other, while nodes connected by indirect paths or unconnected nodes are mapped at a distance. Various kinds of spring embedders are currently the most used algorithms, whereas multivariate statistical procedures such as factor analysis, correspondence analysis, and SVD (singular values decomposition) are other tools employed to produce spatial embeddings (Freeman, 2000, 2005).

Network maps

For centuries the humanities had a very distant relationship to any form of graphic representation of scientific knowledge, and cartography was among the first sciences to represent information in visual form. Cartographic maps inform us about "what is where."

Cartographers in the sixteenth century knew how to use triangulations to represent places in maps. In the plane, the distance from location A to location C can be computed by measuring the distance between AB and the *angles* of the lines connecting A and B to C. Mapping streets, shipping routes, trade networks, and movements between places with graphical symbols has proved to be a very informative way of proceeding, which has many uses in social life.

Because many social phenomena exhibit a more or less strong dependence on physical distance, geographical space is a natural frame of reference for social networks. Trade networks have been mapped into geographical maps for more than 200 years (Playfair, 1807; see also Friendly, 2008); mobility patterns are another form of information that has been extensively studied by geographers, mapping their flows to geographical space (Tobler, 1987, 2004).

The comparison of geographical and network mappings has much potential for helping us understand how social activities change the world by overcoming geographical distance by means of modern communication and transport technologies. Surprisingly, the field has not been intensively studied, though it seems to offer a great opportunity for understanding human behavior in a changing world.

Algorithms

Various planar encodings of network data can carry different messages. Figure 37.2 depicts the capital ties of the largest hundred German companies in 1996 with the help of a spring embedder (Höpner and Krempel, 2004). Visualizing the capital ties in this way produces a layout in which companies are placed close when company A holds shares in B. A second layout of the same data in Figure 37.9b encodes status differences and displays these with a radial layout. Companies with a high status are found at the center of the drawing, while the distance to companies on the periphery corresponds to their status differences, with the result that strongly linked companies are not necessarily placed close to each other. Additionally, the location of companies with a similar status (same distance from the center) is optimized so that companies with ties are placed closely together.

The invention of statistical procedures to represent similarities and distances in statistical and network data goes back to the pioneering work of Torgerson (1958) and Kruskal (1964) at Bell Labs in the 1960s and 1970s. In light of observations on similarities or distances, they designed algorithms that allowed them to embed observations in metric space (Kruskal and Wish, 1984). Inconsistencies in the distance data were resolved by a type of least squares procedure. This statistical treatment follows many of the ideas on how cartographers map geographical distance into 2D maps. The fit of these mappings can be inspected with the Torgerson diagram, which relates the distances in the image to the data distances.

Today, the placement problem is typically solved by employing various kinds of spring embedders (Eades, 1984; Fruchterman and Reingold, 1991; Kamada and Kawai; 1989), which arrange the nodes of a graph by translating links into mechanical forces that are counterbalanced by repulsive forces that mimic the repulsion of "electrical fields" to enforce a minimal distance around each of the nodes. The repulsive forces can be scaled, which leads to smaller or larger distances in the image: close neighbors are spread, while large distances are shrunk. The scaling does not affect the readability of a layout as long as the neighborhoods around the nodes are preserved. Central nodes are found at the center of such drawings, while nodes with low or only local connectivity are placed at the periphery.

While the algorithm of Fruchterman and Reingold draws networks using direct links, the Kamada and Kawei algorithm requires distance data. Typically the *geodesic distances*, the shortest paths connecting any pair of nodes, are used to compute the layout. Depending on the weights of

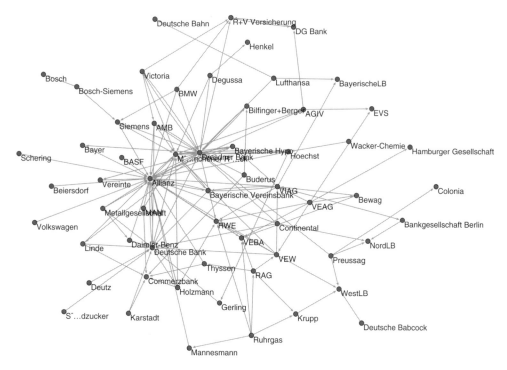

Figure 37.2   A spring-embedded layout of German capital ties for 1996

the links, a single strong link can outperform many weak links attached to a node that moves strongly linked nodes closer to each other.

The relative attractiveness of spring embedders results from their ability to achieve very different representations. Layouts can approach metric space but also achieve gridlike layouts when the repulsing forces are increased. The main characteristic of the embedders' layouts is, however, that spring algorithms provide information about the *local connectivities*, that is, who is linked to whom and the strength of this linkage. Connected nodes are typically placed close to each other.

Many more planar spaces

Because spatial embeddings are the most effective graphical means to map network metrics, many approaches seek to use planar space to convey network properties.

Traditional statistical displays map bivariate relations as scatter plots. The *x* and *y* coordinates in the image depict two attributes of an observed unit measured on a sequential (metric) scale. These scales determine the spacing of the *x* or *y* axis and the location of the observed instance in a drawing. As observations in statistical surveys are sampled, there is no information about how any units are linked.

Relational data, however, describe connections between observed units. A mapping that preserves the *local environments* of the linked units allows us to trace who is connected to whom: friends are placed closer to each other than to friends of friends. *Direct influences* can be read by examining close nodes that are directly linked.

To view the systemwide *potential* of social action, network metrics, such as *centralities* (closeness or betweenness) or *status measures*, are needed. These measures evaluate not only the direct links but also *the indirect links* to access the potential global impact of social action. This shifts the focus of the analysis from *bilateral action* to a *system perspective*: actors occupying higher ranks in a distribution are considered to be more influential.

The *Graph Drawing Community* explores mathematical graphs with algorithms that produce *planar, orthogonal, grid-based, hierarchical,* or *circular* layouts. Other types are graphs with *curved* or *orthogonal* lines. These algorithmic approaches seek to explore meaningful representations under all sorts of different constraints. Aesthetics that are known to enhance the overall readability of a visual representation such as crossing minimizations are additionally performed at certain stages of the algorithms.

Drawings can be simplified if the image space is confined to a number of equidistant points defining a grid in 2D or 3D space. Reducing the resolution of an image by means of grids produces rank orders of connectivity. Dense centers are spread while large distances are shrunk. Such transformations, however, limit the visibility of links when dense graphs are displayed.

A layout that approaches hierarchies in networks is the layered map: the y axis is used to convey information about actor status, while nodes are placed on the x axis so that connected nodes are positioned close (Brandes et al., 2002).

Centrality maps are radial orderings that group nodes around the center of a drawing, where the distance from the center reflects difference in centrality, authority, or other network metrics. Nodes with lower values are placed on more distant concentric circles. Given these constraints, links between the units can still be optimized so that connected nodes on different circles are positioned close.

VISUAL LAYERS OF NETWORK ATTRIBUTES

Translating numerical information visually does not just provide a researcher with a more complete multivariate view, enabling them to observe how actors are embedded in the global structure and facilitating communication of structural findings to scientific and nonscientific audiences. As Jacques Bertin (a French cartographer) notes in his "Semiology of Graphics" (1983), the advantage of using the visual system is that it permits several pieces of numerical information to be communicated simultaneously, whereas numbers, mathematical formulae, and written language have to be read sequentially.

From a more general perspective, visualizations translate numerical information into the visual sign system. Encoding numerical information into visual layers is best thought of as using independent communication channels, each of which transmits a separate piece of information. Choosing various visual modes to map network properties allows properties of the network to be studied with respect to the ordering principles of a given layout. Efficient data visualization requires knowledge of both computer graphics (how to encode information) and properties of human visual perception (how humans decode graphical information) and when this decoding is very fast.

Encoding

Efficient map making is described by Bertin (1983) as the encoding of numerical data into elementary perceptual tasks. Applying the "natural orders" of human perception makes visual communication almost automatic. If universal codes are used, the graphic language becomes instantaneous and international. If there are strict translation rules that enforce a bijective mapping (so that a visual representation maintains the order and the relations between the observations), visual signs can be decoded into human impressions that exactly match the information that is contained in the numerical data.

Human impressions of visual stimuli have been studied in psychology for more than a hundred years. Psycho-physical scaling and psychometric functions describe how physical dimensions of visual stimuli are related to human impressions (Stevens, 1975). To efficiently encode information into visual signs it is necessary to know how observers can read (decode) given graphical information. Apart from the depiction of lines, most of these functions are nonlinear.

Decoding

Visualizations are more effective if they can be interpreted more quickly, enable us to discern more distinctions, and offer fewer errors than alternative presentations. Rules that allow an observer to retrieve the encoded visual information very fast make visualizations effective. As has been noticed from the reports of many practitioners, certain visual encodings can be read almost instantaneously (Tufte, 1983, 1990), while others create visual puzzles.

That certain perceptual tasks can be read extremely fast is explained by the fact that the human brain processes elementary perceptual tasks in parallel through specialized centers. Pre-attentive perception needs less time than the movement of the human eye (less than 200 milliseconds). Complex graphical symbols, however, which may combine several pieces of information as icons or use metaphors, are typically much less efficient. Their meaning is also limited to specific cultural domains, while elementary perceptual tasks are not.

VISUAL ALPHABET FOR NETWORKS

Nodes and lines can be of different sizes, can have different colors or textures, and can be rendered with *2D* or *3D cues*. Most of these are already found in Bertin's list of elementary perceptual tasks (locations, sizes, textures, colors, shapes, directions, angles). A more complete list, as identified by more recent vision research, identifies 2D versus 3D cues, movement and flicker, which are read *pre-attentively*. Combinations of several of these tasks, however, are not pre-attentive but need a longer time to be decoded.

Sizes

How depictions of graphical signs are translated into sense impressions has been the subject of research in psycho-physics for more than 100 years. Stevens (1975) proposed a general relationship between the magnitude of a *physical stimulus* and its *perceived intensity* or strength, which is described as a power law: $f(I) = kI^a$, where I is the magnitude of the physical stimulus, $f(I)$ is the psycho-physical function relating to the *subjective magnitude of the sensation* evoked by the stimulus, a is an exponent that depends on the type of stimulation, and k is a proportionality constant that depends on the type of stimulation and the units used. This permits many kinds of physical stimuli and how they are related to corresponding impressions to be explored.

While the human impression of lines is linear (and has an exponent of 1), the "visual area" of a marker is related to the physical area scaled by an exponent of 0.7 – a rule that has been independently discovered in cartographic praxis and is regularly applied when depicting the sizes of cities on a map.

Shapes and symbols

Classes of nodes can be rendered onto a layout using *shapes, icons*, or *symbols. Color codes* are an alternative. Elementary shapes such as *circles, triangles, quadrangles, stars*, or 3D elements such as *cubes or cones* are shapes that can be used to communicate different classes of nodes. Symbols and trademarks are other ways of marking entities in network representations, but their meaning is limited to specific cultural domains.

Pictograms are used today in many public sign systems to communicate information. Such signs originated with the Vienna school of image statistics and the work of Otto Neurath and Gerhard Arntz in the 1920s, who developed simplified symbols ("isotypes"), signs designed to provide everyday people with insight into complex social phenomena (Neurath, 1936, 1937; Hartmann, 2002).

Lines

Lines can have different sizes (widths), which can easily lead to overlapping if graphs are dense. This can be compensated for to a certain degree if lines are arranged by size, so that strong (short) lines are drawn on top of weak (long) links.

Color-coded lines can be derived from node attributes of the source or target nodes, but they can also represent attributes of the links themselves. If links have quantitative attributes, it is possible to use quantitative color schemes that assign equidistant colors to numerical ranges.

Color

Encoding attributes with *color* is a very complex topic, which can hardly be sketched in this article, but it has enormous potential. Even today *color perception* is only understood at very basic levels. Colors can be used to create *distinguishable and ordered impressions*. On higher levels of color perception, colors are also related to aesthetical impressions, cultural meanings, and physiological reactions.

Human color impressions are organized according to three dimensions: *hue, lightness,* and *saturation*. This provides three *layers* to communicate information. Each of these visual cues can carry its own signal.

Although there are many perception-oriented color systems that differentiate colors according to tone, brightness, and saturation, almost all of these systems fail to describe uniformly perceived gradations. The Munsell color system in Figure 37.3 is considered to be perceptually uniform. Today's psychometric colors "unbeknownst to many" have already gained entry into our everyday life. In 1976 these colors were introduced as international standards (CIE Lab). They are the results of not only decades of quantification by an ambitious group of colorimetricians but also the identification of mathematical functions by means of which the psychometric Munsell System can be applied to the physical model of colors.

Colorimetricians have been exploring color phenomena since the beginning of the twentieth century and have succeeded in mapping the physical properties of light (red, green, blue) into human color sensations (hue, lightness, and saturation). After a century's effort, they have identified complex formulae that describe how combinations of physical light waves are related to (barely) noticeable differences in human color perception (Wyszecki and Stiles, 1982).

To make things more complicated, the appearance of single colors is modified by additional variables, most importantly by the *contrast to the*

Figure 37.3   The Munsell System differentiates between nine levels of lightness and 10 hues, which are organized radially on each of the vertical levels. Colors with identical saturation (chroma) are equidistant to the center. It is a perceptually uniform color system

background of a drawing. The impressions of a color scheme vary greatly in their contrast to the surrounding background (Jacobson and Bender, 1996). A dark background lets color appear brighter, while white backgrounds dim the appearance of the same color scheme. Communicating information with colors is thus highly dependent on the overall composition of a drawing, and the use of *hue*, lightness, and *saturation contrasts* as well as the *contrast to the background* of a drawing.

Psychometric color systems describe levels of *color* that are perceived in the human brain as *equidistant*. They are the key to using color to communicate *ordered* and *quantitative* information. Modern perceptually equidistant color systems like CIE Lab have been international standards since 1976 and allow grades of hues, saturation, and lightness to be chosen so that the values encoded appear *equidistant* to human beings. This enables color schemes to be developed that communicate nominal, ordinal, and even metric information. HSB and HSV are related standards that display color in similar dimensions but do not scale the dimensions in a perceptual way.

If attributes are to be communicated with colors, it is worth taking a look at the work of Cynthia Brewer (1994, 1999), a geographer at Penn State who has put much effort into devising color schemes for geographical maps that are very well informed about the potential of modern color systems. Not only has she developed color schemes that allow *qualitative*, *sequential*, or *diverging* distributions of attributes but she also addresses special topics such as color blindness. Her color schemes are a good starting point when quantities or distributions of exogenous data have to be mapped onto layouts of networks (cf. Figure 37.4).

The requirements for encoding statistical information into color schemes have been spelled out by Rogowitz and Treinish (1996): to encode *nominal* classes, colors should not be too dissimilar. For rank orders, colors should be perceived as *ordered*. To encode quantitative information, *color gradients* are needed where the *different levels appear equidistant*.

MAPPING GRAPH PROPERTIES

A second type of picture emerges when the effort is made to depict the special qualities of a

27	217	117	231	102	230	166	102		
158	95	112	41	166	171	118	102		
119	2	179	138	30	2	29	102		
0.448	0.475	0.474	0.426	0.517	0.667	0.48	0.4		

179	253	203	244	230	255	241	204		
226	205	213	202	245	242	226	204		
205	172	232	228	201	174	204	204		
0.821	0.846	0.831	0.852	0.924	0.934	0.894	0.8		

247	222	198	158	107	66	33	8	8	
251	235	219	202	174	146	113	81	48	
255	247	239	225	214	198	181	156	107	
0.981	0.911	0.842	0.75	0.62	0.5	0.378	0.264	0.166	

255	254	253	253	253	241	217	166	127	
245	230	208	174	141	105	72	54	39	
235	206	162	107	60	19	1	3	4	
0.968	0.919	0.848	0.746	0.649	0.534	0.422	0.321	0.241	

158	213	244	253	254	255	230	171	102	50	94
1	62	109	174	224	255	245	221	194	136	79
66	79	67	97	139	191	152	164	165	189	162
0.216	0.428	0.568	0.742	0.877	0.972	0.903	0.783	0.64	0.455	0.363

103	178	214	244	253	247	209	146	67	33	5
0	24	96	165	219	247	229	197	147	102	48
31	43	77	130	199	247	240	222	195	172	97
0.134	0.283	0.507	0.724	0.89	0.968	0.879	0.723	0.503	0.349	0.158

Figure 37.4 Color schemes for the communication of qualitative, sequential, and divergent distributions (Cynthia Brewer, www.colorbrewer.org)

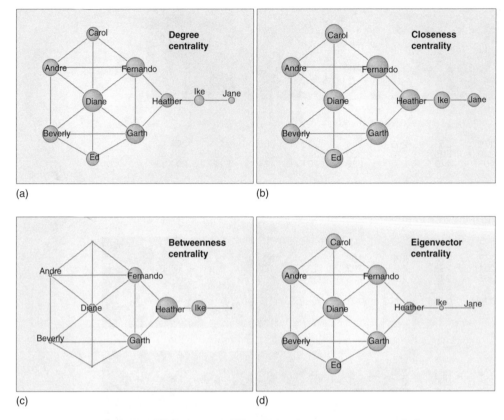

(a)   (b)   (c)   (d)

Figure 37.5   Using size to different centralities makes it easy to compare their distributions (compare to Figure 37.1). (a) Degree; (b) Closeness; (c) Betweenness; (d) Eigenvector centrality

network, its component entities, or certain subsystems in the form of additional graphic features. This necessitates the use of additional graphic attributes: *sizes, colors,* or *forms* that graphically ascribe these characteristics to the layout of the network. In this way, graphical-theoretical qualities derived from the linkages are integrated into the depiction and can thus be read simultaneously.

If the *centrality* of the particular entities is portrayed by means of the *size* of the symbols, then a reading of the graphic representation provides additional information about who is involved in an especially large number of relationships (*degree*), who can reach many agents via particularly short *paths* (*closeness*), and who controls an especially large number of the *shortest linkages* to an adjacent network (*betweenness*). Coding node properties using the sizes of the symbols makes for a simple way to study global and local positions.

Figures 37.5 a–d map different centralities onto the schematic layout of Figure 37.1 through the sizes of the nodes. This permits us to analyze their distributions in detail and to read which actors are considered important by means of a specific type of centrality.

Mapping graph properties as a second layer of information onto the planar layout of a network produces information-rich landscapes, which allow us to explore the layout in greater depth. They provide orientation in a similar way to geographical maps. The fascinating thing about these charts is that they fit together a multitude of observations, like pieces of a jigsaw puzzle, into a picture of the system as a whole. The human eye can discover particular patterns in them with relative ease.

Of special interest are *all intermediate levels* of social structures. *Dense areas* are subsets of nodes that are closely connected. A zoo of concepts exists that can be applied to identify *cohesive subsets* in networks (*components, cores, cliques, n-cliques, clans,* and *clubs*).

To demonstrate how various network metrics can be mapped simultaneously onto the layout of a network, we use the classic "Southern Women" network data set (Davis et al., 1941). This data set describes the interaction patterns of 18 women participating in 14 informal events over a period of nine months. This bipartite graph has often been used to demonstrate the usefulness of new network algorithms in the literature (Breiger, 1974; Freeman, 2003). Figures 37.6 and 37.7 demonstrate how various properties of this well-studied graph can be mapped with different graphical layers onto the layout, which has been produced with the help of a spring embedder.

Figure 37.6a displays the two types of nodes (women and events) using two different colors (in the original version, yellow and blue) and maps the degrees of the women and events with sizes.

Positions and *roles describe* sets of structurally equivalent actors, that is, actors who have similar profiles of connections and certain comparative advantages: high levels of autonomy or competition. As long as intermediate structures such as cores or blocks are used to detect subgraphs, the nodes are decomposed into nonoverlapping subsets (partitions). To display these classes, it is sufficient to use different hues. A computation of a two-mode block model for the Southern Women dataset yields three structurally equivalent blocks for the events and two for the women. Mapping the block membership with colors (in the original version, dark green, yellow, and dark blue for the events; light green and light blue for the women) onto the layout of Figure 37.6a results in Figure 37.6b.

Pie charts allow the connections of the women to the different event blocks to be viewed in greater detail. They depict the number of links to different blocks and reveal which women are connected to a particular event block. Figure 37.7a shows that all women are only connected to two of the event blocks (in the original version, either the yellow/blue or yellow/green). The yellow events are central and are visited by both groups.

Another graphical element is the *convex hull*, which is useful for identifying sets of actors in a given layout. A *convex hull* is a concept from computational geometry and is used here to observe how partitions of the nodes are distributed in a network layout. A *hull* wraps all nodes of a given class by identifying the *area* that is covered by these nodes. If *hulls* are computed for all node sets of a classification, their *intersections* identify areas where members of different sets are placed close to each other, while indicating exclusive

areas that only contain members of a specific set (cf. Johnson and Krempel, 2004). Mapping the blocks for the Southern Women data set yields Figure 37.7b. In this case, we find that the spring embedder layout has positioned all blocks in separate areas of the drawing. Reading the pie charts of the women also allows us to discover that Dorothy and Pearl are both connected to the central block of events only and therefore hold a distinct position in the network (cf. Doreian et al., 2005: 257–65).

Whereas visual approaches to single networks allow us to examine the complete distributions of the nodes and their properties in a layout, comparisons of different networks need additional normalizations, correcting for the number of nodes or lines. Comparisons of different networks typically make heavy use of traditional statistical methodologies. Exceptions to this are dynamic networks that trace network changes over time.

If the focus is to compare *systems*, a whole range of statistics can be used. Graphs can be compared on the system level by their *density, their degree,* their *transitivity and clustering*, and the *number of dense areas or positions.*

MAPPING EXPLANATIONS

A third class of "analytical graphics" emerges if, in similar fashion, external information about the component units or their interrelationships (e.g., theoretical classifications or independently gathered data) is introduced into the representation. In mapping explanations, typically *color schemes* are used.

Attributes of the links can greatly help to understand how relations between different subsets of external classes of actors ("*catnets*" as defined by White, 2008) are organized. Color codes of partitions and color schemes derived from these external classifications can be used to display who is connected to whom and to what extent.

Mapping exogenous attributes onto the layout of a graph makes it possible to explore how actors of a certain kind interact in the network and how a given pattern of external attributes relates to the layout of a graph (Figure 37.8). Again, correlations will appear as local patterns that may allow us to understand the possible causes of emergent social processes.

In an analysis of equity capital interrelationships, for example, classifying firms as industrial enterprises, banks, and insurance companies, and selecting a different color for each category facilitates recognition of particular concentrations in the network, with any preponderance of units

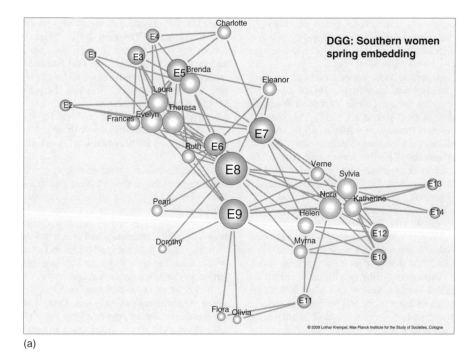

(a)

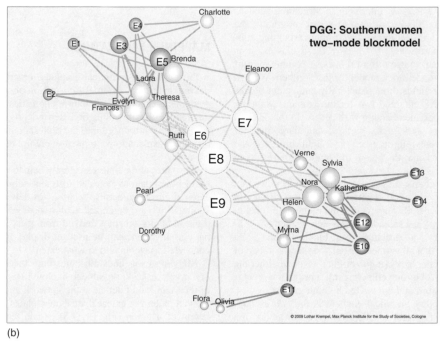

(b)

Figure 37.6   A bipartite graph: Davis Southern Women. (a) Layout, degrees and sets; (b) A two-mode blockmodel: two women and three event blocks

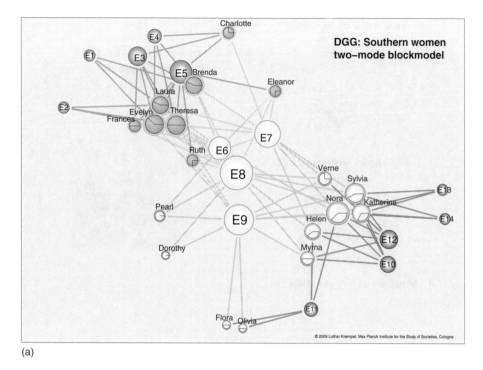

(a)

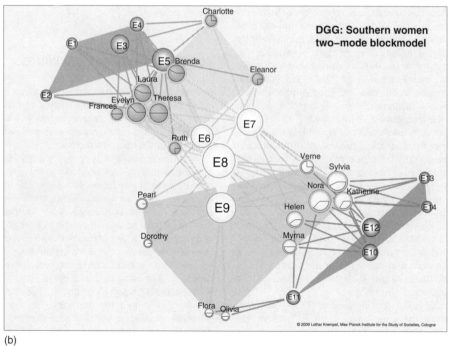

(b)

Figure 37.7   A block model: Southern Women. (a) Pie charts as node symbols; (b) Using convex hulls

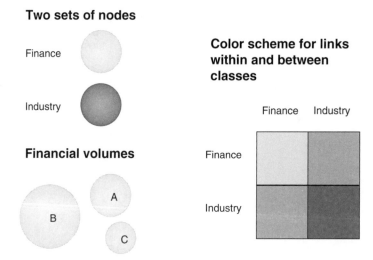

Figure 37.8   Mapping external attributes

of the same color displayed indicating internal interrelationships.

These can be examined more closely by means of lines in a *derivative color scheme*: the extent to which such investments are held exclusively by banks and industrial enterprises or whether the majority of the interrelationships consists of equity capital interpenetration by banks and industrial enterprises. In this case, utilizing different colors projects a theoretically significant classification onto the arrangement of a network.

The depiction makes it possible to ascertain whether the theoretical process of differentiation exhibits systematic patterns in the optimized arrangement of the network. In contrast to a purely statistical treatment, weak local interconnections also emerge in networks. They indicate the structure's potential for development.

The spring embedder solution reveals a central core formed of cross-linked banks, which (in the original color version of this image) appear as a yellow pattern in the center of the drawing and a second (dark) industrial cluster in the north-east of the drawing (Figure 37.9a).

In the radial drawing (Figure 37.9b), which is based on the same data, status differences are encoded. Such a drawing rests on the assumption that the bilateral control rights that are affiliated with a capital link go beyond direct control. Here the insurer Allianz holds the most dominant position in the center, whereas the other cross-linked banks appear on the semi-periphery (i.e., they have lower status). Looking at the color patterns, it is easy to see that the banks hold the most

dominant positions, while the industrial cluster can be detected in the north-north-west of the outer circles.

COMPLEX AND LARGE DRAWINGS

Networks of several thousands of nodes are not easily displayed, even if large output formats are used. The analysis of large networks has to use *formal* or *substantial strategies* that illuminate processes in the overall structure.

A common strategy is to apply some *sort of filtering*, which reduces networks to the *most connected nodes* or *most dominant lines*. The idea is to discern some sort of *backbone* to the overall structure. *Node-cuts* or *line-cuts* are two strategies that can help to identify the most important parts of a network. A *node-cut* results from a decision to keep only nodes that surpass a certain *threshold* – for instance, nodes with a certain degree or centrality. The subgraph will contain only lines between the selected elements. If, however, we impose a threshold for the lines (*line-cut*), the subgraph is defined by all nodes that are connected by lines that surpass a certain threshold. Only nodes that are linked by at least one of the selected lines are contained in the subgraph.

Another approach is to select *dense areas* that surpass a certain threshold of connectedness. *Cores* are node sets that are linked by a certain number of ties. While many definitions of dense clusters generate overlapping cliques, cores are

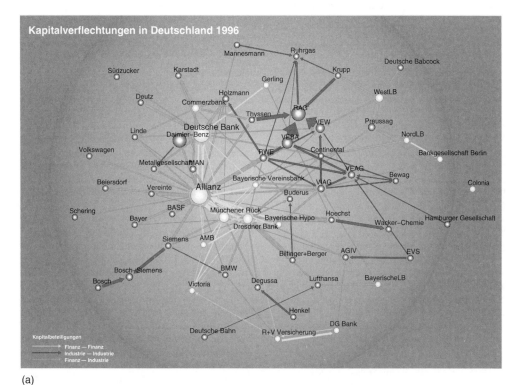

(a)

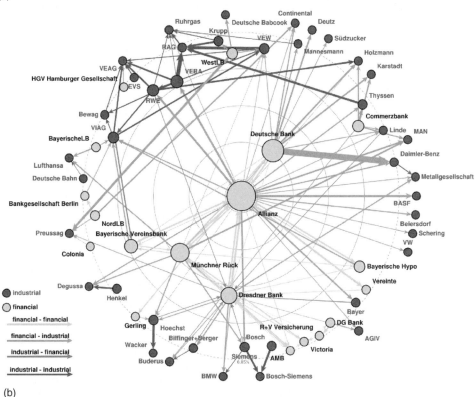

(b)

Figure 37.9 Capital ties and attributes. (a) Attributes and spring layout; (b) A radial layout of status differences (Baur et al., 2008) (*Capital Ties and Attributes: A Radial Layout of Status Differences.* Baur, Brandes and Wagner)

nested hierarchically, which results in nonoverlapping network partitions.

Blockmodeling is the traditional approach to analyzing social networks and allows graphs to be reduced to block structures (partitions of the nodes), which provides information on who is connected to similar actors in the system. *Structural equivalence* seeks to identify *positions* (sets of the nodes) that are connected to (identical) actors. Social positions need not be densely connected; they describe actors that are engaged in the same contacts. *Aggregating* nodes and ties for blocks yields a reduced graph (simplified structure and image) that describes interrelations between *positions* (Krempel, 2005).

Multigraphs are composed of different kinds of links. In such a case, a *peeling approach* is advised. Which type of link achieves the highest levels of connectivity? Which type of link contributes to the overall connectivity once the most dominant ties have been removed?

Temporal networks are one of the frontiers of today's network research and visualization.

> The combined use of timing and relational information is usually named "Dynamic Network Analysis.". . . Confusingly, the term "dynamic network" is often used in the literature to describe various specific subclasses:
>
> - Networks in which the edge and node sets remain fixed, but values of attributes on nodes and edges may vary in time (transmission models)
> - Networks in which edges are added or deleted over time (computer networks, friendship relations)
> - Networks in which the weights of edges change over time (neural networks, exchange networks)
> - Networks in which nodes are added or removed in time (ecological food webs, organizations)
>
> Clearly these categories are not exclusive (Bender-deMoll et al., 2008).

Many real-world problems, however, exhibit more complicated dynamics: if we trace capital ties between companies over time, we find that new firms *emerge*, companies *cease* to exist, pairs of companies *merge* into *new legal entities*, while others *split* or *spin off* into new companies.

Temporal networks, which describe graph changes diachronically, are attracting growing research interest in their analysis (Moody et al., 2005, de Nooy, 2008). As *time* adds an additional dimension to the data, there is also a tendency to use 3D drawings. 2D representations can be an alternative if *sequences of drawings* are used, when there is only a small turnover in the population over time.

Structural growth processes represent simple cases, where a growing number of relations reshape a population of nodes over time. Links attach to an early core and produce snowflake-like growth. New links (that do not decay) connect an increasing number of nodes over time. Looking at the development of collaborations among graph-drawing scientists, Graphael (Forrester et al., 2004) present a network that has developed around an initial core.

To trace networks diachronically, *sequences of drawings* can be used. However, if the layout changes too much between single points in time, it becomes too difficult to trace what happens. The Graph Drawing Community deals with this problem by implementing algorithms that preserve *mental maps*, limiting changes to the nodes between different points in time in the overall layout (Purchase et al., 2006). One strategy is to compute the layout for the *supergraph* (the union of all graphs in sequence) and to display only active elements at certain points.

Skye Bender-deMoll and McFarland (2006) present various ways of how to visualize network processes as *sequences of images* or as *films*. The authors use *smoothing techniques* such as *moving averages* that aggregate network information in larger *time frames*, or the *interpolation* of layouts between discrete points in time, to achieve easier readable results.

A temporal extension of radial drawings can be found in GEOMI (Ahmed et al., 2006).

> The 2.5 D method is one of the solutions to represent temporal network data. In such a method, a graph snapshot at a particular time is placed on a 2D plane, in which a layout algorithm can be applied; a series of such planes are stacked together following time order to show the changes. In order to identify a particular node in a different time plane, same nodes in different planes are connected by edges. Combined with navigation tools in GEOMI, users can trace the change of each individual node's relationship to others and also can evaluate the evolution of the whole network in general.

As an example, Figure 37.11 shows the email connections of a certain research group. Each plane represents one month, while each node is one person. The edges between nodes on the same plate depict the e-mail traffic between persons. In addition, degree centrality is mapped to node size, while node color represents betweenness centrality.

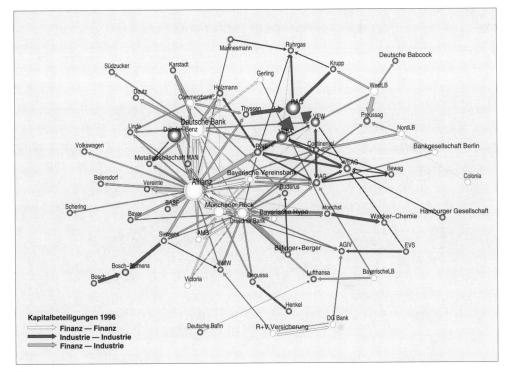

(a)

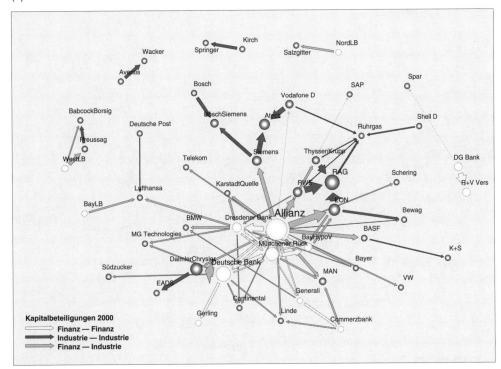

(b)

Figure 37.10 Visualizing the comparative static development of the German company system (1996–2006). (a) 1966; (b) 2000

(Continued)

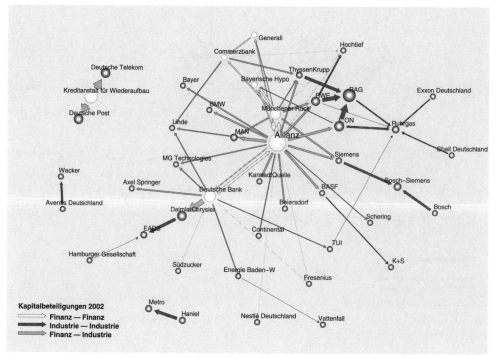

(c)

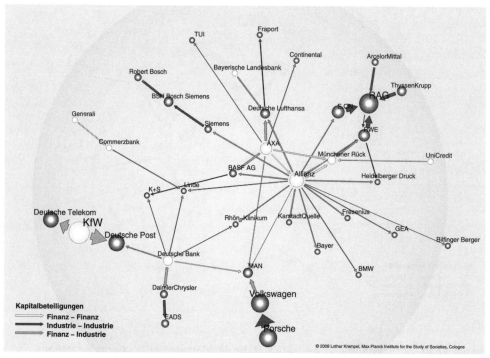

(d)

Figure 37.10 Cont'd (c) 2002; (d) 2006

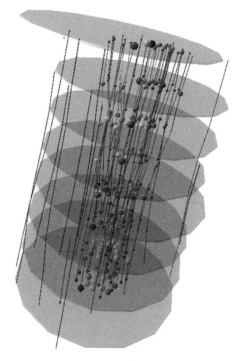

Figure 37.11   Geomi: Emails between scientists over time (*emails between Scientists Over Time: A Temporal Extension of Radial Drawings can be Found in GEOMI, GEOMI*) Image courtesy Seok-Hee Hong

SUMMARY

The potential of such "visual statistics" is strongly dependent upon the resolution of a series of additional questions. How can quantitative information be communicated? In what cases can depictions of manifold information be interpreted especially easily and quickly? French cartographer Jacques Bertin already provided an important key to understanding such fundamental problems of information processing in his 1983 work "The Semiology of Graphics."

What distinguishes visual symbols from other systems of signs (writing, language, and music) is their ability to simultaneously communicate different types of information. Converting numerical information is a process of translation into elementary graphic signs. With the elementary graphic attributes of size, color, and form, multiple sets of information can be communicated independently of each other and at the same time. If the natural categories of human perception are exploited in doing this, then the translation is especially effective.

If relational observations are ordered according to systematic rules and additional external information is pictorially projected onto these orderings in a way that takes psycho-physiological principles into consideration, then the results are highly optimized, graphical information landscapes – artificial worlds that fit together manifold descriptions of the same objects and reconstruct these objects. This makes it possible to view local, multidimensional patterns and to study the positioning of the elements that have been multiply described in this way within the system as a whole.

The use of colors in particular expands the possibilities of discovering within these structures concentrations of characteristics that identify multivariate linkages. Both the technologies for automatically generating colors and the facility for utilizing different technologies to evoke similar color impressions on the part of different people are based upon an enormously improved understanding of the human perception of color. Although the use of these color technologies has quickly become very widespread in our everyday lives, the scientific use of colors in the investigation of complex issues is still pretty much in its formative phase.

The extent to which we are able to better understand and apply these rules will determine how well we can exploit the natural attributes of human perception for scientific purposes. To this end, ergonomically optimized graphics use the particular capabilities of human perception in a systematic way. This makes it possible to combine the potential of automatic procedures with the special capacities of human perception.

The historical concern that visual mappings create artifacts can be overcome if we apply systematic encoding rules to represent numerical information and choose encodings that can be almost automatically decoded. Along with procedures that let us map social space into meaningful planar representations, a new world of scientific images becomes available. If done well, these images are bijective mappings that depict nothing else but the information that is encoded in the numerical data. If this is the case, the researcher can move back and forth between the numerical data and their visualizations, making comparisons that offer many new insights. Combining more traditional statistical exploration with exploratory visual inspection is especially promising when it comes to generating new knowledge.

Visualizations can supplement statistical procedures to capture local events, which are typically undetected in statistical analysis because the observed local regularities only result in medium effects if computed on a systemwide scale. The potential of visualizations is that they can identify local combinations of external attributes, which are linked into clusters that are forerunners of emerging social processes. Visualizations of multi-dimensional network data are more sensitive than traditional statistical approaches: while linear statistics identifies causalities by revealing all the instances of certain combinations of exogenous variables, the visual layers disclose *maximal connected local patterns* that are *homogeneous* for a specific combination of external variables. Such patterns need more attention because they are candidates for emerging social processes – processes that are currently not completely understood because our knowledge and information is too limited. Visualizations can hint at where additional information is needed and help to direct our attention to domains that need further exploration. Mapping network data provides a starting point for all sorts of inquiries, no matter whether they are quantitative or qualitative.

NOTES

1 A large number of publications are referenced under http://www.graphdrawing.org.

2 Color versions of the figures in this chapter are available from http://www.mpifg.de/people/lk/downl_de.asp.

REFERENCES

Ahmed, A., Dwyer, T., Forster, M., Fu, X., Ho, J., Hong, S.-H., Koschützki, D., Murray, C., Nikolov, N.S., Taib, R., Tarassov, A. and Xu, P. (2006) 'GEOMI: GEOmetry for maximum insight', In P. Healy and Eades (eds), *Proceedings on Graph Drawing*. Springer Verlag. pp. 468–79.

Ars Electronica. (2004) 'Language of networks'. Conference and exhibition on networks, curated by Gerhard Dirmoser, Lothar Krempel, Ruth Pfosser, and Dietmar Offenhuber, http://www.aec.at/en/festival2004/programm/LON_folder_lowres.pdf.

Baur, M., Ulrik B. and Dorothea W. (2008) 'Attribute-based visualization in Visone', at the 15th International Symposium on Graph Drawing, Sydney, Australia, September 2007.

Bender-deMoll, S., Morris, M. and Moody, J. (2008) 'Prototype packages for managing and animating longitudinal network data: Dynamic networks and RSonia', *Journal of Statistical Software*, 24(7), http://www.jstatsoft.org.

Bender-deMoll, S. and McFarland, D.A. (2006) 'The art and science of dynamic network visualization', *JOSS Journal of Social Structures*, 7(2).

Bertin, J. (1983) *Semiology of Graphics*. Diagrams Networks Maps: The University of Wisconsin Press.

Borgatti, S. and Everett, M.G. (1997) 'Network analysis of 2-mode data', *Social Networks*, 19: 243–69.

Brandes, U. and Erlebacher, T. (eds) (2005) *Network Analysis: Methodological Foundations*. Heidelberg: Springer.

Brandes, U., Raab J. and Wagner, D. (2002) 'Exploratory network visualization: Simultaneous display of actor status and connections', *JOSS Journal of Social Structure*, 2(4).

Breiger, R.L. (1974) 'The duality of persons and groups', *Social Forces*, 53: 181–90.

Brewer, C.A. (1994) 'Guidelines for use of the perceptual dimensions of color for mapping and visualization', in J. Bares (ed.), *Color Hard Copy and Graphic Arts III*, Proceedings of the International Society for Optical Engineering (SPIE), San José, Vol. 2171. pp. 54–63.

Brewer, C.A. (1999) 'Color use guidelines for data representation', Proceedings of the Section on Statistical Graphics, American Statistical Association, Baltimore. 55–60.

Chen, C., Härdle, W. and Unwin, A. (eds) (2008) *Handbook of Data Visualization*. Berlin: Springer-Verlag.

Davis, A., Gardener, B.B. and Gardener, M.R. (1941) *Deep South*. Chicago: University of Chicago Press.

Diesner, J. and Carley, K. (2004a) 'AutoMap 1.2 Extract, analyze, represent, and compare mental models from texts', *CASOS Technical Report*, January 2004 CMU-ISRI-04–100.

Diesner, J. and Carley, K. (2004b) 'Revealing social structure from texts: Meta-matrix text analysis as a novel method for network text analysis', in *Causal Mapping for Information Systems and Technology Research: Approaches, Advances, and Illustrations*. Harrisburg, PA: Idea Group Publishing.

Dorein, P., Vladimir, B. and Ferligoj, A. (2005) *Generalized Blockmodeling*. Cambridge University Press.

Eades, P. (1984) 'A heuristic for graph drawing', *Congressus Numerantium*, 42: 149–60.

Forrester, D., Kobourov, S., Navabi, A., Wampler, K. and Yee, G. (2004) 'Graphael: A system for generalized force-directed layouts', Department of Computer Science, University of Arizona, http://graphael.cs.arizona.edu.

Freeman, L.C. (2005) 'Graphic techniques for exploring social network data', in Peter J. Carrington, John Scott, and Stanley Wasserman (eds), *Models and Methods in Social Network Analysis*. pp. 248–69.

Freeman, L.C. (2003) 'Finding social groups: A meta-analysis of the Southern Women data', in Ronald Breiger, Kathleen Carley and Philippa Pattison (eds), *Dynamic Social Network Modeling and Analysis*. Washington, DC: National Academies Press, 2003.

Freeman, L.C (2000) 'Visualizing social networks', *JOSS Journal of Social Structure*, 1(1).

Friendly, M. (2008) 'Milestones in the history of thematic cartography, statistical graphics, and data visualization', http://www.math.yorku.ca/SCS/Gallery/milestone/milestone.pdf.

Fruchterman, T.M.J. and Reingold, E.M. (1991) 'Graph drawing by force directed placement', *Software-Practice and Experience*, 21(11): 1129–64.

Hartmann, F. and Bauer, E.K. (eds) (2002): *Bildersprache, Otto Neurath: Visualisierungen*. Vienna: WUV Universitätsverlag.

Höpner, M. and Krempel, L. (2004) 'The politics of the German company network', *Competition and Changem,* 8(4): 339–56.

Jacobson, N. and Bender, W. (1996) 'Color as a determined communication', *IBM Systems Journal,* 36(3 and4): 526–38.

Johnson, J.C. and Krempel, L. (2004) 'Network visualization: The "Bush team" in Reuters news ticker 9/11–11/15/01', *JOSS Journal of Social Structure,* 5(1).

Kamada, T. and Kawai, S. (1989) 'An algorithm for drawing general undirected graphs', *Information Processing Letters,* 31(1): 7–15.

Krempel, L. (2005) *Visualisierung komplexer Strukturen. Grundlagen der Darstellung mehrdimensionaler Netzwerke.* Frankfurt: Campus.

Kruskal, J.B. and Wish, M. (1978) *Multidimensional Scaling.* Beverly Hills, CA: Sage.

Kruskal, J.B. (1964) 'Nonmetric multidimensional scaling: A numerical method', *Psychometrika,* 29(2): 115–29.

Moody, J., McFarland, D.A. and Skye Bender-deMoll. (2005) 'Dynamic network visualization: Methods for meaning with longitudinal network movies?' *American Journal of Sociology,* 110: 1206–41.

Neurath, O. (1937) *Basic by Isotype.* London: K. Paul, Trench, Trubner.

Neurath, O. (1936) *International Picture Language: the First Rules of Isotype.* London: K. Paul, Trench, Trubner.

de Nooy, W., Mrvar, A. and Batagelj, V. (2005) *Exploratory Social Network Analysis with Pajek.* Structural Analysis in the Social Sciences. New York: Cambridge University Press.

de Nooy, W. (2008) 'Signs over time: Statistical and visual analysis of a longitudinal signed network', *Journal of Social Structure,* 9(1).

Playfair, W. (1807) *An Inquiry into the Permanent Causes of the Decline and Fall of Powerful and Wealthy Nations* London: W. Marchant for Greenland and Norris.

Purchase, H., Hoggan, E. and Görg, C. (2006) 'How important is the "mental map"? – an empirical investigation of a dynamic graph layout algorithm', in Proceedings of 14th International Symposium on Graph Drawing, Karlsruhe, Germany, September 2006.

Rogowitz, B.E. and Treinish, L.A. (1996) 'Why should engineers and scientists be worried about color?' http://www.research.ibm.com/people/l/lloydt/color/color. HTM.

Scott, J. (2000) *Social Network Analysis.* London: Sage.

Spence, I. and Wainer, H. (1997) 'Who was Playfair?' *Chance,* 10: 35–37.13

Stevens, S.S. (1975) *Psychophysics. Introduction to Its Perceptual, Neural, and Social Prospects.* New York: John Wiley.

Tobler, W. (2004) 'Movement mapping', http://csiss.ncgia. ucsb.edu/clearinghouse/FlowMapper.

Tobler, W. (1987) 'Experiments in migration mapping by computer', *American Cartographer.*

Tufte, E.R. (1990) *Envisioning Information.* Cheshire, CT: Graphics Press.

Tufte, E.R. (1983) *The Visual Display of Quantitative Information.* Cheshire, CT: Graphics Press.

Torgerson, W.S. (1958) *Theory and Methods of Scaling.* New York: John Wiley.

Wasserman, S. and Faust, K. (1994) *Social Network Analysis: Methods and Application.* Cambridge: Cambridge University Press.

White, H. (2008) *Identity and Control. How Social Formations Emerge.* 2nd ed. Princeton, NJ: Princeton University Press.

Wilkinson, L. (2008) 'Graph-theoretic graphics', in C. Chen, W. Härdle, and A. Unwin (eds), *Handbook of Data Visualization.* Berlin: Springer-Verlag. pp. 122-–50.

Wilkinson, L. (2005) *The Grammar of Graphics.* New York: Springer Science and Business Media.

Wyszecki, G. and Stiles, W. S. (1982) *Color Science. Concepts and Methods, Quantitative Data and Formulae.* 2nd ed. New York: John Wiley.

38

A Reader's Guide to SNA Software

Mark Huisman and Marijtje A.J. van Duijn

INTRODUCTION

Where can I find a comprehensive list of software applications for social network analysis? This seems a likely question, especially for a researcher who is new to social network analysis (SNA) or who is not familiar with software for SNA. The answer to the question of whether such a list exists[1] is not a simple yes or no. Yes, there are several lists available in the literature and, more importantly, on the Internet, but no, none of these lists are complete or comprehensive.

Two good starting points in the search for SNA software can be found, however: the comprehensive collection of SNA tools publicly available on the software pages on the International Network for Social Network Analysis (INSNA) Web site and the software articles about social network analysis in Wikipedia. And, with this chapter, we hope to have created a third starting point: The list of programs and toolkits reviewed here are also available on an accompanying Web site (http://www.gmw.rug.nl/~huisman/sna/software.html; URLs of all Web sites mentioned in the text are provided in Table 38.5 in the references).

Making an overview of software is a seemingly hopeless task in a fast-changing field of research. By definition, a software list becomes outdated soon if not immediately after publication. Still, we feel the need for information on software packages, in such a way that readers may obtain a general sense on the usefulness of particular packages for their own research (Erickson, 2005; Butts, 2007). We have provided the reader with an overview of 56 selected programs and toolkits for SNA.

The selection of software is based on the two comprehensive lists mentioned before: the INSNA list and the Wikipedia list, leaving out the programs merely aimed at visualization and highly specialized programs not directly suitable for the analysis of social networks. Searching the Internet, we found software that was suitable for review but not mentioned in the two lists. We stress at this point that our list is probably not complete either, as it is a selection of available software (i.e., software we were able to find up to January 2010) to analyze (certain aspects of) social networks. However, we do think that it contains the most prominent and important programs in the field.

We will not review programs in detail, but we give a global description and categorization of their characteristics, highlight new developments, and make general comparisons between packages. The focus is on social network *analysis*, although we do inspect visualization routines in analysis tools. Network visualization is the topic of investigation of Krempel's chapter (this volume). Applications for social networking like Facebook, Twitter, or LinkedIn (boyd and Ellison, 2007) are not discussed either.

Table 38.1 Major SNA packages reviewed in the last 20+ years. Reviews by Freeman (1988), Wasserman and Faust, (1994), Degenne: and Forsé (1999), Scott (2002), Huisman and van Duijn (2005a), and Loscalzo and Yu (2008) and Kirschner (2008)

Program	F 1988	WP 1994	DP 1999	S 2002	HvD 2005	LY,K 2008
SONIS	M					
SONET	M					
GRADAP	M	M		*M*	*m*	
STRUCTURE	M	M	P	*M*	M	
SNAP		M			*m*	
NEGOPY/FATCAT/MultiNet	M	M		M	M	
UCINET	M	M	P	M	M	M
KrackPlot		M		*m*	*m*	
Pajek				M	M	*m*
NetMiner					M	M
StOCNET					M	*m*
Other packages				1	19	17

M = considered a major package in the corresponding review.
m = considered a minor package in the corresponding review.
P = considered a popular package in the corresponding review.
Italics indicate no change in the program with respect to previous review.

For ordering the selected software we chose the three general introductory texts on social network analysis, by Wasserman and Faust (1994), Degenne and Forsé (1999), and Scott (2002). The three books together give a brief review of seven computer programs for social network analysis (see also Scott, 1996). These seven programs, which can be considered the major SNA programs of the 1990s, are listed in Table 38.1.[2]

Table 38.1 almost presents a brief history of SNA software (Freeman, 1988, gives a history of tools up to 1988; Hummon and Carley, 1993, present a history of major events in SNA, including software packages, up to 1990) and contains four extra programs besides the seven mentioned in the textbooks: the older, and by now discarded, programs SONIS and SONET (reviewed by Freeman in 1988), and the two more recently developed packages NetMiner and StOCNET (reviewed in 2005 by Huisman and van Duijn, and in 2008 by Loscalzo and Yu and Kirschner). Most programs are general programs containing many routines and analysis methods, with two exceptions: KrackPlot, one of the first graph-drawing programs, and StOCNET, aimed at statistical modeling of cross-sectional and longitudinal network data. Three of the major general programs were no longer updated in 2002 (GRADAP and STRUCTURE) or 2005 (SNAP). Only one program, UCINET, is present in all reviews, is still regularly updated, and can be considered the most prominent SNA package of the last 20+ years.

In the early 1990s (and in the 1980s), GRADAP and STRUCTURE were major programs like UCINET, but their position was taken over by the programs Pajek and NetMiner. MultiNet should be positioned between the early programs (it emerged from the even older programs NEGOPY and FATCAT) and the recent developments, and it had its peak around 2006. This classification of programs is supported by the number of (software) workshops organized at the INSNA Sunbelt conferences on social networks since 2000. All 11 Sunbelt conferences (including the one in 2010) featured workshops on UCINET and SIENA (one of the main programs in the StOCNET package). Pajek workshops have been organized for the last nine years, starting in 2002, and MultiNet workshops were held in four years (2000, 2003, 2005, 2006). The workshop schedules also reveal two emerging major software packages: statnet/sna (workshops since 2006), and ORA (2009, 2010).

AN OVERVIEW OF SNA PACKAGES

The 56 software packages selected for our review are presented in Tables 38.2 and 38.3. Most of these packages are listed on the INSNA Web site and in the articles about social network analysis in Wikipedia. Table 38.2 lists 42 standalone software programs, and Table 38.3 contains 14 software toolkits and libraries. Both tables describe the

Table 38.2 Overview of programs for social network analysis: objectives, version number, data format (type, input format)}, functionality (visualization, analysis methods), and support (availability, help)

Package	Objective	Version	Data		Functionality		Support	
			Type[a]	Input[b]	Vis.	Analyses[c]	Avail.	Help[d]
General packages								
Agna	Applied graph/network analysis	2.1.1[e]	c	m	Yes	d,sl	Free	h,m
Blue Spider	Network analysis	0.8.2	c,e	m, ln	Yes	d,sl	Com	h,m
DyNet (SE/LS)	Knowledge visualization	1.1	c,e	ln	Yes[i]	dc,d,sl,rp	Com[k]	h,m,t
GRADAP	Graph definition and analysis	2.0[ef]	c	ln	No	d,sl,dt	Com	m
GUESS	Visual exploration	1.0.3	c	ln	Yes[i]	d,sl	Free[m]	m,t,u
InFlow	Analysis and visualization	3.1	c,e,a,l	ln, n	Yes	d,sl,rp	Com	h,m,t
MDLogix solutions	Analysis and visualization	–[g]	c,e	m, ln	Yes	dc,d,sl,rp	Com	h,m
MuitiNet	Contextual and network analysis	5.24	c,l	ln	Yes	d,sl,rp,dt,s	Free	h,m,t
NetMiner 3	Visual exploration and analysis	3.4.0	c,e,a	m, ln	Yes	d,sl,rp,dt,s,dy	Com[k]	h,m,u
NetVis	Dynamic visualization	2.0[e]	c,e,a	m, ln	Yes	d,sl	Free[m, n]	h,t
Network Workbench	Analysis, modeling, visualization	1.0.0	c,e	m, ln	Yes	d,sl	Free[m]	h,m,t,u
ORA	Dynamic network analysis	1.9.5	c,e,a,l	m, ln	Yes[i]	dc,d,sl,rp,dt,dy	Free	h,m,t,u
Pajek	Network analysis and visualization	1.26	c,a,l	m, ln	Yes[i]	d,sl,rp,dt,dy	Free	m,t,u
Sentinel Visualizer	Link analysis and visualization	4.0	c,e	ln	Yes[i]	sl,dt	Com[k]	h,m
SocNetV	Analysis and visualization	0.6	c,c	m, ln	Yes	d,sl	Free[m]	h,m
STRUCTURE	Structural analysis	4.2[ef]	c,a	m	No	sl,rp	Free	m
UCINET 6 (+NetDraw)	Network analysis and visualization	6.220	c,e,a,l	m, ln	Yes	d,sl,rp,dt,s	Com[k]	h,m,t,u
visone	Analysis and visualization	2.4	c,e,a,l	m, ln	Yes	d,sl,rp,dt	Free	m,u

Specialized packages

CID-ABM	Propagation of information	1.0	c	m,ln	No[j]	dy	Free	m
C-IKNOW	Knowledge networks	–	e,l	n	Yes	dc,d,sl	Free	h,m
Commetrix	Dynamic network visualization	1.4	c,e,l	ln	Yes[i]	dc,d,sl,dt,dy	Com[k,l]	h
MetaSight	Knowledge and email networks	4.16	c,e,a,l	ln	Yes	dc,d,sl	Com	h
Referral Web	Exploration of Internet networks	2.0[e]	e,l	ln	Yes	dc,d	Free	h,m
SONIVIS	Virtual information spaces	0.8	c,a	ln	Yes[i]	dc,d,sl,dy	Free[m]	h,m,t,u
UNISoN	Message networks	1.0	c,e,l	ln	Yes	dc	Free	m
CiteSpace	Citation networks	2.2	e	ln	Yes[i]	d,sl,dy	Free[n]	h,t,u
E-Net	Egocentric network analysis	0.022	c,e	m,ln	Yes	d,sl	Free	m
Ego Net	Egocentric networks	–	c,e	m	No[j]	dc,sl	Free[m]	u
VennMaker	Actor-centered network analysis	0.9	c,e	m	Yes	dc,d	Free	m,t
Financial Network Analyzer	Statistical analysis of financial data	1.2	c	ln	No	d,sl	Free[m]	h,m
PGRAPH	Marriage network analysis	2.7[e]	c	ln	Yes	d,rp	Free	m[o]
Puck	Analysis of kinship data	0.7	c	ln	No	dc,d,sl,rp	Free[m]	h,m

(continued)

Table 38.2 (Continued)

Package	Objective	Version	Data		Functionality		Support	
			Type[a]	Input[b]	Vis.[i]	Analyses[c]	Avail.	Help[d]
Blanche	Network evolution	4.8.1	c	m	Yes[i]	s,dy	Free	h,m
PermNet	Permutation tests	0.94[e]	c	m	No	dt,s	Free	h
PNet	Exponential Random Graph Models	1.0	c,a,e	m	No	s,dy	Free	m,t
Snowball	Hidden populations	–[e][f]	e	m	No	s	Free[m]	m
StOCNET (+SIENA)	Advanced statistical analysis	1.8	c	m,ln	No	d,dt,s,dy	Free[m]	h,m,t,u
CFinder	Dense groups and visualization	2.0.1	c,l	ln	Yes	sl	Free	h,m
KeyPlayer	Identifying nodes for interventions	1.45[h]	c,e	m,ln	No[j]	sl	Free	h,m
KliqFinder	Cohesive subgroups	0.11	C	m,ln	No[j]	sl,s	Free[m]	m,t
Network Genie	Design and manage network surveys	–	c,e	m,ln,n	No	dc	Com[n]	h,m,t
ONA surveys	Organizational network surveys	–	c,e	m,ln,n	No	dc	Com[k,n]	m,t

[a] c = complete, e = ego-centered, a = affiliation, l = large networks (>10k nodes).
[b] m = matrix, ln = link-node list, n = node list.
[c] dc = data collection, d = descriptives, sl = structure/location, rp = roles/positions, dt = dyadic/triadic methods, s = statistical models, dy = dynamics.
[d] h = build-in help function, m = manual, t = tutorial/demo, u = user group/mailing list.
[e] Version number has not changed since previous review of 2005.
[f] MS-DOS program.
[g] Collection of several stand-alone programs.
[h] KeyPlayer 1; there are two versions, see section on UCINET.
[i] Supports visualization of network evolution.
[j] Uses or calls on other paclcages for network visualization.
[k] An evaluation/demonstration/trial version is available.
[l] Free research collaboration: free software for a limited set of research projects.
[m] Open-source software.
[n] Internet program/Webstart available.
[o] Manual is available after registration and payment of administration costs.

Table 38.3 Overview of software toolkits and libraries for social network analysis: objective, language/environment version number, data format (type, input format), functionality (visualization, analysis methods), and support (availability, help)

Package	Objective	Data				Functionality		Support	
		Environment	Version	Type[a]	Input[b]	Vis.	Analyses[c]	Avail	Help[d]
NodeXL	Analysis and visualization	Excel/.NET	1.0.1	c,e	ln	Yes	dc,sl	Free[h]	h,u
MatMan	Matrix manipulation and analysis	Excel	1.1[e]	c	m	No	d,sl,s	Com	h,m
SNAP	Social network analysis	Gauss	2.5[e]	c	m	No	d,sl,rp,dt,s,dy	Com	m
JUNG	Modeling, analysis, visualization	Java	2.0	c	m,ln	Yes[f]	d,sl,rp,dt	Free[h]	m,t,u
yFiles	Network visualization	Java/.NET	2.6/3.2	c,e	ln	Yes[f]	d,sl	Com[i]	m,t
LibSNA	Social network analysis	Python	0.32	c,l	ln	No	sl	Free[h]	
NetworkX	Complex networks	Python	0.99	c,a	ln	Yes	d,sl	Free[h]	m,t,u
UrlNet	Web mining for networking data	Python	0.83	c,e	ln	No[g]	dc	Free[h]	m
igraph	Creating and manipulating graphs	R/Python/C	0.5.1	c,e,l	ln	Yes	d,sl,rp,dt	Free[h]	h,m,t,u
latentnet	Latent position aud cluster models	R	2.2.3	c	m,ln	Yes	d,s	Free[h]	h,m
RSiena	Evolution of network and behavior	R	4.0	c	m,ln	No	d,s,dy	Free[h]	h,m,t,u
sna	Social network analysis	R	2.0	c,e,a,l	m,ln	Yes	d,sl,rp,dt,s	Free[h]	h,m,t
statnet	Statistical modeling of networks	R	2.2	c,e,a,l	m,ln	Yes	d,s,dy	Free[h]	h,m,t,u
tnet	Weighted and longitudinal data	R	0.1.0	c	ln	No	d,sl	Free[h]	h,m

[a] c = complete, e = ego-centered, a = affiliation, l = large networks (>10k nodes).
[b] m = matrix, ln = link-node list, n = node list.
[c] dc = data collection, d = descriptives, sl = structure/location, rp = roles/positions, dt = dyadic/triadic methods, s = statistical models, dy = dynamics.
[d] b = build-in help function, m = manual, t = tutorial, u = user group/mailing list.
[e] Version number has not changed since previous review of 2005.
[f] Supports visualization of network evolution.
[g] Uses or calls on other packages for network visualization.
[h] Open-source software.
[i] An evaluation/demonstration/trial version is available.

main objective or characteristic of each program, the current version number (and whether it was updated since 2005), and for toolkits and libraries the environment for which they are developed. The data format distinguishes the types of data the program can handle and the input format. Next, functionality is presented: availability of network visualization options and information on the type(s) of network analysis featured in the program. Based on the network terminology and categorization of Wasserman and Faust (1994), we defined the following types of analysis (cf. Huisman and van Duijn, 2005a):

- data collection (e.g., survey design or Web searches);
- descriptive measures (for both links and nodes);
- structure and location (approaches to groups and subgroups, for example, centrality or cliques);
- roles and positions (notions of social role, status, and position, for example, structural equivalence or blockmodeling);
- dyadic and triadic methods;
- statistical probability models (for example, QAP or exponential random graph models);
- network dynamics (models for network evolution and longitudinal network data).

The final property of the programs listed in the tables is the amount of support: the availability of the package (free or commercial, not listing prices) and the type of help available (built-in help functions, manuals, tutorials, user/mailing lists).[3]

In Table 38.2, two types of programs are distinguished: general and specialized packages. We define packages as *general* if they contain ample procedures for general exploration and analysis of network data. General packages are not designed merely to perform some specialized analysis, although some of them were originally developed for network visualization (e.g., visone) or succeeded (older) specialized programs (e.g., MultiNet). Table 38.2 lists 18 general programs, which are presented in alphabetical order. In addition, 24 *specialized programs* are distinguished. Packages are categorized as *specialized* if they contain a few distinctive procedures for network analysis (for example, KliqFinder to find cohesive subgroups), or a range of analysis procedures to perform a specific type of analysis (for example, StOCNET for statistical analysis). The packages are (roughly) grouped according to specialization: communication networks (knowledge/information/message), citation networks, egocentric networks, financial networks, kinship networks, statistical methods, analysis of subgroups, and network surveys. Within specializations, the programs are ordered alphabetically.

Table 38.3 presents 14 toolkits and libraries, without a distinction between general and specialized. The packages are grouped according to their environment (software packages/development environment or programming language). References of all programs can be found in the references section. URLs of individual packages are not listed in the references. Instead, the Web sites and URLs of all packages in Tables 38.2 and 38.3 are presented on a Web site accompanying this chapter. The Web site also lists software aimed at network visualization and some programs for the analysis of specific applications other than social network data, such as network text analysis.

In the following subsections we briefly discuss the three types of packages presented in Tables 38.2 and 38.3. In each case, we refer to the review of 2005 (Huisman and van Duijn, 2005a) with respect to the number of packages that were taken into account. Even though neither list is complete, the comparison serves to illustrate the increase in the sheer number of packages during the last 5 to 10 years.

General packages

In the review of 2005, 22 programs were presented,[4] of which 12 were general packages. The current list of general programs displayed in Table 38.2 contains 10 of them. Two programs are not listed because they are unavailable (both the program and Web site were unavailable) or embedded in a newer package and no longer updated as a separate program. Eight new general programs are presented. The major programs listed before in Table 38.1 (except those before 1994) are included in this overview, although two, GRADAP and STRUCTURE, are no longer updated. The packages MultiNet, NetMiner, Pajek, and UCINET are among the programs with the largest number of different SNA procedures (column *functionality* in Table 38.2), making them the most comprehensive programs. Another program with a comprehensive analysis list is ORA, which is new in the overview (developed after 2004).

All programs (except GRADAP and STRUCTURE) contain visualization routines. Almost all use link-node input files, especially the more recent packages, which is not surprising considering the need for software capable of analyzing large networks (for example, as available via the Internet). Considering functionality, the more recent packages often include routines and functions that facilitate data collection or network dynamics (often also including visualization of network dynamics or evolution). Because of this increased functionality, the number of different types of analysis is larger in some of the newer packages, although within a certain type of analysis the number of measures may be reduced compared to the older programs. Approximately half of the programs are freely available, and some kind of support (in the form of a manual or built-in help) is always available (except for Blue Spider).

Table 38.1 shows that the popular, major programs of the last 5 to 10 years, MultiNet, NetMiner, Pajek, and UCINET, are still among the most comprehensive programs. This is especially true with respect to the number of different routines that are included in the programs. In order to compete, the newer packages should at least have routines in all analysis categories, and preferably they also include some new types of analysis. Such a program is visone, with strong graphical procedures, as is DyNet, which includes data collection options. It appears that ORA has specific potential to become a major package, because it contains routines for data collection and network dynamics, coupled with the advantage of being freely available and having strong support functions.

Specialized packages and toolkits

The list contains 24 specialized packages, belonging to one of the following categories: communication networks, citation networks, egocentric networks, financial networks, kinship networks, statistical methods, analysis of subgroups, and network surveys.

Eight of the 10 programs in the 2005 list of specialized packages appear in the current list whereas two programs are not listed anymore because they are included in another (collection of) program(s): FATCAT in MultiNet, and SM LinkAlyzer in the MDLogix solutions package. Some of the programs have not been updated since 2005 but are still available for analysis.

The columns in Table 38.2 related to functionality show that the specialized programs were developed to perform specific types of analysis. About half of the programs do not have visualization routines, especially those aimed at statistical modeling or at network surveys. In the other categories, where visualization is an important exploratory tool (for example, for the detection of subgroups or analysis of egocentric networks), graph-drawing routines are available or the program facilitates visualization through other packages. As is the case with the general programs, the most recently developed programs contain data collection routines: Network Genie and ONA Surveys are developed to collect network data via surveys, and most packages in the category communication networks support the collection of Web-based data. Almost all packages are freely available.

Table 38.3 contains an overview of software toolkits and libraries. Five of the 14 packages were already included in the 2005 review. Most new developments are libraries with procedures for Python and R, but collections for Excel and Java are also available. The R packages especially cover a wide range of analysis methods, where we consider the statnet suite together with the sna package to be a general package for social network analysis, and therefore one of the major (collection of) packages (as was already indicated in in the first section, discussing the Sunbelt conference workshops). One of the major statistical analysis programs, SIENA (in the StOCNET package), was recently replaced by the R package RSiena, and together with the two packages mentioned before, sna and statnet, as well as igraph, latentnet, and tnet, a comprehensive collection of (statistical) analysis procedures for SNA has become available in R.

Almost all toolkits and libraries in Table 38.3 are freely available and are open-source software. This makes them especially useful in a programming environment (such as Java, Python, or R), where the routines cannot only be freely used but also can be modified according to a researcher's interest.

GENERAL SNA PROGRAMS: A CLOSER LOOK

In this section, the separate general packages presented in Table 38.2 are briefly discussed. We start the overview with the major programs UCINET, Pajek, NetMiner, and MultiNet, which have been available for many years and were investigated in detail in the 2005 review (Huisman and van Duijn, 2005a). Next, one more recent program (ORA) is presented, and we end with a brief overview of the other programs listed in Table 38.2. As the programs are comprehensive general packages, they experience many (and sometimes large) revisions on a yearly basis. Fortunately, for all programs detailed overviews of changes and updates can be found, and we mention some major updates when deemed appropriate.

UCINET

UCINET 6 (Version 6.220; Borgatti et al., 2002) is a comprehensive package for the analysis of social network data as well as other one-mode and two-mode data. It can handle reasonably large networks and contains a large number of social network analysis methods. In addition, the program has strong matrix analysis routines. Manuals and a tutorial (Hanneman and Riddle, 2005) are available, and integrated within UCINET is the program NetDraw for visualization of social networks. Some other programs are distributed with UCINET: KeyPlayer for identifying nodes for interventions (see Table 38.2), Eicent for extending centrality measures to include node attributes, and Pajek, which can be launched from within UCINET. Hanneman and Riddle's chapters (this volume) give examples of analyses performed with UCINET.

UCINET is a menu-driven Windows program that "is built for speed, not for comfort" (Borgatti et al., 2002). The menus open parameter forms to specify the input for the procedures, and output is displayed on the screen as well as saved in log files. The program is matrix oriented and data are stored and entered in UCINET (matrix) format. For this purpose, the built-in spreadsheet can be used, or the import and export functions, which process several types of network formats[5] (including the link-node Pajek format). In addition, network generation procedures (e.g., Erdös-Rényi) are available.

Network visualization is supported by the program NetDraw. NetDraw has advanced graphic properties and updates can be downloaded separately (at the time of writing, version 2.084 was the latest). Figure 38.1 shows an example of the NetDraw program presenting the Krackhardt high-tech managers' advice network (Krackhardt, 1987; these data were used in Robins's chapter, this volume). UCINET contains a large amount of analytic routines for the detection of cohesive subgroups and regions, (group) centrality measures, egocentric networks, and analysis of structural holes. It contains scaling routines (multidimensional and two-mode scaling), procedures for cluster analysis, equivalence (structural, role, and regular), and core-periphery models. Although the number of statistical techniques (based on probability models) is limited, the program has strong permutation-based testing procedures, especially the QAP procedures. Recent updates include QAP correlation and regression based on the method of Dekker et al. (2007), of which an example is given in van Duijn and Huisman's chapter (this volume). The program also has a routine for estimating Holland and Leinhardt's (1981) p_1 model (see Robins, this volume).

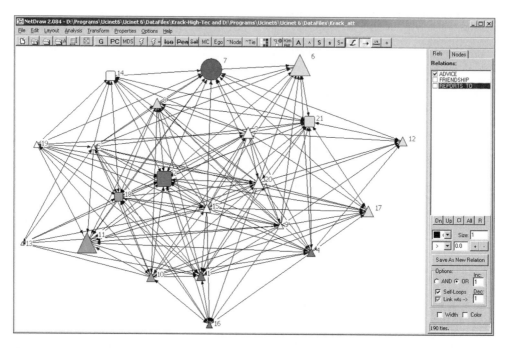

Figure 38.1   NetDraw user interface presenting the graph of the Krackhardt high-tech managers' advice network

Pajek

Pajek (Version 1.26; Batagelj and Mrvar, 1998, 2010) is a program for the analysis and visualization of large networks (Batagelj et al., this volume). Its main goals are to facilitate the reduction of large networks into smaller networks that can be analyzed using more sophisticated methods, to provide powerful visualization tools, and to implement a selection of efficient network algorithms (Batagelj and Mrvar, 1998). The program is freely available via the Pajek Wiki, which provides news, updates, resources, help, and more. A reference manual is available, as well as an introduction on exploratory network analysis with Pajek (de Nooy et al., 2005). Because a built-in help function is not available and handling the program is sometimes complicated, we find the textbook very useful for novice users.

Pajek is developed to analyze very large networks (millions of nodes), but it is probably best known for its powerful visualization tools. The implemented algorithms are based on six different data structures (networks, partitions, permutations, clusters, hierarchies, and vectors) in order to support abstraction by decomposing large networks into several smaller ones. The structure of the program is entirely based on the data objects and the transitions among the objects. Menu items are ordered according to the data objects, and output of analysis is also often presented using the data structures so that it can be easily used as input of further analysis procedures. Data are entered using node and link (arcs/edges) lists (for small networks, adjacency matrices can be used), or they can be simulated or defined inside the program. Pajek has ample manipulation options and descriptive methods for all the data structures and it facilitates nonstatistical analysis of longitudinal network data. The program contains procedures for detecting structural balance and clusterability, hierarchical decomposition, and blockmodeling. And although it does not contain statistical procedures for networks (there are some standard procedures for vectors and partitions), there is the option to call the statistical packages R and SPSS from Pajek. If the program is available, Pajek will open it and generate a script or syntax file to open the data object (usually networks or vectors) in the selected program.

Pajek's graphical options are advanced. It contains several layout procedures, ranging from simple layouts (circle, random) to more complicated procedures based on eigenvectors and spring embedders, for both 2D and 3D visualizations. These procedures create network visualizations according to the following rules: not too many crossing lines, not too many small angles among lines that have one vertex in common, approximately the same length for lines, and vertices not too close to lines. All graphs can be improved by hand, and partitions and vectors representing attributes of vertices can be included. Graphs can be saved in several output formats (for example, BMP or EPS) by using the export function.

NetMiner 3

NetMiner 3 (Version 3.4.0; Cyram, 2009) is a program for exploratory network analysis and visualization of network data. The program allows users to explore network data interactively, integrating analysis and visualization methods, and it helps to detect underlying patterns and structures of the network. NetMiner is a commercial product (next to the basic module, specialized modules can be purchased separately), but a four-week evaluation version is available. NetMiner offers good support with online help, a user's manual, and a message board on the Web site.

NetMiner has adopted a network approach that is optimized for integrating analysis and visualization. Data can be entered via the built-in spreadsheet editor or by opening data sets in various formats (NetMiner NTF files, Excel spreadsheets, UCINET data sets), or data can be simulated using different algorithms. The program can handle large data sets, with many data manipulation options, a matrix calculator to manipulate matrices, and a data manager to track the transformation history. It contains procedures for the inspection of the connectivity and neighborhood structure of networks (e.g., structural holes, assortativity) and subgraph configurations, shortest path routines, and routines to analyze cohesion (for example, components, cliques, or clans) and calculate centrality measures. Procedures for multidimensional scaling, cluster analysis, matrix decompositions, and blockmodeling are available, as well as routines to explore the role-set structure of networks (structural, role, and regular equivalence).

More than UCINET and Pajek, NetMiner supports a reasonably large number of statistical procedures. Some standard statistical routines are available, like correlation (including autocorrelations), regression analysis (including logistic regression), and permutation tests (including QAP permutation). Moreover, the p_1 model can be fitted to network data, as well as the p^* or exponential random graph model (ERGM; see Robins, this volume). This latter routine is based on the procedure implemented in MultiNet and uses pseudo-likelihood estimation, which gives biased results and can only be approximate at best (van Duijn et al., 2009). Recent updates of NetMiner include procedures to fit power law models (Clauset et al., 2009).

Like Pajek and NetDraw, NetMiner has advanced graphical properties. Almost all results are presented both textually and graphically. Network drawing can be based on several spring-embedding algorithms or multidimensional scaling. Clustered, circular, and simple layouts are also available. The program supports 3D visualizations and all visual displays can be manually improved and saved in a wide variety of formats. Several other types of (standard) graphical displays can be generated, such as pie charts, matrix diagrams, box plots, scatter plots, or contour plots.

MultiNet

MultiNet (Version 5.24; Richards and Seary, 2009) is a program designed for exploratory data analysis of networks. It can handle large data sets and large numbers of variables. It combines attribute data and structural data into a single model to perform contextual analyses: analyses of attributes in the context of the structure of the network and vice versa. Results are always presented both textually and in interactive visualizations, and the program has excellent online help. MultiNet is freely available and has a comprehensive user's manual (Seary, 2005).

Some of the analysis methods and procedures in MultiNet were originally contained in separate programs, as was mentioned before. FATCAT can be used for categorical social network analysis, and PSPAR can fit the $p*$ model for adjacency matrices (in link-node format) based on pseudo-likelihood (like NetMiner). More recently NEGOPY, a program for finding cohesive subgroups, was embedded in MultiNet.

Like Pajek, MultiNet is designed for the analysis of large networks. It has routines to calculate network descriptives (for example, betweenness, closeness, triad census for sparse networks), to perform categorical network analysis (for example, contingency tables), and to analyze the structure of networks using eigenspace methods. These eigenprocedures create visual displays of the network such that the location of the actors reveals the structure of the relationships and their patterns. A number of standard statistical analysis (for example, ANOVA) of the links in the network are available; these results should be interpreted with caution as the assumption of independency of all relations will generally be violated.

ORA

ORA (Version 1.9.5; Carley, 2009) is described as "a risk assessment tool for locating individuals or groups that are potential risks given social, knowledge, and task network information." It is designed to analyze a large variety of networks including social networks, activity networks, knowledge networks, communication networks, and more. The program is capable of analyzing large-scale multimode, multilink network data and can assess changes in network structure over time, that is, it is a package for analyzing complex systems as dynamic social networks. Good support is offered via a comprehensive manual, tutorials, and a mailing list.

The main unit of input in ORA is the so-called meta-network, an ecology of interlinked networks that represents complex systems like organizations. A meta-network can be opened from ORA-files (XML) or comma delimited files (CSV; from Excel), or it can be created by importing networks of various data formats (including UCINET and Pajek files). Data can also be imported using CEMAP II, a tool that allows input of data from a wide and expandable set of real-world data sources (often Web-related, like networks extracted from emails, but also networks extracted from text files), or networks can be generated using a variety of models and procedures. The program has a meta-network manager, and basic information on the active meta-network is provided in an editor and tool panel, which allows quick access to three important tools: the ORA Visualizer, the reports tool, and the chart tool. Analyses are performed on (partitions of) the network data by generating reports for the selected meta-networks. Via the drop-down menu, statistics can be chosen that are used to generate reports. This abundance of measures include amongst others (various forms of) centrality, clusters, components, congruence, triad counts, cliques, and key actors. Other types of (statistical) analysis available are latent semantic analysis, correspondence analysis, spatial autocorrelations (Geary's C and Moran's I) with randomization tests, and QAP analysis. Moreover, ORA can (visually) analyze changes in these statistics by performing a "view measures over-time analysis."

Three types of (standard) charts are available in ORA: bar charts, scatter plots, and histograms. The charts are used to graphically display the selected network measures. Next to the usual options, ORA has some unique graphical properties. Measurements and networks can be viewed over time, and network drill-down plots can be made, as well as geospatial networks and node clouds. Visualizations of networks are rendered in the interactive ORA Visualizer. Different layouts can be chosen (amongst others spring-embedded,

MDS, tree, or circle), and 2D and 3D visualizations are possible, with good options to (manually) improve the graphs. The program also has graphical procedures for ego-networks and a group viewer to separate nodes into distinct groups. Figure 38.2 gives an illustration of the ORA Visualizer, presenting the graph of the Krackhardt high-tech managers' advice network, using the spring-embedded layout.

Other packages

The five programs described in the previous sections can be regarded as the major general packages with respect to functionality. Right behind these programs are the medium-sized packages, which still have many analysis or graphical procedures. DyNet is one of these medium-sized programs. It is a package for the analysis of network data unveiling relations and interconnections via graphical and textual outputs. The package MDLogix solutions is a medium-sized package containing the programs VisuaLyzer, to graphically analyze networks; EgoNet, for ego-centric data; and linkAlyzer, to construct networks from hidden populations. The program visone is developed with the aim to integrate and advance the analysis and visualization of networks. It has advanced graphical properties facilitating a wide range of graph layouts, and it contains some

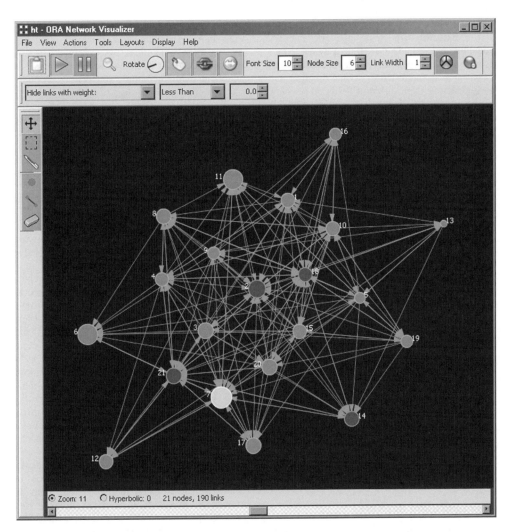

Figure 38.2   ORA Visualizer user interface presenting the graph of the Krackhardt high-tech managers' advice network

standard analysis routines that can be performed on multiple networks simultaneously. Moreover, the statistical package SIENA is integrated to perform longitudinal network analysis.

Somewhat smaller packages are GUESS, InFlow, and the Network Workbench. GUESS is an exploratory analysis and visualization tool for graphs and networks. It supports the export of static images and dynamic movies. It is Java-based open-source software (and it also uses open-source software like JUNG), has many graphical options, and has an interface to R, which makes the statistical R packages (see Table 38.3) available for analyses. InFlow is a commercial program for network mapping, especially aimed at organizational applications. It features some descriptive and procedure-based routines, and it carries out network analysis and visualization simultaneously. Finally, the Network Workbench is a toolkit for large-scale network analysis, modeling, and visualization. It is designed to be a resources environment to provide an online portal for researchers interested in a wide range of networks, coming from different fields of research, and it supports the integration and dissemination of SNA algorithms. It contains some advanced analysis and modeling procedures and has contributions from JUNG and GUESS for network visualization.

The DOS-based programs GRADAP and STRUCTURE are outdated programs, which have some unique features that are not or not easily available in other software. Agna, Blue Spider, SocNetV, and Sentinel Visualizer are small programs (containing few routines), of which the latter two were originally developed for network visualization. NetVis, an open-source Web-based tool, is also one of the smaller packages with strong visualization options.

SPECIALIZED PACKAGES AND TOOLKITS: A CLOSER LOOK

In this section, we briefly discuss the specialized packages and toolkits presented in Tables 38.2 and 38.3. We present the programs within their specialization or environment without the aim to compare or rank them, as this depends very much on the purpose the researcher has in mind.

Communication networks

A large number of packages for the collection and analysis of (often large-scale) networks and network data on the Web have been developed over the last five years. Some of these programs focus on special types of communication networks, like email networks or knowledge networks; others are more general, with the aim to collect data from the Web even though they can handle all kinds of networks.

One of the most comprehensive programs in Table 38.2 is Commetrix, an exploratory analysis tool for dynamic network data. The program reads all sources of accessible network data via the Internet but is especially designed to analyze (large) communication networks. It uses SNA together with dynamic graph visualization to explore social networks, thus potentially qualifying as a general program with procedures in almost all analysis categories in Table 38.2. The number of different measures and routines Commetrix contains in these categories, however, is (yet) small, with only a few options for identifying subgroups, eliciting core structures, or analyzing network dynamics (for example, stability or integration of two networks). The focus is on analyzing evolving patterns of electronic communication like email or discussion lists. Specially designed dynamic spring embedders are used to visualize the large heterogeneous and evolving networks. Therefore, we consider Commetrix to be a specialized program with which "the detailed lifecycle of a communication network of thousands of simultaneously changing relationships becomes observable" (Trier, 2008).

Other programs that analyze Web-based data are C-IKNOW, MetaSight, ReferralWeb, SONIVIS, and UNISoN. C-IKNOW is the extension of the older package IKNOW, which maps, measures, and, if desired, modifies the knowledge and information flows in networks. It has automated data collection techniques that include Web-administered network surveys and procedures to upload publicly accessible network data from the Web. These data can be analyzed and mapped, either in the form of egocentric network visualizations or displays of (parts of) the complete network. MetaSight is a commercial package that maps business expertise and relations using networks generated from email data. SONIVIS is open-source Java-based software that can analyze and visualize so-called virtual information spaces on the Web. The focus is on wiki-based information spaces (Weblogs and social networking sites are also examples of intended virtual spaces), where different kinds of networks (for example, social, knowledge, information, or event) are investigated to explore and map knowledge processes in a wiki. A Java-based package that can access and analyze messages from usenet, a worldwide-distributed Internet discussion system, is UNISoN. After selecting a newsgroup on usenet, messages are downloaded and visualized. They can be saved as Pajek network data for further analyses. ReferralWeb is the oldest program for searching the Web. It is used for the exploration of researchers' social networks in order to find short referral chains between the researcher (ego) and others. Information on the network is obtained from publicly available documents on the Internet.

CID-ABM is a somewhat different package. It does not use Internet data but is a package that allows a researcher to investigate the propagation of information through a network, taking into account the network structure and the actor (agent) characteristics. The program uses simulation models that use the network structure and decision models to simulate the transmission of information through the network.

Another program that uses the Web to collect network data is CiteSpace. Listed in Table 38.2 as a program for citation networks, it is used to detect and visualize trends and patterns in scientific literature. It uses the Web of Science as its primary source of information. Other sources can be used as well (for example, PubMed) or are under construction (for example, Scopus). The networks are visualized and can be decomposed into mutual exclusive groups by spectral clustering.

Egocentric networks

Egocentric network data reflect the relations of one actor (ego) with others (alters), as opposed to data on the complete network (full-network data). For a discussion and analysis methods, see Hanneman and Riddle's chapters (this volume). Most of the generalized programs can handle egocentric data, and there are specialized packages as well.

E-Net is such a program, made by the developers of UCINET and, therefore, it has strong links with this package. It uses attribute data of ego and alters, as well as ties among the alters. Measures of composition of the network, heterogeneity, homophily, and structural holes are calculated for all selected egos, and the ego-networks can be visualized. EgoNet is a package for the collection and analysis of egocentric network data. It contains routines that facilitate questionnaire development and data collection, and it calculates general network measures as a first step in data exploration. For further analysis, the data can be saved in formats that are readable by other SNA software. VennMaker is a software tool for collecting egocentric network data. One of the main features of the program is questionnaire development, using name generators, and providing a framework to configure and perform a survey interview. The collected network data can be visually explored, manually altered, or be exported to other programs (for example, Excel or UCINET).

Statistical methods

The field of statistical methods is one in which major developments have taken place in the last decade (an overview of software for statistical network analysis was given by Huisman and van Duijn, 2005b). This has resulted in a large increase in statistical routines and software packages. Recent developments are found for p^* exponential random graph models (ERGMs). Starting from the p_1 models of Holland and Leinhardt (1981), and the Markov random graph models proposed by Frank and Strauss (1986), the p^* model was introduced by Wasserman and Pattison (1996). To estimate the models, pseudo-likelihood estimation was originally used and implemented in the software. This procedure, however, gives biased results (van Duijn et al., 2009). New procedures based on Markov chain Monte Carlo (MCMC) methods were developed, also resulting in new model specifications and software tools (for more details and examples, see Robins, this volume).

There are several programs that have routines to estimate ERGMs. Of the general packages, NetMiner and MultiNet contain (older) procedures to estimate the p^* model using pseudo-likelihood. As this method is known to give incorrect results, we advise not to use these routines. New estimation methods that give unbiased estimates of model parameters and standard errors are implemented in several (newly developed) packages. The programs SIENA and PNet are based on the method proposed by Snijders (2002); the R package statnet uses the method proposed by Hunter and Handcock (2006). A review of these programs is given by Robins et al. (2007).

SIENA is a program for the analysis of longitudinal network data (see Snijders, this volume) that is implemented in the StOCNET package. StOCNET is a package for advanced statistical analysis of social networks. It was designed to be a platform for easy distribution of statistical methods and allows new routines to be easily implemented. Besides SIENA, it contains modules for stochastic blockmodeling (BLOCKS), estimating latent transitive structures using ultrametrics (ULTRAS), determining probability distributions of random graph statistics (ZO), fitting structural models based on partial algebras (PACNET), and estimating the p_2 exponential random graph model (P2) and the p^* exponential random graph model (PNet and SIENA). The p_2 model is a random effects model with the dyadic ties as the dependent variables (van Duijn et al., 2004). The model and software are recently updated with improved MCMC estimation methods (Zijlstra et al., 2009). In the chapter by van Duijn and Huisman (this volume) some procedures are discussed in more detail and examples are presented.

SIENA is designed to analyze longitudinal data of networks and behavior (i.e., the co-evolution of networks and behavior; see the tutorial by Snijders et al., 2010). In the StOCNET package, the SIENA module can also be used for cross-sectional network data to estimate ERGMs. Recently SIENA was replaced by the R package RSiena, in which only the longitudinal analysis procedures are implemented. The older version implemented in StOCNET will not be updated anymore.

PNet is a program for the simulation and estimation of exponential random graph (p^*) models (ERGMs). There are six different versions of the program for single networks, multivariate networks, longitudinal analysis, bipartite networks, social influence models, and snowball sampling. There is also a version of PNet that can be run as a module within the StOCNET package. The program offers simulation of network distributions (with known ERGM parameter values). Goodness of fit of an estimated model is tested by simulating the network distribution using the parameter estimates of the model.

Other (older) programs for statistical analyses are Snowball, a DOS program for estimating the size of a hidden population from a one-wave snowball sample; PermNet, which provides a set of permutation tests for valued social network data (for example, symmetry tests or transitivity tests); and Blanche, which creates and simulates models of network dynamics by using nonlinear difference equations that describe the change in the strength of links and the attributes of nodes over time.

Analysis of subgroups

For the analysis of subgroups, three packages are listed in Table 38.2. CFinder is a package for finding subgroups in large sparse networks. It is based on the clique percolation method of Palla et al. (2005) to find overlapping dense groups of nodes (k-clique communities). The program has several procedures to visualize and explore the (overlapping) communities found in the networks. The second program is KeyPlayer, distributed together with UCINET for identifying the key actors in a network. The programs uses two definitions of key actors: (1) the optimal set of nodes that cripple the network if they are removed, or (2) the optimal

set of nodes to keep under surveillance or try to influence through an intervention. The program uses these node sets to inspect the vulnerability of the network and to identify well-connected nodes that possess a lot of information. Finally, KliqFinder is aimed at identifying subgroups based on the maximization of the log-odds of ties (connectivity) within the groups and minimization of connectivity between groups (Frank, 1995) or based on structural equivalence. It has recently been updated with an export function to NetDraw for visualization of the position of the actors within groups and the distances between actors and groups.

Surveys and data collection

In the discussion of the general packages we already mentioned a trend in new developments: procedures for data collection are often included in new packages. The same was seen in the specialized packages for communication networks. Almost all programs in this category contain procedures to collect data, either by designing surveys or (most often) by searching the Web (almost all programs were developed during the last five to six years). There are two packages that are developed for data collection via surveys only (not searching the Web). These programs are Network Genie and ONA surveys.

Network Genie is a Web-based package to design and manage social network survey projects. It facilitates the design of online survey questionnaires, including both network items (for example, social ranking, social nomination, or social peer perception) and person-centered items (demographics or behavior topics). The questionnaires are used to collect network data through the program. Network Genie distinguishes three types of data: egocentric, complete networks, and snowball samples. The collected data can be exported to other network software (for example, UCINET, MultiNet, or InFlow) for additional analyses or visualization.

ONA surveys is a program for organizational network analysis. It can be used to design Web-based network surveys and collect and process survey data. Surveys can be either person-centric, consisting of a number of questions for each participant, or question-centric, to assess relationships for each question. The approach can be "bounded," assessing the relations within a predefined group, or "snowball," where an initial group is asked to nominate its contacts, who are then asked to nominate their contacts. Surveys can be tested and published, and there are export functions to other software.

Other specialized programs

Table 38.2 presents two programs to analyze kinship data. PGRAPH is software for kinship and marriage networks that works with so-called *p*-graphs, a representation of networks in which the nodes are the intersections between individuals (e.g., marriage) instead of the individuals themselves (see the chapters by White and Hamberger et al., this volume). This representation using *p*-graphs is also available in Pajek (see White et al., 1999). Puck is a program for analyzing genealogical and other kinship-related data that can visually explore elements from kinship network theory.

Financial Network Analyzer is an open-source package for the analysis of financial networks. It constructs networks from payment/trade data, with links that indicate payment/trade between banks. The program contains options to edit and transform networks and to calculate some basic SNA measures (for example, betweenness, eigenvector centrality, average shortest paths, reciprocity, or eccentricity).

R

Over the past few years, the number of packages for social network analysis available in R has rapidly increased. It all started with sna, a package developed by Carter Butts in S (the precursor of R; see Butts, 2008b). The R package sna contains a wide range of tools and functions for visualization and analyses (Figure 38.3 gives an example, presenting the Krackhardt high-tech managers' advice network). Although it can still be used on its own, sna has now merged into statnet, which is built around the function ergm to estimate

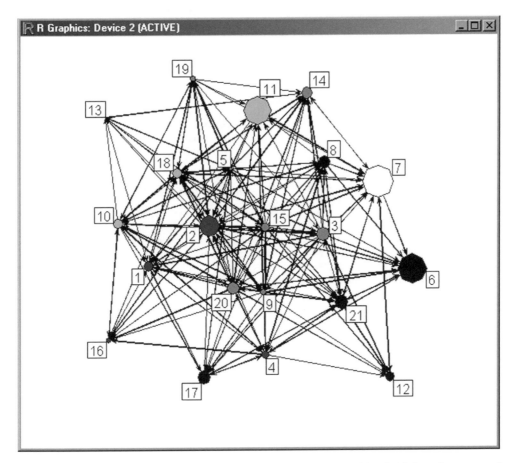

Figure 38.3   R Graphics window presenting the graph of the Krackhardt high-tech managers' advice network made with SNA

exponential random graph models. The statnet tutorial (Goodreau et al., 2008) provides a good introduction to estimating ERGMs using the package.

The suite of software tools for social network analysis statnet (Handcock et al., 2008) requires network (Butts, 2008a), providing the R class for relational data (roughly network data in the form of adjacency matrices or link-node lists, with attribute information on links or nodes if available). The network class is related to the graph class also used by the package igraph (see Table 38.3). Two more packages related to statnet through its developers are degreenet (Handcock, 2003), modeling skewed count distributions (as is typical for degree distributions), and networksis (Admiraal and Handcock, 2008), for simulating bipartite networks with fixed marginals.

Another class of statistical models for social network analysis is implemented in latentnet, also in the statnet suite. It can be used to estimate a type of stochastic blockmodels or latent position models (Hoff et al., 2002; Handcock et al., 2007; see also Krivitsky and Handcock, 2008). Two more recent additions to the R packages are RSiena and tnet. RSiena is the successor of the SIENA module in StOCNET, with similar functionality with respect to the longitudinal procedures. The package tnet features functions for the analysis of weighted (or valued), two-mode, and longitudinal network data.

Other packages

Some other packages and libraries are available for Excel, GAUSS, Java, and Python. The GAUSS package SNAP contains general analysis procedures but has not been updated since 2005. This is also true for the Excel package MatMan, for social dominance and correlational analyses. NodeXL is a more general template for Excel 2007, which has built-in connections to import networks from Twitter, Flickr, YouTube, and local email, and it has strong visualization options.

The Java library JUNG provides a common and extendible language for modeling, analysis, and visualization of graphs. The routines of this open-source package are used, among others, in GUESS and Network Workbench. The other Java library, yFiles, provides efficient and effective visualization algorithms and has routines for descriptive analysis. It also provides components for the .NET platform, as does NodeXL.

Three packages in Table 38.3 are libraries for Python, a general-purpose programming language whose design philosophy emphasizes code readability. Like other dynamic languages, Python is often used as a scripting language. LibSNA is a small general package. NetworkX is developed for the creation, manipulation, and exploration of the structure, dynamics, and functions of complex networks. The UrlNet library is intended to provide a powerful, flexible, easy-to-use, "spider"-like mechanism for generating networks from the Web.

RECOMMENDATIONS

We conclude this chapter with a summary and comparison of some of the packages presented in Tables 38.2 and 38.3, and we offer some general recommendations.

General programs

Comparing the different programs and giving recommendations are difficult (maybe even impossible) tasks, as the objectives of the packages and therefore their functionalities are often very different. Still, we think it worthwhile to make a comparison of the general packages we discussed

Table 38.4 Scores for some general packages

	Functionality						Support		User-friendly
	Data	Vis.	Desc.	Proc.	Stat.	Dyn.	Doc.	Help	
MultiNet	+ −	+	+ −	+	−	0	+	+ +	+
NetMiner 3	+ +	+ +	+ +	+ +	+ −	+ −	+	+	+ +
ORA	+ +	+ +	+	+ +	+	+	+	+	+ −
Pajek	+	+ +	+	+ +	0	+ −	+	0	+ −
statnet/sna	+ +	+	+ +	+ +	+ +	+	+ +	+	+ −
UCINET + NetDraw	+ +	+ +	+ +	+ +	+	0	+ +	+	+

in more detail: MultiNet, NetMiner 3, ORA, Pajek, statnet/sna, and UCINET. We scored the software on nine criteria:[6] (1) data manipulation, (2) network visualization, (3) network descriptives (for example, centrality), (4) procedure-based methods (for example, cluster analysis or eigendecompositions), (5) statistical methods (for example, exponential random graph models or QAP procedures), (6) network dynamics, (7) availability of documentation (manuals, tutorials), (8) online help, and (9) user friendliness.

Table 38.4 contains the ratings for the general packages. A + is used to indicate that it is good (at least suffcient), ++ that it is very good or strong. A – indicates that the program has shortcomings, a 0 that the aspect considered is absent, and a + – that it is undecided (having both good and bad parts). We will explain the ratings per criterion further below, giving special attention to the critical (– and + –) scores.

With respect to data manipulation, only MultiNet obtained a score + – because it contains relatively few options. All other programs score + (good) or ++ (strong). Pajek has many options, but its data structures make the program hard to use. ORA uses complicated data structures as well, but it is the only program that supports data collection (by searching the Web). Visualization options are good in all packages. Although MultiNet, again, has the lowest score, it has some unique visualization routines based on eigendecompositions. These are, however, not as strong as the routines in other packages. statnet/sna requires knowledge of the programming language R and does not have an interactive user interface for visualizations.

The scores for the descriptive, procedure-based, and statistical methods are indicative of the number of different features. The descriptive methods are strong in almost all packages. Only MultiNet contains relatively few methods. All programs contain many procedure-based methods. Statistical methods are strong in statnet, which has more methods, and more advanced methods than the other programs. The statistical methods in Pajek are so limited that they score a 0 (although R packages can be called from Pajek). ORA and UCINET contain some up-to-date procedures. NetMiner does contain a number of statistical methods, but they are presented uncritically, whereas some warning would definitely be warranted for the estimation of the p^* model and QAP regression. The same holds for MultiNet, whose statistical methods, especially the ANOVA and p^* procedures we advise not to use.

MultiNet and UCINET contain so few (or no) procedures for network dynamics that they score a 0. Pajek offers descriptive analysis of series of cross-sectional networks using time indicators, but the options are few. This is also true for NetMiner. Only the newer packages ORA and statnet/sna have some good (graphical) routines for network dynamics.

The documentation of statnet/sna is relatively strong with the special (tutorial) issue of the *Journal of Statistical Software* and for UCINET with the step-by-step tutorial by Hanneman and Riddle (2005). It should be noted that the documentation of the other programs, although in some cases comprehensive, almost always consists of a long list of procedures, which is not always instructive or easy to use. Built-in help is strong in MultiNet and absent in Pajek.

Three of the programs score + – on user friendliness. For ORA this is due to the complex data management using meta-networks. Although menu-driven, the program does not allow an intuitive finding of procedures and methods. Compared with, for instance, NetMiner and UCINET, we find that ORA is not a program suitable for novice users. Pajek scores + – on user friendliness for more or less the same reason. The different data structures for which the program is developed make finding the right procedures and analyzing data sets difficult (the book by de Nooy et al., 2005, is very helpful but is not a tutorial). Compared to the menu-driven general packages, the R packages statnet and sna require a larger effort on the part of the user, especially if they are new to R as well. Therefore we rate statnet/sna with a + –. The R package RSiena is an exception, because it more or less mimics the interface and stepwise modeling approach used in StOCNET.

Final observations

From Table 38.4 (functionality) it follows that the newer packages score + (good) or ++ (strong) on all analysis types. This is especially true for ORA, which has procedures for collecting data from the Web and network dynamics. The routines to search the Internet and collect longitudinal network data, and algorithms for statistical modeling of networks or network dynamics, have only become available in the last 5 to 10 years. This is an advantage for the newer packages, because they can develop frameworks in which these new technologies are included. The existing (older) programs were developed in a time when these procedures were scarcely available, making their implementation a much harder task.

Although almost all programs score + (good) or ++ (strong) on descriptive and procedure-based methods, this does not imply that all packages feature the same summary statistics. Xu et al. (2010) compared the overlap in procedures available in six packages, among them Pajek, statnet,

Table 38.5 URLs of all websites mentioned in the text

Website	URL
This chapter	http://www.gmw.rug.nl/~huisman/sna/software.html
INSNA	http://www.insna.org/software/index.html
	http://www.insna.org/software/software_old.html
Wikipedia	http://en.wikipedia.org/wiki/Social_network_analysis_software
Formats diagram	http://mdround.blogs.com/usingnetworks/2009/07/sna-tools-and-formats-diagram-updated.html

and UCINET, and found that the packages complement each other in the sense that they have (slightly) different implementations of general network concepts. A new user should, therefore, know exactly what kind of analysis or procedure he or she wants to perform and should then look for the right software. In research areas with specialized applications of social network analysis, this choice will be straightforward and can therefore easily lead to choosing a specialized package.

Researchers from an area in which social network analysis is not yet a common method may face a more difficult task. Before embarking on complex analysis methods, we would strongly advise them to study the literature, for instance, using one of the earlier mentioned textbooks, in order to get to know the concepts and applications in social network analysis. An important distinction between research areas is the size of the network under study. With the increasing availability of tools to automatically collect large networks (for example, Web-based) the software also needs to be able to deal with increasing memory demands. Xu et al. (2010) found that Pajek especially scored quite well on this aspect, whereas UCINET and statnet did not score well at all, probably at least partly due to the programming language.

Researchers new to social network analysis who want general and relatively easy-to-learn packages are advised to use UCINET or NetMiner.[7] NetMiner stands out with respect to user friendliness because of the integration of visualization, data management, and data exploration. To a lesser extent this is true for UCINET, whose menu-driven procedures have the same intuitive appeal as those of NetMiner, however, without the same visual exploration properties. For researchers who are more experienced with data analysis and different software packages, and maybe less hesitant to spend some (or a lot of) time to learn new programs, the packages ORA and Pajek offer many possibilities. For researchers who have experience with programming or who are willing to invest time in learning the R language, the packages statnet and sna (and all other SNA and non-SNA packages available in R) offer a large range of routines.[7]

We started this chapter with the question of whether there is a comprehensive list of software for social network analysis. Tables 38.2 and 38.3 give such a comprehensive list, but as we already mentioned in the introduction, maintaining such a list is a difficult task. A suggestion was given on SOCNET, in January 2010, to employ the software articles about SNA in Wikipedia to this end, because the "social network community" would contribute. We support this suggestion to add and update the SNA packages on this list to make and maintain the comprehensive list of SNA software. Such a list is desirable and useful, maybe even necessary, because choosing a program to perform SNA is not easy or straightforward. It depends to a large extent on the type of analysis and data to be analyzed. It will remain difficult to compare the different packages, as we already pointed out at the beginning of this section. We hope to have given some useful criteria and advice for making a choice, but ultimately we have to leave it to the readers of this chapter to decide which software to use for social network analysis.

NOTES

1 In January 2010, such a request was actually posted on SOCNET, the email list-server of INSNA.

2 We will not give references to each software package mentioned in the text. All package references can be found in the software reference list at the end of the chapter.

3 All developers of the software in Tables 38.2 and 38.3 were given the opportunity to check the contents of the tables with respect to their packages.

4 Not counting NetDraw, as this is a visualization program included in the UCINET package.

5 Mark Round (2009) gives a comprehensive (graphical) overview of data formats in the SNA tools and formats diagram on his Web site (see Table 38.5).

6 In the 2005 review, the programs StOCNET and STRUCTURE were included in the comparison using eight of the nine criteria (except network dynamics). These two programs are not used in the current comparison because they are not a general package (StOCNET) or have become outdated (STRUCTURE).

7 This advice is shared by Loscalzo and Yu (2008) and Kirschner (2008).

REFERENCES

Admiraal, R. and Handcock, M.S. (2008) 'networksis: A package to simulate bipartite graphs with fixed marginals through sequential importance sampling', *Journal of Statistical Software*, 24(8).

Batagelj, V. and Mrvar, A. (1998) 'Pajek: A program for large network analysis', *Connections*, 21(2): 47–57.

boyd, D.M. and Ellison, N.B. (2007) 'Social network sites: Definition, history, and scholarship', *Journal of Computer-Mediated Communication*, 13(1): article 11.

Butts, C.T. (2007) 'Book review: Carrington, P.J., Scott, J., Wasserman, S., 2005'. *Models and Methods in Social Network Analysis*. Cambridge: Cambridge University Press, *Social Networks*, 29(4): 603–8.

Butts, C.T. (2008a) 'network: A package for managing relational data in R', *Journal of Statistical Software*, 24(2).

Butts, C.T. (2008b) 'Social network analysis with sna', *Journal of Statistical Software*, 24(6).

Clauset, A., Shalizi, C.R. and Newman, M.E.J. (2009) 'Power-law distributions in empirical data', *SIAM Review*, 51(4): 661–703.

Degenne, A. and Forsé, M. (1999) *Introducing Social Networks*. London: Sage.

Dekker, D., Krackhard, D. and Snijders, T.A.B. (2007) 'Sensitivity of MRQAP tests to collinearity and autocorrelation conditions', *Psychometrika*, 72(4): 563–81.

de Nooy, W., Mrvar, A. and Batagelj, V. (2005) *Exploratory Social Network Analysis with Pajek*. Cambridge: Cambridge University Press.

Erickson, B.H. (2005) 'Book Review: Carrington, P.J., Scott, J., Wasserman, S., 2005. *Models and Methods in Social Network Analysis*. Cambridge: Cambridge University Press', *Canadian Journal of Sociology Online* Sept.-Oct.

Frank, K.A. (1995) 'Identifying cohesive subgroups', *Social Networks*, 17(1): 27–56.

Frank, O. and Strauss, D. (1986) 'Markov graphs', *Journal of the American Statistical Association*, 81(395): 832–42.

Freeman, L.C. (1988) 'Computer programs and social network analysis', *Connections*, 11(2): 26–31.

Goodreau, S.M., Handcock, M.S., Hunter, D.R., Butts, C.T. and Morris, M. (2008) 'A statnet tutorial', *Journal of Statistical Software*, 24(9).

Handcock, M.S. (2003) 'degreenet: Models for skewed count distributions relevant to networks', statnet Project, http://statnetproject.org/, Seattle, WA.

Handcock, M.S., Raftery, A.E. and Tantrum, J.M. (2007) 'Model-based clustering for social networks. With discussion', *Journal of the Royal Statistical Society A*, 170(2): 301–54.

Handcock, M.S., Hunter, D.R., Butts, C.T., Goodreau, S.M. and Morris, M. (2008) 'statnet: Software tools for the representation, visualization, analysis and simulation of network data', *Journal of Statistical Software*, 24(1).

Hanneman, R.A. and Riddle, M. (2005) *Introduction to Social Network Methods*. Riverside: University of California. http://faculty.ucr.edu/~hanneman/.

Hummon, N.P. and Carley, K. (1993) 'Social networks as normal science', *Social Networks*, 15(1): 71–106.

Hunter, D. and Handcock, M.S. (2006) 'Inference in curved exponential families for networks', *Journal of Computational and Graphical Statistics*, 15(3): 565–83.

Hoff, P. D., Raftery, A.E. and Handcock, M.S. (2002) 'Latent space approaches to social network analysis', *Journal of the American Statistical Association*, 97(460): 1090–98.

Holland, P.W. and Leinhardt, S. (1981) 'An exponential family of probability distributions for directed graphs', *Journal of the American Statistical Association*, 76(373): 33–50.

Huisman, M. and van Duijn, M.A.J. (2005a) 'Software for social network analysis', in P.J. Carrington, J. Scott and S. Wasserman (eds), *Models and Methods in Social Network Analysis*. Cambridge: Cambridge University Press. pp. 270–316.

Huisman, M. and van Duijn, M.A.J. (2005b) 'Software for statistical analysis of social networks', in C. van Dijkum, J. Blasius and C. Durand (eds), *Recent Developments and Applications in Social Research Methodology, Proceedings of the RC33 Sixth International Conference on Social Science Methodology*, August 17–20, 2004, Amsterdam, the Netherlands. Leverkusen: Budrich-Verlag.

Kirschner, A. (2008) *Overview of Common Social Network Analysis Software Platforms* (presentation). San Francisco: Monitor Institute.

Krackhardt, D. (1987) 'Cognitive social structures', *Social Networks*, 9(2): 104–34.

Krivitsky, P.N. and Handcock, M.S. (2008) 'Fitting latent cluster models for networks with latentnet', *Journal of Statistical Software*, 24(5).

Loscalzo, S. and Yu, L. (2008) 'Social network analysis: Tasks and tools', in H. Liu, J.J. Salerno and M.J. Young (eds), *Social Computing, Behavioral Modeling, and Prediction*. New York: Springer. pp. 151–59.

Palla, G., Derényi, I., Farkas, I. and Vicsek, T. (2005) 'Uncovering the overlapping community structure of complex networks in nature and society', *Nature*, 345: 814–18.

Robins, G.L., Snijders, T.A.B., Wang, P., Handcock, M.S. and Pattison, P. (2007) 'Recent developments in exponential random graph (p^*) models for social networks', *Social Networks*, 29(2): 192–215.

Round, M.D. (2009) 'SNA tools and formats diagram', http://mdround.blogs.com/.

Scott, J. (1996) 'A toolkit for social network analysis', *Acta Sociologica*, 39(2): 211–16.

Scott, J. (2002) *Social Network Analysis: A Handbook*. 2nd ed. London: Sage.

Seary, A.J. (2005) 'MultiNet: An interactive program for analyzing and visualizing complex networks', Unpublished Ph.D. thesis, Simon Fraser University.

Snijders, T.A.B. (2002) 'Markov chain Monte Carlo estimation of exponential random graph models', *Journal of Social Structure*, 3(2), http://zeeb.library.cmu.edu:7850/JoSS/snijders/Mcpstar.pdf.

Snijders, T.A.B., Steglich, C.E.G. and van de Bunt, Gerhard G. (2010) 'Introduction to actor-based models for network dynamics', *Social Networks*, 32(1): 44–60.

van Duijn, M.A.J., Snijders, T.A.B. and Zijlstra, B.J.H. (2004) 'p_2: A random effects model with covariates for indirected graphs', *Statistica Neerlandica*, 58(2): 234–54.

van Duijn, M.A.J., Gile, K. and Handcock, M.S. (2009) 'A framework for the comparison of maximum pseudo-likelihood and maximum likelihood estimation of exponential family random graph models', *Social Networks*, 31(1): 52–62.

Wasserman, S. and Faust, K. (1994) *Social Network Analysis: Methods and Applications*. Cambridge: Cambridge University Press.

Wasserman, S. and Pattison, P. (1996) 'Logit models and logistic regression for social networks: I. An introduction to Markov graphs and p^*', *Psychometrika*, 61(3): 401–25.

White, D.R., Batagelj, V and Mrvar, A. (1999) 'Analyzing large kinship and marriage networks with PGRAPH and Pajek', *Social Science Computer Review*, 17(3): 245–74.

Xu, K., Tang, C., Ali, G., Li, C., Tang, R. and Zhu, J. (2010) 'A comparative study of six software packages for complex network research', paper presented at the 2010 International Conference on Communication Software and Networks, Singapore, http://cs.scu.edu.cn/~tangchangjie/paper doc/2010/XKKcomparision.pdf.

Zijlstra, B.J.H., van Duijn, M.A.J. and Snijders, T.A.B. (2009) 'MCMC estimation for the p_2 network regression model with crossed random effects', *British Journal of Mathematical and Statistical Psychology*, 62(1): 143–66.

SOFTWARE REFERENCES

Agna: Benta, I. Marius (2003) Agna. Cork: University College Cork, Ireland.

Blanche: Hyatt, A., Contractor, N. and Jones, P.M. (1996) 'Computational organizational network modeling: Strategies and an example', *Computational and Mathematical Organization Theory*, 2(4): 285–300.

BLOCKS: Nowicki, K. and Snijders, T.A.B. (2001) 'Estimation and prediction for stochastic blockstructures', *Journal of the American Statistical Association*, 96(455): 1077–87.

Blue Spider: Blue Spider Analytics (2009) *Blue Spider*. King George: Blue Spider Analytics.

CFinder: Adamcsek, B., Palla, G., Farkas, I.J., Derényi, I. and Vicsek, T. (2006) 'CFinder: Locating cliques and overlapping modules in biological networks', *Bioinformatics*, 22(8): 1021–23.

CID-ABM: Elbrit, B. (2009) 'Competing idea diffusion ABM (CID-ABM)', ET Software and Consulting.

C-IKNOW: Contractor, N. (2009) 'C-IKNOW cyber-infrastructure for inquiring knowledge networks on the Web'. Evanston, IL: Science of Networks in Communities (SONIC), Northwestern University.

CiteSpace: Chen, C. (2006) 'CiteSpace II: Detecting and visualizing emerging trends and transient patterns in scientific literature', *Journal of the American Society for Information Science and Technology*, 57(3): 359–77.

Commetrix: Trier, M. (2008) *Commetrix. Dynamic Visualization and Analysis*. Berlin: Technical University Berlin.

DyNet: ATA SpA (2007) *DyNet (SE and LS)*. Lucca, Italy: ATA SpA Advanced Technology Assessment.

EgoNet: EgoNet Development Team (2009) *EgoNet*. http://sourceforge.net/projects/egonet/.

Eicent: Borgatti, S.P. (2002) *Eicent. Attribute-Based Partitioning of Centrality*. Harvard: Analytic Technologies.

E-Net: Borgatti, S.P. (2006) *E-Net Software Package of Ego-Network Analysis*. Harvard: Analytic Technologies.

FATCAT: Richards, W.D. and Seary, A.J. (1993) *FATCAT. Version 4.2*. Burnaby: Simon Fraser University.

Financial Network Analyzer: Soramaki, K. (2010) *Financial Network Analyzer v1.2*. http://www.financialnetwork analysis.com.

GRADAP: Sprenger, C.J.A. and Stokman, Frans N. (1989) *GRADAP: Graph Definition and Analysis Package*. Groningen: iec. ProGAMMA.

GUESS: Adar, E. (2006) 'GUESS: A language and interface for graph exploration', paper presented at CHI 2006, April 22–28, 2006, Montreal, Canada.

igraph: Csérdi, G. and Nepusz, T. (2009) *The igraph Project*. Budapest: Hungarian Academy of Sciences.

InFlow: Krebs, V.E. (2003) *InFlow*. Cleveland: Orgnet.com.

JUNG: JUNG Framework Development Team (2009) *JUNG: The Java Universal Network/Graph Framework*. http://jung.sourceforge.net/.

KeyPlayer: Borgatti, S.P. (2003) *KeyPlayer*. Harvard: Analytic Technologies.

KliqFinder: Frank. K.A. (1995) 'Identifying Cohesive Subgroups', *Social Networks*, 17(1): 27–56.

latentnet: Krivitsky, P.N. and Handcock, M.S. (2008) 'Fitting latent cluster models for networks with latentnet', *Journal of Statistical Software*, 24(5).

LibSNA: Usher, A. (2008) *libsna: The Library for Social Network Analysis*. Washington, DC: Sharp Ideas LLC.

MatMan: Noldus (2004) *MatMan: Software for Matrix Manipulation and Analysis*. Wageningen, The Netherlands: Noldus Information Technology.

MDLogix - EgoNet: mdlogix (2007) *EgoNet*. Baltimore, MD: Medical Decision Logic.

MDLogix - LinkAlyzer: mdlogix (2007) *LinkAlyzer*. Baltimore, MD: Medical Decision Logic.

MDLogix - VisuaLyzer: mdlogix (2007) *VisuaLyzer*. Baltimore, MD: Medical Decision Logic.

MetaSight: Morphix (2009) *MetaSight*. Crowthorne, UK: The Morphix Company.

MultiNet: Richards, W.D. and Seary, A.J. (2009) *MultiNet for Windows*. Burnaby, Canada: Simon Fraser University.

NEGOPY: Richards, W.D. (1995) *NEGOPY. Version 4.30*. Burnaby: Simon Fraser University.

NetDraw: Borgatti, S.P. (2002) *NetDraw: Graph Visualization Software*. Harvard: Analytic Technologies.

NetMiner 3: Cyram (2009) *Cyram NetMiner 3*. Seoul: Cyram Co., Ltd.

NetVis: Cummings, J.N. (2009) *NetVis Module—Dynamic Visualization of Social Networks*. Cambridge: Massachusetts Institute of Technology.

Network Genie: Hansen, W.B. and Reese, E.L. (2008) *Network Genie*. Greensboro, NC: Tanglewood Research.

Network Workbench: NWB Team (2006) *Network Workbench Tool*. Indiana University, Northeastern University, and University of Michigan.

NetworkX: Hagberg, A.A., Schult, D.A. and Swart, P.J. (2008) 'Exploring network structure, dynamics, and function using NetworkX', in G. Varoquaux, T. Vaught and J. Millman (eds), *Proceedings of the 7th Python in Science Conference (SciPy2008)*, August 2008, Pasadena. pp. 11–15.

NodeXL: NodeXL Development Team (2009) *NodeXL: Network Overview, Discovery and Exploration for Microsoft Excel 2007*. http://nodexl.codeplex.com/.

ONA surveys: Optimice (2009) *ONA surveys*. Sydney: Optimice Pty.

ORA: Carley, K. (2009) *ORA. The Organizational Risk Analyzer*. Pittsburgh, PA: Carnegie Mellon University.

P2: Van Duijn, M.A.J., Snijders, T.A.B. and Zijlstra, B.J.H. (2004) 'p_2: A random effects model with covariates for indirected graphs', *Statistica Neerlandica*, 58(2): 234–54.

PACNET: Pattison, P., Wasserman, S., Robins, G. and Kanfer, A.M. (2000) 'Statistical evaluation of algebraic constraints for social networks', *Journal of Mathematical Psychology*, 44(4): 536–68.

Pajek: Batagelj, V. and Mrvar, A. (2010) *Pajek—Package for Large Networks*. Ljubljana: University of Ljubljana.

PGRAPH: White, D.R. and Skyhorse, P. (1997) *PGRAPH: Representation and Analytic Program for Kinship and Marriage Networks*. Irvine: University of California.

PermNet: Tsuji, R. (1997) 'Permutation tests for symmetry and transitivity in real-valued data', paper presented at JAMS 24th Conference, November 10, 1997, Hokkaido University, Saporro.

PNet: Wang, P., Robins, G. and Pattison, P. (2008) *PNet: Program for the Simulation and Estimation of p* Exponential Random Graph Models*. User manual. Melbourne: University of Melbourne.

PSPAR: Seary, A.J. (1999) *PSPAR: Sparse Matrix Version of PSTAR*. Burnaby: Simon Fraser University.

Puck: Research Group TIP (2007) *Puck: Program for the Use and Computation of Kinship Data*. Paris: Centre National de Recherche Scientifique, Research Group TIP (Traitement Informatique de la Parenté).

ReferralWeb: Kautz, H., Selman, B. and Shah, M. (1997) 'The hidden web', *American Association for Artificial Intelligence Magazine*, 18(2): 27–36.

RSiena: Ripley, R.M. and Snijders, T.A.B. (2010) *Manual for SIENA Version 4.0*. Oxford, UK: University of Oxford.

Sentinel Visualizer: FMS (2009) *Sentinel Visualizer. The Next Generation of Data Visualization*. Vienna, VA: FMS Advanced Systems Group.

SIENA: Snijders, T.A.B., Steglich, C.E.G, Schweinberger, M. and Huisman, M. (2009) *Manual for SIENA Version 3.2*. University of Groningen/ICS, University of Oxford.

Snowball: Frank, O. and Snijders, T.A.B. (1994) 'Estimating the size of hidden populations using snowball sampling', *Journal of Official Statistics*, 10(1): 53–67.

sna: Butts, C.T. (2008b) 'Social network analysis with sna', *Journal of Statistical Software*, 24(6): 51 pp.

SNAP: Friedkin, N.E. (2001) *SNAP: Social Network Analysis Procedures for GAUSS*. Maple Valley, WA: Aptech Systems, Inc.

SocNetV: Kalamaras, D.V. (2009) *SocNetV*. http://socnetv. sourceforge.net/index.html.

SONET: Seidman, S.B. and Foster, B.L. (1980) 'SONET-1: Social network analysis and modeling system', *Social Networks*, 2(1): 85–90.

SONIS: Pappi, F.U. and Stelck, K. (1987) 'SONIS: Ein Datenbanksystem zur Netzwerkanalyse', in F.U. Pappi (ed.), *Techniken der empirischen Sozialforschung. Methoden der Netzwerkanalyse*. Munich: Oldenbourg Verlag. pp. 253–66.

SONIVIS: SONIVIS:Team (2009) *SONIVIS:Tool*. http://www. sonivis.org/.

statnet: Handcock, M. S., Hunter, D. R., Butts, C. T., Goodreau, S. M. and Morris, M. (2003) *statnet: Software Tools for the Statistical Modeling of Network Data. Version 2*. Seattle, WA: Statnet Project.

StOCNET: Boer, P., Huisman, M., Snijders, T.A.B., Steglich, C.E.G., Wichers, L.H.Y. and Zeggelink, E.P.H. (2006) *StOCNET: An Open Software System for the Advanced Statistical Analysis of Social Networks. Version 1.8*. Groningen: ICS, University of Groningen/SciencePlus.

STRUCTURE: Burt, R.S. (1991) *STRUCTURE. Version 4.2*. New York: Columbia University.

tnet: Opsahl, T. (2009) *tnet. Analysis of Weighted and Longitudinal Networks*. London: Queen Mary University of London.

UCINET 6: Borgatti, S.P., Everett, M.G. and Freeman, L.C. (2002) *UCINET 6 for Windows: Software for Social Network Analysis*. Harvard, MA: Analytic Technologies.

ULTRAS: Schweinberger, M. and Snijders, T.A.B. (2003) 'Settings in social networks: A measurement model', in M.E. Sobel (ed.), *Sociological Methodology 2003*. London: Basil Blackwell. pp. 307–41.

UNISoN: Leonard, S. (2008) 'UNISoN: A tool to aid evaluation of sociability in on-line discussion boards', unpublished MSc thesis. London: City University.

UrlNet: Hunscher, D. (2009) *UrlNet: A Python Class Library for Generating Networks for Analysis*. Ann Arbor: University of Michigan Medical School.

VennMaker: Schoenhuth, M., Gamper, M. and Stark, M. (2009) *VennMaker*. Trier, Germany: University of Trier.

visone: Brandes, U. and Wagner, D. (2004) 'visone—Analysis and visualization of social networks', in M. Jünger and P. Mutzel (eds), *Graph Drawing Software*. New York: Springer. pp. 321–40.

yFiles: yWorks (2009) *yFiles Graph Visualization Library*. Tübingen, Germany: yWorks GmbH.

ZO: Snijders, T.A.B. (1991) 'Enumeration and simulation models for 0–1 matrices with given marginals', *Psychometrika*, 56(3): 397–417.

Index